THE OXFORD HANDBOOK OF

SLAVERY IN THE AMERICAS

The Oxford Handbook of Slavery in the Americas offers penetrating, original, and authoritative essays on the history and historiography of the institution of slavery in the New World. With essays on colonial and antebellum America, Brazil, the Caribbean, the Indies, and South America, the Handbook has impressive geographic and temporal coverage. It also includes a generous range of thematic essays on comparative slavery, the economics of slavery, historical methodology in the field, slavery and the law, for instance.

While obviously indebted to the foundational works of the 1960s and 1970s, current writing on the history of slavery and forms of unfree labor in the Americas has taken decidedly original, new, often ingenious turns. A younger generation of scholars has shown a healthy respect for that tradition while posing new, often interdisciplinary, and theoretically informed questions, considering, for example, the nature and definition of slave resistance in the Americas, evolving meanings of gender and race under slavery, the complicated nature of class formation in unfree societies, the elaboration of proslavery and antislavery ideologies, the origins and subsequent elaboration of race-based slavery, and mechanisms of emancipation.

Written by an international team including some of the field's most eminent historians and the most innovative younger scholars working today, *The Oxford Handbook of Slavery in the Americas* seeks to explain the enduring importance of the earlier historiography, identify current trends and developments, and offer suggestive but informed commentary on future developments in the field for a global scholarly audience.

Robert L. Paquette is Publius Virgilius Rogers Professor of American History at Hamilton College and co-founder of the Alexander Hamilton Institute for the Study of Western Civilization in Clinton, New York. He has published extensively on the history of slavery and his *Sugar is Made with Blood* won the Elsa Goveia Prize given by the Association of Caribbean Historians for the best book in Caribbean history.

Mark M. Smith is Carolina Distinguished Professor of History at the University of South Carolina. He is author or editor of a dozen books, including *Mastered by the Clock: Time, Slavery, and Freedom in the American South*, winner of the Organization of American Historians' Avery O. Craven Award and South Carolina Historical Society's Book of the Year in 1997. He is the current President of The Historical Society.

'brings together leading scholars in the field who re-examine and present new perspectives on old and new themes, successfully reviews the main debates in broad geographic regions, considers indigenous slavery as well as African slavery, reassesses aspects of comparative and economic history regarding slavery, and presents articles that bring important reflections on new and understudied sources'

Fabricio Prado, *Labor: Studies in Working-Class History in the Americas*

THE OXFORD HANDBOOK OF

SLAVERY IN THE AMERICAS

Edited by

ROBERT L. PAQUETTE

and

MARK M. SMITH

OXFORD
UNIVERSITY PRESS

OXFORD
UNIVERSITY PRESS

Great Clarendon Street, Oxford, OX2 6DP,
United Kingdom

Oxford University Press is a department of the University of Oxford.
It furthers the University's objective of excellence in research, scholarship,
and education by publishing worldwide. Oxford is a registered trade mark of
Oxford University Press in the UK and in certain other countries

Published in the United States of America by Oxford University Press
198 Madison Avenue, New York, NY 10016, United States of America

British Library Cataloguing in Publication Data
Data available

Library of Congress Cataloging in Publication Data
Data available

ISBN 978–0–19–922799–0 (Hbk.)
ISBN 978–0–19–875881–5 (Pbk.)

For our children,
Alex and Natalie
Bennett and Sophie

ACKNOWLEDGMENTS

One of ancient Rome's most celebrated moralists after exiting the house of bondage deposited wisdom as a freedman on the relations that precept our obligations. "When you are eating with another," Epictetus observed, "remember to look not only to the value for the body of the things set before you, but also to the value of the behaviour toward the host which ought to be observed." For inviting us to the table, we would like to thank Christopher Wheeler, History Publisher at Oxford University Press. His fine staff—Matthew Cotton, Carol Bestley, and Jackie Pritchard—helped us diligently each step of the way through the various courses necessary to finish the meal.

Work at Paquette's end of the operation benefited repeatedly from the generous support of the independent Alexander Hamilton Institute for the Study of Western Civilization (AHI). He would like to thank in particular Carl B. Menges without whom the AHI would have remained in 2007 little more than a dream of a cranky traditionalist.

A volume of this sort—a decidedly multi-year endeavour—requires, above all, time. Mary Anne Fitzpatrick, Dean of the college of Arts and Sciences at the University of South Carolina, and Lacy K. Ford, Jr., Chair of USC's Department of History, understood the importance of time and granted Smith the flexibility he needed to conclude his labors, he remains grateful for their support. Both editors thank Robert Ellis for invaluable help in preparing the index.

CONTENTS

List of Contributors   x

INTRODUCTION

Slavery in the Americas   3
ROBERT L. PAQUETTE and MARK M. SMITH

PART I: PLACES

1. Spanish Hispaniola and Puerto Rico   21
   FRANCISCO A. SCARANO

2. Mexico and Central America   46
   K. RUSSELL LOHSE

3. Spanish South American Mainland   68
   PETER BLANCHARD

4. Cuba   90
   MATT D. CHILDS and MANUEL BARCIA

5. Brazil   111
   ROBERT W. SLENES

6. British West Indies and Bermuda   134
   TREVOR BURNARD

7. Dutch Caribbean   154
   HENK DEN HEIJER

8. French Caribbean   173
   JOHN GARRIGUS

9. Colonial and Revolutionary United States   201
   DANIEL C. LITTLEFIELD

10. Early Republic and Antebellum United States   227
    JEFF FORRET

PART II: THEMES, METHODS, AND SOURCES

11. The Transatlantic Slave Trade   251
    STEPHEN D. BEHRENDT

12. The Origins of Slavery in the Americas   275
    JOHN J. MCCUSKER and RUSSELL R. MENARD

13. Biology and African Slavery   293
    KENNETH F. KIPLE

14. Indian Slavery   312
    ALAN GALLAY

15. Race and Slavery   336
    TIMOTHY LOCKLEY

16. Class and Slavery   357
    JONATHAN DANIEL WELLS

17. Religion and Slavery   378
    DOUGLAS AMBROSE

18. Proslavery Ideology   399
    JEFFREY ROBERT YOUNG

19. United States Slave Law   424
    PAUL FINKELMAN

20. Slave Resistance   447
    DOUGLAS R. EGERTON

21. Slave Culture   465
    KEVIN DAWSON

22. The Economics of Slavery   489
    PETER COCLANIS

23. Gender and Slavery   513
    KIRSTEN E. WOOD

24. Masters   535
    EUGENE D. GENOVESE and DOUGLAS AMBROSE

25. Abolition and Antislavery   556
    JOHN STAUFFER

26. Emancipation   578
    CHRISTOPHER SCHMIDT-NOWARA

27. Slavery and the Haitian Revolution   598
    STEWART R. KING

28. Internal Slave Trades   625
    MICHAEL TADMAN

29. Demography and Slavery   643
    RICHARD H. STECKEL

30. Comparative Slavery   664
    ENRICO DAL LAGO

31. Finding Slave Voices   685
    KATHLEEN HILLIARD

32. Archaeology and Slavery   702
    THERESA SINGLETON

EPILOGUE

33. Post-Emancipation Adjustments   727
    STANLEY L. ENGERMAN

Index   745

List of Contributors

Douglas Ambrose co-founded the Alexander Hamilton Institute for the Study of Western Civilization in Clinton, New York, and is Professor of History at Hamilton College.

Manuel Barcia lectures in Latin American Studies at the University of Leeds.

Stephen D. Behrendt serves as Senior Lecturer, School of History, Philosophy, Political Science & International Relations at Victoria University of Wellington, New Zealand.

Peter Blanchard is Professor of History at the University of Toronto.

Trevor Burnard is Professor of the History of the Americas, History, and Comparative American Studies at the University of Warwick.

Matt D. Childs is Associate Professor in the Department of History at the University of South Carolina.

Peter Coclanis is Albert R. Newsome Professor in the Department of History at the University of North Carolina, Chapel Hill, where he also serves as Associate Provost for International Affairs.

Enrico Dal Lago is Lecturer in American History at the National University of Ireland in Galway.

Kevin Dawson is Assistant Professor in the Department of History at the University of Nevada, Las Vegas.

Douglas R. Egerton is Joseph C. Georg Professor in the Department of History at Le Moyne College in Syracuse, New York.

Stanley L. Engerman is John Munro Professor of Economics and Professor of History at the University of Rochester.

Paul Finkelman teaches at the Albany Law School where he is President William McKinley Distinguished Professor of Law and Public Policy and Senior Fellow, Government Law Center.

Jeff Forret is Associate Professor in the Department of History at Lamar University in Beaumont, Texas.

Alan Gallay holds the Warner R. Woodring Chair in Atlantic World and Early American History at the Ohio State University.

John Garrigus is Associate Professor in the Department of History at the University of Texas at Arlington.

Eugene D. Genovese, a retired historian, works as an independent scholar from his home in Atlanta, Georgia.

H. J. (Henk) den Heijer teaches history in the Faculty of Humanities, Institute for History, at the University of Leiden.

Kathleen Hilliard is Assistant Professor in the Department of History at Iowa State University.

Stewart R. King is Professor of History at Mount Angel Seminary in Benedict, Oregon.

Kenneth F. Kiple is Distinguished Professor in the Department of History at Bowling Green State University.

Daniel C. Littlefield directs the Institute for African American Research at the University of South Carolina where he is also Carolina Professor of History in the Department of History.

Timothy Lockley is Associate Professor in the Department of History at the University of Warwick.

K. Russell Lohse is Assistant Professor in the Department of History at Penn State University.

John J. McCusker is the Ewing Halsell Distinguished Professor of American History and Professor of Economics at Trinity University, San Antonio, Texas.

Russell R. Menard is Professor in the Department of History at the University of Minnesota.

Robert L. Paquette co-founded the Alexander Hamilton Institute for the Study of Western Civilization in Clinton, New York, and holds the Publius Virgilius Rogers Chair in American History at Hamilton College.

Francisco A. Scarano is Professor in the Department of History and in the Chicana and Latina Studies Program at the University of Wisconsin, Madison.

Robert W. Slenes is Professor in the Department of History, University of Campinas (Unicamp) in Brazil.

Christopher Schmidt-Nowara is Professor in the Department of History and a member of the Latin American & Latino Studies Institute at Fordham University.

Theresa Singleton teaches in the Maxwell School of Syracuse University where she is Associate Professor in the Department of Anthropology.

Mark M. Smith is Carolina Distinguished Professor of History at the University of South Carolina.

John Stauffer is Chair of History of American Civilization and Professor of English and African and African American Studies at Harvard University.

Richard H. Steckel is SBS Distinguished Professor of Economics, Anthropology, and History at the Ohio State University as well as Research Associate, National Bureau of Economic Research in Cambridge, Massachusetts.

Michael Tadman serves as Senior Lecturer in the School of History at the University of Liverpool.

Jonathan Daniel Wells is Associate Professor of History at Temple University.

Kirsten E. Wood is Associate Professor in the Department of History at Florida International University in Miami.

Jeffrey Robert Young is Associate Director of the Undergraduate Honors Program at Georgia State University.

INTRODUCTION

SLAVERY IN THE AMERICAS

ROBERT L. PAQUETTE

MARK M. SMITH

THOMAS Reade Rootes Cobb, the proslavery Georgian architect of the Confederate Constitution, and José Antonio Saco, the antislavery Cuban patriot, both reared and educated among slaves, stood almost alone among the intellectuals of the nineteenth century in combining sufficient interest, boldness, and erudition to undertake the daunting task of writing a serious global history of slavery. Although they ultimately reached different conclusions about the institution's morality, they concurred on the problem of its history. "A detailed and minute inquiry into the history of slavery," Cobb observed in the preface to his magnum opus, *An Inquiry into the Law of Negro Slavery* (1858), would force the historian "to trace the history of every nation of the earth." Slavery's beginnings, he suggested, date at least to Noah and the flood, and probably before. From that darkened moment in biblical time, slavery spread out across the habitable continents of the earth to become "more universal than marriage, and more permanent than liberty."[1] Like Cobb, Saco in his multi-volume *Historia de la esclavitud* (1875–7) investigated slavery around the world "from the times most remote." He examined not only bound and documentary sources, but also ancient sculptures, inscriptions, and monuments. "Nations, whether barbarous or civilized, great or small, powerful or weak, pacific or warlike, under the most diverse forms of government, professing the most antagonistic religions, and without distinction of climate and ages," he concluded, "all have carried the poison of slavery in their womb."[2]

At first blush, the thirty-three essays that comprise *The Oxford Handbook of Slavery in the Americas* suggest that slavery ranged so ineffably wide across continents with such remarkable regional diversity that generalizations about the institution from a hemispheric or even global perspective might seem to obscure more than they reveal about the significance of slavery in a particular location. Slavery, wherever it existed, evolved with no predictable trajectory under dynamic pressure from a complex battery of internal and external forces. They stamped each New World slaveholding society with a distinctive profile so that, for example, the countenance of slavery in Brazil, the country that imported African slaves in numbers that approached half of the total, was, in any number of important ways, quite different from that in the United States, the Dutch Caribbean, or the slaveholding societies established and fostered by the French and the Spanish.

Slavery in the Americas pre-dated Columbus, but once taking root in the Americas under western European auspices, acquired a predominantly commercial character whose benefaction to the sustained economic growth of the Western world no serious scholar can any longer doubt. Some regions began—Britain's colonies on the North American mainland, for example—as societies with slaves. Slavery there existed as one particularly extreme, ignominious form of dependency in a continuum of others. In other regions or countries slavery quickly developed into the cornerstone of the economy and the very essence of social life, as it did in northeastern Brazil by the end of the sixteenth century or in Barbados by the mid-seventeenth century. Colonial Cuba remained a society with slaves for several centuries after the Spanish conquest. But with the boom in coffee and sugar production during the first half of the nineteenth century, the island became one of the hemisphere's most conspicuous slave societies and one of the world's wealthiest colonies, importing more African slaves in a fifty-year period than did the United States during its entire colonial and national history.[3]

If, as the classicist Moses Finley and the sociologist Orlando Patterson would have it, the proper cross-cultural definition of slavery connotes the idea of social death, then slaves throughout the world have struggled at ground level to redeem themselves from non-humanity or chattelhood through persistent artifice.[4] They married, forged families, worshiped together, staged funerals, engaged in market activity, and initiated legal actions in courts. In the process slaves also differentiated among themselves: by status, occupation, ethnicity, gender, and color. In the Americas, slave revolts, gestures toward manumission, important demographic shifts in the ratio of female to male slaves, and the reconfiguring of slavery from a patriarchal institution with the emphasis on brute force to a paternalistic one that sought to translate power into authority changed the shape, flavor, and meaning of slavery not only to the enslaved and their masters, but to nonslaveholders as well. The definition of slavery also proved mildly plastic. Laws, whether constructed from the ground up by a ruling class of masters or imposed from the top down by nonslaveholding metropolitan officials, reiterated and reconfigured slavery throughout the New World. At different times and in some places slavery was indexed to "race"; at other times, genealogy furnished the proper metric. Even the common tendency to enslave "outsiders" proved subject to compromise when those deemed to be "natural" slaves began to share, especially in maturing slave societies, some of the values and cultural norms of their masters.[5]

If slavery itself were a highly variable and differentiated condition, so too were the many institutions and classes to which it gave rise. The introduction of slavery into the New World affected indigenous peoples in many ways, sometimes drawing them into the orbit of slave society, sometimes alienating them from it, and sometimes augmenting a preexisting commitment to different types of slavery already practiced by some of those societies. On the one hand, Tapuya auxiliaries in seventeenth-century Brazil helped Portuguese forces after decades of struggle put an end to Palmares, the largest community of runaway slaves in the history of the hemisphere. In 1811 Tunica trackers helped French-speaking planters above New Orleans hunt down the routed remnants of the largest slave insurrection in United States history. On the other hand, in 1729 African slaves joined the Natchez in attempting to cleanse lower Louisiana of French colonists. During the Second Seminole War (1835–42) Creeks and runaway slaves fought together against US troops in the swampland of central Florida.

Free people of color inhabited slaveholding societies in different proportions, the result largely of varying rates of manumission and natural increase. Like indigenous peoples, they tended to live in studied ambiguity, sometimes acting as agents of slave liberation, sometimes acting as agents of slave repression, and sometimes acting as both depending on the time of day and perceived changes in the balance of forces. Slavery affected nonslaveholding whites, most often the numerical majority in New World slave societies, in ways not always predictable by phenotype. Some remained peripheral to the cultural imperatives of the institution but benefited from the economic system to which it gave rise; others, such as the aspirant yeomen farmers of the antebellum southern United States, frequently joined the ranks of the slaveholding class even as they remained skeptical and critical of many of the master class's political initiatives and cultural pretensions. With the prices for slaves rising and the percentage of slaveholders declining in the South in the 1850s, nonslaveholding farmers in Mississippi figured prominently in the movement to reopen the Atlantic slave trade. Rural poor whites known as *monteros* or *guajiros* in Cuba hunted down runaway slaves for big planters and mustered as an irregular cavalry after outbreaks of slave insurrection. Although sometimes politically independent of slaveholders, nonslaveowning whites lived in societies where slaveholding was the norm, where owning slaves was considered desirable and empowering, and where the general desirability for social order and hierarchy was seemingly preserved by making white men, slaveholding or no, the arbiters of power.

As several of the essays presented in this collection point out, slavery gave rise to classes that looked rather conventional within modernizing, industrializing societies. Slavery did not, for example, prove incompatible with the emergence of a small, often urban, middle class; nor did it preclude the existence of a class of poor whites who had, in material terms, a standard of living more in common with that of enslaved field-hands than with that of slaveholding planters. How these multiple classes functioned, how they accommodated to and challenged the prevailing cultural and political authority of the masters, also varied but, in most instances, the cultural, economic, and political sway of slavery proved sufficiently strong to prevent the emergence of class consciousness and conflict. The ideology and general authority of the master class as well as the heavy emphasis on racialized slavery tended to preclude the sort of class consciousness among the dispossessed and the middle class that was beginning to emerge in nineteenth-century nations that had abandoned bondage in favor of various forms of free or wage labor, the defining feature, according to various proslavery and antislavery thinkers, of capitalism itself.

Master classes also varied. Brazil and the United States typically produced resident masters; the French and British Caribbean had high rates of master absenteeism. Cuban masters tended to sojourn on their rural estates, preferring residence in a townhouse. Those looking for a full-blown formal defense of slavery in the eighteenth-century will find it largely absent, courtesy of a general agreement among elites of all persuasions in a patriarchal age, that organic social relations and hierarchy structured all good societies. During and after the Enlightenment masters throughout the hemisphere found common ground in targeting Rousseau as a primary source of all manner of things profane and radical to established hierarchies. Beginning mainly in the early nineteenth century slaveholding elites in the Americas began to articulate a more systematic and thoroughgoing defense of the institution, principally in response to an emerging modernist critique that conjoined religious and secular ideas. United States slaveholders who congealed as a class with formal political power in that great experiment in republican government developed the most sophisticated proslavery argument by arguing in a way that transcended race that slavery was the proper relation between capital and labor. The intellectual premises of the proslavery defense varied, however, and elaborated in tension with each other. Scattershot sociological and scriptural defenses frequently collided, and defenses of bondage grounded in the precepts of political economy seemed far removed from the biological defenses of race-based enslavement pushed by a rising tide of nineteenth-century ethnologists and natural scientists. Although lawless filibustering activities like those of William Walker in Nicaragua drew sharp criticism in the antebellum South itself, only antebellum southern slaveholders embarked in conspicuous numbers on a civilizing mission to the tropics by attempting to regenerate allegedly inferior others through enslavement.[6]

The experiences of the enslaved throughout the Americas also depended on a rich assortment of particulars in any given place: the ethnic origins of the slave, the timing of his or her forced relocation to the Americas, the type and size of plantation, the particular proclivities and personalities of the master and mistress, the age of the slave, the region and sub-region where they lived, type of crop produced, climate, stage of economic development, demographics, gender, disease, and locus of political power to list a few of the more obvious variables in the formula. As many of the essays in *The Oxford Handbook* make clear, such forces decisively shaped the lived experience of slaves and influenced how they managed their lives in a tension-filled, conflict-ridden dialectic of resistance and accommodation. For some slaves, whether they lived in Canada, Chile, or somewhere in between, life resembled Thomas Hobbes's famous description of the natural condition of mankind: a state of "continuall feare and danger of violent death," where "the life of the man [is] solitary, poore, short, nasty, and brutish," as, indeed, was also the case—as proslavery advocates were quick to point out—for many of the working poor in ostensibly free and industrializing societies.[7] For other slaves, happenstance, skin color and tone, and a variety of other factors enabled them to carve out slightly better lives. Some even became slaveholders themselves and bought bondspeople either by way of introducing them to a nominal form of slavery or for reasons very similar to the master class. The French colony of Saint-Domingue, for example, gave rise to one of the most powerful classes of free colored slaveholders in the Americas, and in the South Province, before the outbreak in 1791 of a rebellion that would become a revolution, mulatto slaveholders may have outnumbered white slaveholders.[8]

Yet with all the variegating factors shaping slavery, slaveholding societies in the hemisphere held a good deal in common. The idea that both practice and theory interwove human bondage together inextricably with freedom prevailed among slaveholders from Buenos Aires to Boston. The wedding of slavery and freedom had an ancient genealogy in Western civilization. Slavery in various forms flourished throughout antiquity and in no way compromised the idea of social freedom. Nor was Edmund Burke the first Western thinker to conceive that slaveholders regarded freedom more preciously than other men, that "a vast multitude of slaves" made "the spirit of liberty still more high and haughty" in Virginia than in Massachusetts.[9] One need only look at Justinian's *Digest* of Roman Law and the citations of, say, Gaius, Florentinus, or Marcian on human status to appreciate the extent to which in Western culture the ideas of slavery and freedom proved mutually constitutive.[10] Only members of antiquity's "fringe" groups, like the "occasional eccentric Stoic," called into question slavery as a viable and, indeed, necessary and desirable institution. "It is no accident," Orlando Patterson has explained, that the "first and greatest mass democracies of the ancient and modern worlds" were ancient Athens and eighteenth-century America, both nourishing a "profound commitment of both cultures to the inspired principle of participative politics" from the soil of slavery. Political freedom, then, could and did demand the existence of bondage.[11]

The experience of the enslaved throughout the Americas suggests the intricacy of the relationship between bondage and freedom. More than ten million slaves arrived in the Americas through such major slave trading ports as Cartagena (New Granada), Salvador (Brazil), Cap Français (Saint-Domingue), Bridgetown (Barbados), Havana (Cuba), Kingston (Jamaica), and Charleston (South Carolina). These and other towns and cities exported a wide variety of profitable plantation staples: sugar, rice, coffee, hemp, cotton, tobacco, cacao, and indigo. But these very urban areas so dependent on plantation slavery tended to muddle it by granting the enslaved room for maneuver. They enhanced opportunities to earn money, acquire property, obtain manumission, communicate with friends and patrons, and plug into information from the outside world. Although masters and government officials were prone to exaggerate the dangers posed by urban environments to slavery, slaves from Spanish-controlled Buenos Aires to French-controlled New Orleans to English-controlled Richmond gambled, fought, conspired, engaged in illicit as well as licit economic trade, cultivated distinctive forms of cultural expression, consorted with free blacks and poor whites, and used the relative anonymity of the city to press their bounds and "normalize" their claims to quasi-independence. Although authorities fought back, the peculiar economic and social structure of cities animated the tension between slavery and freedom and, indeed, fostered ambiguity in the conditions of bondage.[12]

Even as racial slavery was being consolidated in the Americas and increasingly underwritten by slave codes in maturing slave societies, slaves found ways to carve out degrees of freedom from their bondage by working the system, by negotiation, and, on occasion, by violence. As slaves attained a degree of autonomy, they gathered, met, paraded, and achieved a public presence. Slave assemblages and mobilizations, always a concern for slaveholders, continued despite harsh laws designed to restrict them. Legal and statutory efforts to control the behavior of the enslaved were only partially effective and did not foreclose the creation of new patterns of African-American culture as generations passed.[13] Crackdowns and repression rolled back gains at any given moment. But enforcement of the laws had seasonal temperatures, and slaves took advantage of lax times and issued renewed challenges in the fields, in fraternal organizations, in places of worship, and in the marketplace to the masters' visions of plantation political economy and social order. To be sure, masters got much of what they wanted, but a good deal less than the abstract, absolutist dominion of their dreams. Although "a degree of order was obtained" it was necessarily fragile because "the culture of power rested uneasily upon a continuous dialectical process of contention and concession" between master and slave.[14] Slaves' involvement with market transactions, for example, their ability to sell crops they had grown and circulate goods they had acquired, enabled them to garner a degree of autonomy that was, theoretically at least, inconsistent with the practice of bondage. Slaves' participation in the market was empowering and exposed the dependency masters had developed on slave labor.

Slave resistance took many forms, passive and active, and bloody insurrections occasionally broke the surface calm, exposing swirling undercurrents of unrest and discontent for all to see. Masters, however, did not usually discern what they saw, and blamed outside agitators for an uprising that was home-grown in the shadows. From one point of view, the whole question of why slaves rebelled, as the Marxist historian Herbert Aptheker declared a half century ago in a classic study of slave revolts in the United States, has a rather simple, blunt answer: slavery. "The fundamental factor provoking rebellion against slavery was the social system itself, the degradation, exploitation, oppression, and brutality which it created, and with which, indeed it was synonymous."[15]

Since the publication of Aptheker's book painstaking research configured by imaginative minds has deepened and broadened the debates about slave resistance in the Americas and the nature of the master–slave relation. Specialists have identified conditions that favored slave revolts; they have discovered the importance of rumor and shifting troop movements in precipitating them; they have illuminated the broad array of tools at the master's disposal to enforce the terms of bondage; they have distinguished between ethnic revolts of African slaves and those dominated by creole slaves; they have examined the problems of rebellious slave leaders in recruiting and mobilizing followers and coordinating their movements; they have probed the role of ritual and religion in binding rebels into collective solidarity; they have noted the timing of slave revolts to take advantage of darkness and heightened moments of white distraction; they have explored the slaves' weapons and modes of warfare; they have scrutinized the identity of rebellious slaves, soldiers, and chieftains, to account for origin, occupation, ethnicity, status, gender, and color; and they have speculated about the goals of the insurgents (since most slave plots were betrayed or preempted and most slave insurrections were crushed within a day or two of their outbreak, scholars have had to speculate).[16]

By definition, slaves lived tenuous, vulnerable lives. Sometimes they did what they wanted to do; most of the time they did what they had to do. Although Plato's ideal slave eluded masters like the will-o'-the-wisp, they did wield a monopoly of force that when applied on a plantation in a closely managed, tightly supervised system of gang labor typically yielded a handsome return on investment. Adam Smith in *Wealth of Nations* delighted subsequent generations of antislavery advocates by pronouncing the labor of slaves to be "the dearest of any," a costly relation rooted in the "pride of man" and his "love to domineer." But in a neglected passage in the very same section on agriculture Smith also observed without a trace of explanation that profits on British West Indian slave-based sugar plantations were "generally much greater than those of any other cultivation that is known either in Europe or America."[17] That said, the slaves' accommodation to gang labor or any other imposition by the master neither implies acceptance of slavery nor denies resistance to it. That privileged slaves—drivers, artisans, preachers, domestics—led many of the largest slave insurrections in the history of the Americas speaks to the point.

Insurrections in the United States or what became the United States broke out less frequently and with a generally lesser magnitude than those in Brazil, Cuba, or Jamaica. But insurrections anywhere revealed powerfully the tension between freedom and order and the universality of resistance to enslavement. In colonial South Carolina, for example, the Stono Rebellion, the largest slave revolt in the history of the colonial British North American mainland, erupted in a slave society burgeoning under the impetus of rice cultivation. The revolt involved up to one hundred slaves, some of whom had already converted to a syncretic form of Kongolese Catholicism years before their enslavement in West-Central Africa. Inspired by a thirst for religious and social freedom, the rebels attempted to reach St Augustine, in slaveholding Spanish Florida, and claim freedom under a welcoming decree, designed to undermine foreign rivals, from Spanish officials. Although unsuccessful, the Stono rebels nevertheless highlighted the determination of the enslaved to enjoy a particularist kind of liberty, the freedom from forced labor that they experienced on a daily basis in South Carolina.[18]

Resistance to slavery as a social system, a historically specific phenomenon, registered a qualitative leap, a crossing of a threshold, in the patterns of slave resistance. However much particularistic grievances mobilized the mass of Saint-Domingue's slaves, African and creole, to pick up the sword against their masters in the colony's sugar heartland during the summer of 1791, the revolution that created Haiti, a modern black nation-state, bore witness to an age of democratic revolution. Inflammatory ideas about the universal rights of Man circulated in transatlantic trading networks like combustible freight. In this "age of possibilism," to borrow the historian Robert Darnton's telling term for this period, the adoption by a former slave like Toussaint Louverture of the word "citizen" to prefix his name or the use by one of his literate lieutenants of stationery embossed with the words "liberté, égalité, fraternité" spoke not just to resistance to enslavement, a fact of life wherever slavery existed, but to a historically specific crusade against the system of slavery itself: something wrong for anyone, anywhere.[19]

Supporters of plantation slavery, on their part, persistently argued in their defense that some of the most impressive civilizations of the past, notably Greece and Rome, had rested on mass enslavement. Glimmers of the positive-good argument could be seen in the eighteenth-century transatlantic world, decades before antebellum southern thinkers in the United States articulated a full-blown proslavery argument. Slaveholders throughout the Americas could draw on ample pre-nineteenth-century Western precedent.[20] "The idea that there is something wrong with [slavery]," observes Orlando Patterson, "is one of the peculiar products of Enlightenment rationalism."[21] But the specific nature of the tension between bondage and freedom has challenged the best historical minds. Christianity remained largely indifferent to slavery for nearly two millennia or at best had a modest ameliorating influence. Why beginning in the eighteenth century did certain evangelical Protestant denominations rise to fore and begin to understand the institution as not just an evil but a sin? How did religious influences conjoin with Enlightenment rationalism and other secular modes of thinking to animate deadly criticism of such an ancient and pervasive institution? Why was slavery evermore an affront to liberty, progress, democracy, and civilization?

The Quakers deserve pride of place as the first religious denomination to come out systematically against the institution. The seeds of abolitionist immediatism, like the seeds of the positive-good proslavery argument, began to germinate long before the United States Civil War. Wrestling with the problem of slavery in a letter to other Friends in 1767, a rather nondescript Pennsylvania Quaker named Thomas Nicholson nicely encapsulated for posterity four lines of attack that would be exploited under changing political circumstances with different emphases by future generations of emancipationists throughout the Americas: First, Nicholson believed that the slave trade and slavery were "wicked and abominable" practices "contrary to the natural Rights and Privileges of all mankind, and against the Golden Rule of doing to others as we would be done unto." Second, the relation itself, full of "evils and difficulties," functioned to corrupt the master, nurturing in him "pride, Idleness and a Lording Spirit over our Fellow Creatures" that could easily augment with any provocation into brutalization of the slave. Third, since many acts of enslavement originated in violence—war, kidnapping, brigandage, and the like—slavery appeared to Nicholson to contradict Quaker principles of pacifism and benevolence toward their fellow men. Robbing fellow human beings of "their own free will and Consent" would naturally lead slaves to rise and rebellion, forcing Quakers to violate their own faith in acting to subdue them or in helping others to do so. Fourth, since enslavement by its very nature breeds discontent and resistance to bondage, it impedes the slaves' own salvation; degraded and unhappy slaves do not easily admit "the Principles of true Religion, Piety and Virtue."[22]

Several intellectuals, including Montesquieu, Francis Hutcheson, and especially Adam Smith in *The Theory of Moral Sentiments* (1759), popularized the idea that benevolence and capitalism promoted "sympathy" among distant strangers and, in turn, rendered the idea that slavery and freedom were incompatible. Christian religion, especially its Protestant variant, alerted some intellectuals to the tension between slavery, morality, and emerging notions of individual liberty.[23] But the triumph of the emancipation was by no means certain. Slavery and unfree labor, whether in the Americas or around the world, looked by 1800 and after to most observers as very much part and parcel of the human condition, something that had always existed and always would exist. Britain—itself home to some of the most articulate and strident opponents of slavery—did not begin its emancipation project until the 1830s. By the mid-nineteenth century slavery was still economically robust in places like Peru's Chicama Valley and other agricultural zones scattered about South America. Cuba's slave-based sugar boom continued apace, generating a demand annually for thousands of illegally imported African slaves. Southeastern Brazil was receiving African slaves in record numbers to satisfy the demand for labor on coffee plantations. At least some proslavery southerners in the United States were contemplating reopening the Atlantic slave trade and restoring slavery in certain tropical areas where it had been abolished. Serfdom and various forms of bonded labor abounded in nineteenth-century Europe.[24]

Analysis of emancipation must proceed at several levels. At one level, slaveholding countries traveled different roads to achieve a common end: A slave revolution ended slavery in Saint-Domingue; bloody sectional warfare at the cost of more than 600,000 lives brought slavery to an end in the United States; slavery unraveled in Cuba in the context of a lengthy anti-colonial rebellion against Spanish rule; Great Britain legislated emancipation in its colonies gradually and with compensation to slave owners; France's slaveholding colonies had two emancipations legislated from the metropolis, one in 1794 and one in 1848. At another level, the ending of slavery everywhere in the Americas represented a seismic shift in moral sensibility. If, as T. S. Eliot maintained, "The culture of a people [is] an incarnation of its religion," then the point bears repeating that over millennia all of the world's great religions had given slavery authoritative sanction.[25] By the end of the nineteenth century, however, a momentous breakthrough had occurred in the West. Preachers began preaching the sinfulness of slavery. Political commentators increasingly spoke of freedom as a natural right of man. Economic thinkers labeled slavery inferior to wage labor. Nationalists proclaimed slavery a barbarism and an impediment to human progress and greatness as a civilization. Few scholars now believe that slavery died a market death anywhere in the Americas. Slavery remained a profitable investment at the time it was abolished regardless of country. Thus, the more sophisticated scholarship on emancipation has focused on the interplay of economics, morality, politics, and ideology in explaining why the slave trade and slavery ended in the Americas.[26]

In the United States, some of the most clearly articulated positions on the relationship between liberty and bondage derived from those who formally supported slavery as well as from those who formally did not, and both groups began framing the intellectual coordinates of their argument in the eighteenth century. Eighteenth-century opponents of slavery and their antebellum abolitionist heirs were a diverse group, to be sure. Some were convinced of innate black biological inferiority and championed black "freedom" by advocating their colonization outside of the United States. Others, especially in the antebellum period, embraced a more racially egalitarian philosophy and lobbied for the immediate and unequivocal emancipation of American slaves. Some objected to slavery on moral grounds, some in the context of Enlightenment ideals promoting the importance of individual liberty, still others, especially during and after the 1840s, on the grounds that slavery was economically deleterious to the economic welfare of the United States. But whatever their differences, they tended to agree that slavery was regressive and archaic and should be ended.[27] Slavery did, of course, end in the United States in 1865 thanks to the first of the constitutional amendments passed after the northern triumph in the Civil War. Masters in Cuba and Brazil looking on had no intention of fighting a death struggle for the institution but wanted essentially an ordered, gradual, compensated process that at the end of the day would guarantee a cheap and reliable labor force in a coercive form other than slavery.

During the last four decades or so, the profession of history has witnessed a remarkable outpouring of scholarship on slavery, remarkable not only in quantity but in quality. The field brims with distinguished practitioners, boasts some of the world's best-known historians, and continues to attract some of the most talented younger scholars working today. A glance at award-winning books reflects both the deep pedigree of the field and its continued esteem. By our count, since 1976, sixteen books dealing with some aspect of slavery and freedom in the New World have won the Bancroft Prize. Eight books on the topic have won the Pulitzer Prize for History in the same period. The essays that comprise *The Oxford Handbook of Slavery in the Americas* reflect the enduring importance of the topic and offer various blueprints for its future elaboration. We hope the *Handbook* will serve as a source consulted by the next generation of historians working on the history of slavery and by teachers who must deal in their classrooms with a complex subject that has a painful legacy and defies easy generalization.

In initiating the project, we handed our contributors an impossible assignment: In about 8,000 words describe in the richest possible terms the key historical and historiographical issues related to the assigned topic with an eye also to playing Sherpa in the field by guiding readers to fruitful areas of future inquiry. In their essays, some contributors leaned more toward the historiographical; other contributors leaned more toward the historical. While each topic has its riches, not all historical and historiographical traditions have equal wealth. Instead of imposing a rigid set of guidelines on our contributors, we preferred to allow their creative juices to flow. In an effort to reflect the scope, depth, breadth, and trajectory of old and new work on slavery in the Americas, we have divided the *Handbook* into two parts with an epilogue: Part I focuses on slavery in specific locations. Part II focuses on themes, methods, and sources in the study of slavery. The epilogue looks at the aftermath of slavery and its legacy in a number of post-emancipation societies.[28]

We have enlisted some of the most distinguished historians in the field and attracted some of the best young talent to write the essays. While obviously and necessarily indebted to the foundational works of the 1960s and 1970s, current writing on the history of slavery and forms of unfree labor in the Americas has taken decidedly original, new, often ingenious turns. The *Handbook* seeks to explain the enduring importance of the earlier historiography, identify current trends and developments, and offer suggestive but informed commentary on future developments in the field. A younger generation of scholars has shown a healthy respect for that tradition while also posing new, often interdisciplinary, and theoretically informed questions concerning, for example, the nature and definition of slave resistance throughout the New World, evolving meanings of gender and race under slavery, the complicated nature of class formation in unfree societies, the elaboration of proslavery and antislavery ideologies, the origins and subsequent elaboration of race-based slavery, and mechanisms of emancipation, to identify just a few key developments. In other words, each essay and author, in his or her own way and with varying degrees of emphasis, attempts to trace the historiographical genealogy of their subject while, at the same time, remaining sensitive to the preeminent importance of historical context.

In scope, scale, and organization, the *Handbook* attempts to detail sensitively with historiographical trends and to map out future trajectories within the pages of a single (if large) volume. We make no claim to utter comprehensiveness. Like Thomas R. R. Cobb and José Antonio Saco, we find any attempt to write the American side of the story, much less the global history of slavery, humbling. But we believe that the *Handbook* offers good coverage and thoroughness and will contribute to further advances in the field.

NOTES

1. Thomas R. R. Cobb, *An Inquiry into the Law of Negro Slavery in the United States of America. To Which Is Prefixed, An Historical Sketch of Slavery* (Philadelphia, 1858), pp. xxxv–xxxvi.
2. José Antonio Saco, *Historia de la esclavitud desde los tiempos más remotos hasta nuestros días*, 6 vols. (2nd edn. Havana, 1936–45), i. 5–6 (Paquette's translation). The first three volumes of the first edition were published in Paris from 1875 to 1877.
3. The comparative calculations and many others can be readily performed by consulting "The Trans-Atlantic Slave Trade Database," http://slavevoyages.org/tast/index.faces put together over the last several decades by a team of specialists headed by David Eltis of Emory University.
4. Finley and Patterson, in a sense, are probably the most notable twentieth-century heirs of the global project undertaken by Cobb and Saco. See, for example, M. I. Finley, "Slavery," in David L. Sills (ed.), *International Encyclopedia of the Social Sciences*, 17 vols. (New York, 1968), xiv. 307–13; M. I. Finley, *Ancient Slavery and Modern Ideology* (New York, 1980); Orlando Patterson, *Slavery and Social Death: A Comparative Study* (Cambridge, 1982); Orlando Patterson, *Freedom*, i: *Freedom in the Making of Western Culture* (New York, 1991).
5. For a thick compendium of primary and secondary sources that provide insight into these questions from a hemispheric and global perspective, see Stanley Engerman, Seymour Drescher, and Robert Paquette (eds.), *Slavery* (Oxford, 2001).

6. On the mixed opinion about filibustering in the pre-Civil War South, see Elizabeth Fox-Genovese and Eugene D. Genovese, *Slavery in White and Black: Class and Race in the Southern Slaveholders' New World Order* (Cambridge, 2005), 221–3; and William W. Freehling, *The Road to Disunion*, ii: *Secessionists Triumphant, 1854–1861* (New York, 2007), 145–67.

7. Thomas Hobbes, *Leviathan, or The Matter, Forme, & Power of a Common-wealth Ecclesiastical and Civil* (London, 1651), 95.

8. Philip Curtin makes this point in *The Rise and Fall of the Plantation Complex: Essays in Atlantic History* (Cambridge, 1990), 160. During the slave revolution, mulatto and white slaveholders in battling each other made the mistake of arming their slaves.

9. Edmund Burke, *Burke's Speech on Conciliation with America*, ed. Hammond Lamont (Boston, 1897), 22.

10. *The Digest of Justinian*, ed. Theodor Mommsen, Paul Krueger, and Alan Watson, 4 vols. (Philadelphia, 1985), i. 16.

11. Patterson, *Freedom*, 321, 405.

12. The literature on urban slavery and American port cities within the transatlantic plantation complex is large and growing. See, e.g., Frederick P. Bowser, *The African Slave in Colonial Peru, 1524–1560* (Stanford, Calif., 1974); Thomas N. Ingersoll, *Mammon and Manon in Early New Orleans: The First Slave Society in the Deep South* (Knoxville, Tenn., 1999); Claudia D. Goldin, *Urban Slavery in the American South* (Chicago, 1976); Richard C. Wade, *Slavery in the Cities: The South 1820–1860* (New York, 1964); Mary Karasch, *Slave Life in Rio de Janeiro, 1808–1850* (Princeton, 1987); Franklin W. Knight and Peggy Liss (eds.), *Atlantic Port Cities: Economy, Culture, and Society in the Atlantic World, 1650–1850* (Knoxville, Tenn., 1991); Anne Pérotin-Dumon, *La Ville aux Iles, la ville dans l'île: Basse-Terre et Pointe-à-Pitre, Guadeloupe, 1650–1820* (Paris, 2000).

13. Ira Berlin, *Many Thousands Gone: The First Two Centuries of Slavery in North America* (Cambridge, 1998), 60–1, 369–70. For ethnic backgrounds of American slaves, see Gwendolyn Midlo Hall, *Slavery and African Ethnicities in the Americas* (Chapel Hill, NC, 2005); Linda M. Heywood and John K. Thornton, *Central Africans, Atlantic Creoles, and the Foundation of the Americas, 1585–1660* (New York, 2007). For evidence suggesting that new, albeit highly attenuated, cultural relationships were formed among a variety of Africans from quite different societies even on slave ships and during the Middle Passage, see Stephanie E. Smallwood, *Saltwater Slavery: A Middle Passage from Africa to American Diaspora* (Cambridge, 2007); Marcus Rediker, *The Slave Ship: A Human History* (New York, 2007).

14. Robert Olwell, *Masters, Slaves & Subjects: The Culture of Power in the South Carolina Low Country, 1740–1790* (Ithaca, NY, 1998), 13.

15. Herbert Aptheker, *American Negro Slave Revolts* (New York, 1943), 139.

16. Eugene D. Genovese, *From Rebellion to Revolution: Afro-American Slave Revolts in the Making of the Modern World* (Baton Rouge, La., 1979) remains the only volume analyzing slave plots and insurrections in the Americas within a comparative framework. See also Robert L. Paquette, "Revolts," in Seymour Drescher and Stanley L. Engerman (eds.), *A Historical Guide to World Slavery* (New York, 1998), 334–44.

17. Adam Smith, *An Inquiry into the Nature and Causes of the Wealth of Nations*, 2 vols. (London, 1776), i. 471–2.

18. Mark M. Smith, "Remembering Mary, Shaping Revolt: Reconsidering the Stono Rebellion," *Journal of Southern History*, 67 (3) (August 2001): 513–34; John K. Thornton,

"African Dimensions of the Stono Rebellion," *American Historical Review*, 96 (4) (October 1991): 1101–13; Darold D. Wax, "'The Great Risque We Run': The Aftermath of Slave Rebellion at Stono, South Carolina, 1739–1745," *Journal of Negro History*, 67 (2) (Summer 1982): 136–47; Peter H. Wood, *Black Majority: Negroes in Colonial South Carolina from 1670 through the Stono Rebellion* (New York, 1975).

19. Genovese argues for the Saint-Domingue Revolution as "The Turning Point," in chapter 3 of *From Rebellion to Revolution*, 82–125. David Patrick Geggus has extended the discussion in a number of articles and anthologies. See, e.g., David Barry Gaspar and David Patrick Geggus (eds.), *A Turbulent Time: The French Revolution and the Greater Caribbean* (Bloomington, Ind., 1997); David Patrick Geggus (ed.), *The Impact of the Haitian Revolution in the Atlantic World* (Columbia, SC, 2001); David Patrick Geggus, *Haitian Revolutionary Studies* (Bloomington, Ind., 2002); David Patrick Geggus and Norman Fiering (eds.), *The World of the Haitian Revolution* (Bloomington, Ind., 2009). See also Laurent Dubois, *Avengers of the New World: The Story of the Haitian Revolution* (Cambridge, 2004), which is now the best single-volume treatment in English of the revolution. On the age of "possibilism," see Robert Darnton, "What Was So Revolutionary about the French Revolution," *New York Review of Books*, January 19, 1989, p. 10.

20. Larry E. Tise, *Proslavery: A History of the Defense of Slavery in America 1701–1840* (Athens, Ga., 1987). For a study that stresses the continued economic importance of race-consciousness and slavery to New England, see Joanne Pope Melish, *Disowning Slavery: Gradual Emancipation in New England 1780–1860* (Ithaca, NY, 1998). For a reminder as to the meaning of Western precedent in early encounters with African slaves in colonial Spanish America, see Alonso de Sandoval *De instauranda aethiopum salute: historia de Aethiopia: naturaleça, policia sagrada y profana, costumbres, ritos y cathecismo evangelico de todos les aethiopes* (Madrid, 1647), a must read, especially now that Enriqueta Vila Vilar has ably edited a new Spanish edition *Un tratado sobre la esclavitud* (Madrid, 1987). Sandoval, a Jesuit priest in Cartagena, baptized and otherwise tended to Africans debarking slave ships.

21. Patterson, *Freedom*, 4. See also David Brion Davis, *The Problem of Slavery in Western Culture* (Ithaca, NY, 1966); David Brion Davis, *The Problem of Slavery in the Age of Revolution 1770–1823* (New York, 1999), 46–7, esp. 255–468. See also Edmund Morgan, *American Slavery, American Freedom: The Ordeal of Colonial Virginia* (New York, 1975); David Brion Davis, *Inhuman Bondage: The Rise and Fall of Slavery in the New World* (New York, 2006); David Brion Davis, *Slavery and Human Progress* (New York, 2004).

22. Thomas Nicholson, "To any judicious and enquiring Friend," June 1, 1767, Historical Society of Pennsylvania, Philadelphia, Miscellaneous Collection, Box 11a, file 16.

23. Davis, "The Perils of Doing History by Ahistorical Abstraction," in Thomas Bender (ed.), *The Antislavery Debate: Capitalism and Abolitionism as a Problem in Historical Interpretation* (Berkeley, 1992), 290. See also Elizabeth B. Clark, "Pain, Sympathy, and the Culture of Individual Rights," *Journal of American History*, 82 (September 1995): 463–93. Davis's interpretation has not gone unchallenged, and it is worth noting competing—if sometimes not altogether incompatible—interpretations. See Thomas L. Haskell, "Capitalism and the Origins of Humanitarian Sensibility, Parts I and II," *American Historical Review*, 90 (April and June 1985): 339–61, 457–566; John Ashworth, "The Relationship between Capitalism and Humanitarianism," *American Historical Review*, 92 (October 1987): 813–28. See also David Brion Davis, "Reflections on

Abolitionism and Ideological Hegemony," *American Historical Review*, 92 (October 1987): 797–812.

24. Peter Kolchin, "In Defense of Servitude: American Proslavery and Russian Proserfdom Arguments, 1760–1860," *American Historical Review*, 85 (October 1980): 809–27; Peter Kolchin, *Unfree Labor: American Slavery and Russian Serfdom* (Cambridge, 1987); Shearer Davis Bowman, "Antebellum Planters and Vomarz Junkers in Comparative Perspective," *American Historical Review*, 85 (October 1980): 779–808; Mark M. Smith, "Old South Time in Comparative Perspective," *American Historical Review*, 101 (December 1996): 1432–69; Manuel Moreno Fraginals (ed.), *Between Slavery and Free Labor: The Spanish-Speaking Caribbean in the Nineteenth Century* (Baltimore, 1985); Michael Twaddle, *The Wages of Slavery: From Chattel Slavery to Wage Labour in Africa, the Caribbean and England* (London, 1993); Franklin W. Knight, *Slave Society in Cuba during the Nineteenth Century* (Madison, 1970); Rebecca J. Scott, *Slave Emancipation in Cuba: The Transition to Free Labor, 1860–1899* (Princeton, 1985); Thomas C. Holt, *The Problem of Freedom: Race, Labor, and Politics in Jamaica and Britain, 1832–1938* (Baltimore, 1992); Carl N. Degler, *Neither Black Nor White: Slavery and Race Relations in Brazil and the United States* (Madison, 1986); Rebecca J. Scott, *Abolition of Slavery and the Aftermath of Emancipation in Brazil* (Durham, NC, 1988); Robert Brent Toplin, *Freedom and Prejudice: The Legacy of Slavery in the United States and Brazil* (Westport, Conn., 1981).

25. T. S. Eliot, *Notes Toward the Definition of Culture* (New York, 1949), 32.

26. A good starting point for comparing emancipations would be David Brion Davis, *The Problem of Slavery in the Age of Revolution, 1770–1823* (Ithaca, NY, 1975); Davis, *Inhuman Bondage*, 231–322; Robert William Fogel, *Without Consent or Contract: The Rise and Fall of American Slavery* (New York, 1989), 201–417; Seymour Drescher, "Brazilian Abolition in Comparative Perspective," *Hispanic American Historical Review*, 68 (1988): 429–60; Seymour Drescher, *Abolition: A History of Slavery and Antislavery* (Cambridge, 2009); Rebecca J. Scott, *Degrees of Freedom: Louisiana and Cuba after Slavery* (Cambridge, 2005).

27. On abolitionist movement in the United States, see Ronald G. Walters, *The Antislavery Appeal: American Abolitionism after 1830* (Baltimore, 1977); William Lee Miller, *Arguing about Slavery: John Quincy Adams and the Great Battle in the United States Congress* (New York, 1998); Julie Roy Jeffrey, *The Great Silent Army of Abolitionism: Ordinary Women in the Antislavery Movement* (Chapel Hill, NC, 1998); John Stauffer, *The Black Hearts of Men: Radical Abolitionists and the Transformation of Race* (Cambridge, 2002). Also see Winthrop D. Jordan, *White over Black: American Attitudes toward the Negro 1550–1812* (Chapel Hill, NC, 1968).

28. In addition to the thirty-three essays in the volume, we designed to have two others (on the yeomanry and on the Danish Virgin Islands) as well. But lacking the monopoly of force inherent in slavery, we ultimately could not extract from certain free laborers delivery of the promised goods.

PART I

PLACES

CHAPTER 1

SPANISH HISPANIOLA AND PUERTO RICO

FRANCISCO A. SCARANO

INTRODUCTION

Santo Domingo, the Spanish colony that became the Dominican Republic, and Puerto Rico, its island neighbor to the east, rank as two of the Western hemisphere's most racially mixed societies. In 1792, Puerto Rico's free colored population stood at 41 percent of the total population, more than double that of Cuba. Santo Domingo's free persons of color in 1788 numbered 80,000, more than four times the size of the colony's slave population. Little wonder that Pedro Andrés Pérez Cabral, a Dominican political scientist, has called his native land, albeit with a touch of derision, a "mulatto community" (*comunidad mulata*), and that historian Jay Kinsbruner has described San Juan, Puerto Rico's capital, as possibly the most racially integrated of Latin American cities in the midst of one of the hemisphere's most highly miscegenated populations.[1]

Historical factors related in one way or another to slavery account for the high degree of racial admixture. Both countries experienced enslavement and the Atlantic slave trade intensely in the sixteenth century. This was followed by a long period of economic declension during which slave imports were low and the exploitation of slave labor fell into relative obsolescence. In the seventeenth and early eighteenth centuries, virtual economic autarchy in both colonies allowed for greater rates of miscegenation than in almost every other New World society significantly influenced by the institution of slavery. Toward the latter years of the slave regime, however, these societies experienced racialized enslavement differently. The self-liberation of hundreds of thousands of slaves in the neighboring colony of French Saint-Domingue during the Haitian Revolution (1791–1804) unleashed powerful forces throughout Hispaniola. The hurricane of social revolution eventually toppled slavery in Santo Domingo, the eastern two-thirds of the island, which had been established as the independent country of the Dominican Republic on 1 December 1821, following a revolt led by Lieutenant-Governor José Núñez de Cáceres. Occupation by Haitian forces in February 1822 dashed plans for a union with the Republic of Gran Colombia. At the same time, and in sharp contrast to the Dominican experience, Puerto Rico, like Cuba, underwent a "second slavery"—a cycle of sugar production for export that prompted the smuggling of tens of thousands of additional slaves before the sinister trade in humans effectively ceased around 1850.[2]

The rise, decline, reconstitution, and eventual abolition of slavery frame the closely parallel histories of Santo Domingo and Puerto Rico as Afro-American societies. Slavery lasted approximately 325 years in Santo Domingo before it ended in 1822. It survived 375 years in Puerto Rico, until a Spanish emancipation decree passed in 1873 and the last of the slaves gained freedom three years later. In the 1600s and 1700s, when the slaveholding societies of the British, French, and Dutch in the Caribbean were booming as sugar-and-slavery complexes, Santo Domingo and Puerto Rico underwent an economic and demographic contraction that resulted in the depletion of their slave labor force and a relaxation of racial barriers. Those boundaries would be drawn more boldly, and the specter of intensifying racial discrimination augmented, however, at a later time; in Santo Domingo by the slave revolution in Haiti in the late eighteenth century and in Puerto Rico by the renewal of the African slave trade in the first half of the nineteenth. Yet, neither of these colonies would again experience the heavy dependence on slave labor they had witnessed in the decades after effective Spanish colonization.

Socio-historical factors specific to each society favored miscegenation and Afro-descended majorities in the long run. In Santo Domingo, for example, the French and Haitian occupations of 1802–9 and 1822–44, respectively, resulted in greater interaction with Haitians, many of them former slaves, and in the emigration of members of the white elite. In Puerto Rico in the nineteenth and twentieth centuries, high rates of internal labor migration fostered intermixing. Capitalist forces pulling Puerto Rico into Atlantic circuits of trade and investment fostered large-scale immigration of Africans, Europeans, and other Caribbeans in the 1800s. Such events reinforced the early colonial patterns favoring racial intermixing, a process some have called *mulatización* (mulattoization). Thus, while the practice of enslavement may not have pervaded Dominican and Puerto Rican societies as it did in neighboring Cuba or the non-Hispanic islands, enslavement *plus* the immigrant flows it entailed left a profound demographic and cultural imprint on the former. The implications of this history for the development of contested constructions of racial and national identities remain strong to this day. A recurring theme in the literature on the slave systems of both Santo Domingo and Puerto Rico from the institution's early sixteenth-century origins to its demise in the 1870s is that national mythologies peculiar to the two nations, especially those that reflect the intersection of race and racial identities with concepts of nationhood, have shaped our views of important social and cultural processes that attended the institution of slavery. Many aspects of slavery covered thoroughly for other Caribbean contexts—especially for Cuba and the British West Indies—remain unexplored or underexplored for Santo Domingo and Puerto Rico.

HISTORIOGRAPHICAL AND POLITICAL CONTEXTS

By the 1970s, the notion that slavery in Spanish America had been accidental or perhaps absent-minded, once a historical cliché, was largely discredited. This view had owed some of its credibility to Spain's marginal presence in Africa as a slave trading country for most of the duration of the slave trade. In *Slave and Citizen: The Negro in the Americas* (1946), Frank Tannenbaum, a leading historian of Latin America in the United States, had bolstered its scholarly credentials when he suggested, in a sweeping review of how slaves were treated in the Americas, that powerful legal and church precepts and traditions in the Iberian-American colonies had essentially resulted in a milder, less brutal form of enslavement there.[3] By the 1960s, however, many historians had begun to criticize Tannenbaum for his emphasis on normative and institutional factors, rather than on what actually happened on the ground as labor conditions evolved. The shift away from idealism to an interpretation inflected by a materialist skepticism was especially evident in Cuba, where a number of monographs on slavery—none more important than Manuel Moreno Fraginals's 1964 study *El ingenio*, a Marxist interpretation of Cuba's nineteenth-century sugar boom—radically changed the terms of the debate.[4] Moreno Fraginals argued that cultural and institutional restraints on the practices of enslavement failed to derail the economic logic of an increasingly capitalistic system of slave exploitation. In raising objections to the Tannenbaum thesis, he built upon a strong current of twentieth-century historiography on Cuba, which included important contributions from such scholars as Fernando Ortiz, Ramiro Guerra y Sánchez, Raúl Cepero Bonilla, and Julio LeRiverend Brusone.[5]

The materialist turn in scholarship about Cuba, the Caribbean's largest and most important slave society in the nineteenth century, inevitably influenced the manner in which historians of the other two Spanish colonies, Santo Domingo and Puerto Rico, approached the slave past there. The connection between what transpired in Cuban scholarship, inspired after 1959 by the triumph of a socialist revolution, and what ultimately happened in Cuba's "sister" nations was at once direct and indirect, simple and complex. Among Dominican and Puerto Rican scholars who were inspired by the Cuban Revolution, some turned their attention to economic and social history for political and ideological reasons; the past, after all, was like a high-powered lens focused on injustices not yet redressed. Of those historians, a few consciously followed the examples of Moreno Fraginals and other scholars of Cuban slavery, such as the historians Franklin W. Knight and Juan Pérez de la Riva and the anthropologist Verena Stolcke.[6] The mere emulation of Cuban scholars was not the only factor accounting for the historical revisionism of the late 1960s and after. Worldwide anti-colonial and civil rights movements and other forms of international or transnational turmoil influenced and inspired historians of the Caribbean region. Even processes home-grown in the Caribbean, like the Cuban Revolution, resonated internationally. Caribbean intellectuals, especially on the left, reacted with a renewed sense of purpose and mission. A sense of protagonism on a worldwide scale, not experienced since the emancipation struggles of the previous century, re-energized the writing of history. Marxism and its dialectical method of historical materialism became more alluring to intellectuals as a conceptual framework for investigating the past, not necessarily as part of a political allegiance to any particular socialist project but as a way to analyze specific historical problems, such as the interconnected history of slavery and sugar plantations. The turn toward economic and social history may also be explained by national circumstances and events: in the Dominican Republic, the intellectual revival that accompanied the end of Rafael L. Trujillo's thirty-one-year dictatorship (1930–61), and in Puerto Rico, the loss of faith after the mid-1960s in Governor Luis Muñoz Marín's populist program.

THE "THIRD ROOT"[7]—OR PERHAPS THE FIRST

With regard to slavery and race, perhaps none of the Spanish Caribbean's national historical literatures underwent as much revision in the wake of Moreno Fraginals's *El ingenio* as did colonial Santo Domingo's. Political circumstances dictated an intellectual renewal, which the historical literature mirrored. Under Trujillo's repressive regime, Dominican intellectuals resisted discussing the slave past other than to celebrate the alleged "mildness" with which slaves were treated in the colonial period. Inspired by Tannenbaum's thesis of a more benign slave regime under Catholic constraints and Iberian legal precepts, the few historians who undertook any serious consideration of slavery in Hispaniola usually contrasted the milder character of Dominican master–slave relations to the severe exploitation of slaves in French Saint-Domingue on the western third of the island. Tannenbaum's thesis resonated with two of the prevalent themes of Trujillo's dictatorship: Hispanophilia and anti-Haitianism.[8] Trujillo and the intellectuals who justified his regime advanced the notion that colonial Santo Domingo had stood as a beacon of Hispanic civilization and Catholicism in the New World. The celebration of the Dominicans' Hispanic roots drew psychological strength from the search by national elites for a historical narrative that would not only demonstrate racial harmony and consensus across time (in sharp contrast to the revolutionary violence that had given birth to Haiti), but also gave historical credence to the notion that Dominican society had been undergoing a *whitening* process across time.[9] Standard bearers, in their self-image, of white, Catholic *hispanismo* in the Americas, many Dominicans believed their society to be the racially mixed product of a consensual colonialism, and the Dominican people the lighter-colored offspring of a peaceful encounter between superior white bodies and inferior black ones. The resulting ("whitened") population would have cast off its "inferior" (black) traits as it acquired "superior" (white) ones.[10]

The racial dogma of the *trujillato*, as Trujillo's regime was known, became so deeply etched in Dominican intellectuals' consciousness—with the assistance of a highly repressive state machinery—that they rarely questioned the dictatorship's historical narrative. Even *mestizaje* or race-mixing and its phenotypic results were topics considered off limits by intellectuals aligned with the dictatorship's knowledge agenda. Magnus Mörner's 1962 assessment of the scholarship on Dominican *mestizaje* illustrates this point well. "With regard to the Dominican Republic," he noted from the relative bibliographic isolation of Sweden, "it appears that no studies have yet been published on this fundamental aspect in the history of the Dominican people."[11]

Avoidance and distortion of topics associated with the colonial racial regime also characterized scholarship at the end of the *trujillato*. In 1967, six years after Trujillo's assassination, Carlos Larrazabal Blanco published *Los negros y la esclavitud en Santo Domingo*, a general history of slavery in colonial Santo Domingo that still reflected the passing dogma. In assessing human interactions during slavery, Larrazabal Blanco concluded,

Relations between masters and slaves that obtained solely from authority and hierarchy, plain human relations, and social relations differed in Spanish Santo Domingo from those in French Saint-Domingue. This is why in the former there was a melding and evolution toward a common purpose. On the French side, however, there was profound discord and violent altercation: slaves rose up against their masters, dominating and defeating them. Moreau de Saint-Mery refers to the "mild" regimen of slave control in Spanish Santo Domingo; that laws which worked against the slaves were frequently overlooked while those that favored them were strictly observed. Personal relations were likewise "mild." Truly treated in a Christian way, slaves came to be like members of the families to which they belonged.[12]

This disingenuous view of slavery prevailed for decades among Dominican historians, many of them members of the country's prestigious Dominican Academy of History (Academia Dominicana de la Historia). Indeed, so embossed in the dominant discourse had this view become that the topic itself rarely appeared in work published in *Clío*, the Academy's official journal. Similarly, the *Boletín del Archivo General de la Nación*, the parallel journal from the National Archives, first published in 1938, had almost nothing to say about slavery.

A decade would pass after the publication of Larrazabal Blanco's book on Dominican slavery before a new generation of historians mounted a challenge to the prevailing orthodoxy. In a 1976 anthology about eighteenth-century Santo Domingo, Rubén Silié confronted the issue directly. The different demographic performance of the slaves on both sides of the French–Spanish border of Hispaniola (i.e., slaves of the French lived shorter lives and emigrated to the Spanish side whenever possible), he claimed, had nothing to do with the superior "morality" with which slaves were allegedly treated on the Spanish side. Instead, economic considerations predominated. On the French side, where slaves were more numerous and cheaper, masters sought to exploit them as much as possible in as short a time as possible. On the less developed Spanish side, however, where slaves were dearer and labor exactions less intense on account of the predominant cattle-grazing economy, masters recognized the advantage of keeping their slaves alive as long as possible and reproducing them naturally.[13]

While Silié and other scholars, like Frank Moya Pons, one of the country's most celebrated historians, had suggested since the early 1970s a revisionist interpretation of the colony's slave past, the turning point in Dominican slavery scholarship came with Carlos Esteban Deive's two-volume *La esclavitud del negro en Santo Domingo(1492–1844)*, published in 1980.[14] Deive's patient investigation into published primary sources as well as archival material in the Dominican Republic, Spain, and Cuba countered the *trujillista* narrative and its whitening prejudice. A historian and ethnologist, Deive described the history of enslavement in Santo Domingo as a struggle over labor power, with the masters seeking to extract as much of it as possible from their chattels, and they, in turn, resisting the masters' effort at every turn. This was a mild assertion that nonetheless would have unsettled the tightly controlled environment of Trujillo's Dominican Republic. Like Cuba's Moreno Fraginals some years before, Deive placed economic considerations above moral ones in determining the character of the slave regime. He described social relations in the colony as fraught with conflict and violence. Regarding relations between colonial poverty and enslavement, he inverted the usual theorem that poverty had mitigated the master–slave bond to insist that "the colony's poverty led masters to exploit their day-laborer slaves (*esclavos jornaleros*), especially females, to the maximum."[15] On the critical issue of the Church's role in "humanizing" the practices of control and punishment, Deive's words sounded skeptical and, for many in the Dominican Republic, almost subversive:

If the Church accepted African slavery it was allegedly because it [the Church] needed to rescue him [the slave] from pagan darkness and to elevate him through baptism to the category of a human being. The slave's body was put in chains in order to offer him, as a reward, a soul that could be saved. In this way the white man obtained as much forced labor as he could get, or even wanted, because in accepting the Church's preachings, he accepted the obligation of collaborating with it in the education of his chattel. This obligation was, however, not more than a declaration of intent. The facts would demonstrate that, with only a few exceptions, religious education mattered nil to the master.[16]

In this unsentimental view of the Catholic Church's role in buttressing slavery, Deive had garnered some company in the Dominican Republic, for by the 1980s scholarship on colonial Santo Domingo, inspired by developments in revolutionary Cuba, had reached consensus on the primacy of economic factors in slave treatment and on the complicity of the Church in slave exploitation, especially in times of high labor demand.[17]

ENSLAVED AFRICANS: COLONIAL SANTO DOMINGO'S ESSENTIAL WORKFORCE

Several Dominican historians working from the 1970s onward joined Deive in discrediting the *trujillista* narrative. They revisited the Spanish colonial period to uncover the foundations of Dominican society, successfully applying theories and methods from economics and the social sciences. In several major studies on the colonial period, Frank Moya Pons examined the labor systems that undergirded the gold, sugar, and cattle economies of the Spanish period. Inevitably, he revisited slavery and the lives of the enslaved, although these themes were not his sole focus.[18] In *La dominación haitiana, 1822–1844* (1972), a study of Haitian President Jean-Pierre Boyer's twenty-two-year occupation of the eastern portion of Hispaniola, he dealt soberly with the Haitians' 1822 decree that abolished slavery in the fleeting Dominican nation-state, just recently taken over by its neighbor to the west. The book also analyzed the consequences of the emancipation decree, especially in the area of landholding. In this book and in a succeeding conference essay, Moya Pons skillfully wove a narrative of increasing elite discomfort with and opposition to Haitian rule with the jolting suggestion that many among the Dominican masses, especially those who descended from slaves, had actually opened their arms to Haitian rule.[19] Support for Haitian rule was strong, not only among freedpeople, but also among the previously free who benefited from laws redistributing the lands confiscated from the Church and exiled landowners. It was particularly so among the more established peasant groups, like the tobacco growers of the Cibao valley, for whom the Haitian regime's policies of rationalizing landholding (via cadastral surveys and systematic redistribution schemes) and opening markets for the peasants' produce proved especially beneficial.

Several Marxist-inspired historians emerged alongside Moya Pons in the 1980s to challenge the prevailing orthodoxy about the relative insignificance or marginality of Dominican slavery. Genaro Rodríguez Morel, for example, a long-time resident of Seville, Spain, spent years mining the city's rich colonial archives for documentation on sixteenth-century Santo Domingo and other early Spanish Caribbean settlements. Perhaps best known for his carefully transcribed documents of the appeals tribunal (*Real Audiencia*), city council (*cabildo*), and ecclesiastical council of the bishopric (*cabildo ecclesiástico*), all based in the capital city of Santo Domingo, Rodríguez Morel published, beginning in the 1990s, a host of suggestive articles and book chapters on the economic and social history of the mining and sugar economies of sixteenth-century Hispaniola and of neighboring Puerto Rico.[20] The culmination of these efforts was his 2009 unpublished doctoral dissertation on Hispaniola's sixteenth-century sugar plantation system.[21] His research revealed that enslaved Africans formed the backbone of the colonial labor force much earlier than other historians had thought. Hispaniola's sugar plantations during the middle decades of the sixteenth century possessed a significantly larger slave population than standard accounts had indicated. The colony's enslaved Africans numbered some 15,000 in the 1540s and 25,000 or more by mid-century, while the European population numbered fewer than 5,000.[22] Under these conditions, the threat of slave rebellion was a constant challenge for the Spanish colonists and their allies, one they had to meet often and at a very high cost.

In collaboration with Roberto Cassá, Rodríguez Morel published in 1993 a forceful reinterpretation of slave resistance in Santo Domingo by bringing to light new documentation on a spate of sixteenth-century slave insurrections, some of which combined Indian and African protagonists.[23] Southeastern Hispaniola near the city of Santo Domingo gave rise in 1521, for example, to one of the hemisphere's earliest revolts of African slaves, an ethnic rebellion of enslaved Wolofs who erupted on a plantation named Nueva Isabela owned by Diego Columbus, Christopher Columbus' eldest son. According to Cassá and Rodríguez Morel, previous historians had seriously neglected multiple expressions of class solidarity and consciousness manifest in the documentary record on these rebellions. These earliest instances of rebellion in the hemisphere exhibited what Eugene Genovese has called a "restorationist" purpose. Rather than trying to undermine Spanish authority on the island, as officials always feared they might, the rebels "tried to build a sociocultural identity based on the behavioral patterns of the tribal groups to which they belonged."[24] This identity, however, was also predicated on practices learned on Hispaniola's sugar estates and cattle-grazing open ranches (*hatos*). For example, rebels took advantage of horseback-riding skills and their deft use of iron spears, leather vests, and guns, whose proper deployment in warfare they had learned while working as farmhands in a frontier environment. Slaves and maroons learned to challenge enslavement so well that Hispaniola became, especially after about 1540, a veritable war zone, a colony always on the brink of some internal commotion. To defend Spanish settlements from such attacks, the Crown devoted a fixed budget to internal security and maintained a standing militia. By the latter decades of the century and the early 1600s, when the island's economy collapsed and the Spanish population, especially in the northern and western fringes, was forced to move closer to the capital city of Santo Domingo, maroons filled many of the spaces abandoned by the Spanish *vecinos* (citizens). Undoubtedly, the epoch of widespread marronage that followed was a direct result of the resistance to slavery carried out during the boom decades of the plantation system in the sixteenth century.

Historians of Santo Domingo have also made strides recently in interpreting other facets of the slaves' social history. Celsa Albert Batista's *Mujer y esclavitud en Santo Domingo* (1990) speaks to the growing importance of gender and the experience of female slaves in bondage.[25] Like other recent studies of slave women elsewhere in the Caribbean, Albert Batista's book presents a global picture of women's experiences in slavery. Stories of arrival, labor, violence, love, resistance, and cultural expressions occupy discrete chapters. Although successful in presenting a previously neglected side of the story of enslavement, this narrative comes at the expense, perhaps, of detail and nuance. "Normal" stories attract more attention, for obvious reason, than the lives and circumstances of exceptional women. In the study of the slave experience, however, we have learned that contexts in which slave women lived and struggled as women are as valuable to analyze as those in which they acted as instruments of production. Enslaved women lived enmeshed in a pyramidal grid of power in which their status and conditions were mutually constituted by other attributes, such as skin color, ethnicity, and even class. Still, while not accounting for these factors, Albert Batista's fresh scholarship on colonial Santo Domingo represented a vital first step toward a more subtle understanding of gender ascriptions as part of a larger system of race-based, class-based, and ethnic-based exploitation.

SLAVERY IN PUERTO RICO'S NEW HISTORY

While the historiographic renewal was in full swing in the Dominican Republic, in nearby Puerto Rico a revisionist tide was also sweeping the country. Especially critical for this intellectual renewal was a period in the early 1970s when Puerto

Ricans were preparing to commemorate the emancipation centennial in 1973.[26] At the start of this period, Luis M. Díaz Soler's erudite general history of Puerto Rican slavery, first published in 1953 and reissued by the University of Puerto Rico Press in 1970, still dominated the field.[27] Díaz Soler had applied to Puerto Rico's almost four-century experience with enslavement many of the same insights that Tannenbaum had spelled out in *Slave and Citizen*, viewing Spanish law and Catholic doctrine as effective barriers against excesses and abuses seen elsewhere. The *Historia* recognized that there had been two main cycles of enslavement, one in the sixteenth century and the other in the nineteenth. In between, the long pause in slavery's importance as an economic and social institution allegedly softened the brutality of the experience for its victims. Díaz Soler's book was a more scholarly treatise than Larrazabal Blanco's on Santo Domingo, but like the latter, it made the centuries of imperial isolation and economic autarchy the distinguishing feature of a slave regime believed to have been "milder" than most others and thus more conducive to cordial interracial relations and miscegenation.

By the early 1970s, scholars began to express skepticism about these views. The doubters included members of an older generation of historians who now recognized the importance of economic contexts for a more nuanced interpretation of the slave experience. Arturo Morales Carrión was the key person in this cohort. A leading Puerto Rican historian and educator who served as John F. Kennedy's Deputy Assistant Secretary of State for Inter-American Affairs, he used a National Endowment for the Humanities grant to lead a team of researchers in constructing a documentary collection that would highlight the economic, social, legal, and cultural processes of emancipation. This research made clear that the Tannenbaum-inspired narrative of benign slavery embraced by Díaz Soler needed considerable revision. The resulting two-volume documentary collection, *El proceso abolicionista en Puerto Rico* (1974), demonstrated the need to reconsider the re-emergence of plantation slavery in the nineteenth century, when Puerto Rico followed Cuba's lead in relying on gangs of tightly supervised slaves to efficiently produce sugar for world markets.[28] The collected documents portrayed the enslaved workers not only as objects of property, to be bought and sold and used for long hours of intense, regular labor, but as people who protested their conditions, fled westward to Haiti (a country that from 1822 to 1844 encompassed Spanish-speaking Santo Domingo) in small vessels under cover of darkness, rebelled openly against abusive masters and against the system of slavery itself in more revolutionary times (e.g., in 1848, when neighboring slaves in the French colonies of Guadeloupe and Martinique and in the Danish colony of St Croix engaged in a "riotous but surprisingly bloodless" rebellion).[29] When emancipation finally arrived in 1873, it came with strings. Former slaves found employment as apprentices, but they used their new-found spatial mobility to reconstruct ties with children, parents, and siblings from whom they had been separated under slavery.[30]

Morales Carrión's collection and the academic conferences held in commemoration of the centennial set the critical tone that would infuse much of the revisionist scholarship, which, collectively known as Puerto Rico's New History, would yield dividends over the next decade.[31] Salient themes included many that were at the forefront of the international literature on slavery at the time: the profitability and productivity of slavery, marronage, rebellion, and the demography of slave populations, for example.[32] The question of the comparative profitability and productivity of export agriculture was at the heart of the debate about Puerto Rican slavery, for many scholars assumed, following Díaz Soler, that Puerto Rican producers could not compete with other Caribbean agriculturalists, especially the Cubans, and hence were unlikely to rely on the expensive labor of imported Africans. By the same token, historians were disinclined to compare the Puerto Rican experiences of enslavement, resistance, and emancipation with those in surrounding colonies, believing, as Díaz Soler had framed the issue, that on the Spanish island the experience of enslavement had been attenuated by the institution's low significance as a labor system.

Several doctoral dissertations submitted to United States universities in the late 1970s and early 1980s probed these themes on the basis of new types of documents—notarial records, local correspondence and trial records on slave conspiracies, population censuses, official reports on local economic conditions, and others—available for the first time when the Archivo General de Puerto Rico opened in 1973. Guillermo Baralt's work on slave rebelliousness, for instance, underscored the volatile nature of slave control in the nineteenth century. While the standard accounts had treated slave conspiracies and rebellions during the nineteenth-century apogee of the plantation system as anomalies in an otherwise peaceful history of master–slave relations, Baralt argued differently. Slaves resisted openly and often, he wrote, and the methods of struggle they selected had much to do with local demographic, economic, and political conditions as well as with Caribbean geopolitics. Baralt counted twenty-two slave conspiracies that shook the island between 1795 and 1848, of which five alone occurred during the apogee of the slave trade during the governorship of Miguel de la Torre (1823–37). The most serious of the conspiracies took place in Bayamón (1821), Ponce (1826 and 1848), and other districts where newly imported slaves were concentrated, mostly on sugar plantations. Eventually, Baralt argued, the period of open conspiracies and revolts subsided after the ending of the slave trade from Africa around mid-century. But even in the latter years of the regime, slaves resisted their oppression actively and violently. During the remaining quarter century of the slave regime, however, this resistance took on a less collective character, with subversions of the established order occurring more commonly as individual acts against the excesses of owners and overseers.[33]

José Curet, for his part, opened new vistas on the economic and political processes of emancipation.[34] The main question underlying his doctoral dissertation was drawn from the classic issue posed for Cuba by Manuel Moreno Fraginals: to what extent was slave emancipation a result of declining profitability of the slave regime? Curet estimated that slave productivity on sugar haciendas in the important Ponce region registered declines during the final decades of slavery. Shifts like these help explain the masters' embrace of emancipation with reparations for the loss of the slaves' value. For Curet, Puerto Rican emancipation in 1873 (extended to 1876 by an apprenticeship system) must therefore be understood in the context of declining profitability and evolving capitalist relations in agriculture, which overtook enslavement as the preferred labor nexus.

The third of the so-called "new historians" of slavery to present an American dissertation on Puerto Rico's slave regime, Francisco A. Scarano, also investigated the leading sugar district of Ponce. He described not only the central role that the Atlantic slave trade and slave labor played in economic growth, but also the importance of the district's embeddedness in regional and Atlantic circuits of capital (both human and physical), labor, and exchange.[35] The story he told of Ponce's transformation into a slave society is uncannily familiar to students of Caribbean economic and social history. When international commodity prices rose as a result of the Haitian Revolution beginning in the 1790s, Ponce was one of several Puerto Rican coastal districts that emerged as thriving sugar producers. Significant importations of enslaved Africans soon followed, and in the 1820s to the 1840s the sugar regions saw a steep rise in the number of enslaved workers. By 1845, out of 4,216 workers on Ponce's 86 sugar estates, 3,460 (82 percent) were enslaved. Similar proportions held in other newer sugar-and-slavery districts, like Guayama and Mayagüez.

The thrust of these studies paralleled the Cuban and Dominican revisions then taking place: that the Puerto Rican slave regime was not governed simply by the legal and moral constraints that Tannenbaum posited for all of Spanish America, but rather was influenced by changing labor demands and market conditions more so than by legal and ecclesiastical traditions. In 1860, Puerto Rico had 41,738 slaves who comprised 7 percent of the total population; in 1862, Cuba had 370,553 slaves who comprised 27 percent of the population. While a smaller slave population and substantial peasant sector might not justify Puerto Rico's designation as a "slave society," that is, as a society in which the master–slave relation decisively shaped the island's politics and culture, slave labor drove sugar production, which was the most dynamic economic sector of the colony until the Puerto Rican coffee boom of the 1880s. Thus, when slaves took flight, conspired to rebel, purchased their freedom, killed a master or an overseer, demanded their customary rights to Sundays off, and accused a particularly abusive master of violating the laws that protected them from such abuse, they struck at the very heart of a prospering plantation economy that had turned both Puerto Rico and Cuba, the nineteenth-century remnants of Spain's once vast empire, into a kind of fulsome milk cow feeding the Spanish state.[36]

Puerto Rico's labor requirements in the nineteenth century took shape within an economic system on the periphery of capitalist financial and commodity markets and under the influence of substantial technological change and innovation. In view of this dynamic process, one could reasonably argue that the island's nineteenth-century plantation cycle, dependent as it was on a revamped form of chattel slavery, describes one of the Western hemisphere's most modern chapters of slave exploitation. On this issue, Moreno Fraginals's Cuban case provides insights about Puerto Rico: The entrepreneurial class of planters that emerged in Puerto Rico (and Cuba) grew into an important agent in the world economy, adopted some of the most advanced technology anywhere, promoted some infrastructural development and scientific and technical advances, and renegotiated the colonial pact with the Spanish metropole under terms that included demands for greater self-government and liberal rights.[37] These entrepreneurs, who set up some of the most efficient mechanisms ever devised to maximize labor efficiency and labor control, turned their backs, however, on international treaties that abolished the slave trade in order to purchase hundreds of thousands of illegally imported slaves. These classes, at once exploitative of their private property in human beings and liberal in their politics within the empire, engaged in processes that left little room for the kind of intimate, paternalistic interaction between masters and slaves that Tannenbaum had hypothesized as the hallmark of the Iberian variant of slavery in the Americas.

Although the tide of revisionist scholarship on slavery in Puerto Rico slowed after 1980, important contributions to the history of Puerto Rican slavery appeared. One of the issues they tackled was the importance of enslaved labor and of African immigrants in general at the beginning of the Spanish colonial period. Nineteenth- and early twentieth-century scholars of the conquest and colonization period had affirmed on the basis of substantial documentary evidence the growing presence of African slaves in the Puerto Rican population after the 1520s or 1530s. The 1530 "census" ordered by Governor Francisco Manuel de Lando rendered a fascinating portrait of the insular population at a crucial moment of transition. Slightly more than two decades after the initial Spanish conquest, there were only 333 Spanish *vecinos* (enfranchised adult Spaniards), 510 Indians distributed as *encomendados* (given to a Spaniard for labor exaction), 1,043 enslaved Indians, and 2,284 enslaved Africans. Whereas the original Indian population may have been around 100,000, the total population had declined sharply to well below one-tenth that number, of whom Africans constituted the largest group.[38]

Because the island lost its earlier prominence as a center of Spanish colonization and gold production shortly after those decades, historians had not paid much attention to the remainder of the sixteenth century, which appeared to some of them as "a blank slate." But sugar cane had arrived in Puerto Rico with the island's conqueror, Juan Ponce de León, and the first sugar mills were established in 1523. In the mid- to late 1500s, slave importations increased markedly in order to satisfy labor demands in agriculture, particularly in the thriving sugar zones. Only

Hispaniola supplied more sugar to Spain than Puerto Rico during the middle third of the sixteenth century. In these years, Puerto Rico imported thousands of enslaved Africans. These workers provided the key labor (but not the only one, as Indians also contributed) to develop some thirteen sugar plantations, most of them located on the northern coast not too far from the port of San Juan. They even boasted a larger average size than the forty or so plantations erected in Hispaniola. According to Elsa Gelpí Baíz, data for seven of Puerto Rico's ingenios in the 1570s shows that the average size of slaveholdings was forty-two—comparable to, if slightly higher than, in the neighboring colony.

Filling a crucial void in the literature about the early colonial period, Gelpí Baíz has richly documented the economic and social dimensions of the sugar economy between 1540 and 1620. Slave importations proved so numerous during this period that in Puerto Rico, as in neighboring Hispaniola, blacks became the overwhelming majority of the island's total population; it is quite likely, as Gelpí Baíz and others have suggested, that the preponderance of Africans in the population noted for 1530 continued throughout the century.[39] Her work complements that of Rodríguez Morel's on the early Spanish Caribbean's sugar economy during the mid-sixteenth-century boom and of Francisco Moscoso on early colonial agriculture. Moscoso revised the pioneering work on the subject by the Spanish historian Juana Gil-Bermejo García. Gelpí Baíz's findings on the depth of the African imprint in early Puerto Rican history accord with those of Jalil Sued Badillo and Ángel López Cantos, in *Puerto Rico negro* (1986), while giving it empirical backing.[40] Their book includes compelling biographical accounts of persons of African descent whose lives and achievements had been largely overlooked by earlier historians; Gelpí Baíz's provides a richly textured narrative of Puerto Rico's agrarian history during the first cycle of sugar's predominance, one that lasted into the first decade of the seventeenth century. "In that world," she concluded, "blacks were [tantamount] to sugar."[41]

Nineteenth-century slavery and emancipation have also been the subject of enlightening new work since 1990. Joseph Carroll Dorsey's 2003 book on the slave traffic into Puerto Rico has filled an important vacuum in our understanding of the slave trade—its sources, dimensions, routes, practices, and cultural consequences. Basing his insights primarily on diplomatic sources, Dorsey asserts that Puerto Rico's nineteenth-century trade was essentially different from and independent of Cuba's, insofar as regional traders (French-, Dutch-, and Danish-based merchants) supplied the plantation districts with enslaved laborers and the captives were from multiple West African ethnicities. Thus, unlike in Cuba, where large shipments brought directly from Africa were the norm and Yoruba speakers predominated, arrivals into Puerto Rico came in smaller groups, aboard smaller vessels, and along a supply chain that almost always involved intermediaries in the Lesser Antilles.[42]

While Dorsey has thrown light on the slave trade, Luis A. Figueroa has worked on a number of important questions regarding the Puerto Rican experience with enslavement and emancipation. The book provides a sweeping account of Guayama (a district along the southern coastal plains) before, during, and after its intense cycle with sugar and slavery. It contains cogent discussions of the debates prompted by the adoption of slavery as a preferred mode of labor exaction in opposition to the enlistment of peasant workers through state coercion. Figueroa's *Sugar, Slavery, and Freedom in Nineteenth-Century Puerto Rico* deepens and enriches the discussion of the multiple ways in which the enslaved workers carved out spaces of autonomy for themselves before and during emancipation, the latter a process that in Puerto Rico took place in 1873 and was followed by a short period (three years) of compulsory contracts. Because Guayama was the quintessential Puerto Rican plantation district, Figueroa's study complements the earlier work of Mariano Negrón and Raúl Mayo Santiago on the slave population of the capital city, San Juan, a set of studies partially based on a statistical analysis of the 1872 slave register.[43]

Analysis of slavery scholarship on Santo Domingo and Puerto Rico between the early 1960s and the present yields four conclusions. First, as economic and social history with a strong Marxist or materialist bent came of age in these countries, students of slavery targeted Tannenbaum's thesis for qualification or outright repudiation. Spanish American slavery, they stressed, made significantly milder by legal traditions and church practices, was applicable only in specific historical circumstances. Economic forces drove the character of slave–master relations; the Catholic Church essentially played a role supportive of the master class and its need to squeeze out as much labor as possible from their slaves.[44] Second, the focus on slavery as a system diverted attention away from slave agency and slave culture, although there were in this period a few important studies, like those of Nistal Moret in Puerto Rico, that probed the slaves' capacity and willfulness to resist bondage and create spaces of freedom whenever possible. Third, the complexities of African ethnicity, slave culture, and the formation of *creole cultures* generated little scholarly interest before the 1980s, notwithstanding the pioneering ethnographic work of, for example, Alonso de Sandoval, a Jesuit priest who ministered to African slaves imported into Cartagena in the seventeenth century, and Fernando Ortiz, a Cuban anthropologist, in the twentieth century.[45] Fourth, concerns over class formation within the slave regime diverted attention away from other kinds of identity such as gender and race. In fact, except for Stolcke's pathbreaking book on race and gender in nineteenth-century Cuba, which dealt with slavery only in passing, the literature of the period remained silent about the manner in which gender and race were mutually constitutive in slave society and how both were also ultimately integral to the process of class formation and to the reproduction of systems of domination. The next generation of scholars would grapple with these themes but not nearly as systematically as would scholars of other parts of the Caribbean. Although Cuban scholarship, particularly Moreno Fraginal's *El ingenio*, profoundly influenced the work of Caribbean historians of the slave economy, Hispanic scholarship on slavery generally during the last quarter century lagged behind that produced for the British Caribbean and for other areas of western European colonialism in the Americas.

A MATERIALIST NARRATIVE MEETS ITS LIMITS

With the growing use of poststructuralist approaches and sensibilities by the current generation of Caribbean historians, the shortcomings of the Hispanic scholarship have become all the more obvious. With its strong materialist bent, "new historians" of both the Dominican Republic and Puerto Rico failed to take into account—or perhaps did not emphasize enough—the roles of culture, gender, political consciousness, and individual agency in structuring communities built around the sugar complex. Moreover, with the notable exception of Fernando Picó's fine-grained books on the *jornaleros* of Utuado and the small coffee farmers of Puerto Rico's interior highlands, the so-called New History contained a Gordian knot: although claiming to write the history of workers, peasants, slaves, and women, "new historians" in fact did so primarily in the idiom of statistics and other forms of aggregate representation, all the while registering the lives of persons in dominant positions on a more individual and first-name basis.[46] The New History limned the life of this or that *gran hacendado* in Ponce or influential merchant in San Juan, and, to be sure, the working class and its leaders received coverage, but this scholarship left out the workers. Slavery attracted attention, but not the slaves.[47] Even in masterful representations of the lives of the *gente sin historia* (people without history), like Picó's, one would eventually miss the conceptual innovations of gender studies and discourse analysis that a younger generation of historians began practicing with verve in the 1980s and 1990s.[48]

Although post-modernist trends of the last two decades have diverted energy away from research into the sugar-and-slavery complex of the nineteenth century, valuable new studies have appeared on Puerto Rico's sixteenth-century experiment with slave-produced sugar, on the island's colonial agriculture and animal husbandry, and on the twentieth-century expansion of the corporate land-and-factory combines (*centrales*).[49] For the period in the 1800s, however, when hundreds of slave-based haciendas arose throughout the island's plains, not much new research has surfaced in the past couple of decades.[50]

Historians of other New World slave societies have recently made strides in several areas, all of which would be fruitful to explore for Santo Domingo and Puerto Rico. These include investigations on slave women and gender; on slaves' participation in a so-called "proto-peasant" adaptation; on the reproduction of African cultural patterns alongside of and in creative tension with processes of creolization; on slaves' engagement in modes of everyday resistance; slave religiosity; and on the contribution of slaves and freed people to a radical understanding of liberal concepts of freedom and civic participation. A promising agenda for further research would be slave-centered on purpose, as a partial corrective to the planter-centered work that many historians carried out in the 1970s and 1980s.

Perhaps no questions are crying out for analysis more than those surrounding relations between women and men, gendered discourses of hierarchy and power, and constructions of femininity and masculinity inside the boundaries of the slave regime. Research in this area over the last twenty years for other Caribbean societies has almost turned on its head our understanding of the slave plantation complex. Few studies of slave women in Puerto Rico exist outside the pioneering work of Félix Matos Rodríguez on the city of San Juan and of Celsa Albert Batista on the colony of Santo Domingo.[51] Research in Jamaica, Barbados, and elsewhere in the British Caribbean has shown how vital gender was to slave management and control, to the maintenance and reproduction of master–slave relations of power and privilege. Planters maintained, for example, labor discipline on large sugar estates with hundreds of slaves by organizing the working "careers" of slaves according to binary hierarchies that made male slaves superior to women, creole slaves superior to the African born, and lighter-skinned slaves superior to the darker skinned. In the ultimate analysis, the overall hierarchy—and with it, the system's reproduction and stability—depended on exploiting women most of all and making male slaves aware of their condition of relative privilege.[52] Moreover, the exploitation of slave women—as cane cutters, wet nurses, domestic servants, sexual partners, and more—so thoroughly violated English notions of femininity that they made a convenient foil with which to elaborate strict controls over European women who found themselves in the Caribbean colonies, controls much more strict than those that prevailed in the metropole.

In thinking about Santo Domingo and Puerto Rico in light of these findings, one wonders how the sugar plantation complex at various points in time may have buttressed itself on the backs of slave women and how notions of slave womanhood may have influenced ideals of femininity for others in the society, especially the women of the middle and upper classes. Roberto Cassá and Genaro Rodríguez Morel have emphasized the frequency and seriousness of slave resistance in sixteenth-century Santo Domingo. By contrast, Guillermo Baralt found for Puerto Rico that plantation slaves curbed their acts of collective violence after the 1840s.[53] Did this latter trend reflect stability in the plantation workforce, and if so, did the structuring of work regimes to underscore male dominance reinforce it? And how did the debasement of slave womanhood affect conceptions of mid-nineteenth-century bourgeois femininity?

A second neglected area of research involves the economic life of slaves outside of the planters' control. Scholars of other Caribbean slave societies, especially of Jamaica's, have shown that with the passage of time slaves grew more secure in their control and exploitation of plots or provision grounds allotted to them by the planters. What masters claimed as a privilege, the conditional use of their property by the slaves, the slaves themselves claimed as a customary right. In Jamaica, these "proto-peasants," to borrow the term of the anthropologist Sidney Mintz, especially the women, organized and controlled the colony's internal marketing system. This so-called slave economy formed the basis of the peasant adaptation that flowered in the country after emancipation.[54] The significance of enslaved Africans to the development of Dominican *campesino* culture remains understudied; the question of how a proto-peasant adaptation may have emerged and developed after emancipation is still a matter for speculation.[55] For Puerto Rico, Luis A. Figueroa has recently found that in the sugar-producing district of Guayama, a proto-peasant adaptation was rendered difficult but not impossible by the planters' insistence on labor control and, especially after emancipation, the ecological limitations of this very dry region. Although Figueroa believes it likely that some form of peasant adaptation emerged there during slavery, he finds it difficult to document conclusively.[56] Other students of the Puerto Rican sugar complex in the nineteenth century have not determined whether assigning plots was a practice followed in other areas, and if so, under what conditions and with what specific consequences. In a late-blooming sugar complex like Puerto Rico's, where as many as half the estate slaves were recent African imports as late as 1850 and where land on or near plantations was relatively expensive, not enough time had passed for the peculium to have become institutionalized. Even if it had to some degree, the costs associated with it (for the planters) would have restricted its growth. Moreover, Puerto Rico's internal marketing system was well developed and in the hands of the *jíbaro* peasantry by the time the sugar complex took off in the 1810s and 1820s, a fact that would have limited the attraction of plots as a means for slaves to produce surpluses and obtain supplementary income. Perhaps for this reason Victor Schoelcher, France's most famous abolitionist, expressed surprise in 1841 when he visited the estate of Cornelius Kortright on Puerto Rico's north coast where slaves were "completely given over to the discretion of the master." Without the slaves' command of time of their own, the provision grounds system could not flourish.[57]

If indeed the proto-peasant adaptation was underdeveloped both in the early colonial Dominican context and in Puerto Rico's nineteenth-century sugar complex, one might appropriately ask: Was this a sign that slaves had limited opportunities for their own economic life, or simply that the "slaves' economy" took on a different form in these two colonies?[58] One of Andrés Ramos Mattei's most important findings for Puerto Rico was that as planters began to require more "free" workers in the period between the cholera epidemic of 1855–6 and full emancipation in 1876, they instituted a division of labor between slaves and hired hands. Estate slaves and even rented slaves, typically more skilled in the industrial tasks of the sugar mills, labored in these higher-reward tasks. Planters employed hired peasants to supplement the fixed workforce in the more unskilled agricultural occupations.[59] If this pattern reproduced across Puerto Rico, one would expect slaves to have received monetary income and other incentives during the period of slavery and higher wages after emancipation. Thus, it is possible (albeit not yet studied sufficiently) that Puerto Rican slaves engaged in a proto-proletarian adaptation rather than a proto-peasant one, a possibility that Gervasio L. García and Angel G. Quintero Rivera suggested in their short history of the labor movement. They observed that some of the earliest strike activity in Puerto Rico took place among slaves, *emancipados*, and *libertos* during the transition between slavery and freedom.[60]

The third area of research opportunity centers on the cultural implications of the rekindled slave trade of the nineteenth century in Puerto Rico. Joseph Carroll Dorsey has recently provided compelling details about the Puerto Rican slave trade in the nineteenth century, showing it to have been different, in several ways, from Cuba's—in the nationality of the traders, the ethnic and tribal origin of the captives, and the brokerage and intermediary roles played by merchants in regional centers like the Danish and French islands. Earlier studies of plantation communities had offered us glimpses of these differences, but the recent revelations have filled large and important gaps.[61]

Yet, our coverage of the African diaspora in Santo Domingo and Puerto Rico as cultural phenomenon and human drama is still spotty. The cultural contexts of slaves and free people who labored in the sugar complex need to be put in dialogue with other cases of American societies substantially influenced by the African diaspora. Largely unmentioned by Dominican and Puerto Rican historians is a debate rekindled in recent years among students of African and New World histories about the cultural dynamics of communities of individuals of African descent.[62] In some ways, this debate replicates the 1930s controversy in the United States between the sociologist E. Franklin Frazier and Melville Herskovits, a specialist in African anthropology, on the impact of Africa on slave cultural formation in the Americas. Fernando Ortiz's concept of "transculturation," the process by which different cultures mix and synthesize, raised a similar question about the extent to which New World cultures derived in part from Africa may be deemed to be entirely "new cultures" or cultures constructed to one degree or another from African survivals. The chief point of contention these days is no longer between the negation or recognition of African influence, but rather the extent to which African cultures were recreated more or less autonomously in the New World by children of Africa, and the degree to which that autonomy was denied by the systems of domination like slavery. On one hand, then, the "diasporists" posit cultural survival via re-creation and reformulation of specific African expressions. On the other hand, proponents of creolization argue for a power-laden and contingent process of cultural mixing that gave rise to cultures in essence neither African nor European.

Puerto Rico, like Cuba, developed the slave-based sugar plantation system in the nineteenth century. The belatedness of that development relative to other slave societies forms an interesting case study of the process of creolization. It had to occur in the long term, for sooner or later African cultural expressions would be overwhelmed by an entrenched *criollo* culture. But, in the short term, concentrated communities of Africans would likely play out the drama of recomposition and reconstitution that some historians of the African diaspora have observed in locales where populations of African origin were quantitatively superior to all others, such as in colonial Brazil or eighteenth-century Saint-Domingue. In the middle decades of the nineteenth century, the lowland barrios of Guayama, Ponce, Mayagüez, and other island districts had African and Afro-Creole *majorities*. How did these highly condensed communities of immigrant workers relate to the world outside the plantations? How were communal bonds created between the *jíbaro* peasant majorities of surrounding areas and the African and Afro-Creole majorities of the sugar barrios? Twentieth-century ethnographies reveal that intense racial distrust characterized relations between highland peasants who came to work in sugar and the darker-skinned residents of the coastal lowlands, many of them descendants of slaves imported before 1850. But it stands to reason that in addition to hostility there would be interaction and even *integration*. What cultural forms did these take? Only further work on the laboring communities of sugar cane plantations will allow us to answer questions of this sort and begin to insert Puerto Rico's case into the conversations now taking place around the subject of culture building in the African diaspora.

Notes

1. Pedro Andrés Pérez Cabral, *La comunidad mulata: el caso socio-político de la República Dominicana* (Caracas, 1967); Jay Kinsbruner, *Not of Pure Blood: The Free People of Color and Racial Prejudice in Nineteenth-Century Puerto Rico* (Durham, NC, 1996).
2. Arturo Morales Carrión, *Auge y decadencia de la trata negrera en Puerto Rico (1820–1860)* (San Juan, 1978).
3. Frank Tannenbaum, *Slave and Citizen: The Negro in the Americas* (New York, 1946).
4. Manuel Moreno Fraginals, *El ingenio: complejo socioeconómico cubano del azúcar* (1964; Havana, 1978).
5. Fernando Ortiz, *Contrapunteo cubano del tabaco y el azúcar (advertencia de sus contrastes agrarios, económicos, históricos y sociales, su etnografía y su transculturación)*, prologue by Herminio Portell Vilá, introd. Bronislaw Malinowski (Havana, 1940); Ramiro Guerra y Sánchez, *Azúcar y población en las Antillas* (Havana, 1927); Raúl Cepero Bonilla, *Azúcar y abolición: apuntes para una historia crítica del abolicionismo* (Havana, 1948); and the chapters on economic history by Julio LeRiverend Brusone in Ramiro Guerra y Sánchez et al., *Historia de la nación cubana* (Havana, 1953).
6. Franklin W. Knight, *Slave Society in Cuba during the Nineteenth Century* (Madison, 1969); Verena Stolcke, *Marriage, Class, and Colour in Nineteenth-Century Cuba: A Study of Racial Attitudes and Sexual Values in a Slave Society* (New York, 1974); and Juan Pérez de la Riva, *El barracón y otros ensayos* (Havana, 1975).

7. This notion of the "third root" refers to a common platitude that metaphorically depicts the racial origins of Spanish Caribbean societies as three roots: European (Spanish), Indian, and African. Some scholars have directly challenged the implicit devalorization of African-ness, which is always deemed the third influence and accordingly termed "the third root." See Various, *La tercera raíz: catálogo acompañando la exposición* (San Juan, 1992).

8. Tannenbaum, *Slave and Citizen*; Ernesto Sagás, "The Development of *Antihaitianismo* into a Dominant Ideology during the Trujillo Era," in Juan Manuel Carrión (ed.), *Ethnicity, Race, and Nationality in the Caribbean* (Río Piedras, 1997), 96–121.

9. Meindert Fennema and Troetje Loewenthal, "La construcción de raza y nación en la República Dominicana," *Anales del Caribe*, 9 (1989): 191–227.

10. Pedro San Miguel, "Discurso racial e identidad nacional en la República Dominicana," *Boletín del Centro de Investigaciones Históricas*, 7 (1993): 67–120, and *La isla imaginada: historia, identidad y utopía en La Española* (San Juan and Santo Domingo, 1997).

11. "Informe sobre el estado de la investigación elaborado por Magnus Mörner," in Silvio Zavala, Magnus Mörner, et al., "El mestizaje en la historia de Ibero-América," *Revista de historia de América*, 53/54 (June–December 1962): 127–69, 171–218. The quote is on p. 134.

12. Carlos Larrazabal Blanco, *Los negros y la esclavitud en Santo Domingo* (Santo Domingo, 1975), 178.

13. Rubén Silié, *Economía, esclavitud y población: ensayos de interpretación histórica del Santo Domingo español en el siglo XVIII* (Santo Domingo, 1976), 83.

14. See, for example, Pérez Cabral, *La comunidad mulata, passim*; and Frank Moya Pons, "Notas sobre la primera abolición de la esclavitud en Santo Domingo," *Eme Eme*, 3 (13) (1974): 3–26; "Azúcar, negros y sociedad en la Española en el siglo XVI," *Eme Eme*, 1 (4) (1973): 3–18; *Historia colonial de Santo Domingo* (Santiago, 1973); and *Manual de historia dominicana* (Santiago, 1978).

15. Carlos Estevan Deive, *La esclavitud del negro en Santo Domingo (1492–1844)* (Santo Domingo, 1980), i. 310.

16. Ibid.

17. Another virtue of Deive's work was its comprehensive character and wide-angled approach. In this sprawling book, in which the author engaged in wide-ranging historical reflections on topics as diverse as slavery as an economic system and the moral bases of European and American abolitionist sensibilities, Dominican slavery was placed in the larger context of worldwide slavery and emancipation.

18. Frank Moya Pons, *Historia colonial de Santo Domingo* (3rd edn. Santiago, 1973); *La Española en el siglo XVI, 1493–1520: trabajo, sociedad y política en la economía del oro* (Santiago, 1971); and *Manual de historia dominicana* (Santiago, 1978).

19. Frank Moya Pons, *La dominación haitiana, 1822–1844* (Santiago, 1972). Moya Pons also wrote more specifically on this theme in "The Land Question in Haiti and Santo Domingo: The Sociopolitical Context of the Transition from Slavery to Free Labor, 1801–1843," in Manuel Moreno Fraginals, Frank Moya Pons, and Stanley L. Engerman (eds.), *Between Slavery and Free Labor: The Spanish-Speaking Caribbean in the Nineteenth Century* (Baltimore, 1985).

20. For an example of his edited documentary collections, see Genaro Rodríguez Morel (ed.), *Cartas de los cabildos eclesiásticos de Santo Domingo y Concepción de la Vega en el siglo XVI* (Santo Domingo, 2000).

21. Genaro Rodríguez Morel. "Los orígenes de la economía de plantación en América: la Española en el siglo XVI" (Ph.D. diss., Castellón, 2009).

22. Also see Rodríguez Morel's contribution in Stuart B. Schwartz (ed.), *Tropical Babylons: Sugar and the Making of the Atlantic World, 1450–1680* (Chapel Hill, NC, 2004), a book that challenges the chronology of the New World's sugar-and-slavery cycle and argues for the importance of Spanish-Caribbean, and primarily Dominican, experiments with sugar and slavery in the sixteenth century. For a discussion of population figures and trends, see Rodríguez Morel, "Desarrollo económico y cambio demográfico en la Española: siglos XVI–XVII," *Boletín del Archivo General de la Nación*, 22 (117) (2006): 79–144.

23. Roberto Cassá and Genaro Rodríguez Morel, "Consideraciones alternativas acerca de las rebeliones de esclavos en Santo Domingo," *Anuario de estudios americanos*, 50 (1) (1993): 101–31.

24. Eugene Genovese, *From Rebellion to Revolution: Afro-American Slave Revolts in the Making of the Modern World* (Baton Rouge, La., 1979); Rodríguez Morel, "Los orígenes," 85.

25. Celsa Albert Batista, *Mujer y esclavitud en Santo Domingo* (Santo Domingo, 1990). On marronage in Spanish Hispaniola, see Carlos Esteban Deive, *Los guerrilleros negros: esclavos fugitivos y cimarrones en Santo Domingo* (Santo Domingo, 1989).

26. The emancipation decree for Puerto Rico was passed by the Spanish Parliament (*cortes*) in 1873. Final emancipation took place three years later, after a largely failed apprenticeship period of three years.

27. Luis M. Díaz Soler, *Historia de la esclavitud negra en Puerto Rico* (1953; Río Piedras, reprint 1970).

28. Francisco A. Scarano, *Sugar and Slavery in Puerto Rico: The Plantation Economy of Ponce, 1800–1850* (Madison, 1984).

29. I borrow this evocative phrase from Neville A. T. Hall, *Slave Society in the Danish West Indies: St. Thomas, St. John & St. Croix*, ed. B. W. Higman (Baltimore, 1992), 208.

30. For an analysis of these struggles to reunite freedpeople's families, see Ileana Rodríguez-Silva, "A Conspiracy of Silence: Blackness, Class, and Nation in Post-Emancipation Puerto Rico, 1850–1920" (Ph.D. diss., University of Wisconsin-Madison, 2004).

31. Centro de Investigaciones Históricas, *El proceso abolicionista en Puerto Rico: documentos para su estudio* (San Juan, 1974). See also Arturo Morales Carrión, "El centenario de la abolición: una visión histórica," *La Torre*, 21 (81–2) (1973): 1–21. For an introduction to the development of Puerto Rican historiography during the 1970s, see Francisco A. Scarano and Carmelo Rosario Natal, "Bibliografía histórica puertorriqueña de la década de los setentas, 1970–79," *Homines, revista de ciencias sociales*, 6 (1) (1982): 193–219. Also, Allen L. Woll, *Puerto Rican Historiography* (New York, 1979); and Arcadio Díaz Quiñones, *La memoria rota: ensayos sobre cultura y política* (Río Piedras, 1993).

32. A selection of the most significant works of this "boom" in slavery scholarship would have to include the following: Andrés A. Ramos Mattei, *La hacienda azucarera: su crecimiento y crisis en Puerto Rico* (San Juan, 1981); Scarano, *Sugar and Slavery*; Guillermo Baralt, *Esclavos rebeldes: conspiraciones y sublevaciones de esclavos en Puerto Rico (1795–1873)* (Río Piedras, 1981); Benjamín Nistal Moret (ed.), *Esclavos prófugos y cimarrones: Puerto Rico, 1770–1870* (Río Piedras, 1984); and by the same author, "Problems in the Social Structure of Slavery in Puerto Rico during the Process of Abolition, 1872," in Manuel Moreno Fraginals, Frank Moya Pons, and Stanley L. Engerman (eds.), *Between Slavery and Free Labor: The Spanish-Speaking Caribbean in the Nineteenth Century* (Baltimore, 1985), 141–57.

33. Baralt, *Esclavos rebeldes*. An English translation exists: *Slave Revolts in Puerto Rico: Conspiracies and Uprisings, 1795–1873*. Translated from Spanish by Christine Ayorinde (Princeton, 2007).

34. José Curet, "From Slave to Liberto: A Study on Slavery and its Abolition in Puerto Rico, 1840–1880" (Ph.D. diss., Columbia University, 1979); Baralt, *Esclavos rebeldes.*
35. Scarano, *Sugar and Slavery.*
36. On the matter of Cuba and Puerto Rico's joint weight in the Spanish economy of the nineteenth century, see Jordi Maluquer de Motes Bernet, "El mercado colonial antillano en el siglo XIX," in *Agricultura, comercio colonial y crecimiento económico en la España contemporánea* (Barcelona, 1974), 322–57, Luis Martínez-Fernández, *Torn between Empires: Economy, Society, and Patterns of Political Thought in the Hispanic Caribbean* (Athens, Ga., 1994), and Christopher Schmidt-Nowara, *Empire and Antislavery: Spain, Cuba, and Puerto Rico, 1833–1874* (Pittsburgh, 1999).
37. Francisco A. Scarano, "Liberal Pacts and Hierarchies of Rule: Approaching the Imperial Transition in Cuba and Puerto Rico," *Hispanic American Historical Review,* 78 (4) (November 1998): 583–601.
38. For every Spanish *vecino* there were several dependants: women, children, and servants. In 1774, the ratio of persons per *vecino* was 5.8. "Memorial con que el Illmo. Sor. D. D. Fr. Manuel Jiménez Pérez dio cuenta a Su Majestad de todos los acontecimientos y providencias que tomó en su santa pastoral visita, extensiva a los anexos de esta diócesis. Año de 1774," *Boletín histórico de Puerto Rico,* 7 (1920): 36–48.
39. Elsa Gelpí Baíz, *Siglo en blanco: estudio de la economía azucarera en el Puerto Rico del siglo XVI (1540–1612)* (San Juan, 2000).
40. Moscoso, *Lucha agraria en Puerto Rico, 1541–1545: un ensayo de historia* (San Juan, 1997) and *Agricultura y sociedad en Puerto Rico, siglos 16 al 18: un acercamiento desde la historia* (San Juan, 1999); Gil-Bermejo García, Juana, *Panorama histórico de la agricultura en Puerto Rico* (Seville, 1970); and Sued Badillo and López Cantos, *Puerto Rico negro* (Río Piedras, 1986).
41. Gelpí Baíz, *Siglo en blanco,* 210.
42. Joseph Carroll Dorsey, *Slave Traffic in the Age of Abolition: Puerto Rico, West Africa, and the Non-Hispanic Caribbean, 1815–1859* (Gainesville, Fla., 2003).
43. Luis A. Figueroa, *Sugar, Slavery, and Freedom in Nineteenth-Century Puerto Rico* (Chapel Hill, NC, 2005); Mariano Negrón Portillo, *La esclavitud urbana en San Juan de Puerto Rico: estudio del Registro de Esclavos de 1872* (Río Piedras, 1992), and by the same author with Raúl Mayo Santana and Manuel Mayo López, *Cadenas de esclavitud . . . y de solidaridad: esclavos y libertos en San Juan, siglo XIX* (Río Piedras, 1997).
44. It should be mentioned that not all recent work has contradicted the Tannenbaum thesis. David M. Stark's study of parish registers in various localities of eighteenth-century Puerto Rico before the onset of the plantation system shows convincingly that regardless of locale, many slaves married in the Church and engaged in family relationships that were as stable as those of the non-slave population. See especially Stark, "Discovering the Invisible Puerto Rican Slave Family: Demographic Evidence from the Eighteenth Century," *Journal of Family History,* 21 (4) (October 1996): 395–418.
45. See Alonso de Sandoval's wonderfully detailed description of the slaves he tended to in the Caribbean port city of Cartagena at the time of this city's preeminence in the transatlantic slave trade; Sandoval, *Un tratado sobre la esclavitud,* introd. Enriqueta Vila Vilar (Madrid, 1987). In the twentieth century, of course, the studies of Cuba's Fernando Ortiz stand out as some of the most important anthropological work on African cultures in the New World: Ortiz, *Hampa afro-cubana: los negros brujos (apuntes para un estudio de etnología criminal)* (Madrid, 1906); *Hampa afro-cubana: los negros esclavos. Estudio*

sociológico y de derecho público (Havana, 1916); and especially his masterpiece, *Contra-punteo cubano.*

46. Some historians complained that many works published in the 1970s and 1980s on slavery treated people as if they were mere statistics; as if enslaved Africans were all body and no mind. In addition to being applicable to the studies of the sugar economy already cited, the critique extended to studies of other dimensions of agrarian society, such as the coffee sector. Laird Bergad's *Coffee and the Growth of Agrarian Capitalism in Nineteenth-Century Puerto Rico* (Princeton, 1983) was singled out by some scholars as a valuable, yet flawed, analysis of the economy, not of the flesh-and-bone workers.

47. See especially Fernando Picó, *Libertad y servidumbre en el Puerto Rico del siglo XIX (Los jornaleros utuadeños en vísperas del auge del café)* (Río Piedras, 1979); *Registro general de jornaleros: Utuado, Puerto Rico (1849–50)* (Río Piedras, 1976); and *Amargo café (los pequeños y medianos caficultores de Utuado en la segunda mitad del siglo XIX)* (Río Piedras, 1981).

48. Antonio Gaztambide Géigel and Silvia Alvarez Curbelo (eds.), *Historias vivas: histor-iografía puertorriqueña contemporánea* (San Juan, 1996).

49. Gelpí Baíz, *Siglo en blanco*; Francisco Moscoso, *Agricultura y sociedad*; and César J. Ayala, *American Sugar Kingdom: The Plantation Economy of the Spanish Caribbean, 1898–1934* (Chapel Hill, NC, 1999).

50. On the decline of scholarly interest on the sugar industry during this period, see Astrid Cubano Iguina, "El azúcar en Puerto Rico, siglo XIX: fuentes y problemas," *América Latina en la historia económica*, 11 (January–June 1999), 51. Published work during this period about sugar and slavery has tended to follow closely the economicist line established by earlier studies. See, for example, Elí D. Oquendo Rodríguez, "Una noticia histórica de las haciendas de caña del barrio Tibes de Ponce, 1840–1940," *Horizontes*, 39 (76) (1997): 95–116.

51. See his "'¿Quién Trabajará?': Domestic Workers, Urban Slaves, and the Abolition of Slavery in Puerto Rico," in *Puerto Rican Women's History: New Perspectives* (Armonk, NY, 1998), 62–82; and the more comprehensive study of urban women: *Women and Urban Change in San Juan, Puerto Rico, 1820–1868* (Gainesville, Fla., 1999). A notable exception to the observed dearth of studies on rural women in slavery is Ivette Pérez Vega, "Juana María Escobales, liberta 'liberada,' " *Homines*, 11 (1–2) (March–February 1987–8): 397–402.

52. See especially Richard S. Dunn, " 'Dreadful Idlers' in the Cane Fields: The Slave Labor Pattern on a Jamaican Sugar Estate, 1762–1831," *Journal of Interdisciplinary History*, 17 (4) (1987): 795–822; and by the same author, "Sugar Production and Slave Women in Jamaica," in Ira Berlin and Philip D. Morgan (eds.), *Cultivation and Culture: Labor and the Shaping of Slave Life in the Americas*, Carter G. Woodson Institute Series in Black Studies (Charlottesville, Va., 1993), 49–72. See also Michael Craton, *Searching for the Invisible Man: Slaves and Plantation Life in Jamaica*, in collaboration with Garry Greenland (Cambridge, Mass., 1978).

53. Cassá and Rodríguez Morel, "Consideraciones"; Baralt, *Esclavos rebeldes.*

54. Sidney W. Mintz, "Slavery and the Rise of Peasantries," *Historical Reflections*, 6 (Summer 1979): 213–42. See also Jean Besson, *Martha Brae's Two Histories: European Expansion and Caribbean Culture-Building in Jamaica* (Chapel Hill, NC, 2002).

55. On Dominican peasants' early history, see Roberto Cassá, "El campesinado dominicano," *Boletín del Archivo General de la Nación*, 30 (112) (May–August 2005): 213–61; essays by Carlos Esteban Deive and Rubén Silié in Bernardo Vega (ed.), *Dominican Cultures: The Making of a Caribbean Society* (Princeton, 2007); Roberto Cassá, "Transformaciones del

régimen agrario," *Boletín del Archivo General de la Nación*, 30 (113) (September–December 2005): 447–533; and Richard Lee Turits, *Foundations of Despotism: Peasants, the Trujillo Regime, and Modernity in Dominican History* (Stanford, Calif., 2003).

56. Luis A. Figueroa, *Sugar, Slavery, and Freedom in Nineteenth-Century Puerto Rico* (Río Piedras, 2008).

57. Cited in Scarano, *Sugar and Slavery*, 29.

58. I borrow this term from Ira Berlin and Philip D. Morgan, "Labor and the Shaping of Slave Life in the Americas," introduction in *Cultivation and Culture*, 1–45.

59. Andrés Ramos Mattei, *Apuntes sobre la transición hacia el sistema de centrales en la industria azucarera: contabilidad de la hacienda "Mercedita," 1861–1900*, vol. iv of *Cuadernos*, Centro de Estudios de la Realidad Puertorriqueña (1975).

60. Gervasio L. García and Angel G. Quintero Rivera, *Desafío y solidaridad: breve historia del movimiento obrero en Puerto Rico* (Río Piedras, 1982).

61. Dorsey, *Slave Traffic*.

62. Angel G. Quintero Rivera, "La música puertorriqueña y la contra-cultura democrática: espontaneidad libertaria de la herencia cimarrona," *Folklore Americano*, 49 (January–June 1990): 135–67; and by the same author, *¡Salsa, sabor y control! Sociología de la música tropical* (Mexico, 1998).

Select Bibliography

Albert Batista, Celsa. *Mujer y esclavitud en Santo Domingo*. Santo Domingo: Centro Dominicano de Estudios de la Educación, 1990.

Baralt, Guillermo. *Esclavos rebeldes: conspiraciones y sublevaciones de esclavos en Puerto Rico (1795–1873)*. Río Piedras: Ediciones Huracán, 1981.

Cassá, Roberto, and Genaro Rodríguez Morel. "Consideraciones alternativas acerca de las rebeliones de esclavos en Santo Domingo," *Anuario de estudios americanos*, 50 (1) (1993): 101–31.

Centro de Investigaciones Históricas. *El proceso abolicionista en Puerto Rico: documentos para su estudio*. San Juan: Centro de Investigaciones Históricas e Instituto de Cultura Puertorriqueña, 1974.

Deive, Carlos Estevan. *La esclavitud del negro en Santo Domingo (1492–1844)*. Investigaciones Antropológicas no. 14. 2 vols. Santo Domingo: Museo del Hombre Dominicano, 1980.

Díaz Soler, Luis M. *Historia de la esclavitud negra en Puerto Rico*. 1953. Río Piedras: Editorial Universitaria, 1970.

Figueroa, Luis A. *Sugar, Slavery, and Freedom in Nineteenth-Century Puerto Rico*. San Juan; Chapel Hill: University of Puerto Rico Press; University of North Carolina Press, 2005.

Moya Pons, Frank. *La dominación haitiana, 1822–1844*. Santiago: Universidad Católica Madre y Maestra, 1972.

——— *La Española en el siglo XVI, 1493–1520: trabajo, sociedad y política en la economía del oro*. Santiago: Universidad Católica Madre y Maestra, 1971.

Nistal Moret, Benjamín, ed. *Esclavos prófugos y cimarrones: Puerto Rico, 1770–1870*. Río Piedras: Editorial de la Universidad de Puerto Rico, 1984.

Scarano, Francisco A. *Sugar and Slavery in Puerto Rico: The Plantation Economy of Ponce 1800–1850*. Madison: University of Wisconsin Press, 1984.

CHAPTER 2

···

MEXICO AND CENTRAL AMERICA

···

K. RUSSELL LOHSE

INTRODUCTION

···

Two pervasive myths have long stifled research on slavery in Mexico and Central America. First, scholars stereotyped Mesoamerica as an "Indian" area of Latin America, where Africans were numerically and culturally insignificant. Second, those who did study slavery in the region tended to downplay its economic and social significance. For decades, few scholars other than anthropologist Gonzalo Aguirre Beltrán (1908–96), the don of Afro-Mexican studies, showed much interest in slavery in the region. Even today, many Mexicans and Central Americans express surprise or disbelief on hearing that African slavery even existed in their countries. Since the 1990s, however, encouraged by such projects as "Nuestra Tercera Raíz" (Our Third Root), sponsored by the National Council for Culture and the Arts in Mexico (CONACULTA), and the UNESCO Slave Route Project, a growing number of Mexicanist and Central Americanist historians have turned their attention to the subject. Almost unanimously, a new generation of researchers concludes that slaves (and people of African descent generally) played a far greater role in both Mexico and Central America than previously assumed or acknowledged. Although a minority of the population in most areas, black and mulatto slaves provided the bulk of the workforce in several key colonial industries. Even as a small minority of laborers, slaves often occupied critical roles in production as skilled workers and supervisors. The catastrophic decline of the native population in the sixteenth and early seventeenth centuries forced Spanish colonists to search for another viable source of labor. In the first century after the conquest, Mexico imported nearly one-half of all Africans brought to Spanish America—more than any other colony. A few areas such as the cane fields of Veracruz and Morelos in Mexico, the tropical forests of Belize, and the cacao haciendas of Costa Rica came to rely heavily on African slaves. In urban centers such as Mexico City, Puebla de los Angeles, Santiago de Guatemala, or even Realejo, Nicaragua, slaves could be seen working not just in elite homes, but at every conceivable task. In plantation areas and cities, critical masses of Africans formed, making possible the formation of African ethnic communities.

In most areas of Mexico and Central America, however, small numbers of slaves provided an essential, supplementary source of labor rather than the primary one. The temporary closure of the African slave trade to the region in the 1640s resulted in a self-reproducing population. By the late seventeenth century, creoles out-numbered Africans in Mesoamerica, and by the mid-eighteenth century, most slaves in the region were mulattos. By then, the recovery of the Indian population and the phenomenal growth of the mestizo and free mulatto populations through-out Mexico and Central America gradually eliminated the need for slave workers in most regions. Although a few areas experienced a resurgence in slave imports in the late colonial period, slaves and their children passed increasingly into the free mixed-race population. Yet abolition in the 1820s resulted not just from the growth of the free population, nor from the commitment of creole patriots to Enlighten-ment ideals, but in part from the slaves' own efforts at liberating themselves.

INDIGENOUS SLAVERY AND THE
INDIAN SLAVE TRADE

Various institutionalized forms of lifelong, involuntary servitude existed through-out Mesoamerica before the arrival of the Spanish invaders, although these labor regimes exhibited considerable diversity. People called *tlacotin* in Nahuatl and *munib* in K'iche' Maya were forcibly separated from their communities of origin and subjugated to masters who could buy them, sell them, use them sexually, or kill them as they chose. Individuals became enslaved when relatives sold them into bondage; when they sold themselves to pay debts; when they were purchased at regional markets; when they were punished for crimes such as murder and adul-tery; or, most commonly, when they were captured in battle. In Mesoamerican societies, tributary peasants, not slaves, did most agricultural work, but slaveholding was widespread among the nobility in urban centers such as Tenoch-titlán or Utatlán (highland Guatemala). War captives destined only for sacrifice were distinguishable from slaves participating in production, but a master could sacrifice his slaves at any time and many were buried alive with their deceased masters. Slaves enhanced their lords' prestige as well as grinding corn, gathering wood, cooking, serving food, washing, and performing other daily tasks. Important differences existed between slavery as practiced by the Nahuatl- and Maya-speaking peoples. Among the Mexica (Aztecs, Central Mexico), Pipil (El Salvador), and Nicarao (Nicaragua), children of slaves were born free, but among the Yucatec and K'iche' Maya, they inherited their parents' condition. Among the Maya, free people who married slaves forfeited their liberty; among the Mexica, they remained free.[1]

Hernando Cortés and his companions set about enslaving the native inhabitants immediately upon arrival in Mexico in 1519. Royal decrees issued in 1522 and 1523 distinguished two types of Indian slaves: "slaves of war" (*esclavos de guerra*) and "slaves of rescue" (*esclavos de rescate*). Slaves of war lost their freedom when they refused the famous "Requirement" (*Requerimiento*) to accept Christianity and surrender to Spanish rule. Reputed cannibals also fell into this category. The law also permitted Spaniards to "rescue" Indians by enslaving them to prevent Indian lords from using them in human sacrifice. Twisting the evidently benign intent of this law, conquistadors forced conquered Indian nobles to round up droves of free individuals, whom they could then "rescue." Just as frequently, the conquerors simply seized Indians at random, searing the brands that marked them as slaves into their faces without any pretense of legal justification. Although figures offered by the early chroniclers are notoriously unreliable, the number of indigenous captives taken by Cortés and his men within a decade of their arrival in Mexico must have reached the tens of thousands.

A thriving trade in Indian captives emerged as the first profitable trade estab-lished by the Spanish conquerors in Central America. By 1526, Spaniards in Honduras and Nicaragua had begun exporting enslaved Indians to replace those who had died in the mines and plantations of the Caribbean and on the Isthmus of Panama. Central America's highest royal officials dominated the trade, including Governors Diego López de Salcedo and Andrés de Cerezeda of Honduras and Pedrarias Dávila, Francisco de Castañeda, and Rodrigo de Contreras of Nicaragua. The Indian slave trade contributed significantly to the exceptionally severe depop-ulation of Honduras and Nicaragua. Linda Newson, the most careful historical demographer of the region, has estimated that between 100,000 and 150,000 Honduran Indians were enslaved and exported, amounting to between one-fifth and one-quarter of the total population of western and central Honduras. Nicar-agua suffered even more; estimates range from 200,000 to 500,000 enslaved and exported out of a total of 825,000 to 1 million people. The Indian population in areas of Nicaragua under Spanish rule fell by up to 98 percent in the quarter century before 1550—one of the highest depopulation ratios in all the Americas.[2]

As conquest society took shape, Spaniards in Mexico and Central America put vast numbers of Indian slaves to work, abusing them as a seemingly inexhaustible natural resource. By 1530, Hernando Cortés owned more than 500 Indian slaves working his mines and sugar mills in Cuernavaca and Oaxaca; Pedro de Alvarado was mining gold in Guatemala with around 330 Indian slaves by 1538. Besides brutal overwork and physical coercion, pointless tortures and killings of Indians were common. In his celebrated *Brief Account of the Destruction of the Indies*, the Dominican friar Bartolomé de Las Casas described atrocities against Indians throughout Spain's new empire, including in Mexico, Guatemala, Nicaragua, and Panama. Although some of Las Casas's information was second-hand and exaggerated, his grim portrayal of brutality and population decline had a basis in fact and contributed to the Crown's growing concern for the Indians.

In response to the demographic disaster, the Crown issued the famous New Laws for the Good Treatment and Preservation of the Indians on 22 November 1542. Among other provisions, these prohibited the future enslavement of Indians for any reason and mandated the liberation of slaves whose owners could not provide legal proof of ownership. Slaveholders in Guatemala, however, ignored the law until Alfonso López de Cerrato arrived as new President of the Audiencia in 1548. In New Spain, Viceroy Antonio de Mendoza delayed even announcing the laws for almost a decade. By 1552, only 170 of Mexico's Indian slaves had been liberated; some were not freed until the early 1560s. By then, the indigenous population in conquered areas had dropped disastrously; the laws simply reflected the fact that there were few Indians left to enslave. Colonists on New Spain's frontiers where government control was tenuous clung for centuries to the doctrine of "just war" to legitimize their enslavement of unconquered Indians. In New Mexico, for example, they continued to seize, own, and sell Apache captives long into the nineteenth century. In core areas, however, most Indian slaves had been freed by the late 1550s. As the *cabildo* (city council) of Mexico City pleaded to the Crown in 1562, "Since the personal services of the Indians have been taken away suddenly . . . there is a great need for labor in the haciendas, mines, sugar refineries, ranches and other businesses in the land, and the remedy cannot justly be other than to bring large numbers of negroes to this land."[3]

THE RISE OF AFRICAN SLAVERY

Black men participated in virtually all—if not every one—of the earliest Spanish expeditions to Mexico and Central America. "Diego el Negro," one of the first black men to reach Central America, arrived in Honduras on 14 August 1502 aboard the caravel *Capitana,* one of four ships commanded by Christopher Columbus on the latter's fourth voyage to the New World. Nuflo de Olano, a black man probably free, accompanied Vasco Núñez de Balboa in Panama when the two "discovered" the Pacific Ocean in 1513. Six years later the black slave Juan Cortés and perhaps five other blacks joined his master Hernán Cortés in the conquest of Tenochtitlán, reportedly frightening the Indians who first saw them. A number of sixteenth-century chroniclers asserted that Francisco de Eguía, another black man, introduced smallpox to New Spain—a claim historian Matthew Restall suspects is "classic Spanish scapegoating." Pedro de Alvarado brought black slaves with him when he set out to conquer Guatemala, and Cortés took them to Honduras in 1524. A forced member of Pánfilo de Narváez's ill-fated expedition to Florida in 1527, the Moroccan-born "Estevanico," became the first African to set foot in what is now the United States.

A few of these "black conquistadors" succeeded in attaining freedom, recognition, and rewards for their contributions to the Spanish conquest. African-born ex-slave Juan Garrido, already a seasoned veteran of the Caribbean conquests, arrived and fought with Cortés in Mexico in 1519. He subsequently planted the first wheat in the colony and was rewarded with a home in Mexico City's new center (*traza*), otherwise reserved for the Spanish elite. "Juan el Negro" and "Benito el Negro" received *encomiendas* in what is now San Luis Potosí. Juan Bardales, another black freedman, obtained an annual pension for his role in the conquest of Honduras.[4]

As raging epidemics claimed tens of millions of Indian lives during the sixteenth and early seventeenth centuries, Spanish colonists confronted an acute need for laborers. With the union of Spain and Portugal in 1580, the Crown promoted a massive expansion of the slave trade to its New World colonies by institutionalizing the *asiento,* a contract that granted a monopoly on the slave trade to Spanish America. Portugal held the *asiento* from 1580 to 1640. When they founded the Angolan port of Luanda in 1575, the Portuguese tapped into a flood of hundreds of thousands of captives who had fallen victim to wars in the West-Central African hinterland. Veracruz became one of only a handful of ports in Spanish America authorized to receive African slaves. Among the first slave ships was the *Buen Jesús,* which arrived there from Angola with 210 captives in 1596. Between 1601 and 1640 up to 70,000 enslaved Africans arrived at Veracruz, more than any other port in Spanish America.

Between 1580 and 1620, Mexico imported nearly half of all African slaves brought to the New World. By 1600, according to Colin Palmer and others, people of African descent outnumbered Spaniards in Mexico and Central America. One 1645 report to the King estimated 80,000 slaves in Mexico. Central America had far fewer. The slave trade to Guatemala peaked in the early seventeenth century. Between 1613 and 1628, at least ten slave ships legally brought perhaps 1,100 captives. Although the Crown periodically authorized Guatemalan and Honduran ports to receive shipments of African slaves, these dispensations always proved ephemeral, and to the disappointment of prospective slave buyers, contracts often went unfulfilled. Only a few hundred Africans legally arrived in Costa Rica and Nicaragua, where buyers purchased slaves primarily from markets in Portobello and Panama City rather than Veracruz. As elsewhere in Spanish America, however, high taxes on imported Africans encouraged smuggling. In remote areas such as Tabasco, Campeche, and Costa Rica, probably as many African slaves arrived illegally as legally.

The ethnic origins of Africans imported to Mexico and Central America closely mirrored trends in the Atlantic slave trade as a whole. The earliest arrivals, including a handful of "white" Spanish Muslims (*moriscos*), came from the Iberian Peninsula itself. For much of the sixteenth century, Africans from Senegambia and the Guinea-Bissau region predominated. A significant minority, usually called *mozambiques*, came from East Africa; a few captives arrived from Portuguese India (Goa), and several thousand "chinos" from the Philippines arrived by way of Acapulco. Between 1580 and 1640, women and men called *angolas* and *congos* from West-Central Africa accounted for 80 percent or more of the enslaved Africans brought to Mexico and Central America.

When Portugal struck for independence in 1640, the Spanish Crown halted the slave trade to its colonies. When the trade reopened in the 1660s, new Dutch, British, and French suppliers brought captives from the Gold Coast, Slave Coast, and Bight of Biafra regions as well as West-Central Africa; a roughly equal number of slaves from the same areas came by way of Jamaica and Curaçao. The African slave trade to Mexico never again rose to its previous volume; about 2,100 captives arrived in Veracruz between 1663 and 1674, for example, and about 3,000 between 1716 and 1739. Regional economic demands, however, reinvigorated imports from time to time. The demand for African slaves in Córdoba, for instance, unlike in most of Mexico, did not reach its peak until the first decade of the eighteenth century. Campeche legally imported more than 800 captives between 1725 and 1739. A sugar boom there and in Tabasco in the late eighteenth and early nineteenth centuries led to a last-minute surge in slave imports before the closure of the trade. Colonial Mexico and Central America preceded the colonial United States by decades in developing slave populations with a majority of American-born slaves. With the effective, though temporary, closure of the Atlantic slave trade to Mexico in 1640, natural reproduction and gender parity were rapidly achieved. By the 1740s, 78 percent of the slaves sold in Córdoba, for example, were Mexican born.[5]

SLAVE WORK

The first black slaves arrived in Mexico and Central America as personal servants of wealthy Spaniards. By the early seventeenth century black "domestic" slaves could be seen all over the large cities of Mexico City, Puebla de los Angeles, and Santiago de Guatemala, but also in much smaller towns such as Mérida (Yucatan), Granada (Nicaragua), or even Cartago (Costa Rica). In Mexico City's Zócalo, black slaves sold chickens, produce, and prepared foods. At fountains, they collected water and washed clothes. Luxuriously dressed enslaved attendants and pages trailed men and women of the Spanish elite. Slave criers announced the slave auctions that were held in the central plazas. Slave children made lively gifts for ruling-class children, who were nursed and cared for by enslaved nannies and who ate meals prepared by enslaved cooks. Slaves waited on friars and nuns bound by vows of poverty and humility; they even saved the mendicant "slaves of God" the work of flagellating themselves. The wealthiest Spaniards in the Mexican capital counted twenty or more slaves in their retinues.

Even Spanish shopkeepers and artisans aspired to own one or two slaves. Some masters (and especially mistresses) relied on their slaves for their entire incomes. A few placed slave boys as apprentices to master craftsmen, viewing them as investments for the future. Once trained, slave artisans could turn their substantial earnings over to their masters, and if sold, bring a handsome price. More commonly, masters rented out their slaves for manual labor. Some slaves who worked outside the home managed to save a portion of their earnings; they might even live away from their masters, and some succeeded in purchasing their freedom.[6]

Mexico and Central America never became full-blown plantation societies like Brazil or the Caribbean islands, but Spaniards introduced sugar cane soon after the conquest and developed an extensive industry for the domestic market. Although most prevalent in the modern Mexican states of Morelos, Veracruz, and Oaxaca, *ingenios* (sugar mills) were scattered through much of Mexico and Central America. Few sugar complexes approached the size of San Jerónimo in Guatemala, where the Dominican Order held between 550 and 700 men, women, and children in slavery. Labor forces of 80 to 100 slaves more typically worked on the *ingenios* of Morelos and Veracruz. Most sugar in Mexico and Central America, however, was made in small animal-, human-, or water-powered mills called *trapiches*, which were operated by about ten slaves. Although early scholars assumed that free workers began to replace enslaved sugar workers by the mid-seventeenth century, more recent research by Juan Manuel de la Serna Herrera and Frank T. Proctor shows that, at least in some places, slaves remained crucial to the industry at least until the last third of the eighteenth. Slave women, as on Caribbean sugar plantations, tended to work in the fields. Slave men predominated in processing the extracted cane juice. During the harvest, masters might also hire free workers to cut cane in the fields. Masters invariably preferred slaves, however, in the specialized work of grinding, boiling, crystallizing, and refining sugar. The whole elaborate process depended on a "sugar master" who timed the precise moment when successive boilings crystallized syrup into granulated sugar. Slaves usually handled this exacting job right up to the end of the colonial period and numbered among the estate's most valuable slaves.[7]

Spaniards introduced cattle, sheep, and pigs as soon as they arrived in the New World. Estates devoted to agriculture and livestock breeding (haciendas and *estancias*), mainly oriented toward domestic markets, soon arose and came to dominate large areas of Mexico and Central America. Usually a minority among Indian, free mulatto, and mestizo workers, slaves not only worked alongside dependent laborers of higher status, but frequently supervised their work in the livestock industry. Hacienda owners—especially absentees—usually secured these slave men's loyalty by positive incentives such as extra rations, cash salaries, their own herds, allowing them their choice of wives from the women on the hacienda, and occasionally, the offer of freedom. Slave cowboys of necessity enjoyed a great deal of freedom of movement, participating in semiannual roundups and even joining long cattle drives (*sacas*) over hundreds of miles. Slave "men on horseback" exercised significant authority, responsibility, and freedom of movement.[8]

In Mexico's crucial silver mines, slaves formed an important minority of the labor force. In a few mines, as many as 800 black slaves toiled. But, as historian Colin Palmer emphasizes, "Slaves never arrived in numbers adequate to solve the acute labor problem" and never made up more than one-fifth of the total work-force in major mining areas such as Taxco, Guanajuato, Zacatecas, or San Luis Potosí. Only a few mines used them exclusively. Contrary to Spanish expectations, Africans survived the mines little better than Indians. Pneumonia, silicosis and other respiratory diseases, mercury and carbon monoxide poisoning, and roof collapses led to staggering mortality rates among all workers, and from a master's perspective, the cost of slaves was prohibitive. In the lucrative Honduran placer mining economy in the early colonial period, black slaves dominated by the 1530s. As many as 1,500 slaves toiled in the streams near Olancho in 1542, when they rebelled and briefly drove Spanish colonists from the area. The high price of African slaves acted to discourage further investment, but the use of African slaves in mining continued. The role of slaves in the all-important mining industries, whether underground or placer mining, awaits comprehensive study.[9]

Slaves also played a major part in Mexico's extensive textile industry, which concentrated in and around the capital, Puebla, Valladolid (now Morelia, Michoacán), and Querétaro, as well as in indigo production in Chiapas and Central America. In airless, hot, humid, fly-infested compounds choked with noxious fumes, Indians recruited by labor draft (*repartimiento*), debt peons, slaves, and convicts all toiled in coerced conditions that historian Javier Villa-Flores has characterized "a living hell." Frank T. Proctor, taking issue with previous scholarship, has produced convincing evidence that slaves in Mexican textile manufactories from the mid-seventeenth to the mid-eighteenth centuries provided the "backbone of the labor force." A number of seventeenth-century workshops (*obrajes*), which were typically operated by fifty to seventy workers, used only slaves. Enslaved laborers, unlike Indians, could be worked mercilessly under the shadow of the lash without attracting official intervention. By the late eighteenth century, however, slaves concentrated in such skilled occupations as master weaver, and wages and the promise of freedom were replacing simple coercion as the motivation for labor.[10]

Slaves worked in Mesoamerica's important cacao industry from the early sixteenth century. All along the Pacific coast of Mexico and northern Central America, they tended large haciendas and smaller *huertas* (groves). Slaves also grew cacao in areas of the Gulf Coast, and in Central America, renewed slave imports made Costa Rica's short-lived cacao boom possible in the late seventeenth and early eighteenth centuries.[11] In addition to these larger industries, black and mulatto slaves often worked in small, local enterprises. Black slaves mined lime from a quarry on a Jesuit-owned estate in Oaxaca, for example. In the Pacific coast state of Colima, enslaved black men oversaw the Indian work crews who mined the salt flats. In Nicaragua and Nicoya, slaves cut timber, manufactured pitch, and built and caulked ships in the yards of Realejo and Nandayure. Off the Pacific coast of Costa Rica and Panama, slaves made their masters' fortunes through their skill in diving for pearls.

In a few areas, a stark gender division of labor emerged. Logging dominated Belize's slave-based economy, and only male slaves cut logwood and mahogany. Gangs of enslaved woodcutters, generally consisting of between ten and twelve men but occasionally as many as fifty, spent months encamped in the forests. African slaves of the British "Baymen" vastly outnumbered the one or two white overseers who typically supervised them in the logging camps. In contrast, women, children, and elderly slaves worked as domestic servants in the homes of white or free colored masters in Belize Town. Similarly, in Costa Rica only enslaved men lived on the cacao haciendas of the Matina, Barbilla, and Reventazón valleys, several days' journey from Cartago, the capital, where most slave owners lived. Female slaves and their children worked as "domestic" slaves, there or elsewhere. Masters visited the haciendas rarely, leaving day-to-day operations in the hands of their African slaves. In both Belize and Costa Rica, enslaved men enjoyed exceptional freedom of movement and minimal interference from whites, but they suffered from long stretches of time away from their families. The status of wives and children as de facto hostages in white households goes far toward explaining the relatively low incidence of slave flight and resistance in those colonies.[12]

FAMILY, COMMUNITY, AND CULTURE

Cultural expressions for slaves in Mexico and Central America varied according to place, time, and work. Africans found their greatest opportunities for contact with men and women of similar ethnic backgrounds in major cities and on some large estates such as sugar plantations. In small towns and in districts dominated by industries such as mining or textile manufacturing, slaves might also be clustered in substantial numbers. More commonly, a mere handful of slaves lived and labored among a much greater number of Indians, mestizos, free mulattos, and Spaniards. With the decline of the slave trade after 1640, Africans throughout the region found themselves increasingly isolated among creoles. Widespread *mestizaje* (racial mixture) meant that by the eighteenth century, slaves in Mexico and Central America were not only American born but, increasingly, mulatto. By the end of the eighteenth century, having merged with the much larger free mulatto population, in many areas blacks had all but disappeared as a distinct group.

In the late sixteenth and early seventeenth centuries, tens of thousands of West-Central Africans arrived in Mexico and Central America. Their relative cultural homogeneity allowed them to form new "ethnic" identities reflecting both their Old World origins and New World experiences. Describing oneself as an *angola*, for example, bespoke an identity that transcended both slavery and geography. In seventeenth-century Mexico City, long-term, stable relationships as "lovers, family, and friends" were the rule, not the exception. *Angolas* and other Africans forged strong communities based in both similar ethnic background and in their appropriation of Christian institutions such as marriage and godparentage.[13]

Christian teaching formed an essential part of the reduction to slavery. Urban slaves lived close to churches, and their masters invited disapproval or even prosecution if they failed in their spiritual duty to instruct their servants. Although Africans surely practiced other religions rooted in their homelands, to date researchers have found little direct evidence to substantiate this generalization. All slaves were made to accept Christianity at least nominally, but their understandings and practice of the faith often diverged from orthodoxy. In provocative recent works, Joan Bristol, Laura Lewis, Martha Few, and others have mined the archives of the Inquisition for the hundreds of descriptions of unsanctioned ritual practices among slaves and free blacks and mulattos in Mexico and Guatemala which they contain. Much work remains on this subject, but indigenous and European elements prove far more evident than African. Persons of African descent by and large navigated the same spiritual universe as colonial Indians, mestizos, and Spaniards. Lewis and Few have shown that black women and *mulatas* showed a particular affinity for indigenous ritual practices, and women of African descent were the single group most likely to be denounced before the Holy Office.[14]

Enslaved and free blacks and mulattos throughout the region also founded and actively participated in vibrant Catholic confraternities (*cofradías*). Historian Nicole von Germeten studied dozens of black confraternities in colonial Mexico. Of the predominantly slave confraternities of the early seventeenth century, Von Germeten's research shows several distinctive characteristics, including prominent female leadership, a reliance upon alms for income, and a highly public identification with the sanctity of humility and suffering, reflected in extravagant flagellant processions.[15]

As Catholics, slaves could claim certain rights before the Church, such as the right to marry. The Church required slaves (as well as other married couples) to live together as husband and wife, and the law required masters to allow them to do so. In theory, slave marriages should have been inviolate, but slaves claimed their rights with varying degrees of success. In Mexico City during the early seventeenth century, as Herman Bennett has pointed out, Africans learned the legal system quickly and proved adept at using it to protect their marriages and families. Yet Proctor's more recent research for a slightly later period revealed only two cases in which married slaves had successfully petitioned to prevent their separation by sale. In any case, laws protecting slave marriages benefited only a tiny minority of enslaved couples simply because so few slaves married in the Church. Up to 90 percent or more of children born to enslaved mothers in some areas of Mexico and Central America were born out of wedlock. Unless legitimized by the sacrament, slave unions enjoyed no legal protections.

On large properties, slave families tended to be more stable whether or not they were sanctioned by the Catholic Church. Although some plantation slaves lived in large, barracks-like compounds, most seem to have lived, often with family, in small houses or huts (*jacales*). The historian Patrick Carroll has shown that over time, slaves on the plantations near Xalapa also benefited from greater family stability. Between 1575 and 1615, 60–70 percent of the persons listed in plantation inventories had no apparent family ties. After the decline of the slave trade, between 1645 and 1720, that proportion fell to less than half, and by 1780, 81 percent of adult slaves lived with family members. Sex ratios during this period had become more balanced on the plantations, and the number of families separated by sale appears to have dropped. On some estates, slave communities spanning several generations developed.

Religious orders such as the Jesuits and Dominicans especially encouraged slaves on their properties to marry, and most adult slaves there eventually did. Although legally married slaves could invoke the law to protect their marriages, security from separation might not extend to their children. Regular clergy cared less about keeping slave families together than about preventing licentious behavior on the estates. The late historian Herman Konrad showed, for example, that Jesuits at the Santa Lucía hacienda in the Valley of Mexico avoided potential scandals by systematically selling away girls who had not married by their mid-teens. Dominicans at the huge San Jerónimo sugar complex in Guatemala sold children and adolescents so frequently that by the end of the colonial period, San Jerónimo was the single most common birthplace of slaves throughout the country. The large properties of some religious orders, in fact, became de facto "breeding farms" that helped perpetuate slavery in areas which otherwise had no steady access to slave traders.[16]

RESISTANCE

Just as some slaves served their Spanish masters loyally in the conquest, others rebelled and escaped almost from the moment they arrived on the soil of the Americas. Flight was always the most common form of slave resistance. Creoles and mulattos often tried to pass as free persons, especially in large cities and mining areas. Africans, less likely to pull off the charade, more commonly sought refuge in communities of fugitive slaves (*cimarrones*) beyond Spanish control. By the 1560s, *cimarrones* were terrorizing the near north from Guadalajara to Zacatecas, burning ranches and robbing travelers, sometimes with the help of Indians. In the 1570s the Crown issued a string of royal *cédulas* aimed at the maroons, including penalties of castration or death for slaves absent from their masters for more than six months. These decrees, however, did nothing to discourage the runaways. Settlements of *cimarrones* multiplied in the Valley of Mexico around the capital, along the road between Puebla and Veracruz, near the silver mines of Pánuco, in the *tierra caliente* of Michoacán, on the Pacific coast around Acapulco, and throughout the future state of Veracruz. Fugitive slaves also formed a few hideouts in Guatemala. In the early decades of the seventeenth century, up to 300 *cimarrones* lived in the mountains along the road between Santiago and Guatemala's Golfo Dulce (Lake Izabal), preying on passing mule trains and enticing enslaved members of the caravans to join them.

By attacking New Spain's mines and trade routes, maroon bands posed a serious threat to Spanish colonialism. Authorities invariably attempted to exterminate maroon communities through military action. When unable to do so, they sometimes reluctantly negotiated treaties with the runaways. Yanga, a man probably born in Guinea-Bissau who escaped slavery around 1570, founded the best known of Mexico's *cimarrón* communities. After decades of failed attempts to conquer the settlement, the Viceroy signed a treaty with the maroons in 1609, guaranteeing their freedom and legally incorporating their town as San Lorenzo de los Negros.[17]

Spanish colonial authorities also had to deal with numerous slave conspiracies— or with rumors of them. In late 1537, Viceroy don Antonio de Mendoza informed the Crown that he had foiled a large-scale slave rebellion planned to break out in and around Mexico City. He ordered the ringleaders tortured and publicly hanged (a scene recorded by an indigenous artist in the Telleriano-Remensis Codex). In 1542, another attempted rebellion in the capital failed, and in 1546, yet more black slaves in Tenochtitlán and Tlatelolco attempted to revolt, but they, too were captured, tortured, and executed. In 1608, investigating judge don Luis López de Azoca insisted that slaves had planned a rebellion for the Festival of the Epiphany on 6 January (*Día de los Reyes*). Although lacking firm evidence of the plot, Viceroy don Luis de Velasco ordered the public flogging of the alleged plotters.

Neither colonial authorities nor historians have proven the reality of these alleged conspiracies. Mexico City's most serious incident occurred in 1612, following a year of unrest among the city's slaves. According to indigenous historian Chimalpahin's Nahuatl-language account, the enslaved members of a religious confraternity planned an uprising to establish a "black monarchy" by killing or enslaving the whites and Indians of the city. The conspiracy began to fall apart when visiting Portuguese merchants overheard an *angola* slave woman refer in her native language to an uprising set to break out on the Thursday before Easter. In this plot, as in others, as historian María Elena Martínez contends, "it is simply impossible to distinguish fact from fiction." Colonial authorities cancelled holiday celebrations, prohibited blacks and mulattos from bearing arms or meeting in groups of more than four people, and imposed a curfew on slaves. When weapons were found in the homes of the suspected leaders, they were condemned to death. On 2 May 1612, thirty to thirty-five people were hanged, up to a third of them women. As a grisly warning, six of the bodies were drawn and quartered, and the body parts were displayed on pikes along the city's streets.

Slave insurrections, some involving up to 2,000 slaves, broke out in the Córdoba and Orizaba region in 1725, 1735, 1741, 1749, and 1768. The largest of these understudied revolts broke out in 1735, when Miguel Salamanca, a free mulatto, initiated the rumor that the King had freed the slaves. The hacendados' out-of-hand denial of the rumor only confirmed the slaves' belief that the planters were concealing the King's decree. On 19 June 1735, about 500 slaves revolted on the San Juan de la Punta hacienda near Córdoba. Spreading to the plantations of the coastal lowlands around the port of Veracruz, the uprising continued for five months. Slaves vented their hatred by killing and injuring planters, attacking travelers, burning cane fields and sugar houses, and stealing the copper cauldrons used in the boiling process. The 1735 rebellion destroyed the region's sugar industry, inflicting 400,000 pesos in damage to buildings and equipment alone; when the planters added the loss of their human property, the rebellion cost them more than one million pesos. The hacendados captured and executed the leaders of the revolt in Córdoba's public square in 1737, but many more of the rebels escaped to the nearby mountains of eastern Oaxaca, where they founded six settlements and continued to plague the haciendas with raids and attacks. One of these *palenques*, Mandinga, acquired legal recognition years later as the free black town of Nuestra Señora de Guadalupe de Amapa.[18]

TOWARD FREEDOM

By the late seventeenth century, Mexico's and Central America's free blacks and mulattos outnumbered slaves, making up the largest population of free people of African descent in the New World. Under Spanish law, slaves had greater opportunities for manumission than their counterparts in most other European colonies. Most frequently, slaves were manumitted without payment or condition after their master's death. As elsewhere, women and children most frequently benefited from manumission. Urban slaves won their freedom more often than rural slaves, and mulattos were manumitted more frequently than blacks. Scholars have often interpreted the prominence of mulatto women and children among those freed as evidence that masters favored their enslaved lovers and children. In some cases they did, but Proctor has now shown that just as many mistresses as masters freed slaves, demonstrating the need to consider other kinds of intimate relationships as well.

Male African slaves between 20 and 35 years of age, who worked in the country-side—especially on plantations—faced the greatest odds against manumission. They had few opportunities to cultivate the relationships with masters and mistresses that could lead to manumission, although some of these valuable slaves were able to purchase their freedom for a price. Several African-born men in eighteenth-century Costa Rica, for example, negotiated their manumission in return for quantities of cacao which they managed to grow over a period of years or decades. Free family members and friends often proved critical to effecting manumission. Some masters accepted incremental payments toward freedom over a period of time or made liberation conditional on the slave's fulfillment of additional years of service.[19]

Legal manumission affected only a small minority of slaves and had a minimal impact on the overall growth of the free population of African descent. Much more consequential was the practice that historian Paul Lokken has called "marriage as slave emancipation." By the late seventeenth century, in most places, slave men married free women more often than not; slave women rarely married legally at all. Few black women were free, and enslaved black men practiced exogamy by marrying a woman of lighter skin color, usually a free *mulata*, but sometimes an Indian or mestiza. The growth of the free population of color went hand in hand with racial mixture (*mestizaje*) and a progressive "whitening" (*blanqueamiento*), which ultimately led to the disappearance of people of African descent as a phenotypically distinct group.

Traditionally, historians attributed the marked proclivity of slave men to choose free women as wives to a shortage of enslaved women as potential mates. It is now clear, however, that after the decline of the Atlantic slave trade in the 1640s, a balanced sex ratio among slaves was soon achieved in Mexico and Central America. The number and proportion of marriages between two slaves was actually higher at the height of the slave trade, when many more male Africans than females were being imported, than after its decline, when the gender ratio among slaves equalized. The argument that black slave men married free women because of a gender imbalance among slaves, as Proctor contends, is a myth that "should be laid to rest."[20]

One reason marriage was more prevalent in the earlier period is that Africans (especially *angolas*) used Christian marriage as a means of reinforcing ethnic ties and building community, as Bennett has illustrated for slaves in Mexico City. For creoles legal condition and possibly "race" became more important criteria in choosing a spouse. Enslaved mulatto men usually enjoyed considerably greater success in attracting free mates than did black slave men, and they married free *mulatas* far more than woman of any other group. As *mulata* slaves were presumably also available, free legal status rather than skin color seems to explain the preference. Black slave men also married *mulatas* more frequently than other free women. In other areas such as the sugar regions of Xalapa (Veracruz), Amatitlán (Guatemala), or Antequera (Oaxaca City), enslaved black men more often married indigenous women. By the eighteenth century, people of African descent came to see their communities as rooted in location (urban neighborhoods, towns, plantations), and tended to choose spouses with whom they had grown up, regardless of race. Interracial marriages, especially between mulattos and mestizas, became increasingly common, and thus the free population of African descent was overwhelmingly of mixed descent.[21]

Fanciful names for people of mixed ancestry (*castas*) such as *tente en el aire* (remain in the air), *saltapatrás* (jump back), and *no te entiendo* (I don't understand you), illustrated in the eighteenth-century "*casta* paintings" fashionable among the Spanish elite, were probably not much used in other contexts. Rather, as R. Douglas Cope argues, people of mixed ancestry tended to be identified as either mestizo or mulatto. The applicability of the concepts of "race" and "racism" to colonial Spanish America, with their modern connotations, continues to ignite controversy among historians. Documents from colonial Mexico and Central America hardly ever use the word "race" (*raza*), but frequently refer to *casta* and *calidad*, terms which might reflect cultural practices, social and family connections, upbringing or "breeding," clothing styles, occupation, and legal condition—among other traits— as well as skin color, hair texture, and genealogy. However Spaniards referred to them, blacks and people of mixed ancestry unquestionably suffered more severe restrictions and punishments than Spaniards, and sometimes Indians, socially and legally.[22]

Many free blacks and mulattos (as well as runaway slaves) left the cities for frontier areas where they found less conflict with the legal system. Authorities throughout Mexico and Central America expressed alarm over the proliferation of free black and mulatto "vagabonds" who lived beyond effective Spanish control. Stereotyped as bandits, cattle rustlers, and outlaws in general, these *castas* nevertheless provided essential seasonal labor for the haciendas and ranches. Many eventually gravitated to the estates; others gathered in semi-autonomous "pueblos de mulatos," often next to *pueblos de indios*, where they tended to be strongly influenced by indigenous cultures. Some of these communities, such as San Pedro

Metapa, Nicaragua (now Ciudad Darío), gained legal recognition and their own all-mulatto municipal governments.[23]

Beginning in the seventeenth century, colonial authorities sought to co-opt potentially troublesome free blacks and mulattos by drafting them to military service in free colored militias. To free men of African descent, membership in the militias conferred a respectable, legally recognized, corporate identity, which they succeeded in extending to their families and communities. Citing brave military exploits, militiamen of color persistently and often successfully petitioned the Crown for special privileges for themselves and their communities. The foremost scholar of Mexico's free colored militias, Ben Vinson III, has argued that the militias provided a key site for the formation of "racial consciousness," a contingent, strategic, and ambivalent identity that could be abandoned if and when it presented more disadvantages than advantages. In addition to fighting hostile Indians, heretic pirates, and other foreign invaders, free colored militiamen routinely captured runaway slaves and participated in expeditions against maroon communities. Some of the free colored elite, many of them militia officers, acquired slaves of their own. But despite the mobility offered by military service, free men of color faced discrimination right up to the end of the colonial period.[24]

THE END OF SLAVERY

In the course of the eighteenth century, a combination of factors made slavery less and less viable as an economic system in most parts of Mexico and Central America. The Indian population reversed its decline, and people of mixed ancestry became the large majority in the core areas of the region. The population explosion at mid-century led to a land shortage that forced indigenous and free *casta* villagers into the labor market. In major slaveholding areas such as Córdoba, slave rebellions and *cimarronaje* devastated the local sugar industry. An epidemic of slave flight both reflected and contributed to the breakdown of discipline on the plantations and haciendas as well as in the cities. Slaves no longer reliably provided labor; free workers had grown to abundance; and the price of slaves declined. A growing number of masters became willing to contemplate freeing their slaves, especially when offered a reasonable price. Manumissions increased. The pattern of overall decline in the eighteenth century is clear enough, but the trend was far from uniform at the national, regional, or even local level.

Historians including Dennis Valdés and Catherine Komisaruk have argued that the pull of growing cities played a critical role in bringing slavery to its end. Thousands of slaves in Mexico and Guatemala, by the late colonial period mostly mulattos, greatly enhanced their opportunities for freedom by migrating to the capitals. Often aided by free family and friends, many simply disappeared into urban communities of free people of African descent. In Guatemala City, high-paying construction jobs attracted male fugitives after an earthquake destroyed Santiago in 1773. Spaniards there constantly complained of a shortage of domestic servants, and offered runaway slave women room and board in exchange for their labor. The option of flight also contributed to a rise in legal manumissions, as it gave slaves "some leverage" when negotiating the price of self-purchase with their owners. If an acceptable deal could not be struck, slaves simply ran away, rarely returning to their masters.[25]

In 1810, when Father don Miguel Hidalgo y Costilla first ordered Mexican slaveholders to free their slaves on pain of death, probably no more than 10,000 people remained enslaved in Mexico. Perhaps half that number remained enslaved in Central America. On 14 September 1813, the National Constituent Congress of Chilpancingo, led by José María Morelos, confirmed that slavery, along with caste distinctions, was abolished in Mexico. These declarations, however, applied only to areas controlled by the insurgents. Agustín de Iturbide's Imperial "Commission on Slaves," which convened on 24 October 1821, did not free most slaves, but it prohibited the slave trade to Mexico and freed all children born to slave mothers since the proclamation of independence on 24 February 1821. On 13 July 1824, during the administration of President Guadalupe Victoria, the Sovereign Constituent Congress of Mexico declared slavery as well as the slave trade abolished forever. Despite the clear text of the law, however, numerous loopholes, designed to appease predominantly Anglo-American settlers in Texas, allowed slavery to continue in Mexico's far north. President Vicente Guerrero's proclamation of 15 September 1829 finally made abolition a reality in Mexico (excepting Coahuila and Texas). Beginning in the 1820s, hundreds of slaves fled the United States to Mexico's northern border states. Similarly, slaves from Belize fled to Yucatan, Guatemala, and Honduras.[26]

In Córdoba, unlike most other parts of Mexico, planters clung to slavery tenaciously, and slaves played a major role in the wars for independence. The movement begun by Hidalgo reached Córdoba in 1812, and the following year, Morelos sent agents including free mulatto Juan Bautista to recruit fighters on local plantations. Slaves swelled the ranks of the insurgents, joining them in guerrilla attacks on their former masters. Even slaves who remained on the plantations transformed the nature of their service by demanding payment for their work. "The law has not declared [the slaves] free but since the year 1812 they are in fact and they are paid for their work," complained a local Córdoba writer.[27] When the Crown offered amnesty to insurgents in 1816, many withdrew from the area. But once fighting cooled, local hacendados savagely repressed the remaining slaves, killing rebels, burning down slave quarters, raping enslaved women, and withholding rations from almost all the slaves in the district. Slaves who had joined the insurgency refused to return and retreated to hideouts in the nearby foothills. Continuing to attract slave rebels and runaways to their settlements for more than a decade, they began to trickle back to the towns only after final abolition in 1829. Córdoba's sugar industry did not recover from the destruction of infrastructure and the loss of labor until the 1840s.[28]

The five countries of the United Provinces of Central America emancipated the several hundred remaining slaves in Guatemala, El Salvador, Honduras, Nicaragua, and Costa Rica on 17 April 1824. The law provided for the compensation of slaveholders by a council—the Junta Piadosa de Indemnización de Esclavos. It continued periodically to issue payments as funds became available until the Federal Republic of Central America dissolved in 1838 and 1839. In Guatemala City, a mere fifty-seven people appeared for official liberation; nineteen of them were children younger than 14 years old. In Costa Rica, fewer than 100 slaves were freed by the law, virtually all of them female domestic servants and their children, who most likely continued to work in the same Cartago elite households after abolition.[29]

Independence brought the end of legal racial distinctions as well as slavery. The official abolition of racial classifications (for non-Indians), continuing *mestizaje*, and a persistent denigration of black people led to the eventual disappearance of people of African descent as an identifiable group. In time, people of African descent were simply erased from Mexico's mythical narrative of the mestizo "cosmic race," which represented a perfect blend of Spaniard and Indian. In Guatemala, persons of African descent vanished into the ill-defined but decisively non-Indian *ladino* group; and in Costa Rica, a national discourse of racial homogeneity whitened them, like the Indians, out of existence. With the exception of a few enclaves, much studied by anthropologists, such as the "Afro-Mexican" communities of Veracruz and the Costa Chica or the Garífuna villages of Caribbean Central America, the descendants of the African people of the colonial period have largely become invisible. Historians have scarcely begun to investigate their past.

Notes

1. Robert D. Shadow and María Rodríguez-Shadow, "Aztec Slavery: A Historical Panorama of Anthropological Perspectives," in Rüdiger Zoller (ed.), *Amerikaner wider Willen: Beiträge zur Sklaverei in Lateinamerika* (Frankfurt, 1994), 321–45; Robert M. Carmack, *The Quiché Mayas of Utatlán: The Evolution of a Highland Guatemalan Kingdom* (Norman, Okla., 1981), 151–2.

2. Silvio Zavala, *Los esclavos indios en Nueva España* (Mexico, 1967); Linda A. Newson, *The Cost of Conquest: Indian Decline in Honduras under Spanish Rule* (Boulder, Colo., 1996); Newson, *Indian Survival in Colonial Nicaragua* (Norman, Okla., 1987).

3. Colin Palmer, *Slaves of the White God: Blacks in Mexico, 1570–1650* (Cambridge, Mass., 1976), 77 (quoted); William L. Sherman, *Forced Native Labor in Sixteenth-Century Central America* (Lincoln, Nebr., 1979), chs. 8–9; Zavala, *Esclavos indios*, chs. 1–2; James F. Brooks, *Captives and Cousins: Slavery, Kinship, and Community in the Southwest Borderlands* (Williamsburg, Va., 2002).

4. Matthew Restall, "Black Conquistadors: Armed Africans in Early Spanish America," *The Americas*, 57 (2) (October 2000): 171–205.

5. Palmer, *Slaves of the White God*, ch. 1; Marisa Vega Franco, *El tráfico de esclavos con América (Asientos de Grillo y Lomelín, 1663–1674)* (Seville, 1984), 184–8; Colin Palmer, *Human Cargoes: The British Slave Trade to Spanish America, 1700–1739* (Urbana, Ill., 1981), chs. 4, 6; Christopher H. Lutz, *Historia sociodemográfica de Santiago de Guatemala, 1541–1773* (Antigua, 1982), 85, 22; Kent Russell Lohse, "Africans and their Descendants in Colonial Costa Rica, 1600–1750" (Ph.D. diss., University of Texas at Austin, 2005), chs. 2–3; Gonzalo Aguirre Beltrán, *La población negra de México, 1519–1810: estudio etno-histórico* (2nd edn. Mexico, 1972). For creolization of the slave population, see Frank T. Proctor III, "Slavery, Identity, and Culture: An Afro-Mexican Counterpoint, 1640–1763" (Ph.D. diss., Emory University, 2003), 146–7, 156; Adriana Naveda Chávez-Hita, *Esclavos negros en las haciendas azucareras de Córdoba, Veracruz, 1690–1830* (Xalapa, 1987), 44–8; Matthew Restall, *The Black Middle: Africans, Mayas, and Spaniards in Colonial Yucatan* (Stanford, Calif., 2009), 26–33.

6. Herman L. Bennett, *Africans in Colonial Mexico: Absolutism, Christianity, and Afro-Creole Consciousness, 1570–1640* (Bloomington, Ind., 2003); Lourdes Mondragón Barrios, *Esclavos africanos en la Ciudad de México: el servicio doméstico durante el siglo XVI* (Mexico City, 1999).

7. Lowell Gudmundson, "Los afroguatemaltecos a fines de la colonia," in Rina Cáceres (ed.), *Rutas de la esclavitud en África y América Latina* (San José, 2001); Beatriz Palomo de Lewin, "Perfil de la población africana en el Reino de Guatemala, 1723–1773," in Cáceres (ed.), *Rutas de la esclavitud*; Martin, *Rural Society in Colonial Morelos*, ch. 6; Gisela von Wobeser, *La hacienda azucarera en la época colonial* (Mexico, 1988); Ward Barrett, *The Sugar Hacienda of the Marqueses del Valle* (Minneapolis, 1970); Naveda Chávez-Hita, *Esclavos negros en las haciendas azucareras*.

8. Lolita Gutiérrez Brockington, *The Leverage of Labor: Managing the Cortés Haciendas in Tehuantepec, 1588–1688* (Durham, NC, 1989), ch. 7; Pedro Gómez Danés, *Negros y mulatos en el nuevo reino de León 1600–1795* (Monterrey, 1996); Restall, *Black Middle*, ch. 4.

9. Palmer, *Slaves of the White God*, 75–82, quoting p. 78; Melida Velásquez, "El comercio de esclavos en la Alcaldía Mayor de Tegucigalpa, siglos XVI al XVIII," *Mesoamérica*, 42 (December 2001): 199–222.

10. Juan Manuel de la Serna H., "Bregar y liberar: los esclavos de Querétaro en el siglo XVIII," in Adriana Naveda Chávez-Hita (ed.), *Pardos, mulatos y libertos: sexto encuentro de afromexicanistas* (Xalapa, 2001), 99–116; Frank T. Proctor III, "Afro-Mexican Slave Labor in the Obrajes de Paños of New Spain, Seventeenth and Eighteenth Centuries," *The Americas*, 60 (1) (July 2003): 33–58, quoting p. 44; Javier Villa-Flores, "Voices from a Living Hell: Slavery, Death, and Salvation in a Mexican Obraje," in Martin Austin Nesvig (ed.), *Local Religion in Colonial Mexico* (Albuquerque, NM, 2006).

11. Juan Carlos Reyes G., "Negros y afromestizos en Colima, siglos XVI–XIX," in Luz María Martínez Montiel (ed.), *Presencia africana en México* (Mexico, 1994), 291–3; Juan

Andrade Torres, "Historia de la población negra en Tabasco," in Martínez Montiel (ed.), *Presencia africana en México*, 437–8; Lohse, "Cacao and Slavery in Matina, Costa Rica, 1650–1750," in Lowell Gudmundson and Justin Wolfe (eds.), *Between Race and Place: Blacks and Blackness in Central America* (Durham, NC, forthcoming).

12. O. Nigel Bolland, "Timber Extraction and the Shaping of Enslaved People's Culture in Belize," in Verene A. Shepherd (ed.), *Slavery without Sugar: Diversity in Caribbean Economy and Society since the Seventeenth Century* (Gainesville, Fla., 2002), 36–62; Lohse, "Cacao and Slavery."

13. Herman Lee Bennett, "Lovers, Family and Friends: The Formation of Afro-Mexico, 1580–1810" (Ph.D. diss., Duke University, 1993); Bennett, *Africans in Colonial Mexico*, chs. 4–5; Colin A. Palmer, "From Africa to the Americas: Ethnicity in the Early Black Communities of the Americas," *Journal of World History* (Honolulu), 6 (2) (1995): 223–36.

14. Lewis, *Hall of Mirrors: Power, Witchcraft, and Caste in Colonial Mexico* (Durham, NC, 2003); Joan Cameron Bristol, *Christians, Blasphemers, and Witches: Afro-Mexican Ritual Practice in the Seventeenth Century* (Albuquerque, N. Mex., 2007); Martha Few, *Women Who Live Evil Lives: Gender, Religion, and the Politics of Power in Colonial Guatemala* (Austin, Tex., 2002); Javier Villa-Flores, "Talking through the Chest: Divination and Ventriloquism among African Slave Women in Seventeenth-Century Mexico," *Colonial Latin American Review*, 14 (2) (December 2005): 299–322.

15. Nicole Von Germeten, *Black Blood Brothers: Confraternities and Social Mobility for Afro-Mexicans* (Gainesville, Fla., 2006).

16. Bennett, *Africans in Colonial Mexico*; Proctor, "La familia y la comunidad esclava en San Luis Potosí y Guanajuato, Nueva España, 1640–1740," in Cáceres (ed.), *Rutas de la esclavitud*, 223–50; Herman W. Konrad, *A Jesuit Hacienda in Colonial Mexico: Santa Lucía, 1576–1767* (Stanford, Calif., 1980), ch. 10; Gudmundson, "Los afroguatemaltecos."

17. Naveda Chávez-Hita, *Esclavos negros en las haciendas azucareras*, ch. 3; Adriana Naveda Chávez-Hita, "De San Lorenzo de los Negros a los morenos de Amapa: cimarrones veracruzanos, 1609–1735," in Cáceres (ed.), *Rutas de la esclavitud*, 157–74; Paul Lokken, "A Maroon Moment: Rebel Slaves in Early Seventeenth-Century Guatemala," *Slavery and Abolition*, 25 (3) (December 2004): 44–58.

18. María Elena Martínez, "The Black Blood of New Spain: Limpieza de Sangre, Racial Violence, and Gendered Power in Early Colonial Mexico," *William and Mary Quarterly*, 61 (3) (July 2004); Patrick J. Carroll, "Mandinga: The Evolution of a Mexican Runaway Slave Community, 1735–1827," *Comparative Studies in Society and History*, 19 (4) (October 1977): 488–505.

19. Proctor, "Gender and the Manumission of Slaves in New Spain," *Hispanic American Historical Review*, 86 (2) (May 2006): 309–36; Lowell Gudmundson, "Mecanismos de movilidad social para la población de procedencia africana en Costa Rica colonial: manumisión y mestizaje," in *Estratificación socio-racial y económica de Costa Rica, 1700–1850* (San José, 1978), 17–78.

20. Proctor, "Slavery, Identity, and Culture," 143–4, quoting p. 156; Paul Lokken, "Marriage as Slave Emancipation in Seventeenth-Century Rural Guatemala," *The Americas*, 58 (2) (October 2001): 175–200.

21. R. Douglas Cope, *The Limits of Racial Domination: Plebeian Society in Colonial Mexico City, 1660–1720* (Madison, 1994), 81–2, 82, table 4.10; Bennett, "Lovers, Family and Friends"; Bennett, *Africans in Colonial Mexico*; Lokken, "Marriage as Slave

Emancipation"; María de los Angeles Acuña León and Doriam Chavarría López, "Endogamia y exogamia en la sociedad colonial cartaginesa," *Revista de historia* (Heredia, Costa Rica), 23 (1991): 107–44; Restall, *Black Middle*, ch. 3.

22. Aguirre Beltrán, *Población negra*, ch. 9; Cope, *Limits of Racial Domination*, chs. 3–4; Ilona Katzew, *Casta Painting: Images of Race in Eighteenth-Century Mexico* (New Haven, 2004); Lewis, *Hall of Mirrors*; Restall, *Black Middle*, ch. 3; Robert McCaa, "Calidad, Clase, and Marriage in Colonial Mexico: The Case of Parral, 1788–1790," *Hispanic American Historical Review*, 64 (3) (August 1984): 477–501.

23. Magnus Mörner, "La política de segregación y el mestizaje en la Audiencia de Guatemala," *Revista de Indias*, 24 (1964): 137–51; Brígida von Mentz, *Pueblos de indios, mulatos y mestizos, 1770–1870* (Mexico, 1988); Paul Lokken, "Génesis de una comunidad afro-indígena en Guatemala: la villa de San Diego de la Gomera en el siglo XVII," *Mesoamérica*, 29 (50) (January–December 2008): 37–65; Germán Romero Vargas, *Las estructuras sociales de Nicaragua en el siglo XVIII* (Managua, 1988).

24. Ben Vinson III, *Bearing Arms for His Majesty: The Free-Colored Militia in Colonial Mexico* (Stanford, Calif., 2001); Rina Cáceres, *Negros, mulatos, esclavos y libertos en la Costa Rica del siglo XVII* (Mexico, 2000).

25. Carroll, *Blacks in Colonial Veracruz*, ch. 6; Juan M. de la Serna H., "Bregar y liberar"; Dennis N. Valdés, "The Decline of Slavery in Mexico," *The Americas*, 44 (2) (October 1987): 167–94; Catherine Helen Komisaruk, "Women and Men in Guatemala, 1765–1835: Gender, Ethnicity, and Social Relations in the Central American Capital" (Ph.D. diss., University of California, Los Angeles, 2000), ch. 2, quoting p. 25.

26. Theodore G. Vincent, *The Legacy of Vicente Guerrero, Mexico's First Black Indian President* (Gainesville, Fla., 2001); Sean Kelley, "'Mexico in his Head': Slavery and the Texas–Mexico Border, 1810–1860," *Journal of Social History*, 37 (3) (Spring 2004): 709–23; O. Nigel Bolland, *Formation of a Colonial Society: Belize, from Conquest to Crown Colony* (Baltimore, 1977), 77–80.

27. Quoted in Naveda Chávez-Hita, *Esclavos negros en las haciendas azucareras*, 159. For an analogous example of slave resistance at the Ingenio San Jerónimo in Guatemala, see Komisaruk, "Women and Men," 32–48.

28. Carroll, *Blacks in Colonial Veracruz*, 99–101; Naveda Chávez-Hita, *Esclavos negros en las haciendas*, 153–61.

29. Agustín Estrada Monroy, *Datos para la historia de la Iglesia en Guatemala* (Guatemala, 1974), ii. 519–520; Tatiana Lobo Wiehoff and Mauricio Meléndez Obando, *Negros y blancos: todo mezclado* (San José, 1997), 71–6, 145–6, 146 A; Franklin Alvarado Quesada (ed.), "Documentos relativos a la población afroamericana," *Revista de historia* (Heredia, Costa Rica), 39 (January–June 1999): 277–94.

SELECT BIBLIOGRAPHY

AGUIRRE BELTRÁN, GONZALO. *La población negra de México, 1519–1810: estudio etno-histórico.* 1942. Mexico: Fondo de Cultura Económica, 1972.

BENNETT, HERMAN L. *Colonial Blackness: A History of Afro-Mexico.* Bloomington, Ind.: Indiana University Press, 2009.

CARROLL, PATRICK J. *Blacks in Colonial Veracruz: Race, Ethnicity, and Regional Development*. Austin, Tex.: University of Texas Press, 1991.

LOHSE, KENT RUSSELL. "Africans and their Descendants in Colonial Costa Rica, 1600–1750." Ph.D. diss., University of Texas at Austin, 2005.

MARTÍNEZ MONTIEL, LUZ MARÍA, ed. *Presencia africana en México*. Mexico: Consejo Nacional para la Cultura y las Artes, 1994.

NAVEDA CHÁVEZ-HITA, ADRIANA. *Esclavos negros en las haciendas azucareras de Córdoba, Veracruz, 1690–1830*. Xalapa: Centro de Investigaciones Históricas, Universidad Veracruzana, 1987.

PALMER, COLIN A. *Slaves of the White God: Blacks in Mexico, 1570–1650*. Cambridge, Mass.: Harvard University Press, 1976.

PROCTOR, FRANK T., III. "Slavery, Identity, and Culture: An Afro-Mexican Counterpoint, 1640–1763." Ph.D. diss., Emory University, 2003.

RESTALL, MATTHEW. *The Black Middle: Africans, Mayas, and Spaniards in Colonial Yucatan*. Stanford, Calif.: Stanford University Press, 2009.

VINSON, BEN, III, and MATTHEW RESTALL, eds. *Black Mexico: Race and Society from Colonial to Modern Times*. Albuquerque, N. Mex.: University of New Mexico Press, 2009.

CHAPTER 3

....

SPANISH SOUTH AMERICAN MAINLAND

....

PETER BLANCHARD

THE subject of slavery in Spanish South America has long prompted calls for further research. In 1944 the Peruvian historian Fernando Romero wrote: "Latin America is virgin territory for the investigation of this subject." That same year, James Ferguson King, an American specialist in the history of Colombia, echoed the point, urging scholars to focus on the survival of African cultural patterns in the Americas. In assessing the field, King also presented an evaluation that continues to affect slavery studies to the present day. "The most disinterested evidence available," he maintained, "indicates that slavery in continental Spanish America was relatively mild" in comparison with other regions in the Americas.[1]

This argument lies at the heart of Frank Tannenbaum's influential book *Slave and Citizen: The Negro in the Americas* (1946) and has subsequently been repeated by others writing about specific countries. Josefina Plá, for example, in 1972, described slavery in Paraguay as "softer" (*mas dulce*) than elsewhere in Latin America and "the gentlest in the panorama of Latin American slavery." Norman Meiklejohn, writing in 1974 on eighteenth-century New Granada (modern Colombia), concluded that conditions unique to that area—including a shortage of slaves, difficulties in securing replacements, frequent manumissions, and pro-slave court decisions—"made the slave institution more humane." Indeed, these factors helped foster "the evolution of a system of slavery that was more akin to contractual labor than it was to slavery."[2] But other historians have not been persuaded by the Tannenbaum thesis and have used their own studies to present a harsher picture of Spanish American slavery. The debate produced such a significant outpouring of slave studies that in 1972 when Frederick Bowser examined the "research achievements and priorities" for the African in colonial Spanish America, he produced a long list of the works that had appeared in the past forty years and covered "all facets of the African experience in the Western Hemisphere." Bowser added, however, that much work remained to be done.[3]

The same could be said today, despite an impressive addition to our knowledge since Bowser's article. That much still needs to be done is evident in the small number of general surveys that exist for both the region as a whole and its component parts. Among the former, the most comprehensive are still the works published decades ago by Leslie Rout, Jr., and by Rolando Mellafe. Both cover the history of African slaves in all of Spanish South America from their arrival in the area in the early sixteenth century until slavery's demise 300 years later. The 2005 survey by the Spanish historian José Andrés-Gallego taps into more recent publications on the subject and contains numerous examples of slave responses. But he is primarily concerned about the treatment of slaves, and his examples are drawn primarily from Peru and Argentina in the second half of the eighteenth century. Book-length studies exist for Argentina, Bolivia, Paraguay, Peru, Uruguay, and Venezuela, but the list is short and the quality, which tends toward the descriptive rather than the analytical, varies widely.[4] Historians have preferred to concentrate on particular regions, periods, and aspects of slavery, even though their books and articles provide the wherewithal for quite sophisticated general studies.

The history of African slaves on the South American mainland began with the Spanish conquistadors in the early sixteenth century. Already present in the West Indies and Mexico following the Spanish conquest and settlement of those areas, slaves now became involved in the expansion of Spanish rule southward. Small numbers accompanied the conquistadors along the Pacific coast. They participated in Francisco Pizarro's legendary expedition into the heartland of the Inca empire in the 1530s and in the subsequent quests for El Dorado, the fabled city of gold, that led to the exploration and settlement of much of the continent. Slaves helped suppress the indigenous uprisings against the new rulers at mid-century, notably the Manco Inca rebellion of 1535–6 around Cuzco, and they played an active role in both the civil wars that broke out among the conquistadors as well as the conquistadors' rebellions against the authorities that bloodied Peru between 1542 and 1554.[5]

While most of the African slaves and slaves of African descent who participated in the conquest were soon freed, thereby establishing the roots of a growing and important free colored population, thousands more arrived in their footsteps. In the process the role of the African slave changed significantly. Initially, the majority of the slaves had been retainers and servants of the conquistadors who used some of the looted wealth of the Incas to acquire what was essentially an expensive status symbol. Many subsequently filled a similar position for the prominent members of society who were granted through the *encomienda* system the right to derive income and labor from specified indigenous communities. And while the slave as status symbol remained a constant throughout the history of slavery in Spanish South America, the vast majority of the new imports were destined to occupy far more demanding and onerous positions as manual laborers and domestic servants.

The importation of thousands of African slaves was tied to the demographic disaster that befell the indigenous population. The indigenous decline, which amounted to 90 percent and more in some areas, created an obvious need for a supplementary or alternative labor force. Numerous laws designed to protect the Indians reinforced the decision to import enslaved Africans. Of these the most important were the reformist New Laws issued by Charles V in 1542 that, among other prohibitions, ended the enslavement of Indians. *Encomiendas* continued to remove indigenous workers from the pool of available laborers, as did their assignment to particular economic sectors, especially the silver mines of the central Andes. Since the Spanish Crown had already permitted the importation of African slaves to the Antilles as a solution to its earlier labor crisis, officials had little reason to prevent African slaves from being assigned to the newly conquered areas as replacement workers.

Importing large numbers of slaves from Africa, however, created a dilemma. On the one hand, Spanish officials believed that relying on African slaves would protect the natives from gross abuse and permit their conversion to Christianity, which was central to the papal recognition of Spain's claim to most of the Western hemisphere. Moreover, numerous commentators, including clerics such as the Dominican friar Bartolomé de Las Casas, favored replacing the Indians with African slaves, although Las Casas and others soon came to change their views. On the other hand, the African slave trade was in the hands of Portuguese traders, so that acquiring slaves meant diverting American silver into foreign pockets, which ran counter to the Crown's mercantilist economic policies. Furthermore, the religious issue aroused concerns about cultural contamination, in particular the fear that imported slaves would "infect" the indigenous population with their own religions and thereby hinder the process of conversion. As a result, the Crown agreed to the trade, but insisted upon strict controls that until late in the colonial period severely limited imports. Restrictions produced frequent complaints, as demand exceeded supply in many areas, and led to a substantial contraband trade in slaves that frustrated the Crown by reducing potential revenues from the taxes levied on legitimate slave imports. Furthermore, because of the extent of the smuggling, historians have been unable to calculate exactly the number of slaves imported to the mainland during the colonial period. Philip Curtin's figure of 522,000 is probably low.[6] One other effect of the restrictions was that prime slaves, meaning young adult males, constituted the majority of the imported *bozales* or African-born slaves. While the Crown insisted that one-third of cargoes were to be women in order to relieve concerns about meeting the male slaves' sexual needs, traders frequently ignored the regulation.

To try to enforce its wishes with regard to the slave trade, the Spanish Crown introduced late in the sixteenth century a monopoly system known as the *asiento* that granted companies a contractual right to supply a defined number of slaves to delineated areas. It replaced the previous system of licenses that had been granted first to conquistadors to allow them to bring small numbers of slaves with them and later to settlers to import more substantial quantities. Portuguese slave traders controlled the *asiento* through the late sixteenth and early seventeenth centuries and then were replaced by traders from France and England. They viewed it as a profitable investment in its own right as well as a means to gain access to Spanish American ports where they could engage in other forms of trade—often illegally— and acquire more of the area's fabled silver.[7] The monopoly was never complete, however, as the Crown was willing to grant concessions and licenses as its financial needs grew and new areas developed, permitting traders from other nations to engage in the trade. But the monopolists' determination to protect their interests resulted in frequent legal battles that constitute an important part of the documentary evidence on slavery in Spanish South America.

With the establishment of the trade from Africa, Cartagena, founded in 1533 on the northern coast of New Granada, became the principal port on the mainland for offloading slaves before transshipment to the viceregal capital of Lima in Peru and distribution throughout the hemisphere. Buenos Aires, founded in 1580, developed as a secondary port of entry in the late sixteenth century, but smuggling and concerns about the loss of silver from highland Upper Peru (modern Bolivia) resulted in the route being closed by the mid-seventeenth century, although the prohibition was only partially successful. Some 3,000 slaves passed annually through Cartagena during the period of the Portuguese *asiento*, having survived the horrors of the Atlantic crossing with its diseases and high mortality rates that David Chandler has described in detail. More recently, Linda Newson and Susie Minchin have found that for the early seventeenth century the place of origin and the conditions in Africa were more important in explaining slave deaths than the shipboard conditions during the Middle Passage. They also point out that slaves who were not properly registered tended to be treated much more harshly than legal imports once they arrived, which also increased mortality rates, as did the American diseases which they now faced. At the same time, efforts to reinvigorate the slaves and make them saleable resulted in a surprisingly wholesome and nutritious diet, both in Cartagena and on the journey to Panama and then on to Lima. Chandler notes that mortality rates in Cartagena dropped significantly from the late seventeenth century, as slaves were first disembarked for "refreshing" in Jamaica and other Caribbean islands before being sent on to Cartagena. His description of the subsequent distribution of slaves and the difficulties of the internal slave trade, which resulted in more deaths, has no counterpart in other areas that might indicate if the trade elsewhere was as deadly as that of New Granada. Evidence may be not be readily available, however, for the internal trade seems to have involved large numbers of illegal sales, at least in the case of Venezuela, where owners sought to avoid the taxes imposed by the Crown.[8]

Those slaves who survived the several legs of the long journey and reached their eventual destination were valuable property. The Crown initially set the selling price for slaves when they were brought to the colonies at about seven or eight times what the *asiento* contractors paid for each slave license. But market forces quickly undermined Crown wishes. On the one hand, prices varied according to time, gender, age, skills, place of labor, availability of alternative workers, and the potential profitability of the land. Where small and medium-sized farms competed with big estates and reduced the planters' profits, for example, slave labor was less attractive, keeping slave prices low. On the other hand, distance, as in the case of bringing slaves to Bolivia, drove up prices. The route, too, had an impact. Slaves transported to Chile and Peru via Buenos Aires were cheaper than those brought through Panama and Lima because of the longer distance and, consequently, extra cost of transportation, medicines, clothing, food, and other essentials that were required en route. In Colombia in the early seventeenth century, the important variable seems to have been the job to which the slave was assigned. Thus, mining workers fetched higher prices than domestic slaves. Yet, female slaves in this area tended to be more expensive than men, and even the elderly were valuable. Availability was a further factor affecting prices. The simultaneous arrival of several slave ships could create a glut that depressed prices. In the case of Paraguay, prices tended to be higher during the colonial period than after independence when the number of slaves rose as a result of natural reproduction. Another glut occurred with the expulsion of the Jesuits in the late eighteenth century as the Crown sought to divest itself of the many slaves it had acquired. This period marked the beginning of a general decline in slave prices that lasted until abolition, although the cost of individual slaves could still be very high, and local conditions could produce short-term spikes.[9]

The nature of slave employment in Spanish South America challenges some of the commonly held assumptions about chattel slavery in the Americas. For one thing, in most areas slaves did not constitute the predominant labor force. Despite the staggering decline in the size of the indigenous population, sufficient numbers remained to satisfy many of the demands of the small white population. In some areas, such as Paraguay and the highlands of Ecuador, Peru, and Bolivia, the surviving Indians and their descendants as well as a growing mixed-blood population were adequate to meet requirements so that only small numbers of African slaves were imported. The Andean silver mines, the centre of economic activity in the Spanish American colonies, also relied on labor other than slaves. The authorities certainly considered them for the task, but cost and the harsh climate of the Andean highlands deterred their widespread use. Instead, Indians provided most of the work through the notorious forced labor system known as *mita*, with slaves relegated to a secondary role in the most important silver-mining area of Potosí in Upper Peru where they served as foremen and workers in the refining, minting, and transportation sectors. In other mining regions, such as the gold workings of Chile and Colombia and the copper mines of Venezuela, they were more prominent from as early as the mid-sixteenth century. Initially they may have worked alongside Indian slaves, but in Venezuela and the Colombian Popayán and Chocó regions, they in time came to replace the indigenous workers. The numbers were not large: in the Popayán region fewer than 300 African slaves were employed in 1628, growing to 1,000 over the next fifty years, while in the more northern Chocó, slaves arrived later and expanded in number from 600 in 1704 to over 7,000 in 1782. Slaves remained a minority of the population, less than 6 percent for all of Colombia in 1778, but their labor was vital, and in the case of Popayán, according to Sherwin Bryant, what developed was a "classic slave society."[10]

The description also applies to certain agricultural areas where black slaves came to constitute the principal labor force. Agriculture was the major economic activity in many parts of the mainland, and, again, slaves worked alongside the indigenous population in some areas, while in others, such as the cacao plantations of Venezuela and the farms and haciendas of the central highlands of Bolivia, they came to replace the native population.[11] Slaves were particularly prominent on the plantations of lowland and tropical areas where the Indian population virtually disappeared and where the cultivation of luxury crops offset the slaves' high prices. They predominated in the cultivation of sugar cane and also worked on estates producing cacao, indigo, and cotton as well as grapes and livestock. Indeed, agricultural estates incorporated the largest groupings of slaves under a single owner. Urban slave owners may have outnumbered their rural counterparts, but they tended to own only a few slaves, while individually the latter owned far more slaves. In some cases that number could be in the hundreds. The Catholic Church was the single largest owner of slaves, while within the Church, the Jesuit order ranked as the pre-eminent owner. The Jesuits and their relations with their slaves have consequently attracted the attention of numerous historians, notably Nicholas Cushner who has examined the subject in Argentina, Ecuador, and Peru. Other areas of Spanish South America require companion pieces, as do the slaveholding activities of the Jesuits' fellow orders, such as the Augustinians, Dominicans, and Mercedarians. Similarly, Jean-Pierre Tardieu's two-volume description of the Catholic Church and its slaves in Peru calls for similar studies for other South American countries. With their extensive and growing holdings, the Jesuits emerged as major buyers of African slaves by the early seventeenth century. They considered slaves more economic and productive than wage-earning indigenous labor and employed them in both their rural and urban properties. At the same time, they encouraged marriage among their slaves in order to promote childbearing, both to reduce the need for imports as well as to satisfy moral concerns and ensure stability on their estates. In fostering marriage the Jesuits were complying with a Crown directive from the late seventeenth century that there should be no impediment to slave marriages. As a result, some Jesuit properties achieved gender equilibrium among their slaves. Yet, because of high mortality rates from disease and low fertility rates, they continued to depend on the African slave trade to replenish their stock, in common with other slave owners.[12]

While this picture of rural labor fits preconceived notions of slavery in the Americas, according to Frederick Bowser's impressively researched and influential work *The African Slave in Colonial Peru, 1524–1650* (1974), slavery, at least in Peru, was largely an urban phenomenon.[13] Not every historian has agreed, suggesting that Bowser's focus is too narrow. Yet others have supported his argument, concentrating as he did on the viceregal capital of Lima, which was founded in 1535 and flourished from the late sixteenth century with the wealth derived from the viceroyalty's silver mines. The city became the center of the mainland slave trade, and its inhabitants were major purchasers of African slaves through much of the colonial period. According to an official census of Lima in 1614, blacks (most but not all of whom were slaves) numbered 10,386, constituting more than 40 percent of the total population of 24,454. Female blacks outnumbered males 5,857 to 4,529. Owners used their human property in various occupations, ranging from common laborer to skilled artisan to domestic servant, so that by the end of the colonial era, slaves were ubiquitous in all aspects of urban labor and vital to the whole process of colonial urbanization. Nancy van Deusen's work on Lima in the latter part of the seventeenth century complements Bowser's research by describing how slaves in the artisan trades assisted in the construction of the city's buildings, including its hospitals where many slaves ended their days. During this period they tended to retain their African surnames and mixed with an increasingly diverse population that included large numbers of free blacks and mulattos.[14] Many lived away from their owners, operating on their own as they earned wages from which they had to pay a predetermined amount to their owners as well as meet their own subsistence requirements. Less well-to-do owners relied for their daily necessities on the income of their one or two slaves. The sense of freedom derived from working away from the owner must have been attractive to slaves. It also led, however, to charges of slaves having too much freedom, that they were prone to anti-social behavior, such as gambling and drinking. Charges such as these aroused concerns among officials and owners as both were determined to maintain a system that functioned without serious problems, which meant a quiescent slave population.

Control of the growing slave population was a central issue throughout the colonial period, and royal authorities tried to achieve it through a complex combination of fear and incentives. Underlying the system was the understanding that slavery was not a permanent state and that the soul of the slave was equal to that of the free person. Slaves, consequently, had certain rights, and owners dangled emancipation as a reward for those who remained loyal and obedient. The prospect of freedom, coupled with the imbalance of forces ranged against them, convinced many slaves to accommodate themselves to the system. At the same time, those in authority promoted divisions among the slaves as a further means of control. For example, they sought to keep apart those from the same linguistic regions in Africa, believing that left together ethnically homogeneous slaves would more likely conspire against their owners. They also fostered a hierarchy among slaves in assigning them to different occupations. Masters ranked a domestic higher than a field slave, while those who had a skill were considered superior to common laborers. Over time the slaves came to accept these divisions, just as they seemed to accept the racial hierarchy of this stratified society that was committed to purity of blood. With color determining status, further divisions developed along racial lines, as mulattos claimed higher rank than blacks. A revealing episode occurred during the early Independence period in Cartagena, when free people of color with the assistance of slaves helped to take control of the government from the royalist authorities. But they then refused to reward their allies by calling for an abolition decree. The Swiss historian Aline Helg points to the limited intermixing and marriage between the two groups as additional evidence of the effect of racial policies in the city.[15] Cartagena, however, may have been unusual in this regard, for elsewhere racial divisions between free people of color and slaves do not seem to have been as pervasive.

Central to the establishment and maintenance of control over the slave population was the Catholic Church. Clergy had the task of ensuring that the newly arrived slaves were converted to Catholicism and that they then complied with Hispanic norms, including attending Mass and celebrating the other sacraments.[16] An arm of the Church in promoting these goals was the Church brotherhood or *cofradía*. Established for the purpose of caring for a particular church or religious statue, the brotherhoods in return provided members with a form of mutual assistance. For slaves, the *cofradía* also offered a sense of community, a means to deal with concerns about the afterlife, an opportunity to practice their culture and even aspects of their African religions, and an environment for a degree of personal enjoyment. Some brotherhoods restricted their membership to particular African tribal groups, while others were less exclusive, accepting members who were black or mulatto, free or slave. Thus, while the religious and secular authorities may have hoped that the *cofradías* would help to convince slaves that they should accommodate themselves to their position in society, the organizations also served as a momentary release from the harsh realities of daily life.[17]

Initiatives such as these often proved ineffective, and all slave owners, including the Church and its orders, were prepared to resort to more forceful measures to maintain control. Daily life could be extremely harsh for the slaves of the Spanish American mainland, challenging those who have described slavery in the area as "benign" compared to that of other parts of the Americas. The whip was always present and used by both masters and authorities to indicate clearly who was in charge. Running away usually resulted in a whipping, as did affronts to anyone in positions of authority. The whipping could be quite vicious, amounting to 100 lashes or more despite rules against excessive punishment. Less serious crimes such as theft, assaulting another slave, and drunkenness might be similarly punished, or could result in assignment to some public works project or confinement in a jail or bakery, where the offender might also be shackled. Female slaves could be incarcerated in jails, bakeries, or convents, depending on the offense. Slaves who committed more serious crimes, such as murder, faced the prospect of hanging, but could be sent to the galleys or into perpetual exile. Killing an owner or rebellion, however, almost guaranteed execution. Although not written into any criminal code as a punishment, slaves also could be sold away from their family or to a distant place, which may have seemed like a greater punishment to them than many of those sanctioned by law.

In attempting to control the slave population, particularly in the first century after the conquest, Spanish officials paid particular attention to the relationship that developed between slaves and the indigenous population, a relationship that has attracted growing academic interest. According to earlier studies based largely on official documentation or *cédulas*, the authorities were determined to keep the two communities separate, in large part to satisfy religious concerns. They were also keen to prevent sexual relations between the two groups, consequently passing laws that prohibited slaves from living in Indian villages and even mandating castration for slaves who were found guilty of raping Indian women. While officials justified their measures on religious grounds, some historians have argued that the real goal was to prevent these two exploited groups from allying against the Spaniards, a view which may have had some justification since Indians continued to be enslaved in Chile, Paraguay, Venezuela, and perhaps elsewhere well into the colonial period.[18] Charles Beatty Medina and Jean-Pierre Tardieu suggest, however, that the authorities were overreacting to the problem, for in their view relations between the two groups were anything but harmonious. From the time of the conquest, indigenous leaders accused slaves of taking advantage of their position as associates of the conquistadors or representatives of their owners to abuse the Indians. In the words of Matthew Restall, the black population "lived and worked in and for the Spanish world, rather than the native one." Similarly, Tardieu notes that "oppressed, the slaves became oppressors."[19] Just as slaves played an important military role at the time of the conquest, subsequently they helped the new rulers prevent indigenous unrest and maintain control over what was still the largest sector of the population. Their involvement in suppressing the Inca rebellions in the Peruvian highlands in the mid-sixteenth century foreshadowed similar actions throughout the colonial era. For example, runaway slaves in the Esmeraldas region of Ecuador in the late sixteenth century offered to assist in subjugating local bellicose Indians who were resisting Spanish settlement. Two hundred years later, in November 1777, plantation slaves armed with lances and machetes helped end an

Indian insurrection in northern Ecuador.[20] Indians, on their part, had no reservations about responding in kind. They were prominent in capturing runaway slaves, and members of the Indian nobility became slaveholders once the slave trade developed.

Yet evidence exists that slaves and Indians managed to surmount the apparent divisions and establish close relations at different times and in different places, as economic and human realities rendered the prohibitions ineffective. The appearance of a growing mixed black-Indian or *zambo* population was clear proof of racial mixing. Some blacks, particularly runaways, settled among natives in Ecuador, Venezuela, and Colombia, and on the northern coast of Peru. Leo Garofolo and Kathryn Joy McNight have provided a more nuanced indication of the close relationship by delineating the Africans' role in transferring not just their own culture but also native ritual practices and skills via witchcraft and magic to all sectors of society. In other words, slaves acted not simply as conduits for Hispanic culture and values, but added—at least in Lima and Cartagena—their African traditions to a mix of Christianity and indigenous religious practices. One further indication of some sort of connection is the fact that in the late eighteenth century on one estate near Córdoba in Argentina, the slaves spoke Quechua among themselves, not Spanish.[21]

The slaves' developing relationship with the native inhabitants was one aspect of the colonies' shift from the conquest culture of the sixteenth century to the less dramatic settlement culture of the seventeenth and early eighteenth centuries. The later period was marked by the growth of the American-born population that included creole slaves. Their appearance attests to the presence of significant numbers of female slaves of childbearing age, despite the predominance of male slaves in the slave trade. A few female slaves had accompanied the conquistadors, and their numbers grew subsequently, explaining the increasing numbers of slave children who, according to legal dictates, followed the status of the mother. Some of these were mulatto children indicating the occurrence of sexual relations between white owners and their African slaves. This natural reproduction helps to explain why female slaves came to predominate in some areas, and especially in urban centers.[22] They filled a variety of urban and rural occupations that ranged from domestic servant and street vendor, to wet-nurse and prostitute, to farmhand and field worker, although the details for many areas are still scanty. One particular role, as *curandera* or healer, has attracted some academic interest, as it often had African roots and seems to have involved as much witchcraft and sorcery as healing skills. *Curanderas* dispensed their services to all sectors of society, even though their activities occasionally brought them to the attention of the Inquisition for what were perceived to be blasphemous or heretical actions. In some cases this led to harsh punishments. Female slaves everywhere commonly suffered mistreatment in much the same way as male slaves, perhaps even more so, for they also had to contend with sexual exploitation at the hands of their masters. Yet, in rare instances slave women managed to overcome their status and to be accepted by even the highest levels of society. Nancy van Deusen's examination of the ex-slave Ursula de Jesús reveals the life of a mystic residing in a Lima convent who, like the *curanderas*, had influence far beyond the black community, although in this case it was because of her piety and good works rather than her healing skills.[23]

Ursula's experiences were, of course, exceptional, but her life points to the fact that some slaves managed to obtain their freedom, a goal to which most if not all slaves aspired. The general pattern seemed to be that females, along with the elderly (at least in Lima), the locally born, and mulattos, were in an advantageous position where manumission was concerned. While some white fathers freed their mulatto children, the continuing presence of mulatto slaves indicates, however, that many, probably the majority, did not. Records also show that the number of slaves freed was small during both the colonial and national periods. Lyman Johnson's study of manumission in Buenos Aires between 1776 and 1810 found that the possibility for slaves obtaining their freedom improved during the period but that the number still amounted to only 1.3 percent of the slave population in the latter year. Self-purchase was the most common route to freedom, although in some areas wills and deathbed declarations freed significant numbers. The opportunity for self-purchase explains why valuations were so important to slaves, as they established how much they needed to save in order to buy freedom for themselves or for members of their families. Both urban and rural slaves managed to obtain funds in various ways, although the former tended to have more options by having access to wage-earning jobs. In the rural sector some slaves had the right to sell produce grown on estate plots. Those who worked in the gold fields, such as the Colombian Chocó region, enjoyed a particularly advantageous position since they had access to a resource that they could exchange directly for their freedom. The large number of accusations that slaves were stealing from the mines suggest that some, at least, were tempted, and harsh punishments were imposed to try to prevent it. Slaves seemed willing to take the risk, however, indicating the precious valuation that many slaves placed on freedom.[24]

Indeed, stealing from mines to become free was only one example of a characteristic that was true of slaves everywhere in the Americas: "slavery," in the words of historian Lolita Gutiérrez Brockington, "was synonymous with resistance." Carlos Eduardo Valencia Villa, a student of Colombian slavery, adds that, given an opportunity, slaves did what they could "to subvert the rules of domination."[25] Slave resistance covered a wide range, from passive, individual, day-to-day acts to open acts of collective violence, although only the most overt tend to appear in the historical record. Slave insurrection before the mid-eighteenth century seems to have been rare, probably because of the difficulties in fomenting this sort of organized, collective resistance.[26] More frequently, slaves turned to the less dangerous method of appealing to the courts to protect what they believed were their rights, even if decisions were not always in their favor. Sherwin Bryant has noted that this particular form of resistance had a long history, as slaves demonstrated their "fortitude, legal savvy, and social awareness" from an early date.[27] Everywhere they used the courts to try to improve their lot, change owners, or secure their freedom. Another form of resistance that led to court cases, although in a starkly different way, was the practice of infanticide. The Canadian historian Renée Soulodre-La France has uncovered a case of a slave in eighteenth-century New Granada who stabbed her 5-year-old daughter to death, fearing that her owner intended to separate them. The authorities were unwilling to blame slavery for her act, concluding instead that she was either irrational or crazy or intoxicated. Slaves were already considered a group "without honour," but this went beyond what was expected even of them.[28]

If the courts could not provide some sort of relief, many slaves resorted to one of the most common forms of active resistance that seemed to promise freedom: they simply ran away. Official reports of runaways appeared almost from the time that slaves first arrived on the mainland. Groups of fugitives frequently established communities called *palenques* that aroused even greater official concern. As María del Carmen Borrego Plá has pointed out in her study of Cartagena at the end of the seventeenth century, the problem of runaways was multifaceted, involving the loss of their labor and value, the example they set for other slaves, their possible alliance with enemy pirates who appeared on occasion in these coastal waters, their attacks on rural travelers and rural property, and their threats to the city. In some areas there was the fear that they would join with indigenous communities and rebel against Spanish rule. As a result, the presence of runaways and *palenques* was an important factor behind the issuance of controls on urban slave movements, the imposition of brutal punishments such as whipping, mutilation, and execution, and the mounting of expeditions to try to suppress the communities. The Crown was willing on occasion, however, to offer freedom to the runaways in order to eliminate them, indicating both the fears as well as the difficulty in suppressing them. In 1679, for example, the authorities granted freedom and land to runaways in the Colombian province of Santa Marta to eliminate the perceived threat. *Palenques* remained a common feature in Colombia where in the eighteenth century, according to Anthony McFarlane, African ethnic elements as well as European influences were evident. He concludes that while the inhabitants were active and they sometimes plotted to establish wider alliances with the aim of overthrowing slavery, there is little to indicate that they contemplated a general slave rebellion or that their actions at this time can be seen as a factor advancing the cause of abolition. But runaway slaves remained a threat, both in Colombia and elsewhere in Spanish South America, as they linked with indigenous groups in some places and bandits in others, and even secured assistance from local white communities that permitted them to avoid recapture for many years.[29]

Slave resistance continued and, according to some historians, intensified in the late colonial period as slavery, along with the whole colonial structure, began to experience a long period of unsettling changes that led eventually to independence and abolition.[30] The changes began in the mid-eighteenth century when Spain's Bourbon monarchs introduced the first of a series of economic and administrative reforms designed to restore Spain's power internationally and royal absolutism at home and abroad. Underlying some of these changes were the enlightened ideas of the times that were spreading throughout the region, including those that would lead to the American and French revolutions and to the slave revolt in the French colony of Saint-Domingue. To implement the economic reforms in the colonies workers were needed, and African slaves were viewed as the logical choice. As a result, the Crown ended the *asiento* system and began to liberalize the slave trade. In 1789 it issued a royal order permitting Spanish subjects to trade slaves in selected ports in Venezuela, Cuba, Santo Domingo, and Puerto Rico, an order that was extended elsewhere over the following years. A surge of new imports followed, introducing once again mostly young men who remembered what it was like to be free. The reforms saw peripheral areas, such as Venezuela and the Río de la Plata, become increasingly important, as cacao production stimulated the economy of the former, while Potosí silver supplemented by exports of cattle hides and other agricultural produce boosted the latter. Thousands of newly arrived slaves provided the labor for much of the transition. Elena de Studer has described the slave trade to Argentina at this time, but for other areas details of the trade have to be gleaned from works that deal more broadly with the economic reforms.[31] The Bourbon reformers in their attempts to establish a more centralized and absolutist system also became suspicious of any institution or body that seemed to challenge their goals. Consequently, the Jesuits, with their wealth and independence, fell under suspicion, leading to their expulsion from all Spanish territory in 1767 and the transference of their extensive holdings, including their slaves, to the Crown.

All of these developments had a dramatic impact on Spanish South America, provoking unrest among various sectors of the population that on occasion involved slaves, notably those previously owned by the Jesuits. One result of the Crown's assumption of Jesuit property was that it had become the major slave owner in Spanish South America. Already it possessed some slaves, the so-called "negros del rey," through intestate deaths, legal acquisition, and purchase. In Chile they labored on public works, while in Peru, among other tasks, they served on royal ships sailing along the Pacific coast. But the Crown had little desire to retain ownership of its newly acquired property and eventually put much of it up for sale. That decision was often unsettling for the slaves. In parts of Argentina new owners divided slave families and redistributed individuals, some from as far away as Peru. The disruption, along with efforts to implement a new work regime, aroused hostility that took the form of indiscipline, a rejection of authority, flight, and, in the cases of Ecuador and Peru, violent risings on individual estates, as Jean-Pierre Tardieu and Wilfredo Kapsoli have shown.[32]

The slaves' readiness to agitate was also apparent in their response to a number of the major rebellions that erupted on the mainland during the late eighteenth century. Some slaves seemed to share the views of the leaders of these movements who, in response to the reforms and the enlightened ideas of the time, charged that their rights were being ignored and made demands that included the abolition of slavery. Thus, in the early 1780s a few slaves joined the Túpac Amaru and Túpac Katari rebellions in the Andean highlands of Peru and Bolivia. An even larger number supported the Comunero rebels in New Granada in 1781, and they played a more prominent role in the Coro rebellion of western Venezuela in 1795. Led by José Leonardo Chirino, a free *zambo*, the latter movement can be traced to the spread of French revolutionary slogans, as well as an awareness of the slave revolt then occurring in Saint-Domingue, as it called for the abolition of slavery and the dismantling of racial and social hierarchies. Failing to win widespread support, however, the movement was crushed in a matter of days, and its leaders were executed.[33]

In the face of the growing discontent, the Crown sought to address what it saw as problems associated with slavery by issuing legislation that laid out the rights and obligations of slaves and slaveholders alike. In 1783–4 Charles III drew up a comprehensive *Código Negro* or Black Code, modeled on the French legislation of the same name. The initiative led to a royal *cédula* or decree in 1789 that the Argentine historian Mario Rufer has described as one further example of the Crown's efforts to impose absolutism on the colonies. According to the code, the state, in Rufer's view, would have assumed a more active role in overseeing the slaves, in contrast to the past when the owner had complete control. But slaveholder resistance prevented the code's implementation, even though elements of it were introduced in different areas over the following years. For example, branding was abolished and attempts were made to control whipping. In Ecuador violation of the rules actually resulted in some owners being fined. But the Crown had still not managed to establish its authority over slaveholders in much of Spanish America. The latter maintained their right to discipline their human property and did not hesitate to punish or mistreat their slaves. Only on those rare occasions when public order was subverted did the state in the person of Crown officials manage to impose itself.[34]

Nevertheless, because of the attempts to implement the *Código Negro*, as well as the other developments of this revolutionary era, slaves had acquired a better idea of their rights and were displaying a willingness to defend them, particularly through the courts. While this may not have been something new, as Sherwin Bryant argues, studies of the late colonial period give the sense of a surge of judicial appeals. The cases seemed to originate largely among urban slaves, a scenario that is understandable since they had easier access to the authorities and the courts than their rural cohorts. But the result is, perhaps, a somewhat skewed picture of slave response. Renée Soulodre-La France, who sees a shift in the focus of slave resistance at this time from owners toward the state—marking in her view the beginning of pressure for abolition—describes how slaves turned to the authorities for redress of grievances. They accepted their status as slaves and the right of enslavement, but they charged that owners were not complying with the King's rules, a reference to the *Código Negro*. They were, thus, once again using the system to try to improve their situation, selecting an option that was less dangerous to themselves than flight, but one that in its own way was equally rebellious.[35]

Female slaves appear in the historical record as playing a prominent role in initiating these legal challenges. It may have reflected their greater numbers in many urban centers as well as their continuing privileged position where manumission was concerned. One Ecuadorian slave who tried to secure her freedom and that of her daughter at this time was María Chiquiquirá Díaz. María's life points to the fluidity of slavery in late colonial Guayaquil, a city where the opportunities for slaves to obtain their freedom seemed to have been improving. Married to a freeman who was a tailor, she lived with her family with the permission of her owner, a priest, in a separate part of his house. Both María and her daughter had received some education.[36] María's efforts to free her daughter indicate in addition to the abiding desire for freedom, a concern common to slave women to protect their children and the family unit in general. According to David Chandler, marriage and family life were vital to slaves in Colombia throughout the colonial period, and the same was true of Lima in the late colonial and early republican eras, as Christine Hünefeldt has shown. Challenging the view that slavery destroyed or permanently enfeebled family life, they point out how slaves sought to maintain the family intact. In the case of Lima, female slaves used marriage as a tool to gain control over their own lives, as they carefully selected their marriage partners with an eye to freedom, preferring freemen over slaves and creoles over *bozales*. Patterns, however, varied throughout Spanish South America, even in parts of Colombia, for Rafael Antonio Díaz Díaz has found that in early eighteenth-century Bogotá, few slaves married, although marriage became more frequent subsequently. In contrast to Chandler, he argues that the nuclear family was less common here, as owners had no reservations about ignoring legal prohibitions and separating slave children from their parents.[37]

The agitation that marked the late colonial period further intensified during the long years of the independence wars of the early nineteenth century, which proved to be another watershed for Spanish American slavery. The wartime destruction of property, the migration of slaveholders, and the recruiting of slaves by both sides in return for their freedom provided unprecedented opportunities for slaves to challenge both their owners and the system. So, too, did the antislavery legislation that the new patriot governments passed. The laws reflected their commitment to liberal goals as well as their desire to garner backing within the slave community. The most important of these laws ended the African slave trade and declared that all children born from a certain date would be free, the so-called free womb laws. The legislation proved successful in winning slave support, as did the offer of freedom in return for military service. Thousands came to serve, primarily as conscripts but also as volunteers. In the process they played a vital role in the patriot victory and established a reputation as valiant and skillful soldiers. The war years also saw other instances of slave resistance that continued after independence was won. They ranged from a serious rebellion in Venezuela (1811–16), to flight by slaves everywhere, to demands for improvements in their conditions. Once again female slaves joined male slaves in this agitation, with a few taking their demands directly to the new leaders. One was the Ecuadorian slave Angela Batallas, who in 1823 appealed to Simón Bolívar for her freedom on the grounds of a sexual relationship with her owner. In the process she equated her personal freedom with the freedom of the new nations, adopting the language of the time, just as others were doing.[38]

The continuing slave agitation proved important, for despite the various war-time attacks on slavery that pointed the way toward abolition, the institution survived. Slaveholders remained too powerful and the new governments were too weak to challenge them. Indeed, the new states, having inherited the Jesuit properties that the Crown had confiscated earlier, were often slaveholders themselves. Most governments tried to divest themselves of their slaves, but state ownership in Paraguay actually increased after Independence along with the numbers of slaves.[39] The new governments also tended to ignore promises made during the wars. The African slave trade was supposed to end, yet, as James Ferguson King has shown, Britain's attempts to suppress the trade had only partial success. Significant numbers of illegal imports continued to arrive, especially to Uruguay and Argentina via Brazil. Slaveholders and their political allies also attempted to reopen the intracontinental slave trade, thereby securing needed slaves while remaining technically in compliance with treaty obligations. During the late 1830s and 1840s, for example, slave traders shipped more than 600 slaves, along with their free children, from Colombia to Peru's Pacific coast.[40]

Abolition, thus, may have unfolded gradually, and even been a "non-event" in the case of Venezuela, as John Lombardi has claimed. But elsewhere, as Harold Bierck, Jr., has argued, it involved a lengthy "struggle." Officials and slaveholders had to be convinced that slavery should be abolished, and a generation passed in all but one country before they were. The exception was Chile where legislators, in response to the liberal ideas of the Independence period and the country's small population of 4,000 slaves, issued an abolition decree in 1823, the first Latin American country to do so. Elsewhere the gradualist struggle that culminated in a spate of abolition decrees in the 1850s required pressures from other quarters, with slaves often in the forefront. In Colombia slaves agitated because of the ineffective-ness of the manumission juntas that were set up at the time of Independence to facilitate the move toward abolition. In Peru, whose abolition process has been the most thoroughly examined of all of the South American republics, slaves purchased their own freedom, ran away, engaged in banditry, and even rebelled, all helping to reduce the number of slaves still in bondage as well as the number of slaveholders committed to slavery. British pressure, changing economic factors, the movement of slaves from countryside to urban centers, and the availability of alternative workers and funds for compensation also helped to undermine slavery both here and elsewhere. Nevertheless, the institution managed to stagger on, requiring more forceful actions in some cases. Warfare or the threat of warfare determined the dates of abolition in Peru, Uruguay, and even in Venezuela, while Paraguay, the last of the mainland Spanish American countries to abolish slavery, had it imposed by Brazilian occupying forces in 1869 during the War of the Triple Alliance.[41]

The above case studies and examples indicate that historians have uncovered many new aspects of slavery in Spanish South America since Frederick Bowser assessed the state of the field in 1972. Yet much remains to be done. While providing new details of an old subject, recent articles are often limited in time and place. Similar studies are needed for other regions and different periods in order to make comparisons and to understand slavery's transformation and resilience in the hemisphere. Statistics are still largely missing for much of Spanish South America despite the existence of notarial archives that contain information about the ethnic origin, age, value, marriage status, children, and other details of the lives of slaves. The same source can also be used to clarify the relations between slaves, their owners, and other members of their community, as well as the intricacies of a slavery system that was not simply a relationship between whites and blacks. One particular aspect that has colored slave studies in recent years has been researchers' stress upon the agency of slaves. They have indicated that slaves enjoyed a great deal of control over their own lives, that they had opportunities to address their own concerns, even to limit the effects of slavery. While the evidence certainly supports this to a point, the overall impression at times is that the writer has validated the Tannenbaum thesis, that slavery on the Spanish American mainland was comparatively benign, as many writers in the past claimed. The impression is not deliberate, for all students of slavery invariably include in their works details of the horrors of slavery and the various forms of mistreatment that slaves suffered. Yet, perhaps a greater emphasis on the latter aspect needs to be made, for slavery in this vast area was often as dehumanizing as it was elsewhere, despite what some have written and despite the best efforts of Spanish South America's slaves to challenge and mitigate the undeserved burden that they bore for over 300 years.

Notes

1. Fernando Romero, "The Slave Trade and the Negro in South America," *Hispanic American Historical Review*, 24 (3) (August 1944): 368–86; James Ferguson King, "Negro History in Continental Spanish America," *Journal of Negro History*, 29 (1) (January 1944): 7–23, esp. 17.

2. Frank Tannenbaum, *Slave and Citizen: The Negro in the Americas* (New York, 1947); Norman A. Meiklejohn, "The Implementation of Slave Legislation in Eighteenth-Century New Granada," in Robert Brent Toplin (ed.), *Slavery and Race Relations in Latin America* (Westport, Conn., 1974), 197–8; Josefina Plá, *Hermano negro: la esclavitud en el Paraguay* (Madrid, 1972), 74, 77, 147. For similar claims about slavery in Colombia and Argentina, see David L. Chandler, "Family Bonds and the Bondsman: The Slave Family in Colonial Colombia," *Latin American Research Review*, 16 (2) (1981): 108; Elena F. S. de Studer, *La trata de negros en el Rio de la Plata durante el siglo XVIII* (Buenos Aires, 1958), 331–2.

3. Frederick P. Bowser, "The African in Colonial Spanish America: Reflections on Research Achievements and Priorities," *Latin American Research Review*, 7 (1) (1972): 77–94.

4. Leslie B. Rout, Jr., *The African Experience in Spanish America: 1502 to the Present Day* (Cambridge, 1976); Rolando Mellafe, *La esclavitud en Hispanoamérica* (Buenos Aires, 1964); José Andrés-Gallego, *La esclavitud en la América española* (Madrid, 2005). National studies include Miguel Acosta Saignes, *Vida de los esclavos negros en Venezuela* (1967; Havana, 1978); Carlos Aguirre, *Breve historia de la esclavitud en el Perú: una herida que no deja de sangrar* (Lima, 2005); Alfredo Boccia Romañach, *Esclavitud en el Paraguay: vida cotidiana del esclavo en las Indias Meridionales* (Asunción, 2004); Alberto Crespo, *Esclavos negros en Bolivia* (La Paz, 1977); Plá, *Hermano negro*; Angelina Pollak-Eltz, *La esclavitud en Venezuela: un estudio histórico-cultural* (Caracas, 2000); Carlos M. Rama, *Los afro-uruguayos* (Montevideo, 1967); William F. Sater, "The Black Experience in Chile," in Toplin, *Slavery and Race Relations*, ch. 1.

5. Frederick P. Bowser, *The African Slave in Colonial Peru, 1524–1650* (Stanford, Calif., 1974), 7–10; Rolando Mellafe, *La introducción de la esclavitud negra en Chile* (Santiago, 1959); Matthew Restall, "Black Conquistadors: Armed Africans in Early Spanish America," *The Americas*, 57 (2) (October 2000): 171–205.

6. Taken from table 11, Philip D. Curtin, *The Atlantic Slave Trade: A Census* (Madison, 1969), 46.

7. Acosta Saignes, *Vida*, ch. 2.

8. David L. Chandler, *Health and Slavery in Colonial Colombia* (New York, 1981); Linda A. Newson and Susie Minchin, "Slave Mortality and African Origins: A View from Cartagena, Colombia, in the Early Seventeenth Century," *Slavery and Abolition*, 25 (3) (December 2004): 18–43; Linda A. Newson and Susie Minchin, "Diets, Food Supplies, and the African Slave Trade in Early Seventeenth-Century Spanish America," *The Americas*, 63 (4) (April 2007): 517–50.

9. Carlos Eduardo Valencia Villa, *Alma en boca y huesos en costal: una aproximación a los contrastes socio-económicos de la esclavitud. Santafé, Mariquita y Mompox 1610–1660* (Bogotá, 2003). For eighteenth-century Colombia, see Rafael Antonio Díaz Díaz, *Esclavitud, región y ciudad: el sistema esclavista urbano-regional en Santafé de Bogotá, 1700–1750* (Bogotá, 2001).

10. Sherwin K. Bryant, "Finding Gold, Forming Slavery: The Creation of a Classic Slave Society, Popayán, 1600–1700," *The Americas*, 63 (1) (2006): 81–112; William F. Sharp, *Slavery on the Spanish Frontier: The Colombian Chocó, 1680–1810* (Norman, Okla., 1976), chs. 7–10, table 7, 199; Renée Soulodre-La France, *Región e imperio: El Tolima Grande y las reformas borbónicas en el siglo xviii* (Bogotá, 2004), table 1-A, 31. See also Liliana Crespi, "Utilización de mano de obra esclava en áreas mineras y subsidiarias: apuntes sobre su comercio y distribución desde el puerto de Buenos Aires (siglos XVII y XVIII)," in Dina V. Picotti (ed.), *El negro en la Argentina: presencia y negación* (Buenos Aires, 2001), 127–61; Kris Lane, "Captivity and Redemption: Aspects of Slave Life in Early Colonial Quito and Popayán," *The Americas*, 57 (2) (2000): 225–46; Acosta Saignes, *Vida*, ch. 7.

11. Lolita Gutiérrez Brockington, "The African Diaspora in the Eastern Andes: Adaptation, Agency, and Fugitive Action, 1573–1677," *The Americas*, 57 (2) (October 2000), 207–24; Robert J. Ferry, "Encomienda, African Slavery, and Agriculture in Seventeenth-Century Caracas," *Hispanic American Historical Review*, 61 (4) (November 1981): 609–35.

12. Nicholas P. Cushner, *Farm and Factory: The Jesuits and the Development of Agrarian Capitalism in Colonial Quito, 1600–1767* (Albany, NY, 1982); Nicholas P. Cushner, *Jesuit Ranches and the Agrarian Development of Colonial Argentina, 1650–1767* (Albany, NY, 1983); Nicholas P. Cushner, *Lords of the Land: Sugar, Wine, and Jesuit Estates of Coastal Peru, 1600–1767* (Albany, NY, 1980); Nicholas P. Cushner, "Slave Mortality and Reproduction on Jesuit Haciendas in Colonial Peru," *Hispanic American Historical Review*, 55 (2) (May 1975): 177–99; Jean-Pierre Tardieu, *L'Église et les noirs au Pérou: XVIe et XVIIe siècles*, 2 vols. (Paris, 1993). Other works that detail Jesuit relations with their slaves include Jean-Pierre Tardieu, *Noirs et nouveaux maîtres dans les "vallées sanglantes" de l'Équateur 1778–1820* (Paris, 1997); Jeanette C. de la Cerda Donoso de Moreschi and Luis J. Villarroel, *Los negros esclavos de Alta Gracia: caso testigo de población de origin africano en la Argentina y América* (Córdoba, 1999).

13. Bowser, *The African Slave*.

14. Nancy van Deusen, "The 'Alienated' Body: Slaves and Castas in the Hospital de San Bartolomé in Lima, 1680 to 1700," *The Americas*, 56 (1) (July 1999): 1–30.

15. Aline Helg, "The Limits of Equality: Free People of Colour and Slaves during the First Independence of Cartagena, Colombia, 1810–15," *Slavery and Abolition*, 20 (2) (August 1999): 1–30.

16. Margaret M. Olsen, *Slavery and Salvation in Colonial Cartagena de Indias* (Gainesville, Fla., 2004).

17. Bowser, *The African Slave*, chs. 7–9.

18. Acosta Saignes, *Vida*, 167–9; Mellafe, *La introducción*, 34–6; Plá, *Hermano negro*, 34–5.

19. Restall, "Black Conquistadors," 199; Jean-Pierre Tardieu, *Noirs et indiens au Pérou (XVIe–XVIIe siècles): histoire d'une politique ségrégationniste* (Paris, 1990), 72.

20. Charles Beatty Medina, "Caught between Rivals: the Spanish-African Maroon Competition for Captive Indian Labor in the Region of Esmeraldas during the Late Sixteenth and Early Seventeenth Centuries," *The Americas*, 63 (1) (July 2006): 113–36; Tardieu, *Noirs et nouveaux maîtres*.

21. Leo J. Garofalo, "Conjuring with Coca and the Inca: The Andeanization of Lima's Afro-Peruvian Ritual Specialists, 1580–1690," *The Americas*, 63 (1) (July 2006): 53–80; Kathryn Joy McNight, "'En su tierra lo aprendió': An African Curandero's Defense before the Cartagena Inquisition," *Colonial Latin American Review*, 12 (1) (July 2003): 63–84; de la Cerda Donoso and Vallarroel, *Los negros esclavos*, 93. See also Rachel Sarah O'Toole, "'In a War against the Spanish': Andean Protection and African Resistance on the Northern Peruvian Coast," *The Americas*, 63 (1) (July 2006): 19–52.

22. Mellafe, *La introducción*, 45–51; Plá, *Hermano negro*, 25.

23. Ursula de Jesús, *The Souls of Purgatory: The Spiritual Diary of a Seventeenth-Century Afro-Peruvian Mystic, Ursula de Jesús*, trans. and ed. Nancy E. van Deusen (Albuquerque, N. Mex., 2004); Mario Rufer, *Historias negadas: esclavitud, violencia y relaciones de poder en Córdoba a fines del siglo XVIII* (Córdoba, 2005), ch. 6; McNight, "'En su tierra lo aprendió'".

24. van Deusen, "The 'Alienated' Body"; Lyman L. Johnson, "Manumission in Colonial Buenos Aires," *Hispanic American Historical Review*, 59 (2) (May 1979): 258–79; Díaz Díaz, *Esclavitud, región y ciudad*; Sharp, *Slavery on the Spanish Frontier*, 141–7.

25. Gutiérrez Brockington, "The African Diaspora," 217; Valencia Villa, *Alma en boca*, 162.

26. Pollak-Eltz, *La esclavitud en Venezuela*, 71–4; William F. Sharp, "Manumission, *Libres*, and Black Resistance: The Colombian Chocó 1680–1810," in Toplin, *Slavery and Race Relations*, 102–3.

27. Sherwin K. Bryant, "Enslaved Rebels, Fugitives, and Litigants: The Resistance Continuum in Colonial Quito," *Colonial Latin American Review*, 13 (1) (June 2004): 29. See also David L. Chandler, "Slave over Master in Colonial Colombia and Ecuador," *The Americas*, 38 (3) (January 1982): 315–26.

28. Renée Soulodre-La France, "'Por el amor!' Child killing in colonial Nueva Granada," *Slavery and Abolition*, 23 (1) (April 2002): 87–100.

29. María del Carmen Borrego Plá, *Palenques de negros en Cartagena de Indias a fines del siglo XVII* (Seville, 1973); Anthony McFarlane, "*Cimarrones* and *palenques*: Runaways and Resistance in Colonial Colombia," *Slavery and Abolition*, 6 (3) (December 1985): 131–51; Carlos Lazo García and Javier Tord Nicolini, *Del negro señorial al negro bandolero: cimarronaje y palenques en Lima, siglo xviii* (Lima, 1977); Acosta Saignes, *Vida*, chs. 13 and 14.

30. George Reid Andrews, *Afro-Latin America, 1800–2000* (New York, 2004), 95; Renée Soulodre-La France, "'Whites and Mulattos, our Enemies': Race Relations and Popular Political Culture in Nueva Granada," in Matthew Restall (ed.), *Beyond Black and Red: African–Native Relations in Colonial Latin America* (Albuquerque, N. Mex., 2005), 150; Lyman L. Johnson, "'A Lack of Legitimate Obedience and Respect': Slaves and their Masters in the Courts in Late Colonial Buenos Aires," *Hispanic American Historical Review*, 87 (4) (November 2007): 634.

31. de Studer, *La trata de negros en el Río de la Plata*.

32. de la Cerda Donoso de Moreschi and Villarroel, *Los negros esclavos de Alta Gracia*; Florencia Guzmán, "El destino de los esclavos de la Compañía: el caso riojano," in Dina V. Picotti (ed.), *El negro en la Argentina: presencia y negación* (Buenos Aires, 2001), 87–108; Tardieu, *Noirs et nouveaux maîtres*; Wilfredo Kapsoli Escudero, *Sublevaciones de esclavos en el Perú. s. XVIII* (Lima, 1975).

33. Crespo, *Esclavos negros*, 160–1; José Marcial Ramos Guédez, "La insurección de los esclavos negros de Coro en 1795: algunas ideas en torno a posibles influencias de la revolución francesa," *Revista universitaria de ciencias del hombre . . . Universidad José María Vargas*, 2 (2) (1989): 103–16.

34. For the *Código Negro* and its effects, see Manuel Lucena Salmoral, *Sangre sobre piel negra: la esclavitud quiteña en el contexto del reformismo borbónico* (Quito, 1994); Rufer, *Historias negadas*, 45–9; Tardieu, *Noirs et nouveaux maîtres*, 172.

35. Renée Soulodre-La France, "Socially not so dead! Slave identities in Bourbon Nueva Granada," *Colonial Latin American Review*, 10 (1) (June 2001): 87–103; Bryant, "Enslaved rebels"; Meiklejohn, "Implementation of Slave Legislation"; Johnson, "'A Lack of Legitimate Obedience,'" 631–57. For Buenos Aires, see also Carmen Bernand, "La población negra de Buenos Aires (1777–1862)," in Mónica Quijada, Carmen Bernand, and Arnd Schneider, *Homogeneidad y nación con un estudio de caso: Argentina, siglos xix y xx* (Madrid, 2000), 93–140, as well as the numerous works by Marta B. Goldberg, including "Mujer negra rioplatense (1750–1840)," in Lidia Knecher and Marta Panaia (eds.), *La mitad del país: la mujer en la sociedad argentina* (Tucumán, 1994), 67–81.

36. María Eugenia Chaves, *María Chiquinquirá Díaz: una esclava del siglo XVIII. Acerca de las identidades de amo y esclavo en el puerto colonial de Guayaquil* (Guayaquil, 1998). An

extended version of this work is María Eugenia Chaves, *Honor y libertad: discursos y recursos en la estrategia de libertad de una mujer esclava (Guayaquil a fines del periodo colonial)* (Göteborg, 2001). See also Camilla Townsend, "'Half my body free, the other half enslaved': The Politics of the Slaves of Guayas at the End of the Colonial Era," *Colonial Latin American Review*, 7 (1) (June 1998): 105–28.

37. Chandler, "Family Bonds," 107–31; Christine Hünefeldt, *Paying the Price of Freedom: Family and Labor among Lima's Slaves, 1800–1854* (Berkeley, 1994); Díaz Díaz, *Esclavitud*, 156–8.

38. Peter Blanchard, *Under the Flags of Freedom: Slave Soldiers in the Wars of Independence in Spanish South America* (Pittsburgh, 2008); Núria Sales de Bohigas, *Sobre esclavos, reclutas y mercaderes de quintos* (Barcelona, 1974), 57–135; George Reid Andrews, *The Afro-Argentines of Buenos Aires, 1800–1900* (Madison, 1980), ch. 7; Seth Meisel, "From Slave to Citizen-Soldier in Early Independence Argentina," *Historical Reflections*, 29 (1) (2003): 65–82; Rama, *Los afro-uruguayos*, ch. 4; Townsend, "'Half my body free'"; Peter Blanchard, "The Language of Liberation: Slave Voices in the Wars of Independence," *Hispanic American Historical Review*, 82 (3) (August 2002): 499–523.

39. Plá, *Hermano negro*, ch. 6, 37–44, 141–3.

40. James Ferguson King, "The Latin-American Republics and the Suppression of the Slave Trade," *Hispanic American Historical Review*, 24 (3) (August 1944): 387–411; John W. Kitchens, "The New Granadan-Peruvian Slave Trade," *Journal of Negro History*, 64 (3) (1979): 205–14.

41. John V. Lombardi, "The Abolition of Slavery in Venezuela: A Non-event," in Toplin, *Slavery and Race Relations*, ch. 8. Other studies of abolition include Alberto González Arzac, *Abolición de la esclavitud en el Río de la Plata* (Buenos Aires, 1974) on Argentina; Guillermo Feliú Cruz, *La abolición de la esclavitud en Chile: estudio histórico y social* (2nd edn. Santiago, 1973) on Chile; Harold A. Bierck, Jr., "The Struggle for Abolition in Gran Colombia," *Hispanic American Historical Review*, 33 (3) (August 1953): 365–86; Russell Lohse, "Reconciling Freedom with the Rights of Property: Slave Emancipation in Colombia, 1821–1852, with Special Reference to La Plata," *Journal of Negro History*, 86 (3) (Summer 2001): 203–27 on Colombia; Carlos Aguirre, *Agentes de su propia libertad: los esclavos de Lima y la desintegración de la esclavitud, 1821–1854* (Lima, 1993); Peter Blanchard, *Slavery and Abolition in Early Republican Peru* (Wilmington, NC, 1992); Hünefeldt, *Paying the Price*; Jean-Pierre Tardieu, *El decreto de Huancayo: la abolición de la esclavitud en el Perú 3 de diciembre de 1854* (Lima, 2004) on Peru; Jorge Pelfort, *150 años: abolición de la esclavitud en el Uruguay* (Montevideo, 1996) on Uruguay; and John V. Lombardi, *The Decline and Abolition of Negro Slavery in Venezuela, 1820–1854* (Westport, Conn., 1971) on Venezuela.

SELECT BIBLIOGRAPHY

ACOSTA SAIGNES, MIGUEL. *Vida de los esclavos negros en Venezuela*. 1967; Havana: Casa de las Américas, 1978.

AGUIRRE, CARLOS. *Breve historia de la esclavitud en el Perú: una herida que no deja de sangrar*. Lima: Fondo Editorial del Congreso del Perú, 2005.

BLANCHARD, PETER. *Under the Flags of Freedom: Slave Soldiers and the Wars of Independence in Spanish South America*. Pittsburgh: University of Pittsburgh Press, 2008.

BOWSER, FREDERICK P. *The African Slave in Colonial Peru, 1524–1650*. Stanford, Calif.: Stanford University Press, 1974.

CHANDLER, DAVID L. *Health and Slavery in Colonial Colombia*. New York: Arno Press, 1981.

FELIÚ CRUZ, GUILLERMO. *La abolición de la esclavitud en Chile: estudio histórico y social*. 2nd edn. Santiago: Editorial Universitaria, 1973.

LUCENA SALMORAL, MANUEL. *Sangre sobre piel negra: la esclavitud quiteña en el contexto del reformismo borbónico*. Quito: Ediciones Abya-Yala, 1994.

ROUT, JR., LESLIE B. *The African Experience in Spanish America: 1502 to the Present Day*. Cambridge: Cambridge University Press, 1976.

STUDER, ELENA F. S. DE. *La trata de negros en el Rio de la Plata durante el siglo XVIII*. Buenos Aires: Universidad de Buenos Aires, 1958.

CHAPTER 4

···

CUBA

···

MATT D. CHILDS
MANUEL BARCIA

THE subject of Cuban slavery has attracted scholars for more than four centuries. A list of conspicuous authors on the subject would include Bartolomé de Las Casas, the celebrated sixteenth-century Dominican friar and Spanish chronicler of Indian mistreatment; Alexander Von Humboldt, the renown German naturalist, scientist, and explorer; José Antonio Saco, one of nineteenth-century Cuba's foremost educators and patriots; Fernando Ortiz, whose nationalistic anthropology elevated him to international stature during the first half of the twentieth century; and Miguel Barnet, one of Ortiz's students, a revolutionary intellectual who like hundreds of other Cuban scholars entered the field of slavery studies after consummation of the Cuban Revolution in 1959. The famous Cuban dictum *"sin azúcar no hay país"* ("without sugar there is no country") could well serve as a concise expression of both the modern historians' concentration on slavery during the island's nineteenth-century sugar boom and the related neglect of the first 300 years of Cuban slavery.

During the last century such thematic issues as demography, economics, the slave trade, ethnography, race, the colonial and imperial dimensions of Cuban slavery, urban slavery, and slave resistance have commanded considerable scholarly attention. Marxism has exercised a decisive theoretical and political influence on Cuban scholarship, particularly in the aftermath of the Cuban Revolution. Thus, economic interpretations with an emphasis on slavery as a mode of production have framed the interpretation of various aspects of Cuban slavery; the dialectical interplay of domination and resistance at the core of the master–slave relation prefigured class tensions and class struggle. Cuban historians approached the past with a revolutionary call to arms to create a new history most powerfully stated by Manuel Moreno Fraginals as "*la historia como arma*," to recover "*la historia de la gente sin historia*." In that spirit, Cuban scholars such as José Luciano Franco, Juan Pérez de la Riva, Pedro Deschamps Chapeaux, and others constructed vital scaffolding for modern historians by publishing an impressive body of work on the history of colonial Cuba's slaves and free persons of color. In aggregate, modern historians from Cuba, Spain, and the United States have produced a body of work on Cuban slavery that in volume and quality approaches that produced by modern historians in the United States and Brazil on slavery in their respective countries.[1]

CONQUEST (1511–53)

As Alejandro de la Fuente has most recently emphasized for understanding sixteenth-century Cuban slavery, at the time of conquest, enslaved sub-Saharan Africans could be found in Spain, and in major cities such as Seville, where they may have comprised as much as 10 percent of the population. Africans crossed the Atlantic and accompanied Diego Velásquez and other Spanish conquistadors in the first expeditions sent to subjugate Cuba. Spain's familiarity with African slavery on the Iberian Peninsula served to allocate legal rights—but most certainly not legal equality—to the enslaved population through such influential Spanish legal codes as *Las siete partidas* (*c.*1263). Africans served in post-conquest Cuba as enslaved assistants to powerful military and political officials or as domestic servants. Some toiled alongside indigenous persons in the coercive *encomienda* system, which legally ended in 1553 but continued much longer in practice. Indians allotted to Spaniards in *encomienda* initially performed most of the arduous labor in the mines and in the fields. Disease and warfare, however, rapidly reduced Cuba's indigenous population to isolated pockets of "conquered" and "unconquered" Indians.[2]

By the mid-sixteenth century many Spaniards had left the island for opportunities on the mainland, leaving behind several hundred enslaved Africans, a small minority of the total population. They worked mainly in domestic and urban tasks. Spanish colonists, like their counterparts in Hispaniola, had tried to expand sugar production using slave labor. To that end, they petitioned in the 1520s and 1530s for royal largesse in constructing sugar mills and in importing African slaves duty free. Spain, however, denied the requests. Cuban gold production collapsed from 112,000 pesos in 1519 to 8,000 pesos in 1539. The economic history of Cuba for the first half of the sixteenth century could be summed up as a meager boom followed by an extended bust. Few masters in Cuba owned more than five slaves in the first half of the sixteenth century; enslavement and racial identity had yet to become inextricably linked.

Alejandro de la Fuente has carefully constructed from disparate sources the demographic history of Cuba for the sixteenth and seventeenth centuries. An indigenous population that may have numbered as many as 500,000 at the time of the conquest declined by 90 percent from 1519 to 1539. With dying Indians and little gold, Cuba looked unattractive to Spaniards like Hernando de Soto, who, in 1538, vacated the island for the lure of a more lucrative future on the mainland. As one resident remarked that same year, the island had become "the mother to populate New Spain and to supply Tierra Firme."[3] By the 1550s the European population had reached its lowest points since the conquest, declining to less than 200 heads of households. Indians and Africans responded to brutal working and living conditions by flight and, occasionally, by rebellion. Las Casas's writings on the conquest immortalized the 1511 rebellion of Hatuey—reputed to be a cacique from Hispaniola—as the first anti-colonial uprising in Cuban history. Similar Indian rebellions periodically occurred through the 1550s, often marked by short-lived raids on Spanish towns and settlements. African slaves and slaves of African descent also engaged in violent acts of resistance. Reports of slaves running away and attacking masters filled correspondence between Spain and Cuba. Documents indicate that during the first half of the sixteenth century slaves and Indians often made common cause by engaging in *cimarrón* (runaway) activities and by forming maroon encampments (*palenques*).[4] For scholars studying slavery and coercive labor relations that went hand in hand with the conquest of the New World, the literature for the first half of sixteenth-century Cuba remains an open field and calls out for more detailed analysis.

EARLY MODERN CUBAN SLAVERY (1553–1789)

The first volumes of Leví Marrero's fifteen-volume *Cuba: economia y sociedad* (1972–92), an ambitious synthesis compiled from published sources and from manuscripts in the Archivo General de Indias, remains a good starting point for the study of slavery in Cuba's lengthy and understudied early modern period. Havana and other port cities serviced the Atlantic fleet system, and plantation agriculture slowly and unevenly rolled back the frontier for settlement. Historians have recognized but have yet to build upon the important observations made decades ago by Cuban scholars Julio Le Riverend and Juan Pérez de la Riva about the diversity and flexibility of Cuba's early modern economy. In most accounts about the rise of Cuban slavery, the period 1553–1789 served simply as a "precursor," "preface," or "prehistory" to the nineteenth-century sugar boom.[5]

Gold and silver shipments transported from mainland Latin America to Spain and protected by the Spanish fleet (*flota*) system stopped in Havana twice a year. Wind patterns, the Gulf Stream, and a deep-water, pocket-like harbor elevated Havana into a position of vital strategic importance for ships crisscrossing the Atlantic. Ancillary economies in shipbuilding, food provisioning, artisanal trades, and military fortifications developed in response to Havana's growing population and bureaucracy. Abolition of the *encomienda* system in 1553 encouraged the use of enslaved Africans. During the unification of the Spanish and Portuguese monarchies (1580–1640), employment of the *asiento* system, whereby the slave trade to Spanish America was contracted out to individuals, resulted in a slow increase of Cuba's slave population. By 1600 Africans comprised roughly one-third of Havana's inhabitants and the city ranked among the ten largest urban settlements in the Americas and the largest in the Caribbean. Nearly "every important economic activity," Alejandro de la Fuente has concluded, "benefited from their [slaves'] labor." Slaves' knowledge of urban social dynamics allowed them to build valuable networks and many worked on their own as *ganadores* who contracted out their labor in exchange for a daily wage, which was paid to their owners. Some slaves operated taverns, inns, and slaughterhouses for their masters; others labored as artisans in carpentry, blacksmithing, stonemasonry, woodcutting, and shoemaking, among other trades. A few slaves not only accumulated wealth, as evidenced by their wills and testaments, but also loaned money to persons both slave and free. Whites took notice and complained to Havana's town council. Multiple regulations concerning slaves appear in the first comprehensive set of ordinances for Cuba, issued in 1574 by Alonso de Cáceres, a judge on the *audiencia* of Santo Domingo. These ordinances and others on runaway slaves in 1600 suggest the increased reliance in Cuba on enslaved Africans.[6]

The Spanish Crown ranked as the single largest slave owner in Havana during the seventeenth and eighteenth centuries. Beginning in the 1570s, the Crown owned a workforce of 200 slaves, supplemented by perhaps another 100 rented slaves, for the construction and maintenance of forts and public works projects. These "royal slaves" lived and worked together. They acquired a unique collective identity at a time when most slaves in Havana were owned in groups of two to three and lived and worked in their owner's household as domestic servants. Royal slaves, by contrast, lived in separate quarters under the care of a medical official. When work lagged on forts or public works, the crown rented out royal slaves to raise revenues. More scholarship needs to be done on Cuban slave hiring practices throughout its colonial history and recent research shows the practice was far more common than previously thought. Royal slaves often took advantage of their flexible work schedule to earn additional income from multiple employers. In particular, female royal slaves earned income by tending to the needs of the garrison and to ships that docked in the harbor by doing laundry and providing meals to Havana's transient population.[7]

A community of royal slaves that formed around the El Cobre copper mines in eastern Cuba speaks to the diversity and ambiguity of slavery during the seventeenth and eighteenth centuries. Historians María Elena Díaz and Olga Portuondo have studied in Cuban and Spanish archives the voluminous legal documents that pertain to this peculiar group of state-owned slaves, known as *cobreros*. The Spanish Crown seized control of the mines and 271 enslaved, mostly male, African miners from a private contractor in 1670. Over the next century, the community grew to more than 1,000 and the demographic profile shifted: African slaves turned into creoles; females outnumbered males. Next to the mines, the *cobreros* constructed a sanctuary in honor of the apparition of the Virgin that would be recognized by the Catholic Church and eventually adopted as the patron saint of Cuba. The *cobreros* used their status as royal slaves and as guardians of the sanctuary to acquire a corporate land grant on which they founded their own *pueblo* (officially recognized town), complete with a town council as well as a local militia staffed and operated by slaves and free people of color. In 1780 the Spanish Crown sold the mine and the slaves to private investors. But by this time, the *cobreros* no longer considered themselves "slaves." As the new owners attempted to assert dominion over them, they resisted by revolting, running away, and, more effectively, by using the courts to press their claims through litigation. Deftly navigating colonial and imperial courts, the *cobreros* compiled a lengthy list of loyal actions on behalf of the Spanish Crown and the Virgin of Charity. In response, King Charles IV in 1800 issued a royal edict declaring the community free.[8]

Historians Julio le Riverend, Juan Pérez de la Riva, Alejandro de la Fuente, Mercedes García Rodriguez, and Gloria Garcia also stress variation in characterizing the agricultural labors of enslaved Africans during the seventeenth and eighteenth centuries. Cuba's agricultural economy first developed around food and livestock production to support the inhabitants of Havana and the fleet system. The *estancias*—as these small farms and plantations were known—produced cassava, yucca, plantains, corn, and various fruits. The first sugar and tobacco plantations grew out of the *estancias*. They contrast with nineteenth-century sugar plantations in that they were relatively self-sufficient and far more diversified; many had no slaves at all because of the dearth of imports. Quantifying the Cuban slave trade remains difficult as legal imports for the entire seventeenth century under the *asiento* system probably numbered no more than 5,000 African slaves. Indicative of how little historians know about the seventeenth-century transatlantic slave trade to Cuba is that the second edition of the most comprehensive database on the slave trade compiled by David Eltis et al. documents only 434 slaves arriving in Cuba. The largest sugar plantations on the island in the seventeenth century employed upwards of thirty slaves, with most employing less than ten. Low-capital, land-extensive agricultural activities such as cattle ranching and pig farming proliferated. Only during the second half of the seventeenth century did sugar and tobacco exports to Spain generate considerable revenues for Cuban colonists, but even then these commodities remained a close second to the export of hides.[9]

Cuba's development as a slave-based plantation economy during the eighteenth century benefited from a fortuitous conjunction of external and internal events. Beginning in the 1700s, the regulations and procedures for the ownership and use of land shifted away from the Crown toward local officials, who sold plots of land to individuals for use in sugar and tobacco production. While the *asiento* system continued to generate complaints for failing to meet the demands of Cuban slave owners, cargoes shipped under contract by British firms such as the South Sea Company after the War of the Spanish Succession (1701–14) helped to increase the growing slave population on the island. The Seven Years War (1756–63) and in particular the 1762 seizure of Havana by the British resulted in Spain's becoming much more attentive to the economic interests of its Caribbean colonies. The same year Spain regained Havana in the Treaty of Paris (1763) 7,000 slaves entered Cuba, more than the *asiento* brought to the island for the entire seventeenth century. During the eighteenth century Cuba's slave population grew from thousands to tens of thousands, making up more than a third of the population by 1800. Taking advantage of these new opportunities to expand slavery, masters devised creative strategies in expanding agricultural production. Cuban historian Mercedes García Rodríguez has shown how elite planters of the eighteenth century continued to operate diversified agricultural holdings in which tobacco and sugar production often complemented each other rather than existing in "counterpoint," as Fernando Ortiz had emphasized in his widely read *Contrapunteo cubano* (1940). Cuban planters, for example, often used their tobacco yields as credit to purchase slaves to work on their expanding sugar plantations. A coherent master class began to form in Cuba during the eighteenth century. Its members pushed for commercial, political, and economic reforms to strengthen their position as slaveholders, yet they remained ambivalent in defining themselves as Cuban creoles or Hispanic Iberians.[10]

Havana's sizeable free colored class had benefited early on from a liberal policy of manumission. Under Roman law slaves had the right to purchase themselves or have a third party purchase freedom for them. Medieval Spain incorporated this practice into *Las siete partidas*, and throughout Latin America the customary practice of self-purchase became enshrined into positive law as *coartación*, a word that connotes the process of cutting relations with the master. Over the last decade historians have analyzed how slaves understood and exercised their legal rights with a special interest in the practice of *coartación*. Slaves would first make a down payment towards their freedom often supervised by a legal official appointed by the town council. Then, over a specified period of time agreed on by a notarized contract, the slave would make yearly installments until he or she had paid off the balance. To be sure, slaves working in urban areas (where female slaves typically predominated) and those with family members already freed had advantages in this legalistic, drawn-out process, for they could tap into the urban service economy to accumulate savings and draw upon relatives for assistance. The pronounced urban bias of the manumission process resulted in a gendered division among the freed black community with women outnumbering men as they played a more prominent role in city markets and offered a wide variety of domestic services for the town's population. Additional avenues to manumission included the occasional master who rewarded a slave by freeing them upon his death and freeing illegitimate children upon being recognized as legitimate heirs.[11]

More than any other historian, Cuba's Pedro Deschamps Chapeaux brought attention to Cuba's free colored class in a series of books and essays published during the second half of the twentieth century. More recently, Maria del Carmen Barcia has built upon and exceeded the work of Deschamps Chapeaux with two impressive books focused on the close, ambivalent, and all too often contradictory relations between free persons of color and slaves. The absence in Cuba of a large class of poor Europeans and the inclination of whites to avoid tasks associated with persons of African descent resulted in slaves and free people of color dominating such artisanal trades as shoemaking, coopering, and stonecutting. Some freedmen and freedwomen became significant landholders in their own right and owned cattle ranches, pig farms, tobacco and sugar plantations. Free people of color actively participated in the Catholic Church and the militia. By the early seventeenth century, the freed population of Havana had the financial resources to support two confraternities made up of black and mulatto members: Our Lady of the Remedies and the Holy Spirit. As their numbers increased in the eighteenth century, free people of color formed additional black brotherhoods that made them regular features of Cuba's religious landscape. Black and mulatto militias first formed in the sixteenth century to protect Havana and other Cuban ports from foreign attacks. Free men of color eagerly joined the militia because membership provided special privileges and distinction within Cuban society. Militia rights (*fueros*) included access to military courts, exemptions from certain taxes, tribute payments, and labor levies, and the right to bear arms. Because Cuba's late colonial society had become dependent on the services offered by free persons of color, some whites called for their removal, and laws passed to circumscribe their freedom.[12]

NINETEENTH-CENTURY PLANTATION SLAVERY (1789–1867)

Cuban social and political life centered on the master–slave relation during the nineteenth-century heyday of plantation slavery. During this period, foreign capital and foreign political pressure—British abolitionism and United States annexationism, for example—began to shape Cuban slavery beyond the contours of Spanish colonialism alone. The transatlantic slave trade lasted longer to Cuba than to any other New World slave society with final abolition coming only in 1867. Production of coffee, tobacco, and, most notably, sugar soared in the aftermath of the Haitian Revolution (1791–1804) and transformed Cuba into one of the hemisphere's largest slave societies and one of the world's most valuable colonies. While no consensus has emerged over exact figures for total imports from 1789 to 1867, David Eltis, the leading quantitative historian of the Atlantic slave trade, has estimated that more than 700,000 slaves entered Cuba, nearly doubling the number of slaves imported into the United States during its entire colonial and national history.

The Spanish Crown made two important decisions in 1789 that would bear on the development of Cuban slavery in the nineteenth century. First a royal order liberalized Spanish participation in the Atlantic slave trade by abolishing the *asiento* and allowing Spanish subjects to trade slaves in select ports in Cuba, Santo Domingo, Puerto Rico, and Venezuela. Foreigners could now import slaves into these designated ports duty free. African imports to Cuba increased to thousands per year. As they did, Cuban culture increasingly manifested West African influences, and a creole economic elite tied to slavery and the plantation system congealed into formidability. For Cuban slaveholders the Crown's ability to influence and shape their future revealed both the benefits and limitations of Spanish colonialism. A liberalized slave trade suggested the advantages to planter prosperity of a totally free slave trade. Yet over time Cuban slaveholders grew more dependent on the Spanish Crown for delivering slaves and for defending the transatlantic trade against foreign pressure to shut it down. In the span of fifteen years from 1789 to 1804 the Crown issued altogether eleven decrees aimed at expanding the slave trade.[13]

Cuba's growing dependence on the transatlantic slave trade emerged during a tumultuous moment in the history of slavery in the Americas. The Haitian Revolution (1791–1804) had destroyed the most valuable slave-based economy in the Caribbean and liberated 400,000 slaves from bondage. Yet it was precisely the results of the Haitian Revolution that drove sugar and coffee prices upward and thereby provided Cuban entrepreneurs with promising economic opportunities. Great Britain's radical volte-face at this time from being the largest transporter of slaves in the eighteenth century to abolishing the British slave trade in 1807 and championing the abolitionist cause in the nineteenth century complicated matters. David Murray's *Odious Commerce* (1980), better than any other source, details the political history of Britain's subsequent efforts to end the importation of enslaved Africans to Cuba. Britain pressured Spain into signing the Treaty of Madrid (1817), which prohibited the trade from Africa in slaves after 30 May 1820. The Spanish Crown retained the allegiance of many Cuban slaveholders, however, by turning a blind eye towards its treaty obligations and supporting slavery in the island.[14]

Dovetailing with new studies of *coartación*, historians inside and outside of Cuba have shown renewed interest in the history of slave laws and how slaves could use the legal system to advance their interests. At the same time Spain liberalized the transatlantic slave trade to Cuba, the Crown approved the *Código Negro Español*, a Spanish Black Code that received high marks from outside observers as well as modern historians for its humanitarian provisions. This and subsequent slave codes issued by the Crown revealed that as subjects of Spain, rather than as citizens of their own independent country, Cuban masters, even in matters of slave treatment, were still legally beholden to their own "master" on the other side of the Atlantic. The 1789 code specified food and clothing provisions, set daily work hours, required religious instruction, protected marriages, and limited punishments for slaves. Writing in the 1970s, Franklin Knight and Gwendolyn Midlo Hall demonstrated that the rosy picture of slave rights provided by the legislation rarely conformed to reality. Indeed, Cuban slaveholders gathered to resist enforcement and forced the Spanish Crown to rescind various provisions of the Black Code that would limit slaveholders' ability to discipline and command their slaves. More recently, historians have returned to these laws not to analyze how masters simply ignored the laws as was common of scholarship in the 1970s, but rather how slaves employed the laws to assert rights and use the courts in addressing relations with their masters.[15]

The Spanish Crown and its colonial officials in Cuba took note of master protests to the 1789 law and when composing subsequent slave codes sought input from well-known slave owners on the island. Jeanne-Pierre Tradieu has recently devoted a monograph to the making of the slave code of 1842. Captain-General Gerónimo Valdés, a Spanish general intent on suppressing the illegal slave trade to Cuba, solicited input from elite masters such as the Marqués de Arcos, Rafael O'Farrill, and Domingo de Aldama. Valdés asked them to report on labor, housing, health, religious instruction, marriage, clothing, and other topics related to slave life on the plantations. Even though most of the consulted planters accepted the idea of a new code of rules to govern their slaves only reluctantly, Valdés pushed ahead. The resulting 1842 slave code, although disturbing to planters, did not bring about the same degree of protest elicited in 1789. Nor was it regarded as a direct assault on masters' authority. The shift from a code dictated by the Crown in 1789 to one that solicited input from elite colonial slaveholders in 1842 suggests cooperation between Spain and its Cuban subjects over slavery at a heady political moment when the pressure of British abolitionism from without and slave rebellion from within was mounting. This attempted inclusiveness, however, was short-lived. Barely two years later, Leopoldo O'Donnell, Valdés's more draconian successor to Cuba's captain-generalcy, undermined the 1842 code by issuing his own set of ordinances.[16]

In assessing Cuba's nineteenth-century sugar boom, Manuel Moreno Fraginal's multi-volume *El ingenio* (1964) stands out as one of the most influential works ever written on the subject. A Cuban historian influenced by Marxist theory, Moreno Fraginals explored colonial Cuba's sugar economy along the lines of the *histoire total* of the French *Annales* school. In depicting the life and labor of plantation slaves, he connected the intensification of the slave's work regimen to the application of the steam engine in the mill by entrepreneurial Cuban planters. In fact, Cuba possessed a railroad before Spain did. Railroads and other industrial, capital-intensive technologies concentrated production in large sugar mills (*ingenios*). Economies of scale resulted in expanding sugar plantations, pushing out small producers, marginalizing the diversified estancias of previous centuries, and enslaving more and more Africans for arduous, regimented fieldwork. The profits generated by Cuban sugar production and the ability to buy and replace enslaved Africans through imports from the transatlantic slave trade forced slave mortality high enough and slave fertility low enough so that the slave population could not reproduce itself naturally. Although Moreno Fraginals's Marxian economic and technological determinism tended to turn Cuba's slaves into rather wooden instruments of production, *El ingenio* has achieved classic status in the historiography of Cuban slavery.[17]

Cuban coffee and tobacco have yet to receive the same detailed scholarly treatment as Cuban sugar despite a significant literature that extends back to Francisco Pérez de la Riva and Fernando Ortiz in the 1940s. Ortiz's romanticized treatment of tobacco production in *Contrapunteo cubano* paid little attention to the use of slave labor. Cuba's tobacco industry, he argued, fostered the growth of an independent peasantry, artisanal pride and craftsmanship, and harmonious labor relations. In truth, tobacco remained the second most important sector of the Cuban economy over the course of the nineteenth century after sugar and calls out for more detailed scholarly analysis. From 1827 to 1862 tobacco production grew from 6.5 percent to 15 percent of the value of total agricultural output. In terms of labor relations, tobacco production showed the greatest variations from small tobacco farms employing three to four slaves often supplemented by wage and seasonal labor to the occasional large tobacco plantation that employed twenty to thirty slaves.[18]

Sugar has also overshadowed coffee in the literature on Cuban slavery. In the early decades of the nineteenth century, Coffee planters rivaled sugar planters in building Cuba's slave society. The Haitian Revolution not only presented a golden opportunity for Cubans to fill the void in the world sugar market, but also the world coffee market as well, for the price of coffee doubled between 1792 and 1796. French refugees from Saint-Domingue migrated to nearby Cuba and set up scores of coffee plantations (*cafetales*). From the 1790s through the 1820s coffee production flourished with dramatic increases in the jurisdictions of Havana in western Cuba and Santiago in eastern Cuba. In 1827 coffee actually competed with sugar and represented 23 percent of the total value of agricultural production on the island compared to sugar's 26 percent. By the 1840s, however, Brazilian competition, the profitability of sugar production, and destructive hurricanes in the 1840s that flattened coffee groves sent Cuba's coffee industry into rapid decline. Suffering coffee planters who lacked the financial resources to rebuild opted to sell their land

and enslaved laborers to big sugar planters. By 1862 coffee had declined to only 2 percent of the total value of agricultural production on the island, and by the end of the century, Cuba would be a net importer of coffee, mostly from nearby Puerto Rico.[19]

Over the last twenty years historians have increasingly paid attention to the African ethnic communities that emerged in nineteenth-century Cuba as the Atlantic slave trade replenished the slave population with hundreds of thousands of slave imports from very specific embarkation points in West Africa. As a result of collaborative efforts, computer assistance, and the construction of data sets, it has become easier for scholars to eschew the generic non-descriptive terms "Africa" and "African," and identify more precisely the origins of slaves and their New World destinations. David Eltis, David Richardson, Stephen D, Behrendt, and Herbert S. Klein compiled an easily accessible CD-ROM database of more than 27,000 slaving voyages in the late 1990s, which has subsequently been updated and made accessible as a free web-based source that now makes it possible to trace the Old World origins and American destinations of Africans with greater precision than ever before.[20] From a cultural standpoint, the substantial African presence that derived in particular from the Bight of Biafra (Carabalí), Bight of Benin (Lucumí), and the Congo/Angolan cultures of West-Central Africa stamped Cuban society with a vibrant African imprint that remains to this day. Historians such as Philip Howard, Matt Childs, and Rafael Lópz Valdés have analyzed how these African ethnic associations emerged and manifested themselves in Cuba through culturally organized mutual aid and religious societies, which overtime became known as *cabildos de nación*. They thrived in urban areas such as Matanzas, Santiago, and Havana where they numbered well over 100 by the mid-nineteenth century. The *cabildos de nación* participated in Afro-Catholic religious festivals, most notably the Day of the Kings (Epiphany) on January 6; hosted festivities of their own; sponsored patron saints from local churches; and pooled resources to provide educational services and artisanal training and even to purchase the freedom of enslaved members.[21]

During the nineteenth century slave rebellions became larger, more frequent, and more sophisticated. In 1812 a series of conspiracies and rebellions occurred throughout the island that have since been known collectively as the Aponte Rebellion after its leader, José Antonio Aponte, a free black artisan and militiaman from Havana. The Aponte Rebellion, as Matt Childs has demonstrated, involved connections between free people of color and slaves, both urban and rural, who sought to destroy slavery and end Spanish colonialism. The urban leaders of the rebellion capitalized on the large presence of Africans on plantations, most notably those outside of Havana, and circulated rumors that the slaves had been declared free as a strategy to enlist support for the uprising. Colonial officials brutally suppressed the rebellion by executing the leaders, imprisoning and punishing hundreds, and deporting others to Spanish colonies in Florida, Central America, and South America. The Aponte Rebellion surfaced during mainland Latin America's wars of independence from Spain. Cuba's white elite, increasingly worried about the dangers of expanding slavery, turned with renewed enthusiasm to Spain and colonialism rather than risk the instability that could emerge if they made a bid for an independent Cuba.[22]

The Cuban historian José Luciano Franco devoted much of his scholarly life to documenting and publishing work chronicling Cuban slave resistance. During the first half of the nineteenth century, Cuba, especially its western department, recorded more slave insurrections than any other place in the Atlantic world. A series of events in Africa including the fall of the Oyo empire changed the demographics of the slave trade to Cuba. Manuel Barcia has recently brought attention to the surge of African-led rebellions in the western countryside around Havana and Matanzas. Former subjects of Oyo emerged as leaders in some of the most notable revolts: the 1825 rebellion in Guamacaro, the 1833 uprising in Guanajay, and the two large outbreaks of March and November 1843 in Bemba and La Guanábana, respectively. In the first four years of the decade of 1840 acts of collective slave resistance were so frequent that even elite slave owners like Juan Montalvo and Ricardo O'Farrill began to ask for the end of the slave trade to the island. A climax occurred in 1844 when thousands of slaves, free persons of color, and even white people were accused by the colonial authorities of planning a large revolt to overthrow Spanish rule in the island.[23]

The largest slave conspiracy in the nineteenth century and one of the most controversial events in Cuban history occurred in 1843–4, later known to history by the gruesome title of La Escalera (the Ladder), a reference to the ladders to which hundreds of slaves and free persons of color were tied face down and then whipped mercilessly during arrest and questioning. Ever since the mid-nineteenth century La Escalera has generated historical controversy. The plot inculpated not only slaves and free people of color, but also Cuban whites and British abolitionists. Authorities executed Plácido (Gabriel de la Concepción Valdés), a gifted mulatto poet, as one of the revolutionary chieftains.

Much of the debate has focused on who was mastermind of the movement. Historians have reached various conclusions about the role of British abolitionists like David Turnbull; of sympathetic but naive white intellectuals like Domingo del Monte who lobbied against Cuba's illegal slave trade; and of free people of color like Plácido, who because of their intermediate position in Cuban society could make alliances with slaves and whites. A series of slave rebellions broke out in 1843 in the sugar-producing regions east of Havana in Matanzas and Cárdenas. The increase in the levels of slave unrest provoked panic among the authorities and planters. By December 1843 a female slave named Polonia denounced to her owner the existence of an extensive plot among the slaves and free colored of Matanzas and Havana. Captain-General Leopoldo O'Donnell ordered investigations that unleashed one of the bloodiest repressions in the history of the island. The Cuban state focused their repression on the free people of color and singled out Turnbull as the "prime mover" of a revolutionary plot. Current scholarship on the insurrection over the last twenty years led by historians Robert Paquette, Rodolfo Sarracino, and Gloria García has reached the judicious conclusion that rather than one single coordinated movement or a movement that was fabricated by the state to crack down on its subject populations and tighten the reins of colonialism, La Escalera represented a series of overlapping conspiracies that originated in different circles of constituents with different degrees of involvement. Recent scholarship on Cuban slave rebellions has emphasized the need to decipher content, to appreciate African ethnic influences, to understand slave rebels on their own terms, with their own goals and political ideas, rather than seeing them as simply manipulated extensions of outsiders. In that vein, modern scholars who have creatively sought to recapture the voice of the subaltern have built a veritable cottage industry around the prose and poetry of one of La Escalera's notable victims, Juan Francisco Manzano, whose voice was silenced after imprisonment by authorities. A literate, privileged slave, Manzano wrote his own autobiography at the behest of white patrons, who eventually raised the money to purchase his freedom in 1836. Evelyn Picon Garfield and Ivan A. Schulman have published a useful bilingual edition of Manzano's singular narrative.[24]

In the aftermath of La Escalera, Cuban slavery began a slow but gradual transition in response to changing politics in the Atlantic world. By 1850, Cuba had become one of the wealthiest colonies in the world. But slavery, the foundation of that wealth, had been abolished for more than a decade in the British empire; the Revolution of 1848 had ended slavery in the remaining French colonies; and most Latin American countries had either abolished slavery or were on the way to doing so. Sectional politics of the 1850s in the United States indicated to many Cuban slave owners, notwithstanding the influence of such annexationists as Narciso López, that slavery did not have a secure future in the United States. Cuban masters might find solace in Brazil, where slavery would last until 1888. But even in Brazil, British warships had put an end to the transatlantic slave trade by 1850. For many mid-century Cuban slave owners abolition loomed large on the horizon, but one to which they could accommodate if the process of getting there was gradual, orderly, and compensated.

Beginning in the 1840s, Cuban plantation owners participated in the international Chinese coolie labor market that brought indentured laborers to the United States, Mexico, South America, and other destinations. From 1847 to 1874, Cuba imported roughly 125,000 Chinese contract laborers. They primarily worked cutting cane alongside enslaved Africans on some of the largest sugar plantations in Cuba. In additional to agricultural tasks, many also found employment in domestic service and the artisanal trades in urban areas. Labor-hungry Cuban planters also purchased perhaps 2,000 indigenous laborers coughed up by the 1848 Caste War in Yucatan before Mexican President Benito Juárez indignantly outlawed the trade in 1861. For Cuban planters, finding a satisfactory substitute for enslaved African labor proved difficult.[25]

Christopher Schmidt-Nowara has ably reconstructed the origins of Spanish abolitionism and its bearing on the politics of slavery in both metropolis and colony. The Spanish Abolitionist Society began work in 1865 and embraced Spaniards, Cubans, and Puerto Ricans. Following the example of British abolitionists earlier in the century, they focused on abolishing the transatlantic slave trade before turning to the institution of slavery itself. Reform politics in Spain further created an atmosphere of abolition. In 1865 Spain formed the Junta de Información, a council composed of Cuban, Puerto Rican, and Spanish representatives, to discuss and formulate economic and social policies for the Caribbean colonies. Many abolitionists won seats on the Junta, including long-time Cuban anti-slave trade advocate José Antonio Saco. As slavery grew increasingly insecure in the island, many slaveholders showed an inclination to invest in machinery over purchasing enslaved Africans. Under pressure to pacify abolitionists, to buy time to reform slavery, and to foster the growth of Cuba's slave population by natural increase, Cuban slaveholders finally conceded to abolish the transatlantic slave trade in 1867.[26]

ABOLITION AND INDEPENDENCE (1868–86)

The ending of slavery in Cuba became inextricably intertwined with the island's Wars for Independence. The historians Ada Ferrer, Rebecca Scott, and María del Carmen Barcia, most notably, have provided detailed analysis of the importance of slaves in entering the struggle and advancing their own liberationist agenda. Indeed, during the Ten Years War (1868–78), Cuban slaves helped transform a separatist struggle led by white slaveholding elites in eastern Cuba into a war for personal liberation. The unraveling of slavery, as both sides attempted to coax slaves into their ranks, not only led to final abolition in 1886, but helped spread the independence movement westward throughout the most dynamic plantation zones.

The reform politics that emerged in Spain in the 1860s did not end with the abolition of the Cuban slave trade in 1867. The inability of the Junta de Información to resolve colonial issues was indicative of larger political problems and divisions in Spain. In September of 1868 naval officers revolted in Cádiz and shortly thereafter revolutionaries took Madrid, proclaiming a liberal republic. The unwillingness of the new Spanish government to extend reforms to its most valuable Caribbean colony resulted in the *Grito de Yara*, the call by creole planter Carlos Manuel de Céspedes from Bayamo for independence. Capitalizing on the opportunity created by political divisions in Spain between monarchists and republicans, the movement for Cuban independence quickly gained momentum in the eastern portion of the island, where slavery was weakest.[27]

In launching the Ten Years War on October 10, 1868, Céspedes symbolically and strategically gathered slaves on his La Demajagua sugar plantation and granted them their freedom. Addressing them as "citizens," he told them they were now "free" to join the fight to "conquer liberty and independence" for Cuba. Ada Ferrer has deftly analyzed the slavery "problem" that plagued the movement for independence, emphasizing that Céspedes from the very beginning insisted that the goal of the movement was ending colonial rule, not abolishing slavery. Some Cuban masters shared Céspedes's ideological convictions and individually emancipated their slaves in public ceremonies when they joined the cause. The early leaders of the independence movement came from eastern districts where the slave population numbered less than 10 percent of the total population. Thus, their own decision to individually free their slaves did not appear that radical or financially costly. In the western portion of island, however, where slave populations remained heavily concentrated, such actions would indeed threaten the planter class. Consequently, as a strategy to win over recruits from the powerful planter class in the west to their cause and not alienate the economic elite, Céspedes and others adopted a policy of gradual abolition after independence with indemnification for masters.[28]

The politics on the ground confounded attempts to draw neat distinctions between a war to abolish colonialism and a war to postpone abolition. First, the independence army needed soldiers. As cane fields turned into battlefields, slaves did not hesitate to join the rebel cause, regardless of their master's position on slavery. The enslaved and freed population of African descent eagerly joined the cause if it meant both personal and political freedom. Detailed statistics on the content of the rebel army remain elusive, but units comprised of persons of African descent expanded during the war among the soldiery and within the officer corps. Declarations by white leaders that discussion of slavery and abolition would have to wait until independence had been achieved increasingly fell on deaf ears. Spanish officials and loyalists who wanted to discredit the movement by portraying it as a race war to destroy slavery emphasized slave participation. The slaves themselves insisted that freedom was precisely what the war meant to them as they fled the plantations and flocked to rebel army encampments.

In the east central town of Puerto Príncipe, desertions and surrenders between 1870 and 1872, most prominently among white members and leaders of the rebel army, resulted in a shifting of the perceived racial identity of the movement from multiracial to black. By 1873, surrenders and desertions had become so numerous that Spain had firmly regained control of the area. In Santiago and Guantanamo, however, where the white population made up only 25 percent of the total population, opportunities abounded for slaves and free people of color to join the movement. The highest-ranking officers of color came from these regions, most notably the mulatto Antonio Maceo who proved to be the decisive military leader in engineering the campaigns that won the rebel army a stronghold in the region. In response to Maceo's achievements, however, rumors spread that he conspired to take over the movement and turn

Cuba into another Haiti. Whether as a result of white desertion and surrender, or the inability to acknowledge the achievements of people of color on the battlefield, the rebel army remained divided by race and slavery.

The rebel army largely failed to break their struggle outside the confines of the eastern department. The fractured leadership neither adopted a clear and unified position on abolition, nor surmounted racial prejudice. Declining morale; disintegrating units; and stalemated fighting undermined the movement and forced negotiations. In February 1878 Spanish officials and a delegation of rebel leaders signed the Pact of Zanjón. This peace treaty provided a political pardon for insurgents and recognized the legal freedom for slaves in the insurrection. More than 16,000 slaves received their freedom according to the terms of the treaty. Thus slaves who had rebelled to overthrow Spanish colonialism were awarded freedom; those who had demonstrated loyalty by not joining the insurgency remained enslaved. Not all rebel leaders accepted the pact. Antonio Maceo, most notably, rejected it and issued his "Protest of Baragua" in response. He vowed to continue fighting for independence and abolition, even though he and other insurgent chieftains were forced into exile.[29]

Cuban slavery survived the Ten Years War weakened and unraveling. Shortly before the onset of the war slaves numbered 363, 288. The 1877 census counted 199,094 slaves (14 percent of the total population), which in a year was reduced by 16,000 more by the terms of the Pact of Zanjón.[30] Few historians have studied the transition from slave labor to free labor with the care of historian Rebecca Scott. In 1870 the abolitionist Segismundo Moret, a Spanish delegate to the Cortes, introduced a bill into parliament for the "gradual abolition of slavery." The law most certainly was a response to counter the moral high ground the rebel army had claimed in recruiting slaves to their cause. The Moret Law—as the bill became known—freed all children born to slave mothers since September 1868 and all slaves upon reaching the age of 60. Slaves' actions reveal they understood the legal foundations for slavery as system were crumbling around them. Scott has shown that in the wake of the Moret Law slaves called upon the state more frequently to exercise certain rights that they had been granted since the early colonial period. Cuban authorities recorded, for example, an increase in complaints against abusive masters, an increase in *coartacíon* agreements to earn their freedom, and day-to-day acts of resistance increased as well. If Cuban masters attempted to minimize the impact of the Moret Law through subterfuge such as changing the birth dates and ages of their labor force, slaves fought valiantly for its implementation.[31]

The second legal change in slavery that made gradual abolition possible was the passage of the *patronato* in 1880. The law left in place the fundamental labor relations between masters and slaves, but changed them legally to something akin to an apprenticeship system that marked the final years of slavery in the British Caribbean. The law redefined master–slave relationships and renamed owners *patronos* and slaves *patrocinados*. Its most important provision was that one-quarter of the *patrocinados* held by each master in 1884 were to be freed at the end of the year. This emancipation by one-fourth would then be followed over the next three years so that by 1888 all *patrocinados* on the island would be emancipated and slavery abolished. The passage of the law also empowered a series of local and regional boards (*juntas*) to oversee the process. These local committees also had powers to oversee and regulate self-purchase, and if slaves could document abuse they could be given their freedom under article 4 of the *patronato* law. The intent of the *patronato* was to guide Cuba peacefully from slave labor to free labor without disrupting the plantation system and maintaining a disciplined and subordinated labor force.

The *patronato* specified slavery's expiration date and many slaves did not wait around for eight years for it to go into effect. Like Brazilian slaves after the Rio Branco Law (1871), Cuban slaves began fleeing the plantations in droves. With only limited years of labor before final abolition, many masters simply calculated it was not worth it to hunt their slaves down and have them returned. *Coartación* agreements became easier to achieve with the local juntas now charged to oversee the process. Masters had no choice but to work out relationships for post-emancipation labor while they still had some coercive sway over their laborers. Many relinquished their legal control over laborers in exchange for a commitment to continue working for them once emancipated. Scott found that emancipation by "mutual accord" between masters and slaves outnumbered all other avenues for freedom under the *patronato*. As with the Moret Law, now that there was an intervening legal force between masters and slaves, slave complaints for abusive masters increased dramatically, especially since documented abuse could result in freedom according to article 4 of the *patronato*. Collectively, these changes empowered the *patrocinados* to simply make the disciplined relations masters held over slaves obsolete and the system unworkable. Two years before the system was scheduled to come to an end, Cuban masters conceded that the system was unworkable and agreed to end the *patronato* by royal decree on October 7, 1886. In effect, slaves' actions most decisively sped up the emancipation process.[32]

Notes

1. For an overview of the historiography of Cuban slavery, see the following: Tomás Fernández Robaina, *Bibliografía de temas afrocubanos* (Havana, 1985); Ernesto Ruiz, "Bibliografía acerca de la esclavitud en Cuba," in Instituto de Ciencias Históricas, *La Esclavitud en Cuba* [no editor] (Havana, 1986), 196–266; Alejandro García Álvarez and Antonio Santamaría García, "El azúcar y la historiografía Cubana," in *O açucar e o quotidiano* (Funchal, 2005), 489–528; and for succinct analysis of Cuban historiography more broadly, see Oscar Zanetti, *Isla en la historia: la historiografía de Cuba en el siglo xix* (Havana, 2005).
2. Alejandro de la Fuente, with the collaboration of César García del Pino and Bernardo Iglseias Delgado, *Havana and the Atlantic in the Sixteenth Century* (Chapel Hill, NC, 2008).

3. Quoted ibid 3.

4. For indigenous and slave resistance in the sixteenth century see Leví Marrero, *Cuba: economía y sociedad* (Rio Pedras, 1972), i. 184–8, ii. 367–9; and Estrella Rey Betancourt and César García del Pino, "Conquista y colonización de la isla de Cuba (1492–1553)," in *La colonia: evolución socioeconómica y formación nacional de los orígines hasta 1867* (Havana, 1994), 91–100.

5. Julio Le Riverend, *Problemas de la formación agraria de Cuba, siglos xvi–xvii* (Havana, 1992); Juan Pérez de la Riva, "Una isla con dos historias," in *El barracón y otros ensayos* (Havana, 1975), 75–89.

6. De la Fuente, *Havana and the Atlantic*, ch. 6, quote p. 151.

7. For a discussion of royal slaves in Havana, see the recent work by Evelyn Powell Jennings, "War as the 'Forcing House of Change': State Slavery in Late-Eighteenth-Century Cuba," *William and Mary Quarterly*, 62 (3) (July 2005): 411–40.

8. María Elena Díaz, *The Virgin, the King, and the Royal Slaves of El Cobre: Negotiating Freedom in Colonial Cuba, 1670–1780* (Stanford, Calif., 2000); Olga Portuondo Zúñiga, *La virgen de la Caridad de Cobre: símbolo de cubanía* (Santiago, 1995).

9. For accounts of Cuban agriculture in the seventeenth and eighteenth centuries, see Le Riverend, *Problemas de la formación agraria de Cuba, siglos xvi–xvii*, especially 164–75; Juan Pérez de la Riva, *El barracón y otros ensayos* (Havana, 1975); Alejandro de la Fuente, "Sugar and Slavery in Early Colonial Cuba," in Stuart B. Schwartz (ed.), *Tropical Babylons: Sugar and the Making of the Atlantic World, 1450–1680* (Chapel Hill, NC, 2004), 115–57; Mercedes García Rodríguez, *La aventura de fundar ingenios: la refacción azucarera en La Habana del siglo xviii* (Havana, 2004); Gloria García, "El auge de la sociedad esclavista en Cuba," in *La colonia: evolución socioeconómica y formación nacional de los origines hasta 1867* (Havana, 1994), 225–64; David Eltis et al., the Trans-Atlantic Slave Trade Database, http://www.slavevoyages.org/tast/assessment/estimates.faces?yearFrom=1601&yearTo=1700&disembarkation=701 (accessed 10 July 2008).

10. García Rodríguez, *La aventura de fundar ingenios*; Fernando Ortiz, *Cuban Counterpoint: Tobacco and Sugar*, trans. Harriet de Onís (1947; reprint Durham, NC, 1995).

11. For the practice of *coartación* see Hubert S Aimes, "Coartación: A Spanish Institution for the Advancement of Slaves into Freedom," *Yale Review*, 17 (1909): 412–31; Alejandro de la Fuente, "Slaves and the Creation of Legal Rights in Cuba: *Coartación* and *Papel*," *Hispanic American Historical Review*, 87 (4) (November 2007): 659–92.

12. Pedro Deschamps Chapeaux, *El negro en la economía Habanera del siglo xix* (Havana, 1971); Pedro Deschamps Chapeaux, *Los batallones de pardos y morenos libres* (Havana, 1976); María del Carmen Barcia Zequeira, *La otra familia: parientes, redes, y descendencia de los esclavos en Cuba* (Havana, 2003); María del Carmen Bracia Zequeira, *Los ilustres apellidos: negros en La Habana colonial* (Havana, 2009).

13. For the slave trade to Cuba after 1789 see Sherry Johnson, "The Rise and Fall of Creole Participation in the Cuban Slave Trade, 1789–1796," *Cuban Studies*, 30 (1999): 52–75; David Murray, *Odious Commerce: Britain, Spain and the Abolition of the Cuban Slave Trade* (Cambridge, 1980).

14. For the international politics of the Cuban slave trade see Murray, *Odious Commerce*; Rodolfo Sarracino, *Inglaterra: sus dos caras en la lucha cubana por la abolición* (Havana, 1989); Christopher Schmidt-Nowara, *Empire and Antislavery: Spain, Cuba, and Puerto Rico, 1833–1874* (Pittsburgh, 1999).

15. Franklin Knight, *Slave Society in Cuba during the Nineteenth Century* (Madison, 1970); and Gwendolyn Midlo Hall, *Social Control in Slave Plantations Societies: A Comparison of St. Domingue and Cuba* (Baltimore, 1971); For the most recent debate about slave law in Cuba see Alejandro de la Fuente, "Slave Law and Claims-Making in Cuba: The Tannenbaum Debate Revisited," *Law and History Review*, 22 (2) (Summer 2004): 339–70; Maria Elena Díaz, "Beyond Tannenbaum," *Law and History Review*, 22 (2) (Summer 2004): 371–6; Christopher Schmidt-Nowara, "Still Continents (and an Island) with Two Histories?," *Law and History Review*, 22 (2) (Summer 2004): 377–82; Alejandro de la Fuente, "Slavery and the Law: A Reply," *Law and History Review*, 22 (2) (Summer 2004): 383–8; and Manuel Barcia, "Fighting with the Enemy's Words: The Usage of the Colonial Legal Framework by Nineteenth-Century Cuban Slaves," *Atlantic Studies*, 3 (2) (October 2006): 159–81.

16. For the 1842 slave code see Manuel Barcia Paz, *Con el látigo de la ira: legislación, represión y control en las plantaciones cubanas* (Havana, 2000); and Jean-Pierre Tardieu, *"Morir o dominar": en torno al reglamento de esclavos de cuba (1841–1866)* (Frankfurt, 2003).

17. Manuel Moreno Fraginals, *El ingenio: complejo económico social Cubano del azúcar*, 3 vols. (Havana, 1978); an abbreviated English translation appeared as Manuel Moreno Fraginals, *The Sugarmill: The Socioeconomic Complex of Sugar in Cuba* (New York, 1976).

18. Ortiz, *Cuban Counterpoint*; for an analysis of the Cuban economy at mid-century and tobacco and sugar in particular, see Gloria García and Orestes Gárciga, "El inicio de la crisis de la economía esclavista," in *La colonia: evolución socioeconómica y formación nacional de los origines hasta 1867* (Havana, 1994), 369–78.

19. For the emergence and decline of the coffee industry see the foundational work of Francisco Pérez de la Riva, *El café: historia de su cultivo y explotación en Cuba* (Havana, 1944); for the role of sugar in overtaking coffee in Mantanzas, see Laird Bergad, *Cuban Rural Society in the Nineteenth Century: The Social and Economic History of Monoculture in Matanzas* (Princeton, 1990); and for how hurricanes in the 1840s transformed coffee plantations to sugar plantations, see Louis A. Pérez, Jr., *Winds of Change: Hurricanes & the Transformation of Nineteenth-Century Cuba* (Chapel Hill, NC, 2001).

20. David Eltis, David Richardson, Stephen D. Behrendt, and Herbert S. Klein (eds.), *The Trans-Atlantic Slave Trade: A Database on CD-ROM* (Cambridge, 1999); and the 2nd edn. of the Trans-Atlantic Slave Trade Database by Eltis et al. can be found at: http://slavevoyages.org/tast/index.faces

21. For the ethnic and cultural diversity of the enslaved population and the *cabildos de nación*, see Philip A. Howard, *Changing History: Afro-Cuban Cabildos and Societies of Color in the Nineteenth Century* (Baton Rouge, La., 1998); and Matt D. Childs, "'The Defects of Being a Black Creole': The Degrees of African Ethnicity in the Cuban Cabildos de Nación," in, Jane A. Landers (ed.), *Slaves and Subjects: Blacks in Colonial Latin America* (Albuquerque, N. Mex., 2006), 209–45; Rafael López Valdés, *Pardos y morenos esclavos y libres en Cuba y sus instituciones en el Caribe hispano* (San Juan, 2007).

22. For an account of the Aponte Rebellion, see José Luciano Franco, *La conspiración de Aponte* (Havana, 1963); Gloria García Rodríguez, *Conspiraciones y revueltas: la actividad política de los negros en Cuba (1790–1845)* (Santiago, 2003), 55–74; Matt D. Childs, *The 1812 Aponte Rebellion in Cuba and the Struggle against Atlantic Slavery* (Chapel Hill, NC, 2006).

23. For slave resistance in Cuba, see David P. Geggus, "Slave Resistance in the Spanish Caribbean in the Mid-1790s," in David Barry Gaspar and David P. Geggus (eds.), *A Turbulent Time: The French Revolution and the Greater Caribbean* (Bloomington, Ind., 1997), 131–55; García Rodríguez, *Conspiraciones y revueltas*; and Manuel Barcia, *Seeds of Insurrection: Domination and Resistance on Western Cuban Plantations* (Baton Rouge, La., 2008).

24. The literature on La Escalera is extensive and polemical; for judicious treatment, see Paquette, *Sugar is Made with Blood*; Sarracino, *Inglaterra: sus dos caras*; Gloria García Rodríguez, "A propósito de la Escalera: el esclavo como sujeto político," *Boletín del Archivo Nacional* (Havana), 12 (2000): 1–13; García Rodríguez, *Conspiraciones y revueltas: la actividad política de los negros en Cuba (1790–1845)* (Santiago, 2003), 127–32; Juan Francisco Manzano, *Obras* (Havana, 1972); Juan Francisco Manzano, *Autobiography of a Slave*, trans. Evelyn Picon Garfield (Detroit, 1996).

25. For the use of Chinese laborers, see Lisa Yun, *The Coolie Speaks: Chinese Indentured Laborers and African Slaves in Cuba* (Philadelphia, 2008); for the importation of Yucatecan laborers, see Paul Estrade, "Los colonos yucatecos como sustitutos de los esclavos negros," in Consuelo Naranjo Orovioand Tomás Mallo Gutiérrez (eds.), *Cuba la perla de las Antillas: actas de las I Jornadas sobre "Cuba y su historia"* (Madrid, 1994), 93–107.

26. For the final abolition of the trade, see Murray, *Odious Commerce*, 298–326; and Schmidt-Nowara, *Empire and Anti-Slavery*, 100–8.

27. For a succinct treatment on the politics in Spain in 1860s and its repercussion for Cuban slavery, see Schmidt-Nowara, *Empire and Anti-Slavery*, 126–35.

28. For an excellent and concise overview of slavery during the Ten Years War, see Ada Ferrer, "Armed Slaves and Anticolonial Insurgency in Late Nineteenth-Century Cuba," in Christopher Leslie Brown and Philip P. Morgan (eds.), *Arming Slaves: From Classical Times to the Modern Age* (New Haven, 2006), 304–29. More extensive and in-depth treatments can be found in Ada Ferrer, *Insurgent Cuba: Race, Nation, and Revolution, 1868–1898* (Chapel Hill, NC, 1999), esp. chs. 1–2; Rebecca J. Scott, *Slave Emancipation in Cuba: The Transition to Free Labor, 1860–1899* (Princeton, 1985), 45–62; and María del Carmen Barcia, *Burguesía esclavista y abolición* (Havana, 1987), 138–48.

29. Ferrer, *Insurgent Cuba*, 40–69.

30. For slave population figures, see Kiple, *Blacks in Colonial Cuba*, 7–8, 65–71; and in particular the careful interpretation of these figures in Scott, *Slave Emancipation*, 72–87.

31. Ibid. 63–83.

32. Ibid. 127–97.

Select Bibliography

BARCIA, MANUEL. *Seeds of Insurrection: Domination and Resistance on Western Cuban Plantations*. Baton Rouge, La.: Louisiana State University Press, 2008.

BARCIA ZEQUEIRA, MARÍA DEL CARMEN. *Los ilustres apellidos: negros en La Habana colonial*. Havana: Ediciones Boloña, 2009.

CHILDS, MATT D. *The 1812 Aponte Rebellion in Cuba and the Struggle against Atlantic Slavery.* Chapel Hill, NC: University of North Carolina Press, 2006.

DE LA FUENTE, ALEJANDRO, with the collaboration of César García del Pino and Bernardo Iglseias Delgado. *Havana and the Atlantic in the Sixteenth Century.* Chapel Hill, NC: University of North Carolina Press, 2008.

DÍAZ, MARÍA ELENA. *The Virgin, the King, and the Royal Slaves of El Cobre: Negotiating Freedom in Colonial Cuba, 1670–1780.* Stanford, Calif.: Stanford University Press, 2000.

FERRER, ADA. *Insurgent Cuba: Race, Nation, and Revolution, 1868–1898.* Chapel Hill, NC: University of North Carolina Press, 1999.

GARCÍA RODRÍGUEZ, GLORIA. *Conspiraciones y revueltas: la actividad política de los negros en Cuba (1790–1845).* Santiago: Editorial Oriente, 2003.

MANUEL, MORENO FRAGINALS. *El ingenio: complejo económico social Cubano del azúcar.* 3 vols. Havana: Editorial de Ciencias Sociales, 1978.

PAQUETTE, ROBERT L. *Sugar is Made with Blood: The Conspiracy of La Escalera and the Conflict between Empires over Slavery in Cuba.* Middletown, Conn.: Wesleyan University Press, 1988.

SCOTT, REBECCA J. *Slave Emancipation in Cuba: The Transition to Free Labor, 1860–1899.* Princeton: Princeton University Press, 1985.

CHAPTER 5

....

BRAZIL

....

ROBERT W. SLENES

THE debate on slavery in Brazil at the beginning of the 1970s largely reflected the influence of the so-called São Paulo School of Sociology. Four assumptions guided the work of this eclectic group of Marxian scholars that strove to demonstrate the deleterious impact of slavery and racism on Brazilian history. First, mercantilist structures imposed by the "absolute monarchy" in Portugal in the colonial period (1500–1822) decisively configured Brazil's society. Second, masters and slaves confronted each other in Brazil predominantly on those sites—plantations and mines—valued by the metropolis, since the internal market created by the export economy was small and not profitable enough to compete for bonded labor. Third, the slaveholders, presumed usually to be masters of many persons, ruled virtually unchallenged over their subalterns. The slaves and the free poor, respectively victimized to the extreme and marginalized in the subsistence sector, suffered from anomie and alienation; thus, they were generally unable to contest the dominant order effectively through concerted action or to rise socially as individuals, beyond low-level clientage to a powerful patron. Fourth, large merchants resident in Portugal (or in England and other North Atlantic nations after Independence) and their agents in Brazil dominated commerce to such an extent that most capital accumulated in the New World slave system was transferred abroad, hindering internal economic development. Based on these assumptions, the São Paulo School articulated common arguments in the international bibliography of the time about the nature of slavery: that it was a precapitalist system, less rational than free labor even for the employer, and that the progressive expansion of capitalist rationality in the North Atlantic—and its late but inevitable entry into

Brazil—determined the process of abolition, from the closing of the African slave trade in 1850 to the end of slavery itself in 1888.[1]

An outpouring of scholarship based on intensive archival research has overturned all of these assumptions and arguments. In moving beyond the 1970 paradigm, historians have opened up new lines of inquiry, especially regarding questions of culture, identity, and subaltern agency. They have also redirected attention to older problems, such as the incidence of manumission and the degree to which masters imposed hegemony through patriarchal ideology and practice. In doing so, they have restructured the classic debate between the pioneering sociologist Gilberto Freyre and the São Paulo School, which regarded Freyre as its main opponent—the prime defender of the idea that Brazil was, historically, an "ethnic democracy."[2]

The turn to the archive was encouraged by the São Paulo School itself. Sociologist Florestan Fernandes, the "dean" of this group, his students Octávio Ianni and Fernando Henrique Cardoso, and associated scholars such as historians Emília Viotti da Costa and Fernando Novaes and philosopher Maria Sylvia Carvalho Franco produced significant monographs in the 1960s and early 1970s on colonial Brazil and on the export economy and society of the center-south (the region comprising Rio de Janeiro, São Paulo, Minas Gerais, and Espírito Santo) as well as on Brazil's non-plantation south (Paraná, Santa Catarina, and Rio Grande do Sul), during the nineteenth century.[3] Other scholars at the University of São Paulo, which at the time was Brazil's only center for doctoral study in history, also published important archival research on their state's agricultural and demographic history during the slave period.[4] In the United States, beginning in the late 1950s, historians of Brazil published model social histories of slave plantation areas or their port cities based on micro-level sources, particularly notarial and judicial records. Stanley Stein focused on the nineteenth-century coffee zone in Rio's Paraíba Valley; Warren Dean on coffee plantations in western São Paulo, 1820–1920; Peter Eisenberg on Pernambuco's coastal sugar region from the mid-nineteenth to the early twentieth century; Stuart Schwartz on sugar plantations in Bahia's *Recôncavo* (the region of the bay on which the city of Salvador is located) from 1550 to 1835; and Mary Karasch on the social history of slavery in the city of Rio de Janeiro, the emporium of the rising coffee economy, from the transfer of the Portuguese court to Brazil (1808) to 1850. British historians C. R. Boxer and Kenneth Maxwell turned their attention to Minas Gerais during the rise and decline of the gold and diamond booms in this central Brazilian region from 1695 to the early nineteenth century.[5]

The opening of new graduate centers of history in Brazil from the late 1970s, along with the influence on the Brazilian academy of the French *Annales* school, further stimulated regional and local histories, even of areas that had not emerged as export centers. A theoretical debate in Marxist historiography also proved important in directing attention inward. Against the argument that colonial slavery was a precapitalist mode of production, or, contrariwise, that it was capitalist because its "movement" was determined by the expansion of the European "world system," historian Ciro Flamarion Cardoso and political activist/independent scholar Jacob Gorender propounded the concept of the "colonial slave mode of production," "colonial" here understood in an economic, not strictly political sense. In their formulations, external market forces and internal relations of production combined to create a complex new society in Brazil that had a peculiar economic and social dynamic, neither "quasi-feudal" nor "capitalist." In Cardoso's essays, in particular, this idea of a hybrid "mode of production" became a heuristic tool that pointed to the need for research in local history, even in "peripheral" areas, to understand the systemic whole.[6]

From this beginning, a rush of studies appeared. The new research demonstrated that Brazil possessed a more varied slave economy with a much larger sector producing for the internal market than scholars had previously thought. The Brazilian economic historian Roberto Borges Martins showed that the already large slave population of Minas Gerais increased dramatically from 168,543 in 1819 to 381,893 in 1872—that is, during a period presumed by historians to be characterized by depression in the region's mining sector and overall economy. Martins could attribute only a small part of the increase to plantation agriculture. Subsequent work established that this "new" Minas Gerais consisted of an intricate mercantile system based on slave labor that not only supplied foreign markets with hides, tobacco, and the products of a revived mining and incipient coffee sector, but also satisfied the domestic demand of Minas and of the rapidly growing Rio de Janeiro and São Paulo plantation complex (including its urban centers), for cheese, hogs, cattle, and homespun cotton cloth. Historian Hebe Maria Mattos (de Castro) likewise demonstrated the intensive use of slaves in a non-plantation county to grow provisions for the nearby city of Rio. Other scholars documented the importance of forced labor in the cattle-raising interior of the northeast and far south (Rio Grande do Sul) as well as in the mixed farming and ranching *agreste* area, located between the dry northeastern interior and the coastal sugar zones. Historians had considered these regions rather marginal sites of slave labor, even while giving them some recognition as sources of provisions, cattle, and pack animals for the northeastern sugar complex, the mining sectors of eighteenth-century Minas Gerais, and the later sugar and coffee economy of the center-south. Similarly, B. J. Barickman demonstrated the surprisingly extensive use of slaves in the production of cassava and other products for rural and urban markets in the Recôncavo.[7]

Parallel research established that virtually everywhere in Brazil in the eighteenth and nineteenth centuries, even in plantation centers, small slave owners formed the large majority of masters. Likewise, a substantial proportion of Brazilian households (one-fourth to one-half may be taken as typical) held slaves. Even in plantation regions usually only a small percentage of slaves (11.6 percent in the sugar parishes of the Recôncavo in 1816–17) resided in holdings of 100 bondspeople or more, although there were exceptions where the figure was much higher, for instance the coffee counties of the Paraíba Valley and of western São Paulo from c.1840 to the end of slavery. Brazil's slaveholding patterns, as Stuart Schwartz noted, more closely resembled those in the antebellum southern United States than those in the major nineteenth-century slave societies of the Caribbean. In both Brazil and the antebellum South, masters and slaves typically interacted on properties where face-to-face contact could occur on a daily basis.[8]

These findings complemented discoveries that merchants resident in Brazil were active in internal markets, frequently combining production with trade. Indeed, as João Fragoso, Manolo Florentino, and their associates and students at the Federal University of Rio de Janeiro and elsewhere have shown, an elite group of merchants in the ports—often descendants of representatives of Portuguese mercantile houses who had married into large landowning and slaveholding families—came to dominate Brazil's trade with Africa as well as its coastal commerce (using ships made in Brazil). These elite merchants benefited as well from tax-collecting contracts and maintained far-flung commercial contacts with agents and peers in Brazil and elsewhere in the Lusitanian empire. Their ascent occurred not just because of the internal possibilities of capital accumulation, but because Brazilian-based merchants had a virtual monopoly on the products that were most in demand in Africa in the exchange for slaves: Bahia's tobacco, Rio's *cachaça* (raw sugar cane rum), and cotton cloth received directly from India, not via Portugal (a reminder that the empire extended beyond the Atlantic). Earlier historians, it seems, took Portuguese mercantilist laws at face value, rather than as attempts to reverse processes that were making Brazil the economic center of the empire well before the transfer of the court to Rio. Indeed, the absolute monarchy with absolute power did not exist; the Portuguese court constantly had to "negotiate" with local elites.[9]

The slave trade from West and West-Central Africa, an administered commerce as Luis Felipe de Alencastro has stressed, served as the linchpin of this whole system. Portugal's slave trade in its initial stages mostly supplied the labor demands of the Spanish colonies, but the Crown promoted it early on because it could be taxed. From the end of the sixteenth century, however, Brazil's thirst for workers in sugar production (in a slave plantation/factory system first essayed by Portugal in the African-Atlantic islands of São Tomé and Cape Verde) was the prime mover of this commerce. Enslaved Indians (to be discussed later in this essay) predominated in the initial stages of sugar production but quickly gave way to the growing number of Africans at the turn of the seventeenth century.

Estimates of the Atlantic slave trade to Brazil have risen since the historian Philip Curtin, in a groundbreaking quantitative study published in 1969, placed the number of imports at 3,646,800. Specialists now estimate that 4,864,400 Africans disembarked in Brazil during the course of the transatlantic trade, 45.5 percent of the total to the Americas and the Old World. About seven-tenths of these people originated in Bantuphone West-Central Africa (roughly present-day Angola and the Zaire River basin), a common culture area. Most of the rest came from West Africa (the area from Senegambia to the Bight of Biafra), the greater part shipped from the Bight of Benin, although Bantu-language speakers from East Africa formed a significant minority (greater than the contingent of West Africans) in the slave trade to Rio de Janeiro after 1810. The end of forced labor in Saint-Domingue and then of the African slave trade and slavery in the British Caribbean, along with Portuguese policies for increasing Brazilian exports, triggered the rapid expansion and diversification of the slave-based plantation complex (including production for the domestic market), especially in the center-south. (The Cuban slave economy was the other major "beneficiary" of these Caribbean abolitions.) As a result, the influx of new Africans to Brazil peaked at an annual average of 37,400 between 1811 and 1856, giving a total for these forty-six years of 1,720,500—35.4 percent of Brazil's overall sum since the beginning of the trade. This new estimate, 50 percent higher than Curtin's for the same period, has led Dale Tomich to speak of the "second slavery" (the parallel is to the "second serfdom," which grew in eastern Europe as western serfdom declined), and to call attention to its more "industrial" nature, that is, its greater mobilization of capital and regimentation of labor.[10]

This South Atlantic system, which included Portugal (Angola's metropolis) even after Independence, embraced an intensive movement of ships' crewmen, freed people of color, and even (up to 1822) government officials who occupied successive posts. Transatlantic exchanges also included black and mestizo soldiers sent from Brazil to fight in Portugal's African wars. Alencastro, however, sees the system as characterized above all by the interlocking production of goods on the Atlantic's western (American) shore and the reproduction of labor on the eastern (African) shore. Indeed, with a few sub-regional exceptions (that of Paraná in the early nineteenth century and perhaps that of São Paulo somewhat earlier) the slave population in Brazil depended on the influx of Africans to grow. To be sure, debate continues about the nineteenth-century slave population of Minas Gerais, certainly a large sub-system within Brazil; yet, the modest decline in the proportion of Africans among slaves in Minas between 1805–9 and 1845–9—the figure goes from 38 to 32 percent—suggests that the rapid increase of the total mineiro slave population during that period was substantially, or (since Africans' children were creoles) even entirely, the result of slave imports. In sum, natural increase in Minas, if it existed, must have been far less vigorous that that of the United States slave population during the same period. In any case, the generally huge and unbalanced nature of the trade (characterized by far more men than women) meant that in most places and periods sharp population decline would have initially set in if slave imports had ended—as indeed it did, nationally, after 1850.[11]

At the same time that historians were discovering a diversified forced labor system characterized by widespread slave ownership and by a redoubtable and varied group of elites, fresh scholarship was also revising stereotypes about slaves and the free(d) poor. A paradigm shift in slavery studies in the United States in the 1970s (particularly as expressed in books by the historians Eugene Genovese and Herbert Gutman and by the anthropologists Sidney Mintz and Richard Price) acted in Brazil as a catalyst of change by portraying the enslaved as bearers and creators of culture, capable of improving their situation by weighing experiences and devising strategies of action. Monographs on Brazilian slavery by Stanley Stein, Warren Dean, Mary Karasch, and other American scholars—who either antici-pated this change or accompanied it—were a further influence. Perhaps even more important was the work of the British Marxist historian E. P. Thompson, intro-duced to Brazilian readers through Portuguese and Spanish translation of some of his essays. The "rebellious" culture of Thompson's eighteenth-century English "plebeians," hidden behind outward deference towards "patricians," had particular resonance in Brazil in the early 1980s at the end of the military dictatorship, especially for students of slavery, who tended to share the São Paulo School's vision of the harshness of forced labor, but who also wished for more than a theory of victimization. Thompson, together with Gutman (a "Thompsonian" who had debunked theories of anomie in his research on both the industrial working class and slaves in the United States), also provided the impetus, especially for historians at the São Paulo "State University of Campinas" (Unicamp), to begin dismantling the "wall" in Brazilian historiography that then separated the pre- and the post-1888 periods (the first seen as "precapitalist," with "pre-political" African and native-born laborers, the second as essentially "capitalist," with European immi-grants as the prototypical—and most studied—"political" workers).[12]

In this context, the notion of slave anomie, the idea that shattered social norms impeded "links of interdependence, responsibility and solidarity" among bonded workers, could not escape criticism. One line of attack, represented, for example, by the work of João José Reis, Maria Helena Machado, Silvia Hunold Lara, and Sidney Chalhoub (the latter having already published a study of largely black urban workers post-1888), relied on notarial, police, and trial records to analyze master–slave encounters. These historians documented the alliances that slaves made with peers, including kin (for instance, by pooling resources to purchase manumission). Furthermore, they demonstrated how slaves continually "negotiated" with their masters, using deference, the mediation of elite sponsors, or direct confrontation: for instance, to induce or block transfer to another owner. Slave flight, often viewed by earlier historians as inconsequential or even pernicious since it supposedly drained away potential rebels against the system, also came under revisionist interpretation. Case studies by Flávio dos Santos Gomes demonstrated the frequent symbiosis between the runaway group (usually located near settled areas in order to trade for necessities) and the "quartered" community, each providing support for the other and thus potentially altering the balance of power in slave–master negotiations. In sum, slave agency was political action in the broadest sense: the mobilization of allies and the calculated use of both resistance and accommodation to obtain advantage, the very negation of anomie.[13]

Another approach focused on the meaning slaves gave to kinship ties. Since the notion of anomie centered on the idea that slavery (and slaveholders, acting deliberately) had, in the first instance, destroyed the family institutions of bonds-people, questions about the slave family became a central issue for researchers. The São Paulo School, to build its argument, had drawn in part on E. Franklin Frazier's sociological studies of the "Negro family" in the United States. Thus, the new United States bibliography on slavery, by rejecting Frazier's insistence that enslavement had utterly deculturated the ancestors of African-American families, bore directly on revisionist history in the Brazilian case. The critique of the Brazilian version of Frazier's argument began in the late 1970s and continued in the 1980s and after with a spate of studies, accompanied by theoretical and historiographical criticisms, on the demography of slave families and on fictive kinship (*compadrio*), the godparentage and co-parentage ties created at baptism.[14]

The demographic studies indicated that slave families, particularly those on smaller estates, were often severely disrupted. Between 1850 and 1881, for example, a large internal slave trade, driven particularly by a coffee boom in Brazil's center-south, replaced the Atlantic slave trade and reallocated tens of thousands of slaves from small properties to plantations.[15] Yet, slave behavior under propitious conditions belied a loss of motivation for association, for on middling and large properties in areas of economic expansion and stability over time, slaves demonstrated strong interest in forming and maintaining real and fictive kinship ties. Debate exists as to the deeper meaning of slave family networks, particularly as regards the plantation areas of nineteenth-century Rio and São Paulo. Did the slave family "pacify" an unruly, ethnically divided quarters, strengthening masters' control? Did it encourage creoles, with access to garden plots and manumission, to look towards freedom while turning away from Africans, thus undermining the unity of the slave quarters? Or, given the uncertainty of manumission (a topic to be discussed shortly), did the slave family strengthen a rebellious identity marked by the West-Central African culture shared by the majority of slaves in the quarters of the center-south?[16] These diverse approaches recognize that family strategies were linked to slaves' reflections about the possibilities of manumission, post-freedom mobility, and identity formation in the broader society.

With respect to the free(d) poor, a similar deconstruction of received ideas about "marginalization" has occurred. Scholars had taken evidence of low marriage rates and intense internal migration to diagnose a social pathology produced by slavery's relegation of free(d) workers to the subsistence sector. Historian Sheila de Castro Faria, however, discovered that marriage rates among rural populations in the center-south were considerably higher than in the capitals and mining towns described by earlier studies. More importantly, she and Hebe Maria Mattos (de Castro) demonstrated the linkage between migration and family strategies among the poor in early nineteenth-century Rio. Young male migrants from older settled areas moved to a mercantile frontier where, through insertion into large land-owners' clienteles, they married (thereby forming horizontal ties with peers), often gained access to land (as retainers of the wealthy if not proprietors themselves), and sometimes entered the ranks of small slaveholders.[17]

This latter group included surprising numbers of people of color, especially in Minas Gerais, probably the region with the highest proportion of non-whites among the free at the end of the colonial period. For instance, in one mineiro parish in 1795 (analyzed by Douglas Libby and Clothilde de Paiva) and in two mineiro counties in 1831 (studied by Francisco Vidal Luna and Herbert S. Klein), the percentage of all slaveholding heads of household that was non-white was respectively 34, and 12 and 43. For the case with the middle value (34 percent), the parish of São José del Rey in 1795, the data are broken down by holding size; there, 44 percent of owners with 1–5 slaves were free(d) people of color. To be sure, when one turns this analysis around and looks at the percentage of white-headed and non-white-headed households that had slaves, the results are more sobering. In the county above that has the highest proportion—43 percent—of slave owning heads of household classified as free(d) people of color (the data are for Sabará in 1831), only 16 percent of households headed by non-whites owned slaves, in contrast to 65 percent of white-headed households. In forty-one counties of São Paulo in 1829 (where only 6 percent of all household heads with slaves were non-white), the equivalent figures—respectively 6 and 34 percent—showed an even greater slave-holding gap between the two groups.[18]

Clearly, non-whites' very visible presence among slaveholders in some parts of Brazil (a reflection, in part, of their demographic weight in the population) stands in stark contrast to patterns observed in the southern United States. Yet, at the same time, blacks and mulattos faced a much greater barrier to slave ownership than whites, although to a substantial extent this barrier was probably the result of accumulated income and social-network disparities between the two groups, one formed ultimately of descendants of slaves, the other containing many descendants of slaveholders. This contrast certainly must be kept in mind when evaluating stories of non-white upward mobility (see the detailed biographies of mobile people of color presented by Zephyr Frank, Júnia Furtado, and Roberto Guedes), particularly since success leaves more traces in the archive than failure. Still, the work of these authors, like that of Hebe Maria Mattos (de Castro) and Sheila Faria as well as the demographic studies sampled above, do suggest that the Brazilian slave system, at least in the late eighteenth and early nineteenth centuries, allowed much greater integration into the monetary economy and more upward mobility to free(d) non-whites than the rigid "estate" society with virtually zero mobility that had been imagined by the São Paulo School.[19]

Indeed, a large class of *pardos*—a term that denoted persons of partial African descent and connoted social distance from slaves and ex-slaves—had come into existence and become politically expressive (and socially threatening to some dominant groups) by Independence. This subject has begun to receive the attention it deserves from historians, as books by Silvia Hunold Lara, Larissa Vianna, and Ivana Stoltz Lima attest. Mattos (de Castro) argues, however, that with the closing of the frontier (c.1830–50 in Rio de Janeiro, São Paulo, and Minas Gerais and perhaps earlier in the densely populated northeast) and the ending of the African slave trade (1850), social mobility declined as access to land and slave labor became increasingly difficult. Then, too, the citizenship and voting rights gained by non-whites in the 1824 Constitution, which made no distinction between people on the basis of color, began to be eroded after the rise to power in the 1830s of the Conservative Party (representing coffee planters, who rode the crest of the "second slavery"), despite opposition by some high-placed *pardos* in politics like Antônio Pereira Rebouças.[20]

The memory of this "birthright" from Independence, however, seems to have encouraged blacks and mulattos to embrace the ideal of equal citizenship, particularly during the last years of slavery and following abolition, when white racism and discrimination were on the rise. Note particularly, in this regard, the electoral law of 1881, which moved the country from a relatively generous income-based suffrage that allowed about half of male heads of household to vote, to a literacy-based system that drastically reduced the proportion of this group thenceforth eligible— an apparently non-racialized measure that, like analogous laws in the United States South in the years that followed, hit free(d) people of color especially hard. Mattos [de Castro] and Tiago de Melo Gomes have argued that the identity politics of blacks and mulattos anticipated Gilberto Freyre's formulation of the idea of ethnic democracy, but as a demand to be implemented, not as a celebratory representation of the past.[21] Indeed, the unprecedented new bibliography that extends the history of African Brazilians into the post-abolition period—a result of breaking down the historiographical "wall" of 1888—makes it clear that there was increasingly little to celebrate. To be sure, as late as 1940, census data indicate that, with respect to several socioeconomic indicators, there was a smaller gap between the situation of whites and non-whites in Brazil than in the United States. Yet, by 1980 the comparison had come to be in the latter's favor. Much more research is needed to understand the timing and the details of this downward slide in the condition of African Brazilians in free society, but the bibliography reviewed here suggests that it began, not in 1940 or 1888, but in the three decades following Independence, when the "second slavery" reached its apogee.[22]

What about the question of mobility from slavery to freedom? The São Paulo School tended to minimize the possibilities of manumission or claim that it was reserved largely for old and infirm slaves. Population data, particularly the three to one ratio of free(d) people of color to slaves in 1872, make this argument questionable. Today, a number of monographs on manumission have shown how widespread the practice was and have pointed to common patterns among the freed: in general, proportionately more women than men, more children than elders, more Brazilian-born people than Africans, more persons from the Bight of Benin than from West-Central Africa. Studies differ, however, in their evaluation of manumission's frequency and social impact, although they generally concede the practice was more common in Brazil than in the antebellum southern United States. One problem with this bibliography is that the sources almost always used— the *cartas de alforria* (writs of freedom) registered in notarial archives—probably greatly under-represent the *cartas* that were conceded privately. Lizandra Meyer Ferraz pointed out another difficulty: that only a small proportion of the many freedoms that occurred in wills and in inheritance proceedings were included in the notary books. A third problem is that manumission rates apparently varied strongly and inversely with holding size, according to studies that have linked freedoms in wills, *cartas de alforria*, and baptism records to the lists of slaves in inheritance proceedings.[23]

The seven monographs that have established such linkages for ten area-periods (all focusing on Rio, São Paulo, and Minas in the eighteenth and nineteenth centuries) show arresting results. Among all slave owners dying testate or intestate, small proprietors consistently freed a far greater percentage of their slaves (in wills and subsequent inheritance proceedings) than large ones. Yet, smallholders showed a huge variation. A large proportion of them manumitted no slaves at all; a minority freed an extraordinary number. Take, for example, slave owners in the Rio das Velhas mining district in eighteenth-century Minas Gerais. When those who actually left wills are examined, the gap between the proportions freed by small and large owners proves enormous: 42.1 versus 1.8 percent (the respective figures are for holders of 1–5 slaves and those with more than forty).[24] The single study linking manumissions at baptism to slave lists in inheritance proceedings, as well as the only monograph doing the same with writs of freedom, point strongly in the same direction.[25] One may conclude from this data that manumission from all sources was considerably more common than most studies have shown; yet, the rate at which it occurred (in wills and inheritance proceedings and perhaps also in baptisms and writs of freedom) varied greatly. While slaves of some smallholders (those leaving wills) had very substantial chances for manumission, slaves of large owners in general seem to have had little chance at all.

This pattern sheds light on recent work involving the wills of successful freed-women, predominantly of Mina origin, in Brazil's center-south (where "Mina" designated West Africans shipped predominantly from the Bight of Benin). Faria demonstrates that many such women who died single and without heirs freed most of their few slaves—frequently Mina women—in *cartas* and wills, often leaving them property as well. This pattern of behavior, presumably the result of long negotiation between the parties involved (note that small holders surely had less leverage on their slaves than large ones), speaks, in addition, to broader questions. João Fragoso and his colleagues tend to argue that the South Atlantic system not only permitted the transfer of the *ancien régime*'s hierarchy of estates to the tropics, but also strengthened its social and ideological base by enabling at first some non-noble Portuguese and then some free people of color to move up the hierarchy through relatively easy access to slave laborers. A society of estates, according to this scenario, proved quite capable of absorbing considerable upward mobility but in such a way that it retained its exclusionary ethos. The system also allowed some slaves, predominantly those Brazilian born, to initiate the same rise in sufficient numbers so as to defuse the danger of unrest from below by convincing many Africans that their children might benefit from this mobility. The picture thus drawn, while differing in the logic that frames it (a logic that asserts the agency of subalterns, but also the success of dominant groups in "persuading" subordinates to accept their hegemony), recalls Gilberto Freyre's portrayal of Brazil as a society in which social tensions were muted by the relatively cordial ties between patriarchal masters in the big house and their slave "dependents" in the quarters. The manumission studies reviewed here, however, suggest a more complicated picture. Slaves of smallholders prone to manumit may have opted for strategies of integration into the broader society, while perhaps most slaves on larger properties, unconvinced by their owners' posturing as benevolent patriarchs, did not. To be sure, manumission (gratis, purchased, or conditional) was not the only "gift" that owners had in their arsenal, for they also applied positive incentives like cash payments for work on holidays and job promotions within slavery. Nor did "freedom" for most slaves mean radically escaping from subordination to a patron. Yet, Ricardo Salles has presented telling data on Rio's coffee region, suggesting the importance of prospects for freedom in slaves' reflections on their condition. Large properties manumitted slaves during inheritance proceedings at a much lower rate than small ones, but their estate evaluation lists, which identify absent runaways, show a higher incidence of flight.[26]

These results may help explain two tendencies in recent studies that might otherwise suggest contrasting "Africanist" and "creolist" assumptions (i.e., African cultural continuity versus intense African/European interchange) about the results of colonial encounters.[27] On the one hand, monographs that focus on plantation areas, particularly during the period from the late eighteenth century to 1850 when the influx of Africans was at its height, often see slave agency expressed especially by resistance and by identity politics mobilizing African cultural markers.[28] On the other hand, those concerned with urban and non-plantation rural areas, characterized by smaller holdings, sometimes portray agency primarily in terms of integrative strategies, cultural hybridity, and go-between or mestizo identities.

Studies of slave uprisings, plots, and runaway communities figure prominently in the first group. The bibliography on Palmares, the large *quilombo* community or group of communities in the hinterland of Pernambuco's sugar region that survived for most of the seventeenth century, has particularly come to emphasize the continuity there of West-Central African cultural traditions, indeed political institutions, as principles of governance. This bibliography accords with James Sweet's research on Portuguese Inquisition trial records, largely involving residents of Brazil, which also details specific religious and healing practices that can be traced to Africa, particularly West-Central Africa. For the Bahian Recôncavo, where diverse peoples from the Bight of Benin predominated among African slaves in the early 1800s—but alongside a large West-Central African group—and where creoles of varying ancestry formed a near majority of bondspeople, João José Reis has documented frequent African ethnic-based slave uprisings between 1807 and 1830, although ethnic tensions, particularly between Africans and creoles, seem generally to have impeded concerted action. In the nineteenth-century center-south, where West-Central Africans, coming from a common cultural area, formed a large majority of slaves and where creoles tended to be their children, recent studies have not found such ethnic cleavages in slave revolts. Indeed, according to Robert Slenes, the region's slaves had defined a common religion by 1850—a forerunner of the later African-Brazilian religions, Macumba and Umbanda—centered on ceremonies reminiscent of those of the community "cults of affliction" (cults seeking the cure of social ills) among the Kongo and related people of the lower Zaire River basin. This common religion often underlay plans of rebellion, even into the 1880s. The Christian icons in these cults—St Anthony in particular—seem to have been reinterpreted along West-Central African lines, as they had been previously in the Kingdom of Kongo.[29]

In the post-1850 center-south, slaves in mining and on plantations became increasingly assertive, running away or rebelling. The historian Walter Fraga Filho has found the same for plantations in the Recôncavo. With slavery losing its legitimacy and with opportunities for the free(d) poor becoming scarcer, the elite's patriarchal pretensions seem to have become ever less convincing to their subordinates—something satirized, according to Chalhoub, by the literary genius of Joaquím Maria Machado de Assis (1839–1908), one of the world's most celebrated novelists. Looking backward, Stanley Stein's *Vassouras*, particularly its groundbreaking pages on slave *jongos*—satirical call-and-response songs of Central African origin still sung in the Paraíba Valley today—seems to have prefigured this portrait of an insurgent *senzala* with its own deeply rooted traditions.[30]

The second group of studies concentrates on the strategies of slaves and free(d) people of color to better their condition, ostensibly within the system. A high point here is Júnia Furtado's study of Chica da Silva, who rose from slavery to wealth and power in the eighteenth-century diamond region of Minas, through her relationship as mistress, then common-law wife to a high colonial official. Although Chica was exceptional, Furtado documents significant mobility among many women like her. Also noteworthy are recent studies of urban black religious brotherhoods by Mariza de Carvalho Soares, Marcelo Mac Cord, Anderson J. Oliveira, and others, which have gone well beyond the limited official documentation usually available on these groups (and earlier scholars' assimilationist portraits of them) to interrogate their political alliances, internal disputes, and memories of Africa. Indeed, a close look at both sets of research results indicates that the underlying processes of cultural re-signification that they describe, if not the outcomes, were the same. The religious brotherhoods, for example, displayed a bewildering variety of ethnic alliances and oppositions, which can only be the result in each case, as João José Reis has emphasized, of on-the-ground reconfigurations of diverse African and creole identities. In the same way, the Hausa of the "Hausa-based" revolts in the Recôncavo had negotiated an identity that joined people of similar language and culture, but that was not a copy of a specific community sentiment in the homeland.[31]

Analyses of the local remaking of cultures and identities that give close attention to African backgrounds, yet focus on the situational interplay of historical actors, often using the method of biography, are particularly notable in studies on the cities of Rio de Janeiro and Salvador. Mary Karasch's book on slave life in Rio, 1808–50, set a high standard, particularly her nuanced chapter on slave religion, which used recent Africanist insights to understand how Central Africans came to terms with Catholic Christianity and its saints. João José Reis's study of the 1835 *Malê* rebellion in Salvador was another model work. An expanded edition (2003) of the book stresses even more the ethnic (*nagô*-centered) character of this predominantly slave movement and the non-jihadist goals of its Islamic leaders. Subsequently, other exemplary studies appeared, focused on social and cultural interchanges within funereal customs, in popular festivals, in the martial art *capoeira*, and between the followers of popular healers. Luís Nicolau Parés, a specialist in African Brazilian religion, detailed the dialogue between the *jeje* and the *nagô* ("nations" formed in Brazil from, respectively, diverse Gbe- and Yoruba-speaking groups), in the making of the *Candomblé* religion. Others have analyzed the central place of Candomblé, as well as that of its increasingly female leadership, in the construction of a Bahian black identity during the second half of the nineteenth century. Nominative record linkage in judicial and notarial archives has resulted in two impressively detailed and contextualized biographies (by João José Reis and by Reis with Flávio dos Santos Gomes and Marcos de Carvalho) of peripatetic religious leaders, a practitioner of Candomblé and a Muslim, who linked Africa and Brazil in their travels.[32] All of these works on urban contexts document the strong continuity in Brazil of diverse African traditions. Yet, carrying forward the classic work of French anthropologist Roger Bastide on the "interpenetration of civilizations," most of this recent scholarship also confirms the intense interchanges between these traditions and with European ones as well, particularly in healing practices that evoked other-worldly forces. Just as in plantation contexts, the particular form these continuities and exchanges took depended on each individual's complex evaluation of lived experience, including, surely, his or her perceived chances for manumission and subsequent mobility.[33]

The growing perception that a multitude of actors occupied the historical stage, each engaged in daily micro-politics, has changed the way historians conceive of the process of abolition. For the São Paulo School, the prime internal agent of change from slave to free labor was a new group of planters in western São Paulo that supposedly had more diversified investments, a more capitalist mentality, and less attachment to slavery than peers elsewhere. Research on the slave market and the profitability of the plantation "firm" has disproved this argument. Slavery in Brazil, like slavery in other areas of the Americas, did not die a market death in any strict accounting sense. Western São Paulo planters, even more than their counter-parts in Rio, Bahia, and Pernambuco, purchased slaves vigorously—because they perceived it was profitable—until 1881, when fear about the political future of forced labor caused the slave market to crash. Even with regard to the administra-tion of their labor force, nineteenth-century planters give the impression of being thoroughly "modern." Rio coffee planters' strategies for managing and directing their slaves showed clear parallels with those applied in Cuba and in the southern United States. In all cases they were patterned after European principles enunciated by Enlightenment thinkers and liberal political economists, according to a study of planter manuals in the three regions over the long term (1660–1860) by Rafael Bivar Marquese.[34] This is not to say that planters did not have specific practices or beliefs grounded in particular cultural and situational contexts. The new bibliography has also given slaveholders their due as "agents," particularly with respect to family precepts and practices, with studies ranging from demographic inquiries into marriage patterns (within an institutional context that required strict equality in the division of estates between all children) to analyses of changing attitudes regarding female choice in marital alliances and of the intersection of family and politics.[35]

Contributing to the perception that the crisis of slavery was political in nature are studies that show the impact of national or even international politics on the actions of the quarters and, vice versa, of local subaltern movements on the deliberations of parliaments and government counselors. Thus, as Dale Graden, Robert Slenes, and others have argued, the 1850 abolition of the slave trade was the result, not just of escalating British pressure, which in the late 1840s seemed to threaten the possibility of a naval blockade, but also of increased unrest on the part of slaves. The latter, taking advantage of the international context, sharpened masters' long-standing fears of "Haitianization," already made acute by the 1835 *Malê* rebellion and by the specter raised by the unprecedentedly large slave trade from 1845.[36] Likewise, Brazilian statesmen exerted much less control of the gradual process of abolition on which Brazil embarked from the late 1860s than previously thought. In formulating the Rio Branco Law (1871) that freed children born of slave mothers, in prohibitively taxing the internal slave trade to the center-south (1880–1), in passing the Dantas-Saraiva-Cotegipe Law (1885) that freed elderly slaves, and in finally ending slavery itself with the so-called Golden Law of 1888, the national and provincial legislatures were forced to take into account the internal agitation of the slaves—runaways, rebels, plaintiffs who brought freedom suits to the courts—and their middle- and working-class sympathizers. In explaining emancipation, recent scholarship has assigned primary roles to ideological changes, the international decline of forced labor, the decreasing political commitment of most regions to slavery as bonded workers drained away to more productive estates in the center-south, broad-based mobilizations against the institution, and the ultimate ability of planter factions in Pernambuco and São Paulo to meet the impending crisis through technological change and the promotion of immigration.[37]

In conclusion, Indian slavery, as it relates to African slavery, deserves mention. The rapid increase in scholarship on Indian history since the 1980s has greatly refined knowledge about the enslavement of native people in the northeast and the Amazon in the sixteenth and seventeenth centuries. Dramatic population decline among Indians forced into slavery on northeastern sugar plantations—the result of European and African disease vectors—along with the rise in Africa of Portuguese slaving, oriented at first towards other European colonies, shifted Brazilian sugar production to a reliance on African labor by the early 1600s. To the mix of causes, Alencastro adds the weak structure of Indian political leadership compared to African, seeing it as an impediment to a large, indigenous slave trade. He cites as well the Crown's greater ease in taxing transatlantic labor shipments. Forced Indian labor now appears as more widespread and long-lasting than once thought. It was present, for instance, in São Paulo in the seventeenth century, producing wheat for the rest of Brazil during and after the Dutch wars; in Rio in the seventeenth and early eighteenth; and in Minas Gerais and Goiás as a by-product of frontier wars of extermination from the eighteenth century into the nineteenth century. Like enslaved Africans, enslaved Indians acted within the constraints of bondage as resistant "negotiators." Along these lines, historians like John Monteiro and Maria Regina Celestino de Almeida examined Indians' running away and rebelling in, respectively, seventeenth-century São Paulo and colonial Rio; Alida Metcalf explored Indian cultural and religious exchanges with both Europeans and Africans; and Maria de Leônia Chaves de Resende and Hal Langfur shed light on Indian slaves who defended themselves against often unspeakable exploitation by seeking redress in Brazilian courts.[38]

NOTES

1. For this synthesis, see Florestan Fernandes, *A integração do negro na sociedade de classes*, 2 vols. (São Paulo, 1965), vol. i; Octávio Ianni, *Raças e classes sociais no Brasil* (Rio de Janeiro, 1966), chs. 4–5; Fernando Henrique Cardoso, *Mudanças sociais na América Latina* (São Paulo, 1969), 186–98; and *Autoritarismo e democratização* (2nd edn. Rio de Janeiro, 1975), 104–15.
2. Gilberto Freyre, *The Masters and the Slaves: A Study in the Development of Brazilian Civilization* (New York, 1946), translation of *Casa grande e senzala: formação da família*

brasileira sob o regime da economia patriarcal (1st Brazilian edn. 1933). Freyre preferred the term "ethnic democracy" to "racial democracy": Gilberto Freyre, "A atitude brasileira," *Quilombo*, 1 (December 1948): 8, in Abdias do Nascimento and Elisa Larkin Nascimento (eds.), *Quilombo (. . .): edição fac-similar do jornal dirigido por Abdias do Nascimento, Rio de Janeiro, nos. 1–10, dezembro de 1948 a julho de 1950*, introd. Antonio Sérgio A. Guimarães (São Paulo, 2003), 26.

3. Fernandes, *A integração do negro*; Octávio Ianni, *As metamorfoses do escravo: apogeu e crise da escravatura no Brasil meridional* (São Paulo, 1962); Fernando Henrique Cardoso, *Capitalismo e escravidão no Brasil meridional* (São Paulo, 1962); Emília Viotti da Costa, *Da senzala à colônia* (São Paulo, 1966); Fernando A. Novais, *Portugal e Brasil na crise do antigo sistema colonial (1777–1808)* (São Paulo, 1979; a 1973 Ph.D. thesis). Maria Sylvia de Carvalho Franco, *Homens livres na sociedade escravocrata* (São Paulo, 1969). A forerunner: Caio Prado Júnior, *The Colonial Background of Modern Brazil* (1942; Berkeley, 1967). An important foreign influence: Eric Williams, *Capitalism and Slavery* (Chapel Hill, NC, 1944).

4. See especially Maria Luiza Marcílio, *Crescimento demográfico e evolução agrária paulista, 1700–1836* (São Paulo, 2000; originally a post-doctoral (*livre-docência*) thesis, 1974).

5. Stanley J. Stein, *Vassouras, a Brazilian Coffee County, 1850–1900* (1958; 2nd edn. Princeton, 1985); Warren Dean, *Rio Claro: A Brazilian Plantation System, 1820–1920* (Stanford, Calif., 1976); Peter L. Eisenberg, *The Sugar Industry in Pernambuco: Modernization without Change, 1840–1910* (Berkeley, 1974); Stuart B. Schwartz, *Sugar Plantations in the Formation of Brazilian Society: Bahia, 1550–1835* (Cambridge, 1985); Mary Karasch, *Slave Life in Rio de Janeiro, 1808–1850* (Princeton, 1987), a revision of her 1972 doctoral dissertation; Charles Boxer, *The Golden Age of Brazil* (Berkeley, 1962); Kenneth R. Maxwell, *Conflicts and Conspiracies: Brazil and Portugal, 1750–1808* (Cambridge, 1973).

6. Ciro F. S. Cardoso, "O modo de produção escravista colonial na América," in Théo Araújo Santiago (ed.), *América colonial: ensaios* (Rio de Janeiro, 1975), 89–143, and *Agricultura, escravidão e capitalismo* (Petrópolis, 1979); Jacob Gorender, *O escravismo colonial* (1978; 4th edn. São Paulo, 1985).

7. Roberto Borges Martins, "Growing in Silence: The Slave Economy of Nineteenth-Century Minas Gerais, Brazil" (Ph.D. diss., Vanderbilt University, 1980); Amilcar Martins Filho and Roberto B. Martins, "Slavery in a Nonexport Economy: Nineteenth-Century Minas Gerais Revisited," *Hispanic American Historical Review*, 63 (3) (August 1983): 537–68; Douglas Cole Libby, *Transformação e trabalho em uma economia escravista: Minas Gerais no século XIX* (São Paulo, 1988); Afonso de Alencastro Graça Filho, *A princesa do Oeste e o mito da decadência de Minas Gerais: São João del Rei, 1831–1888* (São Paulo, 2003); Hebe Maria Mattos de Castro, *Ao sul da história* (Rio de Janeiro, 1987); Diana Soares de Galliza, *O declínio da escravidão na Paraíba, 1850–1888* (João Pessoa, 1979); Luiz R. B. Mott, *Piauí colonial: população, economia e sociedade* (Teresina, 1985); Helen Osório, *O império português no sul da América: estancieiros, lavradores e comerciantes* (Porto Alegre, 2007). B. J. Barickman, *A Bahian Counterpoint: Sugar, Tobacco, Cassava and Slavery in the Recôncavo, 1780–1860* (Stanford, Calif., 1998).

8. Schwartz, *Sugar Plantations*, 439–67; Francisco Vidal Luna and Herbert S. Klein, *Slavery and the Economy of São Paulo, 1750–1850* (Stanford, Calif., 2003); Iraci del Nero da Costa, Francisco Vidal Luna, and Herbert S. Klein, *Escravismo em São Paulo e Minas Gerais* (São Paulo, 2009); Ricardo Salles, *E o Vale era o escravo: Vassouras, século XIX. Senhores e escravos no coração do Império* (Rio de Janeiro, 2008), 157.

9. João Luís Ribeiro Fragoso, *Homens de grossa aventura: acumulação e hierarquia na praça mercantil do Rio de Janeiro (1790–1830)* (1992; 2nd edn. Rio de Janeiro, 1998); João Fragoso and Manolo Florentino, *O arcaísmo como projeto: mercado atlântico, sociedade agrária e elite mercantil em uma economia colonial tardia (Rio de Janeiro, c.1790—c.1740)* (1993; 2nd edn. Rio de Janeiro, 2000); João Fragoso, Maria de Fátima Bicalho, and Maria de Fátima Gouvêa (eds.), *O Antigo Regime nos trópicos: a dinâmica imperial portuguesa (séculos XVI–XVIII)* (Rio de Janeiro, 2001); Roquinaldo Ferreira, "Dinâmica do comércio intracolonial: gerebitas, panos asiáticos e guerra no tráfico angolano de escravos (século XVIII)," in João Fragoso et al. (eds.), *O Antigo Regime nos trópicos*, 339–78.

10. Luíz Felipe de Alencastro, *O trato dos viventes: formação do Brasil no Atlântico Sul* (São Paulo, 2000), esp. chs. 1–5; Philip Curtin, *The African Slave Trade: A Census* (Madison, 1969), 268; Tables and Maps on Disembarkations and Embarkations of Africans, www.slavevoyages.org (accessed 2 April 2010); Dale Tomich, "The 'Second Slavery': Bonded Labor and the Transformation of the Nineteenth-Century World Economy," in *Through the Prism of Slavery: Labor, Capital, and World Economy* (Lanham, Md., 2004), 56–71.

11. Alencastro, *O trato dos viventes*, chs. 6–7; Jaime Rodrigues, *De costa a costa: escravos, marinheiros e intermediários do tráfico negreiro de Angola ao Rio de Janeiro (1780–1860)* (São Paulo, 2005). Horacio Gutiérrez, "Crioulos e africanos no Paraná, 1798–1830," *Revista brasileira de história*, 4 (16) (March–August 1988), 161–88; Luna and Klein, *Slavery and the Economy of São Paulo*, 133–57; Laird Bergad, *Slavery and the Demographic and Economic History of Minas Gerais, Brazil, 1720–1888* (Cambridge, 1999); Douglas Cole Libby and Clotilde de Paiva, "Caminhos alternativos: escravidão e reprodução em Minas Gerais no século XIX," *Estudos econômicos*, 25 (2) (1995): 203–33. I use Bergad's own data here (pp. 125, 253), to question his argument that the trade contributed negligibly to slave population growth during the period cited.

12. Eugene D. Genovese, *Roll, Jordan, Roll: The World the Slaves Made* (New York, 1974); Herbert G. Gutman, *The Black Family in Slavery and Freedom, 1750–1825* (New York, 1976); Sidney W. Mintz and Richard Price, *An Anthropological Approach to the Afro-American Past: A Caribbean Perspective* (Philadelphia, 1976); E. P. Thompson, *A miseria da teoria, ou um planetário de erros: uma crítica ao pensamento de Althusser* (Rio de Janeiro, 1978, containing only the title essay), and *Tradición, revuelta y consciencia de clase: estudios sobre la crisis de la sociedad preindustrial* (Barcelona, 1979). Translations into Portuguese of other books by Thompson, of half of Genovese's book (the second of two projected volumes never appeared), and of the second edition of Mintz and Price's work, followed. For a retrospective on breaking down the 1888 "wall," see Sidney Chalhoub and Fernando Teixeira da Silva, "Sujeitos no imaginário acadêmico: escravos e trabalhadores na historiografia brasileira desde os anos 1980," *Cadernos AEL* (Arquivo Edgard Leuenroth, Unicamp), 14 (26) (2009): 13–57. On slaves and free poor workers before 1888 as not even "pre-political": Cardoso, *Autoritarismo e democratização*, 104–15.

13. Fernandes, *A integração do negro*, 38 (quotation). João José Reis, *Rebelião escrava no Brasil: a história do levante dos Malês em 1835* (1986; 2nd Brazilian edn., revised and expanded from the English-language version of 1993, São Paulo, 2003); Maria Helena Machado, *Crime e escravidão: trabalho, luta e resistência nas lavouras paulistas, 1830–1888* (São Paulo, 1987); Silvia Hunold Lara, *Campos da violência: escravos e senhores na Capitania do Rio de Janeiro, 1750–1808* (Rio de Janeiro, 1988); João José Reis and Eduardo Silva, *Negociação e conflito: a resistência negra no Brasil escravista* (São Paulo, 1989); Sidney Chalhoub, *Visões da liberdade: uma história das últimas décadas da escravidão na*

Corte (São Paulo, 1990). Katia Queiroz Mattoso, *Ser escravo no Brasil* (São Paulo, 1982) was a pioneering work. Flávio dos Santos Gomes, *Histórias de quilombolas: mocambos e comunidades de senzalas no Rio de Janeiro—século XIX* (1995; revised and expanded edn. São Paulo, 2006); João José Reis and Flávio dos Santos Gomes (eds.), *Liberdade por um fio: história dos quilombos no Brasil* (São Paulo, 1996).

14. Schwartz, *Sugar Plantations*, ch. 14; *Estudos econômicos*, 17 (2) (1987), issue on the slave family; Alida Metcalf, *Family and Frontier in Colonial Brazil: Santana de Parnaíba, 1580–1822* (Berkeley, 1992), ch. 6. Sidney Chalhoub, *Trabalho, lar e botequim: o cotidiano dos trabalhadores no Rio de Janeiro da Belle époque* (Rio de Janeiro, 1986), 35–58; George Reid Andrews, *Blacks and Whites in São Paulo, Brazil, 1888–1988* (Madison, 1991), 54–89.

15. Richard Graham, "Another Middle Passage? The Internal Slave Trade in Brazil," and Robert W. Slenes, "The Brazilian Internal Slave Trade, 1850–1888: Regional Economies, Slave Experience and the Politics of a Peculiar Market," both in Walter Johnson (ed.), *The Chattel Principle: Internal Slave Trades in the Americas* (New Haven, 2004), 291–324, 325–70.

16. See, respectively: Manolo Florentino and José Roberto Góes, *A paz das senzalas: famílias escravas e tráfico atlântico, Rio de Janeiro, c.1790–c.1850* (Rio de Janeiro, 1997); Hebe Maria Mattos (de Castro), *Das cores do silêncio: os significados da liberdade no sudeste escravista—Brasil, século XIX* (1995; 2nd edn. Rio de Janeiro, 1998); Robert W. Slenes, *Na senzala, uma flor: esperanças e recordações na formação da família escrava—Brasil Sudeste, século XIX* (Rio de Janeiro, 1999). See also José Flávio Motta, *Corpos escravos, vontades livres: posse de cativos e família escrava em Bananal (1801–1829)* (São Paulo, 1999); Sandra Lauderdale Graham, *Caetana Says No: Women's Stories from a Brazilian Slave Society* (Cambridge, 2002), part I; Cacilda Machado, *A trama das vontades: negros, pardos e brancos na construção da hierarquia social do Brasil escravista* (Rio de Janeiro, 2008), on slave families in small holdings in Paraná.

17. Sheila Siqueira de Castro Faria, *A colônia em movimento: fortuna e família no cotidiano colonial* (Rio de Janeiro, 1998); Mattos (de Castro), *Das cores do silêncio*.

18. Douglas Libby and Clotilde A. de Paiva, "Manumission Practices in a Late Eighteenth-Century Brazilian Slave Parish: São José d'El Rey in 1795," *Slavery and Abolition*, 21 (1) (2000): 117; Luna and Klein, *Slavery and the Economy of São Paulo*, 164.

19. Zephyr L. Frank, *Dutra's World: Wealth and Family in Nineteenth-Century Rio de Janeiro* (Albuquerque, N. Mex., 2004); Júnia Ferreira Furtado, *Chica da Silva: A Brazilian Slave of the Eighteenth Century* (Cambridge, 2009); Roberto Guedes, *Egressos do cativeiro: trabalho, família, aliança e mobilidade social (Porto Feliz, São Paulo, c.1798–c.1850)* (Rio de Janeiro, 2008), ch. 5. For more biographies see Eduardo Silva, *Prince of the People: The Life and Times of a Brazilian Free Man of Colour* (London, 1993); Regina Célia Lima Xavier, *A conquista da liberdade: libertos em Campinas na segunda metade do século XIX* (Campinas, 1996) and *Religiosidade e escravidão, século XIX: Mestre Tito* (Porto Alegre, 2008). On the barriers to mobility faced by poor single women: Elizabeth Anne Kuznesof, *Household Economy and Urban Development: São Paulo, 1765 to 1836* (Boulder, Colo., 1986). On discriminatory taxation against freed Africans in Bahia: Manuela Carneiro da Cunha, *Negros, estrangeiros: os escravos libertos e sua volta à África* (São Paulo, 1985).

20. Silvia Hunold Lara, *Fragmentos setecentistas* (São Paulo, 2007); Larissa Vianna, *O idioma da mestiçagem: as irmandades de pardos na América portuguesa* (Campinas, 2007); Ivana Stoltz Lima, *Cores, marcas e falas: sentidos da mestiçagem no Império do Brasil* (Rio de Janeiro, 2003); Keila Grinberg, *O fiador dos brasileiros: cidadania,*

escravidão e direito civil no tempo de Antonio Pereira Rebouças (Rio de Janeiro, 2002); Leo Spitzer, *Lives in Between; Assimilation and Marginality in Austria, Brazil, West Africa, 1780–1945* (New York, 1989), ch. 4.

21. Sidney Chalhoub, "The Politics of Silence: Race and Citizenship in Nineteenth-Century Brazil," *Slavery and Abolition*, 27 (April 2006): 71–85; Mattos [de Castro], *Das cores do silêncio*; Tiago de Melo Gomes, *Um espelho no palco: identidades sociais e massificação da cultura no teatro de revista dos anos 1920* (Campinas, 2004). On nineteenth-century stereotypes and debates over "race": Lília Moritz Schwarcz, *Retrato em branco e negro: jornais, escravos e cidadãos em São Paulo no final do século XIX* (São Paulo, 1987) and *O espetáculo das raças: cientistas, instituições e questão racial no Brasil, 1870–1930* (São Paulo, 1993); Célia Maria Marinho de Azevedo, *Onda negra, medo branco: o negro no imaginário das elites—século XIX* (Rio de Janeiro, 1987); Valéria Lima, *J.-B. Debret, historiador e pintor: a viagem pitoresca e histórica ao Brasil (1816–1839)* (Campinas, 2007). On blacks and mulattos in the military: Ricardo Salles, *Guerra do Paraguai: escravidão e cidadania na formação do exército* (Rio de Janeiro, 1990); Hendrik Kraay, *Race, State, and Armed Forces in Independence-Era Brazil: Bahia, 1790s–1840s* (Stanford, Calif., 2001).

22. See particularly: Walter Fraga Filho, *Encruzilhadas da liberdade: histórias de escravos e libertos na Bahia, 1870–1910* (Campinas, 2006); Hebe [Maria] Mattos [de Castro] and Ana Lugão Rios, *Memórias do cativeiro: família, trabalho e cidadania no pós-abolição* (Rio de Janeiro, 2005); Olívia Maria Gomes da Cunha and Flávio dos Santos Gomes (eds.), *Quase cidadão: histórias e antropologias da pós-emancipação no Brasil* (Rio de Janeiro, 2007); Andrews, *Blacks and Whites in São Paulo* and "Racial Inequality in Brazil and the United States: A Statistical Comparison," *Journal of Social History*, 26 (2) (1992): 229–63.

23. Kátia M. de Queiroz Mattoso, "A propósito de cartas de alforria—Bahia, 1779–1850," *Anais de história* (Assis, São Paulo), 4 (1972): 23–52; Stuart B. Schwartz, "The Manumission of Slaves in Colonial Brazil: Bahia, 1684–1745," *Hispanic American Historical Review*, 54 (4) (November 1974): 603–35; Manuela Carneiro da Cunha, "Sobre os silêncios da lei: lei costumeira e positiva nas alforrias de escravos no Brasil do século XIX," in *Antropologia do Brasil: mito, história, etnicidade* (São Paulo, 1986), 123–44; Maria Inês Cortes de Oliveira, *O liberto: o seu mundo e os outro. Salvador, 1790/1890* (São Paulo, 1988); Marcus J. M. de Carvalho, *Liberdade: rotinas e rupturas do escravismo. Recife, 1822–1850* (Recife, 1998); Kathleen J. Higgens, *"Licentious Liberty" in a Brazilian Gold-Mining Region: Slavery, Gender and Social Control in Eighteenth-Century Sabará, Minas Gerais* (University Park, Pa., 1999); A. J. R. Russell-Wood, *Slavery and Freedom in Colonial Brazil* (2nd edn. Oxford, 2002); Mariana L. R. Dantas, *Black Townsmen: Urban Slavery and Freedom in the Eighteenth-Century Americas* (New York, 2008), on Baltimore and Sabará; Paulo Roberto Staudt Moreira, *Os cativos e os homens de bem: experiências negras no espaço urbano. Porto Alegre—1858–1888* (Porto Alegre, 2003). Lizandra Meyer Ferraz, *Testamentos, alforrias e liberdade: Campinas, século XIX* (Campinas, 2008).

24. Márcio de Sousa Soares, *A remissão do cativeiro: a dádiva da alforria e o governo dos escravos nos Campos dos Goitacases, c.1750–c.1830* (Rio de Janeiro, 2009), 91–2 (on two periods); Guedes, *Egressos do cativeiro*, 192; Salles, *E o Vale era o escravo*, 291; Ferraz, *Testamentos* (on Campinas, two periods); Jonis Freire, "Escravidão e família escrava na Zona da Mata mineira oitocentista" (Ph.D. diss., Universidade Estadual de Campinas, 2009), 313–25; Eduardo França Paiva, *Escravidão e universo cultural na Colônia: Minas Gerais, 1716–1789* (Belo Horizonte, 2001), 175–6 (on two sub-regions), 175 for data cited.

25. Cristiano Lima da Silva, "Como se livre nascera: a alforria na pia batismal em S. João Del-Rei (1750–1850)" (master's thesis, Universidade Federal Fliminense, 2004); Freire, "Escravidão e família escrava," 313–25.

26. Sheila de Castro Faria, "Damas mercadoras: as pretas minas no Rio de Janeiro (século XVIII–1850," in Mariza de Carvalho Soares (ed.), *Rotas atlânticas da diáspora africana: da Baía do Benim ao Rio de Janeiro* (Niterói, 2007), 103–34; João Luís Ribeiro Fragoso, "Fidalgos e parentes de pretos: notas sobre a nobreza principal da terra do Rio de Janeiro (1600–1750)," in Fragoso, Carla Maria Carvalho de Almeida, and Antonio Carlos Jucá de Sampaio (eds.), *Conquistadores e negociantes: histórias de elites no Antigo Regime nos trópicos. América lusa, séculos XVI a XVIII* (Rio de Janeiro, 2007), 33–120; Salles, *E o Vale era o escravo*, 291 (data on slaves freed in other ways than by dispositions in wills—e.g., self purchase, gift from heirs).

27. See Richard Price, "O milagre da crioulização: retrospectiva," *Estudos afro-asiáticos*, 25 (3) (2003): 383–419.

28. On the origins of Africans in Rio de Janeiro: Karasch, *Slave Life*, ch. 1; Manolo Florentino, *Em costas negras: uma história do tráfico de escravos entre a África e o Rio de Janeiro (séculos XVIII e XIX)* (1995; 2nd edn. São Paulo, 1997). On Salvador and Recife: Pierre Verger, *Fluxo e refluxo do tráfico de escravos entre o golfo do Benin e a Bahia de Todos os Santos, dos séculos XVII a XIX* (São Paulo, 1987); Maria Inês Cortes de Oliveira, "Quem eram os 'negros da Guiné'? A origem dos africanos na Bahia," *Afro-Ásia*, 19/20 (1997): 37–73; Manolo Florentino, Alexandre Vieira Ribeiro, and Daniel Domingues da Silva, "Aspectos comparativos do tráfico de africanos para o Brasil (séculos XVIII e XIX)," *Afro-Ásia*, 31 (2004): 83–126; Luís Nicolau Parés, *A formação do Candomblé: história e ritual da nação jeje na Bahia* (Campinas, 2006), ch. 2.

29. Stuart B. Schwartz, "Rethinking Palmares: Slave Resistance in Colonial Brazil," in *Slaves, Rebels and Peasants: Reconsidering Brazilian Slavery* (Urbana, Ill., 1993), 103–36; John K. Thornton, "Les États de l'Angola et la formation de Palmares (Brésil)," *Annales: histoire, sciences sociales*, 63 (July–August 2008): 769–97; Silvia Hunold Lara, "Palmares e Cucaú: o aprendizado da dominação" (unpublished thesis, Unicamp, 2009); James H. Sweet, *Recreating Africa: Culture, Kinship, and Religion in the African-Portuguese World, 1441–1770* (Chapel Hill, NC, 2003); Reis, *Rebelião escrava*, part I; Gomes, *Histórias de quilombolas*, ch. 2; Marcus Ferreira Andrade, "Rebelião escrava na comarca do Rio das Mortes, Minas Gerais: o caso Carrancas," *Revista Afro-Ásia*, 21/2 (1998–9), 45–82; Ricardo Figueiredo Pirola, "A conspiração escrava de Campinas, 1832: rebelião, etnicidade e família" (master's thesis, Universidade Estadual de Campinas, 2005); Robert W. Slenes, "L'Arbre nsanda replanté: cultes d'affliction kongo et identité des esclaves de plantation dans le Brésil du Sud-Est entre 1810 et 1888," *Cahiers du Brésil contemporain*, 67/8 (2007): 217–313.

30. Isadora Moura Mota, "O 'vulcão' negro da Chapada: rebeliões escravas nos sertões diamantinos (Minas Gerais, 1864)" (master's thesis, Universidade Estadual de Campinas, 2005); Azevedo, *Onda negra*; Maria Helena P. T. Machado, *Crime e escravidão* (São Paulo, 1987), and *O Plano e o pânico: os movimentos sociais na década da Abolição* (Rio de Janeiro, 1994); Fraga Filho, *Encruzilhadas da liberdade*; Sidney Chalhoub, *Machado de Assis: historiador* (São Paulo, 2003); Silvia Hunold Lara and Gustavo Pacheco (eds.), *Memória do jongo: as gravações históricas de Stanley J. Stein. Vassouras, 1948* (Rio de Janeiro, 2008).

31. Furtado, *Chica da Silva*; Mariza de Carvalho Soares, *Devotos da cor: identidade étnica, religiosidade e escravidão no Rio de Janeiro, século XVIII* (Rio de Janeiro, 2000); Elizabeth W. Kiddy, *Blacks of the Rosary: Memory, and History in Minas Gerais, Brazil* (University

Park, Pa., 2005); Marina de Mello e Souza, *Reis negros no Brasil escravista: história da festa de coroação de rei Kongo* (Belo Horizonte, 2002); Marcelo Mac Cord, *O Rosário de D. Antônio: irmandades negras, alianças e conflitos na história social do Recife, 1848–1872* (Recife, 2005); Anderson José Machado de Oliveira, *Devoção negra: santos pretos e catequese no Brasil Colonial* (Rio de Janeiro, 2008); João José Reis, "Identidade e diversidade étnicas nas irmandades negras no tempo da escravidão," *Tempo*, 2 (3) (June 1997): 7–33.

32. Karasch, *Slave Life*; Reis, *Rebelião escrava*; João José Reis, *Death is a Festival: Funeral Rites and Rebellion in Nineteenth-Century Brazil* (1991; Chapel Hill, NC, 2003); Martha Abreu, *O Império do Divino: festas religiosas e cultura popular no Rio de Janeiro, 1830–1900* (Rio de Janeiro, 1999); Carlos Eugênio Líbano Soares, *A negregada instituição: os capoeiras na Corte imperial, 1850–1890* (Rio de Janeiro, 1998); Gabriela dos Reis Sampaio, *Juca Rosa: um pai-de-santo na Corte imperial* (Rio de Janeiro, 2009); Parés, *A formação do Candomblé*; Rachel E. Harding, *A Refuge in Thunder: Candomblé and Alternative Spaces of Blackness* (Bloomington, Ind., 2000); João José Reis, *Domingos Sodré: um sacerdote africano. Escravidão, liberdade e Candomblé na Bahia do século XIX* (São Paulo, 2008); João José Reis, Flávio dos Santos Gomes, and Marcus J. M. de Carvalho, "África e Brasil entre margens: aventuras e desventuras do africano Rufino José Maria, c.1822–1853," *Estudos afro-asiáticos*, 26 (2) (2004): 257–302.

33. Roger Bastide, *The African Religions of Brazil: Toward a Sociology of the Interpenetration of Civilizations* (1960; Baltimore, 1978); Laura de Mello e Souza, *O diabo e a terra de Santa Cruz: feitiçaria e religiosidade popular no Brasil colonial* (4th edn. São Paulo, 1994); Luis Mott, *Rosa Egipcíaca: uma santa africana no Brasil* (Rio de Janeiro, 1993). On connections between the city and the countryside, João José Reis, "La Révolte haussa de Bahia en 1807: résistence et contrôle des esclaves au Brésil," *Annales*, 61 (2) (March–April 2006): 383–419.

34. Slenes, "Brazilian Internal Slave Trade"; Pedro Carvalho de Mello, "The Economics of Labor in Brazilian Coffee Plantations, 1850–1888" (Ph.D. diss., University of Chicago, 1977); Bert J. Barickman, "Persistence and Decline: Slave Labour and Sugar Production in the Bahian Recôncavo, 1850–1888," *Journal of Latin American Studies*, 28 (1996): 581–633; Rafael Bivar Marquese, *Feitores do corpo, missionários da mente: senhores, letrados e o controle dos escravos nas Américas, 1660–1860* (São Paulo, 2004). For "biographies" of planters and their properties: Eduardo Silva, *Barões e escravidão: três gerações de fazendeiros e a crise da estrutura escravista* (Rio de Janeiro, 1984); Hebe Maria Mattos de Castro and Eduardo Schnoor (eds.), *Resgate: uma janela para o oitocentos* (Rio de Janeiro, 1995). On Pernambuco's economy and its sugar sector: Eisenberg, *Modernization without Change*; Evaldo Cabral de Melo, *O norte agrário e o Império* (Rio de Janeiro, 1984).

35. Carlos de Almeida Prado Bacellar, *Os senhores da terra: família e sistema sucessório entre os senhores de engenho do Oeste paulista, 1765–1855* (Campinas, 1997); Alida Metcalf, *Family and Frontier in Colonial Brazil*, ch. 4; Silvia Maria Jardim Brügger, *Minas patriarcal: família e sociedade (São João del Rey—séculos XVIII e XIX)* (São Paulo, 2007); On elite patronage: Richard Graham, *Patronage and Politics in Nineteenth-Century Brazil* (Stanford, Calif., 1990).

36. On English pressure: Leslie Bethell, *The Abolition of the Brazilian Slave Trade: Britain, Brazil and the Slave Trade Question: 1807–1864* (Cambridge, 1970); Luis Felipe de Alencastro, "Le Versant brésilien de l'Atlantique-Sud: 1550–1850," *Annales*, 61 (2) (March–April 2006): 339–82. On slave pressure: Dale Graden, "An Act 'Even of Public Security': Slave Resistance, Social Tensions and the End of the International Slave Trade

to Brazil, 1835–1856," *Hispanic American Historical Review*, 76 (2) (May 1996): 249–82; Slenes, "L'Arbre *nsanda* replanté." A dissenting view: Jeffrey Needell, *The Party of Order: The Conservatives, the State, and Slavery in the Brazilian Monarchy, 1831–1871* (Stanford, Calif., 2006), 138–55.

37. Azevedo, *Onda negra*; Elciene Azevedo, *Orfeu de carapinha: a trajetória de Luiz Gama na imperial cidade de São Paulo* (Campinas, 1999); Eduardo Spiller Pena, *Pajens da casa imperial: jurisconsultos, escravidão e a lei de 1871* (Campinas, 2001); Chalhoub, *Machado de Assis* (on the 1871 law); Joseli Mendonça, *Entre a mão e os anéis: a Lei dos Sexagenários e os caminhos da abolição no Brasil* (Campinas, 1999); Machado, *O plano e o pânico*. On mainstream abolitionism: Célia Maria Marinho de Azevedo, *Abolitionism in the United States and Brazil* (New York, 1995). For new light on abolitionist Joaquim Nabuco: Izabel Andrade Marson, *Política, história e método em Joaquim Nabuco: tessituras da revolução e da escravidão* (Uberlândia, 2008). Still useful: Robert Conrad, *The Destruction of Brazilian Slavery, 1850–1888* (Berkeley, 1972).

38. Schwartz, *Sugar Plantations*, 28–72; Alencastro, *O trato dos viventes*, 117–54; *The Americas*, 61 (3) (January 2005), issue on "Rethinking Bandeirismo in Colonial Brazil" (ed. A. J. R. Russell-Wood); John Manuel Monteiro, *Negros da Terra: índios e bandeirantes nas origens de São Paulo* (São Paulo, 1994); Maria Regina Celestino de Almeida, *Metamorfoses indígenas: identidade e cultura nas aldeias coloniais do Rio de Janeiro* (Rio de Janeiro, 2003); Alida Metcalf, *Go-betweens and the Colonization of Brazil, 1500–1600* (Austin, Tex., 2005); Maria de Leônia Chaves de Resende and Hal Langfur, "Minas Gerais indígena: a resistência dos índios nos sertões e nas vilas de El-Rei," *Tempo*, 12 (23) (July–December 2007), 15–32; Hal Langfur, *The Forbidden Lands: Colonial Identity, Frontier Violence and the Persistence of Brazil's Eastern Indians, 1750–1830* (Stanford, Calif., 2006).

Select Bibliography

Alencastro, Luíz Felipe de. *O trato dos viventes: formação do Brasil no Atlântico Sul.* São Paulo: Companhia das Letras, 2000.

Barickman, B. J. *A Bahian Counterpoint: Sugar, Tobacco, Cassava and Slavery in the Recôncavo, 1780–1860.* Stanford, Calif.: Stanford University Press, 1998.

Chalhoub, Sidney. *Visões da liberdade: uma história das últimas décadas da escravidão na Corte.* São Paulo: Companhia das Letras, 1990.

Fragoso, João, Maria de Fátima Bicalho, and Maria de Fátima Gouvêa, eds. *O Antigo Regime nos trópicos: a dinâmica imperial portuguesa (séculos XVI–XVIII).* Rio de Janeiro: Civilização Brasileira, 2001.

Furtado, Júnia Ferreira. *Chica da Silva: A Brazilian Slave of the Eighteenth Century.* Cambridge: Cambridge University Press, 2009.

Gomes, Flávio dos Santos. *Histórias de quilombolas: mocambos e comunidades de senzalas no Rio de Janeiro—século XIX.* 1995; revised and expanded edn. São Paulo: Cia. das Letras, 2006.

Karasch, Mary. *Slave Life in Rio de Janeiro, 1808–1850.* Princeton: Princeton University Press, 1987.

MATTOS (DE CASTRO), HEBE MARIA. *Das cores do silêncio: os significados da liberdade no Sudeste escravista—Brasil, século XIX*. 1995; 2nd edn. Rio de Janeiro: Nova Fronteira, 1998.

REIS, JOÃO JOSÉ, *Rebelião escrava no Brasil: a história do levante dos Malês em 1835*. 1986; 2nd Brazilian edn., revised and expanded from 1993 American edn. São Paulo: Companhia das Letras, 2003.

SCHWARTZ, STUART B. *Sugar Plantations in the Formation of Brazilian Society: Bahia, 1550–1835*. Cambridge: Cambridge University Press, 1985.

....

CHAPTER 6

BRITISH WEST INDIES AND BERMUDA

....

TREVOR BURNARD

IN 1998, Ira Berlin published a comprehensive study of slavery in colonial mainland British North America. He assumed that slavery was a negotiated relation that varied considerably not only over space but also over time. Slavery should not be viewed as a timeless, unchanging institution, he insisted, but had to be seen as continually changing in accord with circumstances of contestation and cooperation between owners and enslaved people.[1] Although Berlin did not deal with slavery in the British West Indies and Bermuda—half of the twenty-six British slaveholding colonies in the Americas in 1776—his four-staged evolutionary model proves useful for understanding the dynamic development of chattel slavery in what became the epicenter of British slavery in the Americas.

Berlin locates the origins of slave life and culture in mainland North America in a "charter generation" of Africans and persons of African descent—"Atlantic creoles"—who forged a composite identity from encounters and exchanges within an increasingly commercialized transatlantic littoral. Atlantic creoles established the lineaments of slave life in societies where the master–slave relation did not yet stand at the center of economic production. The length of this initial phase of slavery varied. In Bermuda, the charter period was considerable; in Barbados and in the smaller islands of the British Leewards (St Christopher, Nevis, Antigua, and

Montserrat), the charter period was relatively short; in Jamaica and later settled islands, a charter period could hardly be said to have existed.

The British West Indies differed from other places colonized by the British in the Americas in the rapidity by which slavery became central to the workings of society. In this process, Barbados, the easternmost island in the Caribbean, stands out both for the qualitative leap taken by entrepreneurial Barbadian sugar planters in integrating the factors of production—Barbadian land, African slaves, and London capital—into an impressively efficient operation under a single owner and for the influence of Barbados's slave society on English and non-English colonies. Colonized by the English in 1627, the island underwent a sugar boom beginning in the 1640s. The speed by which the integrated plantation developed in Barbados and the alacrity by which it was transferred throughout the English Caribbean and the southern colonies of mainland North America has led historians, such as Richard Pares, to term it a "plantation revolution." Recent scholarship, notably by John McCusker and Russell Menard, suggests that it took some time for a mature plantation system to emerge. About a generation passed between the transformation of English Caribbean societies into slave societies and the development of large plantations with gangs of several hundred slaves each. The making of the plantation system was, therefore, a distinctive phase in the enslaved experience in the English West Indies. By the eighteenth century English inventiveness in Barbados and elsewhere had helped mature slavery in the Americas into what Philip Curtin, a prominent historian of Africa, has called the "full blown plantation complex" where "the agricultural enterprise was organized in large-scale capitalist plantations" based on non-self-sustaining forced labor from Africa.[2]

The plantation period itself, lasting from the last third of the seventeenth century until the end of slavery, can be divided into two periods, one marked by the continual importation of African slaves to maintain enslaved population numbers, and one, starting after the abolition of the British slave trade in 1807, that relied on a growing creole, or native-born, enslaved population. In the first period, African influences predominated. Not only were the great majority of enslaved people recent arrivals from West Africa, but also the cultural patterns established by slaves were strongly African in form. When enslaved people resisted their bondage, African ideas and culture invariably informed alternative, restorationist visions to the white-controlled plantation world. African influences in Caribbean slavery never disappeared but were modified considerably as the abolitionist campaign against the slave trade forced slave owners to adopt ameliorationist policies towards their slaves and as both abolitionists and enslaved people began to agitate for the ending of slavery. Gradually, enslaved populations through natural reproduction began to become more creole, both in composition and in cultural orientation. That creole character was manifested most markedly in the adoption of evangelical Protestantism by enslaved persons and by their impatient aspirations for freedom. Although metropolitan actors played the leading role in making emancipation a reality in the 1830s, increasing restlessness and rebellion among creole slaves unwilling to wait for the gradual granting of freedom shaped significantly the emancipation process.

OVERALL DIMENSIONS: VOLUME AND ETHNIC ORIGINS

By the 1620s, when English colonizers began to make permanent settlements in the Caribbean, slavery had long disappeared in England. Learning from the example of Iberian colonists to the Caribbean, however, English colonists, from the beginning, associated the New World with slavery. Many of the first slaves were Amerindians: Henry Powell, captain of the first ship to disembark Englishmen at Barbados, also freighted to Barbados in 1627 thirty-two Indians—Arawaks from the Wild Coast of mainland South America—to be used as slaves. In 1626, the prominent London merchant Maurice Thompson had organized sixty Africans to be deposited at St Christopher. It was West and West-Central Africans who comprised the great majority of enslaved people in the English Caribbean and Bermuda, although Indians were still being enslaved until the beginning of the eighteenth century (from 1707, the English Caribbean became the British Caribbean, following the union of Scotland and England).

Indeed, Africans made up the great majority of migrants to the British Caribbean. The best estimates suggest that 2,238,700 Africans arrived before 1807. Of these, the British retained 1,973,200 (around 25 percent of all slaves sent to Jamaica were transshipped to Spanish America). In 1807, the total number of slaves in the British West Indies (defined to include colonies around as well as in the Caribbean) was 776,105, indicative of the enormous demographic wastage (low fertility and high mortality) involved in plantation slavery. By 1830, the number of slaves had declined to 684,600, which accounted for 81.2 percent of the total population. If freed people are included in the calculations, then the total number of people in 1830 in the British West Indies who were of African descent was 783,035 or 93.7 percent of the total population. Jamaica alone accounted for 46.6 percent of British West Indian slaves. British Guiana accounted for 13 percent; Barbados for 12 percent; and the Leewards, the Windward Islands (Dominica, St Lucia, St Vincent, Grenada, and the Grenadines), and Trinidad and Tobago accounted for 25.5 percent of British West Indian slaves. The small colonies of the British Virgin Islands (of which Tortola is the largest and most important), British Honduras, the Cayman Honduras, the Bahamas, Anguilla, and Barbuda had 2.9 percent of the slaves.[3]

Recent scholarship has helped clarify the African origins of British West Indian slaves. David Eltis, an economic historian, has led the way in constructing rich data sets for the seventeenth-century traffic and for the last years of the slave trade. Identifying the sources of slave supply sheds light on the ability of enslaved Africans to recreate African cultural patterns in the New World. If Africans tended to come from one particular area of Africa and were sold to planters in large parcels containing people from a single area, then it seems logical to assume that there would be enough cultural commonality between enslaved Africans that they could create societies that resembled the cultures from which they originated. If, however, the regions of provenance for Africans were both diverse and also changing in importance over time and if enslaved Africans were sold to planters individually or in small parcels, suggesting a considerable degree of randomization in the distribution process, then enslaved people would find it hard to recreate the specific cultures from which they came.

The evidence about the regional origins of Africans sent to the Americas supports both interpretations. On the one hand, the anthropologists Sidney Mintz and Richard Price argued that Africans came from such a diversity of places in Africa that Africans who reached the New World did not arrive as communities but "as *crowds* and very heterogeneous crowds at that." The British were the most expert slave traders in the Atlantic world, with wide contacts throughout West and West-Central Africa (they took very few slaves from beyond the Cape of Good Hope). Consequently, they shipped slaves from a number of different regions. Compared with other traders, they took relatively few Africans from the Bight of Benin or from Upper Guinea and acquired comparatively numerous Africans from the Bight of Biafra and from the Gold Coast. But shipments from all regions were sizeable, and the British changed their shipping patterns frequently. Thus, in the late seventeenth century, as the Bight of Biafra slipped in popularity, the Bight of Benin ascended, becoming the source of the largest shipments. In the early eighteenth century, the Gold Coast and West-Central Africa became important sources of slaves until the Bight of Biafra overtook them after 1750. In the 1760s and 1770s, peak periods of shipments to Jamaica and Grenada, Sierra Leone equaled the Bight of Biafra as the region from which the British collected most captives.

Even within a single region, British slave traders purchased slaves gathered together by African suppliers from a large spatial area, so that it was unlikely that shipmates would come from the same area. The ways in which slaves were sold upon arrival also militated against their coming together on any one plantation from a single area of West or West-Central Africa. Becoming a slave in the West Indies evolved in a two-stage process. The majority of Africans were sold to merchants for a wholesale price. They kept these slaves in urban yards before selling them at retail prices, usually individually or in small parcels of two to five slaves, to planters or other purchasers. Consequently, any large plantation, from the late seventeenth century onwards, tended to contain enslaved people from many regions of Africa. Frequent slave sales on plantations increased not just the likelihood of constant flux in an enslaved person's life but also the certainty of slave gangs containing slaves from diverse ethnic and regional origins. Thus diffusion and dispersal proved to be key features of the slaves' experience in the British West Indies.[4]

On the other hand, a good deal of evidence exists that slaves came from contiguous regions of Africa where pronounced cultural commonalities and shared language, ideas, and memories bound people from similar backgrounds together. Especially in the seventeenth century, when the lineaments of Afro-Caribbean culture in the British West Indies were first elaborated, nearly four-fifths of the slaves arriving in Barbados, nine-tenths of slaves arriving in Antigua, and three-quarters of Africans shipped to Jamaica came from the adjacent regions of the Gold and Slave Coasts and the Bight of Biafra, a stretch of coast only 200 miles long. Moreover, age and sex patterns were such among these captives that establishing family life just as in Africa was much easier than it was for slaves from other African regions or, indeed, for English migrants.

The pre-colonial African historian John Thornton argues for a relatively homogeneous Africa of three culturally distinct zones and seven sub-zones. For David Eltis, West African regional geographical, cultural, and political connections proved so strong that slaves in Barbados and Jamaica were as distinctively Akan/Aja in cultural orientation as European settlers were distinctively English. That Akan/Aja dominance receded as Africans from the Bight of Biafra and Angola became the dominant migrant groups. But conceptions of "Africanness" in the major West Indian colonies of Barbados, Antigua, and Jamaica suggest fundamental components of Coromantee (or Gold Coast) culture, as evidenced by such diverse practices as funerals and rebellion. A major conspiracy uncovered in Antigua in 1736, for example, revealed a Coromantee leadership that sought to replace white authority with a Coromantee kingdom.[5] Still, a sizeable number of Africans shipped to the British Caribbean also came from the Angola coast, where cultural traditions were quite different from those in Lower Guinea. West-Central Africans were especially well represented among the slaves coming to the West Indies before 1650 and may have been influential in the early formation of Afro-Caribbean cultures.[6]

Recent scholarship has revised understanding of the impact of the Middle Passage on the development of Afro-American societies in the Americas. For some scholars, such as Orlando Patterson, the transit to America and the travails of enslavement led to cultural debasement, to a hollowing out of culture where enslaved people could merely mimic in desultory fashion dominant European cultural motifs. For other scholars, such as Edward Braithwaite, enslavement harmed but did not debilitate slaves into mere ciphers. To be sure, slaves confronted a host of restrictions and regulations that impeded cultural sharing, but the daily grind of enslavement notwithstanding, friction between black and white operating in the interstices of the plantation complex created vibrant new African-American social and cultural patterns.[7] In looking at the formation of African culture in the New World, as the historian James Sweet has insisted, "we should not start from a premise of creolization . . . [but rather] we should assume that specific African cultural forms and systems of thought survived intact."[8] Ethnicity is therefore more important than race in shaping early cultural patterns. These negotiations reflect the extent to which the first arrived African-born members of slave communities, be they Yoruba in Trinidad or Akan/Aja in Jamaica or Barbados, were able to impose their cultural predilections on later generations of slaves.

Consequently, scholars now underscore the need to explore the African backgrounds of Caribbean slaves because early Afro-Caribbean culture should be seen as extensions of African ethnic alliances into the New World. Not until relatively late in the history of slavery in the British West Indies—probably around the mid-eighteenth century and perhaps not until the abolition of the slave trade—did Africans and creoles come to accept European assumptions that the major division in Caribbean societies was between white and black. Only then did ethnicity begin to be defined almost entirely in terms of skin color. This approach has greatly expanded understanding of the African roots of British West Indian culture. It is curious, however, how investigations into the formation of Afro-Caribbean culture diverge from concurrent investigations into the transfer of European cultures into the New World, where stress is placed in Europeans' creative adaptations to new environments and on the cultural heterogeneity that resulted from these adaptations. If environment significantly constrained Europeans in their re-creation of European culture in the New World, then how much more so must environment have significantly constrained Africans, given the coercive conditions in which they were placed, in their attempted re-creation of Africa in the West Indies?

CHARTER PERIOD

Arguing that African slaves surmounted their conditions of bondage to recreate African cultural patterns in Britain's Atlantic possessions requires much more intensive research into the history of the Atlantic creoles who formed the charter group in societies where slavery was not yet the norm. These Africans and persons of African descent, free people as well as slaves, tended to be multilingual, cosmopolitan residents of port communities in the Atlantic rim and acted as cultural brokers between Africans and Europeans. In the Caribbean, Atlantic creoles probably arrived with the first settlers. Barbados, for example, contained 40 African and Amerindian slaves among its 140 residents in 1628, one year after English settlement. But that ratio soon declined. In 1638, there may have been only 200 Africans in the island and around 6,000 whites. These slaves left behind only a faint footprint, which was largely effaced in the next two decades by the sugar boom and the attendant arrival on the island of 60,000 African slaves.

In Bermuda, the charter generation of Africans, possibly from West-Central Africa, arrived early (by 1620, the island had around 100 African slaves) and lasted for several generations. Bermuda tried—and for a time succeeded—in establishing an economy based on tobacco, but this tiny archipelago, one-eighth the size of Barbados, never made the transition to a mature plantation society. By the turn of the eighteenth century Bermuda had become transformed into a maritime economy, specializing in shipbuilding, trade, and salvage. The number of slaves in the population proved substantial by the standards of New England and of pre-plantation Virginia and Barbados. By the 1680s and 1690s, slaves accounted for between one-fifth and one-third of the population. Without a plantation generation to overwhelm them, however, Bermudian slaves were quintessential Atlantic creoles, often attaining a measure of independence denied to slaves elsewhere in a fluid society where slavery closely resembled indentured servitude. Indeed, in 1739, Governor Alured Popple estimated that at least one-quarter of all sailors who crewed Bermuda's celebrated sloops were black.

England's main West Indian colonies, unlike Bermuda, had a brief charter period. In the British Leewards and in Jamaica, slavery on the model established in Barbados in the 1640s had become typical by the 1660s. Even if whites outnumbered blacks for twenty years in Jamaica and were the bare majority of the population in the Leewards until the 1690s, little latitude for enslaved people existed. In 1661 Barbados's legislature passed a harsh, comprehensive, and influential slave code. Colonists in both Jamaica and the British Leeward Islands, by that time working their slaves hard on small farms making tobacco, cotton, indigo, and sugar, drew on the Barbadian code for their own laws against slaves. Africans subsequently transported to these islands showed few of the characteristics of Atlantic creoles.[9]

THE MAKING OF THE PLANTATION

The limited importance in the seventeenth century of Atlantic creoles in England's principal West Indian colonies does not mean that the plantation system immediately took hold there. Although Barbadian planters broke new ground in the establishment of the integrated plantation with hundreds of slaves working in gangs to produce sugar, Russell Menard's research on the rise of Barbadian sugar culture argues for evolutionary rather than revolutionary transformation in which the emergence of a sugar monoculture evolved out of previous attempts at market-oriented agricultural diversification. The dispersed system of sugar production, customary in Brazil, where tenant farmers grew cane for their landlord's mill, coexisted with the integrated plantation in Barbados until at least the 1680s. By then, however, most Barbadian slaves lived in plantations of 100 slaves or more and worked in sugar, possibly in gangs, although detailed evidence on slave labor management remains scarce until well into the eighteenth century. Small slave-holdings typified Jamaican agriculture until the 1690s, and in the British Leewards large plantations did not predominate until the early eighteenth century. Some of the delay in the making of the big sugar plantations can be explained by the need, especially in Jamaica, to clear land for cultivation and by small landowners' continuing attraction to other profitable crops besides sugar. One reason why the integrated plantation emerged slowly is that planters did not immediately turn to gang labor with its lock-step discipline and liberal use of the whip. A factory-like labor regimen that demanded intense, regular labor from slaves took time to develop as planters' attempts to impose gang-labor discipline clashed with the slaves' understanding of a proper moral economy, informed both by their African past and by the American conditions of bondage. To manage slave gangs, big planters often appointed one or more head persons or foremen to supervise the distribution of tasks among their fellow slaves. Even more important, however, was finding whites willing to do the hard work necessary to keep a workforce, dispro-portionately composed of restive adult African men, in check. Such white supervi-sory personnel were difficult to find as long as opportunities existed for smallholding. But as land aggregation proceeded and small planters were driven off the land, many found employment as overseers on plantations with expanding slave forces. At the same time that the integrated plantation became the norm, the number of whites listed as servants on inventories declined. If slaves were to be controlled, then there needed to be a firm division between supervisors who were white and workers who were black. It is also probable that many of these white overseers had military experience or had worked on slave ships. The gang system on large plantations represented a revolution in working practices and resembled the regimentation in armies that had emerged in Britain at the end of the seven-teenth century. Men used to the severe discipline that marked late seventeenth-century European armies would have found the integrated plantation a familiar environment.[10]

Africans may have had more latitude and autonomy in their lives before the triumph of large estates and the integrated plantation system. But that latitude, however expansive, confronted the quotidian reality of racially prejudiced English-men who were ready, willing, and able to use their monopoly of force in brutal displays of violence against slaves. Thus the seventeenth century generated a supreme irony: while Englishmen fought battles with their rulers to establish fundamental liberties for themselves, they established in the colonies a system of enslavement that in its bigotry, cruelty, and tyranny had no counterpart in England.[11] Early visitors to Barbados, including such leading Quakers as George Fox and Benjamin Lay, recoiled at the viciousness of the emerging slave system. Isaac Berkenhead, an English military officer in Barbados during the mid-seventeenth century, noted that it scarcely bothered planters to kill their slaves, "dogs and they being in one ranke with them." The French priest Antoine Biet who visited Barbados in 1654 recorded how Protestant masters, surprisingly tolerant of his Catholicism, treated slaves "with a great deal of severity." One whipped a slave caught stealing a pig "until he was all covered with blood" and then "cut off one of his ears, had it roasted, and forced him to eat it." Though Biet agreed that planters "must keep these kinds of people obedient," he thought it "inhuman to treat them with so much harshness."[12]

The making of the plantation system in seventeenth-century Barbados and Jamaica engendered various forms of slave resistance, including plots and revolts. In 1692, for example, Barbadian officials claimed to have uncovered a sophisticated, island-wide conspiracy led by skilled and privileged creole slaves who had ambitiously recruited Africans into the fold. In suppressing such movements, anxious whites often mixed frightened comments about the "heathenish" ways and savagery of the coadjutors with genuine respect for their fortitude in facing torture and death. Christopher Codrington, the largest planter in the Lesser Antilles, called Akan rebels "Intrepid to the last degree, not a man of them but will stand to be cut to pieces, without a sigh or a groan." It is in these executions of rebels that we begin to hear slaves speak for the first time. After a revolt in Barbados in 1675, a slave named Tony refused to name others before he was burnt to death. When a spectator heckled him, Tony replied insouciantly, "If you Roast me today, you cannot Roast me tomorrow." The most poignant words, however, were uttered by another slave facing execution: "the devil was in the Englishman that he makes everything work; he makes the Negro work, he makes the horse work, the ass work, the water work, and the wind work." The slave's predicament showed the relentlessness of the plantation system.[13]

AFRICAN SLAVES IN THE PLANTATION SYSTEM

The twin maturations of the integrated plantation system and the British transatlantic slave trade in the early decades of the eighteenth century were the period of greatest degradation for African slaves and their descendants. Untroubled by metropolitan opposition to their actions and encouraged by the wealth that plantation commodities, especially sugar, brought them, planters refined and perfected their systems of control over plantation slaves until the plantation became one of the most efficient economic systems for the production of wealth that man had yet devised. Slaves suffered from the system's exacting means of allocating resources to their most highly valued uses. Isolated, atomized, usually employed in backbreaking labor on plantations patrolled by planters and their operatives who treated them with terrible cruelty, slaves experienced desperate, uncertain lives that resembled nothing less than the Hobbesian vision of the state of nature, a *bellum omnium contra omnes*, in which slaves' nasty, short, and brutish existence was compounded by hunger and despair.

The easiest way to get a measure of the hellish existence many slaves experienced in the eighteenth-century British Caribbean is through demography. The demographic facts of slavery in the British West Indies tell their own story. Only Barbados, of the sugar colonies, managed to achieve natural increase in the slave population and that was only achieved around 1810, after the ending of the slave trade.[14] In Jamaica, the importation of 575,000 Africans during the eighteenth century resulted in a population of 348,825 by 1807. Demographic conditions were probably worse earlier on before some limited ameliorative policies were adopted from the 1780s. In the century before 1750, the British West Indies had imported almost 800,000 Africans but deaths so far exceeded births that the slave population stood at less than 300,000. Although population data before the nineteenth century remains sketchy, the result was a dramatically imbalanced population, with relatively few children and young people and with the age structure skewed towards productive adults in their twenties and thirties. The health of these young adults was poor. Listings of slaves in inventories suggest that the percentage of adult slaves in workforces deemed by planters to be unhealthy amounted to around 20 percent. Slaves were generally malnourished, lacking sufficient amounts of thiamine, calcium, and Vitamin A to do their jobs properly.

Kenneth Kiple estimates that Caribbean slaves received around 1,500 to 2,000 calories a day when they probably needed around 3,000 calories to work as a field laborer. Evidence is scarce but it is probable that malnourishment was especially prevalent among children, as planters reserved food supplies for healthy field workers. The ways in which food was distributed aggravated malnourishment among the weak, the young, and the unhealthy. In most British West Indian islands, masters required slaves to grow their own food to feed themselves. For healthy enslaved persons who did not have large families to support, having individual provision grounds proved beneficial, allowing them sufficient food for their own needs and for sale of surplus when harvests were good at slave markets. Some slaves derived from their provision grounds money and goods to make their lives more enjoyable. But for slaves who were diseased, old or young, or burdened with a large family to support, the inadequacy of masters' rations and difficulties in cultivating provision grounds kept them hungry. Most slaves, even healthy ones, lived close to subsistence. If conditions deteriorated, through drought, as a result of hurricanes, or consequent to wartime disruptions, as in the American Revolutionary War when cereals and fish from North America stopped coming to the Caribbean, then famine resulted. The devastating hurricanes of 1780 in Barbados and Jamaica led to thousands of slaves dying of hunger as food supplies were disrupted. The Jamaica Assembly estimated that 15,000 slaves died of "Famine or of Diseases contracted by scanty and unwholesome diet, between the latter end of 1780 and the beginning of 1787." One should not overemphasize nutritional stress— poor people in Europe and Africa suffered as much as slaves from inadequate diets—but one standard measure of well-being—height—suggests that slaves, especially children, in the British West Indies were at the low end of nutritional health. Slave children were smaller in stature than poor children working in the exacting mills of industrializing England.[15]

Sugar made the Caribbean a slave graveyard. Abundant demographic evidence suggests that slaves employed on sugar plantations had worse health, were worked more onerously, were punished more savagely, and died earlier and in greater numbers than slaves working in other agricultural occupations. Sugar culture took a severe toll not just in the British West Indies but also in nineteenth-century Louisiana, Cuba, and Brazil.[16] The regimen on sugar plantations was not conducive to slave fertility, and it was low fertility, especially among African-born women working in sugar, not high mortality, that was mostly responsible for demographic failure. Historians, notably B. W. Higman and Stanley Engerman, have debated the causes of such low fertility. Slave women may have deliberately chosen not to have children as a means of biological resistance against enslavement. Others have argued that African cultural practices such as long lactation led to relatively lengthy gaps in childbearing. But the demands of working in sugar, especially for planters who preferred to buy rather than to breed and who were indifferent at best to the needs of pregnant women, are sufficient to explain the limited reproduction of slave women in the eighteenth century. As Kenneth Morgan argues, "among the many causes of low reproduction among Jamaican slaves, the material circumstances of overwork, dietary deficiencies and physical punishment provided a lethal cocktail."[17]

On the quotidian existence of slaves in eighteenth-century Jamaica, the diaries of Thomas Thistlewood, an English migrant who came to the island in 1750, yield disturbing riches. Thistlewood was a tough man in a tough place and knew that the only way that he could force slaves to do his will was through a combination of force and psychological pressure. Most male slaves were whipped for some small infraction and some slaves faced the indignity of being forced to eat excrement as a punishment. Female slaves suffered sexual exploitation. Having on 27 February 1758, purchased a young girl he named Abba, Thistlewood deflowered her on 19 April. He noted in his diary that the sex was "non bene," which is not surprising given Abba's youth and recent trauma on the Middle Passage. For some slaves, living under such brutality induced despair. Sally was so traumatized by her mistreatment that she gave up.

Originally from the Congo, she was bought in 1762 when she was 9. Flogged and repeatedly raped by Thistlewood and other white men, she became a habitual thief. By the 1770s, she had become a persistent runaway and was put in a collar "as she will not help herself, but attempts to run away." Disliked by fellow slaves, indifferent to her welfare, with no partner or family to help her, she lost the will to survive and was transported off the island in 1784. For slaves under Thistlewood's control, suicide ranked as one of the leading causes of death.

Nevertheless, slaves did gain some measure of self-expression within social structures characterized by fierce repression and constant uncertainty. They developed a rich cultural life, exemplified by their language, music, and religion. Many aspects of plantation life, not least the sexual exploitation that many whites employed against slave women, militated against the creation of stable family life, but it is clear that families did emerge and formed a bulwark against the rigors of enslavement. For many slaves, living on large plantations allowed them to find both emotional sustenance and alternative sources of meaning to those provided them by masters. Thistlewood's diaries reveal how slaves adapted to enslavement. Re-creating the life story of Lincoln, the first slave whom Thistlewood purchased, reveals a determined survivor. Lincoln had his faults—he was as compulsive a womanizer as his master and was given to violence against other slaves. But through will power and the assiduous manipulation of his master for his own benefit, Lincoln established himself as a leader in his community. He worked himself into positions of authority as a driver; enjoyed a degree of autonomy as the slave sent on messages outside the plantation; and made himself the head of a large and polygynous household. He used his intimacy with Thistlewood to become an African patriarch and an economically autonomous individual, able, after Thistlewood's death in 1786, to hire himself out for pecuniary gain.[18]

Given the harshness of slavery in this period when slave owners were unconstrained in their actions and when an increasingly streamlined transatlantic slave trade enabled them to concentrate on production with little concern for the humans whose labor and lives they consumed, it is unsurprising that slaves tried to resist bondage. They did so either through individual acts of disobedience and sabotage or, less frequently, through insurrection. The British West Indies experienced only two major acts of collective slave resistance in the eighteenth century: a sophisticated conspiracy in Antigua in 1736 and an insurrection in Jamaica in 1760. Led by Tacky in the north and Apongo in the southwest, the Jamaican rebels, mostly Coromantee, made a concerted attack upon white planters, aiming to "extirpate" all the whites and replace white rule with an African kingdom. Tacky's revolt was put down only with the help of regular British troops and Jamaica's maroon allies. Although temporarily unnerving the Jamaican plantocracy, the insurrection inflicted little lasting damage on the plantation system and only about sixty whites and free coloreds respectively were killed.[19] By contrast, Jamaican whites, after crushing the rebellion, followed by waging a brutal campaign of terror designed to keep disaffected slaves in their place. As the historian Bryan Edwards wrote, it was "thought necessary to make a few terrible examples of some of the most guilty of the captives." Rebels were starved in gibbets, burnt to death by slow fire, and hanged. Nearly 400 slaves were killed during the revolt, a further 100 were executed, and 500 were transported to British Honduras. The planters' power was undisturbed and the plantation system continued to eat up its laborers. Tacky's revolt merely confirmed that in the plantation system the monopoly of force lay with whites. The gross imbalance of forces in every British West Indian slave society made frontal assaults by slaves against their enslavement acts of virtual suicide. After 1736, slaves in Antigua did not mount a major revolt until 1831, and Barbadian slaves did not rise up in a major insurrection against masters before Bussa's rebellion in 1816. Whites had good reason to trust in the stability of their slave system, maintaining an interest in their homeland security that paralleled their efficiency in sugar production.[20]

CREOLES AND THE COMING OF FREEDOM

White self-confidence in slavery, an institution, in Voltaire's words, "as ancient as war," made the abolitionist onslaught against it from the 1780s until 1838 seem all the more astonishing. Metropolitan opposition to planter pretensions and growing creole dominance within slave populations after 1807 made beaten down slaves suddenly optimistic about their chances for freedom. The great age of slave rebellions in the British Caribbean came at the end of slavery, with serious rebellions in Barbados in 1816, Demerara in 1823, and Jamaica in 1831/2. Both more violent and more politically focused than previously and put down with characteristic white brutality, these revolts, especially in Jamaica, had a considerable impact on metropolitan thinking and probably hastened the abolition of slavery. One reason for their comparative success was that they took place in slave societies with American-born slaves in the majority. Many of these creole slaves had become evangelical Protestants, able to articulate their resistance to enslavement in Christian terms easily understandable to Britons increasingly concerned about the humanitarian implications of slavery.

Nevertheless, if much changed between 1807 and 1834, much remained the same. Conditions on sugar plantations may have become somewhat easier as imperial officials insisted that the worst excesses of slavery were reined in, but work remained onerous, tedious, and dangerous to health. Planters continued to try and maximize production at all costs, meaning that, except in Barbados, natural increase did not occur. On Montpelier estate in Jamaica, where excellent records exist for the early nineteenth century, birth rates continued to be less than death rates, leading to a slow decline in total slave numbers. Gradually the number of slaves who were creole increased until by 1832 they comprised 82 percent of the slave population. Male slaves held most of the supervisory positions, leaving females dominant in the field. Montpelier slaves lived in three kinds of households. About 30 percent of slaves, mostly African-born men, lived alone or with friends. A majority of the 70 percent of slaves with family links lived in simple, nuclear households. The small remainder, mostly creoles, lived in a variety of extended households. The nuclear family mattered most. They lived in houses reminiscent of West African compounds but with significant resemblances in form and function to houses in villages in lowland Britain. The physical patterns on Montpelier suggest both slave manipulations of the built environment and also planter power in imposing their models on slaves. Slave housing was poor and slave possessions were minimal. Nevertheless, by the end of slavery, slaves at Montpelier had established genuine small communities. These were not idyllic, stable places, but they did support "a fragile system of sharing and exchange that provided a common focus." This community was "rooted in material culture associated with the spirituality attached to particular places and largely contained within the boundaries of the plantation village, yet riven by conflict."[21]

The decibel level of slave voices rises during this period, amplified both by slave conversion to Christianity and by the antislavery white amanuenses who begin to record slave complaints. One source of slave testimony comes from the abundant records kept in Demerara, a colony acquired from the Dutch in 1803, by an official, probably derived from Spanish colonialism, called the fiscal. Like its Spanish counterpart, the fiscal investigated slaves' complaints. The British kept the office and recorded thousands of pages of testimony given by slaves about their treatment. The fiscal was a white official who tended to side with planters. When the slave Lewis complained that the overseer did not give slaves time to eat, the fiscal took the manager's side after the manager explained that his slaves were dissatisfied because they were now cultivating sugar rather than cotton. But the cases, coming as they did during a period when the metropolis enacted policies to ameliorate colonial slavery, suggest the limits of reform. Parents of Elizabeth, a recently deceased child, complained to the fiscal that their 10-year old daughter had been raped. The rape had been discovered when she was taken to the sick house. The slave nurse examined her and thought she had been raped. Pressed by her mother, the child blamed an adolescent slave boy for the rape (although doctors claimed in testimony that her physical condition suggested that penetration had not occurred). But when questioned more intensively, she put the blame for rape on her master, telling him when he confronted her that "It was you, master." The case was inconclusive, but the matter of fact way in which rape was discussed suggests that such treatment of slave girls was normal. The persistence of the parents in seeking justice, however, shows how determined these parents were to see justice done on behalf of their deceased daughter.

The records of the fiscals speak to how differently slaves and masters understood the system's moral economy. Masters wanted obedience; slaves wanted fairness. Slaves assumed that masters and slaves shared an unspoken contract, in which they had rights—such as getting sufficient food and clothing, not being forced to work unusually hard, and not being punished if they completed their tasks. Slaves in Demerara believed that they should perform to their abilities and that all should be provided for according to their needs.[22] When this moral economy was violated, they felt entitled to rebel, as thousands of slaves did in 1823, alleging violations of their "rights." What was so dangerous about this revolt in the eyes of the authorities was that the Christian slaves who dominated the leadership of the rebels rebelled according to evangelical Christian principles and posited a vision of a free Demerara society in which slaves would be free to practice their Christian religion. British missionaries such as John Smith in Demerara and William Knibb in Jamaica, although instructed not to preach rebellion to slaves, did preach liberating messages that validated slaves' dreams of freedom and thus legitimized their rebellion. As the historian Emilia Viotti da Costa notes for Demerara, missionaries gave slaves dignity, autonomy, and a sense of being part of a community of brethren that encouraged them to rise up against a slave system predicated on humiliating slaves and on destroying group solidarity.

The slave leaders who led these revolts were prominent Christians. Quamina, the nominal leader of the Demerara uprising, was senior deacon at Bethel Chapel. Samuel Sharp, the leader of the Baptist revolt in Jamaica in 1831/2, was a fervent evangelical whom the missionary Henry Bleby thought "the most intelligent and remarkable slave I had ever met with." Sharpe asserted "the natural equality of man" rooted in "the holy Scriptures." He told Bleby before his death on 23 May 1832 that "he learnt from his Bible, that the whites had no more right to hold black people in slavery, than black people had to make the white people slaves." If he were like most slaves, he would have combined his evangelical Christianity with traditional African beliefs, as West Indian Christianity was a fusion of European and African value systems. But his Christianity differentiated Sharpe and other nineteenth-century slaves from their ancestors. Slaves adopted evangelical Protestantism for a variety of reasons, especially because they were receptive to the intense emotionality of its theology and because they could shape their Christian beliefs so as to allow for expressive ritual behavior, ecstatic behavior, and strongly participatory worship. It also served as a principal form of resistance to masters. Ironically, the more that masters persecuted missionaries and their followers, the more likely it was that slaves would become attracted to evangelical religion.[23] With widespread conversion to Christianity after 1820, Afro-Caribbean people entered into a new phase, stretching but not breaking the bonds that had linked the British West Indies with West Africa that had lasted 200 years.

FUTURE NEEDS

It is scarcely possible to write a history of any place in the Americas without mentioning slavery. It is impossible to do so for the British West Indies and Bermuda. Slavery represents the engine that drove world commerce, "the principal cause," in Abbé Raynal's words, "of the rapid motion which now agitates the universe." It was also, in the words of Derek Walcott, "some open passage that has cleft the brain, some deep, amnesiac blow." For British West Indians, the vast majority of whom are of African descent and thus connected intimately at some generations' remove to the Africans who toiled in the hot sun as slaves, the legacy of slavery is still "laid wide like a wound . . . and in its swaddling cerements we are still bound."[24]

Yet work still needs to be done on recovering the history of slavery in the region. The origins of enslavement deserve revisiting, in the light of work done by literary scholars, such as Mary Floyd-Wilson, that cast doubt on the instinctual racism of the English and by historians, such as David Eltis and Hilary Beckles, that stress the significance of local contingencies and the experience of white indentured servitude in shaping the introduction of slavery in Barbados.[25] An even more urgent need is a study of the transition from small-scale slavery to large-scale slavery in the late seventeenth century. We know very little about the process whereby slaves became part of slave forces that contained hundreds of slaves, working in lock-step producing sugar under very harsh conditions. British West Indian slavery was transformed in the first half of the eighteenth century as the average size of slave forces greatly increased, as the Atlantic slave trade became more efficient and more able to provide thousands of captive Africans each year for a burgeoning plantation economy, and as African cultural patterns became entrenched into West Indian society. The British West Indies was never more African than in the first half of the eighteenth century. Yet virtually nothing is known about this period and about the slaves who toiled without much chance of freedom, producing tropical commodities for an increasingly affluent British and colonial British American populace. A first step would be in-depth studies of the structure of slavery in the major British West Indian slave societies—Jamaica, Barbados, Antigua—in the first half of the eighteenth century. Indeed, more empirical studies of slavery in individual slave societies would be welcome. Relatively little is known, for example, about slavery in Grenada, one of the primary destinations of enslaved Africans in the years following the Seven Years War, or in early nineteenth-century British Guyana, a slave society acquired by the British from the Dutch in the Napoleonic Wars that had the potential, if the abolition of the slave trade had not occurred, to replace Jamaica as the leading slave colony in the British West Indies.

The greatest gap in the literature is, as is common in studies of slavery, an appreciation of the ordinary lives of enslaved people. Recovering the lives of illiterate, poor people from the condescension of posterity is, of course, extremely difficult, especially in the African period of slavery before the abolition of the slave trade, ameliorative policies, and the adoption of Christianity by enslaved people changed the character of West Indian slavery. But sufficient sources exist about what enslaved Africans believed and about how they behaved to suggest that some of our interpretative paradigms are in need of revision. In particular, historians might reconsider whether it makes sense to view slavery in the British West Indies as much through the lens of resistance as is done at present. The West Indian slave is portrayed as always striving for freedom, with freedom described in unthinking ways as being the kind of freedom espoused during the great revolutions of the late eighteenth century. But to see West Indian slaves as always resisting and seeing their actions and behavior entirely within a framework that led to freedom diminishes the lives of those many slaves who neither resisted nor contemplated freedom in the ways that were customary for western Europeans and African-Americans in the nineteenth century. Most West Indian enslaved people came to the Caribbean from African societies committed to monarchy and hierarchy and entered into societies in which the possibilities of individual freedom were extremely limited. In order to understand these people and their lives, we need to imaginatively recreate the "deep, amnesiac blow" that they suffered as enslaved people by using a compass that includes, but is not limited to, the small amounts of direct resistance to overwhelming power that enslaved people were able to exercise.

NOTES

1. Ira Berlin, *Many Thousands Gone: The First Two Centuries of Slavery in North America* (Cambridge, Mass., 1998).
2. Philip Curtin, *Rise of the Plantation Complex: Essays in Atlantic History* (Cambridge, 1998), 10–12.
3. David Eltis, "The Volume and Structure of the Transatlantic Slave Trade: A Reassessment," *William and Mary Quarterly*, 3rd ser. (January 2001): 45; B. W. Higman, *Slave Populations of the British Caribbean 1807–1834* (Baltimore, 1984), 417–18, 433.
4. Sidney W. Mintz and Richard Price, *The Birth of African-American Culture: An Anthropological Perspective* (Boston, 1992), 18, 43; David Richardson, "The British Empire and the Transatlantic Slave Trade, 1660–1807," in P. J. Marshall (ed.), *The Oxford History of the British Empire*, ii: *The Eighteenth Century* (Oxford, 1998), 450–2; Trevor Burnard, "The Atlantic Slave Trade and African Ethnicities in Seventeenth-Century Jamaica," in David Richardson et al., *Liverpool and Transatlantic Slavery* (Liverpool, 2007), 138–63.
5. David Eltis, *The Rise of African Slavery in the Americas* (Cambridge, 2000), 252–7; John Thornton, *Africa and Africans in the Making of the Atlantic World, 1400–1800* (Cambridge, 1992), 184–92; David Barry Gaspar, *Bondmen and Rebels: A Study of Master–Slave Relations in Antigua* (Baltimore, 1985).
6. Linda M. Heywood and John K. Thornton, *Central Africans, Atlantic Creoles, and the Foundation of the Americas, 1585–1660* (Cambridge, 2007); Maureen Warner-Lewis, *Central Africa in the Caribbean* (Kingston, 2003).

7. Orlando Patterson, *The Sociology of Slavery* (London, 1967); Edward Braithwaite, *The Development of Creole Society in Jamaica, 1770–1820* (Oxford, 1971); Mintz and Price, *Birth of African-American Culture*; Mervyn C. Alleyne, *Roots of Jamaican Culture* (London, 1988).

8. James H. Sweet, *Recreating Africa: Culture, Kinship and Religion in the Portuguese World, 1441–1700* (Chapel Hill, NC, 2003), 229.

9. Berlin, *Many Thousands Gone*, 17–28; Heywood and Thornton, *Central Africans*, 248–50, 255–8. Bermuda fits uneasily into this chapter, as it followed a different trajectory not only from the West Indian islands that became plantation colonies but also from marginal, small colonies such as British Honduras and the Bahamas. Bermuda did, however, have strong links with several marginal colonies through its maritime activities, through salt-raking on the Turks and Caicos islands and through logging on the Mosquito Shore of present day Honduras. See Michael Jarvis, *In the Eye of All Trade: Bermuda and Bermudians in the Maritime Atlantic World, 1680–1820* (Chapel Hill, NC, 2010).

10. Russell R. Menard, *Sweet Negotiations* (Charlottesville, Va., 2006), 91–105; Eltis, *Rise of African Slavery*, 193–223; Robin Blackburn, *The Making of New World Slavery: From the Baroque to the Modern 1492–1800* (London, 1997), 332–44; Gary Puckrein, *Little England: Plantation Society and Anglo-Barbadian Politics, 1627–1700* (New York, 1984), 82–3.

11. Susan Dwyer Amussen, *Caribbean Exchanges: Slavery and the Transformation of English Society, 1640–1700* (Chapel Hill, NC, 2007), 142–4.

12. Larry Gragg, *Englishmen Transplanted: The English Colonisation of Barbados 1627–1660* (Oxford, 2003), 129.

13. Craton, *Testing the Chains*, 100, 110; Puckrein, *Little England*, 77.

14. Natural increase among slaves also seems to have existed in marginal West Indian colonies such as the Bahamas, Anguilla, and Barbuda during the eighteenth century. Higman, *Slave Populations*, 307.

15. Matthew Mulcahy, *Hurricanes and Society in the British Greater Caribbean, 1624–1783* (Baltimore, 2006), 113–14; Richard B. Sheridan, *Doctors and Slaves* (Cambridge, 1985); Kenneth F. Kiple, *The Caribbean Slave: A Biological History* (Cambridge, 1984); Philip D. Morgan, "The Poor: Slaves in Early America," in David Eltis et al., *Slavery in the Development of the Americas* (Cambridge, 2004), 302–6.

16. Michael Tadman, "The Demographic Cost of Sugar: Debates on Slave Societies and Natural Increase in the Americas," *American Historical Review*, 105 (December 2000): 1534–75.

17. Kenneth Morgan, "Slave Women and Reproduction in Jamaica, c.1776–1834," *History*, 91 (April 2006): 251.

18. Trevor Burnard, *Mastery, Tyranny, and Desire* (Chapel Hill, NC, 2004).

19. Compare the revolt to the Gordon riots of 1780 in London, in which 60,000 people overturned public order for nearly a week and where the destruction of property and the extensive loss of life caused a real challenge to established authority. Nicholas Rogers, *Crowds, Culture, and Politics in Georgian Britain* (Oxford, 1998).

20. More serious than slave rebellions was maroon opposition. Maroons threatened white control in Jamaica before 1739 and in 1795–6 and in Dominica and St Vincent in the second half of the eighteenth century. Also very serious was a revolt in Grenada in 1795–6 when francophone forces, including many slaves, rebelled under free colored planter Julien Fedon against anglophone whites. Michael Craton, *Testing the Chains* (Ithaca, NY, 1982); Gaspar, *Bondmen and Rebels*; and Mavis Campbell, *The Maroons of Jamaica, 1655–1796* (Granby, Mass., 1988).

21. B. W. Higman, *Montpelier, Jamaica* (Kingston, 1998), 293, 304 (quotes).

22. Emilia Viotti Da Costa, *Crowns of Glory, Tears of Blood* (New York, 1994), 65–73.

23. Craton, *Testing the Chains*, 319–21; Sylvia R. Frey and Betty Wood, *Come Shouting to Zion* (Chapel Hill, NC, 1998), 137–43, 181, Vincent Brown, *The Reaper's Garden* (Cambridge, Mass., 2007).

24. Abbé Raynal, *Philosophical and Political History of the East and West Indies*, 6 vols., trans. J. O. Justamond (New York, 1969), v. 107; Derek Walcott, "Laventille," *The Castaway* (London, 1965), 35.

25. Mary Floyd-Wilson, *English Ethnicity and Race in Early Modern Drama* (Cambridge, 2003); Hilary M. Beckles, *White Servitude and Black Slavery in Barbados, 1627–1715* (Knoxville, Tenn., 1989); Eltis, *Rise of African Slavery*.

SELECT BIBLIOGRAPHY

BECKLES, HILARY M. *White Servitude and Black Slavery in Barbados, 1627–1715.* Knoxville, Tenn.: University of Tennessee Press, 1989.

BERNHARD, VIRGINIA. *Slaves and Slaveholders in Bermuda, 1616–1782.* Columbia, Mo.: University of Missouri Press, 1999.

BRATHWAITE, EDWARD. *The Development of Creole Society in Jamaica, 1770–1820.* Oxford: Ian Randle Publishers, 1971.

BROWN, VINCENT. *The Reaper's Garden: Death and Power in the World of Atlantic Slavery.* Cambridge, Mass.: Harvard University Press, 2007.

BURNARD, TREVOR. *Mastery, Tyranny, and Desire: Thomas Thistlewood and his Slaves in the Anglo-Jamaican World.* Chapel Hill, NC: University of North Carolina Press, 2004.

BURTON, RICHARD D. E. *Afro-Creole: Power, Opposition and Play in the Caribbean.* Ithaca, NY: Cornell University Press, 1997.

CRATON, MICHAEL. *Testing the Chains: Resistance to Slavery in the British West Indies.* Ithaca, NY: Cornell University Press, 1982.

DA COSTA, EMILIA VIOTTI. *Crowns of Glory, Tears of Blood: The Demerara Slave Rebellion of 1823.* New York: Oxford University Press, 1994.

DUNN, RICHARD S. *Sugar and Slaves: The Rise of the Planter Class in the English West Indies 1624–1713.* Chapel Hill, NC: University of North Carolina Press, 1972.

ELTIS, DAVID. *The Rise of African Slavery in the Americas.* Cambridge: Cambridge University Press, 2000.

FREY, SYLVIA R., and BETTY WOOD. *Come Shouting to Zion: African American Protestantism in the American South and British Caribbean to 1830.* Chapel Hill, NC: University of North Carolina Press, 1998.

GOVEIA, ELSA V. *Slave Society in the British Leeward Islands at the End of the Eighteenth Century.* New Haven: Yale University Press, 1965.

HANDLER, JEROME S., and FREDERICK LANGE. *Plantation Slavery in Barbados: An Archaeological and Historical Investigation.* Cambridge, Mass.: Harvard University Press, 1978.

HIGMAN, B. W. *Montpelier, Jamaica: A Plantation Community in Slavery and Freedom 1739–1912*. Kingston: University of the West Indies Press, 1998.

MENARD, RUSSELL R. *Sweet Negotiations: Sugar, Slavery, and Plantation Agriculture in Early Barbados*. Charlottesville, Va.: University of Virginia Press, 2006.

SHERIDAN, RICHARD B. *Doctors and Slaves: A Medical and Demographic History of Slavery in the British West Indies, 1680–1834*. Cambridge: Cambridge University Press, 1984.

WARD, J. R. *British West Indian Slavery, 1750–1834: The Process of Amelioration*. Oxford: Oxford University Press, 1988.

CHAPTER 7

DUTCH CARIBBEAN

HENK DEN HEIJER

INTRODUCTION

Dutch participation in the Atlantic slave trade ended legally by royal decree in 1814. Much of the modern scholarship on Dutch slavery has concentrated on delineating the contours of this odious commerce. Pioneering research began rather late, after the Second World War, both inside and outside the Netherlands, in the wake of rancorous debate about decolonization. The first Dutch historian to delve deeply into the relevant archival records was W. S. Unger. In the 1950s, he published two articles on the slave trade of the Dutch West India Company (WIC) and the Middelburgse Commercie Compagnie (MCC). The WIC, a government-sponsored joint-stock company, enjoyed a monopoly in the Dutch transatlantic slave trade until 1730. The MCC was the largest private Dutch company trading slaves in the second half of the eighteenth century. Beginning in the 1970s, Johannes Postma and Piet Emmer dramatically extended Unger's work. Postma focused on the operation and magnitude of the Dutch Atlantic slave trade, and after twenty years of research, published *The Dutch in the Atlantic Slave Trade, 1600–1815* (1990), the most important quantitative study on the subject to date. Emmer, who completed his doctoral dissertation in 1974 on the struggle in the nineteenth century against the illegal slave trade, published *De Nederlandse slavenhandel 1500–1850* (2000), a broad overview of the slave trade and of Dutch attitudes toward slavery. This book, translated into English in 2006, disposes of a number of hoary presuppositions about the economics of the Dutch slave trade and its reputed profit-ability.[1] Although Postma and Emmer carefully examined the scale and organization of the Dutch slave trade, much work remains to be done on certain aspects such as the treatment of slaves aboard Dutch slave ships. The illegal Dutch slave trade between 1621 and 1730, the period in which the WIC had a monopoly on the slave trade, also requires further investigation. This illegal traffic may prove far more extensive than had been previously believed. The archive of the MCC, which contains a wealth of information about slave ships, offers excellent possibilities for such research.

Research into slavery in the Dutch plantation colonies on the coast of Guiana and the Dutch islands in the Caribbean started hesitantly in the early 1970s, despite the efforts of Harry Hoetink, a Dutch anthropologist, who had published groundbreak-ing work, beginning in 1958, on race relations in the Dutch Caribbean both before and after emancipation in 1863. Several of the first significant studies of Dutch slavery deal with the lengthy process of slave emancipation, aptly called the "long good-bye" by the United States historian Seymour Drescher.[2] Drescher's work in particular advances a much larger debate on the role of capitalist development and markets in the genesis of the humanitarian values and sensibilities associated with the world's first ecumenical antislavery crusade. In the 1980s, interest in Dutch slavery grew steadily, and fresh research has yielded a substantial body of literature, albeit not of the same size as that for slavery in the British and French colonies. Of the Dutch possessions, Curaçao, which emerged as a major slave trading entrepôt in the second half of the seventeenth century, and Suriname, the Netherlands' most important plantation colony, have garnered far more attention than the tiny islands of Aruba, Bonaire, St Eustatius (Statia), Saba, and St Maarten/St Martin.

Archives on both sides of the Atlantic have yielded little information on the intimacies of slave life on Dutch plantations. In a recent issue of *Oso*, a journal devoted to Suriname's history, the Dutch historian Gert Oostindie lamented the dearth of archival information about the lives of ordinary Surinamese slaves.[3] Oostindie did uncover an abundance of quantifiable economic information since plantations were large enterprises that kept meticulous accounts of profit and loss. Although these sources say little about the lives and culture of slaves, recent studies have shown that more information about slavery from the slaves' point of view can be squeezed from written and graphic sources than previously supposed.

SLAVE TRADE AND SLAVERY

In 1596, Dutch privateers in the venerable commercial city of Middelburg in southwestern Netherlands offered 130 African slaves captured from a Portuguese vessel for sale. The auction so shocked the city's burgomaster Adriaen ten Haeff that he ordered the slaves' immediate release. In his eyes, slave trading and slave owning designated sins perpetrated by the Catholic Spaniards and Portuguese, not by the Protestant inhabitants of the Dutch Republic. Ten Haeff could not have guessed then that his countrymen would become guilty of the same sins only a few decades later.[4] His antislavery inclinations can be easily explained. Dutch seafarers, like their English counterparts, first ventured across the Atlantic without the intention of enslaving anyone. They went looking largely for supplies of salt sufficient to keep the profitable Dutch herring trade up and running. Only in the last decades of the sixteenth century, about a century after the Spanish and Portuguese had established slaveholding colonies in the Americas, did Dutch sailors undertake scouting and trading expeditions to West Africa, South America, and the Caribbean. By the beginning of the seventeenth century, they had established the Netherlands' first trading posts and colonies in the "Wild Coast," the area of mainland South America between the Orinoco and Amazon rivers. Repeated Dutch attempts during the first half of the seventeenth century to settle this insalubrious frontier failed for the most part, although some of these settlements before vanishing may have contained a few slaves. The merchant Abraham van Pere from the port of Vlissingen founded Fort Nassau, a colony on the Berbice River in Guiana in 1627. He received a patent from the WIC that stipulated the company's obligation to deliver as many black slaves to the colony as needed. On several eastern Caribbean islands, the Dutch also built trading posts and plantations that may have employed slave labor before the middle of the seventeenth century. Although archival sources about the first Dutch colonies in the Caribbean prove scarce, these early settlements would not have generated significant demand for slaves since they engaged largely in barter with Indians, not in plantation agriculture.[5]

The Dutch embraced the slave trade and slavery on a large scale for the first time in Brazil. It had developed a booming zone of sugar production under Portuguese auspices within a century of Pedro Alvares Cabral's unexpected landfall in 1500. Even before the end of the Twelve Years Truce in 1621 and the related creation of the WIC that same year, the region was attracting the gaze of Dutch merchants. Dutch forces in the service of the WIC and under Hendrick Corneliszoon Loncq, a decorated Dutch naval commander, occupied Recife in 1630 and from there extended Dutch control over the sugar-rich province of Pernambuco and the other captaincies of northeastern Brazil, renaming it New Holland. The WIC's directors determined that the colony could only make a profit if they succeeded in acquiring a sufficient supply of slaves to Brazil to work on the sugar plantations. After pacification of the conquered area and the resumption of the sugar production, the Dutch energetically entered the Atlantic slave trade. The WIC shipped around 25,500 slaves from the Gulf of Guinea and Angola to Brazil between 1636 and 1651. Most of the slaves were sold on the slave market in Recife to Portuguese planters and owners of sugar mills. Inhabitants of Recife and nearby Mauritsstad, however, purchased slaves primarily for household labor. In 1645, nearly 2,000 slaves were living in both cities. Many of these slaves found themselves pressed into service in the defense of New Holland as the Portuguese gradually took back this valuable portion of Brazil from the Dutch.[6] After the fall of the last stronghold of Recife in 1654, the remaining Dutch and Jewish colonists departed, taking their slaves with them to the Caribbean, including areas not under Dutch control, where they helped spur the spread of the plantation system generally and sugar culture particularly.

The loss of Brazil started a new phase in the history of the Dutch slave trade and slavery. The WIC seized Curaçao from the Spanish in 1634. Strategically located north of Venezuela and possessed of a superb deep-water port at Willemstad, the island would develop in little more than a decade into an important transit port for slaves destined for sale in the Spanish colonies. Portuguese traders had brought mainland Spanish America most of its slaves under contract (the *asiento*) during the first decades of the seventeenth century. But the Portuguese overthrow of Hapsburg rule in 1640, which ended the personal union between the crowns of Spain and Portugal, closed this traffic. The Dutch proved particularly well positioned to fill the void. Their ships had the carrying capacity; the WIC owned a number of forts and trading posts in West Africa; and several Dutch islands in the Caribbean would serve as transit centers. During the third quarter of the seventeenth century the Dutch slave traders carried almost 100,000 slaves to the Americas, far surpassing Portugal's contribution to the Atlantic slave trade and challenging England's for overall supremacy in the trade. The slave trade of the WIC through Curaçao grew rapidly during this period.[7] The linguist Charles Gehring of the New York State Library as part of his ambitious New Netherland Project uncovered and translated a treasure trove of documents that while not directly focused on Dutch participation in the Atlantic slave trade reveal Curaçao's centrality in the seventeenth century to the transit trade in slaves to the Americas.[8] Between 1650 and 1700 an estimated 50,000 slaves passed through Curaçao to Spain's colonies on the mainland. After the War of the Spanish Succession (1701–14), the English became the most important slave suppliers for the Spanish colonists, and, as a consequence, Curaçao's stature in the American slave market plummeted. Curaçao was, however, not the only Dutch slave market in the Caribbean where slaves were provided for sale to other nations. St Eustatius also filled the role. During the last quarter of the seventeenth century, Dutch interlopers from West Africa supplied most of the slaves offered for sale there. Tens of thousands of slaves may have found their way through St Eustatius to the surrounding Danish, English, and French islands. Between 1719 and 1727 the WIC organized the island into an open slave market. During this period alone perhaps 10,000 slaves exchanged hands.

Although the transit trade passed most slaves through the Dutch islands on the way to other locations, insular inhabitants also purchased Africans for agricultural labor. Soil infertility and lack of rainfall hindered the cultivation of sugar cane and other profitable export crops on the Dutch Leeward Islands of Aruba, Bonaire, and

Curaçao. But slaves raised maize and other crops for local consumption. Slaves also tended cattle, extracted sea salt, and performed domestic tasks. Very little research exists on the size of the slave populations in the Dutch Leeward Islands and the circumstances in which their slaves labored. Specialists presume the existence of a relatively mild slave regime because of the lack of a plantation economy. On the small plantations—better described as farms—a patriarchal ethos prevailed in regulating the master–slave relation, at least according to W. E. Renkema's work on Curaçao plantations in the nineteenth century.[9] Research on the Dutch Wind-ward colonies—St Eustatius, St Maarten, and Saba—remains in its infancy, but they possessed climates suitable for the growth of tropical export crops. There Dutch colonists built dozens of small sugar plantations that used slave labor. The meager literature shows that tiny St Eustatius, whose total area amounted to eight square miles, had no less than seventy-six plantations in 1775.[10]

Until now, historians have mostly focused on the Dutch plantation colonies on the Wild Coast, which before the end of the seventeenth century utilized slaves on a large scale to cultivate sugar cane and other tropical export crops. In the eighteenth century, the Netherlands owned the plantation colonies of Suriname, Berbice, Demerara, and Essequibo, the last three named after rivers in what is today Guyana. Suriname, the most important Dutch plantation colony in the Americas, has generated the most scholarship on slavery. Before the mid-eighteenth century, Suriname alone had hundreds of large sugar plantations with more than 100 slaves each and, of all the Dutch colonies in the Americas, was attracting the most Dutch investment. On the eve of the Fourth Anglo-Dutch War (1780–4) these four colonies together had about 880 plantations with 87,500 slaves.[11] Most of the slaves worked in the fields, the sugar mills, and the coffee drying houses. Initially, planters concentrated on growing sugar cane, but in the second half of the eighteenth century the number of coffee and cotton plantations also expanded rapidly. Before the end of the century the plantation area in the colonies had reached its maximum size and started to decline; Berbice, Demerara, and Essequibo—obtained by the British from the Dutch by the Treaty of London (1816) and then combined under British rule in 1831 to form British Guiana—began to decline after their capture by the British during the Napoleonic Wars.

TREATMENT, PUNISHMENT, AND RELIGION OF SLAVES

Voltaire's *Candide* contains a memorable depiction of the cruelty of Dutch slavery in Suriname, and, indeed, until recently the idea prevailed in the scholarly litera-ture that slaves in Suriname and in the other Dutch colonies on the Wild Coast suffered a more abysmal fate than their counterparts in the Caribbean. John Gabriël Stedman, a soldier of Scot and Dutch parentage, reared in the Netherlands, reinforced Voltaire's depiction in 1796 by publishing a widely read *Narrative of a Five Years' Expedition against the Revolted Negroes of Suriname.* The book, seeded with gruesome illustrations by Stedman's friend the famous English artist and abolitionist William Blake, describes in considerable detail not only Stedman's service in a campaign against runaway Surinamese slaves, but also the abuse of Surinamese slaves by planters. Stedman undoubtedly saw with his own eyes what he recorded, but the excesses of which he spoke hardly single out Suriname or Dutch slavery for special condemnation.[12]

Historical research shows that the treatment of slaves could differ widely depending on time, place, and occupation. The life of a field slave was usually harder than the life of a house slave. But also the kind of plantation made a difference. Field slaves on cotton plantations in Dutch colonies on the Wild Coast at the end of the eighteenth century did not have the backbreaking responsibility of digging irrigation canals as did field-hands on coffee and sugar plantations. Cotton slaves tended to maintain the fields and pick cotton during the day. Slaves on coffee plantations during the harvest, by contrast, had to break the beans they picked during the day and wash them at night. Work on sugar plantations taxed slave bodies even more. To prevent soil exhaustion, slaves regularly had to clear new fields. During harvest time they had to work day and night. During the day, field slaves cut the sugar cane that had to be processed in the sugar mills and cookeries after dusk.

To keep the production process running smoothly during harvest time, supervisory personnel such as overseers and drivers (enslaved agricultural foremen called *bastiaan* or *bomba*) spurred slaves to work regularly and intensively in gang labor. The severity of the work also had consequences for the slaves' life expectancy. Slaves on cotton plantations lived longer on average and under better circumstances than their fellow slaves on coffee and sugar plantations.[13] Improvements in the living and working conditions in the decades before slave emancipation in 1863 did increase the life expectancy of the field slaves on coffee and sugar plantations. Research into slave demography on Dutch plantation colonies is at present limited to Suriname in the period of 1750–1863.[14] Fragmented sources about the number of slaves in the Dutch colonies make difficult meaningful conclusions about slave demographic performance before 1750.

Slaves in the Dutch colonies, unlike those in the antebellum United States, showed a natural rate of decrease until the beginning of the nineteenth century. To counter the consequences of this surplus of deaths over births, new slaves had to be imported from Africa. No one has as yet found a conclusive explanation for the natural decrease of the slave population, although the combination of low fertility and high mortality certainly factor into the equation. Slaves clustered together in gangs and close quarters made ripe targets for epidemic disease. Poor living and working conditions and harsh punishments undoubtedly exacerbated the situation.[15] The continual import of slaves skewed the slave population's age structure, toward the upper age brackets, in effect ageing it. Conversion of slave populations subject to substantial in- and outmigration into stable populations suitable for precise demographic analysis remains difficult because of the paucity of reliable data and the problematic application of model life tables from the life experience of non-slaves.

Slaves imported from Africa, called salt-water negroes or *bozales* (from the pejorative Spanish word for newly arrived slaves), ran the greatest risk of dying prematurely. Forced acculturation to new surroundings, to different food, hard labor, and unknown diseases, a process known as seasoning, killed perhaps more than 10 percent of the newcomers within a year. Slaves who survived the first year in the colony had a life expectancy of around thirty years in the second half of the eighteenth century. In the nineteenth century longevity would increase to around forty. Planters knew the risks for newcomers and treated them with a certain amount of care. After branding they were allowed to rest for two weeks to help adapt to their new environment. Three months of light work usually followed. During this period the newly imported Africans stayed with experienced slaves who familiarized them with the work and the relations on the plantation. After this process of adjustment these slaves were fully included in the gang-labor regimen.[16]

Creole slaves, who were a minority of the slave population until the end of the eighteenth century, lived longer and fetched higher prices than the newly arrived Africans. Dutch planters considered creoles and slaves of mixed descent more capable, malleable, and reliable than *bozales*. Creoles disproportionately filled skilled and privileged positions. On the plantations they served as carpenters, masons, coopers, blacksmiths, and sugar boilers. Those regarded by masters as the best and most reliable slaves could advance to a supervisory position on the plantation. They carried out instructions from the white owner, director, or overseer of the plantation and reminded their fellow slaves, with a lash if necessary, to work harder. These enslaved officers or foremen typically had to receive white permission—from a master or his surrogates—to impose or enforce penalties on the slaves.

Whites composed no more than 10 percent of the population in the Dutch colonies on the Wild Coast. Their minority status made them chronically anxious about slave rebellion. To prevent outbursts of violence and calm their own fears, officials imposed strict rules and applied hard punishments. Like masters in every other slave society in the Americas, Dutch planters pursued a divide-and-conquer strategy in dealing with their slaves. Skilled slaves, drivers, and house slaves usually escaped field labor. They received better rations and more consumer goods than the field slaves. As long as the favored slaves served their masters loyally, they enjoyed these privileges. Slaves who failed to work hard enough or broke the rules could expect swift punishment whose severity might not be proportional to the nature of the misdeed. For small incidents of misbehavior, slaves might lose allowances or privileges, the daily dram, for example, or the ability to attend a dance or travel to see a loved one. A variable number of lashes punished misdeeds of varying kinds. Slaves dreaded the Spanish Buck, a punishment that began by bending a slave's arms to his knees, then fastening them together with a stick underneath in preparation for a beating on the backside until not a swatch of skin was left. As the colonies matured, fears mounted that gross abuse could lead to dangerous eruptions of slave violence. Colonial law, beginning notably in the middle of the eighteenth century, began to rein in the private power that masters exercised over their slaves, by attempting to regulate slave punishment. Crimes that carried severe disciplinary measures or the death penalty could only be executed by the colonial government. Nineteenth-century laws gradually replaced cruel corporal punishments with more humane forms of punishment.[17] In practice, however, planters still took the law into their own hands on their estates.

The most enlightened masters learned to rely on the carrot as well as the stick to regulate slave behavior. Planters offered incentives and rewards to preserve the peace and improve productivity. They gave their slaves Sunday off, increased food rations, and permitted amusements. Dancing, the so-called "baljaren," took place on Sunday or in the evening after work. The dancers stood in two rows facing each other and were surrounded by a ring of spectators. Dancing, drumming, and singing parties were the most important forms of relaxation for slaves but such festivities, often elaborate and highly ritualistic, could also have religious meanings and accompanied slave funerals. Whites permitted but also regulated many of these celebratory events, fearing that outright prohibition might spark rebellion. The so-called *Watra Mama* dance (the goddess who led the water gods) caused such concern, however, that Suriname's colonial government banned it in 1776.[18]

The horrors of the Middle Passage did not denude survivors of their African past, and, indeed, it informed and shaped slaves' religious practices to varying degrees throughout the Americas. Surviving documents for the Dutch colonies from the seventeenth and eighteenth centuries, however, reveal little about slave religion. Not until the nineteenth century with the advent of serious missionary activity do relevant sources become more abundant. With creolization of the slave population, different African religions merged in complicated, syncretic patterns, and Afro-American religions developed in almost all plantation colonies. Many slaves and free persons of color in Curaçao, a thoroughfare for Spanish influences, had become at least nominal Catholics since the beginning of the eighteenth century. Of the limited research on slaves' religious beliefs in the Dutch colonies, those of Surinamese slaves have received the most attention.[19] In the eighteenth century, the Winti, an animistic Afro-Suriname faith, developed that is still adhered to by many Surinamese. The slaves acknowledged an upper god or *Gran Gado*, the creator of heaven and earth, and believed in the existence of lesser gods and spirits that manifested themselves in the elements and in the woods. Slaves believed that the dead returned to the land of their ancestors as spirits and made regular offerings to their pantheon of gods and spirits.

Serious efforts at Christian missionary outreach to the slaves did not begin in the Dutch colonies until the nineteenth century. In the seventeenth century, Dutch slave traders and slaveholders, like other western Europeans involved in the plantation complex, frequently resorted to the Curse of Ham to justify racial slavery. In *The City of God*, St Augustine referred to the biblical verses Genesis 9: 18–27, on which the curse is based, as the first justification for slavery in Scripture. Ham, the son of Noah, viewed his father Noah drunk and naked in his tent and committed some unstated misdeed. His sin caused Noah to place a curse on Ham's son Canaan: "a servant of servants shall he be unto his brethren." Only with the increasing enslavement of blacks, however, did these verses become interpretatively twisted by Muslims and Christians into an explicitly racial justification for slavery. With the curse in mind, many Dutch colonists refrained from converting these allegedly doomed people to Christianity. Clergymen did from time to time try to convert slaves to Christianity, but encountered opposition from the planters, and the authorities balked.[20] The Moravians, a pietistic German denomination that had been particularly active in Christianizing slaves in the Danish Virgin Islands during the eighteenth century, had opened missions to Suriname's free blacks as early as 1735. In the nineteenth century, Moravian missionaries received permission to preach to Suriname's slaves. Maria Lenders's *Strijders voor het Lam* (*Warriors of the Lamb*) splendidly documents these activities. After the abolition of the slave trade many planters changed their mind about missionary work, thinking that the Christianization of slaves might actually help turn their slaves into a more disciplined and obedient workforce. In the run up to emancipation, the conversion of slaves to Christianity undoubtedly narrowed but did not eliminate the considerable cultural distance between black and white in Suriname. Christianity for the slaves was not a replacement for the Winti but a separate second belief.[21] Missionaries were already working among the slave population on the Dutch Leeward Islands in the eighteenth century, where Catholicism among persons of color, slave and free, had the most influence. According to a report from 1828 almost the entire slave populations of Aruba, Bonaire, and Curaçao were baptized and converted to the Catholic faith. On the Dutch Windward Islands, where the Methodist faith gained the upper hand from the beginning of the nineteenth century, conversion did not have a particularly high priority, and many slaves remained faithful to a creolized Afro-American faith.[22]

SLAVE RESISTANCE AND SLAVE REVOLTS

The recent historiography of Dutch slavery parallels that for other American slave societies in having dissolved crusted stereotypes of slave docility by detailing a range of ways, from passive resistance to open rebellion, that slaves countered dehumanization and altered the terms of their bondage. Familiar forms of non-violent protest included slowdowns and work stoppages, whether in the field, the sugar mills, or during the processing of the coffee harvest. Planters could counter such behavior by using a whip, but its indiscriminate application could make matters worse. Thus, masters frequently worked through enslaved surrogates like the drivers to re-establish order. Another form of disobedience was stealing food or supplies. Slaves could also run away, as a protest against mistreatment or against the prospect of being sold. They usually hid in a nearby forest or on another plantation. But life in the forest was hard and uncertain; therefore most runaways chose to absent themselves from the plantation temporarily.[23]

In some cases, slaves exposed to frequent, random, and cruel behavior or forced into sexual relations retaliated with deadly violence against their master or a white overseer. Given the intimidating array of forces at the masters' disposal, slaves rarely translated plotting into insurrection. One noteworthy exception, however, erupted in Suriname on the Commewijne River in February 1750 and ultimately embraced more than 100 slaves. They seized the Bethlehem plantation, executed its owner—allegedly a brutal fellow who had taken the wife of one of his slaves as a concubine—and his white administrator, and moved on to destroy several other estates. Whites in Paramaribo mustered a company of burghers that eventually suppressed the rebels, who had fled into the forest. Several dozen captured rebels faced a quick trial, and those executed were put to various forms of gruesome death such as breaking on the wheel and burning.[24]

Dutch colonists first confronted impressive displays of slave collective resistance among maroons or runaway slaves in northeastern Brazil. Under Portuguese rule runaway Angolan slaves had founded in the surrounding country several villages or *quilombos* (from the Bantu word for war camp) from where they undermined the stability of the colony. Several expeditions were dispatched to stamp them out, but failed to do so.[25] The anthropologist Richard Price and others have produced an impressive body of scholarship on Suriname's maroon communities, the largest of which as *imperium in imperio* presented a serious problem to white rule. By the mid-eighteenth century perhaps as many as one in ten of all of Suriname's plantation slaves qualified as deserters. The colony's extensive jungle provided favorable terrain in which to secure enclaves based on hunting and subsistence agriculture. Villages formed from which the maroons conducted hit-and-run operations on plantations to acquire females, weapons, tools, and other necessities for survival. The Dutch islands in the Caribbean, in contrast, without a bush, lacked sizeable enclaves of runaways, although they did yield maritime maroons. The anthropologist Wim Hoogbergen estimates that around 250 slaves escaped annually from Suriname's plantations, of which a third established themselves permanently in the forest. Colonial officials repeatedly organized expeditions to root out organized maroon activity. But their very lack of success led in the second half of the eighteenth century to an alternative course of action: the conclusion of peace treaties with several groups of maroons. With freedom inscribed in these treaties, the affected groups promised to lend white authorities a helping hand tracking down and returning newly escaped slaves to planters in return for goods and firearms. But not all maroons chose peace. In the border area between Suriname and French Guiana a group of maroons under the leadership of the legendary chief Boni continued the attacks on plantations. Not until 1860, three years before the abolition of slavery in the Dutch colonies, did this group of rebels finally make peace with the Dutch.[26]

The history of Dutch slavery records two major uprisings, both of which were led by skilled and privileged slaves. In Berbice, a number of small slave revolts, largely confined to one or few plantations, preceded a major insurrection in 1763 that almost destroyed the colony. In July 1762, for example, several dozen slaves, led by a *bomba* (driver), revolted on plantation Goed Fortuin while their master, a government official, was off site engaged in political duties. They pillaged firearms and reduced the estate house to ashes. The governor of Berbice, fearful of a spreading contagion, had considerable difficulty defeating the rebels who resisted stoutly from defensive positions in the forest against white volunteers sent against them. No one has adequately investigated the cause of this "small mutiny," to borrow the term of the nineteenth-century Dutch scholar P. M. Netscher, and others like it. Deplorable living conditions—the lack of provisions and epidemics (a recurring problem after the 1750s)—probably played a role in precipitating the violence and preconditioning the largest and longest lasting slave revolt in the circum-Caribbean region before the outbreak of the revolution on Saint-Domingue in 1791. This uprising began in Berbice on the Magdalenenburg plantation on 23 February 1763. The revolt spread rapidly from there as slaves burned buildings and killed whites, whose own ranks at that time had been decimated by epidemic disease. At the time of the uprising, slaves openly complained of their rough treatment by "Christians." They outnumbered whites in Berbice by ten to one (3,850 to 350). Two African-born, Akan-speaking slaves led the revolt: a cooper named Coffy from the Leliënburg plantation was proclaimed governor; his partner Accara, also from Leliënburg, was made captain. They sent to Governor W. S. Van Hogenheim a letter that sought partition of the colony. The rebels organized themselves in a disciplined, military fashion, killed around forty whites, and drove most of the remainder from the colony. To regain it, outside help from Essequibo and Suriname, including Indian mercenaries, had to be called in. During this servile war, which lasted ten months, more than 1,800 slaves were killed.[27]

Curaçao's slave society had a reputation for mildness relative to the Netherlands' mainland plantation colonies, although recurring drought brought on by provision crises unsettled the slave population. Nearby Coro on what is today the Venezuelan mainland attracted runaways, but Spanish officials returned many of them to the island. A list of slaves that had fled to Coro and other areas from 1729 to 1775 shows them to be overwhelmingly male (85 percent) with field hands

(26 percent) and seamen (16 percent) comprising the main occupations, although slave artisans—carpenters, shoemakers, and tailors, for example—were disproportionately represented. Laundresses and seamstresses comprised 32 percent of the eighty-five female runaways identified.[28] Curaçao's first major slave uprising erupted in the summer of 1750 on the plantation Hato, owned by the WIC. About a hundred, mostly African slaves revolted. These so-called Mina slaves (named, it appears, after the Dutch trading castle Elmina on the Gold Coast) stole weapons, torched buildings, and killed several whites as well as some slaves who refused to be recruited to the cause. A militia of whites, free mulattos, and free blacks organized by Governor Isaac Faesch eventually crushed the uprising. Some slaves preferred suicide to surrender. They threw themselves into the sea off the cliffs at Hato. More than thirty others, including thirteen female slaves, were brutally tortured and executed.[29]

Fallout from the great slave revolution in the French colony of Saint-Domingue helped spark in August 1795 the largest insular slave revolt in the history of the Dutch Caribbean. This insurrection followed an emancipation decree issued in 1794 for France's colonies by the Jacobin regime and the overthrow a few months later of the Dutch Republic by French revolutionary forces. In fact, whites in Curaçao had made themselves vulnerable by splitting into Orangist and pro-French factions. Rumors spread among Curaçao's slaves of their own impending liberation. Despite efforts of the colonial government to restrict movements of slaves and free persons of color, enslaved rebels concerted in nightly gatherings to plot a course of action.[30] The revolt started on plantation De Knip in western Curaçao with a work stoppage by about fifty slaves. Led by Tula (alias Rigaud, after a leader of the Saint-Domingue Revolution), the rebels left De Knip to recruit slaves from other plantations. Whites scrambled to Willemstad for safety, leaving slaves to confiscate weapons left behind. After two days, the number of rebels increased to 2,000 slaves, about a third of the slave population of Curaçao. To prevent an island-wide conflagration, the colonial government deployed regular troops in an attempt to seal off western Curaçao. Tula and other leaders, including one who called himself Toussaint, sang French songs and demanded their freedom. A Franciscan priest, acting as a go-between, tried unsuccessfully to get them to surrender their weapons and return to work. The military, which included free colored militiamen, eventually counterattacked and drove the rebels into a corner of the island. Only after a few weeks did they succeed in clearing up the last pocket of resistance. The uprising cost the lives of more than 100 slaves and three whites. In the trial that followed 31 rebels were sentenced to death. As a warning, the rebel leaders Tula, Varpetta, and Wacao were first broken on the wheel and then beheaded while the other convicts were hanged. The aftermath of the insurrection did lead in November 1795, however, to legal reforms that promised the slaves better food and clothing, shorter working hours, and more humane punishments.

THE LONG ROAD TO ABOLITIONISM

Scholars have often portrayed the Netherlands as a country largely indifferent to emancipation, one that lagged decades behind other European nations in ending both the Atlantic slave trade and slavery. This image, enshrined in the historiography, prompted a major conference in 1993 that yielded the anthology *Fifty Years Later* (1996), the most comprehensive study of the Dutch road to abolition and emancipation.[31] This volume underscores the peculiarity not of the Netherlands, but of Great Britain with respect to organized antislavery. Only in Great Britain had opponents of the slave trade and slavery succeeded by 1800 in mobilizing a large-scale, popular movement whose values had begun to penetrate into the marrow of the political establishment.

The lack of a public debate and popular mobilizations against slavery in the Netherlands did not mean total silence. Even in the beginning of the seventeenth century various authors in the Republic had damned the slave trade and slavery as iniquities. The theologian Festus Hommius (1576–1642), a pietistic Calvinist influenced by Puritanism, spoke out against slavery in *Schat-boeck der Christelycke Leere* (1602), a translation of the Heidelberg Catechism produced by the German theologian Zacharias Ursinius. Hommius, like Ursinius, took a firm stand based on Exodus 21: 16 that the slave trade and slavery derived from unchristian acts of theft, perpetrated primarily by Spanish and Portuguese papists. In 1602, of course, the Dutch had not yet become deeply involved in the slave trade, but at least some Dutch theologians and clergymen railed against the slave trade from the mid-seventeenth century until its abolition. Cornelius van Poudroyen (d. 1662), for instance, the student of Gisbertus Voetius (1589–1676), one of the country's most influential Dutch Reformed theologians, published a new *Catechizatie over den Heidelbergschen Catechismus* (1653) in which he maintained that the Bible unequivocally rejected slavery. The celebrated jurist Hugo Grotius (1583–1645) argued that under certain circumstances slavery was legal, but Poudroyen attempted to rebut these arguments with the Ten Commandments. Bernard Smytegelt (1665–1739), a Calvinist minister from Middelburg, and the Hoorn Predikant Jacobus Hondius (1629–91) also preached against slavery.[32]

In the Dutch Republic the entrepreneurial spirit finally won out over conscientious objections, and the slave trade and slavery became generally accepted. As Thomas Lynch, Jamaica's governor during the Third Anglo-Dutch War (1672–4), said of Dutch priorities, "Jesus Christ was good, but trade was better." Nonetheless opposition to slavery and the slave trade never died. In the second half of the eighteenth century French and English antislavery tracts translated into Dutch reached the elite. And popular writers such as Betje Wolff (1738–1804), Aagje Deken (1741–1804), and Elisabeth Maria Post (1755–1812) attacked slavery in their novels. The Netherlands' educated upper class was well informed about slavery in the colonies but chose nonetheless to tolerate it silently.[33]

Not all Africans and creoles, mulattos and blacks, in the Dutch Caribbean lived in bondage. Over time, a sizeable intermediate class of free mulattos and blacks emerged in the colonies. From the beginning of slavery in the Dutch colonies, slaves attained freedom with the permission of their masters. They frequently manumitted female slaves with whom they had sexual relations as well as the resulting progeny of such unions. Loyal domestic slaves also benefited from manu-mission. That Dutch masters manumitted old and infirm slaves to relieve themselves of economic burdens is revealed by eighteenth-century laws designed to regulate the practice. Curaçao, which allowed slave self-purchase, had a much more liberal manumission policy than Suriname. After 1733, for example, the colonial government of Suriname permitted the emancipation of slaves only if they could look after themselves. After 1788, a certificate of manumission in Suriname required a payment of 100 guilders, a levy that was increased several times. The Dutch islands, in contrast, issued no restrictive regulations on manumission, although laws were passed to abate the nuisance caused by free mulattos and free blacks. Restrictive regulations or not, the number of free persons of color increased rapidly in the second half of the eighteenth century in all Dutch colonies in the Caribbean. In 1738 Suriname had 2,133 whites and 598 free persons of color; in 1831 Suriname had 2,696 whites and 5,154 free persons of color. On the Dutch Windward and Leeward Islands the number of free non-whites also increased steadily. Whereas in Suriname in 1863, at the moment of abolition, slaves amounted to about 55 percent of the total population, they amounted to about 35 percent of the total population of the islands.[34]

Whatever the manumission practices, during the last quarter of the eighteenth century, Dutch ships carried more than 40,000 slaves to the Americas and thousands of the imported slaves ended up in the Dutch colonies. During the Napoleonic era, the great slave revolution in Saint-Domingue chilled debate about slave trade abolition in France and in the Netherlands. Popular pressure in Great Britain, however, succeeded in moving Parliament in March 1807 to pass the "Act for the Abolition of the Slave Trade." Under British pressure, King Willem I of the new Kingdom of the Netherlands acted in 1814 without any discussion or involve-ment of the Dutch States-General to end the Dutch slave trade after 180 years of operation.

Looking back, the British antislavery movement developed an effective strategy of public pressure that disaggregated the related issues of the slave trade and slavery to reach their desired goals successively not simultaneously. When the British Parlia-ment passed the Emancipation Act in August 1833, the Netherlands had abolitionists, but lacked an organized, mass-based antislavery movement. To be sure, the Dutch Parliament discussed abolition and emancipation but largely in practical, economic terms. The issue became particularly topical after 1848 when France abolished slavery (for the second time) in its colonies. The ending of French slavery meant that Suriname was now hemmed in to the east and west by French Guiana and British Guiana, respectively, free colonies that could harbor runaway slaves.

In 1840 Minister of Colonies J. C. Baud asked J. C. Rijk, governor of Suriname, to investigate the possibility of slave emancipation. He replied that the abolition of slavery in the long run was inevitable but also that the elevation of slaves to freedom necessitated careful planning and management. In British Guiana plantation production had dropped dramatically after emancipation; Surinamese officials like Rijk wanted to avoid a similar fate. His plan lobbied for a long transitional period during which the slaves would have to earn their freedom. The government would buy the slaves' freedom and then rent out the freedmen and freedwomen to the planters for several years to earn back the purchase price.[35]

Years of discussion in the Dutch States-General about the end of slavery followed Rijk's proposal and centered on the amount of the compensation to Dutch slave owners and on the specifics of an ordered process of gradual emancipation. A few Members of Parliament, like the liberal W. R. van Hoëvell, adopted a moralistic, ideological tone in the debate, but most approached emancipation from a purely commercial point of view. Ironically, money earned in the Dutch East Indies by forced labor helped purchase the freedom of slaves in the Dutch Caribbean. On July 1, 1863, twenty-one cannon shots in Paramaribo, the capital of Suriname, announced the abolition of slavery in the colonies: the freeing of 33,621 slaves in Suriname and 11,654 slaves in the Dutch Antilles. Freed persons on the plantations, however, had to remain there as wage laborers for ten years before they were allowed to opt out of the gang system and choose other work. Much work remains to be done on emancipation in the Dutch Antilles. But A. F. Paula's recent dissertation describes what happened in St Maarten/St Martin. Emancipation in 1848 on the French side of this divided island with its many valuable salt ponds forced the hand of Dutch masters to follow suit that same year.[36] Failure to liberate, they recognized, would not only lead to a rapid exodus of Dutch slaves to the French side, but scattered violence following the French emancipation raised the specter of a general insurrection if Dutch masters did not act expeditiously to free their slaves.

Conclusion

Research into Dutch slavery started slowly during the last quarter of the twentieth century but has gained strength in recent decades. Significant geographical and chronological gaps exist, however, in the literature. Curaçao and Suriname have generated far more scholarly interest than the other Dutch colonies. The most thorough history of Essequibo, Demerara, and Berbice dates from the nineteenth century, when slavery was not at the center of attention.[37] Because of Britain's capture of these colonies, its National Archives in Kew holds relevant sources that may well remedy the neglect. Slavery on the Dutch Leeward Islands of Aruba and Bonaire and on the Dutch Windward Islands of Saba, St Eustatius, and St Maarten remains understudied. Much of the work on Dutch slavery has concentrated on the nineteenth century because of the relative abundance of sources. Ruud Beeldsnijder and Frank Dragtenstein, however, in their studies of slavery in Suriname, have proven that intrepid and painstaking archival research can bear fruit on the history of Dutch slavery for the eighteenth century and even for the seventeenth century. The subjects of the Dutch slave trade, slave resistance, and abolitionism have a firm foundation in the historiography. Studies by Alex van Stipriaan and Gert Oostindie on Suriname's plantation economy at both the macro and micro levels have provided penetrating insights into the lives and work of plantation slaves. Interest in the history of Dutch slavery in the Netherlands has grown in recent decades, and Dutch universities are training more specialists in the field. After a slow start, scholars have erected the scaffolding necessary for the construction of a rich and comprehensive picture of Dutch slavery.

NOTES

1. W. S. Unger, "Bijdragen tot de geschiedenis van de Nederlandse slavenhandel," part I, *Economisch-Historisch Jaarboek*, 26 (1956): 133–74; part II, *Economisch-Historisch Jaarboek*, 28 (1958): 3–131; J. M. Postma, *The Dutch in the Atlantic Slave Trade 1600–1815* (New York, 1990); P. C. Emmer, *De Nederlandse slavenhandel 1500–1850* (Amsterdam, 2000). In 2006 Emmer's book was translated into English, see the Selected Bibliography.

2. The first Dutch scholar who carefully reconstructed the Dutch debates preceding the Emancipation Act of 1863 was J. P. Siwpersad, *De Nederlandse regering en de afschaffing van de Surinaamse slavernij (1833–1863)* (Groningen, 1979). S. Dresher, "The Long Goodbye: Dutch Capitalism and Antislavery in Comparative Perspective," in G. Oostindie (ed.), *Fifty Years Later: Antislavery, Capitalism and Modernity in the Dutch Orbit* (Leiden, 1995), 25–66.

3. G. Oostindie, "Slaaf van de bronnen: De reconstructie van het onherroepelijk verlorene," *Oso. Tijdschrift voor Surinaamse Taalkunde, Letterkunde en Geschiedenis*, 7 (1988), 135–46.

4. V. Enthoven, "Early Dutch Expansion in the Atlantic Region, 1585–1621," in J. Postma and V. Enthoven (eds.), *Riches from Atlantic Commerce: Dutch Transatlantic Trade and Shipping, 1585–1817* (Leiden, 2003), 40.

5. P. M. Netscher, *Geschiedenis van de koloniën Essequebo, Demerary en Berbice van de vestiging der Nederlanders aldaar tot op onzen tijd* (The Hague, 1888), 58 and 353; H. den Heijer, 'Over warme en koude landen: Mislukte Nederlandse volksplantingen op de Wilde Kust in de zeventiende eeuw', *De zeventiende eeuw*, 21 (2005), 79–90. According to C. C. Goslinga, *The Dutch in the Caribbean and on the Wild Coast 1580–1680* (Assen, 1971), 435, the WIC was obliged to supply the colony with slaves.

6. E. van den Boogaart and P. C. Emmer, "The Dutch Participation in the Atlantic Slave Trade, 1596–1650," in H. A. Gemery and J. S. Hogendorn (eds.), *The Uncommon Market:*

Essays in the Economic History of the Atlantic Slave Trade (New York, 1979), 367–9. According to the latest research, done by Jelmer Vos, the Dutch shipped approximately 30,900 slaves from West Africa to Brazil of which 25,500 survived the transatlantic passage. Vos's findings will be incorporated in the Trans-Atlantic Slave Trade Database, compiled under the direction of David Eltis. http://slavevoyages.org/tast/index.faces; jsessionid=EF27C2F2EA51C14E9448C1B6EEE250CD

7. The Dutch share in the total Atlantic slave trade was approximately 5%. Only in the second half of the seventeenth century did the Dutch played a mayor role. By exporting nearly 501,500 slaves from West Africa in two centuries the Dutch were the fourth nation in the Atlantic slave trade. J. Postma, "A Reassessment of the Dutch Atlantic Slave Trade," in Postma and Enthoven, *Riches from Atlantic Commerce*, 137, table 5.7.

8. Charles T. Gehring and J. A. Schiltkamp (eds.), *Curaçao Papers, 1640–1665*, p. xvii: *New Netherland Documents* (Interlaken, 1987).

9. W. R. Renkema, *Het Curaçaose plantagebedrijf in de negentiende eeuw* (Zutphen, 1981), 112–43.

10. L. Knappert, *Geschiedenis van de Nederlandsche Bovenwindsche eilanden in de 18e eeuw* (The Hague, 1932), 229–30.

11. C. C. Goslinga, *The Dutch in the Caribbean and in the Guianas 1680–1791* (Assen, 1985), 492–3; A. van Stipriaan, *Surinaams contrast: Roofbouw en overleven in een Caraïbische plantagekolonie 1750–1863* (Leiden, 1993), 28, table 1, and 33; J. P. van de Voort, *De Westindische plantages van 1720 tot 1795: Financiën en handel* (Eindhoven, 1973), 204; E. W. van der Oest, "The Forgotten Colonies of Essequibo and Demerara, 1700–1814," in Postma and Enthoven, *Riches from Atlantic Commerce*, 329, table 12.1.

12. Emmer, *De Nederlandse slavenhandel*, 179–81; G. Oostindie, *Het paradijs overzee: De "Nederlandse" Caraïben en Nederland* (Amsterdam, 1997), 68–107.

13. Van Stipriaan, *Surinaams contrast*, 327–8.

14. Ibid. 310–11; H. E. Lamur, "Fertility Differentials on Three Plantations in Suriname," *Slavery and Abolition*, 8 (1987): 313–35; G. J. Oostindie, *Roosenburg en Mon Bijou: Twee Surinaamse plantages, 1720–1870* (Dordrecht, 1989), 131–46, 251–9.

15. Richard Price and other researchers argued that an unbalanced sex ratio (a large surplus of male slaves) in the colonies was due to the negative demographic curve, but recent scholarship has called this explanation into question. R. Price, "De marrons van Suriname: Een historische inleiding," *Mededelingen van de Stichting Surinaams Museum*, 28 (1979), 20; Van Stipriaan, *Surinaams contrast*, 314–15.

16. R. Beeldsnijder, *"Om werk van jullie te hebben": Plantageslaven in Suriname, 1730–1750* (Utrecht, 1994), 117–19.

17. Ibid. 236–53; Van Stipriaan, *Surinaams contrast*, 370–5.

18. E. Klinkers, *Op hoop van vrijheid: van slavensamenleving naar creoolse gemeenschap in Suriname, 1830–1880* (Utrecht, 1997), 58–9; J. A. Schiltkamp and J. T. de Smidt, *West Indisch Plakaatboek. Suriname*, deel II (Amsterdam, 1973), 896.

19. C. J. Wooding, *Winti. Een Afroamerikaanse godsdienst in Suriname: een cultureel-historische analyse van de religieuze verschijnselen in de Para* (Meppel, 1972).

20. J. M. van der Linde, *Over Noach en zijn zonen: De Cham-ideologie en de leugens tegen Cham tot vandaag* (Utrecht, 1993); J. M. van der Linde, *Jan Willem Kals: leraar der Hervormden; advocaat van indiaan en neger* (Kampen, 1987); F. L. Schalkwijk, *The Reformed Church in Dutch Brazil (1630–1654)* (Zoetermeer, 1998), 151.

21. M. Lenders, *Strijders voor het Lam: Leven en werk van Hernhutter-broeders en zusters in Suriname, 1735–1900* (Leiden, 1996); Klinkers, *Op hoop van vrijheid*, 60–1.

22. W. R. Menkman, *De Nederlanders in het Caraibische zeegebied waarin vervat de geschiedenis der Nederlandsche Antillen* (Amsterdam, 1942), 208–9.

23. Michael Craton, *Testing the Chains: Resistance to Slavery in the British West Indies* (Ithaca, NY, 1982); Eugene D. Genovese, *From Rebellion to Revolution: Afro-American Slave Revolts in the Making of the New World* (New York, 1979); Beeldsnijder, "*Om werk van jullie te hebben,*" 216–21.

24. G. W. van der Meiden, *Betwist bestuur: Een eeuw strijd om de macht in Suriname 1651–1753* (Amsterdam, 1987), 110–11.

25. J. A. Gonsalves de Mello, *Nederlanders in Brazilië (1624–1654): de invloed van de Hollandse bezetting op het leven en de cultuur in Noord-Brazilië* (Zutphen, 2001), 188–90.

26. W. Hoogbergen, "*De Bosnegers zijn gekomen*": *slavernij en rebellie in Suriname* (Amsterdam, 1992), 1–19. See for the early period of marronage F. Dragtenstein, "*De ondraaglijke stoutheid der weglopers*": *maronnage en koloniaal beleid in Suriname, 1667–1768* (Utrecht, 2002).

27. Goslinga, *The Dutch in the Caribbean and in the Guianas*, 461–94; Netscher, *Geschiedenis van de koloniën*, 188–241.

28. Calculated from Wim Klooster, "Subordinate but Proud: Curaçao's Free Blacks and Mulattoes in the Eighteenth Century," *New West Indian Guide*, 68 (1994): 285.

29. Goslinga, *The Dutch in the Caribbean and in the Guianas*, 113.

30. A. F. Paula (ed.), *De slavenopstand op Curaçao, 1795: een bronnenuitgave van de originele documenten* (Curaçao, 1974).

31. The first historian who made a comparison of the antislavery debate in the Netherlands and in Great Britain was P. C. Emmer, "Anti-Slavery and the Dutch; Abolition without Reform," in Roger Anstey, Christine Bolt, and Seymour Drescher (eds.), *Anti-Slavery, Religion, and Reform: Essays in Memory of Roger Anstey* (Folkestone, 1980), 80–98.

32. G. J. Schutte, *Het Calvinistisch Nederland: mythe en werkelijkheid* (Hilversum, 2000), 27–45.

33. A. N. Paasman, *Reinhart: Nederlandse literatuur en slavernij ten tijde van de Verlichting* (Leiden, 1984), 209–16; A. Sens, "*Mensaap, heiden, slaaf*": *Nederlandse visies op de wereld rond 1800* (The Hague, 2001).

34. L. Dalhuisen et al. (eds.), *Geschiedenis van de Antillen* (Zutphen, 1997), 54–6; G. Oostindie, "Perspectives on Slavery and Slaves in Suriname and Curaçao," in Oostindie, *Fifty Years Later*, 158.

35. J. R. Bruijn, H. J. den Heijer, and H. Stapelkamp, *Julius Constantijn Rijk: Zeeman en minister 1787–1854* (Amsterdam, 1991), 68–9; Siwpersad, *De Nederlandse regering*, 84–6.

36. A. F. Paula, "*Vrije*" *slaven: een sociaal-historische studie over de dualistische slavenemancipatie op Nederlands Sint Maarten 1816–1863* (Zutphen, 1993), 153–7.

37. Netscher, *Geschiedenis van de koloniën*.

SELECT BIBLIOGRAPHY

BEELDSNIJDER, R. "*Om werk van jullie te hebben*": *Plantageslaven in Suriname, 1730–1750.* Utrecht: Bronnen voor de studie van Afro-Suriname, deel 16, 1994.

DRAGTENSTEIN, F. "*De ondraaglijke stoutheid der weglopers*": *marronage en koloniaal beleid in Suriname, 1667–1768.* Utrecht: Bronnen voor de studie van Suriname, deel 22, 2002.

EMMER, P. C. *The Dutch Slave Trade, 1500–1850*. New York: Berghahn Books, 2006.

GOSLINGA, C. C. *The Dutch in the Caribbean and in the Guianas 1680–1791*. Assen: Van Gorcum, 1985.

HOOGBERGEN, W. *The Boni-Maroon Wars in Suriname*. Leiden: Brill, 1990.

OOSTINDIE, G., *Roosenburg en Mon Bijou: twee Surinaamse plantages, 1720–1870*. Dordrecht: Floris Publications, 1989.

OOSTINDIE, G., ed. *Fifty Years Later: Antislavery, Capitalism and Modernity in the Dutch Orbit*. Leiden: KITLV-Press, 1996.

PAULA, A. F. *"Vrije slaven": een sociaal-historische studie over de dualistische slavenemancipatie op Nederlans Sint Maarten*. Zutphen: Walburg Pers, 1993.

POSTMA, J. M. *The Dutch in the Atlantic Slave Trade 1600–1815*. New York: Cambridge University Press, 1990.

RENKEMA, W. E. *Het Curaçaose plantagebedrijf in de negentiende eeuw*. Zutphen: Walburg Pers, 1981.

STIPRIAAN, A. *Surinaams contrast: Roofbouw en overleven in een Caraïbische plantagekolonie 1750–1863*. Leiden: KITLV-Press, 1993.

CHAPTER 8

FRENCH CARIBBEAN

JOHN GARRIGUS

INTRODUCTION

Pierre d'Esnambuc, a Norman sailor, planted France's first Caribbean colony on the tiny Lesser Antillean island of St Christopher in 1625. The settlement, as d'Esnambuc himself noted, contained several dozen slaves. Although Great Britain removed this French foothold at the end of the War of the Spanish Succession (1701–14), slavery expanded under French auspices, albeit in fits and starts, to other islands during the seventeenth century. Guadeloupe and Martinique, colonized in 1635, became France's two most important Lesser Antillean possessions, boasting slave majorities before the last quarter of the seventeenth century. Slavery peaked in the French Caribbean during the eighteenth century as French slave traders carried more than one million slaves to the Americas. Indeed, Saint-Domingue, the western third of the island of Hispaniola, received roughly 800,000 slaves (about 70 percent of the total to the French Americas) and ranked in the 1780s as perhaps the world's most valuable colony with more than 450,000 slaves. In 1789, Martinique and Guadeloupe possessed around 81,000 and 89,000 slaves, respectively. France and the Netherlands jointly occupied the tiny island of St Martin/St Maarten, dotted with valuable salt ponds, after the Spanish were driven off in the mid-seventeenth century. By 1780, perhaps 600 slaves worked there raking salt and growing tobacco. French Guiana (Cayenne), on the South American mainland, which had a temporary French presence as early as 1626, had approximately 10,000 enslaved people in the 1780s, rising to 19,000 in the 1830s.[1] When the Provisional Government of the Second French Republic decreed the abolition of slavery throughout the French empire on 27 April 1848, bondage ended in the French Caribbean for 174,000 slaves.

France also controlled a half dozen other slave territories at various times in the seventeenth and eighteenth centuries, though slavery in most of these societies has until recently received little historical attention. In the Indian Ocean island of Mauritius, French colonists enslaved some 60,000 people from 1715 to 1809, before British rule began. In the Caribbean, France ceded a number of island territories to Britain, and in nearly all of them, French colonists had first introduced slavery. In 1778, French Dominica had 14,309 slaves; St Lucia had 13,784 in 1788. Grenada had 11,991 slaves in 1753, a decade before France ceded it to the British. On the North American mainland, Louisiana, a French possession from 1699 to 1763, had little more than 5,000 slaves when it was turned over to the Spanish after the end of the Seven Years War. Metropolitan France, by contrast, contained between 4,000 and 5,000 free and enslaved people of African ancestry when the French Revolution began in 1789.[2]

Four important themes have emerged from the scholarship on slavery in the French Caribbean.[3] First and foremost, historians have sought to describe the material nature of the peculiar institution. How many people were enslaved? What was their experience in the slave trade? What were the physical conditions in which they lived, worked, and died in the French Antilles? Second and more recently, the cultural nature of French slavery has attracted scholarly attention. Historians like Pierre de Vaissière in the early twentieth century examined white creole culture in French Caribbean slave societies, but academic historians did not consider the cultural ramifications of French slavery on the slaves themselves until the late 1940s, when historians in the United States began to study the legacies of plantation slavery throughout the New World. In the 1970s. David Brion Davis in the USA, Michèle Duchet in France, and others began to analyze the relationship between the Enlightenment and colonial slavery.

Scholarship on the political nature of French slavery constitutes a third major theme, one which cannot be neatly separated from the theme of "revolution," for Saint-Domingue gave rise during the French Revolution to a momentous slave revolution that produced the world's first black nation-state. In studying the preconditions of the Saint-Domingue Revolution (1791–1804) an important debate has surfaced about the character of French colonial slavery, about changing patterns of resistance, and about the apparent lack of organized rebellion in the French Antilles before the great uprising in August 1791. The fourth theme, the ostensible disappearance of race and especially slavery in France's national experience and memory, has emerged since 1998, as social tensions within metropolitan France have challenged the idea of a colorblind French Republic.

PLANTATION SLAVERY AND
ITS HISTORIOGRAPHY

Most slaves in the French Caribbean labored on plantations and in other commercial enterprises. The surviving records of those institutions often contain information about the material aspects of slaves' lives: their numbers and ages, their genders and ethnic identities, and their transportation to the New World. To a lesser extent slaves' working conditions and approximate survival rates can be reconstructed from these sources. The difficulty has been that these records were often in private hands, sometimes held by individuals who were unaware of their scholarly value or embarrassed by this aspect of their family history.

French Caribbean agriculture began in St Christopher (St Kitts) after 1625 and continued with the establishment of colonies in 1635 on the larger but still relatively small islands of Martinique and Guadeloupe. The tobacco that colonists grew for export in this early period required minimal processing after harvest and was, at first, highly valuable. Two or three men could grow enough to make a good profit and French servants were far less expensive than enslaved Africans. In the early 1630s there were only fifty black captive workers in French St Christopher, outnumbered by 500 colonists.

By the end of the decade, the price of Caribbean tobacco had fallen some 80 percent and even though it revived a bit in the 1640s and 1650s, French colonists began looking for more valuable exports. Cacao, the base ingredient in chocolate, was one alternative for small farmers. But it was highly susceptible to disease, and the chocolate market in Europe grew slowly until sugar to sweeten the product became more affordable. For ex-tobacco farmers, the problem with sugar was that it required extensive on-site manufacturing, since the syrup pressed from the sugar cane spoiled quickly. To pay for these installations, farmers required extensive land, and then, considerable labor to work the fields and factory. Although there were experimental sugar plantations in the 1640s, it was only after 1654, when refugees from a failed Dutch attempt to conquer Portuguese sugar territories in northern Brazil arrived in the Caribbean, that colonists in Martinique, St Christopher, and Guadeloupe had access to the technical knowledge to successfully manufacture brown sugar. Because it required more land, labor, and processing equipment than any previous crop, sugar eventually transformed French Caribbean society. Martinique was the fastest to move to sugar; Guadeloupe and St Christopher took more time. All these colonies were far behind the English West Indies, in large part due to France's fledgling slave trade. French planters had to buy many of their African captives from Dutch and English traders.

This slow start was even more true for the tobacco-planting colonists on the western coast of Santo Domingo, abandoned by the Spanish. The French called this territory "Saint-Domingue," and they sent governors there who by the 1650s had convinced the preexisting buccaneer populations to accept their authority. Tobacco was still the main crop for colonists, but in the 1670s many would start to plant indigo, a bush that produces a blue dye when soaked in water. But indigo planters needed masonry soaking vats, and considerable technical knowledge to distill the dye. They also needed a dozen or more workers to grow and tend enough plants to produce saleable quantities of high-quality dye.

Thanks in large part to Dutch traders who provided slaves, credit, and technical knowledge, Martinique had become by the 1660s a majority black society. Guadeloupe reached this point in the early 1670s, and Saint-Domingue did not reach it until the 1690s. In 1700 there were fewer slaves in the entire French Caribbean than in either Barbados or Jamaica. Still, in Martinique that year the slave population outnumbered masters, 15,266 to 6,774. Guadeloupe lagged behind with 6,855 slaves and 4,466 whites. But in 1700 Saint-Domingue, where indigo cultivation was taking off, had two times as many slaves as free people, 9,082 to 4,560.[4]

Recent scholarship argues that talk of a "sugar revolution" in either the English or French Caribbean in the seventeenth century exaggerates the rate of social and agricultural change.[5] But as aspiring sugar planters gradually bought up tobacco farms and acquired African workers, immigration from France slowed to a trickle. In the early 1700s French colonists struck out for new lands in the islands of Dominica, St Lucia, and St Vincent, islands that were still partly occupied by warlike Carib people whom the French had driven from Martinique and Guadeloupe by the 1650s.

Shortly after Spain recognized Saint-Domingue as a French possession in 1697, the colony experienced economic take-off. From 1685 to 1700, thanks to indigo, the enslaved population tripled, surpassing that of whites. It tripled again from 1700 to 1715 and doubled up to 1730. In the 1730s, after the French slave trade was thrown open to merchants from France's largest Atlantic ports, sugar plantations began to flourish in Saint-Domingue's rich alluvial plains. The rise of major irrigation projects in the 1750s swelled the enslaved population even more, although the commercial blockades of the Seven Years War slowed slave imports, as did growing British power on the West African coast. But French slave traders, as described below, moved to other African ports, farther south.

The introduction of a profitable new product, coffee, into the French Caribbean in the 1720s and 1730s accelerated the growth of slavery there. Coffee plantations expanded rapidly in Martinique after 1727 when an earthquake and years of fungus wiped out the island's cacao plantations. Coffee, unlike sugar, thrived on cooler hillsides where sugar could not grow and had little of the time-sensitive milling and distilling that required sugar planters to employ a workforce of at least 100 slaves. A coffee plantation required more labor than a cacao grove, but a small estate could subsist on the labor of one or two dozen people.

From Martinique, coffee spread to Saint-Domingue in the mid-1730s, causing a flurry of activity in the 1750s and 1760s. Sugar planters expanded into coffee and new immigrants from France, as well as farmers and ranchers, turned to the new product. In the Lesser Antilles colonies, those who could not find land in well-established Martinique and Guadeloupe staked claims and built coffee estates in the 1740s in the nearby islands of Dominica, St Lucia, St Vincent, and Grenada, even though France and Great Britain disputed possession of these islands. As coffee cultivation spread, so did French slave imports. By the 1770s, the enslaved populations of Martinique and Guadeloupe were largely creole, or island born. But new estates demanded new workers, and these demands intensified especially in Saint-Domingue, where the coffee phenomenon, coming on top of an extraordinarily high death rate on sugar plantations, required ever-greater infusions of new African workers. The end of the American Revolutionary War in 1783 brought the French slave trade and the enslaved population of the French Caribbean to its highest levels ever by the time of the outbreak of the Haitian Revolution in 1791.

The earliest retrospective writings about French slavery were produced in the aftermath of that revolution, as Haitian intellectuals like the Baron de Vastey defended their new state's rejection of France and French officials and ex-colonists like Pierre-Victor Malouet argued that France should recapture Saint-Domingue. But these authors focused on the revolution far more than on slavery itself, despite the title of books like Gastine de Civique's 1819 antislavery *Histoire de la république d'Haïti ou Saint-Domingue, l'esclavage et les colons.* In 1825 Charles X ended this era by recognizing Haitian independence. Nevertheless, when Haiti's most important early historians like Thomas Madiou and Beaubrun Ardouin published multi-volume works they remained far more interested in preserving the memory of their nation's revolution than in dissecting the slave period that preceded it.

A similar polemic style characterized a second wave of publications, this time about the future—and the past—of slavery in Martinique and Guadeloupe. In 1847, the year before France finally ended slavery in its territories, the Guadeloupean planter Adrien Dessales published a five-volume history designed to defend his class and explain the colonial society they had created. Victor Schoelcher, France's leading abolitionist in the 1830s and 1840s, described himself as a "historian of slavery" but, even more than the planters, he wrote for political audiences.[6]

The first scholarly historians of French slavery wrote in the era of "new imperialism," which for France was launched after 1871 as the Third Republic sought to recover from the humiliation of the Franco-Prussian War. These pro-colonial works reflected the "scientific" racism of that period. At a time when imperial administrators in France were systematizing the colonial archives, these historians specialized in maritime history, and their greatest contribution to the field was in analyzing the slave trade. In 1897, for example, Lucien Peytraud produced a volume about slavery, based on state papers, mostly laws, administrative correspondence, and official memoranda on the colonies.

Peytraud's work was thorough and deep, covering the slave trade, and topics like slavery in France itself that were ignored by later historians. Although he described Saint-Domingue, Peytraud scarcely mentioned the revolution against slavery, for his real goal was to provide historical context for French colonial administrators struggling to understand and govern Martinique, Guadeloupe, or La Guyane. Like the Antillean planter-historians of the nineteenth century, Peytraud believed France had forced slavery on its territories, creating great wealth but also setting up long-term consequences for economic development. Peytraud's readers could craft better policies for the empire if they understood his views: Slavery destroyed the colonial work ethic, suppressed economic innovation, and prevented the emergence of a middle class. Without understanding the impact of slavery, Peytraud suggested, one might believe that France had failed in the "civilizing mission" it used to justify its post-1870 expansion into Africa and Asia. In addition to slavery's corrupting influence, the new racial "science" of Peytraud's time offered other explanations for what he described as the economic and cultural stagnation of the Antilles. Apparently referring to the racial hybridity that some theorists believed sapped the energy and creativity of "pure" races, Peytraud noted the mixture of African and European people in the Antilles posed great problems for those societies and for France.[7]

In 1935, the French empire celebrated its 300-year anniversary of colonization in Martinique and Guadeloupe. In that year the young historian Louis-Philippe May, who had completed a 1930 doctoral dissertation on the economic history of the *ancien régime* in Martinique, coauthored with Alfred Martineau, a colonial governor-general, *Trois siècles d'histoire antillaise, Martinique et Guadeloupe*. On the one hand, the authors interpreted slavery in a way that, today, seems unusual for an economic historian like May; they described it as a source of cheap labor and said little about planters' chronic indebtedness to French merchants and slave traders. They portrayed these colonial slave societies as divided by racial rather than economic tensions and celebrated the benevolence of the royal government, which after 1763, they claimed, was trying to end slavery gradually. The authors blamed planters for defeating reforms that would have accelerated emancipation. The era of the French and Haitian revolutions was an even greater disaster, for it "set back by 50 years the reforms prepared by the monarchy." Like Peytraud, essentially, the authors described slavery as an economic, moral, and political obstacle that the colonies had to overcome. On the other hand, they were more optimistic than Peytraud about racial mixture, hailing the French emancipation act of 1848 as "the origin of another civilization." They called on the *Antillais*, natives of the West Indies, "to brew together their blood, self-interest, and aspirations and, with the help of time and the sun, to form gradually a single half-tone race."[8]

The Second World War opened a new period in the historiography of French slavery. From the 1940s until well after the 1970s, the French-born historian Gabriel Debien dominated the field. Although his predecessors had recognized that slavery shaped colonial society, they were writing to educate future colonial administrators. Moreover, they approached their study of the institution largely through government documents. Debien, in contrast, was not writing to justify French imperialism and in any event he was more interested in agriculture than administration. One of his great achievements was to unearth a wealth of plantation papers in private and local archives throughout western France. He used these to write dozens of plantation case studies, the first of which appeared in 1941.[9] Inspired by the social science methodology of France's *Annales* school and by the plantation studies being produced in the United States, Debien revealed the remarkable diversity of French slavery in the Caribbean. He documented the high mortality rates on French plantations, the range of estate sizes and profit margins, their organization of labor, and the immense cultural variety among their enslaved African-born and American-born work crews. But without computers to help him analyze this data, he never produced a synthesis that matched the subtlety and range of his case studies. He himself described his 450-page *Les Esclaves aux Antilles françaises* (1974) as "a sheaf of notes."[10] Although Debien was quite aware of the new English-language scholarship on the slave trade, plantation demographics, slave culture, and resistance, his best-known and most comprehensive volume on French Caribbean slavery did not engage this literature.

By the time of Debien's posting to the University of Nantes (1967–72), a small group of other scholars, some of them his students, had begun publishing similar work on the plantation system. In the 1970s and 1980s, French scholars, under Debien's influence, began using notarial documents, parish registers, and other kinds of records to further illuminate the intricacies of slave life. The most original among these researchers was Arlette Gautier, who published a nuanced history of enslaved women in the French Antilles in 1985. Looking at the place of women in French slavery, Gautier went beyond traditional legal, administrative, and travelers' texts to work through thousands of notarized contracts from eighteenth-century Saint-Domingue and Guadeloupe. These documents allowed her to show, for example, how enslaved women remained excluded from skilled plantation jobs; the sales of female housekeepers, who managed a plantation's domestic staff, showed that they were priced far below top-ranking male workers. Countering the evidence that enslaved women were two to three times more likely to be manumitted than men, she calculated that less than 3 percent of Martiniquan and 10 percent of Saint-Domingue slave concubines received freedom. She showed that French authorities made only limited attempts to encourage the birth and survival of enslaved children, and that these "pro-natalist" policies constituted new burdens for enslaved women.

A serious challenge to Debien's plantation-centered vision of French Antillean history did not emerge until 2000, when Anne Pérotin-Dumon called for a rethinking of French Caribbean history that would recognize the importance of colonial port cities as well as plantations.[11] In the 1980s, David Geggus, a historian trained in England and working in the United States, assumed Debien's mantle as the leading historian of French slavery and of the Haitian Revolution.[12] By 1989 he had assembled a database with information on more than 13,000 enslaved people living on more than 400 plantations. In a host of tightly argued articles stressing the scale and complexity of French Caribbean slavery, Geggus, unlike Debien with his case studies, succeeded in extracting critical patterns from this data. He compared slave sex ratios and birth rates on sugar, indigo, and coffee plantations to show how the heavy work routines of a sugar estate appeared to be responsible for the extraordinary low birth rate in Saint-Domingue. The fertility index for enslaved women on coffee and indigo estates was about 50 percent lower than eighteenth-century European rates or twentieth-century African rates. It was 66 percent lower for enslaved women on sugar plantations.[13] In coffee and indigo estates then, enslaved women were notably more able to produce surviving children.

Despite these welcome advances, neither Debien nor Geggus was able to deliver a single number on slave mortality in the French Caribbean, which varied in different case studies from 5 to 6 percent to 10 percent and even higher.[14] Debien estimated that half of all newly arrived Africans would die within eight years of beginning plantation work but he, Geggus, and other researchers have been forced to note the enormous diversity of slave conditions, even in sugar plantations, which were not uniformly massive, as some authors have maintained. Even in Saint-Domingue's North Province, known as the colony's center of sugar production, Geggus found the mean size of sugar estates in his sample amounted to 182 slaves.

Acknowledging that planters' notations on slave ethnicities are dauntingly difficult to interpret, Geggus also shed new light on this source of information, comparing plantation records with data on the Atlantic slave trade. He showed that the ethnic numbers, sex ratios, and adult/child ratios were comparable between the two data sets. He documented that Saint-Domingue's coffee planters, building estates in the second half of the eighteenth century with limited funds, staffed their workforces with enslaved Africans from the Kongo, or West-Central, region of Africa; wealthier sugar planters, in contrast, purchased more desirable enslaved workers from the West Africa coast, especially the Bight of Benin. Sex ratios differed as well between these types of plantations, with greater parity between women and men on coffee plantations. He then linked these conclusions backwards to the slave trade, suggesting, for example, that sex ratios were a product of African, not European slave preferences. By investigating the ethnic profile of Saint-Domingue's northern plain where the 1791 insurrection broke out, Geggus revealed the impressive political achievement of the revolt's enslaved creole planners, many of them enslaved agricultural foremen (*commandeurs*), in crafting a rebel alliance with newly arrived Africans.[15]

THE FRENCH SLAVE TRADE

France never developed a strong abolitionist movement like that of England and, for this reason, its role as a major slave trading power remains, to this day, largely unknown by the French public. Yet the attempts of the French state to build its maritime power in the 1700s did create an extraordinarily complete set of documents, tracking the departures and arrivals of French vessels, including slave traders. Historians' exploitation of these sources has created a picture of French slave trading activity that today is more complete than that of almost any other nation.

The first recorded French vessel involved in the slave trade sailed from Le Havre in 1571 and was captured while selling African captives to Spanish colonists at Margarita, off the Venezuelan coast. Although Martinique and Guadeloupe had thousands of African captives by 1660, many of them were carried across the Atlantic by Dutch traders. In 1664, Louis XIV's government gave monopoly rights over the trade with Africa and the Caribbean to the royally chartered French Company of the West Indies. Hoping to build up French maritime power vis-à-vis the Dutch, France remained committed to this mercantilistic approach into the early eighteenth century, despite the failures of nearly all these companies. This strategy meant that for much of the seventeenth century private slave voyages by French merchants were illegal and thus went largely unrecorded. In 1716 the royal government allowed merchants from four major French port cities to buy captives in Africa and to sell them to French Caribbean colonists. Not until 1725, however, did the trade truly open up to private traders.

France carried about one-eighth of all Africans traded across the Atlantic, but French colonists also bought captive workers from smugglers, especially in Saint-Domingue, whose dynamic plantation economy and high mortality rates outstripped the ability of French merchants to supply them with slaves. In the eighteenth century the British navy routinely shut down all French Atlantic commerce in wartime. But the French slave trade grew dramatically from twenty-eight voyages in the year 1715 to sixty-five in 1741. After the American Revolutionary War (1776–83) the trade doubled in size to 114 slave trading voyages in 1787, hitting an unprecedented peak of 149 in 1790. The French and Haitian revolutions stopped the legal trade entirely until the end of the Napoleonic Wars in 1815. By this time the British were pressuring the French to end the trade, but the updating and rebuilding of plantations in Guadeloupe and Martinique brought fifty-three voyages in 1822 and thirty-six voyages in 1825. The last recorded French voyage was in 1864, for French smugglers continued to bring captured Africans to slave societies like the southern United States and Cuba long after 1831, when France began to enforce its 1818 anti-slave trading laws.

The centralization of French maritime administration created records that have made France the most thoroughly researched of all the western European slave trading nations at least in terms of the overall number of voyages. Much of the early scholarly work in this field, as was the case with the early research into plantation records, proved more important for finding and publicizing these sources than for interpreting them. Although Peytraud devoted roughly one-third of his 1897 book to the slave trade, it was in 1931 that Gaston Martin began the quantitative analysis of the commerce, using Admiralty records for 787 voyages from Nantes, France's leading slave trading port. In 1938 Father Dieudonné Rinchon published more Admiralty data from Nantes, but still gave only a partial set. Rinchon made greatest use of records from individual firms to argue that slave traders were respected merchants and notable members of society during the *ancien régime*.[16]

The real value of these Admiralty records became obvious in 1969 when the American scholar Philip Curtin published his pathbreaking "census" of the Atlantic slave trade in 1969. For France, Curtin used Rinchon's publications and checked their accuracy against Debien's analysis of African ethnicities in plantation slave lists. The attention given to Curtin's work attracted the Canadian scholar Robert Stein to the Admiralty archives in Nantes. His 1979 survey followed the path laid by Rinchon and others in depicting the French slave trade as a respected trade and "old regime business." But the most extensive analysis of all Nantes merchants, not only slave traders, came in the 1969 book by Jean Meyer. His analysis of account books showed the extraordinary profits of French slave traders and colonial merchants in Nantes, where one major trading family doubled its capital every decade. But Meyer also showed how the slave trade became less profitable by the end of the eighteenth century, as colonial planters became progressively more indebted and slower to pay for their human merchandise.

Jean Mettas attempted to follow Meyer's analytic lead with a monumental thesis on the French slave trade. But his premature death meant that his great accomplishment, made possible by his colleague Serge Daget, was to compile a nearly complete set of slave trade data for others to analyze. Published in 1978 and 1984, the Mettas–Daget volumes captured most of the existing French Admiralty documents, especially from the eighteenth and nineteenth centuries.[17] Although Nantes, with 40 percent of the French slave trade, was by far the most important, in 1995 Eric Saugéra showed that Bordeaux, France's largest Atlantic port, was also deeply involved in the slave trade, especially after the Seven Years War (1756–63). In the nineteenth century Bordeaux led France's slave trade as this commerce dwindled.

In 1999 a team of scholars affiliated with Harvard University's Du Bois Institute published a database combining the data earlier researchers had compiled on the slave trades of all the major trading nations. With records from an estimated two-thirds of all Atlantic slaving voyages the database, transformed into a website in 2008, made it possible to rank France as the third leading carrier of slaves to the Americas during the entire history of the Atlantic slave trade, moving 13 percent of all captives, compared to Portugal's 46 percent and Britain's 29 percent. Saint-Domingue received a few hundred thousand fewer slaves than the one million or so that went to Jamaica, but the French colony out-produced the British island in sugar and coffee, revealing the high level of French capital investment in irrigation and sugar mills. The British Caribbean received far more slaves than their French counterparts, but Saint-Domingue's chief port, Cap Français, was the third largest debarkation area for Africans in the New World and the largest in the Caribbean.[18]

The Dubois database allowed historians to trace the shifting flow of the French slave trade. Despite France's long historical association with Sénégal, where in 1659 France established Saint-Louis, the oldest European-founded city in Africa, most of the French slave trade in the first half of the 1700s came from Africa's Gold Coast or the "Slave Coast" region, especially the major African slave trading city of Ouidah, in modern-day Benin. In the second half of the century, traders drew heavily from far down the coast in modern-day Angola and Congo. In the late eighteen and early nineteenth centuries, French traders bought captives from as far as East Africa. Overall, about a quarter of all French slave purchases came from the Ouidah and other ports in the Bight of Benin and 36 percent came from Angola or Kongo ports.

A counterpart to the highly quantitative study of the trade is Robert Harms, *The Voyage of the Diligent* (2002), which follows, in extraordinary detail, a single slave trading voyage from western France to West Africa, to Martinique and back to France in 1731–2. Based on the on-board journal of a junior officer, Harms's book illustrates the many unique events that shaped a single voyage, from political turmoil in the African kingdoms of Jakin and Ouidah to a cacao plague in Martinique that devastated demand for new Africans at the moment of the *Diligent's* arrival there.

Although the French signed a treaty with Great Britain in 1818 ending the slave trade, an illegal French slave trade thrived for several more decades, as economic protection from Paris breathed new life into the French Antillean sugar industry. Serge Daget remains the leading historian of this illegal trade, which brought another 85,000 Africans to the Antilles after the treaty date. Christopher Miller's literary study *The French Atlantic Triangle* (2008) described how the marginal importance of nineteenth-century French abolitionism resulted in numerous popular novels in the nineteenth century romanticizing the slave trade as a form of piracy and opposition to British naval power. Miller describes how France's most popular "abolitionist" novel, Prosper Mérimée's *Tamango* (1830), is actually profoundly dismissive of Africans' humanity.

Even after the slave trade withered away, subsidies and an expanding world market for sugar into the mid-1830s led planters in Martinique and Guadeloupe to expand production, apply new techniques of fertilization to depleted soils, adopt new technologies, and acquire more slaves. At the same time, coffee and cotton growing collapsed. In 1990 the Marxisant sociologist Dale Tomich described the ways in which lower sugar prices on the world market after the 1830s gave more autonomy to Martinique's plantation slaves, even while political forces continued to support the plantation system. Financial pressures on planters forced some of them to change from gang labor to task labor and to increase the size of slaves' gardens or provision grounds so that slaves could produce more of their own food. Some slaves improved their lives by earning income from surpluses produced from these plots and marketed.[19]

RACE AND CULTURE

Attempts to describe the cultural nature of French slavery have attracted a broader range of scholars than those focused on the study of plantation registers and slave trading voyages. Historians who wrote during the imperial period condemned slavery but disparaged the emergence of African-influenced cultures in France's colonies and glorified the achievements of colonial administrators. In 1909 the French historian Pierre de Vaissière devoted the longest of his four chapters on Saint-Domingue to the colony's "Black World." Despite attention to the details of slave torture cases, Vaissière concluded that "there is a tendency to exaggerate the misery" of the slaves. He described mixed marriages as "deplorable" and noted that there was still a debate over the "true nature of blacks." In the late 1920s Jules Saintoyant, a French army officer who had served in the Congo, concluded that France's 1685 Code Noir, the first comprehensive slave code ever issued by the Crown, limited masters' power over slaves to an extent unmatched by any other empire's slave law. He echoed Vaissière in rebuking abolitionists for overstating the harshness of slavery. In a work published in 1948, Gaston Martin followed in the imperial tradition of using history to explain what colonial administrators might have regarded as the flaws in "our islands." For Martin, not only had wealth and slavery created deep social tensions in the French Caribbean, they had created a unique set of creole vices—drunkenness, laziness, jealousy, cruelty—to which the mix of African cultures had decisively contributed. Like the colonial administrators of his generation, he believed that racial science might explain what history could only describe. Somewhat puzzled that the islands' long history of racial mixture "has nevertheless never resulted in creating a stabilized and homogenous standard [racial] type," Martin hoped that racial anthropology would someday provide the key to understanding colonial society.[20]

By the 1960s, Gabriel Debien had begun writing about slavery in ways that shared none of the imperial preoccupations of the men who had trained him. For one thing, Debien's case studies discredited the notion of a relatively humane French slavery, a point that Haitian authors had been disputing since 1804. Early nineteenth-century Haitian scholars had emphasized not only the harshness of French slavery, but also the virulence of French racism, especially its impact on Saint-Domingue's large free population of mixed European-African descent. In the 1840s Thomas Madiou and Beaubrun Ardouin, the most important of Haiti's first generation of historians, contended that free people of color had initiated the revolution that overthrew slavery and colonialism. Writing between 1853 and 1863, Beauvais Lespinasse produced a deeply researched work to argue that "France used every resource to instill color prejudice in Saint-Domingue." By the second half of the 1800s, the historiography of the Haitian Revolution had shifted to emphasize the role of enslaved black leaders, rather than mulatto elites. Until the 1950s, however, Haitian historians did not closely examine the history of slavery beyond noting it as a cause of their great revolution.[21]

The question of how French culture shaped Caribbean slavery did attract scholarly interest in the United States. In 1946 Frank Tannenbaum, a historian of Latin America, published *Slave and Citizen*, an explicitly comparative essay that contrasted United States racism with its "one-drop" rule of black identity with Latin America's more nuanced and flexible racial categories. For Tannenbaum, Catholicism and the Roman law traditions of Spain and Portugal forced masters to recognize the humanity of their slaves and provided them with certain rights sanctified by positive law. In such cultural systems, he suggested, slaves had more ways to defend themselves from abuse and enjoyed greater access to freedom through, for example, manumission or self-purchase than in the Protestant Anglo-American colonies based on the common law. The elites of these Iberian colonies, claimed Tannenbaum, accepted large free populations of African descent and were generally more accepting of racial mixture than elites in British America.[22]

Tannenbaum overlooked French slavery and racism in his analysis, and, in truth, even African-American intellectuals in the United States knew little of the eighteenth- and nineteenth-century writers that Mercer Cook described in *Five French Negro Authors* (1943). In 1966, as African-Americans struggled for civil rights, Shelby McCloy broke ground by examining the history of slavery and racial categories in the French Antilles. He observed a striking difference between racial attitudes in the United States and France. Across the Atlantic, however, intellectuals living through the dismantling of France's empire remained less sure that France and the USA had a different racial history. Indeed, in 1967 the French sociologist Yvan Debbasch produced a deeply researched study of what he described as "segregationism" in the French Antilles.[23] Debbasch described how racism against colonial free people of color grew increasingly rigid over the course of the 1700s.

In the 1970s, detailed studies of French slavery and racism joined an emerging comparative literature in testing Tannenbaum's thesis of "cultural determinism." In a 1971 book Gwendolyn Midlo Hall compared racism and slavery in Saint-Domingue and Cuba. The following year, David Cohen and Jack Greene published *Neither Slave Nor Free*, a collection of essays comparing the conditions of life for free and enslaved people of color in ten different New World slave societies, including Martinique, Guadeloupe, and Saint-Domingue. These comparative studies argued that economic and demographic factors, not culture, determined the conditions of slave life and attitudes towards African ancestry. Societies with highly profitable and ever-expanding plantation economies, especially in sugar, where enslaved workers vastly outnumbered Europeans and their descendants, shared similar patterns: harsh slave punishments, a low proportion of manumissions to the total enslaved population, and intensifying racial discrimination against free people of African ancestry. For Hall, as for Cohen and Greene and their contributors, the presence or absence of Catholicism and Roman law traditions seemed to make no difference in slave treatment.[24]

Nevertheless, scholars of cultural history continued to wrestle with the ways France's European culture interacted with Caribbean slavery. In 1971, Michèle Duchet's history of Enlightenment anthropological thought convicted French *philosophes*, colonial administrators, and Antillean slave owners of constructing a racialist discourse that counterposed Western civilization to non-Western savagery. While otherwise excellent accounts of colonial science ignored how the Enlightenment reified racial categories, scholars on both sides of the Atlantic traced the growth of racial thinking among scientists and jurists in metropolitan France. In a series of insightful articles, the Canadian historian Pierre H. Boulle dissected how political and scientific concerns of the Enlightenment reinforced colonial racism and contributed to the origins of modern racial thinking. Like Duchet, Boulle showed that Antilles planters, enlightened biologists, and colonial bureaucrats shared the same goal of ensuring the safety and long-term profitability of colonial slave society.[25]

In 1965 Antoine Gisler examined the relations between slavery and French ecclesiastical culture. He explained how in the Antilles, even among priests and missionaries, the church fathers' view that slavery could teach Christian virtues like obedience and humility gave way to a racial theory of slavery that recognized masters' need to terrorize their heathenish bondsmen. By the 1830s, attempts by pious Parisian elites to draft legislation that would "moralize" slaves while humanizing their living conditions were opposed as fiercely by some colonial priests as by planters. Philippe Delisle, who has examined the missionary activities of the Church in Martinique in the last years of slavery, shows that even in the late 1830s, when the French government and Church finally began to try to build rural chapels and primary schools for the slaves, planters blocked their efforts.[26]

In 1987, the philosopher Louis Sala-Molins's book on the Code Noir rejected Gisler's juxtaposition of theory and practice. He exposed the racist and dehumanizing assumptions in this 1685 codification of French slave law, suggesting that there was no significant evolution in institutional attitudes from the 1600s to the 1700s. Alan Watson, however, a legal scholar, sided with Gisler. He argued that Roman slave laws did shape the Code Noir and French slave society by giving masters wide power to free their slaves. Colonial administrators tried but were unable to eliminate this practice.

In fact, by the end of the eighteenth century, France's slave colonies did have a free population of African descent that was larger, wealthier, and more self-confident in legal matters than that in any other slave society in the New World. By the late 1980s, surveys of slavery in the New World reflected this view.[27] According to the best estimates, Saint-Domingue had nearly as many free people of color as whites, making people of African ancestry roughly 45 percent of the free population. In the comparable British colony of Jamaica, free coloreds made up only 19 percent of the free population. In Martinique and Guadeloupe, free coloreds made up 26 percent of the free population, far more than the 4.9 percent found in the similarly sized British colony of Barbados. Dominique Rogers, working with the judicial archives of Saint-Domingue, showed that, despite the complaints of their leaders, free men and women of color there were quite able to use the colonial law courts in the 1770s to bring charges against whites, and win cases. Rogers argued that in the context of old regime society, free people of color enjoyed nearly full civil rights, including the ability to inherit and transmit property.

As historians tried to understand the development of racism within the French Atlantic empire, Guillaume Aubert published in 2004 an innovative article that described the connections between racism in French Canada and the Caribbean. Denying that the French were less prejudiced than contemporary English colonists about Indians and Africans, Aubert showed how sixteenth- and seventeenth-century concerns about noble purity and *mésalliance*, or mixed noble–commoner marriages, shaped attitudes about marriages between French colonists and Indians on the North American mainland and between French colonists and Africans in the Caribbean. He showed that colonial administrators disagreed over whether to encourage colonists to marry non-Europeans and whether the children from such unions should be considered French. By the 1730s, officials in French America had outlawed interracial marriages, everyplace but in Saint-Domingue.

Another new development in this debate over whether France had distinctive racial attitudes was historians' use of local rather than imperial records to examine racial practices. In an article in 1989, John Garrigus used notarial records to illustrate that through the 1760s colonial society considered many of Saint-Domingue's most prominent free people of color to be "white"; it was only after 1769 that colonists began to apply racial labels to them. In a later work he argued that the new obsession with "white" and "non-white" categories in Saint-Domingue derived from political tensions within the empire after Britain defeated France in the Seven Years War. In other words, racism within the free population was not a pressing factor early in colonial history; racism became important later on because the idea of white "purity" could unite both rich and poor colonists from France with island-born whites, ostensibly strengthening France's hold on the colony. At the same time these new racial laws put wealthy slave owning free-born people of color, a group that was at most composed of 300 individuals, into the same social group as ex-slaves. During the early 1790s, these wealthy light-skinned men would make racism, not slavery, into the central colonial controversy in the French Revolution, destabilizing Saint-Domingue. Stewart King also used notarial records to suggest the existence of a free colored "military leadership class" in Saint-Domingue, distinct from the colony's wealthy free colored planters. Though he did not look at the colony's revolutionary period, King suggested that up to 1789 the close social and cultural ties among free colored militiamen and enslaved workers made these men logical rebel leaders during the Haitian Revolution. One of the most provocative examples of the way free persons of color provided military leadership to slave rebels emerged in the discovery, published in 1977 by Debien (with Marie-Antoinette Ménier and Jean Fouchard), that the future Toussaint Louverture, the most conspicuous leader of Saint-Domingue's slave revolution, had been a free man for over a dozen years before 1791 and even, for some time, a slave owner.[28]

Frédéric Régent's work on race and slavery in revolutionary Guadeloupe began with a deep investigation of pre-revolutionary society. Reconstructing families from parish registers, he found that the royal census dramatically undercounted free people of color. Similarly Dominique Rogers used Saint-Domingue's notarial archive to produce a rich portrait of the free colored populations of Port-au-Prince and Cap Français. She suggests that white and free colored populations were becoming more, not less integrated, into society, despite racial laws. Even more than King and Garrigus, she illustrated that free women of color played important economic roles, accumulating capital in urban real estate.

Other scholars have adopted a more theoretical perspective on questions of race and gender. Garrigus argued that when colonial racial stereotypes shifted in the late 1760s whites began portraying people of mixed African and European ancestry, both women and men, as highly sexual and effeminate. Doris Garraway analyzed accounts of life and travel in French Caribbean slave societies to demonstrate that a more open attitude towards sexuality and a tendency to break with European social mores were important aspects of French colonial culture in this region.[29] In *Haiti, History, and the Gods* (1998) Joan Dayan looked at colonial society from the other direction. Claiming that "vodou practices must be viewed as ritual reenactments of Haiti's colonial past," Dayan tried to grasp how slaves understood their experiences by analyzing the stories and rituals preserved in Haitian Vodou, and comparing them with traditional colonial texts. Like Garaway, she found that the sexual and emotional turmoil experienced by enslaved and free women of color were especially powerful themes in this oral literature.

Appreciation of cultural tensions within the world that the slaves made has come belatedly to the academy. David Geggus has used French slave trade data in combination with his own database of plantation slave lists to explore ethnic diversity among slaves. The slave trade literature shows that French merchants shifted from Senegambia and the Bight of Benin in the late seventeenth century, to the Bight of Benin and West-Central Africa—the Congo region—in the early eighteenth century. Then in the late eighteenth century they came to rely far more heavily on those West-Central African ports. By the very end of the century and in the early 1800s, they were also buying captives from Mozambique in southeast Africa. In the 1960s, Debien's analyses of planters' slave lists drew attention to the numerical importance of Kongo slaves in Saint-Domingue and of African-born slaves generally, who made up about two-thirds of the slave population before the revolution. Geggus's database, plus similar work on plantation lists in Guadeloupe by Nichole Vanony-Frisch, allowed him to clarify the distinctive ethnic profiles of various regions and plantation types in the French Caribbean. The number of Biafrans in the colony's isolated southern peninsula, for example, suggests the importance of British contraband slave trading there. The dominance of Kongo people in the newer coffee plantations of Saint-Domingue's mountains, as well as in the colony's smaller and less valuable indigo estates, stands in contrast to the mixture of different African ethnicities and creole slaves on the colony's sugar plantations.

These profiles have generated a better understanding of the cultural lives of enslaved people in Saint-Domingue. Students of Haitian Vodou, which has many theological similarities to the Benin religion of the same name, had believed until the 1980s that enslaved people from the Bight of Benin dominated Saint-Domingue's slave population. Geggus's work showed how Kongos from West-Central Africa contributed to Saint-Domingue's culture, a finding borne out by anthropologists and other scholars of Haitian Vodou.[30]

For the post-revolutionary era, Françoise Thésée examined the fate of a group of Africans imported to Martinique in 1822, four years after the official end of the French slave trade. Her account of how the colonial government used the surviving free Africans to rebuild the island's capital and its port in the aftermath of the Napoleonic War illustrates how reluctant the French were to abolish the slave trade. In 2000, Arlette Gautier, inspired by debates about slave families in the United States and in the English-speaking Caribbean, published an analysis of a sample of 550 names from the emancipation registers of two parishes in Martinique and from one parish in Guadeloupe. She argued that slave conditions helped produce distinct patterns of family life in today's Antilles, like the lack of two-parent nuclear families. In 2005 Caroline Oudin-Bastide picked up an old theme of imperialist historians, who had argued that the long existence of slavery had created a negative attitude towards work in the French Antilles. After examining a wide variety of texts from Martinique and Guadeloupe in the slave period, especially from the nineteenth century, Oudin-Bastide demonstrated that this was essentially correct; colonial society did disparage manual work and associate it with slavery.[31]

RESISTANCE AND REVOLUTION

One area in the historiography of slavery where Haitian scholars have staked out an important position is the theme of resistance. Unlike neighboring Jamaica, which according to one calculation experienced five revolts and three slave conspiracies between 1730 and 1791, Saint-Domingue had no slave revolts or wars between colonists and maroons between 1730 and 1790. The one slave conspiracy in this same period was a wave of poisonings in 1756 and 1757 attributed to a charismatic maroon known as François Makandal, but contemporaries and some scholars debate whether slaves plotted to carry out these killings.

Since Independence in 1804, Haitians have rejected the idea that the French Revolution was the reason their ancestors were the only enslaved population in the Americas to successfully overthrow white rule. Haitian scholars have emphasized that slaves fought against their condition in everyday acts. Alexis Beaubrun Ardouin, a Haitian politician and historian who published a multi-volume history of Haiti in 1865, maintained, "the blacks proved in all periods that the love of liberty was as strong in them as among other men." The eruption of the Haitian Revolution in 1791 was not the beginning of resistance in Saint-Domingue; it was rather the most successful of enslaved workers' constant struggles against their masters. In describing that pre-revolutionary struggle, nearly all Haitian authors argue that the maroon bands and slave poisoners of the eighteenth century were the forerunners of the 1791 uprising.[32]

The US occupation of Haiti from 1915 to 1934 led Haitian intellectuals to renew their insistence on the deep roots of their revolutionary struggle. At the same time, but for different reasons, French imperialist writers trying to explain the roots of colonial social tensions were also locating resistance at the core of slave life. Jules Saintoyant described slave flight or marronage as a "scourge" and wrote about the use of poison "among the blacks," meaning not only people enslaved in the eighteenth-century Caribbean, but the early twentieth-century colonial subjects of French Congo as well. Gaston Martin wrote that maroons were critical to the success of the revolution, though he did not substantiate this claim.[33]

In 1961–2, the French sociologist Yvan Debbasch published a long essay that he claimed corrected both the nationalistic views of Haitian intellectuals and the long refusal of French historians to study marronage seriously. Drawing on the writings of colonists and administrators, he described a specific set of conditions that motivated slaves' attempts to escape their masters: overwork, unfair punishment, and malnutrition. For Haitian readers and those sympathetic to their position, his observation that African slaves fled bondage more frequently than creole slaves suggested that one could be properly socialized into accepting slavery and that most of Saint-Domingue's enslaved people had come to accept their fate.[34] Debien, in an essay published five years later and based on scores of estate records, agreed with Debbasch's basic position: The principal cause of marronage was mismanagement, often by paid surrogates of absentee owners. Nevertheless he did acknowledge cases in which the motives of these mostly male fugitives could not be reduced to a set of grievances. Slaves did flee the plantations of so-called "good masters." Nor were all poorly managed estates plagued by runaways.[35]

In 1972 the Haitian scholar Jean Fouchard, the best-known Haitian historian to focus on the slave period, "defend[ed] the honor of the Haitian historiography." Fouchard challenged the depiction of pre-revolutionary Saint-Domingue as a relatively peaceful plantation colony. He went through the underexplored history of Saint-Domingue year by year, listing reports of marronage, rebellions, and poisonings. He scoured colonial newspapers from 1764 to 1793, collecting some 48,000 notices of runaway slaves to illustrate the ubiquity of resistance to bondage. He admitted that newly arrived Africans dominated the lists of captured maroons, but pointed out that this was because they were more likely than acculturated creole slaves to be arrested. The omnipresence and diversity of maroons suggested that their desire for freedom transcended specific management practices. Fouchard's thesis, however, has generally not persuaded those who follow his own insistence that "only facts can henceforth count in this debate."[36] David Geggus, chief among the skeptics, examined Fouchard's claims and sources and compared them with his collection of plantation records from the North Province. He concluded that Fouchard probably over-counted maroons and that he incorrectly identified many revolutionary-era leaders with pre-revolutionary maroons of similar name. Although Geggus agreed with Fouchard that the relevant primary sources would never provide reliable statistics on marronage, Geggus maintained contra Fouchard that "marronage [was] primarily an alternative to rebellion, a safety-valve that helps explain the remarkable absence of slave revolts in eighteenth-century Saint Domingue."[37]

Haitian scholars have explored connections between religion and slave resistance. The ethnologist Jean Price-Mars, architect of Haitian *négritude*, which advocated pride in the African roots of Haitian folk culture, argued in 1928 that the Revolution was "born of Vodou." But many anthropologists doubt that the spiritual practices of enslaved people in eighteenth-century Saint-Domingue can be so categorized since the word "Vodou" suggests the existence of a shared body of religious rituals and beliefs. The best-documented historical study of Vodou was a 1987 book by the French historian Pierre Pluchon. His most important findings came in a deep study of the Makandal "conspiracy" of 1757–8 that many historians, Haitian and otherwise, have described as the forerunner of the great 1791 uprising. Pluchon highlighted that top administrators estimated the mysterious poisonings had killed between 6,000 and 7,000 slaves, as well as an even greater number of livestock. Authorities never precisely identified how many whites died, but they agreed this number was much less. Although many planters believed there was a conspiracy to drive the whites from the island, the governor and intendant rejected this idea and Pluchon agreed with their conclusion. Did slaves have access to poison? Contemporaries debated this point but Pluchon did not contest the ability of Makandal and others to kill so many slaves. Nor did he did address the troubling question of why one enslaved man would kill so many others who were also in bondage. Karol Weaver's *Medical Revolutionaries* (2006) came at the question of resistance from a technical, rather than spiritual, perspective. Weaver argued that slave healing practices in Saint-Domingue both allowed slaves to survive their living conditions and, in the case of Makandal, to strike back at whites with poison. Weaver did not, however, challenge the powerful documentation Pluchon had uncovered.

Besides illuminating the scale and nature of the poisoning deaths, Pluchon used testimony from the poisoning cases to illuminate the Afro-creole spiritual practices that some colonists blamed for the mysterious deaths. Generally siding with those who describe Vodou as a belief system that emerged coherently only during or after the Haitian Revolution, Pluchon nevertheless showed the importance of spiritual leaders in the lives of the interrogated slaves. For him these practices "represent more than resistance to the colonial order." While many historians have seen the enslaved population as the sum of the work crews of all the plantations, Pluchon argued that it was "a complex yet coordinated mosaic of confraternities, sects, groups, and ethnic associations where blacks gathered.[who whites] hastily assumed were criminals." For Pluchon, French colonial culture played a key role by giving lip service to the Christianization of slaves. But planters and others prevented the Jesuits from effectively evangelizing the slave population when they realized that enslaved people believed priests possessed extraordinary power.[38]

Sue Peabody has shown the influence that missionaries seem to have had on enslaved people before the Saint-Domingue Revolution. But in focusing attention on the Kongo roots of many of the religious practices of Saint-Domingue's slaves, David Geggus found no evidence to support the idea that Vodou practices were becoming more uniform or were helping to unite slaves before 1791. The situation would be different once the Haitian Revolution began, and some experts see Vodou as a product of this cataclysmic event. Others find its genesis in the nineteenth century, after Haitian Independence. With the help of the Africanist Robin Law, however, Geggus did suggest how creole slave leaders planning the insurrection fused ritual oath-taking practices found in the Dahomey, Gold Coast, and Gulf of Biafra regions of West African coast with Kongolese African practices to bring the Haitian Revolution to life.[39]

For the period after the revolution, work on the political currents associated with slavery in Martinique and Guadeloupe has examined the tensions between masters and slaves. In English, Laurent Dubois is the best-known contributor to this literature. He showed how enslaved Guadeloupeans not only grasped the political ideals enunciated by French revolutionaries, but knowingly proclaimed their own revolutionary identity, from 1794, the date of France's first emancipation, to 1802, when French troops successfully fought a bloody but little known war to restore slavery on the island. Dubois's work followed the path blazed by Anne Pérotin-Dumon, Jacques Adélaïde-Merlande, and Frédéric Régent. John Savage exposed the near hysteria with which Martinique's planters reacted to a wave of slave poisoning cases in the 1820s. Savage described these cases, harshly punished by colonial judges, as a reaction to white fears about the approaching end of slavery. An insurrection, apparently connected to the July Revolution in France and embracing hundreds of slaves, followed in 1831. The use by the rebels of Republican symbols and language, including a tricolor flag inscribed with "liberty or death," raise important questions about the impact of transatlantic political and ideological currents in shaping the content and character of collective slave resistance in the aftermath of the Haitian Revolution. Carrying on the work of Guadeloupean historians on the political actions of slaves during the revolutionary era, Josette Fallope's work on post-revolutionary Guadeloupe analyzed the transition of enslaved people into freedom and eventually citizenship. Emphasizing the interplay of resistance and integration, she charted the ways slaves fought the plantation system and at the same time were gradually pulled into French colonial society. Following Guadeloupe's history from 1802 to 1910, Fallope devoted considerable attention to the colony's free population of color and the emergence of a mixed race and then of a black bourgeoisie. She argued that these groups helped smooth the transformation of the colony's working classes from slaves to citizens.[40]

From the 1960s, as the work of Debien and others led to a greater focus on plantation slavery and the revolutionary era, histories of the French Antilles rarely devoted more than a small fraction of their pages to France's final abolition of slavery. Decreed in Paris during the Revolution of 1848, emancipation, according to the early imperial authors, emanated from the metropolis as the logical culmination of France's republican values, as a process largely unaffected by the enslaved people themselves. This Eurocentric interpretation enshrined the central role of Victor Schoelcher, the author of the decree. In the nineteenth and twentieth centuries, "Schoelcher worship" extended to the point that his birthday became an official holiday in Martinique. But as Lawrence Jennings has pointed out, French abolitionism, unlike its British counterpart, received little popular support and was driven by a gradualist elite. To be sure, Schoelcher was France's most visible and energetic abolitionist, but his vision, which included distributing land to ex-slaves, proved so radical that even his fellow revolutionaries rejected much of it. After 1848 his commitment to socialism and his ongoing work to improve French Caribbean society solidified his image as "the savior of the colonies."[41]

In the 1990s, as the celebration of abolition's sesquicentennial approached, this interpretation of emancipation began to change in the Antilles. Even as French scholars were producing new, more nuanced accounts of Schoelcher and his circle, Jennings drew attention to the importance of colonial free people of color, most notably the Martiniquan Cyril Bissette, who worked in both France and the colonies to end slavery. The question of whether a French savior had liberated Antillean people or whether they had freed themselves surfaced notably in the debate over whether the Antilles should celebrate 27 April or 22 May as the true date of emancipation. Schoelcher's decree dated 27 April; unofficial news of the decree reached Martinique ahead of metropolitan commissioners on 22 May. Martiniquan slaves wasted no time in mobilizing by the thousands to claim their freedom. They burned buildings, killed whites, and pressured the provisional governor of the colony in the port of Saint-Pierre to proclaim emancipation publicly. The governor of Guadeloupe, also under duress, performed similarly.[42]

SLAVERY AND HISTORICAL MEMORY

Since 1998, this *prise de conscience* or historical awakening has spread to metropolitan France, launching a fourth theme in the historiography: the place of slavery in French society and historical memory.[43] Around this time the interpretation and commemoration of French slavery became central issues in a debate about whether the long-standing Jacobin ideal of a single, secular, race-blind French civic identity should cede before the reality of multiple cultural identities in French society. In 1999 there were 1.8 million people of African descent living in French overseas territories and departments and 400,000 more living in metropolitan France. In 1998 Jacques Chirac agreed to hold in metropolitan France on April 27 an official government ceremony that commemorated the 1848 emancipation decree. But the debate about how to interpret slavery and emancipation had already begun. By this time, in fact, historians of French slavery had documented, to the surprise of many French laypersons, that in the eighteenth century thousands of black people had lived in slavery within metropolitan France itself. In the late 1990s public and scholarly interest in colonial slavery grew. Most of the scholarship on slavery in French Guyana—a priority neither for Atlantic slave traders nor for historians of slavery—and in France's Indian Ocean colonies was published after 1998. The government in 1999 established a historical research center devoted to the study of slavery.[44]

On 10 May 2001, the French Parliament designated slavery a crime against humanity by passing the Toubira Law, named for the sponsor, Christiane Toubira, a deputy from French Guyana. On 10 May 2006, France observed for the first time an annual government holiday commemorating the victims of slavery, whose date was carefully chosen to ratify neither the anniversary of the Schoelcher decree nor the Saint-Pierre revolt. Not by coincidence the preceding year had been marked by heated debate and even violence over questions of colonization, racism, and French identity. On 23 February 2005, Parliament passed a law that required school textbooks to consider the positive contributions of French colonial presence overseas. Later that year, Claude Ribbe, a popular historian of Antillean descent, published *Le Crime de Napoléon*, arguing that Napoleon's re-establishment of slavery in 1802 was the equivalent of the Nazi genocide. Since 1990, denial of the Holocaust has been a crime in France, and in late November 2005 a group of activists began a lawsuit against the academic Olivier Pétré-Grenouilleau for claiming in a book on the Atlantic slave trade that however odious the commerce, it does not qualify as genocide. The lawsuit was eventually thrown out. But earlier that month, the deaths of two teenagers of immigrant ancestry after an encounter with the police sparked ten days of rioting in the gritty suburbs around Paris and in other major French cities. In early 2006, President Chirac struck down the February 2005 law about teaching the positive aspects of colonial history.

On a positive note, in 2006–7 the evening soap opera *Tropiques amers* (*Bitter Tropics*), about planters and slaves in revolutionary-era Martinique, became a national hit. It depicted a relatively new if heavily romanticized vision of Antillean slavery and freedom to the viewing public. That same year the French National Archives published a thick and useful research guide. It detailed the public and private archival collections around the nation with materials that related to the slave trade and to slavery.[45] "The issue of slavery—unknown to most Frenchmen until the 1990s," observed the French political scientist Jean-Yves Camus, "is now a matter of public debate.... 'Black consciousness' has emerged around the issues of slavery and cultural/racial domination and today it plays an important role in the fundamental transformation of French society from an assimilationist into a multicultural society."[46]

NOTES

1. Frédéric Régent, *La France et ses esclaves: de la colonisation aux abolitions (1620–1848)* (Paris, 2007), 337. For Saint Domingue, see David P. Geggus, "The Major Port Towns of Saint Domingue in the Later Eighteenth Century," in Franklin W. Knight and Peggy K. Liss (eds), *Atlantic Port Cities: Economy, Culture, and Society in the Atlantic World, 1650–1850* (Knoxville, Tenn., 1991), 102.
2. Colonial numbers from the chart in Régent, *La France et ses esclaves*, 335–8; numbers on metropolitan France are from Erick Noël, *Être noir en France au XVIIIe siècle* (Paris, 2006), 95–7.
3. This essay is much indebted to the deep and perceptive reviews of the literature in the following articles: David P. Geggus, "Slavery and Emancipation in the French Caribbean: Recent Scholarship," in Juanita Debarros, Audra Diptee, and David Trotman (eds.), *Beyond Fragmentation: New Directions in Caribbean Scholarship* (Princeton, 2006), 3–34; Anne Pérotin-Dumon, "Historiography of the French Antilles and French Guiana. Part A: Martinique and Guadeloupe," in Barry W. Higman (ed.), *Methodology and Historiography of the Caribbean* (London, 1999), 631–64; Michel-Rolph Trouillot, "Openness and Closure in Haitian Historical Discourses," in Higman (ed.), *Methodology and Historiography of the Caribbean*, 451–77.

4. Philip P. Boucher, *France and the American Tropics to 1700), 230; Tropics of Discontent?* (Baltimore, 2007), 238–9.
5. Boucher, *France and the American Tropics to 1700), 230;* John J. McCusker and Russell R. Menard, "The Sugar Industry in the Seventeenth Century: A New Perspective on the Barbadian 'Sugar Revolution,'" in Stuart B. Schwartz (ed.), *Tropical Babylons: Sugar and the Making of the Atlantic World, 1450–1680* (Chapel Hill, NC, 2004), 289–330.
6. For the creole historians and those who followed them, see Pérotin-Dumon, "Historiography of the French Antilles"; Victor Schoelcher, *Histoire de l'esclavage pendant les deux dernières années* (Paris, 1847); Victor Schoelcher, *Vie de Toussaint-Louverture* (Paris, 1889). Schoelcher's history of Toussaint, the most traditionally historiographical of his books, focuses primarily on the revolutionary period.
7. Lucien Peytraud, *L'Esclavage aux Antilles françaises avant 1789, d'après des documents inédits des archives coloniales* (Paris, 1897).
8. Alfred Martineau and Louis May, *Trois siècles d'histoire antillaise, Martinique et Guadeloupe, de 1635 à nos jours* (Paris, 1935); May, *Histoire économique de la Martinique (1635–1763)* (Paris, 1930).
9. Gabriel Debien, *Une plantation de Saint-Domingue: La Sucrerie Galbaud du Fort (1690–1802)* (n.p., 1941). For an overview of Debien's career, see David P. Geggus, "Gabriel Debien (1906–1990)," *Hispanic American Historical Review,* 71 (1) (February 1991): 140.
10. Gabriel Debien, *Les Esclaves aux Antilles françaises, XVIIe–XVIIIe siècles* (Basse-Terre, 1974).
11. Arlette Gautier, *Les Sœurs de Solitude: La condition féminine dans l'esclavage aux Antilles du XVIIe au XIXe siècle* (Paris, 1985); some of the other scholars working after Debien include Myriam Cottias, "Mortalité et créolisation sur les habitations martiniquaises du XVIIIe au XIXe siècle," *Population,* 44 (1) (1989): 55–84; Arlette Gautier, "Les Origines ethniques des esclaves déportés à Nippes, Saint-Domingue, de 1721 à 1770 d'après les archives notariales," *Canadian Journal of African Studies/Revue canadienne des études africaines,* 23 (1) (1989): 28–39; Jacques de Cauna, *Au temps des isles à sucre: Histoire d'une plantation de Saint-Domingue au XVIIIe siècle* (Paris, 1987); Lucien-René Abénon, *La Guadeloupe de 1671 à 1759: Étude politique, économique et sociale* (Paris, 1987); Nicole Vanony-Frisch, *Les Esclaves de la Guadeloupe à la fin de l'ancien régime d'après les sources notariales (1770–1789)* (Guadeloupe, 1985). Pérotin-Dumon, *La Ville aux îles, la ville dans l'île: Basse-Terre et Pointe-à-Pitre, Guadeloupe, 1650–1820* (Paris, 2001).
12. Pierre Pluchon and Robert Louis Stein were the two other historians who have published important work on both French slavery and the Haitian Revolution since Debien's retirement. But neither of them shared Debien's focus on plantation records, which has been one hallmark of Geggus's scholarship. See Robert Louis Stein, *French Slave Trade in the Eighteenth Century: An Old Regime Business* (Madison, 1979); Robert Louis Stein, *Leger Felicite Sonthonax: The Lost Sentinel of the Republic* (Rutherford, NJ, 1985); Robert Louis Stein, *The French Sugar Business in the Eighteenth Century* (Baton Rouge, La., 1988)
13. David P. Geggus, "Slave and Free Colored Women in Saint Domingue," in Darlene Clark Hine and David Barry Gaspar (eds.), *More than Chattel: Black Women and Slavery in the Americas* (Bloomington, Ind., 1996), 267.
14. Debien, *Les Esclaves aux Antilles françaises,* 345.

15. David P. Geggus, "Sex Ratio, Age and Ethnicity in the Atlantic Slave Trade: Data from French Shipping and Plantation Records," *Journal of African History*, 30 (1) (1989): 23–44; David P. Geggus, "Indigo and Slavery in Saint Domingue," *Plantation Society in the Americas*, 5 (1998): 189–204; David P. Geggus, "Sugar and Coffee Production and the Shaping of Slavery in Saint Domingue," in Ira Berlin and Philip D. Morgan (eds.), *Cultivation and Culture: Labor and the Shaping of Slave Life in the Americas* (Charlottesville, Va., 1993), 73–100. David P. Geggus, "The Demographic Composition of the French Caribbean Slave Trade," in Philip Boucher (ed.), *Proceedings of the Thirteenth and Fourteenth Meetings of the French Colonial Historical Society* (Lanham, Md., 1990), 21.

16. Gaston Martin, *Nantes au XVIIIe siècle: L'ère des négriers (1714–1774)* (Paris, 1931); Dieudonné Rinchon, *Les Armements négriers au XVIIIe siècle* (Brussels, 1956).

17. This characterization is from David Eltis, "The Volume and Structure of the Transatlantic Slave Trade: A Reassessment," *William and Mary Quarterly*, 58 (1) (January 2001): 20; Philip D. Curtin, *The Atlantic Slave Trade: A Census* (Madison, 1969); Jean Mettas and Serge Daget (eds.), *Répertoire des expéditions négrières françaises au XVIIIe siècle: Nantes* (Paris, 1978); Stein, *French Slave Trade*; Jean Meyer, *L'Armement nantais dans la deuxième moitié du XVIIIe siècle* (Paris, 1969).

18. Eltis, "Volume and Structure," 37, 43; Philip D. Morgan, "The Cultural Implications of the Atlantic Slave Trade: African Regional Origins, American Destinations and New World Developments," *Slavery and Abolition*, 18 (1) (1997): 124.

19. Serge Daget, *La Répression de la traite des noirs au XIXè siècle: L'action des croisières* (Paris, 1997); Daget, *Répertoire des expéditions négrières françaises à la traite illégale (1814–1850)* (Nantes, 1988); Daget, Hubert Gerbeau, and Eric Saugéra, *La Dernière Traite: Fragments d'histoire en hommage à Serge Daget* (Paris, 1994); Dale Tomich, *Slavery in the Circuit of Sugar: Martinique and the World Economy, 1830–1848* (Baltimore, 1990).

20. Pierre de Vaissière, *Saint-Domingue: La société et la vie créoles sous l'ancien régime* (Paris, 1909); Jules Saintoyant, *La Colonisation française sous l'ancien régime* (Paris, 1929), i. 254, 260; Gaston Martin, *Histoire de l'esclavage dans les colonies françaises* (Paris, 1948), 120.

21. Trouillot, "Openness and closure"; Alexis Beaubrun Ardouin, *Études sur l'histoire d'Haïti* (Port-au-Prince, 1958); Thomas Madiou, *Histoire d'Haiti* (Port-au-Prince, 1847); Beauvais Lespinasse, *Histoire des affranchis de Saint-Domingue* (Paris, 1882), 14; David Nicholls, *From Dessalines to Duvalier: Race, Colour and National Independence in Haiti* (Cambridge, 1979).

22. Frank Tannenbaum, *Slave and Citizen: The Negro in the Americas* (New York, 1946).

23. Mercer Cook, *Five French Negro Authors* (Washington, DC, 1943); Carter G. Woodson, "Review of Cook, Five French Negro Authors," *Journal of Negro History*, 28 (4) (October 1943): 494–7; W. E. B. Du Bois, "Mercer Cook," *Phylon (1940–1956)*, 5 (2) (1944): 189–90; Yvan Debbasch, *Couleur et liberté: Le jeu de critère ethnique dans un ordre juridique esclavagiste* (Paris, 1967); Shelby McCloy, *The Negro in the French West Indies* (Lexington, Ky., 1966).

24. Gwendolyn Midlo Hall, *Social Control in Slave Plantation Societies: A Comparison of St. Domingue and Cuba* (Baltimore, 1971); see articles by Hall and Léo Élisabeth as well as the editors' introduction in David W. Cohen, and Jack P. Greene (eds.), *Neither Slave Nor Free: The Freedman of African Descent in the Slave Societies of the New World* (Baltimore, 1972).

25. Michèle Duchet, *Anthropologie et histoire au siècle des lumières* (Paris, 1971); James E. McClellan III, *Colonialism and Science: Saint Domingue in the Old Regime* (Baltimore, 1992); Pierre H. Boulle, "In Defense of Slavery: Eighteenth-Century Opposition to Abolition and the Origins of Racist Ideology in France," in Frederick Krantz (ed.), *History from Below: Studies in Popular Protest and Popular Ideology in Honour of George Rudé* (Oxford, 1988), 219–46; Pierre H. Boulle, "La Construction du concept de race dans la France d'Ancien Régime," *Outre-Mers: Revue d'histoire*, 2 (2002): 155–75; Pierre H. Boulle, "François Bernier and the Origins of the Modern Concept of Race," in Tyler Stovall and Sue Peabody (eds.), *The Color of Liberty: Histories of Race in France* (Durham, NC, 2003), 11–27; Pierre H. Boulle, "Racial Purity or Legal Clarity: The Status of Black Residents in Eighteenth-Century France," *Journal of the Historical Society*, 6 (1) (March 2006): 19–46.

26. Philippe Delisle, *Renouveau missionnaire et société esclavagiste: La Martinique, 1815–1848* (Paris, 1997).

27. Antoine Gisler, *L'Esclavage aux Antilles françaises (17e–19e siècle)* (Fribourg, 1965); Louis Sala-Molins, *Le Code Noir, ou, le calvaire de Canaan* (Paris, 1987); Alan Watson, *Slave Law in the Americas* (Athens, Ga., 1989); Herbert S. Klein, *African Slavery in Latin America and the Caribbean* (New York, 1986), 226.

28. John D. Garrigus, "Blue and Brown: Contraband Indigo and the Rise of a Free Colored Planter Class in French Saint-Domingue," *The Americas*, 50 (2) (1993): 233–63; Garrigus, *Before Haiti: Race and Citizenship in Saint-Domingue* (New York, 2006); Stewart R. King, *Blue Coat or Powdered Wig: Free People of Color in Pre-Revolutionary Saint Domingue* (Athens, Ga., 2001); Debien, Jean Fouchard, and Marie Antoinette Ménier, "Toussaint Louverture avant 1789: légendes et réalités," *Conjonction: Revue franco-haïtienne* (1977): 65–80.

29. Frédéric Régent, *Esclavage, métissage, liberté: La révolution française en Guadeloupe, 1789–1802* (Paris, 2004); Dominique Rogers, "Les Libres de couleur dans les capitales de Saint-Domingue: Fortune, mentalités et intégration à la fin de l'Ancien Régime (1776–1789)" (diss., Université de Bordeaux III, 1999); Garrigus, "'Sons of the Same Father': Gender, Race, and Citizenship in French Saint-Domingue, 1760–1792," in Jack R. Censer, Lisa Jane Graham, and Christine Adams (eds.), *Visions and Revisions of Eighteenth-Century France* (University Park, Pa., 1997), 137–53; Doris Garraway, *The Libertine Colony: Creolization in the Early French Caribbean* (Durham, NC, 2005).

30. David P. Geggus, "The French Slave Trade: An Overview," *William and Mary Quarterly*, 58 (1) (January 2001): 123; Vanony-Frisch, *Les Esclaves de la Guadeloupe à la fin de l'ancien régime d'après les sources notariales (1770–1789)* (Guadeloupe, 1985); Terry Rey, "Kongolese Catholic Influences on Haitian Popular Catholicism: A Sociohistorical Exploration," in Linda Heywood (ed.), *Central Africans and Cultural Transformations in the American Diaspora* (Cambridge, 2002), 265–85.

31. Françoise Thésée, *Les Ibos de l'Amélie: Destinée d'une cargaison de traite clandestine à la Martinique, 1822–1838* (Paris, 1986); Gautier, "Les Familles esclaves aux Antilles françaises, 1635–1848," *Population*, 55 (6) (December 2000): 975–1001; Caroline Oudin-Bastide, *Travail, capitalisme et société esclavagiste: Guadeloupe, Martinique (XVIIe–XIXe siècle)* (Paris, 2005).

32. The most accomplished historian adopting this position today is Canadian, not Haitian: Carolyn E. Fick, *The Making of Haiti: The Saint Domingue Revolution from Below* (Knoxville, Tenn., 1990); Beaubrun Ardouin, *Études sur l'histoire d'Haïti*, i. 49 on

the tensions between *mulatriste* and *noiriste* schools of Haitian historiography; see Nicholls, *Dessalines to Duvalier*, 95–101.

33. Martin, *Histoire de l'esclavage dans les colonies françaises*, 128. Saintoyant, *La Colonisation française sous l'ancien régime*, i, 256–7; Jules Saintoyant, *L'Affaire du Congo 1905* (Paris, 1960).

34. Yvan Debbasch, "Le Marronage: Essai sur la désertion de l'esclave antillais, première partie," *L'Année sociologique*, 11 (1961): 1–112; Debbasch, "Le Marronage, seconde partie," *L'Année sociologique*, 12 (1962): 117–95.

35. Gabriel Debien, "Le Marronage aux Antilles françaises aux XVIIIe siècle," *Caribbean Studies*, 6 (3) (October 1966): 13–43.

36. Jean Fouchard (ed., rev., corr., and augm.), *Les Marrons de la liberté* (Port-au-Prince, 1988), 138. Fouchard, *Les Marrons du syllabaire* (Port-au-Prince, 1953).

37. Geggus, "On the Eve of the Haitian Revolution: Slave Runaways in Saint Domingue in the Year 1790," in Gad Heuman (ed.), *Out of the House of Bondage: Runaways, Resistance and Marronage in Africa and the New World* (London, 1986), 112–28. The quote is from David P. Geggus, "Marronage, Voodoo and the Saint-Domingue Slave Revolution of 1791," in Patricia Galloway and Philip P. Boucher (eds.), *Proceedings of the Fifteenth Meeting of the French Colonial Historical Society* (Lanham, Md., 1992), 27.

38. Pierre Pluchon, *Vaudou, sorciers, empoisonneurs: De Saint-Domingue à Haïti* (Paris, 1987), 279–80, 282.

39. Geggus, *Haitian Revolutionary Studies* (Bloomington, Ind., 2002), 91; Robin Law, "La Cérémonie du Bois Caïman et le 'pacte de sang' dahoméen," in Laënnec Hurbon (ed.), *L'Insurrection des esclaves de Saint-Domingue (22–23 août 1791)* (Paris, 2000), 131–47; Sue Peabody, "'A Dangerous Zeal': Catholic Missions to Slaves in the French Antilles, 1635–1800," *French Historical Studies*, 25 (1) (2002): 53–90; Karol K. Weaver, *Medical Revolutionaries: The Enslaved Healers of Eighteenth-Century Saint-Domingue* (Urbana, Ill., 2006).

40. John Savage, "'Black Magic' and White Terror: Slave Poisoning and Colonial Society in Early 19th Century Martinique," *Journal of Social History*, 40 (3) (Spring 2007): 635–62; Josette Fallope, *Esclaves et citoyens: Les noirs à la Guadeloupe au XIXe siècle* (Basse-Terre, 1992).

41. Édouard Delépine, "À propos du 22 mai 1848: Contre le neo-révisionnisme tropical," in Marcel Dorigny (ed.), *Les Abolitions de l'esclavage: De L. F. Sonthonax à V. Schoelcher* (Paris, 1995), 355–358; Lawrence C. Jennings, *French Anti-Slavery: The Movement for the Abolition of Slavery in France, 1802–1848* (Cambridge, 2006).

42. Nelly Schmidt, *Victor Schoelcher et l'abolition de l'esclavage* (Paris, 1994); Patricia Motylewski, *La Société française pour l'abolition de l'esclavage: 1834–1850* (Paris, 1998); Jennings, "Cyrille Bissette, Radical Black French Abolitionist," *French History*, 9 (1) (1995): 48–66.

43. Much of what follows is drawn from Jean-Yves Camus, "The Commemoration of Slavery in France and the Emergence of a Black Political Consciousness," *European Legacy*, 11 (6) (October 2006): 647–55. Delépine, "À propos du 22 mai," 357–58.

44. Pluchon, *Nègres et juifs au XVIIIe siècle: Le racisme au siècle des lumières* (Paris, 1984); Sue Peabody, *There Are No Slaves in France: The Political Culture of Race and Slavery in the Ancien Régime* (New York, 1996); Noël, *Être noir en France*; Serge Mam Lam Fouck, *L'Esclavage en Guyane française: Entre l'occultation et la revendication* (Guyane, 1998); Mam Lam Fouck, *La Guyane française au temps de l'esclavage, de l'or et de la francisation* (Petit-Bourg, 1999); Marie Polderman, *La Guyane française, 1676–1763: Mise en place et*

évolution de la société (Petit-Bourg, 2004). See Centre International de Recherches sur les Esclavages. Acteurs, systèmes, representations, http://www.esclavages.cnrs.fr/

45. Claire Sibille, *Guide des sources de la traite négrière, de l'esclavage et de leurs abolitions* (Paris, 2007).

46. Camus, "The Commemoration of Slavery," 656.

Select Bibliography

Boucher, P. Philip. *France and the American Tropics to 1700: Tropics of Discontent?* Baltimore: Johns Hopkins University Press, 2007.

Debien, Gabriel. *Les Esclaves aux Antilles françaises, XVIIe–XVIIIe siècles.* Basse-Terre: Société d'histoire de la Guadeloupe, 1974.

Fallope, Josette. *Esclaves et citoyens: Les noirs à la Guadeloupe au XIXe siècle dans les processus de résistance et d'intégration: 1802–1910.* Basse-Terre: Société d'Histoire de la Guadeloupe, 1992.

Fouchard, Jean. *Les Marrons de la liberté.* Paris: Éditions de l'École, 1972.

Garrigus, John D. *Before Haiti: Race and Citizenship in Saint-Domingue.* New York: Palgrave Macmillan, 2006.

Geggus, David P. "Sugar and Coffee Production and the Shaping of Slavery in Saint Domingue," in Ira Berlin and Philip D. Morgan (eds.), *Cultivation and Culture: Labor and the Shaping of Slave Life in the Americas.* Charlottesville, Va.: University of Virginia Press, 1993, 73–100.

——"The French Slave Trade: An Overview," *William and Mary Quarterly*, 58 (1) (2001): 119–38.

——*Haitian Revolutionary Studies.* Bloomington, Ind.: Indiana University Press, 2002.

Peabody, Sue. *There Are No Slaves in France: The Political Culture of Race and Slavery in the Ancien Régime.* Oxford: Oxford University Press, 1996.

Régent, Frédéric. *Esclavage, métissage, liberté: La révolution française en Guadeloupe, 1789–1802.* Paris: B. Grasset, 2004.

Vergès, Françoise, and Comité pour la mémoire de l'esclavage. *Mémoires de la traite négrière, de l'esclavage et de leurs abolitions: Rapport à monsieur le premier ministre.* Paris: Découverte, 2005.

CHAPTER 9

COLONIAL AND REVOLUTIONARY UNITED STATES

DANIEL C. LITTLEFIELD

EUROPEAN overseas expansion occurred during an age of hierarchy, when nearly everyone assumed a natural ordering of people in various rankings from high to low. There were and ought to be kings (or occasionally queens), nobles, the middling sort, and servants or laborers of one kind or another. Nor were these lines expected to be very frequently crossed. Many if not most of the complex societies Europeans met in Asia, Africa, or the Americas reflected that assumption. Slavery was just one form of bound labor that encumbered many at the lowest rank and, though it often involved stigma, it was not always ineradicable nor so strange a condition as it would later appear. When Iberian societies established or transported slavery to their New World colonies, however, it had already developed a racial component that attached an ineradicable stain and while it was not as strong or exclusive as it would later become, it was an enduring precedent.

But until the 1960s, people generally approached the study of slavery in the United States from the perspective of the nineteenth century and other precedents scarcely ever came to mind. Slavery was a southern American institution associated primarily with cotton and a divinely ordained labor force of blacks. Southerners in the Chesapeake might realize that slaves once produced tobacco, and in low-country South Carolina and Georgia that they once grew rice, and in southern Louisiana that they once raised sugar cane, but most people, when they thought about slavery at all, thought about the growing of cotton and reckoned that an African workforce required no explanation. Few knew that at one time slavery lived in Massachusetts, Rhode Island, and Connecticut, that it had been vibrant in New York and Pennsylvania, and that slaves still worked in New Jersey in 1860. Even in the South, where the presence of a significant African-American population made the heritage of slavery undeniable and people generally recognized the meaning of that fact, most understood neither slavery's age nor its origins. This naivety is suggested by the query of an American history graduate student historian Peter Wood encountered in the South Carolina archives when he began his study of the colony: "Did they have slaves in those days?"[1] Reading slavery backwards from the perspective of the nineteenth century meant that scholars engaged in what anthropologists call "upstreaming," imposing on an earlier period unwarranted assumptions based on a later reality, failing to see evidence that adduced a contrary interpretation, and neglecting to look where they thought there should be no evidence at all, as in New England, whereby the nineteenth-century abolitionist William Lloyd Garrison had come to represent the region's stereotypical face and spirit.

Without providing the extended historiographical discussion the subject deserves, one can note Peter Wood's comment that slavery scholarship "is often organized thematically rather than chronologically, leaving the impression that the institution was a static one and that the records for studying its evolution from the beginnings of settlement do not exist."[2] Scholars like Michael Mullin and Willie Lee Rose took up the challenge and undertook documentary studies as a preface to extended treatments of changes in slavery over time. What these scholars, and more recently Ira Berlin, have made clear is that slavery as it existed in the colonial period was not the same institution as developed in the nineteenth century or even the same in the eighteenth as in the seventeenth century.[3] To do the subject justice, one needs to consider slavery in discrete regions and epochs before making necessary generalizations and seeing how the practice evolved from one stage or time to another. Moreover, many things happened during the revolutionary era, somewhat slighted here in deference to limitations of time and space, that served as a necessary prelude to the early national and antebellum periods and require further exploration. In this regard, nothing is more important than the working out of regional conflicts between economics and ideology and enslaved peoples' role in the process.

What became the nineteenth-century South was several different "Souths" during the colonial period, even within the British empire, and was a "North," "East," or "West," depending on the imperial viewpoint of contending European powers who inhabited the geographical stage, and was something else again from the outlook of powerful native actors already in play when Europeans and Africans arrived. What seemed preordained from the later perspective appeared highly contingent at an earlier time. Systems of bondage are everywhere oppressive but they were not everywhere and for all times the same; and studying American slavery in comparative and evolutionary perspective shows that societies which used bound labor did not always operate the same way or end with precisely the same results and that the nineteenth-century institution did not come out of thin air.

Iberian colonization set an example that English leaders did not always imitate but could not ignore. Indeed, they sometimes acted in opposition and envisioned a contrast to it, but historical precedent, labor requirements, and philosophical outlook conditioned them to regard slavery as an acceptable institution. Despite that fact, Englishmen did not come to the Americas with the necessary expectation of establishing slave societies. In nearly all their early settlements, in the Caribbean and on the mainland, English leaders desired to establish English societies, and if race was a consideration at all, it initially hindered rather than aided the development of slavery. The need for labor eventually determined the importation of Africans and, once that happened, race affected the type of slavery that evolved.

In Virginia, where historians can view the development of slavery with relative ease, they see that the plantation system, focused eventually on the production of tobacco, was worked throughout the seventeenth century mainly by white indentured servants. Although some Africans came early, a few even in English ships, their formal importation is traditionally traced to the arrival of a Dutch ship that happened upon the colony in 1619. The Dutch were already involved in the slave trade and the Africans imported were sold to the leaders of the Virginia colony making their status, for all practical purposes, that of slaves, even though the condition was not formally recognized in the colony at the time. One might note that the indentures of servants were also sold, permitting a conflation of the *servant* and the *indenture*, suggesting that servants, like slaves, were sold; servants, however, were protected by contracts which did not cover slaves. If they sometimes worked together amicably, maybe even doing the same things, one had protection that the other did not. They may have associated without antagonism while nevertheless maintaining a consciousness of difference. Certainly, early Virginia laws made racial distinctions before the colony made slavery legal. Yet as slavery evolved in law and practice in seventeenth-century Virginia, economic considerations hampered its development as much as race and precedent may have facilitated it. First, slaves cost more than servants and epidemiological conditions were such that either might die before he repaid his cost but with the slave the loss was greater. Secondly, the restrictive nature of the English slave trade before the end of the century meant that slavers, preferring a more certain market in the West Indies, seldom had many slaves left to sell on the continent. Better health conditions and more slave carriers were both necessary before slavery became viable in Virginia. In addition, there had also to be a desire for them over indentured servants and this did not exist until servants became scarce.[4] When slaves could live long enough to make them an economic advantage over servants, when they could be had with some confidence, and when their availability exceeded that of indentured servants, slaves became the preferred commodity. In this equation race was coincidental but not unimportant. It was not unimportant because existing racial attitudes determined that slaves could be worked harder than servants, that black women could be put to tasks eventually spared English women, and that black men and women could be more closely observed and regulated. All of these features made slavery an attractive alternative to indentured servitude. Moreover, slavery was inheritable while servitude was not: The slave could reproduce himself. All of these considerations made slavery advantageous.

By the eighteenth century race and slavery in Virginia were increasingly intertwined and by the nineteenth century regarded as almost immutable but the process and reasoning of that development is still somewhat contested. Successive generations of scholars continue to revisit the issue. This may be because race relations remain a modern concern and one that extends beyond the United States as the world becomes smaller, populations intersperse, and societies even in Europe become multiracial if not quite multicultural. People look to the past for answers. It might be safe to say that while historian Winthrop Jordan has adumbrated the features of English culture that predisposed towards racism, it is also clear that these features were not predeterminative whether in England or America. Otherwise, the evidence would point all in one direction. When Francis Drake captured Spanish treasure in Panama in the 1570s he did so in alliance with *cimarrones*, black Africans who had run away from the Spanish. As historian Edmund Morgan explains: "In spite of the fact that Drake had engaged in the slave trade, in spite of the fact that the English in Ireland were at that very moment subjecting the natives to a treatment not much different from what the Indians of Hispaniola received from Columbus, the English in Panama had cast themselves as liberators and had allied with blacks against whites." Moreover, Morgan continues, the "alliance seems to have been untroubled by racial prejudice." The English were in no position "to assume airs of superiority, but the accounts suggests a camaraderie that went beyond the mutual benefits of the alliance."[5] Therefore, while one might conclude, as has Alden Vaughan, that "the primary sources of early Virginia" suggest that "white Virginians' and other Anglo-Americans' perception was even more thoroughly racial" than he had suspected, he had reason to think otherwise and, anyway, Virginians did not move immediately towards the racially repressive society achieved by the nineteenth century.[6] Blacks in early Virginia, even as slaves, could make contracts with white people, could work their way out of bondage, could contest with their white neighbors in court, could buy and sell white indentured servants, could intermarry with white people, could assimilate to English norms, and could come pretty close to being accepted as English people whose skin just happened to be dark. But coming "close" is not the same thing as absolute acceptability and all these rights were denied the small number of free people of color as the seventeenth century advanced. Their scarcity and relative acculturation is significant because their world began to constrict before the increasing importation of more and less acculturated Africans helped to justify such restrictions at the end of the century. By that time, black slaves were replacing white servants in plantation labor and Virginia's rulers evinced a disposition to associate free colored people with this new class and confine both to the lowest social realm. This happened gradually and maybe even speedily, depending on how one judges such things, but not inevitably. It is conceivable that without the increasing importance of slavery race would have remained a considered but not crucial element of Virginia society. Indeed, Ira Berlin has recently gone in opposition to the trend of focusing on English racism, which views race relations in Virginia as virtually foreordained despite the historical cross-currents, and looks at what he calls the "charter generation" of Africans in America, whose presence complicated the march towards racial slavery in the colony. They were often sophisticated, occasionally Christian, frequently multilingual, and sometimes skilled. Their capabilities were definitely inconsistent with the image of slaves and slavery that evolved. He therefore writes about slavery making race and vice versa, harking back to an earlier view and indicating that in spite of continued study, the subject remains complex. As it happened, English racial attitudes in North America and the Caribbean were distinctive from Iberian in terms of the degree to which they were willing to accept interracial marriages as opposed to less formal liaisons and to acknowledge appearance over genes in assessing status but still had recognizable connections to these other slave societies. Consequently, John Cobb countered the accusation that he was a mulatto in eighteenth-century Virginia "by arguing that he had collected plenty of debts, often gave evidence in controversies 'between other white persons and free subjects,' and possessed the goodwill and esteem of his neighbors and others. By implication, a mulatto could claim none of these things in Northampton County in 1748."[7] This sounds very much like the stereotype of mulattos in Latin America where in seventeenth-century Mexico, for example, the story circulated of a clergyman who offered to canonize a mulatto he encountered because "a Mulatto who seems to be honorable and who has grown as much white hair without being hanged or stabbed to death, must be a Saint."[8] In other words, the greater racial tolerance supposed for Latin America did not always result in radically different racial assumptions. In all racially based societies, the stain of race was not easily effaced and Iberians had a head start in connecting race and slavery.

    In the seventeenth-century Caribbean, where the English settled beginning in the 1720s after years of conflict with the Spanish, they established small farming societies which, following the English example in the Chesapeake, raised tobacco, along with cotton, indigo, and other crops, worked by white indentured servants. The period from 1627 to 1740 has been called the "Tobacco Age" and declining profits caused settlers to seek other crops. The transformation of those societies into plantation colonies whose labor source was enslaved Africans was gradual. The usual story links the transition to African labor in Barbados, the first successful and most populous colony, with a switch from tobacco and cotton to sugar, animated by Dutch knowledge and money; and it was accompanied by a process of land consolidation that brought to power a small elite of wealthy planters. But that story has been revisited. The process of land consolidation, signaling a change from a farming society to a plantation economy, occurred during the 1740s in association with cotton, and the importation of servants continued apace. It seems to have been funded largely by English entrepreneurs and a successful local economy. African importation also became significant in the 1740s and by the middle of the decade slaves outnumbered servants; at the same time, sugar was becoming important. Rather than learning from the Dutch how to make sugar, the English most likely learned from Africans brought from Brazil. But the increase in slaves came before sugar was a major crop and most came to work cotton or tobacco or indigo before sugar engrossed their labors; moreover, although they outnumbered servants by the end of the decade, the number of servants did not decrease. The pace of African importation, intensified by sugar, soon made Africans the dominant labor force but, as one historian expresses it, "Sugar did not bring slavery and plantation agriculture to Barbados."[9] Slavery and plantation agriculture were already happening before sugar became important and one function of that was increasing economic inequality and a rise in plantation size and elegance. What historians have called the "sugar revolution," Russell Menard prefers to call a "sugar boom" because the new crop quickened a process of economic transition that was already in operation and change occurred at a measured pace. It was a vital rather than moribund economy that turned to sugar. Moreover, despite the Brazilian example, the one closest at hand, whose sugar estates were run largely by black labor, Englishmen did not assume only black slaves could produce sugar until they had difficulty securing adequate white labor. Servants continued to be in demand until their price rose relative to slaves, making slaves more attractive to planters. Slaves were also cheaper to keep as they were neither fed nor clothed as well as servants. On the other hand, increasing Africanization and the stringency of labor made Barbados less desirable to servants, so the island moved to slaves.

While Virginia was first settled, slavery was first important in Barbados and while one may explain some features of the tobacco regime in Barbados with reference to Virginia, one can see slavery developing in Virginia within the context of the Barbados experience. When Barbadians were elaborating a successful slave society in the 1740s, Virginians were just beginning to consider the institution, or, more accurately, to casually and informally practice it, and Barbados became a "cultural hearth," transporting features of its system across the Caribbean and to North America. Of the colonists recorded as leaving Barbados in 1679, almost twice as many went to Virginia as to South Carolina, though settlement in the southern region was just getting under way, and they clearly brought ideas about slavery as it had already developed with them.[10] Some came to grow tobacco in a region where the crop had a much better reputation and made more money then the place they left. Yet most Barbadians settled south of the James River in an area noted for livestock production, facilitating a trade in meat and other products with the island. Barbadians came when Virginians were beginning to codify slavery and doubtless influenced the process; it is probable that the spectacle of what was going on in other parts of the New World, including the influence of their Caribbean cousins, had greater effect on Virginia's developing labor system than any aspect of the English background because so much of that background was irrelevant to the new labor conditions. Even English ideas about servitude were severely modified in the Americas.[11] Virginia's slave laws were not adopted lock, stock, and barrel from Barbados as was the case in South Carolina and other West Indian islands but the correspondence between them is significant. So are laws and outlooks regarding race mixture and white solidarity across class lines. If that is the case, pivotal events in Virginia history viewed in isolation might not be as significant otherwise in determining the colony's course towards slavery and a racially based society, though those events may have vindicated the justice of the Barbadian model already proffered. In other words, many of the intriguing features of race and slavery in early Virginia appear less contingent when viewed within a wider perspective. Indeed, creole Africans, enslaved and free, sometimes from New England and the New Netherlands, brought their own views and modified local ideas about slavery and race relations. Attitudes originating in the Caribbean and elsewhere and reinforced in Virginia spread to Maryland and other regions adjoining the Chesapeake.

What has been dubbed the "Barbadian Plantation Complex," so influential in English America, consists of four features: the large-scale, integrated plantation, which brought the cultivation and processing of sugar cane together on one estate; the gang system, which organized enslaved laborers into highly regimented units, driven by the whip; the slave economy system, which required slaves to be responsible for supplying much of their own subsistence but allowed them a minimum of time and acreage to do it; and the commission system, whereby planters sent their raw sugar to Europe for sale on their own accounts. The integrated plantation was a distinct departure from the Brazilian example where sugar was raised by peasant farmers, sometimes on land owned by a large planter, and they took their cane to his estate for processing. In this system, growing and refining sugar were separate operations under different responsibilities. For commercial production the sugar mill was the most important component and helps to explain why sugar estates in the Iberian world were identified in terms of the mill, or *ingenio* (Spanish) (*engenho* (Portuguese)), while the English term "plantation" referred to the whole "integrated" unit. Of course, the meaning, significance, and evolution of "plantation" in the English world has a history unrelated to sugar cultivation and came to mean any large-scale agricultural enterprise but the contrast to the Iberian terminology is still meaningful, especially as related to developments in Barbados. It may be important to note that although by the eighteenth century the term referred to large units of cultivation worked by black labor, in the seventeenth century the same kinds of units were worked by white labor, or a combination of white, red, and black. The origin of gang labor is more problematic. Russell Menard argues that gang labor, like the integrated plantation, appeared first in Barbados and evolved over time, congealed by the need to increase productivity brought about by falling prices. It was not fully operational until the eighteenth century. He rejects the explanation, offered by one scholar, that racial difference permitted the English to apply such a system only to Africans, and the suggestion, tendered by another, that the nature of the crop demanded it. It was a choice made by individuals within a specific historical context. Yet descriptions of African labor in Brazil sound very much like the way they worked in Barbados and may be part of the reason that Michael Craton considers what occurred in Barbados as the "culmination of a process" rather than something qualitatively new as Menard contends. April Hatfield, following Edmund Morgan, even perceives gang labor in early Virginia associated with white indentured servants, and David Eltis finds it earlier in Barbados than Menard does.[12] Morgan's description of the harsh mistreatment of indentured servants in Virginia (and Richard Dunn's in Barbados) make it clear that neither race nor nationality prevented English masters from the cruel exploitation of their laborers but Eltis may have a point in that only racial difference permitted it to be sustained and supported by an elaborate defense. Perhaps it was the sustained intensity of the feature, energized by an omnipresent whip, and imparting a mechanistic overlay, that separated the Barbadian practice from what had gone before and imbued it with a qualitative difference. Whatever the precise dating or lines of evolution, gang labor was characteristic of Barbados sugar cultivation by the eighteenth century and spread to other islands.

The slave economy system, devised in an attempt to prevent hunger and stave off slave unrest, is frequently associated with Jamaica but was also practiced in Barbados. The smaller island did not have as much excess land but enough for slaves to produce a few garden crops and to supply a market dominated by enslaved women. It is possible, however, that the system was prompted as much by Africans out of their own experience, in an attempt to maintain or recreate some portion of their background or to guard some measure of autonomy, as by the master class in an effort to contain them. In that case, it had West African as well as local antecedents.

When, almost sixty years after the settlement of Virginia, and forty after they located in the West Indies, English proprietors envisioned a settlement in the Carolinas, they had a wealth of colonial experience from which to profit. They took their model partly from the islands in desiring to produce commodities for the home market and seeking settlers therefrom and partly from New England in preferring settlement in towns rather than dispersed as in the Chesapeake. They forsook the Spanish pattern of a search for precious metals and envisioned agricultural wealth. They planned an aristocratic set-up that included a provision for slaves and an expectation of religious toleration. The *Fundamental Constitutions* (1669) even allowed slaves to "be of what Church or profession any of them shall think best," permitting their Christianization and indicating that the proprietors saw no contradiction between slavery and Christian worship, which had been a concern for early Virginians, and that they regarded slavery as a perfectly reasonable and practical institution. It may be that there was a larger number of Barbadians but clearly a smaller percentage of the total population in Virginia than South Carolina by the 1680s and their influence, significant enough in Virginia, was proportionately greater in South Carolina. Most colonists by that decade had come from Europe but as many as 40 percent were from the island and brought with them ideas about how slavery should work.[13]

As in Virginia, many seventeenth-century South Carolina slaves also came from the West Indies, often with migrating planters, and they, too, brought notions about how slavery had worked and perhaps their hopes to modify it. The colder winters in North America created some disadvantages for them because they were more susceptible than Europeans to pulmonary disorders but they were better equipped in terms of their resistance to malaria and yellow fever and in their ability to recognize the usefulness of native plants to adapt to South Carolina's semitropical environment. The coastal pharmacopoeia was not as referential to an African background as the tropical islands and, anyway, Barbados was no longer the primeval paradise it might once have been by the time most Africans arrived, but there was enough similarity in either case to make prior learning relevant. Africans brought a familiarity with tropical herbs, an ability to move along inland waterways using canoes or pirogues, skill in fishing utilizing not only nets, harpoons, or other implements, but also in drugging or stunning fish with poisons, and could live off the land much more easily than their masters could. In the first years of Carolina's settlement, the colonists concentrated on sustaining themselves and proved quite receptive to the foodways of native and enslaved peoples. Consonant outlooks towards land and nature, and comparable facets of material culture, facilitated African contact with native peoples. The African use of gourds, for example, could be related to the Native American use of calabashes. Both had basket-weaving traditions, and both were skilled in the use of small watercraft on inland rivers. Africans were among the first to appropriate native languages and were often used as translators. They excelled as guides and boatmen. As often as not, Africans were the mediators of knowledge between red men and white men.

Africans also brought experience in cattle raising, an important enterprise in early Carolina when the colonists had to feed themselves and sent beef and other foodstuffs to Barbados while they shipped deerskins and naval stores to England. Peter Wood suggests that the practice of free grazing, night-time penning for cattle protection, and seasonal burning to freshen pastures all had West African ante-cedents. Max Edelson responds that they had British and West Indian precedents as well, not to mention Native American practices. These considerations point to similarities in the way peoples in Africa, the Americas, and Europe did certain things and suggest the possibilities of mutual reinforcement rather than a need to pose one group against another. Nor is it necessary to flatten out humanity and allege that everyone is everywhere the same in order to acknowledge an essential human spark and the potential for human interchange.

African expertise as well as rough pioneer conditions of a new settlement facili-tated a degree of what some have called "sawbuck equality" in the seventeenth century—a term derived from the image of a slaveholder who worked all day sawing wood with his slave, each facing the other on opposite sides of a whipsaw. This situation did not mask the slaves' servile status but doubtless enhanced their self-esteem. This would be all the more the case because, unlike in Barbados, slaves had places to run and greater room to negotiate their situation. African knowledge and capability may have created conditions analogous if not quite similar to those existing for the relatively few blacks in early Virginia regarding treatment if not in access to freedom. In both cases, an inchoate society permitted rough equality among working blacks and whites. The South Carolina slave code of 1696, based on the Barbadian code of 1688, announced an end to this relatively benign period. The colony increasingly embraced rice as a staple, the most remunerative on the conti-nent at the time, whose reach extended to lowcountry Georgia after the middle of the eighteenth century. At the same time, the colonists brought in more Africans, now directly across the Atlantic, and carried the black population above the white by the beginning of the eighteenth century. This demographic disproportion made South Carolina look more like Barbados than Virginia and helped to make the replication of slave codes appropriate. Indigo joined rice as a Carolina staple after 1740. It was complementary, being grown in higher, more sandy soils than rice with a work regime that was also coincident, needing most attention when rice did not, though most plantations did not grow both of them.

As events in Barbados, South Carolina, and even Virginia suggest, historians have moved away from looking at the development of institutions only from the top down and now pay closer attention to the actions of working-class peoples whose activities have great influence on the way societies operate. In particular, they consider that Africans had some say in how slavery evolved and crops were cultivated in view of the fact that hoe agriculture was practiced in most slave societies and many of the crops raised were familiar in an African setting. Even when Africans had not grown at home the crops they tended in America, they often learned how to grow and process them before their English masters and these masters were not so blind or proud as to deny themselves the advantage. Conse-quently, Englishmen from Barbados traveled to Brazil to learn the secrets of sugar cultivation and doubtless brought back Africans who possessed the skills. April

Hatfield suggests that Virginia planters may have sought out acculturated Africans from the Spanish Caribbean who knew the cultivation of tobacco despite the fact that Native Virginians grew it too (theirs "differs in the Leaf from the sweet scented, and Oroonoko, which are the Plants we raise and cultivate in America," eighteenth-century explorer John Lawson explained, and was also cured differently), and South Carolina planters asked for Africans knowledgeable in rice cultivation.[14] In all of these cases the ruling planters ultimately directed and controlled production but remained dependent upon the disposition of their laborers to effectuate it. The whip could drive but could not ensure performance; at least its effectiveness in that direction was limited. The greater skill required, the less effective was force. When new plantation economies were in the making slavemasters paid more attention to the doings of their slaves and were more open to their expertise but even after plantations developed successful planters realized they could never make decisions without taking into account the possible reaction of their bondspeople. These assertions are not meant to imbue the enslaved with a degree of "agency" that undercut the sting of enslavement, to highlight their "contributions" to the making of New World society in such a way as to de-emphasize the circumstances within which these activities occurred, or to mitigate the weight of domination. The facts do suggest that slavery was a relationship of human beings despite all the attempts of the rulers to deny it, and quotidian interactions forced many of them to acknowledge this reality even while they rejected its implications. Moreover, the knowledge and image of competence among slaves helped to counter the propaganda of ignorance and incompetence and modified the efforts at dehumanization that slavery entailed. If slaves recognized the trappings of power, acquiesced in its brutal exercise, and suffered physical and psychological torture as a result of it, they also knew that it might not touch every aspect of their being; that there were flaws in both theory and practice that permitted them to develop a self-image of their own. They were not all equally adept at avoiding being warped by the system, and some regions provided more leeway than others, but everywhere there were alternative possibilities.

But if, in physics, for every action there is an equal and opposite reaction, the same is true in scholarship and some object to what they see as an unaccountable attempt to level the playing field between master and slave by attributing to Africans too much knowledge or influence. It is, they believe, a perversion to see enslaved Africans as being willing or capable of forwarding a plantation enterprise from which they reaped few advantages, and results, they feel, from the mushy outlook of a politically correct, multicultural, and/or African nationalist perspective.[15] Never mind that many of the new ideas developed within a relatively conservative scholarly community and come from an unjaundiced look at old documents prompted by a changing intellectual climate.

This situation may be clearest in South Carolina where scholars have argued that the African experience in rice cultivation was crucial to its success as a colony. The notion that Africans taught English people how to grow rice is intriguing and has evidence to support it but the case is circumstantial. It revolves around the difficulty Englishmen had in getting the crop to grow, the coincidence between successful cultivation and African importation, and the fact that South Carolinians expressed a preference for people from rice-growing regions, acknowledging that the background was useful. There are also correspondences between the way it is cleaned and planted in Africa and South Carolina and even, during some periods, in the way fields were laid out. Critics counter that there were other places where the English could have gone to learn rice cultivation, including Asia and southern Europe, and that there is little evidence that Africans from the most advanced rice-producing African regions were in the colony during the crucial stage.[16] Yet the argument against the case is no more conclusive than the one for it though it is healthy to the extent that it cautions against replacing one dogma with another. It is unfortunate to the extent that it fails to recognize the conceptual and philosophical breakthrough the idea represents, the significance it has had on the historical profession in encouraging scholars to look to Africa and elsewhere as well as Europe for the sources of American developments, and the way in which the tenor of opposition suggests a return to an earlier imperial outlook. Whether or not one accepts the notion of African tutelage in rice cultivation, most scholars now agree that Africans had a significant influence on the way rice was cleaned and planted. Moreover, their descendants often managed production even after it had, under Euro-American auspices, evolved far beyond its beginnings. The signal contribution is to be found in the way recognition of the circumstances of rice cultivation in South Carolina shifted attention to the people who labored to raise it rather than those who received most of the profits from it, and scholars have taken this perspective to other colonial regions.

Beginning with some similarities in the seventeenth century, the plantation societies in the Chesapeake and the Carolina region were distinctive by the eighteenth century. Chesapeake planters fancied themselves as lords of the manor, living on large estates housing barns, stables, and storehouses to support an elegant mansion and containing wharves that fronted the rivers that connected them to the Atlantic world. They acted as middlemen to surrounding smaller planters and operated autarkic plantation wherein they attempted to produce locally as many of their needs as possible. The home estates were supported by smaller units, "quarters," raising tobacco, livestock, and other produce for use of the whole, manned by a score or more of the enslaved. The planters regarded themselves as patriarchs, heading large families composed of white and black dependants, whose well-being, determined by their own lights, they sought to ensure. But they demanded perfect allegiance and brooked no contestation of their authority. They cultivated a lavish lifestyle, placed great store by their honor, and were extremely sensitive to slights. They took intense interest, extending to interference, in the lives of the enslaved, particularly those with whom they lived in close personal contact on home estates.

But because crops were worked in small farming units, comprising scores rather then hundreds of slaves, even though the owner claimed hundreds, contact between black and white people was common. While slaves developed a divergent culture, the nature of interaction between blacks and whites, together with the longer span of importation from diverse sources, meant a greater variety of influences on slave culture than in places where the slaves came in greater numbers over a shorter time span from Africa. Slaves sometimes worked in gangs but not of the size or intensity in the Caribbean.

Carolina planters also maintained an aristocratic manner and sumptuous lifestyle but focused it on the urban environment of Charlestown, where they supported townhouses to anchor their social life. They conceived of themselves as businessmen as well as aristocrats and many of them were or had been merchants while they engaged in, or before they retired to, planting. They were very much involved in the world of commerce. Except for the bondspeople in their townhouses, their personal servants, or in estates close to Charlestown, in whom they took a casual interest, they were unconnected with the majority of their laborers, who often worked on specialized plantations some distance from the city. These were often inelegant work camps where the enslaved had few comforts and received infrequent visits from the planter. Work was more strenuous than in the Chesapeake, especially after the movement of rice cultivation from inland swamps to fields geared to the tide flow. Cultivation by this method required the construction of massive dikes and wooden trunks or sluices to regulate the flooding or draining of the fields. Letting water onto the fields minimized weeding but it had to be performed in damp conditions when it did occur. Moreover, difficult to construct in the first place, having been claimed from swampy, thickly-grown, reptile-infested wetlands, these works had to be maintained, requiring the attention of men and women. The areas were often disease infested, as standing water encouraged the breeding of mosquitoes and caused various maladies, which the owners could escape but the workers could not. On the other hand, the slaves had most contact with black drivers and an occasional white overseer, and, composing a majority of the population on the work unit, and having a significant presence in the city, developed an important, more African-influenced slave culture. They created a distinctive creole language, related to similar developments in the Caribbean, and a slave economy and female-dominated urban market reminiscent of Africa and the West Indies.

These features were made possible partly by a distinctive labor method, known as the task system, wherein the driver assigned a certain amount of work to be done and, if accomplished, the workers had the rest of the day for themselves. This was in contrast to the dawn-to-dusk routine of gang labor. Although there have been various theories advanced to explain the task system, Max Edelson suggests the most reasonable. He posits that it grew out of the seventeenth-century practice of allowing slaves time to produce most of their own livelihood and continued even as their days became more routinized, tied to staple production. Although planters eventually tried to claim all the time of their slaves by furnishing most of their needs, the custom of allowing them to produce for themselves if they could perform a set amount of work became one that planters could not change without more trouble than it was worth in terms of disrupting production. By the third or fourth decade of the eighteenth century it had become accepted practice.

Wealthy South Carolina planters often spent part of the year in New England, particularly Newport, Rhode Island, where they also maintained townhouses. By the nineteenth century they left a slave state to go where laborers were free, but in the eighteenth century Newport had proportionately one of the largest urban slave populations in the North. A global perspective is especially significant in considering slavery's existence in northern regions not normally considered to be part of what Philip Curtin has styled the "plantation complex" but which were related to it by political, economical, and other connections. In this regard, trade and conflict between England and the Dutch are perhaps as important as precedents established by the Spanish and Portuguese, and while the Dutch may not have been as significant as formerly thought in bringing sugar and slavery to Barbados, they remained a prime supplier of slave labor. Accordingly, it is not strange that among the places whence blacks came into the Chesapeake was the New Netherlands. Settled by the Dutch as a trading post in the 1620s, the Dutch West India Company relied on enslaved Africans to support its settlement, considering them cheaper and more dependable than indentured servants. As a significant naval power with interests throughout the Atlantic world, the Dutch brought in Africans with a variety of experiences, many of them "creoles" whose attitudes and expectations shaped the way slavery evolved. Enslaved Africans performed most of the agricultural labor for the colony, as well as constructing fortifications and engaging in trade with native peoples. By the middle of the century, there were more Africans in the Dutch colony than anywhere else in North America. The West India Company instituted a practice of "half-freedom," authorizing blacks to live on their own and support themselves in return for an annual tribute and a contracted amount of labor. Their children remained enslaved, however, a situation the Africans protested. Nevertheless, society was flexible enough that many families did gain their freedom in New Netherlands, contributing to a noticeable if not large free African population by the time of the English conquest, and, in fact, slavery under the Dutch was customary rather than legally established. When the English claimed what they called New York in the 1660s they legalized the institution, and, in line with what was happening in the Chesapeake and the Caribbean, made it more rigid, abolishing the status of "half-freedom." But the enslaved continued to possess some of the rights granted under the Dutch, including the right to own property. Barbadians fleeing their transforming island who came to New York soon learned that local conditions did not permit slavery as it was developing on the island. As one New Yorker wrote to a West Indian friend, "The Custome of this

Country will not allow us to use our Negroes as you doe in Barbados," a situation that likely also permitted slaves to insist on the task system in South Carolina.[17]

In New England, although much has been made of the debate between John Saffin defending slavery and Samuel Sewall opposing it, the Puritan experience on Providence Island off the coast of Nicaragua in the 1630s, where planters drove slaves to raise cotton and tobacco, imported an African majority, and prompted English's first slave revolt, indicates there was nothing in the Puritan background that conditioned them to reject the harshest form of servitude. The Providence experience may have encouraged colonists in Virginia as well as New England to value a racially homogeneous society, considering the problems slavery brought, though it convinced neither region to turn against it. That background may have been part of the reason Sewall, even while defending the right of Africans to freedom, argued for their exclusion from New England society. Laws against interracial marriage, though not miscegenation, appeared in Massachusetts before South Carolina. Slavery was developing in New England in the 1630s and 1640s at the same time Puritans began fleeing Providence Island and some refugees went to New England. Slaves came into New England from various places in the Americas, including New Netherlands and the West Indies, often as an adjunct of New England trading activities. When Saffin and Sewall debated the issue at the beginning of the eighteenth century it was an accepted though obviously not unquestioned practice. Even Sewall who argued against it probably owned slaves. The nature of New England slavery helped to bring the debate before the public. Slaves in New England could own property, make contracts, and earn wages, and had access to the courts through the intervention of prominent people like Sewall because custom in New England, like elsewhere in North America, barred red and black people from testifying in court against white people. All of these rights, however, were dependent upon the master's permission and willingness to honor them and Saffin had reneged on a promise. As in Saffin's case, masters often had little honor and slaves had little recourse unless others were willing to take their case and even then the odds were stacked against them. However, even in the vitiated fashion that they existed in New England and the Middle Colonies, these rights were denied slaves in plantation regions.

Most slaves in northern regions as in the plantations engaged in agricultural labor. In the North, however, they more often worked on farms rather than the expansive units of production in the South and raised crops that did not require large work gangs; sometimes they worked by task.[18] They raised vegetable and other crops and a few planters in the Narragansett region of Rhode Island and in eastern Connecticut grew tobacco in imitation of the Chesapeake. Most slaves, even in those colonies, did not raise tobacco. They worked on dairy farms and raised horses, cattle and other livestock and provisions for trade in the region and to the West Indies. In Pennsylvania slaves worked iron furnaces and elsewhere in tanneries and salt works. Disproportionately they worked in cities. All the important

northern urban centers—New York, Philadelphia, Boston, Newport—had significant black populations, who did various kinds of work around the house or garden,
on the wharves, as teamsters or wagoners, as sailors or at other jobs connected with
the shipping industry, ran errands, or were hired out to work for others. As
Lorenzo Greene noted for New England the slave "had to be equally at home in
the cabbage patch and in the cornfield; he must be prepared . . . not only to care for
stock, to act as servant, repair a fence, serve on board ship, shoe a horse, print a
newspaper, but even to manage his master's business."[19] Although Ira Berlin,
following Moses Finley, has classified northern communities as "societies with
slaves" rather than slave societies, meaning that slavery was not the prime engine
of the economy, and, in any case, enslaved blacks often worked with equally bound
Indians, or with indentured whites and Indians, he suggests that the blacks'
economic importance exceeded their numbers. In some places blacks were a
third or a half of the working population. Moreover, he argues, at the mid-
eighteenth century slavery "edged toward the center of the northern economy."[20]

Whether in town or country, most northern slave owners did not have much
space. Slaves lived in cramped quarters in the garrets or basements of buildings, in
narrow spaces in outbuildings, or slept on the floors of small houses. Shortage of
space placed a limit on slavekeeping and also on the ability of slaves to set up their
own households as most slave owners did not want to raise children or maintain
families. As a consequence, however, they frequently permitted slaves to live on
their own, providing slaves met contracted obligations, and thereby lightened their
own responsibilities while increasing the responsibilities and opportunities for
slaves. An urban environment that was relatively welcoming in the early eighteenth
century, where a roughly equal sex ratio allowed the black population to reproduce
itself, became less so at mid-century as direct African importation skewed the black
population towards males and reduced reproductive possibilities. Close living
quarters made personality an essential consideration in purchasing slaves and
also in whether the arrangement lasted. For this reason slaves were often permitted
to find a new master if the current situation proved mutually disagreeable. This
practice, among other conditions, provided slaves some measure of negotiation
though constrained by available choices. However, as John Sweet warns, "archaeological evidence from the African Burial Ground in New York City reveals the
grinding brutality of slavery in northern places; bones were enlarged and damaged
by routine, heavy work, and there is evidence of more malnutrition, less cultural
autonomy, and more surveillance than slaves experienced on contemporary plantations in the Chesapeake region."[21]

Slavery brought people in the North—red, black, and white—into close personal
contact and affected slave culture and common relationships. Africans absorbed a
significant proportion of Euro-American culture at the same time that increasing
African importation allowed them to preserve or amalgamate a significant African
dimension. Echoing festivals in the West Indies and Latin America, blacks in New

England celebrated "Negro Election Day," which combined African and Anglo-American customs, and in New York, Pinkster, which combined African and Dutch. In these celebrations whites often participated, demonstrating simultaneously the mixing of cultures, whites' amused condescension towards their servitors, and their sense of political and demographic superiority. Africans were not granted similar leeway in South Carolina and the Chesapeake where their labor was crucial and their numbers daunting. Africans also had intense interactions with native peoples, sometimes when they worked together in houses or on farms and sometimes when they ran away. John Sweet, following Kenneth Porter, points out that Indian enclaves in New England acted like maroon communities where black fugitives found shelter and protection. Despite colonial authorities' efforts to divide the two groups, "their own bitter experiences of servitude in English households" provided Native Americans an opportunity to "feel solidarity with blacks, even at the expense of foregoing financial rewards from whites for helping to identify and return runaways."[22] Intermarriage between the two groups sometimes made it difficult to establish precise identities and individuals might claim one or the other depending on which was most advantageous at the moment.

Indeed, the presence of strong native populations as well as contesting European powers influenced the dynamics of slavery and race everywhere in early America. Coastal peoples in direct contact with Europeans in New England and the Chesapeake had mostly suffered defeat by the end of the seventeenth century, many having been enslaved, sold out of the region, or forced to work in local homes, on farms, or plantations. Usually considered too dangerous for permanent captivity, men were either killed or shipped off, leaving women and children most frequently to labor in colonial establishments. There they met Africans, commonly male, which contributed to racial mixture but also to issues of identification because colonials were seldom consistent in the labels they applied to these or other mixed-race people, and complicated investigation into the endurance and influentiality of native as well as African peoples. In the Carolina region, settled later, there were strong interior groups with whom the colonials interacted. Among other things, they developed an important Indian slave trade in which native peoples participated, similar to what occurred on the African coast. Native peoples were generally middlemen in this trade, funneling peoples to the coast where Carolinians shipped them off to the islands or other continental colonies. Alan Gallay argues, in fact, that up until 1715 there were more native peoples shipped out of Charlestown than there were Africans shipped in.[23] As in other places, some, generally women and children, were retained for labor in the colony and interacted with black workers.

South Carolinians began importing large numbers of Africans directly across the Atlantic at the end of the seventeenth century and brought them in over a relatively short time period. They brought in a population that viewed resistance in a communal fashion and tended to run away in groups. As in South America and on the larger Caribbean islands, marronage became a problem as fugitives sought the safety of the wilderness, sometimes for temporary escape and sometimes to form their own settlements, and marronage was a far more significant practice here than elsewhere along the coast. But the American wilderness was not uninhabited and native peoples sometimes aided and sometimes hindered the process. Colonial authorities had an obvious interest in keeping the two groups divided against each other, and while native peoples who specialized in enslaving other natives might not be supposed to sympathize with people from another continent already enslaved, they nevertheless did find affinities with runaways depending on a plethora of local circumstances. Traditional rivalries, complicated by development of a Native American slave trade, were intensified further by European competition and Africans found advantage among the complexities. The Spanish at St Augustine promised sanctuary to enslaved Africans who escaped the English and likewise encouraged native peoples to resist. Of course, native peoples had their own interests and the Spanish set up Gracia Real de Santa Teresa de Mosé as a black settlement outside of St Augustine as a buffer between the city and the depredations of hostile English and Native Americans. Yet Africans in the settlement adopted a material culture closely related to and influenced by surrounding native peoples. Cultural interchange was mutual: Both groups were largely dependent upon wild sources of food and the settlement at Mosé secured and prepared foods in fashions similar to those of nearby villages and apparently under their tutelage. At least one Native American village in the region, on the other hand, was more strongly fortified in a design developed by a self-liberated African.[24] There were also interracial sexual liaisons between the two groups although historians Jane Landers and Kevin Mulroy both suggest that these were not as common as sometimes assumed. The physical and material connections facilitated a disposition among both groups to encourage and shelter subsequent runaways and to that extent local Native Americans were part of a "southern railway" system subversive of slavery and strongly objected to by the planter class. To reach this area, however, slaves had to run a gauntlet of not always friendly native peoples.

In the second half of the eighteenth century when most of the local Florida tribes had expired or moved away to be replaced by members of the lower Creeks, known as Seminoles, runaway slaves lived among them quite openly as allies and vassals. By the end of the century Seminole rather than Spanish territory became a haven for runaway slaves, particularly after the Spanish ended their policy of sanctuary in 1790. Under African influence, Jane Landers argues, Seminoles switched from being enemies of the Spanish to allies against the English. All three saw a convergence of interest: "The Spaniards stood to lose their colony, the blacks their freedom, and the Seminoles their rich lands and cattle herds."[25] Of course, from the Anglo-American point of view, this collaboration made the region all the more dangerous and reinforced their determination to secure the area which extended into the nineteenth century. The War of 1812 and the Creek War it subsumed (1813–14) marked the beginning of a sustained effort to push the Creeks, Seminoles, and

Africans out of their settlements in central and western Florida and also to drive out the Spanish. The main aim of the First Seminole War (1817–18) was to destroy black settlements. The American commanding general told the Seminoles that if they would let him pass to get to the blacks he would not harm Seminole property. But the Seminoles, recognizing a community of interests, refused. The issue of slavery and of Native Americans sheltering or cooperating with slaves was perhaps even more prominently involved in the Second Seminole War (1835–42). General Thomas Jesup declared in December 1836 that "This, you may be assured is a negro not an Indian war; and if it be not speedily put down, the south will feel the effects of it before the end of next season."[26] Despite their cooperation, with Africans settling occasionally among native peoples, the two groups generally lived separately, with villages of Africans neighboring villages of Native Americans, and the African ones can be viewed as maroon communities similar to those existing elsewhere in the Americas. Their neglect in this regard is emblematic of the extent to which the story of African and Native American resistance, particularly when they acted together, has been slighted and helps explain why maroon communities in North America seldom come to mind when one considers the history of marronage.

The Spanish at St Augustine helped also to spark the largest slave rebellion in English colonial North America at the Stono River in South Carolina in 1739. Although they practiced slavery, the Spaniards were nowhere near establishing a plantation economy in the locale and their settlement was similar to the Dutch West India one in New Netherlands, in form if not in function, considering that the Dutch settlement was an expansive arm of their seaborne empire while the Spanish settlement was an outpost in a far-flung empire whose ultimate purpose was to forestall French and English expansion. In their region, Atlantic creoles had unusual influence, protected as they were by Spanish law in conditions favorable to its benevolent expression, and by Spanish need. News of a Spanish promise of sanctuary reached the ears of local Africans, many from the Congo-Angola region who dominated South Carolina's enslaved population at the time. They viewed the Spanish as co-religionists as well as possible protectors, having adopted Catholicism from Portuguese activities in the Kingdom of Kongo. Their revolt failed but it highlights a number of considerations regarding Carolina's eighteenth century African population. Many were conscious of a regional if not ethnic identity; they demonstrated the cultural syncreticism that took place on the African coast and affected some captives before they reached the Americas (reflected in this case in their knowledge of Portuguese and/or a creole variant, their religious outlook, and their military organization which combined African and European weaponry with African tactics), and they viewed resistance communally.[27]

These features, apparent elsewhere among Africans in English North America, were even more prominent among the French in Louisiana where Gwendolyn Midlo Hall argues strongly against the notion that African captives arrived atomized, bereft of cultural underpinnings, and incapable of social cohesion. Slaves in Louisiana quite clearly were able to "regroup themselves in language and social communities derived partly from the sending cultures."[28] Among other things, the French preserved slave records in terms of the slaves' ethnicity and some maintained an African identity years after their importation. Most slaves in early Louisiana came from the Senegambia region and many of these were Bambara (a contested but convenient generic), who, in concert with Native Americans, were prominent in a rebellion that posed a serious threat to the colony in 1729.[29] Moreover, they ensured defeat of a later rebellion based partly on an ethnic outlook that prevented cooperation with other Africans at the end of the century. As in English America, Africans in French settlements came into contact with native peoples as bound labor, and, as in South Carolina, the French engaged in an Indian slave trade to their West Indies colonies though it was not as significant as the Carolina enterprise. The Sieur de Bienville sought to foster an island exchange of two Indians for every African despite French authorities' prohibition of a trade in native peoples. As in English colonies, Africans and Native Americans ran away together, formed occasional maroon communities, and periodically intermarried. The French as the English attempted to keep the two groups at odds, promising rewards to Indians who returned African slaves and sending armed Africans on occasion to attack native villages. These policies were not entirely successful but they complicated an already intricate situation and Africans sometimes fought with native peoples against the French and sometimes did the reverse. Often, Africans fought on both sides of any local conflict, as, on the larger stage, Africans and Native Americans fought on each side as contending parties of Spanish, English, and French attempted to contain their rivals' expansion. This was especially when the English and their native allies tried to extend the Indian slave trade.

Early French Louisiana was a harsh place and, although Africans were not treated especially well, they found advantages in a thinly settled, inchoate society similar to the one that obtained in early South Carolina. Indeed, like the English province, Gwendolyn Hall remarks, "French Louisiana was a chaotic world where the cultural materials brought by Africans often turned out to be the most adaptive."[30] In other respects, the situation of Africans in French Louisiana was significantly different. They raised livestock and garden crops, engaged in regional exchange, and grew tobacco and indigo for an overseas market. However, they were soon governed, at least in theory, by the Code Noir, which sought to regulate relations between masters and slaves, providing standards for housing, clothing and nutrition, limiting physical abuse, and acknowledging slave families. It was perhaps more often breached than observed but slaves and free people of color sometimes made use of it and authorities occasionally tried to enforce it. Despite Ira Berlin's suggestion to the contrary, Hall argues that French Louisiana was not a plantation colony. It was largely a colony of small farms and, as with the Dutch in New Netherlands, the Company of the Indies owned most of the slaves. Of course, there were a few planters who owned twenty or more slaves and the distinctive view-points of the two authors can be explained by their different emphases. Hall looks at the region holistically while Berlin operates from a model that stresses transformation, in this case, from slave society to society with slaves. In Berlin's view, the French intended but did not accomplish a plantation society because the hypothetical march from social flexibility and independent African initiative towards planter hegemony and social stratification was checked by slave and native unrest in 1729 and 1731. By the last date, the black outnumbered the white population and Louisiana, like South Carolina, had a black majority.

Although the Code Noir outlawed interracial marriage and concubinage, French settlers practiced both and Louisiana society was characterized by a racial fluidity that was uncommon in English North America, though colonists in South Carolina openly practiced if they did not formally acknowledge race mixture. Indeed, New Orleans was fabled in the nineteenth century for its racial caste system that provided a separate space for mixed-race people. Such people in Charleston had a much more circumscribed position. Yet they had a prominence in Charleston exceeding that of the free colored population in any other city outside of the Gulf Coast. The foundation for this state of affairs began in the eighteenth century and distinctions can be explained partly by a French, and subsequent Spanish, need to maintain an African military presence. Black militias fed the free black or colored populations and affected the tenor of society by modifying sharp divisions between black and white. Indeed, some historians applaud the French in colonial Louisiana for being extraordinarily oblivious to race, suggested among other things by the fact that black or colored women in conjugal relations with white men were frequently identified as white. It may be, however, that this situation prefigured a later time when separate black and white marriage registers obliged a man to choose if he solemnized the connection. In that case, the French were close to their English rivals on the continent in a bi-racial view of society, though none of these societies was bi-racial. One purpose of black militias, for example, was to overawe native peoples among whom French and Africans lived and they all practiced some measure of cultural and biological blending while their societies intertwined. If the French and English shared some outlooks, their practices nevertheless diverged.

When Spanish replaced French in Louisiana, they placed the first strictures on a racially fluid environment, imposing what Hall calls a "corporatist" conception of race relations, dividing black from white and brown and red and providing each with a particular role and social space. They separated the militia into black and brown regiments and curbed, in an attempt to abolish, Indian slavery. The caste of mixed-race people expanded, as the Spanish paid more attention to degrees of racial blending though their calculations were scarcely accurate. In particular, many people of African and Native American descent were classified as black or mulatto to escape Spanish restrictions on Indian slavery. The *Siete partidas*, like the Black Code it displaced, accorded slaves some protection, most important of which was the right to confront their masters at law. An acceleration of African importation and intensification of plantation agriculture brought Louisiana closer to a plantation economy and adversely affected slave treatment. But Spanish officials had to balance the concerns of enslaved peoples against the threat of disloyalty among French settlers unreconciled to their authority and these considerations brought benefits to enslaved Africans as well as to free people of color.

By the last quarter of the eighteenth century, slavery existed throughout colonial North America. Britain had ousted France from the continent and pushed Spain, excepting its outpost at New Orleans, west of the Mississippi River. The two nations had plantation colonies in Louisiana, the Carolina region, and the Chesapeake (to use general terminology rather than specific political demarcations) and Britain had societies with slaves in the Floridas and the region northward from Delaware. The British seriously attempted to extend their plantation economy to the Gulf Coast and along the Atlantic in East Florida. Carolina planters coveted the latter, though indigo proved more viable than rice, and other settlers, along with slaves and indentured servants, moved west and south into West Florida, raising tobacco, rice, cotton, corn, indigo, livestock, and various garden crops. They engaged in trade with their powerful Indian neighbors, across the border with Spanish and French setters in Mexico and Louisiana, and, as much as possible, across the Atlantic. A strong native presence, vibrant maroon communities, and sparse settlement in frontier conditions for much of the region made it very much a work in progress. In addition, Spain reconquered West Florida during the American War of Independence and regained the whole region thereafter but the war brought loss, unrest, and disorder. A plantation regime would have to await the nineteenth century.

The American Revolution accelerated a movement of British settlers to the Floridas and disrupted plantations in those colonies that resisted British authority. Africans, enslaved and free, fought alongside both of the contending parties, with the singular aim of gaining their liberty and respectability, but often also in interracial paramilitary groups that raided opportunistically. This was especially the situation in the Lower South, which was perhaps more seriously fractured by local disputes and divided loyalties than other regions, and where partisan fighters like Francis Marion had enslaved and free Africans among his band. Thomas Sumpter, by contrast, offered slaves as bounties to attract fighters. Many planters, particularly in the Chesapeake, moved their bondspeople as far away as possible from the fighting and continued their routine as best they could. More widespread fighting in the Lower South meant fewer safe havens, and planters were content if slaves remained on the plantation and supported themselves. Disorder and social uncertainty made this course of action attractive also for many slaves. They raised cotton for their own use and garden crops for their personal consumption and

Joyce Chaplin has noted with irony the fact that cotton at this stage represented the enslaved's temporary autonomy while it would come to symbolize their children's bondage.[31]

As important as anything else, the American Revolution marked division of the emerging nation into a northern region dominated by free labor and a southern region where slavery reigned supreme. The rhetoric of freedom and fervor of evangelicalism affected master and slave alike in the Chesapeake causing some to offer and many to seize their personal independence. One historian suggests, in fact, that the scale of absconding from the plantations could be viewed as a kind of slave rebellion, so widespread was the rejection of bondage, and one that affected Upper and Lower South alike.[32] Only in the Upper South, however, did a few planters move actively to extinguish their claim on slaves. Others passively accepted the slaves' initiative in fleeing and still others provided one or another means for self-liberation—such as self-purchase or acting as a substitute in military service. Ultimately, economic and social habits proved too strong to erode and the region remained dependent upon slaves. This was even more the case in the Lower South, where, despite a proposal to free a few slaves in return for their military service and some increase in manumissions during the era, planters showed themselves to be largely immune to revolutionary altruism.[33] Indeed, consideration of the military proposal indicated how committed they were to their customary labor practices. But enslaved Africans imbibed the tenor of the age and an aggrieved Charleston slavemaster ordered the chastisement of a man he claimed as property because "he has the audacity to tell me, he will be free, that he will serve no Man, and that he will be conquered or governed by no Man."[34]

In the North, where slavery was not so essential to the economy, the ideology of freedom was more corrosive but even there it did not always die quickly or easily and African-Americans did not hesitate to press the issue. Enslaved New Englanders, more likely to be literate than servitors elsewhere, frequently proclaimed their case in the extant language of the revolution. Thus black New Hampshire petitioners declared: "Freedom is an inherent right of the human Species, not to be surrendered, but by Consent, for the sake of social Life."[35] And a black man in Philadelphia expressed in equal measures a longing for social equity, a calculation of the effect of black military activity, and personal bravado when he responded to a white woman in Philadelphia who upbraided him for not giving way to her: "stay . . . 'till Lord Dunmore and his black regiment come, and then we will see who is to take the wall."[36] Although it may not be fashionable to note, the revolutionary crisis caused many ordinary folk to reflect seriously upon the nature of their society, to find it wanting, and to react with resolve or resignation to the inconsistency of bound labor with a cry for the rights of man. Some did so apprehensively, as the Philadelphia woman who "dream'd of our Negroes and cou'd not get them out of my Mind . . . am Uneasy about them . . . had no rest."[37] Others did so forthrightly, as the Massachusetts pamphleteer who proclaimed: "many will object to the freeing of the *Slaves* among us, by saying, If they are set at Liberty they will turn Vagrants, and thereby become a Pest to Society; that our Streets will be filled with Robbers, House-breakers, etc. In Answer to which I would ask this Question, What Right had we to bring those People among us, or to encourage so iniquitous a Trade?"[38]

Eventually, slavery died and laid the basis for two competing economic systems within the nation. The revolution also removed the constraints of a European nation among whose global concerns the North American colonies were but one calculation and brought to power a planter elite of more limited aspirations, who responded favorably to the settler clamor for movement west and creation of the cotton kingdom that dominated the nineteenth century.

NOTES

1. Peter H. Wood, *Black Majority: Negroes in Colonial South Carolina from 1670 through the Stono Rebellion* (New York, 1974), p. xvi n. 3.
2. Ibid., p. xiii. Also see Gerald W. Mullin, "Rethinking American Negro Slavery from the Vantage Point of the Colonial Era," *Louisiana Studies* (Summer 1973): 398–422.
3. See Michael Mullin (ed.), *American Negro Slavery: A Documentary History* (Columbia, SC, 1976), Willie Lee Rose (ed.), *A Documentary History of Slavery in North America* (New York, 1976), and Ira Berlin, *Many Thousands Gone: The First Two Centuries of Slavery in North America* (Cambridge, Mass., 1998).
4. See, for example, Russell R. Menard, "From Servants to Slaves: The Transformation of the Chesapeake Labor System," *Southern Studies*, 16 (Winter 1977): 355–90; and Timothy Breen, "A Changing Labor Force and Race Relations in Virginia 1660–1710," *Journal of Social History*, 7 (Autumn 1973): 3–25.
5. Edmund S. Morgan, *American Slavery, American Freedom: The Ordeal of Colonial Virginia* (New York, 1975), 13.
6. Quotation in Alden T. Vaughan, *Roots of American Racism: Essays on the Colonial Experience* (New York, 1995), 174.
7. Douglas Deal, "A Constricted World: Free Blacks on Virginia's Eastern Shore, 1680–1750," in Lois Green Carr et al. (eds.), *Colonial Chesapeake Society* (Chapel Hill, NC, 1988), 280.
8. Magnus Mörner, *Race Mixture in the History of Latin America* (Boston, 1967), 56–7.
9. Russell R. Menard is responsible for reinterpreting the relationship between sugar, the Dutch, and plantation development in Barbados. See his *Sweet Negotiations: Sugar, Slavery, and Plantation Agriculture in Early Barbados* (Charlottesville, Va., 2006), quotation p. 35.
10. Richard S. Dunn, *Sugar and Slaves: The Rise of the Planter Class in the English West Indies, 1624–1713* (Chapel Hill, NC, 1972), 110–11.
11. April Lee Hatfield, *Atlantic Virginia: Intercolonial Relations in the Seventeenth Century* (Philadelphia, 2004), 140–1.
12. Ibid. 142; Morgan, *American Slavery*, 127–30, 296–8; Menard, *Sweet Negotiations*, 96–7.
13. S. Max Edelson, *Plantation Enterprise in Colonial South Carolina* (Cambridge, Mass., 2006), 43; Hatfield, *Atlantic Virginia*, 143 ff.

14. Hatfield, *Atlantic Virginia*, 138; John Lawson, *Lawson's History of North Carolina* (London, 1714; reprint Richmond, Va., 1937), 182–3.

15. See, for example, Laurence Shore's review of Daniel Littlefield's *Rice and Slaves: Ethnicity and the Slave Trade in Colonial South Carolina* in the *Journal of Ethnic Studies*, 12 (1984): 121–6.

16. David Eltis et al., "Agency and Diaspora in Atlantic History: Reassessing the African Contribution to Rice Cultivation in the Americas," *American Historical Review*, 112 (December 2007): 1329–58.

17. Quotation in Berlin, *Many Thousands Gone*, 54.

18. Lorenzo J. Greene, *The Negro in Colonial New England* (1942; New York, 1968), 106.

19. Ibid. 101.

20. Berlin, *Many Thousands Gone*, 178.

21. John W. Sweet, *Bodies Politic: Negotiating Race in the American North, 1730–1830* (Baltimore, 2003), 62.

22. Ibid. 88.

23. Alan Gallay, *The Indian Slave Trade: The Rise of the English Empire in the American South, 1670–1717* (New Haven, 2002), 7–8.

24. Ibid. 272.

25. Jane Landers, *Black Society in Spanish Florida* (Urbana, Ill., 1999), 72–3.

26. Kevin Mulroy, *Freedom on the Border: The Seminole Maroons in Florida, the Indian Territory, Coahuila, and Texas* (Lubbock, Tex., 1993), 29.

27. See, among other things, John Thornton, "African Dimensions of the Stono Rebellion," *American Historical Review*, 96 (October 1991): 1101–13.

28. Gwendolyn Midlo Hall, *Africans in Colonial Louisiana: The Development of Afro-Creole Culture in the Eighteenth Century* (Baton Rouge, La., 1992), p. xiv.

29. Peter Caron, "'Of a nation which others do not understand': Bambara Slaves and African Ethnicity in Colonial Louisiana, 1718–60," *Slavery and Abolition*, 18 (April 1997): 98–121 offers cautions regarding use of the term "Bambara."

30. Hall, *Africans in Colonial Louisiana*, 2.

31. Joyce E. Chaplin, *An Anxious Pursuit: Agricultural Innovation and Modernity in the Lower South, 1730–1815* (Chapel Hill, NC, 1993), 219.

32. See Sylvia R. Frey, *Water from the Rock: Black Resistance in a Revolutionary Age* (Princeton, 1991).

33. For the suggested increase in manumissions see Robert Olwell, "Becoming Free: Manumission and the Genesis of a Free Black Community in South Carolina, 1740–90," in Jane G. Landers (ed.), *Against the Odds: Free Blacks in the Slave Societies of the Americas* (London, 1996), 5.

34. Quoted in Daniel C. Littlefield, *Rice and Slaves: Ethnicity and the Slave Trade in Colonial South Carolina* (Urbana, Ill., 1991), 165.

35. Littlefield, *Revolutionary Citizens: African Americans, 1776–1804* (New York, 1997), 32.

36. Ibid. 42.

37. Ibid.

38. Quoted in Timothy H. Breen, "Making History: The Force of Public Opinion and the Last Years of Slavery in Revolutionary Massachusetts," in Ronald Hoffman et al. (eds.), *Through A Glass Darkly: Reflections on Personal Identity in Early America* (Chapel Hill, NC, 1997), 93.

Select Bibliography

Berlin, Ira, and Ronald Hoffman, eds. *Slavery and Freedom in the Age of the American Revolution*. Charlottesville, Va.: University Press of Virginia, 1983.

Brown, Richmond F., ed. *Coastal Encounters: The Transformation of the Gulf Coast in the Eighteenth Century*. Lincoln, Nebr.: University of Nebraska Press, 2007.

Curtin, Philip D. *The Rise and Fall of the Plantation Complex: Essays in Atlantic History*. Cambridge: Cambridge University Press, 1990.

Davis, David B. *Inhuman Bondage: The Rise and Fall of Slavery in the New World*. New York: Oxford University Press, 2006.

Fogel, William F. *Without Consent or Contract: The Rise and Fall of American Slavery*. New York: W. W. Norton and Company, 1989.

Hodges, Graham R. *Root and Branch: African Americans in New York and East Jersey, 1613–1863*. Chapel Hill, NC: University of North Carolina Press, 1999.

Innes, Stephen, ed. *Work and Labor in Early America*. Chapel Hill, NC: University of North Carolina Press, 1988.

Jordan, Winthrop D. *White over Black: American Attitudes towards the Negro, 1550–1812*. Chapel Hill, NC: University of North Carolina Press, 1968.

Kulikoff, Allan. *Tobacco and Slaves: The Development of Southern Cultures in the Chesapeake, 1680–1800*. Chapel Hill, NC: University of North Carolina Press, 1986.

Littlefield, Daniel C. "John Jay, the Revolutionary Generation and Slavery," *New York History*, 81 (January 2000): 91–132.

——"Slavery in French Louisiana: From Gallic Colony to American Territory," in John Lowe (ed.), *Louisiana Culture from the Colonial Era to Katrina* (Baton Rouge, La.: Louisiana State University Press, 2008), 75–99.

Menard, Russell R. "The Maryland Slave Population, 1658 to 1730: A Demographic Profile of Blacks in Four Counties," *William and Mary Quarterly*, 3rd ser., 32 (January 1975): 29–54.

——"From Servant to Freeholder: Status Mobility and Property Accumulation in Seventeenth-Century Maryland," *William and Mary Quarterly*, 3rd ser., 30 (January 1973): 37–64.

Parent, Anthony S. *Foul Means: The Formation of a Slave Society in Virginia, 1660–1740*. Chapel Hill, NC: University of North Carolina Press, 2003.

Thornton, John. *Africa and Africans in the Making of the Atlantic World*. Cambridge: Cambridge University Press, 1998.

CHAPTER 10

....

EARLY REPUBLIC AND ANTEBELLUM UNITED STATES

....

JEFF FORRET

DESPITE a history of African slavery on British mainland North America dating back to the seventeenth century, a disproportionate share of slave scholarship has focused on the antebellum era, broadly defined as the last six decades prior to emancipation. The disparity can be traced to the relatively more abundant and available sources on antebellum slavery as well as the connection between slavery and the sectional tensions culminating in the Civil War. During the colonial period, slavery was present in varying degrees throughout what would become the United States. In the wake of the American Revolution, however, slavery became the "peculiar institution" of the South. In the North, where the slave population was small and less crucial to the functioning of the economy, states took the revolutionary ideals of liberty and equality to their logical conclusion, each passing either an immediate or gradual emancipation law by 1804. Further south, especially in the Chesapeake, slavery was weakened as revolutionary-era runaways and manumissions depleted the slave population. Yet, with the fading of the revolution's egalitarian rhetoric and the invention of the cotton gin that made it possible to extract safely and efficiently the delicate fibers from short-staple cotton, the institution of slavery would not only persevere but become entrenched and expand across the southern United States. The antebellum decades witnessed the movement of slaves south and west with the advance of the cotton frontier. Although tobacco, rice, and sugar were cultivated in portions of the

South, slave-grown cotton drove the southern (and American) economy in the antebellum decades. Because the United States ceased its participation in the transatlantic slave trade in 1808, most antebellum-era slaves claimed the American South as their birthplace. Through natural reproduction, their numbers increased from approximately 1.1 million in 1810 to almost 4 million by 1860. Over the course of the antebellum decades, the vast majority of slaves converted to evangelical Christian faiths and forged a distinctly African-American culture. Many of the standard works in slave studies examine this mature slave society of the antebellum South. Since the 1990s, scholars have increasingly peered further back in time to produce a proliferation of studies on colonial-era slavery. The antebellum period, no longer the dominant temporal framework it once was, is anything but moribund, however. New subjects of study, innovative historical approaches, and a greater sensitivity to time and place demonstrate the vitality of slave studies in the antebellum era.

CLASSIC AND REVISIONIST WORKS ON ANTEBELLUM SLAVERY

Many classic works on American slavery implicitly adopted the antebellum period as their era of interest. Little significance, however, was attached to periodization. Widely recognized as the twentieth century's first scholarly authority on slavery, Ulrich Bonnell Phillips published *American Negro Slavery* in 1918, a pioneering book that held sway for nearly four decades. Reflecting a southern white perspective, Phillips portrayed antebellum slaveholders as benevolent masters who cared for their bondspeople and the plantation as a school in civilization for enslaved pupils. Planters molded the allegedly malleable African into a "predominant plantation type." According to Phillips, "The traits which prevailed were an eagerness for society, music and merriment, a fondness for display whether of person, dress, vocabulary or emotion, a not flagrant sensuality, a receptiveness toward any religion whose exercises were exhilarating, a proneness to superstition, a courteous acceptance of subordination, an avidity for praise, a readiness for loyalty of a feudal sort, and . . . a healthy human repugnance toward overwork."[1]

The next two monumental works in the historiography of slavery, Kenneth M. Stampp's *The Peculiar Institution: Slavery in the Ante-Bellum South* (1956) and Stanley M. Elkins's *Slavery: A Problem in American Institutional and Intellectual Life* (1959), responded directly to *American Negro Slavery*. Compared to Phillips, Stampp and Elkins wrote in a radically changed racial climate. As the Civil Rights Movement in the United States gained momentum in the 1950s, Stampp made clear in his preface the fundamental premise behind *The Peculiar Institution*. "I have assumed," he explained, "that the slaves were merely ordinary human beings, that innately Negroes *are*, after all, only white men with black skins, nothing more, nothing less." Although the reverse (that whites are black people with white skins) may be as easily suggested, Stampp rejected the racism that undergirded antebellum slavery and lamented slavery's effects on bondspeople. He portrayed an institution that was exploitative, oppressive, and cruel. Challenging Phillips, Stampp denied masters' paternalism, characterizing slaves as victims of abuse and neglect, robbed of their African culture in exchange for nothing but vocational training. "The average bondsman," he concluded, "lived more or less aimlessly in a bleak and narrow world." With its emphasis on the tragedy of antebellum slavery, *The Peculiar Institution* supplanted *American Negro Slavery* as the standard work in the field.[2]

Stanley M. Elkins's *Slavery* took U. B. Phillips to task for his explanation of the "predominant plantation type" among slaves, the docile, childlike, and dependent Sambo. Elkins accepted the Sambo personality as real. He argued, however, that Sambo was not the product of innate racial inferiority as Phillips had suggested but, rather, of the "closed system" of antebellum slavery in the United States. Compared to the "open system" of slavery in Latin America, where the Church and the state purportedly intervened in the master–slave relationship and mitigated the worst abuses of slavery, in the United States no such institutions interfered with masters' control over their slaves or restrained the powerful forces of capitalism. Thus, Elkins explained, like prisoners in Nazi concentration camps during the Second World War, slaves in the American South identified with the oppressors who wielded absolute power over them and internalized their values. The infantilized Sambo, then, represented a psychic response to harsh conditions rather than an inherently racial trait. Taken together, Elkins and Stampp successfully refuted Phillips's racial assumptions and exposed the destructive power of antebellum slavery. Their depictions, however, characterized southern slaves as victims of white treatment. An effort to counter the victimhood model lay at the heart of the next wave of scholarship on antebellum slavery. Revisionist historians, reflecting the growing radicalism of the Civil Rights Movement, attacked the Elkins thesis by emphasizing the agency of bondspeople.[3]

The revisionist scholarship beginning in the early 1970s relied on previously untapped sources to draw new conclusions about antebellum slavery. Whereas Phillips, Stampp, and others had crafted their works on the basis of antebellum plantation journals and diaries that reflected the perspective of the master, historians such as John W. Blassingame, Eugene D. Genovese, and Lawrence W. Levine increasingly turned to sources emanating from the slaves themselves, including the narratives collected from Works Progress Administration interviews in the 1930s, autobiographies, and folklore. Such sources permitted practitioners of the New Social History to craft their studies "from the bottom up." Not surprisingly, the resulting portrait of antebellum slavery differed markedly. In this new generation of scholarship, slaves were no longer the passive objects of white treatment but active agents in shaping their own lives. Despite the brutality of slavery, bondspeople demonstrated autonomy, resilience, and a remarkable ability to resist oppression. Within the slave quarters, close familial and kinship networks, a strong sense of community, and a rich African culture insulated slaves from the brutal excesses of bondage. Religion and superstition, music and dance, folksongs and folktales all provided slaves means of self-expression and avenues through which to carve out lives for themselves, independent of the master. This was anything but the dehumanizing "closed system" of slavery Elkins described. Sambo was real, John Blassingame concluded, but merely a mask, a ritual expression of deference performed in the master's presence. Acting like Sambo served as a defense mechanism—a means of coping with bondage—and did not signal any genuine psychic damage inflicted by the institution of slavery. The revisionist scholarship continually emphasized slavery's inability to dampen bondspeople's creativity, ingenuity, and adaptability. Despite enslavement, slaves retained a sense of autonomy and control over their own lives.[4]

Another theme historians in the 1970s pursued was the relationship between antebellum slavery and capitalism. Eugene D. Genovese broached this subject in *The Political Economy of Slavery* (1965). His snapshot of the antebellum South uncovered a region distinctly premodern compared to the North. Genovese argued that slavery was an economically irrational system in which an unmotivated labor force kept productivity low. Because capitalism represented not only an economic but also a social system, slavery was best characterized as "precapitalist." In the peculiar social system embraced by the South, Genovese explained, slaveholders' aristocratic ethos subsumed their drive for profits in favor of a preoccupation with honor and luxury. Genovese's monumental *Roll, Jordan, Roll* (1972), still arguably the single most significant volume ever published on antebellum southern slavery, pursued and elaborated upon this theme but from the perspective of those in bondage. Within the precapitalist system of slavery, paternalism defined the master–slave relationship. Genovese defined paternalism as an organic relationship that bound master and slave together in a complex web of reciprocal duties and obligations. Through paternalism, masters established hegemony over their slaves. Yet paternalism betrayed an ambivalence Genovese captured in the dialectic of "accommodation and resistance." Within the framework of paternalism, slaves asserted their own expectations, sometimes accepting and sometimes rejecting masters' efforts to manage them. As a result, the master–slave relationship was constantly negotiated and renegotiated. Through this complex bargaining process, slaves successfully forged their own cultural space, most evident in bondspeople's religious views and expression. For paternalist masters, then, with responsibilities to their broad plantation family, the crass demands of the market alone could not determine slaveholders' actions. The contours of the master–slave relationship Genovese described made the Old South distinct from the antebellum North, where values of the liberal capitalist marketplace predominated.[5]

Criticism of Genovese's argument proceeded along two fronts: quantitative and qualitative. At least as controversial as *Roll, Jordan, Roll*, Robert William Fogel and Stanley L. Engerman's cliometric study *Time on the Cross* (1974) brought statistical data to bear on most major questions scholars of antebellum slavery were actively debating. Unlike Genovese, Fogel and Engerman found antebellum slavery economically rational, efficient, and profitable. Slaveholders' use of rewards and incentives as alternatives to punishment made them much like the capitalist businessmen of the North. Analyzing the papers and diaries of antebellum planter families, James Oakes, too, uncovered an entrepreneurial ethos among southern slaveholders. In *The Ruling Race,* he argued that paternalism, present in the colonial-era South, declined in the face of rising market forces. In the antebellum decades, paternalism's sense of reciprocal obligations was overwhelmed by slaveholders' quest for profit and material gain. Only in the older, more established regions of the South that valued stability and hierarchy did paternalism remain. For the small slaveholders Oakes studied, hopes for the future hinged on the belief that hard work and thrift promised upward social mobility. They were not Genovese's paternalistic aristocrats but acquisitive capitalists, men on the make who sought to create "factories in the field" for pecuniary gain. They maintained a commitment to paternalism only in the rhetoric they employed to defend slavery. Differing definitions of "capitalism" and understandings of "paternalism" offer some explanation for the divergence of opinion between Genovese and Oakes. In addition, they examined different categories of slaveholders in different locations. In reality, the dichotomy between precapitalist and capitalist interpretations was not as sharp as it initially appeared. Subsequent scholarship revealed a convergence in their views. In *Slavery and Freedom* (1990), Oakes maintained that slavery existed within a capitalist world but conceded that "master and slave formed what was, at bottom, a nonmarket relationship." Genovese and Elizabeth Fox-Genovese meanwhile described the antebellum South as "in but not of" the capitalist world. *Fruits of Merchant Capital* (1983) expanded the temporal scope of Genovese's earlier works to embrace the eighteenth century as well as the antebellum period. Placing the Old South in broader context enabled the Genoveses to recognize better the sweeping forces of capitalist development under way and to situate the slaveholding South within that framework. Both sides of the debate, in short, acknowledged a more "ambiguous relationship between slavery and liberal capitalism" than they had previously posited.[6]

POST-REVISIONIST WORKS ON ANTEBELLUM SLAVERY

The sweeping, magisterial tomes common in the 1970s have since yielded to more manageable and narrowly focused volumes. One hallmark of post-revisionist literature is its diversity. Recent studies of slavery examine in remarkable depth an impressive range of topics, including slave law, slave literacy, and slaves' relationships with non-elite whites.[7] Whereas 1970s revisionism collectively sought to refute the Elkins thesis, post-revisionist scholarship lacks such a clear, common goal. Rather than overturning older interpretations, it seeks to refine and complicate the previous generation's findings. Post-revisionist works on antebellum slavery also illustrate contrasting trends toward periodization. Some literature stretches the antebellum time frame to forge links to the colonial or postwar periods, whereas other works reveal a continued commitment to a traditional "antebellum" era. Still others take the tack of examining smaller, meaningful decades within the antebellum years.

Slave autonomy continued as a predominant theme in post-revisionist scholarship, but unlike historians of the 1970s who rooted it in slave culture, post-revisionists of the 1980s and 1990s saw slave autonomy as emerging from the slaves' economy. In a pair of landmark articles, Philip D. Morgan uncovered a thriving internal economy in the Carolina and Georgia lowcountry. There, slaves laboring in rice fields under the task system had the opportunity to use their free time at the end of the day as they saw fit. Many enterprising slaves cultivated provision grounds allotted them by the master, tended horses or livestock, and sold the commodities they grew or raised. Morgan's pioneering investigation into Southern Claims Commission records revealed that some antebellum slaves accumulated impressive amounts of property. Outside the lowcountry, other scholars discovered, conditions were not as favorable for the development of a slave economy. Where slaves labored in gangs from sunup to sundown, or where masters lacked sufficient land to provide slaves garden plots, bondspeople lacked the time and resources of their lowcountry counterparts. Nevertheless, historians have shown that, even outside the lowcountry, slaves' own efforts made them visible participants in the antebellum marketplace. Masters concerned over the sense of independence the slave economy engendered among their bondspeople took steps to curtail it by purchasing slaves' commodities themselves and by prohibiting slaves' marketing activities by law, but their efforts could not entirely prevent slaves' access to markets or exposure to commercial values. Emphasizing slaves' autonomy, historians were slower to realize that the slave economy and property accumulation also generated friction in the quarters.[8]

Much post-revisionist literature contends with the legacy of the "slave community" paradigm of the 1970s, in which family, religion, and culture helped slaves resist the dehumanization of bondage. Although a necessary corrective to the image of Sambo, the "slave community" exaggerated the strength and cohesion of the quarters. As Peter Kolchin observed, the revisionist scholarship came "dangerously close to replacing a mythical world in which slaves were objects of total control with an equally mythical world in which slaves were hardly slaves at all."[9] Any romanticization of the slave community is rapidly drawing to a close. Research now demonstrates that it proved no more immune to conflict than white society. Bridging scholarship on the slave economy and the slave community, Dylan C. Penningroth's insightful analysis of economic relations among slaves reveals frequent disputes over property possession and ownership. Such disagreements internal to the slave quarters, Penningroth contends, dispel the myth of a unified slave community but are not entirely incompatible with a sense of community. Indeed, community recognition was crucial to the validation of slaves' claims to property. For Penningroth, conflict inside the slave community resulted from bondspeople negotiating their own power relationships within the quarters.[10] Anthony E. Kaye goes further in challenging the unity and harmony implicit in the notion of the "slave community." Kaye introduces the interpretative framework of "neighborhood" to explore the question of slave identity. Slave neighborhoods consisted of adjoining plantation spaces in which slaves socialized, forged kinship networks, worked, and resisted bondage. By Kaye's formulation, antebellum slave society consisted of innumerable neighborhoods throughout the South rather than a single, monolithic slave community. His concept of neighborhood explains both solidarity and division among slaves by embracing some bondspeople as "insiders" but rejecting others as "outsiders" or "strangers." Kaye acknowledges briefly, however, a collective identity among slaves broader than neighborhood. Although the general thrust of recent work undermines the revisionist portrayal of a flat, static, and unnaturally harmonious slave community, issues of slave consciousness and identity invite further scholarship.[11]

If historians have recognized the limits of the antebellum slave community, they have also tempered their view of the slave family. For two decades, Herbert G. Gutman's *The Black Family in Slavery and Freedom* (1976) stood as the classic work on the subject. Gutman rejected Daniel Patrick Moynihan's controversial governmental report of 1965, "The Negro Family: The Case for National Action," which attributed the "pathology" of the contemporary black family to the weakness of a matriarchal family structure that dated back to slavery. Gutman portrayed the typical enslaved family as stable, nuclear, and a source of strength for slaves coping with bondage. Neither powerless nor emasculated, slave fathers were important figures in their children's lives. Without denying the centrality of family as an instrument for slaves' survival, scholars have more recently suggested that Gutman overestimated the number of two-parent slave households and exaggerated the stability of the enslaved family. Current research recognizes both the variety of family structures under slavery and the ways in which bondage undermined the family and imposed incredible strains on enslaved husbands and wives. Masters sometimes interfered in bondspeople's choice of marital partners, whipped one enslaved spouse in the presence of the other, and appropriated female slaves' bodies for their own sexual purposes. Southern law withheld legal recognition of slave marriages. The pressures slave couples faced at times erupted in marital strife and discord "within the slave cabin." Although not a majority, many slave families were necessarily matrifocal. Enslaved women in cross-plantation, or abroad, marriages accepted primary responsibility for raising children as their husbands resided on nearby holdings all or most of the week. Slaveholders also tended to respect a slave mother's bond to her child more than that of the father.[12]

Perhaps most important, the ever-present threat of sale and disruption loomed over slave families, especially those living in the slave-exporting states of the Upper South. The thriving interstate slave trade of the late antebellum decades divided enslaved spouses, parents and children, and brothers and sisters, and the forced migration of slaves with their masters to fresh lands on the cotton frontier wrought similar devastation. Whether carried off by the trader or the master, relocation created hardships for slaves and generated irreparable feelings of sorrow and loss. The uprooting of slaves took a particular toll on abroad marriages and the extended kinship and other social networks cultivated across plantation bound-aries. Victims of forced migration described themselves, tellingly, as "stolen." Those separated from friends and loved ones next confronted the challenging task of rebuilding social ties, often in newly settled regions where unbalanced age or sex ratios made family formation difficult. The disruptions of the slave trade and forced migration guaranteed that the construction and maintenance of slave family structures remained an ongoing and dynamic process.[13]

Post-revisionist scholarship on the slave economy, community, and family illustrates the morphology of the term "antebellum," a word with flexible and imprecise meanings. Depending upon the user, it referred to the last three, four, or even six or seven decades prior to the Civil War and emancipation. Most works on slavery published in the 1970s and 1980s employed "antebellum" traditionally, referring to a mature form of southern slavery from 1820 or 1830 to the war. Beginning in the 1990s, scholars took greater interest than ever in colonial-era bondage, producing landmark works in the historiography of American slavery.[14] A relative neglect of slavery in the first two decades of the nineteenth century remains, but historians have increasingly produced studies bridging the colonial and antebellum eras, pursuing themes common to both periods and trends that spanned the American Revolution. Religious developments and cultural processes, for instance, honored no periodization determined by political events. Philip Morgan's study of the slave economy also broke free from the constraints of the antebellum decades, locating the origins of slaves' independent economic activities in the colonial period. In consequence, the once strict division between studies of colonial slavery and those of antebellum slavery is dissolving.[15]

By the same token, recent works on the antebellum South are more likely to extend into Reconstruction and the postwar world as well. Whereas most studies of antebellum slavery offer only a cursory conclusion or epilogue offering a glimpse at the Civil War and its aftermath, growing numbers of scholars are gazing further into the nineteenth century in a substantive and meaningful way. For example, just as Morgan's work embraced the colonial era, his analysis of Southern Claims Commission records also permitted him to venture beyond 1860 and into the postbellum period. Dylan Penningroth and Anthony Kaye offer other studies in which the Civil War served not as a logical conclusion but instead as an engine for change. Extending their studies into the war years and beyond, they showed, respectively, that emancipation rewrote the rules governing slave property and removed the restrictive boundaries imposed on slave neighborhoods. Studies of the slave family have long traversed the Civil War that so many works treat as a barrier. In the wake of war, ex-slaves struggled to reunite families torn asunder, renegotiate household relationships of power, and survive economically. Slavery persisted for centuries on the North American mainland, but it was not a static institution. "Antebellum" retains a distinct if inexact meaning, but looking chronologically backward and forward from those decades alerts historians to change over time. A greater challenge for historians of slavery comes in discerning change over time *within* the customary bounds of the antebellum rubric.[16]

That difficulty is evident in scholarship on enslaved women. As the picture of slave families has come into sharper focus, the condition of women in slavery has become clearer. Like historians before them, the revisionist scholars of the 1970s paid little attention to enslaved women. Their works usually discussed androgynous "slaves" but invoked masculine pronouns when referring to individuals. Even Herbert Gutman's examination of the slave family neglected women, concentrating instead on refuting the alleged "emasculation" of enslaved men. The women's movement and feminist theory at last paid dividends in the study of antebellum southern slavery in the mid-1980s, when gender truly emerged as a category of analysis within the field. Deborah Gray White's pathbreaking *Ar'n't I a Woman?* offered the first study dedicated to the lives of female slaves. She found that, while race distinguished bondswomen in significant ways from white women, their sex made their experience of enslavement notably different from that of enslaved black men. Their reproductive capacity meant that childbearing and childrearing responsibilities determined the course of their lives. Masters rewarded fecund slave women and were more likely to sell the infertile. Because the cycle of pregnancy and childbirth interrupted work routines in the field, female slaves put in their most grueling work routines once their reproductive years had passed but before old age. Throughout their adult lives, after the day's work for the master, slave women faced the added burden of completing domestic chores back in the quarters. As house servants, they suffered the master's constant scrutiny and enjoyed little privacy.[17]

Above all, enslaved women's vulnerability to sexual exploitation by southern white men—masters, masters' sons, and overseers—set their lives apart from those of slave men. As Catherine Clinton explained, slavery represented a system of both production and "reproduction." A cultural double standard permitted sexually predatory southern white men liberties denied white "ladies." Southern law granted tacit permission for the rape and sexual coercion of bondswomen in the quarters, liaisons that sometimes produced offspring to augment the master's wealth. Recent scholarship has exposed the wide range of interracial sexual contacts possible in the South, including apparently long-term relationships such as the widely publicized Thomas Jefferson–Sally Hemings affair, but forced sex always figured more prominently. The sexual menace masters posed to female slaves had wide repercussions on the plantation, not only affecting the enslaved women but also tormenting the black men in the slave quarters as well as plantation mistresses. Slaveholding wives sometimes vented their own frustrations on their husbands' favorite slave women, exacerbating the brutality of a system that induced, in Nell Irvin Painter's memorable words, "soul murder."[18] The sexual violence endemic to the slave system belied notions of planter paternalism, yet southern whites constructed the image of the Jezebel to rationalize white men's sexual adventures in the quarters. Symbolizing the purportedly libidinous black woman, the Jezebel was the antithesis of the southern white lady. She craved sex and invited liaisons with the master. To counterbalance the Jezebel, a contrasting image of black womanhood, the nurturing, devoted, and asexual mammy, reassured masters the slave system was just. Mammy cared for the white family, and the white family reciprocated. According to Deborah Gray White, enslaved women's unique burdens forged among them a distinct identity as women. From the time they joined the predominantly female "trash gang" in their early teens, a network of enslaved women found support in one another.[19]

Despite their enormous contributions to slave scholarship, historians studying enslaved antebellum women have tended to offer broad treatments of the prewar period, likely an unwitting by-product of their reliance on slave narratives. As sources, slave narratives liberate historians from the master's bias, yet, because they are weighted heavily in favor of the late antebellum era, they are not conducive to precise periodization. A truly pivotal moment for enslaved women came when the United States ended its legal participation in the transatlantic slave trade in 1808. Although the slave population had long been rising through natural increase, the reproductive capacity of female slaves now made them instrumental to the survival of the antebellum slave regime. Masters took greater interest than ever in enslaved women's offspring.

The children so crucial to the maintenance of antebellum slavery were slow to gain historians' attention, however. Just as women experienced slavery differently from men, childhood marked a phase of slave life distinct from adulthood. Although some scholars—and slave autobiographers such as Frederick Douglass—suggested that slavery spared enslaved children the worst abuses of the institution, Wilma King's study of slave youth argued that bondage was traumatic for slave children and deprived them of their childhood. Despite some opportunities for play and leisure and the support of community, enslaved children were not spared the horrors of bondage. Masters put them to work as early as was physically possible, punished them, and separated them from parents. According to King, children suffered greatly as the weakest and most vulnerable members of slave society. Rather than gauge the severity of bondage for enslaved youth, Marie Jenkins Schwartz broke down their early lives into developmental stages. From birth to infancy to young adulthood, she contends, masters vied with enslaved parents for authority over slave youngsters. Determined slave parents struggled to minimize white interference in childcare and childrearing, and slave children learned to balance the conflicting expectations of two contrasting sets of authority. Acting as a buffer between master and slave child, enslaved parents socialized their children and instructed them in techniques of survival, including proper racial etiquette, rituals of deference, and the ability to work well. But as children grew into teenagers and gained competence at their tasks, their likelihood of sale increased. In the works of King and Schwartz, age joined gender as a meaningful category of analysis in slave studies. The growing appreciation of age suggests that an examination dedicated exclusively to elderly slaves should be in the offing.[20]

While gender and age have offered new lenses through which to view the experiences of antebellum bondspeople, slave studies have also taken what Edward E. Baptist and Stephanie M. H. Camp describe as a "cultural turn." Building on the social history of the 1970s and 1980s, historians beginning in the 1990s delved deeper than ever into slaves' inner lives, culture, and identity. Analyzing the most personal and profound experiences and events of slaves' lives unlocks their views of the world they inhabited, and bondspeople's values, beliefs, and emotions come into sharper focus. As with other post-revisionist works, the new cultural history of slavery pursues different trajectories in its treatment of the antebellum years. While some studies maintain a commitment to the broad antebellum era as a heuristic device, others parcel the period into narrower segments of time with a precision absent from most previous scholarship.[21]

Dealing with the antebellum era generally, investigations into slave health illustrate the possibilities of the new cultural history of slavery. Whereas historians taking a biomedical approach concentrated on diseases and slaves' susceptibility to them, Sharla M. Fett examines the experience and meaning of illness in the quarters. Health and healing emerged as contested terrain between masters and slaves. While masters concerned themselves with slave health for reasons of plantation productivity and slaves' market value, bondspeople recognized connections between the physical and spiritual well-being of the patient and between the patient and the broader enslaved community. These contrasting approaches to illness translated into conflicting treatment regimens. White medical doctors represented and collaborated with masters to administer—often without a slave's consent—invasive, coercive, and "heroic" treatments sometimes worse than the diseases they attempted to cure. Prioritizing instead the needs and wishes of the patient, slave healers relied upon their own diagnoses and remedies of African, Native American, and European origins. They identified a spiritual dimension to health and willingly harnessed the regenerative power of both natural and supernatural worlds, drawing as appropriate upon medicinal roots, herbal remedies, and conjuration. Masters interfered particularly in the medical care of enslaved women. Female slaves' reproductive powers invited the unwelcome intervention of white doctors concerning issues of infertility, menstruation, pregnancy, childbirth (and its complications), and a range of gynecological maladies. Justifiably distrustful of white medical professionals, enslaved mothers preferred the prescribed treatments of the elderly female slaves and midwives whose expertise they consulted, often secretly. As respected members of slave society, African-American midwives navigated a complex cultural course as they mediated black and white meanings of childbirth, social spaces, and medical knowledge.[22]

Contests between slaves and masters over childbearing, reproductive health, and the treatment of disease point to the enslaved body as a site of struggle. Studies of "resistance" to the master's authority once referred only to the slave revolts so much more common in Latin America than in the southern United States. Between the revolution and the Civil War, only two actual slave rebellions erupted in the South. Nat Turner's 1831 revolt in Southampton County, Virginia, easily overshadows the lesser known and enigmatic rebellion along Louisiana's German Coast in 1811. Far more common were the countless slave plots and conspiracies (some of which existed only in the active imaginations of anxious whites) that were uncovered and frustrated before any blood was shed, most famously those of Gabriel (1800) and Denmark Vesey (1822). By the 1970s, Eugene D. Genovese and others called attention to the various forms of "day-to-day" resistance slaves employed, including work slowdowns, breaking or "losing" tools, theft, arson, and running away.[23] Resistance studies, however, were gendered masculine. Female slaves did not actively participate in the few violent slave rebellions the South witnessed and composed only a small fraction of all runaways. Enslaved midwives notwithstanding, women in bondage lacked the mobility of slave men. Their working lives and childrearing responsibilities limited enslaved women's ability to travel openly and made escape virtually impossible. Women in slavery therefore engaged in more covert forms of resistance than enslaved men, such as feigning illness or poisoning the master's family. Female slaves could also resist white authority by seizing control of their bodies. When they relied upon their own means of regaining health, utilizing the expertise of the black doctors widely respected in the quarters, they implicitly issued a political statement in defiance of the master.[24]

Stephanie M. H. Camp observes that enslaved women's resistance extended to the manipulation and use of their bodies in plantation space. The cultural history of slavery has identified space and movement as important themes in slaves' lives. Even though planters exercised domination over the black female body, Camp observes, it was also a site of "pleasure and resistance." While masters made concerted efforts to restrict and confine their slaves through the use of chains, passes, and patrols, enslaved women countered this "geography of containment" with a "rival geography" of their own. They created distinct, segregated spaces for relaxation and leisure, holding illicit parties deep in the woods for drinking, music, and dancing. At these events, enslaved women's fancy clothing, hairstyles, and jewelry all symbolized personal expression. Another less visible means through which women in bondage resisted the terms and conditions of enslavement was truancy, or temporary absenteeism. Although slave men made up a majority of both runaways and truants, enslaved women frequently absconded from the confines of plantation space for brief periods. Contests over slaves' movement also played out in bondspeople's intimate, romantic lives. Many slaveholders opposed relationships between slaves from different plantations because cross-plantation unions undermined their mastery. By custom, enslaved men rather than women did the traveling during courtship, and slave husbands ventured across plantation boundaries to visit their wives. An apparent preference among many bondspeople for abroad marriages demonstrated the competition between slaves and masters over movement within plantation spaces.[25]

The cultural history of slavery's sensitivity to gender has deepened our understanding of enslaved women's lives, but the gendered experiences of slave men require further study. For decades, scholars accepted the experiences of male slaves as normative and therefore functionally genderless. Whereas work on slave women has shown that sex as well as race uniquely shaped their world, few attempts have been made to view the lives of enslaved men from the same gendered perspective. Edward E. Baptist has opened the exploration of slave men's definition of manhood. White men in the antebellum South constructed their sense of masculine identity in part with respect to slaves—by dominating slave men and denying them their manhood. Certainly slave men lacked the ability to protect and defend their wives and families from white interference, but they nevertheless found ways to prove themselves men. Baptist's work detects different models of slave manhood on the cotton frontier of the antebellum South. Some enslaved men acted heroically, either by running away, fighting, or otherwise defying white authority. Others served as caretakers for new families cobbled together from the shards of broken ones. Still others acted as atomized individuals, rejecting ties to other slaves. All represented attempts to forge a masculine identity amid the chaos of forced migration. Baptist's preliminary findings indicate the need for cultural historians to fill this lacuna in the literature.[26]

As the works of Fett, Camp, and others make clear, the cultural history of slavery recognizes the importance of the enslaved body. But while slavery was fundamentally a system of labor, slaves' bodies also represented a peculiar form of capital. In his rich portrait of the New Orleans slave market, Walter Johnson describes the callous commodification of bondspeople at auction and the meanings of the market for traders, buyers, and slaves. His study departs from the tendency to view the antebellum era broadly by concentrating on the decade of the 1850s. As the interstate slave trade flourished, deception permeated the slave pens. Sellers altered slaves' appearance, instructed them to behave according to script, and concealed or created past histories for those on the block. To gaze beyond the façade of deceit, knowledgeable, savvy purchasers carefully read the coded messages embedded in slave bodies: the color of their skin; their teeth and gums; their scars. But if buyers read slaves, so, too, did slaves read buyers. Bondspeople cut into the dance between buyer and seller, projecting an image of their own choosing at auction. They shared versions of their pasts and answered questions in ways that could manipulate buyers. Reduced to a market value, slaves as capital helped determine the likelihood of sale. New research promises to uncover the many roles of slaves as capital—as payment for debt, as inherited property, as profitable resource for hire, as mortgaged collateral for loans, as insured commodity. These studies must surely demonstrate an increasing sensitivity to time.[27]

If historians have identified any particular defining decade within the antebellum era, it is surely the 1830s. Slavery had erupted as a politically divisive issue in the Missouri crisis between 1819 and 1821. In turn, debate over Missouri's admittance into the Union informed allegations of the Vesey conspiracy of 1822. Rather than simply a culmination of latent tensions, however, events of the early 1820s portended the even more serious developments of the 1830s. With the dissemination of David Walker's *Appeal to the Coloured Citizens of the World* and the publication of William Lloyd Garrison's *The Liberator*, the early 1830s witnessed the rise of a small but vocal and potent abolitionist movement. Not coincidentally, many panicked southern whites linked Nat Turner's bloody rebellion of 1831 to the appearance of *The Liberator* earlier in the year. With John C. Calhoun at the lead, slaveholders mobilized in defense of the peculiar institution by refashioning the proslavery argument. No longer the "necessary evil" that slaveholders inherited from their ancestors, slavery emerged as a "positive good" for the South, for the nation, and for bondspeople themselves. In debates over the federal tariff, meanwhile, Calhoun advanced the theory of nullification that laid the constitutional foundation for the political defense of slavery. Feeling besieged by the growing power of the national government, southern states determined to find recourse.

The 1830s emerges as the pivotal decade in Mark M. Smith's examination of time in the Old South. Among other factors, the transportation revolution of the early nineteenth century and the accompanying rise of steamboats, railroads, and telegraphs complicated traditional southern understandings of time. By the 1830s, masters adopted clock time to measure slaves' productivity, help maximize profits, and instill discipline. Though slaves lacked watches, they grew familiar with clock time by the bells or horns that called them to the fields and learned to arrive punctually to avoid a whipping. Slaves never fully internalized clock time, however, and like industrial workers in the North, resisted its imposition through their own preindustrial conception of time firmly grounded in the seasonal rhythms of plantation agriculture. According to Smith, masters' implementation of clock time permitted them to stake a claim to modernity without embracing the free labor ideology of the capitalist North. Both capitalist and precapitalist features coexisted in the slaveholding South.[28]

The temporal boundaries of antebellum slavery studies have, then, both expanded and become more focused. Scholarship on antebellum slavery now more frequently reaches back into the colonial era or extends forward to the postwar years, yet some studies highlight the significance of particular decades. Limited by the types and availability of sources, works on certain facets of antebellum slavery reflect the more traditional approach to periodization even as they guide the scholarship down uncharted paths.

In their geographic coverage, too, historians of antebellum slavery are branching out to investigate regions long overlooked by past studies. Significant works like *Roll, Jordan, Roll, Time on the Cross*, and others paid little heed to the importance of location within the antebellum South. Sensitivity to place proved more important in the works of such scholars as Charles W. Joyner, William Dusinberre, and Brenda Stevenson, all of whom produced important local studies of antebellum slave communities in South Carolina or Virginia. Likewise, David S. Cecelski has examined maritime slaves in North Carolina who enjoyed remarkable liberties. A careful accounting of place demonstrates the diversity of experiences in antebellum slavery. These works, however, all focus on slavery in the older states of the Atlantic seaboard.[29] Increasingly historians are taking an interest in the emergence of slavery in the Old Southwest, from Florida to Alabama and Mississippi. Louisiana, with its complex political history in the colonial era and early Republic, has attracted more interest from historians of eighteenth-century slavery, but scholarship on the antebellum era is also on the rise.[30] As attention turns to the Old Southwest, the literature on forced migration and the internal slave trade that conveyed a bound workforce to the cotton fields has surged. This work confirms the objectification of bondspeople and lays bare the horror of the domestic traffic, but the concentration on the interstate slave trade underscores the continuing need for more extensive studies of forced separations through inheritance or through local sale.[31]

Despite the growing attention to geography in works on antebellum southern slavery, genuinely transnational comparative studies occupy a more tangential place in the historiography than they once did. Stanley M. Elkins's contention that the closed system of southern slavery exceeded Latin American slavery in brutality and oppression prompted works that traced the broad contours of difference between the two regions. Other scholars compared antebellum southern slavery to various forms of bondage in non-Western societies. Arguably the best of these works remains Peter Kolchin's *Unfree Labor*, which compares southern slavery and Russian serfdom. His analysis revealed a greater sense of community among serfs than slaves that translated into collective resistance in Russia and individual acts of resistance among southern bondspeople. Arrestingly, Kolchin's set of unfree laborers neutralized the factor of race, but his research design had the benefit of controlling for time, given the chronology of the rise and fall of the two labor systems. Any transnational comparative work poses inherent challenges, requiring expertise in not one but two geographic regions, societies, cultures, economies, political systems, and, often, languages. The daunting task is not often executed successfully. Paradoxically, scholars today recognize more than ever the value of comparative work, yet no renaissance of truly comparative studies has materialized. Noteworthy slavery anthologies pursuing common themes across space have tremendous merit, but the collected essays are implicitly rather than explicitly comparative. Direct comparisons and contrasts between slavery in the antebellum South and other regions are less common than they were in the 1960s and 1970s. Long an advocate and practitioner of comparative history, Kolchin recently renewed his call for more works either externally or internally comparative. Much may yet be gained from comparisons of the South to foreign nations or to the North, but comparisons of different locations within the South also prove valuable in highlighting the region's diversity.[32]

From an emphasis on the brutality and dehumanization of enslavement to an overstated stress on slave agency, the pendulum of antebellum slave studies has swung from one extreme to another. Current scholarship provides a more balanced, nuanced assessment of bondage than in generations past. The antebellum period no longer monopolizes studies of slavery in the American South. It now shares the spotlight with exciting scholarship on colonial slavery but nevertheless remains a vibrant field of study. The discovery of new sources and rediscovery of old ones have kept the scholarship alive. In the 1970s historians first turned to sources from the slaves themselves, such as the Federal Writers' Project narratives and slave autobiographies. By the 1980s, records of the Southern Claims Commission fell under historians' scrutiny. Scholars continue to uncover sources from the Civil War and immediate postwar years to read backward into the antebellum era. Pension Bureau files for soldiers of the US Colored Troops, interviews from the American Freedman's Inquiry Commission, and applications for accounts in the Freedmen's Saving and Trust Bank have all provided clues into the lives of antebellum slaves. Renewed appreciation for the Works Progress Administration narratives of the 1930s, often maligned for their shortcomings, has fueled some of the most innovative new gendered and cultural studies of southern slavery. Much can yet be gleaned from church and court records as well. With careful reading and rereading of the available evidence, studies of antebellum southern slavery will be distinguished by increasing creativity, imagination, and sophistication.

NOTES

1. Ulrich Bonnell Phillips, *American Negro Slavery: A Survey of the Supply, Employment and Control of Negro Labor as Determined by the Plantation Régime* (1918; New York, 1952), 291.
2. Kenneth M. Stampp, *The Peculiar Institution: Slavery in the Ante-Bellum South* (New York, 1956), pp. vii, 361.

3. Stanley M. Elkins, *Slavery: A Problem in American Institutional and Intellectual Life* (1959; 3rd edn. Chicago, 1976). Elkins's work drew heavily upon that of Frank Tannenbaum, *Slave and Citizen: The Negro in the Americas* (New York, 1947).

4. Although this scholarship is extensive, an abbreviated list of noteworthy works includes John W. Blassingame, *The Slave Community: Plantation Life in the Antebellum South* (1972; rev. edn. New York, 1979); Eugene D. Genovese, *Roll, Jordan, Roll: The World the Slaves Made* (1972; New York, 1976); George P. Rawick, *From Sundown to Sunup: The Making of the Black Community* (Westport, Conn., 1972); Herbert G. Gutman, *The Black Family in Slavery and Freedom, 1750–1925* (New York, 1976); Leslie Howard Owens, *This Species of Property: Slave Life and Culture in the Antebellum South* (New York, 1976); Lawrence W. Levine, *Black Culture and Black Consciousness: Afro-American Folk Thought from Slavery to Freedom* (New York, 1977); Albert J. Raboteau, *Slave Religion: The "Invisible Institution" in the Antebellum South* (1978; updated edn. New York, 2004); and Sterling Stuckey, *Slave Culture: Nationalist Theory and the Foundations of Black America* (New York, 1987). On the revisionist scholarship, see Peter Kolchin, "American Historians and Antebellum Southern Slavery, 1959–1984," in William J. Cooper, Jr., Michael F. Holt, and John McCardell (eds.), *A Master's Due: Essays in Honor of David Herbert Donald* (Baton Rouge, La., 1985).

5. Eugene D. Genovese, *The Political Economy of Slavery: Studies in the Economy and Society of the Slave South* (1965; New York, 1967); Genovese, *Roll, Jordan, Roll*. For a far more extensive and detailed discussion of the debate over the relationship between slavery and capitalism, see Mark M. Smith, *Debating Slavery: Economy and Society in the Antebellum American South* (Cambridge, 1998).

6. Robert William Fogel and Stanley L. Engerman, *Time on the Cross: The Economics of American Negro Slavery* (1974; New York, 1989); James Oakes, *The Ruling Race: A History of American Slaveholders* (1982; New York, 1998); Oakes, *Slavery and Freedom: An Interpretation of the Old South* (New York, 1990), 54, 79; Elizabeth Fox-Genovese and Eugene D. Genovese, *Fruits of Merchant Capital: Slavery and Bourgeois Property in the Rise and Expansion of Capitalism* (New York, 1983). See also Douglas R. Egerton, "Markets without a Market Revolution: Southern Planters and Capitalism," *Journal of the Early Republic*, 16 (Summer 1996): 207–21.

7. On slave law, see Michael Stephen Hindus, *Prison and Plantation: Crime, Justice, and Authority in Massachusetts and South Carolina, 1767–1878* (Chapel Hill, NC, 1980); Mark V. Tushnet, *The American Law of Slavery, 1810–1860: Considerations of Humanity and Interest* (Princeton, 1981); Edward L. Ayers, *Vengeance and Justice: Crime and Punishment in the 19th-Century American South* (New York, 1984); Philip J. Schwarz, *Twice Condemned: Slaves and the Criminal Laws of Virginia, 1705–1865* (Baton Rouge, La., 1988); Thomas D. Morris, *Southern Slavery and the Law, 1619–1860* (Chapel Hill, NC, 1996); Ariela J. Gross, *Double Character: Slavery and Mastery in the Antebellum Southern Courtroom* (Princeton, 2000); and Christopher Waldrep and Donald G. Nieman (eds.), *Local Matters: Race, Crime, and Justice in the Nineteenth-Century South* (Athens, Ga., 2001). On slave literacy, see Janet Duitsman Cornelius, *"When I Can Read My Title Clear": Literacy, Slavery, and Religion in the Antebellum South* (Columbia, SC, 1991); and Heather Andrea Williams, *Self-Taught: African American Education in Slavery and Freedom* (Chapel Hill, NC, 2005), ch. 1. On slaves' relations with non-elite whites, see Timothy James Lockley, *Lines in the Sand: Race and Class in Lowcountry Georgia, 1750–1860* (Athens, Ga., 2001); and Jeff Forret, *Race Relations at the Margins: Slaves and Poor Whites*

in the Antebellum Southern Countryside (Baton Rouge, La., 2006). On post-revisionist scholarship, see the afterword in Peter Kolchin, *American Slavery, 1619–1877* (rev. edn. New York, 2003), 239–49.

8. Philip D. Morgan, "Work and Culture: The Task System and the World of Low Country Blacks, 1700–1880," *William and Mary Quarterly*, 3rd ser., 39 (October 1982): 563–99; Morgan, "The Ownership of Property by Slaves in the Mid-Nineteenth-Century Low Country," *Journal of Southern History*, 49 (August 1983): 399–420. For another important work on the lowcountry, see Betty Wood, *Women's Work, Men's Work: The Informal Slave Economies of Lowcountry Georgia* (Athens, Ga., 1995). On areas outside the lowcountry, see John Campbell, "As 'A Kind of Freeman'? Slaves' Market-Related Activities in the South Carolina Up Country, 1800–1860," *Slavery and Abolition*, 12 (May 1991): 131–69; John T. Schlotterbeck, "The Internal Economy of Slavery in Rural Piedmont Virginia," *Slavery and Abolition*, 12 (May 1991): 170–81; Loren Schweninger, "The Underside of Slavery: The Internal Economy, Self-Hire, and Quasi-Freedom in Virginia," *Slavery and Abolition*, 12 (September 1991): 1–22; Joseph P. Reidy, "Obligation and Right: Patterns of Labor, Subsistence, and Exchange in the Cotton Belt of Georgia, 1790–1860," in Ira Berlin and Philip D. Morgan (eds.), *Cultivation and Culture: Labor and the Shaping of Slave Life in the Americas* (Charlottesville, Va., 1993), 138–54; Roderick A. McDonald, "Independent Economic Production by Slaves on Antebellum Louisiana Sugar Plantations," in Berlin and Morgan (eds.), *Cultivation and Culture*, 275–302; and Larry E. Hudson, Jr., *To Have and to Hold: Slave Work and Family Life in Antebellum South Carolina* (Athens, Ga., 1997), ch. 1. On a more clandestine, underground economy rooted in theft, see Alex Lichtenstein, "'That Disposition to Theft, with Which They Have Been Branded': Moral Economy, Slave Management, and the Law," *Journal of Social History*, 21 (Spring 1988): 413–40. Lawrence T. McDonnell, "Money Knows No Master: Market Relations and the American Slave Community," in Winfred B. Moore, Jr., Joseph F. Tripp, and Lyon G. Tyler, Jr. (eds.), *Developing Dixie: Modernization in a Traditional Society* (Westport, Conn., 1988), 31–44, first indicated the negative implications of the slave economy on relationships in the quarters.

9. Kolchin, *American Slavery*, 148–9. See also Kolchin, "Reevaluating the Antebellum Slave Community: A Comparative Perspective," *Journal of American History*, 70 (December 1983): 581. For a penetrating critique of the persistence of "agency" in slave studies, see Walter Johnson, "On Agency," *Journal of Social History*, 37 (Fall 2003): 113–24.

10. Dylan C. Penningroth, *The Claims of Kinfolk: African American Property and Community in the Nineteenth-Century South* (Chapel Hill, NC, 2003); Penningroth, "My People, my People: The Dynamics of Community in Southern Slavery," in Edward E. Baptist and Stephanie M. H. Camp (eds.), *New Studies in the History of American Slavery* (Athens, Ga., 2006), 166–76.

11. Anthony E. Kaye, *Joining Places: Slave Neighborhoods in the Old South* (Chapel Hill, NC, 2007). For a more detailed historiographical discussion of the slave community and its conceptual limitations, see Kaye, "Neighbourhoods and Solidarity in the Natchez District of Mississippi: Rethinking the Antebellum Slave Community," *Slavery and Abolition*, 23 (April 2002): 1–24.

12. Brenda Stevenson, "Distress and Discord in Virginia Slave Families, 1830–1860," in Carol Bleser (ed.), *In Joy and in Sorrow: Women, Family, and Marriage in the Victorian South, 1830–1900* (New York, 1991), 103–24; Ann Patton Malone, *Sweet Chariot: Slave Family and Household Structure in Nineteenth-Century Louisiana* (Chapel Hill, NC, 1992), ch. 8;

Stevenson, *Life in Black and White: Family and Community in the Slave South* (New York, 1996); Christopher Morris, "Within the Slave Cabin: Violence in Mississippi Slave Families," in Christine Daniels and Michael V. Kennedy (eds.), *Over the Threshold: Intimate Violence in Early America* (New York, 1999), 268–85; Wilma A. Dunaway, *The African-American Family in Slavery and Emancipation* (New York, 2003); Emily West, "Tensions, Tempers, and Temptations: Marital Discord among Slaves in Antebellum South Carolina," *American Nineteenth Century History*, 5 (Summer 2004): 1–18; West, *Chains of Love: Slave Couples in Antebellum South Carolina* (Urbana, Ill., 2004), ch. 2.

13. Edward E. Baptist, *Creating an Old South: Middle Florida's Plantation Frontier before the Civil War* (Chapel Hill, NC, 2002), ch. 3; Baptist, "'Stol' and Fetched Here': Enslaved Migration, Ex-slave Narratives, and Vernacular History," in *New Studies in the History of American Slavery*, 243–74.

14. Ira Berlin, *Many Thousands Gone: The First Two Centuries of Slavery in North America* (Cambridge, Mass., 1998); Philip D. Morgan, *Slave Counterpoint: Black Culture in the Eighteenth-Century Chesapeake and Lowcountry* (Chapel Hill, NC, 1998).

15. See, for example, Sylvia R. Frey and Betty Wood, *Come Shouting to Zion: African American Protestantism in the American South and British Caribbean to 1830* (Chapel Hill, NC, 1998); and Michael A. Gomez, *Exchanging our Country Marks: The Transformation of African Identities in the Colonial and Antebellum South* (Chapel Hill, NC, 1998). One notable work on the neglected period before 1820 is Adam Rothman, *Slave Country: American Expansion and the Origins of the Deep South* (Cambridge, Mass., 2005).

16. On the family, see Gutman, *The Black Family in Slavery and Freedom*; Leslie A. Schwalm, *A Hard Fight for We: Women's Transition from Slavery to Freedom in South Carolina* (Urbana, Ill., 1997); and Amy Dru Stanley, *From Bondage to Contract: Wage Labor, Marriage, and the Market in the Age of Slave Emancipation* (Cambridge, 1998).

17. Deborah Gray White, *Ar'n't I a Woman?: Female Slaves in the Plantation South* (1985; rev. edn. New York, 1999). For another early look at slave women, see Jacqueline Jones, *Labor of Love, Labor of Sorrow: Black Women, Work, and the Family from Slavery to the Present* (New York, 1986), ch. 1. Dated but still worthwhile is the historiographical discussion of enslaved women in Patricia Morton, "Introduction," in Patricia Morton (ed.), *Discovering the Women in Slavery: Emancipating Perspectives on the American Past* (Athens, Ga., 1996), 1–26.

18. On the sexual exploitation of enslaved women, see Catherine Clinton, "'Southern Dishonor': Flesh, Blood, Race, and Bondage," in Bleser (ed.), *In Joy and in Sorrow*, 52–68 (quotation 54); Catherine Clinton, "Caught in the Web of the Big House: Women and Slavery," in Walter J. Fraser, Jr., R. Frank Saunders, Jr., and Jon L. Wakelyn (eds.), *The Web of Southern Social Relations: Women, Family, and Education* (Athens, Ga., 1985), 19–34; Nell Irvin Painter, *Southern History across the Color Line* (Chapel Hill, NC, 2002), ch. 1; Thelma Jennings, "'Us Colored Women Had to Go through a Plenty': Sexual Exploitation of African American Slave Women," *Journal of Women's History*, 1 (Winter 1990): 45–74; Melton A. McLaurin, *Celia, a Slave* (Athens, Ga., 1991); and Carolyn J. Powell, "In Remembrance of Mira: Reflections on the Death of a Slave Woman," in *Discovering the Women in Slavery*, 47–60. On interracial sex in the antebellum South, see Hélène Lecaudey, "Behind the Mask: Ex-Slave Women and Interracial Sexual Relations," in *Discovering the Women in Slavery*, 260–77; Martha Hodes, *White Women, Black Men: Illicit Sex in the Nineteenth-Century South* (New Haven, 1997); Joshua D. Rothman,

Notorious in the Neighborhood: Sex and Families across the Color Line in Virginia, 1787–1861 (Chapel Hill, NC, 2003); Diane Miller Sommerville, *Rape and Race in the Nineteenth-Century South* (Chapel Hill, NC, 2004); Peter W. Bardaglio, *Reconstructing the Household: Families, Sex, and the Law in the Nineteenth-Century South* (Chapel Hill, NC, 1995).

19. White, *Ar'n't I a Woman?*
20. Wilma King, *Stolen Childhood: Slave Youth in Nineteenth-Century America* (Blooming-ton, Ind., 1995); Marie Jenkins Schwartz, *Born in Bondage: Growing Up Enslaved in the Antebellum South* (Cambridge, Mass., 2000). On the relative mildness of slave child-hood, see Thomas L. Webber, *Deep Like the Rivers: Education in the Slave Quarter Community, 1831–1865* (New York, 1978).
21. Baptist and Camp, *New Studies in the History of American Slavery*, 3–5.
22. Sharla M. Fett, *Working Cures: Healing, Health, and Power on Southern Slave Plantations* (Chapel Hill, NC, 2002); Marie Jenkins Schwartz, *Birthing a Slave: Motherhood and Medicine in the Antebellum South* (Cambridge, Mass., 2006); Schwartz, *Born in Bondage*, ch. 1; Fett, "Consciousness and Calling: African American Midwives at Work in the Antebellum South," in *New Studies in the History of American Slavery*, 65–86. For the biomedical approach, see Todd L. Savitt, *Medicine and Slavery: The Diseases and Health Care of Blacks in Antebellum Virginia* (Urbana, Ill., 1978).
23. Though valuable in destroying the myth of the submissive, obedient, and "happy" slave, Herbert Aptheker, *American Negro Slave Revolts* (New York, 1943) overestimated the number of revolts that took place. On the obscure Louisiana revolt of 1811, see Roth-man, *Slave Country*; and Junius Rodriguez, "Rebellion on the River Road: The Ideology and Influence of Louisiana's German Coast Slave Insurrection of 1811," in John R. McKivigan and Stanley Harrold (eds.), *Antislavery Violence: Sectional, Racial, and Cultural Conflict in Antebellum America* (Knoxville, Tenn., 1999). On Gabriel, see Douglas R. Egerton, *Gabriel's Rebellion: The Virginia Slave Conspiracies of 1800 and 1802* (Chapel Hill, NC, 1993). For the controversy over the alleged Denmark Vesey conspiracy, see Michael P. Johnson, "Denmark Vesey and his Co-Conspirators," *William and Mary Quarterly*, 3rd ser., 58 (October 2001): 915–76, and the subsequent forum in *William and Mary Quarterly*, 3d ser., 59 (January 2002): 135–202. For the first full-length study of slave runaways, see John Hope Franklin and Loren Schweninger, *Runaway Slaves: Rebels on the Plantation* (New Yorks, 1999).
24. On the politics of the female slave body in the antebellum decades, see Fett, *Working Cures*; and Stephanie M. H. Camp, *Closer to Freedom: Enslaved Women and Everyday Resistance in the Plantation South* (Chapel Hill, NC, 2004).
25. Camp, *Closer to Freedom*. On slave patrols, see Sally Hadden, *Slave Patrols: Law and Violence in Virginia and the Carolinas* (Cambridge, Mass., 2001); and on African-American expressive culture, see Shane White and Graham White, *Stylin': African American Expressive Culture from its Beginnings to the Zoot Suit* (Ithaca, NY, 1998). On courtship, see Schwartz, *Born in Bondage*, ch. 7; West, *Chains of Love*, ch. 1; and Rebecca J. Fraser, *Courtship and Love among the Enslaved in North Carolina* (Jackson, Mo., 2007).
26. Edward E. Baptist, "The Absent Subject: African American Masculinity and Forced Migration to the Antebellum Plantation Frontier," in Craig Thompson Friend and Lorri Glover (eds.), *Southern Manhood: Perspectives on Masculinity in the Old South* (Athens, Ga., 2004), 136–73. See also Darlene Clark Hine and Earnestine Jenkins (eds.),

A Question of Manhood: A Reader in U.S. Black Men's History and Masculinity, i: "Manhood Rights": The Construction of Black Male History and Manhood, 1750–1870 (Bloomington, Ind., 1999).

27. Walter Johnson, *Soul by Soul: Life inside the Antebellum Slave Market* (Cambridge, Mass., 1999); Richard Holcombe Kilbourne, Jr., *Debt, Investment, Slaves: Credit Relations in East Feliciana Parish* (Tuscaloosa, Ala., 1995); Jonathan D. Martin, *Divided Mastery: Slave Hiring in the American South* (Cambridge, Mass., 2004); Sharon Ann Murphy, "Securing Human Property: Slavery, Life Insurance, and Industrialization in the Upper South," *Journal of the Early Republic*, 25 (Winter 2005): 615–52.

28. Mark M. Smith, *Mastered by the Clock: Time, Slavery, and Freedom in the American South* (Chapel Hill, NC, 1997). Increasingly, historians agree that the South contained both capitalist and precapitalist features. In Warren County, Mississippi, for example, residents did not immediately adopt cotton production for market, but rather carefully weighed the benefits of such a move. Safety-first agriculture coexisted with more market-oriented production in Warren County, and planters played the paternalist in their households and neighborhoods while proving astute capitalists in their dealings with the wider commercial world. See Christopher Morris, *Becoming Southern: The Evolution of a Way of Life, Warren County and Vicksburg, Mississippi, 1770–1860* (New York, 1995), 34–6, 171–2. Walter Johnson, "The Pedestal and the Veil: Rethinking the Capitalism/Slavery Question," *Journal of the Early Republic*, 24 (Summer 2004): 299–308, urges historians to jettison the slavery/capitalism dichotomy to examine instead the political economy of the broad Atlantic world in which slavery and capitalism thrived simultaneously.

29. Charles W. Joyner, *Down by the Riverside: A South Carolina Slave Community* (Urbana, Ill., 1984); William Dusinberre, *Them Dark Days: Slavery in the American Rice Swamps* (New York, 1996); Stevenson, *Life in Black and White*; David S. Cecelski, *The Waterman's Song: Slavery and Freedom in Maritime North Carolina* (Chapel Hill, NC, 2001). Although not exclusively a study of slavery, see also Drew Gilpin Faust, *James Henry Hammond and the Old South: A Design for Mastery* (Baton Rouge, La., 1982), chs. 5–6.

30. Baptist, *Creating an Old South*; Daniel S. Dupre, *Transforming the Cotton Frontier: Madison County, Alabama, 1800–1840* (Baton Rouge, La., 1997); Morris, *Becoming Southern*; Rothman, *Slave Country*. On antebellum Louisiana, see Judith Kelleher Schafer, *Becoming Free, Remaining Free: Manumission and Enslavement in New Orleans, 1846–1862* (Baton Rouge, La., 2003); and Richard J. Follett, *The Sugar Masters: Planters and Slaves in Louisiana's Cane World, 1820–1860* (Baton Rouge, La., 2005).

31. Michael Tadman, *Speculators and Slaves: Masters, Traders, and Slaves in the Old South* (Madison, 1989) reopened scholarly inquiry into the domestic slave trade, a subject of little concern since the 1930s. He was followed by Johnson, *Soul by Soul*; Robert H. Gudmestad, *A Troublesome Commerce: The Transformation of the Interstate Slave Trade* (Baton Rouge, La., 2003); Walter Johnson (ed.), *The Chattel Principle: Internal Slave Trades in the Americas* (New Haven, 2004); and Steven Deyle, *Carry Me Back: The Domestic Slave Trade in American Life* (New York, 2005). Deyle, *Carry Me Back*, and West, *Chains of Love*, ch. 5, offer initial looks at local sales.

32. Important comparative works on the South and Latin America include Herbert S. Klein, *Slavery in the Americas: A Comparative Study of Virginia and Cuba* (Chicago, 1967); Carl N. Degler, *Neither Black Nor White: Slavery and Race Relations in Brazil and the United States* (New York, 1971); and Eugene D. Genovese, *From Rebellion to*

Revolution: Afro-American Slave Revolts in the Making of the Modern World (Baton Rouge, La., 1979). For comparisons outside the Western hemisphere, see Peter Kolchin, *Unfree Labor: American Slavery and Russian Serfdom* (Cambridge, Mass., 1987); and Shearer Davis Bowman, *Masters and Lords: Mid-19th Century U.S. Planters and Prussian Junkers* (New York, 1993). Valuable edited collections that break down geographic boundaries include Berlin and Morgan, *Cultivation and Culture*; David Barry Gaspar and Darlene Clark Hine (eds.), *More than Chattel: Black Women and Slavery in the Americas* (Bloomington, Ind., 1996); and Baptist and Camp, *New Studies in the History of American Slavery*. Notable comparative studies published recently include Enrico Dal Lago, *Agrarian Elites: American Slaveholders and Southern Italian Landowners, 1815–1861* (Baton Rouge, La., 2005), in which laboring people are not the focus, and David Brion Davis, *Inhuman Bondage: The Rise and Fall of Slavery in the New World* (New York, 2006). Kolchin, *American Slavery*, 248; Peter Kolchin, *A Sphinx on the American Land: The Nineteenth-Century South in Comparative Perspective* (Baton Rouge, La., 2003).

SELECT BIBLIOGRAPHY

BAPTIST, EDWARD E., and STEPHANIE M. H. CAMP, eds. *New Studies in the History of American Slavery*. Athens, Ga.: University of Georgia Press, 2006.

BLASSINGAME, JOHN W. *The Slave Community: Plantation Life in the Antebellum South.*, rev. edn. New York: Oxford University Press, 1979.

CAMP, STEPHANIE M. H. *Closer to Freedom: Enslaved Women and Everyday Resistance in the Plantation South*. Chapel Hill, NC: University of North Carolina Press, 2004.

FETT, SHARLA M. *Working Cures: Healing, Health, and Power on Southern Slave Plantations*. Chapel Hill, NC: University of North Carolina Press, 2002.

GENOVESE, EUGENE D. *Roll, Jordan, Roll: The World the Slaves Made.* 1972. Reprint. New York: Vintage, 1976.

GUTMAN, HERBERT G. *The Black Family in Slavery and Freedom, 1750–1925*. New York: Pantheon Books, 1976.

JOHNSON, WALTER. *Soul by Soul: Life inside the Antebellum Slave Market*. Cambridge, Mass.: Harvard University Press, 1999.

KOLCHIN, PETER. *American Slavery, 1619–1877*. Rev. edn. New York: Hill and Wang, 2003.

LEVINE, LAWRENCE W. *Black Culture and Black Consciousness: Afro-American Folk Thought from Slavery to Freedom*. New York: Oxford University Press, 1977.

PENNINGROTH, DYLAN C. *The Claims of Kinfolk: African American Property and Community in the Nineteenth-Century South*. Chapel Hill, NC: University of North Carolina Press, 2003.

PART II

THEMES, METHODS, AND SOURCES

CHAPTER 11

....

THE
TRANSATLANTIC
SLAVE TRADE

....

STEPHEN D. BEHRENDT

THE foundations of a slave trade historiography date to the late eighteenth-century abolition movements in North America, Britain, and France. Before then, occasional voices sounded in protest. The Dominican friar Tomás de Mercado, for example, published in 1569 an anti-slave trade tract based on his observations of slave sales in Seville and of the institution of slavery in Mexico. He also attacked the cruelty of the Portuguese slave trade. In 1627 Alonso de Sandoval, a Jesuit priest who baptized slaves in the Spanish colonial port city of Cartagena, condemned the slave trade while also providing historians with detailed information on names and origins of enslaved Africans landed in the city.[1] Other writers examined the slave trade within the context of mercantilism, debating whether to restrict slaving to chartered companies. From 1698 to 1714, 198 pamphlets concerning the Royal African Company's monopoly were published in England.[2]

With the founding of the world's first antislavery crusade, antislavery advocates came to predominate among the researchers who were seeking information on the slave trade. They searched libraries and bookstores for African travel literature. They also tried to locate slaving journals or accounts, to find state records that concerned the trade, or to identify sailors or former slaves who could offer testimonies. Abolitionist energies coalesced in 1787–9 in London with the formation of anti-slave trade committees and the subsequent British parliamentary inquiries. In this three-year period at least twenty-five British, American, and French authors wrote about the slave trade, a total that would not be reached again until the 1970s, when academics organized the first major conferences on Atlantic slaving. During 1750–1808, antislavery and proslavery tracts and published parliamentary evidence produced a substantial body of material upon which future scholars would rely.

The most important early abolitionist researcher, Quaker Anthony Benezet (1713–84), resided near the Library Company of Philadelphia—the first public library in the Americas. Benezet argued that the European slave trade fostered warfare by citing evidence, albeit selectively, from well-known and recently published African travel literature, available from his local library or from acquaintances in town. In particular, he had access to a series of British and French accounts about Africa compiled in collections of voyages by John Churchill (1732) and Thomas Astley (1745). Relying on Quaker connections, he was able to view a Liverpool slaving surgeon's journal, penned in 1724 on the Windward Coast of Africa, and one written by a surgeon on a New York slaving vessel c.1750. He published extracts from these journals telling readers that, to meet the demand for slaves on the Atlantic coast, African rulers went to war against their "enemies" in the interior, burning towns and enslaving entire communities of men, women, and children.[3]

Whereas Benezet's investigations occurred later in his life, Thomas Clarkson was the first English postgraduate student who studied the slave trade and slavery. He earned his BA (1783) and MA (1785) from Cambridge University, and during his MA studies researched and wrote a prizewinning Latin essay on slavery and the slave trade, which he translated, expanded, and published in 1786. Though not part of his degree requirements, one can consider Clarkson's essay to be the first formal academic study on the Atlantic slave trade. Drawing on Benezet, Clarkson cited African travel literature from the 1690s to 1740s. He also had access to the papers of an unnamed slaving merchant and located other new sources about the slave trade, such as the crew lists of Liverpool slave ships. In 1787, working on behalf of the London committee to abolish the slave trade, Clarkson took the first of his four tours to interview officers and sailors, to extract additional evidence from muster rolls, to collect dyestuffs, pepper, cotton, and manufactures from Africa, and to purchase shackles and torture devices used in the slave trade. Letters of introduction from Charles Middleton, Comptroller of the Navy, enabled the young scholar to board navy vessels and interrogate sailors.[4]

Clarkson numbered as one of 100 witnesses who submitted evidence about the Atlantic slave trade to Members of Parliament during the first hearings in 1788–9. In February 1788 King George III ordered a Privy Council committee to investigate the "present state of the African Trade" and its impact in Britain, Africa, and the Americas. From April 1788 to March 1789 the committee heard testimony about the British slave trade, foreign slave trades, imports from Africa, and slavery in the Americas. Evidence from witnesses appeared in the 890-page *Report of the Lords of* the Committee of Council, published in May 1789, a volume that would, until the 1930s, remain the most important collection of eighteenth-century Atlantic slaving information. The Report broached five topics about the trade. First, officials wanted to know its size and geographic distribution. Second, they sought to establish the impact of the slave trade on African societies and to learn how people became enslaved in Africa. Third, following Clarkson's initial research, they wanted to determine mortality rates of enslaved Africans and sailors and whether shipboard crowding related to health. Fourth, they sought information on the profitability of the trade and its contribution to the British treasury. Fifth, to investigate whether abolition would hurt English manufacturing and shipping, they assessed the importance of the slave trade to domestic and colonial economies.

From 1790 to 1808 Parliament and abolitionists published further evidence about the slave trade. Additional hearings before the Commons occurred in 1790 and 1791. Beginning in 1792 customs officials extracted and printed lists of British slaving vessels. These summary shipping lists, tabled as Parliamentary Papers, document 1,971 British slaving voyages, 1789–1807, and include information on sailors, slaves, and ports of trade. Growing public awareness and interest in the slave trade produced a market for poems, placards, sermons, pamphlets, and longer monographs. One important work was Olaudah Equiano's autobiographical Interesting Narrative (1789). The book recalls Equiano's enslavement, as a child, in Africa, forced marches to the coast, Middle Passage imprisonment, and life in Barbados, Virginia, and Montserrat. Recently historians have debated whether Equiano was born in Africa or colonial British America; some contemporaries also challenged Equiano's authenticity as an African-born Briton. Strong sales of the Interesting Narrative, which went through nine editions from 1789 to 1797, demonstrate nonetheless the popularity of travel literature, the African narrative, and topics concerning the slave trade and abolition.[5]

THE ABOLITIONIST LEGACY, 1808–95

The abolitionist legacy loomed large after Parliament's passage of "An Act for the Abolition of the Slave Trade" in March 1807. Especially after the Congress of Vienna (1815), many studies of the Atlantic slave trade continued to focus on the question of suppression and on the international abolition of Atlantic slaving. In the 1820s and 1830s a new generation of abolitionists, most importantly Thomas Fowell Buxton (1786–1845), publicized the expansion of transatlantic slaving in Africa (particularly south of the equator) and in the Americas (particularly in Cuba and Brazil). Less obvious, Buxton and other authors relied upon the same types of sources—travel literature, published state records, and the occasional journal or account book—as did earlier slave trade historians. They also cited the two major works generated during the 1788–1808 British campaign: the *Report of the Lords* (1789) and Clarkson's *History of Abolition* (1808). The final study concerning abolition written in the nineteenth century, W. E. B. Du Bois's Harvard Ph.D. thesis "The Suppression of the African Slave-Trade to the United States of America, 1638–1870" (1895), anticipated new developments in historical scholarship.

Historians have placed most writings on the slave trade from 1815 to 1850 in the context of Europe's creeping imperialism in Africa, notably Buxton's *African Slave Trade and its Remedy* (1840), written during the early Victorian reassessment of empire. Buxton, a supporter of the Niger Expedition in 1841–2, is regarded both as an abolitionist saint and an early imperialist.[6] But his monograph proved that subsequent to British abolition, the Atlantic slave trade had continued unabated, in spite of interdiction efforts, largely because of the demand for slaves in Cuba and Brazil. Suppression activities north of the equator shifted the trade to new regions of Africa. Buxton's comprehensive chapter on African mortality in the slave trade was the first such study since the 1780s. Following Clarkson and inquiries from the Privy Council in 1788, Buxton examined mortality in five stages: seizure into slavery in Africa; the forced march to the coast and detention in barracoons; the Middle Passage; confinement in harbor and port; and the "seasoning" process during initial years as plantation laborers. Scholars would not again systematically research transatlantic slave mortality until the 1960s and 1970s.

Buxton built upon the evidentiary base mined by pioneering abolitionist historians of the eighteenth century. Travel literature again provided rich veins: Buxton cited sections on Brazil and Cuba by Alexander Caldcleugh, an English businessman and plant collector, in his *Travels in South America* (London, 1825). Published Parliamentary Papers on the slave trade, distilling information from British vice-consuls in Havana and Rio de Janeiro, proved to be his crucial research. In Brazil, alone, Buxton cited official slave imports into Rio de Janeiro totaling 148,940 individuals from July 1827 to June 1830—now believed to be the peak three-year period in the history of the Atlantic slave trade. He also cited letters from Captain McLean, governor of Cape Coast Castle, about the movement of vessels past Gold Coast forts to the Bights of Benin and Biafra to estimate the number of slaves who would have been embarked. *Reports* from the African Institute, a London-based organization created by abolitionists in 1808, summarized various state records, and each year increased in size and comprehensiveness. So too did the Parliamentary Papers. Indeed, by 1845 one Paper documented 2,765 non-British slaving voyages, 1808–43.[7]

As abolitionists kept the transatlantic slave trade in the spotlight, historical societies and journals grew apace to facilitate public conversations. In the United States, local and state societies that developed in the first half of the nineteenth century began publishing in the second half of the century. One finds discussions on the slave trade in early volumes of the *New York Colonial Tracts* (1867), *American Historical Record* (1873), *Proceedings of the Worcester Society of Antiquity* (1886), *Proceedings of the American Antiquarian Society* (1886), *Collections of the Virginia Historical Society* (1887), and *Papers of the New Haven Colony Historical Society* (1888). The New York work translated Dutch material on two mid-1600s Dutch slaving ventures, redressing historian George Bancroft's remark in his US history survey (1858): "Of a direct Voyage from Guinea to the Coast of the United States no Journal is known to exist." In Europe, the slave trade featured in a range of new and established academic periodicals. An overview on the Danish slave trade appeared in 1850 in the ten-year-old *Nyt Historisk Tidskrift* (*New Historical Journal*). Works also appeared in the *Journal of the Statistical Society of London* (1868); volume 1 of the *Bulletin de la Société de Géographie d'Anvers* (1877); the *Journal des économistes* (1879); and in 1892 the century-old *Revue maritime et coloniale* published information on a Bordeaux slaving voyage.[8]

When W. E. B. Du Bois, Harvard's first African-American Ph.D., completed his dissertation at Harvard University in 1895 on the suppression of the slave trade to the United States, he signaled that the topic had become a legitimate research area in the emerging discipline of history. Germany was the center of the historical profession: at Harvard, Du Bois worked with Dr Albert Bushnell Hart (Ph.D. Freiburg, 1883), who had introduced the German research seminar to the Harvard history faculty. Following Hart's method, Du Bois searched for material on the Atlantic slave trade by plowing through colonial statutes, state records and the *Congressional Record*. He presented his research in Harvard seminars and in early 1892 at a meeting of the American Historical Association (AHA)—published subsequently as a paper in the AHA's *Annual Report*. Based on available primary sources, Du Bois necessarily focused on political, diplomatic, and legal efforts to end the Atlantic slave trade. "[F]acts and statistics bearing on the economic side of the study," he noted, "have been difficult to find." After studying in Berlin for two years thanks, in part, to further grants from Harvard, Du Bois submitted his dissertation in 1895—the first Ph.D. on a slave trade topic. In 1896 it was published as volume 1 of the *Harvard Historical Series*.[9]

THE HISTORICAL PROFESSION, SOURCE MATERIAL, AND SLAVE TRADE SCHOLARSHIP, 1895–1960

In 1895, the same year that Du Bois presented his thesis to Harvard, John Franklin Jameson became a founding editor of the *American Historical Review* and urged the AHA to collect and publish key American historical source materials. The AHA then established the Historical Manuscripts Commission (HMC) and appointed Jameson as Chairman. In 1905, the HMC became part of the Carnegie Institute in Washington, DC, and ten years later Jameson's professional researchers began collecting documents on slavery and the slave trade. Meanwhile advances in archive management and a strengthened historical discipline in the United States and Europe gave postgraduate students improved access to professorial expertise, source material, funding, and publication outlets. More historical theses appeared about the slave trade, but it would be anthropologists who began in earnest to study Africa, African slavery, and Africa's cultural contribution to the Americas. Indirectly, works on the economics of the slave trade and slavery also brought African history into the nascent discipline of Atlantic slave trade studies. By 1960 and the launch of African history, research on the slave trade had begun to look beyond imperial history.

Some of the earliest history theses in the United States, France, and Britain researched the Atlantic slave trade. Following Du Bois's dissertation, Edward Day Collins (Yale) completed in 1899 his Ph.D. thesis on the Royal African Company, as did George Frederick Zook at Cornell fifteen years later. Yale granted the Ph.D. in 1905 and 1911 to Hubert Aimes (on the Cuban slave trade) and Frank Klingberg (on the abolition of British slaving). In 1905, at the École Libre des Sciences Politiques in Paris, Georges Scelle completed a prizewinning thesis on the Spanish slave trade to the West Indies. In 1906 Waldemar Christian Westergaard, working on his master's thesis at the University of California, examined documents on the Danish West Indies that had been acquired the previous year in the Hubert Howe Bancroft Collection. Granted a fellowship in 1907, Westergaard studied at Cornell University and later traveled to Copenhagen to gather archival material. His 1915 dissertation on the Danish West Indies included a groundbreaking chapter on the Danish slave trade. At the University of London, Arthur P. Newton supervised MA theses by Kate Elliot (1915), Thora G. Stone (1921), and Eveline C. Martin (1922), each study examining how English monopoly companies in the seventeenth century organized the slave and gold trades. In 1922 and 1923 the Universities of Liverpool and Bristol approved their first MA theses on topics concerning the rise of these two respective outports in the eighteenth-century slave trade.[10]

Though neither Elizabeth Donnan nor Gaston-Martin produced dissertations on the Atlantic slave trade, by the early 1930s the two had become experts on the British and French slave trades, respectively. Donnan's four-volume *Documents Illustrative of the History of the Slave Trade to America* (1930–5) stands as a landmark of scholarly research. Following earlier thesis researchers, Donnan, an economist, honed her skills as a researcher under John Franklin Jameson's tutelage at the Carnegie Institution.[11] She examined the African Company records and Calendars of State Papers, which she supplemented with documents from every record class available. In the British Library she trawled through the major manuscript collections from the sixteenth to the eighteenth century, and she was the first historian of the slave trade to research extensively eighteenth-century British and colonial newspapers. In total, Donnan's four volumes contain 1,295 documents (2,290 pages), and include comprehensive bibliographic and historiographical information and indexes. Though the volumes focused on the British and North American slave trades, the collection, republished in 1965, 1969, and 2002 and now on-line, has continued to provide source material for all historians working on the slave trade.[12]

In the late 1920s Gaston-Martin shifted his research from the French Revolution to the commercial rise of eighteenth-century Nantes. He discovered the rich trove of slaving records in the Admiralty archives in the département de Loire-Inférieure (now Loire-Atlantique). Nantes ship captains were required to present declarations to the Admiralty, and Gaston-Martin located 787 reports about slaving voyages, 1714–74, as well as a dozen slaving journals and thousands of inventories, manifests, musters, passports, registrations, and other documents pertaining to individual voyages. His *Nantes au XVIIIe siècle: L'ère des négriers, 1714–1774* (1931) was the most wide-ranging study on the Atlantic slave trade published to date. Gaston-Martin based his information almost entirely on shipping documents from Admiralty archives. "[T]hough not giving the original documents," Gaston-Martin "does in a more restricted manner for the French slave-trade what Miss Donnan's work does for the British," cultural anthropologist Melville Herskovits astutely noted.[13] Analyzing ships' outfit, Gaston-Martin demonstrated that French merchants sold a great variety of expensive manufactured items, Asian textiles in particular, to African slaving dealers, destroying the myth that slaves were purchased largely with trinkets, baubles, or shoddy second-hand goods. Gaston-Martin also presented new information on the geography of Nantes slaving, slaving ships, slave and crew mortality, insurrections, and variability in profits. "In short," as Donnan remarked, "it would be difficult to think of any question pertaining to the slave traffic on which [Gaston-Martin] has not extracted material from his documents."[14]

Herskovits and Eric Williams, two scholars who benefited from Donnan and Gaston-Martin's collections, would radically redirect slave trade studies towards Atlantic-wide issues. Herskovits added the newly available British and French slave trade data to his fieldwork notes from Africa and to his anthropological studies on African cultural traits in the Americas, such as those from Fernando Ortiz, a pioneering Cuban ethnologist. He also located new information, for example, on slaving ship arrivals from specified African regions listed in the *Royal Gazette* (Kingston, Jamaica, 1803) and the *Essequibo and Demerary Gazette* (1803–7). Herskovits emphasized the prevalence of African cultural traits in many regions of the Americas, and his research and insights anticipated and stimulated future scholarly inquiries. Fieldwork along the Gold Coast led him to conclude "that the conception of an Africa depopulated by the slave trade, without the numbers necessary to support a drain that is to be figured in the millions, stands in need of drastic revision."[15] The slave trade's volume and demographic impact would be addressed by scholars a generation later, as would the importance of planter preferences for enslaved Africans from certain ethnicities or specific coastal regions of Africa.

Whereas Herskovits was interested in the slave trade as a cultural bridge from Africa to the Americas, Eric Williams, a Caribbean-born Marxist historian, wanted to understand the Atlantic slave trade's broader position in British colonial and economic development and the link between capitalism, slavery, and abolition. In *Capitalism and Slavery* (1944), one of the most influential books on slavery ever written, Williams substantially rewrote and condensed his Oxford Ph.D. thesis, adding new material on the pre-1780 rise of British slavery and the slave trade. He built in particular on Donnan's *Documents* and Stock's five-volume *Proceedings and Debates of the British Parliaments Respecting North America* (1924–41). Williams linked the rise of slaving and the rise of capitalism in Britain and speculated that the link would apply to France as well by citing Gaston-Martin's remark that all major Nantes shipowners, 1714–89, invested in slaves. Williams contended that slavery and the slave trade fueled British industrialization and that slaving's post-1783 decline explained the timing of Britain's abolition of the slave trade in 1807 and of slavery in 1833. His linking of slaving and capitalism challenged prevailing scholarly opinion that relegated both African and Caribbean history to the periphery. In explaining the end of Britain's slave trade, Williams's Marxian emphasis on economic forces as decisive agents of historical change elevated market forces over a moral crusade led by a handful of "saints."[16]

Herskovits and Williams aside, between Gaston-Martin's work on Nantes in 1931 and the formal development of African history in 1960,[17] Atlantic slave trade studies generally built upon the foundations established by earlier scholars. Dieudonné Rinchon's *Trafic négrier* (1938) added details on the organization of Nantes slaving voyages. It spotlighted sailors from Ghent and allocated sixty pages to tables on individual slaving voyages. Journalist Maurício Goulart's *A escravidão africana no Brasil* (1949) suggested that between 3,500,000 and 3,600,000 African slaves disembarked in Brazil. His estimate, based upon Brazilian population data and labor productivity and some export totals from Africa, proved to be a useful corrective to exaggerated slave import totals that reached as high as fifteen million.[18] Drawing upon European archival sources, historians Simone Berbain (1942), K. G. Davies (1957), and Abdoulaye Ly (1958) discussed the business and political activities of trading companies, as did works by Zook and Martin written a generation earlier.[19] Aspects of antislavery featured in twenty-two of twenty-three honors, MA, and Ph.D. theses produced in England and the United States from 1941 to 1960. Only one focused on economic history: the profitability of some British slaving voyages, a topic that recently had engaged a few historians of accounting.[20]

EXPANSION OF TERTIARY EDUCATION AND ATLANTIC SLAVE TRADE STUDIES SINCE 1960

The expansion of tertiary education and the growth in African history, Latin American studies, and quantitative history energized scholarship on the Atlantic slave trade and widened its geographic scope. Most importantly, the new field of African history injected into scholarly discussions "the African side of the Atlantic slave trade," as Philip D. Curtin noted in the preface to *Africa Remembered* (1967), a volume that compiled ten "accounts by Africans" on the trade. The "African side" would be told not only from first-hand narratives, but also by understanding slavery in Africa, the organization of trade in the hinterland and Atlantic coast, and how the trade impacted upon African societies and peoples. One significant problem facing researchers examining the Atlantic trade's impact was that, as Curtin and Jan Vansina wrote in 1964, "Estimates of the number of slaves exported each year or decade are mainly educated guesses."[21] But by the early 1970s, a "critical mass" of young scholars with expertise on Africa, the Atlantic slave trade, and slavery in the Americas had formed. Membership in the African Studies Association, for example, increased from 200 to 1,800, and by 1970 historians of Africa had replaced anthropologists as those Africanists most concerned with researching the Atlantic slave trade.[22] With greater public and private funding in hand, these younger scholars organized conferences and workshops that would help to shape the future direction of Atlantic slave trade studies.

Curtin's *Atlantic Slave Trade: A Census* (1969) answered the need for more accurate estimates on the volume of Atlantic slaving and provided a platform that helped to trigger four decades of scholarship. Curtin based his *Census* on the best secondary source estimates, such as those by Goulart for Brazil, and on published primary sources in monographs or collections. He relied, for example, on Donnan's documents regarding the slave trade to North America and Rinchon's list of Nantes slaving vessels. Where shipping sources were lacking, he examined demographic data on slave populations in the Americas. A comparative work, Curtin's *Census* surveyed all Atlantic slave trades from the mid-1400s through the 1860s and examined the geographical distribution of the slave trade by African and New World regions over time. To students of American slavery, his most important conclusion was that fewer than 5 percent of all Africans forced into the Atlantic slave trade arrived in North America. Yet, by 1950, about one-third of all people of African descent in the Western hemisphere lived in the United States. To those interested in the history of Atlantic migration, more Africans than Europeans crossed the Atlantic from 1492 to 1770. In acknowledging that his estimates of 9.4 million slave imports in the Western hemisphere might be 20 percent too high or too low, he nonetheless created benchmark data that other scholars could challenge and refine, and established the preferred method of projecting estimates by using shipping-based sources.[23]

In estimating the volume and geographical distribution of the Atlantic slave trade across time, Curtin's *Census* directed attention again to levels of Middle Passage mortality, a major concern of the first abolitionist-scholars. For the late seventeenth-century British slave trade, Curtin used Davies's Royal African Company data (1672–87) that indicated a 23.3 percent "loss in transit" of enslaved Africans. To help analyze French slave trade data, he created a machine-readable data file, "coded and punched on IBM cards," of the Nantes data (910 voyages) compiled by Rinchon and determined that African mortality on the Passage averaged 15–17 percent over the period 1748–92. Curtin's "Postscript on Mortality" compared slave and crew mortality data, republicizing the pioneering research undertaken by abolitionist-historian Thomas Clarkson in the late 1780s.[24] Shipping evidence from British, Dutch, and French slave traders revealed that Middle Passage slave and crew mortality rates differed significantly by the coastal African location of trade. Examining the "African side" of the Atlantic slave trade again proved vital to understand issues, in this case mortality, broached centuries earlier from a European perspective.

As Curtin was completing his *Census*, Herbert S. Klein began a decade of quantitative work on shipping patterns and mortality on the slave trades to Brazil, Cuba, the West Indies, and North America. Klein, first a Bolivian history specialist (Ph.D. 1963, University of Chicago), was one of the first formally trained students of Latin American history and with Curtin, one of the first to use punch cards and mainframe computers in quantitative research. Klein's important comparative studies from 1969 to 1976, republished in *The Middle Passage* (1978), demonstrated that there were broad similarities in ship types and sizes, slave-per-ton ratios, sailing times, and Middle Passage mortality among the Portuguese, Brazilian, British, French, and North American slave trades. Klein concluded that in each slave trading nation there was a long-term decline in Middle Passage slave mortality, due mostly to a reduction in shipboard epidemics, and while time at sea increased mortality rates, the varying skills of surgeons or slave-per-ton ratios—degrees of "tight packing"—did not. To explain the reason for this uniformity among European slave traders, Klein suggested, one must turn to the constraints imposed on the trade by conditions in Africa. Similarly, local African disease environments and food supplies impacted significantly upon the shipboard health of enslaved Africans. In the late eighteenth and early nineteenth centuries, slave mortality rates from the Angolan ports Luanda and Ambriz, Klein pointed out, doubled the rates from ports near the mouth of the Zaire River, only a few hundred miles to the north.[25]

Two of the first conferences in the United States on the Atlantic slave trade featured papers that illustrated the influence of Curtin's *Census*, developments in quantitative history, and the continuing growth of African studies. In 1972 the

University of Rochester hosted a conference, "An International Comparison of Systems of Slavery," out of which came a volume rich in slave trade data. Essays refined the scale and African distribution of the British and Dutch slave trades, provided new data on European mortality on the African coast, and gauged the economic impact of British antislaving suppression policies after 1815. By 1975 interest in the economics of slaving led to another major conference, "The Economic History of the Transatlantic Slave Trade," in Colby, Maine. Specialists in African history, including three young scholars—Patrick Manning, Joseph Miller, and Paul Lovejoy—all recent Ph.D.s from the University of Wisconsin mentored by Curtin or Vansina, wrote four of the papers that were subsequently published. The conference also featured a paper by David Richardson, a British economic historian, on "West African Consumption Patterns." Based on shipping cargo evidence contained in the business papers of British merchants William Davenport and James Rogers, Richardson argued that African demand for European and Asian goods varied by coastal market and dictated how merchants outfitted their slaving vessels.[26]

Since Curtin's *Census*, efforts to organize slave trade documents and catalogue voyages, initiated by the British government during abolition debates and then by Elizabeth Donnan, have been continued by, among others, Jay Coughtry (Rhode Island slave trade), Jean Mettas and Serge Daget (French slave trade), David Richardson (Bristol slave trade), David Eltis (early English and nineteenth-century slave trades), Stephen D. Behrendt (late British slave trade), and James McMillin (US slave trade). Along with the first digitalized slaving data sets by Curtin and Klein, these endeavors, supported by the microcomputer and internet revolution in the 1980s and 1990s and by university and government funding, have aided the creation of the consolidated Atlantic slave trade database.[27] Released first on CD-ROM (1999), since December 2008 the public can access the database on the website *Voyages*.[28] Whereas the CD-ROM set of 27,233 slaving voyages catalogued the large majority of British, French, and Dutch slaving voyages, the subsequent decade of work in Portuguese, Spanish, Angolan, and Brazilian archives more than doubled the sample of slaving voyages sailing to Brazil, 1601–1825, and to the Spanish Americas, 1525–1640. Four decades after Curtin's *Census* established baseline data by Atlantic slaving region, the on-line database of 34,940 voyages—sampling 95 percent of the total trade from 1525 to 1866[29]—enables researchers to fine-tune their inquiries to individual years or Atlantic ports. One now can discuss the slave trade from Liverpool rather than England, Bonny rather than the Bight of Biafra, and Kingston rather than Jamaica. These efforts have furthered studies on individual African ports, such as Ouidah, Bonny, and Lagos, ports whose histories have been published recently.[30] The *Voyages* database sample and corresponding estimates of the trade by Eltis have raised Curtin's global volume of the transatlantic slave trade by 11–12 percent and refined the scale of the trade by national carrier, African region of embarkation, and American region of disembarkation (see Table 11.1).[31]

The first generation to specialize in African history followed British and French abolitionists of the latter eighteenth century by exploring the impact of the Atlantic slave trade on African societies. Though scholars now can draw upon comprehensive slave trade data, African population data from censuses are lacking. Thus, an important question remains: Did the overseas demand for slaves cause an African demographic catastrophe? Historians generally accept that three centuries of continued slaving raids drained population and resources in West-Central Africa, pushing the Angolan slaving frontier inward. In other major slaving regions, such as along the coast of modern-day Nigeria, nineteenth- and twentieth-century visitors remarked upon dense populations, suggesting that natural growth rates offset population losses. In West Africa, a map of coastal languages today mirrors that in the early sixteenth century, leading scholars to infer that communities, even stateless societies, could defend themselves. Both the transfer of new protein-rich foodstuffs through the Columbian Exchange and the retention of female slaves would have helped sustain populations in polygamous societies. As abolitionists learned, European demand widened manners of enslavement; over time more and more debtors or adulterers or thieves were forced into bondage. Africans importing European and Asian textiles, metal goods, firearms, and alcohol did not destroy their domestic manufacturing bases, which historians now know to be more developed than many European visitors believed. The wealth to be gained from overseas trade, though, enriched some African elites, transformed religious shrines, and created complex commercial networks from hinterland to coast.[32]

Scholarship on the Atlantic slave trade's impact on the Americas continued efforts by Eric Williams and Melville Herskovits regarding the economic and cultural contribution of African peoples. The regimented backbreaking work of enslaved African workers enabled plantation colonies to be the most productive and wealthiest agricultural enterprises in the world. Reflecting productivity increases, prices for enslaved Africans on the African coast and in the New World rose in the eighteenth century, rising faster than prices of agricultural commodities. Rather than arguing, as Williams did, for a decline in the productivity and wealth of slave-based agriculture after 1783, this recent research furthers the argument that Atlantic slaving expanded in many regions through the first half of the nineteenth century.[33] Scholars searching for African roots in the New World have drawn upon the increasingly refined slave trade shipping data that estimate numbers embarked in coastal ports. Shipping records, though, usually lack the information needed on ethnicities to help map African cultural carryovers in the Americas, and different groupings of African peoples entered the African diaspora at different times. Scholars have had more success charting African cultural carryovers in Haiti and those parts of Brazil that drew heavily on the slave trades from the Bight of Benin and West-Central Africa over long periods.[34]

Table 11.1. The volume and regional distribution of the transatlantic slave trade, 1525–1866

A. Volume by national carrier

	Portugal/Brazil[a]	Britain	France	Spain[b]	Netherlands	USA[c]	Baltic states[d]
1. 1525–1640	565,248	2,444	66	231,373	9,972	0	0
2. 1641–1807	3,067,992	3,247,693	1,188,314	44,498	542,635	292,170	111,042
3. 1808–66	2,208,228	9,306	193,025	779,495	1,729	13,151	0
Slave exports	5,841,468	3,259,443	1,381,405	1,055,366	554,336	305,321	111,042
12,508,381	(46.7%)	(26.1%)	(11.0%)	(8.4%)	(4.4%)	(2.4%)	(0.9%)

B. Volume by African region of embarkation

	West-Central Africa	Bight of Benin	Bight of Biafra[e]	Upper Guinea[f]	Gold Coast	Southeast Africa
1. 1525–1640	621,102	5,517	13,478	168,594	68	345
2. 1641–1807	3,264,663	1,613,597	1,203,016	1,074,250	1,194,658	144,162
3. 1808–66	1,808,176	379,943	378,067	225,991	14,598	398,163
Slave exports	5,693,941	1,999,057	1,594,561	1,468,835	1,209,324	542,670
12,508,388	(45.5%)	(16.0%)	(12.7%)	(11.7%)	(9.7%)	(4.3%)

C. Volume by American region of disembarkation

	Brazil	West Indies	Spanish Central/South America	North America	Guianas
1. 1525–1640	290,693	667	326,474	100	0
2. 1641–1807	2,741,034	3,718,447	147,558	381,594	289,713
3. 1808–66	1,832,647	783,947	4,818	7,052	4,938
Slave imports	4,864,374	4,503,061	478,850	388,746	294,651
10,529,682	(46.2%)	(42.8%)	(4.6%)	(3.7%)	(2.8%)

a Most vessels departed from Brazil after 1640; Brazilian flagged from 1822.
b Includes eight Uruguay-flagged ships from the 1830s.
c Includes pre-1783 slavers that departed from North America (principally from Rhode Island).
d Mostly Denmark.
e Includes São Tomé and Île de Príncipe.
f Includes Senegambia, the Sierra Leone region, the Windward Coast, the Canaries, and the Cape Verde Islands.
Source: http://www.slavevoyages.org/tast/assessment/estimates.faces (totals differ due to rounding).

Significant advances in research on the Brazilian slave trade, helped along by reforms in higher education and by improved library facilities, have dramatically advanced the study of African cultures in Brazil.[35] The first postgraduate students to focus on bilateral African–Brazilian links wrote dissertations in France, but since the 1980s several public universities in Brazil have created new courses that bear on African and Afro-Brazilian history and culture, and the past decade has seen an expansion in postgraduate programs, research and conference funding, and study-abroad programs.[36] Slavery and the slave trade, central themes in the history of Brazil, now engage research interests of formally trained students; contact and exchange of information among Brazilian and international researchers has increased accordingly. Researchers now may photograph documents in the reno-vated National Archives; the National Library has been digitalizing manuscripts and making them available on-line. Catalogues for both repositories have im-proved. In 1996 officials launched Projeto Resgate, a joint venture between Brazil and Portugal to start digitalizing the 340,000 documents (three million manuscript pages), held in the Arquivo Histórico Ultramarino in Lisbon, concerning Portu-guese captaincies in the Americas. The Lisbon archive houses the largest collection of colonial Brazilian material.[37]

Developments in Brazil remind historians about the dominance of the South Atlantic slave trade and that ongoing digitalization of primary and secondary sources will play a major stimulus for future studies of Atlantic slaving. The expansion in Atlantic history since 1990 has furthered interest in the slave trade, now a required chapter in any Atlantic history reader.[38] This supposedly new specialization has in fact shifted from the "White Atlantic" to the "Black Atlantic," thanks to Curtin's *Census* and important comparative migration studies by Eltis, and now the Black Atlantic is understood to be more a feature of the New World colonial system south of the equator. Not only is the West-Central Africa-to-Brazil pathway the largest and most enduring in the history of the Atlantic slave trade, but the only slaving ships manned by significant numbers of enslaved black and free African sailors mustered from Brazil.[39]

When future scholars from their vantage point look back at the growth in Atlantic slave trade scholarship, they will point to times when scattered materials shifted to centralized repositories and were catalogued, when private and public monies became available to fund scholarly activity, and when, via the microcom-puter and internet revolution, the cost to research, collect, analyze, and disseminate information shrank dramatically. Developments such as Projeto Resgate and *Voyages*; the University of Virginia's website "The Atlantic Slave Trade and Slave Life in the Americas: A Visual Record"; the on-line database "Afro-Louisiana History and Genealogy, 1718–1820"; the creation of the Wilberforce Institute for the Study of Slavery and Emancipation (University of Hull); the Harriet Tubman Resource Centre on the African Diaspora (York University, Canada); the recently funded African Origins on-line project (Emory University); the growth of on-line books and journals; and initiatives by publishers to digitalize slave trade documents, predict a true democratization of learning and a near future when the internet will permit research on the slave trade from anywhere in the world.[40]

REFLECTIONS AND RESEARCH OPPORTUNITIES

Antislavery campaigns in the eighteenth century triggered scholarship on the Atlantic slave trade, which continued, with some pauses, until today. It is no surprise that the number of studies has increased after 1960 as higher education has expanded. In the United States and Britain, 1960–2008, students have written sixty-five Ph.D. dissertations largely concerning the Atlantic slave trade, about three every two years—about the same number, per student, as the first wave of theses, 1895–1923. Abolition or antislavery suppression is still a popular topic, though it has declined in the past decade. Few students attempt comparative studies, which can yield the most interesting insights into the history of the Atlantic slave trade.[41] History dissertations focusing on the slave trade and slavery in Africa and Latin America now appear, as do Ph.D.s in literature on Atlantic slaving. Economic history has dropped off, maritime history on the slave trade has never developed, but the most noticeably understudied area is medical history, a curious gap since the morbidity and mortality of slaves and crew in Africa, the Middle Passage, and the Americas were important research areas to abolitionist-historians.[42] That there are few slaving studies written today by formally trained medical, economic, or maritime historians reflects the rise of social and cultural history, the continued geographically centered focus of postgraduate programs, and the difficulty in obtaining permanent posts in academia.

In the conference-driven wave of slave trade scholarship initiated in 1972, none of the papers on mortality yielded a monograph on the medical history of the Atlantic slave trade, which would begin by assessing the pre-embarkation health conditions of enslaved Africans. Why Africans embarked at Old Calabar and Cameroon, for example, died at the highest rates—and at much higher rates than those individuals shipped from the eastern Niger Delta—requires a detailed study of work, nutrition, and exploitation in the Bight of Biafra hinterland. Many surgeons' journals survive for the French, Portuguese, Dutch, and Danish slave trades, and some are sufficiently detailed to allow calculations of daily death rates.[43] In the Danish National Archives are surgeons' journals (written in German) that include diagnoses made and medicines administered. For all slave trading nations, one can analyze the social origin of surgeons to test whether the trade attracted young, impoverished, poorly trained men, as British abolitionists contended in the late 1780s. In an age of "heroic medicine" (blood-letting and leeches), few historians believe that surgeons could provide medical care and treat illness. But merchants, supposedly rational economic actors, paid surgeons handsome monthly wages and bonuses, and captains often attributed low or high mortality to the skills of their doctors. There is more to be learned on diet and disease in Africa and on ship, the comparative management of health care, and disease transmission between shipboard population groups and from ship to shore.

There is also a need to place the Atlantic slave trade in comparative maritime perspective and comprehensively examine sources such as captains' logbooks and ship registers. What were the navigation skills of captains and mates? Captains needed to calculate precisely their anticipated sailing time to determine daily rations they allotted slaves and crew. They sailed, as logbooks indicate, by dead reckoning, employing geometry or trigonometry in creating sailing triangles. Since they linked rainfall to the seasons and position of the sun, their celestial observations may have influenced water rationing. It is said that slaving captains sailed craft built for the Guinea trade, a claim not tested by examining detailed ship registers, such as those that survive for Liverpool. Slaving vessels may have been no more "specialized" than boats in other trades. Historians need to consider ship construction, which was "more material than the tonnage" in determining a vessel's carrying capacity, as one British captain remarked in 1789. In the British slave trade, for example, above-deck structures (quarterdecks, roundhouses) were used to imprison African children, but the enclosed spaces in the structures were not measured for tonnage until the New Measurement Act of 1836.[44]

Slaving merchants, too, are an understudied group whose interests might be no more specialized than the ships they purchased. "Merchants who made side investments in the slave trade" might be a phrase one would read if we knew business portfolios. The names of shipowning partners appear in the *Voyages Database*. Locating probate records to gauge wealth is a first step toward determining profits from the slave trade and other investments. William Davenport (d. 1797), for example, a Liverpool merchant, had an estate valued at £34,000. Initial research suggests that Davenport earned £10,500 in slaving profits, 1757–84 (one-fifth of that sum on one voyage during the American War of Independence), and £1,500 in ivory profits, 1763–85—and then £8,000 through speculation in financial securities during the last decade of his life.[45] How did the heirs of slaving merchants manage their wealth? Reflecting upon the last generation of Liverpool slave traders and their descendants, Richard Brooke (b. 1791) wrote in 1853:

It is a remarkable fact that of the large number of Liverpool persons who made fortunes in the African slave trade, and some of them acquired by that odious traffic considerable wealth, it only remained in very few instances in their families until the third generation, and in many cases it was dispersed or disappeared in the first generation after the death of the persons acquiring it.[46]

Charting the occupations and incomes of slave trading families over generations could help ascertain whether, for example, monies from maritime commerce financed industrial enterprises.[47]

Similarly, historians should continue to look for information on African merchants who, over the eighteenth century, sold more and more slaves directly to ship captains. As early as 1775 political economist John Campbell noted how the slave trade increased in areas where Europeans maintained no permanent coast facilities. Referring to the British slave trade along the eastern Bight of Benin and the Bight of Biafra, he remarked:

In this long tract of coast there are the rivers of Benin, New Callabar, Bonny, Old Callabar, and several others, and notwithstanding that in these we have not either fort or settlement, yet our African traders send thither more ships, and purchase more negroes thereon, than in any of the several coasts we have mentioned.[48]

The ability of slaving ship captains from Liverpool, Bristol, and Nantes to trade profitably with hard-bargaining African businessmen in numerous African Atlantic markets helps to explain the dominance of these three ports. How these African merchants along the Bights and in other coastal communities entered and profited from the Atlantic slaving business—African entrepreneurship—is worth exploring.[49]

Future studies on the Atlantic slave trade may be advanced by the discovery of new sources. Researchers will continue to add slaving ventures to the *Voyages Database*, most likely by finding some to the Spanish Americas (1525–95) or to Brazil (1560–1700), or by locating Dutch voyages (1621–30, 1651–73), London- or Barbados-based voyages (1640–98), French voyages (1670–1710), or some Liverpool voyages (1720s–1740s).[50] Some Arabic business papers, written in northwest Africa, may have survived, perhaps ones similar to the paragraph-long slaving contract found among the De Wolf family papers in Rhode Island.[51] Documents (most likely from colonial collections in Central or South America) should shed further light on African ethnicities in the Americas. It is unlikely that African travel narratives written in a European language have escaped scholarly pursuit, though some may survive written in non-European languages. Merchants' records, unrecognized for their historical value, may remain, however, with families or among lawyers' papers.

For students unsure whether there are discoveries to be made, one needs simply to recall a story from a decade ago. In 2000, twelve leather-bound volumes of a merchant's account book and thirteen bundles of his letters were discovered in a chest in a Cheshire barn. A year later the BBC's *Antiques Roadshow* telecast their existence to the public. What were they? The chest contained the business papers of

Liverpool merchant William Davenport. They supplemented sixteen volumes of materials from Davenport discovered fifty years earlier.[52]

NOTES

Thanks to Bernhard Bierlich, Daniel Barros Domingues da Silva, David Eltis, Stanley L. Engerman, Roquinaldo Ferreira, Linda R. Gray, David Northrup, and Craig Watterson for help with research questions.

1. On Mercado, see A. J. R. Russell-Wood, "Iberian Expansion and the Issue of Black Slavery: Changing Portuguese Attitudes, 1440–1770," *American Historical Review*, 83 (1) (February 1978): 35. Sandoval, in *De instauranda Aethiopum salute* ("concerning what needs to be done to minister for the health of the Africans"), provides the best early documentary evidence of the early Atlantic slave trade to Spanish territories in the Americas (Vincent P. Franklin, "Alonso de Sandoval and the Jesuit Conception of the Negro," *Journal of Negro History*, 58 (3) (July 1973): 349–60).
2. Kenneth Morgan, "Introduction," in Morgan (gen. ed.), *The British Transatlantic Slave Trade*, 4 vols. (London, 2003), ii, p. xviii. See also William A. Pettigrew, "Free to Enslave: Politics and the Escalation of Britain's Transatlantic Slave Trade, 1688–1714," *William and Mary Quarterly*, 3rd ser., 64 (1) (January 2007): 3.
3. Jonathan D. Sassi, "Africans in the Quaker Image: Anthony Benezet, African Travel Narratives, and Revolutionary-Era Antislavery," *Journal of Early Modern History*, 10 (1–2) (2006): 95–129. See also Maurice Jackson, *Let This Voice Be Heard: Anthony Benezet, Father of Atlantic Abolitionism* (Philadelphia, 2008).
4. Ellen Gibson Wilson, *Thomas Clarkson: A Biography* (2nd edn. York, 1989). Clarkson was not the first to write a thesis on slavery, however. In 1742 African-born Jacob Capitein completed his thesis at the University of Leiden on the theology of slavery (Grant Parker (ed. and trans.), *The Agony of Asar: A Thesis on Slavery by the Former Slave, Jacobus Elisa Johannes Capitein, 1717–1747* (Princeton, 2001)).
5. Vincent Carretta, *Equiano, the African: Biography of a Self-Made Man* (Athens, Ga., 2005), pp. xii, 301. Regardless of Equiano's birthplace (Africa or South Carolina), he marketed himself as an African-born Briton.
6. J. Gallagher, "Fowell Buxton and the New African Policy, 1838–1842," *Cambridge Historical Journal*, 10 (1) (1950): 36–58. For a work looking at the "African Question" before the Victorian period, see Michael J. Turner, "The Limits of Abolition: Government, Saints and the 'African Question,' c.1780–1820," *English Historical Review*, 112 (446) (1997): 319–57.
7. British Parliamentary Papers, 1845 XLIX, 593–633, the most important single source documenting the nineteenth-century Atlantic slave trade.
8. E. B. O'Callaghan (ed. and trans.), *Voyages of the Slavers St. John and Arms of Amsterdam, 1659, 1663* (Albany, NY, 1867), p. xxvii; Peter C. Hogg, *The African Slave Trade and its Suppression: A Classified and Annotated Bibliography of Books, Pamphlets and Periodical Articles* (London, 1973), 61–2, 96–8. Unless noted otherwise, all pre-1970 academic works on the slave trade and abolition, included theses, are referenced by Hogg.

9. Francis L. Broderick, "The Academic Training of W. E. B. Du Bois," *Journal of Negro Education*, 27 (1) (1958): 14–16; W. E. B. Du Bois, *The Suppression of the African Slave-Trade to the United States of America, 1638–1870* (New York, 1970), pp. v–x. For information on the British slave trade, Du Bois stated that he relied on information from the *Report of the Lords* published in 1789 (1).

10. Georges Scelle, *La Traite négriére aux Indes de Castille: Contrats et traités d'assiento*, 2 vols. (Paris, 1906). He summarized his findings in Scelle, "Une institution internationale disparue: l'assiento des négres," *Revue générale de droit international public*, 13 (1906): 357–97; Scelle, "The Slave-Trade in the Spanish Colonies of America: The Assiento," *American Journal of International Law*, 4 (3) (1910): 612–61. For Westergaard, see *University of California: In Memoriam (1964)*, available from the University of California History Digital Archives. For the London theses, A. D. Roberts, "The British Empire in Tropical Africa: A Review of the Literature to the 1960s," in W. Roger Louis (gen. ed.), *The Oxford History of the British Empire*, 5 vols. (Oxford, 1999), v. 464–7, and additional London MA theses from 1923, 1930, and 1934 are cataloged in David M. Williams and Andrew P. White (comps.), *A Select Bibliography of British and Irish University Theses about Maritime History, 1792–1990*, Research in Maritime History 1 (St John's, 1991, 11–12).

11. Morey Rothberg (ed.), *John Franklin Jameson and the Development of Humanistic Scholarship in America*, iii: *The Carnegie Institution of Washington and the Library of Congress, 1905–1937* (Athens, Ga., 2001), 236). Jameson earned the first history doctorate from Johns Hopkins University (1882).

12. Donnan's documentary collection is sufficiently rich and varied that it sustained one Ph.D. study: Tommy Todd Hamm, "The American Slave Trade with Africa, 1620–1807" (Ph.D. diss., Indiana University, 1975). The Carnegie Institute also published Helen Tunnicliff Catterall's *Judicial Cases Concerning American Slavery*, 5 vols. (1926–37), which include some cases regarding slaving voyages.

13. M. J. Herskovits, "On the Provenience of New World Negroes," *Social Forces*, 12 (2) (1933): 249 n. 9. An earlier work by Dieudonné Rinchon, *La Traite et l'esclavage des Congolais par les Européens* (Brussels, 1929), contained important listings of French slaving voyages, but it was less known outside France and lacked the analysis of Gaston-Martin's study.

14. Elizabeth Donnan, review of Gaston-Martin, *Nantes au XVIIIe siécle: L'ére des négriers, 1714–1774*, *American Historical Review*, 38 (1) (October 1932): 103. Klein considers *Nantes au XVIIIe siécle: L'ére des négriers, 1714–1774* "without question, the one book that can be said to have created the modern study of the slave trade" (see Herbert S. Klein, *The Atlantic Slave Trade* (Cambridge, 1999), 214).

15. Herskovits, "On the Provenience," 247–62; M. J. Herskovits, "The Significance of West Africa for Negro Research," *Journal of Negro History*, 21 (1) (January 1936): 15–30; Melville Jean Herskovits, *Myth of the Negro Past* (New York: Harper, 1941), 33–53, 304–5, quote on p. 36. Regarding slave preferences, Herskovits, *Myth of the Negro Past*, 50.

16. Eric Williams, *Capitalism & Slavery* (Chapel Hill, NC, 1944); Howard Temperley, "Eric Williams and Abolition: The Birth of a New Orthodoxy," in Barbara L. Solow and Stanley L. Engerman (eds.), *British Capitalism and Caribbean Slavery: The Legacy of Eric Williams* (Cambridge, 1987), 236–7; Richard B. Sheridan, "Eric Williams and *Capitalism and Slavery*: A Biographical and Historiographical Essay," ibid. 319.

17. The launch of the *Journal of African History* in 1960, published by Cambridge University Press, marked the formal development of African history.

18. Dieudonné Rinchon, *Le Trafic négrier: L'organisation commerciale de la traite des noirs* (Brussels, 1938); Maurício Goulart, *A escravidão africana no Brasil: das origens à extinção do tráfico* (São Paulo, 1949).

19. Simone Berbain, *Comptoir français de Juda (Ouidah) au XVIIIe siécle* (Paris, 1942); K. G. Davies, *The Royal African Company* (London, 1957); Abdoulaye Ly, *La Compagnie du Sénégal* (Paris, 1958).

20. James E. Merritt, "The Liverpool Slave Trade" (MA thesis, University of Nottingham, 1959); Bradbury B. Parkinson, "A Slaver's Accounts," *Accounting Research*, 2 (1951): 144–50; Francis Hyde, Bradbury B. Parkinson, and Sheila Marriner, "The Nature and Profitability of the Liverpool Slave Trade," *Economic History Review*, ser. 2, 5 (1953): 368–77. Historians of accounting recently have returned to studying the slave trade. See Cheryl S. McWatters and Yannick Lemarchand, "Accounting Representation and the Slave Trade: The *Guide du commerce* of Gaignat de L'Aulnais," *Accounting Historians Journal*, 33 (2) (2006): 1–37; C. S. McWatters, "Investment Returns and La Traite Négriére: Evidence from Eighteenth-Century France," *Accounting, Business and Financial History*, 18 (2) (2008): 161–85.

21. Philip D. Curtin and Jan Vansina, "Sources of the Nineteenth Century Atlantic Slave Trade," *Journal of African History*, 5 (2) (1964): 185.

22. Craig Watterson, "The Development of African History as a Discipline in the English-Speaking World: A Study of Academic Infrastructure" (MA thesis, Victoria University of Wellington, 2008); Philip D. Curtin, "African Studies: A Personal Assessment," *African Studies Review*, 14 (3) (December 1971): 358–9.

23. Curtin estimated that slaving vessels transported 9,391,000 enslaved Africans to the Americas. In addition, 175,000 arrived in the Old World—50,000 to Europe, 100,000 to São Tomé, and 25,000 to Madeira, the Canaries, and the Cape Verde Islands. Thus, Curtin's estimated global imports totaled 9,566,100 Africans, 1451–1870 (Curtin, *Census*, 268).

24. Curtin, *Census*, 167 n. 2, 275–86.

25. Herbert S. Klein, *The Middle Passage: Comparative Studies in the Atlantic Slave Trade* (Princeton, 1978), 228–35.

26. Stanley L. Engerman and Eugene D. Genovese (eds.), *Race and Slavery in the Western Hemisphere: Quantitative Studies* (Princeton, 1975); Henry A. Gemery and Jan S. Hogendorn (eds.), *The Uncommon Market: Essays in the Economic History of the Atlantic Slave Trade* (New York, 1979), both funded by the National Science Foundation and sponsored by the Mathematical Social Science Board.

27. For a timeline of advances in computer and internet technologies, see www.columbia.edu/acis/history/index.html#ibmpc

28. *Voyages Database*, www.slavevoyages.org which lists sources documenting each slaving voyage.

29. The first transatlantic slaving voyage was probably the *S. Maria de Begoña*, which sailed from Lisbon to São Tomé to Hispaniola, arriving in 1525 (António de Almeida Mendes, "The Foundations of the System: A Reassessment of the Slave Trade to the Spanish Americas in the Sixteenth and Seventeenth Centuries," in David Eltis and David Richardson (eds.), *Extending the Frontiers: Essays on the New Transatlantic Slave Trade Database* (New Haven, 2008), 64; www.slavevoyages.org voyage 46473).

30. Robin Law and Silke Strickrodt (eds.), *Ports of the Slave Trade (Bights of Benin and Biafra)* (Stirling, Scotland, 1999); Robin Law, *Ouidah: The Social History of a West African Slaving "Port,"* 1792–1892 (Athens, OH, 2004); Paul Lovejoy and David Richardson, "'That Horrid Hole': Royal Authority Commerce and Credit at Bonny, 1690–1840," *Journal of African History*, 45 (3) (2004): 363–92; Kristin Mann, *Slavery and the Birth of an African City: Lagos, 1760–1900* (Bloomington, Ind., 2007).

31. David Eltis and David Richardson, "A New Assessment of the Transatlantic Slave Trade," in Eltis and Richardson (eds.), *Extending the Frontiers*, 1–60.

32. Joseph C. Miller, *Way of Death: Merchant Capitalism and the Angolan Slave Trade, 1730–1830* (Madison, 1988); David Northrup, *Trade without Rulers: Pre-colonial Economic Development in South-Eastern Nigeria* (Oxford, 1978); P. E. H. Hair, "Ethnolinguistic Continuity on the Guinea Coast," *Journal of African History*, 8 (2) (1967): 247–68; Walter Hawthorne, *Planting Rice and Harvesting Slaves: Transformations along the Guinea-Bissau Coast, 1400–1900* (Portsmouth, NH 2003); John Thornton, *Africa and Africans in the Making of the Atlantic World, 1400–1800* (2nd edn. New York, 1998); Robert C. Baum, *Shrines of the Slave Trade: Diola Religion and Society in Precolonial Senegambia* (New York, 1999).

33. David Eltis, Frank D. Lewis, and David Richardson, "Slave Prices, the African Slave Trade, and Productivity in the Caribbean, 1674–1807," *Economic History Review*, 58 (4) (2005): 673–700.

34. Philip D. Morgan, "Cultural Implications of the Atlantic Slave Trade: African Regional Origins, American Destinations and New World Developments," *Slavery and Abolition*, 18 (1) (April 1997): 122–45; James H. Sweet, *Recreating Africa: Culture, Kinship, and Religion in the African-Portuguese World, 1441–1770* (Chapel Hill, NC, 2003); José C. Curto and Paul E. Lovejoy (eds.), *Enslaving Connections: Changing Cultures of Africa and Brazil during the Era of Slavery* (Amherst, Mass., 2004). For a succinct summary about the main debates on cultural formations in the Americas, see David Eltis, Philip Morgan, and David Richardson, "Agency and Diaspora in Atlantic History: Reassessing the African Contribution to Rice Cultivation in the Americas," *American Historical Review*, 112 (5) (December 2007): 1329–32.

35. Manolo Florentino, *Em costas negras: uma história do tráfico atlântico de escravos entre a África e o Rio de Janeiro (séculos XVIII e XIX)* (Rio de Janeiro, 1995); Luiz Felipe de Alencastro, *O trato dos viventes: formacão do Brasil no Atlântico Sul, séculos XVI e XVII* (São Paulo, 2000) helped to refocus scholarship on the South Atlantic. New contributions to the growing literature on the Brazilian slave trade and slavery may be found in Eltis and Richardson (eds.), *Extending the Frontiers*.

36. Self-taught French photographer Pierre Verger (b. 1902) began studying links between Africa and Brazil in the late 1940s. In 1966 he defended successfully his dissertation "Flux et reflux du trafic des esclaves entre le Golfe du Bénin et la Baie de Tous les Saints" at the Sorbonne, and received his Ph.D. in African Studies. His work was published in French in 1968, in English in 1976, and then in Portuguese in 1987 by the Brazilian publishing house Corrupio (www.pierreverger.org). Luiz Felipe de Alencastro published his Paris doctoral thesis "Le Commerce des vivants: traite d'esclaves et 'Pax Lusitana' dans l'Atlantique Sud" (1985–6) in Portuguese in 2000. Brazilian-born Manolo Florentino was one who entered the new graduate programs emerging in Brazil during the 1980s. He obtained his BA in 1981 at the Universidade Federal Fluminense, received his MA in African Studies in 1985 at El Colégio de México, but returned to

Brazil to continue his studies at the Federal University Fluminense, where he received his Ph.D. in 1991. Thanks to Daniel Barros Domingues da Silva, Emory University, for this information.

37. Personal communication with Daniel Barros Domingues da Silva (www.cmd.unb.br/ rhistorico.html). In a recent study, Klein discusses the flood of slavery studies in Brazil since the centenary of the abolition of slavery in Brazil in 1888 (Herbert S. Klein, "American Slavery in Recent Brazilian Scholarship, with Emphasis on Quantitative Socio-economic Studies," *Slavery and Abolition*, 30 (1) (March 2009): 111–33).

38. For example, material on the slave trade features in Thomas Benjamin, Timothy Hall, and David Rutherford (eds.), *The Atlantic World in the Age of Empire* (Boston, 2001); Wim Klooster and Alfred Padula (eds.), *The Atlantic World: Essays on Slavery, Migration, and Imagination* (Upper Saddle River, NJ, 2005); Douglas R. Egerton et al. (eds.), *The Atlantic World: A History, 1400–1888* (Wheeling, W. Va., 2007); and Tayin Falola and Kevin David Roberts (eds.), *The Atlantic World, 1450–2000* (Bloomington, Ind., 2008).

39. David Eltis, "Free and Coerced Migrations: Some Comparisons," *American Historical Review*, 88 (2) (1983): 251–80; David Eltis, "Free and Coerced Migrations from the Old World to the New," in Eltis (ed.), *Coerced and Free Migration: Global Perspectives* (Stanford, Calif., 2002), 36. For African and African-Brazilian sailors, see Herbert S. Klein, "The Trade in African Slaves to Rio de Janeiro, 1795–1811: Estimates of Mortality and Patterns of Voyages," *Journal of African History*, 10 (4) (1969): 543; Liliana Crespi, "Negros apresandos en operaciones de corso durante la guerra con el Brasil (1825–1828)," *Temas de Asia y Africa*, 2 (1994): 109–22; Jaime Rodrigues, *De costa a costa: escravos, marinheiros e intermediários do tráfico negreiro de Angola ao Rio de Janeiro (1780–1860)* (São Paulo, 2005); João José Reis, Flávio dos Santos Gomes, and Marcus J. M. de Carvalho, "Rufino José Maria (1820s–1850s): A Muslim in the Nineteenth-Century Brazilian Slave Trade Circuit," in Beatriz G. Mamigonian and Karen Racine (eds.), *Human Tradition in the Black Atlantic, 1500–2000* (Lanham, Md., 2010), 65–75. Paul Gilroy's *The Black Atlantic: Modernity and Double Consciousness* (Cambridge, 1993) has popularized the term "Black Atlantic."

40. British slaving merchants' papers from the Merseyside Maritime Museum are available in *Slavery, Abolition and Social Justice, 1490–2007* (Adam Matthew Digital); those from the Liverpool Record Office are available on the British On-line Archives (Microform Academic Publishers) website.

41. Klein, *Middle Passage*; David Eltis, *The Rise of African Slavery in the Americas* (New York, 2000).

42. On-line searches: ProQuest, *Dissertation Abstracts International*; *Index to Theses: A Comprehensive Listing of Theses with Abstracts Accepted for Higher Degrees by Universities in Great Britain and Ireland since 1716*. David Chandler's "Health and Slavery: A Study of Health Conditions among Negro Slaves in the Viceroyalty of New Granada and its Associated Slave Trade, 1600–1810" (Ph.D. diss., Tulane University, 1972) is the one medical history thesis with substantial material on the slave trade.

43. Simon J. Hogerzeil and David Richardson, "Slave Purchasing Strategies and Shipboard Mortality: Day-to-Day Evidence from the Dutch African Trade, 1751–1797," *Journal of Economic History*, 67 (1) (2007): 160–90, based on analysis of Middelburg Commercial Company voyages. Niels Van Manen, "Preventive Medicine in the Dutch Slave Trade, 1747–1797," *International Journal of Maritime History*, 18 (2) (2006): 129–85 is a recent valuable study.

44. Evidence of Sherwood, 8 December 1789, reprinted in Sheila Lambert (ed.), *House of Commons Sessional Papers of the Eighteenth Century*, 145 vols. (Wilmington, Del., 1975), lxx. 205; David R. MacGregor, *Fast Sailing Ships: Their Design and Construction, 1775–1875* (Annapolis, Md., 1988), 98.
45. Nicholas J. Radburn, "William Davenport, the Slave Trade, and Merchant Enterprise in Eighteenth-Century Liverpool" (MA thesis, Victoria University of Wellington, 2009), 36, 90, 97, 106.
46. Quoted by Gomer Williams, *History of the Liverpool Privateers and Letters of Marque with an Account of the Liverpool Slave Trade* (London, 1897), 485.
47. For the British slave trade, future studies on merchants will build on David Pope, "The Wealth and Social Aspirations of Liverpool's Slave Merchants in the Second Half of the Eighteenth Century" and Jane Longmore, "'Cemented by the Blood of the Negro'? The Impact of the Slave Trade on Eighteenth-Century Liverpool," in David Richardson, Suzanne Schwarz, and Anthony Tibbles (eds.), *Liverpool and Transatlantic Slavery* (Liverpool, 2007), 164–226 and 227–51.
48. John Campbell, *A Political Survey of Britain*, 4 vols. (Dublin, 1775), iv. 630–1.
49. Joseph E. Inikori, "The Development of Entrepreneurship in Africa: Southeastern Nigeria during the Era of the Trans-Atlantic Slave Trade," in Alusine Jalloh and Toyin Falola (eds.), *Black Business and Economic Power* (Rochester, NY, 2002), 41–79.
50. Eltis and Richardson, "New Assessment," 8–25.
51. George E. Brooks and Bruce L. Mouser, "An 1804 Slaving Contract Signed in Arabic Script from the Upper Guinea Coast," *History in Africa*, 14 (1987): 341–7.
52. *BBC News*, 19 December 2001; *Liverpool Echo*, 15 August 2007.

Select Bibliography

Bailey, Anne C. *African Voices of the Atlantic Slave Trade*. Boston: Beacon Press, 2006.
Brown, Christopher Leslie. *Moral Capital: Foundations of British Abolitionism*. Chapel Hill, NC: University of North Carolina Press, 2006.
Christopher, Emma. *Slave Ship Sailors and their Captive Cargoes, 1730–1807*. New York: Cambridge University Press, 2006.
Curto, José C., and Renée Soulodre-La France, eds. *Africa and the Americas: Interconnections during the Slave Trade*. Trenton, NJ: Africa World Press, 2005.
De Corse, Christopher R., ed. *West Africa during the Atlantic Slave Trade: Archaeological Perspectives*. Leicester: Leicester University Press, 2001.
Diouf, Sylviane A., ed. *Fighting the Slave Trade: West African Strategies*. Athens, Oh.: Ohio University Press, 2003.
Eltis, David. *The Rise of African Slavery in the Americas*. New York: Cambridge University Press, 2000.
Howard-Hassmann, Rhoda E., with Anthony P. Lombardo. *Reparations to Africa*. Philadelphia: University of Pennsylvania Press, 2008.
Inikori, Joseph E. *Africans and the Industrial Revolution in England: A Study in International Trade and Economic Development*. Cambridge: Cambridge University Press, 2002.

MILLER, CHRISTOPHER L. *The French Atlantic Triangle: Literature and Culture of the Slave Trade*. Durham, NC: Duke University Press, 2008.

SHAW, ROSALIND. *Memories of the Slave Trade: Ritual and the Historical Imagination in Sierra Leone*. Chicago: University of Chicago Press, 2002.

WALLACE, ELIZABETH KOWALESKI. *The British Slave Trade and Public Memory*. New York: Columbia University Press, 2006.

CHAPTER 12

....

THE ORIGINS OF
SLAVERY IN THE
AMERICAS

....

JOHN J. MCCUSKER

RUSSELL R. MENARD

AN air of inevitability pervades the history of the rise of African slavery in the Americas.[1] By the middle of the eighteenth century, African slavery and Europe's American colonies had become so thoroughly intertwined as to seem inseparable. Much of European America consisted of Africanized slave societies. Before 1750, and even as late the 1820s, imported enslaved Africans far outnumbered settlers from Europe as migrants to America.[2] "From Brazil and the Caribbean to Chesapeake Bay," David Brion Davis observes, "the richest and most coveted colonies—in terms of large-scale capital investment, output, and value of exports and imports—ultimately became dependent on black slave labor."[3] The identification of blacks and bondage was eventually so central a feature of American history that it takes a major effort of imagination to envision other outcomes.

Such an effort is essential, however, for nothing predestined either the Africanization of slavery or the entrenchment of African slavery in the Americas. Several well-known facts establish the point. White slavery, an old and well-established institution in much of the West, persisted in the early modern era around the Mediterranean and in eastern Europe, and did not disappear (indeed, at some times and places it flourished concurrently with the rise of the Atlantic slave trade).[4] Several American colonies never depended on African slaves; some did so only briefly before turning to other peoples and other methods of organizing labor. Finally, and most importantly, many colonial societies that eventually became dependent on Africans did so only after an initial period of reliance on white indentured servants or on Native American Indians. Again, an observation from David Brion Davis proves helpful: "the Africanization of large parts of the New World was not the result of concerted planning, racial destiny, or immanent historical design but of innumerable local and pragmatic choices made in four continents" over an extended period of time.[5]

This essay offers an overview of the rise of African slavery in English America.[6] Several propositions are useful in ordering the historical record. The most important is that transitions to African slavery in the several colonies of England's emerging empire can be better understood if Britain's Atlantic world is approached as a single if imperfect and fragile labor market and if variations in the composition of the workforce among colonies and within particular colonial regions over time are approached through a focus on the supply and demand for labor.

Some scholars contend that transitions to African slavery are more profitably approached through an examination of politics and culture, especially of planter attitudes toward various types of workers. In these studies, attention to racial ideologies trumps analysis of labor markets.[7] Planters, the argument goes, turned to African slaves because they thought blacks better suited to the plantation regimen, more vigorous, easier to control, better able to withstand the climate, diseases, and the work than whites or Indians. One does find clear expressions of such preferences in British America, but most of them seem to have appeared after the Africanization of the workforce rather than before. In lowcountry South Carolina, for example, the belief that the region was not capable of being cultivated by white men because of "their utter ineptitude . . . for the labour requisite in such a climate and soil," that it "must long have remained a wilderness," in the absence of Africans "whose natural constitutions were suited to this clime and work," was central to the ideology of the great planters by the revolutionary era.[8] Such attitudes emerged, however, only after the lowcountry had become a thoroughly Africanized slave society, receiving clear expression for the first time around 1740, during the debate over the introduction of slavery into Georgia.[9]

Earlier in the process of Africanization little evidence exists that planters preferred blacks to Indians or whites. Rather, planters took what workers they could get. An abundance of probate inventories, for example, lists servants, African slaves, and enslaved Indians. These documents reveal that many planters thought of English indentured servants and African and Indian slaves as interchangeable substitutes for one another.[10] In an extreme version of the cultural argument, the historian David Hackett Fischer has concluded "that race slavery did not create the culture of the southern colonies; that culture created slavery."[11] While some attention to culture is clearly important in understanding the rise of slavery,

Fischer's pronouncement seems of little help in making sense of the specifics of the rise of African slavery in the several colonies of British America.

That said, planter predispositions did contribute to the growth of slavery in at least two ways. First, planters had to be willing to substitute Africans for Europeans or Indians and then be willing to treat Africans differently: to reduce them to lifelong enslavement, and to subject them to a severe, harsh, and degrading system. Second, profit-conscious planters had to be persuaded that Africans could be disciplined successfully to fulfill the tasks assigned. Acceptance of such ideas may explain why British Americans adopted slavery so quickly, without hesitation, and with such apparent enthusiasm. But predilections cannot account for the timing of changes in the workforce; timing can be understood only by close attention to labor markets, to the supply of workers available from various sources, and to the demand for labor. On the whole, the political-cultural approach to the rise of African slavery awkwardly confuses consequence and cause and lacks the explanatory power of the materialist approach.

Challenges to the materialist approach can be found in the recent scholarship of Lorena Walsh and April Hatfield. In an important but yet unpublished paper, Walsh reports that, in colony after colony, local elites made a conscious choice to invest in African slaves well in advance of the events—an increase in demand for labor or a decline in the alternative sources of supply, be they British indentured servants or Indian slaves—that the materialist approach has claimed drove the transition to slavery.[12] April Hatfield shows that the growth of slavery in both South Carolina and Virginia was driven by migrants from Barbados interested in recreating the kind of plantation agriculture familiar to them on the island.[13] The challenging work of Walsh and Hatfield complicates the materialist argument, but does not refute it.

The behavior of elites who first invested in African slaves should be understood as having paved the way for the large-scale transitions to African slavery that followed. Elites knew of the successes that planters elsewhere had with Africans: mainlanders drew on the crucial example of Barbados; Barbadians had learned from sugar producers in Brazil and in the Atlantic islands. Moreover elites had the means to pay for slaves, either out of their own pockets or with capital borrowed from their contacts among London merchants eager to invest in plantation agriculture.[14] Their early investments in African slaves provided a demonstration, showing others that Africans could be employed profitably in plantation agriculture. Furthermore, elites in the English colonies were particularly well positioned in their representative assemblies to create the legal systems necessary to protect their new investment. So, when smaller-scale planters faced rising prices for dwindling supplies of Indians and British servants, they chose enslaved Africans with little hesitation. Elites had already shown, after all, that African slaves could be profitably turned to the tasks at hand and had created the needed legal framework for the transition to slavery in the form of various slave codes. Of these, "An Act for the better ordering and governing of Negroes," the infamous Barbadian slave code of 1661, the first comprehensive slave code in English America, proved most influential in shaping the law of slavery in other English colonies.[15]

A more detailed discussion of the transition to African slavery in any of the major plantation districts of British America requires a preliminary examination of the population data assembled in Tables 12.1 and 12.2. (Table 12.1 shows the change in the percentage of African-Americans over time by region. Table 12.2 shows the percentage of African-Americans for selected colonies.) As these data suggest, Africanization was a general process in seventeenth-century British America. There were relatively few Africans in the colonies before the middle of the seventeenth century, but their numbers and their share of the population grew impressively by the late seventeenth and early eighteenth century, until, by 1750, Africans accounted for more than a third of the inhabitants of British America.

Although Africanization was a general phenomenon, the particulars of the process varied by region and colony as some places committed to African slavery earlier and more intensely than others. These variations point to an explanatory dilemma facing students of the rise of African slavery in European America. African

Table 12.1. Percentage of African–Americans in the population of British America, 1640–1770

	British West Indies (%)	Lower South (%)	Upper South (%)	British America (%)
1640	3.6		1.5	2.7
1650	27.0		3.0	15.2
1660	42.1	2.0	4.8	22.2
1670	54.2	4.4	6.6	26.5
1680	63.9	6.2	7.5	29.1
1690	72.5	15.7	14.9	31.9
1700	78.2	20.1	22.3	34.3
1710	82.6	26.0	23.3	34.7
1720	83.6	37.4	25.4	35.0
1730	85.6	43.3	25.4	33.3
1740	87.6	47.4	28.3	32.4
1750	89.2	45.9	39.9	34.3
1760	90.1	44.1	37.8	32.2
1770	90.4	45.1	38.7	32.6

Sources: By "Lower South" is meant the colonies of North Carolina, South Carolina, and Georgia; the "Upper South" is Maryland and Virginia. British America includes the Thirteen Continental Colonies, the British West Indies, and British North America. The African-American population of the last of these three was minuscule through 1750. For the Continental Colonies, see John J. McCusker, "Colonial Statistics," in Susan B. Carter et al. (eds.), *Historical Statistics of the United States* (4th edn. Cambridge, 2006), v. 651–3. Compare the tables in McCusker and Russell R. Menard, *The Economy of British America, 1607–1789* (2nd edn. Chapel Hill, NC, 1991). The data for the British West Indies and British North America were originally compiled and presented in McCusker, *Rum and the American Revolution: The Rum Trade and the Balance of Payments of the Thirteen Continental Colonies, 1650–1775*, 2 vols. (New York, 1989; Ph.D. diss., University of Pittsburgh, 1970), ii. 548–767 (appendix B). Data have been revised somewhat on the basis of additional research. See also the source note for Table 12.2.

Table 12.2. Percentage of African-Americans in the population of selected colonies in British America, 1640–1770

	Virginia (%)	Barbados (%)	Maryland (%)	South Carolina (%)
1640	1.4	3.6	3.4	
1650	2.2	29.9	6.7	
1660	3.5	50.8	9.0	
1670	5.7	64.3	9.0	15.0
1680	6.9	68.7	9.0	16.7
1690	17.6	72.8	9.0	38.5
1700	28.0	76.5	10.9	47.9
1710	26.0	80.1	18.6	55.3
1720	30.3	76.9	18.9	64.5
1730	30.3	78.2	18.9	66.7
1740	33.3	80.2	20.7	72.3
1750	45.3	82.1	30.8	66.2
1760	41.4	83.0	30.2	60.9
1770	42.0	84.2	31.5	60.5

Sources: For Virginia, Maryland, and South Carolina, see John J. McCusker, "Colonial Statistics," in Susan B. Carter et al. (eds.), *Historical Statistics of the United States* (4th edn. Cambridge, 2006), v. 651–3. For Barbados, see McCusker and Russell R. Menard, *The Economy of British America, 1607–1789* (2nd edn. Chapel Hill, NC, 1991), 153, revised on the basis of ongoing research. The data were originally compiled and presented in McCusker, *Rum and the American Revolution: The Rum Trade and the Balance of Payments of the Thirteen Continental Colonies, 1650–1775*, 2 vols. (New York, 1989; Ph.D. diss., University of Pittsburgh, 1970]), ii. 644–5, 699. Compare P[eter] F. Campbell, "Barbados: The Early Years," *Journal of the Barbados Museum and Historical Society*, 35 (3) (1977): 155–77; Campbell, "Aspects of Barbados Land Tenure, 1627–1663," ibid. 37 (2) (1984): 112–58; and Campbell, *Some Early Barbadian History* (St Michael, Barbados, 1993), 84–9.

slavery's very commonality in the Americas has attracted historians to single factor explanations. The free land hypothesis, for example, argues that slavery flourished in the Americas because the abundance of resources and a shortage of workers made wages high and free workers hard to control.[16] An epidemiological argument stresses the greater resistance of Africans to certain tropical diseases as the key variable in the Africanization of the Americas.[17] The close association of slavery with certain plantation crops has led to an emphasis on the work requirements of some crops as critical to the rise of slavery.[18] The persistent power of racism in our own time has provided support for explanations rooted in racial prejudice and ethnic differences.[19] All of these arguments have something to recommend them, and each of these factors probably played some role in the growth of one or another American slave society. But all encounter significant exceptions that upset their claims as general explanations for the origin of African slavery. All of these arguments encourage an ahistorical approach that reduces the existence of African slavery to an inevitable outcome; none of them accounts for the particulars in the rise of the several slave systems of British America.

Similarly, Marxist interpretations of the origin of African slavery as a necessary component of the rise of merchant capitalism in Europe describe more than they explain. In perhaps the most influential formulation of this approach, the sociologist Immanuel Wallerstein interpreted American slave regimes as part of the division of labor in the rise of a new "world-system" during the early modern era. Peripheral areas such as the Americas and eastern Europe, he maintained, were relegated to the production of minerals and crops by coerced workers in order to ensure the surplus which enabled capitalism and free labor to thrive in the core areas of northwestern Europe. Whether by central design or by local response to specific conditions, this explanation makes coerced labor the logical consequence of an exchanged-based capitalist system, but it does not explain why slavery was the preferred form of coercion, or why Africans were the major victims. And, like the other previously discussed single factor explanations, such grand generalizations offer little help in sorting out the particulars of the transition to slavery in the Caribbean, in the Carolina lowcountry, or along the Chesapeake Bay, not to mention in places farther afield.[20]

Concern with the particulars of enslavement has led many historians to develop *ad hoc* accounts of the rise of each slave society. They tell a story of the growth of slavery in, say, Barbados, South Carolina, or Virginia that abstracts the development from the more general process of which it is a part. Such stories have the advantage of identifying the temporal and geographic specifics of the growth of slavery and of providing a wealth of empirical detail. Their emphasis on the particular, however, leaves those concerned to account for the more general Africanization of the Americas awash in a sea of empirical detail, unable to offer arguments that can relate one case to another, to impose order on the vast amount of evidence, or to provide direction to further research.[21]

What is needed is an integration of the two approaches, an analytical model that recognizes the common elements of the growth of African slavery in English America, without suppressing local variations, an approach that acknowledges the concrete particularity of each process without burying the common pattern under a mountain of local detail. How might such a melding be accomplished? It should begin by sketching the structure of the labor market in British America. It should describe the constraints in which planters in the several colonies operated and identify key variables that shaped choices concerning the organization of labor.

Economists Henry A. Gemery and Jan S. Hogendorn have argued that changes in the composition of colonial workforces are best approached by looking at interactions between the supply and demand for labor.[22] Their major insight concerns differences in supply between African slaves and all other sources of labor available to colonial employers. The planters of English America had several options in recruiting and organizing a workforce. They could draw on free workers; on indentured servants or convicts from England, Ireland, and Scotland; on Indians from the vast North American interior; or on colonial-born youths not yet established in households of their own.[23] Such workers usually moved in small markets, circumscribed by geography and political divisions, and characterized by sharp, unpredictable fluctuations in volume and price. As long as demand for labor remained low, one of those sources was often adequate to meet the need for workers.[24] Hence, New England, where the failure to develop a major staple export meant a sluggish economy and relatively low levels of labor productivity, furnished a sufficient supply of workers from its own sons and daughters to maintain the ethnic homogeneity of its workforce.[25]

Regions where demand for labor was higher quickly ran into difficulty if they relied on a single source. The price of workers in those small, localized markets rose sharply, pressed against profit margins, and set off a scramble by suppliers who often exhibited considerable ingenuity in developing new sources of labor. Consequently, in the Middle Colonies, where a lively agricultural export sector and linked commercial development created a more expansive economy and higher levels of labor productivity, there appeared a complex and rapidly changing labor market that helps explain the ethnic diversity of that population.[26]

A different pattern materialized in the southern continental colonies and on the islands of the West Indies. Those regions experimented with workers drawn from a range of sources early in the development of each area, but high productivity and increasing demand quickly stretched those small and localized supplies to their capacity and drove planters toward coerced, non-free labor. They had two choices: either use Europeans hired on contract as indentured servants; or use Africans, captured and enslaved. After a dalliance with the former, American planters turned decisively toward enslaved Africans. These workers, caught in a much wider net, little more than commodities in a relatively stable, large-scale, international labor market, became the victims of choice in the rapidly expanding plantation colonies of European America.[27]

African slavery in British America cannot be understood apart from indentured servitude. Although the principle behind this early, major alternative to African slavery in the plantation colonies was articulated as early as the 1580s, the Virginia Company devised indentured servitude in the late 1610s to finance the recruitment and transport of workers to its colony. Even though some historians view indentured servitude as an entirely new development, most consider it as an adaptation of the traditional English institution of apprenticeship to a new set of circumstances. Servitude and apprenticeship resembled each other but also differed significantly. Servitude was largely an agricultural institution, designed to move people into fieldwork; apprenticeship was urban, aimed toward trade, crafts, and professions. Servitude attracted those too poor to purchase passage across the Atlantic; apprenticeship was for those prosperous enough to pay an entry fee in exchange for training. Servants could be sold from one master to another without consent, or even consultation; apprentices could not. Despite the contractual promise that servants would be instructed in "the mystery, art, and occupation of a planter" and however much servants learned simply by doing, indentured servitude was a labor system, not an educational institution.[28] Apprenticeship was.

These considerations led David Galenson to suggest quite different antecedents for indentured servitude: English farm servants, or "servants in husbandry." Farm servants were numerous in seventeenth-century and eighteenth-century England. They accounted for perhaps 10 to 15 percent of the population, appeared in a quarter to a third of all households, and made up about half of all hired, full-time agricultural workers. Boys and girls from poor families predominated in this category of servants. They left home in their early teens to work for more prosperous farmers until they could marry and set up on their own. They usually lived in the master's household; agreed to annual contracts for wages, food, and lodging; and moved from place to place frequently, often every year. The very pervasiveness of this form of life-cycle service makes it a likely antecedent for indentured servitude and a major source of recruits for American plantations.[29]

According to Galenson, the major differences between indentured servitude and service in husbandry followed from the distances indentured servants traveled on leaving home. Distance proved "a sufficiently important economic difference to necessitate several modifications in the institution," all of which made "the indenture system more rigid and formal than its English counterpart."[30] The major changes concerned length of term, the sale of contracts, and discipline. Servants in husbandry served short terms. They seldom remained with a master for more than a year or two and usually renegotiated their contracts annually. Indentured servants served longer periods under fixed terms negotiated at departure from England. Despite the fact that four years was the usual term for servants who had reached maturity, the length of the contract varied with the time needed to repay the borrowed passage fare. Greater distance and longer terms led to transferable contracts. Planters would have been less willing to lay out the substantial sum required to purchase a servant, if they had to commit themselves to that investment for the entire term, without the possibility of sale, while the trade in indentured servants could not have functioned had ship captains, merchants, and recruiting agents not been able to transfer contracts to colonial masters.[31] To sell an English man or woman "like a damnd slave" was at first shocking to some contemporaries, but it was essential to the success of the indenture system.[32]

These changes, Galenson argues, introduced "a new adversary status . . . into the relationship between master and servant."[33] Longer terms joined with the inability of servants to renegotiate contracts and change masters to produce tension and conflict, evident in the frequency with which servants ran away and were hauled before magistrates.[34] Unlike English servants in husbandry, who were often integrated into their master's family and treated as added children or poor relations, colonial servants were simply workers and investments. While Galenson may underestimate the potential for affection and mutual trust between master and servant, colonial servitude was clearly a harsher institution than its English counterpart.

At least four distinct forms of indentured servitude emerged in British America, three of them voluntary in character.[35] Under the most common mode, before their departure across the Atlantic British servants signed a contract (an indenture) that specified the length of term and conditions of service. That contract—and with it the man or woman—was sold to a master when the servant reached the colonies. Many servants, however, perhaps 40 percent of those who migrated to the seventeenth-century Chesapeake, arrived without written contracts. In such cases, "the custom of the country" structured arrangements, custom gradually specified in each colony by a developing body of legislation.[36]

These two modes of service had systematic differences. Customary servants were younger, about 16 years of age on average, when they immigrated; servants with contracts were usually in their early twenties. Customary servants also "served longer terms than those who arrived with indentures, even if age is held constant, perhaps reflecting that, from the planter's perspective, they were less productive than those with written contracts." Customary servants may also have been "less often skilled, more likely to be illiterate," without prior work experience, "of lower social origins, more often without living parents or guardians to look out for their interests, [and] easier marks for an unscrupulous 'crimp,' and generally less sophisticated about labor relations and opportunities in the New World."[37]

The third form of voluntary servitude appeared in the eighteenth century with the German migration to the Middle Colonies. German redemptioners promised to pay the fare for their passage upon arriving in the colonies, a promise that shifted much of the risk for the trade from merchants and shippers to the migrants. If the passengers proved unable to pay, they were sold as servants to satisfy the debt.[38] In addition to these voluntary systems, penal servitude, a minor institution in the seventeenth century, became an important source of labor later in the colonial period.[39]

Servants played a central role in the development of British America. During the seventeenth century, roughly 250,000 indentured migrants reached the colonies, the majority going to the West Indies and the tobacco coast. Servants were especially important in the plantation colonies. Roughly 70 to 85 percent of the European migrants to the Chesapeake region in the seventeenth century arrived as servants, and the share to the Caribbean was probably even higher.[40]

Some historians may object to the characterization of servants as voluntary migrants, especially to the implication that servants were able to choose among the several available destinations. Gary Nash, for example, maintains that servants "were not making the choices, for power in the commercial transactions that brought bound labor across the Atlantic resided in the hands of the supplier and the buyer."[41] Similarly, James Horn contends that "the servant's individual desires played little part in determining where he eventually ended up. Instead, it was the trading community that was responsible for directing and regulating migration in response to the needs of the colonies."[42]

To be sure, instances of outright coercion occurred in the formation of indentures; uneducated rural youth stood at a disadvantage in negotiations with shrewd, experienced merchants. But servants were hardly passive victims of a process beyond their control. The best evidence on the issue comes from David Galenson's analysis of indenture contracts. Older servants with skills and work experience who could read and write served shorter terms than younger, unskilled, inexperienced, illiterate boys and girls. Servants clearly discriminated among destinations. Those who went to Barbados, where death rates were high, opportunities slender, the work hard, and treatment severe, contracted to serve shorter terms than those who went to the mainland.[43] The variations in the length of term were not trivial. Among servants who left London in the 1680s, for example, those who could write their names signed on for a term seven months shorter on average than those who could not; those who went to Maryland served nine months more than those to Barbados. Given a typical term of five or six years, these variations amount to substantial differences. The patterns only make sense if migration was voluntary and servants struck bargains and made choices among competing destinations.[44]

Another type of evidence permits a test of the proposition that the choices servants made helped shape the pattern of migration to the colonies. On the one hand, if servants made the decision, one would expect that they would pay just as close attention to opportunities and incomes at home and that the size of the migrant stream would be inversely related to English real wages. On the other hand, if the choices of merchants and planters controlled the volume of migration, there would be little relation between real wages and the number of migrants. A comparison of annual fluctuations in the number of indentured servants who left Bristol in the seventeenth century with an English real wage index shows a strong inverse relationship. Servants left in greater numbers when wages were low, strong evidence that they made the decision to move. A comparison of the volume of customary servants arriving in several Chesapeake counties with real wages shows the same pattern, indicating that even servants who came without contracts, who one might expect were the least likely to be in control of the situation, made the decision informed by an assessment of their prospects at home.[45] While significant variations certainly existed across time and space, this analytical approach to labor markets in understanding the choices made in English America not only provides a comprehensive way of configuring a coherent account of the process of Africanization of labor in English America, but it also has enough explanatory power to be useful as a model for the rest of European America—and, just maybe, elsewhere. That, at least, is our argument—and our expectation.

SUMMATION

Even though historians have made considerable progress in understanding the roots of American slave regimes, there are too many loose ends, too many issues that need further work.

We are persuaded that the model of the transition to slavery described above is an accurate description of the process in the Upper South, but we wonder how far it can be generalized. Did elites lead the way in all the plantation colonies of British America? In Brazil? Elsewhere?

What did those who prepared the way by demonstrating slavery's profitability and creating the necessary legal and institutional structures have in mind? Were they thinking only of profits, or did they imagine the gentry-dominated race-based plantation regimes that eventually emerged?

We also need to know more about how the rise of slavery was financed. Building slave economies was expensive and colonies were chronically short of capital.[46] Although one could pay for slaves out of current income, that was a slow process, too slow to account for the speed with which slave populations grew.

Given that the gang system was the source of slavery's productivity and thus its advantage over other forms of labor, we need to understand the origins of that method of labor organization. David Eltis offers a cultural explanation for the origins of the gang system, whilst others have advanced a materialist account of its roots.[47]

Often, the transition to slavery is described as a shift from a society in which there were slaves to a slave society.[48] We are unhappy with that characterization. As a simple dichotomy it is inadequate to describe the variety of slave regimes in the plantation colonies of British America. Even casual students of the subject will know that there were vast differences between the slave societies of the Chesapeake region, the Lower South, and the West Indies. There were also major changes over time. The slave society of the Chesapeake colonies in the late seventeenth century, when only a third of the free householders owned slaves and Africans accounted for only 15 percent of the population, differed vastly from that of the 1770s, when 75 percent of the free householders had slaves and Africans made up almost 40 percent of the population.

Clearly we need to develop a more sophisticated typology to capture the variety of the slave experience in the plantation colonies.

NOTES

1. This essay builds on several of Russell R. Menard's articles which explore the rise of slavery in various plantation colonies. The articles are assembled in Russell R. Menard, *Migrants, Servants and Slaves: Unfree Labor in Colonial British America*, Variorum Collected Studies Series, CS 699 (Aldershot, UK, 2001). For earlier summaries of this

work, see Menard, "Transitions to Slavery in British America, 1630–1730: Barbados, Virginia and South Carolina," *Indian Historical Review: Journal of the Indian Council of Historical Research*, 15 (1–2) (July 1988–June 1989): 33–49; and Menard and Stuart B. Schwartz, "Why African Slavery? Labor Force Transitions in Brazil, Mexico, and the Carolina Lowcountry," in Wolfgang Binder (ed.), *Slavery in the Americas*, Studien zur "Neuen Welt" 4 (Würzburg, 1993), 89–114.

2. David Eltis, "Free and Coerced Transatlantic Migrations: Some Comparisons," *American Historical Review*, 88 (April 1983): 278 (table 3).

3. David Brion Davis, *Slavery and Human Progress* (Oxford, 1984), 51. For a sweeping view of the origins of slavery, see Stanley L. Engerman, *Slavery, Emancipation and Freedom: Comparative Perspectives*, Louisiana State University, Walter Lynwood Fleming Lectures in Southern History 67 (Baton Rouge, La., 2007), 1–36.

4. William D. Phillips, Jr., *Slavery from Roman Times to the Early Transatlantic Trade* (Minneapolis, 1985), surveys the literature on slavery in the early modern Mediterranean.

5. Davis, *Slavery and Human Progress*, 52.

6. We concentrate our attention on English America for two reasons, leaving open the question—as a challenge to others—about how well our arguments might apply to different peoples and other places. The first reason is that this is the time and place we know best. In spite of the fact that we can and do make the occasional reference to elsewhere, our expertise, such as it is, is rooted in early British America. The second reason is that our argument ("the materialist tradition"), essentially an economic explanation for the emergence of and increasing dependence upon the enslavement of Africans, finds a deep resonance among the peoples and places about which we know best. What we know about neighboring economies and societies encourages us to extend this argument to them. (In this regard, see, again, Menard and Schwartz, "Why African Slavery?") The alternative argument ("the political-cultural tradition") involves matters that are not our strong suit, even in early British America, and for those matters we tend to rely on other scholars. Indeed, the more we read of the work about the culture of early British America, the more confirmed we are in the correctness of our cautious stance. Thus we are doubly unwilling to extrapolate from the cultural values and institutional outlooks of early British America to neighboring colonial societies. "Shoemaker, mind your last" seems the proper caution to invoke at this juncture in the discourse. For a general discussion of the colonial American labor force, see John J. McCusker and Russell R. Menard, *The Economy of British America, 1607–1789* (2nd edn. Chapel Hill, NC, 1991), 236–57.

   For a European perspective on this question, see Jochen Meissner, Ulrich Mücke, and Klaus Weber, *Schwarzes Amerika: Eine Geschichte der Sklaverei* (Munich, 2008).

7. The most important work in this tradition is Winthrop D. Jordan, *White over Black: American Attitudes toward the Negro, 1550–1812* (Chapel Hill, NC, 1968). Others have chosen different tacks. Seminal statements that set out the terms of the debate are Oscar Handlin and Mary F. Handlin, "Origins of the Southern Labor System," *William and Mary Quarterly*, 3rd ser., 7 (April 1950): 199–222; Kenneth M. Stampp, "The Historian and Southern Negro Slavery," *American Historical Review*, 57 (April 1952): 613–24; Carl N. Degler, "Slavery and the Genesis of American Race Prejudice," *Comparative Studies in Society and History*, 2 (October 1959): 49–66; and Winthrop D. Jordan, "Modern Tensions and the Origins of American Slavery," *Journal of Southern History*, 28

(February 1962): 18–30. For a review of the debate, see William (A.) Green, "Race and Slavery: Considerations on the William Thesis," in Barbara L. Solow and Stanley L. Engerman (eds.), *British Capitalism and Caribbean Slavery: The Legacy of Eric Williams* (Cambridge, 1987), 25–49; and Alden T. Vaughan, "The Origins Debate: Slavery and Racism in Seventeenth-Century Virginia," *Virginia Magazine of History and Biography*, 97 (July 1989): 311–54. Green's reference is, of course, to Eric Eustace Williams, *Capitalism & Slavery* (Chapel Hill, NC, 1944). For an important effort to tie the growth of slavery to an emerging racial ideology, see Theodore W. Allen, *The Invention of the White Race*, 2 vols. (London, 1994–7). A major contribution to the discussion is David Eltis, "Europeans and the Rise and Fall of African Slavery in the Americas: An Interpretation," *American Historical Review*, 97 (December 1993): 1399–1423.

8. Alexander Hewat, *An Historical Account of the Rise and Progress of the Colonies of South Carolina and Georgia*, 2 vols. (London, 1779), i. 120. For Revd Hewat, see Elmer D. Johnson, "Alexander Hewat: South Carolina's First Historian," *Journal of Southern History*, 20 (February 1954): 50–62; and Geraldine M. Meroney, "Alexander Hewat's *Historical Account*," in Lawrence H. Leder (ed.), *The Colonial Legacy*, 4 vols. (New York, 1971–3), i. 135–63. Readers interested in the debates on this issue will definitely find it useful to contrast Betty Wood's cultural approach to the rise of slavery with our materialist understanding of the question in *The Origins of American Slavery: Freedom and Bondage in the English Colonies* (New York, 1997).

9. Russell R. Menard discussed these attitudes in more detail in "Slavery, Economic Growth, and Revolutionary Ideology in the South Carolina Lowcountry," in Ronald Hoffman et al. (eds.), *The Economy of Early America: The Revolutionary Period, 1763–1790* (Charlottesville, Va., 1988), 244–74. Concerning the Georgia debate, see Betty Wood, *Slavery in Colonial Georgia, 1730–1775* (Athens, Ga., 1984).

10. There are numerous examples in the probate inventories of South Carolina among the Records of the Secretary of the Province (RSP), Recorded Instruments, Miscellaneous Records, Proprietary Series, 1671–1725, South Carolina Department of Archives and History, Columbia, South Carolina. Conveniently, Peter H. Wood has reprinted one such example, the February 1682/83 inventory of the estate of John Smyth, in *Black Majority: Negroes in Colonial South Carolina from 1670 through the Stono Rebellion* (New York, 1974), 332 (RSP (1675–1695), 21–2). For examples at the same time from the Chesapeake Bay region, see Gloria L. Main, *Tobacco Colony: Life in Early Maryland, 1650–1720* (Princeton, 1982), 128–32. Wood draws the lesson (*Black Majority*, 54–5): "Even though such dependants [i.e., Smyth's nine Africans, four Indians, and three whites] were not all engaged in the same tasks or accorded equal status, they must have fulfilled complementary functions at close quarters." John C. Coombs, "Building 'The Machine': The Development of Slavery and Slave Society in Early Colonial Virginia" (Ph.D. diss., College of William and Mary, 2003), 96–8, argues that the use of Native American Indians as slaves helped alleviate the diminished numbers of indentured servants in the southwestern counties of Virginia during the last third of the seventeenth century.

11. David Hackett Fischer, *Albion's Seed: Four British Folkways in America* (Oxford, 1989), 812.

12. Lorena S. Walsh, "A Thinking Decision? Colonial Elites, Slavery, Emigration and Staples" (unpublished paper presented at the 39th Annual Meeting of the Association of Caribbean Historians, Mona, Jamaica, 8 May 2007). Compare Walsh, "Thinking Decisions? Migration, Servitude, and Slavery in the British North American Mainland Colonies" (unpublished paper presented at the McNeil Center for Early America

Studies Seminar, David Library, Washington's Crossing, Pennsylvania, 8 September 2006). See also her: "The Differential Cultural Impact of Free and Coerced Migration to Colonial America," in David Eltis (ed.), *Coerced and Free Migration: Global Perspectives* (Stanford, Calif.., 2002), 117–51; "Mercantile Strategies, Credit Networks, and Labor Supply in the Colonial Chesapeake in Trans-Atlantic Perspective," in David Eltis, Frank D. Lewis, and Kenneth Lee Sokoloff (eds.), *Slavery in the Development of the Americas* (Cambridge, 2004), 89–119 and *Motives of Honor, Pleasure, and Profit: Plantation Management in the Colonial Chesapeake, 1607–1763* (Chapel Hill, NC, 2010). Coombs, "Building 'The Machine,' " provides important empirical support for Walsh's argument.

13. April Lee Hatfield, *Atlantic Virginia: Intercolonial Relations in the Seventeenth Century* (Philadelphia, 2004). Barbadians also played a leading role in bringing slavery to Maryland. See Russell R. Menard, *Sweet Negotiations: Sugar, Slavery, and Plantation Agriculture in Early Barbados* (Charlottesville, Va., 2006).

14. John J. McCusker and Russell R. Menard, "The Sugar Industry in the Seventeenth Century: A New Perspective on the Barbadian 'Sugar Revolution,'" in Stuart B. Schwartz (ed.), *Tropical Babylons: Sugar and the Making of the Atlantic World, 1450–1680* (Chapel Hill, NC, 2004), 289–330.

15. Passed September 27, 1661. "Barbados: A Booke of the Acts Lawes and Statutes of the said Island ... [1649–1682]," CO 30/2, 16–26, Public Record Office/The National Archives, London. There are excerpts from this statute in Stanley L. Engerman, Seymour Drescher, and Robert L. Paquette (eds.), *Slavery* (Oxford, 2001), 105–13. For its influence, see Richard S. Dunn, *Sugar and Slaves: The Rise of the Planter Class in the English West Indies, 1624–1713* (Chapel Hill, NC, 1972), 238–42; and Kenneth J. Morgan, *Slavery and the British Empire: From Africa to America* (Oxford, 2007), 113–14. See also David Barry Gaspar, "With a Rod of Iron: Barbados Slave Laws as a Model for Jamaica, South Carolina, and Antigua, 1661–1697," in Darlene Clark Hine and Jacqueline McLeod (eds.), *Crossing Boundaries: Comparative History of Black People in Diaspora* (Bloomington, Ind., 1999), 343–366. Compare Bradley J. Nicholson, "Legal Borrowing and the Origins of Slave Law in the British Colonies," *American Journal of Legal History*, 38 (January 1994): 38–54; Gaspar, "'Rigid and Inclement': Origins of the Jamaican Slave Laws of the Seventeenth Century, in Christopher, L. Tomlins and Bruce H. Mann (eds.), *The Many Legalities of America* (Chapel Hill, NC, 2001), 78–96, esp. 79, n.2.

Hilary M. Beckles, "Social and Political Control in the Slave Society," in Franklin W. Knight (ed.), *The Slave Societies of the Caribbean*, vol. iii of P(ieter) C. Emmer et al. (eds.), *General History of the Caribbean* (London, 1997), 201, makes the point that it was the revised and "more elaborate" Barbadian "Act for the governing of Negroes" of August 8, 1688 that applied afterwards there and provided the pattern copied by others from its inception forward. For it see Richard Hall (Sr.) and Richard Hall (Jr.) (eds.), [Barbados (Colony), Laws and Statutes], *Acts, Passed in the Island of Barbados. From 1643, to 1762, Inclusive; Carefully Revised, Innumerable Errors Corrected; and the Whole Compared and Examined, with the Original Acts, In the Secretary's Office* ... (London, 1764), 112–21 (No. 82). South Carolina's first slave code (1690) was derived from the 1688 Barbadian statute. Alan Watson, *Slave Law in the Americas* (Athens, Ga., 1989), 68.

16. Evsey D. Domar, "The Causes of Slavery or Serfdom: A Hypothesis," *Journal of Economic History*, 30 (March 1970): 18–32.

17. Philip R. P. Coelho and Robert A. McGuire, "African and European Bound Labor in the British New World: The Biological Consequences of Economic Choices," *Journal of*

Economic History, 57 (March 1997): 83–115; and Kenneth F. Kiple and Kriemhild C. Ornelas, "After the Encounter: Disease and Demographics in the Lesser Antilles," in Robert L. Paquette and Stanley L. Engerman (eds.), *The Lesser Antilles in the Age of European Expansion* (Gainesville, Fla., 1996), 50–67.

18. Carville V. Earle, "A Staple Interpretation of Slavery and Free Labor," *Geographical Review*, 68 (January 1978): 51–65.

19. See the works cited above, n. 7.

20. Immanuel (M.) Wallerstein, *The Modern World* System, 3 vols. (New York, 1974–89). Our assessment of Wallerstein has been shaped by Steve J. Stern, "Feudalism, Capitalism, and the World-System in the Perspective of Latin America and the Caribbean," *American Historical Review*, 93 (October 1988): 829–72.

21. Several of Russell R. Menard's essays fall into this category. See the pieces on the transition to African slavery in the southern mainland colonies collected in Menard, *Migrants, Servants and Slaves*.

22. Gemery and Hogendorn, "The Atlantic Slave Trade: A Tentative Economic Model," *Journal of African History*, 15 (2) (1974): 223–46. For a more formal statement, see David W. Galenson and Russell R. Menard, "Approaches to the Analysis of Economic Growth in Colonial British America," *Historical Methods: A Journal of Quantitative and Interdisciplinary History*, 13 (Winter 1980): 3–18.

23. Thus Alexander Cluny argued the wisdom of befriending the Native American Indians because they could provide a source of free workers who "would take the Labour upon them, which from the Difference of Climates, we are unequal to." (Alexander Cluny), *The American Traveller: Or, Observations on the Present State, Culture and Commerce of the British Colonies in America* . . . (1st edn. London, 1769), 112. This would diminish or obviate the enslaving of Africans, he believed.

24. And, as Gemery and Hogendorn remind us (*Atlantic Slave Trade*, 229), for some countries the option of metropolitan laborers did not exist at all. "Unlike England, neither Spain nor Portugal . . . could provide workers who were prepared to emigrate at any price." Caio Prado, Jr., *The Colonial Background of Modern Brazil*, trans. Macedo, Suzette (Berkeley, 1967), 19. Compare Stanley L. Engerman and Kenneth L. Sokoloff, "Once Upon a Time in the Americas: Land and Immigration Policies in the New World," paper presented at "Understanding Long Run Economic Growth: A Conference Honoring the Contributions of Kenneth Sokoloff," Los Angeles, 7 November 2008.

25. On the New England economy, see McCusker and Menard, *Economy of British America, 1607–1789*, 91–116.

26. See Lucy (Lucile L.) Simler, "Hired Labor," in Jacob Ernest Cooke et al. (eds.), *Encyclopedia of the North American Colonies*, 3 vols. (New York, 1993), ii. 3–15. Compare Simler, "The Landless Worker: An Index of Economic and Social Change in Chester County, Pennsylvania, 1750–1820," *Pennsylvania Magazine of History and Biography*, 114 (April 1990): 163–200. See also Farley Ward Grubb, "Immigration and Servitude in the Colony and Commonwealth of Pennsylvania: A Quantitative and Economic Analysis" (Ph.D. diss., University of Chicago, 1984); and Marianne S. Wokeck, *Trade in Strangers: The Beginnings of Mass Migration to North America* (University Park, Pa., 1999).

27. Richard S. Dunn surveys the labor systems of the several colonies and provides a guide to the literature in "Servants and Slaves: The Recruitment and Employment of Labor," in Jack Greene and J(ack) R. Pole (eds.), *Colonial British America: Essays in the New History of the Early Modern Era* (Baltimore, 1984), 157–94.

28. The quotation is from the agreement between Edward Rowzie (d. *c.*1675), planter of Virginia, and Bartholomew Clarke, 6 June 1659, Order Book, 1664–73, 21, Records of (Old) Rappahannock County, Library of Virginia, Richmond, as quoted in Philip Alexander Bruce, *Economic History of Virginia in the Seventeenth Century: An Inquiry into the Material Condition of the People, Based upon Original and Contemporaneous Records*, 2 vols. (New York, 1896), ii. 2 n. The debate over the relationship between servitude and apprenticeships is summarized in David W. Galenson, *White Servitude in Colonial America: An Economic Analysis* (Cambridge, 1981), 6. Abbot Emerson Smith, *Colonists in Bondage: White Servitude and Convict Labor in America, 1607–1776* (Chapel Hill, NC, 1947) remains a useful study.

29. Galenson, *White Servitude in Colonial America*, 6–8. Ann (S.) Kussmaul, *Servants in Husbandry in Early Modern England*, Interdisciplinary Perspectives on Modern History (Cambridge, 1981) is the best analysis of this form of labor in England. See also Kussmaul, "The Ambiguous Mobility of Farm Servants," *Economic History Review*, NS 34 (May 1981): 222–35. Compare Alan Everitt, "Farm Labourers [1500–1640]," in H(erbert) P. R. Finberg et al. (eds.), *The Agrarian History of England and Wales* (Cambridge, 1967), iv. 396–465.

30. Galenson, *White Servitude in Colonial America*, 7.

31. Ibid. 7–8.

32. Excerpt from a letter from Thomas Best, an indentured servant in Virginia, to his brother and cousin in England, April 12, 1623, among "Notes Taken from Letters Which Came from Virginia in the 'Abigail,' " June 1623, Manchester Papers, PRO 30/15, nos. 338–9, Public Record Office, London, as printed in Susan Myra Kingsbury (ed.), *The Records of the Virginia Company of London*, 4 vols. (Washington, DC, 1906–35), iv. 235. Compare Edmund S. Morgan, *American Slavery, American Freedom: The Ordeal of Colonial Virginia* (New York, 1975), 128. The Manchester Papers, deposited in the PRO in 1880, are no longer part of the collections of the Public Record Office, The National Archives, London. Although there as recently as the 1960s—see *Guide to the Contents of the Public Record Office*, rev. edn., 3 vols. (London, 1963–8), ii. 249—they were withdrawn in 1970 and sold at auction. We were unable to locate where these documents can now be found, but we have established that they are not part of the Manchester Papers among the collections of the Huntingdonshire Archives, Cambridgeshire Archives and Local Studies, Huntingdon, Cambridgeshire.

33. Galenson, *White Servitude in Colonial America*, 8.

34. Although as Christine Daniels persuasively argues, indentured servants were far from powerless before the law: " 'Liberty to Complaine': Servant Petitions in Maryland, 1652–1797," in Tomlins and Mann (eds.), *Many Legalities of Early America*, 219–46.

35. Kenneth J. Morgan has recently surveyed the growing literature on indentured servitude in *Slavery and Servitude in Colonial North America: A Short History* (New York, 2001). In the United Kingdom this book was published as Morgan, *Slavery and Servitude in North America, 1607–1800*, British Association for American Studies Paperbacks (Edinburgh, 2000). It contains an impressively comprehensive bibliography. See also his more recent *Slavery and the British Empire*.

36. For which, see Smith, *Colonists in Bondage: White Servitude and Convict Labor in America*; and Galenson, *White Servitude in Colonial America*. Compare Gabriel Debien, *La Société coloniale aux XVIIe et XVIIIe siècles: Les Engagés pour Les Antilles (1634–1715)* (Paris, 1952).

37. On differences between customary and indentured servants, see Lorena S. Walsh, "Servitude and Opportunity in Charles County, Maryland, 1658–1705," in Aubrey C. Land, Lois Green Carr, and Edward C. Papenfuse (Jr.) (eds.), *Law, Society, and Politics in Early Maryland*, Studies in Maryland History and Culture (Baltimore, 1977), 111–15; and Russell R. Menard, "British Migration to the Chesapeake Colonies in the Seventeenth Century," in Lois Green Carr, Philip D. Morgan, and Jean B. Russo (eds.), *Colonial Chesapeake Society* (Chapel Hill, NC, 1988), 126–7 (quotations).

38. Studies of the redemptioner system include Grubb, "Immigration and Servitude"; and Wokeck, *Trade in Strangers*.

39. On the system of convict labor, see Wilfrid Oldham, *Britain's Convicts to the Colonies*, ed. W(ilfrid) Hugh Oldham (Sydney, 1990). On its application to the British American colonies, see A(rthur) Roger Ekirch, *Bound for America: The Transportation of British Convicts to the Colonies, 1718–1775* (Oxford, 1987).

40. For estimates of the number of servant migrants, see Nicholas P. Canny, "English Migration into and across the Atlantic during the Seventeenth and Eighteenth Centuries," in Nicholas P. Canny (ed.), *Europeans on the Move: Studies on European Migration, 1500–1800* (Oxford, 1994), 39–75; and T(homas) C. Smout, N(ed) C. Landsman, and T(homas) M. Devine, "Scottish Emigration in the Seventeenth and Eighteenth Centuries," 76–112. Compare Dunn, "Servants and Slaves." For the proportion of migrants to the Chesapeake that arrived as servants, see Menard, "British Migration to the Chesapeake Colonies," 121. See also Henry A. Gemery, "The White Population of the Colonial United States, 1607–1790," in Michael R. Haines and Richard H. Steckel (eds.), *A Population History of North America* (Cambridge, 2000), 143–90.

41. Gary B. Nash, *The Urban Crucible: Social Change, Political Consciousness, and the Origins of the American Revolution* (Cambridge, Mass., 1979), 111.

42. James (P. P.) Horn, "Servant Emigration to the Chesapeake in the Seventeenth Century," in Thad W. Tate and David L. Ammerman (eds.), *The Chesapeake in the Seventeenth Century: Essays on Anglo-American Society* (Chapel Hill, NC, 1979), 92.

43. On the conditions servants faced in Barbados, see Menard, *Sweet Negotiations*. For conditions on the mainland, see McCusker and Menard, *Economy of British America*, especially 236–57, and the literature cited there.

44. Galenson, *White Servitude in Colonial America*, 102–13.

45. For details of both these statistical tests, see Menard, "British Migration," 108, 118–19.

46. There is a growing literature on financing the growth of slavery, but the place to start is Jacob M. Price, "Credit in the Slave Trade and Plantation Economies," in Barbara L. Solow (ed.), *Slavery and the Rise of the Atlantic System* (Cambridge, 1991), 293–339.

47. For the debate over the origins of the gang system, see David Eltis, *The Rise of African Slavery in the Americas* (Cambridge, 2000), 202–3; and Menard, *Sweet Negotiations*, 91–105.

48. There is also a large literature on the concept of a slave society. A good place to start is Phillip D. Morgan, "British Encounters with Africans and Afro-Americans, circa 1600–1780," in Bernard Bailyn and Philip D. Morgan (eds.), *Strangers within the Realm: Cultural Margins of the First British Empire* (Chapel Hill, NC, 1991), 157–219.

SELECT BIBLIOGRAPHY

BERLIN, IRA. *Many Thousands Gone: The First Two Centuries of Slavery in North America.* Cambridge, Mass.: Harvard University Press, 1998.

DAVIS, DAVID BRION. *The Problem of Slavery in Western Culture.* Ithaca, NY: Cornell University Press, 1966.

ELTIS, DAVID. *The Rise of African Slavery in the Americas.* Cambridge: Cambridge University Press, 2000.

GALENSON, DAVID W. *White Servitude in Colonial America: An Economic Analysis.* Cambridge: Cambridge University Press, 1981.

JORDAN, WINTHROP D. *White over Black: American Attitudes toward the Negro, 1550–1812.* Chapel Hill, NC: Published for the Institute of Early American History and Culture at Williamsburg, Va., by the University of North Carolina Press, 1968.

McCUSKER, JOHN J., and RUSSELL R. MENARD. *The Economy of British America, 1607–1789.* 2nd edn. Chapel Hill, NC: Published for the Institute of Early American History and Culture, Williamsburg, Va., by the University of North Carolina Press, 1991.

MENARD, RUSSELL R. *Migrants, Servants and Slaves: Unfree Labor in Colonial British America.* Variorum Collected Studies Series, CS 699. Aldershot, UK: Ashgate, 2001.

MORGAN, EDMUND S. *American Slavery, American Freedom: The Ordeal of Colonial Virginia.* New York: Norton, 1975.

SCHWARTZ, STUART B., ed. *Tropical Babylons: Sugar and the Making of the Atlantic World, 1450–1680.* Chapel Hill, NC: University of North Carolina Press, 2004.

SOLOW, BARBARA L., ed. *Slavery and the Rise of the Atlantic System.* Cambridge: Cambridge University Press, 1991.

VAUGHAN, ALDEN T. *Roots of American Racism: Essays on the Colonial Experience.* Oxford: Oxford University Press, 1995.

CHAPTER 13

BIOLOGY AND AFRICAN SLAVERY

KENNETH F. KIPLE

GEOGRAPHY, SLAVERY, AND RACE

"It is evident," declared John Williamson in 1817, after spending more than a decade practicing medicine in Jamaica, "that the Negro system is materially different from ours. It could not have escaped observation how diseases differ in their respective colours of white and black."[1] More than a century later, the historian Kenneth Stampp in prefacing his *Peculiar Institution* (1956), a now classic reversal of the U. B. Phillips interpretation of slavery in the antebellum southern United States as benign, paternalistic, and unprofitable, decried the racism that informed Phillips's work. "The black man," Stampp declared, "is nothing more or less than a white man with a dark skin."[2] Even though Stampp meant well, the statement has a gratuitous ring about it, making blacks honorary biological whites and dismissing their own biological heritage—a heritage that more recent scholars, not just historians, but specialists in such emerging subfields as bioeconomics, anthropometry, and auxology, are finding vital to any holistic understanding of slavery.

This biological heritage brings scholars immediately and unavoidably to the slippery slope of "race," a slope littered with a literature, ancient and modern, that tries to account for noticeable biological differences in humankind. In plant biology race serves as a convenient term that is taken to mean a population that differs from others of the same species in the frequency of hereditary traits. New plant races are regularly born, often in greenhouses. In human terms, however, the term "race" is generally not so convenient, seldom so straightforward, and, at times, downright dangerous, especially when intended to connote an actual biological subspecies. Racialist thinking in previous generations rested on a construction of race that confused broad human groupings whose distinctiveness merely reflects different geographic origins. No races exist within the human race. Scientists make clear that at least 99.9 percent of the DNA of an individual is identical to that of any other individual regardless of "race." Moreover genetic variability proves greater within the so-called races than between them. Thus, there can be no subspecies of *Homo sapiens*.[3]

Every geographic region of the globe equips those born into it to survive their unique environmental circumstances. Sometimes scholars view this equipment as products of "adaptation," and much adapting took place long ago as local conditions such as temperature, humidity, solar ultraviolet radiation, disease environment, and food availability molded human body shape and size, skin color, hair type, and metabolic and immunologic characteristics.[4] This adaptation seems to be what a post-Second World War historian like Kenneth Stampp was trying to get at in first premising his views on race before entering into his discussion of slavery, even though he may have added to the confusion by not understanding or, perhaps better, by not making it clear that those of African ancestry have many traits—besides a dark skin—that have set them apart historically. Not surprisingly then, history (and historiography) teems with racial (and racist) concepts that have been employed to explain what at bottom are traits engendered by geographic environment.

SLAVERY AND DISEASE RESISTANCE

Immunology is one such trait, which can have striking historical consequences. More than a quarter century ago, Philip Curtin, one of the foremost historians of Africa of his generation, suggested the importance of biology and epidemiology to the history of the Atlantic world by providing data that dramatically underscored the ability of blacks (but not whites) during the era of the transatlantic slave trade to survive the tropical fevers that flourish within West Africa, one of the most hostile disease environments in the world. This data derived from the experience of the British military in nineteenth-century Sierra Leone, where white soldiers died at the incredible rate of between 500 and 800 per thousand per year. By contrast their black counterparts died at a rate of thirty per thousand per year.[5] None of this admittedly extreme example of differential mortality has a racial explanation (although black disease refractoriness has been given one). But differential mortality in a pathogenic environment like the tropics does help to explain in stark biological terms why the western Europeans who traveled to West Africa prior to the twentieth century clung to its coasts, seldom ventured inland, and did not establish colonial zones of flourishing African plantations. Rather western Europeans prudently chose to move Africa to the Americas via the Atlantic slave trade.

Phenotypical characteristics of Africans constitute another set of traits. Skin color and hair type, for example, have, as Winthrop Jordan has conspicuously argued in delving into the origins of white supremacy in the United States, helped to set Africans apart in the white mind, and this "apartness"—this "otherness"—in turn, helped to justify their enslavement.[6] Europeans could not have known then that all human beings were roughly the same color when some of them left Africa to out-compete several other Old World hominid species in their rise to the top of the food chain. Skin color changed with geographic location: The descendants of those who moved into northerly latitudes became lighter because they had no need for protection against excessive ultraviolet (UV) radiation and because a lighter skin promoted the absorption of sunlight required to trigger vitamin D production; those humans remaining in Africa became darker, as their part of the world became more tropical, whereas those in Asia retained the color of their ancestors who originally hived out of the mother continent.[7] Immunology and "otherness" together, then, go a long way toward accounting for why western Europeans nominated the African for New World slavery, although Africa's offering of an apparently endless supply of slaves cannot be discounted from a purely economic standpoint. Of the explanations of the origins of African slavery in the Americas, immunology remains the least examined despite Curtin's groundbreaking work.

William McNeill's *Plagues and Peoples* (1976), a pioneering synthesis of medical, biological, and epidemiological literature that showed the often profound influence of pathogens on human affairs, devoted several pages to the impact of "African infections" malaria and yellow fever in the New World. Africans who became slaves in the Americas were Old World people whose ancestors had experienced (and survived) those pathogens that beset other Old World peoples. That experience began long ago with humankind inventing and then settling into sedentary agriculture and animal domestication. As hunter-gatherers they had drifted about in small bands—small so that they would not exhaust the food offered by a new area too quickly. When a band became too large, some members split off to form another one, but bands probably tended to be fairly stable. Nomadic life limited the number of children because the very young proved awkward for people frequently on the move and compelled to carry everything they owned. Circumstances made them a tidy lot. They did not remain in one place long enough to foul their water supply and encourage the proliferation of waterborne pathogens, or pile up refuse to attract rodents and insect disease vectors.[8]

This pattern of behavior changed with the rigors of sedentary agriculture, when our ancestors established a permanent address and built their barnyards.

Sedentism fostered the growth and proliferation of deadly diseases. Domesticated animals not only gave their masters meat, milk, eggs, wool, and hides, but also a vast array of exotic pathogens. Disease vectors settled in with the settlers to propel these and still other pathogens from animals to masters and back to animals in those crowded dwellings that sheltered them all. Human beings and pathogens live in a constantly changing pattern of engagement that is not merely biological, but is also dramatically affected by the specifics of social and cultural formations. Human illnesses took early forms that researchers will probably never fully understand. Eventually, however, these illnesses evolved into such modern, familiar, and contagious diseases as smallpox, measles, diphtheria, whooping cough, which have also frequently yielded epidemic plagues.[9]

These phenomena of ricocheting pathogens crossing the species barrier in the Old World probably first occurred in the earliest centers of agriculture: Mesopotamia, Egypt, the Indus Valley, and China. But when Africans south of the Sahara left hunting and gathering for sedentary agriculture, they, too, became a part of this fearsome and monumental transformation. Traffic across the desert linked them to the growing pool of Old World diseases. But Africans had a couple of illnesses of their own with which to deal: the great tropical killers, yellow fever and falciparum malaria.[10] In the case of the latter (the deadliest of the malarial types), biology tempered the worst of its ravages by bestowing genetic mechanisms on those living in endemic areas that limit the number of those blood cells that permit the protozoan parasite *Plasmodium falciparum* to prosper. The most potent defense against yellow fever is simply to host the virus at a young age (when it is least devastating) and gain a lifetime immunity from any further assaults of the pathogen. In addition to this acquired immunity, however, persons of West African descent appear to possess some, as yet unidentified, yellow fever protection, which is evident in their New World experience with the disease. Black people long removed from Africa fared much better with the disease than did whites or Indians.[11]

Skeletal remains promise a mother lode of information about human health over the ages. Scientists continue to surmount the challenges posed by extracting DNA from bones long dead and buried, and as a result, much new information will be coming to the fore on how Africans and other human groups evolved historically and prehistorically with pathogens. Before Columbus, Indians faced no such life-threatening diseases that would have permitted the development of immunity at an early age, let alone encouraged the development of mechanisms to survive them. They had reached the New World via the Bering Straits and by Polynesian canoes prior to the Old World's invention of agriculture, thus eluding the pathogenic forge that became part of that invention because, save for the dog which had been a part of the last waves of Asian pioneers, they had no domesticated animals with which to share diseases. Moreover, when the original Americans brought off their own Neolithic revolution later on, they added only a few animals to their barnyards and, consequently, managed to continue to elude the kind of epidemiological tempering that had taken place in the Old World. It was not that the Americas existed disease free, but pre-Columbian illnesses seem to have been mostly of a gastrointestinal nature.[12] The Americas harbored none of the contagious diseases that brought an epidemiological reckoning to the Americans when the Europeans and Africans arrived. A vast literature exists on the demographic meltdown of the New World's native populations; Alfred W. Crosby's *Columbian Exchange* (1972) and Noble David Cook's *Born to Die* (1998) remain good places to start.[13]

This reckoning—the price of long isolation from Old World plagues—involved after 1492 a massive die-off of millions that some scholars have estimated eventually reduced the Indian population by 90 percent. Such a holocaust seems almost unimaginable and, at the same time, leaves little sympathy for the Iberian settlers who had been counting on those natives to do the hard work of colonizing the Americas. Equally cataclysmic, however, was the Iberian resolution of their dilemma. Contemporaries noticed that those blacks born in Spain (*ladinos*) who had served side by side with the Spaniards in exploration and conquest fared no worse than their masters from the epidemic illnesses that were mowing down the natives. There is no mystery here. The same epidemiological agents in the Old World had buffeted *ladinos* along with everyone else. But an understanding of immunology lay centuries in the future, and the conclusion reached then—that black people were "racially" much sturdier than Indians—coupled with a desperate need for labor led directly to Spain's beginning of the transatlantic slave trade to the Americas in 1518.[14]

Thus, one holocaust—the American die-off—led inexorably to another, the transatlantic slave trade and African slavery in the Americas. The link might not have been so inexorable had the importation of slaves directly from Africa done some damage to the European's conviction of black sturdiness. But it did not. As products of an Old World disease environment Africans proved about as immunologically tough as their *ladino* predecessors against Old World pathogens in the New World. And what also became apparent was the Africans' incredible ability to ward off the tropical fevers that had begun to smolder in the West Indies soon after the Atlantic slave trade had gotten under way.

Both the pathogens and the (mosquito) vectors of falciparum malaria and yellow fever had accompanied the Africans on the Middle Passage, and these two tropical killers would spectacularly change the course of New World history. Neither red nor white people had ever suffered these plagues, and as a consequence, both populations stood immunologically helpless against them. Both diseases joined in the pathogenic assault that engulfed Indians, inflicting at the same time such morbidity and mortality on the Europeans—and particularly on their white indentured servants—as to ratchet up the belief in black sturdiness to the conviction that only black people could survive hard work in hot places. Peter Wood stands out as one of the first historians in the United States to incorporate biological scholarship in understanding the origin of racial slavery in the United States. In his 1974 study of slavery in colonial South Carolina, he investigated how the resistance of Africans to swampland fevers fueled the justification for black enslavement and perhaps contributed as well to the development of the task system of labor on the plantations of the disease-ridden South Carolina lowcountry.[15]

To be sure, whites had experienced the chills and fevers of malaria. But vivax malaria, a generally (but not always) benign illness caused by *Plasmodium vivax*, had produced the kind of "ague" suffered by whites in Europe.[16] As a rule, vivax malaria is a self-limiting disease because the plasmodium injected into the human body by a mosquito enters only young erythrocytes (red blood cells). *Plasmodium malariae*, another malarial type resident in Africa, enters only mature erythrocytes. But *Plasmodium falciparum* is not so finicky, invading both young and mature blood cells indiscriminately, and the much higher parasite count it achieves makes it extremely dangerous. Moreover, the blood cells parasitized by *Plasmodium falciparum* tend to adhere to one another, forming clumps that block blood vessels that lead to internal organs. These clumps, in turn, bring about internal hemorrhaging, including that of the brain.[17]

Such frequently occurring lethal complications in Africa had led millennia ago to the selection of innate protective traits for those living in close proximity to the disease. Only recently have medical researchers begun to understand them. The long mysterious sickle trait, for example, became less mysterious when its carriers were associated geographically with areas where falciparum malaria is or has been endemic. If both parents possessed the trait then a quarter of their offspring were cursed with deadly sickle cell anemia. As a rule, natural selection should have eliminated such an apparent genetic flaw, but it persisted because the trait saved substantially more lives than it claimed. Researchers discovered that sickle-shaped blood cells are resistant to the invasion of *Plasmodium falciparum*, making the sickle trait what geneticists call a balanced polymorphism, that is, a situation in which selective factors create a balance in a population of different alleles.

In addition to the sickle trait, which protected only a minority of a population (less than 25 percent) from the disease, scientists have also turned up other genetic mechanisms of malarial protection. Foremost among these is the inherited condition glucose-6–phosphate-dehydrogenase deficiency (G6PD deficiency), caused by the lack of an enzyme crucial to red blood cell metabolism. This deficiency—another balanced polymorphism—creates a condition that, like sickle trait, discourages parasite proliferation. Researchers have also linked other genetic conditions, such as hemoglobin C disease and thalassemia traits, to malarial protection. At the risk of belaboring the point, then, natural selection seems to have relatively well outfitted those born into areas of endemic falciparum malaria to survive the disease.

One says "relatively" because malaria, especially falciparum malaria, remains a major killer in Africa particularly among the young. Malarial deaths in Africa fall off dramatically, however, after age 5 as youngsters develop some tolerance for malaria parasites. This highlights the importance of still another form of resistance—acquired immunity—which would have also protected slaves in the

Americas.[18] West Africans also apparently acquired the equipment to survive vivax malaria, the most common form of malaria and probably the oldest. Today the disease is not the sort of killer able to call up genetic immunologic mechanisms and is not even much of a problem in Africa, although it undoubtedly ravaged African populations in the distant past. Today most African-Americans, as well as most Africans, possess red blood cells without the Duffy group antigenic determinates Fy^a and Fy^b, which act as erythrocyte receptors for *Plasmodium vivax*. Researchers suspect that African erythrocytes may also be refractory to falciparum malaria.[19]

While plenty of genetic evidence exists to help us understand why Africans in the New World could weather malarial assaults that devastated whites and Indians, immunological questions continue to surround yellow fever. The disease derives from a virus that principally infects monkeys but can be transmitted to humans (making it a zoonosis) when carried by the female *Aedes aegypti* mosquito. Both the virus and the mosquito appear to be immigrants to the Americas, although specialists cannot say precisely when yellow fever arrived because many of its symptoms (like hemorrhaging) resemble those produced by *Plasmodium falciparum*. Recent phylogenetic analysis of yellow fever virus isolates from diverse geographic regions argues, however, for the likely African origin via the Atlantic slave trade of yellow fever in the Americas.[20] Although much work remains to be done on the biological history of slaves on discrete Caribbean islands, Jerome Handler, an anthropologist, has investigated the origin of yellow fever and the medical history of slaves in the English colony of Barbados. The first recognizable yellow fever epidemic in the Americas took place on the island in 1647 during the onset of the island's sugar boom with its attendant importation of thousands of African slaves. The epidemic killed thousands of whites but apparently no blacks.[21] The following year the virus showed a similar preference for whites as it invaded nearby Guadeloupe and St Kitts, and then moved on to Cuba and the Yucatan Peninsula. In the latter location it also sought out Indians but invariably spared blacks.[22]

Kenneth Kiple and Sheldon Watts have recently debated the origin of yellow fever and the nature of the immunity possessed by Africans who survived the Middle Passage. Most of this apparently uncanny exemption from fatality is explained easily enough by immunity acquired by those blacks born in Africa (as were almost all of those imported to Barbados during much of the seventeenth century) who had experienced yellow fever when very young. Since the disease treats the young much more gently than adults, it, like other viral illnesses, immunizes survivors against future attacks. But acquired immunity cannot account for the relative absence of black yellow fever mortality in Cuba when the disease reigned during the months of August and September of 1649. Cuba at this time was a Caribbean backwater. It had never before experienced a yellow fever epidemic; it had no slave trade worthy of the name; and most, if not all, of the slaves on the island would have been creoles (American born). Thus circumstances afforded neither blacks nor whites the opportunity to acquire immunity. Yet the disease killed close to 500 whites but only twelve blacks.[23]

From the beginning of yellow fever's documented Caribbean career to its end more than two centuries later, both blacks and whites had experienced the same opportunity to acquire yellow fever immunity. But in Antigua between 1857 and 1895, whites accounted for an astounding 84 percent of its yellow fever deaths even though blacks comprised 96 percent of the island's population.[24] Interestingly enough, the same sort of protection was afforded black people outside of the Caribbean. In one example from the Cape Verde Islands, yellow fever had apparently not reached out to Boa Vista, the easternmost island in the archipelago, prior to 1845. Consequently, save for a few individuals who may have visited the African coast or the West Indies, the population was "immunologically naïve." Nonetheless, when the disease did strike in the epidemic of 1845–6 it inflicted a death rate of 46.4 percent on the Europeans, but killed only 6.5 percent of the Cape Verdeans.[25] It seems clear enough then, that something besides acquired immunity was at work in protecting Africans from an African disease not just in Africa, but in the West Indies and off the coast of West Africa. Researchers on the human genome may be on the verge of shedding light on resistance to yellow fever. At Yale University, for example, scientists have recently identified a number of genes that inhibit infections by the West Nile Virus, a cousin to the flavivirus that causes yellow fever.

Although identifying the protector remains elusive, it is certainly not "racial." Africans with long residence outside of yellow fever's normal range have proven highly susceptible to yellow fever when that range momentarily expanded. Thousands of Ethiopians, for example, died during an epidemic in 1961, and northwestern Nigerians have had continual brushes with the disease, most notably in 1986. By contrast, whites born in the New World in places infested by yellow fever have revealed steadfast resistance because they had hosted the virus and survived it—most likely as children. In New Orleans, Havana, Rio de Janeiro, and Kingston they called yellow fever "Strangers Fever" because it unerringly claimed the lives of itinerant businessmen, sailors, soldiers, and newly arrived citizens. In the Spanish colonial port city of Cartagena, where during the War of Jenkins's Ear (1739–42) yellow fever shattered British Vice-Admiral Edward Vernon's attacking forces, the disease became known as "Patriotic Fever."[26]

If African fevers were an important reason for the continuing enslavement of Africans, they also promoted employment of malaria-resistant Caribbean blacks after slavery. Conversely, the plague of African fevers in certain tropical areas discouraged white employment. Certainly such was the case during the construction of the Panama Canal in the twentieth century, and centuries before, yellow fever had chased away white indentured servants from Barbados. Yellow fever not only helped to terminate the indenture system, but discouraged whites from settling anywhere close to African fevers. Barbados, as a case in point, counted 37,000 whites in 1643 before its first yellow fever epidemic, but only 12,500 in 1712, a decline of 66 percent.[27]

The same demographic pattern recurred throughout the Caribbean as noted by the eighteenth-century French *philosophe* Abbé Raynal who wrote that "of ten men that go into the Islands, four English die, three French, three Dutch, three Danes, and one Spaniard."[28] Popular wisdom, which held that 30 to 40 percent of the northern Europeans who ventured into the West Indies could write themselves off as mortality statistics, had to be a bit daunting. Yet, one cannot but wonder why Spaniards were reputed to have fared substantially better than the other Europeans and if their tendency to interbreed with Africans had anything to do with their apparent resilience.

Resistance to hookworm disease also ranks as another important, if generally overlooked, relative immunity of blacks in the Americas, and scientific research continues on precisely how hookworms interact with the immune system. During the early twentieth century, organizations funded by John D. Rockefeller launched campaigns for hookworm eradication in the southern United States, the Caribbean, and Brazil. Indeed, future researchers might well begin with the Rockefeller Archive Center in Sleepy Hollow, New York, which houses a wealth of information on the subject gathered during these ultimately unsuccessful but expansive efforts. The culprit *Necator americanus* responsible for the disease should more properly have been dubbed *Necator africanus*, since this hookworm turned out to be one more African pathogen that had survived the Middle Passage in the bodies of people who had a millennia-long history of experience with it. That experience did not prevent invasion by the pathogen. But as a rule, Africans tolerated infection so well that they did not develop the anemia symptomatic of the illness.[29] This fact came to light during the Rockefeller campaigns, when it was shown that blacks in the Caribbean and Brazil had lighter hookworm loads than both their white and East Indian neighbors.[30] The same held true in the southern United States where the stereotypical image of a lazy, hookworm-infested individual centered on, despite a raging racism, a poor white man rather than a poor black man. But, again, the resistance was not racial. Rather, it attests, as in the case of yellow fever and malaria, to eons of coexistence with the pathogens—a history denied to the more susceptible Caribbean whites and East Indians.[31]

NUTRITION, DISEASE SUSCEPTIBILITIES, AND SLAVE DEMOGRAPHY

What about a reverse situation in which whites, not blacks, were veterans of a long-term acquaintanceship with an illness? As already pointed out, Old World Africans shared many disease immunities with Old World whites—immunities that stood out while Indians were dying out. But Africans suffered from a few ailments—

tuberculosis and bacillary pneumonia foremost among them—with which they had little experience in their homelands. These diseases set upon blacks only after they had reached the Americas and thus before they had time to build resistance. Because of urbanization, Europeans had become painfully familiar with both tuberculosis and bacillary pneumonia and could generally weather them. Yet, as New World morbidity and mortality data indicate, these two diseases subjected Africans (and Indians) to a brutal initiation. During slavery their susceptibility to pulmonary illnesses was credited to "weak lungs," and sometimes diagnosed as "scrofula." But as statistics and diagnoses improved, "weak lungs" became mostly tuberculosis (consumption), which emerged as a major killer of blacks. It is a difficult disease to identify on the plantations but easy enough as blacks headed for the cities after slavery. In Havana during the years 1872 to 1890, blacks died at the astronomical annual rate of 800 per 100,000 population.[32] In Savanna, Charleston, and New Orleans, during the same rough time frame, the rate reached a still incredible 300 to 500 per 100,000, although at about the same time Indians in Alberta and Saskatchewan, Canada, were tragically demonstrating an almost total susceptibility to tuberculosis by dying from it at a rate of close to 9,000 per 100,000.[33]

A lack of experience with tuberculosis governs susceptibility to the illness. But it is also a function of poor nutrition. Scholarship on the nutritional history of slaves in the Americas has taken a giant step since the publication of Robert Fogel and Stanley Engerman's *Time on the Cross* (1974). This challenging econometric study contained a wealth of statistical data that portrayed slaves in the antebellum southern United States as generally well treated in a material sense by the standards of the time.[34] Since human growth registers nutritional input, researchers have dug into archives on both sides of the Atlantic to find data on height so as to measure the net nutrition of select populations. Richard Steckel, the leading figure in this field, has underscored the importance of assessing height data for slaves in the context of diet, work regimen, and exposure to disease. For slaves in the antebellum United States, he detailed a more complex picture of the slave's relative well-being that depended to a great degree on stage in the life cycle. Malnourishment characterized the lives of slave children; slave teenagers, with more protein in their diet, experienced a period of rapid, indeed "phenomenal," catch-up growth, largely as a result of an improving diet supervised by masters.[35] Recent scholarship has reconstructed diets for various slave populations in the Americas, but more work is needed on what West African peoples during the era of the slave trade did and did not consume. In an age when little was known about nutrition, people viewed food as fuel, and planters who supplemented the foods that slaves grew for themselves on the peculium—a provision ground or garden plot permitted by the master—provided the cheapest fuel possible. As a rule, in the United States South the master's supplements consisted of salt pork and cornmeal; in Brazil masters dispensed manioc and dried beef; and in the British West Indies masters or their surrogates frequently issued salt fish and rice, although in Cuba dried beef (*tasajo*) from Argentina and cornmeal were often dietary staples.[36]

In Brazil and the Caribbean slaves would probably have suffered mass starvation without their provision grounds where they grew most of their own food. Because such plots were often located at some distance from the plantation, on soil that could be spared from sugar cultivation, slaves expended precious calories in walking to and from these plots, let alone in tending them. In the islands, planters much preferred slaves to plant below-ground crops such as cassava and yams (*malanga*, *yautia*, and coco) because of the risk of hurricane damage. But the slaves, "perversely" according to some planters, preferred foods that grew above ground, such as bananas, plantains (*plátanos*), beans (kidney, pigeon peas, black beans), and sorghum (guinea corn), as well as chilli peppers, okra, onions, papayas, avocados, guavas, pineapples, and, after their late eighteenth-century arrival, mangoes. Slaves entered markets and exchanged at least some of this produce for other foodstuffs and non-food items. Still, as the historian Barry Higman has pointed out in assessing the dietary adequacy for slaves in the British Caribbean, "the basic slave diet was monotonous even when it was substantial in terms of quantity."[37] Slaves in the southern United States depended less on their own gardening efforts in part because their masters, who were blessed with more land than was available in the islands or coastal Brazil, proved more inclined to furnish dietary staples. In addition to pork and cornmeal, they included foremost sweet potatoes and cowpeas (field peas, black-eyed peas, Crowder peas) and molasses.[38]

Slave codes throughout the hemisphere prescribed a core diet for slaves, and, indeed, slave owners claimed to uphold legal standards by giving their workers weekly allotments of three pounds of meat or fish and six or seven pints of rice, corn meal, or manioc flour to make up their core diet. These rations, plus adequate supplementation, would have constituted a kind of ideal diet, which, in truth, slaves seldom received.[39] Slaves throughout the Americas grumbled regularly about inadequate rations, and provision crises sparked occasional slave rebellions. Malnourishment goes a long way in explaining the disproportionate deadliness of cholera to slaves. The bacterium *Vibrio cholerae*, encouraged by poverty and spread by sewage, causes severe diarrhea and dehydration. One of the deadliest epidemics struck Cuba in 1833, when slaves numbered perhaps 40 percent of the population. Of the diseases 23,000 victims in and around Havana, more than 80 percent (19,000) were black. About 8 percent of the island's entire slave population died during the epidemic. A person's normal stomach acidity serves as a main line of defense against the disease. Yet malnutrition produced slaves with low gastric acid, thereby making them especially susceptible to both contracting the disease and dying from it.[40]

More vivid proof of the problem of slave malnourishment lies in the widespread diseases of nutritional origin that reigned in slave quarters from northeastern Brazil to North Carolina. In Brazil the major deficiency disease was beriberi (a deficiency of thiamine); in the southern United States, it was pellagra (a deficiency of niacin); and in the Caribbean both were prevalent.[41] Diets deficient in these B-complex vitamins by focusing too closely on rice and dried beef or fat pork and cornmeal brought on the proximate causes of beriberi and pellagra. Pellagra has tended to hound peoples whose diet has a substantial maize component, for the niacin in the food comes chemically bound and must be treated in certain ways to be released to benefit consumers. In the United States northerners looked at pellagra as a southern disease, and, indeed, it took a heavy toll, particularly during the winter or spring months, on antebellum slaves, who in lean times supped monotonously on the three Ms, meat, (corn)meal, and molasses. In recognition of one of the more obvious symptoms, white physicians labeled the disease "black tongue." Needless to say, differential susceptibilities and mortality fed racial thinking. The swellings, sicknesses, odd behavior, and much infant and child mortality that such deficiencies as beriberi and pellagra occasioned suggested to the white community that their black counterparts were indeed something else—in many cases, something loathsome.

Dirt-eating or pica, one such repellent illness, unsettled masters to the point that they cautioned one another that this mania for consuming earth could erupt into fatality, killing gangs of slaves on a plantation practically overnight. But, interestingly enough, dirt-eating was a secret mania. Few masters had ever witnessed this "horribly disgusting" practice, first mentioned by Caribbean slave owners, because it was done "secretly and clandestinely," and the slaves would "never acknowledge it."[42] Yet, despite (or maybe because of) the secrecy shrouding pica, planters and physicians had plenty of names for the affliction: *struma Africana, mal d'estomach* (common in the Caribbean), *hatiweri*, and *cachexia Africana* (probably the most common in the United States). This rather extensive list seems (suspiciously) to have been an effort to make the disease real by giving it a name.[43] Nineteenth-century medical literature abounds on the subject. Some West Indian doctors thought that African slaves, in despair from the loss of their homeland, suffered in greater proportions from the disease than did creole slaves. Slaves on sugar estates supposedly showed greater susceptibility to dirt-eating than did their fellow fieldhands on other estates. Large numbers of slave women and slave children allegedly engaged in the practice. But was the disease real? Today researchers know that dirt-eating seldom kills anyone and, in fact, can go far toward supplying minerals lacking in a given diet, making the practice especially important for pregnant and lactating women.[44] Far from being a disease, dirt-eating could serve as its remedy. The question follows, however, as to what precisely was the affliction of slaves that not only prompted masters of some plantations to outfit suspected dirt eaters with iron masks, but to move a frustrated physician in Jamaica to proclaim that whoever discovered its cause "would deserve a statue"?[45]

Symptoms began with "a great deal of torpor," a tiredness and inability to work accompanied by a "loss of appetite." Next came "breathlessness on the least motion, attended with visible pulsations of the carotids or arteries of the neck," and the victim became "bloated." Or alternatively, he likely developed a kind of "giddiness" or "vertigo," along with a "peculiar gait," and an "inability to go uphill."[46] But these very distinctive symptoms, accusatory of pica by nineteenth-century slaveholders, would have alerted tropical physicians in the next century to the presence of beriberi instead. Victims that became bloated were suffering its "wet" or cardiac variety; whereas those with walking difficulties were experiencing its "dry" or paralytic form.[47]

A deficiency of thiamine that provokes both sets of symptoms proved wide-spread in both the Caribbean and Brazil in the eighteenth and nineteenth centuries, yet was much less of a problem in the antebellum southern United States where the slave diet contained more good-quality protein. This single factor may have played a significant role in the relative inability of tropical slave populations to grow demographically.[48] For in addition to the "wet" and "dry" kinds of beriberi a third type—infantile beriberi—exists, and it develops when a thiamine-deficient mother passes along that deficiency through her milk to a nursing child. Since infantile beriberi is almost always fatal for youngsters who generally have no other source of thiamine, and since slave populations do not appear to have reproduced their numbers wherever dietary and epidemiological circumstances indicate that beri-beri prevailed, one might reasonably assume that thiamine deficiency was a part of the adverse demographic equation in the slave societies of the Caribbean and Brazil.[49] Most of these deaths would have fallen under the rubric of child mortality, as opposed to infant mortality, causing the cohort of slaves 1 to 4 years of age to bulk abnormally large in mortality data. Yet, "abnormal" is relative. As Sir Stanley Davidson, a distinguished British physician, pointed out in his pioneering *Human Nutrition and Dietetics* (1961), "while the infant mortality in a poor community may be 10 times higher than in a prosperous one, the mortality in the 1 to 4 years of age group may be 50 times higher."[50]

Historians now know that slaves' lactation practices varied between the United States (where about one year was the normal nursing period) and West Africa and the Caribbean (where two or more years on the breast was not uncommon). Prolonged breastfeeding, as West Indian masters correctly surmised, reduces fertili-ty. For the Nobel laureate Robert Fogel, narrowness of the birth interval along with length of childbearing span explains the relatively high rate of natural reproduction of the slave population in the antebellum United States.[51] Resolving grim questions of slave childhood mortality will require, however, further research on the discrete nutritional history of slave mothers in various slaveholding regions in the Americas.

Numerous diseases contributed to the unhealthiness of slave children. Questions of childhood mortality invariably led to questions about infant mortality, that other major component of the adverse demographic equation in the slave societies not only of the Caribbean and Brazil but in the United States as well. Steckel has shown that those readers of Fogel and Engerman's *Time on the Cross* who had jumped to the conclusion that in matters of health and diet slave children and slave adults in the antebellum South fared similarly had erred. Slave infant mortality rates of 350 per thousand or higher appear to have been widespread throughout the Americas. Scholars of different stripes have focused on low birth weight as a culprit and on the demands masters placed on pregnant slaves. Physical anthropologists and other scientists are even exploring the possibility that the rigors of bondage may have resulted in a kind of "fetal programming" that would have passed through the mother as a kind of "epigenetic" inheritance to maintain relatively high infant mortality rates in African-American populations from one generation to another.[52]

Infantile tetanus appears to have been one of the most prevalent killer of slave infants. By the 1840s, it had caught the attention of physicians throughout the southern United States who called it "no uncommon disease" and one of the most serious obstacles to the survival of slave infants. Those Africans who in their West African homeland became slaves were largely unfamiliar with tetanus thanks to the tsetse fly (genus *Glossina*), the bug that transmits trypanosomes (which causes sleeping sickness) to humans and especially to livestock. In fact, its partiality for large domesticated animals had historically ensured that there were few horses and oxen in Africa south of the Sahara to scatter tetanus spores about in their manure.[53] As a consequence, tetanus, including neonatal tetanus, was rare or non-existent in that part of the world and, therefore, could not discourage the practice among midwives of cutting the umbilical cord of a newborn with a rusty tool or anything else handy, then applying a mixture of charcoal and dirt to the stump and binding the wound with leaves or an old piece of cloth.[54]

On New World plantations where oxen and horses ranged ubiquitously, such a procedure would almost certainly lead to disaster, which regularly appeared in infants within ten days after birth as the "jawfall," the "nine-day-fits," trismus, and "locked jaw" in the British Islands, *mal à mâchoir* in the French Caribbean, *mocezuelo* in Puerto Rico, and *tetanos neonatorum* in Cuba.[55] In fact, the words of a Jamaican midwife, "till nine days over, we *no hope* of them" (the slave infants), suggests the ubiquitousness of the malady, and many observers credited it alone with extinguishing hope for around 25 percent of the newborn.[56] The problem with this number is that until infants had weathered their first ten days or so of life they were not regarded as "fully part of the terrestrial world."[57] So witnesses to this staggering post-partum mortality would also have probably lumped infanticide, neonatal tetany, and a host of other causes of death under the "locked jaw" rubric, and thus no one can never know with any certainty the toll that neonatal tetanus exacted. But the real point here is the explanation for slave populations in the Caribbean and Brazil not reproducing themselves naturally: Their numbers reflected not so much low fertility (which is often blamed for the problem) as an extraordinarily high infant and child mortality. As the English novelist Matthew Gregory (Monk) Lewis, who also doubled as a Jamaican planter, lamented in 1816, "the instances of those [slave mothers] who have had four, five, six children, without succeeding in bringing up one, in spite of the utmost attention and indulgence, are very numerous."[58]

Summary and Conclusions

Mother Africa ensured that her sons and daughters could tolerate a disease environment sufficiently harsh that it served as a barrier to European outsiders for many centuries, keeping them confined to the coast and, save for some notable exceptions, away from the interior. Falciparum malaria and yellow fever, however, the chief ramparts in this barrier, did not remain confined to Africa. Rather, they reached the Americas with the Atlantic slave trade to rage among non-immune white and red people alike. But they largely spared blacks who were relatively resistant to these African illnesses, as well as to the bulk of those Eurasian diseases whose ravages were mostly directed at indigenous peoples. The sum of these pathogenic susceptibilities and immunities added up to the elimination of the latter (and white indentured servants) as contenders for tropical plantation laborers, and placed that onus squarely on the shoulders of the Africans.

Yet, such a nomination in an age of rationalism bore with it the notion that black people, because of their ability to resist fevers, were sufficiently different biologically from Europeans as to constitute a separate branch of humankind and a lower one at that—after all, dogs, horses, and other domestic animals also did not get yellow fever.[59] Moreover the symptoms of black disease difficulties also counted against them: Dirt-eating, weak lungs, and a holocaust of infant and child mortality all buttressed the conviction that blacks constituted a decidedly different species. From a demographic standpoint the nutritional and disease factors that caused infantile beriberi, neonatal tetanus, and a host of other diseases brought about such excessive infant mortality that slaves were prevented from reproducing their numbers. This grim experience, in turn, ensured the perpetuation of the Atlantic slave trade and, most likely, its corollary—planter carelessness with slave lives.[60]

Notes

1. John Williamson, *Medical and Miscellaneous Observations Relative to the West India Islands*, 2 vols. (Edinburgh, 1817), i. 248.
2. Kenneth M. Stampp, *The Peculiar Institution: Slavery in the Ante-Bellum South* (New York, 1956).

3. D. J. Witherspoon et al., "Genetic Similarities within and between Human Populations," *Genetics*, 176 (2007): 351–9.

4. Tony McMichael, *Human Frontiers, Environments, and Disease* (Cambridge, 2001), 61.

5. Philip D. Curtin, "Epidemiology and the Slave Trade," *Political Science Quarterly*, 83 (June 1968): 190–216.

6. See Winthrop D. Jordan, *White over Black: American Attitudes toward the Negro, 1550– 1812* (Chapel Hill, NC, 1968).

7. G. Chaplin, "Geographic Distribution of Environmental Factors Influencing Human Skin Coloration," *American Journal of Physical Anthropology*, 125 (November 2004): 292–302.

8. This discussion is based on Kenneth F. Kiple, "The History of Disease," in Roy Porter (ed.), *The Cambridge Illustrated History of Medicine* (Cambridge, 1996), 16–51, and William H. McNeill, *Plagues and Peoples* (Garden City, NY, 1976), 51.

9. McNeill, *Plagues and Peoples*, 51–3 and *passim*.

10. Alfred W. Crosby, *Ecological Imperialism: The Biological Expansion of Europe, 900–1900* (Cambridge, 1986), 137–9.

11. Kenneth F. Kiple, *The Caribbean Slave: A Biological History* (Cambridge, 1984), 20.

12. For Indian health, before and after Columbus see Richard H. Steckel and Jerome Rose (eds.), *The Backbone of History: Health and Nutrition in the Western Hemisphere* (Cambridge, 2002).

13. Alfred W. Crosby, *The Columbian Exchange: Biological and Cultural Consequences of 1492* (Westport, Conn., 1972); Noble David Cook, *Born to Die: Disease and New World Conquest, 1492–1650* (Cambridge, 1998).

14. Kiple, *Caribbean Slave*, 12–13.

15. Ibid. 20; Peter H. Wood, *Black Majority: Negroes in Colonial South Carolina, from 1670 through the Stono Rebellion* (New York, 1974), 63–91.

16. Unless otherwise indicated the following discussion of malaria is based on Kiple, *Caribbean Slave*, 14–17.

17. Kenneth F. Kiple and Virginia H. King, *Another Dimension to the Black Diaspora: Diet, Disease, and Racism* (Cambridge, 1981), 15–16.

18. Kiple, *Caribbean Slave*, 32.

19. Kiple and King, *Another Dimension*, 21–2.

20. Juliet E. Bryan et al., "Out of Africa: A Perspective on Yellow Fever Virus," *PloS Pathogens*, 3 (May 2007): 668–73.

21. Jerome S. Handler, "Disease and Medical Disabilities of Enslaved Barbadians, from the Seventeenth Century to around 1838, Part 1," *Journal of Caribbean History*, 40 (2006): 18–19.

22. Kiple, *Caribbean Slave*, 20.

23. Sheldon Watts, "Yellow Fever Immunities In West Africa and the Americas in the Age of Slavery and Beyond: A Reappraisal," *Journal of Social History*, 34 (Summer 2001): 955– 67; Kenneth F. Kiple, "Response to Sheldon Watts," *Journal of Social History*, 34 (Summer 2001): 969–74. Kiple, *Caribbean Slave*, 161–3.

24. H. K. Uttley, "The Mortality of Yellow Fever in Antigua, West Indies, since 1857," *West Indian Medical Journal*, 9 (1960): 185–8.

25. K. David Patterson, "Epidemiology in the Mid-Nineteenth Century: The Case of the 1845–1846 Yellow Fever Epidemic," in Yosio Kawakita et al. (eds.), *History of Epidemiology* (Tokyo, 1993), 63–4, 72.

26. Kiple, *Caribbean Slave*, 166.

27. Leslie B. Rout, Jr., *The African Experience in Spanish America, 1502 to the Present Day* (New York, 1976), 274–5; Gordon Harrison, *Mosquitoes, Malaria, and Man* (New York, 1978), 4; Kiple, *Caribbean Slave*, 179.

28. Abbé Guillaume Raynal, *A Philosophical and Political History of the Settlements and Trade of the Europeans in the East and West Indies*, 8 vols., trans. J. O. Justamond (London, 1788), v. 502.

29. Reinhard Hoeppli, *Parasitic Diseases in Africa and the Western Hemisphere: Early Documentation and Transmission by the Slave Trade* (Basel, 1968).

30. For an overview, see W. P. Jacobs, "Hookworm Surveys and Resurveys, 1910–1915, 1920–1923," in, Rockefeller Archive Center, Sleepy Hollow, New York, Sanitary Commission, Series 200, box 3, folder 21; See also John Ettling, *The Germ of Laziness: Rockefeller Philanthropy and Public Health in the New South* (Cambridge, Mass., 1981).

31. For blacks and hookworm, see Hoeppli, *Parasitic Diseases, passim*.

32. "Dr. Frederick L. Hoffman's Collection of Statistics, Havana Cuba," Rockefeller Archive Center, Sleepy Hellow, New York, International Health Board, Series 2, 315, Cuba, box 30, folder 178.

33. Data for tuberculosis among blacks in the United States has been drawn from Kiple and King, *Another Dimension*, 139–46; and René Dubos, *Man Adapting* (New Haven, 1965), 165–6, 170.

34. Robert William Fogel and Stanley L. Engerman, *Time on the Cross: The Economics of American Negro Slavery* (Boston, 1974).

35. Richard H. Steckel, "Slave Height Profiles from Coastwise Manifests," *Explorations in Economic History*, 16 (1979b): 363–80; Richard H. Steckel, "A Peculiar Population: The Nutrition, Health, and Mortality of American Slaves from Childhood to Maturity," *Journal of Economic History*, 46 (September 1986): 421–41.

36. For Caribbean slave diets, see Kiple, *Caribbean Slave*, 76–9. See also Robert William Fogel, *Without Consent or Contract: The Rise and Fall of American Slavery* (New York, 1989), 132–47.

37. Fogel, *Without Consent or Contract*, 86–8; B. W. Higman, *Slave Populations of the British Caribbean, 1807–1834* (Baltimore, 1984), 217.

38. For the slave diet in the American South, see Kiple and King, *Another Dimension*, 79–95 and Fogel, *Without Consent or Contract*, 132–47.

39. Kiple, *Caribbean Slave, passim*.

40. Ibid. 146; "Cholera in Cuba," *Medical Magazine*, 1 (1833): 668–74.

41. Kenneth F. Kiple, "The Nutritional Link with Slave Infant and Child Mortality in Brazil," *Hispanic American Historical Review*, 69 (4) (November 1989): 677–90; Kenneth F. Kiple and Virginia H. Kiple, "Black Tongue and Black Men: Pellagra in the Antebellum South," *Journal of Southern History*, 43 (August 1977): 211–28; Kiple, *Caribbean Slave*, 93–103.

42. P. Dons, "Recherches sur la cachexi africaine," *Gazeta medicale de Paris*, 6 (1838): 289–95; Thomas Dancer, *The Medical Assistant or Jamaica Practice of Physic . . .* (2nd edn. Kingston, 1809), 174; Thomas Roughley, *The Jamaica Planter's Guide, or, A System for Planting and Managing a Sugar Estate, or Other Plantations in that Island and throughout the British West Indies in General* (London, 1823), 118–19.

43. Kiple, *Caribbean Slave*, 99: Kiple and King, *Another Dimension*, 119–22.

44. John M. Hunter, "Geophagy in Africa and the United States: A Culture-Nutrition Hypothesis," *Geographical Review*, 63 (April 1973), 170–95.

45. Williamson, *Medical and Miscellaneous Observations*, i, 170.
46. Robert Collins, *Practical Rules for the Management and Medical Treatment of Negro Slaves in the Sugar Colonies* (London, 1811), 29: John Stewart, *An Account of Jamaica, and its Inhabitants* (London, 1808), 273.
47. Robert R. Williams, *Toward the Conquest of Beriberi* (Cambridge, 1961), 67 and *passim*.
48. Kiple, Caribbean Slave, 96–103, 125–9, and "Nutritional Link," 677–90: Kiple and King, *Another Dimension*, 122–3.
49. Derrick B. Jelliffe, *Infant Nutrition in the Subtropics and Tropics* (2nd edn. Geneva, 1968), 98–9.
50. Sir Stanley Davidson et al., *Human Nutrition and Dietetics* (6th edn. Edinburgh, 1975), 6.
51. Fogel, *Without Consent or Contract*, 148–51.
52. Grazyn Jasienska, "Low Birth Weight of Contemporary African Americans: An Intergenerational Effect of Slavery?," *American Journal of Biology*, 21 (2009): 16–24.
53. Sally G. McMillen, "'No Uncommon Disease': Neonatal Tetanus, Slave Infants, and the Southern Medical Profession," *Journal of the History of Medicine and Allied Sciences*, 46 (July 1991): 291–314. T. Winterbottom, *An Account of the Native Africans in Sierra Leone*, 2 vols. (London, 1803), ii. 220; Charles Wilcocks and P. E. C. Manson-Bahr, *Manson's Tropical Diseases* (Baltimore, 1972), 546; Oscar Felsenfeld, *The Epidemiolgy of Tropical Diseases* (Springfield, Ill., 1966), 174.
54. Winterbottom, *Account*, ii. 220.
55. Kiple, *Caribbean Slave*, 120–1.
56. Matthew Gregory Lewis, *Journal of a West India Proprietor* (London, 1934); Joshua Steele et al., *Mitigation of Slavery, in Two Parts* (London, 1814), 249.
57. Michael Craton, "Hobbesian or Panglossian: Two Extremes of Slave Conditions in the British Caribbean, 1783–1834," *William and Mary Quarterly*, 35 (April 1978): 343.
58. Lewis, *Journal*, 97.
59. See the citations for this sort of biological racism in Kiple, *Caribbean Slave*, 256 n. 5.
60. Williamson, *Medical and Miscellaneous Observations*, ii. 262–3.

Select Bibliography

Higman, B. W. *Slave Populations of the British Caribbean, 1807–1834*. Baltimore: Johns Hopkins University Press, 1984.
Hoeppli, Reinhard. *Parasitic Diseases in Africa and the Western Hemisphere: Early Documentation and Transmission by the Slave Trade*. Basel: Verlag für Recht und Gesellschaft, 1968.
Kiple, Kenneth F. *The Caribbean Slave: A Biological History* Cambridge: Cambridge University Press, 1984.
—— "A Survey of Recent Literature on the Biological Past of the Black," *Social Science History*, 10 (Winter 1986): 343–67.
—— and Virginia H. King, *Another Dimension to the Black Diaspora: Diet, Disease, and Racism*. Cambridge: Cambridge University Press, 1981.
McNeill, William H. *Plagues and Peoples*. Garden City, NY: Anchor Press, 1976.

MADRIGAL, LORENA. *Human Biology of Afro-Caribbean Populations.* Cambridge: Cambridge University Press, 2006.

MARGO, ROBERT A., and RICHARD H. STECKEL. "The Heights of American Slaves: New Evidence on Slave Nutrition and Health," *Social Science History,* 6 (1982): 516–38.

SAVITT, TODD L. *Medicine and Slavery: The Diseases and Health Care of Blacks in Antebellum Virginia.* Urbana, Ill.: University of Illinois Press, 1978.

STECKEL, RICHARD H. *The Economics of U.S. Slave and Southern White Fertility.* New York: Garland, 1985.

—— "A Peculiar Population: The Nutrition, Health, and Mortality of American Slaves from Childhood to Maturity," *Journal of Economic History,* 46 (September 1986): 421–41.

CHAPTER 14

INDIAN SLAVERY

ALAN GALLAY

INTRODUCTION

Most people associate slavery in the early modern world with Africa and Africans. This arose because of the many millions of Africans shipped from Africa to the Americas, the centrality of African enslavement to the economic development of the West, and the long struggles to end the international slave trade and slavery. The ongoing struggle for civil rights, and to ensure freedom and equality for all, had its roots in the overthrowing of slavery, while the racism and economic exploitation on which slavery flourished remain embedded in the body politic of many nations. It is imperative to continue to study slavery's character and evolution not only to remember the past, but to help us understand the present. But it is equally imperative that we recognize and explore the simultaneous history of the enslavement of non-African peoples, whose stories and experiences are worth recounting on their own terms, and which will help us further contextualize and understand the enslavement of Africans, the evolution of racial ideologies, and the meaning of exploitation of humans by humans.

Slavery was a ubiquitous institution in the early modern era. Contemporary to the rise of African slavery in the Americas, millions of non-African peoples were enslaved. Over a million Europeans, for instance, were kept as slaves in North Africa, and perhaps more in the Ottoman empire.[1] As this collection of essays is on slavery in the Americas, the story of European enslavement in Africa and Asia will not be recounted here. But this essay will examine the history of the millions of Native Americans enslaved in the Americas. Contrary to popular perception,

Indian slavery was neither fleeting nor secondary to the story of colonialism, imperialism, and economic exploitation in the Americas. Persisting for centuries, it both pre-dated African slavery in the Americas, and survived African slavery's abolition in the United States. Not until the American government's five-year program to eradicate Indian slavery in Colorado and Utah *after* the American Civil War did slavery officially end, though it likely persisted in several areas of the American West.

The history of Indian slavery is only beginning to receive the attention it deserves. It largely has been ignored because its extent chronologically and geographically has been underestimated. Until recently it was widely assumed that enslavement of Native Americans occurred only for the relatively brief half century after the arrival of Columbus on the island of Hispaniola, then was replaced by African slavery owing to the large numbers of indigenous Americans falling prey to the diseases carried by Europeans to the New World. This line of thinking posited that European planters and mine owners in the Americas considered African slaves a more reliable and profitable workforce than American Indians. Moreover, Indians were deemed too savage to be confined as slaves, with the implicit assumption held by contemporaries (and many modern peoples) that Indians loved freedom too much to bear enslavement, while Africans were more easily domesticated to a life of bondage.[2]

This essay examines the contours of Indian slavery in the Americas, its evolution and character, the varieties of labor systems implemented to control Indian labor and lives, and the existence of Indian slave trades that paralleled African slave trades. No attempt will be made to produce 'numbers' designating the *entire* impact of Indian slavery—the historiography is still too primitive to hazard such a guess—but where estimates can be made for particular regions and times, these will be offered.

INDIAN SLAVERY BEFORE EUROPEAN ARRIVAL

Slavery existed among the indigenous peoples of the Americas before the European arrival. Its character varied from place to place. In societies that practiced human sacrifice, slaves were captured from enemies for ritualistic purposes. This occurred, for instance, among the Aztecs in Mexico and the Indians of the Pacific Northwest. More commonly, native peoples captured enemies to procure slave laborers for agricultural production and public works projects, particularly in Central and South America. Captivity, however, was not the only rationale for enslavement. In Guatemala, a male who received the death penalty for crimes also was punished by having his wife and children enslaved. When the Spanish established their own forms of slavery in the Americas, and wrestled with the issue of "who" could be enslaved, they readily permitted Spanish ownership of *esclavos de rescate*—those individuals who previously had been enslaved by Indians, some of whom they identified by the physical markings imposed by native societies on their slaves: in Nicaragua, slaves were branded, while in the Yucatan slaves' heads were shorn of hair.[3]

Not all Native American societies kept slaves, or if they did, primarily held slaves for their labor or ritualistic sacrifice. In many areas of the Americas, where hunting and gathering predominated for subsistence, slavery was not a significant economic institution. Hunter-gatherers received little economic advantage from owning slaves. Some of these societies ritually killed male captives taken in war, and either assimilated the females and children, exchanged them for their own captives, or kept small numbers as slaves. These slaves could be forced to labor, but their labor was not essential to their captors. These slaves were socially dead, people without kin connection and social status. They served as a reminder that the individual without kinship lacked an essential component of humanity. Native societies in the American South, for instance, considered their people who had been captured and enslaved as having lost their kinship with them; if they rejoined their natal communities through escape or exchange they had to go through ceremonies of rebirth.[4]

SPANISH SLAVING IN THE WEST INDIES AND CENTRAL AMERICA

The Europeans introduced an entirely new scale of slave trading to the New World. In many regions, the indigenous population was almost completely removed by slave raiders, transported to distant places to work on plantations, in mines, and in other economic enterprises. This slaving began shortly after the landing of Columbus on the island of Hispaniola. Familiar with the slave markets of Spain and elsewhere in the Mediterranean world that dealt in Africans, and cognizant that Europeans were sold in the slave markets of northern Africa, it was natural for Columbus to consider slaving as a way to earn profits. He authorized enslaving Indians to labor for the Spanish in Hispaniola, but also shipped slaves to Spain to generate funds. At least 1,500 were sent by February 1495. Others, including, Columbus' brother Bartolomé, followed suit. Quite simply, if the Spaniards did not have enough gold to fill their ships, they added Indian captives. Queen Isabella of Spain vociferously opposed Indian enslavement, but her husband King

Ferdinand refused to halt it entirely, though he supported instituting alternative ways to control Indian labor.[5]

Once the Spanish discovered significant stores of gold in the West Indies they ceased shipping Indians to Spain and kept them as slave laborers. With the dramatic decline of the native population of Hispaniola (from upwards of one million to 30,000 by the early 1530s),[6] they scoured new places for slaves, particularly locations judged as lacking in precious natural resources. By 1511, the governor of Puerto Rico, Juan Ponce de León, undertook slaving raids into Cuba. Later he led an onslaught into the Bahamas almost entirely depopulating these islands of upwards of 40,000 people. When Ponce de León entered Florida seeking Indians to enslave, the local natives apparently knew what had happened on the nearby Bahamas, and, for the first time, the Spanish faced resistance from Americans who had not previously met Europeans.[7]

By 1514 the Spanish had extended their slaving forays to the islands off the coast of Venezuela, including Curaçao, Trinidad, and Aruba, followed by raids on the mainland of Central America. Many of the victims were shipped to Hispaniola, Cuba, Jamaica, and Puerto Rico, and later to New Spain and Peru. The devastation of slavery, disease, abuse, and warfare continued on the Central American mainland through the sixteenth century. The native population declined an incredible 97 percent in Pacific Nicaragua and the Nicoya Peninsula in Costa Rica, mostly from disease, with up to one half million enslaved. Many thousands also died in the slaving raids. The population of much of Honduras was reduced from an estimated 600,000 to 32,000, again, mostly from disease, with approximately 150,000 enslaved.[8]

Enslavement of Indians conflicted with the Pope's charge to Spanish and Portuguese colonizers to convert indigenous Americans to Christianity. Many Iberian political and religious leaders thus opposed enslavement, but generally agreed that to bring natives to Christianity they must be organized into religious communities, and that Indians owed tribute and/or labor as compensation to the Europeans for converting and civilizing them. The Europeans rationalized that labor discipline would eliminate or reduce the Indians' savagery, making successful conversion possible. As the Spanish developed new ways for controlling Indian labor, they also developed rationales for keeping some Indians as slaves. Thus, they continued to enslave Indians who previously had been enslaved by Indians—for these were presumably not deprived of preexisting freedom by the Spanish, and if anything, would allegedly enjoy an elevated status under Spanish rulers. Natives classified as cannibals (though most were not cannibals) or who resisted Spanish dominance also were enslaved. This included the Caribs, and any Indians who used poisoned arrows (who often were labeled Caribs) though the Spanish initially avoided these Indians of the Lesser Antilles as too dangerous to capture. When the Spanish crown offered tax relief to those who would subdue the Caribs, they were hunted down and enslaved.

No rationale but the desire for labor was behind enslavement of Indians as *naborias* and *tamemes*. *Naborias* was a term used with vagueness. It generally described the widely distributed Indians that Spanish colonists took into personal service. Often these were displaced people unconnected to local Indian communities. Several laws provided they could return to their homeland, if they so desired, but this almost never happened—the expense was too great. Instead, they worked without pay in Spanish households. Though not legally slaves—laws barred their branding, as well as their sale to new masters—they often were both branded and sold.

Tamemes were Indians forced to labor by the conquistadors. They carried the Spaniards' baggage over long distances, and died at high rates from abuse—on one journey from Honduras to Nicaragua, for example, but six of an estimated 4,000 *tamemes* made it home. By the 1530s and 1540s Spanish legislation tried to end the involuntary nature of *tameme* service, but new systems were created to recruit, employ, and control Indian laborers to fill the duties of the *tamemes*.[9]

Spain officially outlawed Indian slavery in the New Laws (1542), but large numbers—hundreds of thousands—continued to be reduced into chattel slavery. For instance, outright Spanish enslavement of Indians persisted in Chile and Peru until the 1680s, and well into the nineteenth century in New Mexico and Texas. The legal end to Indian slavery owed to a variety of factors. The Spanish priest Bartolomé de Las Casas, who witnessed first hand the brutalization of Native Americans, extensively wrote, lobbied, and debated to end enslavement. (Later in his life he rued not opposing enslavement of Africans as well.) Ending Indian slavery also made sense to a Crown that witnessed conquistadors operating in the Americas as if they owned independent fiefdoms and resisting imperial authority. Church fathers were permitted by the Spanish government to play a greater role in administering to the native population: converting Indians and organizing their daily life. The Spanish Crown's hands-on approach, particularly under Philip II (reigned 1556–98), led to massive reorganization and regulation of the empire, with a subsequent plethora of new ways to direct and control Indian labor for the benefit of Crown, Church, and colonists, which theoretically, at least, considered the needs of native peoples.[10]

VARIETIES OF SLAVERY AND COMPULSORY LABOR UNDER THE SPANISH

Old and new forms of coerced labor resulted from the Spanish reforms, often differing little from chattel slavery. One form was *yanaconaje*. This system of labor control was adapted by the Spanish from the Incas in Peru and Bolivia, who enslaved Indians removed from their natal communities. Similar to medieval serfdom, *yanaconas* were tied to specific lands—but not to lords. If the land was sold, the Indians did not follow their master, and stayed with the land. Most *yanaconas* engaged in agricultural production. By the end of the sixteenth century, more than a third of the Indians of Peru and Bolivia were classified as *yanaconas*. Some advantages they possessed over chattel slaves included the keeping together of families, and the Crown was more apt to press for their rights.[11]

Another labor system, which began early in the Spanish conquest on Hispaniola and then moved to other islands and the American mainland, was the *encomienda*, a system used in Spain during the Reconquista against Muslims and adapted to the New World. The Crown granted *encomendero* status to individuals—conquistadors illegally did likewise, which the Crown often later approved—who then attached Indians to labor for them or to provide tribute, in exchange for conversion and physical protection. The Indians received no pay for their labor, and were in effect slaves, though the Crown periodically ordered protection and rights for the Indians. The Crown moved towards abolishing the *encomienda* system in the 1540s, but was unwilling to follow through as it benefited from the revenues. In some places the *encomenderos* flourished by claiming the bulk of Indian labor, but the Crown steadily took over economic operations in many areas. Churchmen then took over conversion, while government officials oversaw tribute collection and the forced labor drafts. Usually Indians served in the drafts once every seven years, for six months to a year. *Encomendero* power survived longest in frontier areas, especially in Venezuela, Chile, the Yucatan in Mexico, and in Paraguay, where it lasted until the early nineteenth century.[12]

Influenced by lobbying from the religious orders, the Crown created another labor system, *repartimiento*, which became widespread in Spanish America, combining both tribute and forced labor. *Repartimiento* varied in form from one place to the next, but generally involved compelling Indians to work at low wages to pay tribute, and for communities to provide compulsory laborers to work in the mines, on public works projects, and in agricultural or cloth production for the state, church and colonists. *Repartimiento* was widespread in Mexico and Peru, where it was adapted from Indian forms of corvée labor, whereby communities owed labor to the state. The Indians were not slaves, but they were compelled to labor. *Repartimiento* faded quickly in Mexico, but persisted in Bolivia, particularly to provide workers for the great silver mines at Potosí, which employed as many as 13,000 male laborers at a time. The forced workers received below-market wages, often laboring distant from their homes, though often their families accompanied them. The period of their labor usually extended from a few weeks to many months, with the norm at Potosí of three to four months—three weeks of work, then one week off. There was great variance in the percentage of a community required to fill the labor drafts, which extended from under 5 percent to over one-third. Though males predominated in the labor drafts, women and children occasionally were recruited. *Repartimiento* predominated as the system that organized and channeled unfree labor in the seventeenth and eighteenth centuries in Colombia, Ecuador, Florida, and in Peru and Bolivia, where it survived into the 1820s.[13]

INDIAN SLAVERY IN PORTUGUESE BRAZIL

Portuguese enslavement of Indians in Brazil was more widespread than Spanish enslavement of Indians in their colonies. The Portuguese focused on procuring Indian slaves for plantation agriculture, not mining, public works, or subsistence agriculture. The Portuguese obtained native slaves in two ways—by purchasing Indians' slaves and through raiding expeditions by *bandeirantes* operating out of São Paulo. The *bandeirantes* got their name from the flag or *bandeira* they presumably carried to signify their ethnic affiliation, though most were of mixed blood. They enslaved many thousands of Indians in Brazil and Paraguay—one expedition alone in 1628 may have netted upwards of 60,000 Indians.[14] The Portuguese Crown began to bar slaving in the 1570s, with further laws passed in 1595 and 1609, but the slaving continued. The Jesuits called for prohibition of outright enslavement, though they did not oppose the planters' use of Indian labor by other means. The *bandeirantes* continued their slave raiding well into the eighteenth century.

Slavery was not the only way to exploit native labor, however, and the Portuguese tried other methods. The Jesuits organized native peoples into large villages (*aldeiras*), but disease and escape sharply reduced their numbers in the sixteenth century. Moreover, most of the *aldeiras* were not located in sugar-producing regions where Indian labor was most desired. Nevertheless, large numbers of Indians confined to *aldeiras* were consigned to Portuguese colonists as contract laborers, who at best received paltry monetary compensation. Portuguese planters were willing to employ free waged native laborers in sugar production—the most important and profitable New World crop—if slaves were unavailable, but low pay discouraged Indians from working on the plantations.

As the Brazilian sugar planters accumulated capital they steadily turned to the purchase of African laborers. This occurred for several reasons. Natives succumbed to numerous epidemic diseases making them an unreliable labor force. Moreover, Indians could run away more easily than Africans because of their familiarity with the landscape. When they escaped, Indian slaves could often pass themselves off as non-slaves, while Africans usually had to join maroon communities in distant places, such as Palmares, a confederacy of eleven towns of over 20,000 people that existed from the late fifteenth to late sixteenth century on the northern frontier. Native resistance also was a persistent problem. Indian slaves killed many masters, and a millennial resistance movement that united Indian slaves and non-slaves together in the 1560s, known as the *Santidade*, resulted in the destruction of sugar plantations. The movement lasted into the seventeenth century. Thus, the susceptibility to disease, the relative ease of resistance, the desire to end Indian slavery by the religious orders and the Crown, and the growing availability of African slaves from Portuguese colonies in West Africa led Portuguese planters to increase importation from Africa toward the close of the sixteenth century. But there was another reason as well. Although often outnumbered by Indians on many Brazilian plantations, Africans usually were given the more skilled positions in sugar production. Perhaps this occurred because many of the Africans arrived in Brazil as skilled artisans. Male Indians tended to fill more of the supporting occupations, such as hunters and fishermen and boatmen, while female Indians engaged in producing food crops to feed the labor force. Of course, planter preferences may have been key in assigning work tasks, and prejudice against Indian labor in comparison to African labor could be found throughout the Atlantic world. But natives' ability to escape, unless transferred to areas distant from their homes, may have played the greatest role in planter evaluations of the relative merits of Indian versus African labor. As the Portuguese author Magahães de Gandano noted in his *Histories of Brazil* (*c.*1576), "if the Indians were not so fickle and given to flight, the wealth of Brazil would be incomparable."[15]

To summarize the first period of enslavement of Native Americans in the Spanish and Portuguese empires: though made illegal in the former by the mid-sixteenth century, and the latter by the early seventeenth century, Indian slavery continued despite imperial laws prohibiting it, and was supplemented by new systems of compulsory labor. Tributary status compelled natives to work for low wages, and in forced production of crops and goods (such as items of clothing and other manufactures), and to provide an array of services for the colonizers. Labor drafts removed Indians from their communities to labor for Crown, Church, and colonists in mining, agriculture, and cloth production. African slaves often replaced natives in mining and agriculture, but they also worked side by side in both. Many Europeans expressed preference for Africans as more reliable laborers, especially in sugar production, and the increased availability of slaves from Africa, as well as imperial and church opposition to Indian slavery, meant that African slavery would have a growing prominence within the Iberian empires in the seventeenth and eighteenth centuries, but mainly in the plantation areas of the West Indies and Brazil. Indian labor predominated in many, perhaps most areas of the Latin American mainland.

INDIAN SLAVERY IN THE EARLY FRENCH
AND ENGLISH COLONIES

Permanent French and English colonization began later than the Iberians, in the seventeenth century, focusing on the Caribbean and North America. By the time of initial colonization, the native population had been so severely reduced that the French and English readily turned to African slaves to fill their labor needs on sugar plantations, though significant numbers of European indentured servants were used on the English islands. Both English and French planters imported Native American slaves from the mainland, though the number was small compared to African imports. Nonetheless this was a significant trade that brought much desired capital into the mainland colonies.[16]

Few French and English would have thought about Indian slavery before their arrival in the Americas. At the time of the founding of the first permanent French and English colonies, slavery already was associated with Africans in European minds, and ideas were current in the Western world that the Europeans had the duty to convert indigenous Americans to Christianity and offer them the fruits of European civilization. French and English colonizers received the charge from their governments to convert native peoples—the charter of every English colony stipulated conversion as a reason for, and justification of, colonization. In reality, the English rarely attempted to missionize, while the French sent numerous missionaries to New France (Canada) and their later settlements throughout inland North America. Given this same charge, the Spanish focused on ways to control Indian labor. Despite French attempts to organize Indian communities, sometimes on *reserves*—the prototype for the reservation—and the English creation of "Praying Towns" for converted Indians in New England, both English and French made little attempt to directly control Indian labor through tribute payments or labor levies. In the non-plantation colonies, English and French were more interested in trade. Native peoples would follow traditional economic activities, albeit on an altogether new scale, as the Europeans offered manufactures for the animals pelts that native peoples hunted and processed. The limitations of French and English military power in North America, and notably, their competition with one another, precluded their organization of Native American communities to extract their labor, except to enlist their services as hunters and warriors.[17]

Far more negotiation went into the European–Indian relationship in North America because of the very real limitations on European power. Although French and English had little ability to organize communities of native laborers, they did *actively* engage in the enslavement of native peoples. In the early stages of colonization, as with Columbus in Hispaniola, the enslavement of native peoples was quickly perceived as a relatively easy way to obtain capital. Since the demand for labor was immense in the West Indies, slavers could always find ready buyers for Indian captives there, but even in the mainland ports Indian slaves were easily sold, where the unfortunates could be employed as domestics, farm and unskilled laborers, or trained by artisans to become craftsmen. For decades, American scholars have debated the origins of slavery—meaning African slavery—in the English colonies, failing to notice how the first colonists engaged in slave raiding and ownership of Native American slaves.[18] The Jamestown colonists enslaved local Indians, as did the Puritans in significant numbers in New England, and the Dutch in New Netherland, and so on through the North American landscape. From Canada to Florida, and west through the Great Plains and the Southwest to the Pacific, the buying and selling of native peoples was widespread, and persisted even longer than the enslavement of people of African descent in the United States.

Native American Slavers

The process of enslaving native peoples varied from place to place, and over time, but generally, slave trading in North America above Mexico was more akin to the trade in Africa than to the Iberian slaving against native peoples in South and Central America and the Caribbean. The Iberians tended to conduct their own raids on island and coastal populations. In contrast, in Africa as in much of North America slaving usually was conducted against inland communities, where the Europeans lacked the skills and military power to conduct slaving raids.[19] (In many of the North American coastal areas native numbers had been greatly reduced by disease precluding sustained slaving.) In Africa and North America outside of New England, the Europeans purchased most of their captives from native peoples. The victims were easily transportable—they could be walked great distances to the coast and loaded on ships for transport to other ports. Native Americans participated in slaving for a variety of reasons. They gained European alliance and access to a network of slaving allies. Refusal to engage in slaving left a group vulnerable to becoming enslaved themselves. Simply put, in places where slaving reached frenzied proportions, as in the American South from the 1670s to about 1717, Indians had to choose between becoming slavers or being enslaved. Yet it was not unusual for those engaged in slaving to become victimized themselves, and for victimized groups to become slavers. Slaving broke old friendships and increased the numbers of one's enemies, even as it propagated new opportunities for alliances.[20]

Slaving was not always a matter of survival, and a way to secure a group against enemies. Some slavers' primary motive lay in the desire to obtain European trade goods—and not just weaponry, but labor-saving tools such as metal knives, axes, and pots, as well as woolen blankets and clothing. These slavers not only went against enemies, but sought out distant people they did not know. Arguably, these slavers could have been dependent on European goods, and slaving was the only, or at least the easiest way to obtain commodities, but many natives undertook slaving before dependency had occurred.[21]

Securing alliance and trade goods, and danger of their own enslavement, were the major reasons why natives became slavers for the Europeans, but there were other roots that lay within indigenous societies. As we have seen, the capture and enslavement of humans was not new to most indigenous peoples, but for many part of a larger cultural matrix involving achieving vengeance against enemies. Personal and group motives often took precedence over European market conditions in Indians agreeing to become slavers for them, but likely there was a combination of these and other motives.

Indian Slavery in the American South

In terms of sheer numbers, in the area of the future United States, the American South experienced the greatest amount of slaving of native peoples. Some 30,000 to 50,000 slaves or more were taken in the region below Virginia before 1720. How many were taken by the Virginians is unknown. Groups like the Ocaneechi and the Westo sold slaves to the Virginians in the seventeenth century. The Westo moved south to the Savannah River where they (as well as pirates) preyed on Indians living on Spanish missions on the sea islands of Georgia and Florida. The Westo then raided far and wide on the mainland and established a new trading partnership with the Carolina colony (founded in 1670). The South Carolinians stepped up the enslavement of native peoples as a major money-making enterprise in the colony. After turning on and enslaving the Westo, they enlisted new allies such as the Savannah (Shawnee), and a variety of groups that coalesced into two confederacies, the Yamasee and the Creek, who themselves previously had been victimized by slaving. The Yamasee and Creek, along with their English allies, swept through Florida for over a generation, effectively depopulating much of the peninsula by the early eighteenth century. First they assaulted the Spanish missions of northern Florida, then they captured both missionized and non-missionized Indians all the way to Key West. The Spanish tried to save some of their Christianized Indians by transporting them to Cuba and Mexico, while others, such as the Apalachee, became refugees in French Louisiana (where their descendants remain to this day) or were compelled into becoming "allies" by their forced removal to the Savannah River, where they remained until 1715 before being enslaved or fleeing.[22]

The Carolinians also established an alliance with the distant Chickasaw in northern Mississippi and southwest Tennessee, who enslaved thousands of Indians on both sides of the Mississippi River. Their attacks to the south led to the coalescence of many peoples into the Choctaw confederacy, while their assaults into Arkansas and along the Mississippi River not only resulted in the death and enslavement of large numbers of Indians, but also pushed refugees south and west. The French benefited from English slaving, which pushed many of the trans-Mississippi Indians into French alliance. The French were not opposed to enslaving native peoples, but generally traded for Indian slaves who came from the north and west whom their allies or their own traders brought to French settlements. The French consciously modeled their Louisiana colony on English Carolina, seeing that Indian slaves traded to the West Indies would earn capital for purchasing African slaves to build a plantation society. Even when slaving of southeastern Indians practically died out after the 1720s, the French in Louisiana continued to purchase slaves in significant numbers, particularly from Indian slavers operating in Texas and New Mexico. The Apache and Comanche, for instance, assaulted each other in the southwest and sold their captives to the French in Louisiana, or the Spanish in Texas and New Mexico.[23]

In the Upper South, slaving of Indians declined after the departure of the Westo for the Savannah River in the mid-seventeenth century, and Virginia engaged neighboring Indians to protect the colony's borders. But in 1676, Bacon's Rebellion, understood today as a civil war among colonists in Virginia, was labeled by contemporary Virginians as "The Indian War," a more appropriate description of a conflict that began with Nathaniel Bacon and his frontier supporters assaulting and capturing for enslavement the colonies' native allies. The rebellion against Virginia authorities failed, but most of their native captives remained slaves on tobacco plantations in the colony.[24]

In North Carolina, colonists were too militarily weak to enslave many of their Indian neighbors in the seventeenth century, but most of the European settlers might not have been inclined to do so if they could, given the nature of a colony that attracted the dispossessed who showed little interest in accruing riches and tended to get along well with local natives. But an influx of new settlers in the early eighteenth century led to growing complaints of enslavement by the Tuscarora and other indigenous people in North Carolina, and contributed to the outbreak of the so-called Tuscarora War in 1711. A South Carolina army composed mostly of Indians came to North Carolina's rescue during the war and in the process enslaved many North Carolina natives. North Carolinians joined in as well, and several thousand Indians were enslaved and shipped to other colonies, but mostly to the West Indies.[25]

The slaving of native peoples in the American South greatly declined as a result of the Yamasee War (1715–17). This war united many southern native peoples, particularly those who had been slaving allies of the British, against South Carolina. It not only led the colony to the brink of destruction, but to the death of a generation of Carolina Indian slave traders, about 100 of whom were killed in Indian towns and villages from the Atlantic coast to the Mississippi River. After the war, most southern Indian peoples refused to go "a-slaving" for the British, who had more fully shifted their economy to plantation agriculture based on African slavery. The British became intent on protecting their valuable plantations against hostile Indians, and thus in a weaker position vis-à-vis the powerful confederacies of the South. The Creek, Chickasaw, and Cherokee confederacies had grown stronger by slaving and by assimilating refugees from slaving. Warfare did not disappear from the South with the end of the slaving wars, and remained endemic for almost two generations among the southern Indians, who were less inclined to go on massive slaving raids.[26]

INDIAN SLAVERY IN THE NORTH

In New England there were two stages in the enslavement of native peoples. The first involved the sale of enemy captives (including women and children) taken in war, most notably the Pequot War (1636–7) and King Philip's War (1675–6). (Some remained as slaves in New England, many were sent to the West Indies.) Slaving was prevalent enough in King Philip's War and its aftermath that a few traders dealt mostly or exclusively in Indian slaves, though not anywhere near the number who operated in the South. Roger Williams, who often saw through the racism of his fellow Puritans towards Indians and who supported native land rights and fair treatment, raised objections to Indian slavery, particularly for women and children. But he not only became convinced of its efficacy as a war measure, he actually oversaw a public sale of Indian slaves in Rhode Island.[27]

The New Englanders not only enslaved local Indians, but purchased Indian slaves from the South, whom they often called Spanish Indians. Most Indian slaves in the region lived in urban areas and towns. Ministers, carpenters, rope makers, in fact, a broad range of society, purchased slaves to assist in various professions or as domestic servants. So many Indian slaves were shipped to New England as a result of the Yamasee War that a dangerous situation was created in the urban areas—many were recently captured male warriors understandably unhappy about their new status. Most of the New England colonies passed laws, some in emergency sessions, to bar the import of these slaves. This did not, however, end Indian slavery in New England, which entered a second stage, by which "friendly" and local Indians were increasingly enslaved.[28]

King Philip's War had largely removed independent Indian groups from southern New England. Friendly Indians, often Christian, who remained in southern New England sometimes fell victim to unscrupulous men capturing free Indians and selling them as slaves. (The Puritans also continued to enslave, when they could, Indians from northern New England and Canada.) More common, however, was enslavement by court decision. Local Indians who committed crimes, even small crimes like stealing a handkerchief or a loaf of bread, found courts sentencing them to years of servitude. The Indians were then sold to private individuals. Some were shipped out of the colony, particularly to the West Indies, to face a life of slavery. But even those who remained in New England often became de facto slaves, never earning release from servitude.[29]

Little research has been done on Indian slavery in New York and Pennsylvania. We do know, however, that during the Dutch period there were brutal wars between the Dutch and natives in the vicinity of New Amsterdam (later New York City), and the captives were shipped to the West Indies as slaves.[30] After the English conquest of New Netherland (1664), New Yorkers purchased Indian slaves, who were imported into the colony in small numbers. The New Yorkers probably did not export many slaves because there were relatively few natives available to purchase from inland peoples. The neighboring Iroquois to the north, with whom the New Yorkers traded, captured many Indians from groups in the interior continent, keeping a small number as slaves for themselves but assimilating the majority to boost their numbers. The Iroquois, due to their declining numbers from the six-decade long Iroquois Wars (1641–1701), needed to replace those who had fallen or died from disease.[31] Moreover, the English lacked the military power to induce the Iroquois to sell their captives, and were content to make profits from the Iroquois through the fur trade. Nevertheless, the New York records contain numerous references to Indian slaves in the seventeenth and eighteenth centuries.

In Pennsylvania (founded 1680), Quaker control of government precluded a large trade in Indian slaves. The Quakers were not opposed to slavery, at least before the mid-eighteenth century, keeping and dealing in African slaves, but most were intent on maintaining good relations with native peoples, and by their pacifism were ill disposed to promote military measures to obtain Indian slaves. We know that Indian slavery existed in Pennsylvania because Indians complained to Pennsylvania authorities about it, with the result that the government passed laws to reduce Indian slave importations in 1706 and again in 1712, though Queen Anne rejected the latter bill. When the Quakers lost control of the government in the 1750s, and relations deteriorated on the frontier, white settlers became more intent on killing Indians than enslaving them.

INDIAN SLAVERY IN THE WEST

Further inland, where French traders predominated, Indian slavery was ubiquitous, as many Indians were brought from the west at least as far as the Great Plains and the Southwest by Indian and French traders to the French posts spread over the trans-Appalachian and Mississippian west, and throughout the Great Lakes region. Native peoples in the Missouri country, for instance, were carried as slaves to places as distant and diverse as Montreal, New Orleans, and Santa Fe.[32] Many slaves were called by the French Panis, implying they were Pawnee, but they actually came from any number of peoples, including Sioux, Apache, Ojibwa, and so on. When English traders moved west after French defeat in the Seven Years War (1756–63), they too engaged in Indian slave trading throughout Canada, the Ohio Country, and points west.

In the Spanish Southwest, the enslavement of Indians began as early as the Coronado Expedition (1540–2), and continued through the history of Spanish occupation into the early nineteenth century. Indian slaves from California to the Great Plains were brought by Spain's native trading partners to Santa Fe and other Spanish settlements in New Mexico and later into Texas. Indians were sold at various trade fairs, in a trade so prevalent that some Indians described the month in which the annual fairs occurred as the "month of slaves." The Comanches called September "Mexico Month," because that was when the slaves were moved to New Mexico. The victims often were sold to individuals desiring slave labor in northern Mexico. The Spanish in New Mexico also adapted the Ottoman practice of keeping Janissaries, slaves who were turned into soldiers. The Spanish called their slave-soldiers Genizaros. These were Indian slaves given land in exchange for service to the government as soldiers. Since the Genizaros were Indians from distant places possessing no kin ties with local Indians, and owing their position and land to the government, the Spanish could maintain their loyalty and use them to police local Indians, but they nonetheless were slaves.[33]

Slaving in the West extended far longer than in the East, particularly in Arizona, California, Utah, and Colorado. As late as the early 1850s, an American official in the newly acquired New Mexico territory described the trade in Indian slaves as "'exceedingly pernicious' and the 'greatest curse' on the Indians of the territory."[34] A central axis of the trade was from Utah to New Mexico, maintained largely by the Utes. When Mormons moved into Utah in the 1850s, they were astonished by the scale of slaving, and "redeemed" many children from the Utes, some of whom in effect became indentured servants—quasi-slaves—to pay off their ransom. The Indians who sold these slaves had participated for generations in the trade, and it was not unusual for them to threaten to kill their captives if the Mormons, or the Spanish in New Mexico, or the Navajo did not purchase them.[35] Even with the emancipation of slaves in the United States in 1865, Indian indentured servants and peons (those forced to labor to pay off debts) remained de facto slaves, as their labor service was considered voluntary by their owners. To effect actual emancipation, President Andrew Johnson in 1865 ordered an end to Indian slavery, and the United States government spent five years scouring Colorado and New Mexico to free remaining captives.

INDIAN AND AFRICAN SLAVERY FROM
A EUROPEAN PERSPECTIVE

Despite the ubiquity of Indian slavery in most areas of colonial America, African slavery predominated where large numbers of laborers were desired, as in plantation agriculture in the Southeast. The most cogent reason lay in the availability of Africans. After areas had been "over-hunted" for Indians, who also perished in great numbers from epidemic diseases, the sources for more Indian labor in the East dried up. Moreover, as the colonies grew richer they could ill afford Indian wars that risked plantations, farms, and villages. Colonial governments saw there was more money to be made in plantation agriculture or surplus production of farms than in Indian slavery, and that peace needed to be maintained with Indians who provided the best protection of colonial settlements from hostile Indians and Europeans, and who could also be employed to return runaway slaves and European servants. Enslavement of Indians continued, but not as a point of policy in the East, or through large expeditions, but intermittent and sporadically, except in the huge area from the trans-Mississippi West to California where few African slaves were available.[36]

Comparing the enslavement of Native Americans to Africans will help us better understand the evolution of concepts of race and racism among Europeans. Certainly, Europeans in Europe and the Americas questioned the morality of enslaving Native Americans, whereas before the eighteenth century few gave a thought to the enslavement of Africans. Perceptions of indigenous Americans as "naturals," or in Spanish America as children or neophytes, who could be brought to Christianity and European civilization through conversion, education, and transformation of their way of life and economy, fed European romantic notions of their own munificence in settling the Americas, while rationalizing conquest. Colonists tended to hold much less romantic notions than their counterparts in Europe, but some were squeamish about enslaving Native Americans. Many Euro-Americans held the notion that slavery should be reserved for only those born into slavery or as punishment for crime, or as the just deserts of war captives. It was widely considered reprehensible to enslave free people by the second quarter of the eighteenth century. Europeans in both Old and New Worlds believed that holding Africans as slaves posed no ethical dilemma because they had not enslaved them: they purchased people enslaved by Africans or kept people born into bondage in the Americas. (It became convenient for colonists in post-revolutionary America to forget their own long history of enslaving free Indians.) Colonists and other Europeans came to think that slavery was a natural condition for Africans, since virtually all of the Africans they encountered in the Americas and Europe were slaves, but most Indians were free people. The moral quandary did not prevent enslavement of large numbers of Indians and control of their labor through myriad means, but the discussion of whether Indians *should* be enslaved contributed to the discourse over whether any human should suffer bondage.

INDIAN SLAVERY AND THE
EUROPEAN IMPERIAL POWERS

There needs to be further analysis of the important differences among the Europeans in their views of Indians and slavery. The Spanish and Portuguese governments played a much greater role in attempting to regulate colonial policies regarding Native American labor than did the French and English, though Iberian policies often were unclear, contradictory, and poorly enforced. In the large and varied Spanish empire, the Crown had to contend with an array of interests among the religious orders and colonial groups in creating and enforcing regulation of Indian life and labor. At the other end of the imperial spectrum, the English interfered little with its colonies' Indian affairs. The English Crown and Parliament never tried to bar Indian slavery, as it was considered a local issue, even as it regulated the African slave trade from which it received tax revenues. Likewise, the English government played virtually no role in the conversion of native peoples, which it left to the colonies and charitable organizations in England.

Among the Catholic imperial powers, increased measures were taken to convert both Indians and Africans, with their slaves receiving a variety of rights denied them by the Protestant (English, Dutch, and Danish) powers. Conversion of Indians was undertaken only haltingly by the Protestants, many of whom held Calvinist notions that their efforts would be wasted since heaven, according to the Book of Revelation, held room for only 144,000 souls, and it was highly unlikely that God would preserve space for savages. Nevertheless, missionary efforts were undertaken by Puritans, Anglicans, and later by evangelicals, but with little overall success. By the 1720s and 1730s, disappointed Protestant missionaries (except in Pennsylvania where German Protestant pietists became active) turned their efforts away from converting Native Americans to conversion of Africans. Many British missionaries and colonists had decided that native peoples were irredeemable savages, too resistant or incapable of conversion and civilizing, and could not be assimilated within colonial society, whereas Africans, confined to plantations, in possession of rudimentary English, and more available to convert, were capable of assimilation. Much more attention was then paid by the British to Africans as people, as many worried over the state of African souls, considered the horrors of the "Middle Passage," and raised issues regarding the improvement of their condition as slaves.

The eighteenth century saw the development of an array of racist attitudes towards Native Americans and Africans evolve into an ideology of racism among British North Americans. Africans were deemed peculiarly suited to enslavement, based upon their alleged intellectual inferiority, superior ability to perform agricultural labor in "hot countries," and willingness to follow the directions of a "big man"—the master who directed their lives as slaves—since they presumably could not take care of themselves. Indians, it was argued, made poor slaves because they succumbed too readily to disease, worked poorly in agriculture, and possessed a love for freedom that induced them to run away, commit suicide, or refuse to work under any conditions. All of these racist conceptions were false. Indians were forced to labor as slaves, and many developed antibodies to resist European diseases. (Africans and Europeans also succumbed to an array of diseases, malnutrition, and other factors to perish in large numbers, particularly during the first year of "seasoning" in the New World.) Native populations stabilized in Central and South America, where the Spanish continued to control Indian labor through a variety of means. Only military and political weakness, as well as difficulty enlisting Indian allies, reduced Indian slavery in eastern North America. Africans were no more suitable for enslavement than any other people, but by the eighteenth century European ideology rationalized their enslavement by positing that slavery was the Africans' natural condition.

Future Directions in the Study of Indian Slavery

What remains to be done in studies of Indian slavery? The lives of Indian slaves, especially within the plantations systems of the West Indies and South America, require further analysis. Many of the historical questions applied to the enslavement of Africans can be asked of natives' experience, especially concerning the impact of diaspora on cultural retention and transformation, the psychological and social aspects of free people becoming slaves or being born into slavery, and the prospects and forms of resistance. I have suggested elsewhere that Indians captured in the American South and enslaved in Boston associated with other Indian slaves of the same background and not with New England slaves, whether native or African. This likely was the case elsewhere, but how long did native slaves retain their cultural self-identifications? Did the children of first-generation slaves easily discard their parents' identities and forge ties with others across class lines as slaves, and did they as easily associate with slaves of African descent as those who were Native American.[37]

Study of Native American slavery will help us to better understand African slavery. The process and meaning of conversion or resistance to Christianity, nuclear and extended family dynamics, community formation, and cultural adaptation will all become clearer when we analyze Africans and Indians living in similar circumstances. Plantation records in the West Indies and Brazil will be of great importance in this regard.

More also needs to be done in church and government records to determine European perceptions of African and Native American slaves, which should provide essential clues as to the process of racialization. The evolution of European ideologies of races, which became so prevalent in the eighteenth and nineteenth centuries, took root in the sixteenth and seventeenth centuries. Scholars often speak of racism towards Africans and native peoples as two disconnected ideologies, particularly in anglophone areas, yet they must have been intimately intertwined. Both Indians and Africans were deemed inferior peoples, but the former, it was proclaimed in the eighteenth and nineteenth centuries, were too savage to be tamed through Christianity, Western civilization, or slavery. Instead, colonists and post-Revolutionary War Americans believed that Indians should be removed from their presence, perhaps even eliminated, as an incorrigible danger to their own society. Africans, on the other hand, could be tamed by slavery, elevated by Christianity and exposure to Western culture, though it was assumed they would always occupy the lowest rungs on the social ladder. The divergence in racist ideology towards Africans and Native Americans, when both were kept as slaves, needs to be treated with greater attention and nuance. It could help further divulge the differences between the Iberians, French and English in their construction of racialized societies. The Iberians perceived much more variance in native societies; some Indians could be organized into communities, converted to Christianity, and be forced to labor for the benefit of others and themselves. Others were considered too wild and ignored unless they proved a threat. The Iberians drew sharp distinctions between Africans and Indians, and in many places in Latin America the two largely were segregated, and treated differently both legally and socially. But there was also a great deal of intermixture of Indians, Africans, and Europeans, with a resulting blurring of racial lines. The Iberians put great stake in degrees of skin color—with the darker the skin color the lower the status. The English, on the other hand, sought to create a racial system with sharp divides between Indians, Africans, and Europeans that took no account of individuals bearing mixed parentage. Mulattos, mustees, and others of mixed parentage were relegated to categories such as black, white, or red. The very different experiences of Iberians and English in their construction of slave systems must have played some role in the formation of racial ideologies—these ideologies are part of the legacy of New World slaveries that haunts modern society today.

Notes

1. For European enslavement in North Africa, see Robert C. Davis, *Christian Slaves, Muslim Masters: White Slavery in the Mediterranean, the Barbary Coast and Italy, 1500–1800* (New York, 2003); Linda Colley, *Captives: The Story of Britain's Pursuit of Empire and how its Soldiers and Civilians were held Captive by the Dream of Global Supremacy, 1600–1850* (New York, 2002). Narratives of English enslavement can be found

in Daniel J. Vitkus, *Piracy, Slavery, and Redemption* (New York, 2001). For slavery in the Ottoman empire, consult Bernard Lewis, *Race and Slavery in the Middle East* (New York, 1990); Ehud R. Toledano, *Slavery and Abolition in the Ottoman Middle East* (Seattle, 1998); Daniel Goffman, *The Ottoman Empire and Early Modern Europe* (Cambridge, 2002); Colin Imber, *The Ottoman Empire, 1300–1650: The Structure of Power* (New York, 2002); Cemal Kafadar, *Between Two Worlds: The Construction of the Ottoman State* (Berkeley, 1995).

2. Modern people of European descent make a similar assumption about themselves and their ancestors: that intellectually superior, freedom-loving Europeans would not have tolerated enslavement, thus implicitly ascribing some blame to Africans for their own enslavement. This of course overlooks the millions of Europeans held in bondage at the same time African slavery proliferated.

3. Inga Clendinnen speculates on the Aztec use of slaves for both labor and ritualistic purposes in *Aztecs* (New York, 1991). See also Michael E. Smith, *Aztecs* (Cambridge, 1996). On Aztec conquests and tribute, see Ross Hassig, *Aztec Warfare: Imperial Expansion and Political Control* (Norman, Okla., 1988) and *Trade, Tribute, and Transportation: The Sixteenth-Century Political Economy of the Valley of Mexico* (Norman, Okla., 1985). An excellent account of slavery in the Pacific Northwest is Leland Donald, *Aboriginal Slavery on the Northwest Coast of North America* (Berkeley, 1997). For discussion of Indian slavery in Central America before the European arrival, see William L. Sherman, *Forced Labor in Sixteenth-Century Central America* (Lincoln, Nebr., 1979), 15–17; and Linda A. Newson, *The Cost of Conquest: Indian Decline in Honduras under Spanish Rule* (Boulder, Colo., 1986), 108.

4. Important sociological and anthropological studies of slavery include Orlando Patterson, *Slavery and Social Death: A Comparative Study* (Cambridge, Mass., 1982); Claude Meillassoux, *Anthropology of Slavery: The Womb of Iron and Gold*, trans. Alide Dasnois (Chicago, 1991); James L. Watson (ed.), *Asian and African Systems of Slavery* (Berkeley, 2000). For reintegration of slaves into their natal communities, see Denise Bossy, "Indian Slavery in Southeastern Indian and British Societies, 1670–1730," in Alan Gallay (ed.), *Indian Slavery in Colonial America* (forthcoming).

5. The best examination of Columbus' slaving activities is Troy S. Floyd, *The Columbus Dynasty in the Caribbean, 1492–1526* (Albuquerque, N. Mex., 1973).

6. An excellent discussion of population on Hispaniola, including its historiography, is R. A. Zambardino, "Critique of David Henige's 'On the Contact Population of Hispaniola: History as Higher Mathematics,'" *Hispanic American Historical Review*, 58 (4) (1978): 700–8.

7. Recent examinations of the early stages of Spanish conquest include John H. Elliott, *Empires of the Atlantic World: Britain and Spain in America, 1492–1830* (New Haven, 2006); Hugh Thomas, *Rivers of Gold: The Rise of the Spanish Empire, from Columbus to Magellan* (New York, 2004); and Henry Kamen, *Empire: How Spain Became a World Power, 1492–1763* (New York, 2003).

8. Floyd, *Columbus Dynasty*, 133–5; Sherman, *Forced Labor*, 39–63, 79–82; Newson, *Cost of Conquest*, 4–5, 107–11, 4–5, 126–7, 329.

9. A good discussion of the use of *naborias* and *tamemes* can be found in Sherman, *Forced Labor*, 102–28.

10. For Las Casas, see Bartolmé de Las Casas, *An Account, Much Abbreviated, of the Destruction of the Indies with Related Texts*, ed. and introd. Franklin W. Knight, trans.

Andrew Hurley (Indianapolis, 2003); Juan Friede and Benjamin Keen (eds.), *Bartolomé de Las Casas in History: Toward an Understanding of the Man and his Work* (DeKalb, Ill., 1971); David M. Traboulay., *Columbus and Las Casas: The Conquest and Christianization of America, 1492–1566* (Lanham, Md., 1994). The widely publicized sadism and failure of the De Soto entrada (1539–42), which spread a path of seemingly mindless destruction through the American South from Florida north to the Carolinas, and west across the Mississippi River, helped lead to the end of the era of the conquistadors by buttressing the arguments of those who sought reform of the Spanish empire—and firm policies to bring Indians to Christianity, while protecting them from abuses. For reorganization, early reforms, and the growing involvement of the Church in the Spanish empire, see Lewis Hanke, *The Spanish Struggle for Justice in the Conquest of America* (Philadelphia, 1949); Eugene H. Korth, SJ, *Spanish Policy in Colonial Chile: The Struggle for Social Justice, 1535–1700* (Stanford, Calif., 1968); Ralph H. Vigil, "The Expedition of Hernando De Soto and the Spanish Struggle for Justice," in Patricia Galloway (ed.), *The Hernando de Soto Expedition: History, Historiography, and "Discovery" in the Southeast* (Lincoln, Nebr., 1997). On Philip II, see Geoffrey Parker, *The Grand Strategy of Philip II* (New Haven, 1998).

11. Juan A. Villamarin and Judith E. Villamarin, *Indian Labor in Mainland Spanish America* (Newark, Del., 1975), 1–47, neatly summarizes the various forms of unfree labor in the Spanish empire. But also see Sherman, *Forced Labor.*

12. Good places to begin an examination of the *encomienda* include Charles Gibson, *The Aztecs under Spanish Rule: A History of the Indians of the Valley of Mexico* (Stanford, Calif., 1964); Lesley Byrd Simpson, *The Encomienda in New Spain: The Beginnings of Spanish Mexico* (Berkeley, 1966); James Schofield Saeger, *The Chaco Mission Frontier: The Guaycuruan Experience* (Tucson, Ariz., 2000); Barbara Ganson, *The Guaraní under Spanish Rule in the Rio de la Plata* (Stanford, Calif., 2003); Floyd, *Columbus Dynasty.*

13. Other important works to consult on the early use of unfree Indian labor in Latin America not noted above include Peter J. Bakewell, *Miners of the Red Mountain: Indian Labor in Potosí, 1545–1650* (Albuquerque, N. Mex., 1984); Lolita Gutiérrez Brockington, *The Leverage of Labor: Managing the Cortés Haciendas in Tehunantepec, 1588–1688* (Durham, NC, 1989); Jeffrey A. Cole, *The Potosí Mita: Compulsory Indian Labor in the Andes* (Stanford, Calif., 1985); Linda A. Newson, *Life and Death in Early Colonial Ecuador* (Norman, Okla., 1995).

14. For the *bandeirantes*, see the essays in Richard M. Morse, *The Bandeirantes: The Historical Role of the Brazilian Pathfinders* (New York, 1965).

15. Stuart B. Schwartz, *Sugar Plantations in the Formation of Brazilian Society: Bahia 1550–1835* (Cambridge, 1985) and "Indian Labor and New World Plantations: European Demands and Indian Responses in Northeastern Brazil," *American Historical Review,* 83 (February 1978): 43–79; John Hemming, *Red Gold: The Conquest of the Brazilian Indians* (Cambridge, Mass., 1978). For slavery in Portugal before the settlement of Brazil, see A. C. de C. M. Saunders, *A Social History of Black Slaves and Freedmen in Portugal, 1441–1555* (Cambridge, 1982). A fine recent study of the early African experience in Brazil which also examines the transformation from Indian to African labor is James H. Sweet, *Recreating Africa: Culture, Kinship, and Religion in the African-Portuguese World, 1441–1770* (Chapel Hill, NC, 2006). For the Palmares, see Mary Karasch, "Zumbi of Palmares: Challenging the Portuguese Colonial Order," in Kenneth J.

Andrien (ed.), *The Human Tradition in Colonial Latin America* (Wilmington, Del., 2002), 104–20.

16. The English did not place an imperial tax on Indian slaves, though they did on the importation of Africans.

17. This was not the case in areas where Europeans desired Indians' land, as in English colonization of southern New England, and along the Atlantic coast from New York to Georgia, and in French colonization in scattered inland areas, such as Natchez, Mississippi, portions of the Illinois country, and around Quebec—there removal of Indians and replacement by European and African labor took precedence. On Indian slavery in Canada, see Marcel Trudel, *L'Esclavage au Canada français: Histoire et conditions de l'esclavage* (Quebec, 1960), and Brett Rushforth, " 'A Little Flesh we Offer You': The Origins of Slavery in New France," *William and Mary Quarterly*, 60 (October 2003): 777–808. For Indian slavery in the Mississippi Valley, see Carl J. Ekberg, *Stealing Indian Women: Native Slavery in the Illinois Country* (Champaign, Ill., 2007).

18. Early English colonists did not need to learn how to become slave traders—that was easy enough—but they did need to learn how to become masters of slaves: at the beginning of colonization, the lack of law, tradition, and experience would have made slave owning difficult, confusing, and experimental. Two fine essays by Alden T. Vaughan discuss the origins of African slavery in Virginia, and the historiography surrounding the issue. See "Blacks in Virginia: Evidence from the First Decade," and "The Origins Debate: Slavery and Racism in Seventeenth-Century Virginia," both found in Vaughan, *Roots of American Racism: Essays on the Colonial Experience* (New York, 1995). For the enslavement of Indians in early Virginia, see Chris Everett, " 'They shalbe slaves for their lives': Indian Slavery in Colonial Virginia," in Gallay (ed.), *Indian Slavery in Colonial America*.

19. For the African slave trade, see John Thornton, *Africa and Africans in the Making of the Atlantic World* (2nd edn. New York, 1998); Herbert S. Klein, *The Atlantic Slave Trade* (New York, 1999); David Eltis, *The Rise of African Slavery in the Americas* (New York, 2000); Paul E. Lovejoy, *Transformations in Slavery: A History of Slavery in Africa* (2nd edn. New York, 2000); Patrick Manning, *Slavery and African Life: Occidental, Oriental and African Slave Trades* (Cambridge, 1990).

20. Alan Gallay, *The Indian Slave Trade: The Rise of the English Empire in the American South, 1670–1717* (New Haven, 2002).

21. For example, the peoples who coalesced into the Creek and Yamasee Confederacies scoured the Florida peninsula to its southern reaches to enslave people with whom they had no interactions, and who posed no threat to them.

22. Eric Bowne, *The Westo Indians: Slave Traders of the Early Colonial South* (Tuscaloosa, Ala., 2005), Everett, "They shalbe slaves"; Gallay, *Indian Slave Trade*, 53–69. For slaving in Florida, see Gallay, *Indian Slave Trade*, chs. 3 and 5.

23. For the coalescence of the Choctaw, see Patricia Galloway, *Choctaw Genesis, 1500–1700* (Lincoln, Nebr., 1996). On the impact of slaving in the Arkansas Valley, see Kathleen DuVal, *The Native Ground: Indians and Colonists in the Heart of the Continent* (Philadelphia, 2007). For the impact of slaving on the Mississippi Valley, see Gallay, *Indian Slave Trade*; Robbie Ethridge, "Raiding the Remains: The Indian Slave Trade and the Collapse of the Mississippian Chiefdoms," in Thomas J. Pluckhahn and Robbie Ethridge (eds.), *Light on the Path: The Anthropology and History of the Southeastern Indians* (Tuscaloosa, Ala., forthcoming) and "The Making of a Militaristic Society: The Chickasaws and the Colonial

American Slave Trade," in Gallay (ed.), *Indian Slavery in Colonial America*. For slaving among the Apache and Comanche, see Juliana Barr, "From Captives to Slaves: Commodifying Indian Women in the Borderlands," *Journal of American History*, 92 (June 2005): 19–46; and "A Spectrum of Indian Bondage in Spanish Texas," in Gallay (ed.), *Indian Slavery in Colonial America*; and *Peace Came in the Form of a Woman: Indians and Spaniards in the Texas Borderlands* (Chapel Hill, NC, 2007).

24. Everett, "They shalbe slaves"; April Hatfield, *Atlantic Virginia: Intercolonial Relations in the Seventeenth Century* (Philadelphia, 2003).

25. For North Carolina in its early years, see Noeleen McIlvenna, *"A Very Mutinous People": North Carolina's Struggle for Independence in the Late Seventeenth Century* (Chapel Hill, NC, 2009). The Tuscarora War and the enslavement of its victims is discussed in Gallay, *Indian Slave Trade*, ch. 10.

26. On the Yamasee War, see William Ramsey, *The Yamasee War: A Study of Culture, Economy, and Conflict in the Colonial South* (Lincoln, Nebr., 2008); Stephen J. Oatis, *A Colonial Complex: South Carolina's Frontiers in the Era of the Yamasee War, 1680–1730* (Lincoln, Nebr., 2005); Gallay, *Indian Slave Trade*, ch. 12.

27. Margaret Ellen Newell, "The Changing Nature of Indian Slavery in New England, 1670–1720," in Colin G. Calloway and Neal Salisbury (eds.), *Reinterpreting New England Indians and the Colonial Experience* (Boston, 2004), 106–36, and "Indian Slavery in Colonial New England," in Gallay (ed.), *Indian Slavery in Colonial America*.

28. Almon Wheeler Lauber, *Indian Slavery in Colonial Times within the Present Limits of the United States* (1913; reprint Williamstown, Mass., 1979); Gallay, *Indian Slave Trade*.

29. Newell, "Indian Slavery in Colonial New England."

30. For recent accounts of the wars, see Paul Otto, *The Dutch–Munsee Encounter in America: The Struggle for Sovereignty in the Hudson Valley* (New York, 2006); and Donna Merwick, *The Shame and the Sorrow: Dutch–Amerindian Encounters in New Netherland* (Philadelphia, 2006). For the sale of Indian slaves to the West Indies by the Dutch, see Allen W. Trelease, *Indian Affairs in Colonial New York: The Seventeenth Century* (Ithaca, NY, 1960).

31. For the Iroquois Wars and Iroquois incorporation of captives, see Daniel Richter, *The Ordeal of the Longhouse: The Peoples of the Iroquois League in the Era of European Colonization* (Chapel Hill, NC, 1992).

32. The Indian slaves in the North often were called by the French and their allies "Panis," the French word for Pawnee, but in fact they could come from any native people.

33. For a nuanced study of Indian slavery in New Mexico, which includes discussion of the Genizaros, see James F. Brooks, *Captives and Cousins: Slavery, Kinship, and Community in the Southwest Borderlands* (Chapel Hill, NC, 2002). An excellent overview of Indian slavery in New Mexico—and its extent into Utah into the mid-nineteenth century—can be found in Sondra Jones, *The Trial of Don Pedro León Luján: The Attack against Slavery and Mexican Traders in Utah* (Salt Lake City, 2002), see 26–8, for the trade fairs.

34. Jones, *Trial of Don Pedro*, 81.

35. Ibid. 47–52.

36. A recent essay on Indians kept in bondage in Civil War-era California is Michael Magliari, "Free Soil, Unfree Labor: Cave Johnson Couts and the Binding of Indian Workers in California, 1850–1867," *Pacific Historical Review*, 73 (August 2004): 349–90.

37. Gallay, *Indian Slave Trade*, 302–6.

SELECT BIBLIOGRAPHY

BAKEWELL, PETER J. *Miners of the Red Mountain: Indian Labor in Potosí, 1545–1650*. Albuquerque, N. Mex.: University of New Mexico Press, 1984.

BROOKS, JAMES F. *Captives and Cousins: Slavery, Kinship, and Community in the Southwest Borderlands*. Chapel Hill, NC: University of North Carolina Press, 2002.

DONALD, LELAND. *Aboriginal Slavery on the Northwest Coast of North America*. Berkeley and Los Angeles: University of California Press, 1997.

FLOYD, TROY S. *The Columbus Dynasty in the Caribbean, 1492–1526*. Albuquerque, N. Mex.: University of New Mexico Press, 1973.

GALLAY, ALAN, ed. *Indian Slavery in Colonial America*. Forthcoming.

——*The Indian Slave Trade: The Rise of the English Empire in the American South, 1670–1717*. New Haven: Yale University Press, 2002.

LAS CASAS, BARTOLOMÉ DE. *An Account, Much Abbreviated, of the Destruction of the Indies with Related Texts*, ed. with an introd. Franklin W. Knight, trans. Andrew Hurley. Indianapolis: Hackett Publishing Company, Inc., 2003.

LAUBER, ALMON WHEELER. *Indian Slavery in Colonial Times within the Present Limits of the United States*. 1913. Reprint Williamstown, Mass.: Corner House, 1979.

SHERMAN, WILLIAM L. *Forced Labor in Sixteenth-Century Central America*. Lincoln, Nebr.: University of Nebraska Press, 1979.

VILLAMARIN, JUAN A., and JUDITH E. VILLAMARIN. *Indian Labor in Mainland Spanish America*. Newark, Del.: University of Delaware, 1975.

CHAPTER 15

....

RACE AND SLAVERY

....

TIMOTHY LOCKLEY

THE word "race" has become synonymous in modern parlance with skin color and is often associated with prejudice and violence: news bulletins, for instance, report "racially aggravated" attacks among Asians, whites, and blacks, while the "racial" issues of the United States, South Africa, Zimbabwe, or any other nation for that matter, invariably focus on the different treatment and experiences of those with specific skin tones. A notable exception to this generality was the demarcation of Jews as a racial group by the Nazis. Yet, as biologists and geneticists have conclusively shown, there is only one human race, with the degree of genetic difference among whites the same as between whites and blacks, or between any so-called "racial group." When scholars use "race" as a useful category of historical inquiry they are not suggesting that white people and black people, for instance, belong to different species. Instead they are concerned with the sociological meanings of race, whereby racial terms only have meaning because individuals or groups either attribute a significance to the differences between themselves and others, or impose such a significance on others. The bald fact that a person has designated "white," "black," or any other type of skin "color" is not what is important: it is the way that person was treated *because* of the perceived color of their skin, whether privileged or denigrated, and the mechanisms informing the social construction of color in a given historical context, that is significant. As Barbara Fields has shown us, the social interpretation of "race" has been of critical significance throughout American history because of the constant interaction among different types of people.[1] "Race," and how Americans of various sorts understood it, particularly in relation to slavery, is the subject of this essay.

EARLY CONSTRUCTIONS OF RACE

....

As historians of European expansionism have shown, race was not always synonymous with skin color. In the early modern period, when light-skinned Europeans started to come into regular contact with dark-skinned sub-Saharan Africans, they placed just as much significance on dress, religion, customs, language, and degree of civilization as they did on skin color.[2] Moreover, Mark Smith has recently argued that race was not only determined visually but could also be sensed by noses, ears, fingers, and even tongues.[3] Clearly there were many different ways for Europeans to mark the differences between themselves and the new peoples they encountered. Race in this early period was not only about more than physical differences, it was also a flexible and adaptable identity. It was possible for non-whites to effectively "become white" by adopting Christianity, and by dressing or living like Europeans. English trader Bartholomew Stibbs, visiting the Gambia River in 1723, remarked, without apparent irony, that the local inhabitants were "as Black as Coal; tho' here, thro' Custom, (being Christians) they account themselves White Men."[4] It was equally possible for whites to "go native" by adopting African lifestyles. In the fifteenth and sixteenth centuries, skin color was often perceived to be a simple result of the degree of exposure to the sun. White people who lived in tropical climates became darker skinned, seemingly affirming this idea, though rather more puzzling was the fact that Africans who traveled to Europe remained "black."

The etymology of the word "race" helps to demonstrate its flexible usage. Entering the English language in the sixteenth century from the medieval Italian word "razza" (meaning "group"), "race" was simply a method of classifying any number of things—human, animal, or plant—into groups with ostensibly shared characteristics. Each European nation might therefore be termed a specific "race": Frenchmen, Italians, Germans, Englishmen; but sometimes there were additional races within a nation, such as Basques in Spain, or Bretons in France. None of these "races" was classified according to physiognomy but more often, as Denis Hay and more recently Michael Adas have argued, on custom, history, language and, most importantly, religion.[5] The encounter with sub-Saharan Africans, from the mid-fifteenth century onwards, encouraged Europeans to conceive themselves as part of a broader grouping of white people, in contrast to the black-skinned Africans. Europeans inevitably made comparisons between themselves and Africans, and invariably found Africans inferior and less civilized.

But, if "race" was a construct, why did Europeans begin to "invent" it and, subsequently, denigrate "black" Africans? One answer is that all European elites at the time were obsessed with hierarchy and its preservation, believing that it denoted order in contrast to chaos.[6] Peasants and serfs were meant to pay due homage to their local lords who in their turn were part of a detailed hierarchy of earls, counts, and dukes. Alongside this temporal hierarchy was a spiritual one of people, priests, bishops, archbishops, Pope, and ultimately God. It was understood to be a natural part of life that some were "better" while others were "lesser" and the chances of moving from the lower order to the higher ranks were slim indeed. While status differences were often obvious, many European states passed sumptuary laws regulating the dress of the lower orders to prevent those of a lower social status passing themselves off as members of the elite. Such classificatory impulses, argue Alden T. Vaughan and Virginia Mason Vaughan, were easily imported in the context of European encounters with Africans.[7] Some of the differences noted were physical, especially the hair, nose, lips, and sexual organs, but as often Europeans commented on the strange languages, lack of clothing, and "barbaric" customs of African peoples.

Attitudes such as these were not spontaneous but emerged from a long tradition of negative attitudes towards black-skinned peoples, dating back several centuries before Europeans began to explore the world. The Arab overlords of North Africa generally believed that sub-Saharan darker-skinned peoples were culturally and intellectually inferior, mocking their "wisdom, ingenuity, religion, justice and regular government," and they imported those attitudes with the conquest of most of Spain in the eighth century.[8] During the long Reconquista of the Iberian Peninsula by the Christian kings of Castile and Aragon these negative stereotypes crossed over the cultural divide between Muslim and Christian. Winthrop Jordan was perfectly correct to point out the negative connotations of the word "black" in early modern English, and other tongues, and that people with black skin in effect suffered by association because of it, but the roots of European racism went even deeper than that.[9] There is a clear lineage of negative racial imagery from Arabic to Hispanic to English thought. Arabs enslaved people from many different parts of the world, but tended to treat those with the blackest skin unsparingly, assigning them the most menial positions. Furthermore, it was Arabs who first arrived at the concept of the biblical curse as an explanation for the skin color of blacks. Since it was generally accepted that all humanity stemmed from a common root, namely Noah and his three sons as the only men to survive the flood, then the curse issued by Noah on his son Ham (or more specifically on Ham's son Canaan) (Genesis 9: 21–7), that he should be the "servant of servants" for gazing upon his father's nakedness, became of central importance. Yet, as Benjamin Braude has shown, there was nothing in the Bible that said Canaan was black. In medieval Europe all the descendants of Noah were portrayed as white since the lineage of Noah's sons was somewhat confused; indeed Ham's descendants were often believed to have populated Asia rather than Africa. During the early modern period, however, the Arab version that Canaan's descendants had been "marked" as servants by altered skin color became widespread in Europe as well.[10] This belief fitted in neatly with preexisting negative attitudes towards black people and helped to confirm the idea that black skin was a mark of subordinate and inferior status.

Yet there were also those who commented positively on the black peoples during the seventeenth century: John Ogilby, visiting Africa, commented that "The Natives are very black; but the Features of their faces, and their excellent Teeth, being white as Ivory, make up together an handsom Ayre, and taking comeliness of a new Beauty," while Richard Ligon described a black woman in Barbados "of the greatest beautie" as "excellently shap't, well favour'd, full-eye'd, and admirably grac't."[11] Elite European attitudes towards Africans were therefore mixed, even plastic. They observed mainly with interest, occasionally with disgust, the major differences between whites (Christian, civilized, technologically advanced) and blacks (heathen, uncivilized, technologically backward) and it seems clear that an internal hierarchy of superiority and inferiority was part of the response of whites during these encounters. Yet Europeans were not so foolish as to try to treat all Africans the same, whatever they might have believed about their own elevated status, since they were acutely conscious that without the goodwill of local chiefs and princes their ships would have found trade goods as well as basic supplies hard to come by. Pragmatism, if nothing else, required that early modern Europeans responded to Africans on a case-by-case basis.

THE INTRODUCTION OF SLAVERY
TO THE AMERICAS

Quite how Africans came to be enslaved in America is something that has taxed some of the greatest historians of slavery since a general belief in negative stereotypes did not automatically equate to enslavement. As James Sweet has shown, Iberians had a reasonably lengthy history of enslaving Muslim prisoners of war long before 1492, and records indicate many thousands of slaves were brought to Europe in the second half of the fifteenth century.[12] While the enslavement of prisoners of war needed no justification, the expansion of the slave trade to include those purchased in Africa required, and received, papal sanction on the basis that these "pagans" would be brought into the "Christian family." The vast majority of these slaves had darker skins than those enslaving them, and again this helped to justify and reinforce early modern notions about the suitability of black people for slavery. Having said that, according to Winthrop Jordan, Europeans did not set out in the fifteenth century to explore the world with the express intention of subjugating more than ten million Africans; they were far more interested in securing trade routes to Asia that promised real wealth. After the somewhat accidental European discovery of America (Columbus was seeking China and Japan, and indeed never believed that he had been anywhere but Asia) and the gradual conquest of the larger Caribbean islands and parts of mainland Central and South America, the demand for new labor to clear forests and foster productive land increased dramatically. Since voluntary waged labor was insufficient, the Spanish and Portuguese turned to a type of involuntary labor with which they were familiar: slavery. The various problems associated with the most obvious and convenient source of involuntary labor, Native Americans, led Europeans to seek an alternative. Africans proved more resistant than whites to certain tropical illnesses common to New World plantations. Furthermore, whereas Indian slaves found it relatively easy to escape and blend back into their own tribes, the skin color of blacks marked them readily as slaves and it was far more straightforward for whites to exercise tighter control over them. The fact that slavery existed within Africa, and that African princes were willing to deal in slaves, made the shift towards African slavery in America even easier.[13]

Historians have debated the association between racial attitudes and the introduction of slavery in the Americas, without coming to any clear consensus. Eric Williams first made the case for the primacy of an economic over a racial explanation for slavery in his widely read *Capitalism and Slavery* (1944). Williams's specific focus was the West Indies, but a few years after *Capitalism and Slavery* appeared Oscar and Mary Handlin arrived at a broadly similar conclusion for the infant Chesapeake colonies: that racial discrimination came after not before slavery.[14] Carl Degler, on the other hand, stressed the marginalization and discrimination experienced by blacks in Virginia from the earliest colonial period, evidence he argued of long-standing and preexisting racial prejudices. Degler was later supported by the work of Winthrop Jordan and Alden T. Vaughan.[15] Since the 1970s the economic argument has returned to favor, with Russell Menard pointing out dwindling supply of white servants in the later seventeenth century; Edmund Morgan suggesting that planters only plumped for slavery when the demography of the Chesapeake meant that it made economic sense; and Breen and Innes documenting the vast array of interracial cooperation between white servants and black slaves which tends to undermine the theory that all migrants to Virginia arrived with a fully formed racial consciousness.[16]

It is hard to chart a course between these differing interpretations, and perhaps the evidence simply does not exist to permit historians to make a definitive judgment, but certainly many white settlers did arrive in the Americas with an evolving and ever clearer sense of their own superiority over other people. Interracial cooperation, as outlined by Breen and Innes, does not necessarily mean that lower-class whites lacked any racial sensibility, only that they were capable of prioritizing alliances of convenience when it suited them. English settlers often accepted negative stereotypes about Africans at face value, most especially that they were incapable of the higher reasoning of Europeans, that they acted more emotionally, and that their putatively limited mental capacity coupled with their physical prowess suited them for directed manual labor. Significantly in North

America early European attitudes towards Native Americans were very different. Commentators and travelers praised the "noble" and "aristocratic" bearing of Native Americans, and especially their upright and open stance. As Karen Kupperman has recently argued, native peoples were perceived as heathens yet their lighter skin persuaded many that Indians were in fact born white, and that their skin darkened as adults because of exposure to the sun and tattooing. Indians could only be incorporated into the theory of monogenesis by taking on the mantle of one of the lost tribes of Israel, and as such Europeans sometimes believed that Indians were similar to their own ancestors, living in harmony with nature in an almost Edenic existence. In the early seventeenth century these attitudes protected Native Americans from widespread enslavement in North America, though the comparative military and political strength of native tribes compared to Europeans also made this a highly pragmatic decision.[17] Attitudes towards Native Americans would of course change, particularly after the massacre of a quarter of the white population in Virginia in 1622, and the uprising which whites termed King Philip's War in New England in 1675, but the use of Native Americans as forced labor never reached the scale in North America that it did in Central and South America.[18]

White people's negative racial attitudes were not the only factor that led to the enslavement of millions of Africans in America. Even Degler and Jordan tend to accept that without a pressing economic need it is extremely doubtful that many Africans would have been imported into America. For all the talk about rescuing Africans from heathenism, or cannibalism, enslavement was never altruistic. Instead, it was principally economic and, in the sixteenth and seventeenth centuries, economic imperatives combined neatly with racial prejudice to create a climate where the enslavement of Africans was a perfectly logical decision. Winthrop Jordan has described the development of slavery in English America as an "unthinking decision" in the sense that no one really thought about it very much at all—the English just imitated the systems that had already been put in place by the Spanish and the Portuguese.[19] It is certainly true that the English lacked the long experience of slavery possessed by the Spanish and the Portuguese, and indeed the legal systems to manage a large body of enslaved workers. At least some of the first Africans imported into North America ended up as free landowners, suggesting that there were certain similarities between the status of black workers and white indentured servants. The labor of both sets of workers could be traded, and neither were free to chose whom they worked for. Gradually however, a number of statutes began to appear in Virginia and Maryland regulating gun ownership and ordaining punishments for crimes which marked black workers as different from their white counterparts whose servitude, providing they lived, would eventually come to an end. By c.1660 status was beginning to be synonymous with skin color.

As Africans began to be imported into the Americas in large numbers it became necessary to clearly define who was and, therefore, who was not a slave. The first comprehensive slave code, passed in Virginia in 1705, was a little vague on the subject of race, establishing only that all non-Christian "servants" imported into the colony would be considered slaves "and as such be here bought and sold." Only later in the eighteenth century was it thought necessary to spell out that "Negroes" would "remain for ever hereafter absolute slaves, and shall follow the condition of the mother."[20] In the seventeenth century some argued that it was the Christian faith of whites which exempted them from slavery in the Americas, but this definition quickly slipped out of fashion from fears that Christianized blacks would be able to claim their freedom. By the mid-seventeenth century white skin alone was sufficient to prevent enslavement. Once this principle became established in Spanish and Portuguese territory, where missionaries expended considerable efforts converting the enslaved, it was the template followed by future colonial powers such as the English. With the status and label of "slave" came additional discrimination, including a loss of civil rights and restrictions on sexual relationships with those from a different status group. As slavery and black skin became synonymous the importance of skin and bodily differences grew.

Racial categories, which had remained somewhat flexible during the sixteenth and seventeenth centuries, now became more rigid. Before 1700 it was possible for at least some blacks in the Americas to earn their freedom perhaps by purchase or via manumission, or even to arrive as a free settler, and subsequently own property, vote, and take a full part in civil society. In the eighteenth century, however, as what one historian has described as a "cultural consensus" emerged, racial attitudes hardened, and even free blacks found that their lives were becoming more difficult.[21] New slave codes in the colonies established that all non-whites were to be considered slaves, unless they were able to prove otherwise. Manumission continued to be relatively straightforward, either by deed or by will, even if it was not as widespread in North America as it was in Latin America, and the free black population continued to grow slowly despite the erosion of their civil rights. The changes in racial attitudes can be blamed on enlightenment thinking, and historians such as William Stanton firmly link the emergence of a coherent racial ideology with a new scientific approach to the world.[22] Naturalists began to explore the globe in the eighteenth century, classifying an immense amount of flora and fauna, and naturally they turned their attention to the various "types" of people found around the world. In particular they tried to measure the physical differences between populations, including head size (which they took to indicate intelligence), angle of face (the upright "flat" faces of Europeans being thought typical of those with high intelligence), and size of breasts (the large breasts of African women were interpreted as a sign of their high fertility). Studies by Johann Frederick Blumenbach and Charles White confirmed to Europeans that the physical differences between themselves and non-whites were simply signs of their own superiority and the inferiority of others.[23] Some even began to question whether it was fair to classify Africans as fully human. Edward Long's widely read *History of Jamaica* (1774), for example, suggested that subhuman blacks were "represented by all authors as the vilest of the human kind, to which they have little more pretension of resemblance than what arises from their exterior form." By stressing that black people should be "distinguished from the rest of mankind" Long arrived at a novel conclusion that blacks were "a different species of the same genus" situated somewhere between fully human (whites) and the great apes of Africa.[24] Of course, if black slaves in the Americas were less-than-human "others" it became even easier to justify their harsh treatment. Contemporary with this new scientific thinking was the growth of a philosophy that moved away from monogenesis towards polygenesis, theorizing that God had actually made several different creations. Adam and the biblical creation was the last, and hence most perfect, creation, and less-perfect pre-Adamites populated east Asia, sub-Saharan Africa, and the Americas.[25]

In North America Samuel Stanhope Smith made a link between the physical differences between whites and blacks and their innate characters. He believed that the degraded, ignorant, and barbarous lives of native Africans were a direct cause of their various physical "deformities" whereas the enlightened, graceful, and refined lives of whites were reflected in their upright bearing. In Smith's view blacks could never elevate themselves to the same level as whites, though they could make progress, and he cited the physical improvements of creole slaves born in America as proof.[26] Another good example of these changing racial attitudes is in Thomas Jefferson's *Notes on the State of Virginia*, published in 1787. Jefferson was clearly an educated and intelligent man who considered himself qualified, as a slave owner himself, to describe the attributes of Africans in America. For Jefferson the physical and behavioral differences between black and white were " fixed in nature." Blacks were not only born with black skin, they also "seem to require less sleep" and were "more ardent after their female: but love seems with them to be more an eager desire, than a tender delicate mixture of sentiment and sensation." Yet despite these clearly racialized sentiments, Jefferson conducted a long-term sexual relationship with one of his own mulatto slaves, Sally Hemings, and fathered several children with her.[27] This is evidence not just of Jefferson's own hypocrisy but also of the complex nature of race relations in the Americas. White men were seemingly repelled and attracted in equal measure by non-white women, frequently decrying their supposedly sexualized natures while being unable to resist their allures, especially when compared with the uptight morality that was imposed on white women. The frequent sexual relationships between white men and non-white women, often coerced but not always so, resulted in a large mixed-race mulatto population. In Latin America this population was particularly important since the small numbers of white women meant that significant numbers of white men, particularly from the lower classes, took non-white women as wives.[28] There was no such demographic necessity in North America where interracial marriage was often illegal. Even in places like South Carolina, where it was not banned by statute, social conventions meant that few white men actually married non-white women, though some, like Jefferson, conducted long-term relationships.

THE "MIXED-RACE" PROBLEM

The mulatto population in the Americas posed an interesting dilemma: while they were mainly enslaved because their mothers were enslaved, their white fathers often bequeathed them a lighter skin tone. Were they as inferior as other slaves, or elevated intellectually and morally because of their white blood? Most whites believed mulattos the most intelligent type of slave, in effect crediting white blood with the ability to improve the mind and morals of an individual. When a mulatto woman had mixed-race children herself, the offspring was sometimes able to pass as white, and some notable escapees from slavery used their lighter skin to their advantage in this manner. One of the children of Sally Hemings and Thomas Jefferson (with three white grandparents) was white enough to be described as white by one of the enumerators of the federal census in 1830, reinforcing the importance of personal perception in the description of race. Some master-fathers freed their mixed-race offspring, perhaps believing that their improved capacities no longer suited them for enslavement, but also sometimes out of simple love and desire to help their own children. Certainly mulattos were a disproportionate part of the free black population in the Americas.

While there is some evidence that mulatto slaves received preferential treatment from masters and mistresses, perhaps because of their perceived greater intelligence, and were more likely to be given positions of responsibility in the household or the plantation than darker-skinned slaves, it is not necessarily the case that the rest of the enslaved population accorded mulattos any special status. John Blassingame has suggested that mulattos could be treated with suspicion by other slaves, believing them to be too close to the whites and therefore untrustworthy. Their lighter skin could therefore act against them, excluding them from profiting from covert acts of resistance, such as stealing extra food or clothing, which were common on the plantations. At the very least mulattos would have to earn the trust of other slaves over a lengthy period of time. According to Blassingame true status among slaves was accorded to religious leaders, those with medical and magical skills, and the keepers of folklore, and not to those who whites believed were of higher status such as domestic slaves and drivers.[29]

The existence of mulattos led some states to at least attempt some definition of how white you needed to be in order to qualify as white. A 1705 Virginia statute specified that those with one black great-grandparent were black, even though they might be seven-eighths white, though this rule was redefined after the revolution to allow those with more than 75 percent white ancestry to claim whiteness.[30] Elsewhere in North America the definition of just how much black ancestry was required to make someone black was rarely debated. In many states by the early nineteenth century a single proven black ancestor was sufficient to make you black—the so-called "one-drop" rule—but of course, application of the one-drop rule required a detailed knowledge of the ancestry of every individual, something that was entirely impractical for communities where internal mobility was high. An attempt in Virginia to introduce a form of "one-drop rule" in the 1850s floundered mainly because it was totally unenforceable. Therefore, despite what statute law may have stipulated in any particular location, determining the race of any individual person was often a matter of highly subjective perception. If someone claimed to be white, looked white, spoke like a white person, smelled like a white person (or perhaps more accurately didn't have the peculiar "stink" that whites believed was a defining characteristic of black people), acted like a white person, and, significantly, had the wealth of a white person, then they were often treated by others as white, regardless of their biological ancestry.[31] This was true in Central and South America as well as in North America. Conversely, if someone was known to be of black ancestry they would be treated as black by being denied various rights granted to whites, regardless of their actual skin color. In a revealing example in mid-1830s Virginia a self-styled free black, William Hyden, was taken up as a runaway slave and lacking the correct documentation was put up for public auction when no one claimed him. His extremely light skin saved him from enslavement since no one would buy him at any price—he was "too white," and "so bright that he might easily escape from slavery." When he escaped from jail this particular free black was able to evade capture by successfully passing as a white man.[32]

In 1835 South Carolina judge William Harper confirmed that perception was crucial in determining racial status and that skin color was only part of what made someone white: "We cannot say what admixture of negro blood will make a colored person. The condition of the individual is not to be determined solely by distinct and visible mixture of negro blood, but by reputation, by his reception into society, and his having commonly exercised the privileges of a white man . . . it may be well and proper, that a man of worth, honesty, industry, and respectability, should have the rank of a white man, while a vagabond of the same degree of blood should be confined to the inferior caste. It is hardly necessary to say that a slave cannot be a white man."[33] This last sentence helps to explain why no Virginian would buy William Hyden even though the state believed him to be a slave.

Free mulattos such as William Hyden occupied a confusing middle ground between whites and blacks. In the seventeenth and early eighteenth centuries the relatively small number of free mulattos were relatively easy for whites to ignore but after the American Revolution thousands of mulattos were freed, especially in the Upper South, and a prominent free black community was formed in Baltimore.[34] Free mulattos posed a dilemma for elite whites. On the one hand their non-white skin color resulted in a denial of a number of civil rights, including often the right to vote, testify against whites in court, or engage in certain occupations. Most were required to have white guardians who would act on their behalf. On the other hand, their free status elevated them significantly above the enslaved population. They could live where they liked, worship freely, marry whom they chose, and raise their children without the risk of them being sold away to suit the financial needs of a master. Historians have debated how far mulattos identified themselves with other freemen, and how far with non-whites. In the Caribbean and Latin America, in places like Jamaica, Haiti, and Suriname, where the number of "free coloreds" could outnumber free whites and the enslaved constituted 80 percent of the population throughout the eighteenth century, there was often a conscious effort made by colonial administrations to make allies of elite non-whites, though these efforts often did not filter down to the poorer free blacks. Elsewhere, in Curaçao and Puerto Rico for instance, a more even division between slaves, free blacks, and whites meant such an alliance of convenience did not occur.[35] Nowhere in the Americas did free mulattos consistently and systematically identify themselves with free blacks or with slaves and it seems that mulattos' conception of their own social position depended on their own economic circumstances. Those who owned property, ran businesses, and owned slaves considered themselves on a par with white freemen and could be accepted by white society precisely because they behaved like white people.[36] They created parallel community institutions to those of whites, such as charitable and fraternal societies and, where permitted, schools. Eligibility for charitable assistance was measured partly by status—only free people were able to apply—but also crucially by color. Mulattos were eligible, whereas those considered "black" were not. The Brown Fellowship Society in Charleston (founded 1790) restricted membership to free mulattos and in response free blacks in Charleston founded their own charitable society, the Free Dark Men of Color (1791), thus helping to perpetuate this unusual example of discrimination among non-whites.[37]

THE PROBLEM OF POOR WHITES

Race, as a category of difference in the Americas, did not exist in a vacuum, rather it interacted with class and gender to create very complex and nuanced status gradations within societies. "Whiteness" was of course just as much a social construct as "blackness" but being white was not an automatic passport to wealth and status. Throughout the Americas there were large numbers of whites who lacked property and money, and who were an obvious embarrassment to those who believed that white skin made an individual inherently better than those without it. White skin was meant to endow those fortunate enough to possess it with greater intelligence, capacity for self-improvement, and entrepreneurial spirit. Yet in every slaveholding society there were whites who worked in menial jobs, who lived from hand to mouth, raising families in cramped and squalid housing, who begged on the streets, and who relied on state handouts. They were hardly shining examples of the "master race." Yet even within this large class of non-slaveholding whites there were gradations. Some were perfectly respectable shopkeepers, farmers, and artisans to whom the expense and burden of owning slaves outweighed any potential benefit. It was not the lack of slaves that made you "poor," or indeed a general lack of wealth either. The widow who worked all hours of the day to support her children could be represented as a victim of circumstances, whose thrifty ways were evidence of her true character. Ultimately, therefore, "poor white" was a sociological status rather than a simple economic one. A "poor white" was one who did not behave as white people should, either by fraternizing with non-whites, or failing to improve and elevate themselves as white people were supposed to and as the status of "white" demanded.

Poor whites who interacted with non-whites posed a particular threat to the racial hierarchies of slave societies. Whites who were prepared to deal with non-whites on an almost equal basis, by frequenting the same bars, attending the same churches, trading, and even working alongside them, seemed to be suggesting that race did nothing to differentiate between peoples. Friendships could traverse racial boundaries, and there was more than one white person who assisted in the escape of a slave by writing a pass, or providing a safe haven. Plantation slaves were perfectly well aware of the existence of poor whites throughout the South, and often viewed them as idle and worthless individuals whose presence confirmed to them that whiteness per se did not, contrary to slaveholders' claims, convey any inherent privileges.[38]

From the mid-1830s onwards elite whites in the American South made stronger efforts to draw a clear distinction between whites and blacks. Stung by abolitionists, southerners marshaled the pro-slavery defense which, among other things, argued strongly that blacks were inherently inferior to whites. In an 1833 pamphlet Richard Colfax argued that the shape of black people's heads was sufficient proof of their intellectual weakness, and hence "his want of capability to receive a complicated education renders it improper and impolitic, that he should be allowed the privileges of citizenship in an enlightened country."[39] A few years later Alabama physician Josiah Nott went further, claiming "that the human race is descended from several or many original pairs . . . there is not at present a single unmixed race on the face of the earth."[40] Nott repeated his argument, that whites and blacks were essentially different species, in a number of influential publications. Although this point had been made by Edward Long seventy years previously, Nott attempted to legitimize his conclusions that blacks were inherently inferior by pseudo-science: "The brain of the Negro . . . is, according to the positive measurements, smaller than the Caucasian by a full tenth; and this deficiency exists particularly in the anterior portion of the brain, which is known to be the seat of the higher faculties."[41] Interbreeding produced mulattos who he believed were "certainly more intelligent than the Negro, [but] less so than the white," however Nott claimed that he had never seen a southern mulatto "so fair that I could not instantaneously trace the Negro type in complexion and feature." After all, he commented tellingly, "it is a hard matter to wash out blood."[42]

Elsewhere in the Americas the racial defense of slavery was often not so well articulated, but we should be careful not to infer from this that racial discrimination in the Caribbean and Latin America was less than in North America. While mulattos could sometimes rise to a semi-elite status they were still clearly not of "true" Spanish or Portuguese blood, and were denied important positions in two key institutions: the Church and the army. Furthermore, the systems of slavery enforced in Brazil, Suriname, and Haiti were among the most brutal ever devised, and many masters continued to make the economic calculation that it was easier to work their slaves to death, and then purchase more than to ease workloads and aim to grow the slave population by natural increase. Slavery in Latin America and the Caribbean was still a harsh system of racialized labor exploitation.[43]

By the 1850s in the United States it was no longer sufficient to state that whites were free while blacks were not.[44] There were too many whites enduring living conditions that were worse than those of many slaves, while there were prosperous free blacks who clearly belied the myth of innate racial superiority. The differences between whites and blacks needed to be redefined, and it was to this end that several legal changes were implemented in the American South. Poor whites who traded with slaves were punished more harshly, and where legal sanctions did not work, extra-legal vigilante actions, such as burning down the store of someone who traded stolen goods in return for alcohol, were sometimes used.[45] Those in charge of evangelical churches that were popular amongst non-whites first constructed balconies to physically separate white and black worshipers, then set aside certain times for non-whites to hold their services, and finally built entirely separate buildings for white and non-white congregations.[46] Elite whites also went to increased lengths to persuade poor whites not to overlook racial differences, and emphasized the racial privileges that white people had. Only white people, for instance, had access to publicly funded systems of education (which expanded rapidly in the South during the 1850s), and they also received a disproportionate share of public welfare and a virtual monopoly of private charity.[47]

Despite these changes, racial barriers continued to have something of a plastic quality in slave societies. Strictly policing racial boundaries required a considerable investment of time, effort, and money. Interaction which occurred behind closed doors, and not overtly, was often ignored as posing little threat to the social order. Furthermore, the existence of the legal institution of slavery provided all whites with a comfort blanket of superiority, even if the reality was quite different. No matter how miserable their own lives, poor whites could always tell themselves that at least they were free. Racial barriers became far more important to poor whites once slavery no longer existed to mark a clear distinction between black and white. Several million newly freed people after 1865 in the United States found that their new status was sometimes freedom in name only, and that lynching became more common as a terror tactic to instill fear into the black population.[48]

RACE AND NATIVE AMERICANS

Although the bulk of the existing historiography on race in the Americas concentrates on slavery and especially white attitudes towards Africans and African-Americans and black responses to enslavement, it should not be forgotten that there was a third distinct racial group in the Americans—indigenous people. Interaction between imported Africans, European migrants, and indigenous tribes occurred throughout the Americas, but it was not uniform. While in nearly all areas Native American populations declined rapidly due to disease, and were supplanted by Africans and Europeans, Native Americans did not treat all these newcomers the same. In Latin America, where Native Americans were enslaved in significant numbers, Indians often found common cause with the enslaved Africans who shared their marginal status, and the large maroon communities created in Brazil, Colombia, and Suriname were populated by fugitive slaves from both racial groups. Native tribes in Amazonia which had not been enslaved were also generally willing to assist fugitive slaves, by providing either shelter or food.[49] In general this sort of collusion amongst non-whites did not occur in North America. Native Americans were not widely enslaved in North America, except in early South Carolina, and were as likely to kill runaway slaves who entered their territory as help them. Part of the reason for the abandonment of Native American slavery in South Carolina was the fear that enslaved Indians might form common cause with imported African slaves and show them secret paths leading to safe havens. In order to limit the interaction between Indians and African slaves eighteenth-century whites encouraged the "natural Dislike and Antipathy" that already seemed to exist between their African slaves and Native American tribes. Certainly in North Carolina it was believed that far more slaves would flee into the woods and swamps "were they not so much afraid of the Indians, who have such a natural aversion to the Blacks, that they commonly shoot them when ever they find them in the Woods or solitary parts of the country." South Carolina resident George Milligan Johnston commented matter-of-factly that "it can never be in our Interest to extirpate them [Native Americans], or to force them from their lands; their Ground would soon be taken up by runaway Negroes from our settlements, whose Numbers would daily increase, and quickly become more formidable Enemies than Indians can ever be, as they speak our Language, and would never be at a Loss for Intelligence."[50] Using Indians as slave catchers was deemed a particularly effective way to "strike terrour" into the slave population since first Native Americans were actually very good at finding runaway slaves who had secreted themselves in swamps and woods, and secondly they were often given license to kill and mutilate the bodies of those they found.[51] Most Native Americans believed that as free sovereign peoples they were the equals of whites, and for much of the eighteenth century powerful tribes were treated as such by colonial governments who went to considerable lengths to avoid conflicts. Moreover, Native Americans were perfectly aware of the degraded status of black people in white eyes, and so it is not surprising that some tribes such as the Cherokee, Choctaw, and Chickasaw also accepted the principle of racial slavery and were willing to purchase and trade in black slaves just as whites did. Indeed, owning slaves was one way that tribes tried to demonstrate how "white" they were, though ultimately this did not prevent their forced migration west during the 1830s.[52]

A singular example in North America of cooperation between Native Americans and imported Africans occurred in Florida. Florida had a long history of being a safe haven for runaway slaves from South Carolina and Georgia and, for a time, it was official Spanish policy to welcome runaways since it strengthened the under-populated colony while weakening its northern neighbors. The effective disinte-gration of Spanish power in Florida in the early nineteenth century allowed an alliance to grow between the large Seminole tribe in northern Florida and escaped slaves from United States territory. The United States army fought three wars with the Seminoles and their black allies between 1815 and 1858, never entirely defeating them. Although often termed "black Seminoles" the relationship between the Seminoles and their black recruits was complex. Most blacks lived in their own villages, under their own government, and paid a form of tribute to Seminole chiefs in return for nominal protection. The creole heritage of most blacks, which meant that most spoke at least some English, and perhaps shared a common belief system based loosely on Christianity, set them apart from the Seminoles who generally remained unacculturated. Escaped slaves sometimes acted as translators and inter-mediaries between Seminole chiefs and white authorities, but they also took the lead in organizing military matters, knowing that military defeat would result in re-enslavement. The "black Seminoles" were regarded by American commanders as the more dangerous and effective enemy, inflicting several defeats on American troops.[53]

FUTURE RESEARCH

Our understanding of the relationships between Native Americans and African Americans remains somewhat limited. Apart from the Seminoles there is surpris-ingly little scholarly work on Native American racial thought, and even less on

African-American racial attitudes towards Indians. Far more attention needs to be paid to the variations caused by geography and chronology. How were Native American racial attitudes altered by removal in the 1830s, for instance? Did they finally begin to appreciate that enslaved blacks might be useful allies against white aggression, or did they continue to cling to the hope that if they became sufficiently Americanized they might be treated as "white"? An additional area where there is considerable scope for new and innovative research is on "whiteness" more generally in the Americas. David Roediger published his groundbreaking *The Wages of Whiteness* back in 1991 but only part of that book was on the colonial and antebellum eras, and very little of it dealt with race consciousness and race making in slave societies. What did it really mean to be white in societies based on racial slavery? This question demands serious thought: was "whiteness" principally a negative construct, based on *not* having the skin tone, speech patterns, smell, or behavior of non-whites? Or was being "white" mainly about being "superior" to those considered "inferior"? How important was class and/or gender in influencing how whites thought about themselves? Research in the past decade, my own included, has tended to suggest that whiteness was not as important as one might think, especially in the colonial and early national eras. Examples exist of southern courts acquitting black men accused of raping poor white women; of whites working alongside free blacks or hired slaves without complaint; of interracial couples being tolerated by the community; and of common cause being made by the poor regardless of race against the white elite.[54] But was this the case throughout the history of slavery in the Americas? We know far more now about the importance of race in slave societies in the Americas that we did a generation ago, yet we still could learn far more about how contemporaries understood whiteness in different parts of the South, away from the older East Coast states, as well as elsewhere in the Americas, and how that understanding developed and evolved over time. Moreover there is plenty of serious research that needs to be done to delve deeper into how all types of Americans conceived of other racial groups, as well as how they saw themselves. Indeed is it worth considering whether the term "race" is still helpful. Does our use of the concept help to reinscribe "race" into analysis? If so, are we complicit in perpetuating what is, after all, a social construction?[55] I hope that a new generation of young scholars will continue to explore some of these themes and the key importance of race in slavery.

NOTES

1. Barbara J. Fields, "Ideology and Race in American History," in J. Morgan Kousser and James M. McPherson (eds.), *Region, Race and Reconstruction: Essays in Honor of C. Vann Woodward* (New York, 1982), 143–77; and Barbara J. Fields, "Slavery, Race and Ideology in the United States of America," *New Left Review*, 181 (May–June 1990): 95–118.

2. See for example Roxann Wheeler, *The Complexion of Race: Categories of Difference in Eighteenth-Century British Culture* (Philadelphia, 2000).

3. Mark Smith, *How Race is Made* (Chapel Hill, NC, 2006).

4. "Journal of a Voyage up the Gambia," printed in Francis Moore, *Travels into the Inland Parts of Africa* (London, 1738), 243.

5. Alden T. Vaughan and Virginia Mason Vaughan, "Before Othello: Elizabethan Representations of Sub-Saharan Africans," *William and Mary Quarterly*, 3rd ser., 54 (1) (January 1997): 19–44; Denis Hay, *Europe: The Emergence of an Idea* (Edinburgh, 1957); Michael Adas, *Machines as the Measure of Man: Science, Technology, and Ideologies of Western Dominance* (Ithaca, NY, 1989).

6. See R. H. Tawney, "The Rise of the Gentry, 1558–1640," *Economic History Review*, 11 (1) (1941): 1–38; and J. H. Hexter, "The English Aristocracy, its Crises, and the English Revolution, 1558–1660," *Journal of British Studies*, 8 (1) (November 1968): 22–78. On the English elite's reaction to the mobility of the lower orders, see Paul Slack, "Vagrants and Vagrancy in England, 1598–1664," *English Historical Review*, 27 (1974): 360–79.

7. See the examples cited in Vaughan and Vaughan, "Before Othello," 24.

8. James H. Sweet, "The Iberian Roots of American Racist Thought," *William and Mary Quarterly*, 3rd ser., 54 (1) (January 1997): 146.

9. Winthrop Jordan, *White over Black: American Attitudes towards the Negro 1550–1812* (Chapel Hill, NC, 1968).

10. Benjamin Braude, "The Sons of Noah and the Construction of Ethnic and Geographical Identities in the Medieval and Early Modern Periods," *William and Mary Quarterly*, 3rd ser., 54 (January 1997): 103–42.

11. John Ogilby, *Africa, being an Accurate Description of the Regions* (London, 1670), 318; Richard Ligon, *A True and Exact History of the Island of Barbadoes* (London, 1657), 12.

12. Sweet, "The Iberian Roots of American Racist Thought."

13. Historians have hotly debated the impact of the slave trade on Africa, with some such as J. D. Fage, in *A History of Africa* (London, 1978), suggesting that the money injected into African economies balanced the population loss. Others such as Nathan Nunn, "The Long-Term Effects of Africa's Slave Trades," *Quarterly Journal of Economics*, 123 (1) (February 2008): 139–76, argue that a negative relationship exists between societies heavily involved in the slave trade and subsequent economic growth. For the contours of the debate, see Joseph E. Inikori, "Ideology versus the Tyranny of Paradigm: Historians and the Impact of the Atlantic Slave Trade on African Societies," *African Economic History*, 22 (1994): 37–58.

14. Eric Williams, *Capitalism and Slavery* (Chapel Hill, NC, 1944). Oscar and Mary F. Handlin, "Origins of the Southern Labor System," *William and Mary Quarterly*, 3rd ser., 7 (2) (April 1950): 199–222.

15. Carl N. Degler, "Slavery and the Genesis of American Race Prejudice," *Comparative Studies in Society and History*, 2 (1) (October 1959): 49–66; Jordan, *White over Black*; Alden T. Vaughan "Blacks in Virginia: A Note on the First Decade," *William and Mary Quarterly*, 3rd ser., 29 (3) (July 1972): 469–78.

16. Russell Menard, "From Servants to Slaves: The Transformation of the Chesapeake Labor System," *Southern Studies*, 16 (1971): 355–90; Edmund Morgan, *American Slavery American Freedom: The Ordeal of Colonial Virginia* (New York, 1975); T. H. Breen and Stephen Innes, *"Myne Owne Ground": Race and Freedom on Virginia's Eastern Shore, 1640–1676* (New York, 1980).

17. Karen Ordahl Kupperman, "Presentment of Civility: English Reading of American Self-Presentation in the Early Years of Colonization," *William and Mary Quarterly*, 3rd ser., 54 (1) (January 1997): 193–228; Joyce E. Chpalin, "Natural Philosophy and an Early Racial Idiom in North America: Comparing English and Indian Bodies," *William and Mary Quarterly*, 3rd ser., 54 (1) (January 1997): 229–52. The only colony to enslave significant numbers of Indians was South Carolina, though most were shipped to the West Indies rather than being used in situ. After the Yamasee war in the early eighteenth century, South Carolinians turned away from enslaving Indians fearing that they might ally themselves with the French and the Spanish. See Alan Gallay, *The Indian Slave Trade: The Rise of the English Empire in the American South, 1670–1717* (New Haven, 2002), 345–9.

18. On the impact of the 1622 massacre see Alden T. Vaughan, " 'Expulsion of the Salvages': English Policy and the Virginia Massacre of 1622," *William and Mary Quarterly*, 3rd ser., 35 (1) (January 1978): 57–84; on changing white attitudes more generally, see Alden T. Vaughan, "From White Man to Redskin: Changing Anglo-American Perceptions of the American Indian," *American Historical Review*, 87 (4) (October 1982): 917–53. Also relevant are Gary B. Nash, "The Image of the Indian in the Southern Colonial Mind," *William and Mary Quarterly*, 3rd ser., 29 (2) (April 1972): 198–230; G. E. Thomas, "Puritans, Indians, and the Concept of Race," *New England Quarterly*, 48 (1) (March 1975): 3–27; William S. Simmons, "Cultural Bias in the New England Puritans' Perception of Indians," *William and Mary Quarterly*, 3rd ser., 38 (1) (January 1981): 56–72.

19. Winthrop Jordan, *The White Man's Burden: Historical Origins of Racism in the United States* (New York, 1974), 26–54.

20. An act concerning servants and slaves (1705), *A Collection of all the Acts of Assembly, now in Force, in the Colony of Virginia* (Williamsburg, Va., 1733), 219. An act for the better ordering and governing Negroes (1740), *Acts Passed by the General Assembly of South-Carolina, May 10, 1740–July 10, 1742* (Charleston, SC, 1742), 3. The South Carolina act was later adopted almost verbatim by Georgia, see An act for ordering and governing slaves (1770), Robert and George Watkins (comp.), *A Digest of the Laws of the State of Georgia* (Philadelphia, 1800), 163.

21. Wheeler, *The Complexion of Race*, 240.

22. William Stanton, *The Leopard's Spots: Scientific Attitudes toward Race in America, 1815–59* (Chicago, 1960).

23. Johann Frederick Blumenbach, *De generis humani varietate nativa* (On the Natural Varieties of Mankind) (Göttingen, 1776); Charles White, *An Account of the Regular Gradation in Man, and in Different Animals and Vegetables* (London, 1799). Londa Schiebinger, "The Anatomy of Difference: Race and Sex in Eighteenth-Century Science," *Eighteenth-Century Studies*, 23 (4) (1990): 387–405.

24. Edward Long, *The History of Jamaica. Or, General Survey of the Antient and Modern State of that Island: With Reflections on its Situation, Settlements, Inhabitants* (London, 1774), ii. 353–4, 356–78.

25. See Audrey Smedley, *Race in North America: Origin and Evolution of a Worldview* (Boulder, Colo., 1993); Emmanuel Chukwudi Eze (ed.), *Race and the Enlightenment: A Reader* (Cambridge, Mass., 1997); and Bruce Dain, *A Hideous Monster of the Mind: American Race Theory in the Early Republic* (Cambridge, Mass., 2002).

26. Samuel Stanhope Smith, *Essay on the Causes of the Variety of Complexion and Figure in the Human Species* (Philadelphia, 1787).

27. For an interesting statistics-based analysis that proves beyond a reasonable doubt that Jefferson was the father of Hemings's children, see Fraser D. Neiman, "Coincidence or Causal Connection? The Relationship between Thomas Jefferson's Visits to Monticello and Sally Hemings's Conceptions," *William and Mary Quarterly*, 3rd ser., 57 (1) (January 2000): 198–210.

28. See Verena Martinez-Alier, *Marriage, Class and Colour in Nineteenth-Century Cuba* (Ann Arbor, 1974).

29. John W. Blassingame, "Status and Social Structure in the Slave Community: Evidence from New Sources," in Harry P. Owens (ed.), *Perspectives and Irony in American Slavery* (Jackson, Mo., 1976), 137–51.

30. Joshua D. Rothman, *Notorious in the Neighborhood: Sex and Families across the Color Line in Virginia, 1787–1861* (Chapel Hill, NC, 2003), 204–5.

31. On the importance of non-visual senses to racial identification, see Smith, *How Race is Made*.

32. Rothman, *Notorious in the Neighborhood*, 216–17.

33. Cited in Joel Williamson, *New People: Miscegenation and Mulattos in the United States* (Baton Rouge, La., 1995), 18.

34. Christopher Phillips, *Freedom's Port: The African American Community of Baltimore, 1790–1860* (Urbana, Ill., 1997); for a similar community further south, see Whittington B. Johnson, *Black Savannah, 1788–1864* (Fayetteville, Ark., 1999).

35. See for example Gad Heuman, *Between Black and White: Race, Politics and the Free Coloureds in Jamaica, 1792–1865* (Westport, Conn., 1981); and Arnold A. Sio, "Marginality and Free Colored Identity in Caribbean Slave Society," *Slavery and Abolition*, 8 (1) (September 1987): 166–82.

36. See Michael P. Johnson and James L. Roark, *Black Masters: A Free Family of Color in the Old South* (New York, 1984).

37. Ibid. 212–22; Michael P. Johnson and James L. Roark, "'A Middle Ground': Free Mulattos and the Friendly Moralist Society of Antebellum Charleston," *Southern Studies*, 21 (3) (Fall 1983): 246–65.

38. See Eugene D. Genovese, "'Rather be a Nigger than a Poor White Man': Slave Perceptions of Southern Yeomen and Poor Whites," in Hans L. Trefousse (ed.), *Toward a New View of America: Essays in Honor of Arthur C. Cole* (New York, 1977), 79–96.

39. Richard H. Colfax, *Evidence against the Views of the Abolitionists, Consisting of Physical and Moral Proofs, of the Natural Inferiority of the Negroes* (New York, 1833), 25v.

40. Josiah C. Nott, *Two Lectures on the Natural History of the Caucasian and Negro Races* (Mobile, Fla., 1844), 28.

41. Ibid. 35.

42. J. C. Nott and G. R. Gliddon, *Types of Mankind: or, Ethnological Researches Based upon the Ancient Monuments, Paintings, Sculptures, and Crania of Races, and upon their Natural, Geographical, Philological and Biblical History* (Philadelphia, 1854), 399–400.

43. Tannenbaum was the first to suggest that slavery was not as harsh in Latin America as in the British colonies, but the work of later historians has tended to disprove his assertions. See Frank Tannenbaum, *Slave and Citizen: The Negro in the Americas* (New York, 1946); Rolando Mellafe, *Negro Slavery in Latin America*, trans. J. w. S. Judge (Berkeley, 1975); Leslie B. Rout, Jr., *The African Experience in Spanish America: 1502 to the*

Present Day (New York, 1976); Stuart B. Schwartz, *Sugar Plantations in the Formation of Brazilian Society: Bahia, 1550–1835.* (New York, 1985).

44. For examples of confusions over determining the race of individuals, see Walter Johnson, "The Slave Trader, the White Slave, and the Politics of Racial Determination in the 1850s," *Journal of American History*, 87 (1) (June 2000): 13–38.

45. For more on the interaction between poor whites and slaves, see Timothy James Lockley, *Lines in the Sand: Race and Class in Lowcountry Georgia, 1750–1860* (Athens, Ga., 2001) and Jeff Forret, *Race Relations at the Margins: Slaves and Poor Whites in the Antebellum Countryside* (Baton Rouge, La., 2006).

46. See Christopher H. Owen, "By Design: The Social Meaning of Methodist Church Architecture in Nineteenth Century Georgia," *Georgia Historical Quarterly*, 75 (1991): 221–53.

47. Timothy James Lockley, *Welfare and Charity in the Antebellum South* (Gainesville, Fla., 2007).

48. On the explosion of postwar violence against blacks see W. Fitzhugh Brundage, *Lynching in the New South: Georgia and Virginia, 1880–1930* (Urbana, Ill., 1993); W. Fitzhugh Brundage (ed.), *Under Sentence of Death: Lynching in the South* (Chapel Hill, NC, 1997). See also James H. Madison, *A Lynching in the Heartland: Race and Memory in America* (New York, 2001); and Martha Hodes, *White Women, Black Men: Illicit Sex in the 19th-Century South* (New Haven, 1997).

49. See R. K. Kent, "Palmares: An African State in Brazil," Roger Bastide, "The Other Quilombos," Stuart B. Schwartz, "The Mocambo: Slave Resistance in Colonial Bahia," all in Richard Price (ed.), *Maroon Societies: Rebel Slave Communities in the Americas* (2nd edn. Baltimore, 1979).

50. John Brickell, *The Natural History of North Carolina* (Dublin, 1737), 263. George Milligen Johnston, *A Short Description of the Province of South Carolina* (London, 1770), 26. See also William S. Willis, "Divide and Rule: Red, White and Black in the Southeast," *Journal of Negro History*, 48 (3) (July 1963): 157–76v; James H. Merrell, "The Racial Education of the Catawba Indians," *Journal of Southern History*, 50 (3) (August 1984): 363–84; Gallay, *The Indian Slave Trade*.

51. South Carolina Commons House of Assembly Journal, 14 January 1766. UK National Archives, CO 5/488, 2–4.

52. The best discussion of slave owning amongst Native Americans is Theda Perdue, *Slavery and the Evolution of Cherokee Society, 1540–1866* (Knoxville, Tenn., 1979).

53. On the Florida maroons and their interaction with the Seminoles see Kenneth W. Porter, *The Black Seminoles: History of a Freedom-Seeking People* (Gainesville, Fla., 1996) and Kevin Mulroy, *Freedom on the Border: The Seminole Maroons in Florida, the Indian Territory, Coahuila and Texas* (Lubbock, Tex., 1993).

54. Diane Miller Sommerville, "The Rape Myth in the Old South Reconsidered," *Journal of Southern History*, 61 (1995): 481–518; Lockley, *Lines in the Sand*; Forret, *Race Relations at the Margins*.

55. Thomas C. Holt, "Marking: Race, Race-Making, and the Writing of History," *American Historical Review*, 100 (1) (February 1995): 1–20.

Select Bibliography

Dain, Bruce. *A Hideous Monster of the Mind: American Race Theory in the Early Republic.* Cambridge, Mass.: Harvard University Press, 2002.

Degler, Carl N. "Slavery and the Genesis of American Race Prejudice," *Comparative Studies in Society and History,* 2 (1) (October 1959): 49–66.

Fields, Barbara J. "Ideology and Race in American History," in J. Morgan Kousser and James M. McPherson (eds.), *Region, Race and Reconstruction: Essays in Honor of C. Vann Woodward* (New York: Oxford University Press, 1982), 143–77.

—— "Slavery, Race and Ideology in the United States of America," *New Left Review,* 181 (May–June 1990): 95–118.

Forret, Jeff. *Race Relations at the Margins: Slaves and Poor Whites in the Antebellum Countryside.* Baton Rouge, La.: Louisiana University Press, 2006.

Genovese, Eugene D. " 'Rather be a Nigger than a Poor White Man': Slave Perceptions of Southern Yeomen and Poor Whites," in Hans L. Trefousse (ed.), *Toward a New View of America: Essays in Honor of Arthur C. Cole* (New York: Burt Franklin & Co., 1977), 79–96.

Heuman, Gad. *Between Black and White: Race, Politics and the Free Coloureds in Jamaica, 1792–1865.* Westport, Conn.: Greenwood Press, 1981.

Holt, Thomas C. "Marking: Race, Race-Making, and the Writing of History," *American Historical Review,* 100 (1) (February 1995): 1–20.

Jordan, Winthrop. *White over Black: American Attitudes towards the Negro 1550–1812.* Chapel Hill, NC: University of North Carolina Press, 1968.

Lockley, Timothy James. *Lines in the Sand: Race and Class in Lowcountry Georgia, 1750–1860.* Athens, Ga.: University of Georgia Press, 2001.

Rout, Leslie B., Jr. *The African Experience in Spanish America: 1502 to the Present Day.* New York: Cambridge University Press, 1976.

Schiebinger, Londa. "The Anatomy of Difference: Race and Sex in Eighteenth-Century Science," *Eighteenth-Century Studies,* 23 (4) (1990): 387–405.

Sio, Arnold A. "Marginality and Free Colored Identity in Caribbean Slave Society," *Slavery and Abolition,* 8 (1) (September 1987): 166–82.

Smedley, Audrey. *Race in North America: Origin and Evolution of a Worldview.* Boulder, Colo.: Westview, 1993.

Smith, Mark. *How Race is Made.* Chapel Hill, NC: University of North Carolina Press, 2006.

Stanton, William. *The Leopard's Spots: Scientific Attitudes toward Race in America, 1815–59.* Chicago: University of Chicago Press, 1960.

Vaughan, Alden T. "From White Man to Redskin: Changing Anglo-American Perceptions of the American Indian," *American Historical Review,* 87 (4) (October 1982): 917–53.

Wheeler, Roxann. *The Complexion of Race: Categories of Difference in Eighteenth-Century British Culture.* Philadelphia: University of Pennsylvania Press, 2000.

Williamson, Joel. *New People: Miscegenation and Mulattos in the United States.* Baton Rouge, La.: Louisiana State University Press, 1995.

CHAPTER 16

CLASS AND SLAVERY

JONATHAN DANIEL WELLS

CLASS IN SLAVEHOLDING SOCIETIES

Class has often been a troubling and difficult subject for Americans, and hardly less so for scholars. At least since the Enlightenment, the notion that individual will and strength of character are more important influences on social mobility than the particular class into which one is born has become embedded in Western culture. From well-worn tropes such as the rugged frontier, the hard-working family farmer, the industrious businessman, and the toiling laborer, the notion that the individual determines his or her economic destiny through sheer will and diligence, notions powerful in Western society and especially in American culture, have often blunted class consciousness. The belief that all men are born with equal opportunities to make their way in life, that individual initiative can overcome any obstacle, that hard work and ambition override whatever circumstances into which one enters life, has veined American history. These prevailing cultural constructs have not only suppressed the emergence of class consciousness among white Americans but have surely quelled the potential for African-Americans and economically disadvantaged whites to join together in any shared class identification, especially in slaveholding societies.

Scholars have not infrequently struggled with the notion—and applicability—of class in history, debating whether to consider class as an objective element of the social order defined strictly by indicators such as income, status, occupation, level of slave or land ownership, personal wealth, and other information that might be discerned from quantitative analysis of census data, court records, wills, and similar records or emphasizing the importance of the cultural, subjective construction of class, employing readings of newspapers, pamphlets, personal letters, magazines, and the like to discover a class consciousness that relied not necessarily on shared income levels but a common sense of distinctiveness from other groups in the social structure. A third group of scholars has stressed the value of using both objective and subjective considerations of class to profitably explore the historical evolution of class conflict, class alliances, class formation, and class consciousness. E. P. Thompson, one of the most insightful students of class, argued that class was "a historical relationship shaped by both economic relations of production and cultural modes," but as historian Daniel J. Walkowitz has noted scholars have had a difficult time following and applying Thompson's maxim.[1] In fact, as Geoff Eley and Keith Nield have recently pointed out, the controversy among scholars regarding the various ways to consider the meaning of class "connected with a much broader upheaval in historical studies beginning in the 1980s, namely, the turning away from social history toward cultural history, which was itself was part of a more general crisis of social explanation across the disciplines in the human sciences."[2] The dominance of cultural history and the receding numbers of historians studying class in Western culture was perhaps the surest indication that if the study of class had not been completely eclipsed then certainly greater numbers of younger scholars were turning their attention to other elements of society, particularly race and gender.

Despite political and cultural trends that have inhibited the development of class consciousness, slave societies in the Western world have nonetheless expressed class sentiments that, in the eyes of a growing number of historians, warrant a renewed emphasis on the relevance of class formation and class consciousness. Perhaps the best way to re-inject class into historiographical debates is to reconsider the ways in which the peoples of the past themselves considered the meaning of class.

In the eighteenth and nineteenth centuries, the word "class" usually delimited a social grouping. Often used as a synonym for "category" to delineate differences among all kinds of groupings, particularly varying kinds of cotton, even in the earliest years of the nineteenth century, newspapers, pamphlets, monthly literary journals, and other printed material referred to a specific meaning of class as distinctive constituents of the social order. In the slave states of the antebellum American South, literate peoples employed class to indicate groups, such as a class of lawyers or a class of farmers, in a top-down ordering of civilization. Social hierarchy was certainly accepted as the normal course of all societies, both slaveholding and nonslaveholding. In the eyes of many historians the slave South was especially prone to be deferential to a self-aware and objectively wealthy planter class, whose economic, political, and social authority was so pronounced that it created a cultural hegemony for the region. Most clearly articulated by Eugene D. Genovese, this view holds that in contrast to the more socially fluid antebellum North, the Old South was typical of pre-bourgeois societies which suppressed dissent or class hostility among whites. Genovese has modified his earlier position on this question, but his important body of work clearly argues in favor of a South that was dominated by a largely unchallenged planter class.[3]

Genovese and other scholars are right, of course, in maintaining that the Old South was led by the planter class. Slaveholding societies, like most throughout Western history, have generally been highly unequal in terms of land and wealth distribution, deferential toward the economic elite, and led politically by the upper class. In the slave South and in the slave nations of the Caribbean and South America, class served to maintain a status quo to protect the wealth and power accumulated by elite slaveholders. Large planters along the US Atlantic Coast, especially in the Sea Islands and, further inland, the Black Belt, often governed plantations in a feudal manner, sometimes lording over hundreds of slaves on vast plantations consisting of thousands of acres. As Richard Follett has lately shown, a rigid class hierarchy was observed with brutal consequences on the sugar planta- tions of antebellum Louisiana.[4] Sugar plantations in Cuba and South America were similarly dominated by large-scale enterprises that foreshadowed the agribusi- nesses of the twentieth century. According to Luis A. Figueroa, the sprawling plantations in Puerto Rico were not only tightly controlled fiefdoms, but the oppression of Africans lasted well past emancipation in 1873.[5]

Slaves in Western slaveholding societies cannot be said to have articulated any recognizable class consciousness or any firm notion of belonging to a class hierar- chy. A sense of class, as Eric Hobsbawm has observed, begins to emerge when "a group's awareness and understanding of itself . . . grows out of opposition to other groups."[6] However, to be considered a "class," this group must not only possess at least a nascent self-awareness, but also be able to act in some way to encourage and develop that thinking to a level that can be articulated and acted upon. While slaves beyond any doubt perceived their differences with others in the South, if only by virtue of their black skin and their status as property, the legal, political, and intellectual culture of the region made any attempts to form a class consciousness virtually impossible. None of the mechanisms by which the southern middle class or the planter class developed a sense of distinctiveness in the social order were available to slaves. The professional and commercial middle class, for example, rallied around a set of core ideas they learned about through newspapers and magazines, as well as through their interactions with northerners in personal and professional circles. Although slaves sometimes got wind of current events through occasional readings of newspapers, and though the oral transmission of news in slave communities could be both powerful and substantive, pathways for develop- ing a class consciousness among bondsmen were significantly more fraught with obstacles. The overwhelming force and power of white society and its legal and political means of maintaining slavery, from slave codes to slave patrols, hampered any attempts by slaves to join together to articulate a fully formed class ideology.

Nonetheless, bondsmen and bondswomen were keenly aware of their degraded status and slaves throughout Western history have attempted to exercise their will in ways that were perceived by their white masters as threats to the social order. Slave rebellions in the American South, such as the Stono Revolt (1739) and Nat Turner's insurrection (1831), were enough to cause hysteria among whites but were quickly suppressed. Members of the planter class were ever suspicious of any lower-class white cooperation with slaves or free blacks, and the elite acted swiftly to end any attempts at revolt by either group. Rebellions in the Caribbean, including those in Barbados (1816) and the 1791 revolt led by Toussaint Louverture that established Haiti, were more successful than their American counterparts.[7] Matt D. Childs has recently studied the 1812 Aponte Rebellion in Cuba and discovered a brief but powerful alliance between slaves, creoles, mulattos, and free blacks that created one of the most potent slave rebellions in the Atlantic world.[8] South American slave uprisings, such as the Bahia Rebellions on early nineteenth-century sugar plantations in Brazil, indicate that against overwhelming odds African slaves attempted to overthrow their oppressors.[9] The vast majority of these slave insurrections were unsuccessful and quashed with an alacrity that is testimony to the overwhelming power of the planter class. While the fact that slaves in virtually all societies have attempted to escape their bondage is not necessarily evidence of class consciousness among bondsmen, such revolts nonetheless were perceived by white society as dangerous challenges to the social hierarchy.

To acknowledge the point that the planter class maintained an encompassing power on their plantations and a prominent place in the social hierarchy of slave societies is not to argue that the elite wielded absolute power. On the contrary, a growing body of scholarship indicates that in public and private forums whites in the American South and in other slaveholding societies such as Brazil often sought to counteract the power and dominance of the planters in meaningful ways.[10] In the American South, it is hard to discern any robust sense of class consciousness among middling professionals or laborers, or classes behaving as though their interests and ideology is distinct from other elements of society grouped by wealth or status, at least until the 1850s. And yet in the late eighteenth and nineteenth centuries there were frequent complaints from yeomen farmers, editors, urban merchants, education reformers, and others about planter political power, the dominance of the economic elite, and the pursuit of wealth, complaints suggesting that whites in slave societies did not present a racially united front either in public or private discourse. In the American South, objections to the planter class often emanated from professional and commercial interests who held moderate wealth and who rallied around a set of cultural and economic objectives that they believed separated them from other elements of the social order. Largely urban dwellers, these doctors, lawyers, teachers, merchants, and editors sought public schools, a modernized and diversified economy, and admired many of the features of north-ern cities. These southerners boldly and openly challenged the planter class on a number of fronts, criticizing them sharply for (in the eyes of the middle class) failing to support public money for common schools, internal improvement projects, and cultural advances, such as public libraries. Such criticism also ques-tioned the planter class and its commitment to diversifying the southern economy. Merchants and industrial promoters protested that planters were too consumed with growing cotton and not concerned enough with growing the region's cities and factories. These middling southerners also scorned barbaric relics of a feudal past, especially the practice of dueling to defend one's honor, a practice that they associated with the elite, by forming anti-dueling associations in Savannah and other southern cities. In developing a sense of class distinctiveness, a sense of ideological separation from themselves and the other elements of the southern social structure, middling southerners came together with a class conscious economic and cultural agenda by the 1850s. Though the Civil War would destroy its hopes of remaking the South, the southern middle class had a profound influence on the region's development in the final decade of the antebellum era.[11] In newspapers, magazines, speeches, and private correspondence, middle-class southerners criticized the planters for what they perceived to be the eco-nomic and cultural backwardness of the southern elite. Although the planter class certainly held a significant portion of southern wealth and power, that standing was not unquestioned.

Neither was the slave South unusual in this regard. Scholars of Caribbean and South American slavery have begun to reexamine assumptions about the suppo-sedly truncated nature of class consciousness among whites. Richard S. Dunn, for example, has studied the emergence of a class identity among planters in the West Indies.[12] Luis Martinez-Fernandez has similarly studied the Caribbean and found political and social conflict among the middling and planter classes.[13] Just as scholars of the American South are finding the white social hierarchy to be more complicated than previously held, so too may historians of slaveholding societies elsewhere begin to examine non-planters, and, in the process, reveal emerging class tensions among whites that parallel those in nineteenth-century free wage labor societies.

As Martinez-Fernandez notes, critiques of the planter class in the Caribbean often emanated from white evangelical Protestants, and this is equally true in the American South. The Second Great Awakening that swept the eastern United States in the antebellum era shaped the ideology of whites in the slave states in profound ways. Central to this wave of heightened religious fervor was the evangelical critique of flamboyant displays of wealth.[14] Reminding followers to live simply, evangelical preachers in Sunday sermons scorned those who dressed in a manner they deemed showy or gaudy. Schools for girls and young women drove this point home by requiring a dress code for pupils that emphasized the practical over the pretentious. In sermons, periodicals, and pamphlets working- and middle-class evangelicals leveled critiques at the planter class. Thus, while planters in slaveholding societies can certainly be said to have wielded a great deal of economic and political power, that authority, in particular contexts, could draw condemnation from other whites of the social order, and even occasionally from slaves in the form of potent slave rebellions that broke out in the Caribbean, South America, and the southern United States.

CLASS AND SLAVERY IN THE UNITED STATES: THE STATE OF THE FIELD

The evolution of the historiography on class and slavery is complex, and historians have only recently begun to revisit some of their basic assumptions about class formation, class ideology, and the social structure of the Old South more broadly. New studies raise questions about the ways in which human bondage and class intertwined in slave societies, particularly the American South, and have initiated a discernible shift in the field. While scholars profitably continue to study the plantation and the lives of masters and slaves, many historians now call for a wider view of southern society to take account of life in the region outside the plantation, and the various ways in which different classes of whites interacted with, and were shaped by, the institution of slavery. It is with these new calls that the subject of class is enjoying resurgence.

The modern study of social groupings in slave society began with Ulrich B. Phillips and his innovative work on plantation society. Phillips's landmark study *Life and Labor in the Old South* (1929) was among the first studies of the slave states to focus on the cultural elements of the region, rather than the political leaders and issues that had dominated the historiography. Phillips, a native of Georgia who taught at Yale, the University of Michigan, and the University of Wisconsin, sought to create a vivid sense of what it was like to live on an antebellum plantation. As important as Phillips's study was, however, the Georgia native could not escape his southern upbringing. *Life and Labor* depicted slavery as a largely benevolent institution and claimed that slaves were generally well fed and content. African-American scholars such as Charles H. Wesley criticized Phillips for ignoring the more heinous aspects of slavery, such as the sexual abuse of female slaves and the lynching of innocent blacks.[15]

Despite his positive depiction of slavery as a civilizing influence on Africans, Phillips was sensitive to the fact that the Old South was not simply about life on the plantation and that class was important to the functioning and elaboration of social relations in the region. In *Life and Labor*, Phillips was among the first scholars to consider seriously the history of ordinary white southerners. Toward the end of his study Phillips devoted a short chapter to "The Plain People," in which he briefly considered nonslaveholding whites but did not fully address them as a social class. One senses that later studies in his projected series on the South, of which *Life and Labor* was only the first volume, might have dealt more squarely with the social structure of the slave states. Alas, Phillips died of cancer at age 57 before he could complete any subsequent volumes in the series. As if to bring his innovative study back to more traditional historiographical concerns, Phillips closed *Life and Labor* with a chapter on the gentry. It would be left to later scholars to uncover crucial aspects of the southern social structure.

Phillips's approach remained paramount until Frank L. Owsley and several of his graduate students embarked upon new efforts to understand the role played by ordinary white southerners, whom he called "plain folk," and their relationship to slavery. In *Plain Folk of the Old South* (1949), Owsley sought to provide a voice for nonslaveholding whites. Northern observers of the slave South in the antebellum period, Owsley pointed out, saw just two white classes in southern society: masters and poor laborers. Northern and European travelers to the South such as Frederick L. Olmsted, George M. Weston, and J. E. Cairnes frequently complained that the miserable state of poor whites was evidence of slavery's baneful effect on all elements of the region's population, particularly the nonslaveholders. Owsley believed that an over-reliance on plantation records and accounts of the South by outside, politically motivated observers had distorted both the popular and scholarly interpretations of the region. In *Plain Folk of the Old South*, he emphasized the dividends of combing other historical sources, including wills, county tax records, church documents, minutes from county court proceedings, census data, and older biographies of locally important figures. From a careful examination of such sources, Owsley concluded that the South was far from a society with a bifurcated social structure of planters and "poor white trash," but was instead "a society of great complexity." "The core of this social structure," he argued, "was a massive body of plain folk who were neither rich nor very poor." Rather than directly tied to slavery and the plantation economy, these whites were primarily engaged in "farming and livestock grazing." The plain folk had a complicated relationship with slavery. Owsley was not concerned with demonstrating conflict between the rural plain folk and planters, and he denied the existence of any significant hostility among whites of different levels of wealth and status. Indeed, he maintained that though they shared key characteristics such as religious beliefs, speech patterns, affinity for hunting, and other common folkways, the middling and poor whites "were not class conscious in the Marxian sense, for with rare exceptions they did not regard the planters and men of wealth as their oppressors. On the contrary they admired them as a rule and looked with approval on their success."[16] The rural common people believed that southern society was open enough to allow men of intelligence and ambition to succeed, both financially and politically. This perceived openness blunted any class conflict that might have otherwise emerged in the Old South.

Despite the groundbreaking work in *Plain Folk of the Old South* Owsley slighted the relationship between common whites and the institution of slavery. Content to outline the culture and outlook of rural plain folks, he largely ignored the existence of slavery and the myriad ways in which these common whites might have interacted with bondsmen and bondswomen. Most importantly, he generally declined to discuss the slaves themselves. Thus, while Owsley attempted to reorient the direction of southern studies by exploring class, it was left to later scholars to consider the full meaning of the relationship between class and slavery in the antebellum South.

In the 1960s and 1970s, scholars began to examine the lives of the slaves themselves, helping to spark a historiographical revolution in the ways in which historians thought and wrote about the antebellum South. Richard C. Wade's landmark study *Slavery in the Cities: The South 1820–1860* (1964) was among the first works to examine human bondage away from the plantation setting. Wade argued that in New Orleans, Mobile, Savannah, Richmond, Baltimore, and other important southern cities, slavery was a kind of halfway point between bondage and freedom. Slavery in the urban environment, Wade argued, was more flexible given the busy nature of city life. Most of these slaves were domestic servants who worked as cooks, maids, seamstresses, and nannies.[17] The nature of their work may have been preferable to the toil of a field-hand, but domestic slaves were nonetheless human property and the slave codes guaranteed urban owners a similar degree of control over bondsmen exercised by rural masters. Yet Wade de-emphasized a potentially rich area of inquiry: the interaction among slaves, the poor, and middling whites who lived in southern towns. Indeed, Wade maintained that urban slaves' "contacts with whites were few and seldom lasting."[18] Later scholars would dispute this claim, but Wade had made an important contribution by shedding needed light on urban slavery.

Despite such innovative work, many historians of the 1960s and 1970s continued to view the antebellum South as a pre-bourgeois society that valued rural, almost feudal, characteristics such as honor, deference, and economic tradition. Chief among the studies to make this case was Eugene D. Genovese's seminal *The Political Economy of Slavery* (1965). Genovese acknowledged in his work that the South's precapitalist economy did permit the emergence of a small commercial bourgeoisie but, he claimed, "merchants either became planters themselves or assumed a servile attitude toward the planters. The commercial bourgeoisie, such as it was, remained tied to the slaveholding interest, had little desire or opportunity to invest capital in industrial expansion, and adopted the prevailing aristocratic attitudes."[19] Genovese's characterization of the slave South as precapitalist, and his depiction of a planter hegemony over white society, would remain widely accepted for years to come.

One of the most significant advances of the historiography of the 1960s and 1970s was the shift toward history "from the bottom up," away from studying presidents and prominent white politicians and toward the common folk. In fact, a rising number of black and white younger scholars in these decades argued that studies of the plantation had relied largely upon self-serving accounts left behind by wealthy white masters and ignored the lives of the slaves themselves. This important historiographical shift meant that more attention would be devoted to the lower classes in the southern social structure. John W. Blassingame's *The Slave Community* and Eugene Genovese's *Roll Jordan, Roll*, both published in the 1970s, presented refreshing examinations of slave life that gave agency to, and provided rich discussions of, slave spirituals, survival strategies, family life, and culture.[20] It is difficult to overestimate the impact of these and similar studies on the historiography of the nineteenth-century South. Works by Blassingame, Genovese, and others sparked a remarkably creative and varied history of slavery that culminated in important cultural studies such as Charles Joyner's *Down by the Riverside* (1984).[21] While these important works did not consider slaves as part of a social class, they were nonetheless influential in exploring the history of previously neglected aspects of southern society. Authors like Blassingame, Genovese, and Joyner proved that despite the lack of historical sources in which slaves spoke directly to modern scholars, one could still recover their voices. Inspired by this body of work that brought new and significant insights to our understanding of the slave South, subsequent authors would investigate similarly unstudied groups in the South, including yeomen.

One of the most important monographs to reveal key elements of yeomen society was Steven Hahn's *The Roots of Southern Populism* (1983), which examined the Georgia up country between 1850 and 1890. Hahn discovered that yeomen farmers strongly resisted their switch from independent farmers to sharecroppers dependent upon the market and creditors for their livelihood.[22] Similarly, Lacy K. Ford, in *Origins of Southern Radicalism* (1988), built upon an earlier study by J. Mills Thornton III to investigate the shift in the South Carolina up country from subsistence farming to commercial center. For Ford and Hahn especially, slaveholding and nonslaveholding yeomen, while shy of having developed a class consciousness, were nevertheless fiercely independent and framed that independence through a republican worldview.[23] In the 1990s scholars began to investigate the ways in which lower-class whites lived in the midst of slavery. In *Poor Whites of the Antebellum South* (1994), Charles C. Bolton argued that lower-class whites "remain the most historically obscure social group of the Old South." Superficially characterized as "rednecks," "crackers," and "poor white trash," Bolton claims, these southerners and the details of their difficult lives were barely known to scholars.[24] Bolton found that American mythology to the contrary, the class structure of the nineteenth-century South allowed for very little social mobility. "Despite persistent efforts," Bolton found, "a significant number of poor whites who migrated from their homes in the search for land never broke into the landowning class."[25] The reason why the social structure of the region remained rigid, posited Bolton, can be attributed to the control of wealthy speculators over the open lands of states like Texas, Arkansas, and Mississippi, control to which local government officials were eager accessories. Perhaps even more important than this valuable insight was the refreshing analysis Bolton conducted of the relationship between poor whites and slaves. In fact, white tenants, free blacks, and slaves often intermingled in ways positive and negative. Certainly fights broke out in which white–black violence was the result. But social interaction in the form of playing cards or drinking troubled members of the planter class, who complained about racial intermingling as a threat to social order. Bolton's important insights into the complex intertwining of race and class would help spark later studies of black–white interaction viewed through the lens of class analysis.

The last ten years have been fertile ground for historians working on the intersection of class and slavery. Building upon earlier works, new approaches have greatly enriched our understanding of the southern social structure, though fundamental questions remain. Opening a significant new area of inquiry, Michele Gillespie's study of white artisans in antebellum Georgia, *Free Labor in an Unfree World* (2000), found that working-class whites formed mechanics' associations to influence political discourse and frequently banded together to fight the introduction of slaves into the skilled trades. Her evidence indicated that as early as 1790 white artisans had formulated a political consciousness. However, Gillespie also maintained that artisans were aspiring slaveholders who supported bondage because they held out hope that one day they would enter the planter class.[26] Thus, in Gillespie's view, the interests of the planter class and the incipient white working class were bound together to form a racially united front. "Artisan-leaders," she argues, "chose to conceive of themselves as white men of the dominant social order rather than a distinct class of white artisans."[27] One of Gillespie's most noteworthy contributions was to suggest that the social hierarchy of the slave South remained an underdeveloped field of study.

Since the publication of *Free Labor in an Unfree World*, scholars have devoted considerable attention to teasing out the complicated nature of class in the nineteenth-century South. In *The Origins of the Southern Middle Class, 1800–1861* (2004), I attempted to show that there was indeed a vibrant and active class of middling white southerners that often called into question planter dominance. Far from a precapitalist society in which the commercial bourgeoisie remained shackled to the will of the planter class as Genovese had argued in *The Political Economy of Slavery*, I maintained that in fact merchants, doctors, lawyers, editors, and other commercial and professional southerners of middling means constantly sought to gain preeminence for their distinct vision of the region's future. The southern middle class advocated the construction of public school systems, more factories and economic diversification, cultural improvements such as public libraries, and favored the urban lifestyle they associated with the great cities of the North. In pushing for its agenda, these southerners became increasingly class conscious as they fought against what they perceived as the stubborn resistance to modernization from planters, yeomen, and white laborers. By the eve of the Civil War, the middling southerners had formed a sense of distinctiveness from other groups in the social structure that warranted the term "middle class." Indeed, professional and commercial interests even employed the term "middle class" to describe themselves and their distinct position in southern society. In the South, however, the middle class willingly embraced slavery, not because they were beholden to a planter hegemony but because they believed that slaves could be employed in factories more cheaply and more reliably than skilled white workers, many of whom staged strikes and walk-outs throughout the southern states in the 1850s. Thus, instead of a pre-bourgeois society with a stunted social structure, I saw in the Old South the emergence of a middle class that had a profound effect on the region's culture, economy, and society. In advocating a new and modern South that valued and admired northern cities and industry, in chastising the planters and the yeomen for their perceived failure adequately to support these modernizing efforts, and in offering a different vision of the region's future that joined slavery with a burgeoning capitalistic society, the middle class helped shape the antebellum South.

Two works in recent years take this view of class and slavery in the South to heart. Frank J. Byrne's *Becoming Bourgeois* (2006) adds significantly to the growing body of studies on the southern middle class. Byrne illuminates class hostility within the white South by demonstrating that shopkeepers, grocers, and wholesale merchants were the object of considerable scorn from their fellow southerners. Byrne agrees with some of the fundamental points made in *The Origins of the Southern Middle Class*, particularly the argument that southern merchants adhered to broader, American nineteenth-century middle-class values such as the importance of education for advancement, the value and importance of economic diversification and industrialization, and adherence to particular values with regard to religion and culture. Southern merchants were criticized harshly as "Yankees" who were ideologically marginalized, but they were also openly embraced by like-minded members of the southern middle class.

While Byrne's study contributes much to our understanding of the southern middle class, Tom Downey's book *Planting a Capitalist South* (2006) offers a strident case against the notion of planter hegemony. Building upon earlier important work by James Oakes, Downey finds that rather than a region dominated by the anti-capitalist attitudes of the planter class, as Genovese had argued, the slave South was very much involved in commerce and manufacturing.[28] In *The Ruling Race: A History of American Slaveholders* (1982), Oakes had employed the term "slaveholding middle class" to denote the vast majority of slaveholders who owned fewer than five slaves and especially those who populated the expanding southern frontier. In examining these small slaveholders, Oakes found that they were not aristocratic, anti-modern, or paternalistic as Genovese had maintained. Rather Oakes discovered that small slave owners were anti-aristocratic, modern in their approach to the market and in their cultural outlook, and keen to bring internal improvements to the South.[29] In *Planting a Capitalist South*, Downey helps to support Oakes's interpretation. Focusing on the Savannah River Valley in the western portion of South Carolina, Downey's study examines the effect of the market revolution on the Edgefield and Barnwell Districts. Downey found significant class conflict between merchants and planters, and regional conflicts between urban and rural interests. As Downey writes, "far from assuming 'a servile attitude towards the planters,' merchants in Edgefield and Barnwell actively—and successfully—elevated the place of commerce in the agrarian landscape, seldom with the blessing of district planters and frequently over their vocal opposition."[30] As vociferous advocates for a new South that would build factories, invest heavily in railroads, and encourage economic diversification, these middling merchants and industrialists, Downey concludes, facilitated the shift in South Carolina "from merely being a society with capitalist features toward becoming a capitalist society."[31] Scholars like Oakes and Downey have complicated greatly our understanding of social structures in slave societies. Rather than merely two groups consisting of masters and slaves, historians have discovered that even in a slave economy, the social structure may harbor other groups and classes, from yeoman farmers and white laborers to merchants, teachers, and doctors.

Work has already begun to study neglected elements of slave societies in regions outside the United States. In his recent study *Business Interest Groups in Nineteenth-Century Brazil* (2004), Eugene Ridings argues that typically middle-class, commercial interests played a key role in the development of South America, particularly the modernization of communication systems and agriculture, while also facilitating the development of industries. Importantly, Ridings's findings for Brazil echo those of the southern middle class in America, for Ridings emphasizes the ties between commercial interests in South America and those in the broader Atlantic world. Indeed, he has gone much further than those who study the Old South in analyzing the impact of business and trade associations on the economic development of Brazil, especially in the later nineteenth century. Zeroing in on the minutes and reports from these organizations, Ridings sheds light on the lobbying efforts of merchants, their considerable efforts to standardize weights and measures and thus to provide stability and rationality to the Brazilian economy, and the importance of business associations in transporting European business culture to South America.[32] Still, Ridings concludes (as have scholars of the American South) that business interests in Brazil buttressed rather than challenged the existence of slavery. Race and class shaped one another in a dialectical process in Brazil as in other slave societies.

The comparative influence in slave societies of race and class has attracted renewed interest among scholars, not just in works such as Ridings's study of Brazil but in works on the Old South as well. Timothy J. Lockley's *Lines in the Sand* (2004) examines the mixing of African-Americans and whites in the Georgia lowcountry in the late eighteenth and early nineteenth centuries, focusing upon "social contacts, economic networks, criminal encounters, and shared religious experiences."[33] In contrast to the viewpoints of historians such as Bradley G. Bond, Lockley suggests that race was less of an impediment to interaction among lower-class whites and blacks than the historiography has argued. Nonslaveholding whites and African-Americans (both slave and free) maintained a host of social, religious, and economic ties that often attracted the scorn of the white elite. Thus, from Lockley's perspective, race and racism did not prevent poor whites and blacks from forming a range of relationships. Finally, like Bolton and Lockley, Jeff Forret, in *Race Relations at the Margins* (2006), has recently found that whether at work or in social activities such as gambling, consensual sex, and drinking, blacks and poor whites often intermingled. As Forret explains, "slaves and poor whites overcame racial barriers to mingle in any number of ways that should not have occurred in a society rigidly divided by race."[34] Forret points out that slaveholders often expressed fear of poor whites and their potential to join with slaves and free African-Americans. "Poor whites," Forret posits, "often laid claims to superiority over slaves by virtue of the white skin they shared with wealthy slaveholders; at other times, however, they recognized that their material circumstances differed little from those of slaves. Like slaves, they, too, were social inferiors." Perhaps most importantly, he finds that whites and blacks interacted much more frequently, and on much more friendlier bases, than we have thought previously. "When slaves and poor whites recognized their shared subordinate status," Forret concludes, "camaraderie rather than conflict characterized many of their social encounters."[35]

Parallel to the work of Lockley, Forret, and others in analyzing the culture of poor whites and their interaction with African-Americans has been an equally significant trend of studying southern dissent. In the 1970s, Carl N. Degler's *The Other South* was one of the few studies to spotlight dissent in southern history. In studying trends from the short-lived Constitutional Union Party that sought to keep the slave and free states together in the 1860 election to the Civil Rights Movement of the 1960s, Degler was largely alone in suggesting the significance of conflict within the South.[36] Recently, however, numerous studies, while not necessarily discussing class conflict, have nonetheless challenged the perception of a region dominated by wealthy whites and the rigid ideology of social and racial hierarchy. Instead, new scholarship has underscored the considerable differences among white southerners on a range of issues. William Freehling's *The South vs. the South* (2001), for example, highlights the split between Deep South and Border South states before and during the Civil War. Indeed, Freehling goes so far as to argue that the "anti-Confederate Southerners piled on psychological, economic, and geographic burdens that ultimately helped flatten white Confederates' resiliency" and thus contributed mightily to the South's defeat.[37] Other analyses of the nineteenth-century South, including Margaret M. Storey's *Loyalty and Loss* (2004) and Hyman Rubin's *Southern Scalawags* (2006), have diluted the interpretative preeminence of planter and elite hegemony.[38]

The notion of a closed society that adhered unswervingly to a class and racial hierarchy born of intellectual isolation, a notion that emerged most clearly in Genovese's *The Political Economy of Slavery*, has been dealt further blows by scholars who stress the connectedness of the Old South to a broader intellectual culture. Planter and middle-class southern families subscribed to a wide range of northern newspapers and magazines, including *Harper's Magazine, Atlantic Monthly*, and *Putnam's Magazine*. As recent scholarship has shown, white southerners took advantage of the improved postal system and early nineteenth-century transportation advances to purchase subscriptions to literary and financial periodicals.[39] Antebellum postal records, which are especially detailed for the 1850s, reveal important insight into the reading habits of white southerners. The fact that many periodicals contained abolitionist sentiments did not dissuade southern readers, who oftern supplemented northern publications with subscriptions to periodicals closer to home, such as *The Southern Literary Messenger and DeBow's Review*. Added to these American publications were subscriptions to European periodicals like the *Edinburgh Review*. A planter or educated middle-class professional might subscribe to as many as a dozen periodicals, or even read them in town or college libraries. The diverse nature of nineteenth-century magazines and newspapers meant that southern readers were exposed to a broad range of literary, religious, political, and economic viewpoints.

Taken together, the historiographical trends of the last ten years point to a fundamentally different view of the slave South than the one dominant in the 1970s and 1980s. Previously, thanks to the insightful work of Genovese and others, scholars often thought of planter dominance when they considered the culture, economy, and politics of the Old South. Race seemed to trump class consciousness and whites were taken together as active participants in erecting a racial hierarchy that blurred class distinctions among whites, stunting the formation of class ideology. This line of thinking was perhaps the natural result of the concentrated focus on the plantation, even though the vast majority of white southerners had little connection to or direct involvement in life on a plantation. But the recent studies that take account of the majority of white southerners who did not own a plantation or slaves for that matter have helped us to understand better the complex nature of the southern social structure. Scholars now recognize the importance of telling the story of middle-class and poor whites alongside the continuing explorations into slave life and culture and the master class. Undoubtedly, historians will remain interested in the economic and political elite; *The Mind of the Master Class* (2005) by Elizabeth Fox-Genovese and Eugene Genovese testifies to the rich history still to be written about elite white southerners.[40] The equally significant work on slavery, such as Walter Johnson's *Soul by Soul: Life inside the Antebellum Slave Market* (1999) and Steven Deyle's new study of the slave trade, are evidence that slavery remains a vigorous, essential, and fertile area of historical inquiry.[41] But added to these areas of scholarly inquiry has been a new wave of works that stress conflict with the region, including class and political clashes among whites, as well as neglected groups such as merchants and tenant farmers.

QUESTIONS FOR FUTURE STUDY

Few areas of historical inquiry have undergone more historiographical shifts in the last half century than the study of class and slavery. Studies on race over the past few decades have enriched our understanding of class and slavery in the New World significantly, even as new creative tensions have emerged as to which held sway over the politics and society of the Old South, race or class. And yet, despite the mountain of scholarly work on the Old South, we still have only a tenuous grasp on the southern social structure, how classes differed or were similar in rural and urban areas, how classes evolved over time, and many other possible avenues for historical investigation. Thus while the study of class and slavery has received significant scholarly attention in recent decades, a surprising number of fundamental questions remain regarding the social structure of the South and the institution of slavery.

The study of class in the Old South is complicated significantly by the interplay between Upper South and Deep South, between mountain and lowcountry regions, between the older Atlantic states in the Southeast and the newly founded states of the Southwest such as Texas, Arkansas, and Missouri. And, even more fundamentally, the rural and urban divisions within the South make firm statements about the social structure problematic. For example, it is clear that in the Black Belt counties and along the coasts of South Carolina and Georgia, large planters, often governing plantations with hundreds of slaves, were dominant politically and economically. These planters formed an upper class that contrasted sharply with the lower classes of white laborers, small farmers, and, at the bottom of the order, bondsmen and women. In these rural areas, the yeomen farmers, overseers, and factors can be said to have formed a loose middling class.[42] Added to these categories in the middle class were the rural storekeepers and grocers who might have made a living at a rural crossroads. Until the late nineteenth century, when the Grange movement and other farmer-laborer groups were formed, it is difficult to detect any kind of meaningful, robust, or enduring class awareness. In the South's small towns and cities, however, one can discern a social structure more easily, one that often evinced an incipient class consciousness. At the top of this order stood the wealthy lawyers, large-scale merchants, and industrialists who accumulated significant money through speculation, success in the courtroom, or investment in manufacturing. Not all of these wealthy southerners were urban dwellers; many, such as William Gregg, built factories in the countryside. Still, it is important to note that the slave South spawned a proto-industrialist class that would become more prominent and numerous in the years after the war. Below the wealthy urbanites stood a middle class of professional and commercial southerners, including doctors, small merchants and grocers, middling lawyers, the clergy, editors, teachers, dentists, and white collar workers such as clerks. It has been argued that these southerners formed a class conscious and self-aware group in the years leading up to the war.[43] Below this largely urban middle class in the social structure were white laborers, an increasing number of whom were immigrants from Ireland and Germany, and free blacks. Thus, while one can paint with a broad brush a sense of the rural and urban social structures several fundamental questions remain unanswered. How did the social structures of town and country interact? How was one shaped by the other? How many, in terms of numbers, were there in each category, how much social mobility was there, and to what extent did southerners in each class challenge the social status quo?

Such questions remain unaddressed largely because scholars have been reluctant to consider the Old South a socially complicated region. Arguments often seem to boil down to statistics showing the overwhelming northern advantage in manufacturing and virtually every other category of economic and cultural modernization. These statistics are undeniable. But northern advance in modernization does not obviate a similar, albeit smaller-scale and slower, transition in the slave South. Indeed, leaving aside comparisons between North and South, and examining only the dramatic shifts *within* the slave states in the antebellum period, one sees important changes in the amount of capital invested in manufacturing, in the output of these efforts, in the numbers of banks, schools, railroads, and other internal improvements, in the population growth of cities and towns, and in many other facets of southern society, especially between 1840 and 1860. Stuck in the traditional historiographical rut of sectional distinctiveness, however, some scholars have questioned the relevance of class studies in a region that, it is argued, was "economically backward."

In addition to downplaying the significance and scale of changes within the region over the final antebellum decades, such a perspective also considers class only as a function of internal dynamics. The southern economy was far behind the North's, the argument goes, so therefore must have been its social development. But, as Michael O'Brien and others have recently demonstrated, the Old South and slave societies in South America and the Caribbean were linked in an Atlantic economy with the North and Europe that allowed for the easy transference of ideas. O'Brien demonstrated that elite white southerners, even in the midst of slavery, were well aware of the current intellectual trends emanating from the North and Europe, though southerners did not always embrace these ideas. Southern readers were well acquainted with the works of James Fennimore Cooper and Washington

Irving, and read British and French works avidly.[44] *Conjectures of Order* adds further weight to the argument that scholars who study class formation and the evolution of class consciousness must not only consider the elements that are of internal importance to a society, but, in addition, all such ideas coming from outside as well as inside a given society. Antebellum southerners, after all, were not just familiar with the thoughts of John C. Calhoun, Henry Hughes, and George Fitzhugh. Instead white southerners, including the middle class, were shaped equally powerfully by the works they read from northern and European thinkers, from Ralph Waldo Emerson and Henry David Thoreau to Voltaire and Edmund Burke. Even before the invention of the telegraph, slave societies were connected with free societies, which of course often sparked animosity as well as personal and professional relationships. The importance of this Atlantic network should not be underestimated, for although mails could be unreliable and travel by sea and railroad was often slow, slave and free societies were fully aware of each other's economic, political, and social ideology. Thus, while it is true that the southern economy lagged behind the North, it is also true that whites in the Old South read northern and European newspapers and magazines, cherished the same authors and popular novels, and agreed on most any matter aside from slavery.

Looking at class formation in this new fashion allows scholars to take the lessons learned from the cultural turn of the last few decades and re-inject new life into the debates about class and society. As Geoff Eley and Keith Nield have pointed out in *The Future of Class in History* it will not do for scholars to resurrect the old debates about class and class formation if the social is to be reexamined. Rather, by considering the cultural and intellectual connections throughout the Atlantic world, historians could offer new and important insights into class ideology as it existed in slave societies in the USA, the Caribbean, and South America.[45] Postal records, examination of reading habits, lyceums, debating societies, library records, data from nineteenth-century publishers, all offer potential insights into this Atlantic culture. Through such studies future works may uncover a greater class consciousness in slave societies than was previously believed to exist.

Other basic questions regarding class and slavery remain relatively unexplored. Scholars have examined the yeomen of the rural South as well as the mountain residents but the class resentment between mountain and lowcountry southerners seems underappreciated. In *Roots of Secession* (2003), historian William A. Link discovered significant conflict between eastern and western Virginians in the antebellum period.[46] While others have pointed out the east–west division within southern states, few have understood its full significance better than Link. Although such divisions appear on the surface to be mostly rooted in geography, class resentments between small mountain farmers, many of whom had few or no slaves, and the large-scale planters of the lowcountry are central to southern politics. Similar studies of North Carolina, South Carolina, Tennessee, and Georgia might indeed reveal similar deep-seated animosities among white southerners of varying degrees of wealth.

Finally, a few works have hinted at the social implications of the influx of white immigrants to the slave South, especially in the 1850s. While the numbers of German and Irish immigrants to the slave states were but a fraction of those that settled in northern cities like Boston, New York, and Philadelphia, a substantial number came to the South and helped to transform the region in the 1850s. As Ira Berlin and Herbert Gutman argued in an important but underappreciated article in 1983, immigrants shaped the politics, culture, and economy of southern port cities.[47] Much more work could be done to examine not only the influence of immigrants in the southern social structure, but also the extent to which white laborers formed a collective identity before the Civil War. It is clear that class hostility rose to the surface in the 1850s, as a number of strikes erupted throughout the region. In addition, protests, such as the tax revolt by workingmen in Raleigh in 1859, suggest the possibility of a broader class consciousness among the white laborers of the slave South.

Students of class and slavery have reason to hope that many of the questions posed here will be answered in the coming years. The recent spate of works on the economy and society of the nineteenth-century South provide the basis for optimism that long-standing questions and confusion over the social structure of the region will at last be addressed in greater depth. While scholars will undoubtedly continue to study the plantation and planter culture, fresh examinations of long-neglected groups may illuminate the nexus of class and slavery, and in doing so open new paths to our understanding of the Old South and of slave societies more broadly.

NOTES

1. Daniel J. Walkowitz, *Working with Class: Social Workers and the Politics of Middle-Class Identity* (Chapel Hill, NC, 1999), 6. See also John R. Hall (ed.), *Reworking Class* (Ithaca, NY, 1997); Martin J. Burke, *The Conundrum of Class: Public Discourse on the Social Order in America* (Chicago, 1995); Dror Wahrman, *Imagining the Middle Class: The Political Representation of Class in Britain, c.1780–1840* (Cambridge, 1995); Gareth Stedman Jones, *Languages of Class: Studies in English Working Class History, 1832–1982* (Cambridge, 1983).
2. Geoff Eley and Keith Nield, *The Future of Class in History: What's Left of the Social?* (Ann Arbor, 2007), 10.
3. Genovese modified his earlier arguments in works such as *Slaveholders' Dilemma: Freedom and Progress in Southern Conservative Thought, 1820–1860* (Columbia, SC, 1994), in which he argued that planters were caught between their desire for modernization and their attachment to an archaic system of slavery.
4. Richard Follett, *The Sugar Masters: Planters and Slaves in Louisiana's Cane World, 1820–1860* (Baton Rouge, La., 2007).

5. Luis A. Figueroa, *Sugar, Slavery, and Freedom in Nineteenth-Century Puerto Rico* (Chapel Hill, NC, 2005); Walton Look Lai, *Indentured Labor, Caribbean Sugar: Chinese and Indian Migrants to the British West Indies, 1838–1918* (Baltimore, 2004); Brian L. Moore (ed.), *Slavery, Freedom and Gender: The Dynamics of Caribbean Society* (Kingston, 2003); Kathleen Monteith and Glen Richards (eds.), *Jamaica in Slavery and Freedom: History, Heritage and Culture* (Kingston, 2002).

6. Hobsbawm quoted in Scott G. McNall, Rhonda F. Levine, and Rick Fantasia (eds.), *Bringing Class Back In: Contemporary and Historical Perspectives* (Boulder, Colo., 1991), 7.

7. Laurent Dubois, *Avengers of the New World: The Story of the Haitian Revolution* (Cambridge, 2005). Scholars have offered various reasons for the lack of success for slave revolts in the southern United States in contrast to Haiti and Barbados, but perhaps the most significant reason is the existence of sophisticated mechanisms for maintaining social order established in the American South. See Sally E. Hadden, *Slave Patrols: Law and Violence in Virginia and the Carolinas* (Cambridge, Mass., 2003).

8. Matt D. Childs, *The 1812 Aponte Rebellion in Cuba and the Struggle against Atlantic Slavery* (Chapel Hill, NC, 2006).

9. Laird Bergad, *The Comparative Histories of Slavery in Brazil, Cuba, and the United States* (Cambridge, 2007).

10. New research has suggested that in South America, scholars may have underestimated the level of animosity among whites, suggesting that the social order of slave societies in nations like Brazil may be more complicated than first believed. See, for example, Mieko Nishida, *Slavery and Identity: Ethnicity, Gender, and Race in Salvador, Brazil, 1808–1888* (Bloomington, Ind., 2003) and Jeffrey Needell, *The Party of Order: The Conservatives, the State, and Slavery in the Brazilian Monarchy, 1831–1871* (Palo Alto, Calif., 2006).

11. Jonathan Daniel Wells, *The Origins of the Southern Middle Class, 1800–1861* (Chapel Hill, NC, 2004).

12. Richard S. Dunn, *Sugar and Slaves: The Rise of the Planter Class in the English West Indies, 1624–1713* (Chapel Hill, NC, 2000).

13. Luis Martinez-Fernandez, *Protestantism and Political Conflict in the Nineteenth-Century Hispanic Caribbean* (New Brunswick, NJ, 2002).

14. On evangelical complaints about the pursuit of wealth, see Kenneth Moore Startup, *The Root of All Evil: The Protestant Clergy and the Economic Mind of the Old South* (Athens, Ga., 1997).

15. John David Smith (ed.), *Life and Labor in the Old South* (1929; reprint Columbia, SC: University of South Carolina Press, 2007), p. xli.

16. Frank Lawrence Owsley, *Plain Folk of the Old South* (Baton Rouge, La., 1949), 3–8. Quotations appear on pp. 6, 7–8, and 133. See also Samuel C. Hyde, Jr., *Plain Folk of the South Revisited* (Baton Rouge, La., 1997).

17. Richard C. Wade, *Slavery in the Cities: The South 1820–1860* (New York, 1964), 30.

18. Ibid. 247.

19. Eugene D. Genovese, *The Political Economy of Slavery: Studies in the Economy and Society of the Slave South* (New York, 1965), 20.

20. John W. Blassingame, *The Slave Community: Plantation Life in the Antebellum South* (New York, 1972); Eugene D. Genovese, *Roll Jordan, Roll: The World the Slaves Made* (New York, 1972).

21. Charles Joyner, *Down by the Riverside: A South Carolina Slave Community* (Urbana, Ill., 1984).

22. Steven Hahn, *The Roots of Southern Populism: Yeoman Farmers and the Transformation of the Georgia Upcountry, 1850–1890* (New York, 1983).

23. Lacy K. Ford, *Origins of Southern Radicalism: The South Carolina Upcountry 1800–1860* (New York, 1988); J. Mills Thornton III, *Politics and Power in a Slave Society, 1800–1860* (Baton Rouge, La., 1988).

24. Charles C. Bolton, *Poor Whites of the Antebellum South: Tenants and Laborers in Central North Carolina and Northeast Mississippi* (Durham, NC, 1994), p. ix. See also J. William Harris, *Plain Folk and Gentry in a Slave Society: White Liberty and Black Slavery in Augusta's Hinterlands* (Middletown, Conn., 1985).

25. Bolton, *Poor Whites*, 71. Like Bolton, Bradley G. Bond, in *Political Culture in the Nineteenth-Century South: Mississippi, 1830–1900* (Baton Rouge, La., 1995), offered key insights into the world of the southern yeoman and the shift from independent farming to sharecropping. Bond, however, adds another important dimension: race. In embracing a vision of white democracy, Bond argues, Mississippi farmers used race to blunt the potential for a shared class consciousness among lower-class blacks and whites.

26. Michele Gillespie, *Free Labor in an Unfree World: White Artisans in Slaveholding Georgia, 1789–1860* (Athens, Ga., 2000), 5, 33, 61.

27. Ibid. 64.

28. James Oakes, *Slavery and Freedom: An Interpretation of the Old South* (New York, 1990).

29. James Oakes, *The Ruling Race: A History of American Slaveholders* (New York, 1982).

30. Tom Downey, *Planting a Capitalist South: Masters, Merchants, and Manufacturers in the Southern Interior, 1790–1860* (Baton Rouge, La., 2006), 175.

31. Ibid. 8.

32. Eugene Ridings, *Business Interest Groups in Nineteenth-Century Brazil* (Cambridge, 2004).

33. Timothy J. Lockley, *Lines in the Sand: Race and Class in Lowcountry Georgia, 1750–1860* (Athens, Ga., 2004), p. xvii.

34. Jeff Forret, *Race Relations at the Margins: Slaves and Poor Whites in the Antebellum Southern Countryside* (Baton Rouge, La., 2006).

35. Ibid. 17.

36. Carl N. Degler, *The Other South: Southern Dissenters in the Nineteenth Century* (New York, 1974).

37. William W. Freehling, *The South vs. the South: How Anti-Confederate Southerners Shaped the Course of the Civil War* (New York, 2001), p. xiii.

38. Margaret M. Storey, *Loyalty and Loss: Alabama's Unionists in the Civil War and Reconstruction* (Baton Rouge, La., 2004); Hyman Rubin III, *South Carolina Scalawags* (Columbia, SC, 2006); James Alex Baggett, *The Scalawags: Southern Dissenters in the Civil War and Reconstruction* (Baton Rouge, La., 2003).

39. Michael O'Brien, *Conjectures of Order: Intellectual Life and the American South, 1810–1860* (Chapel Hill, NC, 2004).

40. Elizabeth Fox-Genovese and Eugene D. Genovese, *The Mind of the Master Class: History and Faith in the Southern Slaveholders' Worldview* (Cambridge, 2005).

41. Walter Johnson, *Soul by Soul: Life Inside the Antebellum Slave Market* (Cambridge, 1999); Steven Deyle, *Carry Me Back: The Domestic Slave Trade in American Life* (New York, 2005).

42. On this point, see Stephanie McCurry, *Masters of Small Worlds: Yeoman Households, Gender Relations, & the Political Culture of the Antebellum South Carolina Low Country* (New York, 1995), 40.

43. Wells, *Origins of the Southern Middle Class*.
44. Michael O'Brien, *Conjectures of Order: Intellectual Life and the American South, 1810–1860* (Chapel Hill, NC, 2004).
45. Eley and Nield, *The Future of Class in History*, 12–13.
46. William A. Link, *Roots of Secession: Slavery and Politics in Antebellum Virginia* (Chapel Hill, NC, 2003).
47. Ira Berlin and Herbert G. Gutman, "Natives and Immigrants, Free Men and Slaves: Urban Workingmen in the Antebellum American South," *American Historical Review*, 88 (December 1983), 1175–201. See also David T. Gleeson, *The Irish in the South, 1815–1877* (Chapel Hill, NC, 2001).

Select Bibliography

Bolton, Charles C. *Poor Whites of the Antebellum South: Tenants and Laborers in Central North Carolina and Northeast Mississippi*. Durham, NC: Duke University Press, 1994.

Downey, Tom. *Planting a Capitalist South: Masters, Merchants, and Manufacturers in the Southern Interior, 1790–1860*. Baton Rouge, La.: Louisiana State University Press, 2006.

Figueroa, Luis A. *Sugar, Slavery, and Freedom in Nineteenth-Century Puerto Rico*. Chapel Hill, NC: University of North Carolina Press, 2005.

Forret, Jeff. *Race Relations at the Margins: Slaves and Poor Whites in the Antebellum Southern Countryside*. Baton Rouge, La.: Louisiana State University Press, 2006.

Fox-Genovese, Elizabeth, and Eugene D. Genovese. *The Mind of the Master Class: History and Faith in the Southern Slaveholders' Worldview*. Cambridge: Cambridge University Press, 2005.

Gillespie, Michele. *Free Labor in an Unfree World: White Artisans in Slaveholding Georgia, 1789–1860*. Athens, Ga.: University of Georgia Press, 2000.

Harris, J. William. *Plain Folk and Gentry in a Slave Society: White Liberty and Black Slavery in Augusta's Hinterlands*. Middletown, Conn.: Wesleyan University Press, 1985.

Moore, Brian L. (ed.). *Slavery, Freedom and Gender: The Dynamics of Caribbean Society*. Kingston: University of the West Indies Press, 2003.

Ridings, Eugene. *Business Interest Groups in Nineteenth-Century Brazil*. Cambridge: Cambridge University Press, 2004.

Wells, Jonathan Daniel. *The Origins of the Southern Middle Class*. Chapel Hill, NC: University of North Carolina Press, 2004.

CHAPTER 17

RELIGION AND SLAVERY

DOUGLAS AMBROSE

INTRODUCTION

For most of history, religion has sanctioned slaveholding. All of the world's great religions on the eve of European colonization of the Americas permitted slavery, notwithstanding certain restrictions concerning who could or could not be enslaved. In addition to Christian denominations, traditional religions in Africa and the Americas also allowed slaveholding. By the end of the nineteenth century, however, religion in the West had come to condemn slavery as a *malum in se* (evil in itself). Historians have long recognized that this sea change in religious belief played a vital role in the genesis of the world's first antislavery crusade. Organized abolitionism in England and the United States in the early nineteenth century grew out of Protestant Christian churches, and devout evangelicals filled the movement's rank and file. But the topic of slavery and religion extends beyond the rise and triumph of the Christian antislavery crusade. Much recent scholarship has focused on two issues in particular: the varied processes by which Africans and peoples of African descent responded to and shaped Christianity to qualify the terms of bondage, and the ways defenders of slavery, especially in the American South, elaborated a sophisticated proslavery Christian worldview.

The emergent field of Atlantic history has profoundly influenced scholarship on the response of African slaves to Christianity, the nature of black Christianity in the Americas, and the ways that black Christianity differed from that of whites.

Atlantic history has also contributed to the study of Islam among Africans in both Africa and the New World and among African-Americans. Scholars have not always explicitly engaged the religious dimensions of the material and cultural contexts of slavery. But the crops grown, the master–slave relation, the demographic and ethnic makeup of the enslaved populations, and the character and influence of the white population shaped both the religious beliefs and practices of slaves throughout the New World.

The study of the religious lives of enslaved peoples in the Americas has benefited enormously from the work of historians and anthropologists who have studied Africa during the centuries of the Atlantic slave trade. In articles and books, John Thornton, most notably, a historian of pre-colonial Africa, has argued for the need to understand the religious lives of Africans before their enslavement and forced relocation to the Americas. Thornton's work has focused on West-Central Africa in general, primarily on the kingdom of Kongo, which encountered Portuguese explorers in the mid-fifteenth century. Within a few decades after first contact, missionaries had converted the Kongolese ruling elite to Catholicism. By the mid-sixteenth century, Thornton contends, the number of conversions had extended to the point of turning the kingdom into a Catholic society. For Thornton, the conversions of Kongos reflected the willingness of Africans themselves to embrace Catholicism. Far from having Catholicism imposed on them by Portuguese conquerors and their missionary allies, West-Central Africans adopted Catholicism on their own terms, for their own purposes. This adoption was possible, in large part, because "both cultures [West-Central African and European] accepted the basic reality of religion: that there was another world that could not be seen and that revelations were the essential source by which people could know of this other world." Thornton urges less focus on the "cosmological differences" between traditional West-Central African religions and Catholicism and more on their shared emphasis on "revelation." Catholicism allowed for West-Central Africans to convert "because they received 'co-revelations,' that is, revelations in the African tradition that dovetailed with the Christian tradition. The conversion was accepted because Christians also accepted this particular set of revelations as valid."[1] The specific character of traditional religion in West-Central Africa facilitated the process of conversion to Christianity, producing both Christian Africans and an Africanized Christianity. Although traditionalist priests existed, they exercised considerably less authority than Christian clerics, and that lack of authority prevented the maintenance of a rigid orthodoxy. Without a strong priesthood to interpret the continual revelations received by the laity, those revelations led to a fluid and dynamic religious tradition receptive to such revealed European religions as Catholicism.

Thornton's work underscores that many enslaved Africans were in fact believing and practicing Christians before the Middle Passage. This recognition has implications for the ways in which African Christianity informed slave life and culture in the New World. Both Thornton and Mark M. Smith, for example, have elaborated upon the ways in which Catholicism shaped the Stono Rebellion—an ethnic rebellion of Kongo slaves—in South Carolina in 1739. Hein Vanhee and Terry Rey have examined West-Central African Christian influences on Haitian religion. Scholars of Haitian Vodou, Rey claims, "have succeeded admirably" in their efforts "to uncover [in Vodou] traditional Kongolese 'survivals.'" But this very focus may have "unwittingly de-Catholize[d] seventeenth and eighteenth century Kongolese religious culture in the New World."[2]

The prominent role of laypersons in spreading Christian belief and practice in West-Central Africa entails a reexamination of conversion. It meant less a stripping away of tradition and the imposition of an alien faith than "a spontaneous, voluntary act on the part of Africans convinced by the same types of revelations that had shown them their own gods that the other world was in fact inhabited by a group of beings who were identical to the deities of the Europeans." "African Christianity," Thornton notes, "allowed Africans to retain their old cosmology, their old understanding of the structure of the universe and the place of the gods and other divine beings in it."[3] Thus for some Africans, Christianity was not a "foreign" or exclusively "white" religion that they first encountered in the New World. For these Africans, Annette Laing posits, "it is hardly likely that they would have considered Christianity as part of their oppression in America."[4]

Recognizing the volitional nature of African conversion to Christianity raises questions about what made African religion compatible with Christianity and about what made Christianity acceptable to Africans. The Christianity that Europeans—and Christianized Africans—presented to Africans clearly proved accommodating to traditional African beliefs and practices. Christianity in both Africa and the New World often permitted and even encouraged a degree of syncretism. That syncretism, however, developed organically from the nature of Christianity, especially Catholicism, and not from African "deviation" from a static "orthodoxy." Rather than viewing African-American Christianity as a syncretic religion produced primarily if not exclusively by African initiative and in opposition to European orthodoxy, syncretism represents a process accepted by both Africans and European Christians. Thornton maintains that Africans "were not given hasty instruction in a complex and foreign religion they could barely understand," but entered into voluntary mutually beneficial exchanges with Christian clergy and lay evangelists that led to a legitimized blending of African tradition with "what was 'essential' to being a good Christian."[5]

James H. Sweet, a historian with a transatlantic reach, has leveled the most formidable challenge to Thornton's work. Although agreeing that Africa "must be the starting point for any study of Africans in the diaspora, particularly during the era of the slave trade," Sweet asserts that for most Africans, including the Kongolese, traditional religion, not Christianity, informed "the institutions that Africans created" and provided "them with a prism through which to interpret and understand their condition as slaves and as freed peoples." Focusing primarily on seventeenth-century Brazil, but with implications for other New World regions that depended on steady importations of Africans, Sweet argues that Africans "utilized a variety of specific 'Angolan,' and especially Mbundu, ritual practices and beliefs—divinations, ordeals, ritual burials, dietary restrictions, and cures—as a way of addressing their condition." Not only were Africans able to "replicate specific African institutions in America," but their "African religions were not syncretic or creolized but were independent systems of thought, practiced in parallel to Catholicism."[6]

Sweet and Thornton differ in large part regarding the processes of syncretism and Christianization among Africans in the diaspora. Thornton's emphasis on "revelation over the broader cosmology" of traditional African religion, Sweet argues, "downplays the real essence of Central African religious thought." Although Catholicism did rely on revelation, the Church "considered revelations to be extraordinarily rare and miraculous expressions of God's will on earth." The Kongolese, by contrast, "depended upon continuous revelation for their daily survival." This difference amounted to incompatible cosmologies. Sweet discerns in the "constant dialogue between laypeople and the spirit world . . . the linchpin of African cosmology," and it "became the primary target of Catholic extirpation campaigns" that reveal "the narrowness of the European Catholic conversion project in Central Africa." Although Sweet acknowledges that many Kongolese "adopted Christianity as a fundamental part of their individual and collective identity," he maintains that concepts such as "African Christianity" obscure more than they reveal about the "spiritual" and "cosmological core" of Kongolese faith. At the core, Sweet insists, the "broad Central African cosmology" remained "the dominant religious paradigm for most Kongolese," even though in their religious practices they used "Christian symbols to represent their own deities." Unlike Thornton, Sweet sees Christianity as "at best, a parallel system of belief that served to complement Kongolese worldviews." Thus, Central Africans who arrived as slaves in the New World were not full-fledged Christians; they did not simply bring with them some random "survivals" of traditional religion. Instead, the "functional and structural integrity of specific African rituals and beliefs was sustained from Africa to the Americas." Only "over the course of several genera-tions" did "the blending of various aspects of the two traditions eventually [lead] to the development of a distinctly Africanized form of Christianity that began to be seen as a religious movement independent of traditional Kongolese cosmology." Yet even that Africanized version of Christianity was as much "African" as it was "Christian."[7]

Sweet and others explain the compatibility of certain Christian features with Africans not by shared belief in revelation but by "earth-bound pragmatism."[8] Christianity was adapted as an additional means to realize traditional "African" ends. "Christian thought," argues Michael Gomez, "was incorporated into a means of approaching and experiencing the divine that was totally African."[9] For many Africans, "approaching and experiencing the divine" meant dealing with real-world problems; religion restored "temporal balance through spiritual intervention."[10] African religion's preoccupation with the temporal—as opposed to the heavenly—realm led Africans to approach Christianity "as they approached all potential spiritual tools: selectively and constructively . . . as a means to control their everyday environments."[11] Baptism, for example, marked not so much the initiation of an African into a Christian community, but the use of a spiritual weapon in a battle against earthly ills. "Baptism," Sweet writes, "was understood as an external protection against the evils that plagued Africans. It was very much a temporal remedy, not a prescription for eternal salvation and the washing away of sin." Likewise he views slave adoption of the rosary as a means of acquiring its "object power." As such, the rosary acted "like so many other African talismans."[12] The development in the Americas of such Christian and African syncretic witch-crafts as Vodou, hoodoo, and conjure revealed "two critical continuities: the African perspective of causality and techniques of traditional intercession."[13] Thus slaves adopted Christianity, at least in part, because they understood it as a force to provide "remedies to their worldly ills."[14]

Although Christianity proved compatible with traditional African religions, that fact alone does not explain why so many slaves eventually embraced Christianity and became thoroughgoing Christians. For many scholars who believe that that embrace was sincere and not coerced, feigned, or merely pragmatic, the answer lies in what Christianity provided to slaves psychologically and spiritually. Some scholars posit that these distinctly Christian psychological and spiritual benefits complemented the more traditionally African physical benefits, exhibiting the unique ways African-American Christianity built upon both the African religious inheritance and the New World experience of enslavement. For Gomez, "Christianity provided an explanation for large-scale suffering that could not be found in African religions." Enslavement, the Middle Passage, and slave life in the New World inflicted on Africans shocks and upheavals so profound that "the religions of the ancestors were unable to satisfactorily explain" them.[15] Christianity, in both the story of the Hebrew people and the suffering of Jesus, thus presented slaves with both consolation and explanation. Eugene Genovese pointed out in his magisterial study *Roll, Jordan, Roll* how both the story of the Hebrews and the passion of the Christ resonated for slaves with the theme of deliverance through suffering.[16] Consolation came through knowing that although God's people had suffered in ages past, they had gained deliverance, that God himself, in the person of Jesus, had experienced physical torment but had triumphed over death. As Jon Sensbach's recent study of black Moravians in the Americas notes, "the Gospel would never have spread among the slaves if it taught them only to bow. Its . . . popularity suggests that they took something greater from the Bible, some affirmation, perhaps, that Jesus died for them, a fundamental sense that their affliction made them God's chosen people."[17] Redemptive suffering lies at the heart of Christianity. African slaves in the New World, by embracing that faith, acquired not only the understanding of their own suffering, but also the means of transcending it.

African-American Christianity varied enormously across time and space as did the intrusiveness of masters in their slaves' religious practices. Brazil and the Caribbean sugar islands experienced a more pronounced African emphasis in slave religious life than did the antebellum United States in which Africans comprised a small portion of the slave population. In the British Caribbean, where master absenteeism was rife, the overwhelming black majority, as Sylvia Frey and Betty Wood point out, produced an "almost complete separation of black and white spiritual communities," which "made it possible for Afro-Caribbeans to create a spiritual universe whose primary cultural essence derived from African antecedents."[18] Catholic regions in the Americas differed considerably from Protestant ones, especially prior to the mid-eighteenth-century revivals. Before "the 1730s, to be black and Christian almost certainly meant being Catholic."[19] Not only had Catholicism made inroads among Africans in Africa, its emphasis on the saints, revelation, sacramentals (rosaries, medals, holy water, statues), and iconography provided attractive means to reach traditionalist Africans. Several Catholic religious orders held slaves, including the Benedictines and Carmelites in Brazil and the Jesuits and Vincentians in the United States. Protestantism prior to the eighteenth-century revivals known as the Great Awakening appealed to few Africans. Frey and Wood, in a comparative study of Protestantism in the British Caribbean and the American South before 1830, observe that in British colonies prior to 1730 "the vast majority of bondpeople found little in Anglicanism with which they could or wished to identify; they were offered no convincing, or compelling, reasons to abandon traditional beliefs and rituals in favor of those espoused by the colonial clergy." Although Annette Laing has recently suggested that scholars may have overstated the extent of slaves' rejection of Anglicanism, no one seriously questions the role of the Great Awakening in initiating the widespread conversion of African slaves to Protestantism.[20]

THE DEVELOPMENT OF AFRICAN-AMERICAN EVANGELICAL CHRISTIANITY

In 1830 the slaves of the British colonies and former British colonies in the Americas constituted the largest population of African Protestants in the world. How this transformation—from African traditionalists to Protestants—happened has been the subject of intense study. Most scholars agree that several developments contributed to the conversion of African and African-American slaves to Protestantism. First, a growing creole (native-born) population, especially in North America, lowered linguistic barriers between slaves and white missionaries. More important, these missionaries increasingly came from evangelical sects and denominations, especially Methodists and Baptists, along with some Presbyterians and evangelical Anglicans such as George Whitefield. These evangelical Protestants promulgated "a powerful integrating ideology and an ethos whose emphasis on spiritual equality had the potential for creating the first distinctive changes in African values in relation to Protestant Christianity." Unlike Anglicans, evangelicals de-emphasized formal, literate catechesis in favor of oral communication and a profound, transforming experience of the Spirit. The evangelicals' focus on "the direct operation of the Holy Spirit, which should come to the individual in an overwhelming experience that would immediately change his basic nature," resonated powerfully among slaves.[21] The expressive physicality of conversion, some suggest, proved "entirely consistent with [slaves'] roots in indigenous African religion. They sang, they swayed, but more important, they danced and went into trance."[22] Conversion also emphasized the equality of souls before God; every individual, regardless of class or race, had the chance to be reborn in the Spirit. Membership in evangelical churches depended on whether or not one was reborn, not whether one had mastered a catechism or biblical exegesis. Both theologically, in the emphasis on rebirth through the Spirit, and ecclesiologically, in basing membership on experience rather than formal learning, evangelical churches appealed to slaves of African descent.

Many scholars, while acknowledging the importance of theological and ecclesiological aspects of evangelical Christianity to the spread of evangelical Protestantism, emphasize the vital role that Africans and African-Americans played in spreading the faith. In St Thomas, for example, black lay Moravians "fanned out along the rugged roads to bring their teachings to the people." These "foot soldiers of a spiritual revolution" took "practical control of the mission" to the slaves themselves. They made "Christianity a religion of and for people of African origin, they were the spokeswomen and men of the emerging black church in America." In Jamaica, "a far greater number of Afro-Jamaicans were exposed to Christianity through self-proclaimed black and colored preachers, exhorters, and male and female class leaders than by white missionaries." Charles Irons notes that in eighteenth-century Virginia "one thing that may have attracted black men and women to Baptist and Methodist churches . . . was the growing number of black evangelists within these denominations."[23] Although the emphasis on blacks as carriers of the faith risks minimizing the intrinsic power of the content of the faith in its acceptance, no one can deny that black men and women, both slave and free, proved indispensable to the conversion of people of African descent in the Americas.

The Great Awakening ushered in not only the evangelical emphasis on the new birth and the work of the Spirit but also the denominational divisions that characterized Protestantism in late colonial British North America and the United States. Those denominational divisions, and the lack of state sponsorship, prompted primarily Baptists and Methodists, but also some Presbyterians, Moravians, and even evangelical Anglicans/Episcopalians, to engage in an intense missionary competition for black souls.

However much evangelical Protestantism provided continuities with traditional African religion, becoming Christian entailed fundamental changes among African and African-American converts in both belief and behavior. Although few if any scholars share Jon Butler's controversial but often misunderstood notion of an "African spiritual holocaust," most acknowledge that black conversion to Christianity required more of slaves than simply adding onto their preexisting belief systems.[24] Two of the most important changes that conversion to Christianity brought to African slaves concerned the nature of the afterlife and the notion of sin. As Frey points out, "Most Africans expected neither judgment nor reward in the hereafter." Death, for most traditional Africans, served as "a transition to a hereafter, which they viewed as a continuation, of sorts, of life in its human form."[25] Christianity, therefore, demanded a fundamental reconceptualization not only of death and the nature of the afterlife, but also of life, since how people lived their lives affected, even determined, how they would spend the afterlife. Christian notions of heaven and of judgment, however, did not gain immediate acceptance among Africans, even those attracted to Christianity. Although some black Christians continued to see heaven in traditional African terms as an ancestral home, heaven necessarily evolved into a universal rather than a particular or familial home. In the Christian heaven, all the saved—black and white, male and female, slave and free—resided together for eternity. "The new Christianity," Mechal Sobel observes, "changed the African linkage of close kin and unique afterworld, which had excluded the stranger and the slave from the afterlife of an ethnic group, to a linkage of all Christians to one Heaven."[26]

Hell necessarily attended the Christian notion of heaven. A place of eternal punishment for the wicked was foreign to most Africans. The traditional concept of the afterlife was no respecter of persons; all members of an ethnic group went to the ancestral homeland. "In the slaves' traditional religion," writes Mary Turner, "nothing that happened on earth affected their prospect of feasting with the ancestors in the afterlife." Christianity, however, forcefully inserted ethics into the convert's understanding of his nature and destiny. "Nothing in the slaves' theology prepared them for the idea of God the law giver." And the corresponding notion, "that there was a vital connection between conduct in this world"—obeying or disobeying God's laws—"and fate in the world to come, was completely novel to the slaves."[27] Slaves throughout the Americas proved resistant to the Christian idea of sin, of disobedience to God's law, in part because it located evil within individual persons. "African cosmologies defined evil as that which destroyed health, life, or fortune. The sources of evil were supernatural or mystical forces or the malevolent powers of sorcerers or witches." Christianity redefined the source and the meaning of evil. Rather than something done *to* someone and that had no relation to one's character, sin, to the Christian, became something someone *did*, and it related directly to one's character and ultimate destiny. "Converted Afro-Americans," Sobel concludes, "did begin to take the Christian idea of sin very much to heart and to worry about their own salvation, even after conversion." Accepting the Christian notions of evil, sin, and hell, however, did more than produce fear about salvation. Believing in them both provided slaves with an "enhanced . . . sense of their own worth and laid the foundation for changes in their conduct."[28] These Christian beliefs thus provided slaves with powerful psychological weapons in their struggle with those who held them in bondage.

The concept of sin that prevailed among most black Christians never fully incorporated the Augustinian version of original sin. Rather than emphasizing innate depravity, black Christians conceived of sin as ethical or moral transgression. A paradox resulted: "The slaves admitted to sin only when they had grasped that to acknowledge their sinfulness was to acknowledge, as Christians, their individual spiritual value." By striving to fulfill "the strenuous measures [missionaries] recommended to secure" one's salvation, the individual affirmed his sense of worthiness before God and his fellow sinful but striving Christians.[29] Such a conception of sin located judgment and justice beyond the master and reminded the slave of what was God's and what was Caesar's. Worthiness came from how well one tried to fulfill God's law, not from one's earthly station or earthly authority. Evidence from disciplinary proceedings of evangelical churches suggests that black Christians actively sought to fashion their lives in accordance with the faith's precepts. Evidence indicates that only a "miniscule proportion" of black church members lost their membership because they failed to regulate properly their sexual conduct and family relations. "The vast majority of enslaved church members freely chose and, often in the most harrowing of personal circumstances, did their best to order their sexual morality according to the Christian ideal espoused by their white co-religionists." In choosing to conform to the "ideal espoused by their white co-religionists" black church members affirmed their moral worth as responsible beings before God. Frey and Wood see similar commitment and agency in blacks' willingness to devote "time and resources . . . to what they considered to be their churches," in their faithful "attendance at Sunday services and weeknight meetings," and in their adherence to "strictures against any form of Sabbath breaking."[30] By making Christian morality a code that individuals chose to live by, black Christians resisted the logic of dehumanization inherent in slavery and strengthened their personal and collective sense of human dignity.

Black Christians understood the Christian notions of heaven, hell, and judgment in ways that reflected both their experiences as slaves and their belief in a just and righteous God who punished evildoers. Hell, in the slaves' view, would be populated primarily if not exclusively by masters. As Emily Burke, a northern schoolteacher in Georgia, reminisced in 1850, "I never saw a negro a Universalist; for they all believe in a future retribution for their masters, from the hand of a just God."[31] Although few slaves held such a Manichean view of heaven and hell and of slaves and masters, the belief that God would hold people accountable for their actions on earth provided slaves with a powerful sense of an ultimate, divine justice. If slaves obtained consolation through the suffering servant Jesus, they obtained righteous satisfaction through the wrathful judge Jehovah.

Most research into the religious lives of New World slaves discusses the diverse, uneven, and complex processes by which traditional African religions resisted, mixed with, and embraced Christian beliefs and practices. Islamic slaves in the Americas remain understudied, despite João José Reis's penetrating book on the 1835 Muslim slave revolt in Salvador, Brazil. Although the number of enslaved Muslims transported across the Atlantic defies precise estimation, they were present in every American slave society. As an organized religion, however, Islam faced enormous difficulties in the New World. "For Islam to endure," maintains Sylviane Diouf, "it had to grow both vertically, through transmission to children, and horizontally, through conversion of the unbelievers. Both propositions met a number of obstacles."[32] First, their small numbers within the slave population meant that few could find Muslim spouses, have children, and then raise them in the faith, especially under conditions that rendered families vulnerable to break up through death and sale. Second, slavery severely restricted the ability of Muslim slaves to promote literacy in Arabic to others. Muslim slaves in North America "could not openly maintain Qur'anic schools, nor did they have access to Islamic texts."[33] Without proper education, transmission of the faith even within families proved extremely difficult and it made conversion even more so. Islam never developed a creolized or syncretic variant in the Americas. Although elements of Islam undoubtedly survived in the syncretic religions of Candomblé, Santeria, and Vodou, Islam, in stark contrast to Christianity, never became a dynamic creolized black religion during the slavery era. It became even weaker when the ending of the slave trade stopped the flow of African Muslims into New World slave societies.

WHITE AND BLACK CHRISTIANS IN THE UNITED STATES

The religious lives of American slaves reflected their African origins, demographic factors, and, perhaps most important, the influence of whites: masters, missionaries, and others. Whatever agency slaves exercised, they did so, to varying degrees throughout the New World, within societies dominated by whites. Thus, most historians continue to demarcate the process of slave Christianization in ways that reveal that power. For the area that became the United States, a three-period scheme of black Christianization tends to obtain: the first period, which began in the 1730s and ended around 1785, witnessed the initial efforts by white evangelical missionaries to reach out to slaves; the second, from 1785 to 1830, reveals the consolidation of a growing population of black Christians and their organization in both white and black churches; the third, from 1830 to 1860, marked an aggressive mission to the slaves and the suppression of independent black churches. From the initial efforts to convert slaves to Christianity to the outbreak of the Civil War, white southerners pondered the political and religious meanings of a Christianized slave population and a Christian slave society in a world and a nation increasingly convinced that slavery was a sin. As white southerners confronted their slaves and their antislavery opponents, they developed a religious understanding of themselves and their world that convinced them of both their righteousness before God and the need to defend their Christian social order from enemies who had perverted the Bible's meaning and undermined true Christianity.

To be sure, the first great wave of slave conversions to Protestant Christianity in British North America met initial resistance from colonial masters who feared conversion would undermine their authority over slaves. Indeed, in Virginia before 1667, slaves who could prove they had been baptized often won their freedom, leading the Virginia legislature in that year to pass a law stating that conversion to Christianity did not affect a slave's status. Although every other colony concurred with Virginia, suspicions that conversion would beget unruly slaves, even though it could not free them, persisted. At the heart of these suspicions was the recognition, implicit or explicit, that Christian doctrine contained within it messages subversive of bondage. Religious belief, per se, posed no particular problem. It was Christianity, with its themes of liberation, deliverance, and equality, that frightened masters. For missionaries of all denominations interested in ministering to slaves, calming white fears became an essential prerequisite to their labors.[34]

Most missionaries in the decades before the American Revolution accepted slavery as a system even as they frequently criticized abusive masters and directed harsh language at those who neglected their slaves' spiritual need for the gospel. Missionaries sought not so much to meliorate the material treatment of slaves but to save their souls. Drawing upon a rich Christian tradition that had unequivocally distinguished between the spiritual and civil meanings of liberty and equality, missionaries assured masters that the Christianization of the slaves would not produce social chaos and economic ruin. Rather, they argued, Christianity, properly taught, would render slaves more obedient and productive. Samuel Davies, an emblematic Presbyterian minister in Virginia during the mid-eighteenth century, reminded masters that *"true* Christianity . . . tends to inspire its subjects with modesty, humility, meekness, faithfulness, and every grace and virtue; and that a *good Christian* will always be a *good servant.*"[35] Throughout the entire history of white evangelization among African-American slaves, ministers and missionaries would seek to promote "true" Christianity, to prevent the slaves themselves from "misinterpreting" a message of discipline and obedience into one of rebelliousness.

The decades following the American Revolution posed new challenges to American whites in their efforts to understand the relation between their Christian faith and slavery. A small but vocal antislavery movement within British and American Christianity proclaimed that slavery was inherently sinful, a *malum in se*. Although the Quakers had banished slaveholders from their flock in the 1750s, only when the Methodists, following their leader John Wesley, moved against slaveholding did Christian slaveholders begin to close ranks in response. At the annual meeting of the American Methodist Episcopal Church in Baltimore in 1784 the Church demanded that members free their slaves within two years or face expulsion. Ferocious opposition from the laity, however, forced withdrawal of the rule within six months. Citizens countered Methodist and Quaker efforts to promote emancipation in Virginia with petitions to the state legislature. They reveal, like Davies's sermon, a serious biblical defense of slavery, an insistence on a divine sanction for slaveholding. To substantiate the argument, they cited a multitude of biblical verses—e.g. Genesis 9: 25–7, Leviticus 25: 44–6, and 1 Corinthians 7: 20–4—that would reappear countless times in proslavery sermons and tracts down to the Civil War.[36]

Historians have tended to overstate the significance of the antislavery challenge posed in the post-revolutionary South by Methodists, Quakers, and Baptists. The usual depiction suggests that the combination of revolutionary, natural rights ideology and evangelical Christianity drove slavery in the South to the ropes. Only the co-option of the churches by proslavery planters, who appealed to marginalized but socially ambitious Methodist and Baptist ministers, allowed the continuance of slavery.[37] Recent scholarship has effectively countered this interpretation. "Post-Revolutionary evangelical leaders," as Charles Irons demonstrates, "did not arrest any religious momentum for abolition because no real momentum existed."[38] Instead, evangelical whites followed a path blazed by Davies and other theologians: They concentrated on fulfilling their primary responsibility of saving souls, on spreading the gospel "to all nations," and on reaffirming the divine sanction of slavery. The shepherds increased their flocks. The number of black Christians continued to grow, masters' fears, although never eliminated, tended not to inhibit missionary work, and antislavery Christianity remained muted and marginalized if not totally absent.

To be sure, the growth of independent black churches during this second period of slave Christianization created problems in the South. Although the African Methodist Episcopal (AME) Church, the first independent black church, appeared in the North in 1816 under the leadership of Bishop Richard Allen, several thousand blacks formed a southern branch in Charleston, South Carolina, in 1817. In fact, throughout the slave states blacks gathered in their own congregations in churches, cabins, and fields and listened to fellow blacks proclaim God's word. Whites often ignored laws that restricted black assemblages outside of white supervision and permitted these religious gatherings. The Denmark Vesey conspiracy of 1822 in Charleston, alleged to have been plotted by AME class leaders, began a dramatic crackdown on separate black worship; Nat Turner's revolt in Virginia in 1831 crested a wave of repression. Vesey's plot and Turner's bloody revolt convinced many whites that blacks could not be left to themselves in religious matters, for to do so could turn a religion of peace into a superstitious creed that fostered rebelliousness. Nor did Jamaica's so-called Baptist War (1831), the largest slave insurrection in the history of British America, led by Christianized slaves, put the minds of southern masters at ease. Still, most southern whites remained committed to the proposition that "true" Christianity, administered by whites, would mold slaves into "good Christians" and "good servants."

The Vesey and Turner affairs effectively ended the second period of slave Christianization. That they coincided with organized antislavery's gathering momentum in the North served to galvanize southerners into a more concerted effort at missionary outreach to the slaves. In this effort, Presbyterian minister Charles Colcock Jones of Liberty County, Georgia, stands out. The mission movement characterized much of the final period of slave Christianization and had several main objectives. First, Jones and other southern ministers lamented the persistence in nominally Christian slaves of what they saw as "heathenish" elements, often attributable, whites thought, to the slaves' African inheritance. "They believe," Jones wrote in 1842, "in second-sight, in apparitions, charms, witchcraft, and in a kind of irresistible Satanic influence. The superstitions brought from Africa have not been wholly laid aside."[39] Eradicating the vestiges of traditional religion and enforcing Christian doctrinal orthodoxy required an active white presence during black worship and an ongoing catechesis at other times.

The second objective related to the first and sought to teach slaves the Christian values of "modesty, humility, meekness, [and] faithfulness" that Davies nearly a century earlier had insisted would accompany "*true* Christianity." This need to control the message that slaves derived from Christianity took on special urgency after 1830 because of the unsettling influence of northern and foreign white antislavery Christians. In responding in this way to the rise of Christian abolitionists, white proslavery Christians demonstrated that their mission to the slaves represented a struggle between rival meanings of Christianity itself. As northern abolitionists increasingly invoked Christianity in their denunciations of slavery and occasionally directly called upon slaves to resist the sin of slavery, white southerners rallied around a biblical defense of slavery and labored assiduously if largely in vain to instill it into their slaves. Slaves resisted this message, but their masters drew strength from it, more firmly embracing than ever before the justice of slaveholding and their perception of themselves as the preservers of "true Christianity" against the perverted version of it steadily infecting the North and western Europe.

A biblical, paternalistic, and corporatist worldview framed the white South's understanding of a Christian slave society. Accordingly, southern ministers, echoing a theme that went back to George Whitefield and Samuel Davies, enjoined masters to act like Christian stewards, charged by God with the care of black bodies and black souls. Forcefully rejecting the scientific racism of polygenesis, which posited that blacks were a distinct species that derived from a separate creation, southern ministers affirmed the spiritual equality of blacks as descendants of Adam and Eve even as they maintained their civic inequality and enslavement. God had placed persons in particular stations and from those stations flowed one's rights and one's obligations to others. In countless sermons on the "rights and duties of masters," ministers reminded masters to "give unto your servants that which is just and equal; knowing that ye also have a Master in heaven" (Colossians 4: 1). Only by conforming southern slavery to the divine code of conduct could masters expect God's favor.

One prominent feature of much proslavery Christian thought was the "Curse of Ham," also known as the "Curse of Canaan." Genesis 9: 20–9 relates the story of how Noah's third son, Ham, looked upon his drunken father's naked body and then told his two older brothers, Shem and Japheth, what he had done. Noah, upon discovering Ham's transgression, pronounced "Cursed be Canaan [Ham's son]; a servant of servants shall he be to his brethren" (Genesis 9: 25 KJV). Historians and biblical scholars have intensively studied the curse's meanings through time, noting that although it had functioned as a justification of slavery throughout antiquity and the medieval era, only with the predominance of sub-Saharan Africans in first the Muslim slave trade and subsequently the Atlantic slave trade did the curse come to have a distinct racial meaning. By the early nineteenth century, many white Christians had come to believe that black Africans were Canaanites, destined by God to be "servants of servants."

Although no scholar denies that the curse circulated widely in the antebellum South, a critical question concerns the curse's role in proslavery Christianity. Some, including Stephen Haynes, contend that the curse, by fusing Scripture and racism, provided the justification for not only slavery but also postwar segregation. Others, however, dispute the foundational character of the curse within the proslavery argument. They argue that the curse was of marginal significance to the religious defense of slavery. Some antebellum theologians and ministers recognized that most biblical references to slavery did not mention specific races and, therefore, did not justify enslavement of a specific race. Nor did the Bible establish the genealogical descent of modern black Africans from Ham. The debate highlights a topic that deserves more scholarly attention, namely, the extent to which southern proslavery Christians sought both to defend their particular regime and to abstract general principles of social order and organization from that particular regime. Those who emphasize the curse's role in southern religion tend to neglect the latter effort. Those who minimize the curse's significance highlight the southern clergy's efforts to defend the biblical legitimacy of slavery in the abstract and not simply black slavery in the Americas.[40]

CHRISTIANITY AND THE COMING OF THE AMERICAN CIVIL WAR

Missionary outreach to the slaves did not prevent blacks from meeting separately, although the occurrence of such meetings often required considerable slave ingenuity and discretion. The mission movement failed not only to eradicate African "superstitions" from black Christianity, but also to persuade black Christians that "true" Christianity supported slavery. Yet some northern blacks, including ex-slaves Bishop Richard Allen and Frederick Douglass, also embraced the notion of the "fortunate fall": Enslavement, the slave trade, and New World slavery, whatever their costs, had brought civilization and Christianization to persons of African descent. Christianized African-Americans could then promote God's kingdom by returning to Africa and evangelizing the continent. Scholarship on whether slaves too embraced this thinking is lacking.

The mission movement failed to turn the majority of southern masters into paternalist Christian stewards, but it did contribute to the belief, and the elaborate defense of that belief, that the South's slave society adhered to biblical standards and was increasingly the last best hope on earth of preserving Christian orthodoxy. White southerners vigorously resisted the growing conviction among Christians in the West that slavery violated Christian precepts. The great schisms in the Methodist and Baptist churches in 1844 and 1845, respectively, testify to the depth of white southern Christian resolve. Both schisms resulted from southerners' refusal to accept implications that slaveholding was sinful or in any way necessarily compromised one's Christianity. Southern Methodists, Baptists, and Old School Presbyterians grounded their defense of slavery in a defense of biblical orthodoxy. The debate over the compatibility of slaveholding and Christianity opened up much broader debates regarding biblical exegesis, human nature, the implications of the fall, and the question of authority. These debates demonstrate that the American Civil War was, in a very real sense, a death struggle over the meaning of the Bible and the future of Christianity.[41]

Antislavery appeals to the Golden Rule ("Therefore all things whatsoever ye would that men should do to you, do ye even so to them" Matthew 7: 12) failed to convince southerners that slavery violated biblical principle. Southerners pointed out that the Golden Rule applied not to abstract individuals but to the particulars of established relations: People should treat others as they would expect to be treated if they occupied the others' station. Thus a master should treat his slave as he would want that slave to treat him if their stations were reversed. Southerners also tellingly pointed out that rigid application of the "antislavery" interpretation of the Golden Rule would destroy all unequal human relations, including those of employer/employee, husband/wife, parent/child, even magistrate/criminal. Even more disturbing to southern Christians was the abolitionists' appeal to the "spirit" of the Bible over its literal meaning. Although some antislavery biblical exegesis sought to refute the southern evangelicals' proslavery reading of the Bible, more and more abolitionists insisted that the New Testament's "law of love" trumped all the chapters and verses to which proslavery Christians appealed. As early as 1833, John Rankin, a leading antislavery Presbyterian, declared, "The whole Bible is opposed to slavery. The sacred volume is one grand scheme of benevolence— beams of love and mercy emanate from every page, while the voice of justice denounces the oppressor, and speaks his awful doom!"[42]

Southerners saw in such appeals a pronounced northern tendency of loosely interpreting sacred texts, denying their plain meaning to make them conform to what they wanted them to say. The overriding principle of "benevolence" rendered moot all biblical passages that sanctioned slavery. Perceptive southerners predicted the outcome: Such radical abolitionists as Henry C. Wright and William Lloyd Garrison "were led to repudiate certain [biblical] texts as contrary to God's true intent and to decide that not all of the Bible was inspired." By what authority, southerners asked, could one determine which passages from the Bible were inspired? Without direct divine revelation, "the only alternative was to discard the arbitrary will of God as the determinant of true principles set forth in the Bible, and in its place to hypostatize those principles themselves." Southerners recoiled at the inversion of authority that such an alternative produced. "Christian" abolitionists who "had begun by judging the world by Truth and Right as revealed in the scriptures, ended by judging the scriptures by Truth and Right as revealed by their own reason."[43] The right of private judgment elevated human reason above divine revelation. For southern Christians, this apostasy, not simply the abolitionist agenda it promoted, helped make the religious debate over slavery a minor if significant battle in a holy war that arrayed heresy and atheism against true biblical Christianity. The southerners' right to hold slaves became a defense of the Bible, of Christianity itself.

Julia Ward Howe's "Battle Hymn of the Republic" suggests that many northerners also marched to battle in defense of "His Truth." Much of the excellent recent historical work on the religious dimension of the American Civil War reflects how deeply religious beliefs informed soldiers' and civilians' understandings of the war, slavery, victory, defeat, justice, and a myriad of other ideas. This scholarship also suggests that the experiences of war, in turn, influenced religious belief.[44] Although slavery continued to exist in parts of the Western hemisphere after 1865, the religious debate over slavery, centered as it was in the antebellum United States, effectively ended with the defeat of the Confederacy. The ironic story of how the Civil War's shattering of southern Christian orthodoxy contributed to the rise of a postbellum secular racism more virulent than its antebellum counterpart has yet to be fully told.[45]

For African-Americans, the war and emancipation answered prayers and presented challenges, both physical and spiritual, that revealed the ways that slavery had shaped their Christianity and how Christianity informed their understanding of slavery and freedom. Almost immediately following emancipation, freed slaves, not only in the American South but in the Caribbean and South America as well, established independent churches. There they maintained and developed the traditions and beliefs they had forged in slavery, traditions and beliefs that emphasized their chosen character, their kinship with the ancient Israelites who had also suffered oppression but had been delivered by the God who had not abandoned them. Albert Raboteau concludes his seminal book on African-American slave religion with the 1862 testimony of a contraband slave named Brother Thornton. His words illustrate the distinct perspective of an African-American Christian, a unique product of the suffering of slavery and the redemptive faith of the believer: "We have been in the furnace of affliction, and are still, but God only means to separate the dross, and get us so that like the pure metal we may reflect the image of our Purifier, who is sitting by to watch the process. I am assured that what God begins, he will bring to an end." Affliction, like Christ's suffering, has meaning, and that affliction would not end with emancipation. Brother Thornton then reminded his listeners that the slavery they had finally escaped did not free them from the spiritual slavery that Christians everywhere and always have recognized as far worse than physical enslavement. "If we would have greater freedom of body, we must free ourselves from the shackles of sin, and especially the sin of unbelief. We must snap the chain of Satan, and educate ourselves and our children."[46] Many Christian slaves had struggled to "free themselves" of the "shackles of sin" while enslaved. Their legacy was to remind their descendants of that heroic effort and pass on the faith that helped to make such freedom possible.

NOTES

1. John Thornton, *Africa and Africans in the Making of the Atlantic World, 1400–1680* (New York, 1992), 236, 255. Other important works by Thornton include "The Development of an African Catholic Church in the Kingdom of Kongo, 1491–1750," *Journal of African History*, 25 (2) (1984), 147–67; "On the Trail of Voodoo: African Christianity in Africa and the Americas," *The Americas*, 44 (3) (January 1988): 261–78; and *Kongolese Saint Anthony: Dona Beatriz Kimpa Vita and the Antonian Movement, 1684–1706* (New York, 1998).

2. John K. Thornton, "African Dimensions of the Stono Rebellion," *American Historical Review*, 96 (4) (October 1991): 1101–13; Mark M. Smith, "Remembering Mary, Shaping Revolt: Reconsidering the Stono Rebellion," *Journal of Southern History*, 67 (3) (August 2001): 513–34; Hein Vanhee, "Central African Popular Christianity and the Making of Haitian Vodou Religion," in Linda M. Heywood (ed.), *Central Africans and Cultural Transformations in the American Diaspora* (New York, 2002), 243–64; Terry Rey, "Kongolese Catholic Influences on Haitian Popular Catholicism: A Sociohistorical Exploration," in Heywood (ed.), *Central Africans and Cultural Transformations*, 265–85, quotation from 267.

3. Thornton, *Africa and Africans*, 271; Thornton "On the Trail of Voodoo," 278.

4. Annette Laing, "'Heathens and Infidels'? African Christianization and Anglicanism in the South Carolina Low Country, 1700–1750," *Religion and American Culture: A Journal of Interpretation*, 12 (2) (Summer 2002): 217.

5. Thornton, "On the Trail of Voodoo," 275, 277, 276, 262.

6. James H. Sweet, *Recreating Africa: Culture, Kinship, and Religion in the African-Portuguese World, 1441–1770* (Chapel Hill, NC, 2003), 1, 2, 7.

7. Ibid. 110, 109, 111, 112–13, 116, 113.

8. Ibid. 113.

9. Michael Gomez, *Exchanging our Country Marks: The Transformation of African Identities in the Colonial and Antebellum South* (Chapel Hill, NC, 1998), 268. For a broader argument regarding the African core of beliefs "under cover" of a "protective exterior" of Christianity, see Sterling Stuckey, *Slave Culture: Nationalist Theory and the Foundations of Black America* (New York, 1987), 35 and *passim*.

10. Sweet, *Recreating Africa*, 132.

11. Laing, "'Heathens and Infidels'?," 200.

12. Sweet, *Recreating Africa*, 196, 207.

13. Gomez, *Exchanging our Country Marks*, 284.

14. Sweet, *Recreating Africa*, 152. For similar conclusions, see Charles Joyner, "'Believer I Know': The Emergence of African-American Christianity," in Paul E. Johnson (ed.), *African-American Christianity: Essays in History* (Berkeley, 1994), 18–46; Jon F. Sensbach, *Rebecca's Revival: Creating Black Christianity in the Atlantic World* (Cambridge, 2005), 85–8; and Vanhee, "Central African Popular Christianity and the Making of Haitian Vodou Religion."

15. Gomez, *Exchanging our Country Marks*, 282. Gomez draws upon the seminal works of Howard Thurman, including *Deep Rivers: Reflections on the Religious Insight of Certain of the Negro Spirituals* (New York, 1955) and *Jesus and the Disinherited* (New York, 1949).

16. Eugene D. Genovese, *Roll, Jordan, Roll: The World the Slaves Made* (New York, 1974), 252.

17. Sensbach, *Rebecca's Revival*, 243.

18. Sylvia Frey and Betty Wood, *Come Shouting to Zion: African American Protestantism in the American South and British Caribbean to 1830* (Chapel Hill, NC, 1998), 172.

19. Sensbach, *Rebecca's Revival*, 239.

20. Frey and Wood, *Come Shouting to Zion*, 75. See also Gomez, *Exchanging our Country Marks*, 246. Laing, "'Heathens and Infidels'?"

21. Frey and Wood, *Come Shouting to Zion*, 82; Mechal Sobel, *Trabelin' On: The Slave Journey to an Afro-Baptist Faith* (Princeton, 1979), 90.

22. Gomez, *Exchanging our Country Marks*, 252. Charles Irons cautions against placing too much emphasis on the connection, at least in North America, between evangelical

Christianity and traditional African religion. He notes that "what begins as a thoughtful analysis of continuities across African and Christian theologies often becomes in effect a form of racial essentialism. Black Virginians joined Baptist or Methodist denominations not primarily because elements of the Baptist or Methodist tradition corresponded to remembered fragments of African belief, but because white and black evangelicals recruited them to those denominations." Charles F. Irons, *The Origins of Proslavery Christianity: White and Black Evangelicals in Colonial and Antebellum Virginia* (Chapel Hill, NC, 2008), 45.

23. Sensbach, *Rebecca's Revival*, 69–70; Frey and Wood, *Come Shouting to Zion*, 139; Irons, *Origins of Proslavery Christianity*, 45.

24. Jon Butler, "Slavery and the African Spiritual Holocaust," in *Awash in a Sea of Faith: Christianizing the American People* (Cambridge, 1990), 129–63. Butler restates some of his arguments in "Africans' Religions in British America, 1650–1840," *Church History*, 68 (1) (March 1999): 118–27.

25. Sylvia Frey, *Water from the Rock: Black Resistance in a Revolutionary Age* (Princeton, 1991), 304. See also Sweet, *Recreating Africa*, 108: "[T]he notion of Heaven, in the Judeo-Christian sense, was unknown in African religions."

26. Sobel, *World They Made Together*, 202.

27. Mary Turner, *Slaves and Missionaries: The Disintegration of Jamaican Slave Society, 1787–1834* (Urbana, Ill., 1982), 72–3; 71.

28. Frey and Wood, *Come Shouting to Zion*, 174; Sobel, *World They Made Together*, 216; Turner, *Slaves and Missionaries*, 72.

29. Ibid. 71–2.

30. Frey and Wood, *Come Shouting to Zion*, 189; 204; 206.

31. Emily Burke, *Reminiscences of Georgia* (Oberlin, Oh., 1850), 47.

32. João José Reis, *Slave Rebellion in Brazil: The Muslim Uprising of 1835 in Bahia* (Baltimore, 1993); Sylviane A. Diouf, *Servants of Allah: African Muslims Enslaved in the Americas* (New York, 1998), 179.

33. Gomez, *Exchanging our Country Marks*, 79.

34. A vast literature explores early missionary work in North America and the problems missionaries encountered. For useful examples see Sensbach, *Rebecca's Revival* and Frey and Wood, *Come Shouting to Zion*.

35. Samuel Davies, *The Duty of Christians to Propagate their Religion among Heathens, Earnestly Recommended to the Masters of Negro Slaves in Virginia* . . . (London, 1758).

36. Fredrika Teute Schmidt and Barbara Ripel Wilhelm, "Early Proslavery Petitions in Virginia," *William and Mary Quarterly*, 3rd ser., 30 (1) (January 1973): 133–46.

37. A number of studies follow this pattern, with some variations. See, for examples, Christine Heyrman, *Southern Cross: The Beginnings of the Bible Belt* (New York, 1997); Donald Mathews, *Religion in the Old South* (Chicago, 1977).

38. Irons, *Origins of Proslavery Christianity*, 57.

39. Charles Colcock Jones, *The Religious Instruction of the Negroes in the United States* (Savannah, Ga., 1842), 127–8. On Jones, see Erskine Clarke, *Dwelling Place: A Plantation Epic* (New Haven, 2005).

40. Stephen R. Haynes, *Noah's Curse: The Biblical Justification of Slavery* (New York, 2002). Eugene D. Genovese, in *A Consuming Fire: The Fall of the Confederacy in the Mind of the White Christian South* (Athens, Ga., 1998), argues for the limited role of the curse in antebellum proslavery thought.

41. On the Methodist and Baptist schisms, see C. C. Goen, *Broken Churches, Broken Nation: Denominational Schisms and the Coming of the Civil War* (Macon, Ga., 1985) and Mitchell Snay, *Gospel of Disunion: Religion and Separatism in the Antebellum South* (New York, 1993). On the broader debates, see, especially, Elizabeth Fox-Genovese and Eugene D. Genovese, *The Mind of the Master Class: History and Faith in the Southern Slaveholders' Worldview* (New York, 2005), part iv.

42. John Rankin, *Letters on American Slavery* (Boston, 1833), 112. For a representative example of the southern refutation of the abolitionist application of the Golden Rule, see George D. Armstrong, *The Christian Doctrine of Slavery* (New York, 1857), 115–16.

43. Aileen S. Kraditor, *Means and Ends in American Abolitionism: Garrison and his Critics on Strategy and Tactics, 1834–1850* (New York, 1969), 92.

44. See for examples, Noll, *Civil War as Theological Crisis*; Gardiner H. Shattuck, Jr., *A Shield and a Hiding Place: The Religious Life of the Civil War Armies* (Macon, Ga., 1987); Steven E. Woodworth, *While God is Marching On: The Religious World of Civil War Soldiers* (Lawrence, Kan., 2001); Daniel W. Stowell, *Rebuilding Zion: The Religious Reconstruction of the South, 1863–1877* (New York, 1998); Genovese, *A Consuming Fire*; and Edward J. Blum and W. Scott Poole (eds.), *Vale of Tears: New Essays on Religion and Reconstruction* (Macon, Ga., 2005).

45. Some important work into this topic has been done. See Genovese, *A Consuming Fire*, Sean Michael Lucas, *Robert Lewis Dabney: A Southern Presbyterian Life* (Phillipsburg, NJ, 2005); and Haynes, *Noah's Curse*.

46. *American Missionary*, 6 (2) (February 1862): 33, quoted in Albert Raboteau, *Slave Religion: The Invisible Institution in the Antebellum South* (New York, 1978), 320.

SELECT BIBLIOGRAPHY

BOLES, JOHN B. *Masters & Slaves in the House of the Lord: Race and Religion in the American South, 1740–1870*. Lexington, Ky.: University Press of Kentucky, 1988.

DIOUF, SYLVIANE A. *Servants of Allah: African Muslims Enslaved in the Americas*. New York: New York University Press, 1998.

FOX-GENOVESE, ELIZABETH, and EUGENE D. GENOVESE. *The Mind of the Master Class: History and Faith in the Southern Slaveholders' Worldview*. Cambridge: Cambridge University Press, 2005.

FREY, SYLVIA R., and BETTY WOOD. *Come Shouting to Zion: African American Protestantism in the American South and British Caribbean to 1830*. Chapel Hill, NC: University of North Carolina Press, 1998.

GENOVESE, EUGENE D. *Roll, Jordan, Roll: The World the Slaves Made*. New York: Pantheon Books, 1974.

GOMEZ, MICHAEL ANGELO. *Exchanging our Country Marks: The Transformation of African Identities in the Colonial and Antebellum South*. Chapel Hill, NC: University of North Carolina Press, 1998.

IRONS, CHARLES F. *The Origins of Proslavery Christianity: White and Black Evangelicals in Colonial and Antebellum Virginia*. Chapel Hill, NC: University of North Carolina Press, 2008.

RABOTEAU, ALBERT J. *Slave Religion: The "Invisible Institution" in the Antebellum South.* New York: Oxford University Press, 1978.

SENSBACH, JON F. *Rebecca's Revival: Creating Black Christianity in the Atlantic World.* Cambridge, Mass.: Harvard University Press, 2005.

SWEET, JAMES H. *Recreating Africa: Culture, Kinship, and Religion in the African-Portuguese World, 1441–1770.* Chapel Hill, NC: University of North Carolina Press, 2003.

THORNTON, JOHN K. *Africa and Africans in the Making of the Atlantic World, 1400–1680.* Cambridge: Cambridge University Press, 1992.

CHAPTER 18

PROSLAVERY IDEOLOGY

JEFFREY ROBERT YOUNG

OVER the years, historians of proslavery thought in the Americas have arrived at a bewildering array of contradictory conclusions.[1] Scholars have argued over the manner in which slaveholders justified human bondage, some emphasizing the influence of a dehumanizing brand of racism, others stressing the role of paternalistic rationales for slavery that were predicated on the notion of reciprocal relations between masters and slaves.[2] Scholars have also debated the extent of regional variation, across the Americas, in the slaveholders' values. Even among scholars who agree that there was a significant cultural difference between Latin American and Anglo-American proslavery thought, there has been spirited debate over how best to characterize the proslavery sensibility in these respective zones of settlement.[3] On the question of historical timing, scholars have also disagreed. Some historians emphasize proslavery thought's relatively late appearance and its reactive (and reactionary) character. This school of interpretation locates the genesis of coherent proslavery thought in the turbulent 1820s and 1830s, when antislavery activism required sophisticated cultural and political responses from the caretakers of the slaveholding system.[4] By contrast, others surveying the same sets of historical records have concluded that the proslavery ideology that surfaced in the American plantation environment was rooted in systems of ideas that stretched backward to antiquity. According to this reading, defenders of slavery were merely repeating arguments that had long been available to those seeking to justify unequal social power structures.[5]

Even if one is not inclined to view the historical profession as a vehicle for the recovery of some objectively rendered truth, this state of historiographical affairs is puzzling. It might even go so far as to nurture the suspicion that whatever American slaveholders actually did or did not think about the morality of their masterly endeavors would turn out to be almost irrelevant to the historical profession's subsequent theorizing and debates over this subject. And yet, if one considers certain philosophical and historical contradictions attending the growth of slavery in the modern world system, the contentious state of the historiography concerned with proslavery thought becomes more understandable. At a most elemental level of human psychology, masters and slaves struggled over the meaning of concepts such as freedom, autonomy, and the individual's proper relationship with society and with the world at large. In shaping the specific contours of the master–slave relationship in various historical settings, slaveholders were by definition battling over the meaning of existence itself.

However much slavery as an institution derived from an economic need to marshal labor power, it always introduced philosophical questions that could never neatly be answered by profit–loss calculations. If, as the sociologist Orlando Patterson has argued, an awareness of the constricting nature of the bondservant's identity paradoxically fostered the articulation of a social ideal of freedom over the millennia, then there were ideological ramifications flowing from the institution of human bondage that might even have contradicted the slaveholding elite's obvious and stated desire to effectively deny all freedom to the enslaved population. Moreover, as G. W. F. Hegel contended (during the very era when slavery in the Americas was reaching new levels of economic and political significance), on the level of identity formation itself—the formulation of self-consciousness in relation to other beings—the dynamics of the master–slave relationship could unexpectedly create odd dependencies on the part of the master while carving out for the slave unanticipated kinds of power.[6] The point here is that when analyzing slavery, the scholar cannot avoid a host of questions concerning the biggest historical categories imaginable in the formation of the modern world. Hence, in parsing the meanings and repercussions of proslavery thought in the Americas, twentieth- and early twenty-first-century scholars have been wrestling with a most unwieldy subject. Given the scope and complexity of the swirling political, economic, and religious forces giving rise to New World slavery, one might expect tremendous scholarly disagreement over the influences that shaped the institution's growth and evolution. Factor in the aforementioned philosophical and epistemological concerns and one can begin to appreciate why there has often been so little consensus among scholars. As we shall see, despite this lack of consensus, the same fundamental questions raised by proslavery thought have consistently confronted not only modern scholars but also the very historical actors who battled over slavery's fate in the eighteenth and nineteenth centuries.

Early Proslavery Thought
in the Americas

A rationale in favor of building a New World economy on the backs of enslaved laborers was already surfacing at the very moment when Columbus first set eyes on the Caribbean landscape. His expedition had hardly stepped foot on land when Columbus began to speculate about the suitability of the native population for enslavement. Even at this early moment of proslavery reasoning, one can discern some of the features that would come to define American efforts to justify slavery over the next four centuries. Columbus perceived quasi-racial differences between European and Americans that suggested to him that the native population was, by its nature, well suited for slavery. This assumption, moreover, was neatly reinforced by the religious values inculcated by Catholicism—values that took for granted an uneven social hierarchy and the need for subordinate members of society to be carefully overseen by the proper authorities. Of course, such assumptions were articulated against the backdrop of an economic agenda which already had Columbus scanning the horizon for potential commodities and the labor power to bring them to market. He also anticipated the political institutions that would provide the necessary power to instill order over these interactions—a political system that, not surprisingly, would reinforce the mastery of the future slaveholders, who could easily claim that their ownership of other human beings was sanctioned by God, King, and the attending laws of the state. Throughout this imagined organic society, individuality was consistently tempered by the broadly stated agenda of popular allegiance to the goals articulated by societies' leaders. Individual incentives for profit and upward social mobility certainly informed the choices made by the merchant class that underwrote much of this era's expansionary tendencies. Still, the emerging European bourgeoisie at least initially parlayed its individual successes to gain entry into the elite ranks of their respective societies rather than to attack the existing social framework.[7]

In concrete historical terms, this meant that the American colonies that evolved in the sixteenth and seventeenth centuries were designed, notwithstanding some very different religious and political leanings, with an eye towards establishing effective mechanisms for social control that could be leveraged into economic development that would enrich colonial proprietors and the countries from which they hailed. Slavery's role in this colonial world was significant from the system's inception. When the native population in the New World demonstrated its waning usefulness to the European invaders (after, in some cases, a brutal century of grotesque exploitation and extermination), the architects of the colonial system almost seamlessly adapted to an alternative supply of enslaved laborers who were transported from Africa. The few colonial settings where enslaved labor played a secondary role to indentured or more independent forms of labor were exceptions proving an almost-axiomatic principle of colonial government: the men who aggressively expropriated swathes of territory thousands of miles from their own places of origin did not hesitate to expropriate the labor power of men, women, and children whom they frequently reduced to the level of chattel. The story of European colonization of the Americas was, in this sense, built on a proslavery plot. When the contingencies of early colonial history required would-be imperialists to review policy options, their proslavery logic sometimes surfaced. More often, it went unspoken. Not, one must hasten to add, because of any embarrassment or squeamishness, but rather because the institution—for all the novel ways in which it developed in the modern New World setting—violated few of the deeply held principles by which the European nations dealt with questions of labor and social control.[8]

Hence, from the perspective of those who were building and operating this system on the ground, as it were, a proslavery mentality was the starting and ending point of the entire colonial project. It is no exaggeration to claim that the process by which European nations established themselves as colonial powers in the Western hemisphere was the very process by which they launched the modern institution of transatlantic slavery. Day in and day out, slave-based New World plantations and mines operated without serious ideological challenge. Interestingly, one can make this point even though some early sixteenth-century theologians were beginning to consider the moral implications of unfree labor in the New World. The Spanish missionary Bartolomé de Las Casas, for example, bemoaned the wide-scale abuse of Native American workers whom he wished to protect from extermination. And he was just the first in a long line of Catholic and Protestant religious authorities who spoke out, sometimes at great length, against the hideous abuses inflicted upon the slaves by American masters. Strangely, however, these critics seldom followed the logic of their condemnation of the abuses of particular slaveholding regimes to an abstract endpoint of abolitionism. Indeed, Las Casas advocated African slavery as an alternative to the oppression of Native American workers and his seventeenth- and eighteenth-century successors often interspersed their criticism of slavery with elaborate justifications for its potential accordance with divine and secular law. The dialectic between observations concerning the alleged cruelty of particular slaveholders and counterarguments defending the institution on theological, philosophical, or practical grounds would play a consistent role in the unfolding historical struggle over human bondage.[9]

Fittingly, the historiography concerned with proslavery thought has likewise been shaped by this dialectic—one pitting scholars emphasizing the institution's aggressive entrepreneurialism against scholars concentrating upon the conservative ideological imperative that American slaveholders protect rather than attack traditional values. Even before the institution's demise, defenders and critics of human bondage mapped out the strengths of these respective interpretations. Antislavery

authors such as Frederick Douglass and Harriet Beecher Stowe assailed the institution for elevating fiscal gain into a force that obliterated ethical concerns that might
otherwise have affected the planters' moral compass. Proslavery thinkers countered
with the claim that slavery established enduring moral relationships between
masters and slaves—relationships that were far less conducive to cold-hearted
profiteering than the contractual relationship between employers and their wage
employees. Writers such as Albert Taylor Bledsoe and George Fitzhugh characterized southern mastery in terms of the broader social good delivered by the
institution exactly because it tempered the ability of individuals—particularly
individuals of African descent but, it should be noted, also the slaveholders
themselves—to put selfish, destructive desires before the value system ensuring
social stability and Christian harmony.[10] Far from trampling upon human decency
in an unrestrained pursuit of personal wealth, the slaveholders (as depicted by the
proslavery theorists) were morally as well as economically connected to their
bondservants—bound to respect the ethical obligations enjoined upon the master
class by God, local custom, and state law.

Ironically, given the defeat of the southern Confederacy and the hemisphere-
wide abolition of chattel slavery by the end of the nineteenth century, white
postbellum scholarship of American slavery initially tipped strongly in favor of
the historical logic of the proslavery theorists. Defeated on the battlefield, advocates of slavery earned a strange victory in the textbooks explaining what had
caused—and more important, what had not caused—all of the fighting. Within the
reactionary climate of the post-Reconstruction South—the historical moment
when white supremacy was reinforced through a host of legal and extra-legal
means—historians such as U. B. Phillips resurrected core elements of the proslavery theorists' arguments respecting the humanizing rather than dehumanizing
tendencies of the master–slave relationship. By the early twentieth century, these
paternalistic fantasies about slavery's softer side met with receptive audiences
across the United States.[11]

Only after the Second World War did white liberal sentiment begin to reshape
the historiography concerned with proslavery thought. In the 1950s, progressive
white scholars seemingly discovered the hideous truth about slavery—a truth, of
course, that had been articulated by slaves throughout the ages. To make the
historical case against slavery, authors such as Stanley Elkins turned their scholarly
gaze to the long-neglected other half of the dialectic: the unmitigated and brutally
aggressive profit-seeking mentality that drove the plantation machine in the
Americas. And yet, by the 1960s, the scholarship rejecting the paternalistic plantation myth was followed by (and, on some level, complicated by) a new wave of
studies concerned with planter ideology—a historiographical movement initiated
by the innovative work of Eugene Genovese. Unlike racist scholarly predecessors
such as Phillips who accepted at face value the slaveholders' paternalistic pretensions, Genovese approached slaveholder paternalism less as a means towards

accurately describing the slave experience and more as a window onto the slave-holders' "worldview." Until the last decade of the twentieth century, scholars who focused their reading of slaveholding society on the professed paternalism of American masters battled with scholars who deemphasized the professed conservatism of the master class and concentrated instead on their brutal acumen as businessmen. Even among professionally trained scholars, the old dialectic attending slavery's economic and ethical justifications died hard.[12]

And well it might have given the many centuries during which the "profit vs. paternalism" dialectic shaped the conversation about slavery. One sees evidence of these twin concerns in the religious responses to New World slavery during the colonial era. Ministers from a variety of early modern Christian denominations pointed to scriptural passages in which slaveholders were enjoined to wield their power over their bondservants in a manner that underscored the entire society's fealty to God. Such passages cut in two directions. On the one hand, they served as a potentially powerful limiting factor upon the slaveholders' ability to treat their slaves as non-human objects that could be subjected to any work regimens in order to maximize profit and to any punishments in order to maximize control. On the other hand, this conservative theology linked the slaveholders' earthly stature as masters to other forms of legitimate authority within a universal hierarchy that stretched ultimately to God's towering presence. The ministers who eagerly sought to influence colonial slaveholding society seldom presented the former point without making at least a passing nod—and sometimes much more—to the possibility that there were proslavery scriptural implications. To deny the latter would be to open oneself to the charge of attempting to subvert the labor system on which the colonial order rested, an approach guaranteed to diminish all capacity to achieve reform and, quite likely, to have angry slaveholders speed one's departure from colonial society. In addition to such practical concerns, the theology of reform sought to integrate distant and potentially disparate elements of the imperial system into a cohesive framework of government. To overemphasize the potential liberty and autonomy of the bondservant was to work at cross purposes with the logic by which ministers hoped to convince the slaveholding colonial elite to surrender to metropolitan authorities some of its considerable de facto power.[13]

For a number of rhetorical and religious reasons, then, the problem of slavery as a humanitarian question (not to mention as an institution that might determine the boundaries between moral and immoral political systems and even, for that matter, greater and lesser strands of the human race) initially invited as many proslavery arguments as it did antislavery ones. Indeed, as the historian David Brion Davis has pointed out in a number of brilliant studies, the weight of the Western intellectual tradition was decidedly conducive to arguments in favor of slavery. So much so, in fact, that it was the antislavery cause that required innovative thinking and concerted political action if it was to advance its agenda.[14] Opponents of human bondage could not help but confront proslavery arguments that presented slaveholders as potentially righteous and benevolent stewards engaged in a moral, reciprocal relationship with their bondservants. The kind of paternalistic proslavery rationale that scholars sometimes present as evidence of the shifting ideological ground on which slavery was to be defended in the antebellum era was indisputably articulated centuries (if not millennia, if one considers early Christian texts as relevant sources) earlier. And yet, to frame the slaveholders' ideological development in these terms perhaps distorts the concerns of most New World masters for whom the religious considerations of Christian theologians and ministers were a remote consideration (if they were a consideration at all). The vast majority of slaveholders across the colonies of the Western hemisphere remained largely oblivious to all such reasoning during the initial centuries of the American plantation complex. Their concerns were focused instead on the more immediate proslavery desire to check their slaves' efforts at resistance and to marshal authority over the slaves' labor power into the successful production of commodities that would return sufficient profit so as to make the entire process worthwhile.

PROSLAVERY THOUGHT IN THE AGE
OF REVOLUTION

As the colonial system matured, the European nations that sought to profit from it were racked by rivalry, warfare, and, most significantly, revolution. The impacts that such events had upon political values and attending philosophical notions of just government fostered an environment increasingly conducive to antislavery agitation; and this antislavery activism, in turn, invited greater elaboration of the proslavery perspective. Those profiting from the plantation system could no longer take for granted its ongoing existence. England's experience provides an illuminating case in point. In the seventeenth century, when England finally established its own colonies in the Western hemisphere, it struggled on repeated occasions to ward off the specter of violent uprisings that threatened to undo the entire social order. In England itself, the overthrow of two monarchical regimes led to impassioned debate about civil liberty by theorists such as John Locke. By the turn of the eighteenth century, liberty had emerged as the defining principle of English citizenship, and slavery became the standard metaphor for the unjustly degraded position that improper government would inflict upon insufficiently wary Englishmen. Yet there were obvious limits to the application of this philosophy of liberty to the New World plantation system that, by the late seventeenth century, was operating on the backs of African slaves. The future author of *Two*

Treatises of Government, John Locke, profited from the African slave trade and helped to draft the proslavery Constitution of South Carolina. It would seem that the very social and political currents that sensitized educated English commentators to the relationship between liberty and slavery also pushed them to channel potentially radical antislavery formulations in a very specific and very limited direction.[15]

Time and time again, the evocation of antislavery possibilities prompted the architects of the colonial plantation system to delineate more carefully the legal and cultural edifices on which the slave-based economy rested. When social unrest bubbled over to become a rebellion against Virginia's colonial economy in 1676, for example, the specter of runaway slaves fighting against their former owners did not lead colonial administrators to disavow the labor system that had already begun to replace European indentured servants with African slaves. Instead, the colony accelerated its transition toward a slave-based plantation economy. In the colony of South Carolina, which was being established at this very historical moment, settlers did not look to the north and draw antislavery lessons from the social unrest that literally burned the colonial capital of Williamsburg to the ground. Instead, Carolina's planners (many of whom had experience with slavery in Barbados) anticipated that slave labor would provide the foundation for the colony's future prosperity. They banked their future on slavery, moreover, before they had even located a saleable commodity that could be produced efficiently using enslaved workers.[16]

By the early eighteenth century, Carolina planters were focusing their capital on rice production, a choice that required heavy concentrations of slaves within relatively small geographic areas along the coast. The racially imbalanced population that resulted from these choices heightened the possibility of slave rebellion, an event that came to pass in 1739 in the Stono region just outside Charlestown. Over the years, revolts such as this one and myriad acts of violence against individual slaveholders led to hundreds—perhaps thousands—of deaths and raised the very real possibility that the unequal distribution of power and wealth across colonial society might hasten its destruction. As had been the case more than a half century earlier in Virginia, however, open rebellion against the plantation order did not lead slaveholders to abandon their proslavery convictions. Instead, the Stono Rebellion inspired the 1740 Negro Act, a legislative effort to shore up slavery. The most radical outcome flowing from white fears of such violence was the effort made by some colonial administrators to create a buffer zone free of slavery that might serve to protect the slave-based colonies from incendiary influences introduced by rival colonial powers. Such thinking led the Georgia Trustees to ban slavery over a fifteen-year period early in the colony's history. Whatever the merits of this strategy, the allure of slavery obviously outweighed the fears associated with it. In the face of almost wholesale opposition by white settlers against the ban on slavery, Georgia made the transition to a slave-based plantation system in the 1750s.[17]

The increasing awareness of slavery as a moral and logistical problem during the American Revolution did not lead to a straightforward conclusion that the institution should be abolished. Following the lead of Edmund Morgan's trailblazing work in the 1970s, scholars such as Sylvia Frey and Woody Holton have uncovered a seemingly paradoxical relationship between proslavery considerations and the revolutionary politics of southern slaveholders. Proslavery thinking provided the context for the white southern embrace of liberty as the wellspring for a revolutionary and nationalistic sensibility.[18] The imperial policies that triggered colonial resistance in America were only marginally concerned with slavery, but the resulting debate over the terms of just government was conducted using a political vocabulary that deployed slavery and freedom as highly significant metaphors. As a result, when a Massachusetts lawyer or a South Carolina merchant complained of abuse at the hands of corrupt colonial officials, they complained that they were being reduced to a state of slavery unbefitting for citizens of the British empire. This rhetoric predictably emboldened the actual slave population to voice its own complaints, and in the context of this ideological collision between the power dynamics operating in both imperial and slaveholding contexts, at least a few colonists in this era admitted their own complicity in (what the emerging antislavery camp was now characterizing as) the crime of inflicting slavery on generations of innocent African victims.[19] Once more, however, the ultimate result of these revolutionary challenges to the institution of slavery was a marked proslavery campaign. The sight of African-American slaves chanting their masters' slogans of liberty led slaveholders to defend their claims to mastery. If slavery now carried with it the taint of tyranny, responsibility for the institution's existence could be lodged with the very imperial officials who seemingly threatened to unleash the slave population as a weapon against their ungovernable masters. During this revolutionary era, American slaveholders learned to dissociate their own agenda for liberty and self-government from the moral appeals made by the slaves and their advocates. The former cause could be aggressively pursued with stirring language calling for liberation from English tyrants, while the latter could be viewed with horror, as a possibility that would usher in apocalyptic bloodshed and disorder. In the end, revolutionary slaveholders could reconcile their position as slaveholders with their ideological commitment to liberty by conceptualizing slave ownership first and foremost as a fundamental property right that just government was obligated to protect.[20]

The emergence of the United States as an independent republic whose northern regions were decisively moving away from slavery as a labor system meant that the revolutionary dialectic between anti- and proslavery thought would become a defining feature of the early national era. During the years of actual warfare, slaveholders struggled to keep their plantations from being burned and their slaves from taking flight. They therefore had little use for abstract or theological discussions about the moral dimensions of the system they were directly in the process of defending with force of arms. As they rebuilt the plantation system following the war, however, elite planter politicians and ideologues had both the resources and the motives to develop painstaking arguments respecting slavery's benefits and the moral and practical problems that they anticipated would be the result of emancipation. Given the extent to which antislavery reformers were employing concepts that helped to anchor the very political identity of the United States as a grand experiment in liberty ushering in a newly enlightened era of government, slaveholders discerned that the challenges to their mastery would be persistent and aggressive. In the forum of the new national government, southern politicians attempted unsuccessfully to silence their antislavery critics. They tried to concede bigger questions of abstract morality in order to bring the debate to more immediate moral concerns about the impact of living among a million suddenly unrestrained African-Americans. And they also made grandiose claims concerning the positive benefits associated with slavery and the many principled ways in which the institution served godly and practical purposes. All of these strategies were repeatedly and sometimes haphazardly deployed as early national slaveholders attempted to establish a secure footing for the plantation complex.

The onset of the French Revolution and the subsequent uprising of slaves in Saint-Domingue led many American slaveholders to view the dawn of the nineteenth century with a worried eye. If the American Revolution had promised to set a new standard for government by the people and for the people, and if that revolution had served even partially as a catalyst for the French Revolution, then the antislavery leanings of democratic movements could not safely be ignored by those continuing to wield power as masters. The slaveholding refugees of Saint-Domingue who fled to American ports after 1791 (sometimes having narrowly escaped death at the hands of liberated slaves) provided a stark reminder that the entire social order could be overturned once the movement for emancipation gathered momentum. And the failure of numerous expeditions launched by European powers to regain colonial control of that island demonstrated that once the genie of freedom had broken loose, the bottle of social control would be very difficult to reseal.[21]

By the early decades of the nineteenth century, planters in the American South responded to these global concerns by crafting an ideological solution. To the moral critique against the seeming tyranny of slavery, they elaborated on paternalistic rationales for bondage that cast the master–slave relationship as familial and sanctioned by Christianity. To the accusation that African-Americans were being ruthlessly exploited, white southerners responded with the claim that their slaves received kind treatment and labored in conditions more favorable than those experienced by northern or European wage laborers. And to the campaign made by the American Colonization Society to liberate the slaves and repatriate them to Africa, the slaveholders responded with increasingly racist reasoning that equated emancipation with inevitable black suffering since African-Americans were, according to their masters, incapable of caring for themselves and their children (although they were apparently quite capable of caring for their masters' children not to mention all the backbreaking labor associated with the plantation regime).[22]

THE ROLE OF PROSLAVERY THOUGHT IN SECTIONAL CONFLICT AND POSTBELLUM SECTIONAL RECONCILIATION

Slaveholders across the Americas shared many of the concerns of their counterparts in the American South. Still, only in that region did political and economic conditions foster extreme proslavery formulations that were internalized by sufficient numbers of slaveholders so as to forge a coherent sense of identity predicated upon ostensibly righteous mastery. Ironically, it was that very sense of class purpose that prompted the political decisions that would usher in the utter destruction of southern plantation society. The slaveholders' boldest gesture to protect slavery resulted in the realization of their worst fears about the apocalyptic annihilation of the slaveholding order. Elite slaveholders in Latin America and the British, French, and Danish West Indies, for their part, felt besieged by the growing antislavery clamor in the nineteenth century and fretted over the potential interference with slavery threatened by mediating institutions of Church and state. In the United States alone, however, did slaveholders wield significant control over a government that they themselves had designed with an eye towards protecting slavery. And in the United States alone did that economically secure and politically powerful planter elite have to interact closely with politicians representing nonslaveholding regions, who were increasingly inclined to denounce the institution. This odd mixture of the slaveholders' political empowerment and their direct exposure to the advancing tide of antislavery thought elicited a dramatic proslavery response. Whereas proslavery theorists were largely quiet during Congressional discussion of the closing of the international slave trade in 1807–8, they became noticeably more vocal when Congress confronted the question of whether to ban slavery from Missouri when it entered the Union as a state. Fears about slave insurrection that overtook South Carolina in 1822 and Virginia in 1831 prompted white southerners to invest ever more heavily in a paternalistic, benevolent proslavery image of mastery that provided ideological refuge in a troubled world. By the slaveholders' reading of the history of New World, to make concessions to the antislavery movement was to invite the economic woes that seemingly overtook the British West Indies as those colonies phased in emancipation in the 1830s. Or worse, it was to invite wide-scale slave rebellion as evidenced by the uprisings that convulsed Jamaica and shed blood in Virginia in 1831.[23]

Over the final three decades of the antebellum era, the embrace of intellectual positions justifying slavery as a positive good became the litmus test for wielding cultural, intellectual, and political power in the American South. Ministers, newspaper editors, novelists, poets, politicians, sociologists, and political economists all participated in a dialogue that identified the many ways in which southern slavery supposedly operated to improve the morality and quality of life of the African-American slave population. At the same moment when antislavery reformers were painting the institution as one in which selfish masters sexually tormented and sadistically punished their degraded bondservants, white southern authors retorted that ostensibly "free" wage laborers would consider themselves lucky if they could experience the favorable working conditions enjoyed by the slave population. The tautological assumptions on which this ideology rested made it impervious to contradictory evidence. Inconvenient truths such as the enormous scale of a domestic slave trade that routinely placed slaves on the auction block to face the indignity of being torn from friends and loved ones mattered less to the slaveholders' cultural rendering of the institution than platitudes concerning the love and trust shared between caring white masters and grateful if intellectually limited African-American workers.[24] Rather than a zone of hideous exploitation, the plantation was portrayed as a domestic enterprise that revolved around Christian understandings of organic social hierarchy.[25]

Battling over the fate of slavery in the vast western territory amassed by the United States in the first half of the nineteenth century, antebellum statesmen appreciated that they were playing for the ultimate stakes: the question of whether slaveholders or nonslaveholders would control the future of American society.[26] By the 1850s, the increasingly aggressive proslavery formulations of white southerners clashed ever more fiercely with abolitionist rhetoric that presented slavery as an institution out of step with the moral modern world. Amid this debate, partisans in both camps mobilized the tenet of white racial supremacy. And yet, the broad agreement among white southerners (and, for that matter, white northerners as well) concerning the inferiority of African-Americans masked a swirling constellation of doctrines that sought to define the specific meanings of racial identity as it pertained to slavery. From the colonial through the late antebellum era, slavery's defenders offered theories that ranged from environmental causes for racial differences to innate racial differences that could be traced back to Noah's Old Testament curse upon the descendents of Canaan, son of the disobedient Ham. The argument that specific racial attributes grew in particular environments could be invoked to demonstrate that a well-ordered plantation could positively impact black character and simultaneously be deployed to denounce the supposedly deleterious consequences of black emancipation. On the other hand, innate theories of racial difference offered considerable firepower against antislavery activists who portrayed the slaveholders as enemies of white liberty as well as black. Over the course of the antebellum era, the force of racism in American society intensified as defenders of slavery appealed both to the newly emerging science of racial difference and the time-honored interpretations of the Bible that marked African-Americans as an inferior race. Obviously, to contemplate slavery in the Western hemisphere was to grapple with the boundaries of racial identity.[27]

Nevertheless, historians have engaged in spirited debate over the specific contours of the racism resting at the heart of slaveholding society. Emphasizing paternalism as the hallmark of white slaveholding identity, scholars such as Eugene Genovese have focused on the racist assumptions that tended to humanize as well as to infantilize African-Americans. According to their reading of the evidence, the slaveholder ideology sought to emphasize the "organic" connections between masters and slaves. If the slaveholders' prejudice necessarily cast the slaves into a subordinate position, it also sought to characterize slave character in potentially positive—even redemptive—terms. By contrast, another camp of historians has concentrated upon the considerable evidence that whites conceived of their black slaves as dangerous, bestial outsiders. The point of this form of racism was to deny African-American claims to the natural rights that the Western tradition presented as the birthright of humanity even while it made possible the promise of egalitarian democracy for those inside the pale. In a number of influential studies, historians such as James Oakes depicted the slaveholders less as paternalists than as canny, aggressive businessmen who advocated a brand of political and economic equality of opportunity for white men that necessarily operated at the expense of black claims for inclusion in the body politic. And scholars such as Lacy Ford have revealed how this racially exclusive democratic rhetoric strongly influenced politics in South Carolina, the state where one might have expected to find the political culture to be unapologetically aristocratic in tone.[28]

Still, if white southerners harbored inconsistent views about black racial identity, increasing pressure exerted by sectional politics led them ultimately into a unified camp. By the end of the 1850s, statesmen who had previously been able to manipulate the political system to forestall permanent sectional enmity had run headlong into the slaveholders' strident claims about their region standing culturally apart from the rest of the Union due to the moral superiority of their slave-based economy. Long-standing associations between the defense of slavery and deep suspicion respecting the liberal use of federal power had long since established the foundation for a "state rights" philosophy of government. The same planters who jealously sought to protect the authority of the slaveholder from the interference of the distant antislavery reformer likewise sought to defend the authority of individual state governments to make policies respecting slavery without the meddlesome (and supposedly unconstitutional) efforts of federal institutions to control the fate of the institution. The election of a northern President who had built his political reputation as an opponent of slavery proved to be the final straw for the slaveholding South. No matter how much Lincoln sought to reassure the planter elite that he intended no abolitionist policies as President, his wholly sectional victory and his aggressive rejection of slavery as a morally deformed system of authority rendered him an unsuitable and unacceptable choice as chief executive. The ultimate measure of the power of proslavery ideology over the antebellum South was the willingness of the wealthy, conservative slaveholding leaders of that region to wage war, less to ward off some immediate tangible threat to the maintenance of the slave system and more to protect their image of themselves as honorable, moral men who could no longer bear to be insulted by their fellow Americans. Only in an independent slaveholding republic did the planters believe their proslavery vision for their society could be maintained. Secession from the Union and the resulting destruction of plantation slavery flowed inexorably and paradoxically from the planters' investment in proslavery thought.[29]

Unlike slavery itself, certain strands of proslavery thought oddly survived the American Civil War. This survival had little to do with the lingering presence of the institution in Cuba and Brazil. Although a group of southern planters did seek to reconstruct their culture and economy in Latin America, they quickly grew disillusioned with the project.[30] And without access to their former privileges as masters, many white southerners abandoned the paternalistic conceptions that had informed their understanding of their relationship with black labor power. By the 1880s, chattel slavery had disappeared from the Western hemisphere. Slaveholders in Cuba and Brazil, the final holdouts to the emerging standard of wage labor as the morally and economically superior mode of organizing labor's relationship to capital, were eager to protect their social standing for as long as possible, but were hardly eager to follow the southern slaveholders' example of waging a war that was bound to hasten their own demise.[31]

Nevertheless, certain aspects of the proslavery rationale survived the demise of the institution in the Americas and continued to exert influence over perceptions of planter identity that had formerly existed in the Old South.[32] White nostalgia about slavery reflected the ongoing appeal of paternalistic readings of the slaveholders' motives for holding human property. As Reconstruction tested the ability of former slaveholders to make the economic transition to a plantation economy shorn of slave labor, and as the freedmen pressed their claims for political and economic rights, white southerners yearned for racial control. Paternalism no longer offered much as a measure for conceptualizing postbellum race relations, but it continued to inform the former slaveholders' sense of their own history. Tragically (as the political activist and former slave Frederick Douglass noted), northern politicians did not ultimately require white southerners to disavow the proslavery myth of plantation life.[33] As white political resolve to protect the freedmen's rights withered, northern commentators proved more willing to jettison their own stereotypes of the slaveholders as selfish and twisted sadists. By the turn of the twentieth century, just a few decades after the institution of the Military Reconstruction Act and the forceful federal response to the rise of the Ku Klux Klan, both northern and southern white audiences were enthusiastically applauding D. W. Griffith's *The Birth of a Nation*, a cinematic adaptation of Thomas Dixon's white supremacist novel *The Clansman*.[34] The film's early scenes sketch a portrait of plantation life in which caring white masters presided over an interracial extended household that was harmonious exactly because the different races occupied different social stations. The outbreak of war, in the film's rendering of history, did not result from ideological divergence between the best (white) men in the two regions but rather from politicians' miscalculations and selfish scheming. Early twentieth-century northern audiences accepted the very proslavery premises that their fathers' and grandfathers' generations had rejected as self-interested nonsense spouted by a southern elite bent upon subverting the Constitution to its own ends. The fact that slavery itself had been abolished seemed to permit greater cultural flexibility on the part of white northerners to recognize retro-actively the merits of certain aspects of southern proslavery thought.

As films such as *The Birth of a Nation* made clear, white racism was obviously one of the principal factors enabling certain strands of proslavery thought to outlive the institution of slavery by decades. Imagery of smiling, foolishly earnest African-Americans, alternatively bumbling, dancing, and singing their way through their plantation tasks, played well to postbellum white audiences—even those that were self-consciously attempting to make sense of the history of slavery in scientific terms. Woodrow Wilson famously applauded Griffith's cinematic vision after a screening of the film in the White House, perhaps even referring to it as "history with lightning." Notwithstanding Wilson's southern roots, his approval of the film's historical interpretation of slavery is especially significant if one considers his professional training in the fields of history and political science at Johns Hopkins. Closer consideration of the racial wisdom prevalent in the academic world of the Progressive Era helps to explain how the same person credited with turning Princeton University into a center for the modern, scientific pursuit of knowledge could applaud nostalgia-laced portraits of life on the old plantation. There could be no doubt that Progressive notions of human social development required that slavery be cast into the dustbin of history, a relic of an era not fully awakened to human potential for education and improvement. And yet, the Progressive Era was also the era that gave rise to the Eugenics movement, to a vision of scientific progress and human development that raised the possibility that the detrimental qualities associated with inferior races might somehow be culled altogether from humanity. The traditional proslavery arguments were taking on new meanings in this early twentieth-century context. Whereas the slaveholders themselves claimed their proslavery culture would forever enmesh masters and slaves, whites and blacks, into a symbiotic and stable relationship, Progressive rehashing of the proslavery vision did not constitute an element of an earnest campaign to resurrect the institution or the supposedly intimate interactions that had been a defining feature of the paternalistic vision of plantation life. For all their racism, the Progressives fully applauded the demise of slavery. They merely re-served the right to accentuate the slaveholders' benevolent motives and the very good reasons for them to fear emancipation in an age preceding the advances in science and education that promised to mitigate the dangerous impact that liberated African-Americans might have on American culture.

THE PROBLEM OF PROSLAVERY THOUGHT
IN THE MODERN WORLD AND IN
TWENTIETH-CENTURY HISTORIOGRAPHY

U. B. Phillips towered above the ranks of early twentieth-century historians and decisively influenced the emerging historiography of the subject of American slavery. Like his mentor William Dunning (whose work dominated scholarly interpretation of Reconstruction in the American South), Phillips's starting point for making sense of plantation slavery was his deeply racist notion of the limited capacities of African-Americans to enjoy cultural and economic opportunities for autonomy. To a degree shocking to the modern reader, the racist underpinnings of the proslavery thought he sought to place in historical perspective permeated his own readings of the historical evidence and led him inexorably to the conviction that the vast majority of southern planters struggled earnestly to make the best of their necessary role as guardians of this separate race. His argument concerning the value system of slaveholding southerners can be boiled down to his claim that their society reflected a paternalistic ethos of mastery. For Phillips, the relationship between white planters and their African-American bondservants was one of benevolent and intimate oversight. Although reduced to the state of chattel property, the slaves did not become alienated from their owners, argued Phillips, but rather settled into an unequal yet mutually negotiated system of power and obedience in which each group achieved benefits. It is therefore tempting to lump him with his white historical subjects.

Still, Phillips's overall understanding of history placed him firmly in the ranks of twentieth-century Progressive academics, many of whom likewise built their readings of the world upon a foundation of racial distinctions that were seemingly grounded in scientific observation of carefully collected evidence. For all their hideous embrace of racist doctrines, the Progressives were on the cutting edge of a modern scholarly approach to human history that sought to elevate historical narrative above the realm of sentimentality. Through the careful identification of appropriate evidence, professionally trained historians sought to unlock the deeply held principles that created either inertia or historical movement. Phillips made a concerted effort to differentiate polemical thought from authentic culture, an effort that led him to privilege private correspondence, legal records, and economic evidence and to discount the prepared speeches of politicians and authors speaking directly on the contested issue of slavery and southern political rights. His desire for the creation of a dispassionate scholarly environment in which to arrive at a meaningful interpretation of southern society led him to edit a multi-volume collection of primary sources so as to invite other scientifically minded scholars to peruse the evidence on which he crafted his own interpretation. Phillips was struggling to turn what he deemed the most culturally significant kinds of feelings into a form of knowledge that could be scientifically isolated and examined.[35]

By the 1940s, liberal scholars were beginning to attack the overtly racist agenda of Phillips's scholarly generation. As the Nazis pressed their racist schemes to their genocidal conclusion in Europe, liberal distaste for racial hierarchy energized the scholars who were beginning to treat racial boundaries as a historical problem rather than as a historical explanation. In the 1940s and 1950s, this scholarship brought to light a series of revelations concerning the planter class's methods of control and punishment of the slave population—revelations that rendered an apparent death blow to Phillips's romanticized portrait of a southern culture that rested on warm feelings between master and slave. Taking a hemisphere-wide perspective on the plantation system, Frank Tannenbaum asserted that it was in the Latin American context that powerful institutions of Church and state fostered the slaveholders' recognition of their bondservants' humanity. The southern slaveholders, in his estimation, went to extreme lengths to systematically deny any human connection to their slaves and, instead, to reduce them to the level of livestock who might be bought, sold, and even bred "as if they were mere cattle."[36] This was the historiographical moment when Stanley Elkins painted plantation disciplinary methods as similar in kind to those at work in Nazi concentration camps and when Kenneth Stampp catalogued the slaveholders' avarice and widescale disregard for their slaves' humanity.[37]

This liberal scholarly movement de-emphasized paternalistic proslavery thought as a meaningful element of white southern culture. Instead, the slaveholders chronicled in these historical accounts emerged as profit-obsessed entrepreneurs whose racism enabled them to disregard utterly the notion that they had obligations to their slaves by virtue of a common sense of humanity. The slaveholders obviously remained proslavery and racist in the sense that they unapologetically sought to exploit black workers for maximum financial gain, but, as presented in the liberal scholarship, the planter elite did not utilize conservative, paternalistic thoughts to construct a coherent, proslavery mentality.[38] The term ideology had not yet come into scholarly vogue yet all of these scholars, Progressive and liberal, were systematically searching for the system of values that explained the outcome of the slaveholders' reign over plantation society. Lurking in this historiography, despite the monumental shift from Progressive to liberal paradigms for proslavery thought, was a sustained effort to separate meaningful historical sentiment (of the kind that truly informed political and economic choices) from the empty lip service that those in power often have to pay to ideas for which, on some private, deeper level, they have little use.

From the 1960s through the 1980s, the interpretative divide between paternalistic and capitalistic readings of the southern plantation system opened up analytical possibilities for new generations of historians to insert themselves energetically into the debate over the fundamental meaning of the slaveholders' culture. As we have seen, the scholarship of Eugene Genovese built upon Phillips's paternalistic reading of the slaveholders' ideals and portrayed those idealistic notions of the master–slave relationship as the heart of a powerful ideology of reciprocal relations and organic hierarchy that, in his estimation, permeated southern culture. Unlike Phillips, Genovese recognized that this ideology served the interests, financial and cultural, of the master class and justified their exploitation and oppression of enslaved African-Americans. Nevertheless, in Genovese's estimation, the slave-holders' paternalistic ideology was the expression of authentic principles that differentiated their regime from the capitalistic industrialists and democratic en-thusiasts in the northern states. As Genovese and like-minded scholars developed paternalistic interpretations of southern slaveholding culture in influential books from the late 1960s into the 1980s, alternative schools of interpretation also were taking shape. Historians such as James Oakes were building upon the findings of mid-twentieth-century liberal scholars in order to emphasize the dehumanizing racism and profit-seeking mindset of the southern master class. The debate be-tween these paternalistic and capitalistic schools of interpretation was further complicated by scholars utilizing the newly acquired ability to employ computers to analyze large data sets. Stanley Engerman and Robert William Fogel sought to demonstrate that the plantation system operated profitably and that the entrepre-neurially minded slaveholders offered incentives to their enslaved workforce who responded rationally with effective labor. These scholars found that whatever the rhetorical differences between the prevailing proslavery ideology of the slavehold-ing South and the wage labor ethos of northern businessmen, similar economic motivations prevailed in each region.[39] In different ways, these approaches coun-tered Genovese's claim that by dint of their paternalistic ideology the slaveholders had created a system of social relations that rested outside the current of market capitalism, liberal democracy, and the embrace of individualism.

For all of the very real conflicts between these models for the slaveholders' historical development and for all the passionate criticism that historians from different camps leveled at each other's methodologies, it is fascinating to note the underlying similarities in the questions they were asking. The bitter historiograph-ical battles of these decades were waged over the same fundamental questions: in what manner did the slaveholders justify human bondage and in what ways did those ideas structure their expectations about the moral basis of sound govern-ment, thriving families, and prosperous economies? To unlock the slaveholders' defense of slavery was to gain insight into their most deeply held convictions about power in the modern world. As historians such as Elizabeth Fox-Genovese, Stephen Hahn, J. William Harris, and Stephanie McCurry weighed in on the question of antebellum southern power dynamics, they contemplated how the proslavery logic that colored the master–slave relationship likewise permeated the power dynamic between wealthy whites and yeomen farmers, and between white men and the women and children in their extended households.[40] With the notable exception of

Michael O'Brien's work, the historiography that took shape in the 1980s tended to read a host of complicated intellectual, political, and economic questions about southern culture through the prism of the white defense of slavery.

After decades of scholarly acrimony, historians of the American South moved in the 1990s towards a position that reconciled elements of the capitalistic and paternalistic readings of slaveholding society. Working with Fox-Genovese, Genovese himself staked out a more nuanced position that acknowledged with greater force the slaveholders' relationship with capitalistic markets. By the end of the twentieth century, Genovese and Fox-Genovese were also emphasizing the ways in which concepts of bourgeois individuality and domesticity were coloring the worldview of the slaveholding elite that, in their later accounts, defined plantation society as modern and progressive.[41] Meanwhile, scholars such as James Oakes were also gravitating towards a middle position that found analytical space for both the planters' acumen as entrepreneurs and their discomfort with the cultural influence of unfettered market capitalism.[42] During the 1990s, historians such as Joyce Chaplin, Mark Smith, and Walter Johnson authored influential works that solidified what, with the benefit of hindsight, appears to have been a historiographical armistice.[43] Delving into such diverse topics as the planters' understandings of agricultural technology, their definitions of humanitarianism, their relationship with modern clock time, and their notions of the vast domestic slave trade over which they presided, late twentieth-century scholars embraced the difficult task of contextualizing the contradiction that rested at the heart of the planters' quest to define their mastery in moral terms. This historiographical development enabled scholars to appreciate the extent to which the slaveholders themselves wrestled with the tension between modern capitalistic economic concerns and paternalistic conceptions of organic social hierarchy. Accordingly, historians increasingly agreed that their job was not to resolve this tension and certainly not to pick one side of it to present as the linchpin of southern culture.

The most notable trend in historians' recent approaches to proslavery thought is the emergence of transatlantic analytical paradigms in historical scholarship. Comparative approaches to the slaveholders' ideologies had periodically surfaced in the works of historians ranging from U. B. Phillips in the 1910s, to Frank Tannenbaum in the 1940s, and Eugene Genovese in the 1960s and 1970s. More recently, the brilliant work of Peter Kolchin (who compared southern slavery with Russian serfdom) demonstrated the benefit of adopting a wide chronological and geographic frame of reference with which to make sense of the defining features of mastery in various cultures. Over the past fifteen years, an outpouring of studies—many of them by scholars trained and/or influenced by Jack P. Greene—have offered analytical connections between the regions and cultures which directly intersected as a result of the plantation system.[44] This scholarship has tended to uncover the ways in which cultural concerns which once seemed to grow directly out of the slaveholders' isolated experiences actually grew in dialogue with ideals articulated in metropolitan centers thousands of miles away.[45] In making this point, transatlantic studies have not only undermined earlier scholars' contentions that proslavery thought was the hallmark of social conditions peculiar to the American South, but also illustrated the full range of intellectual interests pursued by the planter and colonial elite across the Americas. The great question of how proslavery thought led slaveholders to craft their relationship with the Western world has been, on some significant level, reversed by scholars who now ask how the slaveholders' relationship with the broader world led them to develop particular defenses of slavery as an element in their larger cultural and economic agenda.

In this sense, the historiography of proslavery might be gravitating towards the model provided by Michael O'Brien's work. The irony here is that O'Brien has always emphasized that southerners were immersed in intellectual currents that could never fully be reduced to simple formulations respecting the morality of slavery. His ability to paint nuanced portraits of southern intellectuals such as Hugh Swinton Legaré has always earned him admiration and respect from other historians, yet these same historians seldom seemed quite to know what to do with his findings amid the clear theoretical choices offered by the historiography of slavery through the 1980s. By the time that he published his opus, *Conjectures of Order*, there existed a historiography willing to grapple with the very complicated ideas and ideals formulated by southern thinkers who were, at once, immersed in a slave system and struggling to find their place in a larger intellectual and political context.[46] Texts dealing with proslavery and racist ideals have been making their way into anthologies of sixteenth- and seventeenth-century English and Caribbean literature.[47] As historians of slavery in the Americas gain greater familiarity with these works and the larger literary and religious debates that prompted them, they will no doubt develop new models for explaining the relationship between the proslavery concepts articulated in the American South, in Latin America, and across the West Indies. And as this scholarship defines the role of proslavery thought in the shaping of particular conversations about history, power, nature, and morality, it will probably further reveal the extent to which the attempt to defend slavery was integrally involved in the making of the modern world.

Notes

1. The interpretation of writings about proslavery thought in the Americas has become something of a cottage industry in historiographical scholarship. For a sampling of other approaches to the vast literature on proslavery thought, see Drew Gilpin Faust, "The Peculiar South Revisited: White Society, Culture, and Politics in the Antebellum Period, 1800–1860," in John B. Boles and Evelyn Thomas Nolen (eds.), *Interpreting Southern History: Historiographical Essays in Honor of Sanford W. Higginbotham* (Baton Rouge,

La., 1987), 78–119; Mark M. Smith, *Debating Slavery: Economy and Society in the Antebellum American South* (Cambridge, 1998); Gordon Lewis, "Pro-Slavery Ideology," in Verine A. Shepherd and Hilary M. Beckles (eds.), *Caribbean Slavery in the Atlantic World: A Student Reader* (Kingston, 2000), 544–79; Lacy K. Ford, *Deliver Us from Evil: The Slavery Question in the Old South* (New York, 2009), a superb recent exploration of these issues.

2. See, respectively, Kenneth M. Stampp, *The Peculiar Institution: Slavery in the Antebellum South* (New York, 1956); and Eugene D. Genovese, *Roll, Jordan, Roll: The World the Slaves Made* (New York, 1974).

3. For example, for the notion that capitalistic slaveholders in the American South constructed a regime that brutally denied acknowledgment of any aspect of the slave's humanity, see Herbert S. Klein, *Slavery in the Americas: A Comparative Study of Virginia and Cuba* (Chicago, 1967); for the opposite interpretation, emphasizing that southern masters were uniquely invested in the notion that their mastery was predicated on the recognition of their slaves' humanity, see Eugene D. Genovese, *The World the Slaveholders Made: Two Essays in Interpretation* (New York, 1969).

4. Manisha Sinha, *The Counter-revolution of Slavery: Politics and Ideology in Antebellum South Carolina* (Chapel Hill, NC, 2000), chs. 1–3; John Patrick Daly, *When Slavery Was Called Freedom: Evangelicalism, Proslavery, and the Causes of the Civil War* (Lexington, Ky., 2002), ch. 2; and Nathalie Dessens, *Myths of the Plantation Society: Slavery in the American South and the West Indies* (Gainesville, Fla., 2003), ch. 4.

5. William Sumner Jenkins, *Pro-Slavery Thought in the Old South* (1935; reprint Gloucester, Mass., 1960).

6. Orlando Patterson, *Freedom in the Making of Western Culture* (New York, 1991); and G. W. F. Hegel, *Phenomenology of Spirit*, trans. A. V. Miller (Oxford, 1977), 111–19.

7. Robin Blackburn, *The Making of New World Slavery: From the Baroque to the Modern, 1492–1800* (London, 1997); Eugene Genovese and Elizabeth Fox-Genovese, *The Fruits of Merchant Capital: Slavery and Bourgeois Property in the Rise and Expansion of Capitalism* (New York, 1983).

8. For consideration of the forces that *did* ultimately lead European economies to make a transition away from chattel slavery, see Pierre Dockès, *Medieval Slavery and Liberation*, trans. Arthur Goldhammer (Chicago, 1982); and Pierre Bonnassie, *From Slavery to Feudalism in South-WesternEurope*, trans. Jean Birrell (Cambridge, 1991).

9. Daniel Castro, *Another Face of Empire: Bartolomé de Las Casas, Indigenous Rights, and Ecclesiastical Imperialism* (Durham, NC, 2007); Francis Augustus MacNutt, *Bartholomew de Las Casas: His Life, His Apostolate, and His Writings* (New York, 1909).

10. Frederick Douglass, *Narrative of the Life of Frederick Douglass, an American Slave*, ed. Deborah E. McDowell (1845; reprint Oxford, 1999); Harriet Beecher Stowe, *Uncle Tom's Cabin, or Life among the Lowly*, ed. Stephen Railton (1852; reprint Boston, 2008); Albert Taylor Bledsoe, *An Essay on Liberty and Slavery* (Philadelphia, 1856); George Fitzhugh, *Cannibals All! Or Slaves without Masters*, ed. C. Vann Woodward (1857; reprint Cambridge, Mass., 1960).

11. Ulrich Bonnell Phillips, *American Negro Slavery: A Survey of the Supply, Employment and Control of Negro Labor as Determined by the Plantation Regime* (New York, 1918).

12. Stanley Elkins, *Slavery: A Problem in American Institutional and Intellectual Life* (Chicago, 1959); Genovese, *Roll, Jordan, Roll*. For fuller consideration of the paternalism/ capitalism dichotomy, see my *Domesticating Slavery: The Master Class in Georgia and South Carolina, 1670–1837* (Chapel Hill, NC, 1999).

13. I discuss this theological tension and offer relevant historical sources in my edited volume, *Proslavery and Sectional Thought in the Early South, 1740–1829* (Columbia, SC, 2006). Also see Leland J. Bellot, "Evangelicals and the Defense of Slavery in Britain's Old Colonial Empire," *Journal of Southern History*, 37 (February 1971): 19–40; and Larry Tise, *Proslavery: A History of the Defense of Slavery in America, 1701–1840* (Athens, Ga., 1987).

14. David Brion Davis, *The Problem of Slavery in Western Culture* (Ithaca, NY, 1966); and *The Problem of Slavery in the Age of Revolution, 1770–1823* (Ithaca, NY, 1975). For the relationship between humanitarianism and the proslavery sensibility, see Joyce E. Chaplin, *An Anxious Pursuit: Agricultural Innovation and Modernity in the Lower South, 1730–1815* (Chapel Hill, NC, 1993).

15. For his pronouncements on the relationship between just government and the principles of freedom and slavery, see John Locke, *Two Treatises of Government*, ed. Peter Laslett (Cambridge, 1960); for his involvement with the Royal African Company and the plantation economy, see Maurice William Cranston, *John Locke: A Biography* (London, 1957), 115, 155.

16. Edmund S. Morgan, *American Slavery, American Freedom: The Ordeal of Colonial Virginia* (New York, 1975); S. Max Edelson, *Plantation Enterprise in Colonial South Carolina* (Cambridge, Mass., 2006).

17. Mark M. Smith (ed.), *Stono: Documenting and Interpreting a Southern Slave Revolt* (Columbia, SC, 2005); Betty Wood, *Slavery in Colonial Georgia, 1730–1775* (Athens, Ga., 1984).

18. Sylvia Frey, *Water from the Rock: Black Resistance in a Revolutionary Age* (Princeton, 1991); Woody Holton, *Forced Founders: Indians, Debtors, Slaves, and the Making of the American Revolution in Virginia* (Chapel Hill, NC, 1999); and Simon Schama, *Rough Crossings: Britain, the Slaves, and the American Revolution* (New Ysork, 2006).

19. Bernard Bailyn, *The Ideological Origins of the American Revolution* (Cambridge, Mass., 1967).

20. In this sense, the revolutionary slaveholders offer support for a "liberal" as opposed to a "Republican" reading of revolutionary ideology (to use the terms employed in the late twentieth-century debate about the fundamental values on which the campaign for American freedom was waged. Daniel T. Rodgers, "Republicanism: The Career of a Concept," *Journal of American History*, 79 (June 1992): 11–38. As we shall see, however, the brand of paternalistic proslavery thought that came into favor during the Early National era dovetailed with the communal sensibility associated with the "Republican" school of interpretation.

21. Eugene D. Genovese, *From Rebellion to Revolution: Afro-American Slave Revolts in the Making of the Modern World* (Baton Rouge, La., 1979).

22. On these points, see especially Willie Lee Rose, "The Domestication of Domestic Slavery," in William W. Freehling (ed.), *Slavery and Freedom* (New York, 1982), 18–36; Ira Berlin, *Many Thousands Gone: The First Two Centuries of Slavery in North America* (Cambridge, Mass., 1998), ch. 5; Frey, *Water from the Rock*, ch. 8.

23. William W. Freehling, *Prelude to Civil War: The Nullification Controversy in South Carolina, 1816–1836* (New York, 1966), ch. 9; and Alison G. Freehling, *Drift toward Dissolution: The Virigina Slavery Debate of 1831–32* (Baton Rouge, La., 1982). On slave resistance in the Caribbean, see Michael Craton, *Testing the Chains: Resistance to Slavery in the British West Indies* (Ithaca, NY, 1982).

24. For consideration of the tensions between the internal slave trade and the slaveholders' self-image as a class, see Walter Johnson, *Soul by Soul: Life inside the Antebellum Slave Market* (Cambridge, Mass., 1999).

25. Drew Gilpin Faust, *A Sacred Circle: The Dilemma of the Intellectual in the Old South, 1840–1860* (Baltimore, 1977); and Clement Eaton, *Freedom of Thought in the Old South* (New York, 1951). Collections of antebellum proslavery texts are available in E. N. Elliott (ed.), *Cotton is King, and Pro-Slavery Arguments* (Augusta, Ga., 1860); and Faust (ed.), *The Ideology of Slavery: Proslavery Thought in the Antebellum South, 1830–1860* (Baton Rouge, La., 1981).

26. Michael A. Morrison, *Slavery and the American West: The Eclipse of Manifest Destiny and the Coming of the Civil War* (Chapel Hill, NC, 1997); and William W. Freehling, *The Road to Disunion*, i: *Secessionists at Bay, 1776–1854* (New York, 1990).

27. As Paul Finkelman succinctly concluded, "in the end, the key to the proslavery argument was *race*." See Paul Finkelman "The Significance and Persistence of Proslavery Thought," in Steven Mintz and John Stauffer (eds.), *The Problem of Evil: Slavery, Freedom, and the Ambiguities of American Reform* (Amherst, Mass., 2007), 110. For relevant scholarship to this effect, see Winthrop D. Jordan, *White over Black: American Attitudes toward the Negro, 1550–1812* (Chapel Hill, NC, 1968); George M. Fredrickson, *The Black Image in the White Mind: The Debate on Afro-American Character and Destiny, 1817–1914* (New York, 1971); Thomas Virgil Peterson, *Ham and Japheth: The Mythic World of Whites in the Antebellum South* (Metuchen, NJ, 1978); and Stephen R. Haynes, *Noah's Curse: The Biblical Justification of American Slavery* (New York, 2002).

28. Genovese's critics have suggested that his historical theories failed to acknowledge the extent to which white southern racism informed the treatment of black slaves. Genovese perhaps fueled these charges when he pointed to the antebellum proslavery theories of George Fitzhugh as the "logical outcome" of the slaveholders' worldview. Fitzhugh, in a highly unusual step for an antebellum proslavery commentator, flirted with the abstract possibility that slavery might be extended on non-racial terms to encompass bondservants who were not of African descent. And in recent work, Genovese referred to southern conservatism as resting on ideas that could potentially be "shorn" of racism and the commitment to slavery. See *The Slaveholders' Dilemma: Freedom and Progress in Southern Conservative Thought, 1820–1860* (Columbia, SC, 1999), 3. See also Genovese and Elizabeth Fox-Genovese's frank acknowledgment that they harbored "respect for the slaveholders" and their "admiration for much in their character and achievements." And yet, their sympathy with some of the slaveholders' principles did not lead them to ignore the slaveholders' willingness to entertain such absurdly and indefensibly racist theories such as the Curse of Ham. See Fox-Genovese and Genovese, *The Mind of the Master Class: History and Faith in the Southern Slaveholder's Worldview* (Cambridge, 2005), 5, 522–6. For the other side of this historiographical divide, see Oakes, *The Ruling Race: A History of American Slaveholders* (New York, 1983), and Ford, *Origins of Southern Radicalism: The South Carolina Upcountry, 1800–1860* (New York, 1988).

29. For evidence of the relationship between proslavery thought and secession, see William W. Freehling and Craig Simpson (eds.), *Secession Debated: Georgia's Showdown in 1860* (New York, 1992); and David B. Chesebrough (ed.), *God Ordained This War: Sermons on the Sectional Crisis, 1830–1865* (Columbia, SC, 1991), ch. 7. At the same time, however, one should note that until secession became a fait accompli a number of prominent proslavery theorists thought the South could best defend its interests in the Union. See

Charles F. Irons, *The Origins of Proslavery Christianity: White and Black Evangelicals in Colonial and Antebellum Virginia* (Chapel Hill, NC, 2008), ch. 6. On the role of honor in the slaveholding South, see Bertram Wyatt-Brown, *Southern Honor: Ethics and Behavior in the Old South* (New York, 1982).

30. James L. Roark, *Master without Slaves: Southern Planters in the Civil War and Reconstruction* (New York, 1977).

31. Rebecca J. Scott, *Slave Emancipation in Cuba: The Transition to Free Labor, 1860–1899* (Princeton, 1985); Robert Edgar Conrad, *The Destruction of Brazilian Slavery, 1850–1888* (Berkeley, 1972); and Laird W. Bergad, *The Comparative Histories of Slavery in Brazil, Cuba, and the United States* (Cambridge, 2007).

32. According to Gordon K. Lewis, the same holds true for the survival of certain proslavery assumptions about the Caribbean plantation system. See *Main Currents in Caribbean Thought: The Historical Evolution of Caribbean Society in its Ideological Aspects, 1492–1900* (Baltimore, 1983), 169–70.

33. David W. Blight, *Race and Reunion: The Civil War in American Memory* (Cambridge, Mass., 2001), ch. 4.

34. Melvyn Stokes, *D. W. Griffith's The Birth of a Nation: A History of "The Most Controversial Motion Picture of All Time"* (New York, 2007).

35. John David Smith and John C. Inscoe (eds.), *Ulrich Bonnell Phillips: A Southern Historian and his Critics* (New York, 1990); Merton L. Dillon, *Ulrich Bonnell Phillips: Historian of the Old South* (Baton Rouge, La., 1985); John Herbert Roper, *U. B. Phillips: A Southern Mind* (Macon, Ga., 1984); and Wendell Holmes Stephenson, *The South Lives in History: Southern Historians and their Legacy* (Baton Rouge, La., 1955), ch. 3.

36. Tannenbaum, *Slave and Citizen* (1946; reprint Boston, 1992), 65–91, quotation 80.

37. Elkins, *Slavery*; and Stampp, *The Peculiar Institution*.

38. On the historiographical movement from Progressive to liberal readings of American slaveholders, see Robert William Fogel, *The Slavery Debates, 1952–1990* (Baton Rouge, La., 2003), 1–12. On the role that liberal thought played in the proslavery and antislavery debates of the antebellum period, see David F. Ericson, *The Debate over Slavery: Antislavery and Proslavery Liberalism in Antebellum America* (New York, 2000).

39. Robert William Fogel and Stanley L. Engerman, *Time on the Cross: The Economics of American Negro Slavery* (Boston, 1974); and Fogel and Engerman (eds.), *Without Consent or Contract: The Rise and Fall of American Slavery*, 2 vols., *Technical Papers* (New York, 1992).

40. Elizabeth Fox-Genovese, *Within the Plantation Household: Black and White Women of the Old South* (Chapel Hill, NC, 1988); Stephen Hahn, *The Roots of Southern Populism: Yeoman Farmers and the Transformation of the Georgia Upcountry, 1850–1890* (New York, 1983); J. William Harris, *Plain Folk and Gentry in a Slave Society: White Liberty and Black Slavery in Augusta's Hinterlands* (Middletown, Conn., 1985); and Stephanie McCurry, *Masters of Small Worlds: Yeoman Households, Gender Relations, and the Political Culture of the Antebellum South Carolina Low Country* (New York, 1995).

41. See especially Genovese, *The Slaveholders' Dilemma*.

42. Oakes, *Slavery and Freedom: An Interpretation of the Old South* (New York, 1990).

43. Chaplin, *An Anxious Pursuit*; Mark M. Smith, *Mastered by the Clock: Time, Slavery, and Freedom in the American South* (Chapel Hill, NC, 1997); and Johnson, *Soul by Soul*.

44. Peter Kolchin, *Unfree Labor: American Slavery and Russian Serfdom* (Cambridge, Mass., 1987). For a notable example of Jack Greene's influence resulting in a scholar taking a

comparative analytical approach, see Philip D. Morgan's *Slave Counterpoint: Black Culture in the Eighteenth-Century Chesapeake and Lowcountry* (Chapel Hill, NC, 1998).

45. See, for example, Robert Olwell, *Masters, Slaves, and Subjects: The Culture of Power in the South Carolina Low Country, 1740–1790* (Ithaca, NY, 1998); and Olwell and Alan Tully (eds.), *Cultures and Identities in Colonial British America* (Baltimore, 2006).

46. Michael O'Brien, *A Character of Hugh Legaré* (Knoxville, Tenn., 1985); *Conjectures of Order: Intellectual Life and the American South, 1810–1860* (Chapel Hill, NC, 2004).

47. Robert Robertson, *The Speech of Mr. John Talbot Campo-bell, c.1730–40*, in Thomas W. Krise (ed.), *Caribbeana: An Anthology of English Literature of the West Indies, 1657–1777* (Chicago, 1999), ch. 7; *A True Relation of the Inhumane and Unparallel'd Actions and Barbarous Murders of Negroes or Moors: Committed on Three English-men in Old Calabar in Guinny, 1672*, in Alan Rudrum et al. (eds.), *The Broadview Anthology of Seventeenth-Century Verse and Prose* (Peterborough, Ontario, 2000), 1266–75; and Derek Hughes (ed.), *Versions of Blackness: Key Texts on Slavery from the Seventeenth Century* (Cambridge, 2007).

Select Bibliography

Bellot, Leland J. "Evangelicals and the Defense of Slavery in Britain's Old Colonial Empire," *Journal of Southern History*, 37 (February 1971): 19–40.

Daly, John Patrick. *When Slavery Was Called Freedom: Evangelicalism, Proslavery, and the Causes of the Civil War*. Lexington, Ky.: University Press of Kentucky, 2002.

Faust, Drew Gilpin, ed. *The Ideology of Slavery: Proslavery Thought in the Antebellum South, 1830–1860*. Baton Rouge, La.: Louisiana State University Press, 1981.

Ford, Lacy K. *Deliver Us from Evil: The Slavery Question in the Old South*. New York: Oxford University Press, 2009.

Fox-Genovese, Elizabeth, and Eugene D. Genovese. *The Mind of the Master Class: History and Faith in the Southern Slaveholder's Worldview*. Cambridge: Cambridge University Press, 2005.

Irons, Charles F. *The Origins of Proslavery Christianity: White and Black Evangelicals in Colonial and Antebellum Virginia*. Chapel Hill, NC: University of North Carolina Press, 2008.

Jenkins, William Sumner. *Pro-Slavery Thought in the Old South*. 1935; reprint Gloucester, Mass.: Peter Smith, 1960.

Lewis, Gordon. "Pro-Slavery Ideology," in Verine A. Shepherd and Hilary M. Beckles (eds.), *Caribbean Slavery in the Atlantic World: A Student Reader*. Kingston: Ian Randle Publishers, 2000, 544–79.

Rose, Willie Lee. "The Domestication of Domestic Slavery," in William W. Freehling (ed.), *Slavery and Freedom*. New York: Oxford University Press, 1982, 18–36.

Tise, Larry. *Proslavery: A History of the Defense of Slavery in America, 1701–1840*. Athens, Ga.: University of Georgia Press, 1987.

Young, Jeffrey Robert, ed. *Proslavery and Sectional Thought in the Early South, 1740–1829: An Anthology*. Columbia, SC: University of South Carolina Press, 2006.

CHAPTER 19

UNITED STATES SLAVE LAW

PAUL FINKELMAN

OVERVIEW

Slave law in the United States developed over 225 years through a complicated mixture of custom, statutes, and court decisions. Before the American Revolution of 1776 England never micromanaged the colonies or promulgated a colonial slave code, as France did for its colonies with the Code Noir (1685). Each of the thirteen colonies that became the United States had its own legislatures and court structures, and thus each colony developed slave law in its own way. This local development continued after the revolution, as each state had its own rules and regulations. The US Constitution, written in 1787, did not interfere with slavery in the states, but had a number of provisions which directly and indirectly impacted slavery throughout the nation. In addition, the Constitution gave Congress the power to govern the District of Columbia and to pass all "needful rules and regulations" for federal territories. Thus, by 1860, there was no truly unified "slave law" in the United States, but rather fifteen separate state legal systems as well as a federal slave law that governed slavery in the District of Columbia and the territories and on a limited number of national issues, such as the African slave trade and the return of fugitive slaves. All slave jurisdictions shared some legal principles, such as the rule that the children of slave mothers would be slaves even if the father was free (or white), that conversion to Christianity did not effectuate a manumission, that slaves were property and could be sold, given away, or bequeathed, and that no slave could testify against a white person. But states differed on many other aspects of slavery, such as the regulation of manumission, what constituted a crime against a slave, or whether a slave gained freedom by being brought to a free state. Thus, in 1860 there was a clearly recognizable general American law of slavery, but not a unified one.

The English legal heritage that the colonists carried with them to the New World both hampered and aided the development of slavery in the Americas. The institution developed slowly in the British mainland colonies in part because the colonists initially brought with them no laws to support the concept of treating people as private property. Colonial self-government with elected legislatures allowed for the development of a legal structure that would support slavery. The creation of a system of slavery was also helped by the flexibility of English common law jurisprudence, which the colonists brought with them. Judges in the colonies were able to make new law for the new circumstances of the colonies and adapt existing English law to accommodate a new form of property. By the time of the American Revolution the colonies had developed a fairly elaborate system of laws that integrated slavery—the legal ownership of human beings—into the English common law system that venerated both individual liberty and private property.

Like the principles of the common law, American leaders and voters of the revolutionary period also venerated both private property and liberty. The ideology of the American Revolution reflected John Locke's notion that the purpose of government was to protect "life, liberty, and property," which Jefferson rephrased as "life, liberty and the pursuit of happiness." This ideology obviously created a tension within American society, as some citizens of the newly independent states struggled with the evident contradiction between slavery and revolutionary liberty. Locke had never denied the legitimacy of slavery, arguing that slaves lived outside the social compact in "the state of war continued."[1] But Locke lived in England and had never seen a slave society. Locke's argument made little sense in the new American Republic, where masters lived in close proximity to their slaves, and after 1776 most slaves were not the victims of the African trade, but had been born and raised in America. At the time of the revolution many masters understood the contradiction between the claims of the revolution and the realities of slavery.

Some Americans resolved this contradiction by voluntarily manumitting their slaves, many of whom then served in patriot armies during the revolution. During and after the revolution some of the new states facilitated manumission through new laws and constitutions. Between 1780 and 1804 all of the northern states took steps to end slavery, either immediately through constitutional provisions or gradually through statutes that respected existing property relationships but provided that the children of all slaves would be born free, thus guaranteeing that slavery would literally die out.

South of Pennsylvania a few Americans also freed their slaves and suggested ways to end slavery. In 1782 Virginia passed legislation allowing masters to privately free some adult slaves, while Maryland and Delaware law allowed even greater opportunity for private manumission. These individual acts led to liberty for some slaves but did not undermine the system of slavery in any of these states. In Virginia Judge St George Tucker, born and raised in Bermuda's peculiarly fluid maritime slave society, proposed a gradual abolition scheme for his adopted state of Virginia, but few Virginian politicians supported it.[2] More southerners accepted slavery and gradually the intellectual leaders of the South constructed from religious and secular sources a sophisticated proslavery ideology that allowed them to defend slavery and let it expand. This process began with Thomas Jefferson's *Notes on the State of Virginia* (1784), which provided a defense of slavery based on pseudo-scientific arguments about race. In the post-revolutionary South new laws created more humane conditions for those in bondage, and some states allowed masters to voluntarily manumit their slaves. The revolutionary influence on slave law in the South was short-lived, however, and in the early 1800s the South began to develop a legal regime that increasingly protected slavery and subordinated all blacks, slave or free. The trend began around 1800, was in full flower by the 1820s, and dominated all southern law after that.

During and after the revolution slave law developed in response to independence, constitutionalism, territorial expansion, and the closing of the African slave trade. The United States Constitution (1787) reflected the importance of slavery within the young nation and also its very peculiar nature. Thus, slavery stands as the only form of privately held property that is explicitly protected by that document. The national Constitution gave important protections to slavery and gave the slave states a permanent veto over amendments that might have harmed their system of bondage. Starting in the post-revolutionary era, and coming to full maturity in the 1830s, a newly emerging ideology of racism influenced the law. This mature legal structure was totally committed to the preservation of slavery as a system. Thus, law helped shape slavery in the colonial period, helped preserve it after the revolution, and allowed the system of slavery to grow and develop until the Civil War.

The law, just as it shaped slavery, also always represented a threat to it because the system of bondage was ultimately in tension with common law and revolutionary principles of individual rights and individual liberties. Thus, while law was necessary to the creation and protection of slavery, law also helped dismantle slavery, both in the northern states during and after the revolution and in the entire nation during and immediately after the Civil War.

Colonial Slave Law

In the Americas, slavery developed in England's twenty-six colonies in the seventeenth century with the aid of legislative enactments and common law decisions. The English who settled in Virginia had no heritage of slavery and nothing in

English law supported slavery. Spanish, Portuguese, Dutch, and French settlers could all turn to their Roman law heritage, which had elaborate rules for slavery. Thus, slavery developed faster in the non-English colonies. While generally seen as a system of labor exploitation, slavery necessarily required a legal system to support it. Slaves were property—but always a peculiar kind of property. Owners needed a special legal system to protect that property because unlike other forms of property, slaves were thinking beings with their own volition. Slavery was not found in England, and was contrary to English law and custom and thus required new rules and regulations. Slavery conflicted with English notions of liberty—legal concepts not found in most of the non-English colonial legal systems—and thus new laws and new legal theories had to be developed in order to accommodate slavery within the structure of English law. Finally, as American slavery became a system based on race, the English in the New World had to develop a legal system that allowed for, and even mandated, discrimination based on race. While some scholars, such as Winthrop Jordan in *White over Black* (1968), have argued that the English brought a well-developed ideology of racism with them, others, such as Edmund Morgan in *American Slavery, American Freedom* (1975), persuasively argue that racism developed as a consequence of slavery.[3] The legal cases and statues of the seventeenth century overwhelmingly support Morgan's conclusions. Some of this new slave law was "borrowed" from the Roman law systems of the Spanish, French, Dutch, and Portuguese slave colonies, as Alan Watson argues in *Slave Law in the Americas* (1989), but much of American slave law developed through common law jurisprudence and statutes that allowed the colonial, and later the state, legislatures to graft slavery onto the English common law heritage.[4]

The earliest legal records in Virginia show how race was not initially a central issue in the colony when blacks began to arrive. In 1624 a Virginia Court allowed "*John Phillip* A negro Christened in *England 12* years since" to be called as witness in a civil lawsuit.[5] The fact that Phillip was a Christian mattered, since he could swear on a Bible in court. That he had lived in England and apparently spoke English made him a legitimate witness. Blacks would continue to testify in Virginia cases until the 1730s, even though in the 1690s the legislature prohibited them from doing so. Similarly, blacks and whites married each other until the end of the century when the legislature banned such unions. The case of Hugh Davis illustrates the complexity of law and race at this time. In 1630 the court ordered that a white man, Hugh Davis, was "to be soundly whipt before an assembly of negroes & others for abusing himself to the dishonr of God and shame of Christianity by defiling his body in lying with a negro. wch fault he is to ack[nowledge]. next *sabbath* day."[6] Historians disagree about the meaning of this text. Some scholars, such as Winthrop Jordan and Thomas D. Morris, argue that Davis's crime was interracial sex.[7] It seems more likely, however, that Davis had been caught in a same-sex relationship with an African man, and the whipping was designed to both punish Davis and instruct the non-English laborers from Africa about the nature of English morality. A decade later, for example, authorities simply ordered a white man to do public penance in church for fathering a child out of wedlock with a black woman, just as white men were forced to do for fathering illegitimate children with white women. These punishments, along with a fair number of interracial marriages, suggest that in this early period non-marital interracial sex was not considered to be more of an offense than same race illicit sex.

In 1640 a Virginia court sentenced a group of runaway servants to serve their master for various periods of time. The one black in the group, John Punch, was sentenced to "serve his said master or his assigns for the time of his natural Life here or elsewhere."[8] This punishment, unique in the colony, may indicate that the colony was moving toward slavery, but it also shows that Punch was not a slave when he ran away and that enslavement was a punishment, rather than an assumed status. By this time, however, other blacks were enslaved. Thus, that same year when "Emanuel the Negro" and six white servants were captured in group flight from Virginia, Emanuel was not given any extra time to his service, presumably because he was already a slave. After 1660 courts increasingly assumed that blacks in Virginia were slaves, but as late as 1672 and 1673 the Virginia court held that two blacks, Edward Mozingo and Andrew Moore, were actually entitled to their freedom.

While the Virginia courts helped create a regime of slavery, the Virginia legislature—the House of Burgesses—adopted numerous laws to preserve, protect, and expand slavery. Elite landowners in the colony, virtually all of whom owned slaves, elected members of the Burgesses, and thus, the legislators helped create slavery in the colony to guarantee a stable labor force to grow the tobacco that would enrich those who ran the colony. While they embraced slavery for economic reasons they soon embarked on creating a legal regime that made race a key component of slavery in the colony. As the black population of the colony and neighboring colonies grew, slavery and the legal system that supported it would become as much a system of racial control as it would be a system of labor exploitation.

A number of acts passed by Burgesses illustrate the radical changes in British common law that led to the creation of a slave system. An act of the 1661–2 session provided for increased service when indentured servants ran away from their masters. Recognizing the growing number of blacks in the colony being treated as slaves, the law also provided that if an "English servant shall run away in company of any negroes who are incapable of making satisfaction by addition of a time," after the English servants served out their own indentures, including time added for running away, the English servants would "serve the masters of the said negroes for their absence soe long as they should have done by this act if they had not beene slaves, every christian in company serving his proportion; and if the negroes be lost or dye in such time of their being run away, the christian servants in company with them shall by proportion among them, either pay fower [four] thousand five hundred pounds of tobacco and caske or fower [four] yeares service for every negroe soe lost or dead."⁹ In this act the legislature used the terms "Christian" and "English" interchangeably. This fact may indicate that the Virginians believed that an African's religion would justify his enslavement. White indentured servants who knew of this law would be reluctant to escape with blacks, because if captured, they would have to serve extra time not only for their absence, but for the time the blacks were absent. Black slaves, however, would have no incentive not to expose runaway plans by whites. The law thus drove a wedge between black and white workers while helping to secure slave property.

In 1662 the legislature, for the first time, dealt with interracial sex and the problem of the inherited status of slaves. Under English law a child inherited the status of the father. But, as African women arrived in the colonies as slaves, they were often the mothers of mixed-race children. The new law noted that "*some doubts have arrisen whether children got by Englishmen upon negro women should be slave or ffree.*"¹⁰ Virginia's House of Burgesses resolved this issue by declaring that "all children borne in this country shall be held bond or free only according to the condition of the mother," rejecting the English common law principle that children followed the status of their fathers. The status of slave was now inheritable through the mother. This law had a number of implications. First, it meant that the government would not care who fathered children born out of wedlock to slave women. When a single, white women had a child local officials would try to find the father to force him to marry the woman or support the children. But, the children of slave women would be the property and responsibility of the owner of the mother, and thus no government official would care about such births. The owner of the mother would not care because he would now have more slaves. Thus, an unintended consequence of this law was to make all slave women more sexually vulnerable because the government would not hold any men responsible for supporting out-of-wedlock slave children. This law also prohibited interracial sex, but that provision of the law would never be enforced against white men. A Virginia act of 1705 also undermined enforcement of this law against whites by providing that "negroes, mulattoes, and Indian servants . . . shall be deemed and taken to be persons incapable in law, to be witnesses in any cases whatsoever."¹¹ With this law in place, even the rape of a slave or a free black by a white man would go unpunished because no black person could ever testify against a white person. Thus, by 1662 the legal structure had set out who could be a slave and made both the labor and sexuality of those slaves exploitable by whites.

The Virginia legislature also grappled with the problem of religion and slavery. In the early seventeenth century many Englishmen believed that conversion to Christianity would free a slave. Such a rule would have either undermined the institution or made it impossible for Christian ministers to convert the "heathenish" slaves. An act of 1667 solved this problem by declaring "that the conferring of baptisme doth not alter the condition of the person as to his bondage or ffreedome; that diverse masters, ffreed from this doubt, may more carefully endeavour the propagation of christianity by permitting . . . slaves . . . to be admitted to that sacrament."[12] The Church could now be enlisted in the spread of slavery, and during the next two centuries southern ministers would use the gospel to give slavery divine sanction and the promise of rewards in the afterlife to encourage slaves to accept their earthly status.

In 1669 the Burgesses undermined the lives of all slaves in the colony with "An Act about the Casuall Killing of Slaves." This law declared that masters would not be punished if they killed their slaves while punishing them or restraining them, because "it cannot be presumed that prepensed malice . . . should induce any man to destroy his owne estate."[13] This law did not specifically allow masters to kill their slaves, but it meant that they could do so if they wished without fear of punishment. A year later Virginia prohibited free blacks in Virginia from owning white indentured servants, thus helping solidify the racial context of bondage. Other laws in this period prohibited slaves from possessing guns, made it a crime for a slave to "lift up his hand in opposition against" his master or any other whites, and allowed the use of lethal force in suppressing insurrections and in the hunting down and capture of "outlying Slaves." In the early eighteenth century, Virginia continued to provide new punishments—including severe whippings, cutting off of ears, and "dismembering"—while prohibiting masters from freeing their slaves except for "some meritorious services" which required the approval of the governor and his council. Other laws in this period banned interracial marriage and reiterated the ban on black testimony, even for blacks who were members of churches.

Other southern colonies adopted similar laws, although South Carolina, deeply influenced in law and culture by slaveholding immigrants from England's first great slave society, the sugar colony of Barbados, proved notoriously more brutal in its treatment of slaves than any other mainland colony. South Carolina was Britain's only mainland colony in North America with a Caribbean-like black majority, and it approached two-thirds of the total population by the 1730s. Thus, as historian Peter Wood documented in *Black Majority* (1974), South Carolina, unlike the other thirteen colonies, allowed particularly horrible punishments until well after the American Revolution, and masters in colonial South Carolina were notorious for their routinely brutal, sadistic, and often lethal treatment of their slaves.[14] Some mainland colonies initially treated slaves as real estate for purposes of inheritance and sale, but by the mid-eighteenth century, all the colonies considered slaves to be moveable personal property—chattels in the language of technical law—and thus slaves could be bought and sold in the same manner as people purchased or sold horses, wagons, or any other property that was not land. Laws in the northern colonies were generally less severe, although after a 1712 slave rebellion New York punished the rebels in ways that were as barbaric as almost anything meted out in the Deep South.

In the northern colonies the day-to-day lives of slaves were less brutal than in the South, and treatment was generally less harsh, but the legal structures were similar.

Slaves could not testify against whites, slave status was inherited through the mother, and conversion to Christianity did not lead to emancipation. Most of the northern colonies allowed masters to privately manumit their slaves, and in some cities, like New York, Philadelphia, and Boston, there was a growing free black population.

SLAVE LAW IN REVOLUTIONARY AMERICA

On the eve of the American Revolution, slavery was legal in every one of Britain's thirteen mainland North American colonies as well as in its thirteen other colonies located elsewhere in the Americas. Before the revolution religious opposition had begun to undermine its viability in Pennsylvania and Massachusetts and among Quakers, Baptists, and Methodists everywhere. Revolutionary ideology, especially in the North, also spurred antislavery ideas. At the beginning of the war, free blacks served in the colonial militias of the North, and many masters, acting on revolutionary ideology, emancipated their male slaves so they could enlist in the army. Significant numbers of black men, including many who had been recently manumitted, served in the Rhode Island and Connecticut militias. Masters often received the enlistment bounty while the slaves received their freedom. The history of blacks in the revolution was detailed in the classic book *The Negro in the American Revolution* (1961) by the great black scholar Benjamin Quarles and has been more recently examined in Sylvia Frey, *Water from the Rock* (1999).[15]

Many northerners recognized the contradiction between fighting for their own liberty and denying it to others. Private manumissions increased while legal action to end slavery intensified. Even before the revolution slaves and free blacks in Massachusetts, led in part by Prince Hall, petitioned for an end to bondage in that colony. This agitation, combined with significant religious opposition and revolutionary ideology, led to a climate that made slavery untenable. As the historian Willi Paul Adams pointed out in *The First American Constitutions* (1980), in 1778 voters in Massachusetts rejected a proposed state constitution, in part because it did not end slavery or give free black men the right to vote. In 1780 voters ratified a state constitution, written mostly by John Adams, that did both these things. Between 1781 and 1783 a series of court cases in Massachusetts confirmed that slavery was no longer legal in the state.[16] As Joanne Pope Melish noted in *Disowning Slavery* (1998), many individual masters in New England resisted an end to slavery, but the overwhelming majority of people in the region ignored or rejected such complaints.[17] In 1783 New Hampshire adopted a state constitution with provisions that ended slavery and allowed free black men to vote.

In 1780 Pennsylvania passed the nation's first gradual emancipation act. The preamble to the law cited revolutionary ideology to explain this legal innovation, noting that slaves were "deprived . . . of the common blessings that they were by nature entitled to" and were "cast . . . into the deepest afflictions, by an unnatural separation and sale of husband and wife from each other and from their children, an injury, the greatness of which can only be conceived by supposing that we were in the same unhappy case."[18] This law did not free any existing slaves. But it did provide that after 1 March 1780 the children of slave women would be born free, subject to an indenture. Thus, the law brilliantly and successfully balanced the twin—and in this case competing—ideologies of the American Revolution that venerated both private property and individual freedom. The law, and a 1788 amendment to it, prohibited masters from removing pregnant slaves to preempt their children from being born in slave states and set up an elaborate registration system to prevent fraud and protect the claims to freedom of black children born after the law went into effect. Gary B. Nash and Jean R. Soderlund demonstrated that Pennsylvania masters opposed these new laws and worked hard to defeat legislators who supported them.[19] Because the ending of slavery was gradual in Pennsylvania, some blacks were held in bondage long after most were free. The gradual nature of abolition in the state, as well as the many southerners who visited the state with their slaves, led to a significant amount of litigation, as Paul Finkelman demonstrates in *An Imperfect Union* (1981).[20]

While the law did not end slavery immediately in Pennsylvania, the institution declined dramatically. About 6,000 slaves lived in the state when the law was passed. By 1790 only 3,700 slaves remained, and by 1810 the slave population had diminished to 795. Meanwhile, the free black population grew from 10,000 in 1790 to over 23,000 by 1810. This population growth came not only from the children of slaves but from significant numbers of private manumissions, as well as from slaves and free blacks moving into the state from elsewhere. Connecticut (1784), Rhode Island (1784), New York (1799), and New Jersey (1804) passed similar laws. By 1830 this process, which Arthur Zilversmit details in his pioneering work *The First Emancipation* (1967), had destroyed the system of slavery everywhere in the North except New Jersey, even though a few people were held in bondage in Connecticut and Pennsylvania into the 1840s. Vermont, the fourteenth state, entered the Union in 1791 with a ban on slavery in its Constitution as did Ohio (1803), Indiana (1816), Illinois (1818), and Maine (1820). By 1830 slavery had all but disappeared in the Northeast. Only New Jersey, with 2,200 slaves and 18,000 free blacks, had any noticeable slave population.[21]

The northern states generally allowed southern masters to bring slaves with them on visits, even as they dismantled slavery. This right of transit, as Finkelman details extensively in *An Imperfect Union*, led to litigation and legislation throughout the North. Pennsylvania generally allowed slaves to be kept in the state for six months, but gave members of Congress the right to keep slaves in the state for the entire length of their Congressional service. Georgia's Senator Pierce Butler lost one of his slaves when he remained in the state beyond six months after he had lost his seat in the Senate. But during the War of 1812, South Carolina Congressman Langdon Cheves was able to keep his slave there, even though the national capital had been moved to the District of Columbia. New York had a similar law, with an exemption of nine months. Starting in the 1830s, however, northern states began to emancipate any slave voluntarily brought into the state by a master. In *Commonwealth* v. *Aves* (1836) Chief Justice Lemuel Shaw of Massachusetts held that a slave became free the moment he or she was brought into the state. In *Lemmon* v. *The People* (1860) New York's highest court applied this concept to travelers who stopped in New York for a day while changing ships. By this time the laws of the North had become universally hostile to slavery.

In 1782 Virginia passed legislation that allowed for private manumission. Other southern states adopted similar laws. Free blacks composed the fastest-growing segment of the population in much of the nation between 1780 and 1810, as thousands of masters implemented the liberationist ideology of the revolution by voluntarily emancipating their slaves. In Virginia, for example, the free black population rose from about 2,000 in 1782 to over 30,000 in 1810. In 1790 there were about 60,000 free blacks in the nation; that number had grown to more than 108,000 by 1800 and to more than 186,000 by 1810. But by this time the revolutionary ideology in the South had begun to fade and new laws and judicial interpretations reflected this. In 1806 Virginia passed legislation requiring that newly manumitted slaves leave the state. By the middle of the century private manumission was increasingly difficult in most states and impossible in some. The changing nature of manumission and the status of free blacks is charted in such books as John Hope Franklin's classic *The Free Negro in North Carolina* (1941), Ira Berlin's *Slaves without Masters* (1974), and Thomas D. Morris's massive study *Southern Slavery and the Law* (1996).[22] More recently, Bernie Jones in *Fathers of Conscience* (2009) has written about masters who emancipated their mistresses and their children. No book, however, offers a comprehensive study of the law of manumission or its implementation.[23]

Beyond manumission and emancipation, slave law changed in the South during and after the revolution in a number of other ways. During the revolution all the slave states either suspended the African slave trade or effectively ended it through prohibitively high taxes. These suspensions were initially part of the revolutionary governments' non-importation policies that ended all trade with Great Britain. In the North ending the trade was the first step to ending slavery itself. On ideological grounds, as well as economic and prudential grounds, including the fear of more African-born slaves, the Chesapeake states also continued the ban after independence. Many Virginia and Maryland masters had a surplus of slaves that they could sell further south at higher prices if there were no new imports from Africa. After the revolution, Georgia and South Carolina briefly reopened the trade but then closed it in the 1790s in response to the slave rebellions in Haiti. South Carolina's legislature, by a bare majority vote in 1803, would reopen the trade the next year, leading to the importation of about 50,000 slaves, the most intense burst of African imports in the country's history, before a federal law passed in 1807 ended the trade on January 1, 1808. There has been no significant book-length study of the closing of the trade since W. E. B. DuBois published his classic, but now quite dated, *The Suppression of the African Slave Trade* (1896).[24] A modern book-length study of the end of the trade is needed. Meanwhile, recent articles by Jed H. Shugerman and Paul Finkelman illuminate the legislative and judicial process of the closing of the trade.[25]

In most of the post-revolutionary South, the laws became more humane, as southern states prohibited their more barbaric punishments, such as dismemberment. In Virginia the state's substantial reduction of the number of capital offenses for whites led to a parallel reduction of capital offenses for blacks, although there were always more capital crimes for slaves and free blacks than for whites. North Carolina criminalized the murder of a slave in 1791, but South Carolina did not do so until 1821. Most other slave states adopted similar rules, either by statute or through common law decisions, in the antebellum period. However, as late as 1851, the Georgia Supreme Court held that it was not a crime to murder a slave, even though a state constitutional provision dating from 1798 declared that murder of a slave was punishable in the same way that murder of a white was punishable. The new laws, such as North Carolina's act of 1791 making murder of a slave a felony, in part reflected some of the liberal thought of the revolution. The closing of the African slave trade by the states during the revolution also helped reduce inhumane treatment because slaves who died from punishment or maltreatment could no longer be easily and cheaply replaced.

In the wake of the revolution, slavery became sectional as it ended in the North and expanded in the South. In 1787 the Congress under the Articles of Confederation passed the Northwest Ordinance, which in article 6 banned slavery in the territories north and west of the Ohio River. The Ordinance did not free the existing slaves in the territory, and some people in Illinois remained in bondage until the 1840s. Despite failure to end all slavery in the territory, the Ordinance did set out a line of demarcation between slavery and freedom. The language of the Northwest Ordinance implied that slavery would be permitted south of the Ohio River; the preservation of slavery in this territory was made explicit in the Southwest Ordinance adopted by Congress shortly after the ratification of the Constitution.[26]

At the Constitutional Convention slave-state delegates successfully argued for special protections for slavery. These issues are dealt with extensively in Finkelman's *Slavery and the Founders* (2001) and Donald L. Robinson's *Slavery in the Structure of American Politics* (1971).[27] The three-fifths clause (article I, section 2, clause 3) gave the South extra power in Congress by adding 60 per cent of the slave population to a state's free population when determining the allocation of representation in Congress. The Convention adopted this provision in order to gain southern support for population-based representation in the House of Represen-tatives. The cost of this compromise, however, was to give the South vastly disproportionate power in Congress until the Civil War. Thus, numerous bills protecting or expanding slavery—such as the Missouri Compromise (1820), the annexation of Texas (1845), and the Fugitive Slave Law of 1850—were passed only because of the extra votes the South got by counting slaves for representation. Because presidential electors were allocated on the basis of Congressional repre-sentation, the three-fifths clause also gave the South extra muscle in the electoral college. In 1800 the slaveholder Thomas Jefferson was elected President because of the electoral votes created by counting slaves. If slaves had not been counted for representation and the electoral college then the nonslaveholding John Adams would have been reelected. Antislavery Federalists like Rufus King hammered away at the South on this point, and abolitionists followed suit.

The Constitution also prohibited Congress from banning the African slave trade until 1808, required that slaves escaping to free states be returned to their masters, and obligated the national government to suppress "insurrections," which south-erners correctly understood to include slave rebellions. Under the Constitution, Congress had no power to end slavery, and the requirement that constitutional amendments be ratified by three-quarters of the states gave the slave states a permanent veto, at least in the foreseeable future, over any amendments to the Constitution. As Charles Cotesworth Pinckney, one of the delegates to the Consti-tutional Convention, told the South Carolina House of Representatives, "We have a security that the general government can never emancipate them [slaves], for no such authority is granted and it is admitted, on all hands, that the general government has no powers but what are expressly granted by the Constitution, and that all rights not expressed were reserved by the several states."[28]

Opponents of the Constitution (Anti-Federalists) complained that the "insur-rections clause" of the Constitution would force them to march south to protect slave owners from their bondsmen. The slave trade clause elicited even more opposition. Many in the North, and some in the South, took a principled stand against the Constitution because of that provision. A New Yorker complained that the Constitution condoned "drenching the bowels of Africa in gore, for the sake of enslaving its free-born innocent inhabitants." An Anti-Federalist Virginian from the western part of the state, where there were few slaves, thought that the slave trade provision was an "excellent clause" for "an Algerian constitution: but not so well calculated (I hope) for the latitude of America."[29]

Northern Anti-Federalists feared more than just the slave trade. In Massachusetts three opponents of the Constitution noted that it bound the states together as a "whole" and that the states were "under obligation . . . reciprocally to aid each other in defense and support of every thing to which they are entitled thereby, right or wrong." Thus, they might be called to suppress a slave revolt or in some other way defend the institution. They could not predict how slavery might entangle them in the future, but they did know that "this lust for slavery, [was] portentous of much evil in America, for the cry of innocent blood . . . hath un-doubtedly reached to the Heavens, to which that cry is always directed, and will draw down upon them vengeance adequate to the enormity of the crime."[30]

Although the new Constitution did not allow Congress to completely close the slave trade until 1808, Congress was able to pass laws that limited the trade and American participation in it. In acts of 1794, 1800, and 1803, Congress prohibited American ships, sailors, and investors from participating in the African slave trade. In 1793 Congress passed the first fugitive slave law, which provided a mechanism for masters to recover slaves who escaped into free states.

Scholars disagree about the nature of these compromises over slavery. Finkel-man, Robinson, David Brion Davis, William M. Wiecek, David Waldstreicher, Eugene D. Genovese, and others argue that the Constitution was essentially a proslavery compact which gave the South enormous political advantages.[31] Don E. Fehrenbacher and William W. Freehling, in the whole corpus of their work, argue that the Constitution was essentially antislavery, although they fail to explain how slavery might have ended either at the state level or the national level under the Constitution.[32] Many constitutional scholars and early national scholars dis-miss the provisions involving slavery, and at the law school level, until very recently virtually all constitutional law casebooks utterly ignored slavery.

SLAVE LAW IN ANTEBELLUM AMERICA

The nature of the law of slavery began to change after 1800. The rapid growth of the cotton industry, and of the slave population itself by natural means, led to a huge migration of whites and their slaves to more productive areas of the Deep South and the Southwest. State laws on slavery varied in small and large ways, but general trends could be found throughout the South. By the eve of the Civil War all of the fifteen slave states had elaborate slave codes that were similar. Delaware, with its tiny slave population, gave free blacks a few more rights than other states, as did Louisiana with its French civil law tradition and its large number of free persons of color. The unique and complex interplay between French and Anglo-American legal traditions is de-tailed in books and articles by Judith Schafer.[33] By the eve of the Civil War, however, the law of slavery in Louisiana increasingly resembled that of the rest of the nation.

Masters could buy, sell, loan, lease, or give away slaves like any other form of property. By 1860 their right to manumit slaves was severely limited or prohibited. In 1806 Virginia effectively repealed its 1782 law allowing private manumissions within the state, requiring newly freed slaves to leave the state. Virginia's new law responded in part to the Haitian Revolution and to the discovery in Richmond of Gabriel's conspiracy in 1800, which may have embraced hundreds of rebellious slaves. Virginia subsequently changed its manumission law a number of times to provide some mechanism that would allow newly manumitted slaves to remain in the state. Finally, in 1852 the state permanently banned manumissions through a constitutional amendment. The slave states in the Upper South, such as Maryland and Delaware, resisted the pressures to ban manumission, but in the Deep South most states made it impossible to free a slave unless the freed person left the state. By 1860 in most of the South the law generally prohibited masters from freeing their slaves without removing them from the state, and in 1859 Mississippi's highest court ruled in *Mitchell* v. *Wells* that it was not even obligated to recognize the freedom of a slave whose master (also her father) had taken her to Ohio where he formally manumitted her. The Mississippi court asserted that even the voluntary manumission of a slave in another state violated its public policy. Here the court was unable to order the reenslavement of Nancy Wells, who remained in Ohio after the death of her father, but the court refused to allow her to inherit his property, maintaining that whatever she might be in Ohio, she would always be a slave in Mississippi.

Every southern state prohibited slaves from ever testifying against whites and, with only a few exceptions, also prohibited free blacks from testifying against whites. These laws meant that whites could commit various crimes against slaves or free blacks and not face punishment unless there were white witnesses or other evidence to convict them. Generally, slaves could not move about without a pass, own guns or other weapons (or even possess them with a master's consent), live on their own, have any private property that did not technically belong to their masters, sue their masters (except on bona fide claim that they were actually free), sign contracts, or in any other way act as free adults might. The laws of the slave states prohibited anyone from teaching slaves (and often free blacks) to read and write. Many masters in violation of the law allowed a few slaves to become literate. Interracial sex was illegal, and black men having sex with white women could be executed. There are no known antebellum examples of white men charged with sexually related crimes involving black women. The laws of the South prohibited whites from possessing antislavery literature or speaking out against slavery. The law of slavery in effect made the South a closed society where free speech and even freedom of religion were undermined by the need to protect slavery.

After the discovery of the Denmark Vesey conspiracy in Charleston, South Carolina, in 1822, the state legislature passed laws to crack down on both slaves and free blacks, including limiting the autonomy of free blacks in attending their own churches and providing for the incarceration of free blacks who entered the state as sailors on any vessel until it was ready to leave port. Laws prohibited slaves and free blacks from gathering in groups or even conducting their own church services without white observers. By the 1850s, most slave states had similar laws.

The slave states also prohibited slaves (and sometimes free blacks) from learning to read or engaging in certain professions, such as those of pharmacists or gunsmiths. In general, the laws of the South were developed to limit the options of slaves, and free blacks, so that they would be subordinate to white society.

Most slave states considered it a crime to murder a slave. In North Carolina a few whites were executed for murdering slaves, including John Hoover, who was hanged for murdering his own slave. In *State* v. *Hoover* (1839) the North Carolina Supreme Court affirmed his conviction and death sentence. A slave owner in Virginia was sent to prison for five years after his slave died from inhumane punishments. Virginia's highest court affirmed this result in *Souther* v. *Commonwealth* (1851) but noted in passing that the sentence was lighter than the justices would have imposed if they had heard the case. Prosecutors charged some whites for assaulting slaves owned by others, and juries often brought in guilty verdicts. The legal theory of these results was not based on the right of the slave to be protected from physical assaults but rather to protect slave property from what the North Carolina court in *State* v. *Hale* (1823) called "offences . . . committed by men of dissolute habits, hanging loose upon society, who, being repelled from association with well disposed citizens, take refuge in the company of coloured persons and slaves, whom they deprave by their example, embolden by their familiarity, and then beat, under the expectation that a slave dare not resent a blow from a white man."[34] The court was concerned with preserving the public peace and protecting the valuable property of slave owners.

Except where statutes expressly prohibited specific forms of punishment—such as mutilation or branding—masters were free, however, to punish their slaves however they chose. In the famous case of *State* v. *Mann* (1829), the North Carolina Supreme Court declared that the courts could never second-guess or question the right of a master to inflict punishment. Chief Justice Thomas Ruffin declared that "The power of the master must be absolute, to render the submission of the slave perfect." "The slave, to remain a slave," Ruffin asserted, "must be made sensible that there is no appeal from his master; that his power is in no instance, usurped; but is conferred by the laws of man at least, if not by the law of God. The danger would be great indeed, if the tribunals of justice should be called on to graduate the punishment appropriate to every temper, and every dereliction of menial duty."[35] This was the rule, in the end, for all southern slave states. The *Mann* case has fascinated commentators. In *The Key to Uncle Tom's Cabin* (1853) Harriet Beecher Stowe used it as evidence for the realistic nature of the portrayal of slavery in her famous novel.[36] More recently, legal scholar Mark V. Tushnet examined the case in both history and literature.[37]

Although slaves could not legally be murdered or assaulted by people who did not own them, they also could never testify against a free person. Thus, assaults on slaves by white strangers when there were no white witnesses willing or able to testify about the event, or the rape of a slave by someone who did not own the slave, could never be punished, because the victim could not be a complaining witness. Thomas R. R. Cobb, the South's most significant proslavery legal theorist and chief architect of the Confederate Constitution, commented in *An Inquiry into the Law of Negro Slavery in the United States of America* (1858)—the only treatise on American slave law written by a southerner—that the lack of laws that prevented the rape of slave was a defect in the law of the South for which there was no obvious remedy. Cobb believed that southern legislatures ought to consider "whether the offense of rape, committed upon a female slave, should not be indictable." But if the master was also the rapist, the only possible remedy he could imagine was forcing the master to sell the slave to a new master. Cobb argued that such a law might be passed "for the honor of the statute-book," since he doubted that the actual offense was very widespread.[38] Part of his reasoning was based on his belief, common among the slaveholding class, that black women were naturally lascivious and always willing to have sex with their masters, and thus sex with them was rarely forced. But Cobb also realized that such a law would be detrimental to slavery because a slave could have no legal "rights or privileges except such as are necessary to protect [his] . . . existence."[39]

In no state in the antebellum South could slaves be legally married. A marriage is a contract, and slaves lacked the legal capacity to sign a contract. Masters often used ministers or even justices of the peace to solemnize slave marriages in order to encourage harmony within the slave community. But masters had no legal obligation to preserve slave families. Slaves lived as couples, in what they considered marriages, but these unions never had the sanction of law and might be obliterated at the whim of a master. Slave parents raised their children, but they always knew that at any moment they might be sold away from their children, or their children might be sold away from them. Although some states prohibited the sale of very young children away from a mother at public auctions, no state prohibited private sales or giving slave children as gifts, which was commonly done to celebrate marriages, birthdays, christenings, or other life-cycle events. No slave could ever count on the sanctity of marriage or family life. When slave husbands tried to protect their wives from punishment, they too were punished or even prosecuted.

The illegality of slave marriage troubled at least some God-fearing southern whites. *The Duties of Christian Masters* (1851), for example, by the Baptist minister A. T. Holmes and the *Report* in 1859 by a group of Episcopalians headed by Christopher Memminger, a leading South Carolina statesman, urged that all slave marriages be performed by clergymen and that masters respect the sanctity of such marriages.[40] But in the end, they did not demand a law prohibiting the separation of spouses by sale, because they understood the utter impracticality of such a law for the master class. The lack of protection for slave marriages, the lack of a legal prohibition against the rape of a slave, troubled T. R. R. Cobb, but the only rule he contemplated was one that prevented a sheriff from breaking up a couple if there was a forced sale of slaves to settle debts or an estate. Abolitionists often focused their critiques of southern slavery on the destruction of black families and the sexual exploitation of slave women by members of the master class. Antislavery iconography often showed a child being torn from a mother's arms to be sold at auction, or showed a partially disrobed slave woman on the auction block. Southern masters who had qualms about breaking up slave families were perhaps comforted by the analysis of many proslavery theorists who argued that blacks were so intellectually and emotionally inferior to whites that they were not affected by the destruction of their families. Thomas Jefferson, for example, wrote in his *Notes on the State of Virginia* (1784) that "they are more ardent after their female," but "love seems with them to be more an eager desire, than a tender delicate mixture of sentiment and sensation. Their griefs are transient."[41] Certainly, no southern legislature considered the problem worthy enough to legislate against it. In general, the statutory and common law of slavery was designed to protect the white community from slave revolts, secure the master's property interest in slaves, and reinforce the racial subordination that was central to the enslavement of African-Americans.

Slavery and the Law at the National Level

Congress passed relatively few laws regulating slavery: a series of statutes suppressing and then banning the African slave trade (1794, 1800, 1803, 1807, 1818, 1819, and 1822) and two fugitive slave laws (1793 and 1850). Congress regulated slavery in the territories, banning it under the Northwest Ordinance (1787) and the Missouri Compromise (1820), and allowing it under the Southwest Ordinance, the Compromise of 1850, and the Kansas–Nebraska Act (1854). In the Missouri Compromise, Congress, on a very close vote, allowed Missouri to enter the Union as a slave state. This margin would not have been possible without the Congressional seats created by counting slaves under the three-fifths clause. At the same time, Congress banned slavery in the territories north and west of Missouri. This ban was the last time Congress limited the growth of slavery in any significant way until the Civil War. The annexation of Texas (1845), Mexico's cession of territory under the Treaty of Guadalupe Hidalgo (1848), the Compromise of 1850, and the Kansas–Nebraska Act all allowed the territorial growth of slavery. In 1857 the Supreme Court, in *Dred Scott* v. *Sandford* (1857), held that Congress could not prohibit masters from taking their slaves to any federal territories, thus technically allowing slavery in Minnesota and the Pacific Northwest. Slavery had already been allowed in all the other federal territories.

The United States Supreme Court heard a variety of cases on slavery that can roughly be divided into five categories: (1) cases appealed from the courts of the District of Columbia; (2) cases involving the African slave trade; (3) suits involving contracts for the sale of slaves between private parties; (4) cases involving the return of fugitive slaves; and (5) cases involving the status of slaves taken to free states or federal territories where Congress had banned slavery.

The first category involved freedom claims of slaves who had lived in free jurisdictions, claimed to be born free, or claimed to have been granted freedom by a former or present owner. Such cases came to the US Supreme Court because it served as the final appellate forum for the District of Columbia. These cases were usually decided under Maryland or Virginia law, which governed the district. The Marshall Court (1801–35) proved generally unsympathetic to claims of slaves seeking their freedom; the Taney Court (1836–64) appears to have been more evenhanded in these DC freedom suits, but that result may simply be a function of the aggrieved slaves having stronger claims to freedom. On other issues involving slavery, however, such as fugitive slaves or the right of Congress to regulate slavery in the territories, the Taney Court remained aggressively proslavery.

A second category of cases involved prosecutions for violations of the ban on the African slave trade. Initially, the court was very lenient in slave trade cases, and often reversed the convictions of traders, but starting in the 1820s, traders usually fared poorly. During the Civil War, the court upheld the death sentence for a slave trader. Slave trade cases that involved foreigners had a mixed reception in the court. *The Antelope* (1825) illustrates the complexity of the slave trade cases. The *Antelope* was a Spanish ship captured by pirates. It contained Africans taken off ships of various nations and had sailed under the command of an American, who was in violation of US laws banning American citizens from participating in the African trade. The United States Coast Guard seized the *Antelope* and brought it to Savannah. There the courts had to sort out the status of the 258 Africans found on board. Some of the blacks on the ship had been taken from Africa by citizens of nations still participating in the international slave trade; others were taken illegally, by citizens whose countries prohibited them from participating in the trade. As Chief Justice John Marshall noted, in this case "the sacred rights of liberty and property come in conflict with each other." Marshall ordered some of Africans sold as slaves and others returned to their homelands. Somewhat similar issues arose in *United States* v. *The Amistad* (1841), which involved Africans who had been illegally taken to Cuba as slaves, but who had then revolted in transshipment from Havana and forced their Cuban owners to take the schooner to Africa. Instead, the Cubans steered towards the United States, and ultimately the ship was seized by a Coast Guard ship off the coast of Long Island and towed to New London, Connecticut. The case eventually reached the Supreme Court, which, in 1841, held that the Africans on the *Amistad* had been illegally enslaved in violation of the Anglo-Spanish treaty of 1817, and thus could not be returned to Cuba. The court refused to require, however, that the Africans be returned to Africa at government expense. The court did order the return of a slave born in Cuba, who had been a cabin boy on the ship. While hailed as an antislavery victory, the case turned entirely on the status of the Africans under various treaties. Justice Story, who wrote the opinion of the court, made it quite clear that he would have ordered the return of the blacks to Cuba, if they, like the cabin boy who was returned, had been legally held as slaves there.

A third category of cases involved private disputes between citizens of different states. In *Groves* v. *Slaughter* (1841), for example, the court sided with the sellers of slaves in a dispute regarding a contract for the purchase of slaves. The private law cases involving slavery did not alter the political issues surrounding slavery, but they did underscore the way slavery was deeply embedded in the American legal and constitutional structure.

Cases involving fugitive slaves were politically and legally more important than the cases in the first three categories. In 1793 Congress passed a federal fugitive slave law to implement the fugitive slave clause of article IV, section 2 of the Constitution. No case on this issue reached the Supreme Court until *Prigg* v. *Pennsylvania* (1842). In *Prigg* the court upheld the Fugitive Slave Law of 1793, in a remarkably proslavery decision written by Justice Joseph Story of Massachusetts. Story in effect nationalized the law of slavery, holding that masters had a right to capture alleged fugitives anywhere they found them, and the states could not act to protect the liberty of free blacks who might have been wrongly seized as fugitive slaves. Had it not been for *Dred Scott*, it is likely that *Prigg* would be considered the Court's most important slavery case. Paul Finkelman, in "Story Telling on the Supreme Court: *Prigg* v. *Pennsylvania* and Justice Joseph Story's Judicial Nationalism," *Supreme Court Review*, 1994, argues that Story's opinion was unnecessarily proslavery, and that he was motivated by his desired to support southern demands for extraordinary protections for slavery and his own desire to increase the power of the national government. The cost of such goals, however, was born not only by fugitive slaves but also by free blacks who could more easily be dragged into bondage after *Prigg*. In this case the court overturned the conviction of Prigg for kidnapping, even though one of the people he removed from Pennsylvania had been born there, and was clearly free under the laws of that state. The court reiterated its willingness to accept the return of fugitive slaves without any due process in *Jones* v. *Van Zandt* (1847), in another proslavery opinion written by Justice Levi Woodbury of New Hampshire. In both cases, New England justices on the court proclaimed that masters had virtually unlimited rights to seize blacks in the North as fugitive slaves and drag them back to the South without any formal hearing or judicial investigation.

Prigg, in effect, struck down all the northern statutes, known as personal liberty laws, designed to prevent the kidnapping of free blacks. This decision meant that blacks could be removed from the free states with only a minimal hearing before a federal judge, or simply taken from the state without any hearing under what Justice Story called a "right of reception." Removing a fugitive slave usually required the help of law enforcement officials and the use of local jails. Northern states responded to *Prigg* with new personal liberty laws that prohibited state officials from participating in the return of fugitive slaves. In 1850, in response to these new laws, Congress passed a new fugitive slave law that created federal commissioners to sit in every county of the nation to enforce the law. Under the law, the courts and commissioners could call on United States marshals and, where necessary, the army or the militia, to help capture and return fugitive slaves. The court upheld this law in *Moore* v. *Illinois* (1852) and *Ableman* v. *Booth* (1859).

The court's most important slavery decision, *Dred Scott* v. *Sandford* (1857), concerned the power of Congress to prohibit slavery in the federal territories. By a 7 to 2 vote, the court held that Congress had no power to ban slavery in the federal territories and that blacks, even if free citizens of northern states, could never be citizens of the United States. In holding that Congress had no power to prohibit slavery in the territories, the court energized the new Republican Party, which soon controlled most of the North. Abraham Lincoln's penetrating critique of the case helped catapult him to the White House, and that in turn led to secession, civil war, and ultimately, an end to slavery. In 1860 almost all commentators agreed that the national government had no power to end slavery or even regulate it in the states. At best, some lawyers and politicians might have agreed that Congress could end slavery in the District of Columbia and the federal territories, although such laws would have been in defiance of the holding in *Dred Scott*. In his first inaugural address, Lincoln reminded the southern states that "I have no purpose, directly or indirectly, to interfere with the institution of slavery in the States where it exists. I believe I have no lawful right to do so, and I have no inclination to do so."

During the Civil War, Lincoln authorized the enlistment of black soldiers and on 1 January 1863, declared that all slaves in the Confederate states were free. He lacked the constitutional power to end slavery in the loyal slave states (Missouri, Kentucky, Maryland, and Delaware), but he urged those states to end the institution. Also during the war, Congress ignored the court's ruling in *Dred Scott* and began to dismantle slavery through the First and Second Confiscation Acts (1861, 1862); the abolition of slavery in the District of Columbia (1862) and the federal territories (1862); the repeal of the fugitive slave laws (1864); and finally the Thirteenth Amendment, which, passed by Congress in January 1865 and ratified by the states in December 1865, banned slavery in the United States. Unlike other aspects of the Constitution, which regulated the national government or the states, this amendment was binding on the states, the national government, and individuals.

NOTES

1. John Locke, *Second Treatise of Government*, ed. C. B. Macpherson (Indianapolis, 1980), 90. See also David Brion Davis, *The Problem of Slavery in Western Culture* (Ithaca, NY, 1966), 118–21.

2. St George Tucker, *A Dissertation on Slavery: With a Proposal for the Gradual Abolition of it, in the State of Virginia* (Philadelphia, 1796).

3. Winthrop D. Jordan, *White over Black: American Attitudes toward the Negro, 1550–1812* (Chapel Hill, NC, 1968); Edmund S. Morgan, *American Slavery, American Freedom: The Ordeal of Colonial Virginia* (New York, 1975).

4. Alan Watson, *Slave Law in the Americas* (Athens, Ga., 1989).

5. H. R. McIlwaine (ed.), *Minutes of the Council and General Court of Colonial Virginia, 1622–1632, 1670–1676, Notes and Excerpts from Original Council and General Court Records, into 1683, Now Lost* (Richmond, Va., 1924), 477.

6. William Waller Hening (ed.), The *Statutes at Large; Being a Collection of All the Laws of Virginia, from the First Session of the Legislature in the year 1619*, 13 vols. (New York, 1809–23), i. 146.

7. Jordan, *White over Black*, 78–9; Thomas D. Morris, *Southern Slavery and the Law, 1619–1860* (Chapel Hill, NC, 1996), 23–4.

8. McIlwaine (ed.), *Minutes of the Council and General Court of Colonial Virginia*, 466.

9. Hening, *Statutes at Large*, ii. 116.

10. Ibid. 170.

11. Ibid. iii. 447.

12. Ibid. ii. 260.

13. Ibid. 270.

14. Peter H. Wood, *Black Majority: Negroes in Colonial South Carolina from 1670 through the Stono Rebellion* (New York, 1974), esp. 271–84.

15. Benjamin Quarles, *The Negro in the American Revolution* (Chapel Hill, NC, 1961); Sylvia R. Frey, *Water from the Rock: Black Resistance in a Revolutionary Age* (Princeton, 1991).

16. Willi Paul Adams, *The First American Constitutions: Republican Ideology and the Making of the State Constitutions in the Revolutionary Era* (Chapel Hill, NC, 1980), 182–5.

17. Joanne Pope Melish, *Disowning Slavery: Gradual Emancipation and "Race" in New England, 1780–1860* (Ithaca, NY, 1998), esp. 50–83.

18. "An Act for the Gradual Abolition of Slavery," Act of March 1, 1780. Sec. 1, The Avalon Project: Documents in Law, History and Diplomacy, http://avalon.law.yale.edu/18th_century/pennst01.asp

19. Gary B. Nash and Jean R. Soderlund, *Freedom by Degrees: Emancipation in Pennsylvania and its Aftermath* (New York, 1991).

20. Paul Finkelman, *An Imperfect Union: Slavery, Federalism, and Comity* (Chapel Hill, NC, 1981).

21. Arthur Zilversmit, *The First Emancipation: The Abolition of Slavery in the North* (Chicago, 1967).

22. John Hope Franklin, *The Free Negro in North Carolina, 1790–1860* (Chapel Hill, NC, 1943); Ira Berlin, *Slaves without Masters: The Free Negro in the Antebellum South* (New York, 1974); Morris, *Southern Slavery and the Law*.

23. Bernie D. Jones, *Fathers of Conscience: Mixed-Race Inheritance in the Antebellum South* (Athens, Ga., 2009).
24. W. E. B. Du Bois, *The Suppression of the African Slave-Trade to the United States of America, 1638–1870* (New York, 1896).
25. Jed H. Shugerman, "The Louisiana Purchase and South Carolina's Reopening of the Slave Trade in 1803," *Journal of the Early Republic*, 22 (Summer 2002): 263–90; Paul Finkelman, "Regulating the African Slave Trade," *Civil War History*, 54 (December 2008): 379–405; and Paul Finkelman, "The American Suppression of the African Slave Trade: Lessons on Legal Change, Social Policy, Legislation," *Akron Law Review*, 42 (2) (2009): 431–67.
26. Paul Finkelman, *Slavery and the Founders: Race and Liberty in the Age of Jefferson* (2nd edn. Armonk, NY, 2001), 37–57.
27. Ibid. 3–36; Donald L. Robinson, *Slavery in the Structure of American Politics, 1765–1820* (New York, 1971), 168–247.
28. Jonathan Elliot, *The Debates in the Several State Conventions on the Adoption of the Federal Constitution*, 5 vols. (1888; reprint New York, 1987), iv. 286.
29. Letters from a Countryman from Dutchess County (letter of January 22, 1788), in Herbert Storing (ed.), *The Complete Anti-Federalist* (Chicago, 1981), vi. 62; essays by Republicus (essay of March 12, 1788), ibid v. 169.
30. Consider Arms, Malichi Maynard, and Samuel Field, "Reasons for Dissent," ibid iv. 262–3.
31. Finkelman, *Slavery and the Founders*; Robinson, *Slavery in the Structure of American Politics*; David Brion Davis, *The Problem of Slavery in the Age of Revolution, 1770–1823* (Ithaca, NY, 1975); William M. Wiecek, *The Sources of Antislavery Constitutionalism in America, 1760–1848* (Ithaca, NY, 1977); David Waldstreicher, *Slavery's Constitution: From Revolution to Ratification* (New York, 2009); Eugene D. Genovese, *Mind of the Master Class: History and Faith in the Southern Slaveholders' Worldview* (Cambridge, 2005), esp. 72–6.
32. Don E. Fehrenbacher, *The Slaveholding Republic: An Account of the United States Government's Relations to Slavery* (New York, 2001); William W. Freehling, *Road to Disunion, i: Secessionists at Bay, 1776–1854* (New York, 1990) and ii: *Secessionists Triumphant, 1854–1861* (New York, 2007).
33. Most notably *Slavery, the Civil Law, and the Supreme Court of Louisiana* (Baton Rouge, La., 1994) and *Becoming Free, Remaining Free: Manumission and Enslavement in New Orleans, 1846–1862* (Baton Rouge, La., 2003).
34. *State v. Hale*, 2 Hawks (NC) 582 (1823).
35. *State v. Mann*, 2 Devereux Law Rep. (NC) 263 (1829).
36. Harriet Beecher Stowe, *A Key to Uncle Tom's Cabin* ... (Boston, 1853), esp. 132–4.
37. Mark V. Tushnet, *Slave Law in the American South: State v. Mann in History and Literature* (Lawrence, Kan., 2003).
38. Thomas R. R. Cobb, *An Inquiry into the Law of Negro Slavery in the United States of America. To Which is Prefixed, An Historical Sketch of Slavery*, ed. Paul Finkelman (1858; reprint Athens, Ga., 1999), 100.
39. Ibid. 86. Cobb's significance in summarizing the law of slavery on the eve of the Civil War is set out in Paul Finkelman, "Thomas R. R. Cobb and the Law of Negro Slavery," *Roger Williams University Law Review*, 5 (Fall 1999): 75–115.
40. A. T. Holmes, *Essay: The Duties of Christian Masters* (Charleston, SC, 1851); C. G. Memminger, *Report of the Special Committee Appointed by the Protestant Episcopal*

Convention, at its Session in 1858, to Report on the Duty of Clergymen in Relation to the Marriage of Slaves (Charleston, SC, 1859).

41. Thomas Jefferson, *Notes on the State of Virginia*, ed. William Peden (Chapel Hill, NC, 1954), 138–9. Jefferson's views of slaves and blacks are discussed at length in Paul Finkelman, *Slavery and the Founders: Race and Liberty in the Age of Jefferson* (Armonk, NY, 2001), chs. 6 and 7.

SELECT BIBLIOGRAPHY

FEHRENBACHER, DON E. *The Slaveholding Republic: An Account of the United States Government's Relations to Slavery.* New York: Oxford University Press, 2001.

FINKELMAN, PAUL. *An Imperfect Union: Slavery, Federalism, and Comity.* Chapel Hill, NC: University of North Carolina Press, 1981.

—— *Slavery and the Founders: Race and Liberty in the Age of Jefferson.* 2nd edn. Armonk, NY: M. E. Sharpe, 2001.

MORRIS, THOMAS D. *Southern Slavery and the Law, 1619–1860.* Chapel Hill, NC: University of North Carolina Press, 1996.

ROBINSON, DONALD L. *Slavery in the Structure of American Politics, 1765–1820.* New York: Harcourt Brace Jovanovich, 1970.

SCHAFER, JUDITH K. *Slavery, the Civil Law, and the Supreme Court of Louisiana.* Baton Rouge, La.: Louisiana State University Press, 1994.

SCHWARZ, PHILIP J. *Slave Laws in Virginia.* Athens, Ga.: University of Georgia Press, 1996.

TUSHNET, MARK V. *The American Law of Slavery, 1810–1860: Considerations of Humanity and Interest.* Princeton: Princeton University Press, 1981.

WAHL, JENNY BOURNE. *The Bondsman's Burden: An Economic Analysis of the Common Law of Southern Slavery.* Cambridge: Cambridge University Press, 1998.

WIECEK, WILLIAM M. *The Sources of Antislavery Constitutionalism in America, 1760–1848.* Ithaca, NY: Cornell University Press, 1977.

CHAPTER 20

....

SLAVE RESISTANCE

....

DOUGLAS R. EGERTON

DEMOGRAPHIC realities and power relations in the British mainland colonies (and later, following Independence, in the United States) militated against the type of large-scale slave conspiracies that shook Spanish, Portuguese, and French colonies in South America and the Caribbean. The presence of a heavily armed white majority in every state except for South Carolina (and, toward the very end of the antebellum period, Mississippi), the lack of an impregnable hinterland in which to create maroon colonies from which runaways could besiege plantations, the relatively dispersed nature and small size of slaveholding, and the existence of a resident (as opposed to absentee) landlord class combined to make massive slave rebellions far less common than day-to-day resistance or individual acts of self-threat. In the years after the American Revolution, as harsher forms of colonial patriarchalism began to metamorphose into paternalism—a complex and ongoing process of negotiation and brutality that many scholars regrettably reduce to a simplistic model of accommodation—slaves achieved enough cultural living space to forge stable families and rich spiritual communities. Given the odds against success, it is hardly surprising that the handful of slaves bold enough to rise for their freedom found their rebellions reduced to unsuccessful conspiracies and their fellows doomed to die in combat or on the gallows.[1]

Despite persistent attempts by historians to force a uniformity of vision and goals on rebel leaders, insurgent slaves in the eighteenth and nineteenth centuries differed from one another fully as much as white revolutionaries in the same era. Jemmy, an Angolan who led an agrarian uprising in 1739 near Stono River, South Carolina, tried to hasten his African followers across the border into Spanish Florida. Caesar Varick, who only two years later in 1741 conspired to burn New York City, lived in one of North America's largest urban centers with an Irish wife. Gabriel, a young, secular rebel who had turned away from African traditions, hoped to remain in Virginia and labor as a freeman in a more egalitarian society. Denmark Vesey, an aged free black who bought his freedom the year before Gabriel was executed in 1800, expected to achieve a limited exodus for his family and followers, out of Charleston to Haiti. Whereas Vesey and his chief lieutenant, "Gullah" Jack Pritchard, an East African priest, fused African theology with the Old Testament God of wrath and justice, Nat Turner relied on Christian millennial themes from the Book of Revelation in hopes of bringing about the day of jubilee for black Virginians. Beyond their obvious abilities as leaders and their equally obvious desire to breathe free, rebellious slaves in the United States fit no simple pattern.[2]

If slave rebellions in North America correspond to any one model, it is that they proliferated during times when the white majority was divided against itself in a crippling fashion. Colonial insurgents in South Carolina and New York City, for example, rose in revolt with their masters engaged in war against France and Spain three times. Gabriel, that most politicized of all the slave rebels, formulated his plans during the divisive election of 1800, when Federalists and Republicans threatened to take up arms against one another. The rebels in the Tidewater area of Virginia, despite the memory of the repression that followed Gabriel's death, began to organize again during the chaos of the War of 1812. Having read of the Missouri debates in Charleston newspapers, Vesey prayed that northern whites would prove tardy in riding to the rescue of the estranged southerners, giving his followers time enough to flee the city. Slaves near Natchez, Mississippi, began to plan for their freedom in 1861, following the outbreak of the Civil War.[3]

Most of all, slaves, who well understood the daunting odds they faced and rarely contemplated suicidal ventures, plotted for their freedom only when safer avenues had been closed to them. For most of the seventeenth century, for example, when the high death rate in the southern colonies made inexpensive white indentured servants far more numerous than costly African slaves, enterprising bondspersons relied more on self-purchase than the sword. The economic possibilities in early Virginia produced more runaways than rebels; the practice of buying one's own body even produced several black entrepreneurs—such as Anthony Johnson, a former slave who became a wealthy planter and who named his estate Angola after the land of his birth. Only after landless whites and hard-used white indentured workers under the command of Nathaniel Bacon burned Jamestown in 1676 did southern planters made a concerted effort to replace white servants with African slaves. The comprehensive Virginia Slave Code of 1705, the first of its kind in colonial North America—which made lawful as punishment the master's dismemberment of any outlying, "incorrigible" slave—crushed the hope of industrious slaves that they might be upwardly mobile.[4]

Only then, as North American racial walls rapidly hardened, did desperate slaves turn to physically hazardous paths toward freedom. During the last days of Queen Anne's War in April 1712, a determined band of twenty-five Coromantee (Gold Coast) Africans burned several buildings in New York City and killed nine whites. (Unfree labor had been legalized in New York by the Duke's Law of 1665.) Having made a commitment to unfree labor, equally determined whites revenged themselves on the rebels. Several rebels committed suicide before they could be captured, but those taken alive were broken on the wheel and hanged in chains as a warning to future rebels. These "cycles of rebellion," as the historian Marcus Rediker has dubbed them, prevailed especially in seaports, where news traveled freely and where enslaved rebels exiled from one colony continued their conspiracies in their new places of captivity. Typical of this group was the slave Will, who participated in hatching a major slave insurrection on the Danish Virgin Island of St John. Despite claims that Will had killed several white men during the 1733 revolt—which came close to establishing an African-style kingdom in the Americas—he was sold to Antigua. There he waited less than two years to band together with Akan-speaking slaves from the Gold Coast region of West Africa in a plot to wrest the island from whites.[5]

By the early eighteenth century, even though the constant threat of war between Britain and its continental neighbors provided endless opportunities for daring slaves, revolts on the British mainland rarely posed much of a threat to the slaveholding regime. Because British participation in the Atlantic slave trade peaked in the eighteenth century, Britain's twenty-six American colonies included large numbers of native Africans who sought to escape from bondage by building isolated maroon communities. Most runaways fled into the hinterland, where they established maroon colonies and tried to recreate the African communities they had lost. Even the mainland's two most significant rebellions of the period—that of Stono, South Carolina, and the subsequent attempt to burn New York City—were led by Africans who dreamed only of ending their own bondage, not of ending unfree labor in general. Aware of Spanish promises of freedom in colonial Florida, Angolan soldiers under Jemmy tried to escape across the border. To the north, bondsmen in New York City planned to torch the place and flee to French Canada, which was then at war with the rebels' masters. The price of failure was high. New York authorities ordered Caesar Varick and twelve of his followers burned alive; eighteen others were hanged—two of them in chains—and seventy more bondsmen were banished from the colony.[6]

Outnumbered and outgunned—if rarely cowed by white authority—most enslaved men and women resisted their condition through other methods. Young men, especially those who had not yet married, ran away, often in homogeneous groups. Before the early nineteenth century, slaves in the southern colonies fled toward Spanish Florida, while those in the North sought freedom in French Canada; with the gradual emancipation of slavery in the northern states and the

American acquisition of Florida, bondsmen journeyed toward the free states or remained truants within the South. Some women, particularly domestic servants, occasionally fought back through poison. Although it is hard to know whether the illness of white masters was due to toxins or natural causes, colonies like South Carolina passed legislation in 1751 against "the detestable crime of poisoning [that] hath of late been frequently committed by many slaves."⁷ One of the most unsettling acts of collective slave resistance in the French colony of Saint-Domingue before the onset of slave revolution in 1791 consisted of a poisoning plot concocted by an African slave named Makandal.

The onset of the American Revolution alternately discouraged and stimulated slave rebellions in Britain's mainland colonies. Although the British invasion and the animosity between patriots and Tories presented slaves with a unique opportunity to organize, most slaves chose instead to take advantage of the dislocation of war to escape with their families into the growing cities or behind British lines. The revolution was the one time in North American history when as many female slaves as males ran away. When the British evacuated Manhattan in 1783, they carried with them 3,000 black Loyalists, many of them battle-hardened veterans of the war. Because the aggressive bondsmen who cast their lots with the military forces of King George were precisely the sort of bold, determined slaves who normally tended to organize slave conspiracies, the bloody fighting in the southern states after 1778 actually diminished the prospect that a mainland counterpart of Toussaint Louverture would rise out of the tobacco plantations.⁸

Nonetheless, as Eugene D. Genovese suggested in his influential study *From Rebellion to Revolution*, the age of revolution, and especially the slave revolt in Saint-Domingue in 1791, marked a change in patterns in black resistance. The American and Haitian revolutions served as a dividing line between older, restorationist movement like the vast maroon colony of Palmares (which sought to recreate lost African societies in Portuguese Brazil) and more explicitly politicized revolts of the age of revolution. The Caribbean rebels under the leadership of "Citizen" Toussaint Louverture sought not only to destroy the power of their Parisian absentee masters but to join the societies in which they lived on equal terms. For black Americans determined to realize the egalitarian promise of the American Revolution, the news from the Caribbean reminded them that if they dared, the end of slavery might be within their reach. Whereas Jemmy and his African recruits hoped only to escape the chains of colonial South Carolina, creole slaves born on the mainland increasingly plotted to join American political society on equal terms by demanding their "rights." As these rebels quickly came to understand, equality, and not merely freedom, was the antithesis of slavery.⁹

This understanding vividly manifested itself in the conspiracy organized in Virginia during the summer of 1800 by the slave Gabriel. Born in the year 1776, Gabriel grew to manhood during the chaos of the revolutionary era. Most likely, he actually laid eyes upon white revolutionary Patrick Henry, a close friend and attorney to his master, Thomas Prosser. Gabriel and his lieutenants, who instigated the most extensive plot in Virginia history, hoped to force the white patriot elite to live up to its stated ideal: that all men were created free and equal. Leading a small army of slaves in Henrico County, the young blacksmith planned to march into Richmond under a banner emblazoned with the words "Death or Liberty." He assured one supporter that "poor white people," who had no more political power than the slaves, "would also join" them in the struggle for equality. Although trial testimony makes little mention of events in Saint-Domingue, white authorities like Governor James Monroe harbored no doubts that Toussaint Louverture's victories had an enormous "effect on all the peoples of colour" in the early national South.[10]

In several cases, bondsmen who had been carried from revolutionary Saint-Domingue by their masters participated in North American slave revolts. In 1792 slaves on Virginia's eastern shore proposed to "blow up the magazine in Norfolk, and massacre its inhabitants." Norfolk County had a white majority, but North-ampton and Elizabeth City counties, just across the Chesapeake Bay, had an enslaved majority. Although the rebel leader Caleb, a favored servant and driver, was evidently American born, several of his recruits were Haitian refugees, and all—according to the trial testimony—had been inspired by the example of Saint-Domingue. Two decades later, in 1811, one of the most extensive conspiracies in the history of the United States erupted in southern Louisiana, thirty miles upriver from New Orleans in the United States' first major sugar-producing zone. A diverse group of slaves led by a mixed-race driver named Charles announced their inten-tion of marching down the east bank of the Mississippi River on the city "to kill whites." Although Charles, contrary to myth, was not Haitian, some of the 200 or more slaves who rose with him had previously resided in the French Caribbean.[11]

After Gabriel's execution and the death of twenty-five of his followers in the fall of 1800, slave rebellions on the eastern seaboard became both less common and less politically conscious. Slaves who worked along the rivers in southern Virginia and Halifax County, North Carolina, under the leadership of Sancho, a ferryman, formed a highly decentralized scheme to rise on Easter Monday of 1802. But Sancho, despite having been involved in Gabriel's plot, shared little of Gabriel's dream of a multiracial republic. The lack of an ideological dimension appeared even when the dislocation brought on by the War of 1812 and a second British invasion of the Chesapeake once more gave bondsmen in Virginia an opportunity to rise for their liberty. Gloucester County authorities jailed ten slaves in March 1813, and the following month found rebels in Lancester County and Williamsburg "condemned on a charge of conspiracy & insurrection." By the late summer and early fall, rumors of revolt unnerved inhabitants of Norfolk and Richmond as well.[12]

If the relative ease with which white authorities crushed these isolated rebellions did not extinguish the desire for freedom, it nonetheless reminded leaders in the slave community that the determined white majority in the American South presented insurgents with a formidable obstacle. Denmark Vesey of Charleston, perhaps the most pragmatic of all the rebel leaders, realized that Gabriel's dream of forcing mainland elites to accommodate blacks' aspirations to freedom and economic justice was impossible. Vesey plotted, therefore, not to end slavery in South Carolina, but instead to lead a mass escape from Charleston to the Caribbean, where he had lived and worked as a boy. Hoping to take control of the city on the night of 14 July 1822, Vesey's recruits—many of them Africans—intended to slaughter the inhabitants of the city and seize bank reserves before fleeing to Haiti, an embattled black republic sorely in need of capital and skilled labor. If Vesey, a prosperous freeman, doomed those who remained behind to renewed repression by whites, he can scarcely be faulted: he understood that his followers had virtually no hope of bringing down the peculiar institution in South Carolina.[13]

Even Vesey's unsuccessful exodus, which may be regarded more as mass flight than a revolutionary movement, indicated the difficulties of planning an effective strategy amidst large numbers of ever-vigilant whites. Like virtually all rebel leaders in the United States, Vesey recognized the danger of openly recruiting in the countryside. Word of the Charleston plot probably reached several thousand slaves—which is not to say that even half that number committed themselves to the struggle—and there was always a danger that a black Judas would hear the whispers and inform the master class. White authorities had long ago perfected the art of dividing the slave community by offering a tempting reward—freedom—to those who would turn their coats. Like Jemmy and Gabriel before him, Vesey, whose army had more officers than soldiers, planned to rise quickly and present the low country's black majority with a fait accompli. The victorious armies would not be recruited or armed in advance but raised by the captains as they marched.[14]

Ironically, the bloodiest slave revolt in the United States took place in the decade after Vesey's failure, at a time when rebellion—as opposed to other forms of resistance—had become virtually suicidal. The slaves in Southampton County, Virginia, who rose with Nat Turner in 1831 shared neither Gabriel's trust in a second American Revolution nor Vesey's hope of fleeing to the Caribbean. Although Turner may have expected to establish a maroon colony in the vast Dismal Swamp, as many white commentators of the time supposed, his plot gave little evidence of planning or rational preparation. Most likely, the messianic Turner hoped that God would protect and guide his army as the Lord had guided the Israelites. At least fifty-seven whites perished in the revolt, but local militiamen easily routed the ill-equipped rebels; three companies of federal artillery, together with seamen from two warships in the Chesapeake, reached Southampton only three days after the insurrection began. Of the twenty-seven slaves tried for involvement in the revolt, seventeen were executed, most of them, including Nat, by hanging. Vengeful whites added to the number by killing roughly thirty to forty slaves without trial.[15]

Turner's bloody revolt stands apart from most other North American slave conspiracies in one other significant way, in that it erupted in rural Southampton County. If there is one constant that links the vast majority of plots and revolts, it is that they matured in seaports and urban areas. Early American towns and cities, with their compact geography, tavern culture, churches, and winding back alleys, provided particularly favorable conditions for men like Gabriel or Vesey to meet in private and plan for black liberation. Even more serious was the fact that too many urban masters, from New York to Charleston, allowed their slaves to use a portion of their time and labor for their own account. It can be no accident that the majority of rebel leaders differed from Nat Turner in that they did not harvest rice or sugar or tobacco but hired their time away from their masters and were able to put a few coins into their pockets.

Because the sums earned by slaves who hired their time were modest even by early American standards, students of slave resistance have largely ignored the connection between slave rebelliousness and the larger economic changes sweeping the Atlantic colonial empires in the late eighteenth and early nineteenth centuries. Historians such as Peter Coclanis who denigrate the small amount of cash slave marketers were able to acquire and emphasize instead that the vast majority of any slave's time was spent laboring for their master—which was certainly true—miss the fact that what little money a bondsperson made conferred a degree of psychological independence on the wage-earning bondsman. In the sugar fields of Louisiana and Jamaica, enslaved men and women dressed in their finest clothes before heading toward urban market squares. By donning decent garments acquired through their own labors, slaves not only put their plantation homes behind them physically, they also, as the historian Roderick McDonald has remarked, "divested themselves of the identifiable accoutrements of slavery that their plantation garb constituted." During the week, the master and overseer and driver defined their existence, but Sunday markets did far more than simply provide slaves with a place to sell their wares. Even if sellers returned to their cabins not one cent richer, they spent the day participating in an independent market economy that they controlled. For at least one day out of seven, McDonald adds, "the markets served to loosen, both physically and psychologically, the bonds of servitude." As North Carolina slave Lunsford Lane observed after he sold his first basket of peaches, "the hope that then entered my mind of purchasing at some future time my freedom, made me long for money; and plans for money-making took the principal possession of my thoughts."[16]

Men like Lane's master, who seized the greater portion of their hired slaves' earnings, rarely noticed that the growing desire for cash on the part of their workers fueled an illicit trade in stolen goods. When they did ponder the question, whites attributed theft to the "proclivities" of African-Americans, or the morally damaging nature of slavery. Quaker Robert Williams suspected that the institution itself led blacks into "lying & thieving, Idleness & deceit." Modern scholars think differently, of course, and most endorse the view of one perceptive observer, who summed up the common slave attitude with, "What I take from my master, being for my use, who am his slave, or property, he loses nothing by its transfer." Yet in some cases it was more complex than that. As historian McDonald adds, many bondsmen regarded theft not as the transfer of goods "but as resistance to slavery [itself], and as the appropriation and redistribution of illicitly accrued wealth." Seen from this perspective, theft stands not simply as a matter of obtaining purloined protein, it bespeaks a clandestine demand for wealth by those who had actually created it.[17]

Evidence indicates that discerning whites understood this other meaning all too well. They regarded urbanization as antithetical to unfree labor, hiring out as destructive to servile control, and contact with the market economy as leading to implicit demands for the reallocation of wealth. As one Annapolis resident phrased it while drafting an advertisement for the sale of three slaves, none had been "corrupted by town habits." Nor was it merely individual masters who understood that paternal social relations could not easily be reconciled with the demands of urban capital. Legislators in slave societies across the Americas correctly noted the corrosive effect that practices typical to town venues had on slave controls. When the assembly in Antigua passed a statute banning the "Custom [of] permitting slaves to go about the Towns" to "hire themselves or take their own Liberty," they all but conceded that the sound of hard money clinking in the pockets of slaves was also the sound of the masters' authority being torn asunder.[18]

When that sound grew too loud, southern assemblies clamped down further with increasingly draconian (albeit often unenforceable) laws inhibiting the economic liberty of bondspersons. It can be little accident that many of these codes immediately followed major slave conspiracies and revolts. South Carolina's comprehensive twenty-four-page code of 1740, commonly dubbed the "Negro Act," was enacted shortly after the Stono uprising. Since permitting slaves "to traffic and barter" not only provided them with "an opportunity of receiving and concealing stolen good[s], but to plot and confederate together, and form conspiracies," the legislature not only allowed for the confiscation of both goods and profits, but held both the slave and master responsible. Shortly after, Georgia lawmakers enacted their own code, which was closely modeled after South Carolina's. Bondspersons could not "buy, sell, or exchange any goods, wares, provisions, grains, victuals, or commodities of any sort or kind whatsoever." Politicians across the South—slaveholders all—had no desire to prevent fellow masters from employing their slaves as they might see fit, but rather to prevent human chattel from participating in the market.[19]

Worse yet, from the perspective of control, the influence of the market economy not only provided new opportunities to slaves, participation in it often eroded class and racial barriers. After a day of bartering in rural towns, or following a day of hired labor in larger urban venues, enslaved artisans and unskilled day laborers of both races fell into the natural habit of retiring together to dine and drink. In the Chesapeake, many grog shops were infamous, according to one Virginia authority, "for the equality which reigned [between] the blacks and the whites—all is hail fellow well met, no matter what the complexion." In most western Atlantic seaport towns, a working-class subculture emerged that cut across racial lines. Apprentice boys, servant girls, bond hirelings, mariners, free blacks, and immigrants banded together in a common cultural domain of street fairs, laboring celebrations, and disorderly houses. Along the Mississippi River, despite the racism that was endemic to the steamboat industry, free blacks and whites labored beside slaves for hire, and on occasion, risked their careers by assisting men they knew to be fugitives. From Richmond to New Orleans, well-heeled urban dwellers were horrified by the "negro den[s] where white, yellow [mulatto], and black congregate[d] to eat, drink and be merry."[20]

What particularly concerned southern whites was the model of black resiliency and even upward mobility that free blacks presented to whites. As the historian Donald R. Wright has observed, the "mere existence of so many fellow humans of African descent who were not in slavery made many African Americans want the same status enough to attempt escape to get it." Southern politicians of the early national era consistently condemned free blacks for "every day polluting and corrupting public morals," but they appeared especially unnerved by the fact that so many of these black "rogues" were drawn to the market. Southern newspapers were filled with stories like that of Charles Oates, a "notorious [free black] villain." Oates was infamous around Williamsburg, Virginia, for breaking and entering; typically, he traded away the fine linens he stole, but he kept "the cash" he made off with "in [his] possession."[21]

As several specialists have noted, this urban subculture was not in itself revolutionary, in that it did not consciously challenge the established class structure of slave societies. But black artisans who shared a tankard with a white craftsman or sailor, or more seriously, entered into a solemn relationship with a white immigrant woman—as Caesar Varick did with "Irish" Peg Kerry in 1740s New York— surely flouted established social conventions. Planter legislators rightly feared that the decidedly undeferential discourse heard in cramped drinking cellars threatened their hegemony, and they labored hard to cut apart these interracial gambols, but often without success. In Brazil, many street actions organized by the urban poor, such as the anti-Portuguese riots of 1831, saw *crioulos* and mulattos protest and riot alongside poor whites and Africans.[22]

Historians like George M. Frederickson and Christopher Lasch have traditionally drawn a neat line of demarcation between day-to-day resistance to slavery—such as truancy, or the destruction of property—and rebelliousness of the sort practiced by Nat Turner and his disciples, which aimed at bringing down the entire system of chattel slavery. Yet it may be that the distinction between resistance and rebellion itself is a misleading one, and not merely because the varieties of rebelliousness were so varied. Scholars do not have to argue that every slave who hired his time or sold eggs at a town market plotted revolution to realize that southern whites were correct in thinking that *any* contact with cash was the first step off a very dangerous precipice. Midori Takagi in a study of slavery in Richmond, Virginia, rightly insists that "self-hiring privileges, cash bonuses, and crowded marketplaces did help slaves resist and rebel." Each time a bondsman launched a "successful challenge," that act of autonomy helped lay the basis "for larger and more politicized forms of resistance." Scholars err in believing that only the act of sharpening a sword constituted rebelliousness, for when slaves invested their cash wages in funding black churches or in "underwrit[ing] underground organizations that helped slaves escape," they were inflicting real damage on the system. But since putting an end to the "spirit of insubordination" would have meant eradicating urban slavery itself, Takagi adds, city authorities were ultimately powerless to act.[23]

If nothing else, routine contact with the urban market brought skilled bondsmen into contact with other slaves who shared their dreams of economic liberty. As historian Walter Johnson concedes, "[c]ollective resistance is, at bottom, a process of everyday organization, one that, in fact, depends upon connections and trust established through everyday actions." Planter polemicists certainly recognized that the underlying danger of hiring out was not that it allowed for petty theft, but that it created an illicit network of trade and communication that had the potential to prove disastrous to white control. As the South Carolina statesman Thomas Pinckney worried after the Vesey plot was uncovered, contact with free blacks, other enslaved artisans, and even unskilled white laborers might transform obsequious bondsmen into the "willing instruments of any delusive plan of mischief which may be presented to them."[24]

The fact that skilled bondsmen recognized a common enemy did not necessarily prove that they recognized themselves to be members of a distinct class with specific economic grievances that could only be resolved through violent rebellion. When analyzing human behavior, no economic model can ever prove infallible. For each slave like bellicose Monday Gell, a skilled harness-maker who lived apart from his Charleston master in "all the substantial comforts of a free-man," there was another like quiescent George Wilson, a blacksmith for hire, who informed on his friend Rolla Bennett. Yet there are compelling hints, as David Barry Gaspar argues with evidence drawn from slave resistance in the British Caribbean island of Antigua, that the "psychological and sociopolitical base for a large-scale plot was perhaps strongest among the many artisans" who hired their time and earned a cash wage. If the economies of the southern states and territories in post-colonial America may largely be described as seigneurial, a crude form of capitalism—a mode of production here defined as being characterized by free wage labor, or on occasion semi-free, and the separation of the labor force from the means of production—began to appear in the towns and cities of the early Republic (as well as along the western Atlantic). On plantations from Virginia to Louisiana, master and slave forged a nearly feudal bond. There the relationship between the two, despite the fact that the enslaved were engaged in forced labor, was primarily social rather than economic. But the transitional roles in which urban slaves found themselves—from the hiring out that was common in Richmond and Baltimore to the drawing of cash wages common to skilled slaves in Buffalo Forge and Brazil—were relationships based largely on market considerations, and they provided the enslaved with a glimpse into a world of mobility and prosperity that even their masters could scarcely understand.[25]

The nearly utopian notion that a different sort of future was possible to slaves courageous enough to pick up a weapon informed most of the revolts and conspiracies that took place in the Americas from the mid-eighteenth century onward. Some of the slaves arrested in 1820 "for conspiring against the white people" in British Demerara appear to have been as concerned with protecting the emerging tradition of having two or three days a week to themselves, so that they could cultivate their provision gardens and go to the market with their produce, as they were with legal freedom itself. Eugene Genovese once argued that slave revolts in the age of revolution "must be understood primarily as part of the most radical wing of the struggle for a democracy that had not yet lost its bourgeois moorings." But perhaps a more precise formulation would be that most enslaved rebels were *only just* beginning to develop a bourgeois sensibility. When, for example, the enslaved blacksmith Gabriel planned to burn the Richmond warehouses in 1800 as a diversionary tactic, the destruction of property troubled some of his artisan recruits. George Smith, a slave who hired his time, said he "was not for burning the [ware]Houses, as he observed they would want the Whole of them for their own use" upon becoming free.[26]

This line of argument does not deny that rural slaves could be rebellious—Haiti's Night of Fire began, of course, on the sugar-producing Plaine du Nord and Turner's revolt exploded in the cotton county of Southampton. Nor is it meant to suggest that urban slaves were perpetually on the barricades. But the fact remains that in most countries, rebel leaders disproportionately came from or had frequent contact with urban areas. The United States is hardly atypical in this regard. The vast majority of slaves on the mainland lived on farms or plantations, yet two revolts matured in New York City, two in or near Charleston, one in Richmond with ties to Norfolk, and one above New Orleans on the heavily commercial sugar plantations of the German Coast. Outside the United States, the pattern was similar. The Demerara rebellion of 1823 began on the estates closest to Georgetown and situated on the highly profitable coast between the Demerara and Mahaica Rivers, and Robert Paquette has demonstrated that the scattered uprisings and plotting that shook Cuba during the 1830s and early 1840s took place on plantations in the commercial heartland of Cuba's western department, in and around the booming ports of Havana, Matanzas, and Cárdenas.[27]

So too does the extant evidence strongly indicate that rebellion was the occupation of skilled slaves, and men who grasped the power of cash. Field-hands, of course, could be found tangled up in the court proceedings that followed slave conspiracies, but they rarely were the instigators of these plots. Admittedly, the extant documentation pertaining to rebellions invariably defies quantitative analysis, since white magistrates almost never asked the sorts of questions that historians would have them ask. But when the occupational status of enslaved rebels can be obtained, it is clear that skilled slaves found their way into courts in numbers that far exceeded their statistical ratio in the overall slave community. In the 1835 Muslim uprising in Salvador, Bahia, for example, official documents designated five of the 186 defendants as peddlers and ten as artisans. Twenty-nine held unspecified urban occupations, and twenty-five more were domestics. Eleven were identified as either mariners or "farm workers." The occupations of the remaining 106 are unknown. Similarly, of the 135 slaves and free blacks put to trial by Charleston magistrates in 1822, occupations may be determined for forty-one of the defendants. Four were carpenters, four were coopers, two were blacksmiths, and five were rope makers. The others were painters, cooks, stonemasons, wheelwrights, ship caulkers, and draymen; not a single man, as far as the evidence indicates, waded Carolina's rice fields.[28]

Those were not isolated cases. Enslaved artisans took the lead in organizing rebellions across the Americas. In the fall of 1736 in British Antigua, a bondman named Court, alias Tacky, orchestrated an island-wide conspiracy with the aid of an enslaved carpenter called Tomboy. Many of those who joined the conspiracy were drivers, but most of the leaders were creole slaves who had never worked the fields. Among the rebels executed were thirteen carpenters, eight coopers, two masons, three domestics, and even three fiddlers, but of the forty-nine men banished from the island, only six were unskilled field workers. The judges who condemned the leaders, in language reminiscent of that later heard in courts in Richmond and Charleston, wondered how such artisans could "complain of the hardship of Slavery; their lives being as easy as those of our White Tradesmen and Overseers." Five years later, a similar group of slaves plotted against authorities in New York City. Although magistrates proved even less concerned in this instance in discovering the occupations of the accused, Leslie M. Harris argues that "the arson attacks were part of an extensive plan among an interracial group from the lower classes that sought to achieve greater economic and political equality."[29]

Despite this evidence, a number of recent studies of the internal or domestic economies of slavery have focused on such entrepreneurial bondsmen, but typically without explicitly connecting such involvement with the first steps toward rebellion. Several decades ago, Gerald W. Mullin suggested a link between assimilation and the development of a skill as laying the basis for overt rebelliousness. Perhaps a more accurate formulation would stress that such skills only led bondsmen to consider organizing for their liberty when combined with the marketplace, and especially with urban centers. Certainly Larry Hudson understood this point when he argued based on his study of slavery in South Carolina that access to cash and "the intrusion of market values" challenged "the more traditional values of the quarters." Across the American South, whites fretted that allowing enslaved sellers into Charleston or Savannah or New Orleans on Sundays weakened the hegemony of the master class by making slaves less reliant upon their owners, or that it provided them with the opportunity to gather and plot. But one of the real dangers, whether masters understood it or not, was "the market's ability to provide slaves with a source of self-esteem and material improvement that did not require them to go cap-in-hand to the great house."[30]

To be sure, most whites frowned on slaves' marketeering, for they tended to associate it with the theft of their own goods. Yet here, too, evidence indicates that most masters—many of whom understood the larger Atlantic marketplace only imperfectly—failed to grasp the larger danger of allowing capitalist market values onto their plantations. Indeed, in discussing this point, the historian Philip Morgan comes dangerously close to echoing Richard Wade's discredited theory that urbanization and economic freedom actually *inhibited* slave rebelliousness by giving bondsmen too much to lose. In explaining why his 703-page tome on slavery in the eighteenth-century Chesapeake and Carolina lowcountry features no separate chapter on rebellions, Morgan asserts that his entire book "is a study of resistance." Yet his claim that "slaves constantly achieved small victories" by working toward labor autonomy may help explain why Morgan now believes that actual slave plots never existed in New York in 1741, in Antigua in 1736, in the Chesapeake in the 1790s, and in Virginia in 1802. Rather than recognizing this "autonomous [labor] culture" as a potential stepping stone toward rebellion, Morgan insists that by "carving out some independence for themselves," enslaved marketers simply "eased the torments of slavery."[31]

The debate over whether slave systems in the Americas were a curious variety of capitalism or a modern form of seigneurialism that rested uneasily within the framework of the Atlantic trading world is an old one that gives no indication of resolution. But whether one chooses to regard the great planters of the Western hemisphere to be calculating agrarian capitalists who operated their "factories in the field" productively and efficiently, or whether one sees them instead as fundamentally pre-bourgeois lords who participated in the larger Atlantic network even as they resisted its values and ideology, there remains the possibility that the sort of slaves who entered into rebellion better understood the power of capital, and its corrosive effect on the plantation regime, than did their masters. Cash, at the very least, allowed for the possibility of self-purchase, or purchase of a spouse. Typical of those involved in rebellions was the aged African Sanim, implicated in the 1835 *Malê* revolt in Salvador and known to his Brazilian masters as Luís. Although he could scarcely speak Portuguese, Sanim was a skilled tobacco roller and an urbanite. He not only saved his meager earnings, he organized a pool or savings fund for other skilled slaves. The practical Sanim divided this pool into three parts: one third went to pay the masters' portions of the slaves' wages, the second third went for the purchase of cloth to make Muslim garments, and the final third was used to buy letters of manumission.[32]

In this regard, Sanim had much in common with Watt Tyler, who rose to the forefront of the English peasant revolt of 1381. Historians need to be sensitive to specific context, of course, as capitalist development—or lack thereof, in many places in the Americas—occurred at different times and at different rates in the Western hemisphere. But as Rodney Hilton demonstrated more than three decades ago, the English peasant revolt diverged from a traditional rural insurrection. The "focus of the rising," he noted, "was London," and artisans like Watt the Tiler resided just outside the city in "the most industrialized and commercialized part of the country," where old feudal relationships had been torn asunder "by the developing market economy." One does not have to argue that these craftsmen in mentality were bourgeois, or even petty capitalists, to suggest that the coming of a cash economy provided these men with a vision of new possibilities that lay beyond their tiny village, or their lord's estate.[33]

This realization should not blind us to other factors that led to slave rebelliousness across the Americas. As Stuart Schwartz has observed, the *Malê* movement of 1835 revealed the "deeply African nature of Bahian slave culture," as well as how little that religiosity fit with the links that scholars from Eugene D. Genovese to Stanley Harrold have drawn between slave rebellions and "the wider political movements of the Atlantic revolution." But many of the Hausas involved in the revolt saw no contradiction between being, as Reis bluntly put it, "good Muslims and good businessmen." Nearly half of the Hausas swept up by authorities in 1835 were artisans or tradesmen who "came to the city to sell tobacco and other goods." As the old Islamic proverb read, "Merchants are the messengers of this world and God's faithful trustees on Earth," and if enslaved rebels in New York and Charleston did not share that faith, the evidence is that they more than shared the sentiment.[34]

Although the secession of the southern states in the winter of 1860–1 presented militant blacks with precisely the sort of division that rebel leaders typically tried to exploit to their advantage, the Civil War channeled black resistance into patterns acceptable to the politicians of the free states. During the first year of the conflict, as Confederate soldiers repulsed northern invaders, militant slaves across the cotton-growing South worked from within to pull down the rebel government. A slave plot in Natchez, Mississippi, led by "a negro named Bill Postlethwaite," but still shrouded in mystery, stands as but one example of collective resistance during the months before the Confederate defeat at Antietam Creek. Rumors of black resistance spread in New Orleans and Columbia, South Carolina. Seven slaves swung from the gibbet in Charleston in April 1861. The Confederate brigadier general R. F. Floyd urged Governor John Milton of Florida to declare martial law in six counties in the hope of eradicating a "nest of traitors and lawless negroes."[35]

Armstead Robinson, in demonstrating how the fear of "servile insurrection" affected Confederate troop deployments, also pointed out how attuned southern slaves were during the war to shifting the balance of forces in planning mass desertions from estates.[36]

Most slaves understood, as Herbert Aptheker suggested in his pioneering *American Negro Slave Revolts* (1943), that "the Army of Lincoln was to be the Army of Liberation." Aged slaves with long memories counseled patience and waited for the arrival of northern forces. Following the Emancipation Proclamation, northern freemen and southern runaways, eager and willing to fight, donned blue uniforms in the name of liberty for blacks. Despite the Confederates' threat to execute black soldiers as slave insurgents, thousands of bondsmen fled the countryside, planning to return and liberate their families. By the end of the war, 180,000 African-Americans (one out of every five males in the Republic) had served in Union forces. Those former slaves who marched back toward the plantations of their birth singing "General Gabriel's Defeat," a song about the "incidents" of Gabriel's plot that had become "popular" as early as 1832 "among the colored *population of the South*," rightly understood themselves to be a part of the largest slave rebellion in the history of the United States.[37]

NOTES

1. Despite its flaws and exaggerations, all modern scholarship on slave resistance begins with Herbert Aptheker, *American Negro Slave Revolts* (New York, 1943).
2. On slave religion in the United States, see Eugene D. Genovese, *Roll, Jordan, Roll: The World the Slaves Made* (New York, 1972), 161–284; Albert J. Raboteau, *Slave Religion: The "Invisible Institution" in the Antebellum South* (New York, 1979).
3. This point was first made by Eugene D. Genovese, *From Rebellion to Revolution: Afro-American Slave Revolts in the Making of the Modern World* (Baton Rouge, La., 1979), ch. 1.
4. T. H. Breen and Stephen Innes, *Myne Owne Ground: Race and Freedom on Virginia's Eastern Shore* (New York, 1980), 101–13; Edmund S. Morgan, *American Slavery, American Freedom: The Ordeal of Colonial Virginia* (New York, 1975), ch. 15; Philip J. Schwarz, *Twice Condemned: Slaves and the Criminal Laws of Virginia, 1705–1865* (Baton Rouge, La., 1988), 17.
5. Graham Russell Hodges, *Root and Branch: African Americans in New York and East Jersey, 1613–1863* (Chapel Hill, NC, 1999), 64–7; Peter Linebaugh and Marcus Rediker, *The Many-Headed Hydra: Sailors, Slaves, Commoners, and the Hidden History of the Revolutionary Atlantic* (Boston, 2000), 201–2.
6. Mark M. Smith, *Stono: Documenting and Interpreting a Southern Slave Revolt* (Columbia, SC, 2005), 108–88; Peter Charles Hoffer, *The Great New York Conspiracy of 1741: Slavery, Crime, and Colonial Law* (Lawrence, Kan., 2003), ch. 8.
7. John Hope Franklin and Loren Schweninger, *Runaway Slaves: Rebels on the Plantation* (New York, 1999); Walter C. Rucker, *The River Flows On: Black Resistance, Culture, and Identity Formation in Early America* (Baton Rouge, La., 2006), 112.

8. Sylvia R. Frey, *Water from the Rock: Black Resistance in a Revolutionary Age* (Princeton, 1991), 225–32; Douglas R. Egerton, *Death or Liberty: African Americans and Revolutionary America* (New York, 2009), ch. 8.

9. Genovese, *From Rebellion to Revolution*, 22–3; David Brion Davis, *Revolutions: Reflections on American Equality and Foreign Liberations* (Cambridge, Mass., 1990), 29.

10. Douglas R. Egerton, *Gabriel's Rebellion: The Virginia Slave Conspiracies of 1800 and 1802* (Chapel Hill, NC, 1993), 169.

11. Douglas R. Egerton, "The Scenes Which Are Acted in St. Domingo: The Legacy of Revolutionary Violence in Early National Virginia," in John R. McKivigan and Stanley Harrold (eds.), *Antislavery Violence: Sectional, Racial, and Cultural Conflict in Antebellum America* (Knoxville, Tenn., 1999), 44–6; Aptheker, *American Negro Slave Revolts*, 249; Robert L. Paquette, "'A Horde of Brigands?' The Great Louisiana Slave Revolt of 1811 Reconsidered," *Historical Reflections/Réflexions historiques*, 35 (Spring 2009): 72–96. On the role of drivers in the history of slave collective resistance in the Americas, see Robert L. Paquette, "The Drivers Shall Lead Them: Image and Reality in Slave Resistance," in Robert L. Paquette and Louis A. Ferleger (eds.), *Slavery, Secession, and Southern History* (Charlottesville, Va., 2000), 31–58.

12. Egerton, *Gabriel's Rebellion*, 119–25; Aptheker, *American Negro Slave Revolts*, 255.

13. Egerton, *He Shall Go Out Free: The Lives of Denmark Vesey* (2nd edn. Lanham, Md., 1999), 126–53. In a review essay of my book on Vesey and two others, the historian Michael Johnson raised questions about whether the Vesey plot, in fact, existed, arguing that it was actually contrived by elite slaveholders. See Michael P. Johnson, "Denmark Vesey and his Co-conspirators," *William and Mary Quarterly*, 58 (October 2001): 915–76 and the responses to it: "Forum: The Making of a Slave Conspiracy, Part 2," *William and Mary Quarterly*, 59 (January 2002): 135–202. For more extensive rebuttals of Johnson's thesis, see Robert L. Paquette and Douglas R. Egerton, "Of Facts and Fables: New Light on the Denmark Vesey Affair," *South Carolina Historical Magazine*, 105 (January 2004): 7–47; and Robert L. Paquette, "From Rebellion to Revisionism: The Continuing Debate about the Denmark Vesey Affair," *Journal of the Historical Society*, 4 (Fall 2004): 291–334.

14. Genovese, *From Rebellion to Revolution*, 9.

15. Donald R. Wright, *African Americans in the Early Republic, 1789–1831* (Arlington Heights, Ill., 1993), 114; Douglas R. Egerton, "Nat Turner in a Hemispheric Context," in Kenneth S. Greenberg (ed.), *Nat Turner: A Slave Rebellion in History and Memory* (New York, 2003), 141.

16. Peter Coclanis, "Slavery, African-American Agency, and the World We Have Lost," *Georgia Historical Quarterly*, 79 (Winter 1995): 880–1. Roderick A. McDonald, "Independent Economic Production by Slaves on Antebellum Louisiana Sugar Plantations," in Ira Berlin and Philip D. Morgan (eds.), *Cultivation and Culture: Labor and the Shaping of Slave Life in the Americas* (Charlottesville, Va., 1993), 289; William L. Williams (ed.), *North Carolina Slave Narratives: The Lives of Lunsford Lane, Moses Grandy, and Thomas H. Jones* (Chapel Hill, NC, 2003), 102.

17. Loren Schweninger, "Slave Independence and Enterprise in South Carolina, 1780–1865," *South Carolina Historical Magazine*, 93 (April 1992): 107; Schwarz, *Twice Condemned*, 119; Alex Lichtenstein, "'That Disposition to Theft, with Which They Have Been Branded': Moral Economy, Slave Management, and the Law," *Journal of Social History*, 21 (Spring 1988), 413–40; McDonald, *Economy and Material Culture of Slavery*, 43.

18. Robert H. Gudmestad, *A Troublesome Commerce: The Transformation of the Interstate Slave Trade* (Baton Rouge, La., 2005), 21; David Barry Gaspar, *Bondsmen and Rebels: A Study of Master–Slave Relations in Antigua* (Durham, NC, 1985), 161.

19. "Negro Act," 1740, in Joseph Brevard (ed.), *An Alphabetical Digest of the Public Statute Law of South Carolina* (Charleston, SC, 1814), i. 238–39; Betty Wood, *Slavery in Colonial Georgia, 1730–1775* (Athens, Ga., 1984), 122–3; Wood, *Women's Work, Men's Work*, 82.

20. Boles, *Black Southerners*, 128; Wade, *Slavery in the Cities*, 85; Buchanan, *Black Life on the Mississippi*, 111; Ira Berlin, *Slaves without Masters: The Free Negro in the Antebellum South* (New York, 1974), 261–2.

21. Wright, *African Americans in the Early Republic*, 121.

22. E. P. Thompson, "Patrician Society, Plebian Culture," *Journal of Social History*, 7 (Summer 1974): 397; João José Reis, *Slave Rebellion in Brazil: The Muslim Uprising of 1835 in Bahia* (Baltimore, 1993), 145; Hoffer, *Great New York Conspiracy of 1741*, 62.

23. A classic statement on this subject can be found in George M. Frederickson and Christopher Lasch, "Resistance to Slavery," *Civil War History*, 13 (December 1967): 315–29. Walter Johnson, "On Agency," *Journal of Social History*, 37 (Fall 2003): 16; Takagi, *"Rearing Wolves to our Own Destruction"*, 117.

24. Johnson, "On Agency," 118; Thomas Pinckney, *Reflections Occasioned by the Late Disturbances in Charleston* (Charleston, SC, 1822), 9.

25. James Hamilton, *An Account of the Late Intended Insurrection among a Portion of the Blacks of the City* (Charleston, SC, 1822), 21; David Barry Gaspar, "The Antigua Slave Conspiracy of 1746: A Case Study of the Origins of Collective Resistance," *William and Mary Quarterly*, 35 (April 1978): 320.

26. Emilia Viotti da Costa, *Crowns of Glory, Tears of Blood: The Demerara Slave Rebellion of 1823* (New York, 1994), 172; Genovese, *From Rebellion to Revolution*, 2; Egerton, *Gabriel's Rebellion*, 57.

27. Robert L. Paquette, *Sugar is Made with Blood: The Conspiracy of La Escalera and the Conflict between Empires over Slavery in Cuba* (Middletown, Conn., 1988).

28. João José Reis, *Slave Rebellion in Brazil: The Muslim Uprising of 1835 in Bahia* (Baltimore, 1995), 167; Egerton, *He Shall Go Out Free*, appendix II.

29. Gaspar, "Antigua Slave Conspiracy of 1736," 317–18; Hodges, *Root & Branch*, 97–8; Leslie M. Harris, *In the Shadow of Slavery: African Americans in New York City, 1626–1863* (Chicago, 2003), 43.

30. Gerald W. Mullin, *Flight and Rebellion: Slave Resistance in Eighteenth Century Virginia* (New York, 1972); Larry E. Hudson, Jr., "All That Cash: Work and Status in the Slave Quarters," in *Working toward Freedom*, 84; Robert Olwell, "A Reckoning of Accounts: Patriarchy, Market Relations, and Control on Henry Laurens's Lowcountry Plantations, 1762–1785," ibid. 38.

31. Philip D. Morgan, *Slave Counterpoint: Black Culture in the Eighteenth-Century Chesapeake and Lowcountry* (Chapel Hill, NC, 1998), p. xxii; Philip D. Morgan, "Conspiracy Scares," *William and Mary Quarterly*, 59 (January 2002): 165–6.

32. Reis, *Slave Rebellion in Brazil*, 132–3; I have waded into this debate in "Markets without a Market Revolution: Southern Planters and Capitalism," in Paul Gilje (ed.), *Wages of Independence: Capitalism in the Early American Republic* (Madison, 1997).

33. Rodney Hilton, *Bond Men Made Free: Medieval Peasant Movements and the English Rising of 1381* (London, 1973), 174.

34. Stuart B. Schwartz, *Slaves, Peasants, and Rebels: Reconsidering Brazilian Slavery* (Urbana, Ill., 1992), 15; Stanley Harrold, "Slave Rebels and Black Abolitionists," in Alton Hornsby (ed.), *A Companion to African American History* (Malden, Mass., 2005), 203; Reis, *Slave Rebellion in Brazil*, 169.

35. Winthrop D. Jordan, *Tumult and Silence at Second Creek: An Inquiry into a Civil War Slave Conspiracy* (Baton Rouge, La., 1993), 240; Aptheker, *American Negro Slave Revolts*, 360.

36. Armstead L. Robinson, *Bitter Fruits of Bondage: The Demise of Slavery and the Collapse of the Confederacy, 1861–1865* (Charlottesville, Va., 2004), esp. 38–57.

37. Ibid. 359; "Gabriel's Defeat," *Liberator*, 17 September 1831; James Sidbury, *Ploughshares into Swords: Race, Rebellion, and Identity in Gabriel's Virginia, 1730–1810* (Cambridge, 1997), 259.

SELECT BIBLIOGRAPHY

APTHEKER, HERBERT. *American Negro Slave Revolts*. New York: Columbia University Press, 1943.

CHILDS, MATT D. *The 1812 Aponte Rebellion in Cuba and the Struggle against Atlantic Slavery*. Chapel Hill, NC: University of North Carolina Press, 2006.

EGERTON, DOUGLAS R. *Gabriel's Rebellion: The Virginia Slave Conspiracies of 1800 and 1802*. Chapel Hill, NC: University of North Carolina Press, 1993.

—— *He Shall Go Out Free: The Lives of Denmark Vesey*. 2nd edn. Lanham, Md.: Rowman and Littlefield, 2004.

FREY, SYLVIA R. *Water from the Rock: Black Resistance in a Revolutionary Age*. Princeton: Princeton University Press, 1991.

GENOVESE, EUGENE D. *From Rebellion to Revolution: Afro-American Slave Revolts in the Making of the Modern World*. Baton Rouge, La.: Louisiana State University Press, 1979.

HODGES, GRAHAM RUSSELL. *Root and Branch: African Americans in New York and East Jersey, 1613–1863*. Chapel Hill, NC: University of North Carolina Press, 1999.

HOFFER, PETER CHARLES. *The Great New York Conspiracy of 1741: Slavery, Crime, and Colonial Law*. Lawrence, Kan.: University of Kansas Press, 2003.

LINEBAUGH, PETER, and MARCUS REDIKER. *The Many-Headed Hydra: Sailors, Slaves, Commoners, and the Hidden History of the Revolutionary Atlantic*. Boston: Beacon Press, 2000.

PAQUETTE, ROBERT L. *Sugar is Made with Blood: The Conspiracy of La Escalera and the Conflict between Empires over Slavery in Cuba*. Middletown, Conn.: Wesleyan University Press, 1988.

REIS, JOÃO JOSÉ. *Slave Rebellion in Brazil: The Muslim Uprising of 1835 in Bahia*. Baltimore: Johns Hopkins University Press, 1993.

WRIGHT, DONALD R. *African Americans in the Early Republic, 1789–1831*. Arlington Heights, Ill.: Harlan Davidson, 1993.

CHAPTER 21

....

SLAVE CULTURE

....

KEVIN DAWSON

HISTORIANS of the American South have had an interest in slavery since the early twentieth century but not until fairly recently, as Peter Kolchin has shown, have they paid sustained attention to the enslaved.[1] Traditional analyses tended to rely on top-down examinations that considered how the institution of slavery shaped regional and national economics and politics and southern white society and culture. More innovatively, historians have begun to examine slaves, providing a bottom-up analysis of how slavery and slaves shaped their culture, daily lives, and southern white culture generally. This more recent emphasis has been sensitive to the importance of variables: how southern slave culture was shaped by time, place, work patterns, source population (the origins of African-born slaves); whether a region was under English, Dutch, Spanish, Spanish, French, or American jurisdiction; whether slaves lived and worked in societies with slaves or slave societies; whether slaves were skilled, toiled under the task system, or were gang labor; whether they produced tobacco, indigo, rice, sugar, and cotton; their proximity to Native Americans or Spaniards; and whether they lived in times of war or peace.

This attention to variables defines the more recent trajectory in the writing of slave culture and the analysis of the slave experience has been greatly advanced by historians' eagerness to employ broader temporal and geographic scopes that often include comparative components. More recently still, revisionists have begun employing Atlantic world and African diaspora approaches, placing slaves at the center of their analysis, often tracing the transmission of African culture to the South, and establishing patterns of cultural continuity throughout the African diaspora. Africanists tracing the cultural heritage of members of the African diaspora as they were forcefully taken to Europe, the Americas, and into the Indian Ocean largely initiated this new approach. These reinterpretations remind us of three important, and obvious, though often neglected, historical phenomena: that New World colonies were established and maintained to generate revenue for European metropolises; that slavery generated most of this wealth; and that most of the people that crossed the Atlantic Ocean from the Old World to the New before the early nineteenth century were from Africa. Treating southern slaves as members of the African diaspora, carrying their culture with them, and not Africans in America cut off from their cultural heritage, has greatly enhanced our understanding of slave culture. Moreover, such an approach facilitates comparative, Atlantic world analysis, enabling historians to draw from scholarship on the slave experience in Latin America, the Caribbean, Europe, and the Indian Ocean and allowing us to more readily to trace and identify cultural patterns that were difficult to perceive when using a more focused temporal and geographic scope that only considers the American South.

A Cultureless People: Early to Mid-Twentieth-Century Analysis

Culture is a slippery term. Its definition and application are usually subjectively and sometimes arbitrarily prescribed. What one group considers a cultural trait another may perceive as a lack of culture—as savagery or barbarism. Sociologist William Whit noted, "there is probably no more problematic term than *culture*. Some refer to it exclusively as the high culture of music and art whereas others define it as only the general belief system of a society." Various definitions of culture have been used to analyze the slave experience. Relying on a narrow Eurocentric definition of high culture, early twentieth-century historians avowed that Atlantic Africans and their New World protégés were cultureless and that slavery was a benevolent institution that thoroughly Christianized, civilized, and Americanized Africans.[2]

In the 1960s and especially the early 1970s historians began employing broader, more inclusive definitions of culture. Generally they regarded culture as a something learned and shared, entailing creative expressions that were passed down through generations of bondspeople. Importantly, such definitions recognized the existence of both African and slave culture. Much of the scholarship on slave culture in the 1970s and early 1980s identified African cultural traits in slave culture. However, it was not until Africanists and some Americanists began placing New World slavery into a broader Atlantic world context and considering slaves as members of an African diaspora carrying their culture with them that historians more fully appreciated the depth and complexities of slave culture, especially its African heritage.

This broader analytical approach and definition of culture has enabled scholars to recognize that slaves were far more successful in maintaining their African heritage than previously assumed and forces us to reconsider creolization. Traditionally, scholars assumed that creolization entailed Westernization—the blending of African and Western customs. Recently, some have replaced this narrow Eurocentric definition of creolization with a broader definition that emphasizes the process of creative adaptation. They insist that creolization did not necessarily involve Western influence and could exclusively entail the braiding of traditions held by Africans from different ethnic, language, and cultural groups.

For decades, our understanding of southern slave culture was hobbled by several factors. An early focus on the institution of slavery and how it shaped regional and national politics and economics and the social and economic politics of the Old South tended to eclipse interest in the lives of the enslaved and, instead, targeted slaveholders. Second, historians of antebellum southern slave culture were reluctant to draw from the scholarship of anthropologists, linguists, and archaeologists and to employ a broader, Atlantic world approach by utilizing the interpretative frameworks of scholars studying African history and slave culture elsewhere in the Americas.[3]

Such frameworks were available to historians of the American slave South long before the 1970s when the study of antebellum slave culture gained a foothold in the historiography. The study of slave culture as a legitimate scholarly endeavor arguably began in 1933 with the publication of Brazilian anthropologist Gilberto Freyre's *The Masters and the Slaves: A Study of the Development of Brazilian Civilization*. *The Masters and the Slaves* provided numerous theories, models, and topics that scholars of southern slavery could have considered. Freyre apparently coined the term "Africanization" to describe the cultural "shadow which the Negro slave cast over the Brazilians..." After visiting the American South, Freyre concluded that bondspeople superimposed their African culinary traditions on the region's cuisine.[4] *The Masters and the Slaves* was first published in English in 1946, yet historians of southern slavery did not begin to systematically consider slave culture until the 1970s. Historians did not have to look as far away as Brazil for scholarship on slave culture. Anthropologist Melville Herskovits extensively documented slaves' African heritage as did English professor and linguist Lorenzo Dow Turner.

Part of this reluctance to take seriously the existence and importance of slave culture is attributable to the fact that several prominent works published before the 1970s contended that slaves largely lacked culture. In *American Negro Slavery* (1918), U. B. Phillips argued that Africans possessed no knowledge, skills, or customs of value to the West. For Phillips, the "plantation was a school" that Westernized, Christianized, and civilized backwards Africans, forcing them to "adapt themselves to the white man's ways . . . In short, Foulahs and Fantyns, Eboes and Angolas begat American plantation Negroes . . . Eventually it could be said the Negroes had no memory of Africa as a home."[5]

Phillips's interpretation did not go entirely unchallenged. Several mid-twentieth-century scholars argued slavery was the antithesis of Phillips's model, stressing that slavery was a brutal, oppressive institution. Ironically, though, like Phillips, they concluded that slavery stripped Africans of their African cultural heritage. In *The Negro Family in the United States* sociologist E. Franklin Frazier contended: "Probably never before in history has a people been so nearly completely stripped of its social heritage as the Negroes who were brought to America." Bondage, maintained Frazier, destroyed slaves' culture, making family units few and far between, matriarchal, unstable, and offering their members little emotional or psychological support.[6]

This line of thinking had its most forceful expression in Stanley Elkins's *Slavery: A Problem in American Institutional and Intellectual Life*, which compared plantation slavery to Nazi concentration camps. He asserted that bondage was so brutal it destroyed bondspeople's African cultural heritage, transforming their personal characteristics into childish, submissive dependence caricatured in the "Sambo" stereotype. The scholarship of Frazier, Elkins, and their followers portrayed slaves as a broken, dysfunctional, socially disorganized, cultureless people. Importantly, several mid-twentieth-century social scientists and policy makers embraced such conclusions because they provided non-racist explanations for the perceived cultural differences of blacks and whites and the socioeconomic conditions suffered by many African-Americans.[7]

Other interpretations similarly concluded that bondage virtually extinguished any memory of slaves' African cultural heritage while preventing the development of slave culture. In *The Peculiar Institution: Slavery in the Ante-Bellum South*, Kenneth M. Stampp challenged Phillips's interpretation of slavery, concluding slavery was "[a]mong the more outrageous forms of human exploitation" and that slaveholders were motivated by greed, not by paternalistic desires. He recognized that some "Africanisms" survived. However, he argued that conversion to Christianity, the harshness of bondage, and slaves' inability to control their personal lives obliterated practically all their African heritage, concluding that slavery completely Westernized Africans.[8]

Even in the midst of these works depicting slaves as cultureless, small interpretative fissures, fissures that were to become extremely important for opening up debate later on, were being formed. Melville Herskovits's 1941 *The Myth of the Negro Past* offered one of the first serious challenges to the burgeoning conventional wisdom that slaves had no culture. Through decades of research Herskovits and fellow anthropologists identified various elements of slaves' African cultural heritage, which they called African "carryovers," "survivals," or "Africanisms." Although much of Herskovits's analysis was later criticized for treating Africa as a single cultural area, his field research in the Caribbean, Suriname, and West Africa enabled him to consider how slavery disseminated African culture throughout the Atlantic world.

The 1972 publication of *The American Slave: A Composite Autobiography*, which was edited by George P. Rawick, was a major impetuous for the study of slave culture and allowed historians and not just anthropologists to begin thinking seriously about the lives of slaves.[9] Fisk University and Federal Writers' Projects' Slave Narrative Collection (FWP) interviews of ex-slaves in 1936–8 were published as *The American Slave*. Commonly called the Works Project Administration (WPA) narratives, the typescript of these interviews was bound and deposited in the rare books room of the Library of Congress in 1941 and later microfilmed for distribution. Fisk University made two volumes of what would become volumes eighteen and nineteen of *The American Slave* available in 1945. That same year B. A. Botkin published a short book containing excerpts from the WPA interviews. These sources provided enough historically significant material to alert scholars of their potential value. However, Phillips helped discourage their use for decades by claiming "ex-slaves narratives in general . . . were issued with so much abolitionist editing that as a class their authenticity is doubtful."[10]

New Interpretations of the Slave Experience during the 1970s

Much of the scholarship of the early 1970s sought to counter Elkins's claim that slaves were emasculated and Philips's assertions that slavery was a benign institution that Westernized Africans. Historians who were increasingly interested in the question of "culture" mined bondspeople's accounts to demonstrate that slaves were not physically defenseless, culturally vacant, and could in fact gain significant amounts of personal autonomy. A growing number of historians began shifting their analysis from the institution of slavery as slaveholders perceived it to the slave experience as told by bondspeople.

In 1972 two significant works were published that reflected this analytical shift: John W. Blassingame's *The Slave Community: Plantation Life in the Antebellum South* and George Rawick's *From Sundown to Sunup: The Making of the Black Community*. Blassingame and Rawick cannot claim full responsibility for legitimizing black-authored sources (which Phillips dismissed) to consider slave culture. However, they were instrumental in debunking the belief that such works were too biased to possess historical merit.

Rawick edited *The American Slave* and wrote volume i, *From Sundown to Sunup*, which was an attempt to demonstrate the value of the WPA ex-slave interviews as historical evidence. Reception was mixed. C. Vann Woodward concluded that Rawick generally failed because the book was "complicated by the abstract and theoretical character of his interest in history." Norman Yetman praised *From Sundown to Sunup*, saying it significantly extended historians' understanding of slave culture by considering it as a form of resistance and providing a "fully developed and persuasive" portrayal of the slave community.[11]

John Blassingame used nineteenth-century slave narratives, and not the WPA or Fisk interviews, to gain access to the social and cultural life of the enslaved.[12] Blassingame found that despite white sexual exploitation and forcible separation, the nuclear family survived and functioned, providing its members with emotional and physical support and guidance for negotiating the brutal world of slavery. Plantations were not concentration camps that reduced slaves to powerless children. Slave quarters afforded slaves numerous opportunities for independent and group creativity and expression, including preservation of a broadly construed African heritage that largely ignored ethnic and regional differences.

Blassingame's boldness in declaring that he was breaking from historiographical tradition was interpreted as a sharp indictment of the historical profession, sparking considerable hostility. *The Slave Community* was criticized for excessive deployment of psychological theory, failing to draw from a wide enough selection of primary sources, especially the WPA and Fisk slave interviews, and portraying slaves as homogeneous.[13] Some historians, such as Mary Frances Berry, believe racism muted the praise of Blassingame, who was an African-American, and stimulated a reactionary backlash against *The Slave Community*.[14]

Some of the scholarship directly following Blassingame and Rawick provided more nuanced analysis of slave culture and began considering how some of the variables of bondage affected the slave experience. Eugene Genovese's *Roll, Jordan, Roll: The World the Slaves Made* meticulously considered virtually every aspect of the antebellum South that slaves helped create. *Roll, Jordan, Roll* is the most comprehensive study of antebellum southern slavery. Geneovese provided a model of a slave society in which slaves and slaveholders were inseparably bound. He employed a Marxist theory of cultural hegemony to describe the power of the planter class, while introducing a complex notion of paternalism to the owner–slave relationship that stressed mutual dependence in which both sides played a ceaseless game of give-and-take involving the expansion and contraction of reciprocal rights and obligation. This relationship, Genovese argued, enabled slaves to continually shape and reshape white society.[15]

Genovese believed slaves maintained African traditions and created new ones as part of a "strategy for the survival of their individuality and some measure of group autonomy." He detailed the various elaborations of slave culture in religion, dances, music, work songs, and foodways and considered how such traditions were insinuated upon a receptive southern white culture. Though whites generally regarded blacks as their inferiors, Genovese explained how, in profound ways, they were consciously and subconsciously shaped by slave culture. Describing whites' willingness to embrace slave traditions Genovese noted, "whites particularly enjoyed participating in slaves' 'plantation balls' and other social events." Slave influences on other traditions were perhaps less obvious to some whites but were, nonetheless, just as enjoyable. Genovese explained how enslaved female cooks so thoroughly interlaced their African-influenced cuisine through southern foodways that "it represented the culinary despotism of the quarters over the Big House." Ironically, it was the plantation mistress and not the enslaved cook that usually received the credit and praise for creating African-influenced slave dishes. Thus, Genovese, contended that much of slaves' culture was appropriated by white southerners who knowingly and unknowingly claimed both authorship and ownership of it, transforming slave culture into more broadly and less racially defined southern culture (a conclusion Freyre reached some forty years earlier).[16]

Some historians considered slave culture as part of broader folk culture. In *Black Culture and Black Consciousness* Lawrence Levine tapped the WPA narratives to recreate the "expressive culture" of African-Americans through the analysis of their folk culture. Using a definition of intellectual history as one that considers a people's thought processes to provide a rich understanding of slaves' folk culture and impressed by the retentions of African motifs in black oral traditions, Levine carefully emphasized the dynamic quality of African-American culture, explaining that slaves' folk culture was "created and constantly recreated through a communal process," which resulted in the casting and recasting of a semi-autonomous culture and worldview.[17] Similarly, Charles Joyner's *Down by the Riverside: A South Carolina Slave Community* extended our understanding of slave culture as both folk culture and intellectual history. Joyner analyzes South Carolina lowcountry slave experience. While most of Joyner's analysis is of the antebellum period, he considers how colonial-era events, like the transmission of an African rice culture, shaped nineteenth-century life and culture. Joyner detailed how slaves shaped their own lives by focusing on the retention of African cultural practices, how slaves worked and lived in a communal African-influenced manner, creolization, and leisure activities, and folk life and culture.[18]

The interest in family and community as a proxy for culture continued in the 1970s. Herbert G. Gutman's *The Black Family in Slavery and Freedom, 1750–1925* argued that, despite the brutalities of bondage and threats of family members being sold, the family was slaves' dominant social institution and primary source of social cohesion and group identity. He contended that the nuclear family was the norm, that bondswomen were not promiscuous, and that networks of extended kin created familial bonds that provided sources of identity spanning several generations. Gutman's analysis dealt with slaves' ability to sustain family units, and the implications of his rigorously documented conclusions were that other cultural, communal traditions were similarly sustained.

OUT OF AFRICA AND INTO
THE COLONIAL SOUTH

During the 1970s, many historians recognized that antebellum bondspeople maintained elements of their African cultural heritage and, adopting the language of Herskovits, called African cultural retentions "Africanisms," "carryovers," and "survivals." When considering the African legacies of slave culture, historians of the antebellum South traditionally assumed slavery largely shattered bondspeople's African heritage, allowing them to only maintain broken shards of their African heritage. During the 1970s few historians sought to trace slaves' African cultural heritage.

In the early 1970s, few historians expressed a rich understanding of colonial slave life and historians of the Old South studied a population comprised largely of American-born, Americanized slaves. Indeed, in "Time, Space, and Evolution of Afro-America Society in British Mainland North America" (1980) Ira Berlin complained that the previous generation of historians oversimplified slave life by not accounting for temporal and geographic dimensions, saying their "view[s] [of] southern slavery from the point of maturity, dissecting it into component parts, comparing it to other slave societies, and juxtaposing it to free societies have produced an essentially static vision of slave culture." Hence, by beginning their analysis in the antebellum period many historians lacked the historical perspective necessary to conduct in-depth examinations of slaves' ability to convey and retain large components of their African heritage to the Americas and the creolization process.[19]

Ironically, the heavy use of both WPA and fugitive slave narratives—the very sources that helped liberate the study of slave culture from the Phillips tradition—constrained some of the analysis of the slave experience by shifting much of its focus to the mid-nineteenth century. These sources enabled slaves to describe their lives but, since they largely spoke of mid-nineteenth-century experiences, they offered only a slice the slave experience. In *Exchanging our Country Marks* (which will be discussed later) Michael Gomez convincingly argues: "By 1830, the number of African-born slaves dropped to the single digits—a clear majority were two or more generations removed from African soil . . . American-born slaves far outnumber those of the native African, and the general patterns of the emerging African American identity are discernable." Though slaves living after the 1830s knowingly and unknowingly maintained African traditions, Gomez explains that this is the decade when culturally they shifted from being African to African-American. Generally speaking, fugitive slave narratives were first published in the late 1830s and usually did not discuss events prior to about 1820. WPA narratives overwhelmingly describe experiences in the 1850s and 1860s. Both the WPA and fugitive slave narratives illustrate life in populations that were largely comprised of American-born slaves, containing few and possibly no African-born slaves. Additionally, their narrators often did not seem aware of the African origins of many of their cultural practices. Instead, they evidently regarded many African traditions as a way of life distinct from that of their owners. In the early 1970s, some historians of American slavery became increasingly aware of the need to examine colonial sources in order to appreciate more fully the African origins of slave culture and how it shaped the lives of black and white antebellum southerners.[20]

Histories of the colonial period, especially those deploying Atlantic world and African diaspora approaches, tended to provide revisionist interpretations that stressed the centrality of profit motivation behind slavery and remind us that until the early nineteenth century the vast majority of the people who crossed the Atlantic Ocean from the Old World to the New came in the hold of a slave ship.[21] But such work also spoke in meaningful ways to the question of slave culture, its origins, continuity, and elaboration in the New World.

An informed understanding of American slave culture, especially its African heritage, was hinged on the compilation of monographs that examined sizeable populations of African-born slaves during the seventeenth and eighteenth centuries. These studies considerably extended our understanding of slave culture, especially the transmission of African cultural practices to the Americas, and laid the foundation for a richer understanding of nineteenth-century slave culture. Importantly, they began placing slaves and slavery in the broader context of the Atlantic world by documenting slaves' attempts to maintain ties to their ancestral homelands through the preservation of African traditions and by considering how events in the Caribbean, Latin America, Africa, and Europe shaped the slave experience.[22]

Peter H. Wood's *Black Majority: Negroes in Colonial South Carolina from 1670 through the Stono Rebellion* helped precipitate the shift towards analyzing colonial slavery while broadening our understanding of slaves' experiences. Wood made slaves the center of his analysis and considered how the retention of broadly construed African cultural practices shaped the lives of white and black South Carolinians. Wood documented African transmissions like animal husbandry, canoeing, fishing, and agriculture and how they contributed to South Carolina's economic success. As Benjamin Quarles noted, Wood demonstrated that slaves were a "major rather than a minor" component and that they were "active rather than passive" players in determining South Carolina's development.[23]

Although studies of the antebellum period recognized "Africanisms," their emphasis on the years 1790–1860, especially from about 1820 to 1860, hampered their understanding of cultural transmission and creolization. Scholars of colonial slaves had the vantage necessary for documenting slaves' ability to transmit what Judith Carney calls "African knowledge systems." Rice cultivation is the best example of how the creation and perpetuation of such systems worked, and scholars such as Peter Wood, Daniel C. Littlefield, Gwendolyn Midlo Hall, and Judith A. Carney have convincingly argued that most of the early knowledge, skills, and technology necessary to reproduce a "rice culture" in colonial America were similar to ones that existed in Africa. This analysis illustrates how African-influenced cultural traditions shaped the institution of slavery, including work patterns and profit margins.[24]

In *Africans in Colonial Louisiana: The Development of Afro-Creole Culture in the Eighteenth Century* Gwendolyn Midlo Hall challenged earlier notions, popularized by Sidney Mintz and Richard Price, that claimed the slave trade and slavery made it virtually impossible for slaves to reconstruct African traditions (other challenges to Mintz and Price will be discussed in more depth later in the essay). She argued that slaves in southern Louisiana created "the most Africanized slave culture in the United States." Asserting that the "Louisiana experience calls into question the assumption that African slaves could not regroup themselves in language and social communities derived from the sending culture," Hall paid particular attention to the specific African origins of slaves, documenting especially how slaves from the Senegambia shaped Louisiana's development. Mutually intelligible African languages and dialects facilitated the development of creolized languages necessary for the retention of African traditions. Hall documents how Senegambians shaped Louisiana's indigo and rice cultures and examines how an African syntax or "grammatical structure" was imposed upon creolized French vocabulary. Importantly, Hall explores how African traditions were passed from African-born slaves to their American-born children.[25]

Historians of the colonial period provide important comparative analysis of the slave experience in different colonies. Philip Morgan's *Slave Counterpoint: Black Culture in the Eighteenth-Century Chesapeake and Lowcountry* examines how slavery transformed both black and white society. *Slave Counterpoint* considers the plantation, black–white relationships, and the construction of black cultural and social institutions. Morgan contends that slave culture was a form of resistance, saying "the creation of a coherent culture" was the product of slave resistance in which bondspeople sought to secure "some independence for themselves, by forcing their masters to recognize their humanity, and by creating an autonomous culture, slaves also eased the torments of slavery, and in that respect, their cultural creativity encouraged accommodation." Comparing two regions within British North America, he stresses that it was not necessarily legal systems, mother countries, or religion that shaped slavery and slave culture; instead, slave systems and their respective societies and cultures were shaped by, among other things, slave-produced staple crops, planters' lifestyles, source populations (where African slaves were from), and the creolization process.[26] Perhaps the book's greatest strengths are its interdisciplinary approach and contribution to our understanding of slaves' daily lives, especially their material culture. Morgan demonstrates the value of tapping anthropological and archaeological studies and mining the analysis of scholars of West Indian and Latin American slavery. Morgan's analysis of the internal economy drew from and elaborated on decades of research in the West Indies by scholars like Sidney Mintz, Douglass Hall, Neville T. Hall, Barry W. Higman, and Dale Tomich.

Other historians have stressed change over time while considering different geographic regions. *Many Thousands Gone: The First Two Centuries of Slavery in North America* by Ira Berlin is the most comprehensive analysis of slave life in colonial America. Synthesizing the research of generations of scholars of African history and New World slavery, *Many Thousands Gone* sought to correct the problems Berlin identified in "Time, Space, and Evolution" by presenting an in-depth interpretation of the complexities and diversities of colonial slave life. Berlin explores evolving traits of slavery, owner–slave relationships, and slave life (including work and culture).[27]

The book's comparative and Atlantic world dimensions facilitate nuanced analysis, while reminding readers that what became the United States was small portions of the Spanish, English, Dutch, and French empires. By considering three chronological periods ("Charter," "Plantation," and "Revolutionary Generations") and four geographic regions (North, Chesapeake, lowcountry, and Lower Mississippi Valley) the book chronicles how time and space shaped slaves' experiences. Berlin demonstrates that the creolization process was not necessarily linear and that the degrees of African and Western traditions in slaves' cultures ebbed and flowed from generation to generation. Borrowing from the scholarship of historians of African history Berlin coined the term "Atlantic creole" to assert that the Westernization of a significant number of American slaves began in Africa. Some were bi-racial, but for Berlin Atlantic creoles were born more out of Westernization in Africa than interracial liaisons. Atlantic creoles arrived in America having adopted aspects of Christianity, Western material culture, and gave or were given European names.

Many Thousands Gone was important for allowing historians to think about the role of place and chronological time in shaping slave culture and, by implication, placing the evolution and elaboration of slave cultural identity firmly within the larger context of Atlantic history. In Berlin's hands, slaves were inextricable from the larger forces of the era—the emergence of capitalism, burgeoning imperialism, and intercontinental colonialism—and slave culture both informed and was formed by these larger processes. Berlin's conceptualization of Atlantic creoles primarily focuses on seventeenth- and eighteenth-century Africans from Senegal to Angola. However, as Africanists Robin Law and Kristin Mann state, "Berlin's analysis arguably exaggerates both the extent of cultural 'creolization' in West African coastal communities in early times and the numerical significance of such 'creoles' among exported slaves." Yet, Berlin's conceptualizations have proven helpful. Law and Mann explain: "Even though the argument may be empirically problematic for the seventeenth century, the conceptual framework that Berlin develops, of a cosmopolitan culture linking seaports on all sides of the Atlantic littoral, can be fruitfully applied to later periods."[28] Indeed, while limiting the term's use to a specific time and region, Linda Heywood and John Thornton use the concept to great profit in their 2007 study *Central Africans, Atlantic Creoles, and the Foundation of the Americas, 1585–1660*. Heywood and Thornton use slave trading records to contend that West-Central Africans were the majority of slaves brought to English and Dutch colonies in North America; many seventeenth-century West-Central Africans were Atlantic creoles who had adopted elements of Christianity and European languages, names, and material culture; and suggest ways that Atlantic creole culture laid the foundation for subsequent slave cultures throughout the Americas.[29]

ENSLAVED WOMEN: NEW IMPERATIVES, NEW ANALYSES

To more fully comprehend slave culture historians have recognized the need to consider the experience of all bondspeople, including female slaves. Indeed, Darlene Clark Hine and David Barry Gaspar contended: "To explore slavery and slave society through the prism of the lives of black women is to come to a better understanding of how much scholars have missed or misconstrued when they have used the term slave without due regard to gender, or with reference specifically to slave men." Historians began rigorously considering the experiences of bondswomen in the mid-1980s yet, as late as 1997, Leslie Schwalm bemoaned, "[d]espite the prominence of debates about slave families in the historiography of slavery, including Deborah Grey White's clarion call in 1984 for greater sensitivity to a life-cycle analysis of women in slavery, the field has lagged in studying the experiences and meaning of maternity, motherhood, infancy and childhood in slavery."[30]

Since Deborah Grey White wrote *Ar'n't I a Woman? Female Slaves in the Plantation South* a number of historians have written works that focus on the experiences of slave women. A growing number of historians, like Hillary Beckles, Barbara Bush, Darlene Clark Hine, Jacqueline Jones, Bernard Moitt, Jennifer L. Morgan, Leslie Schwalm, and Marie Jenkins Schwarts, have documented the experiences of slave women throughout the Americas. The scholarship of most authors focuses primarily on issues of gender, race, natural reproduction, and labor rather than how gender directly affected slave culture. However, an understanding of slave women's experiences considerably extends our understanding of slave culture. Indeed, a common cultural theme throughout this new and expanding body of scholarship is on how mothers passed traditions and life skills, like cooking, sewing, gardening, and respect for white authority, to their children.

Analysis of gender and slave culture have, like the analysis of slave culture itself, benefited enormously from a broadened geographic emphasis. David Barry Gaspar and Darlene Clark Hine's anthology *More than Chattel: Black Women and Slavery in the Americas* seeks to conjoin the studies of bondwomen and comparative slavery. The geographic focus of the volume is on the Caribbean, Brazil, and what became the United States, and the temporal scope is broad, extending from the seventeenth through the nineteenth centuries.[31] *More than Chattel* explores numerous aspects of slave women's lives, demonstrating how discussions of gender can heighten our understandings of bondage and the slave experience, both central to our understanding of slave culture. The collection considers the African heritage of slave families, gendered divisions of labor as a method for reaching a deeper comprehension of bondswomen's experiences and slavery in the Americas, stresses that female slaves in slave societies were largely valued for their abilities to produce commodities, and examines how slave women individually and collectively challenged the dehumanizing, destructive forces inherent to slavery.

How slave women were perceived and treated by broader white society impacted the development of slave culture. In *Laboring Women: Reproduction and Gender in New World Slavery* Jennifer L. Morgan considers how early English perceptions of gender and race (especially those held by South Carolinians and Barbadians) influenced how slave women were viewed and treated. Morgan contends that reproduction, and not the type of labor they performed, was the primary influence in female slaves' lives. It shaped experiences with work, community, and culture. Slaveholders recognized the "speculative value of a reproducing labor force."[32] Morgan asserts that reproduction was central to the creation of a creolized population. Slaveholders preferred slaves born in the Americas, believing that they would be a more tractable workforce than African-born slaves.

The internal economy and how bondwomen informally earned and spent money provides considerable insight upon cultural activities. Betty Wood's *Women's Work, Men's Work: The Informal Economies of Lowcountry Georgia* examines the social function of the informal slave economy by focusing on the working lives of slaves outside plantation slavery. Wood's analysis demonstrates that the informal economy's true significance was not economic, but social and cultural. Slaves' informal economy enabled many to obtain considerable degrees of autonomy. Cultural activities like craft-making, hunting, and fishing enabled slaves to generate incomes, and culture influences, such as purchasing nice clothes to wear to church, shaped how slaves earned and spent their money.[33]

Betty Wood stresses that the informal economy and recreational activities improved the quality of their lives while shaping slaves' relationships with white southerners. She documents the roles of gender and family in the informal production of goods during free time and the exchange of these goods. The slave family was the primary unit of production, cultivating fruits and vegetables in gardens, and members hunted, fished, and made crafts. As in Africa, women dominated marketing activities within the informal economy, providing whites with most of their fresh foods. Many whites felt slaves' monopoly on foodstuffs held them to "ransom" to bondspeople's economic whims.[34] White dependence on slaves for much of their sustenance created power struggles over the degrees of autonomy that the informal economy provided to slaves. Thus, contrary to earlier interpretations that claimed slaves were helpless and dependent on whites, Betty Wood illustrates how cultural practices facilitated considerable slave self-sufficiency and economical independence, while making many whites quite dependent on slaves.

ENSLAVED CHILDREN AND CULTURAL CONTINUITY THROUGH THE GENERATIONS

Just as historians' analyses descended back in time, from the antebellum to the colonial period, to consider the origins of mature slave culture, some historians have shifted from studying adults to children. The antebellum American South is one of the few New World slave societies where a slave population sustained itself through natural reproduction. Most slave societies, and some societies with slaves, had to rely on the "massive importation of Africans to maintain their populations." Enslaved both at birth and by birth, more than half all of nineteenth-century slaves were under the age of 20 and were born in America, not Africa. Despite these interesting and provocative statistics historians have largely ignored the lives of enslaved children and how cultural traditions were passed down through the generations. In the early 1970s historians began including some discussion of slave children in their studies of antebellum bondage. Historians like Willie Lee Rose, John Blassingame, Leslie Howard Owens, Brenda Stevens, and Thomas Webber have considered children within their broader analyses and Herbert Gutman examined them within the context of the family.[35]

A focused examination did not appear until 1995, with Wilma King's *Stolen Childhood: Slave Youth in Nineteenth-Century America*. *Stolen Childhood* considers issues of childbirth, familial dynamics, work patterns, play, religious instruction, literacy, and the transition from slavery to freedom. Enslaved children, argues King, "had virtually no childhood because they entered the work place early and were more readily subjected to arbitrary plantation authority, punishments, and separations." Using prose evocative of Elkins, King compared slave children's lives to those of children in war zones, which "robbed many youngsters of a safe and nurturing childhood." Children were often subjected to the same physical, emotional, and psychological abuses as adults, and if they were not subjected to harsh punishment or sexual exploitation they either witnessed or learned about it. Family members provided guidance and support systems that enabled children to survive their oppression.[36] Nevertheless, slavery forced children to grow up prematurely and face the same brutalities as adult slaves.

Marie Jenkins Schwartz's *Born in Bondage: Growing up Enslaved in the Antebellum South* provides a significantly different interpretation of childhood slavery. *Born in Bondage* examines how children "endured the conditions associated with bondage. Because children could not fend for themselves, particularly at young ages, this book focuses on the adults responsible for children, as well as children themselves and their interactions with one another." Schwartz highlights the resiliency of enslaved children and how adults helped them navigate the tortuous maze of inhumanity that sought to rob them of their childhood.[37]

Both *Stolen Childhood* and *Born in Bondage* argue that the lives of enslaved children cannot be comprehended by separating them from the adult world in which they lived. As both children and slaves they were subjected to dual, sometime contradictory, sets of authority—that of their owners and that of their parent. King and Jenkins reveal that these twin sources of authorities bombarded slave children with what must have been perceived as a disorderly aria of contradictory instructions that, despite their parents' best intentions, conceivably exacerbated anxiety in their young lives.

Importantly, both works detail how African and Western life skills and cultural practices that could make slavery more bearable were passed from generation to generation. Parents taught their children cultural traditions, like hunting, fishing, sewing, gardening, cooking, cleaning, childrearing, swimming, and occupational skills, such as domestic work, folk medicine and midwifery, carpentry, and blacksmithing. Literate parents taught their children to read and write. Oral traditions kept family customs and histories alive, enabling some to recount how their grandparents were enslaved in Africa, cargoed across the Atlantic, and sold in America. Folktales provided children with valuable life lessons, such as avoiding white wrath, tricking white authority figures, and how to avoid becoming the victim of someone else's pranks.

Despite the tremendous contributions of King and Schwartz, considerable research on enslaved children is still required. Sources suggest that at least one-fourth of all slaves brought to what became the United States were children under the age of 14. Surprisingly, no monographs devote considerable attention to the experiences of these African-born children. Just as historians examined colonial adults to better appreciate the experiences of antebellum adults so too should we examine colonial slave children. A study of African-born children would undoubtedly advance our understanding of the acculturation process. The experiences of slaves taken from Africa while children, like Venture Smith, Olaudah Equiano, Zamba, James Albert Ukawsa Gronniosaw, John Jea, Phillis Wheatley, Joseph Wright, Samuel Ajayi Crowther, and Ottaba Cuguano, suggest that age—as much as time and place—influenced how quickly and thoroughly many "saltwater slaves" Westernized.[38]

THE AFRICAN DIASPORA IN
THE ATLANTIC WORLD

Since the 1980s historians of Africa, the Atlantic world, and the African diaspora have made extremely important contributions to our understanding of slave culture throughout the Atlantic world, especially in Latin America and the Caribbean and, increasingly, in the American South. Most important, Africanists in particular have helped sharpen our appreciation of slaves' African heritage while considering them as part of a broad diaspora. In 1981, John Thornton asserted: "Scholars of the United States interested in the African background of American history have usually sought general information about African culture by reading accounts of modern anthropologists and ethnologists, which are not always helpful for understanding specific historical situations."[39] Scholars of the American slave experience are increasingly drawing from the scholarship—and adopting the theoretical models of—scholars of African, the African diaspora, and Atlantic world history.

In 1968, Philip Curtin noted that "The recent trend towards world-historical perspective and away from parochial national history also calls for a new approach to the broader patterns of Atlantic history."[40] While studies of southern slavery and slave culture have traditionally not drawn extensively on scholarship beyond the South's geographic boundaries, historians of Africa, the Atlantic world, and the African diaspora have exchanged concepts, theories, and models so freely that it is often difficult to remember or distinguish to which sub-discipline a historian belongs. John Thornton is perhaps the quintessential example of this cross-fertilization. Trained as a historian of early modern West-Central Africa, or the Congo-Angola region, his scholarship has considered historical events throughout the Atlantic world.

Thornton's 1992 study, *Africa and Africans in the Making of the Atlantic World, 1400–1680* traces the movement of Africans and their culture to the Americas. Seminal because it is the first major work on slave culture to shift its emphasis from the Americas to Africa, Thornton wrote against a prevailing grain that traditionally viewed the transmission of African culture from the West. Instead, Thornton examined the creation of African-influenced cultures from the perspective of Africa, documenting the flow of traditions out of Africa, rather than tracing them back to Africa. This approach was widely applauded by Americanists and Africanists. Gwendolyn Midlo Hall asserted that this framework "will help us move away from Eurocentric interpretations of American culture, which have significantly narrowed our vision during the past two decades." Similarly Paul Lovejoy said: "Thornton's expertise in African history enables him to achieve a level of analysis that makes more sense to me than the speculations of most of the scholarship that has emanated from the specialists of slavery in the Americas."[41]

In *Africa and Africans in the Making of the Atlantic World*, Thornton avows that much of what was thought to have been constructed in the Americas was created in Africa. Much of the analysis for *Africa and Africans in the Making of the Atlantic World* was based on years of primary research, not twentieth-century anthropology, enabling him to engage several debates on slave culture. He convincingly argues against many of Sidney Mintz and Richard Price's assertions, especially claims that Africans were too diverse and slaves too brutalized and deracinated to perpetuate their African heritage, and that similarities between African and slave culture were the result of parallel developments in similar tropical climates. Thornton extends Melville Herskovits's analysis pertaining to common African cultural beliefs and practices and persuasively argues that Africans from the Senegambia to West-Central Africa shared many similar culture practices and beliefs, saying, "at most we have three truly culturally divers areas, and the seven subgroups [within these regions] are themselves often quite homogeneous." He contends that the Atlantic slave trade did not "randomize" slaves to the extent that Mintz and Price stressed through a process called "coasting," in which slave ships purchased slaves at several anchorages along the African coast and sold them in many points in the Americas. Rather, Thornton explains: "Slave ships drew their entire cargo from only one or perhaps two ports in Africa and unloaded them in large lots of as many as 200–1,000 in their new Atlantic homes."[42]

Other scholars agree. Though not necessarily engaging the historiographical debate on coasting and randomization, the scholarship of Gwendolyn Midlo Hall, James Sweet, Daniel Littlefield, Herbert Klien, Robin Law, Walter Rodney, Boubacar Barry, Joseph Miller, James Searing, and others suggests that both have been exaggerated. Shipping records, like those of the Royal African Company of England found on *The Trans-Atlantic Slave Trade: A Database on CD-ROM*, document how European slave traders in Africa concentrated enslaved Africans from a given region in slave castles or barracoons, providing slave ship captains with enough humans from mostly the same region to fill a slave ship's hold, and most slaves were sold at one New World port. Such records are bolstered by primary sources that suggest, and sometimes conclusively indicate, slaves' origins. Slave narratives and plantation records indicate that a significant number of slaves designated the origins or ethnicity of themselves and others.[43]

Scholars also must consider other evidence such as linguistics, scarification patterns, filed teeth, slaveholders' ethnic preferences, and discrete cultural practices in trying to locate the sometimes slippery notion of "ethnic identity." In *Exchanging our Country Marks: The Transformations of African Identities in the Colonial and Antebellum South* Michael A. Gomez examines the evolution of identities among slaves. Primarily trained as an African historian, Gomez considers the retention of African culture and identities in the American South up to the 1830s, when a transition occurred "consistent with the demographic evidence, that delineates the demise of a preponderate African social matrix and the rise of an African American one in its place." While language was often the most obvious sign of one's ethnicity, as the title suggests, "country marks," or facial scarification patterns, were often key indicators. Gomez argues that African ethnicities persisted in the Americas after African-born people became the minority in the slave population and even after they adopted a black racial identity in contrast to the white racial identity of their enslavers. *Exchanging our Country Marks* is also significant because it challenges the notion that American slaves were less successful in retaining African culture than bondspeople in the Caribbean or Latin America.[44]

Along similar lines—and perfectly in keeping with the new, broader, more temporally, geographic, and theoretically robust work of Africanists—Gwendolyn Midlo Hall believes slaves could recreate language and social communities. In *Slavery and African Ethnicities in the Americas: Restoring the Links* she traces how work-related skills and cultural practices of African ethnic groups were recreated in the New World. "Specific groups of Africans made major contributions to the formation of the new cultures developing throughout the Americas," wrote Hall. "The diverse peoples who met and mingled in the Americas all made major contributions to its economy, culture, esthetics, language, and survival skills." Importantly, Hall explains: "Creolization was not the process of Africans melting into a European pot." She stresses that creolization often occurred as slaves blended various African traditions and it affected white culture. The author's research is impressive, including manuscript collections in Spain, France, and Louisiana, and relied heavily on the twenty-some years' research dedicated to the topic of slave culture, and which she provides free to the public on her *Louisiana Slave Database, 1791–1820.*[45]

Others historians consider how members of certain ethnic groups were taken to specific places in America. Lorena Walsh's *From Calabar to Carter's Grove: A History of a Virginia Slave Community* provides a historical interpretation for colonial Williamsburg's eighteenth-century slave quarter at Carter's Grove and illustrates how historians can provide depth to generalized histories of slaves by reconstructing late seventeenth- and early eighteenth-century group experiences.[46] Walsh explains that existing records make it virtually impossible to recreate the lives of enslaved individuals linked to Carter's Grove and, instead, traces the history of a slave community owned by the extended Burwell family in tidewater Virginia. Using shipping records and West African naming patterns Walsh asserts that much of the initial slave population was taken from the Senegambia. She then illustrates how the Burwell slaves were drawn from ever further south, with a considerable number being shipped from either Old or New Calabar situated on the Niger River Delta. Walsh identified work skills and cultural beliefs that were probably conveyed to colonial Virginia. She theorizes that just as African knowledge significantly contributed to "the development of rice culture in the Carolinas" it may have contributed to the development of the Chesapeake's tobacco culture.[47]

CONCLUSION AND FUTURE DIRECTION
OF ANALYSIS

Historians, whether Americanists or Africanists, have increasingly begun their studies of the slave experience in Africa and treated slaves not as peoples cut off from their cultural heritage, but members of a diaspora that sustained and disseminated their cultural heritage throughout the Atlantic and Indian oceans. In this vein, the scholarship of the African diaspora and Atlantic world suggest the framework of future studies of the southern slave experience for the next decade or so. Atlantic world and African diaspora approaches demonstrate that comprehension of the southern slave experience must be built on the foundation of an understanding of Africa and can be heightened through the analysis of slave culture elsewhere in the Americas, as well as Europe and the Indian Ocean.

In "Defining and studying the Modern African Diaspora" Colin Palmer states that studies of the "African diaspora, should in my opinion, begin with the study of Africa. The African continent—the ancestral homeland—must be central to any informed analysis and understanding of the dispersal of its peoples." Palmer stresses that scholars "arguably" should not define themselves as "diaspora specialists" if they have a narrow geographic focus. Rather, they must engage broad, interdisciplinary approaches to studying the African diaspora on several continents.[48] Others have similarly emphasized the need to begin the analysis of slave culture in Africa. In "The African Diaspora: Revisionist Interpretations of Ethnicity, Culture and Religion under Slavery," Paul Lovejoy explained how projecting African history into the diaspora establishes "concrete links with the homeland."

Lovejoy states that this illustrates "how slaves could create a world that was largely autonomous from white, European society" by documenting African cultural continuity in the New World diaspora. Consequently, historians can escape the "Eurocentrism and American-centrism" that have dominated the analysis of slave life.[49] The approaches Palmer and Lovejoy stress obviously require considerable knowledge that encompasses a broad expanse of time and space to include Africa, the Atlantic islands, the New World, Europe, and the Indian Ocean and events dating from medieval African history through 1888, when slavery was abolished in Brazil.[50] By situating American slavery in the context of the Atlantic world and treating it as part of the African diaspora we not only continue to expand our understanding of southern slave life but sidestep the interpretive limitations of "southern exceptionalism" by appreciating the similarities of the African slave experience throughout the world.

NOTES

1. Peter Kolchin, *American Slavery, 1619–1877* (New York, 1993), 134.
2. William C. Whit, "Soul Food as Cultural Creation," in Anne L. Bower (ed.), *African American Foodways* (Urbana, Ill., 2007), 45. Philip Curtin provides excellent analysis of British perceptions of savagery, barbarity, and culture and the subjectivity with which the British applied these concepts to Africans. Philip D. Curtin, *The Image of Africa: British Ideas and Action, 1780–1850*, 2 vols. (Madison, 1964).
3. For historiography of slavery, see Mark M. Smith, *Debating Slavery: Economy and Society in the Antebellum American South* (Cambridge, 1998).
4. Gilberto Freyre, *The Masters and the Slaves: A Study of the Development of Brazilian Civilization* (1933; New York, 1946), 279, 287, 465–6. In the late nineteenth and early twentieth century scholars such as W. E. B. Du Bois and Carter G. Woodson considered slavery; unfortunately, much of their scholarship did not gain considerable traction among white historians.
5. U. B. Phillips, *American Negro Slavery: A Survey of the Supply, Employment and Control of Negro Labor as Determined by the Plantation Regime* (Baton Rouge, La., 1966), 45, U. B. Phillips, *Life and Labor in the Old South* (Boston, 1929), 194, 195, 198.
6. E. Franklin Frazier's *The Negro Family in the United States* (Chicago, 1939), 15; E. Franklin Frazier, *The Free Negro Family: A Study of Family Origins before the Civil War* (Nashville, 1932).
7. United States Department of Labor, *The Negro Family: The Case for National Action* (Washington, DC, 1965); Thomas F. Pettigrew, *A Profile of the Negro American* (Princeton, 1964).
8. Kenneth M. Stamp, *The Peculiar Institution: Slavery in the Ante-Bellum South* (New York, 1956), pp. viii, 340, 362.
9. George P. Rawick (ed.), *The American Slave: A Composite Autobiography*, 18 vols. (Westport: Conn., 1972). The African-American protest movement in the 1950s and 1960s and the neo-abolitionist sentiments of some historians also precipitated a growing interest in

slavery and the belief that slaves' perceptions were at least as important as those of their owners. C. Vann Woodward, "*The American Slave: A Composite Autobiography* by George P. Rawick," *American Historical Review*, 79 (2) (April 1974): 471; Norman R. Yetman, "Ex-Slave Interviews and the Historiography of Slavery," *American Quarterly*, 36 (2) (Summer 1984): 190.

10. B. A. Botkin (ed.), *Lay my Burden Down: A Folk History of Slavery* (Chicago, 1945), Phillips, *Life and Labor in the Old South*, 219. C. Vann Woodward concluded that care in using the narratives was required, but the "necessary precautions, however, are no more elaborate or burdensome than those required by any other types of sources he [a historian] is accustomed to use. They are certainly not great enough to justify continued neglect of this valuable evidence on black history in America." Vann Woodward, "*The American Slave*," 480, Yetman, "Ex-Slave Interviews." Though Phillips was referring to nineteenth-century slave narratives, according to C. Vann Woodward, his comments apparently prejudiced all narratives. Vann Woodward, "*The American Slave*," 471.

11. Vann Woodward, "*The American Slave*," 480, Yetman, "Ex-Slave Interviews," 193–4.

12. John W. Blassingame, *The Slave Community: Plantation Life in the Antebellum South, Revised and Enlarged Edition* (1972; Oxford, 1979).

13. Al-Tony Gilmore (ed.), *Revisiting Blassingame's The Slave Community: The Scholars Respond* (Westport, Conn., 1978); Kenneth Wiggins Porter, "Review: *The Slave Community: Plantation Life in the Antebellum South*, by John W. Blassingame," *Journal of Southern History*, 39 (2) (May 1973): 293–4, James M. McPherson, "Review: *The Slave Community: Plantation Life in the Antebellum South*, by John W. Blassingame," *Journal of Social Science*, 7 (2) (Winter 1974): 208–11; William D. Pierson, "Review: *Revisiting Blassingame's The Slave Community: The Scholars Respond* by Al-Tony Gilmore," *Journal of American History*, 66 (1) (June 1979): 148–9.

14. Fogel and Engerman and Gutman appeared on *The Today Show*. Mary Frances Berry, "The Slave Community: A Review of the Reviews," in Al-Tony Gilmore (ed.), *Revisiting Blassingame's The Slave Community: The Scholars Respond* (Westport, Conn., 1978), 3.

15. Eugene D. Genovese, *Roll, Jordan, Roll: The World the Slaves Made* (New York, 1974).

16. Ibid. 10, 181, 540, 543.

17. Lawrence W. Levine, *Black Culture and Black Consciousness: Afro-American Folk Thought from Slavery to Freedom* (Oxford, 1977), pp. ix, 30. Peter Kolchin argued that the strength and cohesion of the slave community were not as strong and pervasive as historians like Rawick, Blassingame, and Levine suggest. Peter Kolchin, "Reevaluating the Antebellum Slave Community: A Comparative Perspective," *Journal of American History*, 70 (December 1983); Kolchin, *American Slavery*.

18. Charles Joyner, *Down by the Riverside: A South Carolina Slave Community* (Urbana, Ill., 1984).

19. Ira Berlin, "Time, Space, and Evolution of Afro-America Society in British Mainland North America," *American Historical Review*, 85 (1980): 44–78, esp. 44.

20. Michael A. Gomez, *Exchanging our Country Marks: The Transformation of African Identities in the Colonial and Antebellum South* (Chapel Hill, NC, 1998), 194–5.

21. Robin Blackburn, *The Making of New World Slavery: From the Baroque to the Modern, 1492–1800* (New York, 1997); Richard S. Dunn, *Sugar and Slaves: The Rise of the Plantation Class in the English West Indies, 1624–1713* (Chapel Hill, NC, 1972); David Eltis, *The Rise of African Slavery in the Americas* (Cambridge, 2000); S. Max Edelson,

Plantation Enterprise in Colonial South Carolina (Boston, 2006); Stewart B. Schwart (ed.), *Tropical Babylons: Sugar and the Making of the Atlantic World, 1450–1680* (Chapel Hill, NC, 2004); Eric Williams, *Capitalism and Slavery* (1944; Chapel Hill, NC, 1994).

22. Thad W. Tate, "Review: The Neglected First Half of American Slavery," *Reviews in American History*, 3 (1) (March 1975): 59–65.

23. Benjamin Quarles, "Reviewed: *Black Majority: Negroes in Colonial South Carolina from 1670 through the Stono Rebellion* by Peter Wood," *Journal of Negro History*, 60 (2) (April 1975): 332.

24. Judith A. Carney, *Black Rice: The African Origins of Rice Cultivation in the Americas* (Cambridge, Mass., 2001), 2; Gwendolyn Midlo Hall, *Africans in Colonial Louisiana: The Development of Afro-Creole Culture in the Eighteenth Century* (Baton Rouge, La., 1992); Daniel C. Littlefield, *Rice and Slaves: Ethnicity and the Slave Trade in Colonial South Carolina* (Chicago, 1991); Peter H. Wood, *Black Majority: Negroes in Colonial South Carolina from 1670 through the Stono Rebellion* (New York, 1972).

25. Hall, *Africans in Colonial Louisiana*, 159, 161, 188. See also Jane Landers, *Black Society in Spanish Florida* (Urbana, Ill., 1999).

26. Philip D. Morgan, *Slave Counterpoint: Black Culture in the Eighteenth-Century Chesapeake and Lowcountry* (Chapel Hill, NC, 1998), p. xxii.

27. Berlin, "Time, Space, and Evolution," 44; Ira Berlin, *Many Thousands Gone: The First Two Centuries of Slavery in North America* (Cambridge, Mass., 1998).

28. Robin Law and Kristin Mann, "West Africa in the Atlantic Community: The Case of the Slave Coast," *William and Mary Quarterly*, 3rd ser., 56 (2) (April 1999): 310.

29. Linda M. Heywood and John K. Thornton, *Central Africans, Atlantic Creoles, and the Foundation of the Americas, 1585–1660* (Cambridge, Mass., 2007).

30. Deborah Gray White, *Ar'n't I a Woman? Female Slaves in the Plantation South* (New York, 1985; 1999), 4, 17–25, esp. 23, David Barry Gaspar and Darlene Clark Hine, *More than Chattel: Black Women and Slavery in the Americas* (Bloomington, Ind., 1996), p. ix; Leslie A. Schwalm, "Review: *More than Chattel: Black Women and Slavery in the Americas* by David Barry Gaspar; Darlene Clark Hine," *Journal of Social History*, 31 (2) (Winter 1997): 440.

31. Gaspar and Hine, *More than Chattel*.

32. Jennifer L. Morgan, *Laboring Women: Reproduction and Gender in New World Slavery* (Philadelphia, 2004), 2–3. Morgan's analysis of race, gender, and slavery reads well with Kathleen M. Brown, *Goodwives, Nasty Wenches, & Anxious Patriarch: Gender, Race, and Power in Colonial Virginia* (Chapel Hill, NC, 1996).

33. Betty Wood, *Women's Work, Men's Work: The Informal Economies of Lowcountry Georgia* (Athens, Ga., 1995).

34. Ibid. 142.

35. Wilma King, *Stolen Childhood: Slave Youth in Nineteenth-Century America* (Bloomington, Ind., 1995), p. xvii.

36. Ibid., pp. xx–xxi, 13, 97, 129. Also see Thomas L. Webber, *Deep Like the Rivers: Education in the Slave Quarter Community, 1831–1865* (New York, 1980).

37. Marie Jenkins Schwartz, *Born in Bondage: Growing up Enslaved in the Antebellum South* (Cambridge, Mass., 2001), 14.

38. Stephanie Smallwood, *Saltwater Slavery: A Middle Passage from Africa to American Diaspora* (Cambridge, Mass., 2007), 164; David Eltis, Stephen D. Berendt, David

Richardson, and Herbert S. Klein, *The Trans-Atlantic Slave Trade: A Database on CD-ROM* (Cambridge, 1999).

39. John K. Thornton, "African Dimensions of the Stono Rebellion," *American Historical Review*, 96 (4) (October 1991): 1101–2.

40. Philip D. Curtin, "Epidemiology and the Slave Trade," *Political Science Quarterly*, 83 (2) (June 1968): 190.

41. Gwendolyn Midlo Hall, "Review: *Africa and Africans in the Making of the Atlantic World, 1400–1680*, by John Thornton," *Journal of American History*, 80 (3) (December 1993): 1047; Paul E. Lovejoy, "Review: *Africa and Africans in the Making of the Atlantic World, 1400–1680*, by John Thornton," *Journal of Interdisciplinary History*, 26 (1) (Summer 1995): 129; Ira Berlin, "Review: *Africa and Africans in the Making of the Atlantic World, 1400–1680*, by John Thornton," *William and Mary Quarterly*, 3rd ser., 51 (3) (July 1994): 544–7.

42. Thornton, *Africa and Africans in the Making of the Atlantic World*, 191–4, 209–10.

43. Eltis et al., *The Trans-Atlantic Slave Trade*.

44. Michael A. Gomez, *Exchanging our Country Marks: The Transformations of African Identities in the Colonial and Antebellum South* (Chapel Hill, NC, 1998).

45. Gwendolyn Midlo Hall, *Slavery and African Ethnicities in the Americas: Restoring the Links* (Chapel Hill, NC, Press), pp. xv–xvi; 166; www.ibiblio.org/laslave

46. Lorena S. Walsh, *From Calabar to Carter's Grove: A History of a Virginia Slave Community* (Charlottesville, Va., 1997), pp. xvii, 4–5.

47. Walsh speculates that after tobacco was introduced into Africa in the early seventeenth century knowledge of its production was probably carried back to the Americas by slaves. Walsh, *From Calabar to Carter's Grove*, 60; 61; 63–5. See also Douglas B. Chambers, *Murder at Montpelier: Igbo Africans in Virginia* (Jackson, Mo., 2005). Chambers adds a layer of nuance to the "Atlantic creole" model by documenting how a considerable number of African-born slaves arrived in Virginia with little or no previous exposure to European influences.

48. Colin Palmer, "Defining and Studying the Modern African Diaspora," *Journal of Negro History*, 85 (1/2) (Winter–Spring 2000), 30; 31.

49. Paul E. Lovejoy, "The African Diaspora: Revisionist Interpretations of Ethnicity, Culture and Religion under Slavery," *Studies in the World History of Slavery, Abolition and Emancipation*, 2 (1) (1997); also see 21 January 2002, http://www.2.h-net.msu.edu/~slavery/essays/esy9701love.html 4–5.

50. Linda Heywood and James Sweet provide examples of the approaches and methods that will be increasingly employed to study southern slave culture. Linda M. Heywood (ed.), *Central Africans and Cultural Transformations in the American Diaspora* (Cambridge, 2002); James H. Sweet, *Recreating Africa: Culture, Kinship, and Religion in the African-Portuguese World, 1441–1770* (Chapel Hill, NC, 2003).

SELECT BIBLIOGRAPHY

BERLIN, IRA. *Many Thousands Gone: The First Two Centuries of Slavery in North America.* Cambridge, Mass.: Harvard University Press, 1998).

CARNEY, JUDITH A. *Black Rice: The African Origins of Rice Cultivation in the Americas.* Cambridge, Mass.: Harvard University Press, 2001.

GENOVESE, EUGENE D. *Roll, Jordan, Roll: The World the Slaves Made*. New York: Vintage, 1974.

GOMEZ, MICHAEL A. *Exchanging our Country Marks: The Transformations of African Identities in the Colonial and Antebellum South*. Chapel Hill, NC: University of North Carolina Press, 1998.

HALL, GWENDOLYN MIDLO. *Africans in Colonial Louisiana: The Development of Afro-Creole Culture in the Eighteenth Century*. Baton Rouge, La.: Louisiana State University Press, 1992.

—— *Slavery and African Ethnicities in the Americas: Restoring the Links*. Chapel Hill, NC: University of North Carolina Press.

HEYWOOD, LINDA M., and JOHN K. THORNTON. *Central Africans, Atlantic Creoles, and the Foundation of the Americas, 1585–1660*. Cambridge: Cambridge University Press, 2007.

JOYNER, CHARLES. *Down by the Riverside: A South Carolina Slave Community*. Urbana, Ill.: University of Illinois Press, 1984.

KING, WILMA. *Stolen Childhood: Slave Youth in Nineteenth-Century America*. Bloomington, Ind.: Indiana University Press, 1995.

LEVINE, LAWRENCE W. *Black Culture and Black Consciousness: Afro-American Folk Thought from Slavery to Freedom*. Oxford: Oxford University Press, 1977.

LITTLEFIELD, DANIEL C. *Rice and Slaves: Ethnicity and the Slave Trade in Colonial South Carolina*. Chicago: University of Illinois Press, 1991.

MORGAN, JENNIFER L. *Laboring Women: Reproduction and Gender in New World Slavery*. Philadelphia: University of Pennsylvania Press, 2004.

MORGAN, PHILIP D. *Slave Counterpoint: Black Culture in the Eighteenth-Century Chesapeake and Lowcountry*. Chapel Hill, NC: University of North Carolina Press, 1998.

SCHWARTZ, MARIE JENKINS. *Born in Bondage: Growing up Enslaved in the Antebellum South*. Cambridge, Mass.: Harvard University Press, 2001.

THORNTON, JOHN K. *Africa and Africans in the Making of the Atlantic World, 1400–1680*. Cambridge: Cambridge University Press, 1992.

WHITE, DEBORAH GRAY. *Ar'n't I a Woman? Female Slaves in the Plantation South*. 1985; New York: W. W. Norton, 1999.

WOOD, BETTY. *Women's Work, Men's Work: The Informal Economies of Lowcountry Georgia*. Athens, Ga.: University of Georgia Press, 1995.

WOOD, PETER H. *Black Majority: Negroes in Colonial South Carolina from 1670 through the Stono Rebellion*. New York: Alfred A. Knopf, 1974.

....

CHAPTER 22

THE ECONOMICS
OF SLAVERY

....

PETER COCLANIS

WRITING on the economics of slavery is in some ways an impossibly difficult task, for the subject's limits and bounds are viewed by many as virtually coterminous with those of slavery itself. Indeed, such an assignment has become increasingly difficult over time, as economists incorporate more and more areas of human experience into their interpretative clutches. Whereas at one time almost everyone conceded the material realm to economics, but cordoned off spiritual concerns, economists now make claims on such matters as well, bringing the emotions, the psyche, and even the soul under the discipline's dominion. It is thus a long way from the ancient Greeks, whose original sense of economics concerned the rules, customs, and laws (*nomos*) of the house or household (*oikos*), to Nobelist Gary Becker, for whom the decision to bear children is interpretatively akin to the decision to purchase a refrigerator or car, to more recent writers who have written on the economics of attention, interpreted the rise of religion and the origin of fear in economic terms, and linked behavioral expressions ranging from sexual orientation to laughter to cruelty to economic variables.

This said, here we shall focus on issues of traditional concern to economic historians of slavery, to wit: the origins of and motivations/rationales for slavery; pattern and variation in the institution both across space and over time; questions relating to slavery's profitability; the developmental effects of slavery; and the reasons for its demise. One other delimiting qualification, relating to purview, should also be kept in mind. Slavery in some form and in some place has been with us from antiquity to the present day.[1] This essay will focus on slavery in the

Western hemisphere, and, only then, on slavery in societies established therein by European colonizers beginning in the late fifteenth century. Even so, our remit is huge, for the system(s) of slavery in the Western hemisphere during that period drew not only Europe and Africa but also Asia into their powerful embrace.

Although there are several plausible and by no means mutually exclusive explanations for the origins of slavery in the areas being treated here, all of them from today's perspective are explicable through recourse to standard bourgeois economic logic. That is to say, we can safely proceed under the assumption that both slaveholders and those authorizing and legitimizing slavery acted, wittingly or unwittingly, self-consciously or unselfconsciously, in ways consistent with what we would today call economic rationality, most notably, utility-maximizing decision-making criteria. Before we go any further, let me wave a few cautionary flags regarding the interpretative thicket we are about to enter. Scholars can and in fact have disagreed, sometimes sharply, over how to classify in economic terms slavery in the societies organized by Europeans in the Western hemisphere. To simplify a number of complex, often arcane academic debates, the key issues revolve around the relationship between slavery and the system(s) of slavery in such areas, on the one hand, and capitalism, on the other.[2] Complicating this inherently difficult question is a host of considerations: There are various ways to approach, let alone attempt to define capitalism. The criteria employed to ascertain its existence vary enormously from interpretative tradition to interpretative tradition, indeed, from scholar to scholar. Numerous European nation-states organized societies in the Western hemisphere wherein slaves played important roles, and these European nation-states and their geopolitical offspring in the Western hemisphere all followed their own trajectories at least to some degree, leading to considerable variation—temporal and spatial—in slavery both *across* colonial/national regimes and *within* the same (within English/British areas, within Spanish or French or Dutch areas, etc.).

Regardless of epistemological predilections, preferred evaluative criteria, or position on slavery and capitalism, the most convincing scholarly explanations of slavery's origins all associate it in one way or another with available resources or factor endowments in the "New World" during the period of initial colonization and settlement.[3] More specifically, they focus on considerations such as the human–land ratio, "open resources," or free land, and the problem these considerations posed to those interested in, if not fixed on, profitable economic exploitation. Simply put, it appeared difficult, even impossible, in certain places at certain points in time for economically rational Europeans to operate efficiently enough at sufficient scale to accrue impressive profits in the absence of institutional mechanisms that functioned to hold down wages and keep an adequate number of laborers from taking advantage of such "open resources," particularly land, by either moving away or setting up for themselves. In other words, slavery in a sense represented the sanctioning and legitimization by the state of a categorical form of property rights in human beings in order to render profitable exploitation possible, thereby facilitating the accumulation process in otherwise unfavorable labor-market conditions.[4]

Of course, slavery—a labor system wherein workers are "unfree" in legal terms, owned by others, and have little or no enforceable claim either to their progeny or to the principal means of production—was not the only way to solve the labor problems mentioned above. Other "unfree" forms of labor organization were possible, and some were in fact tried—indentured servitude, temporary slavery, tribute or corvée labor, convict labor, etc.—with varying degrees of success. Europeans obviously had had long experience as well with another form of labor organization, serfdom, whereby the labor force is tied to a specific piece of land, which shared some features with slavery. Of such options, however, *chattel* slavery (whereby slaves were defined legally as personalty and thus as moveable property) soon came to be seen as the most effective means of solving the labor problems outlined above, and was to prove the most pervasive and enduring option in areas where some form of "unfree labor" made economic sense.

What constituted economic sense in slavery times? Then, as now, the chance for profits, more than anything else. Generally speaking, slavery became deeply entrenched in those parts of the Western hemisphere where profit possibilities were sufficiently large as to justify the time, cost, and trouble of recruiting, retaining, and defending—whether in a constabulatory or an ideological sense—a bound labor force. A few mining areas could justify such assessments, but the vast majority of places dominated by slavery and slave labor were regions whose economies were based largely on the production, mostly for export, of a limited range of highly profitable agricultural staples.

Of these staples, sugar constituted the bellwether for most of the period treated in this essay, in so doing, making the market for slave labor, as it were.[5] Whether or not other parts of the Western hemisphere came to depend on slave labor was largely determined, that is to say, by the chance that the area in question early on could utilize such labor at least as profitably as it—or, more formally, each marginal unit of which—could be used in the principal sugar-producing regions in Brazil or the Caribbean. The power of sugar in informing the market for slaves/slavery in the Western hemisphere was especially great before a second market maker, cotton, began its rapid ascent in the nineteenth century.

Not surprisingly, such stringent conditions—the imputed opportunity costs of deploying slaves in activities other than sugar or cotton—set sharp limits on the appeal and distribution of slave labor in the hemisphere, limits that were always subject as well to additional conditioning factors, most notably, the availability and price of alternative forms of labor, certain "lock-in" mechanisms associated with early path-dependent/path-influenced decisions regarding labor organization, and, in a much more limited way relatively late in the game, to moral qualms about (or "psychic costs" associated with) holding slaves. As a result, although we find slaves (sometimes in sizeable numbers) in most societies organized originally by Europeans in the Western hemisphere, slave labor came to structure entire societies only in parts of the hemisphere: In the circum-Caribbean especially, but also in parts of Brazil and in the southern region of what came to be known after the American Revolution as the United States. This broader area has usefully been labeled the "extended Caribbean" by one influential scholar—Immanuel Wallerstein—and in forcing us, when thinking about slavery in the Western hemisphere, to recalibrate our metageographies so as better to reflect the position of the Caribbean (and Brazil), the formulation makes a good deal of sense.[6]

Explaining the composition, particularly the *racial* composition of the slave labor forces in various part of the Western hemisphere is another thorny issue, one that has pricked many that have deigned to touch it. We cannot do complete justice to an issue of such complexity here, so it must suffice to say that, although a world of possibilities was possible—scholars of race such as Theodore Allen and Noel Ignatiev have usefully reminded us that some whites plausibly could have been enslaved, especially in the fifteenth, sixteenth, and seventeenth centuries—slavery in the Western hemisphere in the period between the early sixteenth century and the late nineteenth century was confined for all practical purposes to peoples classified either as Native Americans or African/African-American blacks. Of these two groups, blacks came to constitute the vast majority, except in certain mining areas in Spanish America.

But why? A number of reasons have been offered: European racism and notions regarding racial/ethnic/religious hierarchies; the greater experience of African blacks with sedentary agriculture, experience made manifest (and attractive) at times in potentially appropriable knowledge systems and technology; Europeans' prior experience with African slaves in the Atlantic islands off Africa (the Canaries and Madeiras especially) and in Europe itself from the mid-fifteenth century on; the greater difficulty of recruiting/retaining sufficient numbers of Native Americans; the greater elasticity of supply of black Africans; the greater relative resistance of black Africans to various Old World diseases (particularly mosquito-borne diseases) that became major epidemiological threats in many parts of the Americas.[7]

All of these reasons have merit, but, for my money, the first—European racism/ethnocentrism—and the latter two weighed most heavily. First of all, if and when the decision to utilize slave labor was made, it is difficult to believe that during the so-called early modern period the Europeans making such decisions would not have preferred *ceteris paribus* to enslave non-Europeans, non-Christians, etc. And all other things were *not* equal, of course. Indeed, if we approach supply elasticity elastically, so to speak, so as to incorporate not only relative supply responses to changing prices, but also total capacity and "spare" capacity, it is readily apparent that in general the supply response was more robust and more predictable in the African/African-American slave trade than in the Native American slave trade, which was at once less organized, more erratic, and more subject to disruption. Coupled with the partial immunities many Africans/African-Americans had to both malaria and yellow fever—deadly killers and debilitators during slavery times—it made greater economic sense for those involved in slave markets as either buyers or sellers to organize said markets around the purchase and sale of Africans/African-Americans rather than around Native Americans, whose numbers in the Americas dropped drastically after and in large part because of the so-called Columbian exchange.[8]

If slave markets were organized by and large around the buying and selling of Africans/African-Americans, it seems both reasonable and, in fact, necessary next to consider where the human chattel being bought and sold lived (and died), and in what numbers. With this in mind, let us move on to what might be labeled geo-historical/demographic concerns, more specifically, the spatial and temporal patterns informing the history of slavery in the Americas.

Such concerns present something of a conundrum, if not "a riddle wrapped in a mystery inside an enigma," as Winston Churchill famously said of Russia. Why? To cut to the chase: As stated above, sugar and slaves were inextricably linked in the Western hemisphere. The vast majority of the 10.5–12.5 million slaves brought to the Western hemisphere between c.1500 and the late nineteenth century worked either in the cane fields themselves or in sugar-producing areas.[9] Relatively speaking, much smaller numbers of slaves were brought to non-sugar-producing areas. Nonetheless, by the middle of the nineteenth century, non-sugar-producing areas were home to the largest number of slaves, and, long after slavery's demise, and even today, very large populations of descendants of slaves live in such areas. How and why did this situation come about?

There are short and long answers to these questions. Here, the short answer must suffice: For a variety of reasons (some simple, some complex), slave mortality rates were higher and slave fertility rates lower in most sugar-producing areas most of the time than was the case in (most) non-sugar-producing regions most of the time. Any list of factors responsible would include the following: the grueling work regimen in sugar; the highly morbid and mortal disease environment in most sugar-producing areas during slavery times; the age and sex ratios typical of slave imports into sugar-producing areas and the preferred age and sex ratios on sugar production units in these areas; the lactation practices amongst slaves in many sugar-producing regions,; and the natalist preferences and policies of slave owners in sugar regions.[10]

The upshot of these factors, *in toto* or in some combination, was that natural increase among slave populations generally did not occur in sugar regions or, when it did, it occurred at low rates. In contrast, African/African-American slave populations in non-sugar areas (where the above considerations affecting slave fertility and mortality were quite different) generally increased at relatively impressive rates by natural means relatively soon after arrival. As a result, slave populations in sugar areas generally grew only—or at least mainly—through the importation of slaves, while slave populations in other areas grew via both the influx of imported slaves and natural increase. Once the transatlantic and intra-hemispheric slave trades were shut down at various points in the nineteenth century, sugar-producing regions, particularly those in which sugar production was still climbing rapidly, had a hard time maintaining, much less increasing, their slave populations.

In contrast, the closing of the foreign slave trades, by and large, mattered little to regions devoted to other cultivations, where slave populations (and, hence, slave labor forces) had long been growing via natural means. For African-Americans, there were profound long-term consequences to the demographic differences between sugar-producing and non-sugar-producing areas in slavery times. We find, for example, that as late as 1950 the Caribbean, the sugar region par excellence, was home to only about 20 percent of the African-American population in the Western hemisphere, despite having accounted for about 40 percent of the total number of African slave imports into the Western hemisphere. In the same year the United States, a minor player in the sugar industry under slavery, was home to about a third of the African-American population in the hemisphere, despite accounting for no more than 5 percent of the total number of slaves imported via the external slave trade. Brazil, where large numbers of slaves worked sugar, but large numbers of slaves were employed in other economic activities as well, we find a kind of equilibrium, to wit: 38 percent of slave imports and 37 percent of the Western hemisphere's African-American population in 1950. To be sure, establishing "race" is fraught with difficulties, and differential population flows and rates of natural increase during the post-slavery period (among other factors) play some part in explaining the hemispheric figures for 1950, but experts are unanimous that the broad contours were set by and because of the differential demographic experience for slave populations in sugar/non-sugar areas under slavery.[11]

In the section above we have emphasized the place of sugar (and to a lesser extent cotton) in the workings of the slave systems in the Americas between 1500 and the late nineteenth century. In so doing we perforce emphasized the principal sugar-producing regions in the Western hemisphere, which is to say, the Caribbean and Brazil. We have proceeded at a very high level of generalization, obviously: Not every part of the Caribbean or Brazil produced a lot of sugar. Slaves in both the Caribbean and Brazil were involved in many other economic activities. Many slaves lived in other areas, especially in the southern part of what eventually became the United States, and relatively few of those slaves produced sugar. Clearly, we need to drill deeper into the economic workings of the slave systems of the Western hemisphere, and, just as clearly, we need to employ the historian's most important stock-in-trade: change over time.

To say that sugar and, later, cotton made the market for slaves in the Western hemisphere is not to imply that slaves could not be profitably employed in other activities, merely that employing slaves in such activities always had to be gauged against the relative costs/returns of employing other forms of labor in said activities and/or against the returns possible of employing slaves in sugar or, late in the history of slavery, in cotton. In the real world, of course, calculations of this sort were often implicit rather than explicit, and numerous non-economic factors—historical, familial, emotional, psychological, and the like—might also enter into any individual or even societal decision regarding the deployment of a slave or slaves. But, generally speaking, slaves were employed systematically in activities and in geographic areas where their labor earned or at least was expected to earn rates of return comparable to those possible in sugar or cotton.

What types of activities? Our argument thus far—quite properly—has stressed the role of slave labor in agricultural activities, particularly the production/manufacture of sugar, but slaves were central to the production of many other crops as well. Other major export staples grown mainly in tropical and subtropical regions of the Western hemisphere—tobacco, rice, indigo, coffee, and cotton—come immediately to mind in this regard, but a variety of other export crops ranging from wheat to cacao and a vast range of food crops for household consumption were also cultivated by slaves. Moreover, although many view slave labor in agriculture and slave labor on plantations almost as a mathematical equality, it should be pointed out that slaves worked on agricultural units of varying sizes, and as part of labor forces ranging from one into the thousands. Similarly, although slave labor in agriculture is typically associated with field crops, slaves were commonly employed in various ways in animal husbandry, particularly cattle herding, as well. Indeed, some scholars view African/African-American slaves as among the Western hemisphere's first "cowboys."[12]

As suggested earlier, slave labor—both Native American and African/African-American—was also vital to mining operations in the Americas. Slaves were employed in significant numbers not only in the famous silver mines in the highlands of New Spain/Mexico and Peru (particularly in the latter) in the sixteenth century, but, later on, also in the placer mines of New Grenada/Colombia and Brazil. Indeed, according to some authorities—Philip Curtin, for example—there were in fact as many or African/African-American slaves working in the gold mines of southwestern Brazil in the late seventeenth century and eighteenth century as there were in the more celebrated cane fields in the northeastern part of the colony. And in the latter century diamond mining—also the work of slaves—became important in southwestern Brazil as well.[13]

One could go on and on regarding the manifold uses of slave labor in the Western hemisphere: They found extensive employment as sailors and in the fishing industry, in the transport sector, in commerce, as soldiers and military auxiliaries, and, of course, in domestic/personal service. Whereas it was once thought (even by scholars) that slaves could not successfully be employed in manufacturing, the historical record demonstrates otherwise, showing conclusively that slaves were prominently represented in all types of trades and manufactories, from ironworks in Virginia to flour mills in Tennessee, from engine shops in Charleston to sugar *ingenios* in Cuba, from textile works in antebellum Georgia and North Carolina to *obrajes* in the viceroyalty of New Spain and *fazendas* in Brazil.

If the labor market in the Western hemisphere for slaves was broad, it was also well developed and articulated, increasingly so over time. Slaves were bought and sold in sophisticated markets, marked by relatively good information, shrewd bargaining strategies and tactics (employed not just by buyers, but by slaves being sold, as Daina Ramey Berry has recently pointed out), well-calibrated standards, and vigilant state regulation.[14] Moreover, as time passed, risk-reduction instruments such as warranties and insurance were often available in such markets. Slaves could be hired by the day, week, month, or year in various areas—sometimes in ways analogous to "spot markets" today—and slaves sometimes entered into informal contracts with their owners to "hire out" their time in exchange for fixed payments at designated intervals. In some cases, we even find groups of slaves themselves hiring out as teams, almost as business partnerships. And, as we shall see later, slaves throughout the hemisphere often "contracted" with their masters to "sell" their "free" time (or the output produced during their free time) to them in exchange for varying forms of compensation. In no way, then, can slave markets in the Western hemisphere be considered lacking in organization, much less as being rudimentary in nature.

The manner in which slave sales were financed adds further support for the view that slave-labor markets were well developed and relatively sophisticated. This general proposition is true whether we look at the financing of the African slave trade or the buying and selling of individual slaves in rural outposts and way stations in the Western hemisphere. The myriad ways in which multiple layers of European, African, American—and Asian—merchant capital combined to finance the African slave trade has been well documented in recent decades. The fact that banions, dubashes, and shroffs from South Asia, Arab traders from the Maghreb, African generals, Afro-European middlemen at coastal trade factories, drapers from northern England, and merchants in Liverpool, Seville, and Nantes all played roles in the financing of the African side of things only hints at the complexity of what might be called, *faute de mieux*, slave financing.[15]

On the other side of the Atlantic, we find some of these same figures—European merchants and drapers, as it were—involved, but also factors in the major ports of the Americas, back country storekeepers, and the final purchasers themselves (planters, farmers, manufacturers, and the like) through retained earnings, and from the profits derived from land and slave appreciation. Government helped, too, by establishing and/or supporting institutions needed for efficient capital mobilization: the provision of clear titles to land (and thus the facilitation of mortgage markets); support for debt instruments such as bonds and promissory notes; the establishment of state banks and agricultural banks; and the licensing of private banks and insurance companies. And then there was the financial help of what we would now call NGOs—fraternal groups and religious orders and sodalities—which sometimes made money available for the acquisition of haciendas, plantations, *ingenios, fazendas*, and slaves (and sometimes even bought slaves themselves). The moneylending nuns in the convents of Santa Clara and Santa Catalina in seventeenth-century Cuzco, the South Carolina Society and the Vestry of St Thomas and St Dennis in eighteenth-century South Carolina, and the brotherhood of the Misericórdia in eighteenth-century Bahia come to mind in this regard.[16]

In light of the fact that slave-labor markets and slave financing were both well organized and smoothly functioning, it is not surprising that slave labor itself, generally speaking, was reasonably well organized and smoothly functioning *in situ*. This is not to suggest that production platforms whereon slaves labored in the Western hemisphere during slavery times—plantations, small farms, fishing boats, mines, shops, factories, etc.—were marked by "efficiency" in the modern sense, only that possibilities for profitable production, the great desideratum of most slave owners, were not foreclosed by opting for slave labor, which, as we have seen, was often viewed as the best, if not the only viable economic choice by those that chose to buy them.

Making universal or normative statements about slave productivity in the Western hemisphere over a period stretching almost 400 years is in many ways a fool's errand, but, given no honorable alternative, try we must. Keep in mind, though, that occupational variation among slaves was great, and that work routines and rhythms differed century by century, region by region, unit to unit—even for slaves doing the same job or involved in the same cultivation. And then there are the profound data gaps, lacunae, and limitations, not to mention the pregnant silences in the sources impeding exegesis and interpretation.

This said, what can we say about slave productivity, that is, about the relationship between the output of goods and services produced by slaves and the factor inputs necessary to produce the same? This question has generated a considerable scholarly literature over the years, particularly among economic historians of the American South. Although students of slavery—including first-hand observers of slavery in the Americas such as Frederick Law Olmstead and Alexander von Humboldt—had often weighed in on the question (using anecdotal or, at best, non-systematic evidence), it was the publication of Robert William Fogel and Stanley L. Engerman's extremely important and controversial two-volume 1974 study *Time on the Cross: The Economics of American Negro Slavery* that led the scholarly world to focus its attention on the question and for the first time to look at slave productivity in formal terms and to attempt to measure it quantitatively.[17] The details of the firestorm that broke out after the publication of *Time on the Cross*, however interesting, cannot be treated here. To simplify matters rather dramatically, let me just say that whereas Fogel and Engerman (and those in their camp) argued that slave-labor productivity in the American South was relatively high—higher in fact that that of free farmers in the northern part of the United States in the mid-nineteenth century—their many opponents argued not only that slave productivity was decidedly *not* high but also that Fogel and Engerman et al. had misspecified this question and mis-measured the productivity of both slave labor and free labor in any case.[18]

If this scholarly brouhaha got nasty and overly personal at times—particularly in the 1970s and 1980s—it nonetheless forced students of slavery to analyze slave labor much more rigorously. As a result, new sources were discovered, new ways to employ older sources were developed, and new ways to conceptualize and measure slave productivity were devised. Despite considerable sound and fury, however, neither side in the debate over slave productivity ever won a clear-cut victory, and defenders of each camp occasionally lob another non-decisive scholarly grenade.[19] A word or two regarding the difficulties associated with this question may help us to understand why it still remains more or less open.

As any economist will admit straight away, productivity estimation is an extremely inexact science even today. Attempting to measure labor productivity, the relationship between labor hours worked and a given output, is tough enough, and broader productivity measures—particularly total factor productivity, which entails knowing the land, labor, and capital inputs used in the production of a given output, and the relative weight of each factor in said production—is more difficult still. Again, even today. Now try to imagine how difficult it is to estimate, much less measure, slave-labor productivity (let alone total factor productivity) when the labor input is comprised of enslaved workers in a variety of settings all over the Western hemisphere over the course of four (largely pre-statistical) centuries.

Take agriculture, for example. We have different cultivations to consider. In different macro and micro climates. Under different production systems and routines. With workforces of varied characteristics, different age structures and gender profiles, and diverse capabilities. And, of course, all working under management schemes that ranged from proto-scientific to inept, and from barbaric to humane. And that's just to get the labor input. What about output? Here, our information is often quite incomplete, based, as it is, on extrapolation from sketchy data on yields and acreage in use, output figures for one isolated year, interpolation between output estimates for years widely separated in time, on murky export data and assumptions about export/output ratios, etc. And all of the above concerns become more problematic still if we want to estimate total factor productivity rather than labor productivity alone. In that case, we need to know about the quantity and quality of land and capital inputs, their relative intensity (factor proportions) in the production process, and whether or not said intensity was stable over time.

Despite all of these obstacles, intrepid (one can think of other adjectives) economic historians have forged ahead, and, as a result, we have a number of estimates of slave-labor productivity and a few of total factor productivity in agricultural regimes employing slave labor. Most of these estimates are of slave-labor productivity in cotton in the southern part of the United States just before the American Civil War or of slave-labor productivity in the Caribbean sugar industry at various points in time.[20] However, we also have a few studies on the other major agricultural staples in which slave labor was utilized in the Americas, tobacco and rice respectively. Some of the studies referred to above focus on the productivity of slave labor, while a few are comparative in nature, analyzing in various ways the productivity of slaves vis-à-vis agricultural workers in other settings ranging from free farmers in the northern part of the United Sates in the mid-nineteenth century to peasant rice cultivators in Burma in the period 1850–80.[21]

What we can take away from this work? Nothing definitive certainly, but it seems fair to suggest that the extant scholarship on questions relating to slave productivity has demonstrated that slave labor could be relatively productive in *some* agricultural settings and that slave-labor productivity *sometimes* rose over sustained periods of time. The reasons for the levels and growth of slave-labor productivity varied and remain debatable. Some see the shift to slavery from less coercive forms of labor organization as providing a "one-time" boost to labor productivity. Others argue that slavery allowed for economies of scale in some cultivations and for more efficient forms of labor mobilization and direction than were possible under other forms of labor organization. The implications of some exciting recent work by Alan Olmstead and Paul Rhode open up the possibility that slave-labor productivity on larger cotton-producing units in the southern part of the United States in the period c.1800–60 may have had biological origins, relating to the fact that slave-holders who employed large numbers of slaves tended to be wealthier, more interested in agricultural improvement, more immersed in agricultural technology networks, and more willing to invest in and mandate the cultivation of superior, higher-yielding cotton varieties.[22] To be sure, biology, or at least the move to "better" land, has long been seen as one of the reasons for rising output—and perhaps for some part of measured labor productivity—in the so-called Cotton South (and in Cuba and Brazil as well, for that matter), but Olmstead and Rhode offer a much richer, empirically based argument for forces biological. Whether or not the findings these scholars made for cotton also hold for other cultivations is still unknown.[23]

What about the productivity of slave labor in comparative terms? As alluded to above, a long-standing debate—or, to be more precise, set of debates—has existed over the relative productivity of slave labor vs. free labor in agriculture in the United States in the mid-nineteenth century. As yet, no consensus has emerged regarding these debates, and because of the huge differences between the agricultural regions (and cultivations) in the regions characterized by slave labor and free labor in the USA, none may be possible. On the other hand, a 1987 analysis of total factor productivity—in standard Cobb-Douglass form—demonstrated that rice production with slave labor in South Carolina and Georgia in the mid-nineteenth century was somewhat more efficient than rice production by peasant cultivators in Lower Burma between about 1850 and 1880, the period in which Lower Burma became the greatest rice exporter in the world.[24] Regarding slave productivity in comparative terms, then, there is still much to learn. At the end of the day, however, it may just be—as Gavin Wright has recently suggested—that productivity is less important in explaining the origins and persistence of slavery than was another consideration: property rights.[25] For, as we have already seen, the rather absolute property rights associated with slaveholding enabled slaveholders to solve various kinds of labor-supply bottlenecks which in many cases (and many parts of the Americas) could have nipped profitable economic activity in the bud.

If many questions remain regarding the productivity of slave labor, most have now been answered regarding a related scholarly perennial: The profitability of the so-called peculiar institution to individual slave owners. Whereas it was once common for scholars to argue either that slavery was unprofitable to slave owners or that profitability was an incidental consideration to slave owners, who were said to be motivated primarily by other concerns, now virtually all scholars of slavery believe that slavery, broadly speaking, was profitable to slave owners and that the behavior and values of slave owners, by and large, were either animated by—or at least consistent with and explicable via—market logic, considerations relating to the so-called cash nexus, and bare-faced, even blunt profit and loss concerns. The most interesting questions related to "profitability" now revolve not around profits to individual slaveholders, but broader questions, including, most notably, who else profited/benefited from slavery and who lost?

Long-term series on the rising prices of slaves in the Western hemisphere over time and on the overall growth in the stock of wealth held in the form of human beings make it well-nigh impossible to argue that slaveholding was not profitable.[26] In the case of the USA, for example, in 1859 slaves comprised about 44 percent of total wealth in the "Cotton South," and about 18.75 percent of the total wealth in the entire country (more than the total comprised by railroads and manufacturing combined).[27]

To be sure, prices for export staples produced by slaves rose and fell, and industries wherein slaves were utilized sometimes collapsed, but the uses of slave labor were sufficiently varied, and slave-labor markets sufficiently flexible that slaves, by and large, were reallocated to efficient (and profitable) uses most of the time in most of the hemisphere. In the case of the United States, for example, Joshua Rosenbloom has found that during the antebellum period slave-labor markets in the South were quite efficient in reallocating workers to their "best" usages and location, which is to say, away from the older agricultural zones along the eastern seaboard and onto cotton and sugar lands in the west south central census region ("the Old Southwest"). This finding is not particularly surprising, of course: For the most part, the internal slave trade in the region was conducted

by highly specialized commercial middlemen—aka slave traders—who established and maintained marketing channels characterized by good information
and organization, considerable standardization, and well-developed financing
mechanisms.[28]

Moreover, while it is still possible to argue that slavery, for a complex variety of
reasons, held back the US South's urbanization and industrialization, it is difficult
to maintain that, in utilizing slaves on cotton plantations and in cane fields in the
Old Southwest, planters were somehow misguided, let alone economically irrational.[29] Indeed, speaking more broadly: Given the production possibilities available,
supply and demand considerations (particularly relating to agricultural export
staples, gold, and silver in extra-regional and international markets), and the
mentalités of most of those who owned slaves and most of those otherwise
implicated in the slave economies, it is not especially surprising where and how
slaves were deployed in the Western hemisphere or that, generally speaking, such
deployments were profitable to many individuals and groups. Many, but not all,
I hasten to add.

Who (or what) besides individual slave owners stood to profit—or to lose—from
the institution of slavery? The slaves themselves clearly lost—of that there can be no
doubt—and it is likely that Africa lost both in social and economic terms. In a recent
econometric study, Harvard economist Nathan Nunn has estimated just how much
the slave trades cost Africa in terms of economic (and political) development.[30] One
thing lacking in Nunn's analysis, however, is a consideration of how much Africa was
aided in a material sense by the so-called Columbian exchange of biota—particularly
by the introduction of American foodstuffs such as maize and manioc—and how
much (if at all) said introduction was sped up by the slave trade.[31]

Whether or not the European governmental entities that sanctioned slavery and
fostered the development of slave societies in the Western hemisphere profited qua
governmental entities from the slave trade and slavery is still debatable, but,
certainly, both individuals and certain groups, classes, and constituencies in the
metropolises did. Slave traders, merchants, and commercial middlemen come
immediately to mind, and, in some cases and in some ways, European manufacturers and industrial interests may have profited as well, though not necessarily in
the straightforward way suggested by Eric Williams in the 1940s.[32] In a material
sense the biggest winners in Europe and elsewhere were arguably those that
consumed commodities, goods, and services produced by American slaves, particularly those that consumed slave-produced sugar, rice, tobacco, and coffee, those
that purchased articles fashioned out of gold and silver mined by slaves, and those
that bought machine-made textiles produced from slave-grown cotton. Clearly,
some part of the surplus extracted from slave labor in the Western hemisphere was
passed along to consumers in the form of cheap carbohydrates, cheap plate, and
cheap cloth and clothing.

There were other winners, too, most notably, mercantile, financial, and industrial groups throughout the *Western hemisphere* that were implicated in some way in slavery's plot. A number of scholars have argued, moreover, that in slave societies some nonslaveholding farmers benefited, too, by embedding themselves in one way or another in the slave economy. Just as small businesses today often benefit by selling to or providing services for large corporations, in slavery times yeomen and others often pursued similar strategies. Here it is important to remember that large slave plantations and mining operations were among, if not *the* largest business entities in the Western hemisphere for most of the period in which slavery existed.[33] In the US case it is likely that the populations in the free states were winners as well, because their taxes were lower than they would have been without the income from tariffs collected on imported goods financed by exports of southern cotton, tobacco, and rice.[34]

Clearly, then, many profited or at least benefited in broader ways from slavery. Careful readers will note, however, that we have not yet discussed the overall effects of slavery on the economic growth and development of areas where the institution played an important role. It is to this hugely important and controversial topic that we now shall turn.

Economic growth and its sometimes companion, development—a broader concept that incorporates a range of qualitative changes such as a shift toward a more sophisticated economic structure, the establishment, if not institutionalization of a relatively sustainable growth path, and evidence of a host of demographic/ social/political changes that were once subsumed under the rubric of "modernization"—have long been the great desiderata of *homo oeconomicus* (as well as most everyone else!) and the most common measuring sticks for evaluating a given economy's performance. To be sure, it is possible to think of other desirable economic ends, and there are alternative ways to assess an economy's performance—in terms of equality or perhaps even the size of a given economy's carbon footprint, for example—but most specialists still believe that evaluating economies in terms of growth and development can offer us important insights about their overall performance.

Assessing the slave economies of the Western hemisphere on the basis of growth and development is tricky for a variety of reasons: matters of definition, intervening variables, and truncation problems to name but three of the most obvious. Let us start with definitional concerns. Most economists define economic growth as a sustained rise in per capita income or output. Unlike the case in economies organized on the basis of free labor, it is not clear in economies wherein slaves are present how to define "per capita." Put another way, should slaves be considered part of the population denominator when we're dividing up income or output on a per capital basis? The decision we make on this matter matters a lot, increasingly so as the slave proportion of the population grows. The best solution to this problem, arguably, is to define and measure "per capita" in a variety of ways when considering questions relating to economic growth, per capita income, per capita wealth, etc., in slave economies. Unfortunately, relatively few scholars studying such questions have done so, which makes for interpretative problems. To further complicate definitional matters: What do we do about the fact that in slave economies a large, often overwhelming proportion of total wealth consisted of "slave capital," which is to say, human beings? This makes comparison with free labor economies quite difficult, as economists going back at least as far as John Stuart Mill have pointed out, because free laborers do not show up as "wealth" in anyone's portfolio.[35] Here, again, a solution is to define wealth in slave economies in a variety of ways, including and excluding wealth held in the form of slaves, but here, too, few scholars have taken this path.

Then there are the problems relating to causation. One can't necessarily assume that slavery, however powerful, was the only important variable involved in shaping an economy even when the institution clearly played a major role. For one thing, since the slave economies in the Western hemisphere were concentrated in the "extended Caribbean," as we have seen, and, since the human population in much of this broad region was plagued by heavy disease loads, disease rather than (or, more likely, in addition to) slavery was probably an important factor in determining the course of the slave economies located therein. Scholars ranging from Pierre Gourou, writing a half century ago, to Jeffrey Sachs today have pointed out that in the tropics especially, people are often poor because they are sick rather than sick because they are poor, as is sometimes assumed.[36] Those interested in evaluating the performance of the slave economies and the relationship between slavery and said performance must perforce allow for the fact that other factors such as disease (not to mention power relations between and among geopolitical entities with varying degrees of might) helped determine the extent to which growth and development occurred. Slavery, that is to say, was *not* the only independent variable involved.

Let us now turn to the truncation problem mentioned above, which in this case relates not to the well-known set of problems subsumed under that rubric in statistics and actuarial science, but rather one arising from what might be called temporal truncation. Two of the principal slave societies in the Western hemisphere, that is to say—Saint-Domingue and that in the southern part of the United States—were destroyed in full flower, in the first case as a result of the Haitian Revolution (1791–1804) and in the second, between 1861 and 1865, as a result of the American Civil War. In other words, we do not know for sure how these societies would have *evolved* economically in the absence of the unforeseen cataclysmic shocks that ended slavery and fundamentally reshaped not only the regions' economic positions, but also their structures of opportunity and, presumably, long-term economic trajectories. We can, of course, gain certain insights from the experiences of other slave economies wherein the demise of slavery came less abruptly—in the British Caribbean, in Cuba, and in Brazil, for example—but we must nonetheless admit that our conclusions about these two places at least are based largely on inference and informed conjecture rather than upon actual historical experience.

Even with the above qualifications in mind, it seems fair to say that most of the slave economies in the Western hemisphere experienced periods, sometimes relatively sustained periods, of economic growth. A number of them were still growing right up until the end of slavery, which offers some support for Seymour Drescher's famous argument that in the case of the British Caribbean, slavery did not die out because it was unprofitable, but through a self-conscious, morally driven policy of "econocide."[37] This said, it also seems fair to point out that none of the slave economies, however robust, showed strong signs over time of developing economically. The American South probably came closest, but, even in this case, we find that on the eve of the American Civil War this region lagged far behind the free states in the North in almost every developmental indicator—quantitative and qualitative—relating to urbanization, industrialization, transportation, labor force composition, education, technological innovation, and domestic demand.[38] As a result in large part of the cotton boom of the 1850s the region was growing relatively rapidly and accumulating considerable wealth, but the structure and degree of sophistication of the southern economy were not changing in commensurate ways.

Moreover, the American South c.1860 by and large was considerably more advanced economically than the other major slave economies in the Western hemisphere. If recent work, such as that by Laird W. Bergad, demonstrates that the slave economies of Cuba and Brazil were also growing in the 1850s and exhibited a number of the same patterns as the American South, no one argues that these economies, let alone slave economies in the other parts of the circum-Caribbean, were at that time on par with the southern part of the United States.[39] In other words, if the American South was not developing as it grew, neither was any other slave economy in the hemisphere.

Not only did slave economies in the Western hemisphere fail to develop when labor markets therein were organized around the peculiar institution, but in many cases the legacy and long-term effects of slavery impeded growth long after emancipation. Indeed, the structural imbalances, distortions, and asymmetries characteristic of most slave economies, coupled with the deficiencies in capital—financial, human, and cultural—that freedmen and women had to make up after emancipation, often meant that such economies, in the aftermath of slavery, often suffered (again in a path-dependent/path-influenced way) through generations of stagnation, poverty, and inequality. In a few extreme cases, alas, slavery may even have led to what some scholars call "the development of underdevelopment."[40]

Thus far, all this talk of the relationship between slavery, on the one hand, and growth and development, on the other, has been cast largely in the framework of standard economic accounting, as it were, but, in thinking about the economic position of enslaved peoples themselves, other frames can also be useful. For example, the "basic needs" approach, popular among development economists in the 1970s and 1980s, assesses performance on the basis of criteria such as infant mortality, nutritional well-being and overall health, life expectancy, housing, and literacy. Judged along these lines, slaves in most parts of the Western hemisphere did not fare well overall, but even here, there were some anomalies and exceptions. In the American South, a number of anthropometric studies have shown that slaves' diets, clothing, and housing generally were at least minimally adequate, and that their net nutrition was sufficient for *adult slaves* to achieve fairly impressive height levels and normal BMIs.[41] Even here, though, it is chilling to learn (from data assembled by Richard Steckel) that the growth of young slaves was often stunted, which suggests that whatever "catch-up" in growth they were able to achieve came about only after they were old enough to contribute economically to the bottom line of their owners.[42] No such thing, then, as the "priceless" child under slavery.

Moreover, both the adequacy of slaves' diets and the fact that adult slaves were relatively tall often owed much to slaves' own efforts in improve their material living standards by working for themselves on their "own" time. Indeed, such efforts, often subsumed under broad rubrics such as "the slaves' economy" or the "internal economy," have generated a significant literature in recent decades, allowing us to understand more clearly than ever before both the material worlds of slaves and the dynamics of master–slave relations.[43] As a result, we now know a good deal about slaves' economic strategies, their bargaining tactics with their masters, the manner in which the "internal economy" supported, supplemented, and articulated with the external economy, and about slave property holding and wealth accumulation. The most complete data available thus far are for the Caribbean and for the American South, but the picture in other regions is beginning to fill out as well. Although some broad patterns have emerged, a number of important questions relating to the internal economy remain open: Why and at whose behest did it originate? Whose overall interests did it serve: Slaves or masters—or both? Can we use limited quantitative data on slave wealth holding (and sometimes even slave income) via careful extrapolation to estimate wealth or income levels for entire slave populations? What were the internal economy's overall effects both on the material (and spiritual) well-being of slaves and on the economy as a whole?

Just as recent scholarship on the internal economy of slaves has generated new insights into the overall economics of slavery, other new sources, new approaches, and new lines of inquiry have done so as well. In this regard, one can point, for example, to recent work on slavery employing the IPUMS (Integrated Public Use Micro Sample) of the federal censuses of the USA, developed at the University of Minnesota, and to scholarship utilizing GIS tools and technology in innovative ways to map both slavery and economic patterns in slave economies. Several scholars—Stanley Engerman and Kenneth Sokoloff, most notably—have refined our understanding of the relationship between factor endowments and institutions (including slavery) in the Western hemisphere, in so doing, endogenizing cultural patterns to boot.[44] Provocative demographic and anthropometric work continues to enrich our understanding of the economics of slavery, as have studies employing insights from the new microeconomics, particularly the economics of information.[45] And feminist scholars and historians of women, in analyzing sexual divisions of labor and infra-household economics, have done so as well.[46]

This said, there is more work to be done and, by now, more work *should* have been done on the economics of slavery. In recent decades, though, many economic historians have tended to shy away from studying the *economics* of slavery, fearful that studying this topic would seem insensitive to post-modern sensibilities or even that they themselves would be considered insufficiently discomfited by one of history's great enormities. This tendency was aided, too, by the cultural turn in the humanities and social sciences, a turn which in a relative sense devalued quantitative work—the "icy water of egotistical calculation" and all that—if not the entire material world.[47] These developments are unfortunate because the past, as we know, is full of distasteful, even villainous agents, events, processes, and institutions—slavery among them—that need to be understood. In averting our scholarly gaze, we may feel smug and self-righteous but, in so doing, at the end of the day we delude only ourselves.

NOTES

1. See, for example, David Brion Davis, *The Problem of Slavery in Western Culture* (New York, 1966); Orlando Patterson, *Slavery and Social Death: A Comparative Study* (Cambridge, Mass., 1982); Davis, Inhuman *Bondage: The Rise and Fall of Slavery in the New World* (New York, 2006).
2. For still provocative introductions to most of the key issues involved in these debates, see Eugene D. Genovese, "The American Slave Systems in World Perspective," in Genovese, *The World the Slaveholders Made: Two Essays in Interpretation* (New York, 1969), 3–113; Elizabeth Fox-Genovese and Eugene D. Genovese, *Fruits of Merchant Capital: Slavery and Bourgeois Property in the Rise and Expansion of Capitalism* (New York, 1983).
3. Evsey D. Domar, "The Causes of Slavery or Serfdom: A Hypothesis," *Journal of Economic History*, 30 (March 1970): 18–32; Stanley L. Engerman and Kenneth L. Sokoloff, "Factor Endowments, Institutions, and Differential Paths of Growth among New World Economies: A View from Economic Historians of the United States," in Stephen Haber (ed.), *How Latin America Fell Behind: Essays on the Economic Histories of Brazil and Mexico, 1800–1914* (Stanford, Calif., 1997), 260–314; Engerman and Sokoloff, "Institutions, Factor Endowments, and Paths of Development in the New World," *Journal of Economic Perspectives*, 14 (Summer 2000): 217–32; Engerman and Sokoloff, "Factor Endowments, Inequality, and Paths of Development among New World Economies," *Economia*, 3 (Fall 2002): 41–109.

4. On slavery as a form of property rights, see Gavin Wright, *Slavery and American Economic Development* (Baton Rouge, La., 2006).

5. See Philip D. Curtin, *The Rise and Fall of the Plantation Complex: Essays in Atlantic History* (2nd edn. New York, 1998); Richard B. Sheridan, *Sugar and Slavery: An Economic History of the British West Indies, 1623–1775* (Baltimore, 1974); Gavin Wright, "Economics of Slavery," in Randall M. Miller and John David Smith (eds.), *Dictionary of Afro-American Slavery* (updated edn. Westport, Conn., 1997), 200–9.

6. On the phrase "extended Caribbean," see Immanuel Wallerstein, *The Modern World System*, 3 vols. thus far (New York, 1974–89), ii. 103.

7. For discussions of these concerns, see Philip D. Morgan, "Slave Trade: Transatlantic," in Paul Finkelman and Joseph C. Miller (eds.), *Macmillan Encyclopedia of World Slavery*, 2 vols. (New York, 1998), ii. 837–44; Herbert S. Klein, *The Atlantic Slave Trade* (New York, 1999), *passim*; John Thornton, *Africa and Africans in the Making of the Atlantic World, 1400–1800* (2nd edn. New York, 1998), 98–151 esp.; Philip D. Curtin, "Epidemiology and the Slave Trade," *Political Science Quarterly*, 83 (June 1968): 190–216.

8. See Alfred W. Crosby, Jr., *The Columbian Exchange: Biological and Cultural Consequences of 1492* (Westport, Conn., 1972), 35–63; Curtin, "Epidemiology and the Slave Trade." For the now classic account of the entrenchment of African slavery in British North America, see Edmund S. Morgan, *American Slavery, American Freedom: The Ordeal of Colonial Virginia* (New York, 1975).

9. This estimate of the total number of Africans imported as slaves into the Western hemisphere (*c.*1500–1870) is based on figures in Morgan, "Slave Trade: Transatlantic," ii. 837; Klein, *The Atlantic Slave Trade*, 210–11; "Estimates," website: *Voyages: The Trans-Atlantic Slave Trade Database*, Emory University, http://www.slavevoyages.org/tast/assessment/estimates/faces. On the geographical distribution of imports, see Klein, *The Atlantic Slave Trade*, 210–11; "Estimates," on *Voyages* website. Much of the fundamental compilation work on numbers and destinations was done by Philip D. Curtin in *The Atlantic Slave Trade: A Census* (Madison, 1969).

10. For a good discussion of these demographic issues, see Kenneth F. Kiple, *The Caribbean Slave: A Biological History* (New York, 1984). For a closer look at one part of the Caribbean, see Barry W. Higman, *Slave Populations in the British Caribbean 1808–1834* (Baltimore, 1984).

11. Curtin, *The Atlantic Slave Trade*, 89–92.

12. James Lockhart and Stuart B. Schwartz, *Early Latin America: A History of Colonial Spanish America and Brazil* (New York, 1983), 381–3; Herbert S. Klein and Ben Vinson III, *African Slavery in Latin America and the Caribbean* (2nd edn. New York, 2007), 25; Peter H. Wood, *Black Majority: Negroes in Colonial South Carolina from 1670 through the Stono Rebellion* (New York, 1974), 28–33.

13. Curtin, *The Rise and Fall of the Plantation Complex*, 100–2; Klein and Vinson, *African Slavery in Latin America and the Caribbean*, 24–5, 28, 65–6, 77–8.

14. On the economic strategies and bargaining tactics employed by slaves to optimize outcomes at sales and auctions, see Daina Ramey Berry, "'We'm Fus' Rate Bargain': Value, Labor, and Price in a Georgia Slave Community," in Walter Johnson (ed.), *The Chattel Principle: Internal Slaves Trades in the Americas* (New Haven, 2004), 55–71.

15. See, for example, Peter A. Coclanis, "Atlantic World or Atlantic/World?," *William and Mary Quarterly*, 3rd ser., 58 (October 2006): 725–42; Philip D. Curtin, *Cross-Cultural*

Trade in World History (New York, 1984), 15–59; Curtin, *The Rise and Fall of the Plantation Complex,* 29–45, 211.

16. Jacob M. Price, *Capital and Credit in British Overseas Trade: The View from the Chesapeake, 1700–1776* (Cambridge, Mass., 1980); Peter A. Coclanis, *The Shadow of a Dream: Life and Death in the South Carolina Low Country, 1670–1920* (New York, 1989), 102–6; Russell R. Menard, "Financing the Lowcountry Export Boom: Capital and Growth in Early South Carolina," *William and Mary Quarterly,* 3rd. ser., 51 (October 1994): 659–76; Stuart B. Schwartz, *Sugar Plantations in the Formation of Brazilian Society: Bahia, 1550–1835* (New York, 1985), 204–18; Kathryn Burns, *Colonial Habits: Convents and the Spiritual Economy of Cuzco, Peru* (Durham, NC, 1999), 41–69, 132–54, and *passim.*

17. Robert William Fogel and Stanley L. Engerman, *Time on the Cross: The Economics of American Negro Slavery,* 2 vols. (Boston, 1974).

18. See Paul David et al., *Reckoning with Slavery: A Critical Study in the Quantitative History of American Negro Slavery* (New York, 1976); Herbert G. Gutman, *Slavery and the Numbers Game: A Critique of Time on the Cross* (Urbana, Ill., 1975); Fox-Genovese and Genovese, *Fruits of Merchant Capital,* 90–171; Gavin Wright, *The Political Economy of the Cotton South: Households, Markets, and Wealth in the Nineteenth Century* (New York, 1978); Peter A. Coclanis, "Time on the Cross," in William A. Darity, Jr. (ed.), *International Encyclopedia of the Social Sciences,* 9 vols. (2nd edn. Detroit, 2008), viii. 366–8.

19. Robert William Fogel, *Without Consent or Contract: The Rise and Fall of American Slavery* (New York, 1989); Robert William Fogel and Stanley L. Engerman (eds.), *Without Consent or Contract: The Rise and Fall of American Slavery, Technical Papers,* 2 vols. (New York, 1992); Fogel, *The Slavery Debates, 1952–1990* (Baton Rouge, La., 2003); Elizabeth B. Field-Hendry and Lee A. Craig, "The Relative Efficiency of Free and Slave Agriculture in the Antebellum United States: A Stochastic Production Frontier Approach," in David Eltis, Frank D. Lewis, and Kenneth L. Sokoloff (eds.), *Slavery in the Development of the Americas* (New York, 2004), 236–57; Wright, *Slavery and American Economic Development,* esp. 83–122.

20. See the works mentioned in n. 19. Also see David Eltis, Frank D. Lewis, and Kenneth L. Sokoloff, "Introduction," in Eltis, Lewis, and Sokoloff (eds.), *Slavery in the Development of the Americas,* 1–27; David Eltis, Frank D. Lewis, and David Richardson, "Slave Prices, the African Slave Trade, and Productivity in the Caribbean, 1674–1807," *Economic History Review,* 58 (October 2005): 673–700.

21. On tobacco, see Lorena S. Walsh, "Slave Life, Slave Society, and Tobacco Production in the Tidewater Chesapeake, 1620–1820," in Ira Berlin and Philip D. Morgan (eds.), *Cultivation and Culture: Labor and the Shaping of Slave Life in the Americas* (Charlottesville, Va., 1993), 170–99. On rice, see Peter A. Coclanis and John Komlos, "Time in the Paddies: A Comparison of Rice Production in the Southeastern United States and Lower Burma in the Nineteenth Century," *Social Science History,* 11 (Fall 1987): 343–54; Peter C. Mancall, Joshua Rosenbloom, and Thomas Weiss, "Agricultural Labor Productivity in the Lower South, 1720–1800," *Explorations in Economic History,* 39 (October 2002): 390–424.

22. Alan L. Olmstead and Paul Rhode, "Biological Innovation and Productivity Growth in the Antebellum Cotton Economy," *Journal of Economic History,* 68 (December 2008): 1123–71.

23. Fogel and Engerman, *Time on the Cross*, i. 196–9; Laird W. Bergad, *The Comparative Histories of Slavery in Brazil, Cuba, and the United States* (New York, 2007), 132–64.

24. Coclanis and Komlos, "Time in the Paddies."

25. Wright, *Slavery and American Economic Development*.

26. Stanley L. Engerman, Richard Sutch, and Gavin Wright, "Slavery," in Susan B. Carter, Scott S. Gartner, Michael Haines, Alan Olmstead, Richard Sutch, and Gavin Wright (eds.), *Historical Statistics of the United States: Earliest Times to the Present, Millennial Edition*, 5 vols. (New York, 2006), ii. 369–74, esp. 372–3; Schwartz, *Sugar Plantations in the Formation of Brazilian Society*, 190, figure 7–4; Eltis, Lewis, and Richardson, "Slave Prices, the African Slave Trade, and Productivity in the Caribbean, 1674–1807"; Bergad, *The Comparative Histories of Slavery in Brazil, Cuba, and the United States*, 157–64.

27. Roger Ransom and Richard Sutch, "Capitalists without Capital: The Burden of Slavery and the Impact of Emancipation," *Agricultural History*, 62 (Summer 1988): 133–60; James L. Huston, *Calculating the Value of the Union: Slavery, Property Rights, and the Economic Origins of the Civil War* (Chapel Hill, NC, 2003), 65.

28. Joshua L. Rosenbloom, *Looking for Work, Searching for Workers: American Labor Markets during Industrialization* (New York, 2002), 40–7 and *passim*.

29. Claudia D. Goldin effectively countered simple arguments about the (allegedly negative) relationship between slavery and cities in *Urban Slavery in the American South, 1820–1860: A Quantitative History* (Chicago, 1976). In more subtle ways, however, slavery likely did hold back urbanization and industrialization in slave economies by impeding the development of the domestic market. See William N. Parker, "Slavery and Southern Economic Development: An Hypothesis and Some Evidence," *Agricultural History*, 44 (January 1970): 115–25; Robert E. Gallman and Ralph V. Anderson, "Slaves as Fixed Capital: Slave Labor and Southern Economic Development," *Journal of American History*, 64 (June 1977): 24–46.

30. Nathan Nunn, "The Long-Term Effects of Africa's Slave Trades," *Quarterly Journal of Economics*, 123 (February 2008): 139–76. Also see Joseph E. Inikori and Stanley L. Engerman, "Introduction: Gainers and Losers in the Atlantic Slave Trade," in Inikori and Engerman (eds.), *The Atlantic Slave Trade: Effects on Economies, Societies, and Peoples in Africa, the Americas, and Europe* (Durham, NC, 1992), 1–21.

31. Crosby, *The Columbian Exchange*, 185–8.

32. Eric E. Williams, *Capitalism and Slavery* (Chapel Hill, NC, 1944); Heather Cateau and S. H. H. Carrington (eds.), *Capitalism and Slavery Fifty Years Later: Eric Eustace Williams—A Reassessment of the Man and his Work* (New York, 2000); Carrington, *The Sugar Industry and the Abolition of the Slave Trade, 1775–1810* (Gainesville, Fla., 2002); Wright, *Slavery and American Economic Development*, 35–40.

33. Alfred D. Chandler, Jr., *The Visible Hand: The Managerial Revolution in American Business* (Cambridge, Mass., 1977), 62–7.

34. J. Bradford DeLong, "Who Benefited from North American Slavery," paper, Fall 2007, http://delong.typepad.com/113_F07/20070910_cuibono.pdf

35. John Stuart Mill, *Principles of Political Economy...*, ed. W. J. Ashley (1848; 7th edn. London, 1909), 8.

36. Pierre Gourou, *The Tropical World: Its Social and Economic Conditions and its Future Status*, trans. E. D. Laborde (2nd edn. London, 1958), 6–12; Jeffrey D. Sachs, *The End of Poverty: Economic Possibilities for our Time* (New York, 2005), 188–209 and *passim*. Also

see James P. Smith, "Healthy Bodies and Thick Wallets: The Dual Relationship between Health and Economic Status," *Journal of Economic Perspectives*, 13 (Spring 1999): 145–66.

37. Seymour Drescher, *Econocide: British Slavery in the Era of Abolition* (Pittsburgh, 1977); Drescher, *The Mighty Experiment: Free Labor versus Slavery in British Emancipation* (New York, 2002).

38. See, for example, Eugene D. Genovese, *The Political Economy of Slavery: Studies in the Economy and Society of the Slave South* (New York, 1965), esp. 13–39; Coclanis, *The Shadow of a Dream*, 111–58.

39. Bergad, *The Comparative Histories of Slavery in Brazil, Cuba, and the United States*, 132–64. Also see Richard Graham, "Slavery and Economic Development: Brazil and the United States South in the Nineteenth Century," *Comparative Studies in Society and History*, 23 (October 1981): 620–55.

40. See, for example, Roger L. Ransom and Richard Sutch, *One Kind of Freedom: The Economic Consequences of Emancipation* (New York, 1977); Gavin Wright, *Old South, New South: Revolutions in the Southern Economy since the Civil War* (New York, 1986); Alex Dupuy, *Haiti in the World Economy: Class, Race and Under Development since 1700* (Boulder, Colo., 1988); Jay R. Mandle, *Not Slave, Not Free: The African-American Economic Experience since the Civil War* (Durham, NC, 1992); Rebecca J. Scott, "Exploring the Meaning of Freedom: Postemancipation Societies in Comparative Perspective," in Scott et al., *The Abolition of Slavery and the Aftermath of Emancipation in Brazil* (Durham, NC, 1988), 1–21; Pieter C. Emmer, "The Big Disappointment: The Economic Consequences of the Abolition of Slavery in the Caribbean, 1833–1888," History in Focus website, Institute of Historical Research, University of London, Spring 2007, http://www.history.ac.uk/ihr/Focus/Slavery/articles/emmer.html For the classic formulation of the "development of underdevelopment" line, see Andre Gunder Frank, "The Development of Underdevelopment," *Monthly Review*, 18 (September 1966): 17–31.

41. Fogel and Engerman, *Time on the Cross*: i: 109–26; Richard H. Steckel, "Slave Height Profiles from Coastwise Manifests," *Explorations in Economic History*, 16 (October 1979): 363–80; Steckel, "The Nutrition, Health, and Mortality of American Slaves from Childhood to Maturity," *Journal of Economic History*, 46 (September 1986): 721–41; John Komlos, "The Stature of Runaway Slaves in Colonial America," in Komlos (ed.), *Stature, Living Standards, and Economic Development: Essays in Anthropometric History* (Chicago, 1994), 93–116. Note that the "basic needs" approach to development was perhaps most closely associated with the strategies and policies of the United Nations Development Program.

42. See Richard H. Steckel and Robert A. Margo, "The Heights of American Slaves: New Evidence on Slave Nutrition and Health," *Social Science History*, 6 (Fall 1982): 516–38; Steckel, "A Peculiar Population: The Nutrition, Health, and Mortality of American Slaves from Childhood to Maturity," *Journal of Economic History*, 46 (September 1986): 721–41; Steckel, "A Pernicious Side of Capitalism: The Care and Feeding of Slave Children" Working Paper, July 2007, http://web.econ.ohiostate.edu/rsteckel/VITA/2007%20Pernicious.pdf

43. See, for example, the essays in Ira Berlin and Philip D. Morgan (eds.), *The Slaves' Economy: Independent Production by Slaves in the Americas* (London, 1991). Also see Michael Mullin, *Africa in America: Slave Acculturation and Resistance in the American South and the British Caribbean, 1736–1831* (Urbana, Ill., 1992); Stuart B. Schwartz,

Slaves, Peasants, and Rebels: Reconsidering Brazilian Slavery (Urbana, Ill., 1992), 65–101; Roderick A. McDonald, *The Economy and Material Culture of Slaves: Goods and Chattels on the Sugar Plantations of Jamaica and Louisiana* (Baton Rouge, La., 1993); Betty Wood, *Women's Work, Men's Work: The Informal Slave Economies of Lowcountry Georgia* (Athens, Ga., 1995); Dylan C. Penningroth, *The Claims of Kinfolk: Property and Community in the Nineteenth-Century South* (Chapel Hill, NC, 2003); Anthony E. Kaye, *Joining Places: Slave Neighborhoods in the Old South* (Chapel Hill, NC, 2007).

44. See Engerman and Sokoloff, "Factor Endowments, Institutions, and Differential Paths of Growth among New World Economies"; Engerman and Sokoloff, "Factor Endowments, Inequality, and Paths of Development among New World Economies."

45. Peter A. Coclanis, "How the Low Country Was Taken to Task: Slave-Labor Organization in Coastal South Carolina and Georgia," in Robert Louis Paquette and Louis A. Ferleger (eds.), *Slavery, Secession, and Southern History* (Charlottesville, Va., 2000), 59–78; Richard Follett, "Slavery and Technology in Louisiana's Sugar Bowl," in Susanna Delfino and Michele Gillespie (eds.), *Technology, Innovation, and Southern Industrialization: From the Antebellum Era to the Computer Age* (Columbia, Mo., 2008), 68–96.

46. Elizabeth Fox-Genovese, *Within the Plantation Household: Black and White Women of the Old South* (Chapel Hill, NC, 1988); Stephanie McCurry, *Masters of Small Worlds: Yeoman Households, Gender Relations, and the Political Culture of the Antebellum South Carolina Low Country* (New York, 1995); David Barry Gaspar and Darlene Clark Hine (eds.), *More than Chattel: Black Women and Slavery in the Americas* (Bloomington, Ind., 1996); Deborah Gray White, *Ar'n't I a Woman? Female Slaves in the Plantation South* (rev. edn. New York, 1999); Hilary M. Beckles, *Centering Women: Gender Discourses in Caribbean Slave Society* (Kingston, 1999); Brian L. Moore et al. (eds.), *Slavery, Freedom, and Gender: The Dynamics of Caribbean Society* (Kingston, 2001); Mieko Nishida, *Slavery and Identity: Ethnicity, Gender, and Race in Salvador, Brazil, 1808–1888* (Bloomington, Ind., 2003).

47. Karl Marx and Frederick Engels, *The Communist Manifesto*, ed. Joseph Katz, trans. Samuel Moore (1848; New York, 1964), 62.

SELECT BIBLIOGRAPHY

BERGAD, LAIRD W. *The Comparative Histories of Slavery in Brazil, Cuba, and the United States*. New York: Cambridge University Press, 2007.

COCLANIS, PETER A. *The Shadow of a Dream: Economic Life and Death in the South Carolina Low Country, 1670–1920*. New York: Oxford University Press, 1989.

CURTIN, PHILIP D. *The Rise and Fall of the Plantation Complex: Essays in Atlantic History*. 2nd edn. New York: Cambridge University Press. 1998.

DOMAR, EVSEY D. "The Causes of Slavery or Serfdom: A Hypothesis," *Journal of Economic History*, 30 (March 1970): 18–32.

DRESCHER, SEYMOUR. *Econocide: British Slavery in the Era of Abolition*. Pittsburgh: University of Pittsburgh Press, 1977.

ELTIS, DAVID, FRANK D. LEWIS, and KENNETH L. SOKOLOFF, eds. *Slavery in the Development of the Americas*. New York: Cambridge University Press, 2004.

Fogel, Robert William. *Without Consent or Contract: The Rise and Fall of American Slavery.* New York: W. W. Norton, 1989.

Fogel, Robert William and Stanley L. Engerman. *Time on the Cross: The Economics of American Negro Slavery.* 2 vols. Boston: Little, Brown, 1974.

Fox-Genovese, Elizabeth, and Eugene D. Genovese. *Fruits of Merchant Capital: Slavery and Bourgeois Property in the Rise and Expansion of Capitalism.* New York: Oxford University Press, 1983.

Genovese, Eugene D. *The Political Economy of Slavery: Studies in the Economy and Society of the Slave South.* New York: Random House, 1965.

Klein, Herbert S. *The Atlantic Slave Trade.* New York: Cambridge University Press, 1999.

——and Ben Vinson III. *African Slavery in Latin America and the Caribbean.* 2nd edn. New York: Oxford University Press, 2007.

Schwartz, Stuart B. *Sugar Plantations in the Formation of Brazilian Society: Bahia, 1550–1835.* New York: Cambridge University Press, 1985.

Wright, Gavin. *The Political Economy of the Cotton South: Households, Markets, and Wealth in the Nineteenth Century.* New York: W. W. Norton, 1978.

—— *Slavery and American Economic Development.* Baton Rouge, La.: Louisiana State University Press, 2006.

CHAPTER 23

GENDER AND SLAVERY

KIRSTEN E. WOOD

In the last three decades, gender has become an indispensable category of analysis in the study of slavery in the Americas, illuminating both the day-to-day lives of enslaved and enslaving peoples and ideas about race and slavery.[1] While gender has touched nearly all aspects of slavery studies, the application of gender analysis has been particularly fruitful in certain areas. Some are self-evidently gendered, like family, reproduction, and sex. Gender analysis has also reconfigured the study of politics, and, as is increasingly clear, studying gender means much more than studying women. Still, the literature on enslaved women is especially influential, in part because of gender analysis's origins in women's history and in part because of women's central importance in slavery: women and ideas about them shaped slavery from beginning to end.

ORIGINS OF SLAVERY

Gender helped early European explorers and settlers to imagine that Africans (and Native Americans) were distinctly "other" and that these "others" could—and should—be enslaved. Barbara Bush and Jennifer Morgan have shown that references to African women's exposed breasts dominated European texts, denoting animalistic behaviors and lusts to authors and readers alike. Easy parturition, meanwhile, suggested that African women did not share in Eve's curse, and thus that Europeans need not treat Africans as fellow children of Adam and Eve. Europeans also believed that polygamy and female agriculture proved African women's degradation and, correspondingly, the superiority of European culture. (While many European women performed farm labor, elite Europeans often viewed it as normatively masculine work.) Together, African labor patterns, familial organization, and bodies not only made Europeans feel superior but also focused their attention on African women's sexuality and reproductive potential.[2]

Gender shaped the laws defining hereditary slavery in both conception and consequence. The legal prescription that an enslaved woman's child was also a slave both ignored children with free mothers and enslaved fathers and essentially erased black paternity in white eyes. The "partus sequitur ventrem" principle also made interracial sex an aspect of slavery *de facto* and *de jure*. As Hilary Beckles has observed, "non pecuniary returns" to slave owning, "including rape and other forms of physical assault," could be extracted from slaves without legal or social "penalties," especially in English and American slavery.[3]

Even before the hereditary principle, gender shaped colonial experiments with race and slavery. In Virginia, a 1641 law decreed that all men and all "negro women" 16 or older were subject to a new poll tax. This grouping reflected gendered ideas about work: it comprised all the people that lawmakers considered full-time agricultural workers. African women were known to perform agricultural work in Africa, and they clearly did in Virginia, but English women were not supposed to be (in both senses) field workers. Virginians thus fumbled toward a legal definition of race through their ideas about women's work. While gender traced a path toward slavery and race in Virginia, in Georgia, slavery reshaped gender. Georgia's founders expected English women to perform commodity production, as well as domestic work and childrearing. African women in the early colony likewise performed diverse tasks. Within fifty years, however, most female slaves performed monotonous work that whites considered unskilled; middling and poor women had few remaining socioeconomic "niches"; and privileged elites did almost no manual work at all.[4]

THE GENDERED DIVISION OF SLAVE LABOR

Planters across the Americas forced enslaved women and men to perform exhausting work in the fields with little regard for sex. In the West Indies, slaves were assigned to the first (or "great"), second, or trash gang depending primarily on strength and age or life stage rather than sex. In the United States, planters often measured all slaves against the standard of the "prime" slave. Thus, a strong woman might be a three-quarter hand, while an old man or a pregnant woman might be a half hand.[5] Working in sex-mixed groups did not, however, erase gender. For example, planters typically assigned children of both sexes to the trash gang. Because the trash gang also contained elderly, heavily pregnant, and breastfeeding women, time served there helped socialize girls but not boys into adult gender roles. Moreover, while Caribbean women sometimes drove the second gang, and older women there and in the United States ran the trash gang, women rarely drove the great gangs. This preserved men's privileged access to supervisory and disciplinary labor.[6] Equally important, slave societies embraced a profound division of labor between enslaved and white women: enslaved women were expected to show strength and stamina in the fields, while white women ideally did little or no outdoors work.

Beyond the fields, gender continued to shape work. Enslaved men occupied almost all occupations that either they or whites considered as skilled. Men were the mechanics, blacksmiths, carpenters, coopers, masons, carters, carriage drivers, sugar makers, boilermen, and furnacemen. The most highly skilled bondsmen enjoyed some prestige and received extra rations and authority over other slaves. Some also enjoyed much greater freedom of movement: an artisan might be hired out and make his own way from job to job. Women had a smaller range of skilled crafts, like cooking, midwifery, and nursing, and those few conferred less prestige and fewer material rewards on their practitioners than male crafts did upon men, and little or no added mobility. Whites did not consider domestic work—the most common female specialization—as skilled, although house servants sometimes gained privileged access to whites' used clothes and leftover food. Defining skill as the ability to do any task well, Daina Berry has recently argued that planters did recognize the skills of certain field women, narrowing the perceptual gap between skillful workers and skilled occupations. Overall, however, the older findings of Deborah Gray White, Hilary Beckles, Jacqueline Jones, and Marietta Morrissey, among many others, still hold: women had little access to skilled occupations, and a higher proportion of women than men were field workers. On some estates, women made up the majority of the field-hands.[7]

Historians have sometimes seemed uncertain whether these patterns stemmed from ideas about sexual difference or from sexual differences themselves. Jacqueline Jones has suggested that planters excluded women from skilled occupations for pragmatic reasons: "the high cost of specialized and extensive training" made it impractical to train women, since "childbearing and nursing" would interrupt their ability to provide "regular service" on the plantation or be hired out profitably. However, a substantial proportion of enslaved women never had children. If practical factors alone shaped access to skilled work, then some of these women would have been eligible. Their continued exclusion indicates that gender impeded a purely pragmatic response to reproductive biology.[8]

Gender also shaped slaves' "after-hours" work. The tasks that men and women performed for themselves and their families differed. Typically, women cooked, cleaned, sewed, and washed for their families. In the West Indies where slaves had to grow their own provisions, women also performed much of the subsistence horticulture as well. Everywhere, women did most of the childcare. Only women had post-sundown orders to spin for their owners. In contrast, men fished, hunted, and made or repaired furniture. If they lived "abroad," they usually commuted to visit wives and children. They also applied their greater opportunities to earn money or goods to their families' benefit. In the West Indies, many assisted in the provision grounds. Yet no one has called men's work for their families a "second shift," as feminist historians have characterized enslaved women's extra work.[9]

Forcing enslaved women and men to work at the same tasks "de-gendered" neither sex. While slaves may have worked too hard to notice whether the neighboring bodies were male or female, we know that slaves' supervisors—white and black—not only noticed but also perceived some individuals as sexually attractive, available, and vulnerable. Women, not men, were overwhelmingly the targets of drivers' and overseers' sexual opportunism. Only an artificially narrow understanding would remove this aspect of gender relations from considerations of slaves' fieldwork. It is equally important to note that gender is constituted not solely through contrasts between men and women, but also through contrasts *among* men and *among* women. Thus, as long as some women, like slave owning women or enslaved housekeepers, did not perform fieldwork alongside men, enslaved women who did had a distinct gender in relationship to other women.[10] The same, of course, applies to enslaved men, and thus there were many genders, not just two.

REPRODUCTION

As Richard Steckel's essay in this collection suggests, work on reproduction in slavery begins with demography, which illuminates the reproductive catastrophes of American slavery. Staggering rates of infant mortality, low fertility, and low fecundity meant that Africans and their descendants in the Caribbean did not experience natural population growth until after slavery, yet those in Barbados, the southern mainland British colonies, and the United States did. Many factors in this pattern were beyond slaves' control, such as malaria, overwork, grossly inadequate pre- and postnatal care, malnutrition, neonatal tetanus, venereal disease. Sex ratios are not, however, considered quite so definitive as they once were, in part because of changing information about sex ratios early in slavery, and in part because normal sex ratios did not automatically mean population growth. That slave owners used the sex ratio to account for low fertility is further reason to be wary of that explanation. Generally, planters in the major staple-producing areas, especially sugar planters, cared little and did less to improve fertility and reduce infant mortality. It was, quite simply, cheaper and easier to buy new slaves and work them quite literally to death than to rely on childbirth to increase and reproduce the labor force. Even in British North America, where slave populations grew through natural reproduction from the mid-eighteenth century or earlier, there is little evidence that planters were particularly consistent or successfully instrumental.[11]

By the late eighteenth and early nineteenth centuries, colonies across the Caribbean launched amelioration campaigns to fend off abolitionists' attacks and stabilize the slave labor supply. Giving pregnant and postpartum women a respite from work, improved rations, and other incentives might have improved outcomes for both mothers and children, but slave owners sometimes boasted more than their choices actually warranted. Even after the British closed the Atlantic slave trade, Caribbean planters generally had far more success in extracting field than reproductive labor from their bondswomen. However, recent work inverts the common view that enslaved women were always workers first, and reproducers second. Jennifer Morgan argues that even though enslaved women's treatment in Barbados and South Carolina impeded both fertility and infant survival, women's reproductive potential shaped planters' ideas about Africans from the very start. In their wills, slave owners fantasized about future wealth, bequeathing not just living children and fetuses but also women's reproductive potential itself. Because both slave owners and enslaved women recognized the potential value of reproduction, contestation over reproduction was a constant.[12] Taken together, the many local and regional studies of slave reproduction suggest that the exploitation of women's reproductive potential was always a subject of contestation in New World slavery, even in the many instances when planters did little to help enslaved women conceive, bear, and raise healthy children.

SEXUALITY

Through interracial rape, white men asserted their dominance over African and African-American men, as well as over all women. While the fact of interracial sexual exploitation has long been acknowledged—having featured largely in abolitionist propaganda, for example—its impact on gender as well as race relations is a topic of relatively recent study.

Endemic throughout New World slavery and its aftermath, rape and sexual fantasies were particularly virulent in the Atlantic and internal slave trades. Edward Baptist observes that enslaved women in the antebellum South were "desirable purchases because they could be raped," and they were exquisitely "vulnerable to sexual assault . . . because they could be sold." He argues further that by raping light-skinned women, antebellum whites could recapitulate centuries of white domination, suggesting that the fantasy and reality of abuse grew more potent, not less, over time. The overarching claim, however, about the centrality of sexual exploitation to slavery pertains throughout its New World history. Consequently, even sexual acts between slaves could take on the stink of coercion. As Thelma Jennings argued in 1990 and as Daina Berry has recently confirmed, when slave owners instructed two slaves to pair off, they coerced both men and women to perform sexual acts not of their own choosing. At the same time, some enslaved men were potential beneficiaries of breeding: some planters encouraged high-status men, such as drivers, to father children with whichever bondswomen they fancied. Freed-people's own testimony suggests that some bondsmen took full advantage of the privilege. In its varied forms, sexual coercion did a lot of work for slaveholders: it produced new chattels; it marked all slaves' inferiority; it terrorized enslaved women and many enslaved men; and it humiliated and brainwashed many white women, all in ways that reinforced both gender and racial hierarchy.[13]

Even long after the institution ended, fears related to sexuality and race continued to warp gender relations. A classic example comes from the early twentieth-century US South, where Thomas Dixon's novels featuring black men as rapists helped reinforce Jim Crow, mask the continued sexual abuse of freed-women, and uphold patriarchy: white women allegedly remained safe from inter-racial assault only as long as they accepted white men's protective custody.[14] As Jacquelyn Dowd Hall has argued, the subsequent campaign against lynching also became, at least in part, a "revolt against chivalry."[15]

Yet while the history of sexuality within slavery is a twisted and ugly story, it was also more than that, even for enslaved women who bore the worst of it. As Henrice Altink and others have argued, some enslaved women chose to enter sexual relationships with white men in the hope of "material favours," or simply because they found reluctant acquiescence preferable to forcible rape.[16] Overall, these women had but slim chance of gaining their own or their children's freedom, and Deborah Gray White has argued that their choice made it harder for others to resist. In the Old South, such relationships rarely resulted in tangible advantages for enslaved women and their children. In Jamaica, as Hilary Beckles has shown, the scarcity of English women made it common for enslaved women to act as housekeeper-mistresses to the resident planters, but a housekeeper rarely got to choose whether she would also be a concubine. Manumitting one's sexual partner and children was most common in the Spanish West Indies. In the French colonies, planters regularly ignored the Code Noir's requirement that they emancipate their own enslaved children. Across the slave societies, urban areas witnessed an espe-cially wide range of interracial sex, ranging from long-term relationships between elite men and their bondswomen to casual encounters in brothels and taverns.[17]

If consent is a difficult topic in the context of slavery, it is arguably even more difficult to speak of sexual pleasure. Yet neither patriarchal social relations, nor the violent expropriation of labor, nor the classifying of people as things or animals could reserve sexual pleasure for the men of the master class alone. Stephanie Camp's "somatic" understanding of slavery acknowledges enslaved women's plea-sure in fancy clothes, flirtation, and furious dancing, and allows for the possibility of pleasure in sex. Cynthia Kennedy's attention to enslaved and free people of color's own understandings of marriage—legal or not—similarly hints at intima-cies both consensual and pleasurable.[18] While challenging from an evidentiary standpoint, more work on these issues will help determine how sexual abuse affected enslaved men's and women's subsequent sexual experiences and identities, work which will complement Darlene Clark Hine's conclusions about the long-term impact of enslaved women's sexual vulnerability on freedwomen's gender identities.[19] Increased attention to sexuality among slave couples—self-chosen and coerced—will also advance our understanding of enslaved families.

ENSLAVED FAMILIES

Much as efforts to document sexual pleasure must struggle against the nearly crushing weight of scholarship on sexual abuse, the much older historiography of slave families has long battled against the presumption that improper gender relations all but destroyed the possibility of cohesive families among the enslaved. Arguing against the presumption of domineering mothers and absent or weak fathers, most famously articulated in the 1965 Moynihan report, John Blassingame and Herbert Gutman argued in the early 1970s that fathers were emotionally and materially central, and that extended kinship networks, fictive kin, and male-headed nuclear families were all key elements of slave families.[20] In the 1980s, Jacqueline Jones and Deborah Gray White systematically dismantled the sexist assumption that families headed by women were necessarily dysfunctional. They argued that women's networks were as important as conjugal ties to slaves, that slave marriages involved comparative equality and complementarity, and that many mothers had to be the primary caretaker because their families lacked a regularly present father at all due to the custom of abroad marriage.[21]

In the 1990s, scholars of American slave families continued to debate family composition while still rejecting the idea of matriarchy. Ann Malone argued that in

Louisiana, the frequency of nuclear families, married couples, single slaves, and mother-headed families varied over time and largely reflected extrinsic factors like the stage of agricultural development and planter life cycles. Working in Virginia, Brenda Stevenson viewed enslaved women as key elements of families and communities: slave owners' refusal to protect conjugal and paternal ties meant that many slave families were perforce matrifocal.[22] In addition to elaborating family structure, American historians have also explored slaves' ideas about family, documenting what Cynthia Kennedy has called a "counter-ideal" to white nuclearity. In this, they echo Caribbeanists who have long noted the importance of West African precedents for both female autonomy and polygamy in shaping gender relations, family dynamics, and household composition.[23] Now, gender has clearly become an analytical tool in studies of slave family, instead of a problem to be explained away.

RESISTANCE

Resistance has been a particularly fruitful area of research in slavery studies, but its relationship to gender is ambiguous. Clearly, certain types of resistance were more common among bondsmen than bondswomen. Men made up a significantly higher percentage of runaways than did women, and men also figured far more prominently among rebels in both the USA and the Caribbean. Those actions, meanwhile, have often been celebrated, while more covert activities are sometimes deemed "accommodation" rather than genuine resistance. Compounding the problem of understanding gender and resistance is that many more covert forms, like feigning sickness and working slowly, were available to women and men. Where scholars have associated types of resistance with one sex, like poisoning with women, it remains unclear whether the pattern reflects the gendered division of labor, a gendered affinity, or other factors. Yet clear evidence of gendered resistance is emerging. Caribbean scholars like Bernard Moitt and David Geggus have demonstrated women's crucial support for rebellions; for example, women in revolutionary-era Saint-Domingue traded sex for ammunition. Other recent scholarship has sharpened our understanding of gender's role in more covert aspects of direct resistance. Stephanie Camp argues that enslaved women in the antebellum South provided essential food and supplies to runaways, hid truants, and even helped negotiate the terms of their return to work. Their assistance depended in turn upon the gendered division of labor: women's typical confinement to the plantation's ambit meant that they were often available when a runaway needed assistance, while their part-chosen and part-imposed responsibility for cooking allowed them to decide whether and how often to redirect food to a hungry truant.[24]

Perhaps the most obviously gendered resistance involved reproduction. Some enslaved women deliberately resisted childbearing for reasons ranging from the refusal to enrich their owners to the unwillingness to reproduce bondage. Slaves and slave owners alike suggested that women used a variety of methods to control their fertility: abstinence; herbal birth control; herbal and mechanical abortion; and, finally, infanticide. A combination of contraception and postnatal abstinence best explains birth spacing of up to and even over two years, which cannot be explained by lactation and postpartum amenorrhea alone. Ex-slaves—men and women—testified to deliberate contraception to deprive owners of additional capital and labor. Contraception was arguably gendered resistance for men as well as for women: while some enslaved men may have prided themselves on fathering many children—with many different mothers—others supported or even encouraged their wives' efforts to limit their families. Still, no one can estimate with any certainty the frequency or scale of enslaved men's and women's efforts to control their own reproductive lives. Similarly, it is impossible to determine how often women shammed obstetric and gynecological complaints, given the variety of genuine diseases and injuries and the complicated mix of African and European attitudes about bodily health and medical care.[25]

If historians hold up contraception as a form of resistance, they often have more trouble with infanticide. Slaveholders accused women of heedlessly smothering their infants, a kind of murder by neglect that confirmed whites' lowest opinions of enslaved women. Accordingly, some historians have hesitated to accept the diagnosis of infanticide, while others, like Sharon Ann Holt and Deborah Gray White, argue for benevolent motives and sympathetic interpretations: desperate but loving mothers murdered their children in order to spare them lives of bondage. Alternatively, some suggest that infanticide is not a helpful analytical category. Barbara Bush notes the belief, perhaps rooted in West African cultures, that babies only became fully human after their ninth day *ex utero*, which would imply that hastening death before that time involved something less prejudicial.[26] Moreover, biological motherhood was not magical, as Jennifer Morgan has recently argued, and presupposing mother-love minimizes the psychological impact of bondage, sexual abuse, and overwork that enslaved women in particular faced, especially those uprooted by the Atlantic or internal slave trades. It also trivializes the heroism that enslaved women—and men—displayed in daring to love, nurture, and protect their children. In this sense, attention to gynecological resistance brings us back to a related observation about slave families. Forming families, whether by marriage, birth, or adoption, strengthened slaves and enabled some to continue and extend their resistance. However, the very virtues of family also meant they gave slave owners a powerful hold over their bondspeople, which some found far more effective than the use or threat of whippings.[27]

BLACK FEMININITY[28]

Historians of enslaved women have long struggled to distinguish white stereotypes of nurturing Mammy, aggressive Sapphire, and lustful Jezebel from slaves' own gender identities. Arguments about whether women invested more significance in female networks or in conjugal relations, or whether women performed skilled work, also affect debates about women's identities.[29] Compounding the difficulty of understanding enslaved women as mothers, lovers, and workers are long-standing questions about gender's priority for women of the African diaspora. In the twentieth century, many African-American women identified more with the civil rights struggle than the women's rights movement. This reflects both the historic racism of American feminism and the judgment that standing with black men against racism was the first and the greater call. If racial justice took priority, then perhaps racial identity did too. Some scholars have tried to theorize that as an essentially false question, because race and gender are mutually constitutive and inextricable. The bulk of the evidence from slavery makes clear not only that black women and men had more in common than black women and white women, but also that the gendered aspects of bondage must not be underestimated.[30]

Some of the most productive recent scholarship in this area takes a multiply relational approach to gender, recognizing that gender meant something different for enslaved women when they talked with their husbands at night, or hoed with other slaves in the fields, or sewed clothes under their mistress's gaze. For an enslaved girl, puberty usually meant both fieldwork and the possibility of interracial rape, perhaps even before her first flirtation with a fellow slave. If sexual maturity increased a girl's fear for herself, it also likely enhanced her empathy for other women. It also afforded new opportunities for enjoyment: athletic dancing and fashionable clothes provided physical pleasure and, perhaps, the recognition that nights spent dancing could be understood as labor power reclaimed from their owners (sources are understandably stingy but nevertheless suggestive on this point). Maternity, meanwhile, brought new dreads—of seeing one's children separated by sale, lashed, demeaned, overworked, raped, or buried—but it also produced, at least for some, a redoubled protectiveness for vulnerable children that may have made them work even harder to resist their degrading bondage. At the same time, women at the peak of their working lives could take pride in their skill even as they resented its exploitation. Older women faced declining bodies that often rendered them less valuable in white eyes, but their knowledge, whether of medicinal plants, conjuring, planters' moods, or midwifery, could make them figures of great esteem to other slaves and sometimes even to whites. Life cycle, long a major area of analysis for free women, continues to attract scholarly attention, even if the key transitions for free people, like coming of age and marriage, operated very differently for slaves.[31]

BLACK MASCULINITY

From John Blassingame's defense of black manhood in *The Slave Community* forward, scholars have tried to unravel the stereotypes of African-American men's emasculation and hypermasculinity. Work on enslaved fathers' devotion to their families, expressed in after-hours work and "commuting" to abroad families, rejects equally the myth of absent fathers and the myth of the feckless stud. In a different vein, Diane Miller Sommerville has argued that the literal castration of enslaved men convicted of rape had surprisingly little to do with fears of ravening black sexuality. Instead, it reflected a financial and agricultural logic: castration saved the colonial government money (because execution required compensating the slave's owner), and it drew on the common knowledge that castrated bulls and horses became placid work animals. None of this was any comfort for the men involved, but it is profoundly important for scholars trying to pin down black masculinity's evolution in white eyes.[32] Meanwhile, recognizing that slave breeding made men and women "victims of reproductive abuse" is one way of attending to Bertram Wyatt-Brown's warning that historians must examine "the social and psychological tensions that slavery entailed." Also important in this regard is the acknowledgment that some enslaved men, especially powerful or influential men like drivers and conjurers, manipulated and coerced female slaves sexually. The broader implications of sexual aggression for black masculinity are somewhat ambiguous, for it remains to be determined exactly how enslaved men in general viewed the matter.[33]

As for enslaved women, historians have identified a range of white stereotypes—Nat, Sambo, Jack, and Uncle Tom—and a variety of lived black masculinities. Some enslaved men cherished the rebel's heroic call to live free or die, even if they did not achieve it. Others adopted the masculinity of the wanderer-outlaw, who is essentially free because he accepts no ties of obligation with others. Still others adopted an ethic of caring, often anchored in a Christian conversion experience. So far, however, a single version of black masculinity predominates in descriptions of the emancipation generations. African-Americans in the Civil War, for example, staked their claims to full citizenship and manhood alike on the grounds of military service and manly valor.[34]

MASTERY AND WHITE GENDER IDENTITIES

In many ways, white gender identities in New World slavery can be understood if not simply the inverse of whatever whites said about enslaved men and women, then in part as the longing to be that inverse. Thus, white women should be virtuous and pure, while enslaved women were lustful and vicious. White men should be chivalrous and rational, while enslaved men were either infantile or savage. But throughout New World slavery, gender relations, roles, and identities among whites also looked beyond race to questions of class. Thus, working-class and poor white women in the North America, the Caribbean, and Latin America often shared much of the stigma that attached to enslaved and Indian women, while white men's claims to masculinity depended at least in part on their access to the property that would enable them to become householders.[35]

The linkage of race and class in white gender identity lies at the heart of mastery and honor, two potently gendered belief systems among New World elites. Work on white masculinity and mastery in the American South has been especially influential. The desire for mastery profoundly shaped not only white men's relations with their slaves and family members, but also their own identities. Mastery hinged on control over domestic dependants. At the extreme, this was always an impossible goal—because slaves, children, and wives never became perfect channels for their master's will—but it predisposed many white men to take resistance in any form as a personal affront. As Eugene Genovese has suggested, the more paternalistic versions of mastery also prompted some planters, perhaps many, to chase the improbable goal of respectful affection from their bondspeople. In some cases, masculinity became totally entangled not only with discipline but also with commerce: purchasers gambled not just their money but also their masculinity on their ability to judge slaves on the auction block. Gender imposed powerful and occasionally dangerous constraints on white men. Some ingested powerful drugs in their campaign to master *everything*, including their own bowels. Others let themselves be shot at in duels, in the name of manly honor.[36]

While physical domination, sexual and otherwise, remained the hallmark of masculinity for many white men, for some, evangelical faiths moderated the fondness for drinking, hunting, dancing, and fighting often associated with white men in slavery. For them, and for many in the Upper South in particular, masculinity encompassed elements of gentleness and emotional expressiveness that meshed well with new notions of companionate marriage, for example, also found in the bourgeois North. Yeoman farmers, landless men, and artisans, meanwhile, sometimes outdid their planter contemporaries in violent self-assertion, but those who depended upon planters for their livelihoods typically had to find ways to accommodate planter condescension—or move west in pursuit of landed independence.[37]

Scholarship on white women's gender identities beyond the planter class remains limited, in large part for evidentiary reasons, but work to date indicates that the impact of class on white women's identities was equally profound. Elizabeth Fox-Genovese's *Within the Plantation Household* continues to influence debates about slave owning women, a field which is particularly rich for the Old South. Fox-Genovese attributed the Old South's gender relations to its male-dominated productive households, contrasting them to northern bourgeois households, which became increasingly feminized as men left home to work. Southern gender roles and norms left planter women at significant risk for economic dependence and domestic violence. However, class and racial privilege so shaped their gender identities that most either embraced their position or resisted it on a personal rather than systemic level. While this aspect of Fox-Genovese's argument remains largely intact, newer research by Anya Jabour, Kirsten Wood, and others indicates that planter women were not always content with being or even allowed to be purely dependent. Antebellum slave owning daughters prized their girlhood freedom and fought determined delaying actions against marriage. From the early colonies through the Civil War, moreover, while most white women entered coverture—sometimes repeatedly—warfare, politics, travel, business, death, and many other factors forced many women to assume the burdens of household mastery as grass or real widows.[38]

Scholars of working women and farm women, meanwhile, have shown that these groups were not simply in thrall to planter ideals.[39] The busy women Julia Cherry Spruill studied in the colonial South had antebellum descendants: middle-class women worked as printers, writers, editors, and shopkeepers, for example, both in their own right and as essential complements to their husbands. Intriguingly, such women subscribed to—and, as writers, advocated—the separate spheres ideology that supposedly buffered them from the world of money and politics, and that Elizabeth Fox-Genovese had argued could not emerge in the Old South.[40]

In the American South in particular, ideas about white manhood (strength, sexual activity, reason, self-restraint, assertiveness, honor) and about white womanhood (purity, dependence, obedience, industriousness, maternity, piety) fused in ways that bolstered not only patriarchy, but also slavery and white supremacy. Key to both were notions of domestic mastery, whether the dependants to be mastered were slaves, wives, children, or grown white men. Especially in the antebellum South, ideas about mastery also bolstered both socioeconomic inequality and electoral democracy. In the context of slavery, to speak of mastery (male or female) is also to talk of politics.[41]

POLITICS

In the United States, gender met southern planters' pressing need to explain why the nonslaveholding majority should support slavery through their votes, taxes, and shared policing. Planters and yeoman farmers shared not only a commitment to white superiority but also to domestic patriarchy: as fathers and husbands, they were equally the "masters" of their "small worlds," to quote Stephanie McCurry. Campaigns to defeat or defend slavery also relied on gender norms. In the antebellum South, marriage became the governing metaphor for proslavery ideologues, who used it to suggest slavery's benevolence and permanence. Everywhere, slavery's defenders insisted on black women's lasciviousness to justify enslaving black women and their mixed-race children, mask white men's adultery, and deny the existence of rape. Some defenders of slavery also argued, contradictorily, that slavery raised white women to their proper place in society: white women could be ladies—and none need be prostitutes—because degraded black women absorbed white men's baser impulses and motivated them to defend white ladies' delicacy. That mythology of white women's pedestal goes a long way to explain white women's support during and after slavery for social mores that have, in the modern era, impeded the spread of feminism beyond its traditionally white, middle-class following.[42]

Despite the pedestal, white women in slavery did not remain aloof from politics. Their alleged purity—a gendered and racialized trait—made them amenable and important to the American Whig party's reform agenda in the 1840s, as Elizabeth Varon and others argue. White women also worked for benevolent reform, gradual emancipation through colonization, poor relief, and temperance, all highly political campaigns in the antebellum South. A particularly clear instance of white women's impact on politics involves the Civil War. Drew Gilpin Faust maintains that women withdrew their support for the Confederacy when their submission no longer bought the reciprocal provision of protection and material support.[43]

Abolitionists also relied on gender, as Kristen Hoganson, Julie Roy Jeffrey, and Henrice Altink have shown. To engage white sympathies, their propaganda urged (female) readers to imagine themselves violated by the overseer's lash or torn forcibly from their nursing infants. Abolitionists also believed adopting the "middle-class marriage ideal" would help make American freedpeople and Jamaican apprentices into productive wage laborers.[44] Fugitive slaves and black abolitionists spoke bitterly about planters' interference in slave family life and especially about sexual violence, with its enormous if different tolls on enslaved women and men. After slavery, freedpeople's frequent commitment to what look like bourgeois family norms— legal marriage and household-centered work for women—reflected both a desire to enjoy what was denied in slavery and an ongoing struggle to wrest control over black families out of white hands. Gender remained deeply embedded in post-slavery politics, from fights over American freedwomen's wearing of veils to whites' struggles to control black women's and children's labor.[45]

NEW DIRECTIONS

Gender analysis has reshaped scholarship on the thirteen colonies and the United States more than the Caribbean and South America, so closer and more sustained scrutiny of those regions promises additional insights. The Caribbean's wealth of studies of enslaved women is yet unmatched for enslaving men and women, although Hilary Beckles and Trevor Burnard have begun the work. Similarly, the vast history of South American and Brazilian slavery could support many more gendered studies.[46] Relatedly, change over time—long underexamined for the American South in particular—needs more elaboration there and elsewhere. Most research to date explores well-developed plantation systems, but as the work of Kathleen Brown, Laura Edwards, and Leslie Schwalm indicates, for example, the frontier and the emancipation stages of slavery's New World history witnessed significant and sometimes quite rapid change in gender roles, identities, and ideologies.[47]

Thematically, we need to forge clearer links between gender ideologies and day-to-day interactions in the fields, kitchens, cabins, courts, slave marts, and slave ships. We need more data on how European and African precedents and the changing context of plantation slavery itself shaped the gendered division of labor over time. We also stand in need of a more precise conceptual language that will clearly explain why it is *not* true that "gender was obliterated under slavery" and that "as workers, women slaves were rendered equal to men."[48]

The way forward is not entirely clear, however. Some scholars worry that gender history, especially of masculinity, is displacing women's history, just as work on race, and especially whiteness, may overshadow black history. Whiteness and masculinity are essential historical subjects, but interest in them should not submerge research about women in general and black women in particular. By the same token, black women's history should not become solely a means to understand "the systemic nature of racism and sexism."[49] At the same time, some modern historians view black women's history as a means to honor and embolden black women in the present, yet this places these historians in a very different relationship to their subject—and their readers—than those who study slavery as an institution. Even so, precisely because gender is both supremely personal and systemically encoded in society-wide relations of power, rigorous gender analysis can help bridge the gap between personal and institutional, micro and macro approaches to slavery in the New World.

NOTES

1. Joan W. Scott, "Gender: A Useful Category of Historical Analysis," *American Historical Review*, 91 (5) (December 1986): 1053–75.
2. Barbara Bush, "'Sable Venus,' 'She Devil' or 'Drudge?': British Slavery and the 'Fabulous Fiction' of Black Women's Identities, c.1650–1838," *Women's History Review*, 9 (4) (2000): 761–89; Jennifer L. Morgan, "'Some Could Suckle over their Shoulder': Male Travelers, Female Bodies, and the Gendering of Racial Ideology, 1500–1770," *William and Mary*

Quarterly, 54 (1) (1997): 167–92; Barbara Bush, *Slave Women in Caribbean Society, 1650–1838* (London, 1990), 13–14; Hilary M. Beckles, *Natural Rebels: A Social History of Enslaved Black Women in Barbados* (New Brunswick, NJ, 1990), 24. Existing work on gender's role in African slave trade has paid more heed to sex ratios and labor patterns than to gender ideology per se. Useful works include: Trevor Burnard and Kenneth Morgan, "The Dynamics of the Slave Market and Slave Purchasing Patterns in Jamaica, 1655–1788," *William and Mary Quarterly*, 58 (1) (2001) (June 23, 2007); G. Ugo Nwokeji, "African Conceptions of Gender and the Slave Traffic," *William and Mary Quarterly*, 58 (1) (2001): 47–68; Jennifer L. Morgan, "Women in Slavery and the Transatlantic Slave Trade," in *Transatlantic Slavery: Against Human Dignity* (London, 1994), 60–9; David Eltis and Stanley L. Engerman, "Was the Slave Trade Dominated by Men?," *Journal of Interdisciplinary History*, 23 (2) (1992): 237–57; Joseph E. Inikori, "Export Versus Domestic Demand: The Determinants of Sex Ratios in the Transatlantic Slave Trade," *Research in Economic History*, 14 (1992): 117–66; David Geggus, "Sex Ratio, Age and Ethnicity in the Atlantic Slave Trade: Data from French Shipping and Plantation Records," *Journal of African History*, 30 (1) (1989): 23–44.

3. Hilary M. Beckles, "Plantation Production and White 'Proto-Slavery': White Indentured Servants and the Colonisation of the English West Indies, 1624–1645," *The Americas*, 41 (3) (January 1985): 45.

4. Kathleen M. Brown, *Good Wives, Nasty Wenches, and Anxious Patriarchs: Gender, Race, and Power in Colonial Virginia* (Chapel Hill, NC, 1996); Ben Marsh, *Georgia's Frontier Women: Female Fortunes in a Southern Colony* (Athens, Ga., 2007), 10–11, 141, 143; Catherine Clinton and Michele Gillespie (eds.), *The Devil's Lane: Sex and Race in the Early South* (New York, 1997). On gender and early Virginia, see also Mary Beth Norton, *Founding Mothers & Fathers: Gendered Power and the Forming of American Society* (New York, 1996).

5. Bernard Moitt, *Women and Slavery in the French Antilles, 1635–1848* (Bloomington, Ind., 2001), 40–5; Beckles, *Natural Rebels*, 31, 33, 52, 106–7; Jacqueline Jones, " 'My Mother Was Much of a Woman': Black Women, Work, and the Family under Slavery," *Feminist Studies*, 8 (2) (1982): 239, 242.

6. Beckles, *Natural Rebels*, 32, 38, 55; Deborah G. White, *Ar'n't I a Woman? Female Slaves in the Plantation South* (1985; rev. edn. New York, 1999), 94.

7. Beckles, *Natural Rebels*; Daina Berry, *Swing the Sickle for the Harvest is Ripe: Gender and Slavery in Antebellum Georgia* (Urbana, Ill., 2007); Sharla M. Fett, *Working Cures: Healing, Health, and Power on Southern Slave Plantations* (Chapel Hill, NC, 2002), 125; Moitt, *Women and Slavery*, pp. xv, 35–6, 48, 52; Susan M. Socolow, "Economic Roles of the Free Women of Color of Cap Français," in David Barry Gaspar and Darlene Clark Hine (eds.), *More than Chattel: Black Women and Slavery in the Americas* (Bloomington, Ind., 1996), 287; Marietta Morrissey, *Slave Women in the New World: Gender Stratification in the Caribbean* (Lawrence, Kan., 1989), 65–8, 161–3; White, *Ar'n't I a Woman?*, 76, 128–30; Rhoda Reddock, "Women and Slavery in the Caribbean: A Feminist Perspective," *Latin American Perspectives*, 12 (1) (Winter 1985): 65, 74; White, *Ar'n't I a Woman?*; Jones, " 'My Mother Was Much of a Woman' ". For domestic labor, see Stephanie Cole, "Servants and Slaves: Domestic Service in the Border Cities, 1800–1850" (Ph.D. diss., University of Florida, 1994). For women in rice agriculture, see Judith A. Carney, *Black Rice: The African Origins of Rice Cultivation in the Americas* (Cambridge, Mass., 2001); Leslie A. Schwalm, *A Hard Fight for We: Women's Transition from Slavery to Freedom in South Carolina* (Urbana, Ill., 1997).

8. Jones, "'My Mother Was Much of a Woman,'" quotation at 243; Bush, *Slave Women*, 129–31.

9. Morrissey, *Slave Women*, 47, 49–54, 61. For change in women's tasks, see Carole Shammas, "Black Women's Work and the Evolution of Plantation Society in Virginia," *Labor History*, 26 (Winter 1985): 5–28; but compare Marsh, *Georgia's Frontier Women*, 139–41.

10. Cynthia M. Kennedy, *Braided Relations, Entwined Lives: The Women of Charleston's Urban Slave Society* (Bloomington, Ind., 2005); Evelyn Brooks Higginbotham, "African-American Women's History and the Metalanguage of Race," *Signs*, 17 (2) (Winter 1992): 251–74; Elsa Barkley Brown, " 'What Has Happened Here': The Politics of Difference in Women's History and Feminist Politics," *Feminist Studies*, 18 (2) (Summer 1992): 295–312.

11. Beckles, *Natural Rebels*, 9, 94; Bush, *Slave Women*, 36, 122; Morrissey, *Slave Women*, pp. xii, 44, 109; Cheryll Ann Cody, "Slave Demography and Family Formation: A Community Study of the Ball Family Plantations, 1720–1896" (Ph.D. diss., University of Minnesota, 1983).

12. Jennifer L. Morgan, *Laboring Women: Reproduction and Gender in New World Slavery* (Philadelphia, 2004), 12–49, 69–106. On amelioration, see Bush, *Slave Women*, 28–30, 44–5, 113, 135; Beckles, *Natural Rebels*, 38, 99, 104, 117.

13. Edward E. Baptist, "'Cuffy,' 'Fancy Maids,' and 'One-Eyed Men': Rape, Commodification, and the Domestic Slave Trade in the United States," *American Historical Review*, 106 (December 2001): quotation at 1649; Diane Miller Sommerville, *Rape and Race in the Nineteenth-Century South* (Chapel Hill, NC, 2004); Merril D. Smith (ed.), *Sex without Consent: Rape and Sexual Coercion in America* (New York, 2001); Sharon Block, *Rape and Sexual Power in Early America* (Chapel Hill, NC, 2006); Susan Migden Socolow, *The Women of Colonial Latin America* (Cambridge, 2000), 134–5, 152–3; Martha Hodes, *White Women, Black Men: Illicit Sex in the Nineteenth-Century South* (New Haven, 1999); Jacquelyn Dowd Hall, "'The Mind That Burns in Each Body': Women, Rape, and Racial Violence," in Christine Stansell and Ann Snitow (eds.), *Powers of Desire: The Politics of Sexuality* (New York, 1983); Berry, *Swing the Sickle*, 82–4.

14. Electronic editions of Dixon's novels are available at Documenting the American South, along with a useful critique introduction to the trilogy. Andrew Leiter, "Thomas Dixon, Jr.: Conflicts in History and Literature," http://docsouth.unc.edu/southlit/dixon_intro.html. Accessed April 29, 2008.

15. Jacquelyn Dowd Hall, *Revolt against Chivalry: Jessie Daniel Ames and the Women's Campaign against Lynching* (New York, 1979).

16. Henrice Altink, "Deviant and Dangerous: Pro-Slavery Representations of Jamaican Slave Women's Sexuality, c.1780–1834," *Slavery and Abolition*, 26 (2) (August 2005): quotation at 274; Joshua R. Rothman, *Notorious in the Neighborhood: Sex and Families across the Color Line in Virginia, 1787–1861* (Chapel Hill, NC, 2003), 155; Virginia Meacham Gould, " 'A Chaos of Iniquity and Discord': Slave and Free Women of Color in the Spanish Ports of New Orleans, Mobile, and Pensacola," in Clinton and Gillespie (eds.), *The Devil's Lane*, 240–3.

17. White, *Ar'n't I a Woman?*, 38; Morrissey, *Slave Women*, 66, 70–3; Beckles, *Natural Rebels*, 141–51; David P. Geggus, "Slave and Free Colored Women in Saint Domingue," in Gaspar and Hine (eds.), *More than Chattel*, 270; Annette Gordon-Reed, *Thomas Jefferson and Sally Hemings: An American Controversy* (Charlottesville, Va., 1997). For free and freedwomen, see also David Barry Gaspar and Darlene Clark Hine (eds.), *Beyond*

Bondage: Free Women of Color in the Americas (Urbana, Ill., 2004); Kimberly S. Hangar, "Coping in a Complex World: Free Black Women in Colonial New Orleans," in Clinton and Gillespie (eds.), *The Devil's Lane*, 218–31.

18. Kennedy, *Braided Relations*, 95, 167–9; Stephanie M. H. Camp, *Closer to Freedom: Enslaved Women and Everyday Resistance in the Plantation South* (Chapel Hill, NC, 2004), 62. For informal marriage and the changing relationship of race and sexuality in a north American city, see Clare A. Lyons, *Sex among the Rabble: An Intimate History of Gender* (Chapel Hill, NC, 2006).

19. Darlene Clark Hine, "Rape and the Inner Lives of Black Women in the Middle West," *Signs*, 14 (4) (Summer 1989): 912–20.

20. E. Franklin Frazier, *The Negro Family in the United States*, with a new introduction and bibliography by Anthony M. Platt (Notre Dame, Ind., 2001); Daniel P. Moynihan, *The Negro Family: The Case for National Action* (US Department of Labor, 1965); John W. Blassingame, *The Slave Community: Plantation Life in the Antebellum South* (New York, 1972); Herbert S. Gutman, *The Black Family in Slavery and Freedom, 1750–1925* (New York, 1977). For free blacks, see Michael P. Johnson and James L. Roark, *Black Masters: A Free Family of Color in the Old South* (New York, 1984).

21. White, *Ar'n't I a Woman?*; Jones, "'My Mother Was Much of a Woman'"; Katia M. de Queirós Mattoso, "Slave, Free, and Freed Family Structures in Nineteenth-Century Salvador, Bahia," *Luso-Brazilian Review*, 25 (1) (Summer 1988): 69–84.

22. Ann Patton Malone, *Sweet Chariot: Slave Family and Household Structure in Nineteenth-Century Louisiana* (Chapel Hill, NC, 1992). Brenda E. Stevenson, *Life in Black and White: Family and Community in the Slave South* (New York, 1997), 160, 221, 223. On domestic violence among slaves, see White, *Ar'n't I a Woman?*, 151–3; Betty Wood, *Women's Work, Men's Work: The Informal Slave Economies of Lowcountry Georgia* (Athens, Ga., 1995), 185; Emily West, "Tensions, Tempers, and Temptations: Marital Discord among Slaves in Antebellum South Carolina," *American Nineteenth Century History*, 5 (2) (2004): 1–18.

23. Kennedy, *Braided Relations*, quotation at 95; Claire Robertson, "Africa into the Americas? Slavery and Women, the Family, and the Gender Division of Labor," in Gaspar and Hine (eds.), *More than Chattel*, 17; Moitt, *Women and Slavery*, 36; Claire C. Robertson and Martin A. Klein (eds.), *Women and Slavery in Africa* (Madison, 1983).

24. Bernard Moitt, "Slave Women and Resistance in the French Caribbean," in Gaspar and Hine (eds.), *More than Chattel*, 239–58; Geggus, "Women in Saint Domingue"; Camp, *Closer to Freedom*, ch. 2; Verene Shepherd, Bridget Brereton, and Barbara Bailey, *Engendering History: Caribbean Women in Historical Perspective* (New York, 1995); Rosalyn Terborg-Penn, "Black Women in Resistance: A Cross-Cultural Perspective," in Gary Y. Okihiro (ed.), *In Resistance: Studies in African, Caribbean, and Afro-American History* (Amherst, Mass., 1986), 188–209; Elizabeth Fox-Genovese, "Strategies and Forms of Resistance: Focus on Slave Women in the United States," in Okihiro (ed.), *In Resistance*, 143–65.

25. Liese M. Perrin, "Resisting Reproduction: Reconsidering Slave Contraception in the Old South," *Journal of American Studies*, 35 (2) (August 2001): 255–74; Thelma Jennings, "'Us Colored Women Had to Go Through a Plenty': Sexual Exploitation of African-American Slave Women," *Journal of Women's History*, 1 (3) (1990): 45–74.

26. Sharon Ann Holt, "Symbol, Memory, and Service: Resistance and Family Formation in Nineteenth-Century African America," in Larry E. Hudson (ed.), *Working toward*

Freedom: Slave Society and Domestic Economy in the American South (Rochester, NY, 1994), 204; White, *Ar'n't I a Woman?*, 87–9; Bush, *Slave Women*, 143–8, 165–6.

27. Morgan, *Laboring Women.*

28. For Native Americans, gender, and slavery, see, for example, Ramon Gutierrez, *When Jesus Came, the Corn Mothers Went Away* (Stanford, Calif., 1991); Barbara Krauthamer, "Ar'n't I a Woman? Native Americans, Gender, and Slavery," *Journal of Women's History*, 19 (2) (2007): 156–60.

29. Henrice Altink, *Representations of Slave Women in Discourses on Slavery and Abolition, 1780–1838* (London, 2007); Bush, "'Sable Venus'"; White, *Ar'n't I a Woman?*

30. Nancy A. Hewitt, "Compounding Differences," *Feminist Studies*, 18 (2) (Summer 1992): 313–26.

31. Kennedy, *Braided Relations*, 95–110; Camp, *Closer to Freedom*; Marie Jenkins Schwartz, *Born in Bondage: Growing up Enslaved in the Antebellum South* (Cambridge, Mass., 2000). For free women, see for example Suzanne Lebsock, *The Free Women of Petersburg: Status and Culture in a Southern Town, 1784–1860* (New York, 1984).

32. Diane Miller Sommerville, "Rape, Race, and Castration in Slave Law in the Colonial and Early South," in Clinton and Gillespie (eds.), *The Devil's Lane*, 74–89.

33. Berry, *Swing the Sickle*, quotation at 79; Bertram Wyatt-Brown, "The Mask of Obedience: Male Slave Psychology in the Old South," *American Historical Review*, 93 (5) (December 1988): quotation at 1230; Fett, *Working Cures*, 91.

34. Edward E. Baptist, "'Stol' and Fetched Here': Enslaved Migration, Ex-Slave Narratives, and Vernacular History," in Edward E. Baptist and Stephanie M. H. Camp (eds.), *New Studies in the History of American Slavery* (Athens, Ga., 2006), 243–74; Heather Andrea Williams, "'Commenced to Think Like a Man': Literacy and Manhood in African-American Civil War Regiments," in Craig Thompson Friend and Lorri Glover (eds.), *Southern Manhood: Perspectives on Masculinity in the Old South* (Athens, Ga., 2004); Darlene Clark Hine and Earnestine Jenkins (eds.), *A Question of Manhood: A Reader in U.S. Black Men's History and Masculinity* (Bloomington, Ind., 1999–c.2001), 10; Jim Cullen, "'I's a Man Now': Gender and African-American Men," in Catherine Clinton and Nina Silber (eds.), *Divided Houses: Gender and the Civil War* (New York, 1992), 76–91; Joseph P. Reidy, Leslie S. Rowland, and Ira Berlin (eds.), *The Black Military Experience* (Cambridge, 1982), 30–2.

35. Lebsock, *Free Women of Petersburg*; Jane H. Pease and William Henry Pease, *Ladies, Women, and Wenches: Choice and Constraint in Antebellum Charleston and Boston*, Gender & American Culture (Chapel Hill, NC, 1990); Socolow, *The Women of Colonial Latin America.*

36. Friend and Glover (eds.), *Southern Manhood*; Trevor Burnard, *Mastery, Tyranny, and Desire: Thomas Thistlewood and his Slaves in the Anglo-Jamaican World* (Chapel Hill, NC, 2003); Walter Johnson, *Soul by Soul: Life inside the Antebellum Slave Market* (Cambridge, Mass., 1999); Stephanie McCurry, *Masters of Small Worlds: Yeoman Households, Gender Relations, and the Political Culture of the Antebellum South Carolina Low Country* (New York, 1995); Kenneth A. Lockridge, *On the Sources of Patriarchal Rage: The Commonplace Books of William Byrd and Thomas Jefferson and the Gendering of Power in the Eighteenth Century* (New York, 1992); Eugene D. Genovese, *Roll, Jordan, Roll: The World the Slaves Made* (New York, 1974); Anya Jabour, *Marriage in the Early Republic: Elizabeth and William Wirt and the Companionate Ideal* (Baltimore, 1998); Jan Lewis, *The Pursuit of Happiness: Family and Values in Jefferson's Virginia* (Cambridge,

1983); Jane Turner Censer, *North Carolina Planters and their Children, 1800–1860* (Baton Rogue, La., 1984). For paternalism, start with Genovese, *Roll, Jordan, Roll* and then consider, for example, Jeffrey Robert Young, *Domesticating Slavery: The Master Class in Georgia and South Carolina, 1670–1837* (Chapel Hill, NC, 1999); Drew Gilpin Faust, *James Henry Hammond and the Old South: A Design for Mastery* (Baton Rouge, La., 1982), esp. 376–7. On honor, see Lyman L. Johnson and Sonya Lipsett-Rivera (eds.), *The Faces of Honor: Sex, Shame, and Violence in Colonial Latin America* (Albuquerque, N. Mex., 1998); Kenneth S. Greenberg, *Honor and Slavery: Lies, Duels, Noses, Masks, Dressing as a Woman, Gifts, Strangers, Humanitarianism, Death, Slave Rebellions, the Proslavery Argument, Baseball, Hunting, and Gambling in the Old South* (Princeton, 1996); Steven M. Stowe, *Intimacy and Power in the Old South: Ritual in the Lives of the Planters* (Baltimore, 1987); Bertram Wyatt-Brown, *Southern Honor: Ethics and Behavior in the Old South* (New York, 1982).

37. For evangelicals, see Jean E. Friedman, *The Enclosed Garden: Women and Community in the Evangelical South, 1830–1900* (Chapel Hill, NC, 1985); Christine Leigh Heyrman, *Southern Cross: The Beginnings of the Bible Belt* (Chapel Hill, NC, 1997); Monica Elizabeth Najar, "Evangelizing the South: Gender, Race, and Politics in the Early Evangelical South, 1765–1815" (Ph.D. diss., University of Wisconsin, Madison, 2000); Frederick A. Bode, "A Common Sphere: White Evangelicals and Gender in Antebellum Georgia," *Georgia Historical Quarterly*, 79 (4) (1995): 775–809. For tenants and artisans, see Charles C. Bolton, *Poor Whites of the Antebellum South: Tenants and Laborers in Central North Carolina and Northeast Mississipi* (Durham, NC, 1994); Michele Gillespie, *Free Labor in an Unfree World: White Artisans In Slaveholding Georgia, 1789–1860* (Athens, Ga., 2004).

38. Anya Jabour, *Scarlett's Sisters: Young Women in the Old South* (Chapel Hill, NC, 2007); Nikki Berg Burin, "A Regency of Women: Female Plantation Management in the Old South" (Ph.D. diss., University of Minnesota, 2007); Elizabeth Fox-Genovese, *Within the Plantation Household: Black and White Women of the Old South* (Chapel Hill, NC, 1988), 24, 30, 35, 44; Kirsten E. Wood, *Masterful Women: Slaveholding Widows from the American Revolution through the Civil War* (Chapel Hill, NC, 2004); Cynthia A. Kierner, *Beyond the Household: Women's Place in the Early South, 1700–1835* (Ithaca, NY, 1998); Lebsock, *Free Women of Petersburg*; Catherine Clinton, *The Plantation Mistress: Woman's World in the Old South* (New York, 1982); Anne Firor Scott, *The Southern Lady: From Pedestal to Politics, 1830–1930* (Chicago, 1970); Lois G. Carr and Lorena S. Walsh, "The Planter's Wife: The Experience of White Women in Seventeenth-Century Maryland," *William and Mary Quarterly*, 34 (4) (1977): 542–71; Linda Speth, "More Than her 'Thirds': Wives and Widows in Colonial Virginia," *Women & History*, 4 (1982): 5–41. Research on white women in the Caribbean is relatively sparse. Cecily Jones, "Contesting the Boundaries of Gender, Race and Sexuality in Barbadian Plantation Society," *Women's History Review*, 12 (2) (2003): 195–231; Cheryl King, "According to the Law: Women's Property Rights in Bridgetown Barbados, 1800–1834," *Journal of Caribbean History*, 36 (2) (2002): 267–84; Hilary M. Beckles, "White Women and Slavery in the Caribbean," *History Workshop Journal*, 36 (1993): 66–82; Susan E. Klepp and Roderick McDonald, "Inscribing Experience: An American Working Woman and an English Gentlewoman Encounter Jamaica's Slave Society, 1801–1805," *William and Mary Quarterly*, 58 (3) (July 2001): 637–60.

39. Susanna Delfino and Michele Gillespie (eds.), *Neither Lady Nor Slave: Working Women of the Old South* (Chapel Hill, NC, 2002); Victoria E. Bynum, *Unruly Women: The Politics of Social and Sexual Control in the Old South* (Chapel Hill, NC, 1992); Lebsock, *Free Women of Petersburg*; D. Harland Hagler, "The Ideal Woman in the Antebellum South: Lady or Farmwife?," *Journal of Southern History*, 46 (August 1980): 405–18.

40. Jonathan D. Wells, *The Origins of the Southern Middle Class, 1800–1861* (Chapel Hill, NC, 2004); Julia Cherry Spruill, *Women's Life and Work in the Southern Colonies* (Chapel Hill, NC, 1938). For domesticity and female identity, see Marli Frances Weiner, *Mistresses and Slaves: Plantation Women in South Carolina, 1830–80* (Urbana, Ill., 1997).

41. Brown, *Good Wives*.

42. McCurry, *Masters of Small Worlds*.

43. Elizabeth R. Varon, *We Mean to be Counted: White Women and Politics in Antebellum Virginia* (Chapel Hill, NC, 1998); Drew Gilpin Faust, *Mothers of Invention: Women of the Slaveholding South in the American Civil War* (Chapel Hill, NC, 1996); LeeAnn Whites, *The Civil War as a Crisis in Gender: Augusta, Georgia, 1860–1890* (Athens, Ga., 1995).

44. Henrice Altink, "'To Wed or Not to Wed?' The Struggle to Define Afro-Jamaican Relationships, 1834–1838," *Journal of Social History*, 81 (1) (2004): quotation at 81; Julie Roy Jeffrey, *The Great Silent Army of Abolitionism: Ordinary Women in the Antislavery Movement* (Chapel Hill, NC, 1998); Kristin Hoganson, "Garrisonian Abolitionists and the Rhetoric of Gender, 1850–1860," *American Quarterly*, 45 (4) (December 1993): 558–95; Elizabeth B. Clark, " 'The Sacred Rights of the Weak': Pain, Sympathy, and the Culture of Individual Rights in Antebellum America," *Journal of American History*, 82 (2) (September 1995): 463–93; Harriet Jacobs and Farah Jasmine Griffin, *Incidents in the Life of a Slave Girl*, ed. George Stade (New York, 2005).

45. Laura F. Edwards, *Scarlett Doesn't Live Here Anymore: Southern Women in the Civil War Era* (Urbana, Ill., 2000), 100–48; Pamela Scully and Diana Paton (eds.), *Gender and Slave Emancipation in the Atlantic World* (Durham, NC, 2005); Verene A. Shepherd (ed.), *Working Slavery, Pricing Freedom: Perspectives from the Caribbean, Africa and the African Diaspora* (New York, 2002); Carol Lasser, "Slavery, Gender and the Meanings of Freedom," *Gender & History*, 13 (1) (April 2001): 161–6; Laura F. Edwards, *Gendered Strife & Confusion: The Political Culture of Reconstruction* (Urbana, Ill., 1997); Schwalm, *A Hard Fight for We*.

46. A classic source for gender in Brazil is Gilberto Freyre, *The Masters and the Slaves (Casa-Grande & Senzala): A Study in the Development of Brazilian Civilization by Gilberto Freyre*, trans. Samuel Putnam (New York, 1946). See also Kathleen J. Higgins, "Gender and Manumission of Slaves in Colonial Brazil: The Prospects for Freedom in Sabara, Minas Gerais, 1710–1809," *Slavery and Abolition*, 18 (2) (1997): 1–29. The recent Herbert S. Klein and Ben Vinson, iii: *African Slavery in Latin America and the Caribbean* (Oxford, 2007) contains chapters on demography and family, but none devoted to women or gender.

47. Brown, *Good Wives*; Edwards, *Scarlett Doesn't Live Here Anymore*; Edwards, *Gendered Strife & Confusion*; Schwalm, *A Hard Fight for We*.

48. Moitt, *Women and Slavery*, quotation at xiv; Bush, *Slave Women*, xii.

49. Leslie Alexander, "The Challenge of Race: Rethinking the Position of Black Women in the Field of Women's History," *Journal of Women's History*, 16 (4) (2004): 56.

SELECT BIBLIOGRAPHY

BECKLES, HILARY M. *Natural Rebels: A Social History of Enslaved Black Women in Barbados.* New Brunswick, NJ: Rutgers University Press, 1990.

BROWN, KATHLEEN M. *Good Wives, Nasty Wenches, and Anxious Patriarchs: Gender, Race, and Power in Colonial Virginia.* Chapel Hill, NC: University of North Carolina Press, 1996.

BUSH, BARBARA. *Slave Women in Caribbean Society, 1650–1838.* London: James Curry, 1990.

FOX-GENOVESE, ELIZABETH. *Within the Plantation Household: Black and White Women of the Old South.* Chapel Hill, NC: University of North Carolina Press, 1988.

GASPAR, DAVID BARRY, and DARLENE CLARK HINE, eds. *More than Chattel: Black Women and Slavery in the Americas.* Bloomington, Ind.: Indiana University Press, 1996.

———— eds. *Beyond Bondage: Free Women of Color in the Americas.* Urbana, Ill.: University of Illinois Press, 2004.

McCURRY, STEPHANIE. *Masters of Small Worlds: Yeoman Households, Gender Relations, and the Political Culture of the Antebellum South Carolina Low Country.* New York: Oxford University Press, 1995.

MOITT, BERNARD. *Women and Slavery in the French Antilles, 1635–1848.* Bloomington, Ind.: University of Indiana Press, 2001.

MORGAN, JENNIFER L. *Laboring Women: Reproduction and Gender in New World Slavery.* Philadelphia: University of Pennsylvania Press, 2004.

MORRISSEY, MARIETTA. *Slave Women in the New World: Gender Stratification in the Caribbean.* Lawrence, Kan.: University Press of Kansas, 1989.

WHITE, DEBORAH G. *Ar'n't I a Woman?: Female Slaves in the Plantation South.* 1985; rev. edn. New York: Norton, 1999.

CHAPTER 24

MASTERS

EUGENE D. GENOVESE
DOUGLAS AMBROSE

MASTERS AND SLAVES

G. W. F. Hegel, in his great set piece on "Lordship and Bondage," highlighted the essential relational character of master and slave. To be a master requires that another human being be a slave. And, as Hegel asserted, the master understands himself by and through his slave in an even more psychological and culturally significant way than the slave understands himself.[1] The relational, in contradistinction to the legal, character of mastery helps explain the fundamental distinctiveness of the slaveholders of the southern United States between the era of the American Revolution and the culmination of the War for Southern Independence. Nowhere else in the hemisphere did a slaveholding class possess as much political power, internal cohesiveness, class confidence, and class consciousness. No other master class envisioned itself as leading a territorially expansive society that could provide other modern societies with an example of social relations that they could emulate to avoid class war and political despotism. Although the master class of the Old South was neither homogeneous nor free of contradictions, it displayed impressive ideological and political unity. That unity grew out of and derived strength from the paternalistic ethos that functioned as its normative ideal even when it failed to guide actual practice. Bolstered by their conviction that the master–slave relation provided the only realistic basis for a Christian, modern, and republican society, they boldly confronted the rising tide of bourgeois individualism, market relations, and radical egalitarianism that was engulfing the Western world.

Slavery and the relations that comprised it varied widely throughout the Western hemisphere, influenced by a number of factors including national traditions, law, religion, and the personal temperaments of masters. Of special importance was the staple crop. Sugar, in particular, produced a culture that owed far less to the national or religious identity of the master than it did to the crop's specific character. The other important slave-grown crops—rice, tobacco, cotton, indigo—imposed their particular stamp on the relations between the slaves who produced them and the masters who commanded their labor. Philip Morgan and other scholars have powerfully demonstrated that attentiveness to the varying demands of the staples provides insight into aspects of slavery that range from settlement patterns to demography to slave culture to the character of the master class in each slave society. Different slave societies, derived in large part from the staple produced, produced different types of master classes. Morgan has also insisted that any attempt to make sense of those slave societies—and the classes within them—requires that scholars be alert "to process, to development, to the changes wrought by time." Slave societies, like all social formations, evolved through time, and masters, as parts of those societies, changed along with them. In the case of southern slaveholders, the most important change over time was that from patriarchalism to paternalism.[2]

PATRIARCHS AND PATERNALISTS

The transition from patriarchalism to paternalism varied considerably over space and time. Historians have carefully pointed out that the two coexisted not only within the master class, but also within individual masters, and certain broad developments of the process are clear. From the second half of the eighteenth century, masters in the Chesapeake region evinced an attitude toward and treatment of their slaves that marked a significant departure from previous thought and practice. These departures had profound implications for slaves, masters, and southern slavery itself. Paternalism became, for the masters, the basis of their understanding of themselves, their households, and their distinct social order. It turned a system based on power into one based on authority, a relation of enemies into a relation of members of the same "family." Moral doubts receded as Christian masters proudly proclaimed slavery scripturally grounded and divinely sanctioned.

Patriarchialism featured several attributes that distinguished it from the paternalism that eventually succeeded it. Philip Morgan has emphasized three key differences between the two. First, "patriarchalism was a more austere code than paternalism. Patriarchal masters stressed order, authority, unswerving obedience, and were quick to resort to violence when their authority was questioned." Paternalist masters, on the other hand, "were more inclined to stress their solicitude, their generous treatment of their dependents." A second key difference concerned masters' personal interest in the lives of their slaves. "Partriarchalism," Morgan writes, "was a more severe code than paternalism," but "it was also less constricting." Patriarchs tended to pay little if any attention to the domestic lives of their slaves, being concerned mostly with their labor. Paternalists, however, often "spoke in cloying and claustrophobic terms of their kindness or their Christian trusteeship toward their slaves." Such kindness, many paternalist masters concluded, ought to elicit gratitude, and those masters' interest in the religious lives of the black members of their households led them to intervene directly in what had been, under patriarchal rule, the slaves' private realm. Finally, Morgan points out that patriarchs had no illusions about their slaves' capacity to rebel; slaves remained dangerous aliens, "domestic enemies," controlled primarily by violence and force. Paternalists, however, notwithstanding persisting fears of the potential violence of slaves, "created the fiction of the contented and happy slave." The paternalist household would be characterized by sentimental attachments between authoritative but benevolent masters and subservient but loyal slaves.[3]

Several factors contributed to the transition from patriarchalism to paternalism, chiefly the slaveholding unit's staple crop. The staple affected the size of the unit, the ratio between slave and non-slave populations, the wealth of masters, the mix of creole and African slaves, master absenteeism, and other factors that influenced the character of master–slave relations and the dynamics of the farm or plantation. It is not surprising that most historians identify paternalism as developing first in the Chesapeake region among tobacco-producing farms and plantations. These units were considerably smaller than the great sugar estates in the Caribbean and Brazil, making possible an intimacy of contact between masters and slaves not easily realized on sugar estates. The majority of slaves in the Chesapeake resided on units of fewer than forty slaves, and many lived on farms with fewer than ten slaves. The majority of tobacco masters resided on their farms and lived among their slaves, again making possible an intimacy that sugar masters, most of whom did not reside on their estates, could not achieve. Tobacco imposed fewer severe physical demands on slaves than did sugar, allowing slaves to survive longer and reproduce. Tobacco's low profitability, unlike sugar's high profitability, also contributed to masters' attentiveness to their slaves' physical needs and reproduction. Masters simply could not afford, as sugar masters could, to purchase new slaves when their slaves died. Although economic motives may have led tobacco masters to encourage slaves to form families and have children, the creolization of the slave population also narrowed the cultural distance between masters and slaves. Creoles spoke English. They grew up under the eyes of their masters who could more easily see them as members of his household than could masters who purchased adult African slaves. The closing of the African slave trade in 1808 also forced masters to be cognizant of their slaves' material well-being.

The rise of evangelical Christianity, which propelled the transition from patriarchalism to paternalism, is attracting increasing scholarly attention. The conversion of slaves to evangelicalism, which began in earnest in the eighteenth century and continued into the nineteenth, narrowed further the cultural distance between masters and slaves. A common religion, notwithstanding considerable differences between white and black understandings of it, provided both opportunities for collective worship and a qualified sense of unity. For masters, perhaps the more important development that accompanied the rise of evangelical Christianity was its promotion of a Christian slaveholding ethic, which grounded mastery within a religious framework that both emphasized the divine sanction of slaveholding and admonished masters to exercise slaveholding in accordance with biblical precepts. Masters, more and more ministers declared, possessed a "divine trust," and God would judge them on how well they fulfilled what he had entrusted to them. The spread of evangelical Christianity and the slaveholding ethic accelerated the spread of paternalism within plantation households and contributed decisively to the masters' conception of themselves as men occupying a "station in which Providence has placed" them. That station required them to care for all whom Providence had placed in their care.[4]

The transition to paternalism, then, united economics and religion. Reduction to one or the other distorts the ways in which they complemented each other. The result was a system of social relations that rested upon duties, responsibilities, and trusteeship and, thus, differentiated itself from the patriarchal model from which it evolved. But, however much masters emphasized the familial, domestic, and sentimental aspects of paternalism, the system, like patriarchalism, ultimately remained grounded in violence. Paternalism did not imply kindness, love, and benevolence. It rested on the threat and actuality of violence, often including meanness and cruelty. And slaves certainly understood paternalism differently than did their masters. They consciously and unconsciously transformed paternalism into a doctrine of protection of their own rights—a doctrine that negated the very idea of slavery. For masters, however, paternalism, as both the underlying principle of their social system and the foundation of their self-image, "lay at the core of the slaveholders' sense of themselves as men who walked in the ways of the Lord."[5] The study of masters has been and continues to be shaped by the challenges of understanding a historically distinct class that arose with the expansion of global demand for slave-produced commodities and yet developed a worldview that rejected fundamental aspects of the individualistic, egalitarian, and democratic ethos that spread throughout the transatlantic world. The masters' understanding of themselves and the contradictions and dilemmas they endured grew out of both their immediate context—their lives with their slaves—and their broader economic, political, and ideological contexts: their relation to and struggle with a world increasingly at odds with their vision of a proper Christian social order.

PATERNALISM AND THE BUSINESS OF SLAVERY

Like most slave owners throughout history, the slaveholders of the Western hemisphere engaged in commercial transactions. Europeans brought African slaves to the Americas to produce staple crops. Slavery thrived in the tropical and semitropical regions of the Americas because masters profited from the managed use of private human property, primarily supervised in gangs, to produce commodities for a burgeoning number of consumers with growing incomes on both sides of the Atlantic. Historians have long debated the relations between capitalism and slavery, whether the two are in fact compatible, as well as the nature of masters as economic agents and the ways they differed and did not differ from other economic elites in the nineteenth-century transatlantic world. Karl Marx spoke about how the "whirlpool of an international market dominated by the capitalistic mode of production" in western Europe grafted unfree labor systems, including slavery, onto other parts of the world. Joseph Schumpeter, in a way that foreshadowed subsequent debates, centered the existence of a capitalist system on private ownership of "non-personal means of production."[6]

However capitalism is defined, the overly simplistic characterization of masters as either pure capitalists or seigneurial lords will not do. Most historians now recognize that southern masters demonstrated at times impressive economic acumen in their utilization of slave labor, in their adjustments to changing demand for staple crops, and in protecting their households from the vicissitudes that accompanied participation in long-distance commercial transactions and commodity markets. Yet critical questions remain: Were southern slaveholders, notwithstanding their participation in and responsiveness to global markets, in important ways distinct from those elites from societies in which free labor predominated? Were they in but not of the transnational, capitalist-driven market system that increasingly prevailed throughout the transatlantic world? And if they did differ significantly from elites in free labor societies, what were the implications of those differences?[7]

The Georgia-born historian Ulrich Bonnell Phillips dominated the study of slavery in the United States during the first half of the twentieth century. While stressing the paternalistic side of the master–slave relation and acknowledging short-term economic benefits from the use of slave labor, he maintained its long-term unprofitability by wedding the southern economy to a cotton monoculture and by impeding industrialization. The econometric study of slavery led by Robert Fogel and Stanley Engerman during the second half of the century has clearly established that southern slavery was not unprofitable or irrational in any strict accounting sense, that on average investment in slaves yielded returns on a par with the best investments in northern factories. Whether in Mississippi's cotton fields, Jamaica's sugar plantations, or Brazil's coffee fields, slave-based commercialized agriculture yielded—as Adam Smith recognized but failed to explain—high rates of economic growth and profits that "are generally much greater than those of any other cultivation that is known either in Europe or America." Inextricably bound up in the fluctuating world of commodity markets, masters' fortunes ebbed and flowed depending on a variety of factors, not least of which was the business acumen of the masters themselves.[8] That slavery as a system proved profitable suggests that masters, as a class, responded rationally to market fluctuations and other factors that affected profitability. But market responsiveness and the desire for profit did not, in themselves, make masters the same as other modern business-men or slavery simply a variant of capitalism. Slavery, especially during boom times for certain staples, such as the late 1850s for cotton, could generate enormous economic growth. But the masters' tendency to invest their profits primarily in land and slaves—investments that reflected both their business sense and their recognition of the social value attached to those possessions—limited the possibi-lities for economic development. As Peter Parish succinctly states, "the combined forces of cotton and slavery kept not only Southern agriculture but the whole Southern economy on a straight and narrow path which led to rejection of other choices, and consequent retardation. The very success (and the profits) of planta-tion slavery and cotton cultivation removed any incentive to switch from agricul-ture to industrial and urban development."[9]

In choosing to invest as they did masters clearly demonstrated good, short-term economic sense, even if they contributed to their society's long-term economic and political disadvantage vis-à-vis the North. But economic choices are never made in vacuums. Relations of production and exchange anywhere invariably beget ethical dimensions. How property, especially human property, is legally defined and encumbered dramatically affects how markets allocate resources. Paternalism shaped the moral economy of the relations between masters and slaves in the antebellum South, but in ways understood quite differently by both parties. What masters regarded as theft, slaves regarded as taking; what masters considered privilege, slaves seized as right. Antebellum masters committed themselves to slavery because they believed it to be more than a viable economic system of social relations. It took into consideration questions of humanity as well as interest; it was not simply economically rational but also consistent with their understanding of themselves as Christian, moral paternalists. They defended slavery as both profit-able and humane, and they understood themselves as both businessmen and paternalists. Abraham became their model slaveholder. They distanced themselves from early Roman slaveholders whom they saw as exercising an absolute dominion that Christian slaveholders as a class could not tolerate. Indeed, before the War for Southern Independence every southern state enacted positive law, however erratically enforced, that attempted to protect slaves against gross abuse. Slaves seized the logic of paternalism to counter dehumanization and to establish standards that qualified their bondage and held masters accountable for their actions.

Some historians question whether paternalism and profit seeking were as compatible as the masters asserted. Richard Follett contends that masters may have believed the "charade of benevolence and kindly paternalism," but "beneath its comforting promise of idealized mastery, paternalism was a façade for exploitation and a convenient tool for managing labor.... The reciprocity of paternalism provided business-conscious planters with an ideological vocabulary for negotiating a contractual relationship with slaves that aided plantation productivity." Paternalism, according to historians such as Follet, followed from rather than qualified or conflicted with the essentially economic imperatives of the masters. Although considering themselves dutiful, responsible, and benevolent guardians of their "family black and white," masters needed to survive in a competitive economic world that only occasionally allowed "a paternalistic polish to a network of coldly rational economic incentives and to dress exploitation in patriarchal garb."[10]

Other historians, while not denying that masters exploited slaves (as all ruling classes extract a surplus product from labor) and frequently behaved in "coldly rational economic" ways that placed economic necessity above "benevolence and kindness," nonetheless maintain that paternalism was much more than a façade for cold economic calculation. Paternalism, for these historians, flowed from the master–slave relation. It often complemented the economic impulses of profit-seeking masters, but it limited the logic of profit maximization. Thus, paternalism contributed not only to the masters' benign concept of themselves, but also to their conviction that their society was morally superior to free labor society, in which no paternalistic bond linked employer to laborer. In translating power into authority, masters deceived themselves. They believed that slaves accepted the masters' depiction of the master–slave relation as one of mutual benefit. But to the extent that masters took seriously their paternalistic obligations they strengthened their belief that slavery constituted much more than a business operation. Rising slave prices, which Phillips took as a sign of slavery's economic weakness rather than its profitability, acted in many cases to reinforce these obligations by making slave property increasingly valuable. While modern economics might have allowed southern slaveholders to defend their peculiar institution on the narrow ground of profitability and productivity alone, they generally conceded the argument of free labor's economic superiority to northerners, preferring instead to build an apology on biblical and sociological grounds. For self-deceived but generally honest masters, paternalism left them psychologically vulnerable, especially when slaves proved less than grateful. When Edmund Ruffin of Virginia, the militantly proslavery planter and soil scientist, discerned one such moment of truth in the mass desertion of slaves from plantations during the waning of the Confederacy, he still retreated into self-deception. He interpreted the wartime "ingratitude and treachery" of slaves in flight by blaming not slavery, but blue-coated Yankee seducers and incendiaries. Paternalism also made masters ideologically resistant to abolitionist condemnations of them as immoral, inhumane brutes; slavery gave them a model, if not always the practical reality, of social relations with which they could attack the moral basis of free labor society.

MASTERS IN MODERN SOCIETY

Slave ownership in the South varied considerably, from region to region, from farm to plantation, and from settled society to frontier. Unlike their counterparts in the British and French Caribbean, antebellum southern masters tended to be residents not absentees. Unlike their counterparts in nineteenth-century Cuba and Brazil, they presided over an American-born slave population since the mid-eighteenth century. Unlike slaveholding sugar planters throughout the Americas, few owned more than 100 slaves. Although the percentage of slave owners declined from one-third to one-quarter during the 1850s, the widespread practice of slave hiring allowed even those who did not own slaves to exercise at least a taste of "mastery" over slaves. Conflicts arose among masters, who, because of slavery's influence, zealously guarded their liberty and grew especially touchy on questions of honor. The political and social influence of masters as a class tended to keep them in check. To be sure, dueling survived in the antebellum South despite legal prohibitions and theological denunciations, but as a kind of manly, ritualized way of channeling intra-class conflict into a less destructive form that reaffirmed, in a highly public way, the value that southern communities placed on courage and habit of command. On fundamental questions of the maintenance and protection of the slave regime, masters tended to close ranks. Although never a uniform, homogeneous body, the master class, especially after 1830, evinced notable unity on questions of the historical, religious, and social legitimacy of slaveholding and the willingness to protect the South from hostile political forces in the North.

Masters' religious convictions deepened their paternalistic relations to their slaves. Believing that God had placed slaves in their care, masters often considered themselves burdened by the responsibilities that accompanied the private owner-ship of human beings. After purchasing a female slave, Eliza Clitherall commented that "I henceforth feel it to be my duty as I trust thro' divine assistance to be enabled to train her, Religiously and usefully—feeling myself responsible for her soul and well doing."[11] Clitherall's notion of training her slave "religiously and usefully" displays the dual character of slaves in the eyes of masters. The slave was a soul and a worker, and the responsible paternalist had to ensure that he attended to both aspects of his slave's nature. Ministers regularly chastised both themselves and their fellow masters for failing to fulfill their religious obligations to their slaves. Some, who argued that masters should avoid breaking up slave marriages and slave families, struggled to reconcile the claims of their religion with the practical economic exigencies of slavery. The inability to reconcile the competing claims of "humanity and interest" revealed the inescapable dilemma at the heart of the effort to build a Christian slave society. But however inescapable the conflict proved, most masters did not succumb to despair or consider their society evil. They recognized that all social systems remained flawed and asserted that their slave society, notwithstanding its imperfections, remained among the most humane, orderly, and progressive societies in the world. Chancellor Harper of South Carolina succinctly stated, "The condition of our whole existence is but to struggle with evils—to compare them—to choose between them, and so far as we can, to mitigate them. To say that there is evil in any institution is only to say that it is human."[12]

Harper's comment reveals one of the most prominent features of the slave-holders' social thought: suspicion of utopian visions of human perfectibility. Led by the divines, they maintained a belief in the essentially fallen character of mankind. Regardless of religious denomination, most masters accepted the notion of original sin and shaped their social and political thought accordingly. As James Henley Thornwell, a Presbyterian minister and the Old South's most formidable theologian, remarked, "Slavery is a part of curse which sin has introduced into the world, and stands in the same general relations to Christianity as poverty, sickness, disease or death. In other words, it is a relation which can only be conceived as taking place among fallen beings—tainted with a curse. It springs not from the nature of man as man, nor from the nature of society as such, but from the nature of man as sinful, and the nature of society as disordered."[13] The acceptance of human imperfectability made masters virtually Burkean in their suspicion of and resistance to heaven-on-earth social schemes emanating from Europe and the North that envisioned a world without sin and its social consequences: slavery, war, government, poverty. This acceptance also permitted them to live with, however problematically, a social system they knew to be flawed. Their dislike of abstractions, of the untethered flight of Reason from history and experience, and their preference for the "Is" of established, natural hierarchies over the "Ought" of radical egalitarian dreamers fostered a mainstream conservatism political tradition in the South. The relation of the antislavery Burke to that proslavery tradition deserves more scholarly attention.

The recognition that earthly perfection remained beyond human realization did not lead masters into a denial of change or progress or a passive acceptance of a static world let alone a desire to return to some romanticized past age. Many slaveholders eagerly and sincerely embraced the technological and material progress that captivated much of the transatlantic world in the first half of the nineteenth century. Masters supported, in general, the expansion of transportation, including canals and railroads. They enthusiastically followed scientific developments. Many believed that the advance of industrialism would ameliorate the condition of mankind. But the masters' embrace of progress, especially the spread of industrial production and all that accompanied it, had limits.[14] Southern intellectuals recoiled against the utopian visions and fanatical cults, informed by radical individualist and perfectionist premises, that were sweeping the antebellum North. In truth, the fabled individualism of white southern adult males stressed the restrictions imposed by social bonds derived from conscience and moral responsibility in a Christian community of interrelated and interdependent, albeit unequal, parts. These limits demonstrate once again that, however economically rational slaveholders were, they retained certain principles that made them leery of evaluating economic developments solely or even primarily by their quantitative material benefits.

Masters had to confront the tension between the material fruits of modern economic development and the social costs. One telling example of a spokesman for the master class who understood the logic of modern economic development but ultimately qualified it because of its moral and social consequences was Thomas Roderick Dew. President of the College of William and Mary and professor of several subjects there, including history, political economy, and moral philosophy, Dew rose to the fore in the defense of slavery after reviewing the debate in the Virginia legislature about the future of slavery after Nat Turner's revolt. Dew believed that the great age of progress that he and his fellow heirs of Western civilization inherited resulted from the expansion of individual freedom. Economic advances freed more and more people from the drudgery of labor, enabling them to devote leisure time to the cultivation of their talents for the benefit of themselves and others. Yet Dew's study of classical political economy, premised on individual freedom, led him to draw back from full acceptance of the progress that political economy promised. Believing that slavery and other forms of unfree labor disappeared once the cost of free labor dropped below that of slave labor, Dew conceived in ways that recall the logic of the iron law of wages that capitalist development meant that "the living standards of laborers would sink to a subsistence level under a system that offered little or no protection during the periodic plunges below that level. The great mass of mankind would have to live not only with poverty and brutal exploitation but with the threat of starvation."[15] This material misery, Dew feared, would produce social catastrophes. Laborers would never tolerate such conditions, and the French Revolution—Dew died in 1846 and did not witness the Revolutions of 1848—suggested that their insurrection would be bloody, disruptive, and a prologue to a despotism that would, in turn, retard or even roll back the progress of civilization. Dew, John C. Calhoun, George Fitzhugh, and other members of the southern clerisy concluded that the peculiar combination of capital and labor inherent in slavery would spare the South from a cataclysmic class struggle that would inevitably undo the North. Thus, Dew and many southern notables in the generation leading up to the War for Southern Independence "ended by holding up the social system of the South as a model for a future world order. Only slavery or personal servitude in some form could guarantee republican liberties for the propertied, security for the propertyless, and stability for the state and society."[16] Slavery, rather than being a hindrance to progress, would actually preserve the order necessary for progress to continue. Masters did not seek to restore a past world; they sought an alternate route to modernity, one that, through slavery or some form of unfree labor, would preserve the social order and stability on which liberty for some depended. The only alternatives, masters increasingly concluded, were anarchy or despotism.

History and its Lessons

Masters' ambivalence toward the modern age made them both proud to belong to a civilization of enormous, unprecedented wealth and wary of the ways that economic development obliterated the social bonds that had provided stability and order. They revealed that ambivalence in the meanings they derived from their intense and serious study of history. Slaveholders seeking to build a modern slave society recognized that history provided no suitable models or precedents; they were on uncharted ground, forging a slave society within an industrializing world characterized by bourgeois individualism and liberal democracy. History could provide, if not exact precedents, examples of societies grounded in principles that reflected the continuities of history. Masters viewed history as possessed of both linear and cyclical dimensions. Change was ever present, but there remained certain constants, which, if properly understood, ensured stability amidst the tumult of inevitable change. Masters in an age of revolution came to see their slave society as a bulwark against leveling tendencies and democratic excesses that threatened mankind with new forms of despotism.

The slaveholders' study of the Middle Ages demonstrates well both their appreciation of progress, a linear view of history, and their conviction that such study revealed "the divinely inspired, the permanent, and the admirable in the medieval legacy."[17] In many ways, southern masters were thankful to live in a modern world that had progressed out of the material and religious dark ages of medieval Europe. Happy to leave behind the pervasive poverty of feudal society and the alleged superstition of medieval Catholicism, southern slaveholders, more so than their bourgeois counterparts in Europe and the North, nonetheless found much to admire in medieval society. They respected the aristocratic and chivalric values of gallantry, personal and family honor, and courage. Although cognizant that their farms and plantations resembled, in important respects, modern businesses more than medieval manors, they admired the medieval ideal's disdain for money-grubbing. And although harshly criticizing lords for oppressing their serfs and other dependents, they saw the relation of lord to serf as, on balance, morally superior to that of capitalist to wage laborer. As Daniel Hundley stated in 1860, "It may be that the old order of things, the old relationship between landlord and villein, protected the latter from many hardships to which the nominal freemen of the nineteenth century are subjected by the blessed influences of free competition and the practical workings of the good and charitable and praiseworthy English maxim: 'Every man for himself, and the devil take the hindmost.'"[18] As Hundley's sarcasm demonstrates, masters praised the aspects of medieval society akin to southern slaveholding society in contrast to the least attractive and most deleterious features of modern, industrializing, bourgeois society, which was flourishing in England and the northern United States unreformed by the welfare state. In the masters' view, their modern slave society preserved the organic social relations between those who performed and those who commanded labor. Although modern slaveholders eagerly participated in market transactions, they believed that their relations with their slaves, like medieval lords' relations with their serfs, remained largely insulated from the heartless machinations of the market. Ultimately, the slaveholders failed to maintain organic social relations while participating in a volatile world increasingly dominated by the cash nexus. Yet their social relations imparted to them a sense of themselves and their society increasingly at odds with others in that world for which the logic of the market and the sense of possessive individualism constituted the only acceptable basis of social organization.

The masters' understanding of history underscores how much their ideological struggle with their free labor opponents informed and shaped their social thought, their politics, and their psyches. Michael O'Brien, among others, has demonstrated that the intellectual worlds of the masters consisted of much more than defenses of slavery or attacks on capitalism.[19] On any number of topics, slaveholding intellectuals expressed views that had little if any direct or even indirect relation to slavery or the civilizational struggle between slave and free societies. As a historically specific class, however, southern masters found themselves engaged in a life and death struggle against hostile forces that increasingly condemned the foundation of slave society. Indeed, paternalism accelerated in part to counter the intensifying assault by a historically unique antislavery crusade that originated in England and rapidly spread under its auspices throughout the transatlantic world. Not surprisingly, the struggle intervened into even the most intimate aspects of life. The

Presbyterian Reverend Charles Colcock Jones of Georgia, the leading exponent of missionary work among slaves, wrote a letter to his mother Mary Jones, conveying condolences for the death of one of their slaves. He then turned to the matter of the slave's children, remarking, "There is much to be said, however, that with kind masters the orphans are always cared for, which is more than can be affirmed of many poor persons not occupying a similar relation in life. Their children are left to public charity, which is too often meager and beggarly."[20] If masters in private correspondence with members of their own families engaged in such ideological point-scoring, one can imagine how extensive was their engagement in public venues. Masters did not spend every waking moment thinking about the relative merits of free versus slave society, but the stakes were too high and the battle spanned too many fronts for them to ignore the extent to which their beliefs about most matters of social, political, and religious significance related back to those societies and the social relations that grounded them.

THE SOCIAL AND POLITICAL VISION
OF THE MASTER CLASS

Southern slaveholders in the decades before secession developed and refined a social vision that put them at odds with the values and vision that emanated from western Europe and the northern United States. In the first half of the nineteenth century, slavery spread through the southern United States within a republican political system that conferred upon slaveholders formal political power, which they used to protect vital interests.[21] The ambivalent or theoretical antislavery sentiments of some slaveholders in the late eighteenth and early nineteenth centuries, including such notable figures as George Washington and Thomas Jefferson, faded dramatically after 1820 as a new generation of southerners recognized that slavery was not going away and, indeed, was woven into the very fabric of southern culture and social life. That shift, from the notion of slavery as a "temporary expedient" or "necessary evil" to a "positive good," long preceded the momentous debates about Missouri's admission into the Union. The rudiments of a paternalist Christian slaveholding ethos—visible in the South during the eighteenth-century Great Awakening—surfaced conspicuously in Virginia shortly after the American Revolution in response to a resolution of the Methodist General Conference in 1784 to extirpate "the abomination" of slavery. Petitioners to the state legislature countered talk of a general emancipation by repeatedly referencing the Bible and history in defense of slavery.[22]

The elaboration of the proslavery argument in the antebellum period derived in large part from the masters' response to the growth of antislavery and abolitionist attitudes and their political expression. Masters sought to defend themselves from attacks that depicted them as inhumane, sinful, and retrograde. Their response led them from defense to offense. As the political crisis of the American union intensified in the 1850s, southern slaveholders defiantly "launched a counter-revolution against secular rationalism, radical egalitarianism, and majoritarian democracy. They defended hierarchy and authority in political and social life and ended with one or another version of 'slavery in the abstract.'"[23] By abstract they tended to mean general. To those who argued that slavery violated natural law, southern elites countered that slavery was a ubiquitous institution in history, that it had originated in the absence of municipal law, that it had sprung up with the human species itself, traveling before history with nomads and flourishing afterwards in some of the world's greatest civilizations. As the Presbyterian Reverend Benjamin Morgan Palmer, one of the most influential proslavery theologians in the late antebellum period, insisted, "in some one of its many forms, servitude is a permanent relation, in all the conditions of human society." In fathoming the mind of the founding generalization on slavery, Gordon Wood has, in effect, seized on Palmer's point by asserting that the very "ubiquity of servitude in that patriarchal age tended to blur the conspicuousness of black slavery, especially in the North."[24] Since antebellum masters conceded limits—informed by Christian precepts, community standards, positive law, and the general progress of humanity—that reined in their private power over their slaves, "servant" increasingly replaced "slave" in antebellum southern discourse.

Perhaps no aspect of the masters' world revealed more powerfully or fundamentally their profound differences with free society than religion. Ostensibly a conflict over whether God sanctioned slaveholding, the religious debate between slaveholders and free labor advocates extended well beyond the rather narrow question of the morality of owning slaves. As both the supporters and opponents of slaveholding elaborated their biblical and religious arguments, the divide grew wider and deeper. The masters' religious perspective convinced them not only that slavery was divinely ordained, but also that opponents of slavery had moved beyond heresy and toward atheism. The defense of slavery became more than a defense of property or the means of maintaining superiority over an inferior race. It became, in a very real sense, a defense of Christianity and of the unique civilization that Christianity had made possible. Masters thus understood slavery as the only basis on which Christianity could survive in an increasingly hostile world.[25]

Racism had always played a prominent role in the masters' justification of New World slavery. Throughout the history of slavery in the Americas, whites regularly expressed the widespread conviction that "Negroes" were incapable, without white assistance, of living as civilized human beings. Thomas R. R. Cobb, the foremost legal scholar of the Old South, summed up this thinking succinctly: "contact with the Caucasian is the only civilizer of the negro, and slavery is the only condition on which that contact can be preserved." White masters portrayed themselves as the true protectors of blacks; to free them and throw them into competition with racially superior whites would doom them to misery and even extinction.[26] Slaveholders selectively appealed to evidence of the condition of free blacks in the North and elsewhere in the hemisphere to bolster their claims that emancipation would render the mass of blacks worse off materially and spiritually. Bolstered by the popular belief that the so-called "Curse of Ham" applied to sub-Saharan Africans, New World masters comforted themselves with the notion that God himself intended blacks to be slaves. Of all the slaveholding classes in the Americas, only those in the antebellum southern United States embarked on a conscious program of imperialism in attempting to spread slavery into tropical areas of the hemisphere where it no longer existed. Southern filibusters William Walker and others seized upon the secularization of racial thinking by nineteenth-century ethnologists and natural scientists to argue for a southern-led imperialism in the tropical parts of the Western hemisphere to extend civilization by regenerating allegedly inferior races through slavery or one or another form of servitude. Yet, neither Walker's adventurism nor his pseudo-scientific racialist views went unchallenged by leading southerners, especially by southern divines. The slave South's expansionist vision deserves and is receiving more attention. Recent works by historians Robert Bonner and Matthew Pratt Guterl highlight the cosmopolitan character of southern slaveholders who, notwithstanding their intense American identity, cast their eyes not only westward to the Pacific, but southward to the Caribbean and Brazil as they envisioned an expanding empire of unfreedom.[27]

At home, the "natural fittedness" of blacks for slavery allowed masters to avoid or deflect questions about whether or not non-blacks should be enslaved. But the masters' belief, as James Henry Hammond famously stated in his "Cotton is King" speech in the United States Senate in 1858, that "in all societies there must be a class to do the menial duties, to perform the drudgery of life . . . Such a class you must have, or you would not have that other class which leads progress, civilization, and refinement," necessarily led back to the question of how those who performed the "menial duties" ought to relate to the class that "leads progress, civilization, and refinement."[28] Most white southerners simply thanked God that he had provided them with an inferior race specially equipped to do menial labor. George Frederickson, among other historians, believes that racism was not only the basis of proslavery, but also the key to the masters' political and social dominance. Although masters were always a minority of the white population, and a shrinking minority at that, they maintained their prominence and support of nonslaveholders in large part because of their shared commitment to white supremacy.[29] No one denies that racism proved vital to the unification of whites of different classes. Some scholars, however, question whether masters or, at least, the logic of their proslavery arguments supported only black slavery. The masters' repeated claim that slavery provided slaves with better material conditions than free labor did for wage workers led them to endorse slavery, in some form, as the preferred condition of working people everywhere.[30] Although few went as far as proslavery advocate George Fitzhugh and called for the enslavement of white workers, many others implied that the destructive forces of the free labor system made some form of unfree labor the only humane solution for workers who suffered oppression. As Presbyterian minister George D. Armstrong suggested in his influential *The Christian Doctrine of Slavery*, "It may be that such a slavery, regulating the relations of capital and labor, though implying some deprivation of personal liberty, will prove a better defense of the poor against the oppression of the rich, than the too great freedom in which capital is placed in many of the free states of Europe at the present day." Like many masters, Armstrong argued that slavery provided the remedy to the "social question" that increasingly plagued free labor societies: "It may be, " he wrote, that "Christian slavery is God's solution of the problem about which the wisest statesmen of Europe confess themselves 'at fault.'"[31]

The masters' endorsement, however implied, of slavery in some form as the optimal relation between capital and labor represented the logical outcome of the positive good argument that had been developing for decades. If slavery promoted the interests of both labor and capital, if it was sanctioned by the Bible, if it was based on a proper understanding of the nature and destiny of man, then how could masters not recommend it for all societies regardless of racial composition or level of economic development? Yet masters recognized that what they promoted did not resemble what most people still believed constituted slavery. For generations, southern slaveholders had differentiated the slavery they practiced from other forms of slavery, such as that of the Romans. Their Christian sensibilities and beliefs convinced them that slaves were persons with immortal souls. Their legal codes and especially their court decisions insisted that slaves were not subject to the arbitrary will of their masters. Their paternalistic ethos reminded them of their responsibilities and duties to those placed in their charge. Thornwell spoke for many southerners when he defined slavery as "the obligation to labour for another, determined by the Providence of God, independently of the provisions of a contract." Under this definition, he continued, "the right which the master has is a right, not to the *man*, but to his *labour*." Ministers and laymen and women as well often coupled their definitions of slavery with strict admonitions about the limits of the masters' authority over the men whose labor they commanded. The apostles had recognized that slaves— brothers and sisters in Christ—were persons with souls and, as such, "possessed of certain rights, which it was injustice to disregard." It was thus the "office of Christianity to protect these rights by the solemn sanctions of religion—to enforce upon masters the necessity, the moral obligation, of rendering to their bondmen that which is just and equal."[32] Although Thornwell hoped that "the solemn sanctions of religion" would "enforce upon masters the necessity . . . of rendering to their bondmen that which is just and equal," he and others recognized that more than religious sanctions might be needed to make masters do what they ought. Public opinion, fraternal correction, and even the law must restrain the individual master from abusing his God-given but qualified authority. Only by limiting the private power of the master, reformers argued, could the slavery they practiced be deserving of God's favor and appropriate for adoption by other societies.

Many ministers and masters, especially in the years leading up to and extending into the War for Southern Independence, favored laws to limit private power. Some sought to forbid the sale of slave children away from their mothers and the dissolution of slave marriages through the sale of one of the spouses. Some favored more stringent and more vigorously enforced laws against excessive cruelty by masters upon slaves. Some, especially among the clergy, wanted to lift the restrictions on slave literacy. Nearly all of these efforts ended in failure, which did not simply reflect the unwillingness of masters to acknowledge slave "rights" or imply a broad rejection of paternalistic principles. Rather, the desire to reform slavery to make it conform more fully in practice to the paternalistic, humane, and Christian social system that its proponents exalted conflicted with the economic imperatives of a commodity-producing slave society that sought to maintain a competitive position in a world increasingly dominated by the market. The masters' inability to make slavery consistent with their avowed principles reflected less their hypocrisy than the insoluble dilemma that lay at the heart of their project to construct an organic "corporate society adaptable to the exigencies of the modern world."[33]

MASTERS IN A WORLD WITHOUT SLAVES

The masters of the Old South risked everything in their bold attempt to secede from the United States and create an independent slaveholding nation. Their brief experiment with nationhood demonstrated not only the weakness of a slave economy at war with an emerging capitalist industrial power but also the "fatal self-deception" of their paternalist beliefs about their loving and loyal slaves. Paternalism had always meant different things to masters and slaves, but masters had read slave compliance as acceptance. The War for Southern Independence revealed painfully and powerfully how badly masters had misread their slaves. When Union troops pushed through the southern states, slaves by the thousands fled their plantation households for the Union lines, leaving behind masters and mistresses whose reactions combined feelings of betrayal, shock, and disbelief. For many masters, the psychological and emotional consequences of their slaves' actions mattered as much as the defeat of the Confederacy and the immediate and total abolition of slavery that resulted.[34]

The war destroyed both slavery and the master class. Although many former masters in the years after the war were able to resume farming with an impoverished black labor force, the legal and political changes that the war ushered in fundamentally altered the relations between those who worked the field and those who commanded their labor. Historians continue to debate the nature and character of the postbellum economy, but whatever continuities some scholars see between the antebellum and postbellum eras cannot minimize the extent of the changes that masters, as masters, experienced.[35] Economically devastated—even if still holding more resources than other black and white Southerners—and politically circumscribed regionally and nationally, masters were no longer masters. The relation that made them who they were, both individually and as a class, had been shattered. However qualified the relation of master and slave had been before the war, the master could still envision himself as having a direct, non-contractual, personal, and familial relation to his slaves. The master–slave relation had provided the basis for the master's self-identity and his understanding of the principles that ought to inform political, social, cultural, and religious life. The abolition of that relation, not simply of slavery as a legal institution or form of property, destroyed the masters' society, their vision for an alternative modern world, and themselves as a historically distinct class.

Notes

1. G. W. F. Hegel, *The Phenomenology of Mind*, trans. J. B. Baillie (1807; New York, 1964), 228–40.

2. See especially Philip Morgan's *Slave Counterpoint: Black Culture in the Eighteenth-Century Chesapeake and Lowcountry* (Chapel Hill, NC, 1998); Morgan, "Three Planters and their Slaves: Perspectives on Slavery in Virginia, South Carolina, and Jamaica, 1750–1790," in Winthrop D. Jordan and Sheila L. Skemp (eds.), *Race and Family in the Colonial South* (Jackson, Ms., 1987), 37–79; Rhys Isaac, *The Transformation of Virginia, 1740–1790* (Chapel Hill, NC, 1983); Sidney W. Mintz, *Caribbean Transformations* (Chicago, 1974).

3. Morgan, "Three Planters and their Slaves," 39–40. See also his *Slave Counterpoint*. For other accounts of the transition from patriarchalism to paternalism, although not necessarily employing those terms, see Willie Lee Rose, "The Domestication of Domestic Slavery," in her *Slavery and Freedom*, ed. William W. Freehling (New York, 1982), 18–36, and Jeffrey Robert Young, *Domesticating Slavery: The Master Class in Georgia and South Carolina, 1637–1837* (Chapel Hill, NC, 1999).

4. For some of the recent work on the religious dimension of the transition to paternalism, see Sylvia R. Frey, *Water from the Rock: Black Resistance in a Revolutionary Age* (Princeton, 1993), ch. 8; Douglas Ambrose, "Of Stations and Relations: Proslavery Christianity in Early National Virginia," in John R. McKivigan and Mitchell Snay (eds.), *Religion and the Antebellum Debate over Slavery* (Athens, Ga., 1998), 35–67; Charles F. Irons, *The Origins of Proslavery Christianity: White and Black Evangelicals in Colonial and*

Antebellum Virginia (Chapel Hill, NC, 2008); and Jeffrey Robert Young (ed.), *Proslavery and Sectional Thought in the Early South, 1740–1829: An Anthology* (Columbia, SC, 2006).

5. Eugene D. Genovese and Elizabeth Fox-Genovese, *Fatal Self-Deception: Loyal and Loving Slaves in the Mind of Southern Slaveholders* (Cambridge, forthcoming); Eugene D. Genovese, *Roll, Jordan, Roll: The World the Slaves Made* (New York, 1974), 49.

6. Karl Marx, *Capital: A Critique of Political Economy*, 3 vols. (1887; New York, 1967), i. 236; Joseph Schumpeter, "Capitalism," *Encyclopedia Britannica* (1946), reprinted in Schumpeter, *Essays on Entrepreneurs, Innovations, Business Cycles, and the Evolution of Capitalism*, ed. Richard V. Clemence (1951; New Brunswick, NJ, 1989), 189.

7. For useful works on these debates see Elizabeth Fox-Genovese and Eugene D. Genovese, *Fruits of Merchant Capital: Slavery and Bourgeois Property in the Rise and Expansion of Capitalism* (New York, 1983); Fox-Genovese and Genovese, *Slavery in White and Black: Class and Race in the Southern Slaveholders' New World Order* (New York, 2008); Raimondo Luraghi, *The Rise and Fall of the Plantation South* (New York, 1978); James Oakes, *The Ruling Race: A History of American Slaveholders* (New York, 1982); Oakes, *Slavery and Freedom: An Interpretation of the Old South* (New York, 1990); and Young, *Domesticating Slavery*.

8. Adam Smith, *An Inquiry into the Nature and Causes of the Wealth of Nations* (Edinburgh, 1827), 159. For Philips's classic presentation of the economic inefficiency of southern slavery, see *American Negro Slavery* (1918; Baton Rouge, La., 1966). For refutations of Philips, see Kenneth Stampp, *The Peculiar Institution: Slavery in the Ante-Bellum South* (New York, 1956); Robert Fogel and Stanley Engerman, *Time on the Cross: The Economics of American Negro Slavery* (New York, 1974); Fogel, *Without Consent or Contract: The Rise and Fall of American Slavery* (New York, 1989); and Gavin Wright, *The Political Economy of the Cotton South: Households, Markets, and Wealth in the Nineteenth Century* (New York, 1978). See also Mark M. Smith's useful synthesis of the debate, *Debating Slavery: Economy and Society in the Antebellum American South* (New York, 1998).

9. Peter J. Parish, *Slavery: History and Historians* (New York, 1989), 59. See also the classic expression of this conclusion in Lewis Cecil Gray, *History of Agriculture in the Southern United States to 1860* (Washington, DC, 1933). The recent work of John Majewski further demonstrates that although individual southerners rationally employed "shifting agriculture in which a substantial portion of acreage rested in prolonged fallow," the practice "for the South as a whole, however, deterred development. The vast tracks of unimproved land resting in long-term fallow acted as a black hole that sapped the South's economic vitality." Majewski, *Modernizing a Slave Economy: The Economic Vision of the Confederate Nation* (Chapel Hill, NC, 2009), 25.

10. Richard Follett, *The Sugar Masters: Planters and Slaves in Louisiana's Cane World, 1820–1860* (Baton Rouge, La., 2005), 152, 155, 156, 158, 159. For similar arguments that view paternalism as incompatible with profit seeking, see William Johnson, *Soul by Soul: Inside the Antebellum Slave Market* (Cambridge, 2001); William Dusinberre, *Them Dark Days: Slavery in the American Rice Swamps* (New York, 1996); Jonathan D. Martin, *Divided Mastery: Slave Hiring in the American South* (Cambridge, Mass., 2004); and Oakes, *Ruling Race*.

11. Eliza Clitherall Autobiography, 2 April 1853, Southern Historical Collection, University of North Carolina, Chapel Hill, NC.

12. William Harper, "Memoir on Slavery," in Drew Faust (ed.), *The Ideology of Slavery: Proslavery Thought in the Old South* (Baton Rouge, La., 1981), 85. On the often competing claims of "humanity and interest" within southern law, see Mark V. Tushnet, *The*

American Law of Slavery, 1810–1860: Questions of Humanity and Interest (Princeton, 1980).

13. James Henley Thornwell, *The Rights and Duties of Masters* (Charleston, SC, 1850), 33.

14. Eugene D. Genovese, *The Slaveholders' Dilemma: Freedom and Progress in Southern Conservative Thought, 1820–1860* (Columbia, SC, 1992).

15. Ibid. 16.

16. Ibid. 18. Dew's important works on these questions include his *Review of the Debate in the Virginia Legislature of 1831 and 1832* (Richmond, Va., 1832) and his posthumously published masterwork, *A Digest of the Laws, Customs, Manners and Institutions of the Ancient and Modern Nations* (New York, 1852).

17. Elizabeth Fox-Genovese and Eugene D. Genovese, *The Mind of the Master Class: History and Faith in the Southern Slaveholders' Worldview* (New York, 2005), 306.

18. Daniel R. Hundley, *Social Relations in our Southern States* (1860; Baton Rouge, La., 1979), 134.

19. Michael O'Brien, *Conjectures of Order: Intellectual Life and the American South, 1810–1860*, 2 vols. (Chapel Hill, NC, 2003).

20. Charles Colcock Jones to Mary Jones, November 22, 1856, in Robert Manson Myers (ed.), *The Children of Pride: A True Story of Georgia and the Civil War* (New Haven, 1972), 266.

21. See Don E. Fehrenbacher, *The Slaveholding Republic: An Account of the United States Government's Relations to Slavery* (New York, 2001).

22. On the development of the proslavery argument, see Larry Tise, *Proslavery: A History of the Defense of Slavery in America, 1701–1840* (Athens, Ga., 1987); Irons, *Origins of Proslavery Christianity*; Young (ed.), *Proslavery and Sectional Thought in the Early South*; Young, *Domesticating Slavery*; Faust (ed.), *Ideology of Slavery*; Ambrose, "Of Stations and Relations." For the petitions to the Virginia state legislature, see Frederika Teute Schmidt and Barbara Ripel Wilhelm (eds.), "Early Proslavery Petitions in Virginia," *William and Mary Quarterly*, 3rd ser., 30 (January 1973): 133–46.

23. Eugene D. Genovese and Elizabeth Fox-Genovese, *Fatal Self-Deception*.

24. Benjamin Morgan Palmer, *The Family, in its Civil and Churchly Aspects: An Essay, in Two Parts* (1876; Harrisonburg, Va., 1981), 124; Gordon S. Wood, "Reading the Founders' Minds," *New York Review of Books*, June 28, 2007.

25. For elaboration on these points, see Fox-Genovese and Genovese, *Mind of the Master Class* and the "Religion and Slavery" essay in this volume.

26. Thomas R. R. Cobb, *An Inquiry into the Law of Negro Slavery in the United States of America* (1858; Athens, Ga., 1999), 51.

27. On southern imperialism and expansionism, see Robert E. May, *The Southern Dream of a Caribbean Empire, 1854–1861* (2nd edn. Gainesville, Fla., 2002); Robert E. Bonner, *Mastering America: Southern Slaveholders and the Crisis of American Nationhood* (New York, 2009); and Matthew Pratt Guterl, *American Mediterranean: Southern Slaveholders in the Age of Emancipation* (Cambridge, Mass., 2008).

28. James Henry Hammond, "Speech on the Admission of Kansas, U.S. Senate, March 4, 1858," in Eric McKitrick (ed.), *Slavery Defended: The Views of the Old South* (Englewood Cliffs, NJ, 1963), 122.

29. For George Frederickson's views, see his essays in *The Arrogance of Race: Historical Perspectives on Slavery, Racism, and Social Inequality* (Middletown, Conn., 1988).

30. See Fox-Genovese and Genovese, *Slavery in White and Black*; Douglas Ambrose, *Henry Hughes and Proslavery Thought in the Old South* (Baton Rouge, La., 1996).

31. George D. Armstrong, *The Christian Doctrine of Slavery* (1857; New York, 1969), 134.

32. James Henley Thornwell, *Rights and Duties of Masters* (Charleston, SC, 1850), 24, 19.

33. Fox-Genovese and Genovese, *Slavery in White and Black*, 203.

34. See Genovese, *Roll, Jordan, Roll*; Thavolia Glymph, *Out of this House of Bondage: The Transformation of the Plantation Household* (New York: 2008); Harold D. Woodman, *New South, New Law: The Legal Foundations of Labor and Credit Relations in the Postbellum Agricultural South* (Baton Rouge, La., 1995); James Roark, *Masters without Slaves: Southern Planters in the Civil War and Reconstruction* (New York, 1978); Jonathan M. Bryant, *How Curious a Land: Conflict and Change in Greene County, Georgia, 1850–1885* (Chapel Hill, NC, 1996); Julie Saville, *The Work of Reconstruction: From Slave to Wage Laborer in South Carolina, 1860–1870* (New York, 1994).

35. For discussions of the postbellum southern economy, see Gavin Wright, *Old South, New South: Revolutions in the Southern Economy since the Civil War* (Baton Rouge, La., 1996); Thavolia Glymph and John J. Kushma (eds.), *Essays on the Postbellum Southern Economy* (Arlington, Tex., 1985); Bryant, *How Curious a Land*; Woodman, *New South, New Law*; Scott P. Marler and Peter Coclanis, "The Economics of Reconstruction," in Lacy K. Ford (ed.), *A Companion to the Civil War and Reconstruction* (Malden, Mass., 2005); Gerald David Jaynes, *Branches without Roots: Genesis of the Black Working Class in the American South, 1862–1882* (New York, 1986).

SELECT BIBLIOGRAPHY

AMBROSE, DOUGLAS. *Henry Hughes and Proslavery Thought in the Old South.* Baton Rouge, La.: Louisiana State University Press, 1996.

FOGEL, ROBERT. *Without Consent or Contract: The Rise and Fall of American Slavery.* New York: W. W. Norton, 1989.

—— and STANLEY ENGERMAN, *Time on the Cross: The Economics of American Negro Slavery.* New York: W. W. Norton, 1974.

FOX-GENOVESE, ELIZABETH. *Within the Plantation Household: Black and White Women of the Old South.* Chapel Hill, NC: University of North Carolina Press, 1988.

—— and EUGENE D. GENOVESE, *Fruits of Merchant Capital: Slavery and Bourgeois Property in the Rise and Expansion of Capitalism.* New York: Oxford University Press, 1983.

———— *The Mind of the Master Class: History and Faith in the Southern Slaveholders' Worldview.* New York: Cambridge University Press, 2005.

———— *Slavery in White and Black: Class and Race in the Southern Slaveholders' New World Order.* New York: Cambridge University Press, 2008.

GENOVESE, EUGENE D. *Roll, Jordan, Roll: The World the Slaves Made.* New York: Pantheon, 1974.

MORGAN, PHILIP. "Three Planters and their Slaves: Perspectives on Slavery in Virginia, South Carolina, and Jamaica, 1750–1790," in Winthrop D. Jordan and Sheila L. Skemp (eds.), *Race and Family in the Colonial South.* Jackson, Mo.: University Press of Mississippi, 1987, 37–79.

TUSHNET, MARK V. *The American Law of Slavery, 1810–1860: Questions of Humanity and Interest.* Princeton: Princeton University Press, 1980.

....

CHAPTER 25

ABOLITION AND ANTISLAVERY

....

JOHN STAUFFER

INTRODUCTION

....

Abolitionism is an idea, articulated through language, that emerged in the eighteenth century and propelled people to act. It ultimately changed the world. People came to believe that God had endowed all humans with the inalienable right to be free and that slavery was an intolerable evil that must be abolished. Most scholars agree with this basic definition of abolitionism. But they have long disagreed about its significance and the process by which the idea led to action and political change.[1]

The debate over abolitionism has undergone four broad stages of evolution.[1] The first stage, emerging in the early nineteenth century, consisted of histories by abolitionists and their friends, including major works by Thomas Clarkson, William Goodell, and Henry Wilson. They characterized the movement to abolish slavery as a holy war, with God's prophets battling against the forces of evil in order to realize His vision of universal freedom. In the late nineteenth century, this providential understanding began to be replaced by a secular notion of progress that accommodated and contributed to the rise of social Darwinism and anti-black racism. In this second phase, historians led by Sir Reginald Coupland, Charles and Mary Beard, and Allan Nevins defined abolitionists as whites only. They ignored or downplayed the role of blacks and yoked economics to abolitionism, often in deterministic ways. They believed that slavery was incompatible with industrial capitalism and on the road to extinction. And they portrayed abolitionists in one of three ways: as secular prophets, helping to usher in a capitalist utopia; as hopeless idealists who were largely irrelevant amid more powerful material forces; or as irresponsible fanatics who caused the bloodbath of the Civil War. Their histories provided, as the historian Robert Forbes noted, "an explicit rationale for colonialism and imperialism."[2]

The third phase effectively began with Eric Williams's seminal work *Capitalism and Slavery* (1944), which did not gain widespread recognition until the early 1960s. In this phase, historians rejected their immediate forebears' acceptance of white supremacy, imperialism, and colonialism but retained their economic determinism. Williams and his followers argued that slavery fueled capitalist expansion and was abolished only when its contributions to economic growth began to wane. Thus, like many of the second-phase writers, they rendered abolitionists irrelevant as historical actors and humanitarian values as largely derivatives from a defining materialist base.

In the fourth phase of the historiography, which emerged during the civil rights era of the 1960s, scholars recovered the viewpoint of the abolitionists, connected their rhetoric to political action, and understood the relationship between ideas and material forces as a dialectic rather than a Marxian form of determinism. As a result, they acknowledged abolitionists' crucial contributions to world history. Indispensable to this phase is the work and influence of David Brion Davis, who examined abolitionism from a comparative perspective and emphasized the ironies, ambiguities, and moral dimensions of the past. Davis has described abolitionists' contribution as a "*willed* achievement, a century's moral achievement that may have no parallel." In 1770 African American slavery "was legal and almost unquestioned throughout the New World." Just over 100 years later, it had been abolished throughout the Western hemisphere and most people considered it an intolerable evil. This extraordinary success "should help inspire some confidence in other movements for social change."[3] Davis's generation, which includes the work of Stanley Engerman, Robert Fogel, Seymour Drescher, Orlando Patterson, and Eugene Genovese, inaugurated one of the most profound transformations in historical knowledge in more than 100 years.

In the past twenty-five years, many scholars have built upon Davis's and his colleagues' insights. James Brewer Stewart, John Stauffer, Richard Newman, Patrick Rael, Laurent Dubois, and James and Lois Horton have analyzed the mutual lines of influence among black and white reformers and shown how the power of race has shaped their visions and their attempts to realize them. Julie Roy Jeffrey, Jean Fagin Yellin, Julie Winch, and Bonnie Anderson have recovered the contributions of women in the abolition movement. Stewart, Stauffer, Bruce Laurie, Christopher Brown, Steven Mintz, and Lawrence Jennings have shown how abolitionism as an "interest group" shaped and transformed national and international politics. And Brown, Stauffer, Dubois, Jennings, Anderson, and Mintz have analyzed the interrelationships among activists and movements throughout the Atlantic world, exploring how emancipation in one nation shaped the movement to abolish slavery in another.

Ironically, however, abolitionists have once again come under attack. In some respects, there has been a circling back toward the second and third phases of the historiography, in which scholars treat abolitionists either as irrelevant pawns amid larger material forces or as hopeless or crazy idealists. These attacks come not from scholars of antislavery and reform, but rather from those focusing on the related fields of slavery, race, or politics. Some scholars, such as Leslie Harris and Mia Bay, understand abolitionists as part of the white bourgeoisie while portraying their black comrades as rebels, activists, or something other than abolitionists. A number of literary theorists and critics, led by Saidiya Hartman, deride the concept of empathy (or sympathy), which was central to abolitionism and indeed all humanitarian reform movements. In their view, abolitionists' sentimental writings did more harm than good, furthering the oppression of blacks. A few slavery scholars, including Michael Craton, Thomas Holt, and Barbara Jeanne Fields, argue that emancipation stemmed from slave resistance and revolts, not from the efforts of abolitionists. Slaves freed themselves, they argue, with little help from white friends, which accords with these scholars' ideological assumption that social change always begins at the margins and transforms the center. And a few influential writers, particularly Sean Wilentz, have retained a rigid, top-down understanding of history. In their view, politicians stage-managed emancipation, wielding enormous power. These recent attacks reflect in some degree the cultures of identity politics, pragmatism, and a new Gilded Age in which they emerged. They are sustained more by ideological preferences than empirical sources. Perhaps the best way to highlight their flaws, while also suggesting directions for new research, is to offer a brief synthetic history that focuses on America, England, and France, assessing, as it were, the state of the field.

THE AGE OF GRADUAL ABOLITIONISM, 1770S–1820S

It is no exaggeration to say that prior to the eighteenth century, few people could envision a world without slavery. The language for articulating universal freedom did not yet exist. Sin was understood as a form of bondage; and since evil was a basic condition of humanity, people accepted slavery as a fact of life. Even slaves, while resisting bondage, did not condemn slavery as an *institution*, a point borne out by the fact that in all the known slave revolts prior to the eighteenth century, rebels felt no compunction enslaving others in their quest to become free. From the Spartacus revolt of the late 70s BCE in Rome, and the Zanj revolt of 869 CE in North Africa, to the maroon communities of the Caribbean, slave rebels sought to invert the master–slave hierarchy, much as the poor in America today hope to get rich rather than overturn the institution of capitalism.[4]

Indeed, prior to the late eighteenth century, there are only a handful of documents that scholars have construed as containing abolitionist sentiment. The ancient Persian King Cyrus the Great produced the "Cyrus Cylinder" (*c.*530 BCE), which Amélie Kuhrt interprets as outlawing slavery in Babylonia and constituting the world's first civil rights document. According to Davis, the ancient Essenes anticipated the abolitionists in their quest to realize their perfectionist ideals, their belief that slavery was a sin, and their desire to achieve freedom from sin. Jack Greene recently discovered a 1709 pamphlet that contains a letter from a Jamaican merchant and a speech by a black from Guadeloupe, which he interprets as antislavery. The world's first undisputed abolitionist document is a Quaker petition against slavery published by the Germantown, Pennsylvania Friends (consisting of Quakers and Mennonites) in 1688. These isolated instances highlight the degree to which abolitionism was an *idea* that needed to be disseminated by language in a movement that could lead to political action.[5]

Abolitionism emerged because of a profound "change in moral perception," and initially it was limited to North America, Britain, and France. These were the three nations, enmeshed in New World slavery, in which ideas could circulate with less restraint than elsewhere. Four factors contributed to the emergence of abolitionism: a Quaker ethos that led people to believe they could dismantle sin and imagine a perfect world of universal freedom; a new understanding of sympathy that encouraged the perceiver to identify with the sufferings of the oppressed and thus collapse the distinctions between master and slave; Enlightenment philosophy of natural rights, which embraced the idea of self-sovereignty for all adults, coupled with a clearly defined social hierarchy; and an age of political revolutions, where men in power were receptive to radically new ideas and able to implement them. David Brion Davis has eloquently summarized this shift in moral perception: "For some two thousand years men thought of sin as a kind of slavery. One day they would come to think of slavery as sin."[6] This shift undermined thousands of years of Judaeo-Christian religious doctrine. Abolitionists ignored the numerous instances in the Bible that defended slavery, and their enemies understandably accused them of being heretics, atheists, or blasphemers. Indeed, abolitionists usually lost debates with slave owners over the biblical defense of slavery.

Abolitionists declared their first major victory in 1772 with the Somerset case, which was popularly interpreted as outlawing slavery in England. In ruling on the case, Lord Mansfield consulted with the great legal theorist William Blackstone, whose four-volume *Commentaries on the Laws of England* (1765) was required reading for students of law in England and America and "ranked second only to the Bible as a literary and intellectual influence on the history of American institutions."[7] Blackstone's understanding of slavery was richly ambiguous. On the one hand, he argued that only a positive law sanctioning slavery could override the natural law of freedom. On the other hand, he suggested that in certain circumstances natural law could trump positive law. Although Lord Mansfield based his decision in the Somerset case primarily on the precedent of villeinage, arguing that slaves could not be treated worse than villeins and thus could not forcibly be removed from England, Blackstone nevertheless contributed to its antislavery interpretation. British lawyers defending the slave James Somerset relied on Blackstone to argue that slavery was contrary to natural law; and Lord Mansfield acknowledged this while ruling in their favor. Somewhat inadvertently, Lord Mansfield established a precedent for Blackstone's theory that slavery could be sanctioned only by positive law. According to the legal scholar Robert Cover, the Somerset decision "gave institutional recognition to antislavery morality."[8] It influenced the gradual abolition of America's northern states, including Vermont's Constitution of 1777 (the first constitution in history to outlaw slavery), and the Quock Walker case of 1783, which effectively ended slavery in Massachusetts. Blackstone's *Commentaries*, coupled with the Somerset decision, would contribute to the antislavery platforms and ideologies of the Liberty, Free-Soil, and Republican parties.[9]

Blacks helped popularize beliefs in individual freedom and natural rights, and in some cases they revised them, an extraordinary accomplishment given that most blacks in the 1770s were illiterate slaves. In 1773 Massachusetts slaves petitioned the governor and general court, protesting their status: "We have no property. We have no wives! No Children! We have no City! No Country! . . . We desire to bless God, who loves Mankind," but slavery "is in itself so unfriendly to Religion, and every moral Virtue except Patience." In protesting against the idea of property in man and the denial of their right to property, the petitioners urged whites to broaden the concept of citizenship, so that they too could enjoy the inalienable right to freedom and property.[10]

This revolutionary ideology helped spark the American Revolution and Jefferson's language of natural rights in the Declaration of Independence: "all Men are created equal" and "are endowed by their Creator with certain unalienable Rights, that among these are Life, Liberty, and the Pursuit of Happiness." What often gets overlooked in the Declaration is the fact that the justification for declaring independence from England came from "the laws of Nature and of Nature's God." God's law "entitled" the colonists to rebel. In this respect, the Founders were prophets seeking to realize God's law. Even though Jefferson did not have blacks in mind when he penned his famous words, the Declaration became widely interpreted in the North in the decades that preceded the Civil War as a sacred and prophetic antislavery text, a crucial influence and inspiration to abolitionists throughout North America, Britain, and France.[11]

Although most of America's Founders were slave owners—from Jefferson, George Washington, James Madison, and Charles Pinckney to John Jay, John Hancock, and Gouverneur Morris—the vast majority of them were genuinely antislavery. They sought a gradual and congenial end to the evil without uprooting the social order or their own wealth and domestic comforts. Madison, the architect of the Constitution and himself a slaveholder, called slavery America's "original sin."[12] The ideals that flowed out of the revolution led directly to the abolition of slavery in the northern states; the exclusion of slavery from the northwest territories; the end of the international slave trade; and the voluntary manumission of 20,000 slaves by their masters by 1800.

The war itself resulted in more slaves being freed than at any time until the Civil War, but freedom stemmed more from military exigencies than from any ideological opposition to slavery. Blacks constituted 20 percent of the total colonial population and represented a crucial source of power to both armies, which suffered from manpower shortages. Between 15,000 and 20,000 slaves of patriot masters joined the British forces, and about 5,000 slaves served as patriots, a majority of them receiving their freedom.

Nevertheless, the war suggested a way for blacks and whites to live together in the same nation as citizens. George Washington integrated his army, with blacks and whites serving together in the same regiments; a few other states also approved interracial regiments. (Another 170 years would elapse before the nation would again integrate its military.) Alexander Hamilton, another fervent antislavery advocate, linked the military logic of arming slaves to his own antislavery ideology: "An essential part of the plan is to give them [slaves] freedom with their muskets. This will secure their fidelity, animate their courage, and I believe will have a good influence upon those who remain, by opening a door to their emancipation."[13] Some four score years later, Lincoln would add a provision in the final Emancipation Proclamation to arm blacks as soldiers after reading a book by George Livermore on the important role black soldiers had played in the Continental Army; Livermore's book echoed the views of U. S. Grant and other trustworthy generals, who emphasized to Lincoln the military importance of arming blacks.[14] The revolution (and later the Civil War) highlighted the need for blacks and whites to unite in common cause in order to defeat a powerful enemy.[15]

From the framing of the Constitution until the crisis over Missouri entering the Union as a slave state in 1819, most American statesmen were "gradual abolitionists" (a term that would be replaced by "antislavery" a few decades later to characterize gradual and conditional means for ending slavery). Gradualists believed in linear progress and saw the United States as "history's revelation of the future."[16] Economically, the nation was in transition, with slave-grown tobacco in decline and the Cotton Kingdom, which would make southerners the richest men in the country, not yet ascendant in the South and Southwest. During this period a tacit agreement existed between northern and southern statesmen: the North would not interfere with slavery in southern states; and southerners would recognize slavery as an evil that should be discouraged and eventually abolished.

The majority of statesmen also believed that slavery *and* blacks were stains on the fabric of American identity. Slavery was the barrier blocking white Americans' path to a millennium that was defined in nationalist terms. The road would be clear, the new age in sight, were it not for the presence of blacks. These beliefs lay at the heart of the many proposals for shipping blacks to another country. Colonization is usually characterized by scholars as having been wildly impractical. Yet statesmen successfully colonized Indians onto western territories and then reservations; and James Madison concluded, after doing the math, that the federal government could easily raise enough money through the sale of public lands to ship all blacks to Africa over a fifty-year period. The point is that African-Americans, the victims of slavery, became in the mind of whites "the embodiment of sin."[17]

Despite the emphasis on colonization among gradual abolitionists, racial hierarchies were more fluid among the lower classes than they would be in the 1840s and 1850s. In a society based on Enlightenment beliefs in hierarchy, rationality, and social deference, it was comparatively easier for blacks and whites at the bottom of the social ladder "to form alliances based on shared conditions and common purposes."[18]

The Enlightenment faith in hierarchy also helps explain why so many elite whites could embrace gradual abolitionism: they wanted blacks to rise up and become free but not equal. In the minds of most elite whites, blacks would remain at or near the bottom of the social order or be shipped to another country, thus posing little threat to their own white identities. Understandably, there are few known accounts of interracial friendship or comradeship between blacks and white elites from the revolution through the 1820s. The first abolition societies refused to accept African-Americans as members; and Quakers, the first white abolitionists, did not welcome free blacks into their churches and homes. Most white abolitionists embraced black uplift and education, with colonization serving as a chief means for blacks to rise up and achieve independence and autonomy. Their vision of freedom did not uproot or collapse the existing social order. By contrast, whites who championed equality found the idea of emancipation far more threatening, for it implied racial equality. The rise of white male suffrage in the 1810s and 1820s was accompanied by "a sharp upsurge of Negrophobia," reflecting, according to George Fredrickson, a leading historian of race, "an ideological marriage between egalitarian democracy and biological racism."[19]

Most opponents of slavery "were firmly in the camp" of the Federalist (and later Whig) parties, rather than in the camp of the Democratic-Republican and then the Democratic parties. This preference reflected Federalist and Whig advocacy of a clearly defined social hierarchy that emphasized freedom and a strong central government over equality. Opponents of slavery (and desegregation after the Civil War) understood that if a strong federal government could create a national bank and post office and subsidize the nation's infrastructure, it could also interfere with slavery (and race relations) in local communities. Democratic-Republicans and Democrats were more inclined to champion state and local rights over federal rule and equality of opportunity for white men only. Visions of universal freedom often came at the expense of equality, whereas egalitarian ideals typically meant equality for the few and unfreedom for the many.[20]

Until the 1820s, most black abolitionists were also gradualists in outlook and strategy. They, too, had been influenced by the Enlightenment faith in rationality and hierarchy (though the degree to which they shaped it has not been fully explored). They advocated practical and patient measures for ending slavery and respected existing laws and lawmakers. Many endorsed emigration to Africa—though not through the American Colonization Society when it emerged in 1816—as a pragmatic solution to racism and unfreedom. Black leaders tended to act deferentially toward white elites. Their rhetoric emphasized prudence rather than defiance. Prince Hall, a Barbadian-born grandmaster of a Massachusetts Masonic lodge, urged "patience" to his black brethren in attacking slavery. James Forten, the wealthy Philadelphia sailmaker, referred to "white men" as "our protectors" in his pleas for "rational liberty."[21]

This rational, pragmatic approach was smart politics. After all, free soil seemed to be spreading, and the leading statesmen "professed to believe that chattel slavery . . . must inevitably give way to Christian freedom."[22] Blacks thus had good reason to believe in linear progress, to assume that slavery would eventually end throughout the nation. And since many of them could remember the bloodshed and upheaval of the revolution, they strategically chose to compromise with slavery's sin by accepting gradual means in order to prevent more bloodshed.

GRADUAL ABOLITION IN THE BRITISH CARIBBEAN

The American War of Independence transformed the movement to abolish slavery in the British West Indies. It made antislavery immensely popular in England by creating, as Christopher Brown has emphasized, "a crisis of imperial authority" that directed "unprecedented attention to the moral character of colonial institutions." In 1783, at the end of America's revolution, the British antislavery movement was tiny, consisting primarily of a few hundred Quakers. By 1787, the British public seemed to announce, "nearly in unison, that a pillar that long had sustained British wealth and power now must fall."[23]

In many respects, British abolitionists had fewer obstacles to overcome than their American counterparts. Unlike the United States, where the slave population reproduced naturally, slaves in the West Indies died out due to the backbreaking nature of sugar and coffee production and planters' preference for male over female slaves. West Indian planters depended on continual imports from Africa to sustain their labor force and profits. And so when England ended the international trade, people viewed it as a "promissory note" for the eventual end of slavery.[24] In the United States, by contrast, ending the trade impeded neither the growth of the slave population nor of slave territories. Additionally, Britain's slave societies were located thousands of miles from England, and Parliament wielded far greater power than colonial governments. America's seat of power, by contrast, remained comparatively decentralized, with slave states enjoying considerable autonomy. Finally, England had few blacks in comparison to the United States, with fewer fears about emancipating them. Almost every United States black who traveled in the British Isles acknowledged the comparative dearth of racism there. As Frederick Douglass noted after arriving in England in 1845, "I saw in every man a recognition of my manhood, and an absence, a perfect absence, of everything like that disgusting hate with which we are pursued in" the United States.[25]

British society, more conservative than in the United States, made the goal of freedom easier for British abolitionists to reach. In England inequalities of power were vast; suffrage was restricted to a tiny elite until the 1832 Reform Act; and the social order was extremely rigid. Most British leaders believed that "equality was synonymous with tyranny," rigid hierarchy with freedom, and they continually guarded against "popular despotism and tyranny in the name of the majority."[26] This conservative ideology proved well suited to antislavery politics, for British abolitionists, much like American gradualists, did not seek to uproot the social order in England.

In Britain, abolitionists (both blacks and whites) focused their energies on ending the Atlantic trade, which reflected their gradualist approach. In the wake of America's revolution in 1776, the growing concern over the moral character of England's colonies led to the formation in 1787 of the Society for Effecting the Abolition of the Slave Trade. Like America's early abolition societies, it dissuaded blacks from becoming members, though it did include women, who made up 11 percent of the subscribers. As early as 1791, about 30 percent of the adult male population of England, Scotland, and Wales signed anti-slave trade petitions, and the following year, William Wilberforce, the wealthy abolitionist and MP from Hull, persuaded the House of Commons to outlaw the trade by 1796, but the bill was defeated in the House of Lords.[27]

The French Revolution and Reign of Terror temporarily crippled the British antislavery movement. The explosive French and Saint-Domingue revolutions threatened the entire West Indian slave societies, highlighting to British leaders the costs of abolishing slavery. They wanted gradual, and peaceful, abolition, not the social chaos that came with immediate action. Indeed, British forces fought to restore slavery in the French West Indies after France outlawed it during the revolution.

By 1804 popular opposition to the trade revived. Although suffering a monumental defeat by slave revolutionaries in Saint-Domingue, Napoleon had restored slavery and the slave trade elsewhere in the French West Indies, and the British now saw abolitionism as a patriotic response to their French enemies. In 1806 abolitionists strategically downplayed their humanitarian motives and succeeded in passing a bill in Parliament that outlawed the slave trade with foreign colonies only. They argued that the bill bolstered Britain's military, economic, and national self-interest. With an important branch of the trade now ended, abolitionists successfully pushed through a bill in 1807 that prohibited any British ship from trading in African slaves beginning 1 January 1808. Soon the British were policing the seas against illegal slave trading and pressuring other countries to end their trade. Suppressing the trade became a "point of honor" for the British.[28]

GRADUAL ABOLITION IN THE FRENCH CARIBBEAN

The London Society for the Abolition of the Slave Trade, which had emerged in 1787, inspired the journalists Jacques Pierre Brissot and Etienne Clavière to found one year later the French *Société des Amis des Noirs*. Brissot spent time in England befriending London abolitionists, who encouraged him to form a similar society in France. The *Amis des Noirs* followed the British abolitionists in its gradualist approach by focusing on the slave trade, which activists believed would lead to an eventual end to slavery. (French West Indian planters, like their British counterparts, relied on continual slave imports to maintain their labor force.) British abolitionists gave the *Amis des Noirs* money and literature, and the famous British abolitionist Thomas Clarkson became a key advisor. Like their British and American counterparts, the *Amis des Noirs* consisted of elite white men (few blacks lived in France).

But whereas the American and British gradualists achieved broad popular appeal, the *Amis des Noirs* focused its energies in the legislature, "avoided appeals to public opinion, and never had more than 150 adherents." In effect it was a political lobby. It advocated—despite its exclusiveness and unlike British and American gradualists—equal rights under the law for all free blacks and mulattos in France's colonies, which it achieved in 1792, under the new Legislative Assembly. This equal rights law constitutes one of the *Amis des Noirs'* only successes and indeed one of the few notable accomplishments of the French Revolution.[29]

In 1793 the Reign of Terror virtually destroyed the *Amis des Noirs*. Robespierre and his followers condemned the society, and many of its leaders, including Brissot, Clavière, and Condorcet, were guillotined or imprisoned. In 1794, when France emancipated its 700,000 colonial slaves and granted citizenship rights to all men regardless of race, the *Amis des Noirs* played no role in the decision. This first emancipation stemmed from military reasons rather than humanitarian impulse: France was at war with England and Spain; its "crown jewel," Saint-Domingue, had erupted in a massive slave revolution in 1791; and the emancipation decree was designed to persuade Toussaint Louverture and his Jacobins on Saint-Domingue to abandon their Spanish allies and rally to the side of the French Republic. The Republic had no intention of permanently emancipating West Indian slaves. It needed money and trade from its colonies to survive, and the colonial lobby was more powerful than the *Amis des Noirs*. When Napoleon came to power in 1799, he silenced France's abolitionists and made the restoration of slavery in the French Caribbean the center-piece of a grand design to recreate a vast French empire in the Americas.

Napoleon hated abolitionism, as did his wife Josephine, who had been raised on a slave plantation in Martinique. Throughout his fifteen-year reign, he suppressed antislavery sentiment in France through draconian restrictions on speech, press, debate, and assembly. During his last "100 Days" in 1815, he did decree the abolition of the slave trade, but this was to placate the British. Louis XVIII, another foe of abolitionism, also succumbed to British pressure later that year and passed a law against the trade. But the law lacked teeth and was ineffective, and for years the French slave trade continued illegally and virtually unabated. From the Reign of Terror until the 1820s, abolitionist sentiment in France stood at low ebb. The movement had little popular support, and its leaders—the de Staël-Holstein family, Abbé Grégoire, the marquis de Lafayette, Benjamin Constant, and Victor de Broglie—continued to rely on British support. With France having lost some of its colonies during the Napoleonic Wars, "slavery receded into the background in France."[30]

The specter of Haiti further reduced sympathy for blacks. In 1804 Haiti declared its independence from France and became the world's first independent black republic. That year President Dessalines expelled former masters from the island, and in 1805 he ordered the massacre of those who remained. Fourteen years of violence in Saint-Domingue had horrified most whites (who ignored the violence perpetrated against slaves). Indeed, most accounts of the Haitian Revolution focused on white massacres rather than the extraordinary accomplishment of Toussaint and his black Jacobins, who defeated the armies of France, England, and Spain and published a constitution that outlawed slavery forever. The example of Haiti suggested to many observers that emancipation led inexorably to blood-shed and that antislavery agitation incited slave rebellions. For whites "who were obsessed with the problem of freedom and order," whether in France, England, or America, "the Haitian Revolution suggested the unleashing of pure id."[31]

The Haitian Revolution marked a turning point in the history of slave rebellions and abolitionism. It was not only the greatest achievement of the French Revolution, but the first instance of immediate abolitionism. Rebel slaves, having been inspired by the French Revolution and its language of natural rights, refused to compromise with the sin of slavery, repulsed their masters, and declared their society forever free. Indeed Toussaint and his followers revised the Declaration of the Rights of Man and Citizen by resolving the contradiction between universal freedom and the right to own property in humans. In rebelling, they acted as citizens and radically transformed the meaning of republican citizenship.[32] The example of Haiti would inspire American and British abolitionists (especially blacks) to radicalize their movement. But it also highlighted the potential costs of sudden and unplanned emancipation: apocalyptic violence.

THE AGE OF IMMEDIATE ABOLITIONISM, 1820S TO 1860S

By 1824, British abolitionists were becoming restive. The end of slavery in the West Indies seemed nowhere in sight, despite their belief that ending the Atlantic slave trade would lead to emancipation. In 1823, Thomas Buxton, the abolitionist leader who had replaced Wilberforce in Parliament, introduced a plan for gradual abolition throughout the British colonies. But his opponent George Canning, the Tory Foreign Minister and ally of the powerful Society of West India Planters and Merchants, subverted Buxton's bill by recommending a plan to ameliorate the condition of slaves. Abolitionists had long championed amelioration—which included measures ranging from religious instruction and literacy to release from work on the Sabbath and outlawing the flogging of women—as a step toward emancipation. Yet planters had consistently resisted ameliorative measures, and Parliament had done little to enforce them. To many abolitionists, gradualism seemed a feeble strategy for ending slavery.

Meanwhile, slaves took matters into their own hands. In 1823, 10,000 to 12,000 slaves on England's colony of Demerara on the South American mainland rose up in revolt. Sensitive to how their actions would be interpreted in England, they purposefully avoided killing whites (only three died), and instead destroyed property and demanded rights as workers and British citizens, in the hopes of forcing colonial authorities to implement better working conditions. Their uprising was quickly stifled: hundreds of rebels were massacred, and others received punishments of "one thousand lashes" or "were condemned to be worked in chains for the residue of their lives."[33]

The Demerara revolt helped inspire the rise of immediate abolitionism in England. Elizabeth Heyrick, a radical, middle-class Quaker who inaugurated the rhetoric of immediatism with her influential 1824 pamphlet *Immediate, Not Gradual Abolition*, referred to the "insurgents of Demerara" and defended them: "The slave has a *right* to his liberty, a right which it is a crime to withhold—let the consequences to the planter be what they may." Like other abolitionists, Heyrick took comfort in the paucity of violence against whites during the rebellion, invoked the glorious example of Haiti, and repudiated accusations by conservatives that slaves needed time to learn the responsibilities of freedom and that immediate emancipation would induce the massacre of whites: "No instance has been recorded of the emancipated slaves (not the gradually, but the immediately emancipated slaves) having abused their freedom," she emphasized. She urged all abolitionists to boycott slave-grown products and endorse immediatism. Gradualism begat "a *gradual indifference* to *emancipation* itself."[34]

Immediate abolitionism represented both a shift in strategy and a change in outlook. It reflected a loss of faith in patient, indirect, and orderly means for reforming society, such as outlawing the slave trade, ameliorative measures, or colonization. Immediatists demanded a total and swift transformation of society. They dismantled the long-standing cultural dichotomies between master and slave, black and white, heaven and earth, in ways that led them to empathize with, befriend, and listen to blacks as never before. In theory, immediatists defined abolitionism in terms of both freedom and equality, though most of them never lived up to their egalitarian ideals. In the larger sense, immediatism reflected a shift from Enlightenment to Romantic worldviews, from a "detached, rationalistic perspective on history and progress, to a personal commitment to make no compromise with sin." It was an expression of inner freedom and triumph over worldly conventions; it reflected an eschatological leap, a *kairos*, or a sharp break from linear notions of progress and history; and it assumed that a new age was dawning. It was an appropriate doctrine for a Romantic age.[35]

In many cases, British (and French) abolitionists experienced "double vision." By turns they endorsed more practical measures and then demanded unconditional and immediate emancipation. They used inflammatory rhetoric to obtain modest concessions, tried to fit rational, pragmatic strategies onto their vision of a Christian millennium, and linked "redemptive theology with social science." Immediatists and gradualists worked well together, the former making the latter appear more moderate. This coupling of gradualism and immediatism in England (and France) stemmed in large part from the great distance separating the cultural and political centers from the slave societies. It also enabled emancipation to be achieved peacefully. In the United States, where slave owners controlled all three branches of government, a huge chasm "separated immediatist rhetoric from the realities of power," resulting in a stark division between immediatists and gradualists.[36]

Gradualists like Henry Clay (Lincoln's political hero) enjoyed immense esteem, while abolitionists were widely caricatured as monomaniacs and raging fanatics.

In England, immediatism received immense popular support, which would have been unthinkable in the United States until the Civil War. The respectable London Anti-Slavery Society advocated immediate and unconditional freedom for all slaves. By 1833, the groundswell of public support for abolition was so large that signers of petitions calling for emancipation reached 1.3 million, with 30 percent of the signatures coming from women. The number of petition signers exceeded the number of eligible voters! Those supporting immediate emancipation outnumbered opponents by a ratio of 250 to 1. The Reform Act, having been passed in 1832, almost doubled the size of the electorate, to about 700,000 in the UK (roughly 20 percent of the adult male population), pressuring Parliament to pay attention to the voice of the people. Conservative policy makers, including conservative abolitionists, were horrified by the intense public support for immediate emancipation. They rightly saw "germs of democracy in such populist agitation."[37]

The "Baptist War" of 1831–2 in Jamaica, the largest slave rebellion in the history of the British Caribbean, further fueled the British abolition movement. Some 60,000 slaves rose up in revolt to demand their natural rights, and through great self-discipline and restraint, they killed only fourteen whites. Baptist missionaries, whom planters accused of causing the rebellion, escaped to England and spoke out in Parliament and to the multitudes, detailing the cruelty of the planters and the Christian behavior of the slaves. The Baptist War highlighted for countless Britons that they were engaged in a war against barbarism that must be ended immediately.

But, as it turned out, British emancipation was gradual in its implementation. The Emancipation Act of 1833, which emancipated 800,000 slaves on 1 August 1834, called for a period of apprenticeship, in which "freed" slaves worked for former masters without compensation. Radicals protested vigorously and were able to shorten the period of apprenticeship from twelve to four years. England compensated masters by paying them over twenty million pounds sterling (over $100 million). Despite these compromises, British emancipation became immensely influential to American abolitionists. They saw in it a typology or foreshadowing of the American millennium, a Second Coming on a national scale. American blacks began celebrating British West Indian emancipation on 1 August 1834, and within a few years, 1 August became a sacred day for black and white abolitionists, rivaling 4 July. By the 1840s, 1 August celebrations had become fully integrated affairs, suggesting an alternative vision of American democracy inspired by monarchical England. Frederick Douglass summarized the significance of British West Indian emancipation: "There was something Godlike in this decree of the British nation. It was the spirit of the Son of God commanding the devil of slavery to go out of the British West Indies."[38]

The example of British West Indian emancipation raises an important question: Why would so many Englishmen and women fervently support a policy that was so destructive to Britain's economy and in many cases their own pocketbooks? Ending slavery elevated the idea of free labor, often in ways that masked the horrible working conditions of British industrial workers. But ending slavery also gave a sense of dignity to the working classes, inspiring them to fight for better conditions and claim their own full rights as citizens. Where slavery had turned the home into a factory, mothers into prostitutes, ending it ensured the sanctity of the domestic sphere and dignified women's work within it. In short, ending slavery redeemed and revised the centuries' old idea that humans had to sweat and toil for their bread because of Adam's sin. To labor freely, within the home or without, could now be seen as life's greatest source of honor and nobility—even in an aristocratic nation.

THE SECOND FRENCH EMANCIPATION

The French abolition movement never acquired broad public support and with few exceptions was confined to a small number of elites. Memories of the revolutions in France and Saint-Domingue had made policy makers and elites fearful of popular mobilization and democracy in any form. Moreover, French abolitionists lacked the millennialist fervor and faith in God as immanent or indwelling that was characteristic of their British and especially American counterparts. Then too, the French government imposed greater restrictions on freedoms of speech, petition, debate, and assembly than in Britain, and people had little say in their government. During the eighteen years of the July Monarchy (1830–48), less than 1 percent of France's population could vote.

During the July Monarchy, French abolitionists did achieve some minor victories. In 1831 the government finally began to enforce prohibitions against the slave trade by imprisoning traders and seizing their ships. British West Indian emancipation spurred French antislavery sentiment, even though the government never moved beyond the vaguest proposals for ameliorating conditions of slaves, preparing them for freedom, and "insisting on stability and caution in all measures."[39]

Cyrille Bissette, a mulatto born in Martinique, emerged as the lone voice of immediatism in the 1830s and became one of France's most persistent and powerful protest writers. The example of British abolitionists taught him the importance of demanding immediate and unconditional emancipation. Gradualism was ineffective unless accompanied by the countervailing voice of immediatism. Like his British counterparts, he launched a petition campaign and was willing to change tactics according to circumstance, endorsing ameliorative measures one moment, immediate and unconditional emancipation the next.

Despite his presence in the metropolis, Bissette was never invited to become a member of France's abolition society, which continued to function as a professional lobby. French abolitionists did not convert to immediatism until the mid-1840s, after finally recognizing that the idea of preparing slaves gradually for emancipation was "a great and deplorable illusion."[40] By 1847 the small coterie of abolitionists finally united with Bissette in demanding immediate emancipation.

What ultimately destroyed French West Indian slavery, however, was the February Revolution of 1848. Louis Philippe fell from power; the provisional government of the Second Republic immediately granted universal male suffrage; and on 27 April 1848 it decreed, effective within two months, immediate emancipation and the end of slavery. But French emancipation was, like that in Britain, conditional: it compensated masters six million francs in cash and six million in credit for the 250,000 slaves in the French colonies, considerably less than British masters had received; and it encouraged freedpeople to work for wages rather than as subsistence farmers by offering incentives and outlawing vagabondage. In the end, the Second Republic freed France's slaves immediately while compromising with slavery's sin.

THE ROAD TO CIVIL WAR AND EMANCIPATION IN THE UNITED STATES

The Missouri Compromise marked the beginning of a transformation in American society. It pointed to signs of a new era in reform, including a shift in visions of citizenship and community and in definitions of national and cultural boundaries. This transformation took many forms, including the emergence of a national market economy; rapid westward expansion, which became the battleground of slavery; and a blurring of God's law and national law. During the Missouri crisis, the New York politician and reformer Rufus King transformed the debates by applying a "higher law" to slavery; he stated that any law upholding slavery was "absolutely void, because [it is] contrary to the law of nature, which is the law of God."[41] King stunned both northern and southern colleagues by interpreting the Constitution through an abstract reading of the principles of freedom and equality in the Declaration of Independence. The higher law thesis would become a central rhetorical weapon in the writings of a later generation of black and white abolitionists.

Most significantly, the Missouri crisis marked a moment in which Americans became increasingly unwilling to compromise with sin and to accept limits, the rule of law, and traditional boundaries in their quest to realize visions of a new age. After the Missouri Compromise, the tacit agreement between the North and South became untenable. Over the course of the 1820s southerners affirmed proslavery ideology, repudiated the belief, shared by most of their forebears, that slavery was a sin, and began to envision an empire of slavery. At the same time, the North witnessed the rise of "modern" or immediate abolitionism, as it was called by both blacks and whites, which distinguished itself from the earlier generation of abolitionists in its refusal to compromise with sin. Increasingly, abolitionists' most passionate desire was the immediate end of all sin, and they saw slavery as the bolt around which all other evils swung. In the broadest sense, a national rite of passage occurred during the Missouri crisis, reflecting a move away from "gradualism" and toward "immediatism." This shift was linked to signs that the old Republic, defined by Enlightenment beliefs, was disappearing, and that a new empire (masquerading as a republic), defined by Romantic worldviews, was emerging.

Immediatism brought blacks and whites together as allies and friends in radically new ways. Such engagement occurred despite the rise of racism and the hardening of racial hierarchies, which led to mob violence against abolitionists. Immediatists advocated universal freedom and racial equality and some of them took steps toward realizing their egalitarian ideals. William Lloyd Garrison began publishing *The Liberator* in 1831 after interacting with and being inspired by black activists. The American Anti-Slavery Society, founded in 1833, and subsequent abolitionist conventions were thoroughly integrated.[42]

Despite their comparative success in transcending the racism that plagued America, abolitionists faced a number of setbacks. Beginning in the 1830s, southerners revoked the freedoms of speech, debate, petition, assembly, and due process in matters relating to slavery and race, which meant that abolitionists' chief weapon, the power of language, was being muted. Southern legislatures and in some cases Congress suppressed antislavery literature and petitions, and state lawmakers unsuccessfully tried to arrest Garrison, Wendell Phillips, Gerrit Smith, and other leaders for libel, offering rewards of thousands of dollars for their capture. Abolitionists could not travel in a slave state without clear danger of being murdered. The defense of slavery engendered a "freedom-of-thought" struggle in the South, as Clement Eaton noted decades ago, which prevented substantive reform in the South. Had abolitionists focused more of their energies on freedom of thought, they *might* have been able to convince more southerners, especially the non-slave owners who constituted two-thirds of the South's population, that slavery was a sin that ultimately needed to be abolished. Scholars need to build upon Eaton's important work.

Another setback came in 1840, when the American Anti-Slavery Society splintered over differences of opinion about political action and women's rights. Garrison and his followers opposed voting, interpreted the Constitution as a proslavery document, and considered American government incurably corrupt, which led them to advocate disunion from the slave republic. Gerrit Smith helped found the Liberty Party in order to nominate antislavery candidates and seek change through political action. A smaller splinter group, opposing women's rights based on its reading of the Bible, organized the American and Foreign Anti-Slavery Society. As a result of the splintering, there was so much infighting that it sometimes seemed as though abolitionists fought against each other and their antislavery foes more than with proslavery apologists. Perhaps had abolitionists remained united and worked more closely with gradualists, they would have been better able to challenge southerners' belligerence and suspension of free speech, debate, petition, and assembly. After all, diverse groups of immediatists and gradualists freed the *Amistad* captives, overturned the Congressional Gag Rules that tabled discussions of slavery, and desegregated public schools and transportation in Massachusetts. And during the Civil War, slavery's opponents again united to form a national Emancipation League, which pressured the Lincoln administration to free the slaves.

In the 1850s, the growing perception of a slave power fueled alliances between abolitionists and antislavery advocates, leading to a broad northern coalition that included working-class men and women, farmers, and northern industrialists. They perceived the southern ruling elite as despotic by the nature of the master–slave relation and thus undemocratic. In their minds, a small cadre of a few hundred thousand slave owners had taken control of the nation and sought to extend slavery into the northern states; and many believed that the slave power threatened to reduce most northerners—blacks and whites—to slaves. Increasingly, northerners felt themselves fighting to preserve national and personal liberty. This broad antislavery and abolition coalition led directly to the emergence of the Republican Party, which sought to prohibit slavery's spread into the territories and called for its "ultimate extinction."

Three major factors engendered this extraordinary rise of northern antislavery and abolition sentiment. The Fugitive Slave Act of 1850 required northerners to form a posse to round up suspected fugitives, making them feel culpable in the sin of slaveholding. No longer could they act like Pontius Pilate and wash their hands of the evil. The law prompted tens of thousands of men and women to break federal laws in order to protect blacks, and it inspired Harriet Beecher Stowe to write *Uncle Tom's Cabin* (1852), the best-selling abolitionist book whose impact was so profound that it purportedly led President Lincoln to call Stowe "the little woman who wrote the book that started this great war" when he met her at the White House in 1862.[43] The Kansas–Nebraska Act (1854) opened northern territories to slavery, leading antislavery men and women to conclude that their nation's destiny and progress had been altered: the Founders' antislavery dreams had been shattered, and the United States was in a state of decline. The *Dred Scott* decision in 1857 declared the Republican Party's platform of non-extension unconstitutional, and it threatened to extend slavery into every state. In his 1858 debates with Stephen Douglas, Lincoln warned of a "second Dred Scott" that would confirm the ruling of the first, allowing southerners to bring their slaves into northern states under the laws of comity. Southern Unionists such as Thomas Cobb tried to allay such fears, but to no avail. More and more Americans believed, with Lincoln, that the nation would soon become all one thing or all the other, and so one needed to do the right thing right now.[44]

In effect, then, northerners *united* in their quest to fight a common foe that threatened their freedom. The white South, in response to growing abolitionist stridence and militance, became more belligerent; and proslavery apologetics increasingly defended slavery as a positive good that deserved to expand nationally and into other parts of the hemisphere. Abolitionists felt threatened by an anti-democratic, expansionist slaveholding republic, making it easier for them to set aside their differences and work together. They made gradualists appear more moderate, and interracial alliances and friendships among radicals mushroomed. The historian Ira Berlin has described black northerners as maroons living in a slaveholding republic. But white abolitionists and gradualists felt *themselves* to be marooned as well, isolated from the nation's slave laws.[45]

In the 1860 presidential election, a majority of northerners voted to prohibit the spread of slavery in order to achieve its ultimate extinction. This central plank of the Republican party platform contrasted the dignity of free labor with the barbarism of slavery. Lincoln owed his election to fears of the slave power; to the Liberty and Free-Soil parties, out of which his own party grew; and to John Brown and his fellow conspirators, whose raid on Harpers Ferry, Virginia, in 1859 had helped split the Democratic Party and topple the Republican frontrunners William Seward and Salmon Chase.[46] In one sense, black and white abolitionists helped provoke southerners into seceding. They also prodded and pushed Lincoln and Republicans to emancipate the slaves as a war measure.

Emancipation stemmed from a number of factors. Lincoln's Emancipation Proclamation reflected his understanding that in order for him to win the war and thus achieve his goal of preserving the Union, he needed to emancipate the slaves and arm blacks. But his Proclamation also turned the war into "a contest of civilization against barbarism" rather than a struggle for territory, as Frederick Douglass noted, restoring the Declaration to its rightful place at the center of the nation's laws. Henceforth, he believed, 1 January and 4 July would rank as the twin births of liberty. Douglass recognized that neither Lincoln nor any other individual had control over emancipation. Events far greater than the president "had wrung this proclamation from him." Every day slaves fled their masters to Union lines, abolitionists and antislavery advocates spoke out in one united voice, Congressional Republicans worked to dethrone slavery, and Union soldiers killed alleged traitors to the country. They were all part of a providential wave of progress sweeping the globe, abolitionists believed. It was thus absurd to think that one man could emancipate four million.[47]

Emancipation in the United States restored a sense of hope to the transatlantic emancipation movement. By the 1850s, many British and some French writers had concluded that the experiment in universal freedom and free labor had failed, owing to the steep drop in West Indian production. The Civil War revived abolitionists' faith in moral progress and renewed their efforts to end slavery everywhere in the New World. In form and substance, emancipation in the United States most closely resembled that of Haiti: It was immediate and unconditional; and it was accompanied by apocalyptic violence. Had Americans been able to abolish slavery peacefully, without the apocalypse of war, they would have avoided another century of horrible racism and racial oppression. But the violence of war begat more violence: white southerners redeemed themselves by retaliating against blacks and preserving a new order of black unfreedom more heavily dependent on race than ever before. Far more than their British counterparts, American freedpeople lived in a state of terror and intimidation. Thus, if America's example inspired abolitionists in Brazil and Cuba, it also foreshadowed the resurgence of evil in the twentieth century. In this sense, America's "first" emancipation should be seen as a dismal failure.

Notes

1. On the stages of abolitionist historiography, see Robert Forbes's superb essay "'Truth Systemitised': The Changing Debate over Slavery and Abolition, 1761–1916," in Timothy Patrick McCarthy and John Stauffer (eds.), *Prophets of Protest: Reconsidering the History of American Abolitionism* (New York, 2006), 3–22. See also Hugh Tulloch, *The Debate on the American Civil War Era* (Manchester, 1999), 71–103; and David Brion Davis, *Inhuman Bondage: The Rise and Fall of Slavery in the New World* (Oxford 2006), 231–49.
2. Forbes, "'Truth Systemitised,'" 7. Exceptions to this summary of the second stage are Vernon Parrington's brilliant *Main Currents in American Thought: An Interpretation of American Literature*, vol. ii (New York, 1927); Gilbert Barnes, *The Anti-slavery Impulse, 1830–1844* (New York, 1933); and Dwight L. Dumond, *Antislavery Origins of the Civil War in the United States* (Ann Arbor, 1939). Parrington, Barnes, and Dumond acknowledge the religious roots of the abolitionists' reform impulse, and Parrington connects rhetoric to action, suggesting that abolitionists helped bring about emancipation. But he also concludes that emancipation was driven by larger economic forces, thus accepting the economic determinism of Charles Beard and others.
3. Davis, *Inhuman Bondage*, 1, 331.
4. David Brion Davis, *Slavery and Human Progress* (New York, 1984), 5–8.
5. Amélie Kuhrt, "The Cyrus Cylinder and Achaemenid Imperial Policy," *Journal for the Study of the Old Testament*, 25 (1983): 83–97; Marguerite Del Giudice, "Persia: Ancient Soul of Iran," *National Geographic*, 214 (2) (August 2008): 48–67; Jack P. Greene, "'A plain and natural Right to Life and Liberty': An Early Natural Rights Attack on the Excesses of the Slave System in Colonial British America," *William and Mary Quarterly*, 3rd ser., 57 (4) (October 2000): 793–808; Davis, *The Problem of Slavery in Western Culture* (Ithaca, NY, 1966), 81–3; 308–9.
   Christopher Brown argues that antislavery sentiment circulated in the early eighteenth century, but he sometimes interprets writers who highlighted the horrors of slavery as

also being antislavery. Countless people saw slavery as a "necessary evil" without being abolitionists. See Brown, *Moral Capital: Foundations of British Abolitionism* (Chapel Hill, NC, 2006), 37–101.

6. Davis, *Slavery in Western Culture*, 90 (quoted), 291–494.
7. Robert A. Ferguson, *Law and Letters in American Culture* (Cambridge, 1984), 11.
8. Robert M. Cover, *Justice Accused: Antislavery and the Judicial Process* (New Haven, 1975), 98.
9. William M. Wiecek, *The Sources of Antislavery Constitutionalism in America, 1760–1848* (Ithaca, NY, 1977), 38–9; David Brion Davis, *The Problem of Slavery in the Age of Revolution, 1770–1823* (Ithaca, NY, 1975), 507–9.
10. "Petition of Slaves," quoted from James Oliver Horton and Lois E. Horton, *Slavery and the Making of America* (New York, 2004), 50–1.
11. Davis, *Inhuman Bondage*, 156; Pauline Maier, *American Scripture: Making the Declaration of Independence* (New York, 1997), 189–216; Henry Louis Gates, Jr. (ed.), *Lincoln on Race and Slavery* (Princeton, 2009), p. xxiii; Davis, *Slavery in the Age of Revolution*, 169–84.
12. Matthew T. Mellon, *Early American Views on Negro Slavery* (Boston, 1934), 158.
13. Davis, *Inhuman Bondage*, 148.
14. Gates, *Lincoln*, pp. xxxix–xl.
15. Philip A. Klinkner with Rogers Smith, *The Unsteady March: The Rise and Decline of Racial Equality in America* (Chicago, 1999).
16. Davis, *Slavery and Human Progress*, 169.
17. David Brion Davis, *Challenging the Boundaries of Slavery* (Cambridge, 2003), 33–4.
18. James Oliver Horton, "Comment," *Journal of the Early Republic*, 18 (2) (Summer 1998): 24.
19. George M. Fredrickson, *White Supremacy: A Comparative Study in American and South African History* (New York, 1981), 154–5.
20. Paul Finkelman, *Slavery and the Founders: Race and Liberty in the Age of Jefferson* (Armonk, NY, 1996), 100.
21. Richard Newman, Patrick Rael, and Phillip Lapsansky (eds.), *Pamphlets of Protest: An Anthology of Early African American Protest Literature, 1790–1860* (New York, 2001), 47, 67.
22. Davis, *Slavery and Human Progress*, 168.
23. Brown, *Moral Capital*, 1, 27.
24. Thomas C. Holt, *The Problem of Freedom: Race, Labor, and Politics in Jamaica and Britain, 1832–1938* (Baltimore, 1992), 17.
25. John Blassingame (ed.), *The Frederick Douglass Papers*, series 1, vol. ii (New Haven, 1982), 59.
26. Davis, *Inhuman Bondage*, 234, 235.
27. Roger Anstey, *The Atlantic Slave Trade and British Abolition, 1760–1810* (Atlantic Highlands, NJ, 1975), 260–80; J. R. Oldfield, *Popular Politics and British Anti-Slavery: The Mobilization of Public Opinion against the Slave Trade, 1787–1807* (London, 1998), 46–54, 113–37; Davis, *Inhuman Bondage*, 234–6.
28. Davis, *Inhuman Bondage*, 164–6, 236–7; Davis, *Slavery and Human Progress*, 166.
29. Jennings, *French Anti-Slavery*, 2.
30. Ibid. 7.
31. Davis, *Inhuman Bondage*, 172.
32. Dubois, *Colony of Citizens*, 3, 28–9, 106, 162–8.
33. Elizabeth Heyrick, *Immediate, Not Gradual Abolition; or, An Inquiry into the Shortest, Safest, and Most Effectual Means of Getting Rid of West Indian Slavery* (London, 1824), 21; Davis, *Inhuman Bondage*, 214–18.
34. Heyrick, *Immediate, Not Gradual Abolition*, 5, 7, 9, 13, 21–2.

35. David Brion Davis, *From Homicide to Slavery: Studies in American Culture* (New York, 1986), 225.
36. Davis, *Slavery and Human Progress*, 177–8, 184.
37. Davis, *Inhuman Bondage*, 237–8.
38. John Stauffer, "Frederick Douglass and the Politics of Slave Redemptions," in Kwame Anthony Appiah and Martin Bunzl (eds.), *Buying Freedom: The Ethics and Economics of Slave Redemption* (Princeton, 2007), 219.
39. Jennings, *French Anti-Slavery*, 74.
40. Ibid. 236.
41. Davis, *Challenging the Boundaries*, 35–59, quotation by Rufus King from 41–2.
42. McCarthy, "'To Plead our Own Cause': Black Print Culture and the Origins of American Abolitionism," in McCarthy and Stauffer (eds.), *Prophets of Protest*, 114–44.
43. Joan D. Hedrick, *Harriet Beecher Stowe: A Life* (New York, 1994), p. vii.
44. John Stauffer, *GIANTS: The Parallel Lives of Frederick Douglass and Abraham Lincoln* (New York, 2009), 188–201; Paul Finkelman, *An Imperfect Union: Slavery, Federalism, and Comity* (Chapel Hill, NC, 1981), 291–343; Don E. Fehrenbacher, *The Dred Scott Case: Its Significance in American Law and Politics* (New York, 1978), 514–95.
45. Ira Berlin, *Generations of Captivity: A History of African-American Slaves* (Cambridge, 2003), 231–45.
46. William W. Freehling, *The Road to Disunion*, ii: *Secessionists Triumphant, 1854–1861* (New York, 2007), 203–68; Stauffer, *GIANTS*, 161–3, 202.
47. Stauffer, *GIANTS*, 244, 246.

Select Bibliography

Brown, Christopher Leslie. *Moral Capital: Foundations of British Abolitionism*. Chapel Hill, NC: University of North Carolina Press, 2006.
Davis, David Brion. *The Problem of Slavery in Western Culture*. New York: Oxford University Press, 1967.
——*The Problem of Slavery in the Age of Revolution, 1770–1823*. Ithaca, NY: Cornell University Press, 1975.
——*Slavery and Human Progress*. New York: Oxford University Press, 1984.
——*Inhuman Bondage: The Rise and Fall of Slavery in the New World*. New York: Oxford University Press, 2006.
Drescher, Seymour. *Abolition: A History of Slavery and Antislavery*. Cambridge: Cambridge University Press, 2009.
Dubois, Laurent. *A Colony of Citizens: Revolution and Slave Emancipation in the French Caribbean, 1787–1804*. Chapel Hill, NC: University of North Carolina Press, 2004.
Jennings, Lawrence C. *French Anti-Slavery: The Movement for the Abolition of Slavery in France, 1802–1848*. Cambridge: Cambridge University Press, 2000.
McCarthy, Timothy Patrick, and John Stauffer, eds. *Prophets of Protest: Reconsidering the History of American Abolitionism*. New York: The New Press, 2006.
Stauffer, John. *GIANTS: The Parallel Lives of Frederick Douglass and Abraham Lincoln*. New York: Twelve, 2009.

CHAPTER 26

······································

EMANCIPATION

······································

CHRISTOPHER SCHMIDT-NOWARA

INTRODUCTION

·······································

In November 1867, the Spanish colonial administration in Puerto Rico freed José Quiñones from servitude in recognition of his heroism during a hurricane: "the said [slave] Quiñones, ignoring all danger, dedicated himself without rest to the salvation of many persons who would have perished without his help." The governor paid 1,000 escudos out of a special fund to Quiñones's owner "so that he will immediately give him his letter of freedom." Officials in Madrid from the Ministry of Overseas Provinces (*Ministerio de Ultramar*) heartily approved of the action and ordered that it be announced in the government's official publication.[1] These measures had precedent. The Spanish government used individual manumissions as rewards, not only to recognize "virtue," as in the case of José Quiñones, but also to encourage collaboration with the administration. Two decades earlier, for example, the island's military governor, General Juan Prim y Prats, ordered that the freedom of the slave Santiago be purchased from his owner Daniel Laport of Ponce because he had revealed the existence of "a conspiracy prepared by others of his class."[2]

There were other routes to legal freedom in Spanish America and Brazil beyond the largesse or manipulations of the state. Laws and institutions (civil and ecclesiastical) implanted in the colonies during the early stages of Iberian expansion regulated aspects of slavery and spelled out mechanisms for the liberation of individual slaves. Over time, customary rights that expanded the ability of the enslaved to claim various forms of autonomy, to change owners, and to purchase their freedom or that of loved ones took hold in the colonies. One institutionalized custom in colonial Cuba was *coartación*. It allowed male and female slaves to agree with their owners on a legally recorded self-purchase price. Even if sold, the *coartado* slave still carried with him the amount paid toward the agreed upon sum. Moreover, in Cuba, *coartados* over time gained the right to demand that they be sold to another master. Alejandro de la Fuente has detailed the efforts of María, an enslaved woman in Santiago de Cuba in the mid-nineteenth century, who appealed to the official in charge of such matters, the *síndico procurador*. He authorized her request to be sold by her master after she had initiated the process of *coartación*.[3]

Legal mechanisms and religious sanctions that encouraged self-purchase and manumission in the Iberian empires shaped societies in which large enslaved and freed populations coexisted. In 1800 the three largest Latin American slave societies, Brazil, Cuba, and Venezuela, all had large free black and mulatto populations. In none of them were slaves in the majority (see Table 26.1).[4]

Emancipation for individual slaves was thus an ongoing process in Latin America and operated at many levels. Historians following the lead of Frank Tannenbaum once argued that the legal paths to freedom indicated that slavery was more contractual and less physically punishing in the Iberian world than it was in the other European colonial empires.[5] However, historians of Latin American plantation societies disproved these claims. The sugar plantations of Bahia and Matanzas were as deadly as those of Barbados and Jamaica. Moreover, the freedom of some came in the context of the enslavement of many others, for the transatlantic trade in enslaved Africans would thrive for more than three centuries. Though all of the Spanish and Portuguese colonies relied upon slavery and the traffic, Brazil and Cuba ranked as the major recipients. Together they accounted for more than half of all slaves who survived the Middle Passage from the sixteenth to the mid-nineteenth century, when the traffic was finally suppressed (1850 in Brazil, 1867 in Cuba). Almost six million captives were disembarked in Cuba and Brazil, almost five million in Brazil alone, out of the almost 10 million Africans who survived the Atlantic crossing.[6]

Thus, while forms of emancipation flourished throughout the Iberian world, they coexisted with a large-scale slave trade and large enslaved populations. What

Table 26.1. Brazilian, Cuban, and Venezuelan populations in 1800

Colony	Brazil	Cuba	Venezuela
Total population	1,942,000	600,000	898,000
Slaves	718,000	212,000	112,000
Free blacks	587,000	114,000	440,000
Whites	576,000	274,000	185,000
Indians	61,000	n.a.	161,000

altered this equilibrium between slavery and freedom in Latin America? In recent studies, scholars have focused on the legal and religious institutions of Latin American slave societies but without making the vast generalizations found in Tannenbaum's influential work. Instead, they have explored how slaves took advantage of laws and customs to free themselves and to expand their sphere of activity after slavery, even though these actions did not necessarily pose a challenge to slavery's stability. In seeking to explain the destruction of Latin American slavery, historians now emphasize the importance of anti-colonial warfare in the nineteenth century and the claims of citizenship made by slaves and ex-slaves during the lengthy process of gaining independence and constructing new regimes. War and independence, in most cases (but significantly, not in the case of Brazil), destabilized the slave systems and occasioned new challenges to their very legitimacy. Therefore, to explain emancipation in Latin America, we must understand the myriad private claims of freedom over the centuries and how those became more radical in the context of major political and military crises over the course of the nineteenth century, when many slaves did indeed become citizens.

War and Revolution in the Atlantic Empires

Latin American independence was part of a widespread challenge to European colonialism in the Americas beginning in the late eighteenth century with the American Revolution. Historians now recognize that slavery and emancipation were central issues in the struggles over empire and independence. To understand how anti-colonial rebellions in the Iberian world undermined slavery and set the stage for emancipation, it is important to look at them in relation to the earlier wars of independence that transformed the British and the French Atlantic empires.

During the American Revolution, the British promised to free slaves and servants that fled to their side. In Virginia, the colonial governor raised a force called the Ethiopian Regiment composed of former slaves. Colonists were more cautious, if not downright resistant. In the southern plantation societies, they refused to employ slave soldiers, even though General George Washington insisted that the patriots needed the manpower. Southern resistance was a sign of things to come after independence. Slaveholding was strengthened in the new country, as was the slave trade until its abolition in 1808. When the British evacuated the former colonies, they included the many slaves who had supported them during the conflict. Initially settled in Nova Scotia, many of the formerly enslaved men and women formed the bulk of British settlers in the West African colony at Sierra Leone.[7]

Perhaps the most unexpected outcome of the British defeat was the rise of a mass antislavery movement in the metropole spearheaded by evangelical Christians who believed that God had punished the British in America for their sins related to slavery. The first antislavery leaders, such as the minister James Ramsay, a man with ample experience in the slave societies of the British West Indies, were convinced that spreading the gospel to the slaves in the colonies was the suitable act of atonement. In the face of planter resistance, they turned to antislavery politics, orchestrating a mass movement against the slave trade (and against slavery some decades later) so as to create Christian slave societies in the remaining colonies. The Anglican bishop Beilby Porteus imagined the West Indies mellowed by the effective spread of Christianity: "a little society of truly Christian Negroes, impressed with a just cause, and living in the habitual practice, of the several duties they owe to God, to their masters, to their fellow labourers, and to themselves; governed by fixed laws, and by the exactest discipline, yet tempered with gentleness and humanity."[8]

From this small but influential circle of religious reformers, British antislavery grew into a mass movement that became a major force in defining British politics and self-image for the next century. British antislavery drove Parliament to outlaw slave trafficking to the British colonies in 1807 and was a crucial factor in the suppression of British slavery in the 1830s. With success at home, British initiatives against the slave trade expanded, becoming international in scope. Beginning with the Congress of Vienna (1815), the government sought to implement slave trade abolition throughout the Atlantic world by securing treaties to that effect with other governments. At times, Britain was willing to back up its negotiations with military force, as in the case of Brazilian slave trade abolition in 1850. Though the traffic in slaves from Africa to the Americas would persist until the Spanish government ended it in 1867, the rise of British antislavery nonetheless represented a decisive blow against the legitimacy and viability of bonded labor in the New World with far-reaching consequences in Latin America.[9]

THE HAITIAN REVOLUTION

Revolutionary events were also transformative in the French Atlantic empire. In the same era in which popular mobilizations throughout the British Isles were demanding the end of the slave trade, slaves in the French colony of Saint-Domingue were taking direct action to throw off their bonds. Revolutionaries destroyed slavery forever in the former French colony of Saint-Domingue (and eventually on the entire island of Hispaniola). The Haitian events also became a symbol of liberation for enslaved and free people of color around the Caribbean. Yet, the demise of slavery in the world's richest sugar colony galvanized slavery in other corners of the Caribbean and Latin America, especially in Cuba and Brazil where planters, merchants, and governments took advantage of new openings for their goods and new anxieties about the consequences of slave emancipation.[10]

The French colony of Saint-Domingue, the western third of the island of Hispaniola, was at the time of the French Revolution the world's largest producer of sugar and coffee.[11] A small free population, divided between great planters and smaller property owners, shopkeepers, professionals, soldiers, and administrators, ruled alongside a massive slave population, largely African born. The free population consisted of roughly equal numbers of whites and people of color but together, little more than 10 percent of the total population. Many of the latter were freed by European fathers and assumed leading positions in the colony through education and the inheritance of wealth, though they found their prerogatives increasingly curtailed in the second half of the century. Some were planters in their own right, and, indeed, they predominated in coffee production. Others filled positions in the colonial militia (through which some participated in the American Revolution against the British) or the *maréchaussée*, the gendarmerie dedicated to tracking down runaway slaves. Though racial discrimination against free people of color was intensifying during the eighteenth century, they posed no fundamental challenge to the colony's slave society.

When revolution broke out in France in 1789, the *gens de couleur* saw the new regime as a potential ally against the "aristocrats of the skin" who sought to disbar them from the full enjoyment of their liberty. They found numerous advocates for equality in France; but they also confronted a small but influential abolitionist society, the *Société des Amis des Noirs*, founded in 1788 and dedicated to the gradual abolition of colonial slavery. By the later eighteenth century, more and more enlightened Frenchmen had come to see New World slavery as a gross injustice that threatened the future of French rule in the Caribbean.

Revolutionary France equivocated when it came to guaranteeing the rights of free colored citizens in the colonies. Saint-Domingue's whites and their French allies continued to enforce discriminatory policies. Frustrated free colored leaders took up arms in the colony in 1790 and 1791 to force the issue of equality, though they remained staunchly committed to their property in human beings. Yet, openings for action against slavery would quickly present themselves as divisions between colony and metropolis widened. While the dominant groups fought among themselves, slaves in the northern part of the colony apparently saw the opportunity to assert their own demands for freedom; inspired by African and European ideas of justice and freedom, a huge slave rebellion erupted in August 1791 in the sugar-producing heartland of the colony's North Province and eventually spread to other parts of the colony.

France's rivals saw in this colonial unrest a chance to advance their own cause. Both the British and the Spanish hoped to incorporate the rich colony into their own empires. Spain, for example, from the adjoining colony of Santo Domingo, supported Toussaint Louverture, a well-educated former slave, who, according to legend, was a reader of the Abbé Raynal, a *philosophe* who had augured the violent destruction of New World slavery by a heroic black Spartacus. Ultimately, Toussaint defied his Spanish patrons. In 1793, he switched his allegiance from Spain to France when the French commissar Sonthonax decreed the abolition of slavery, a measure then ratified by the Jacobin government in France in 1794. For the next several years, Toussaint was the de facto governor of the colony, which he successfully defended against the Spanish and English. In 1802, France sought to restore slavery in its colonies. Though the French were successful in their other Caribbean colonies and able to capture Toussaint, the generals Henri Christophe and Jean-Jacques Dessalines defeated a large European expedition and proclaimed the independence of the new nation, Haiti, on New Year's Day, 1804.

INDEPENDENCE AND EMANCIPATION IN SPANISH AMERICA

The French and Haitian revolutions and British abolitionism would exert important influence in the Iberian slave societies. Spain was one of the participants in the struggles over Saint-Domingue. Troops, refugees, and allies moved between Saint-Domingue and neighboring Spanish colonies such as Cuba, Puerto Rico, and Venezuela. Rebellions in the Spanish domains—at Coro in Venezuela in 1795 and in Havana in 1812—took explicit inspiration from the events in the French colony. Moreover, when Napoleonic France invaded the Iberian Peninsula in 1808, the empires of Spain and Portugal suddenly found themselves thrown into profound crisis.[12] The invasion had differing effects on slavery in the two empires. The Portuguese court embarked for Rio de Janeiro under British escort and remained there until 1822. With Rio as the new capital of the empire and the protection of the hegemonic economic and naval power, Brazilian ports enjoyed greater freedom, urban and plantation slavery boomed, and political order reigned, at least in the short term.

In contrast to Portuguese continuity, Spain's domestic and colonial order virtually collapsed. The Spanish court fell captive to an imposed regime headed by Napoleon's brother Joseph Bonaparte and violent resistance to the occupying force rocked the country between 1808 and 1814. The overthrow of the Bourbon monarchy led to an acute crisis of political legitimacy in the colonies. Many patriots, initially under elite leadership, saw this as the moment to fight for independence in the name of popular sovereignty; in doing so, they shattered the colonial social order from the Río de la Plata in the south to Mexico in the north. Slaves and slavery figured centrally in the independence struggle. Both loyalist and patriotic forces mobilized slaves to fight on their sides during the protracted wars for independence. Loyalists could draw on old precedents by promising freedom in exchange for a term of military service. Such a compromise had existed throughout the colonial period and recognized the basic legitimacy of slavery as an institution in Spanish America, while also honoring the mechanisms for acquiring freedom enshrined in Spanish law since the Middle Ages. Throughout the nineteenth century, Spain was able to attract military recruits from the slave population, trading freedom for service to the King and nation, as it had done throughout the old regime. Patriot armies often tried to strike a similar bargain, for many of their initial leaders such as Simón Bolívar in Venezuela and Carlos Manuel de Céspedes in Cuba later in the century were slave owners themselves. Yet the persistence of slavery became difficult to defend in the context of liberal and republican aspirations, the breakdown of traditional forms of order, and the spread of the language of liberation.[13]

From all corners of South America, where slavery was most widespread in the Spanish domains and where the battles were fiercest, slaves flocked to patriot armies, using the language of national liberation to forward their demands for liberty. Free people of color also saw great promise in the revolutionary movements. For example, the Afro-Colombian population of Cartagena de Indias, the major depot for the slave trade to Spanish America in the sixteenth and seventeenth centuries, enthusiastically supported the uprising against Spanish rule with the hope of achieving political equality under the new regime.[14] Knowledge of the Haitian Revolution also inspired many Spanish Americans of African descent. Demands for equality pervaded revolutionary and post-colonial Spanish America as popular groups—slaves included—mobilized for independence and embraced liberal and republican ideologies. Under such conditions, efforts to formalize inequality on the basis of lineage as the Spanish colonial regime continued to do or to reinvigorate bonded labor were virtually impossible. Revolutionary leaders such as the Venezuelan Bolívar had to give in to these popular pressures in spite of their own doubts and interests. With the important exception of Brazil, all Latin American states passed emancipation laws and banned the slave trade once they threw off colonial rule in the 1820s, though in most cases they compromised by granting freedom to slave combatants and passing gradual emancipation laws that delayed final abolition until mid-century (see Table 26.2).

One reason why abolition laws took hold in Spanish South America was that the British government effectively enforced the suppression of the Atlantic slave trade to the newly independent republics. In the 1820s, Britain made abolition of the trade a condition of recognizing Spanish American independence. One of the questions that British envoys had to put to new regimes was explicit: "Has it abjured and abolished the Slave Trade?"[15] Though the independent governments banned the trade, in some cases even before opening negotiations with Britain, there

Table 26.2. Abolition of slavery in independent Spanish America[a]

Country	Date of abolition
Argentina	1853
Bolivia	1861
Chile	1823
Central America	1824
Colombia	1852
Ecuador	1852
Mexico[b]	1829
Paraguay	1869
Peru	1854
Uruguay	1842
Venezuela	1854

[a] See George Reid Andrews, *Afro-Latin America, 1800–2000* (New York, 2004), 57.
[b] With the exception of Texas, still part of Mexico but also part of the expanding cotton frontier in the US South.

was pressure after independence to reopen it in some quarters. Peru opened a trade in slaves from Colombia in the 1840s. Peru also turned to the traffic in indentured Chinese workers, while slaveholders advocated the resumption of the African slave trade. Uruguay and Argentina circumvented agreements by allowing Portuguese and Brazilian slavers within their countries to outfit their ships and to fly their flags for illegal expeditions to Brazil. Britain would respond aggressively to these subterfuges by demanding new treaties (including with Spain and Portugal) that permitted the Royal Navy to seize and to destroy ships found with slaving equipment.

With the trade interdicted by international agreements and with British military pressure increasing, the gradual emancipation laws enacted in South America led to slavery's suppression by the 1850s, though the degree to which the enslaved and abolitionists had to fight against recalcitrant slaveholders should not be underestimated. Recent scholarship has shown in detail that men and women still legally enslaved took advantage of new laws and political situations to forward their demands for emancipation even before final abolition.[16] Slaves continued to resort to flight, escaping from rural haciendas to urban centers such as Lima. Or they might win their freedom through lotteries established to liberate a certain number of slaves each year. In several Spanish American cities, emancipation funds managed by political parties and religious associations purchased the freedom of enslaved men, women, and children. In Guayaquil, Ecuador, the local government established a *junta de manumisión* that was to oversee the purchase of freedom. Slaves had shown their commitment to such an undertaking from the moment of independence. In 1822, a group of enslaved men petitioned the new government for the right to establish their own manumission fund, whereby each would contribute a portion of their wages to a common pool to be used to purchase the freedom of all. "Liberty for captives has always been a privileged concept," they wrote in their petition. "We hope it will be even more so under the just, humane and honorable government we now enjoy."[17]

SLAVERY AND EMANCIPATION IN CUBA, PUERTO RICO, AND BRAZIL

While revolution and independence precipitated emancipation in much of Latin America, the conflicts of the era actually strengthened slavery in the region's largest slave societies: independent Brazil, and Spain's last colonies, Cuba and Puerto Rico. Dale Tomich has recently argued that planters in these slave societies took advantage of new market conditions in the Atlantic world and of cutting edge technology to build slave regimes of unprecedented scale and productivity. Rather than a relic of the distant past, as some historians once characterized slavery in the nineteenth century, the slave plantations of Cuba and Brazil were novel experiments in bonded labor that far surpassed their predecessors in their voracity for unfree labor and their ability to provision the booming markets of Europe, Africa, and the Americas.[18]

States that protected slaveholders' interests were also crucial. Both the Brazilian monarchy, born in 1822, and the much reduced Spanish colonial regime in Cuba and Puerto Rico, attracted loyalty from the great planters and traders of the era because they continued to support the slave trade, this in the face of British opposition, and to resist emancipation until the end of the century. Spain had sought to defend slavery throughout its struggle in the wars of independence in South America. Doing so eventually cost it popular support in the colonies because independence leaders were more willing to broker emancipation and to enfranchise freed people. Self-destructive though this policy might have seemed, it repaid the metropole mightily in the last colonies, Cuba and Puerto Rico. Indeed, forging and protecting the slave trade and the sugar plantations there created a vast new source of colonial wealth for the weakened metropole, as the studies of Josep M. Fradera have shown.[19] In Brazil, independence was less violent and disruptive than it was in the neighboring Spanish American countries. Rio de Janeiro's status after 1808 as the center of the Portuguese empire stimulated trade and the export of slave-produced goods. In the confrontation between colony and metropole in 1821, the heir to the Braganza throne pacted with colonial elites and broke from Portugal in 1822 with minimal use of force. One reason why the process was so smooth was that colonial elites were agreed that slavery and the slave trade would remain pillars of the new regime. The close link between Brazil and Africa, especially Angola, was unbroken by independence. Since the mid-seventeenth century Angola, as Luiz Felipe de Alencastro has recently argued with great verve and persuasiveness, was far more important to Brazil than was Portugal because of the huge flow of human captives, largely controlled by Brazilian, not Portuguese, traders and soldiers. The independent Brazilian monarchy, a ferocious slave trading regime, vividly demonstrated this priority.[20]

Yet, even in these staunchly pro-slavery regimes, opposition came to the surface, showing the influence of events and ideas in independent Spanish America, Haiti, and Britain. In Brazil, the 1830s were a contentious decade because of divisions between the Emperor Dom Pedro I and the dominant slaveholding groups caused by the Emperor's efforts to curtail the slave trade in response to British pressure. Until that time, Brazilian planters and merchants maintained the commercial nexus that joined ports in the Brazilian northeast and southeast to Angola, the lifeline of colonial Brazil. Though Portugal had signed an anti-slave trade treaty with Britain after the Congress of Vienna, it had included a most favorable exception for Brazil because trafficking remained legal south of the equator, an exception that the Brazilian monarchy exploited after independence.

Pedro I's acquiescence to British demands, however, threw the new regime into a temporary crisis. When Pedro abdicated his throne in favor of his young son and a regency government, the court loosened its control over the vast Brazilian periphery. What ensued was a decade of turmoil that witnessed numerous revolts of a federalist bent against the central authority in Rio de Janeiro. Slave uprisings, especially the Muslim revolt in Salvador, Bahia, in 1835, one of the largest urban slave insurrections in the history of the Americas, also challenged the dominant order. In response, a new conservative party took shape in the southeastern coffee zones of Rio de Janeiro and São Paulo dedicated to restoring the monarchy's authority and defending the slave trade in the face of British pressure. By the 1840s, the conservatives forged a new partnership with the young Emperor Pedro II upon the pillars of centralized political authority, defense of the slave trade, and slavery.[21]

In Cuba, conspiracies to overthrow slavery punctuated the growth of the slave trade and the spread of the sugar frontier. In 1812, the colonial government responded to slave uprisings around the island by carrying out mass arrests. Among the imprisoned was the free man of color José Antonio Aponte, a militiaman who led the organization of free people and slaves, the goal of which was to abolish slavery. Lengthy interrogations revealed that Aponte's inspirations included revolutionary leaders from the Americas, including George Washington and, most potently, black generals from Haiti, including Toussaint Louverture. In the 1840s, the Spanish government again uncovered a broad conspiracy which it suppressed with great violence, the so-called Conspiracy of La Escalera. Once again, slaves and free blacks combined to oppose slavery, this time with apparent support from British abolitionists present in the island.[22]

The Brazilian and Spanish governments and their slaveholding clients thus faced various forms of opposition and rebellion in the nineteenth century. But they also generally proved capable of turning them back, whether by paying lip service to British demands to end the slave trade or by repressing slave insurrections with extreme violence. How then did slavery finally come to an end in Brazil and the Spanish Antilles? There was no single factor but a combination of political, economic, and military transformations that compelled the Brazilian and Spanish states and the planter classes, under great domestic and international pressure, to relent.

In Brazil, one pillar of the conservative order was shakier than the others: the slave trade. The Brazilian government did little to enforce agreements with Britain, so that the traffic continued to flourish: almost one million slaves reached Brazilian shores from independence until 1850.[23] Some diehard conservatives went so far as to advocate openly the repeal of agreements with Britain. In the face of Brazilian defiance, hardened with the ascendancy of Pedro II and the conservatives, the Royal Navy decided to apply decisive force against slavers. In 1850, British warships entered Brazilian ports to bombard, capture, and burn ships outfitted for slaving voyages. These actions provoked an immediate response from the Brazilian monarchy and Council of State. Weighing its options, the Council decided that the lesser evil was to pass an effective law prohibiting the slave trade so as to preserve national sovereignty in the face of British aggression. Within a few days, the Chamber of Deputies and then the Senate passed a new law with teeth in it for the suppression of the traffic. Brazil's transatlantic trade, the most potent current of enslaved Africans to the Americas since the sixteenth century, was finally coming to a close.[24]

The abolition of the Atlantic slave trade transformed the dynamics of Brazilian slavery though it did not strike an immediate blow against the great coffee planters of the southeast. They were able to adapt, much like their counterparts in the antebellum southern United States, by opening an internal traffic that sent slaves from declining or stagnant regions such as Bahia and Pernambuco in the north to the expanding coffee zones in Rio de Janeiro and São Paulo to the south. Though they experimented with free labor and pondered the viability of mass immigration of Asian and European workers, the southeastern planters stubbornly clung to slaves as the core of their labor force.[25]

Those who saw their fortunes suffer most after 1850 were middling urban slave owners like Antonio José Dutra, a freed African-born slave who established himself in Rio as a barber, musician, and owner by the time of his death in 1849 of some dozen slaves. Zephyr Frank shows that while the slave trade from Africa remained open, slaves represented the most accessible form of property in the Brazilian economy: "Slavery was truly ubiquitous in Brazilian life in the early nineteenth century: slaves made up nearly half of Rio's population, and nearly all wealthholders participated in slaveholding." After the suppression of the slave trade, the price of slaves in Brazil steadily increased, making property in slaves prohibitive to those of modest fortune like Dutra. As markets reallocated labor to those who valued it the most highly, slaveholding became more concentrated within Brazilian society and more regionally concentrated in the southeastern coffee sector. Such changes benefited the southeastern planters, but it also ultimately made them more isolated from other Brazilians, a factor in the struggle for emancipation in the 1880s.[26]

If the suppression of the slave trade in 1850 was a significant benchmark in Brazilian slavery, the decade of the 1860s was the turning point for Antillean slavery. The US Civil War and slave emancipation, along with a renewed British initiative against the slave trade, forced the Spanish government to begin tinkering with the colonial regime put in place after the Spanish American revolutions. Most importantly, discussions of slavery's fate commenced. The Spanish Abolitionist Society, composed mostly of Puerto Rican and Spanish liberals and republicans, organized in Madrid. The government definitively banned the slave trade in 1867. The government also convened a body of Spanish and Antillean experts to deliberate on political, social, and economic reforms in the colonies.[27]

In 1868, the outbreak of revolution in Spain, Cuba, and Puerto Rico pushed the question of emancipation across a political threshold. The Cuban uprising, most notably, erupted in the island's eastern end, where the slave-based plantation system was weaker. Led by slaveholders on the margins of the colonial regime, the rebellion had the unintended effect of crippling slavery in the areas brought under rebel control. Slaves fled from their masters to the insurgency. The language of national liberation became entwined with the idea of liberation from slavery. Ultimately, the rebel leadership grudgingly capitulated to facts on the ground and declared slavery abolished in its territories.[28]

Developments in the colonies had an impact on metropolitan politics. The Bourbon monarch Isabel II fled into exile after the 1868 revolution. Under a new constitutional monarchy led by liberals and republicans, the Spanish government formulated a gradual emancipation law, the Moret Law of 1870, named for the Minister of Overseas Provinces, Segismundo Moret y Prendergast. Moret's balancing act sought to initiate a process of gradual emancipation while assuaging the concerns of Antillean planters, the military, and metropolitan merchants and producers with vested interests in the colonial market. The Moret Law liberated all children born to enslaved women but tempered their freedom by binding them to their mother's owner until they reached adulthood. It also liberated the elderly (those 60 and over) and sought to curb excessive corporal punishment.[29]

Resistance and criticism were immediately forthcoming. The Spanish Abolitionist Society, led by Puerto Ricans and Spaniards (Cubans were virtually absent), attacked the Moret Law as timid, unjust, and impolitic. The abolitionists argued that immediate abolition would undercut the Cuban uprising by winning the loyalty of the enslaved population. They also believed as anti-mercantilists that immediate abolition was in the best interest of the Antillean and Spanish economies. Diehard economic liberals in the Society held that once a free market and individual liberty were introduced in the colonies, wealth would expand significantly. Citing the examples of emancipation in other New World settings, they argued, somewhat misleadingly, that only such radical action would avert a crisis in the Antillean economies.[30]

Colonial planters held divergent views. For them, the Moret Law posed a grave threat to their property and to the productivity of their plantations. Like planters in southeastern Brazil, they clung to a core slave labor force until the final moment of abolition. Laird Bergad has shown that one effect of the Moret Law, which freed tens of thousands of slaves in both islands, was to concentrate enslaved workers in the most productive sugar-producing regions of Cuba. Astrid Cubano-Iguina has shown a similar dynamic at work in Puerto Rico, where planters were generally more amenable to some form of compensated emancipation. The arch-conservative sugar noble José Ramón Fernández, the Marquis of La Esperanza, opened perhaps the largest sugar plantation in the colony in the environs of Manatí in the 1850s. He fought bitterly against the abolitionists through the 1860s and 1870s while he continued to buy slaves to work on his Hacienda Esperanza.[31]

Colonial planters and the Spanish state might be said to have won the battle over emancipation. Though Spain passed an abolition law for Puerto Rico in 1873, conservatives managed to limit the act by requiring *libertos* to serve their former masters for three years. In Cuba, planters and their metropolitan allies delayed a final emancipation law until 1886. Yet, if Spain and its major colonial clients won that battle, they most certainly lost the war over the nature of the post-emancipation colonial regime. The Cuban insurgency not only challenged slavery, but also the boundaries of citizenship and nationality. As Spain sought to uphold slavery and equivocated on the incorporation of the colonies into the metropolitan Constitution on equal terms, defenders of Cuban independence saw the idea and the appeal of nationhood transformed. As had happened in the Spanish American revolutions of the early part of the century, in Cuba the participation of slaves and free people of color in the struggle for independence gave rise to a promised political community based on equality and unity instead of formal discrimination and difference.[32] Planters and the state controlled the emancipation process in Cuba, but their resistance to abolition provided advocates of independence with supporters for an even more broadly based war of independence that broke out less than ten years after the end of slavery.

Brazil, like Cuba, the United States, or Spanish South America, experienced violence on the road to emancipation, but politics, not war, proved decisive in bringing Brazilian slavery to an end.[33] Though southeastern planters adapted successfully to the Atlantic trade's suppression, they faced a serious challenge from an unsuspected quarter in Pedro II, the Emperor whose throne they had strengthened. In response to the war and emancipation in the United States and the Spanish government's tentative first steps toward abolition, the Emperor undertook a campaign within the corridors of power to begin an emancipation process in Brazil. Through parliamentary maneuvering Dom Pedro succeeded in securing the Rio Branco Law of 1871, a free womb law that resembled in many ways

Spain's Moret Law of 1870.[34] The resemblance was no coincidence. The Brazilian government closely followed the emancipation process in both Cuba and Puerto Rico. Brazil's representative in Madrid regularly dispatched copies of Spanish laws and debates, as well as summaries of the latest news from the Antilles. These would come to include the Moret Law (which was also debated actively in elite circles in provincial capitals such as Pernambuco),[35] the law abolishing slavery in Puerto Rico in 1873, and information about the traffic in indentured Chinese workers that flourished in Cuba from the 1840s to the 1870s.[36]

Brazilian planters effectively countered the measure despite being overridden by the Emperor. The Rio Branco Law gave slaveholders the choice of reserving for themselves the labor of those children until they reached adulthood or turning them over to the imperial government when they reached the age of 8. The government would then assume responsibility for their education and compensate the owner. Historians have found that they overwhelmingly opted for the first choice. By 1884, the government reported that of the 363,307 children registered as free only 113 were in the care of the state. Those born free by the letter of law in practice found themselves bound to slaveholders.[37]

The futility of the Rio Branco Law and the 1885 Saraiva-Cotegipe Law that would free the elderly but strengthened certain slaveholder prerogatives (they were entitled to labor from those freed for three years or until the age of 65) ultimately provoked a widespread antislavery movement in Brazil, one not instigated by the monarchy but by frustrated politicians, professionals, and artisans in cities such as Rio de Janeiro, São Paulo, and Santos. Local governments in regions peripheral to the slave economy, such as Ceará, also took matters into their own hands when it became clear that conservative politicians in Rio de Janeiro and southeastern planters were more than able to thwart abolition.

Local actions within the existing legal regime were diverse throughout the Brazilian empire. Many cities had private emancipation funds, such as the Emancipadora of São Paulo, that purchased the freedom of slaves from their owners. Also in São Paulo, the attorney Luiz Gama, who was sold as a child into slavery by his own Portuguese father, specialized in winning the freedom of people illegally enslaved according to the terms of the 1831 agreement with Britain. By 1880, however, these small-scale efforts to liberate some slaves were transformed into attacks on the system as a whole. By that time, such an attack was necessarily aimed at the southeastern coffee plantations where the internal traffic had concentrated the vast majority of the empire's slaves.[38] Ceará and other peripheral provinces abolished slavery within their borders. Abolitionists in the core regions also undertook more aggressive actions, especially those based in São Paulo and Santos. Leaders such as Antônio Bento organized raids on coffee plantations, the goal of which was to encourage mass flight by slaves. Slaves led by groups of abolitionist enablers called *caifazes* escaped on foot or by rail to the cities. The *quilombos* (encampments of runaway slaves) of Santos and Rio de Janeiro burgeoned.

Increasingly isolated and divided and faced with unrelenting civil disobedience by abolitionists and the enslaved, the conservatives of the southeastern provinces finally succumbed. Passage of the Golden Law of 1888, in essence, ratified the fact of general emancipation by bringing Brazilian slavery to a legal end.[39]

As in Cuba, the abolition of slavery brought with it the subversion and overthrow of the regime strengthened in the early nineteenth century to defend slavery. In Cuba, abolition not only failed to put the separatist genie back in the bottle, but magnified his influence in the western plantation districts. The ideal of an egalitarian and independent nation forged over the course of the Ten Years War and the emancipation process remained potent. The parallels to the weakening of slavery during the Spanish American revolutions earlier in the century are clear. The convergence of anti-colonial and antislavery mobilization undermined the colonial regime constructed in the first half of the nineteenth century on the foundations of the slave trade, slavery, and political exclusion of various kinds. For decades, Spanish officials had contrived to obviate their own treaty obligations with Great Britain by promoting a massive contraband slave trade to Cuba. "The fear of the negroes," as the Spanish minister José Maria Calatrava was reported to have said in 1836, "is worth an army of 100,000 men." They "will prevent [Cuban] whites from making any revolutionary attempts." The exigencies of a war for independence surmounted those fears.[40]

The actions of former slaves were essential in ending Spanish rule in Cuba because they undermined slavery and forced separatist leaders to demand a more egalitarian nation. In Brazil the actions of slaves and abolitionists in the 1880s precipitated the political crisis that brought slavery to an end. But it was the backlash by *slaveholders* that brought down the imperial government suddenly. The Crown's efforts since the Rio Branco Law to abolish slavery created a rift with the southeastern planters who had formed the backbone of its legitimacy. The decision to capitulate to the civil disobedience of the 1880s, abolishing slavery immediately and without indemnification, turned the conservative planters against the empire, converting one time monarchists into republicans. When the military rose in 1889 and suppressed the monarchy, it found avid support in the southeastern coffee regions among the former slaveholders and imperial senators.[41]

CONCLUSION

Current research on Latin American emancipation has focused on the crisis of the Atlantic empires of the late eighteenth and early nineteenth centuries and the subsequent construction of new states. The outcomes were diverse. In much of

Spanish America, the wars of independence empowered enslaved people, presenting them with opportunities to escape from servitude and to make claims of equality and citizenship in the new republics, states that were committed, even if hesitantly, to emancipation. In the largest Latin American slave societies, Cuba and Brazil, the situation differed significantly. The Atlantic crisis reinforced commitment to slave labor and the slave traffic in defiance of British abolitionism; coffee and sugar frontiers expanded, worked by enslaved laborers. Thus, what emerged in Latin America by the mid-nineteenth century were republics committed to emancipation and two monarchical regimes—the independent Brazilian monarchy and the Spanish regime in Cuba and Puerto Rico—staunchly committed to slavery. With emancipation, these old regime states also capitulated at century's end. In Latin America, republicanism was incompatible with slavery, though in revolutionary Cuba the effort to overcome the slaveholding past was greater than in republican Brazil.[42] New research takes inspiration from Tannenbaum's hypothesis about the links between slavery and citizenship. As one of the most important recent studies has asked: "Would those liberated from slavery also become citizens?"[43] In Latin America, the answer seems increasingly to be yes, but not because of a smooth transition from Iberian colonialism but rather because of the protracted struggles to achieve independence from Spain and Portugal and the efforts to undo colonial legacies of slavery and formal racial discrimination.

NOTES

1. "Sobre libertad del esclavo José Quiñones, que le ha sido concedida por su comportamiento en los conflictos ocurridos en la Isla," Archivo Histórico Nacional (Madrid), Sección de Ultramar (AHN/U), legajo 5094, expediente 39.

2. "Aprobado gasto extraordinario para liberar esclavo," AHN/U, legajo 1071, expediente 13.

3. See Alejandro de la Fuente, "Slaves and the Creation of Legal Rights in Cuba: *Coartación* and *Papel*," *Hispanic American Historical Review*, 87 (November 2007): 659–61. On the *carta de alforria*, certificate of freedom, in Brazil, see Rafael de Bivar Marquese, "A dinâmica da escravidão no Brasil: resistência, tráfico negreiro e alforrias, séculos XVII a XIX," *Novos estudos*, 74 (March 2006): 107–23.

4. George Reid Andrews, *Afro-Latin America, 1800–2000* (New York, 2004), 41.

5. Frank Tannenbaum, *Slave and Citizen: The Negro in the Americas* (New York, 1946).

6. On the volume of the slave trade, see the database available at www.slavevoyages.org. For a recent evaluation of the Tannenbaum debate, see the contributions of Alejandro de la Fuente, Christopher Schmidt-Nowara, and María Elena Díaz to "What can Frank Tannenbaum still teach us about the law of slavery?," *Law and History Review*, 22 (Summer 2004): 339–87.

7. See Benjamin Quarles, *The Negro in the American Revolution*, introd. Gary Nash, foreword Thad W. Tate (1961; Chapel Hill, NC, 1996); Ira Berlin and Ronald Hoffman (eds.), *Slavery*

and Freedom in the Age of the American Revolution (Charlottesville, Va., 1983); and Simon Schama, *Rough Crossings: Britain, the Slaves, and the American Revolution* (New York, 2006).

8. Quoted in Christopher Leslie Brown, *Moral Capital: Foundations of British Abolitionism* (Chapel Hill, NC, 2006), 362.

9. On British mobilization and the politics of abolitionism, see David Brion Davis, *The Problem of Slavery in the Age of Revolution, 1770–1823* (Ithaca, NY, 1975); and Seymour Drescher, *Capitalism and Antislavery: British Mobilization in Comparative Perspective* (New York, 1987). On British efforts against the major slavers in Portugal, Spain, Brazil, and Cuba, see Leslie Bethell, *The Abolition of the Brazilian Slave Trade: Britain, Brazil and the Slave Trade Question, 1807–1869* (Cambridge, 1970); David R. Murray, *Odious Commerce: Britain, Spain and the Abolition of the Cuban Slave Trade* (Cambridge, 1980); and João Pedro Marques, *The Sounds of Silence: Nineteenth-Century Portugal and the Abolition of the Slave Trade*, trans. Richard Wall (New York, 2006).

10. See David Patrick Geggus (ed.), *The Impact of the Haitian Revolution in the Atlantic World* (Columbia, SC, 2001); and Dale Tomich, *Through the Prism of Slavery: Labor, Capital, and World Economy* (Lanham, Md., 2004).

11. This discussion of the Haitian Revolution relies on C. L. R. James, *The Black Jacobins: Toussaint L'Ouverture and the San Domingo Revolution* (2nd edn. rev. New York, 1963); Robin Blackburn, *The Overthrow of Colonial Slavery, 1776–1848* (London, 1988), 161–264; David Patrick Geggus (ed.), *The Impact of the Haitian Revolution in the Atlantic World* (Columbia, SC, 2003); Laurent Dubois, *Avengers of the New World: The Story of the Haitian Revolution* (Cambridge, Mass., 2004); and Miranda Frances Spieler, "The Legal Structure of Colonial Rule during the French Revolution," *William and Mary Quarterly*, 3rd ser., 66 (April 2009): 365–408.

12. Jeremy Adelman, *Sovereignty and Revolution in the Iberian Atlantic* (Princeton, 2006).

13. Important overviews are Andrews, *Afro-Latin America*, chs. 1–3; and Peter Blanchard, *Under the Flags of Freedom: Slave Soldiers and the Wars of Independence in Spanish South America* (Pittsburgh, 2008).

14. Marixa Lasso, *Myths of Harmony: Race and Republicanism during the Age of Revolution, Colombia, 1795–1831* (Pittsburgh, 2007).

15. James Ferguson King, "The Latin-American Republics and the Suppression of the Slave Trade," *Hispanic American Historical Review*, 24 (August 1944): 390.

16. See Lasso, *Myths of Harmony*; Blanchard, *Under the Flags of Freedom*; Carlos Aguirre, *Agentes de su propia libertad: los esclavos de Lima y la desintegración de la esclavitud, 1821–1854* (Lima, 1993); and Christine Hünefeldt, *Paying the Price of Freedom: Family and Labor among Lima's Slaves, 1800–1854* (Berkeley, 1994); Camilla Townsend, *Tales of Two Cities: Race and Economic Culture in Early Republican North and South America: Guayaquil, Ecuador, and Baltimore, Maryland* (Austin, Tex., 2000); James E. Sanders, *Contentious Republicans: Popular Politics, Race, and Class in Nineteenth-Century Colombia* (Durham, NC, 2004).

17. Camilla Townsend, "In Search of Liberty: The Efforts of the Enslaved to Attain Abolition in Ecuador, 1822–1852," in Darién Davis (ed.), *Beyond Slavery: The Multilayered Legacy of Africans in Latin America and the Caribbean* (Lanham, Md., 2007), 38.

18. Influential works that treated slavery as archaic include Eric Williams, *Capitalism and Slavery* (Chapel Hill, NC, 1944); and Manuel Moreno Fraginals, *The Sugarmill: The*

Socioeconomic Complex of Sugar in Cuba, 1760–1860, trans. Cedric Belfrage (New York, 1976). See Tomich's criticism and revision in *Through the Prism of Slavery*. See also the comments of Rebecca J. Scott, *Slave Emancipation in Cuba: The Transition to Free Labor, 1860–1899* (Princeton, 1985), 3–41.

19. Josep M. Fradera, *Colonias para después de un imperio* (Barcelona, 2005).

20. Luiz Felipe de Alencastro, *O trato dos viventes: formação do Brasil no Atlântico Sul* (São Paulo, 2000). See also Rafael de Bivar Marquese and Márcia Regina Berbel, "The Absence of Race: Slavery, Citizenship, and Pro-slavery Ideology in the Cortes of Lisbon and in the Rio de Janeiro Constituent Assembly (1821–1824)," *Social History*, 32 (November 2007): 415–33.

21. Ilmar Rolhoff de Mattos, *O tempo saquarema* (São Paulo, 1987); José Murilo de Carvalho, *Teatro de sombras: a política imperial* (São Paulo, 1988); João José Reis, *Slave Rebellion in Brazil: The Muslim Uprising of 1835 in Brazil*, trans. Arthur Brakel (Baltimore, 1993); and Jeffrey Needell, *The Party of Order: Conservatives, the State, and Slavery in the Brazilian Monarchy, 1831–1871* (Stanford, Calif., 2006).

22. Robert L. Paquette, *Sugar is Made with Blood: The Conspiracy of La Escalera and the Conflict between Empires over Slavery in Cuba* (Middletown, Conn., 1988); and Matt Childs, *The 1812 Aponte Rebellion in Cuba and the Struggle against Atlantic Slavery* (Chapel Hill, NC, 2006). See also Manuel Barcia Paz, *Seeds of Insurrection: Domination and Resistance on Western Cuban Plantations, 1808–1848* (Baton Rouge, La., 2008).

23. See www.slavevoyages.org

24. Bethell, *The Abolition of the Brazilian Slave Trade*. For a recent assessment of the factors leading to the trade's suppression, see Jaime Rodrigues, *O infame comércio: propostas e experiências no final do tráfico de Africanos para o Brasil, 1800–1850* (Campinas, 2000). See also the assessment of the political situation in Murilo de Carvalho, *Teatro de ombras*.

25. Stanley J. Stein, *Vassouras: A Brazilian Coffee County, 1850–1900* (1957; Princeton, 1985); and Emília Viotti da Costa, *Da senzala à colônia* (4th edn. São Paulo, 1997).

26. Zephyr Frank, *Dutra's World: Wealth and Family in Nineteenth-Century Rio de Janeiro* (Albuquerque, N. Mex., 2004), 41.

27. Arthur F. Corwin, *Spain and the Abolition of Slavery in Cuba, 1817–1886* (Austin, Tex., 1967).

28. Karen Robert, "Slavery and Freedom in the Ten Years' War, Cuba, 1868–1878," *Slavery and Abolition*, 13 (December 1992): 181–200; and Ada Ferrer, *Insurgent Cuba: Race, Nation, and Revolution, 1868–1898* (Chapel Hill, NC, 1999).

29. Rebecca J. Scott, *Slave Emancipation in Cuba: The Transition to Free Labor, 1860–1899* (Princeton, 1985), 63–83.

30. Christopher Schmidt-Nowara, *Empire and Antislavery: Spain, Cuba, and Puerto Rico, 1833–1874* (Pittsburgh, 1999). Puerto Rican abolitionists were instrumental in developing this argument in cooperation with doctrinaire liberals in the metropole. With slavery declining in the island, many reformers, and some planters, believed that abolition with indemnification would benefit the plantation sector. In Cuba, slavery was still robust. Only the threat of British force brought the slave trade to an effective close. Planters there were thus defiant. See Schmidt-Nowara, *Empire and Antislavery*, chs. 1 and 2. On the respective plantation economies, see Francisco Scarano, *Sugar and Slavery in Puerto Rico: The Plantation Economy of Ponce, 1800–1850* (Madison, 1984); and Scott, *Slave Emancipation*.

31. Laird Bergad, *Cuban Rural Society in the Nineteenth Century: The Social and Economic History of Monoculture in Matanzas* (Princeton, 1990); and Astrid Cubano-Iguina,

"Freedom in the Making: The Slaves of Hacienda La Esperanza, Manatí, Puerto Rico, on the Eve of Abolition, 1868–1876," *Social History* (forthcoming).

32. See Ferrer, *Insurgent Cuba*; and Rebecca J. Scott, *Degrees of Freedom: Louisiana and Cuba after Slavery* (Cambridge, Mass., 2005).

33. Historians debate the impact of the Paraguayan War (1864–70) on Brazilian slavery: some argue that it undermined commitment to slavery while others argue that beyond several thousand liberated slaves who saw combat, the impact was minimal. See Hendrik Kraay, "Arming Slaves in Brazil from the Seventeenth Century to the Nineteenth Century," in Christopher Leslie Brown and Philip D. Morgan (eds.), *Arming Slaves: From Classical Times to the Modern Age* (New Haven, 2006), 146–79.

34. Murilo de Carvalho, *Teatro de sombras*, 50–83. See also Roderick J. Barman, *Citizen Emperor: Pedro II and the Making of Brazil, 1825–1891* (Stanford, Calif., 1999), 193–274; and Jeffrey Needell, *The Party of Order: The Conservatives, the State, and Slavery in the Brazilian Monarchy, 1831–1871* (Stanford, Calif., 2006).

35. Celso Castilho, "Brisas atlánticas: la abolición gradual y la conexión brasileña-cubana," in Rina Cáceres and Paul Lovejoy (eds.), *Haití: revolución y emancipación* (San José, 2008), 128–39.

36. See for example the report on the effects of the Moret Law in Cuba dated Madrid, 25 September 1875, Biblioteca Itamaraty, Madri, Oficios 1875–1880, 220/1/15.

37. Sidney Chalhoub, "The Politics of Silence: Race and Citizenship in Nineteenth-Century Brazil," *Slavery and Abolition*, 27 (April 2006): 81. See also Stein, *Vassouras*; and Viotti da Costa, *Da senzala à colônia*.

38. See the memoirs of the abolitionist Antonio Manuel Bueno de Andrada, "A abolição em São Paulo: depoimento de uma testemunha," *O estado de São Paulo*, 13 May, 1918. His mother directed the Emancipadora in cooperation with the Liberal Party. As a student in the Escola Polytechnica in Rio de Janeiro, he moved in abolitionist circles among students and faculty, including the director, Rio Branco, maestro of the 1871 law. For an overview of the many abolitionist initiatives, see Robert Edgar Conrad, *The Destruction of Brazilian Slavery, 1850–1888* (Berkeley, 1972). For a comparative perspective, see Seymour Drescher, "Brazilian Abolition in Comparative Perspective," *Hispanic American Historical Review*, 68 (August 1988): 429–60.

39. Conrad, *The Destruction of Brazilian Slavery*, 239–77; Robert Brent Toplin, "Upheaval, Violence, and the Abolition of Slavery in Brazil: The Case of São Paulo," *Hispanic American Historical Review*, 49 (November 1969): 639–55; and Maria Helena Machado, *O plano e o pânico: os movimientos sociais na década da abolição* (Rio de Janeiro, 1994), 143–73.

40. For a recent reevaluation of the independence war in Cuba, see John Lawrence Tone, *War and Genocide in Cuba, 1895–1898* (Chapel Hill, NC, 2006).

41. See Emília Viotti da Costa, "1870–1889," in Leslie Bethell (ed.), *Brazil: Empire and Republic, 1822–1930* (Cambridge, 1989), 161–213.

42. See Andrews, *Afro-Latin America*, ch. 4; and *Blacks and Whites in São Paulo, Brazil, 1888–1988* (Madison, 1991); and Scott, *Degrees of Freedom*, 253–69.

43. Frederick Cooper, Thomas C. Holt, and Rebecca J. Scott, *Beyond Slavery: Explorations of Race, Labor, and Citizenship in Postemancipation Societies* (Chapel Hill, NC, 2000), 17.

Select Bibliography

Alencastro, Luiz Felipe de. *O trato dos viventes: formação do Brasil no Atlântico Sul*. São Paulo: Companhia das Letras, 2000.

Andrews, George Reid. *Afro-Latin America, 1800–2000*. New York: Oxford University Press, 2004.

Blackburn, Robin. *The Overthrow of Colonial Slavery, 1776–1848*. London: Verso, 1988.

Blanchard, Peter. *Under the Flags of Freedom: Slave Soldiers and the Wars of Independence in Spanish South America*. Pittsburgh: University of Pittsburgh Press, 2008.

De la Fuente, Alejandro. "Slaves and the Creation of Legal Rights in Cuba: *Coartación* and *Papel*," *Hispanic American Historical Review*, 87 (November 2007): 659–92.

Geggus, David Patrick, ed. *The Impact of the Haitian Revolution in the Atlantic World*. Columbia, SC: University of South Carolina Press, 2001.

Schmidt-Nowara, Christopher. *Slavery, Freedom, and Abolition in Latin America and the Atlantic World*. Albuquerque, N. Mex.: University of New Mexico Press, forthcoming.

Scott, Rebecca J. *Slave Emancipation in Cuba: The Transition to Free Labor, 1860–1899*. Princeton: Princeton University Press, 1985.

Stein, Stanley J. *Vassouras: A Brazilian Coffee County, 1850–1900*. Princeton: Princeton University Press, 1985.

Townsend, Camilla. "In Search of Liberty: The Efforts of the Enslaved to Attain Abolition in Ecuador, 1822–1852," in Darién Davis (ed.), *Beyond Slavery: The Multilayered Legacy of Africans in Latin America and the Caribbean*. Lanham, Md.: Rowman & Littlefield, 2007, 37–56.

CHAPTER 27

....

SLAVERY
AND THE HAITIAN
REVOLUTION

STEWART R. KING

....

THE Haitian Revolution (1791–1804) stands as the only revolution in history to have destroyed a society in which slaves performed almost all productive labor and constructed on top of the rubble a nation-state in which slavery was prohibited. This unique phenomenon resonated throughout the transatlantic world, with repercussions in the imperial capitals of western Europe and throughout every slaveholding region in the Americas. The revolution inspired slaves with pride and the hope of ultimate deliverance and freedom, and it encouraged advocates of liberty in Europe. Perceptions of the revolution over the ensuing two centuries have been colored by racial attitudes and by the subsequent experience of independent Haiti. In the last half century, scholars have rediscovered the Haitian Revolution. New data and new methods have advanced understanding of the social and cultural circumstances of the revolution and its preconditions.

THE COLONIAL BACKGROUND

....

Spain ceded the western third of the island of Hispaniola to France in the Peace of Ryswick at the end of the War of the Grand Alliance (1688–97). During the eighteenth century the French colony, known as Saint-Domingue, became the richest colony in the Americas. It had almost 500,000 slaves—almost 90 percent of the total population—most of whom toiled on plantations producing sugar, coffee, indigo, and other crops for export. Saint-Domingue's planters had lower production costs than their counterparts in Jamaica or Brazil. As a result, Saint-Domingue producers dominated the European mainland market for sugar and coffee. The livelihoods of several million French depended on Saint-Domingue's commodities, whose value amounted to perhaps 40 percent of the total of France's foreign trade. French port cities like Nantes and Bordeaux flourished as slave trading ports. Slave traders brought more than 700,000 slaves to Saint-Domingue in less than a century; more than 30,000 African slaves arrived annually in the years that immediately preceded the revolution. Precise numbers cannot be known because a lively smuggling trade with British, Dutch, and American merchants circumvented the French mercantilist *exclusif*. The official figure averaged around 25,000 a year from the end of the American Revolutionary War in 1783 until the outbreak of the Haitian Revolution in 1791.[1] Historian David Eltis estimates total arrivals during the period 1775–1800 at 345,000, which, if one assumes that most of those arrivals came during the nine war-free years, means that more than 35,000 arrived each year.[2] Many of those counted by Eltis may have been imported unlawfully by British or Dutch merchants in violation of the official *exclusif*.

Newcomers of all races had a short life expectancy, as the historians Gabriel Debien and David Geggus have shown, but enough survived so that as many as a half of all slaves on the island were born in Africa. Sources differ on the rate of seasoning deaths among the African imports and thus on the proportion of African-born slaves in the colony at the outbreak of the revolution. Based on plantation records in French regional archives, mostly of sugar plantations, the French scholar Gabriel Debien estimated losses at one-half during the first three years. More recent information on a broader range of work environments reviewed by David Geggus suggest that the rate of mortality may have been lower but was still over one-third within the first few years.[3] In any case, large numbers of Africans lived in Saint-Domingue, often young men with military experience from wars in Africa. Jesuit missionaries had evangelized and educated Saint-Domingue's slaves in the early days of the colony, at least in some areas, but these efforts ended with the expulsion of the religious order by Louis XV in 1763. After that date, masters made only limited efforts to acculturate their slaves, who developed their own culture, complete with a language (*kweyol*) and a religion (*vaudou*) both strongly influenced by African models. Because post-revolutionary Saint-Domingue cut ties with European influences, African elements remained strong in Haitian culture. Anthropologists and ethnologists, most notably Melville Herskovits, Howard Courlander, and Alfred Métraux, studied Haiti in the nineteenth and twentieth centuries and much of scholarly and popular culture understanding of the processes of Afro-Creole culture creation begins with Haitian models. Much of

600 STEWART R. KING

their work drew on the ideas of Haitian ethnographers, especially those of the Haitian intellectual Jean-Price Mars and his circle.[4]

The slave population in Saint-Domingue was divided internally between creole and African-born (*bossale*) slaves and between skilled and unskilled workers. Skilled slaves, especially gang foremen (*commandeurs*), possessed significant influence within the slave population, and, indeed, as Carolyn Fick has pointed out, played a crucial role in plotting the slave insurrection that began in August 1791.[5] Creole slaves, while not necessarily more influential within the slave community, were more valuable to their masters, other things being equal, perhaps better treated by whites, and appear to have enjoyed at least some informal protection against masters' gross abuse. Creole slaves may have looked like collaborators to at least some African-born slaves. Other rebellions in the Caribbean before Saint-Domingue like Cuffe's Rebellion in Berbice (1763), the Stono Rebellion in Georgia (1739), and Tacky's War in Jamaica (1760) were mostly organized around African ethnicities, and members of other ethnicities and creoles were often oppressed by the rebels as well as by the victorious whites. Makandal's conspiracy in Saint-Domingue in 1758 was led by a runaway born in West-Central Africa, and most of those prosecuted for participation who appear to have had anything to do with the plot were fellow Kongos. The rebellion has engaged the Haitian patriotic imagination as the first blow in the creation of a national rebel movement.[6] In *The Making of Haiti* (1990), Carolyn Fick does attribute a broader class consciousness to Makandal, but ultimately portrays him as a transitional figure between the ethnic rebellions of the seventeenth and early eighteenth centuries and the national revolution to come.

In 1791, a free population of little more than 50,000 persons owned and supervised Saint-Domingue's 500,000 slaves. Whites, many of whom were absentee proprietors, owned the largest plantations on the island. A growing and understudied class of poorer whites hoped to become planters. Scholarship on Saint-Domingue's free people of color has burgeoned in recent years. As John Garrigus, Dominique Rogers, and Stewart King have demonstrated, many free coloreds worked as managers on plantations; others operated small businesses or pursued trades, often training slaves in skilled trades.[7] Free persons of color comprised about half the free population. Some free coloreds owned plantations and as a class, owned perhaps as much as one-third of the colony's arable land and about one-fourth of its slaves. Other free coloreds competed with lower-class whites for jobs in plantation management or crafts. All free men of any race had to serve in the militia. Those who were better off, free colored as well as white, served reluctantly. Poorer or less well-connected free colored men saw militia service as a way to build relations with white officers and perhaps to stake a claim to equal citizenship as well. Stewart King, in particular, has detailed the military service of Saint-Domingue's free coloreds.[8] Ultimately free men of color, though they comprised no more than half the free population, numbered almost two-thirds of the colony's indigenous armed forces (not counting metropolitan French troops based there).

Especially in the more highly developed North and West provinces, free colored enlistment in the militia and the rural police (*maréchaussée*) served as an important avenue for social promotion for free men of color. The pool of trained fighters created by such service became an important resource for the rebels when the revolution broke out, a resource that the white elite was reluctant to draw upon because of mistrust caused by racial prejudice. A large class of free colored peasants, some of whom were not juridically free, also lived in rural areas. Some of these peasants had their masters' permission to live "as free"; a small number of others lived in maroon communities as runaway slaves.

An extensive, often romanticized, literature exists on Haitian maroons and their role in the revolution. The traditional interpretation was put forward by *noiriste* Haitian writers in the early twentieth century, most notably Jean-Price Mars.[9] Mars's student Dr François Duvalier built a striking memorial in Port-au-Prince across from the national capital to the "*Marron Inconnu*" (the Unknown Maroon) after he became President in 1957. A more nuanced view of Haitian runaways appeared in the work of Haitian historian Jean Fouchard, who discovered that most runaways neither joined maroon settlements nor remained away from their plantations for long, although he argued that runaways were nonetheless important for establishing a revolutionary consciousness among slaves.[10] Haitian historian Leslie Manigat attempted to refurbish the image of the maroon as a key to the Haitian Revolution in a 1977 article, in which he argued that even though maroons living outside the plantation zones were few in number by the late eighteenth century, they embodied a tradition of resistance.[11]

The most recent scholarship to uphold this position was Carolyn Fick's *The Making of Haiti*, which argued that there was a continuous pattern of resistance throughout the period of French rule, embodied in maroons as well as transitional figures such as François Makandal. This traditional line of argument contrasts with the position of most modern scholarship on the subject, embodied in the work of David Geggus and Laurent Dubois, who point out that in most parts of the colony maroon activity waned after the coffee boom of the mid-eighteenth century.[12] In fact, Geggus argues that the reduction in maroon activity removed a safety valve that helped keep rebel activity low in the mid-eighteenth century. Coffee, unlike sugar, can be grown in the mountainous interior of the colony. Once the back country became economically important, the colony's government devoted the resources necessary to subdue the maroons. Some maroon groups remained active and made agreements with the colonial government; others were wiped out or forced further from population centers. Many ended up on the other side of the frontier, in Spanish Santo Domingo, where they received an official welcome and encouragement to settle down as peasants. Some small groups remained in active resistance up to the time of the revolution, especially in the less developed South Province. Although some of these former maroons did subsequently fight for Haitian independence, free people of color constituted the most important components of leadership of the rebellious slaves.

Saint-Domingue's better-off free people, whites as well as people of color, despised French mercantilism and dealt with smugglers whenever they could. They undermined the French government in other ways as well, rebelling in the 1760s, for example, against increased military obligations. Published memoirs of white planters, such as those collected by Pierre de Vaissière, and social-historical studies of free coloreds, including especially the recent study by John Garrigus, reveal that the wealthier inhabitants of Saint-Domingue were developing a creole identity, much like that developed by white North Americans in the period before the American Revolution and by wealthy Spanish Americans of all races in the 1800s before the wars of independence.[13] In this interpretation, prominent white exiles from Saint-Domingue in the nineteenth century such as Moreau de Saint-Méry and many of lesser prominence conveniently forgot their earlier flirtation with a different national identity. They filed petitions with the French government for aid or for a share in the reparations paid by Haiti in the 1840s, stressing their attachment to France in order to appeal for French help either to restore their position on the island or to extract reparations from the Haitians.[14] De Vaissière's view of an evolving creole identity among whites is reflected in Charles Frostin's study of white anti-militia agitation in the 1760s.[15] Anglo-American historians have more recently begun to accept this interpretation of white attitudes, and the link with free colored planters. John Garrigus, for example, in a recent work on pre-revolutionary Haiti, describes conflict between whites and free coloreds rooted in the tension and conflict between a collective creole identity and balkanizing racial identities.[16]

Saint-Domingue's free society divided on racial and class lines, which sharpened after the 1760s. Garrigus suggested that the metropolitan government fostered racial distinctions as a strategy of "divide and conquer" to drive a wedge between wealthy white and free colored inhabitants. Yet the hero of Garrigus's book, the free colored activist and slaveholder Julien Raimond, one of the wealthiest men in the colony, received considerable sympathy and assistance from the Minister of Marine for his 1780s campaign to gain equal rights for free-born people of color. His campaign is described in Garrigus's *Before Haiti* (2006). France's colonial hierarchy actually divided on this question. Racial attitudes in the colony were indeed hardening before the slave revolution, especially among poorer whites. They felt aggrieved because in defiance of Saint-Domingue's racialized hierarchy free coloreds were monopolizing easily available land in the back country and lower-level managerial jobs on the plantation. Poor whites, a segment of society studied by Frostin but only indirectly by Anglo-American scholars, also resented wealthier white landowners and merchants. When the revolution broke out, poor whites formed representative bodies modeled on the French National Assembly and assaulted the privileges of the planters, whom they saw as the local analogues to the French nobility. Most large planters and merchants were not actually nobles, however, and their attitudes and values were more like those of the French bourgeoisie.

Slaves vastly outnumbered Saint-Domingue's racially divided master class. The fear of slave uprisings in combination with a (possibly) calculated government policy to harden racial lines strengthened white racial solidarity. But the wealth of the planter class also divided its members from poorer whites. At the same time, the need for French troops to provide whites with security meant that wealthy colonists would recoil from the very thought of starting an independence movement in Saint-Domingue. Free coloreds shared fears of slave insurrection with whites but were seen by them as suspect allies on racial grounds. Slaves, for their part, had to contend with divisions in their own ranks, between foremen, artisans, and field-hands, between men and women, and between creoles and the African born. Of all these, as Fick points out, the slaves were the most successful in overcoming their internal divisions, thanks to the development of a common creole identity that could nonetheless incorporate African elements through Afro-Caribbean religion and shared suffering. Many of Saint-Domingue's inhabitants seemed to be counting on the system going on just as it had for half a century, yet the suspicion nagged that slaveholders were sitting on a volcano.

THE OUTBREAK OF THE REVOLUTION

At first, the colonial revolution came as a ripple of the French Revolution. Poor whites in Saint-Domingue rebelled against the domination of the wealthy planter class, and free people of color called for their civil rights. White and free colored planters appealed their discrete cases to the French revolutionary assemblies in 1789. Scholars of the French Revolution have become increasingly aware of the importance of these debates to the larger history of the revolution. Laurent Dubois's first book, *A Colony of Citizens*, dealt primarily with Guadeloupe but brought the attention of scholars of French history in the anglophone world back to the first abolition of slavery in 1793–4.[17] Marcel Dorigny and his collaborators addressed the first French emancipation in an important series of essays.[18] The issues of greater representation for the colonies, civil rights for free people of color, and the freedom of slaves were very different and rose to prominence in the debate at different times. The planters' Club Massiac became an important voting bloc in the National Assembly. Julien Raimond had actually departed Saint-Domingue before the outbreak of the revolution in France in order to appeal to the royal government for increased civil rights for free people of color. After 1789, he and fellow free colored activist Vincent Ogé joined forces with the metropolitan abolitionist *Société des Amis des Noirs* to appeal for better treatment for free coloreds through pamphlets and appearances before the Assembly. Ultimately, after the outbreak of the revolution in Haiti, metropolitan activists focused on the outright abolition of slavery. But the French legislatures avoided the question of civil rights for two years and the question of slavery for an even longer period of time. In this transatlantic cauldron, slaves watched and listened to what was swirling around them.

Two wealthy free colored men, Vincent Ogé and Jean-Baptiste Chavannes, rose up in rebellion, calling for civil rights for free coloreds but—explicitly—not for changes in the slave system. The recent scholarship on free people of color by Garrigus, King, and Rogers discusses the background of these men, but more work remains to be done on their role in the revolutionary period. Their movement, which gained support from hundreds of free colored farmers in the North Province, suffered a crushing defeat, and white officials sentenced Ogé and Chavannes to agonizing deaths. Other free colored movements in the west and south experienced greater success, laying the groundwork for political dominance of those regions by free coloreds that lasted into the national period. With the first shots fired, free coloreds navigated in the ensuing revolution a complicated course of changing goals and shifting alliances.

REVOLUTION FROM BELOW

Saint-Domingue's slaves knew they ought to be free without having to read any French philosophers or political pamphlets or to hear lectures from free colored intellectuals. Slave uprisings and other collective acts of resistance on Hispaniola had occurred since the first Africans arrived, brought by the Spanish in the sixteenth century. After 1697 in Saint-Domingue, the colonial government had sufficient forces at its command thanks in large part to the cooperation of free coloreds in the rural police and militia to crush slave rebellions. Until the 1760s, slaves who might have been potential rebels could flee as maroons to the mountains or across the border into Spanish Santo Domingo. As a result, armed collective slave resistance in Saint-Domingue in the eighteenth century erupted with curious rarity compared to other slave societies in the Caribbean. Divisions within a ruling class have helped precipitate many acts of collective slave resistance throughout the Americas. When Saint-Domingue's masters began to fight among themselves, the slaves discerned opportunity that had not existed before.

Privileged slaves, such as coachmen, foremen, technical specialists, and hunters, together with Vodou religious leaders and some free people of color organized a great uprising among the slaves on the sizeable sugar plantations of the North Province's northern plain, the most heavily populated and richest area of the colony. The slaves rose up the last week of August 1791, burning hundreds of plantations and killing or driving out the masters. Boukman, the runaway who organized at Bois Cayman a famous Vodou ceremony that may have been the signal for the uprising, emerged as an early leader of the rebellion. Other leaders included Jeannot Bullet, the brutal field commander, a skilled slave on the Bullet plantation, and Georges Biassou, the commanding general who had Jeannot put to death for excessive cruelty. Observers described the connection between the outbreak of the slave rebellion and the Bois Cayman ceremony at the time.[19] French revolutionary leader Lazare Carnot called the slave rebellion a "colonial Vendée," accusing the rebels of royalist sympathies and suggesting that the rebellion had been secretly provoked by royalist large planters.[20] This view of the event still has its supporters; a recent best-selling novel of the Haitian Revolution takes this line as its premise.[21] Nonetheless, most historians today follow Carolyn Fick in stressing the popular character of the uprising and its roots in a common culture and shared political consciousness among enslaved workers on the plantations of the North Province.

By 1794 Toussaint Louverture, a free black planter and slave owner, had risen to the fore to become the supreme commander of revolutionary forces. Toussaint has always been a remarkable figure, lauded in Haiti as the father of the nation's freedom, regarded by blacks throughout the Atlantic world as a hero, and respected even by white supremacists throughout the slave societies of the Americas as a great military and political leader. He made a considerable effort to identify himself with the slave rebels, to the extent that his status as a free person at the time of the revolution was not widely known until the 1990s. Classic histories of the revolution, such as that by C. L. R. James, and even modern biographies accepted the traditional interpretation.[22] Toussaint's freedom was known in the French-speaking world from the 1940s but was only rediscovered by Anglo-American scholarship in the 1990s.[23] Controversy remains about the scale of his planting or farming. A recent biography, for example, argues that he was a very low-level operator whose slaves were mostly family members for whom he was seeking freedom. Others such as Stewart King have argued that he was a reasonably large planter, as indeed he acknowledged himself in his appeal to Napoleon shortly before his death.[24] As a freedman, he was required to serve in the colonial militia. Haitian tradition—not supported by documentary evidence—holds that he also served as a volunteer in the French regular army during the American Revolution, fighting in a campaign in Georgia alongside a thousand Haitian free men of color. No documentary evidence for this belief exists, however, and in fact some official documents were executed in his name (at least) in Cap Français while the army was away. But the belief remains important in the Haitian national image of Toussaint. Contemporaries and subsequent generations of scholars have lauded Toussaint for his strategic brilliance, and indeed he brought professionalism and discipline to the mass of slave rebels, converting them into a skilled and determined army.

Toussaint's *Armée de Saint-Domingue* would appear to stand as one of those rarities in military history, an army seemingly created from a mass of disarmed civilians during the struggle in which they triumphed. Other great commanders of history such as Napoleon, Grant, or Caesar inherited professional armies from predecessors and put them to work on large tasks. Toussaint had to create his own army as well as lead it to victory. Historians of pre-colonial Africa, especially John Thornton, have pointed out the importance of African military experience in creating the preconditions for a well-organized army in the colony. Thornton points out that a large percentage of Africans landed in Saint-Domingue in the decade preceding the war were young men from West-Central Africa, Kongo and its neighboring states, who were prisoners taken in a variety of wars fought there during the period. The Kongo armies used firearms and were organized and fought in ways not too unlike those of European armies of the period.[25] Toussaint and his generals appear to have benefited from having many combat veterans with appropriate technological skills and knowledge of military culture among their troops.

Toussaint's soldiers fought from 1791 until 1799 against a shifting variety of enemies: French revolutionary governors, French royalists, British and Spanish invaders, internal opponents within the ranks of the slave rebels, and free colored leaders. At first, Toussaint's slave army fought for the King—first the King of France and then the King of Spain. Both Toussaint and Georges Biassou received commissions as generals from the Spanish. The French government sent metropolitan troops but failed to get sufficient reinforcements through the British blockade, which was imposed in 1793. At home, the French National Convention confronted European counter-revolutionary armies massing on the borders of the motherland. Under Jacobin influence, the Convention lurched leftward, and in doing so proclaimed in 1794 the end of slavery in the empire.[26] Meanwhile, in Saint-Domingue, the colonial government had already abolished slavery.[27] Toussaint's forces changed sides after receiving news of the official abolition in 1794, slaughtering their Spanish allies and signing on to fight as part of the French army. Robert Louis Stein has written a useful biography of Léger-Félicité Sonthonax, the revolutionary commissioner and Girondin leader sent to Saint-Domingue to implement the end of slavery.[28] To save Saint-Domingue as a French colony, Sonthonax allied himself with Toussaint as did Charles-Humbert-Marie Vincent, a colonel from a previous expeditionary force. Toussaint's soldiers proved professional and capable of defeating armies of veteran European troops. British, United States, and French liberals and reformers openly admired him. He pinned defeat after defeat on the British expeditionary force, dispatched in 1793, following desperate pleas from Saint-Domingue's white planters for aid.[29] In the end, Britain lost more troops in the Haitian Revolution than in Spain during Lord Wellington's celebrated Peninsular campaign.

A considerable body of scholarship has appeared recently on the impact of the Haitian Revolution on slaves and slavery in other countries. David Geggus, most notably, has contributed to and edited several anthologies on the subject.[30]

Slave owners in neighboring colonies and countries feared that Saint-Domingue's "black Jacobins"—to borrow the title from C. L. R. James's classic book on the revolution—would spread revolutionary contagion by sending agents to their shores or perhaps even by invasion.[31] James, a Trinidad-born Marxist intellectual, saw the Haitian Revolution as a transformative event in international as well as insular terms. Such influential scholars as the historians Eugene Genovese and Robin Blackburn and the Haitian anthropologist Michel-Rolph Trouillot drew on James for their own assessments. Genovese argued for the Haitian Revolution as a turning point in the history of slave revolts in the New World by marking a decisive turn from resistance to enslavement to resistance to slavery as a social system.[32] For Blackburn, the Haitian Revolution deserves pride of place, for it "redeemed and pushed further" the logic of the rights of man beyond that of any other revolution in an age of revolution.[33] Trouillot called the revolution "unthinkable history" before it happened, for it "challenge[d] the ontological and political assumptions of the most radical writers of the Enlightenment."[34] The Haitian Revolution moved slaveholders in the southern United States to rethink their initial applause for the French Revolution. The "horrors of St Domingo" appear over and over again in slaveholder discourses until the end of the Civil War. Cuba and Jamaica raised special defensive forces and invested in fortifications in anticipation of a Haitian invasion. Toussaint, however, preferred to consolidate his control of Saint-Domingue and never undertook the sort of campaigns in the Greater Antilles that revolutionary forces based in Guadeloupe under Victor Hughes did further east, although Saint-Domingue did serve as a base of operations for French privateers operating against British shipping the Caribbean.

Reassessment of the making of Haiti has renewed interest among diplomatic historians and other scholars on the impact of the revolution on the European balance of power and Napoleon's decision to sell Louisiana to the United States. By 1801, with Napoleon now as First Consul in revolutionary France, French officials began to reconsider the emancipation decree of 1794. The Peace of Amiens (1802) allowed him to stand down with Britain and concentrate on the American theater of his global ambitions. He needed the wealth of Saint-Domingue to pay for his ambitious projects in Europe. He may also have harbored racial antipathy towards blacks, and he certainly had a personal interest in the re-establishment of slavery since his wife and brother-in-law owned plantations in Saint-Domingue. President Thomas Jefferson's concern about the "cannibals of the terrible republic" initially blinded him to Napoleon's larger imperial ambitions in the Americas.[35] In any case, while Toussaint had succeeded in taking military control of the island, he had not been able to restore sugar production to its pre-revolutionary levels. Former slaves resisted gang labor on the plantations, even for wages, despite Toussaint's coercive "rural code," issued in 1801, that required them to return to work for their former masters as paid field-hands (*cultivateurs*). Toussaint also leased plantations confiscated from absentee white planters to his military commanders. The new planters wanted what the old planters had wanted: productivity and profits. They did not want to re-establish slavery, but they certainly wanted the former slaves to work in an intensive regimen as they had before the end of slavery. Toussaint's labor code required *cultivateurs* to return to their plantations and work under government supervision and military discipline for fixed wages. The former slaves, however, wanted to farm their own land. Since former slaves made up the vast majority of Toussaint's army, their voices carried weight. Many former slaves received small grants of land, qualifying them as planters and thus exempting them from the labor regulations. Others simply moved their families to the wild lands in the interior, taking the role of maroons. Some former slaves, often the older and weaker among them, did return to the plantations to obtain the promised regular rations. The transition of independent Haiti from planta-tion agriculture to peasant cultivation awaits comprehensive study, but sociolo-gist Mimi Sheller's comparative study casts some light on the early phases of this process.[36]

Toussaint compounded the threat to Napoleon's regime in 1801 by issuing a new constitution in which he proclaimed his loyalty to France but declared himself governor-general of Saint-Domingue for life. This "contradictory document," as the historian Laurent Dubois has called it, prohibited slavery forever in the colony but "consecrated" the rural code. The Constitution suggests a step towards actual independence, or Toussaint's attempt to nail down power within the French imperial system for himself, or perhaps both.[37] In any case, revolutionary forces in Guadeloupe also attracted unfriendly attention from Napoleon despite their clear intention to remain part of France. With visions of recreating a vast French empire in the Americas with Saint-Domingue as the engine of growth, Napoleon decided to reconquer the island and to restore slavery, although, sensibly, he did not announce the latter intention at the beginning of the campaign. Robert Paquette has detailed the contribution of the Haitian Revolution to the Louisiana Purchase and the expansion of the United States in a recent article.[38] Napoleon elevated his brother-in-law Charles Leclerc in 1801 to command a mighty expedi-tionary force of tens of thousands of soldiers and sailors to take control of the colony from Toussaint and his black and colored legions. Napoleon's armada arrived on 4 February 1802, eight years to the day from the proclamation in Paris of the abolition of slavery throughout the French empire.

THE FINAL STRUGGLE

While most of Toussaint's Army of Saint-Domingue initially submitted to Leclerc's orders, Toussaint and some of his soldiers stoutly resisted. They retreated to the interior of the island and established a strong point in the

West Province at La Crète à Pierrot. A garrison of some 2,000 Haitian soldiers held the fortress for twenty days against the main French force, inflicting hundreds of casualties before withdrawing with few losses. Leclerc's troops, steeled by European victories and supported by significant numbers of battle-tested Haitian troops, ultimately crushed this resistance after significant losses. Toussaint himself was arrested and imprisoned in France, where he died in 1803. But disease and relentless acts of insurgency began to take a toll on the French forces. Many of the rebels who had fled to take up land in the interior of the colony fought guerrilla style as the maroons had fought previous colonial armies. At the same time, soldiers who had surrendered when Leclerc arrived performed a volte-face after they sensed Napoleon's ulterior designs about restoring slavery and suppressing Toussaint and his lieutenants. Leclerc had orders to arrest every person of color who had ever served as an officer, and although he was never able to implement them, Toussaint's former officers soon realized the precariousness of their position. Moreover, a premature proclamation of the re-establishment of slavery in newly recaptured Guadeloupe in May 1802 became known in Saint-Domingue and enlightened Toussaint's soldiers about what they could look forward to under French rule. So Toussaint's generals, led by Jean-Jacques Dessalines, a former slave, renewed the struggle, carrying the revolution to a decisive stage.

Dessalines's uprising led to more than a year of heavy fighting marked by terrible massacres on both sides before the final defeat of the French forces at Vertières on 18 November 1803. Leclerc died from yellow fever before the end of 1802. His successor General Rochambeau pursued a genocidal policy, determined to extinguish all vestiges of rebel sentiment by killing almost all adult blacks on the island. All armed blacks who fell into their hands were killed without mercy, as well as many women and children. Dessalines, who had already engaged in bloody reprisals against free colored opponents of Toussaint's forces in Saint-Domingue's South Province, retaliated against the French by killing or driving out almost all remaining white inhabitants and slaughtering most of his prisoners. Nobody knows precisely the toll of this death struggle. The total population of the island fell between 30 and 50 percent between 1789 and 1804, with most of the decline coming in the last two years of the war. Some of this decrease may be accounted for by emigration, decreased birth rates and child survival in the chaos of war, and natural decrease of the African-born population. But the war must have directly killed over 100,000 Haitians. Dessalines and his generals declared Haitian independence on 1 January 1804 as the remnants of the French forces surrendered to the British and were evacuated by sea.

AFTER INDEPENDENCE

Modern scholarship has not paid nearly as much attention to post-Independence Haiti. The most reliable source for this period is still the nineteenth-century Haitian historian Thomas Madiou.[39] Haiti became an independent nation under Emperor Jean-Jacques Dessalines. He tried to follow the same course that Toussaint Louverture had, requiring former slaves to return to work on plantations (now mostly state owned and operated by senior military officers) for state-approved wages in an attempt to restore the island to its former leadership in the global sugar and coffee markets. The former slaves resisted, and Dessalines's authoritarian style angered subordinates. His rule ended in 1806 in assassination by a group of plotters that included generals Alexandre Pétion and Henry Christophe. Pétion and Christophe could not agree on who was to rule, so they divided the country between them. Christophe became the King of northern Haiti, with his capital near Cap Haïtien (formerly Cap Français, also called Cap-Henry during Christophe's reign); Pétion became the President of southern Haiti, with his capital in Port-au-Prince. Christophe tried to follow the same course as Dessalines, keeping the plantations working with forced labor, while Pétion permitted former slaves to take over unused land in the mountainous interior while using what labor he could hire or get out of his soldiers to cultivate the state-owned plantations at a reduced level. Pétion's model ultimately proved more successful, his followers dubbing him *Pè Bon Kè* (Father Goodheart). Christophe's people fumed and plotted and ultimately overthrew him in 1820.

Haiti evolved into a peasant society with limited production of plantation crops. Anthropologist Sidney Mintz has drawn a picture of the Haitian (and other Caribbean) peasantries as reconstituting themselves alongside the industrial system of the plantation, and successfully starving the plantations of labor power.[40] Historian Carolyn Fick also saw peasant agency as the important factor that determined independent Haiti's fate as a predominantly peasant society.[41] Jean-Pierre Boyer, Pétion's successor, signed a treaty with France agreeing to pay a huge indemnity to the masters of plantations who had lost land and slaves during the revolution. This bargain assured Haiti that it would not be attacked by France, but imposed a crippling financial burden and an excessively liberal trade policy on the Haitian state, as historian David Nicholls has pointed out.[42] Financial pressure imposed by the French indemnity exacerbated existing political instability. At the same time, surrounding nations that still owned slaves feared the Haitian example and did their best to keep the new nation isolated and weak. No European country immediately recognized the independence of Haiti; France did not do so until 1825; the United States waited until during the Civil War in 1862.

HISTORIOGRAPHY AND WIDER IMPACT

The understanding of the Haitian Revolution by writers of various stripes has changed remarkably over time. Scholars and activists have drawn different lessons from the event, but they have always recognized its importance. In the nineteenth century, European observers like Bryan Edwards, a British transplant to Jamaica who supported the slave trade and wrote an influential history of Saint-Domingue, sang the praises of Toussaint Louverture, who was safely dead by the end of the struggle. Even in the antebellum southern United States conspicuous proslavery apologists like George Fitzhugh and Thomas Roderick Dew paid tribute to Toussaint's political and military skills. Southern slaveholders as well as European observers displayed considerably less enthusiasm for post-Independence leaders such as Jean-Jacques Dessalines, who massacred most of the remaining whites in the island shortly after the rebels' victory. Defenders of slave systems in other places in the Americas did their best to prevent news of the revolution from coming to the ears of their slaves. They even managed to deny that it was a struggle for liberty, attributing the slaves' rebellion to French Jacobin agitators, disruptive free coloreds, or counter-revolutionary whites trying to destabilize the revolution (depending on their own politics). They played up reports of the savagery of the struggle and the chaos of the postwar political situation to support their belief that blacks were natural savages who needed to be kept under white rule. Much of this commentary was not published in book form but can be found in contemporary newspapers and pamphlets. Even during the revolution, French observers such as Médéric Louis Élie Moreau de Saint-Méry, a Martiniquan-born lawyer who spent more than a decade in pre-revolutionary Saint-Domingue, were producing propaganda pieces intended to inspire the French government to action, and afterwards, defenders of slave societies sought with increasing success to appropriate the Haitian experience as a negative object lesson.[43]

Declining sugar and coffee exports meant that Haiti was less important to the world economy after 1804. Post-1815 governments in Europe and the Americas effectively ostracized Haiti from the community of nations. Although Haiti was ultimately excluded from Simón Bolívar's inter-American Panama Congress (1826), the prospect of a Haitian presence so unsettled American southern politicians that they obstructed the delegation chosen to attend by President John Quincy Adams. The dominant tone of discussions of the Haitian Revolution in the Western world by the 1830s bespoke a post-revolutionary descent into poverty and savagery and smacked of wistful nostalgia by displaced whites for a lost world of economic prosperity and happy master–slave relations. In the 1790s Moreau de Saint-Méry published the foremost description in the Western world of colonial society in Saint-Domingue, a multi-volume work that he revised while in exile from the colony and working for Napoleon's administration in Europe. He longed for the restoration of what he portrayed as Saint-Domingue's relatively benign pre-revolutionary society, as had been done, at least temporarily, in Guadeloupe. A number of pamphlets and books by former colonists, many associated with an ultimately successful campaign to get reparations out of the Haitian government for their lost property, complemented Saint-Méry's depiction of the colony.[44]

Haitians were beginning to write their own history by the mid-nineteenth century. Thomas Madiou and Beaubrun Ardouin wrote competing histories of Haiti in the 1840s.[45] Madiou's eight-volume revisionist project *Histoire d'Haiti* (1844–8) sought to restore the reputation of Haiti's founding heroes: Louverture, Dessalines, Christophe, and Pétion. In so doing, he resurrected the current of liberal analysis of the revolution that had died with the French Revolution, doing so during the rebirth of liberalism in nineteenth-century Europe. Ardouin's five-volume *Études sur l'histoire d'Haïti* (1853–5) contended that the Haitian Revolution had been a tragedy in that it delayed the rise to power of a Creole, Westernized, and modernizing elite composed of free people of color. Those elites, Ardouin noted, had come to power in the 1840s in Haiti and would, he maintained, lead the country to a prosperous future as another liberal republic of the Western hemisphere. The difference between the two historians paralleled the split in Haiti's ruling class between a light-skinned, Westernizing, commercial, urban elite and a darker-skinned, rural, military group of leaders.

In the nineteenth century, Haiti remained an obscure and rather frightening object lesson for whites in slave societies throughout the Americas and a potent symbol of pride and aspiration for African-Americans. Over generations, many African-American leaders, as diverse as José Caridad González in Venezuela, Denmark Vesey in South Carolina, and Antonio Maceo in Cuba, referenced Haiti or Toussaint or both in organizing political movements. James McCune Smith, arguably the foremost black intellectual in the antebellum United States, published in 1841 a penetrating *Lecture on the Haytian Revolutions* with a "character" of Toussaint.[46] W. E. B. Dubois spoke of the Haitian Revolution as a "flare" that "lighted the night and made the world remember that these, too, were men."[47] The historian Alfred Hunt broke ground by tracing *Haiti's Influence on Antebellum America* (1988), but, in truth, he merely scratched the surface.[48] Black abolitionists and black soldiers in the American Civil War looked to Haiti as progeny would look on forebears. Frederick Douglass, in effect, sealed the connection, by becoming the American ambassador in Port-au-Prince during the Grant administration. While Douglass was there, he oversaw the end of a colonization scheme to settle American blacks in Haiti that, while unsuccessful in establishing a large American presence in the country, did fix Haiti as a destination and a positive role model in the black American public imagination.[49]

THE TWENTIETH CENTURY

The invasion and occupation of Haiti by the United States in 1915 renewed public interest in Haiti around the world. Platoons of former US marines wrote memoirs, ranging from the humorously offensive (e.g. Faustin Wirkus's *White King of La Gonave*) to the thoughtful (Stanley Reser's *Doc Reser in Haiti*).[50] Eugene O'Neill's play *The Emperor Jones* (1920), based loosely on the life of Henry Christophe, captivated audiences and resulted in an important stage role for Paul Robeson that catapulted him to stardom. Haiti also figured in a pioneering work of cultural anthropology, Melville Herskovits's *Life in a Haitian Valley* (1937).[51] C. L. R. James's lyrical *Black Jacobins* (1938) remains, despite its Marxist methodological approach, looseness with facts, and questionable interpretations, one of the most influential books ever written not only about the Haitian Revolution, but also about slave rebellion.[52] American cultural icons as diverse as Martha Graham and Selden Rodman traveled to Haiti, where they encountered and reported on a burgeoning Haitian cultural scene increasingly aware of—and comfortable with—its African-ness and the country's revolutionary roots. In *Ainsi parla l'oncle* (1928) the Haitian intellectual Jean Price-Mars, a leader in the international cultural movement of *noirisme* or black consciousness, performed pioneering work in folklore studies that introduced readers throughout the world to the heroes of Haitian independence.[53]

Price-Mars founded the Haitian Ethnographic Society, which included as one of its members a young doctor named François (Papa Doc) Duvalier. When Duvalier came to power after a chaotic election process in 1957 he gratified many retrograde white racist prejudices about the inability of black people to govern themselves without violence. He imposed a harsh dictatorship on the country, enforced by his private militia, the *Volontaires de la Sécurité Nationale*, better known as Tontons Macoutes. Graham Greene's novel *The Comedians* (1966) chillingly portrays the violence of the Duvalier government and the fatuousness of the opposition and became one of the best-known portrayals of Haiti in the United States.[54] A popular 1967 movie of the same title, starring Richard Burton and Elizabeth Taylor, followed.

As the Duvalier regime was becoming more violent, newly independent nations in Africa faced problems similar to those that Haiti had encountered as the world's first black republic. Haitian history came to be seen by the public as an awful example and role model for independent African countries, and Haiti came to be thought of as more African than Latin American. Yet, by and large, Haiti slipped from the public mind in the United States during the 1970s and 1980s, and scholars ceased to write much about the Haitian Revolution as the political and economic situation there deteriorated. The only general history of Haiti in print in the United States at the time of the collapse of the Duvalier regime in 1986 was Robert and

Nancy Heinl's *Written in Blood* (1978), a political history that stresses the inability of Haitians to govern themselves.[55] In 1986, the collapse of Jean-Claude (Baby Doc) Duvalier's dictatorship generated global headlines and stimulated worldwide scholarly interest in Haiti once again. Haiti had become one of the poorest countries in the world, and for a time was unjustly blamed as the source of the AIDS pandemic. After the fall of the Duvaliers, high hopes for democracy faded into a round of coups d'état, bloodily suppressed democracy movements, and military juntas, although skilled Haitian professionals became a fixture in international development agencies and Haitian immigrants in the United States moved into the middle class. This Haitian diaspora, particularly the coming of many new Haitian migrants in the 1990s to the United States and to Europe, sparked further interest in things Haitian.

CONTEMPORARY HISTORIOGRAPHY

The 200th anniversary of the outbreak of the Haitian Revolution in 1991, and the subsequent bicentennial of independence in 2004, as well as the international (United States-led) interventions of 1994 and 2004, stimulated interest in the Haitian Revolution and the slave society from which it sprang.[56] Haitians, from political activists like Chavannes Jean-Baptiste, who assumed the name of a revolutionary leader as his *nom de guerre*, to intellectuals like Patrick Bellegarde-Smith, reexamined the revolution to further understanding of Haiti's national character and the analysis of the nation's contemporary strengths and weaknesses. A conference held at Brown University in 2004, on the 200th anniversary of independence, brought together most of the top scholars in Haitian studies around the world and resulted in an important collection of essays, *The World of the Haitian Revolution* (2008).[57] In undertaking these tasks and others, scholars inside and outside of Haiti have had to confront a relative paucity of primary sources in comparison to what was left behind by roughly contemporaneous revolutionary movements in western Europe and the Americas. French administrators and the government of Toussaint Louverture kept records for those portions of the colony that he and his administration controlled for the period 1789–1802. But most of these records, whether transferred to France or not, have apparently not survived. Very few French sources exist from any time after the outbreak of the revolution. A few dozen volumes of notarized documents pertaining to Saint-Domingue from the revolutionary period lie in the French National Archives; private archives hold some as well. The French expeditionary force under Leclerc filed reports with headquarters, when they could get a ship through the British blockade to carry them, but most of the army's documents perished when the army surrendered. The Haitian rebels kept few records, though some correspondence between various generals has been preserved. Political disturbances in the Haitian state during the ensuing two centuries have caused the destruction of most records kept in Haitian repositories. So much of what is known about the revolution comes from such unexpected places as the Public Records Office in Britain or the Archives of the Indies in Spain. Historian David Geggus, for example, delved into fresh sources painstakingly uncovered in British archives to produce a richly detailed study of the British occupation of revolutionary Saint-Domingue from 1793 to 1798.[58]

Pierre Pluchon, the dean of French Caribbeanists, helped revive French interest in the Haitian Revolution by publishing a biography of Toussaint Louverture in 1989.[59] In France, Victor Schoelcher and the nineteenth-century abolitionists had largely garnered the credit for ending slavery in the French empire. The work of Pluchon and a new generation of scholars, such as Marcel Dorigny and Laurent Dubois, recovered on both sides of the Atlantic the first French emancipation of 1794 and its connection to the slave revolution in Saint-Domingue, the French Revolution, and the global campaign against slavery.

Laurent Dubois drove home this message to English-speaking scholars in *Colony of Citizens* (2004), a prizewinning book on Saint-Domingue's sister colony of Guadeloupe, which experienced a contemporaneous revolution much less remembered than the Haitian but far better documented.[60] Guadeloupe, like Saint-Domingue, experienced an uprising by poor whites, a movement for civil rights by free persons of color, and a slave insurrection that turned into a servile war to prevent Napoleon's restoration of slavery in the island. Guadeloupe's pro-French faction, unlike its counterpart in Saint-Domingue, was able to keep control of the situation and incorporate the former slaves into a revolutionary army, which unlike Saint-Domingue's revolutionary armies, tried to spread revolution throughout the region. Victor Hughes, a white French officer, governed the colony under the Directory, led the revolutionary army, and attacked British and Spanish slave owners throughout the Caribbean until his recall to France in 1798. Guadeloupe, like Saint-Domingue, experienced the landing in 1802 of a French expeditionary force sent by Napoleon. It fared better, however, than Leclerc's, restoring slavery and crushing the last independent elements on the island, led by the mulatto general Louis Delgrès. Driven to the peripheral subject of revolutionary Guadeloupe by the extensive archival sources available on the island's history during this period, Dubois nonetheless prepared to write a history of the main event. His *Avengers of the New World* (2005), a readable yet comprehensive synthesis, replaces James's *Black Jacobins* as the best history in English of the Haitian Revolution.[61]

UNANSWERED QUESTIONS

The central focus of historical research on the Haitian Revolution remains the quest for archival resources in unexpected places. The Haitian national archives contain few relevant documents. Likewise the French national archives lie almost barren of such traditional sources as notarial documents, court records, or government account books, dated after 1790, although both Geggus and Garrigus found a modest amount of relevant material, especially from the South Province where the revolution took longer to develop. Departmental archives in France house some plantation and business records from the period. Correspondence from the Leclerc/Rochambeau expedition can be found in the French military archives in Vincennes, and a collection of Rochambeau Papers resides at the University of Florida Library.[62] Anthropologists and folklorists have made some progress in understanding the roots of Haitian culture using non-documentary sources, tapping into a rich oral tradition in Haiti—though much of their findings only deals peripherally with the revolution.[63] Historians, however, have had difficulty integrating this problematic testimony into their research. Historians of Africa, following the method of the Belgian anthropologist Jan Vansina, have done a better job.[64] As more "Atlantic" historians enter the field of Haitian Revolution studies with a background in, or at least some exposure to, the Africanist literature, some of these methods of analyzing oral traditions pioneered by Vansina and others might be brought to bear in Haiti in understanding the revolution. Notable in this regard has been the work of John Thornton, a historian of pre-colonial Africa, and Nancy Heywood, an African-Americanist, in tracing the connections between Kongo and Caribbean religious practice in the eighteenth century.[65]

Archaeologists have worked in Haiti off and on since the first American intervention of 1915. Their excavations, however, have largely targeted residue from the pre-Columbian or post-conquest periods. Haitian architect and artist Albert Mangones conducted an exhaustive dig and historical reconstruction project, using UNESCO funds, at the site of the Citadel, a formidable fortress built by Henry Christophe atop a mountain in northern Haiti, and at Christophe's nearby palace in Milot. This restoration project revealed many details of life in Christophe's Kingdom of Haiti in the years after the revolution, but has yet to produce a definitive work in English transmitting this knowledge to the scholarly community.

Who were the avengers of the New World? Modern scholarship on this central question in some ways echoes the debates a century and a half ago between Thomas Madiou and Beaubrun Ardouin. The Haitian nationalist tradition, expressed by Madiou, saw the revolutionaries as the oppressed underclass: slaves and maroons. In re-imagining the revolution as a national uprising of creoles rather than a class struggle, Ardouin stressed the decisive role played by free people of color. Elite Haitians preferred to think of things in Ardouin's way. Hostile observers in the nineteenth and early twentieth centuries stressed the racial aspect as a way to denigrate the movement. The anthropological rediscovery of Haitian popular culture and larger trends in the historiography of slavery have restored agency in the modern scholarship to slaves and free people of color in explaining the many complicated twists and turns of a great revolution that lasted more than a decade. Carolyn Fick's social history of the Haitian Revolution notably evidences this trend.[66] Yet the portrayals of many key leaders and the rank-and-file revolutionary soldier remain obscure and cloudy. John Thornton has focused attention on Kongos, the predominant African ethnicity in Saint-Domingue's pre-revolutionary slave population, in the ranks of the soldiery and to their contributions and those of other Africans to the content and character of the revolution. To be sure, recent scholarship has fleshed out the characters of Toussaint, Christophe, and Pétion drawing on accounts from pre-revolutionary social historical records, and from the accounts of themselves left behind and from reports of various friends and enemies who encountered them. But the thinking of the ordinary foot soldier remains highly speculative.

What motivated a Saint-Domingue slave to become a slave rebel, to participate in a collective movement to overthrow an entire social system, rather than just seek a better life for him or herself? Most slaves throughout the Atlantic world accommodated themselves to what they found around them. They looked for advancement within the system: better working and living conditions, more and better food, clothing, household supplies, marriage and a family, maybe manumission for themselves or their children. If they resisted, their resistance was individual: running away, sabotaging tools, slowing down their work, killing the master or the overseer. Mass resistance of the open violent variety amounted to suicide in most of the slave societies of the Atlantic world. Why did Saint-Domingue's slaves and free persons of color erupt in insurrection and after the initial rush of enthusiasm fight for years to effect social transformation? To what extent did the influence of the revolutionary moment, the liberationist ideologies that were sweeping Europe, affect Saint-Domingue's rebellious officers and soldiers? Surely slaves in 1791 had heard their masters talking about the political earthquake in France. After the outbreak of the slave uprising, rebels were exposed to French Jacobin ideas by the various civil commissions that governed the island from 1793 on. What role did religion play? Vodou was congealing into a distinct religious experience in the late eighteenth century, with its own ideology of individual empowerment through better relations with the *loa*, or gods. The Jesuits, with a strongly collectivist idea of how a godly society should be structured, had told the slaves they were human beings made in the image and likeness of God for half a century up until the 1760s. Had any of these ideas survived?[67] Catholicism had been the state religion of the Kingdom of Kongo since the late fifteenth century; Thornton has argued for Christianity's influence on Kongo soldiers. What was the role of African ideas about kingship, liberty, and proper social order? The cross-fertilization between Haitian studies and African studies has resulted in the growth of "Atlantic world" approaches and perspectives that have advanced the debates about the revolutionary era.[68] Before the revolution, Saint-Domingue had a highly developed plantation economy, particularly in the North Province where the slave insurrection began. The region's central plain contained many of the largest and most productive sugar plantations in the world, where slaves outnumbered whites by more than nine to one. There were many large plantations, especially in the sugar regions, but the most common slaveholding was around a dozen slaves working on a small coffee plantation. Saint-Domingue's plantations were significantly smaller than those found in Jamaica or Cuba at the height of the sugar boom in those islands. Did this high level of capitalist development, the intensification of a factory-like regimen that demanded disciplined, regular labor from closely supervised slaves, lead to a worsening of conditions for the slaves and create a climate in which slaves would see revolution as the only possible escape for themselves? Under these conditions, how did master absenteeism and stratification within slave gangs create a class of slave leaders with sufficient space to plot an insurrection?

Recent scholarship, especially the books by Stewart King and John Garrigus, has richly documented intensifying racial prejudice against free coloreds in the years that led up to the revolution. As the slave insurrection evolved into a social revolution, free colored officers often led slaves into battle. What motivated reasonably well off free people of color such as Charles and Sainte Bélair, a prewar free black couple executed by Leclerc in 1802, to give up their farm and their slaves and their piece of Saint-Domingue's prosperity for the life of hunted rebels, and finally an uncomfortable death at the bleakest moment of the revolution? What convinced a large fraction of the literate, propertied free colored class that revolution was in their interest and to what extent did they in formulating their politics engage European liberal ideas? Toussaint's prefacing of his name with "citizen" in many letters and proclamations surely indicates engagement with an age of democratic revolution. Yet scant evidence has surfaced that free people of color were reading Rousseau or Montesquieu in the eighteenth century. The prevalent white (especially poor white) attitude of increasingly virulent racial hatred might well have convinced the free coloreds that revolution was their only option. Since Saint-Domingue's poor whites were justifying themselves in terms of Rousseau in the early years of the revolution, free coloreds may well have thought of European liberalism as inimical to their interests. Economic arguments for free colored resistance seem unlikely, for free persons of color, as a class, were prospering during the latter half of the eighteenth century. Perhaps a model that delineates rising expectations followed by frustration and sharp reversal may have greater explanatory power in this case. Prospering free people of color may have though that they were not advancing fast enough; certainly they were not as wealthy as the biggest white planters. Thus we might suppose that they rebelled to secure a larger share of the wealth. Revolutionaries have visions but tend not to be prescient. Once the rebellion became a revolution to end slavery the basis of the free coloreds' pre-revolutionary wealth and prosperity was permanently destroyed. Most free people of color, like the Belairs, Toussaint Louverture, and Alexandre Pétion, stuck with the revolution despite great personal economic loss.

Military aspects of the revolution bear further study, despite the attempts by Dubois to integrate some military aspects into his general history of the rebellion, and of Thornton to explore the origins of Haitian military practices in Africa. The Haitian Revolution was the first of the Latin American independence struggles and also perhaps the first modern guerrilla war. Asymmetrical, irregular warfare by maroons and nomadic indigenous people, for example, occurred in the Americas throughout the colonial period. But these struggles reflected pockets of resistance, limited in scope, not the involvement of an entire nation in the state of becoming. The Haitian revolutionaries waged a modern national war using guerrilla tactics when needed. Their opponents pioneered many of the unsuccessful counter-insurgency tactics employed against guerrillas in the nineteenth and twentieth centuries from Spain to Vietnam. The colonial government waged a "war of posts" against Toussaint's forces in the north in 1792–3, surrounding high-value targets such as the sugar planting areas with blockhouses manned by small garrisons of regular troops. Toussaint's men could pick their targets for harassing attacks, infiltrate cadres into the protected areas to spread propaganda and recruit troops, and steal supplies and weapons from isolated garrisons. When the British occupied portions of the colony in 1794–9, they pursued a regional strategy, gaining broad support in the south, occupying a few strategic spots in the north, and waging a war of posts in the west. The French, this time led by Toussaint, adapted their tactics to the enemy's flexibility, pioneering the classic multi-level guerrilla strategy laid out by Mao Zedong in his *On Guerilla War*.[69] Mao's concept of fortified sanctuaries in particular played an important role in Toussaint's campaign against the French invasion force led by General Leclerc in 1802, as the most celebrated battle of the war was the siege of Crète à Pierrot, a sanctuary comparable to Mao's Jianxi soviet area before 1934. Like Mao, when the pressure from the enemy's forces became too strong, Toussaint evacuated Crète à Pierrot with minimal losses, though he was eventually run to ground and forced to surrender. After Haitian independence was achieved, the King of northern Haiti, Henry Christophe, took this lesson to heart when he built the most famous monument in Haiti, the Citadelle Laferrière, on a mountaintop overlooking Milot in the interior of what used to be called the North Province. The citadel was not intended to stop invaders from entering the country but to provide an unassailable base from which guerrilla armies could strike.

The Haitian Revolution can be seen as the first "national" war of independence. Study of the revolution as a stage in the formation of a Haitian national identity has been a feature of debates over historical interpretation almost since the smoke cleared. But scholars have yet to look at the war as an exercise in national mobilization. It would be much easier to do this if we had records from the revolutionary government.

NOTES

1. Philip Curtin, *The Atlantic Slave Trade: A Census* (Madison, 1969); Paul Lovejoy, "Volume of the Atlantic Slave Trade: A Synthesis," *Journal of African History*, 23 (4) (1982): 473–501.
2. David Eltis, "Transatlantic Slave Trade," in Stanley Engerman, Seymour Drescher, and Robert Paquette (eds.), *Slavery* (New York, 2001), 186.
3. Gabriel Debien, *Les Esclaves aux Antilles françaises, XVIIe–XVIIIe siècles* (Basse-Terre, 1974), 84; David Geggus, "Sugar and Coffee Cultivation in Saint Domingue and the Shaping of the Slave Labor Force," in Ira Berlin and Philip D. Morgan (eds.), *Cultivation and Culture: Labor and the Shaping of Slave Life in the Americas* (Charlottesville, Va., 1993), 73–98, 318–24.
4. Jean Price-Mars, *Ainsi parla l'oncle* (Port-au-Prince, 1928); Melville Herskovits, *Life in a Haitian Valley* (New York, 1937). Harold Courlander, *The Drum and the Hoe: Life and Lore of the Haitian People* (Berkeley, 1960); Alfred Métraux, *Voodoo in Haiti* (New York, 1959).
5. Carolyn Fick, *The Making of Haiti: The Saint Domingue Revolution from Below* (Knoxville, Tenn., 1990).
6. As, for example, on the website "Makandal: Black Revolutionary Who Toppled Slavery," http://www.macandal.com/
7. John Garrigus, *Before Haiti: Race and Citizenship in French Saint-Domingue* (New York, 2006); Dominique Rogers, "Les Libres de couleur dans les capitales de Saint-Domingue: Fortune, mentalités et intégration à la fin de l'ancien régime" (Ph.D. diss., Université Michel Montaigne Bordeaux 3, 1999); Stewart King, *Blue Coat or Powdered Wig: Free People of Color in Pre-Revolutionary Saint-Domingue* (Athens, Ga., 2000).
8. King, *Blue Coat*, 52–80.
9. Mars, *Ainsi parla l'oncle*.
10. Fouchard, *Les Marrons de la liberté* (Paris, 1972).
11. Leslie F. Manigat, "The Relationship between Marronage and Slave Revolts and Revolution in St. Domingue Haiti," in Vera Rubin and Arthur Tuden (eds.), *Comparative Perspectives on Slavery in New World Plantation Societies* (New York, 1977), 420–38.
12. Fick, *The Making of Haiti*, 46–75; Laurent Dubois, *Avengers of the New World* (Cambridge, 2005), 54; David Geggus, "Le Soulèvement de 1791 et ses liens avec le marronage et le vaudou," in Michel Hector (ed.), *La Révolution Française et Haïti: Filiations, ruptures, nouvelles dimensions* (Port au Prince, 1995), 60–70; and Michel Hector, *Haitian Revolutionary Studies* (Bloomington, Ind., 2002), 75–7.
13. Pierre de Vaissière, *Saint-Domingue: La société et la vie créoles sous l'ancien régime (1629–1789)* (Paris, 1909).

14. M. L. E. Moreau de Saint-Méry, *Description topographique, physique, civile, politique et historique de la partie française de l'isle Saint-Domingue...*, 2 vols. (Philadelphia, 1797–8).

15. Charles Frostin, *Les Révoltes blanches à Saint-Domingue aux XVIIe–XVIIIe siècles* (Paris, 1975).

16. John Garrigus, *Before Haiti*; Garrigus, "Opportunist or Patriot? Julien Raimond (1744–1801) and the Haitian Revolution," *Slavery and Abolition*, 28 (1) (April 2007): 1–21.

17. Laurent Dubois, *A Colony of Citizens: Revolution & Slave Emancipation in the French Caribbean, 1787–1804* (Chapel Hill, NC, 2006).

18. Marcel Dorigny (ed.), *The Abolitions of Slavery: Légér Félicité Sonthonax to Victor Schoelcher, 1793, 1794, 1848* (New York, 2003).

19. As, for example, Antoine Dalmas, *Histoire de la Révolution de Saint-Domingue* (Paris, 1814), 116–27; and Hérard Dumesle, *Voyage dans le nord d'Hayiti ou révélation des lieux et des monuments historiques* (Cayes, 1824), 85–90; both excerpted and translated in Laurent Dubois and David Geggus (eds.), *Slave Revolution in the Caribbean: A Brief History with Documents* (New York, 2006), 86–94.

20. Quoted in David Bell *The First Total War: Napoleon's Europe and the Birth of War as we Know it* (New York, 2007), 169.

21. Madison Bell, *All Souls Rising* (New York, 1995).

22. C. L. R. James, *Black Jacobins: Toussaint L'Ouverture and the San Domingo Revolution* (New York, 1936), 17–19; and Ralph Korngold, *Citizen Toussaint* (New York, 1944).

23. Gabriel Debien, *À propos du trésor de Toussaint L'Ouverture* (Cairo, 1946), 35.

24. Madison Bell, *Toussaint Louverture: A Biography* (New York, 2007); King, *Blue Coat*, 27–8; Stewart King, "Toussaint Louverture before 1791: Free Planter and Slave Owner," *Journal of Haitian Studies*, 3/4 (1997–8): 61–72; and David Geggus, "Toussaint Louverture: avant et après le soulèvement de 1791," in Franklin Midy (ed.), *Mémoire de révolution d'esclaves à Saint-Domingue: la traite négrière transatlantique, l'esclavage colonial, la Révolution de Saint-Domingue et les droits de l'homme* (Montréal, 2006), 112–29 (2nd rev. edn. (2007), 112–32).

25. John K. Thornton, "'I Am the Subject of the King of Congo': African Ideology in the Haitian Revolution," *Journal of World History*, 4 (1993): 181–214; John K. Thornton, "African Soldiers in the Haitian Revolution," *Journal of Caribbean History*, 25 (1993): 59–80; John K. Thornton, "La Nation angolaise en Amérique, son identité en Afrique et en Amérique," *Cahiers des anneaux de la mémoire*, 2 (2000): 241–56; and David P. Geggus, "The Arming of Slaves during the Haitian Revolution," in Christopher Leslie Brown and Philip D. Morgan (eds.), *Arming Slaves: From Classical Times to the Modern Age* (New Haven, 2006), 209–32.

26. Dorigny, *Abolitions of Slavery*.

27. The decree can be found in English translation with explanatory essay in Dubois and Garrigus, *Slave Revolution in the Caribbean*, 120–5.

28. Robert Stein, *Léger Félicité Sonthonax: The Lost Sentinel of the Republic* (Rutherford, NJ, 1985).

29. Bryan Edwards, *An Historical Survey of the French Colony in the Island of Saint Domingo...* (London, 1797) is a particularly sympathetic portrayal of Toussaint's character even while the British invasion was ongoing.

30. David Geggus, *The Impact of the Haitian Revolution in the Atlantic World* (Columbia, SC, 2002), as well as David Gaspar and Geggus (eds.), *A Turbulent Time: The French*

Revolution and the Greater Caribbean (Bloomington, Ind., 2003); Alfred Hunt, *Haiti's Influence on Antebellum America: Slumbering Volcano in the Caribbean* (Baton Rouge, La., 2006).

31. James, *Black Jacobins*.

32. Eugene Genovese, *From Rebellion to Revolution: Afro-American Slave Revolts in the Making of the Modern World* (Baton Rouge, La., 1992).

33. Robin Blackburn, "Haiti, Slavery, and the Age of Democratic Revolutions," *William and Mary Quarterly*, 63 (4) (October 2006): 643–74.

34. Michel-Rolph Trouillot, *Silencing the Past: Power and the Production of History* (Boston, 1997), 70–4.

35. Letter from Jefferson to Aaron Burr, February 11, 1799, cited in "The Jefferson Encyclopedia" at http://wiki.monticello.org/mediawiki/index.php/St._Domingue_or_Haiti

36. Mimi Sheller, *Democracy after Slavery: Black Publics and Peasant Radicalism in Haiti and Jamaica* (Gainesville, Fla., 2001).

37. Dubois, *Avengers*, 245–6. The Toussaint Constitution, in English translation, can be found at http://thelouvertureproject.org/index.php?title=Constitution_of_1801_%28English%29

38. Robert L. Paquette "Revolutionary Saint-Domingue in the Making of Territorial Louisiana," in Gaspar and Geggus, *Turbulent Time*, 204–25.

39. Thomas Madiou, *Histoire d'Haiti*, 8 vols. (1844–7; Port-au-Prince, 1985–8).

40. Sidney Mintz, *Caribbean Transformations* (Chicago, 1974).

41. Fick, *The Making of Haiti*, esp. 237–50.

42. David Nicholls, *From Dessalines to Duvalier: Race, Color, and National Independence in Haiti* (rev. edn. New Brunswick, NJ, 1996), 65.

43. The essays in David Geggus (ed.), *The Impact of the Haitian Revolution in the Atlantic World* (Columbia, SC, 2001), esp. David Brion Davis, "Impact of the French and Haitian Revolutions," Simon Newman, "The Haitian Revolution and American Political Culture: Nathaniel Cutting and the Jeffersonian Republicans," and David Geggus, "The Caradeux and Colonial Memory," are particularly useful in understanding this phenomenon.

44. Many are collected in Jeremy Popkin, *Facing Racial Revolution: Eyewitness Accounts of the Haitian Insurrection* (Chicago, 2007); and others in Dubois and Garrigus, *Slave Rebellion in the Caribbean*.

45. Thomas Madiou, *Histoire d'Haiti* (1847; Port-au-Prince, 1985); and Ardouin, Beaubrun, *Études sur l'histoire d'Haiti* (Paris, 1853–60).

46. James McCune Smith, *A Lecture on the Haytien Revolutions: With a Sketch of the Character of Toussaint L'Ouverture* (New York, 1841).

47. W. E. B. Du Bois, *John Brown: A Biography* (Philadelphia, 1909), 79.

48. Alfred N. Hunt, *Haiti's Influence on Antebellum America: Slumbering Volcano in the Caribbean* (Baton Rouge, La., 1988).

49. For the history of the various attempts to place American settlements in Haiti, see Chris Dixon, *African America and Haiti: Emigration and Black Nationalism in the Nineteenth Century* (Westport, Conn., 2000).

50. Faustin Wirkus and Taney Dudley, *The White King of La Gonave* (Garden City, NY, 1931). Reser's book is no longer available.

51. Melville J. Herskovits, *Life in a Haitian Valley* (New York, 1937).

52. C. L. R. James, *The Black Jacobins: Toussaint Louverture and the San Domingo Revolution* (New York, 1938).

53. Jean Price-Mars, *Ainsi parla l'oncle*.

54. Graham Greene, *The Comedians* (New York, 1966).

55. Robert Debs Heinl and Nancy Gordon Heinl, *Written in Blood: The Story of the Haitian People* (Boston, 1978).

56. The "intervasion" of 1994 has produced its own literature in political science and journalistic commentary. One very readable account is Bob Shacochis, *The Immaculate Invasion* (New York, 1999).

57. David Patrick Geggus and Norman Fiering (eds.), *The World of the Haitian Revolution* (Bloomington, Ind., 2008).

58. David Geggus, *Slavery War and Revolution: The British Occupation of Saint-Domingue* (Oxford, 1982).

59. Pierre Pluchon, *Toussaint Louverture: Un révolutionnaire noir d'ancien régime* (Paris, 1989).

60. Laurent Dubois, *A Colony of Citizens: Revolution & Slave Emancipation in the French Caribbean, 1787–1804* (Chapel Hill, NC, 2004).

61. Laurent Dubois, *Avengers of the New World: The Story of the Haitian Revolution* (Cambridge, 2004).

62. For the UF library's collection, see Laura V. Monti, *A Calendar of Rochambeau Papers at the University of Florida Libraries* (Gainesville, Fla., 1972). For the French archives *Guide des sources de l'histoire de l'Amérique latine et des Antilles dans les archives françaises* (Paris, 1984).

63. Howard Courlander, *The Drum and the Hoe: Life and Lore of the Haitian People* (Berkeley, 1960); Alfred Métraux, *Voodoo in Haiti* (New York, 1959), 25–57.

64. Jan Vansina, *Oral Tradition: A Study in Historical Methodology* (London, 1961); and *Paths in the Rainforest: Toward a History of Political Tradition in Equatorial Africa* (Madison, 1990).

65. John Thornton, "On the Trail of Voodoo: African Christianity in Africa and the Americas," *The Americas*, 44 (January 1988): 261–78; John Thornton, "African Dimensions of the Stono Rebellion," *American Historical Review*, 96 (October 1991): 1101–13; John Thornton, "Les Racines du vaudou: Religion africaine et société haïtienne dans la Saint-Domingue prérévolutionnaire," *Anthropologie et sociétés*, 22 (1998): 85–104.

66. Fick, *The Making of Haiti*.

67. Leslie Desmangles, *Faces of the Gods: Vodou and Roman Catholicism in Haiti* (Chapel Hill, NC, 1992).

68. An important early study in this regard is an article by Thornton, " 'I Am the Subject of the King of Congo', " 181–214.

69. Mao Zedong, *On Guerilla Warfare*, trans. Samuel B. Griffith II (Garden City, NY, 1978).

Select Bibliography

Dubois, Laurent. *Avengers of the New World: The Story of the Haitian Revolution.* Cambridge, Mass.: Harvard University Press, 2004.

—— and John Garrigus, eds. *Slave Revolution in the Caribbean, 1789–1804: A Brief History with Documents.* Boston: Bedford/St Martin's, 2006.

Fick, Carolyn. *The Making of Haiti: The Saint Domingue Revolution from Below.* Knoxville, Tenn.: University of Tennessee Press, 1990.

GARRIGUS, JOHN. *Before Haiti: Race and Citizenship in French Saint-Domingue.* New York: Palgrave McMillan, 2006.

GASPAR, DAVID BARRY, and DAVID PATRICK GEGGUS, eds. *A Turbulent Time: The French Revolution and the Greater Caribbean.* Bloomington, Ind.: Indiana University Press, 1997.

GEGGUS, DAVID PATRICK, ed. *The Impact of the Haitian Revolution in the Atlantic World.* Columbia, SC: University of South Carolina Press, 2001.

—— and NORMAN FIERING, eds. *The World of the Haitian Revolution.* Bloomington, Ind.: Indiana University Press, 2008.

GENOVESE, EUGENE D. *From Rebellion to Revolution: Afro-American Slave Revolts in the Making of the Modern World.* Baton Rouge, La.: Louisiana State University Press, 1979.

JAMES, C. L. R. *The Black Jacobins: Toussaint L'Ouverture and the San Domingo Revolution.* New York: Dial Press, 1938.

KING, STEWART. *Blue Coat or Powdered Wig: Free People of Color in Pre-Revolutionary Saint-Domingue.* Athens, Ga.: University of Georgia Press, 2001.

TROUILLOT, MICHEL-ROLPH. *Silencing the Past: Power and the Production of History.* Boston: Beacon Press, 1995.

CHAPTER 28

INTERNAL SLAVE TRADES

MICHAEL TADMAN

INTERNAL SLAVE TRADES IN THE AMERICAS

In 1902 on a research trip to Charleston, South Carolina, the historian Frederic Bancroft visited Thomas Ryan's old slave trading jail, and in a yard nearby he talked to a black woman who had been one of the hundreds of thousands sold in the interstate trade. When Bancroft asked whether many children had been separated from their parents and sold to traders, the woman, pointing in front of her to a hen with a brood of chicks, explained: "Dey sell em like de hawks take de little chickens, dah. Dey sen de chilluns out in de street an' yo' nevah see'm agin. De specahlatahs pick up de chilluns, like yo' pick up dese chickens."[1] Internal trading in enslaved people had more impact in some slave regimes and in some periods than in others, but across the Americas vast numbers fell into the hands of professional slave traders who abruptly plucked them from one community and dropped them into the hands of strange new owners, perhaps hundreds of miles from home and family. In some regimes—especially in the United States, and probably too in Brazil after 1850—the internal trade became the lifeblood of the slavery system, driving its economic and territorial growth. Owners might sometimes pretend that slavery was not about "Negro speculation"—that it was not about turning people into money—but enslaved people knew better.

Strictly local selling of slaves was always a part of slave regimes, but internal slave trades are taken in this essay to involve two basic factors—first, price differences that stimulated sales to high-price areas and, second, available surpluses of slaves. In the long-distance and more organized markets, certainly in the USA, the process of selling was very much dominated by professional traders. Sometimes, however, migrant planters, before setting out, chose to supplement their slave gang with the sort of selective purchases that traders made, and occasionally after migrating owners made long-distance buying trips. Apart from long-distance trades, there were also less-reported intra-regional trades, often with small owners selling to the big planters of the region.[2]

Sometimes price differences between regions were themselves enough to encourage trading. Internal trades would, however, have been able to flourish best where a slave population grew naturally, that is as a result of more slaves being born than dying. For our present purposes it is important to note a demographic fundamental—slave natural increase almost never occurred on sugar plantations. It is highly significant, then, that while sugar planting played a crucial role in Caribbean and Brazilian slavery, in North America, even at its peak, it only employed 6 percent of slaves. Demographic factors therefore set up some key contexts for our discussion. First, sugar plantations were never likely to be sources of significant exportation—sugar planters always wanted to maintain a slave force with more male than female workers, and they always wanted new and replacement workers. Second, regions that were not based on sugar (or on mining) had the potential eventually to develop both natural increase and substantial slave exportation. Third, within regions dominated by sugar, the slaves of non-sugar producers were likely to develop a pattern of natural increase. This meant that their owners might sell surplus slaves to local sugar planters, or might export surpluses beyond the region.[3]

Intra-regional slave trades in the Americas have often left few records and have been little noticed by historians. In many cases too, historians have probably ignored significant *inter-regional* trades that pre-dated the era of abolition. The internal slave trades that have been most researched are those long-distance trades that operated under the critical attention of active abolitionist movements, and they are trades that flourished after the supply of slaves from Africa had terminated or been much restricted. The internal trade was most prominent in North America from 1807 (the abolition of the African trade) to 1865, in Brazil from 1850 (the ending of African importation) to 1888, and in the British Caribbean from 1807 (again the abolition of the African trade) to 1833.[4]

TRENDS IN THE LITERATURE ON THE NORTH AMERICAN DOMESTIC TRADE

Many of the key positions later taken by historians of the trade were set out, especially from the 1830s, in the antebellum debates between abolitionists and proslavery writers. Evidence from the trade, often gained from the narratives of escaped slaves, was crucial in making the moral case against slavery. According to abolitionists, the trade was vital for the economic viability and indeed the booming expansion of slavery in the nineteenth-century South. Since slaves lacked positive incentives to work, abolitionists tended to assume that slavery must have been economically flawed and fundamentally inefficient. Southern slavery, they thought, was locked into inefficient staple-crop monocultures which, by year-after-year repetition, tended constantly to exhaust the soil and to demand new land. The secret to the awful persistence of American slavery, they concluded, was the internal slave trade, which brought windfall profits to slave exporters in the "exhausted" old states and brought vital labor to the newer states. But, they argued, economic viability came at a huge moral price. Owners in the selling states developed a mentality of "rearing" or "breeding" slaves for the southern market, and with this came the wholesale undermining of slave families as wife was sold from husband, child from parent. Moral corruption, they argued, ran deep in white society as slave owners compromised the principles of humanity and Christianity in the sordid destruction of black families.[5]

Since the trade raised matters that were difficult for proslavery propagandists to defend, the classic southern propaganda response was denial. Essentially, the proslavery thesis presented the master as the benevolent protector of his "family white and black" and—in propaganda at least—the trader was depicted as an outcast. Abolitionist claims about the inefficiency of the slave economy suited slaveholders quite well, and could be nicely folded into the proslavery argument—an argument which claimed that the real purpose of slavery was not profit but the "civilizing" of black people. Proslavery ideologues were therefore happy to suggest that small numbers of owners, in desperate economic straits, resorted to selling to the trader, and they could also allow that a few chronically troublesome slaves were sold. The proslavery purpose, however, was to foster the benign plantation legend, and typical of the proslavery pitch on the trade was Nathan Lewis Rice's assertion that "The slave trader is looked upon by all decent men in the slaveholding states with disgust . . . None but a monster could inflict anguish upon unoffending [slaves] for the sake of accumulating wealth."[6]

The earliest history of the trade was by Winfield H. Collins in 1904. Collins—who in 1918 also published a vigorous defense of lynching—was a thoroughgoing white supremacist. His text on the trade directly reflected proslavery sources and agendas, and according to him, traders "were accounted the abhorrence of everyone. Their descendants, when known, had a blot upon them and the property acquired in the traffic as well." Collins, as some abolitionists had done, used the census to compare the growth rates of slaves in different states and regions. Unlike the abolitionists, however, he claimed that this great internal movement had come about, not by slave trading, but by the migration of planters, with their slaves, from the older states to new lands further south and west.[7]

Ulrich B. Phillips's treatment of the trade was again built on an ideology of white supremacy. For Phillips, as for Collins, slavery was a benign institution in which slave trading was of only marginal importance and where owners did all they could to avoid the separation of families. As in antebellum proslavery discourses, those ending up in the trader's hands were either unruly slaves in need of a change of master or a few unlucky individuals whose masters could no longer afford to support them. In his *American Negro Slavery* (1918) Phillips confidently declared: "The disesteem in which slave traders were held was so great and general in the southern community as to produce a social ostracism." By 1929, he suggested an interesting modification: "The stigma laid upon them [traders] can hardly have been so stringent as tradition tells, for many a planter and perhaps most of the general merchants turned to a trade on a few occasions, and sundry citizens of solid worth and esteem can be identified as regular participants." Phillips, however, made no attempt to give detailed documentation on these many planters, merchants, and worthy citizens. Indeed, a detailed development of such an argument would have started to unravel the plantation legend which he had always been at such pains to nurture and preserve.[8]

In 1931, Frederic Bancroft published *Slave Trading in the Old South* and with it he aimed a direct challenge to Phillips. Where Phillips had emphasized slaveholder benevolence, Bancroft saw self-interest. With Bancroft, the emphasis switched from proslavery to abolitionist traditions—and switched to the cruelty and immorality of slavery, to family separations and slave breeding, and to the everyday presence of the trader in every corner of the South. The great foundation of Bancroft's research consisted of collecting, from the antebellum newspapers of southern towns and cities, a huge compendium of slave traders' advertisements, and this evidence was supplemented by interviews that he conducted with black and white southerners who remembered the trade. His book provides still unrivalled profiles of great numbers of traders, many of whom he found to have the highest social standing.[9]

Bancroft's work represented a huge step forward in the uncovering of the trade. Still, however, supporters of the Phillips school could resist the full force of Bancroft's conclusions. His extensive evidence established that traders were hugely active in towns and cities, but it did not directly establish the overall scale of the trade or its impact across the South. In the case of South Carolina, for example, he documented the activities of numerous Charleston-based traders, but there was limited evidence for the remainder of the state. One scholar who remained unconvinced by Bancroft was Wendell Holmes Stephenson. Stephenson, a former student of Phillips, was unhappy about what he saw as Bancroft's "overzealous criticisms of Phillips," and he thought that Bancroft had permitted the historical pendulum to swing too far to the left. Stephenson's 1938 study of the trader Isaac Franklin did something to push the pendulum back towards the right. Here Franklin was portrayed essentially as an interesting southern anomaly rather than as Bancroft would have seen him—one of many hundreds of participants in a cruel and omnipresent slave traffic. Stephenson took at face value the evidence of a visitor to one of Franklin's slave depots, and concluded that his firm largely avoided breaking up families. He assumed that public opinion of slave traders was generally low, but Franklin was presented as a special case. According to Stephenson, by seeming to trade with unusual honesty, but more especially by leaving the trade behind to become a planter, Franklin managed to avoid the general stigma which supposedly attached to the trade.[10]

As the Civil Rights Movement began to surge in the 1950s, Kenneth Stampp took a far more critical view of slavery than had Stephenson and Phillips. In Stampp's neo-abolitionist view of slavery, the slave trader became central. Owners might sometimes feel a measure of unease about selling to the trader, except out of "necessity"—but, he added, "most of them had in their lexicons an extremely broad definition of 'necessity.'" Stampp saw American slavery as having been much more profitable than abolitionists had tended to suggest, but his emphasis on the devastating impact of the trade for the slave family was an important echo of the abolitionist tradition. Like the abolitionists, he also emphasized the southern tactic of scapegoating the trader in order to hide the naked commercialism of everyday slave owners.[11]

In their controversial econometric study *Time on the Cross* (1974), Robert Fogel and Stanley Engerman went far beyond Stampp in systematically demonstrating the profitable nature of American slavery. Unlike Stampp, however, they carried forward only the mildest version of the abolitionist critique of slave treatment. According to Fogel and Engerman, American slaves enjoyed surprisingly high living standards, they were diligent workers whose morale was high, and owners generally supported the slave family. Fogel and Engerman's sophisticated quantitative evidence has been widely accepted as establishing the profitability of American slavery—indeed as establishing that slave-based agriculture was profitable not just on virgin land but in the older slave-exporting states too. This evidence has cut much of the ground away from the traditional abolitionist claim that the older states only survived through income from slave breeding and the exportation of their surplus slaves. Many of the inferences that Fogel and Engerman drew about black and white mentalities and relationships were, however, far less convincing.[12]

For Fogel and Engerman's model of high slave morale and protected families to work, it was crucial that the domestic slave trade should be shown to be of minor importance in the lives of enslaved people. To make their case, they relied on data for a particular branch of the trade—the coastal route between the Chesapeake ports and New Orleans—and they relied in particular on the percentages of male and female slaves in that traffic. They were correct in concluding that this route was dominated by male slaves, with traders choosing to ship six males for every four females. The next step, it seemed, was simply to establish the gender composition of the total interstate slave movement (a movement which comprised both the trade and planter migrations). Census-based calculations showed that there were barely any more males than females in this total movement, and so Fogel and Engerman concluded that the apparently male-dominated trade could have had little impact. Indeed, generalizing from their New Orleans data, they argued that trading accounted for at most 16 percent of the total movement. They also found that in their New Orleans data there were only a few instances where a child seemed to have been sold without his or her parents, or where a mother and child were sold without a husband. From this sort of evidence it seemed to Fogel and Engerman that the trade wrecked very few families.

Michael Tadman's *Speculators and Slaves* was the first book-length study of the trade as a whole since Bancroft's in the 1930s. Tadman's conclusions about the significance of the trade were markedly different from those of Fogel and Engerman. First, he showed that in America's domestic slave trade the preference for male slaves was unique to New Orleans and southern Louisiana. In fact, the trade to all areas of the South except southern Louisiana carried roughly equal numbers of males and females. It turned out that the wholly exceptional gender skew of the New Orleans market came because planters in the neighboring Louisiana sugar parishes—the location of virtually all of the South's cane sugar planting—demanded great numbers of strong young males who could immediately be employed in the quite exceptionally exhausting labor of the cane fields. This unique gender skew means therefore that the New Orleans data gives no basis for calculating the scale of the trade as a whole. Not only that, the special nature of the New Orleans trade—being dominated by a demand for young adult males and with an exceptionally low demand for women and for young children—means that Fogel and Engerman's calculations of family separations are of limited use.[13]

In contrast to Fogel and Engerman, Tadman argued that fully 60 to 70 percent of inter-regional slave movements were the result of trading rather than planter migrations. His calculations used three complementary methods. The first method was based on an analysis of age structures. Although the trade was not selective in terms of the *sex of slaves* (except for its New Orleans branch), traders' account books, bills of sale, and advertisements make it clear that it was strongly age selective. Traders focused strongly on teenage and young adult slaves, as well as on young mothers with children. This age selective pattern stands in clear contrast to the essentially non-selective character of planter migrations, where planters usually moved the whole of their slave force to their new land, taking a broad cross-section of ages. Demographic analysis using this basic contrast makes it possible to calculate, state by state, the dominant role played by the trade.[14]

Tadman used two additional methods to provide complementary local case studies. His study of shipping records relating to thousands of slaves brought into New Orleans showed the overwhelming dominance at that port of slaves carried by identifiable traders rather than by planter migrants. More importantly perhaps, his detailed district-by-district documentation of slave trading activity in a sample state, South Carolina, directly documented the activities of 97 slave trading companies active in exporting slaves from that state in the 1850s. Suggestive but not conclusive evidence was also found for many more probable firms. Significantly, this South Carolina documentation showed traders to be intensely active, not just in the urban areas on which Bancroft had concentrated, but throughout every district of the state. Tadman's evidence suggested that the human impact of the trade was huge, with well over three-quarters of a million enslaved people being sold in the long-distance trade between 1790 and 1860. The trade, he argued, wrecked as many as one in five of the marriages of slaves born in the exporting states, and separated one in three of that region's children from one or both parents.[15] It also seems to be clear that those who sold to the trader usually did so, not to stave off economic crisis, but instead to make a profit. Only some 5 percent of traders' purchases came from probate sales or from public sales for debt. Tadman's evidence also suggested that, as well as sales to the trader, enslaved families and communities faced high levels of risk from local sales.[16] Slave trading and family separations, he argued, reveal a profound gulf between the benevolent self-image of slave owners and their actual behavior towards enslaved people. The abundant evidence of white disrespect for slave families and for the feelings of slaves meant, he suggested, a pattern of deep distrust of owners by their enslaved people.

Tadman found that the overland trade, driving coffles of slaves southwards, reached into every corner of the South, and was far more important than the coastal route. He also concluded that traders were generally men of high status. Indeed, he suggested that traders found ready acceptance at the highest levels in society: outcast "bad" traders were rarely anything more than devices available for sectional propaganda. In a society that usually relied on credit, traders paid in cash for their slaves, and indeed laid out for their coffles amounts of cash that can have had few if any parallels in the Old South. Except in the role of paid assistant, the trade was a place for men of wealth and for men of substance who could command the confidence of banks.

While Michael Tadman used a framework of quantification in order to suggest what might be some of the important contexts for understanding the lives and mentalities of slaves and their owners, Walter Johnson in *Soul by Soul* (1999) brought a cultural-history approach. Johnson accepted Tadman's estimates of the scale of the trade and of family separations, but suggested that quantitative aggregates left untold much of the real story of slavery.[17] His innovative study looked at slavery through life inside the New Orleans slave market, reading the stories of traders, buyers, and the enslaved. His book, he explained, is the story of the traders' showrooms: "It is a story of back and forth glances and estimations, of hushed conspiracies and loud boasts, of power, fear and desire, of mistrust and dissimulation, of human beings broken down into parts and recomposed as commodities, of futures promised, purchased, and resisted. It is, in no small measure, the story of antebellum slavery." Johnson wrote of the traders and their imaginings that they could change people into mere dollars and commodities, of the traders' clients and their fantasies of climbing the social ladder by owning more and more black bodies, and wrote of the enslaved and their struggle to disrupt the notion that they were mere things.

Johnson's book ran two themes side by side, the chattel principle and paternalism— the principle of people as property and alongside it the slaveholders' seemingly constant inclination to filter their actions through notions of paternalism. Johnson read slaveholder paternalism as something that was infinitely plastic and capable of being adapted to suit any convenience, but at the same time he thought that owners needed to reconcile the buying and selling of slaves with their default position on paternalism. His primary source base relied a good deal on a set of some 200 cases of traders' disputed sales of slaves, cases which highlighted buyers' claims of dishonest dealings by traders. Perhaps influenced in part by the nature of this source base, he concluded that the traders' social position was awkward. Like several other historians, however, he thought that large-scale successful speculation could somehow ease the trader's stigma. He therefore argued that "Some [traders] became rich and bought a measure of social respectability, their wealth washed clean through its very profusion. Others struggled from trading season to trading season, plying the dusty roads and rural markets of the antebellum South in search of a break that never came."[18]

The idea of white southern unease over the morality of the trade became the central focus in Robert Gudmestad's *A Troublesome Commerce* (2003). According to Gudmestad, the trade had been small in scale and loosely organized before 1820, but significant growth in the 1820s was morally troubling for many white citizens in the slave-exporting states. He argued, however, that in the buying states of the lower South, though they might worry about rising black numbers and unruly slaves, slaveholders put their hunger for new slaves far ahead of any moral concern about the principle of slave trading. According to Gudmestad, two significant things happened in the 1830s to create a southern consensus on the trader: first attacks on slavery by northern abolitionists prompted the white South to close ranks and, second, he claimed that slave traders consciously sought to improve their public image. As a result, he suggested, the South moved to a convenient consensus based on the notion that there were too sorts of traders—the first being an outcast set of "disreputable" itinerant, small-scale operators, and second being "respectable," substantial, urban traders. This formulation, he argued, allowed the whites somehow to internalize the fiction that they acted honorably, dealing only with "good" traders, with those who did not break up families.[19]

Gudmestad's formulation is ingenious and reflects an academic tradition that slaveholders struggled to reconcile an ideal of paternalism with the realities of owning and trafficking in people. It might be, however, that the status of the trader was both more consistent over time and that it was generally far less problematic. It is not at all clear either that the scale of the trade shifted dramatically between the 1810s and 1820s or that Upper South angst about traders affected large numbers of those who actually owned slaves. Gudmestad documented some cases of unease over the trade by church members but it is unclear whether these anxieties came mainly from antislavery voices rather than from slaveholders. He also read certain texts as evidence of a general condemnation of the trader. For example, when in a coastwise shipping manifest, an owner recorded that he was "not a dealer in human flesh," he took this to be indicative of widespread disquiet over traders. In thousands of extant coastal manifests there seem, however, to have been only one or two other such declarations. Similarly, when Pulliam and Co., a firm of prominent Richmond slave auctioneers, declared that they had "no connection with the Negro Trade," he read this as unease over trading. In fact the probable intention was simply to assure clients that there was no clash of interests—the firm did not buy and sell in its own right and therefore could be trusted to auction slaves at fair prices. Gudmestad's purpose in the end was to stress the emptiness of white paternalism: it might be, however, that slaveholders had never felt the need to struggle greatly with their consciences.[20]

In a series of articles published from the late 1980s—and later in his book, *Slavery and the Commerce Power: How the Struggle against the Interstate Slave Trade Led to the Civil War* (2006)—David L. Lightner focused on the significance of the trade in antislavery strategy. Arguing that the trade was "the lifeblood of slavery," he explored the antislavery device of seeking to outlaw the trade by appeal to the federal government's powers to regulate commerce. This strategy was not directly successful in ending the trade, but Lightner argued that the threat to the trade was itself sufficient to spread alarm among slaveholders—and by this to contribute significantly to southern secessionism.[21]

Steven Deyle's *Carry Me Back* (2005) is a valuable work of synthesis, drawing extensively on studies published from the late 1980s on slave trading, local sales of slaves, and on abolitionist attacks on the trade. The book's special contribution is to pull together often familiar arguments and evidence in order to emphasize the importance of the trade in southern and indeed in American life. Deyle began by exploring what he called "the irony of liberty," the fateful growth of the domestic slave trade in the age of the American Revolution. He traced the overwhelming role of the trade in fostering the booming expansion of antebellum slavery across the South. He also pointed to its fundamental role in the soaring value of slavery investments both in the exporting and importing states. Arising out of all of this, he emphasized its role in consolidating the slavery interest and its secessionist mentality. Like Lightner, he argued that distaste for the inhumanity of the trade was crucial in forming northern antislavery opinion and, by extension, in bringing about the great conflict with southern secessionism.[22]

According to Deyle, extensive local as well as long-distance sales built "Negro speculation" into the everyday life of the white South. At the same time, he argued, the "ideal" of paternalism was important in slaveholder mindsets. He noted that in practice the ideal admitted great flexibility and convenient reasons were almost always found to justify the buying or selling of slaves. Still, he suggested, the ideal meant enough that the trader's position in society was not unproblematic and owners who dealt with the trader felt the need to satisfy themselves that they acted honorably. Deyle therefore proposed the following formulation: "For the most part southerners despised slave traders more in the abstract than in reality, and they tended to like or dislike their local speculator more for his personal traits than for his occupation. Southerners also judged real-life slave traders more according to their class than anything else. Therefore, while southern elites usually did scorn the majority of traders (those at the bottom end of the trade), that was primarily because of their working-class status . . . Those at the top of the trade (and possessing greater wealth) were treated with honour and respect."[23]

A recent article by Michael Tadman argued that the position of the trader in southern white society was far less delicate than scholars like Johnson, Gudmestad, and Deyle have suggested. All of these historians have assumed that notions of paternalism must have caused owners to feel a measure of unease in dealing with the trader. Tadman argued, however, that traders found no difficulty in being accepted as respected citizens. He pointed to two key elements in the antebellum proslavery position on the trade—first, the notion of the trader as outcast and, second, the concept that black people were not capable of deep and lasting emotional suffering. He argued that the "trader as outcast" operated at the level of propaganda and was not really believed in the white South: the concept of superficial black emotions operated at a deeper level and was internalized by owners. Notions about shallow black emotions allowed slaveholders to break up families and to deal comfortably with the trader while still maintaining a self-image as benevolent paternalists. Tadman's direct evidence on the position of the trader was derived from petitions and grand jury presentments concerning the trade and from the registers of R. G. Dun & Co., a credit assessment agency that spread across virtually all of the counties of the South during the mid-1840s. The Dun registers provide observations on large numbers of traders, and give detailed eyewitness reports on their creditworthiness, their personal habits, and, most interestingly, on their "moral character" and social standing.[24]

The petitions and presentments studied by Tadman did sometimes show slaveholder anxieties about the trade, but these were not concerns about the effects of the trade on slave families. Some petitions and presentments from Delaware and

Tennessee did condemn the trade, but these were antislavery protests that also condemned the whole institution of slavery. These aside, the petitions and presentments reflected the self-serving concerns of slaveholders in particular situations. No slaveholders lobbied against the *exportation* of slaves from their own state. Slaveholders in net importing states (and in net importing sections within certain other states) were generally keen to defend the right to import slaves and to allow white families to make their fortunes out of enslaved people. Those who lobbied to restrict importation at particular moments were generally citizens who already had all the slaves they needed, were people anxious that excessive speculation might be destabilizing, or more usually were those concerned about the inconveniences that traders might bring—especially the inconveniences of threats to public order and public health from increasing numbers of new slaves. Later in this essay, another set of self-serving sectional reactions will be seen in connection with Brazil's domestic trade.

Of course, for enslaved people the central importance of North America's domestic slave trade was its impact on families and communities. Tadman argued, in the tradition of Herbert Gutman, that the institution of the slave family was strong enough to survive the trade, as well as the pressures of local sales, estate divisions, and other disruptive forces. Increasingly scholars like Nell Painter have been more pessimistic, and have taken a neo-abolitionist position, pointing to the corrosive effects of slavery and the trade on black families, as well as on the morals of a white society brought up with such brutalities.[25]

INTERNAL SLAVE TRADES IN BRAZIL

The internal slave trades of Brazil have not yet attracted specialist monographs, but several article-length studies have been published, including particularly important recent essays by Robert W. Slenes and Richard Graham (2004). As with almost all of the available literature, these recent essays focus especially on the inter-provincial trade from the Northeast and South to the booming coffee plantations of the Center-South. This trade came to prominence in the period between the effective abolition of Brazil's African slave trade in 1850 and the ending of Brazilian slavery itself in 1888. The detailed organization of this trade is not closely researched, but Robert Conrad sketched some of its essentials, with traders, as in the USA, forcibly moving their slaves in overland coffles, by sea, and sometimes by rail. Like all internal trades it was age selective. Like the specialist trades to sugar areas, this traffic—supplying coffee planters with slaves—seems to have been male dominated.[26]

Scholars have debated the scale and significance of this inter-provincial trade. Klein estimated the number traded as between 100,000 and 200,000 over the period 1850–88, and argued that a traffic of this scale would have been too limited to have been of major importance in supplying the labor demands of the Center-South coffee region. Robert Conrad gave a significantly higher estimate (at least 300,000 people traded), and saw the social impact of the trade as being greater. In his detailed calculations, Robert Slenes suggested a trade of some 222,000 slaves. He also argued that the percentage of the slave population affected by the trade would have been comparable to that in the domestic trade of the USA.[27]

Slenes has shown that the slave trading patterns of nineteenth-century Brazil were a good deal more complex than in the US domestic trade. Coffee planters in the Center-South imported great numbers of slaves from the Northeast, but at the same time sugar planters within the northeastern region continued to demand new slaves. The sugar planters' buying policy was, no doubt, adopted so as to compensate for the natural decrease that was characteristic of sugar. In nineteenth-century Brazil, then, there were at least two regional slave markets: the Center-South coffee planters and northeastern sugar planters competed strongly for slaves and both influenced slave prices. Slenes has established, therefore, that, coinciding with the height of inter-provincial exportation to the Center-South, there was also a highly significant trade *within* the Northeast: non-sugar farmers in the Northeast (probably as a result of surpluses through natural increase) sold slaves to the region's labor-hungry sugar planters. So far as the inter-provincial trade is concerned, the traditional assumption has been that it was based on impoverished northeastern sugar planters making their slaves available for exportation to coffee planters. Slenes has established, however, that it was actually the non-sugar producers who were the suppliers.[28]

Although there is some debate over the scale of the inter-provincial trade, it was clearly sufficient that northeastern sugar planters became alarmed that they might be outbid for slaves by the Center-South coffee region. Taxation on exportations did something to ease their fears. Eventually, a different regional concern developed, with some in the Center-South becoming worried that the drain of slaves from the Northeast would weaken the hold of slavery there and as a result would undermine the base of support for the Brazilian slave regime. This second concern echoed anxieties associated with the trade of the USA: some embattled American proslavery ideologues worried that the internal trade, by reducing slave numbers in the Upper South, might eventually separate that region from the slavery cause.[29]

As in the US case, historians of Brazilian slavery have in recent years increasingly emphasized the impact of the trade both on the lives of enslaved people and on the building of antislavery forces. Both Slenes and Graham have recently emphasized the trauma of the trade and the surging hostility of slaves—and the connection of all of this to the mass flight of slaves, to the politics of slavery, and to the fall of the whole slavery regime.[30]

Although most scholarly attention has been focused on the post-1850 period, scholars have also documented far earlier internal trading in Brazil. As Richard Graham noted, by at least the early seventeenth century, great numbers of Indians, especially from the Amazon region, were traded to sugar planters in Bahia and Pernambuco—and trading in Indians continued well into the nineteenth century. Graham also noted that in the seventeenth and eighteenth centuries large numbers of Afro-Brazilians were marched hundreds of miles from the Northeast to be traded to the gold and diamond mines of Minas Gerais.[31]

INTERNAL TRADES IN THE CARIBBEAN

The British Caribbean was mostly but by no means completely dominated by sugar, and this meant that it had only limited scope for the development of areas with surpluses of locally born slaves for possible trading. A new market situation was created, however, with the acquisition of new colonies that had huge potential for growth (Trinidad in 1797 and Demerara in 1803), combined with the cutting off of the Africa supply of slaves in 1807. Slave prices soared in Trinidad and Demerara, establishing special inducements for slaveholders in the old territories to sell some of their slaves. The resulting inter-island trade seems to have permanently moved more than 20,000 slaves to the new colonies in the decade 1815 to 1825. Eric Williams and David Eltis have given sharply differing readings of this trade. Williams argued that the colonial authorities connived with the slavery interest, and he maintained that the trade "reached proportions which could not be reconciled with the high-sounding pretensions of [British] humanitarianism."[32] In contrast, Eltis, who has consistently resisted Williams's economic interpretation of British abolitionism, argued that antislavery reformers were effective in limiting the trade. The trade did wreck great numbers of families and sent many enslaved people to spectacularly harsh condition on the new sugar frontier, but at the same time antislavery restrictions do seem to have meant that the voracious demand for new labor was only partially satisfied. Across the Americas, self-imposed restrictions on the various internal trades were never effective, but it might be that in the British Caribbean case trade restrictions imposed by an external British authority were significant.[33]

Historians of Cuban slavery have paid considerable attention to nineteenth-century sugar plantations and to the importation of Africans (until the fairly effective termination of Cuba's Atlantic importations in 1866), but little work seems to have been done on the possible operation of any internal trades. *The Cuban Slave Market* (1995), by Laird Bergad and his colleagues, provides a special resource and gives a quantitative analysis of 23,000 (mostly African) slaves sold in Havana, Santiago, and Cienfuegos over the period 1790 to 1880. This, however, is a study of slave prices, not of slave trading or slave dealers, nor does it explore the social and political impact of the slave market. The effects of gender, place of origin, and skill on slave prices are extensively discussed, and there is a valuable discussion of self-purchase by slaves. Bergad and his colleagues noted that there was little variance in slave prices between their three chosen markets, and this suggests a lack of incentive for inter-regional trading within Cuba in the period concerned. Manuel Barcia Paz has provided glimpses into slave smuggling from the Bahamas to Cuba, and Joseph C. Dorsey has begun to piece together both smuggling from Puerto Rico to Cuba and other slave trading patterns within the Caribbean.[34]

Patterns and Agendas

In the case of the southern USA, research on the domestic slave trade has already opened up important insights into the lives of enslaved people, the mindsets of owners, and into the economic and political significance of slavery's expansion. There is still, however, much scope for further fruitful research. There is, for example, almost no research on internal slave trading from the northern and middle colonies and states like New York and Pennsylvania to the South, but such trading—in the revolutionary era and even earlier—might turn out to have been highly significant in terms of its impact on enslaved people, and possibly in the relocation and expansion of slavery. Another early internal trade whose scale and significance are very much under-researched is the trade within the South, with colonies and states like Maryland and Virginia selling slaves to Georgia and elsewhere from the later eighteenth century. A further area where research might be especially significant is the financing of the trade. Richard Kilbourne has done much to reveal the use of slaves as collateral and as the basis for a highly flexible system of mortgaging, endorsing, and lending, but an explicit study of traders' business records might reveal a great deal about how customers made their purchases as well as about southern banking and finance.[35]

Beyond North America, research on internal trades in Brazil has brought some important results, but for South America and the Caribbean there still seems to be much important work to be done. Recent studies of Brazilian slavery have pointed both to areas of natural increase among slave populations and to the importance of small slaveholdings as well as big plantations—and all of this forms a basis for further exploration of trading routes and patterns. Even for Brazil, however, there is still no monograph on the men who operated as slave traders, or on their dealings with clients and with enslaved people. Such a study might be possible—perhaps making use of traders' newspaper advertisements, court records, bills of sale, taxes paid on traded slaves, shipping manifests, travel accounts, and ideally using the manuscript collections of traders and slaveholders. For the South American and Caribbean slave regimes generally, work on areas of natural increase and decrease, as well as on regional slave prices, could open up new knowledge on internal trades and their significance. Research on internal trades in various parts of the Americas has been important in revealing some of the key contexts in which master–slave relationships were set, and there is a good deal of scope for more discoveries to be made.[36]

Notes

1. Southern Trip Notes, ii. 104, Frederic Bancroft Papers, Columbia University, New York.
2. For an example of a planter's slave-buying trip, unusually by a black slaveholder, see David O. Whitten, "Slave Buying in 1835 Virginia as Revealed by Letters of a Louisiana Negro Sugar Planter," *Louisiana History*, 11 (3) (Summer 1970): 231–44.
3. See Michael Tadman, "The Demographic Cost of Sugar: Debates on Slave Societies and Natural Increase in the Americas," *American Historical Review*, 105 (5) (December 2000): 1534–5. Mining, another male-dominated slave occupation, also contributed to natural decrease in some phases of slavery's development especially in Latin America.
4. For brief suggestions on early trades, see David Eltis, "The Chattel Principle," *Business History Review*, 79 (4) (Winter 2005): 863–6.
5. On abolitionist arguments, see, for example, Executive Committee of the American Anti-Slavery Society (eds.), *Slavery and the Internal Slave Trade* (London, 1841). For an early antislavery depiction of the trade, see Jesse Torrey, *A Portraiture of Domestic Slavery* (Philadelphia, 1817).
6. Jonathan Blanchard and N. L. Rice, *A Debate on Slavery* (Cincinnati, 1846), 28.
7. Collins, *The Domestic Slave Trade of our Southern States* (New York, 1904), 108; Collins, *The Truth about Lynching* (New York, 1918).
8. Phillips, *American Negro Slavery: A Survey of the Supply, Employment and Control of Negro Labor as Determined by the Plantation Regime* (New York, 1918), 200; Phillips, *Life and Labor in the Old South* (Boston, 1929), 138.
9. Bancroft, *Slave Trading* (Baltimore, 1931). For a discussion of the early reception and of the importance of Bancroft's book, see Michael Tadman's introduction (pp. xi–xxxviii) to the 1996 edition of *Slave Trading*.
10. For the first quotation, see Stephenson, review of Bancroft, *Southwestern Social Science Quarterly*, 12 (1) (June 1931), 88; for the second quotation, see Stephenson, *Isaac Franklin: Slave Trader and Planter of the Old South* (Baton Rouge, La., 1938), 6 n.
11. Stampp, *The Peculiar Institution: Slavery in the Ante-bellum South* (New York, 1956), 240, 267.
12. Robert William Fogel and Stanley L. Engerman, *Time on the Cross: The Economics of American Negro Slavery* (1974).

13. Michael Tadman, *Speculators and Slaves: Masters, Traders, and Slaves in the Old South* (Madison, 1989; enlarged edn. 1996).

14. Jonathan B. Pritchett, in his article "Quantitative Estimates of the United States Interregional Slave Trade, 1820–1860," *Journal of Economic History*, 61 (2) (June 2001): 467–75, used regression analysis to comment on Fogel and Engerman's technique and to comment on Tadman's age structure method. This led him to suggest that 50 percent of inter-regional movements were by the trade.

15. Tadman's core calculations suggested an interstate movement (including planter migrations and trading) of about 1.1 million slaves between 1790 and 1860. He noted, however, that because these calculations simply estimated *net importations* or *net exportations* for each state they undercounted the total movement. As he noted, at any particular time several states would in reality have been hybrids, combining sub-regions of importation with sub-regions of exportation. Perhaps these net rather than gross state totals cancelled out 25 percent or more of actual movements. See Tadman, *Speculators and Slaves*, 7, 12, 42.

16. For important studies of local sales, see articles by Thomas D. Russell, including "South Carolina's Largest Slave Auctioneering Firm," *Chicago-Kent Law Review*, 68 (3) (1993): 1241–2. See also James William McGettigan, "Boone County Slaves: Sales, Estate Divisions and Families, 1820–1865," *Missouri Historical Review*, 72 (2) (January 1978): 176–7; and (3) (April 1978): 271–5.

17. Johnson, *Soul by Soul: Life inside the Antebellum Slave Market* (Cambridge, Mass., 1999), quotation p. 3. Unlike Tadman, Johnson assumed that economic pressure from soil exhaustion was important in prompting Upper South owners to sell to the trader.

18. Ibid. 46.

19. Gudmestad, *A Troublesome Commerce: The Transformation of the Interstate Slave Trade* (Baton Rouge, La., 2003).

20. See ibid. 19–20 and 209–10 on the scale of the trade, and 15, 167 for quotations. For fuller comments on Gudmestad, see Michael Tadman, "The Reputation of the Slave Trader in Southern History and the Social Memory of the South," *American Nineteenth Century History*, 8 (3) (September 2007): 252–4; and on Gudmestad's calculation of the scale of the early trade, see Tadman, review of Gudmestad, *Journal of Southern History*, 72 (3) (August 2006): 664–5.

21. Lightner, *Slavery and the Commerce Power* (New Haven, 2006). This book presents some new material and collects together several of Lightner's earlier articles.

22. Deyle, *Carry Me Back: The Domestic Slave Trade in American Life* (New York: 2005).

23. Ibid. 238–9.

24. Tadman, "The Reputation." On the reputation of the trader, see also Tadman, *Speculators and Slaves*, 179–210; Tadman, "The Interregional Slave Trade in the History and Myth-making of the U.S. South," in Walter Johnson (ed.), *The Chattel Principle: Internal Slave Trades in North America, Brazil, and the West Indies 1808–1888* (New Haven, 2004), 117–42.

25. Gutman, *The Black Family in Slavery and Freedom, 1750–1925* (New York, 1976); Painter, *Southern History across the Color Line* (Chapel Hill, NC, 2002).

26. Slenes, "The Brazilian Internal Slave Trade, 1850–1888: Regional Economies, Slave Experience, and the Politics of a Peculiar Market," and Graham, "Another Middle Passage? The Internal Slave Trade in Brazil," in Johnson, *The Chattel Principle*, 325–70 and 291–324 respectively; Robert Edgar Conrad, *The Destruction of Brazilian Slavery,*

1850–1888 (Berkeley, 1972), 33–47; Conrad, *Children of God's Fire: A Documentary History of Black Slavery in Brazil* (Princeton, 1984), esp. 343–57; Conrad, *World of Sorrow: The African Slave Trade to Brazil* (Baton Rouge, La., 1986), 171–91; Herbert Sanford Klein, *The Middle Passage: Comparative Studies in the Atlantic Slave Trade* (Princeton, 1978), 95–120; Klein, "The Internal Slave Trade in Nineteenth-Century Brazil: A Study of Slave Importation into Rio de Janeiro in 1852," *Hispanic American Historical Review*, 51 (4) (November 1971): 567–85. For a useful early publication on the trade, see Stanley J. Stein, *Vassouras: A Brazilian Coffee County, 1850–1900* (Cambridge, Mass., 1957), 66–73.

27. Klein, *Middle Passage*, esp. 98; Klein, "Internal Slave Trade"; Conrad, *World of Sorrow*, 172–3; Slenes, "Brazilian Internal Slave Trade," 331–2.

28. Slenes, "Brazilian Internal Slave Trade," 338–9.

29. On the attempts of sugar interests in northeastern Brazil to use taxation to limit southward slave exportation, see Graham, "Another Middle Passage?," 301; and on attempts by some in the Center-South eventually to use taxation to limit importations, see ibid. 302, and Slenes, "Brazilian Internal Slave Trade," 359.

30. Graham, "Another Middle Passage?," 291, 307–15; Slenes, "Brazilian Internal Slave Trade," 359–61.

31. Graham, "Another Middle Passage?," 293–4.

32. Williams, "The British West Indian Slave Trade after its Abolition in 1807," *Journal of Negro History*, 27 (2) (April 1942), 178.

33. Williams, "The British West Indian Slave Trade," 175–91; Eltis, "The Traffic in Slaves between the British West Indian Colonies, 1807–1833," *Economic History Review*, 25 (1) (February 1972): 55–64. See also Barry W. Higman, *Slave Populations of the British Caribbean, 1807–1834* (Baltimore, 1984), 76–88; and see articles by Seymour Drescher and Hilary M. Beckles in Johnson, *Chattel Principle*.

34. Laird W. Bergad, Fe Iglesias García, and María del Carmen Barcia, *The Cuban Slave Market, 1790–1880* (Cambridge, 1995). See also Manuel Moreno Fraginals, Herbert S. Klein, and Stanley L. Engerman, "The Level and Structure of Slave Prices on Cuban Plantations in the Mid-Nineteenth Century: Some Comparative Perspectives," *American Historical Review*, 88 (5) (December 1983): 1201–18. On inter-island trading and smuggling, see Paz, "The Kelsall Affair: A Black Bahamian Family's Odyssey in Turbulent 1840s Cuba," in Johnson, *Chattel Principle*, 275–90; Dorsey, "Seamy Sides of Abolition: Puerto Rico and the Cabotage Slave Trade to Cuba, 1848–73," *Slavery and Abolition*, 19 (1) (April 1998): 106–28; Dorsey, *Slave Traffic in the Age of Abolition: Puerto Rico, West Africa and the Non-Hispanic Caribbean, 1815–1859* (Gainesville, Fla., 2003).

35. For a brief note on trading from the northern and middle states, see Robert W. Fogel and Stanley L. Engerman, "Philanthropy at Bargain Prices: Notes on the Economics of Gradual Emancipation," *Journal of Legal Studies*, 3 (2) (June 1974): 393. On an interesting branch of the early trade, see Pen Bogert, "'Sold for my Account': The Early Slave Trade between Kentucky and the Lower Mississippi Valley," *Ohio Valley History*, 2 (1) (Spring 2002): 3–16. For a case study of trading from about 1806, see Michael Tadman, "The Hidden History of Slave Trading in Antebellum South Carolina: John Springs III and Other 'Gentlemen Dealing in Slaves,'" *South Carolina Historical Magazine*, 97 (1) (January 1996): 6–29. Richard Holcombe Kilbourne, *Debt, Investment, Slaves: Credit Relations in East Feliciana Parish, Louisiana, 1825–1885* (Tuscaloosa, Ala., 1995).

36. On demography and slaveholdings, see Slenes, "Brazilian Internal Slave Trade"; Laird W. Bergad, *Slavery and the Demographic and Economic History of Minas Gerais, Brazil, 1720–1888* (Cambridge, 1999); and Francisco Vidal Luna and Herbert S. Klein, "Slave Economy and Society in Minas Gerais and São Paulo, Brazil in 1830," *Journal of Latin American Studies*, 36 (1) (February 2004): 1–28.

SELECT BIBLIOGRAPHY

BANCROFT, FREDERIC. *Slave Trading in the Old South*. Baltimore: J. H. Fürst Co., 1931.

BERGAD, LAIRD W., FE IGLESIAS GARCÍA, and MARÍA DEL CARMEN BARCIA. *The Cuban Slave Market, 1790–1880*. Cambridge: Cambridge University Press, 1995.

CONRAD, ROBERT EDGAR. *World of Sorrow: The African Slave Trade to Brazil*. Baton Rouge, La.: Louisiana State University Press, 1986.

DEYLE, STEVEN, *Carry Me Back: The Domestic Slave Trade in American Life*. New York: Oxford University Press, 2005.

ELTIS, DAVID. "The Traffic in Slaves between the British West Indian Colonies, 1807–1833," *Economic History Review*, 25 (1) (February 1972).

GUDMESTAD, ROBERT. *A Troublesome Commerce: The Transformation of the Interstate Slave Trade*. Baton Rouge, La.: Louisiana State University Press, 2003.

JOHNSON, WALTER, *Soul by Soul: Life inside the Antebellum Slave Market*. Cambridge, Mass.: Harvard University Press, 1999.

—— (ed.), *The Chattel Principle: Internal Slave Trades in North America, Brazil, and the West Indies 1808–1888*. New Haven: Yale University Press, 2004.

KLEIN, HERBERT SANFORD, *The Middle Passage: Comparative Studies in the Atlantic Slave Trade*. Princeton: Princeton University Press, 1978.

LIGHTNER, DAVID L., *Slavery and the Commerce Power: How the Struggle against the Interstate Slave Trade Led to the Civil War*. New Haven: Yale University Press, 2006.

TADMAN, MICHAEL, *Speculators and Slaves: Masters, Traders, and Slaves in the Old South*. 1989; enlarged edn. Madison: University of Wisconsin Press, 1996.

—— "The Reputation of the Slave Trader in Southern History and the Social Memory of the South," *American Nineteenth Century History*, 8 (3) (September 2007): 247–71.

WILLIAMS, ERIC, "The British West Indian Slave Trade after its Abolition in 1807," *Journal of Negro History*, 27 (2) (April 1942).

....

CHAPTER 29

DEMOGRAPHY AND SLAVERY

....

RICHARD H. STECKEL

THE mercantilists who governed Europe from the sixteenth through the eighteenth centuries viewed population as a national asset. An excess of births over deaths strengthened the state by furnishing taxpayers and recruits for the military. In their thinking, age at marriage and the number of women who married, both of which reflected economic conditions, governed the birth rate. Events external to the system, such as wars and plagues, affected mortality. Famine-related deaths may have followed harsh weather or excess population relative to resources, especially land. In this panorama, population size and growth became measures of social performance.

When the campaign against slavery began in the second half of the eighteenth century, debate turned naturally to population size and growth, about which something was known from records kept by colonial administrators. Thinkers such as David Hume in Europe and Benjamin Franklin in the United States argued that low or negative rates of slave population growth implied failure to thrive, which was best explained by the brutality of the institution. In the British sugar colonies, for example, deaths exceeded births; only the importation of slaves from Africa maintained or increased the population. In the past several decades scholars have assembled an impressive array of evidence from sources such as colonial records, censuses, manifests, plantation records, probate documents, and bills of sale. Moreover, they have applied new methods to this evidence to estimate nutritional status as well as rates of birth, death, and importation. New understanding of fertility, health and mortality stems from excursions by historians and economists into epidemiology, human biology, and demography. Thus the field of slave demography has become substantially more interdisciplinary.

The antislavery debates defined several topics of current research. Many abolitionists claimed that slaves endured a particularly harsh combination of material conditions—hard work, insufficient food, inadequate clothing, and ramshackle shelter—a finding consistent with negative rates of natural increase (the birth rate minus the death rate) found in many slave societies. While scholars now agree that living conditions, especially diet and work, were important for health, current explanations prove more complex than envisioned by earlier writers and involve health *in utero* and early childhood, acquired immunities, physical growth (height), intercontinental migration, exposure to new pathogens, and the synergy of nutrition and disease. Nineteenth-century explanations of slave fertility, which were put forward by Zachary Macaulay in England and Theodore Weld in the United States, emphasized brutality and breeding, with the former invoked to understand low birth rates in the Caribbean and the latter to account for high birth rates in the United States. While some debate continues on the importance of these factors, current interpretations of cross-country (or cross-colony) fertility patterns emphasize sex ratios, nutrition, breastfeeding patterns, psychological adjustments to enslavement, and opportunities to find partners.

ORIGINS OF AFRICAN SLAVERY

Making sense of the demographic history of slavery requires background on the rise of African slavery in the Western hemisphere. Explorers representing Portugal, Spain, France, and Britain crossed the Atlantic in the early sixteenth century seeking an all-water route to Asia and access to its tropical products saleable in Europe. This specific effort failed. But in the early 1500s Spanish explorers found gold and silver in Central and South America, and a frenzied—and often fruitless—search for these precious metals by other colonizers ensued. European claims to the Western hemisphere were loosely organized by latitude of origin in Europe. Portugal concentrated in Brazil; Spain concentrated in South America, Middle America, the Caribbean, and the southern portion of what is now the United States. Britain and France, along with smaller players such as the Netherlands and Sweden, vied for the remaining territory, initially by targeting the flanks of Spanish dominions.

While all colonizers initially sought gold and silver, and Spain continued to mine precious metals, by the seventeenth century the economy of the Western hemisphere had transitioned to extractive industries, such as timber, furs, fishing, and naval stores in the northern portion of North America and to tropical and semitropical products elsewhere. By far the largest market existed for sugar, the dominant crop in the Caribbean and Brazil. Tobacco predominated on the plantations of the Chesapeake region, and further south, planters grew indigo and rice along the coast of South Carolina and Georgia. In the Caribbean, coffee thrived in a few colonies such as Saint-Domingue and Cuba, but overall the crop was more of a minor player that helped diversify colonial economies.

Production or extraction of these commodities in volume required a large labor force. Few Europeans desired or were financially able to settle in the Western hemisphere as free workers. In the system of indentured servitude European teenagers and young adults received passage and subsistence by selling their labor for four to seven years. British North America, a non-tropical region, where sugar cane could not readily be grown, served as a relatively popular destination for indentures. Colonizers initially sought native laborers, who might have been employed as free workers, slaves, or, more likely, in a coercive system like the *encomienda* or *mita* that resembled slavery. Scholars have debated the size of the pre-Columbian native population, with some estimates ranging up to 100 million. Archaeological evidence suggests that the number was much lower, perhaps 10 to 20 million. Even numbers in the lower range would have permitted production in volume, but the system proved to be unworkable. Scholars have offered various explanations, the most prominent of which is decimation from European epidemic diseases such as smallpox and measles to which indigenous peoples lacked immunity.

By the middle of the sixteenth century Spanish colonists were searching for an alternative labor source. Although colonizers experimented widely, economic advantage pointed to sub-Saharan Africa, from which slaves had long been exported to the Mediterranean and to the Middle East. Initially the slave trade operated haphazardly, yielding chance encounters along the coast of West Africa. There Europeans bartered cloth, iron, cowries, and armaments for slaves, who were often debtors or captives of war. Soon Europeans established trading territories and forts to which Africans brought slaves from the interior to the coast for systematic export. By the late sixteenth century the African slave trade was well under way to the Western hemisphere. But African diseases like yellow fever and malaria made West Africa a graveyard for Europeans. Few Europeans ventured into the interior until the middle of the nineteenth century when quinine was discovered as an antidote for malaria.

DIMENSIONS OF THE AFRICAN SLAVE TRADE

The Atlantic slave trade was central to the demographic history of the Western hemisphere. In 1969 Philip Curtin, a leading historian of Africa, published *The African Slave Trade: A Census*.[1] The volume, based on wide reading in multiple languages and extensive archival research, became the modern quantitative manifesto of the field. Curtin reconstructed the origins, destinations, and chronological pattern of African slave arrivals from the early 1500s to the mid-nineteenth century. He also addressed mortality rates on the voyage and the age and sex distribution of imports. A remarkable outpouring of research followed, including such major works as Kenneth Kiple, *The Caribbean Slave: A Biological History* (1984) and David Eltis, *The Rise of African Slavery in the Americas* (2000).[2] Herbert Klein summarizes much of the literature in *The Atlantic Slave Trade* (1999).[3] Decades of work by a transatlantic team of slave trade specialists, headed by the economic historian David Eltis, have resulted in a comprehensive, publicly accessible database that provides more quantitative information about the migration of enslaved Africans to the Americas from 1501 to 1867 than currently exists for western European migrants during the same period.[4]

What are the quantitative dimensions of the trade? Before the late 1960s some researchers placed the number of arrivals as high as twenty million over 350 years, an estimate that Curtin revised sharply downward to about 9.5 million. Although the exact number will never be known, the painstaking research by Eltis and his associates have raised the figure to more than 10.7 million. Whatever the quantity, Portugal, Great Britain, France, Spain, and the Netherlands, in rank order of importance, shipped the overwhelming majority of African slaves to the Americas. It is also clear that the trade increased gradually, following an inverted-U shape with a peak from the late eighteenth century to the early nineteenth century. The flow began slowly in the early 1500s with annual arrivals, concentrated in the Spanish Caribbean of a few hundred per year. By the middle of the seventeenth century, Britain and France had entered the picture, and annual numbers grew to some 15,000. The trade more than doubled by the early 1700s and a peak inflow of more than 70,000 per year occurred from 1761 to 1810. Britain ended the African slave trade in 1807; the United States followed a year later. But Cuba and Brazil, most notably, continued to import African slaves in large numbers into the middle of the century. Brazil during its history imported more than four million African slaves—more than 40 percent of all imports into the hemisphere. That the United States imported fewer than 400,000 slaves during its colonial and national history, yet, by 1860, boasted a slave population that exceeded four million—more slaves at that time than were in Brazil—speaks to the significance of differential demographic performance in understanding the institution's rise, growth, and fall. This fact has implications for the comparative study of slave treatment, for slave mortality and fertility, for slave agency and marriage patterns, and for the structure and content of slave families. During the last four decades scholars have begun unraveling some of the demographic mysteries of slave mortality and fertility for various slaveholding countries in the Americas. Much more work remains to be done for discrete countries during certain periods with special attention to changes during stages of the slave's life cycle.

Figure 29.1 gives the geographic distribution of imports in terms of colonial destinations. Fresh estimates for imports into Britain's Caribbean colonies, like those for Brazil, have risen. France's and Spain's colonies in the Americas had roughly equal shares. The United States and other minor players such as Sweden, Denmark, and the Netherlands had less than 10 percent of the total.

Relative to others, the United States entered the slave trade rather late. The first handful of Africans arrived in Virginia in 1619 and by the 1660s the institution of slavery had taken firm root in the Chesapeake region, but the annual imports remained low, usually numbering in the hundreds. A convincing explanation as to

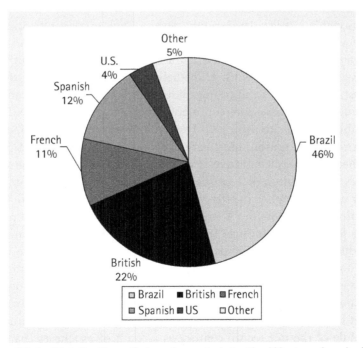

Figure 29.1. Distribution of slave imports into the Western hemisphere, 1500–1860

Source: Tabulated from data in http://slavevoyages.org/tast/assessment/estimates. faces?yearFrom=1651&yearTo=1675&flag=4.3

why the colonial United States was not more receptive to slaves has not yet surfaced, but the relative costs of indentured servants versus slaves as well as geography and related factors such as climate and cropping patterns were probably involved. In the mid-eighteenth century slavery was legal (or at least not illegal) in all thirteen of Britain's mainland North American colonies, although the Chesapeake had become the geographic center of slavery along the East Coast. Very few slaves lived north of Pennsylvania and the lower Hudson Valley, possibly because their mortality rates tended to climb with latitude, as evidenced by bills of mortality maintained by several cities. Some scholars have pointed to cropping patterns that permitted agriculture nearly year round in the South. But in the North slaves required additional training to switch to other activities during the winter. Whatever the explanation, all northern states took legal measures against slavery in the late 1700s or early 1800s. Robert Fogel and Stanley Engerman undertook an economic analysis of these laws, showing that slave owners lost only a few percent of the capital value of their slaves through this legislation.[5] No one has intensively studied the debates and votes over gradual emancipation before the 1830s in southern state legislatures. Votes on the issue failed, albeit by surprisingly narrow margins in some cases.

Unquestionably, slave traders brought slaves to the Americas to work; slave ships freighted few children under the age of 10. Because transportation costs were similar regardless of age, the payback on the transportation investment was highest for those slaves who could work immediately and whose expected work careers were longest, i.e., teenagers and young adults. In this respect, the African slave trade resembled other large-scale intercontinental migrations, such as the flow of Europeans to the United States from 1847 to 1914. Although the ratio varied somewhat by time period and location, most cargos had 60–5 percent males. Scholars have debated whether the explanation rests with supply or demand. On the supply side, many slaves were debtors or captives of war, which disproportionately involved men. They also had higher market value in the Western hemisphere but similar transportation costs across the Atlantic. On the latter point, physical productivity was higher for men than women in fieldwork, the dominant plantation activity. Sugar production in general, especially ditching, digging, and cane cutting, required arduous labor for which male slaves were often preferred. Southern Louisiana after 1820 illustrates the importance of demand. The American sugar industry began in Louisiana shortly before the African slave trade was closed by federal law in 1808. Yet the male–female ratio in sugar parishes stood at approximately 60:40 by the middle of the nineteenth century as a result of purchases (particularly in New Orleans) of slave labor reallocated by markets from slaveholding regions in the east. Relative to the rest of the South, more women were found in the rice counties of South Carolina and Georgia.

DISTRIBUTION OF THE SLAVE POPULATION
IN 1825

Many central questions in the demographic history of slavery can be understood by comparing Figures 29.1 and 29.2, which show the geographic distribution of imports 1500–1860 with that of the population in 1825, at roughly the height of the institution.[6] Although a small importer (5 percent), the United States ranked as the largest slave power in 1825, commanding 36 percent of the total slave population in the hemisphere. Brazil ranked second at 31 percent, followed by the British colonies (15 percent) and Spanish America (11 percent). Because abolitionists thought Brazil a more difficult nut to crack (and in fact the country did not abolish until 1888) the campaign focused on the largest slave power, the United States. By 1850, only the United States, Brazil, and Cuba remained as major slaveholding countries in the Americas.

How could a country with so few imports end up with so many slaves? The answer lies in the slow but powerful consequences of demographic rates of birth and death, as explained with precision by Jack Eblen, a professional demographer,

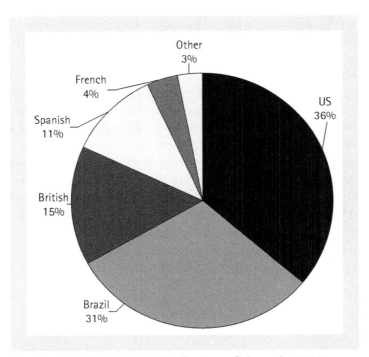

Figure 29.2. Geographic distribution of slaves in 1825

in a groundbreaking essay on the calculation of meaningful birth and death rates in slave populations, which may or may not be subject to the distortions of migration.[7] The rate of natural increase, g, is defined by the following equation:

$$g = b - d$$

where b is the crude birth rate (the number of births divided by the mid-year population) and d is the crude death rate (the number of deaths divided by the mid-year population. Although the figures vary over time and space, the order of magnitude for these rates is given in Table 29.1 for the United States and for the other slave colonies of the Western hemisphere during the eighteenth century.

In the United States the birth rate was approximately 5.5 percent, which is at least one percentage point below the biological maximum found in very high-fertility populations such as the Hutterites of the northern Great Plains. The American death rate of 3 to 3.5 percent is high by modern standards, where figures of approximately 1 percent or slightly less are common, but was somewhat higher than contemporary populations in Europe. On average other slave populations had a birth rate of about 3 percent, which is roughly triple that found in modern industrial countries. The most striking difference between the United States and other slave societies was found in the death rate, which explains approximately two-thirds of the difference in the rate of natural increase.

Before seeking explanations for the pattern of birth and death rates, it is useful to consider the implications of alternative rates of natural increase for population growth. Table 29.2 presents information on doubling time, or the number of years needed for a population to double if births and deaths were the only source of population change. The table draws upon a mathematical formula used for many purposes, including compound interest or growth of a cell culture when compounding occurs continuously. At 1 percent the time is seventy years, but the number declines rapidly as g increases, being thirty-five years at 2 percent, twenty-three years at 3 percent, and only ten years at 7 percent. The numbers also apply if g is negative, but the years refer to halving time. Therefore other slave populations would have shrunk (rapidly) except for imports. Therein lies the crux of the demographic treadmill that dominates sugar production.

Table 29.3 illustrates the implications of rates of natural increase for the course of the slave population in the United States. The American population increased by

Table 29.1. Rates of natural increase of slave populations

Location	b (%)	d (%)	g (%)
US	5.5	3 to 3.5	2 to 2.5
Other WH	3	7 to 10	−4 to −7

Table 29.2. Population doubling time under various rates of natural increase

g (%)	Years
1.0	70
1.5	46
2.0	35
2.5	28
3.0	23
3.5	20
4.0	17
5.0	14
6.0	12
7.0	10

more than fourfold from 1800 to 1860, reaching nearly 4 million at the end of the period. True, imports added to growth between 1800 and 1810, but in the half century after 1810, when the Atlantic slave trade was closed and most scholars believe smuggling was trivial, the gain was 332 percent. This figure corresponds to an annual rate of natural increase of 2.4 percent.

Relative to the United States, why were death rates so high and birth rates so low in other slaveholding countries? Figure 29.3, which reproduces data from Robert Fogel, *Without Consent or Contract* (1989), suggest answers, or at least additional questions to consider.[8] First, the slave population in the United States grew rapidly relative to all other slave societies, but the American white population grew even faster, though not at a biological maximum. Second, most, but not all, slave populations outside the United States had negative rates of natural increase. The pattern did not fit the Bahamas, a Caribbean archipelago where sugar was not grown commercially. Third, some colonies such as Jamaica, where slaves produced sugar, gradually approached but did not achieve a positive rate of natural increase. Fourth, European populations on average doubled in size every century or so during the eighteenth and early nineteenth centuries.

Table 29.3. Slave population in the United States

Year	Population (000)
1790	698
1800	894
1810	1,191
1820	1,538
1830	2,009
1840	2,487
1850	3,204
1860	3,954

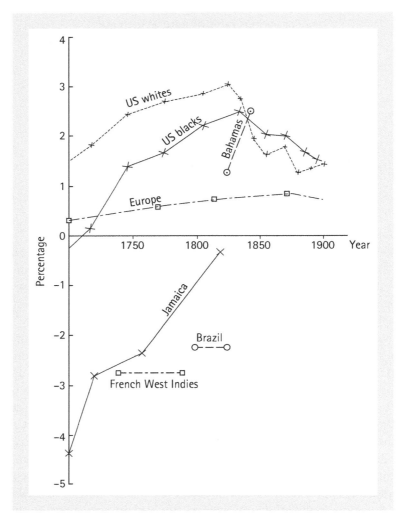

Figure 29.3. Approximate average annual rates of natural increase for various populations, 1700–1900. Negative percentages indicate rates of natural decrease and positive percentages indicate rates of natural increase. Thus in 1700 Jamaica had a rate of natural decrease in excess of 4 percent per year. The closer the line for Jamaica gets to zero, the lower its rate of natural decrease. Since the rate of natural increase of US blacks became positive c.1710, the line representing its growth rate crosses from the negative to the positive portion of the diagram at that point.

Source: Robert William Fogel, *Without Consent or Contract: The Rise and Fall of American Slavery* (New York, 1989), 124.

HEALTH AND MORTALITY

In the past three decades, human biology, nutrition, and epidemiology have provided new insights into the health and mortality of Western hemispheric slave populations.[9] Auxology, a branch of biology that studies human physical growth, has demonstrated that heights and mortality rates are inversely correlated. Think of the body as a biological machine that consumes food as fuel—a blend of calories, protein, micronutrients, and other ingredients. This machine at rest (basal metabolism) expends fuel that amounts to some 1,200 to 1,400 calories per day, depending upon size of the person, to keep him warm, breathing, his blood circulating, and his body growing and fighting infection. In the most arduous activities, such as mushing (guiding a dog sled) in Alaska's 1,100-mile Iditarod dog race, energy expended may amount to 10,000 calories per day. For this reason diets qualify as adequate or inadequate only in relation to demands on the fuel. Infections may consume fuel by raising body temperature or mobilizing the immune system, or both, or through incomplete processing of the diet, especially in gastrointestinal diseases. The body's first priority is to survive, and growth stagnates or takes a back seat under conditions of inadequate net nutrition (diet minus claims on the diet made by work and disease). If good times return, the body may recover much or all of forgone growth through a process of catch-up, whereby velocity exceeds that typical for a given age. Acute malnutrition that is severe retards child growth and can lead to permanent adult stunting if nutritional conditions after the episode do not improve significantly. Chronically poor net nutrition inevitably stunts adult height by as much as ten to fifteen centimeters and possibly more in extreme situations.

A synergy exists between nutrition and infection. Poorly nourished children have weak immune systems and thus are more vulnerable to infections. Moreover, once the poorly nourished children are sick, their illnesses are more likely to progress in severity and end in death, especially from measles, tuberculosis, intestinal parasites, whooping cough, and gastrointestinal and respiratory infections. Thus, physical growth and mortality are opposite sides of the same coin. Given the great importance of variations in mortality rates to differences in natural increase, one would expect average heights to roughly align with the data in Figure 29.3. For the most part, alignment occurs. White men in the United States were the tallest of the lot at roughly 172 centimeters, or 5 feet 7 inches. American slaves followed at 170 centimeters. The height of European men, based on military records, ranged from 164 to 168 centimeters. Creole slaves in St Lucia and Trinidad attained a height of 163 centimeters. The alignment of height and mortality works less well across the sugar colonies because the large share of recent imports within the population led to large numbers of deaths from seasoning.

PLANTATION CONDITIONS IN THE
UNITED STATES

....

Richard Steckel's research on average height by age and sex shed light on decision making at the plantation level in the United States.[10] The raw data stems from legislation that abolished the African slave trade to the United States in 1808. To prove that slaves transported in the coastwise trade were not smuggled from Africa, the ship captain prior to departure from an American port prepared duplicate manifests that described the cargo by name, age, height, sex, and color. After coding data on some 50,000 slaves, Steckel found that the young children were exceptionally small, in fact among the smallest ever measured. From a deficit of approximately six inches relative to modern height standards, the slaves as teenagers gained approximately four inches on these standards.[11] Studies of children from poor countries who were adopted into rich countries prove that catch-up growth of this magnitude is biologically possible, but reconnaissance of historical and contemporary studies shows that it is quite unusual if not unprecedented. Kenneth Kiple's work discusses a number of nutrition-related diseases experienced by slave children at these ages, such as kwashiorkor, tetany, rickets, and pellagra.[12]

Plantation owners in the United States often maintained lists of slave births and deaths, from which one can calculate mortality rates by age. These records show that the mortality rates of young children were very high, approximately 35 percent among infants and nearly 20 percent for children aged 1 to 5, both of which are approximately double the rates for the free population. Mortality rates after age 10 fell dramatically, and by age 20 the excess mortality of slaves was largely eliminated. Additional study of the birth and death lists shows that neonatal mortality (death within the first month of life) was not only high (more than 30 percent of infant deaths on farms with highly detailed lists) but seasonally skewed. Neonatal deaths in late winter and in September–November more than tripled the number found in other months, a pattern consistent with seasonal patterns of net nutritional deprivation for the mother. Possible explanations are diet, work, and exposure to disease. Whereas diet was best from midsummer to late autumn, work was most arduous from late winter to early spring (the plowing and planting season) and from late summer through late fall (harvest). Malarial and other fevers raged during late summer and early autumn. Pounds of cotton picked per day by expectant mothers in relation to date of birth show that women had little or no relief from work prior to a couple of weeks before delivery of the child. Studies of birth outcomes during the Dutch hunger winter of the Second World War indicate that after conception the first trimester was the most vulnerable period of deprivation that affected neonatal deaths. In addition, third trimester deprivation lowered birth weight and raised neonatal mortality. In this deadly process of demographic roulette, the worst period for conception was from late winter to early spring, for the developing fetus would be hit in the first trimester by hard work and poor diet and in the third trimester by the harvest and the fever season.

Attenuated breastfeeding practices aggravated health problems associated with low birth weight. The records on cotton picking show that within a few weeks after delivery the mothers were working full-time. Either they did not nurse or did so very little during the day. In plantation nurseries, older women and young children tended to care for infant slaves by feeding them low-protein paps and gruels. Supplementary feeding per se was not hazardous to health and growth, but the nutritional content was low and commonly the utensils or the food itself were contaminated.

If the child survived infancy, he experienced in the ensuing years minuscule catch-up growth, which was a function of diet or disease or both because work was out of the picture. Letters by planters to southern agricultural journals reveal that meat protein was reserved for working slaves. Longitudinal intervention studies undertaken by INCAP (Institute of Nutrition of Central America and Panama) demonstrate the importance of protein for physical growth. Because nutritionists were debating the importance of protein in the diet, children in Guatemalan villages were randomly assigned to receive, beginning in 1969, rations of a drink fortified with protein, while others received a placebo. Results confirmed the crucial nature of protein for health and growth. Within a few years younger children receiving the fortified drink sometimes overtook their older siblings in stature. Follow-up studies confirm that health and cognitive benefits from protein intake persist into adulthood.

Significant movement toward modern height standards began around age 10, when the young slaves entered the adult labor force, and concluded around age 21 when they reached what was essentially final adulthood. Other things equal, work would have retarded growth. Thus something in the nutritional equation must have improved enough to have stimulated four inches of compensatory growth. Philip Coelho and Robert McGuire have suggested that a lower disease load was responsible, in particular reduced exposure to hookworm.[13] Hookworm eradication programs in the tropics have measurable benefits for growth, but nothing approaching four inches, however. The most powerful explanation is dietary. Diet was not a matter of taste or of a savory reward to workers for diligent service. In letters to southern agricultural periodicals, planters reported that meat rations were essential for slaves to perform a full day's work. The working slaves received about one half pound of pork per day and considerable calories from corn and from various vegetables that were seasonally available. The compensatory growth proves consistent with decline in death rates that gradually eliminated excess mortality relative to the free population.

Labor economists have long argued that employers will provide firm-specific training to their employees but are less willing if not unwilling to invest in general training that is useful to other firms and other industries, lest the employee leave. In other words, why train someone else's workers? Contractual arrangements can reduce the problem if junior workers are paid less than their productive value, but then more if they remain with the firm. But a problem still exists because the junior workers may leave unexpectedly, lowering the return on any firm-specific investments the employer may have made. Slavery eliminates the problem because the planter owns the benefits of human capital investments, i.e., all future labor. By this logic, one would think that slave owners would have invested heavily in early childhood health, but they did not do so. Why?

Preliminary calculations indicate that feeding meat to children was unprofitable. The approximate value of an inch of height is known from slave appraisals: a 1.4 percent increase in price per inch of height. Some assumptions, which are supported by evidence, are required to make the problem tractable, including the amount of the protein deficit relative to modern dietary standards, the protein content of pork, the price of pork, and whether planters faced a "leaky nutritional bucket." The last point means that some protein would have been wasted if the pathogen load diminished the value of the improved diet, thereby reducing the rate of return on the investment. While the issue has yet to be investigated in detail, initial calculations suggest that the rate of return was negative and would have risen to only 1 or 2 percent even if mortality rates declined by half, a figure still well below competitive rates of return on alternative investments.

Some economists may find these economic calculations uncomfortable because it suggests that market rationality failed to protect future workers as children even when their employer owned all future labor. Would parents want their biological children raised by slave owner methods? Is this a dark side of the market, or simply a reflection that the system operates within a biological milieu? Such discussions may quickly approach the philosophical. One can ask a related question, however: Why do parents in free societies typically invest so much in their children? For the most part, children are not profitable in a narrow economic sense, although they may provide considerable nonmonetary compensation. Perhaps a fundamental reason is genetic. Over eons a Darwinian process may have eliminated those family lines that did not make enormous sacrifices to reproduce themselves. If so, economists and other social scientists should recognize these powerful biological forces in devising their explanations for human behavior.

PLANTATION CONDITIONS IN THE SUGAR COLONIES

Historians Barry Higman and Kenneth Kiple have undertaken extensive studies of health and mortality in the sugar colonies, especially the Caribbean. Kiple's work, informed by medical studies, focuses on epidemiological and biological processes.[14] Higman takes more of a social science approach by investigating cropping patterns, plantation size, management, work routines, age distributions, and sex ratios. Taken together their books and articles provide a very useful and informative portrait of demographic conditions. Kiple broadly considers the demographic fate of Africans under slavery in the New World. His explanations emphasize the poor nutritional status of the newly enslaved and the aggravation of their condition in coastal holding forts and depots in West Africa and during the Middle Passage. They arrived with weakened immune systems that left them poorly equipped to confront a host of new pathogens. After arrival, slave diets were inadequate in protein, vitamins, and minerals as a consequence of planter decisions to allocate better land to sugar cane and the high price of food imports from the United States.

Higman based his major work, *Slave Populations of the British Caribbean, 1807–1834* (1984), on an extensive examination of slave registration and compensation records, collected from the end of the Atlantic slave trade to the beginning of emancipation. These records allowed him to investigate the assumption of spatial homogeneity in slave systems. An analysis of patterns of natural increase by using a socioeconomic typology that emphasizes cropping patterns suggests that a sharp demographic distinction existed between sugar and other crops. Across pairs of colonies, there was considerable variation in the extent to which fertility and mortality explained differences in natural increase, depending upon time period, location, and dominant crop. There is little doubt that fertility in the United States was exceptionally high by standards of slavery in the Western hemisphere. On the other hand, the death rate exceeded the birth rate by 1.5 percentage points in early nineteenth century Trinidad; by 2.3 percentage points in Suriname (1826–48); but by only 0.5 percentage points in Jamaica (1817–20). In any event, the demographic costs of sugar are clear from study of patterns by major crop. When dividing the data by major product, differences in natural increase were due heavily to mortality. In particular, the highest death rates were found on large sugar estates.

Future scholarship on slave demography will need to consolidate ideas, bringing together epidemiology, work effort, diet, stature, long-distance migration, and the demand for New World products. Philip Curtin advanced the field by introducing medical knowledge on immune systems in relation to intercontinental migration. He observed that, as children, we train our immune systems to recognize pathogens and create antibodies. Because childhood versions of diseases tend to be mild, but still create the antibodies, mortality rates are low. This training, however, is location specific because subtle yet important variations in pathogens, much less entirely different diseases, existed across regions or continents during the slave era. Therefore people who migrated long distances as adults often faced the deadly consequences of moving into a different disease zone. Though not scientifically understood, the process of "seasoning" was well known to eighteenth-century observers, whereby newcomers were often sick and for a couple of years may have faced annual mortality rates in the neighborhood of 15 percent.

In the sugar colonies, a kind of demographic treadmill existed, driven by the weight of European, African, and New World pathogens which newcomers were poorly prepared to resist. In the tropical and subtropical environments mosquitoes spread malaria, dengue fever, and yellow fever, and flies that were common year round spread gastrointestinal diseases. Parasites or protozoa that caused schistosomiasis, leishmaniasis, Chagas disease, and hookworm were also prevalent. Large numbers of poorly nourished Africans encountered this pathogenic stew. Imports were short, with the men ranging from 160 to 165 centimeters depending upon place of origin. The newcomers not only encountered new diseases but had poorly equipped immune systems further weakened by the psychological stress of enslavement. Hard work on large plantations facilitated the spread of communicable diseases among slaves, and a poor diet worsened the situation. In their allocation of land for cultivation, sugar planters tended to reserve little space for food crops. Thus slaves on Caribbean sugar plantations ate an ample amount of imported food that was not only expensive relative to that eaten by slaves in the United States, but also had lower nutritional value due to processing and storage. Under these conditions, little wonder that slave mortality rates were so high.

The share of the slave population born in Africa plays a central role in the demographic history of the Western hemisphere. In the United States the share of native-born (creole) slaves reached 50 percent by the early 1700s and was nearly 80 percent by 1800. In the sugar colonies the majority of slaves were born in Africa, and the figure approached 80 to 90 percent in places such as late eighteenth-century Barbados. Why was the contrast so great with the United States? A thorough answer would make a good dissertation topic, but the crux of an answer probably lies in the demand for New World products. Tobacco was the most important cash crop in the colonial southern United States, but the demand for this product was low in Europe. Few if any women and children consumed it, and it was popular among men in only a few countries. After the Navigation Act of 1660, England transshipped, principally to the Netherlands and Germany, the vast majority of American tobacco it received. Europeans did, however, readily acquire a sweet tooth. Sugar, a mildly addictive substance, has a very high elasticity of demand. Men, women, and children consumed sugar and molasses (a by-product of sugar processing), and numerous recipes appeared for their use once the products were widely distributed in Europe by the eighteenth century. As prices dropped, Europeans consumed more sugar. Its status descended from a delicacy ingested only by elites to a dietary staple of the masses. Sugar products became so popular that some scholars have linked the Industrial Revolution and increases in agricultural productivity to the abundant, quick energy for workers supplied by sugar.

In the final analysis, geography dealt several of the high cards of slave demographic history in the Western hemisphere. Had climate permitted widespread sugar production in the United States, it seems reasonable to think that sugar plantations would have thrived, and the country would have demographically resembled a sugar colony. Southern Louisiana certainly developed along these lines during the antebellum period. Of course, the land area of the United States was so large that it would have altered the geography of sugar production, perhaps sapping the industry from other colonies endowed with land of lower quality.

FERTILITY

The share of the slave population born in Africa also had a long reach into the history of fertility, by way of sex ratios, reproductive fitness, and psychological adjustments to capture, transportation, and plantation work. Demographic studies indicate that fertility tends to decline as the sex ratio departs from 50:50. Of course, institutional adjustments such as polygamy may occur, but even then the birth rate tends to be lower than that found under equal sex ratios. Since most slave ships carried human cargoes that were 60 to 65 percent males, sugar colonies began their existence at a significant fertility disadvantage. Moreover, over time little movement toward an even sex ratio occurred because growth in demand for sugar led to ever more imports. Height data demonstrate that African-born slave women had lower reproductive fitness than their creole counterparts, especially those slave women born in the United States. The health of the woman as a child and her net nutrition during the childbearing years affect fecundity, her chances of conceiving. Moreover, nutritional status impacts effective fertility or the probability of delivering a live birth that was healthy. On both counts, the sugar colonies were at a reproductive disadvantage.

Richard Steckel has analyzed fertility in the United States by devising a measure of synthetic total fertility, R, as follows:

$$R=\{[\,(L-F)/S\,]+1\}\beta$$

where L and F are the average ages at last birth and first birth, respectively, and their difference equals the average childbearing span; S equals the average spacing interval between births; and β is the proportion of women who eventually have children.[15] The expression in braces, $\{[(L-F)/S]+1\}$, represents the average number of births to women who have at least one child, and multiplication by β converts the equation to the average number of births per woman.

Probate records in the United States sometimes organized the slave property into families, or at least configurations of mothers and their children who were listed by name and age. From these documents one can calculate the elements of R, which were 40.7 and 20.6 for L and F; S averaged 2.92 years between surviving children; and β equaled 0.858. The implied value of R is then 6.76. Of course the interval between live as opposed to surviving births was lower, with a mean of about thirty months based on plantation birth lists. The calculated birth interval is sensitive to the accuracy with which infant deaths were recorded, and it is quite possible their underenumeration occurred to some extent. Values of R were about 50 percent higher on small farms (under twenty-five slaves) as opposed to large farms (seventy-five or more slaves). All elements of R contributed importantly to the difference in the average number of births per woman. But the contrast in age at last birth accounted for somewhat more (37 percent) of the overall difference.

If the probate records are organized by region, the calculated value of R was 8.26 in Virginia and 6.35 in Georgia and Louisiana. In this case, however, values of F were nearly identical (20.5 versus 20.6), and the difference in S was modest (2.78 versus 2.99). The contrast in L was 2.5 years, explaining 47 percent of the difference in R, while β equaled 0.916 in Virginia and 0.837 in Georgia and Louisiana, explaining 31 percent of the difference. What socioeconomic conditions might account for the differences in L, F, S, and β by plantation size and region? The length of the childbearing span and the percentage of women who had children dominate the patterns. Because slaves had no pressing economic reason to practice family limitation, the age at marriage (or partner formation) and whether women eventually found a partner were important for fertility outcomes.

Pension files for dependants of black troops who fought in the Civil War shed light on marriage decisions. To qualify for a pension based on the service of a disabled or deceased former soldier, the law required affidavits by the former owner or owners, stating that a union existed under slavery. Richard Steckel gathered a large sample of these affidavits, which he organized by median plantation size (number of slaves) in the county. In the tobacco-mixed farming areas of Virginia, characterized by small farms (under twenty-five slaves, on which the majority of all slaves in the United States resided), so-called "abroad" marriages (marriages between slaves who resided on different plantations) dominated (69 percent). Across all counties abroad marriages reached 51 percent of the total. Higman, in contrast, reports that the share of mates belonging to different owners ranged from 5.8 percent (Dominica) to 49 percent (Barbados) in the British Caribbean. In the largest colony (Jamaica) the number of abroad marriages reached 28 percent.

Three considerations guided these outcomes: prohibitions against marrying close relatives (siblings or first cousins), commuting (walking) time between farms, and plantation management. In clusters or regions of small farms, commuting time was low, plantation rules were less formal, and slaves on the farm were more likely to have been close relatives. In this setting young adult slaves could search abroad and readily find eligible partners. On large farms, however, commuting times were high because the land area was considerable, and masters imposed strict rules to maintain plantation discipline. Marriage across farms exposed the arbitrary nature of the rules, creating discontent. One might think that large farms had more eligible partners, but restrictions or prohibitions on abroad marriages greatly limited choices. On large farms, it took longer to find a mate and fewer slaves eventually did so.

Fertility patterns speak to the issue of slave breeding, a favorite charge of abolitionists in the United States against southern slaveholders. While most scholars are skeptical, a few claim to have identified breeding farms in the southeast, where birth rates were high, by the existence of a large number of children relative to men. Thus, according to this line of reasoning, some men must have fathered children by more than one woman. The argument cloaks an assumption that unions were limited to slaves on the farm, which was not the case. Moreover the notion of widespread slave breeding clashes with the values of F (average age at first birth), which are several years above the age at which American slave women could have had children.

Unfortunately comparable estimates are unavailable for all elements of R (the measure of synthetic total fertility) in the sugar colonies. Assembling and analyzing such estimates would be a valuable research project. Presumably documents such as probate records and slave registrations, which began in the British Caribbean after 1807, are available for this type of research. At least some of the fertility difference with the United States can be attributed to longer spacing intervals between slave births in the Caribbean, which in turn have been linked to greater duration of breastfeeding and to taboos against intercourse while the child was being nursed. It seems likely that the share of women who readily found mates, which would have lowered F (average age at first birth) and raised β (the proportion of women who eventually bear children), was higher in the United States for two reasons. First, plantations were much smaller, especially in the Old South, giving slaves more options to find compatible mates through cross-plantation marriages. Second, plantation life in the sugar colonies, unlike that in the United States, appears more fragmented by language and culture, which lowered the availability of compatible mates. It remains to be seen how values of L (average age at last birth) fit into the demographic picture, but poorer nutrition may well have reduced the age at which women were biologically capable of having children in the sugar colonies.

David Hume and Benjamin Franklin offered insights into slave demography that survive modern scrutiny: Diet and work mattered for health and fertility. They lacked the evidence, methodologies, and computing power available to modern scholars, however, to understand the complexity of the system. Poor diets and hard work in the sugar colonies aggravated the poor health of imports who encountered an onslaught of unfamiliar pathogens. Hume and Franklin would have been surprised to learn that variations in demand for New World products and geographic conditions heavily drove the demographic regimes of the slave colonies. High fertility in the United States relative to the sugar colonies did not stem from breeding, but from better net nutrition and more widespread availability of partners.

NOTES

1. Philip D. Curtin, *The African Slave Trade: A Census* (Madison, 1969).
2. David Eltis, *The Rise of African Slavery in the Americas* (Cambridge, 2000); Kenneth F. Kiple, *The Caribbean Slave: A Biological History* (Cambridge, 1984).
3. Herbert S. Klein, *The Atlantic Slave Trade: New Approaches to the Americas* (Cambridge, 1999).
4. http://slavevoyages.org/tast/index.faces See also David Eltis and David Richardson (eds.), *Extending the Frontiers: Essays on the New Transatlantic Slave Trade Database* (New Haven, 2008), esp. 1–60.
5. Robert William Fogel and Stanley L. Engerman, *Time on the Cross: Evidence and Methods, a Supplement* (Boston, 1974); Robert William Fogel and Stanley L. Engerman, *Time on the Cross: The Economics of American Negro Slavery* (Boston, 1974).
6. Fogel and Engerman, *Time on the Cross*.
7. Jack Ericson Eblen, "On the Natural Increase of Slave Populations: The Example of the Cuban Black Population, 1775–1900," in Stanley L. Engerman and Eugene D. Genovese (eds.), *Race and Slavery in the Western Hemisphere: Quantitative Studies* (Princeton, 1975).
8. Robert William Fogel, *Without Consent or Contract: The Rise and Fall of American Slavery* (New York, 1989).
9. For a general discussion of methodology and results, see Richard H. Steckel, "Stature and the Standard of Living," *Journal of Economic Literature*, 33 (4) (1995): 1903–40.
10. Richard H. Steckel, "A Peculiar Population: The Nutrition, Health, and Mortality of American Slaves from Childhood to Maturity," *Journal of Economic History*, 46 (3) (September 1986): 721–41.
11. Some of the measured catch-up may have been an artifact of selective survival, which favored taller individuals, or of preferences by traders who favored taller individuals. Investigations to date suggest these effects were small.
12. Kenneth F. Kiple and Virginia Himmelsteib King, *Another Dimension to the Black Diaspora: Diet, Disease, and Racism* (Cambridge, 1981).
13. Philip R. P. Coelho and Robert A. McGuire, "Diets Versus Diseases: The Anthropometrics of Slave Children," *Journal of Economic History*, 60 (1) (2000): 232–46.
14. Barry W. Higman, *Slave Populations of the British Caribbean, 1807–1834* (Baltimore, 1984); Kiple, *Caribbean Slave: A Biological History*.
15. Richard H. Steckel, *The Economics of U.S. Slave and Southern White Fertility* (New York, 1985).

Select Bibliography

Eltis, David. *The Rise of African Slavery in the Americas.* Cambridge: Cambridge University Press, 2000.

—— and David Richardson. *Extending the Frontiers: Essays on the New Transatlantic Slave Trade Database.* New Haven: Yale University Press, 2008.

Fogel, Robert William. *Without Consent or Contract: The Rise and Fall of American Slavery.* 1st edn. New York: Norton, 1989.

—— and Stanley L. Engerman. *Time on the Cross: The Economics of American Negro Slavery.* Boston: Little, Brown, 1974.

Higman, Barry W. *Slave Population and Economy in Jamaica, 1807–1834.* Cambridge: Cambridge University Press, 1976.

—— *Slave Populations of the British Caribbean, 1807–1834.* Baltimore: Johns Hopkins University Press, 1984.

Kiple, Kenneth F. *The Caribbean Slave: A Biological History.* Cambridge: Cambridge University Press, 1984.

—— and Virginia Himmelsteib King. *Another Dimension to the Black Diaspora: Diet, Disease, and Racism.* Cambridge: Cambridge University Press, 1981.

Klein, Herbert S. *The Atlantic Slave Trade, New Approaches to the Americas.* Cambridge: Cambridge University Press, 1999.

—— and Ben Vinson. *African Slavery in Latin America and the Caribbean.* 2nd edn. Oxford: Oxford University Press, 2007.

Steckel, Richard H. *The Economics of U.S. Slave and Southern White Fertility.* New York: Garland, 1985.

—— "A Peculiar Population: The Nutrition, Health, and Mortality of American Slaves from Childhood to Maturity," *Journal of Economic History,* 46 (3) (1986): 721–41.

CHAPTER 30

....

COMPARATIVE SLAVERY

....

ENRICO DAL LAGO

METHODOLOGICAL INTRODUCTION
....

Comparison has long been a favorite method of investigation among historians of slavery in the Americas. For over sixty years, monographs comparing aspects of different slave societies in the New World and more general studies looking at the rise and development of unfree labor in the Americas and elsewhere have contributed significantly to broadening perspectives, shedding new light on controversial issues, and, perhaps most importantly, generating new interpretations concerning the emergence of unfree labor systems, the relation between modernity and agrarian labor (free and unfree), the coexistence of capitalist and precapitalist features in the elites' ideologies and behaviors, and the uniqueness of modern abolitionist movements and of the different processes of emancipation in the Americas. Yet, charting and analyzing the development of the entire comparative historiography on New World slavery suggests that it is very difficult to pinpoint a single, "comparative" methodology. At best, many scholars have relied on two seminal methodological articles by Marc Bloch and by Theda Skocpol and Margaret Somers, while others have preferred to develop their own methodology of comparison.[1]

Recently, valuable help has come from Peter Kochin's *A Sphinx on the American Land*, a book that for the first time has constructed a systematic framework for the understanding of comparative scholarship dealing with the nineteenth-century American South. Kolchin's framework offers an opportunity to think carefully and precisely about the continental scale of New World slavery and allows us to characterize the main methodologies that different comparative historians of slavery in the Americas have employed for the past sixty years. Three main types of comparative analysis appear to have shaped the historiography: (a) comparisons between the slave societies of either specific regions of, or the entirety of, North America on one hand, and Latin America and the Caribbean on the other hand; (b) comparisons between slave societies of different regions of the English-speaking Americas on one hand, or between slave societies of different regions of the non-English-speaking Americas on the other hand; (c) comparisons between slave societies of either specific regions of, or the entirety of, the New World on one hand, and either slave or unfree labor societies in the Old World on the other hand. Still following Kolchin, we can also fruitfully make a distinction between those studies focusing on explicit comparisons—in which a sustained comparative study of two or more cases is the object of the research—and those studies which contain implicit, or "soft," comparisons—in which comparative points are offered but remain largely underdeveloped. Finally, comparison can be synchronic—when the case studies compared are contemporaneous—or diachronic—when the case studies compared belong to different historical epochs.[2]

In this essay, I will first briefly review the historiography of comparative slavery, so as to identify the main trends and changes it went through. I will then provide a summary of the state of the art of comparative studies in the three main historical periods in which slavery flourished in the Americas: the colonial period (sixteenth to late eighteenth centuries), the revolutionary period (roughly 1770–1820), and the nineteenth century. At the heart of the essay will be the different ways in which comparative perspectives have enhanced and can enhance still our understanding of the different historical phenomena—chief among them capitalism—associated with the rise and spread of the Atlantic slave system in the New World. A long debate is still in course on the definition of the relation between slavery and capitalism and on whether we can see this relation as an alternative route to modernity followed by the slave societies in the Americas, especially the Old South. I believe that the comparative perspective helps us also by showing us that capitalist and precapitalist elements were present in different degrees in all the areas characterized by slave labor and that it was this coexistence of different elements that provided New World slavery with features that make it comparable to systems of both free and unfree labor in other parts of the world.

HISTORIOGRAPHY

Generally speaking, the methodology of comparative slavery and the issues on which comparative historians of slavery in the Americas currently focus are a direct result of the developments of a historiographical tradition that started with Frank Tannenbaum's publication of *Slave and Citizen* in 1947. Tannenbaum simultaneously provided the then few comparative historians with a new field of study—that of slavery in the Americas—and slavery historians with a new methodology: comparative history. Brilliantly applying Bloch's central comparative tenet regarding the detection of a similarity between the facts observed and the dissimilarity between the situations in which they had arisen, Tannenbaum sought to explain the now disproven assumption that slavery in the United States, despite its apparent similarity to slavery in Latin America, appeared much harsher than the latter in legal terms, and he found the explanation in the USA's much more exploitative version of capitalism, unmitigated by the Catholic Church. Although not intended as a specifically comparative work, Stanley Elkins's later work *Slavery* did much to reinforce Tannenbaum's idea and led to the so-called "Tannenbaum–Elkins" hypothesis.[3]

Thus, the first steps in comparative slavery in the Americas, significantly taken by a Latin American and a US specialist, led very early to the idea—represented by (a)-type comparative studies—that, methodologically, comparisons were best focused on particular macro features, such as law or race, and that the comparisons' objective was to show the reasons for the different characteristics assumed by the US slave system as opposed to its Latin American counterparts. This main idea, then, informed early comparative works by Herbert Klein and Carl Degler, both of whom used a variant of the method of juxtaposition—in which two cases are juxtaposed and then conclusions are drawn from their comparison—to prove corollaries of the "Tannenbaum–Elkins" hypothesis. Even Eugene Genovese's *The World the Slaveholders Made*, in which he compared diachronically New World slave societies with their European antecedents, reinforced the idea that the US slave system was exceptional.[4]

By the 1970s, as the historiographic revolution centering upon slave agency—the broadly constituted effort to place slaves themselves at the center of the narrative—reached its heyday, US-originated models of interpretation of the origins and main features of slavery were influencing, and were themselves influenced by, research on slave societies in the Caribbean and Latin America. This cross-fertilization led to a proliferation of comparative points in otherwise circumscribed studies on slave life in different parts of the New World, and also to a few explicit (b)-type comparative studies, above all a seminal one by Gwendolyn Midlo Hall on slavery and racism as means to preserve social order in two colonies with large slave populations such as eighteenth-century Saint-Domingue and nineteenth-century Cuba. At the same time, the rereading and rediscovery of older studies by great slavery scholars such as Gilberto Freyre, C. L. R. James, and Eric Williams, which came to be seen as points of departure for comparative research on major themes touching upon all slave societies in the New World, helped create the preconditions for a radical change in the overall interpretative framework of slavery in the Americas. Already Genovese's *From Rebellion to Revolution* referred clearly to a comprehensive interpretation of slave revolts that went beyond the continental American horizon and looked at broader comparative points—thus anticipating later (c)-type comparative studies—as did also an important collection edited by Genovese and Laura Foner. Even more so was the case of David Brion Davis, who, with two crucial works on "the problem of slavery," inaugurated a way of looking at comparative slavery in the New World as an integrated, and very important, part of world history.[5]

Also very important was the parallel growing influence of the new scholarship on the "Middle Passage," whose initiator was Philip Curtin. With his seminal study, published in 1969, Curtin effectively wrote the first comparative treatment of the Atlantic slave trade, analyzing the role of the European colonizing powers, as well as looking at it from the African and American perspectives. Curtin's main focus was on statistics and on the volume of the trade; however, his study provided a model for subsequent studies—such as Herbert Klein's comparative monograph on the "Middle Passage"—that engaged in increasingly deeper comparative analyses of both the different types of Atlantic slave trades and the different effects that the trades had on Africa and on the Americas.[6]

As a result of these developments, by the early 1980s all was in place for slavery in the Americas—meaning the study of the totality of the experiences of slave societies in the New World—to rise to the fore within the emerging historical discipline of Atlantic History—the study of the history of the societies that created an integrated Atlantic world between the sixteenth and the nineteenth century. Though it was going to be still a few years before Atlantic History became an actual historical field in its own right, from then on the main ideas at the heart of that discipline clearly informed all the most important studies of slave societies in the United States, in Latin America, and the Caribbean. In the process, these ideas also provided an innovative, flexible, and well-devised framework within which both explicit comparisons and "soft" comparisons of slave societies in the New World could fit effortlessly.

In the past twenty years, thanks to an impressive body of scholarship made of both interpretative monographs and pathbreaking collections of essays, slavery in the Americas has become progressively an increasingly essential part of Atlantic History, and one with a strong (c)-type comparative component. Monographs by Philip Curtin, Robin Blackburn, Seymour Drescher, and, more recently, David Brion Davis have looked at the entire development of slavery in the Americas—and

thus in a very wide comparative perspective—arguing about the crucial importance of the European background to Atlantic slavery.[7] Also, and more importantly,
all these studies have argued about the novel features of Atlantic slavery's exploitative capitalist system. More restricted in focus, but still very important, have been
also recent (a)-type comparative studies—focusing on comparisons between
North American and Latin American slavery—such Ira Berlin and Philip Morgan's
edited collection on labor, and also monographs by Rafael Marquese, and by Laird
Bergad. In addition, (b)-type comparative works—focusing on either comparisons
within the English-originated slave systems, or comparisons within the non-
English slave systems—include syntheses by James Walvin on slavery in the English-speaking parts of the Americas, and by Herbert Klein and Ben Vinson—this
latter the second edition of a very successful survey of slavery in Latin America and
the Caribbean.[8]

Together with these studies, important recent (b)-type and (c)-type comparative
collections include the ones edited by Barbara Solow, by Joseph Inikori and Stanley
Engerman, by Stuart Schwartz, by David Barry Gaspar and Darlene Clark Hine,
and by Gwyn Campbell, Suzanne Miers, and Joseph Miller. Also as a result of the
editors' and authors' strong links with the increasingly sophisticated scholarship on
the Atlantic slave trade, these collections have come to represent crucial steps in the
attempts at building an overall Atlantic framework within which fruitfully compare, by means of juxtaposition, insightful case studies originating from different
slave societies in the Americas. Moreover, as Atlantic History has grown as a
discipline and the Atlantic framework has become increasingly dominant among
historians of slavery in the Americas, several scholars have begun to investigate
thoroughly, and in comparative perspective, the African backgrounds of the slave
populations of the Atlantic system. Thus, (c)-type comparative studies by Paul
Gilroy, John Thornton, Stephanie Smallwood, and Gwendolyn Midlo Hall have
done much to place the representatives of different African ethnicities at the heart
of those momentous transformations that, in comparable ways all across the
Americas, gave origin to an Atlantic system of slavery. While Paul Gilroy has
argued convincingly in favor of the existence of a shared Black Atlantic culture,
John Thornton has looked at the origins of that same culture analyzing the African
societies' and elites' involvement in the early Atlantic world. Then, building on
Thornton's pioneering work, Smallwood has recently written about the African
perspective on the Atlantic slave trade and the latter's role in erasing and reconstituting African identities, while Midlo Hall has focused specifically on the
persistence of African identity among particular ethnic groups that were brought
to the New World.[9]

Since the beginning of the 1980s, a smaller group of scholars, all of them
comparative historians, has argued in favor of an even wider perspective than
that of Atlantic studies, pointing out the comparability between New World
slavery and other types of labor—mostly "unfree"—spread outside the Americas.

By broadening the geographical scope and employing an innovative methodo-logy, comparison through an enlarged Atlantic perspective, which includes the whole of Europe and also Africa, has proven a particularly fruitful terrain for the writing of explicit (c)-type comparative studies. These have focused particularly on slavery in the nineteenth-century American South and either unfree labor in South Africa (as in George Frederickson's work), Russian and Prussian serfdom (in the case of Peter Kolchin and Shearer Davis Bowman), or, as with my own work, sharecropping and tenancy in southern Italy. Moreover, this enlarged perspective has generated debate on the nature of slavery and serfdom in world history, which in turn has produced highly valuable comparative works— particularly important among them are those by Michael Bush and Dale Tomich—that have argued in favor of the comparability of New World slavery with an ever wider range of case studies of unfree labor in different regions and at different times.[10]

THE RISE OF ATLANTIC SLAVERY
IN COMPARATIVE PERSPECTIVE

Comparison has proven crucial in our understanding of the origins of New World slavery. By investigating similarities and differences across time and space, com-parative historians have established the extent of the continuity and change that slavery in the Americas has represented in world history. Diachronic comparisons with ancient and medieval Europe by William Phillips, Philip Curtin, and David Brion Davis have shown that Atlantic slavery in the New World was the first continental-scale and utterly pervasive, both economically and socially, slave sys-tem since the Roman empire, and yet it differed from the latter—as it differed from all previous slave systems—in being simultaneously capitalist and centered upon racial exploitation.[11] According to Michael Bush, unlike ancient or medieval slavery, "the slave system brought by the Europeans [to the Americas] was heredi-tary, racist, and designed to generate wealth, notably through the mining of precious metals and the cultivation of cash crops."[12] Through diachronic compar-isons, it has been possible to trace the origins both of American racism against Africans and of the particular systems of labor implemented in New World plantations to their late medieval European antecedents. Equally, diachronic com-parisons have also enlightened us on the long story of the different crops—sugar, rice, tobacco—that came from the Mediterranean and from different areas of the Atlantic—notably Africa and the Americas themselves—to make the early fortunes of plantation slavery in the New World.

Yet, it is synchronic comparison that has told us more about the origins of New World slavery between the sixteenth and the seventeenth centuries. Comparisons between different slave societies in the Americas, and between American slavery and eastern Europe's so-called "second serfdom"—notably those by James Walvin, Herbert Klein and Ben Vinson, Peter Kolchin, and Michael Bush—have proven incontrovertibly that the single, most important, factor that led to the making of a massive, and highly racist, Atlantic slave system in the Americas, as well as to the rebirth of a massive serf system in eastern Europe, was a shortage of labor and an availability of land at a time of large-scale economic expansion. In particular, in the Americas, aside from Mexico and Peru with their large native, and agriculturally skilled, population, those areas such as Brazil, the Caribbean, and mainland North America, where cash crop cultivation through plantation slavery became quickly endemic, had sparse native populations which were not nearly as agriculturally advanced. And, as David Eltis has shown, in those New World areas, when the employment of European white servitude became too expensive, the only option left was the transatlantic slave trade of Africans. The Atlantic perspective of different comparative studies—especially those by Stephanie Smallwood, Gwendolyn Midlo Hall, and Lynda Heywood and John Thornton—has, then, been crucial in clarifying how, enslaved and taken by European slave traders from a variety of societies that were at different stages of agricultural and technological advancement, the West and Central Africans of different ethnicities who managed to survive the lethal "Middle Passage" brought with them features of their original African cultures—some of which had been long in contact with Europeans—that had a profound influence on the developing of the Atlantic slave system. In particular, in the different plantation areas of the Americas, African slaves brought with them their invaluable knowledge of plant cultivation—most notably in the case of rice—and, in the process, gave a crucial contribution to the making of New World slave economies and societies.[13]

By the seventeenth century, a fully developed Atlantic slave system had come into being. Broad comparative studies by Immanuel Wallerstein and Eric Wolf have shown how the Atlantic slave system was a central feature of a European-dominated world economy, which, from the very beginning of the early modern era, took advantage of peripheries such as the American colonies—and equally so of eastern and southern Europe, Africa, and Asia—by imposing upon them highly exploitative labor systems for the production of different types of raw materials. In eastern Europe, the dominant crop was grain, while in the Americas, by the seventeenth century, the mechanisms of the European-dominated world market led to a spectacular rise in the importance of sugar, which, until the beginning of the nineteenth century, continued to be the main product of a number of European colonies in the Americas. Both implicit, or "soft," comparative studies, such as Stuart Schwartz's work on early modern Brazil—and also broader, explicit, comparisons by Sidney Mintz—have shown how the truly epochal and novel feature for

the future of the Atlantic slave system was the Portuguese focus on sugar plantations. Adapting techniques already employed by Genoese merchants in the medieval Mediterranean, the Portuguese made heavy use of African slaves in
northeastern Brazil beginning in the 1580s. Also crucial was the later adoption of
sugar plantation and African slavery first by the Dutch, and then by the English—
as shown in Richard Dunn's work—and by the French. Mainly thanks to sugar,
already by the seventeenth century, the Atlantic slave system included several fully
developed "slave societies"—meaning societies in which slavery was at the center of
the economic and social life—mirroring the unfree labor system that had sprung
up everywhere in eastern Europe with the rise of the "second serfdom."[14]

Comparative history has shown clearly how every crop produced in other
regions of the Americas—including Virginian tobacco and South Carolinian
rice—was of secondary importance compared to Brazilian and Caribbean sugar.
Thus, in comparative perspective, the British colonies in North America were at the
periphery of the Atlantic slave system, and yet they were very much part of the
larger British Atlantic network, given the ties between the master classes, and, even
more importantly, their extended commercial exchanges. Atlantic historians such
as Bernard Baylin and Philip Morgan, Nicholas Canny, David Armitage and
Lawrence Braddick, and Kenneth Morgan, by focusing on the early modern British
empire, have done much to help us understand the main features of a shared
northern European culture among the master classes of the different British slave
colonies—a culture within which aggressive Protestantism, obsession with racial
purity and superiority, and mostly unrestrained merchant capitalism all went hand
in hand. At the same time, Latin American historians such as Rafael Marquese and
Michael Zeuske have written important comparative syntheses that have highlighted, together with the similarities and differences, also the many connections
between that culture and the one shared by the Caribbean and Latin American
masters of slave societies that had been established by non-English-speaking
Europeans.[15]

To date, there is still no study that compares systematically the ideologies of all
the different master classes in the Atlantic slave system during the colonial period.
Such a study would be welcome since a sustained comparative examination of the
links between the ideologies and the different European backgrounds of the various
master classes in the New World would help us explain better David Brion Davis's
assertion, shared by many scholars, that "in Brazil . . . the wealthiest [sugar] mill
owners at least posed as patriarchs and community leaders, even though they too
desired to make profit," while British Caribbean planters—seemingly closer to
North American planters—ran a sugar plantation as a "capitalistic enterprise,
not a quasi-seigneurial community with religious and social services that stimulated a surrounding economy," but rather "always on the lookout for cost-saving
devices."[16] While Robin Blackburn's important analysis of comparative links
between the colonial Americas' master classes and their European antecedents in

many ways reinforces Davis's argument regarding British planters, Rafael Marquese's study, instead, provides an important corrective by showing in comparative perspective the presence of shared elements of modernity—specifically the later spread of pamphlets and treatises that advocated reforms of both land and slave management aimed at the goal of rationalization of production—among the slave societies of, equally, North America, the Caribbean, and Latin America. The time is ripe for a wider and systematic comparative work on the New World master classes and their European antecedents, perhaps in the vein of the still pathbreaking, if highly questioned, work by Genovese.[17]

It is important to remember that both broader and more specific comparative studies—especially those by Wallerstein, Kolchin, and Bush—have done much to show us in detail how the rise of New World slavery was contemporaneous to the rise of the "second serfdom" in early modern eastern Europe. Grain became the main staple crop produced by Polish, Hungarian, and Russian masters all over eastern Europe at the same time—the late 1500s—when the Portuguese were making their early experiments in sugar production and African slavery. Both the Atlantic slave system and the eastern European serf system were systems of unfree labor that centered upon production of crops in large landed estates, the plantations and the *latifundia*.[18] In both systems, powerful landed elites ran large-scale agricultural enterprises, either partly or mostly oriented toward a world market. Thus, by some accounts, the origins of the "modern" features of New World slavery ultimately relate to epochal changes that, through the rise of an integrated capitalist world market, led either to the creation, or to the reappearance, of more or less "modern" systems of unfree labor. And, even though historians such as Seymour Drescher have proven little direct connection between the profits from the Atlantic slave trade or the plantation system and the capital that financed the Industrial Revolution (contrary to Eric Williams), a systematic comparative analysis of the rise of systems of unfree labor in the Americas and in eastern Europe in the early modern era would help us understand better also the deeper, global, implications of the making of free and nominally "free" wage labor systems in the West.

THE EURO-AMERICAN WORLD IN THE AGE OF ATLANTIC REVOLUTIONS

Ever since the publication of the now classic studies by David Brion Davis and Eugene Genovese on slavery in the Age of Revolutions, historians of slavery have been thinking comparatively about the Atlantic world in the period 1770–1820, focusing on the links between the Americas and Europe, and on the crucial influence that changes in the latter had on the transformations of the New World slave system as a whole. Though historians still debate the exact nature and origins of Atlantic antislavery, it is now commonplace to think of a Euro-American Enlightenment, of a common Atlantic capitalist doctrine focused on wage—as opposed to slave—labor, and of an equally widespread Quaker and Protestant radicalism as the fundamental ingredients that led to the rise of Anglo-American abolitionism in the Age of Revolutions. At the same time, studies such as Robin Blackburn's *The Overthrow of Colonial Slavery* have shown that it is impossible to understand the true significance of the end of colonial slave systems in the Americas without making constant reference to the economic, political, and social situation in revolutionary and Napoleonic Europe. As a consequence, slavery scholars now see the American Revolution, the French Revolution, and the Haitian Revolution—and their aftermaths—as stages in a massive and interlinked series of upheavals that led to a crisis and then to a readjustment of the New World slave system within an Atlantic context properly understood as essential to a full, textured understanding of the problems of slavery and freedom.[19]

By definition, studies that look at changes in both the Americas and Europe, and at links connecting the former to the latter, are comparative. And yet the fundamental idea at the heart of virtually every work on Atlantic slavery in the Age of Revolutions is that it is particularly important to study changes in Europe, but almost exclusively for the purpose of understanding better the background to the transformations of New World slavery. A more correct approach—close to Christopher Bayly's recent global view of "the birth of the modern world"—would, instead, look at the Americas and Europe in the Age of Revolutions as equally important in a comparative study that would reveal as much about the readjustment of the Atlantic slave system as it would about the establishment of different forms of wage labor—free and unfree.[20] In the mid-eighteenth century, for example, feudalism was widespread in most of Europe, even though its exact features varied from region to region. In areas such as central-eastern Europe, beginning from Austria and Prussia, the status of serf associated to the feudal system was more legally binding and imposed more corvées, while in most of continental western Europe, beginning from France and Italy, the strictest features of feudalism had disappeared, but feudal privileges still weighed heavily on nominally "free" peasants. Still, everywhere in Europe the feudal system was identified with the landed elites' economic and social rule of the countryside, much like the slave system was in the Americas. In order to truly understand the significance of the Age of Revolutions in comparative perspective, it is imperative to recognize that the momentous changes and massive upheavals that led to the transformation and readjustment of the Atlantic slave system in the New World also led to the end of feudalism and its transformation into either free or nominally "free" wage labor in vast areas of the Old World.[21]

To be sure, comparison between the agrarian sectors and labor forces of the American and European economies in the second half of the eighteenth century shows that the main difference between the two regions was that, while in the Americas slavery was prospering as an enterprise with a number of strong capitalist features and as a major factor in the world market, in Europe feudalism had evolved into a parasitic, *rentier*, system which prevented capitalist development. Yet, on both sides of the Atlantic, classical political economists put forward comparable arguments against slavery and feudalism, claiming that, by preventing the formation of either a free labor market or a free land market, the two systems violated the fundamental laws of capitalist development. But while the European feudal system in itself had, without any doubt, very little to do with agrarian capitalism, the Atlantic slave system was very much part of the capitalist world, even though it still retained some precapitalist traits. It is clear, thus, that, economically, it made much sense for the elites of continental western Europe—particularly the rising bourgeois elites with little attachment to the Old Order—to do away with feudalism altogether. Very different was, instead, the situation of the New World elites in regard to slavery, and thus we can say with David Richardson that "factors other than economic ones [meaning moral and political] primarily seem to have determined the shift from enslaved to less coerced forms of labor in the Atlantic world in the century after 1790."[22]

Comparison between the mind of New World slaveholders and the mind of Old World landowners in the second half of the eighteenth century shows that a similar culture of reform—prompted by Enlightenment thought, religious revival, and fear of radicalism—informed the actions of a number of them in regard to management of land and workforce. More efficient systems of production, sometimes accompanied by more contractual forms of rule, based less on simply brutal force, were becoming increasingly popular as the Age of Revolutions began on both sides of the Euro-American world. But, if, as in western Europe, this culture of reform was typical of those agrarian elites who wished to do away with feudalism to create an agrarian economy fully inserted in the mechanisms of the market, in the New World a similar culture of reform was common among slaveholders who wished to ameliorate slavery, by making it an even more efficient and profitable system, but maintaining, at the same time, an ambiguous relationship vis-à-vis their full involvement in capitalist economic and social relations. For this reason, many slaveholders turned to the employment, in different degrees, of more paternalistic forms of rule over their enslaved workforce—forms of rule through which they could, at the same time, obtain higher profits and keep a low level of social conflict, tying even more tightly their crop production to the world market while not changing the fundamental features of their unfree labor system. In both cases, though, the political upheavals of the Age of Revolutions would give a crucial contribution to the elimination of the most outdated features of both feudalism and slavery, while the mechanisms of the world market would ensure that, by the end of that Age, in the early decades of the nineteenth century, European agrarian elites and New World slaveholding elites would be in command of renewed and even more powerful systems of exploitation.

Yet, even though, generally speaking, Euro-American slaveholders and land-owners showed a remarkable ability to continue to wield power even in the face of momentous upheavals, historical comparison highlights the fact that New World slaves and European peasants played a very important role, especially because, through their agency, they contributed significantly in unnerving and disrupting the orderly and organic societies so cherished by masters of unfree labor. Peasant and slave resistance and revolts were common throughout the Euro-American world in the eighteenth century. Resistance, of course, could take many forms both among slaves and among peasants; a lot of it was individually based and it depended on the place, the system of labor, and the opportunities. Revolts, instead, would often lead to massive upheavals and temporary freedom through conflict—as in the case of the 1770s serf rebellion led by Pugachev in Russia, or in the case of the eighteenth-century slave revolts in Jamaica and in Brazil, which gave origin to large maroon communities. All these, however, pale in comparison with the revolution that transformed the French colony of St. Domingue into the free black nation of Haiti between 1791 and 1804. Very fittingly, the Haitian Revolution is now at the very center of a recent wave of Atlantic scholarship—whose best representative is, perhaps, David Geggus—that looks more deeply at ties between the Old and the New Worlds in the Age of Revolutions.[23]

The significance of the Haitian experience for the comparative study of slavery in the Americas is fairly obvious, starting from the fact that it was the only slave revolt that established a permanent legacy in the New World, and in world history in general. Yet, in a comparative perspective which includes Europe, the significance of the Haitian Revolution appears even more striking, since, except for the two years of Jacobin Terror in 1793–5, France, and more generally Europe, was not to live through a radical experience of a comparable level until the 1871 Paris Commune. Even so, both these events ended quickly, so that there truly was no comparable experience to the Haitian Revolution anywhere and at any point in time in the eighteenth- and nineteenth-century Euro-American world. In fact, from C. L. R. James on, historians have analyzed events in Haiti looking not just at the influence that the different phases of the French Revolution had on them, but also at the crucial role that Toussaint L'Overture and the self-liberated Haitian slaves who became "Black Jacobins" had in preserving the most radical French revolutionary principles at a time in which France—and with it the whole of Europe—turned back to conservatism. Thus, this is perhaps the best example of how the comparative perspective helps us appreciate that—in the words of Christopher Bayly—"the European [revolutionary] crisis was not simply passively received by the rest of the world, but 'bounced back' to Europe, where it created further waves of change" within a context that is crucial for our understanding of the transformations New World slavery and Old World feudalism underwent in the Age of Revolutions.[24]

SLAVERY, FREE AND UNFREE LABOR, AND MODERNITY IN THE AMERICAS AND EUROPE

Comparatively speaking, by the 1820s, the Americas and Europe appeared transformed in almost every respect economically and socially. The political upheavals brought by the Age of Revolutions had led to the destruction of a number of old agrarian regimes, while the mechanisms of the world market had led to the rise of new ones. In the Atlantic slave system, a process that had started with the abolition of the slave trade first by Britain (1807) and then by the newly formed United States (1808) reached its peak with the emancipation of slaves in the British colonies in 1833 and in the French colonies in 1848. In Europe, the Napoleonic regime had abolished feudalism in most of the western part of the continent, and in 1848 the legal termination of serfdom reached Prussia and the Habsburg lands. Seen from a comparative perspective—as in Michael Bush's *Servitude in Modern Times*—the Euro-American world at mid-century appeared as a place where freedom was rapidly advancing and was increasingly cornering unfree agrarian labor from every direction. Nonetheless, those places where slave societies continued to flourish in the Americas—the US South, Cuba, and Brazil—and also several places where serf societies disappeared at a later time—notably East Elbia and Hungary—were hardly on the verge of social and economic collapse. Also, the abolition of feudalism and serfdom in areas such as southern Europe, much like the abolition of slavery in the British colonies, had led to the employment of systems of only nominally free wage labor in which emancipated agrarian workers were exploited in some cases to an even greater extent than before.[25]

The nineteenth century saw the peak of the Industrial Revolution led by Britain as the hegemonic world economic power. The demand for new types of raw materials prompted by the Industrial Revolution had comparable effects in the Americas and Europe, and, naturally, both on New World slave and post-slave societies and on European serf and post-feudal societies. Such effects included, in particular, both a movement toward centralization of production around large landed estates and an increase in the level of economic exploitation of agrarian workers, free and unfree, for the purpose of boosting the production of particular items. Thus, in the Atlantic slave system, the nineteenth century—the time that saw the rise of the "second slavery," according to Dale Tomich—became the golden age of cotton production for most of the US South, of sugar for Cuba and Louisiana, and of coffee for Brazil. On the other hand, in the European feudal and post-feudal system, grain production reached very high levels in several eastern European areas, including Prussia and Russia, and partly in southern European regions, such as Italy's south, or *Mezzogiorno*, and Spain's Andalusia. While general works, particularly by Immanuel Wallerstein, Eric Wolf, and Christopher Bayly, have looked at the global context in which these changes have occurred, a few more specific and explicit comparisons between case studies situated in the New and Old Worlds have done much to clarify how these same changes affected areas as diverse as elite ideology, work management, and workers' lives.[26]

Several comparative studies focusing on the ideology of the planter elites in the most profitable slave societies of the nineteenth-century Americas have shown that, from the early 1800s onwards, slaveholders—particularly in the US South, Cuba, and Brazil—sought different ways to improve the productivity of their plantations. As Michael Zeuske has convincingly argued, through "cultural transfers" the New World planter elites learned of particular techniques already successfully tested either in other plantation areas of the Americas or on landed estates in Europe. At the same time—as Rafael Marquese has shown—a plethora of treatises, pamphlets, journals, and other publications often sponsored or actually published by either regional or agrarian institutions, or else written by well-known agricultural reformers, played a very important part in the making of an innovative and forward-looking attitude among the American, Cuban, and Brazilian slaveholding elites. Historians are still debating whether they can consider this innovative attitude in agriculture truly "modern." The crux of the matter here is the fact that the slaveholders' "modern" position vis-à-vis improvement in plantation agriculture—a position which, in the case of the Old South, for Genovese's followers did not affect the paternalistic character of the master–slave relationship, while for neoclassical economic historians was part of a general capitalistic ethos—led to those same slaveholders' reactionary defense of the superiority of the slave system as a whole over systems of free labor. In this sense, the comparative perspective with the post-feudal agrarian regions of Europe can help us by alerting us to the fact that the "modern" concept of agricultural reform was very much widespread in those areas where the landowning elites were more involved in the world market, similarly to the slaveholding elites of the Americas, through their production of particular crops, but were also fiercely committed, despite their "paternalistic" ideas, to keeping the status quo in their relations with the nominally free peasants. As Marta Petrusewicz has shown, in nineteenth-century agrarian Europe, thanks to a very active public opinion and to outstanding figures of agricultural reformers and political economists, agronomy—the "modern" science of improving agricultural performance—was extremely popular among more economically than socially progressive landowners of several regions.[27]

678 ENRICO DAL LAGO

Whether we wish to consider this agronomic culture that characterized the most active and successful slaveholding elites in the Americas and also landowning elites in Europe as a sign of "modernity" or not, the undeniable truth is that the ultimate reason for agricultural improvement in many peripheral areas of the nineteenth-century world economy had much to do with a chain of changes that had spread through the world market as a whole as a result of the Industrial Revolution. The effects of these changes showed particularly clearly in the area of work management, both unfree and free. In the US South, Cuba, and Brazil, the same pamphlets and publications that advised planters on scientific improvements in order to increase productivity also included very detailed instructions on the most efficient way of managing slaves. Though the actual labor system employed depended very much on variables such as the crop, the region, and the individual master, in most of the Americas, and especially on cotton, sugar, and coffee plantations, management was based largely on a system of gang labor. Under the "gang system," slaves were divided, often on the basis of differences in age, sex, or skill, in strictly regimented groups closely supervised by the planter or by an overseer, and sometimes also by a black driver. Instead, particularly—though far from exclusively—on rice plantations, slaves worked under the "task system" by being assigned individually specific tasks to be completed by the end of day. In both cases, it was then up to the individual planter how to effectively manage the workforce in such a way that he was able to obtain the highest productivity with the lowest amount of conflict, and it was then that pamphlets and discussions on agricultural journals would come in, by showing planters the importance of employing a generally paternalistic work ethic with a system of punishments and rewards.[28]

It is a very difficult task to compare explicitly—being fully aware of the enormous differences between them—slave management in the nineteenth-century Americas with post-feudal or even serf management in nineteenth-century Europe, let alone with industrial work management. And yet, comparison can still offer us important insights—especially on the Industrial Revolution's effects on peripheral agrarian areas of the world economy—if we think, for example, of how Mark Smith has been able to demonstrate that the US planters' imposition of strict time schedules over their enslaved workforce was part of a general attempt by the capitalist master classes, including British industrialists, to instill a "clock consciousness" in their workers, whether these were free or unfree. In fact, the comparison could easily extend, with the proper recognition of important differences, to the coffee and sugar plantations areas of Brazil and Cuba in the Americas, and also to several particularly productive agricultural areas of southern and eastern Europe. And to be sure, specific comparative studies between the nineteenth-century US South—often taken as a paradigm, according to Peter Kolchin, for New World slave systems, and even for slavery as a whole—and eastern Europe and southern Italy have, then, widened the contours of the debate over the capitalist vs. non-capitalist character of American planters. These studies have, in fact, tended to take position in the debate by claiming the existence of similarities, amidst significant differences, in the mind and behavior of American planters and either paternalist Russian masters, or capitalist Prussian Junkers, or both paternalist and capitalist southern Italian landowners.[29]

It is, then, an even more difficult task to compare fruitfully the lives and conditions of slaves in the Americas with the lives and conditions of eastern European serfs; even more so in the case of free agrarian laborers, as in southern Europe.[30] Yet, once again, comparison can focus on particular issues in the workers' lives and enlighten us with possible explanations of the inevitable differences discovered between the two case studies. Thus, for example, Peter Kolchin's model comparative study of American slavery and Russian serfdom has been critically important for the appreciation of the mechanisms of both slave resistance and serf resistance and for enhancing our understanding of the characteristics assumed by the slave community and by the serf community. In his now famous thesis, Kolchin argued that, compared to Russian masters, who were few and with large numbers of serfs—whom mostly they did not know—most American masters tended to own fewer slaves and to live in close contact with them. Then, following Eugene Genovese's idea of paternalism and demonstrating how it was possible to test it through comparative history, Kolchin showed that the American masters' paternalistic influence on their slaves' lives was much greater than the Russian masters'. On one hand, American slaves could at least partly benefit from their master's interest in them, while, on the other hand, Russian serfs were able to create much more autonomous forms of serf communities, quite unlike the slave communities in the US South. Even though today the concept of slave community is undergoing intense scrutiny, it would be helpful to see more comparative studies that focus on specific issues related to the lives of unfree, and also nominally free, workers in the Americas and Europe in comparative perspective along the path open by Kolchin.[31]

Among the most important subjects to investigate in comparative perspective, the workers' families would certainly assume a primary importance. In this respect, particularly promising for the future of comparative slavery in the Americas is the current focus of several scholars on possible explicit comparisons between American and African slaves. Important edited collections by Gaspar and Hine, and by Campbell, Miers, and Miller, together with equally significant monographs by Midlo Hall and by Heywood and Thornton, have opened the way in showing us how comparisons focusing on the lives and marriage habits of enslaved women throughout the Atlantic slave system cannot be fully comprehended without making reference to, and ideally making comparison with, the broadly constituted "African" background. More recently, Dylan Penningroth has started an important project that expands on his former study of slaves' claims to family and property and focuses on a helpful and still little practiced type of explicit comparison between the US South and the Gold Coast of Africa. The hope is that scholars will turn their attention also to other types of equally challenging comparisons, such as between New World slaves and eastern European serfs, or even between New World slaves and post-feudal western European peasants, given that a true understanding of the meaning of New World slavery in comparative perspective—and more generally of free and unfree labor in the Euro-American world—can only come from an increase in the number and scope of explicit comparative studies.[32]

Notes

1. Marc Bloch, "Pour une histoire comparée des sociétés européennes," *Revue de synthèse historique*, 46 (1928): 15–50; Theda Skocpol and Margaret Somers, "The Use of Comparative History in Macro-Social Enquiry," *Comparative Studies in Society and History*, 22 (1980): 174–97.

2. Peter Kolchin, *A Sphinx on the American Land: The Nineteenth-Century South in Comparative Perspective* (Baton Rouge, La., 2003).

3. Frank Tannenbaum, *Slave and Citizen* (New York, 1946); Stanley Elkins, *Slavery: A Problem in American Institutional and Intellectual Life* (Chicago, 1959).

4. Herbert Klein, *Slavery in the Americas: A Comparative Study of Virginia and Cuba* (Chicago, 1967); Carl Degler, *Neither Black Nor White: Slavery and Race Relations in the U.S. and Brazil* (New York, 1971); Eugene Genovese, *The World the Slaveholders Made: Two Essays in Interpretation* (New York, 1968).

5. Gwendolyn Midlo Hall, *Social Control in Slave Plantation Societies: A Comparison of Saint Domingue and Cuba* (Baltimore, 1971); Gilberto Freyre, *The Masters and the Slaves* (New York, 1956); C. L. R. James, *The Black Jacobins* (New York, 1938); Eric Williams, *Capitalism and Slavery* (London, 1944); Eugene Genovese, *From Rebellion to Revolution: Afro-American Slave Revolts in the Making of the Modern World* (Baton Rouge, La., 1979); Laura Foner and Eugene Genovese (eds.), *Slavery in the New World: A Reader in Comparative History* (New York, 1969); David Brion Davis, *The Problem of Slavery in Western Culture* (New York, 1966); David Brion Davis, *The Problem of Slavery in the Age of Revolutions, 1770–1825* (Ithaca, NY, 1975).

6. Philip Curtin, *The Atlantic Slave Trade: A Census* (Madison, 1969); Herbert Klein, *The Middle Passage: Comparative Studies in the Atlantic Slave Trade* (Princeton, 1978).

7. Philip Curtin, *The Rise and Fall of the Plantation Complex: Essays in Atlantic History* (New York, 1990); Robin Blackburn, *The Making of New World Slavery, 1492–1800: From the Baroque to the Modern* (London, 1997); Seymour Drescher, *From Slavery to Freedom: Comparative Studies in the Rise and Fall of Atlantic Slavery* (New York, 1999); David Brion Davis, *Inhuman Bondage: The Rise and Fall of Slavery in the New World* (New York, 2006).

8. Ira Berlin and Philip Morgan (eds.), *Cultivation and Culture: Labor and the Shaping of Slave Life in the Americas* (Charlottesville, Va., 1993); Rafael de Bivar Marquese, *Feitores do corpo, missionarios da mente: senhores, letrados e o controle dos escravos nas Americas, 1660–1860* (São Paulo, 2004); Laird Bergad, *The Comparative Histories of Slavery in Cuba, Brazil, and the United States* (New York, 2007); James Walvin, *Questioning Slavery* (London, 1996); Herbert Klein and Ben Vinson, *African Slavery in Latin America and the Caribbean* (New York, 2007).

9. Barbara Solow (ed.), *Slavery and the Rise of the Atlantic System* (New York, 1993); Joseph Inikori and Stanley Engerman (eds.), *The Atlantic Slave Trade: Effects on Economies, Societies, and Peoples in Africa, the Americas, and Europe* (Durham, NC, 1992); Stuart Schwartz (ed.), *Tropical Babylons: Sugar and the Making of the Atlantic World* (Chapel Hill, NC, 2003); David Barry Caspar and Darlen Clark Hine (eds.), *More than Chattel: Black Women and Slavery in the Americas* (Bloomington, Ind., 1996); Gwyn Campbell, Suzanne Miers, and Joseph Miller (eds.), *Women and Slavery, II: The Modern Atlantic* (Athens, Ga., 2007); Paul Gilroy, *The Black Atlantic: Modernity and Double Consciousness* (London, 1993); John Thornton, *Africa and Africans in the Making of the Atlantic World, 1440–1800* (New York, 1998); Stephanie Smallwood, *Saltwater Slavery: A Middle Passage from Africa to American Diaspora* (Cambridge, Mass., 2007); Gwendolyn Midlo Hall, *Slavery and African Ethnicities in the Americas: Restoring the Links* (Chapel Hill, NC, 2007).

10. George Fredrickson, *White Supremacy: A Comparative Study of South Africa and the U.S.* (New York, 1981); Peter Kolchin, *Unfree Labor: American Slavery and Russian Serfdom* (Cambridge, Mass., 1987); Shearer Davis Bowman, *Masters and Lords: Mid-Nineteenth Century U.S. Planters and Prussian Junkers* (New York, 1993); Enrico Dal Lago, *Agrarian Elites: American Slaveholders and Southern Italian Landowners, 1815–1861* (Baton Rouge, La., 2005); Michael Bush, *Servitude in the Modern World* (Cambridge, 2000); Dale Tomich, *Through the Prism of Slavery: Labor, Capital, and World Economy* (Lanham, Md., 2004).

11. William Phillips, *Slavery from Roman Times to the Early Transatlantic Trade* (New York, 1985).

12. Bush, *Servitude*, 69.

13. David Eltis, *The Rise of African Slavery in the Americas* (New York, 1999); Smallwood, *Saltwater Slavery*; Midlo Hall, *Slavery and African Ethnicities*; Thornton, *Africa and Africans*; Linda Heywood and John Thornton, *Central Africans, Atlantic Creoles, and the Foundations of the Americas* (New York, 2007). On rice, see David Eltis, Philip Morgan, and David Richardson, "Agency and Diaspora in Atlantic History: Reassessing the African Contribution to Rice Cultivation in the Americas," *American Historical Review*, 112 (5) (December 2007): 1329–58.

14. Immanuel Wallerstein, *The Modern World-System* (New York, 1974–89); Eric Wolf, *Europe and the People without History* (Berkeley, 1982); Stuart Schwartz, *Sugar and the Rise of Plantation Society in Brazil, 1550–1825* (New York, 1985); Sidney Mintz, *Sweetness and Power: The Place of Sugar in Modern History* (London, 1985); Richard Dunn, *Sugar and Slavery: The Rise of the Planter Class in the British West Indies* (New York, 1972).

15. Bernard Bailyn and Philip Morgan (eds,), *Strangers within the Realm: Cultural Margins in the First British Empire* (Chapel Hill, NC, 1991); Nicholas Canny (ed.), *The Origins of Empire: British Overseas Enterprise to the Close of the Seventeenth Century* (Oxford, 1998); David Armitage and Michael Braddick (eds.), *The British Atlantic World, 1500–1800* (New York, 2002); Kenneth Morgan, *Slavery and the British Empire: From Africa to America* (Oxford, 2007); Marquese, *Feitores do corpo*; Michael Zeuske, "Comparing or Interlinking? Economic Comparisons of the Early Nineteenth-Century Slave Systems in the Americas in Historical Perspective," in Enrico Dal Lago and Constantina Katsari (eds.), *Slave Systems: Ancient and Modern* (Cambridge, 2008), 148–83.

16. Davis, *Inhuman Bondage*, 116.

17. Blackburn, *Making of New World Slavery*; Marquese, *Feitores do corpo*.

18. See Witold Kula, *An Economic Study of the Feudal System* (London, 1976).

19. Davis, *Age of Revolutions*; Genovese, *From Rebellion to Revolution*; Robin Blackburn, *The Overthrow of Colonial Slavery, 1776–1848* (London, 1988).

20. See C. A. Bayly, *The Birth of the Modern World, 1780–1914* (Oxford, 2004).

21. On these issues, see Paul Lovejoy and Nicholas Rogers (eds.), *Unfree Labor in the Development of the Atlantic World* (London, 1994).

22. David Richardson, "Agency, Ideology, and Violence in the History of Transatlantic Slavery," *Historical Journal*, 50 (4) (2007): 973. See also Bush, *Servitude*; and Jerome Blum, *The End of the Old Order in Rural Europe* (Princeton, 1978).

23. See Bush, *Servitude*; and David P. Geggus (ed.), *The Impact of the Haitian Revolution in the Atlantic World* (Columbia, SC, 2001). Compared to Jamaica and Brazil, the American South seems to have witnessed a surprisingly small number of revolts, only two of which—the Stono Rebellion in South Carolina in 1739 and Nat Turner's rebellion in Virginia in 1831—went well beyond the stage of conspiracies and led to the killing of substantial numbers of whites. There is currently a debate in course on the reasons for the scarcity of slave rebellions in the American South; it is worth remembering, though, that, unlike in the Caribbean and Brazil, in most areas of the South whites were the majority, while blacks were fewer and scattered. Also—as Olivier Pétré-Grenouilleau has recently argued—when seen in comparative perspective, day-to-day resistance and especially running away, both ubiquitous in the American South, were just as effective as the most spectacular acts of slave rebellion in harming the productivity, and therefore contributing to a long-term disruption of the slave system as a whole; see Olivier Pétré-Grenouilleau, "Processes of Exiting the Slave Systems: A Typology," in Dal Lago and Katsari (eds.), *Slave Systems*, 233–64.

24. Bayly, *Modern World*, 99. See also James, *Black Jacobins*; Blackburn, *Overthrow of Colonial Slavery*; and Laurent Dubois, *Avengers of the New World: The Story of the Haitian Revolution* (Cambridge, Mass., 2004).

25. See Bush, *Servitude*; Blackburn, *Overthrow of Colonial Slavery*; and Michael Bush (ed.), *Serfdom and Slavery: Studies in Legal Bondage* (London, 1996).

26. See Tomich, *Through the Prism of Slavery*; Wallerstein, *Modern World-System*; Wolf, *Europe*; and Bayly, *Modern World*.

27. See Zeuske, "Comparing or Interlinking?"; Marquese, *Feitores do corpo*; Mark Smith, *Debating Slavery: Economy and Society in the Antebellum South* (New York, 1998); and Marta Petrusewicz, "Agromania: innovatori agrari nelle periferie europee dell'Ottocento," in Piero Bevilacqua (ed.), *Storia dell'agricoltura italiana in età contemporanea*, III: *Mercati e istituzioni* (Venice, 1991), 295–343.

28. See Berlin and Morgan, *Cultivation and Culture*; and Bergad, *Comparative Histories*.

29. See Mark Smith, "Old South Time in Comparative Perspective," *American Historical Review*, 101 (1996): 1432–69; Kolchin, *Sphinx*; Kolchin, *Unfree Labor*; Bowman, *Masters and Lords*; Dal Lago, *Agrarian Elites*.

30. The historians' difficulty in comparing New World slaves and Old World laborers appears even more striking when one thinks that—even though for the purpose of propaganda—southern proslavery ideologues such as George Fitzhugh were very apt at making complex comparisons of that sort; see Genovese's classic analysis in *The World the Slaveholders Made*.

31. See Kolchin, *Unfree Labor*. Excellent general comparative studies include Bush, *Servitude*; and Wolf, *Europe*.

32. See Caspar and Hine (eds.), *More than Chattel*; Campbell, Miers, and Miller (eds.), *Women and Slavery*; Midlo Hall, *African Ethnicities*; Heywood and Thornton, *Central Africans*; and Dylan Penningroth, "The Claims of Slaves and Ex-Slaves to Famly and Property: A Transatlantic Comparison," *American Historical Review*, 112 (4) (2007): 1039–69.

SELECT BIBLIOGRAPHY

BAYLY, C.A. *The Birth of the Modern World, 1780–1914.* Oxford: Blackwell, 2004.

BERGAD, LAIRD. *The Comparative Histories of Slavery in Cuba, Brazil, and the United States.* New York: Cambridge University Press, 2007.

BLACKBURN, ROBIN. *The Making of New World Slavery, 1492–1800: From the Baroque to the Modern.* London: Verso, 1997.

——*The Overthrow of Colonial Slavery, 1776–1848.* London: Verso, 1988.

BOWMAN, SHEARER DAVIS. *Masters and Lords: Mid-Nineteenth Century U.S. Planters and Prussian Junkers.* New York: Oxford University Press, 1993.

BUSH, MICHAEL. *Servitude in Modern Times.* Cambridge: Polity, 2000.

CASPAR, DAVID BARRY, and DARLEN CLARK HINE, eds. *More than Chattel: Black Women and Slavery in the Americas.* Bloomington, Ind.: Indiana University Press, 1996.

CURTIN, PHILIP. *The Rise and Fall of the Plantation Complex: Essays in Atlantic History.* New York: Cambridge University Press, 1990.

DAL LAGO, ENRICO. *Agrarian Elites: American Slaveholders and Southern Italian Land-owners, 1815–1861.* Baton Rouge, La.: Louisiana State University Press, 2005.

DAVIS, DAVID BRION. *The Problem of Slavery in Western Culture.* New York: Oxford University Press, 1966.

——*The Problem of Slavery in the Age of Revolutions, 1770–1823.* Ithaca, NY: Cornell University Press, 1975.

——*Inhuman Bondage: The Rise and Fall of Slavery in the New World.* New York: Oxford University Press, 2006.

DEGLER, CARL. *Neither Black Nor White: Slavery and Race Relations in the U.S. and Brazil.* New York: University of Wisconsin Press, 1971.

DRESCHER, SEYMOUR. *From Slavery to Freedom: Comparative Studies in the Rise and Fall of Atlantic Slavery.* New York: New York University Press, 1999.

ELTIS, DAVID. *The Rise of African Slavery in the Americas.* New York: Cambridge University Press, 1999.

GENOVESE, EUGENE. *The World the Slaveholders Made: Two Essays in Interpretation.* New York: Pantheon, 1968.

——*From Rebellion to Revolution: Afro-American Slave Revolts in the Making of the Modern World*, Baton Rouge, La.: Louisiana State University Press, 1979.

HEYWOOD, LYNDA, and JOHN THORNTON. *Central Africans, Atlantic Creoles, and the Foundations of the Americas.* New York: Cambridge University Press, 2007.

KLEIN, HERBERT. *The Atlantic Slave Trade.* New York: Cambridge University Press, 1999.

KOLCHIN, PETER. *Unfree Labor: American Slavery and Russian Serfdom.* Cambridge, Mass.: Harvard University Press, 1987.

KOLCHIN, PETER. *A Sphinx on the American Land: The Nineteenth-Century South in Comparative Perspective.* Baton Rouge, La.: Louisiana State University Press, 2003.

MARQUESE, RAFAEL DE BIVAR. *Feitores do corpo, missionarios da mente: senhores, letrados e o controle dos escravos nas Americas, 1660–1860.* São Paulo: Editora Companhia das Letras, 2004.

TOMICH, DALE. *Through the Prism of Slavery: Labor, Capital, and World Economy.* Lanham, Md.: Rowman and Littlefield, 2004.

WALLERSTEIN, IMMANUEL. *The Modern World-System.* 3 vols. New York: Academic Press, 1974–89.

WALVIN, JAMES. *Questioning Slavery.* London: Routledge, 1996.

CHAPTER 31

FINDING SLAVE VOICES

KATHLEEN HILLIARD

JOE, Sam, Henry, and Leah must have been nervous as they entered Reid & Simpson's store in May 1851. They were likely familiar with the local institution, as it was one of the few dry goods suppliers in their small community of Anderson Courthouse, South Carolina. Sundries and sweets, tools and tobacco, bolts of cloth and bottles of apothecaries surely lined the walls, tempting them. What had brought them to this place on the fifth day of May 1851? Unlike many of the store's regular customers, the three men and one woman appeared not before clerks but before magistrates. They came not by choice but under guard. They faced not a world of material possibility but the threat of the lash. It was court day in Anderson and Joe and Henry were on trial. By day's end, the threat became reality for them both—convicted of simple larceny, each received "fifty lashes on the bare back with a hickory well laid on."

Much of what we know of that day and the week preceding comes from the records of the trial. J. H. Reid had lost some turkeys a few nights before—the very same fowl, he claimed in an indictment, found in Henry's possession. The voices of four slaves told the story, though not under the white man's oath. As bondspeople, they could not be sworn, yet it was their testimony that ultimately brought down punishment.

In the ongoing search for slave voices, the records of the Court of Magistrates and Freeholders—the body that tried slaves and free blacks in antebellum South Carolina—have provided a promising yet problematic peek into the everyday life and culture of the enslaved. Historians who have searched the hundreds of pages of

indictments, presentments, verdicts, and witness testimony have been richly rewarded. At over 500 cases, the body of records from Anderson and Spartanburg
districts has presented exciting opportunities for explorations of family life, the
master–slave relation, and, notably, economic activity. Slave voices call from
virtually every page—pleading their innocence, defending their brethren, and
indicting their neighbors.[1]

But as eager as historians have been to listen to these voices, they know well to
approach the records from the South Carolina courts with an abundance of
caution. The statements that emerge from the pages of trial documents were not
recorded verbatim. Slaves' words were mediated by a clerk who summarized their
testimony, quoting directly only those statements he found most significant. This
clerk was white, as were all those who stood in judgment of the indicted. The whip
awaited not only those found guilty, but also those who might have displeased their
masters with the words they chose. Judgment, too, was cast by their peers. Loyalty
and self-interest, friendship and jealousy, generosity and greed lay behind pages of
conflicting testimony.

A number of questions, then, face the careful researcher. Are the voices that
emerge from the trial papers authentic? Even if recorded with some degree of
accuracy, was the testimony given under duress? Are the versions of events,
expressions of motivation, and exhibitions of emotion trustworthy? Do the witness
statements truly represent the perspective of the enslaved? The questions are,
indeed, obvious—the records lay bare the power inequities of southern courts,
the potential abuses of the system, and the manifest opportunities for distortion of
the stories the slaves told.

The answers to these questions are less simple. The discourse, however, is a
useful one and has marked scholarly consideration of the sources informing slave
life, culture, and economy for nearly a century. Bold interpretations have prompted
scholars to find new voices and these new voices, in turn, have led to reexamina-
tions of old interpretations. The aims of this essay, then, are twofold. First, it traces
the broad contours of the historiography, examining the myriad ways in which
scholars have come to incorporate the slave perspective in studies of slavery.
Having established the general trajectory of this search through the 1970s, turns
back to Joe, Sam, Henry, and Leah and examines the ways in which voices like
theirs have led scholars to important insights in one particular area of study—the
political, social, and economic implications of the slaves' internal economy.

Any discussion of the sources of slavery must begin with Ulrich B. Phillips and
the first major scholarly considerations of the institution in the southern United
States. The arguments and methodology put forth in *American Negro Slavery* and
Life and Labor in the Old South would hold sway over the profession for nearly
thirty years. That southern slave labor was inefficient but benign became a *sine qua
non* for understanding the South. Future explorations of the region's economic and
social structure would necessarily follow the empirical path Phillips blazed. He

let the voices of the master class guide that path—and his analysis. An avid researcher and collector, Phillips prowled manuscript archives, courthouses, auctions, and private homes for material on which to base his studies of southern life and economy. In his first book-length publication, *Plantation and Frontier*, Phillips published a remarkable collection of documents, chosen for their "rareness, unconsciousness, and faithful illustration." By and large, white voices—from southern newspapers, government papers, and plantation records—met this criterion. Phillips would later explain that, of these, plantation records were most reliable. Researchers could make a "mental journey through the plantation records; and . . . find that planters, overseers and even slaves have more or less unconsciously answered questions of interest and drawn sketches almost as if by interview and request."[2]

Reviewers of *American Negro Slavery* and *Life and Labor in the Old South* lauded the former for its "thorough consultation of the sources" while praising the historian's use of "fresh materials" in the latter. Phillips's work was all the more remarkable, others gushed, because of the author's unfailing objectivity in presenting this material. As Avery Craven noted, "Not only are men allowed to speak for themselves but all parties are given a fair and equal hearing." Not surprisingly, leading African-American scholars found less to admire in Phillips's research methodology. A reviewer for the *Journal of Negro History* warned readers that these sources were "cast in the mind of a man of southern birth and northern environment in manhood" while Carter Woodson maintained that Phillips's "inability to fathom the negro mind" was among the book's greatest shortcomings. In sum, DuBois explained, "a history of slavery would ordinarily deal largely with slaves and their point of view." Phillips, he argued, failed utterly in this task.[3]

But from where was this "point of view" to come? And, what effect would it have on scholars' collective understanding of the peculiar institution? In the years following, historians would echo DuBois's comments but would remain conflicted about just how to define, interpret, and put to use the "point of view" they found lacking in Phillips's accounts. Carter Woodson struck first, publishing hundreds of letters from bondspeople in the documentary collection *The Mind of the Negro*. This body of sources, Woodson argued, would allow readers to "judge hundreds of Negroes as they really expressed themselves." The voices, he imagined, would serve to counter Phillips's characterization of the mental inertness of southern slaves. But because he was concerned with tracking the "mental development" of the race, he avoided a pointed interpretation of slavery itself.[4]

Richard Hofstadter and Kenneth Stampp likewise implored historians to open themselves to the "standpoint of the slave" in 1944 and 1952 assessments of the field. The idea, Stampp argued, was to get at the "mind of the slave," using "clues" plucked from the narratives of fugitive slaves, interviews conducted by travelers to the South, and the WPA narratives. Heeding his own advice, he incorporated these perspectives into his 1956 *The Peculiar Institution: Slavery in the Ante-bellum South*.

Stampp, though, remained hemmed in by Phillips's framework of analysis. The few slave voices that crept into his narrative merely provided new answers to Phillips's old questions. Was slavery profitable to the master class? Yes. Was the system benign? No. In the end, Stampp heard a moral condemnation of the slave system and little more.[5]

In order to move beyond the Phillips debate, historians would have to ask more of their sources and, perhaps more importantly, be prepared to listen differently. But how to do this? Hofstadter made an interdisciplinary plea, arguing that the study of slavery should be undertaken by those who "have absorbed the viewpoint of modern anthropology" and "who have a feeling for social psychology." Stanley Elkins stood ready to shoulder that mantle in his 1959 *Slavery: A Problem in American Institutional and Intellectual Life*. At the outset, he implored his readers to consider "new viewpoints," highlighting, in particular, Frank Tannenbaum's comparative 1946 treatise *Slave and Citizen*. Hailing Tannenbaum's framework as a "breakthrough," he explained that the book did "*not* fit" within an emerging historiography focused on the relative profitability and humaneness of singular regions. He wondered, however, why Tannenbaum and others stopped with mere description of the mechanics of slave life and resources. The more important question was, as he put it bluntly, "*Why?*" Like Stampp, Hofstadter, Woodson, and DuBois before him, Elkins aimed to reveal the mind or, more precisely, the "personality" of the enslaved—not as a tool of moral indictment but as a way to get at the psychology of the warped system itself. Surprisingly, readers heard few slave—or even slaveholder—voices in Elkins's narrative. His controversial discussion of the infantilized Sambo relied not on contemporary evidence but on a more recent analogy, the absolute powerlessness of prisoners in Second World War concentration camps. Reflecting on the much maligned comparison seventeen years later, Elkins defended his method. Though not rooted in empirical evidence, his use of metaphor, he argued, allowed historians to think more imaginatively about the implications of the harsh life Stampp and others took such pains to describe.[6]

That Elkins shunned the sources other researchers were just beginning to consider did not lessen the impact of his work. Scholars hastened to refute Elkins's metaphor, arguing that only the voices of the enslaved could answer the psychological and sociological questions of power Elkins was interested in exploring. Sterling Stuckey, for example, argued that a resistant ethos marked slave communities, mitigating the damaging effects of the plantation system and serving as a means of chipping away the power of the master class. This unique "slave personality and style" could not be understood, Stuckey argued, unless scholars viewed slave life and culture through the "prism of folklore." In a seminal 1968 article, he maintained that the cunning and clever "songs and tales" of the enslaved effectively repudiated the "thesis that Negroes *as a group* had internalized 'Sambo' traits." Countering those who might have doubted the veracity of the abstracted tales,

Stuckey explained, "folklore, in its natural setting, is of, by and for those who create and respond to it, depending for its survival upon the accuracy with which it speaks to needs and reflects sentiments." Time, then, affirmed the validity of the source material as reflective of the black ethos.[7]

Lawrence Levine and Charles Joyner would heed Stuckey's exhortation in their studies of African-American and enslaved folk culture. In his 1977 *Black Culture and Black Consciousness: Afro-American Folk Thought from Slavery to Freedom*, Lawrence Levine sought to "explore and reconstruct the mind of the black folk" through an analysis of the "songs, folktales, proverbs, aphorisms, jokes, verbal games, and . . . toasts" present in African-American written and oral tradition. Like Stuckey, he dismissed concerns about questions of provenance, the practice of folklorists to "censor" black voices, and the inevitable tendency of black folk to censor themselves in the face of outside inquirers. Such problems, Levine noted, were simply a part of the historians' "incessant struggle to overcome imperfect records." The fruits of this struggle, however, were well worth the effort made to engage them. Without the voices of the folk, Levine maintained, scholars are left with descriptions of material deprivation, bondage, and mental and physical abuse. Folklore, however, shows us that the "the sacred world of the enslaved" provided "instruments of life, of sanity, of health, and of self-respect."[8]

As important as the work of Stuckey and Levine was, it took the work of historian and folklorist Charles Joyner to demonstrate fully the utility of folklore in understanding slave life and culture. Joyner was inspired by the Annalistes, seeking less the "mind" of the Negro than to understand the *mentalité* of a community—a specific community, All Saints Parish—in antebellum South Carolina. Part of this process involved using the very records that Phillips and others found so useful—court records, travelers' accounts, plantation records, and the like. But, like Stuckey and Levine, Joyner found folklore spoke most forcefully about the values and traditions enslaved people and their descendants held most dear. Folklore, according to Joyner, was the way "slaves spoke to posterity from their souls". Until scholars analyzed the stories they told each other, "the inner world of slaves' minds" would remain obscured. Joyner, like Stuckey and Levine before him, wanted to impart the importance of folklore. But rather than making a study of folklore itself, Joyner was among the first really to listen to the folk and use their words and traditions to create a nuanced interpretation of community life and culture.[9]

Folklore was but one type of source marshaled against Elkins. By the early 1970s, scholars had developed a growing appreciation for what John Blassingame would call "non-traditional sources." Among the most important of these were the over 2,000 interviews with ex-slaves recorded by the Works Progress Administration in the mid-1930s. Though folklorists Benjamin Botkin and Norman Yetman had published excerpts from the narratives, the vast collection of original material remained hidden deep within the Rare Books Division of the Library of Congress.

George P. Rawick and the Greenwood Press made accessible these voices in 1972 with the publication of *The American Slave: A Composite Autobiography*. Why were these voices important? Masters not only had ruled the plantation, Rawick argued, but they ruled history too, leaving the slaves "murmuring and mumbling" in the background. The interviews brought slave life and culture to the fore, highlighting, in particular, the community bondspeople created from "from sundown to sunup." The interviews related the mundane details of bondspeople's lives—what they ate, where they lived, how they worked, whom they loved, and how and if they were punished. Though Rawick made no claims for a completely accurate representation of slavery, he argued that the "sociological and ethnological" implications for the collection were vast and called on scholars from across disciplines to consider them.[10]

That the veracity of the interviews might be problematic, Rawick, Yetman, and others were well aware. The interviewees were elderly at the time of their interviews and most were mere children during their enslavement. The largely white cadre of WPA interviewers, well-intentioned though they may have been, often hailed from southern communities steeped in Jim Crow law and tradition. Desperately poor interviewees knew well to watch their words and curb their criticisms, lest they face possible retribution from white neighbors. As one Texas freedman noted, many elderly ex-slaves "closes the door before they tell the truth about their days of slavery" but "[w]hen the door is open, they tell how kind their masters was and how rosy it all was." Moreover, because many interviews were not recorded verbatim, WPA staff recreated narratives from scribbled notes, sometimes with considerable editorial and creative license. Post-interview editing at state and regional WPA offices could further muffle freedmen's voices. As John Blassingame would later explain in his own consideration of the slave voice, such "deliberate distortion and interpolation of the views of the WPA staffers pose a serious challenge to those historians who rely heavily on the interviews."[11]

In *The Slave Community: Plantation Life in the Antebellum South,* Blassingame himself argued for the use of "new insights gained from psychology" but maintained that any "investigator of personality development" must rely on voices of the slaves themselves. But, if the voices of 2,000 freedmen were suspect, where, then, might the curious scholar turn for insight on the inner world of the enslaved? Among the most important of these records were slave biographies, Blassingame contended, triangulated with slaveholders' records and travelers' accounts. He explained that, "though there are no absolute guarantees of truth, this three dimensional picture of the plantation at least reveals the complexity of the institution." Blassingame was not the first to use slave autobiographies. Kenneth Stampp and John Hope Franklin, among others, noted their significance. Others were more hesitant. Ulrich Phillips saw possibilities in their use, though, in the end, judged them of "dubious value." His concerns were certainly not without merit. The voices issued as slaves' were often mediated by white abolitionist presses and thus rang with a tone of moral indictment. Perhaps more problematic was the extraordinary nature of their accounts. The men and women who told their stories were those who had—by one means or another—escaped the system. Their stories, then, could speak only to the actions of a lucky and particularly emboldened few rather than the masses who spent their entire lifetimes in chains. Blassingame explored and explained the utility and potential problems of these records in a critical essay on sources appended to *The Slave Community*. Defending their use, he argued that the autobiographies provide researchers with insights on bondspeople's "mental life" and "interpersonal relations." That these accounts were "subjective," Blassingame argued, was a boon to careful researchers. How else were scholars to get at the mind of the enslaved? What other source could provide an account of a man's reaction to bondage? Moreover, these extraordinary men—and some, but not many, women—were witnesses themselves, to their own experiences certainly, but also to the life and culture of the communities from which they came. These "monotonous details of daily routine" not only comprised the evidence most useful to slavery scholars but they also served notice that the account could be relied upon. After all, Blassingame argued, abolitionists were interested in grand escapes from slavery, not the daily routine of bonded life.[12]

Given the profound importance slave autobiographies played in his analysis, it is not surprising then that Blassingame would, five years later, compile and publish a massive documentary volume of "slave testimony." With the same commonsense approach he took to his research for the *Slave Community*, he sagely noted, "Neither the whites nor the blacks had a monopoly on truth, had rended the veil cloaking the life of the other, or had seen clearly the pain and joy bounded by color and caste." Any consideration of slave life would have to use the same triangulation of sources he described in *The Slave Community*. The letters, autobiographies, speeches, magazine and scholarly interviews contained within the current volume's 777 pages testified to those areas in which "only those who had experienced slavery" could answer. As with the slave autobiographies, Blassingame fully disclosed the sources' potential liabilities, but argued that the sources' personal biases were their greatest strengths.[13]

Blassingame's work was published almost contemporaneously with Eugene Genovese's *Roll, Jordan, Roll: The World the Slaves Made*. The title implied a study of a world created, witnessed, and portrayed by slaves themselves. But that title was a misnomer in many respects. Genovese's paternalist thesis described the negotiations undertaken by slaves and masters as they created a world in each other's image. As such, he incorporated a vast array of evidence into his analysis— plantation records, travelers' accounts, agricultural periodicals, and, notably, WPA narratives. He warned his readers that "all the sources are treacherous" and that other historians would likely interpret the voices of master and enslaved differently. In particular, Genovese argued that the careful historian not only had to weigh black sources against white but also against each other. For his own work, Genovese explained that he would rely on his twenty years' experience with slave records to determine "what does and does not ring true."[14]

Concerned as he was with devising a framework for understanding the master–slave relation—not engaging in the increasingly discordant debate over the veracity of the slave voice—Genovese did not elaborate fully on his method of verifying evidence. Critics of the book complained that the voices—slave and free—which informed his analysis skewed his paternalist model. Though he was the first to extensively use the WPA narratives in a major synthetic study, he was excoriated for relying too heavily on them, that the interviews implied a closer relation between master and slave than other sources—for example, slave autobiographies—would allow. Noting the debate over Genovese's evidence, David Thomas Bailey, in a 1980 essay for the *Journal of Southern History*, sought to identify the similarities and differences between these increasingly utilized types of evidence. Comparing portraits of slavery depicted in samples of WPA narratives with a sample of published slave autobiographies, Bailey found substantial differences in descriptions of slave life. In descriptions of the slaves' material world of work and family, the WPA and autobiographies differed substantially. WPA interviewers, by and large, described "great" or "adequate" food supplies which were of "good" quality. Autobiographers, on the other hand, described small quantities of poor quality. The same pattern held true for descriptions of housing and clothing allowances. Punishment, in most WPA narratives, was meted out rarely, usually to "other" slaves, and only to those who "deserved it." Autobiographers argued that beatings were common and almost always drew blood. Interviewees rarely mentioned runaways, stealing, or fighting with whites. The autobiographies—written largely by those who had broken away from the system—were rife with stories of resistance. Finally, the sample of interviewees tended to describe a relatively stable family structure while autobiographers described lives of trauma and instability.[15]

Bailey quantified what many scholars of the peculiar institution had come to realize: there was no harmony to be found among the growing chorus of slave voices. As Peter Kolchin noted in a 1986 review of the historiography, fresh perspectives devolved into cacophony as 1970s revisionists criticized "grave methodological errors and ideological shortcomings" in each other's work. For better or worse, a "general consensus concerning what slavery meant for the antebellum slave" was far from attained. The same could be said for assessments of the availability and utility of the slave voice. While scholars collectively had gathered and made heard enslaved voices from a growing empirical well, there were those still paralyzed by assessments of the veracity contained therein. C. Vann Woodward acknowledged this problem in a 1974 review of Rawick's *American Slave: A Composite Autobiography*, stating, "The norm for historical sources is a mess, a confusing mess." He was not discouraged, however. Despite the "normal shortcomings" of black sources, researchers needed to remember that the "the task of the historian is make sense of it." It was a simple statement and sage advice. As with other sources, scholars needed corroborate to the best of their ability, contextualize where they could, and bear in mind the potential liabilities of each source.[16]

Debates over the veracity of the slave voice did not stand in the way of more focused research as the great synthetic work of the 1970s fragmented into more focused studies of individual aspects of slave life, economy, and culture. Men and women like Joe, Sam, Leah, and Henry increasingly came to play significant roles in such studies—their voices not only acknowledged but eagerly sought out by historians looking to incorporate a valued perspective on bonded life. Among the most important areas of research to emerge more fully in this period was the study of the slaves' internal economy. The four Anderson, South Carolina, slaves would not have been familiar with the term but they would have certainly recognized its importance in their lives. After all, it was their marketing activity—undertaken outside the work they did for their masters—that led them to speak in front of those magistrates in 1851.

Studies of the slaves' internal economy embody both the rewards and the perils of discovering and using the slave voice. At its most basic level, work on the internal economy has involved uncovering the mechanics of slave production, marketing, and consumption of goods and services. Historians and anthropologists of the Caribbean and the United States have used "traditional sources"—planters' records and diaries—as well as sources once considered "non-traditional," including slave autobiographies and interviews. But they have delved into a wide variety of other sources as well—looking for declarations in economic transactions, probing the silences in government legislation, and uncovering conversations in the anxious fretting of the planter elite.

Observations of slaves' marketing activities are nothing new. After all, planters' records are rife with descriptions of and regulations related to slave overwork and provisioning. It took the keen observations of anthropologist Sidney Mintz to bring the focused study of the phenomenon to the fore, however. Significantly, it was not the voices of slaves he heard; it was the voices of their descendants—men and women involved in small-scale cultivating and marketing in contemporary Jamaica. The weekly markets involved thousands of independent producers who transacted large quantities of cash money. These marketers, largely women, preferred to sell the goods themselves, disdaining middlemen and thus potentially achieving higher profit margins. In a brief essay in 1955, Mintz hypothesized that this "fundamental institution" was a crucial component in the transformation of the island labor force from slaves to sturdy peasantry.[17]

Mintz's primary concern was understanding the creation of this peasantry. To do so, he and colleague Douglas Hall argued, scholars had to understand the polink system from which this class emerged. Provision grounds or polinks—large garden plots located high in the Jamaican hills—emerged in the seventeenth century as a means of feeding slaves. By the nineteenth century, bondspeople's excess crops—grown, harvested, and sold apart from the work they did for their masters—fed the entire island. Initially implemented by planters as a means of rationalizing food costs, the system grew "in the absence of compulsion, and under conditions which implicitly acknowledged [slaves'] responsiveness to the same incentives which operated for the free Jamaican." What initially benefited only the master came to be recognized not only as a customary right but also the center of the island's entire subsistence sector.[18]

Mintz and Hall's interpretation was as bold as those offered regarding the peculiar institution in the colonial and antebellum United States. Like Kenneth Stampp, Stanley Elkins, and others, they reviewed plantation records and travelers' accounts. Unlike these esteemed scholars of the American South, however, they avoided Ulrich Phillips's framework of analysis. Their questions were different. Rather than focus on treatment and the psychological effects of enslavement, Mintz, Hall, and others looked for the ways in which enslaved men and women established lives within the system. The slaves they studied were the manifestly human ancestors of the men and women encountered in 1960 Jamaica—the "mind of the negro," so desperately sought after in the American South, was presumed.

But what of the slave voice? Even as historians of the American South began to incorporate folklore, slave interviews, and slave autobiographies into their accounts of slave life and culture, scholars of the internal economy in the Caribbean remained wedded to more "traditional sources." Plantation records, travel accounts, and government legislation and reports formed the empirical basis for most work on slave marketing. Over the next forty years, anthropologists, sociologists, and historians would make the most of these sources, detailing the mechanics of slaves' independent production across the Caribbean. Mintz and Hall, in particular, thoroughly investigated the evolution of Jamaican law, arguing that increasingly specific legislation spoke to a wider acceptance of general slave marketing behavior. Specifically, they noted the shift in negative articulation of the law to a more positive one over the course of the eighteenth century. According to the authors, slaves in 1711 could *not* sell "beef, veal mutton and saltfish." In 1735, they were permitted to market "fresh fish, milk, poultry, and other small stock of all kinds." Mintz and Hall argued that the evolving legal construction of these and other statutes indicate the growing importance of enslaved hucksters to island foodstuff production, allowing them to make "a place for themselves in the free economic activity of the country which would never thereafter be challenged."[19]

Other historians took up Mintz and Hall's work, examining internal economies throughout the Caribbean. Dale Turner's work on Martinique; David Gaspar's research on Antigua; and Woodville Marshall's comparative study of Tobago, Grenada, St Lucia, and St Vincent complemented continuing work on Jamaica by Orlando Patterson, Jerome Handler, and Mary Turner. The law and government reports remained central to each of these analyses, as did travelers' narratives and plantation records. Mary Turner, for example, has compared the "methods of struggle" of Jamaica's wage workers and chattel slaves. "Work on the grounds," she argued, "secured the slaves' foothold in the islands' commercial economy and strengthened their bargaining position on the estate." In slightly more subtle terms, Gaspar found that Antigua's internal economy—and the customary rights and privileges that accompanied it—was among the circumstances that "sharpened [slaves'] awareness of the possibilities to change their lives." This "social and psychological space" allowed them to create a world in which white "resources could be used to challenge the power of the master class." By situating Caribbean slaves within a Marxian struggle for class power, Turner and Gaspar, among many others, were able to see resistance in the records of the colonial elite. A seeming dearth of slave voices did not prevent scholars from exploring "opportunities for [slaves] to express fully their humanity."[20]

Interpretation of the slaves' internal economy in the United States has taken a distinctly different tack. Unlike in the Caribbean studies, interpretative shifts in the historiography of the internal economies of colonial and antebellum American internal economies have largely hinged on the cultivation of specific sources. As in the Caribbean, plantation records and government reports and legislation revealed the contours of these economic systems. Early twentieth-century historians like Ulrich Phillips and Lewis Gray made note of slave gardens and cash exchange in their assessments of plantation labor management. Robert Fogel and Stanley Engerman interpreted them similarly, viewing such economic opportunities as instances of the "rewards and incentives" used by planters to spur efficient production. Blassingame and Genovese noted slave marketing but assigned little significance to its presence. At a time when sociologists, anthropologists, and historians of the Caribbean had made the provisioning system a hallmark of much work on slave life, economy, and culture, historians of the southern United States were seemingly not interested.[21]

It took the voices of ex-slaves to catch Americanists' attention. In exploring the records of the Reconstruction-era records of the Southern Claims Commission, Philip Morgan and the staff of the Freedmen and Southern Society Project at the University of Maryland uncovered a vast repository of testimony about all aspects of enslaved life including the slaves' internal economy. The Federal Government established the Southern Claims Commission in the years following the Civil War as a means of reimbursing loyal southerners who might have lost property during the Union attack and occupation. By 1880, over 22,000 men and women had filed petitions to the commission. Of the 5,004 claims allowed, 602 were made by ex-slaves. Because the commission was concerned with property ownership, the records are uniquely suited to work on the internal economy. As with free white petitioners, commissioners required ex-slaves to outline the provenance of their lost items: from whom they had purchased the items and how long they had been in their possession. It is worth noting the incredulity with which commissioners initially received these petitions. After all, how could enslaved chattels have owned property? Their ignorance has proven the historian's gain, however. In addition to what they acquired, slaves were asked to describe how they could possibly have earned the money to acquire the capital they now claimed they had lost.

Philip Morgan and, more recently, Dylan Penningroth made studies of these eager and detailed explanations of property acquisition. In his seminal 1983 essay on the relationship between property ownership and the task system, Morgan asked readers to "listen" to freedmen's accounts of the task system in coastal Georgia and South Carolina. The "authentic voice of the slave," Morgan argued, articulate a "touching concern for detail...a dash of pride...and an occasional display of emotion." Rather than the unremitting toil described in many WPA accounts and autobiographies, lowcountry ex-slaves described a flexible labor system that allowed blocks of time for leisure or, as often, work for themselves. From these records, Morgan and Penningroth reconstructed not only the mechanics of property acquisition in the lowcountry but also something, they imagined, of the collective ethos of the slave community. Freedmen's voices, Morgan argued, articulated a spirit of "collective solidarity and communal worth." In his *Claims of Kinfolk: African American Property and Community in the Nineteenth-Century South*, Dylan Penningroth took Morgan's research and his interpretation further, probing the "world of social relationships and negotiations" that lay behind property ownership.[22]

The records are not without their drawbacks. Dylan Penningroth ably and carefully parsed the records but understood that the words scribbled on the manuscripts were mediated by a white Union clerk. Likewise, some former bondspeople surely exaggerated their claims, either of their own volition or at the urging of hired lawyers. In keeping with a growing league of Americanists interested in the internal economy, Penningroth took the valuable information gleaned from the SCC records and interrogated WPA interviews, slave autobiographies, travelers' accounts, and plantation records with a new set of questions. As it turns out, descriptions of slaves' marketing activity burst from nearly all of these sources. WPA interviewers often asked slaves whether they had ever seen or used money. Autobiographers chronicled both their efforts to earn cash and the items on which they chose to spend it. Travelers to the South were as surprised as SCC commissioners at the sight of and conversations with property-bearing slaves and often noted such instances in their accounts.

Court records, too, spill with the voices of the enslaved. Lawrence McDonnell, Jeff Forret, Larry Hudson, and Kathleen Hilliard, among others, have plumbed the records of state and county courts, looking for accounts of the slaves' economy. As we have seen, bondspeople—including Joe, Henry, Leah, and Sam—were both indicted and provided testimony in such court proceedings. Because many of these records deal with the transmission of cash and property, their potential rewards match those in the SCC claims. As in the claims records, bondspeople sought to prove—or disprove—their claim to stolen property. Slaves' testimony, then, often winds through complex channels of trade and property acquisition in plantation communities. Enmeshed within these economic networks, the watchful scholar finds not only bondspeople but other largely illiterate groups as well, including free blacks and poor whites. That duplicity and wariness mark this often conflicting testimony, there is no doubt. But even such discordant voices have their value. Whereas Philip Morgan and Dylan Penningroth found examples of community formation in the records of the SCC, Lawrence McDonnell found community degradation and alienation in the conflicting and sometimes harsh words and deeds found in South Carolina court testimony. That each body of records draws from different regions of South Carolina—SCC records from the lowcountry and the Court of Magistrates and Freeholders from the upstate—might explain the discrepancy. More likely, though, these scholars have identified equally relevant characteristics of slave life and culture.[23]

Americanists have learned from their Caribbeanist colleagues as well. Historians have used the records of plantation owners and storekeepers to outline the framework of management within which slave producers and consumers operated. The voices of the enslaved, however, only rarely speak from these pages. Or, do they? The work of Caribbean anthropologists and, more recently, historian John Smolenski indicates other possibilities. Smolenski has suggested that historians heed the lessons of microhistory pioneer Carlo Ginzburg when addressing trad-itional white sources, arguing for an ethnohistory "grounded in narratives of interaction between slave owners and enslaved peoples." Ginzburg's own words are instructive:

They [records of the Inquisition] must be read as the product of a peculiar, utterly unbalanced interrelationship. In order to decipher them, we must learn to catch, behind the smooth surface of the text, a subtle interplay of threats and fears, of attacks and withdrawals. We must learn to disentangle the different threads which form the textual fabric of these dialogues.

So too with the records of the master class. In his own microhistorical analysis of Virginian Landon Carter's colonial diary, Smolenski listened for not monologue but dialogue, and thus was able to discern the "echoes" of the plantation's slaves in Carter's words.[24]

Smolenski's approach is particularly appropriate for historians of the internal economy. Planters across the South produced volumes of prescriptive literature. Agricultural journals served as primers for planting, manuals for management, and, notably, outlets for social anxieties. In her study of antebellum slaves as consumers, Kathleen Hilliard has noted the mental gymnastics undertaken by slaveholders as they assessed the material and moral challenges of slaves as economic actors. Behind seemingly certain offers of advice lay the voices of a planter's "people": a woman explaining why she had exchanged her provisions for a bonnet; a child exclaiming happily as he eagerly took his master's nickel, or a man expressing frustration with a payment not made. Such conversations lay between the columns of credits and debits in store accounts as well. Hilliard—and before her, Ted Ownby and Roderick McDonald—have looked for evidence of slave economic activity in more formal venues of consumption, antebellum general stores. Each has found that bondspeople spent their money in ways that illustrated not simply material need but consumer aspiration. Though a white clerk noted a mere name, purchase, and price, a decision-making process involving quality, quantity, and value (or lack thereof) lay behind every transaction. Discerning this process—and the voices that go with it—admittedly involves some conjecture. But understanding the framework of management the planters established and the risks and rewards of slaves' economic actions provides the context needed to assign significance to the choices made.[25]

The historiography of the internal economy, like the study of slavery in the Americas as a whole, continues to evolve. Scholars will use insights from emerging work to plumb old—and possibly, new—sources. It is worth noting, however, that the problem of evidence for the next generation of scholars is not one of "finding slave voices." A veritable chorus has been found, digitized, publicized, and utilized by researchers from grade school classrooms to ivory tower offices. These text-searchable documents have made even the most obscure projects feasible, permitting the expeditious and thorough compilation and categorization of source material. For this, cash- and time-strapped researchers ought to be grateful. But increased access does not guarantee good history and scholars of slave life, culture, and economy might bear in mind some of the issues addressed by earlier generations. Confounded by the conflicting testimony of black slaves and freedmen, the competing management strategies of white masters, and the varied and often biased reports of travelers and commentators, scholars tried their best to "make sense" of it all. They noted the importance of context, collaboration, and balance. Most importantly, they learned to listen carefully, to the loudest declarations certainly, but also to the deepest silences. The depth and breadth of the field can only expand if this same sense of innovation and consideration is taken by scholars in the emerging digital age.

NOTES

1. Anderson/Pendleton District, Magistrate and Freeholders Court, Trial Papers: *State* v. *Joe, Henry*, 5 May, 1851, South Carolina Department of Archives and History.
2. Ulrich B. Phillips, *American Negro Slavery: A Survey of the Supply, Employment and Control of Negro Labor as Determined by the Plantation Regime* (New York, 1918); U. B. Phillips (ed.), *Plantation and Frontier, 1649–1863* (New York, 1910), i, 95; U. B. Phillips, *Life and Labor in the Old South* (Boston, 1929), 219.

3. C. P. Patterson, review of *American Negro Slavery*, by Ulrich B. Phillips, *Political Science Quarterly*, 33 (3) (September 1918): 456; Avery Craven, review of *Life and Labor in the Old South*, by Ulrich B. Phillips, *Political Science Quarterly*, 45 (1) (March 1930): 136; review of *American Negro Slavery*, by Ulrich B. Phillips, *Journal of Negro History*, 4 (1) (January 1919): 102; Carter G. Woodson, review of *Life and Labor in the Old South*, by Ulrich B. Phillips, *Mississippi Valley Historical Review*, 5 (4) (March 1919): 480; W. E. B. DuBois, review of *American Negro Slavery*, by Ulrich B. Phillips, *American Political Science Review*, 12 (4) (November 1918): 723.

4. Carter Woodson (ed.), *The Mind of the Negro as Reflected in Letters Written during the Crisis, 1800–1860* (Washington, DC, 1926), pp. v–vi.

5. Richard Hofstadter, "U. B. Phillips and the Plantation Legend," *Journal of Negro History*, 29 (2) (April 1944): 124; Kenneth M. Stampp, "The Historian and Southern Negro Slavery," *American Historical Review*, 57 (3) (April 1952): 618–19.

6. Hofstadter, "U. B. Phillip and the Plantation Legend," 124; Stanley M. Elkins, *Slavery: A Problem in American Institutional and Intellectual Life* (3rd rev. edn. Chicago, 1976), 25, 304–7.

7. Sterling Stuckey, "Through the Prism of Folklore: The Black Ethos in Slavery," *Massachusetts Review*, 9 (1968): 419, 435.

8. Lawrence W. Levine, *Black Culture and Black Consciousness: Afro-American Folk Thought from Slavery to Freedom* (New York, 1977), pp. xi–xiii, 80.

9. Charles Joyner, *Down by the Riverside: A South Carolina Slave Community* (Urbana, Ill., 1985), pp. xv–xviii, 172–3.

10. John W. Blassingame, *The Slave Community: Plantation Life in the Antebellum South* (New York, 1972, 1979), p. xii; George P. Rawick, *From Sundown to Sunup*, vol. i of *The American Slave: A Composite Autobiography* (Westport, Conn., 1972), pp. xiv, xix–xx; Benjamin A. Botkin (ed.), *Lay my Burden Down* (Chicago, 1945); Norman R. Yetman (ed.), *Voices from Slavery* (New York, 1970). For extensive analysis of the WPA interviews, see Paul Escott, *Slavery Remembered: A Record of Twentieth-Century Slave Narratives* (Chapel Hill, NC, 1979).

11. Rawick (ed.), *The American Slave*, iv, pt. 2, 189. Quoted in John W. Blassingame, *Slave Testimony: Two Centuries of Letters, Speeches, Interviews, and Autobiographies* (Baton Rouge, La., 1977), p. xlv; Blassingame, *Slave Testimony*, p. xlviii.

12. Blassingame, *Slave Community*, pp. x–xii; Stampp, *Peculiar Institution*; John Hope Franklin, *From Slavery to Freedom: A History of African Americans* (New York, 1947); Phillips, *American Negro Slavery*, 445 n.; Blassingame, *Slave Community*, 367–82.

13. Blassingame, *Slave Testimony*, p. lxv. See also Robert S. Starobin (ed.), *Blacks in Bondage: Letters of American Slaves* (New York, 1974).

14. Eugene D. Genovese, *Roll, Jordan Roll: The World the Slaves Made* (New York, 1974), 675–8.

15. David Thomas Bailey, "A Divided Prism: Two Sources of Black Testimony on Slavery," *Journal of Southern History*, 46 (3) (August 1980): 381–404.

16. Peter Kolchin, "American Historians and Antebellum Slavery, 1959–1984," in William J. Cooper, Jr., et al. (eds.), *A Master's Due: Essays in Honor of David Herbert Donald* (Baton Rouge, La., 1986), 90; C. Vann Woodward, "History from Slave Sources," *American Historical Review*, 79 (2) (April 1974): 475.

17. Sidney W. Mintz, "The Jamaican Internal Marketing Pattern: Some Notes and Hypotheses," *Social and Economic Studies*, 4 (1955): 102.

18. Sidney W. Mintz and Douglas Hall, "The Origins of the Internal Marketing System," *Yale University Publications in Anthropology*, 57 (1960): 4.
19. Ibid. 15, 17.
20. Mary Turner, "Chattel Slaves into Wage Slaves: A Jamaican Case Study," in Malcolm Cross and Gad Heuman (eds.), *Labour in the Caribbean: From Emancipation to Independence* (London, 1988), 14–23; David Barry Gaspar, *Bondmen & Rebels: A Study of Master–Slave Relations in Antigua* (Baltimore, 1985), 256. For an overview of work on Caribbean internal economies, see Ira Berlin and Philip Morgan (eds.), *The Slaves' Economy: Independent Production by Slaves in the Americas* (London, 1991). Woodville K. Marshall, "Provision Ground and Plantation Labour in Four Windward Islands: Competition for Resources during Slavery," in Berlin and Morgan (eds.), *The Slaves' Economy*, 63.
21. Phillips, *American Negro Slavery*, 288–305, 411–14; Lewis C. Gray, *History of Agriculture in the Southern United States to 1860* (1933; reprint New York, 1941), 465, 564–5; Robert Fogel and Stanley Engerman, *Time on the Cross: The Economics of American Negro Slavery* (Boston, 1974), 127, 144–57; Genovese, *Roll, Jordan, Roll*, 538–9; Blassingame, *The Slave Community*, 147–8, 179.
22. Philip D. Morgan, "The Ownership of Property by Slaves in the Mid-Nineteenth Century Low Country," *Journal of Southern History*, 49 (3) (1983): 399, 405, 407; Dylan Penningroth, *Claims of Kinfolk: African American Property and Community in the Nineteenth-Century South* (Chapel Hill, NC, 2003), 12.
23. Lawrence T. McDonnell, "Money Knows No Master: Market Relations and the American Slave Community," in Winfred B. Moore, Jr., Joseph F. Tripp, and Lyon G. Tyler (eds.), *Developing Dixie: Modernization in a Traditional Society* (Westport, Conn., 1988), 31–44; Jeff Forret, *Race Relations at the Margins: Slaves and Poor Whites in the Antebellum Southern Countryside* (Baton Rouge, La., 2006); Larry E. Hudson, Jr., "'All that Cash': Work and Status in the Slave Quarters," in Hudson (ed.), *Working toward Freedom: Slave Society and Domestic Economy in the American South* (Rochester, NY, 1994), 77–94; Kathleen Hilliard, "Spending in Black and White: Race, Slavery, and Consumer Values in the Antebellum South" (Ph.D. diss., University of South Carolina, 2006).
24. Carol Ginzburg, "The Inquisitor as Anthropologist," in *Myths, Emblems, Clues*, trans. John and Anne Tedeschi (London, 1990), 160–1; John Smolenski, "Hearing Voices: Microhistory, Dialogicality and the Recovery of Popular Culture on an Eighteenth-Century Virginia Plantation," *Slavery and Abolition*, 24 (1) (April 2003): 3.
25. Hilliard, "Spending in Black and White," 40–72; Ted Ownby, *American Dreams in Mississippi: Consumers, Poverty, & Culture, 1830–1998* (Chapel Hill, NC, 1999), 33–60; Roderick McDonald, *The Material Culture and Economy of Slaves: Goods and Chattels on the Sugar Plantations of Jamaica and Louisiana* (Baton Rouge, La., 1993).

SELECT BIBLIOGRAPHY

BERLIN, IRA, and PHILIP D. MORGAN, eds. *The Slaves' Economy: Independent Production by Slaves in the Americas*. London: Frank Cass & Co., Ltd., 1991.
BLASSINGAME, JOHN W., ed. *Slave Testimony: Two Centuries of Letters, Speeches, Interviews, and Autobiographies*. Baton Rouge, La.: Louisiana State University Press, 1977.

MINTZ, SIDNEY W. *Caribbean Transformations*. New York: Columbia University Press, 1974.

MORGAN, PHILIP D. "The Ownership of Property by Slaves in the Mid-Nineteenth-Century Low Country," *Journal of Southern History*, 49 (3) (August 1983): 399–420.

PHILLIPS, ULRICH B. *Plantation and Frontier, 1649–1863*. 2 vols. New York: Burt Franklin, 1910.

RAWICK, GEORGE P. *The American Slave: A Composite Autobiography.*, 41 vols. Westport, Conn.: Greenwood Press, 1972–9.

SMOLENSKI, JOHN. "Hearing Voices: Microhistory, Dialogicality and the Recovery of Popular Culture on an Eighteenth-Century Virginia Plantation," *Slavery and Abolition*, 24 (1) (April 2003): 1–23.

STAMPP, KENNETH M. "The Historian and Southern Negro Slavery," *American Historical Review*, 57 (3) (April 1952): 613–24.

STUCKEY, STERLING. "Through the Prism of Folklore: The Black Ethos in Slavery," *Massachusetts Review*, 9 (3) (1968): 417–37.

WOODSON, CARTER G. *The Mind of the Negro as Reflected in Letters Written during the Crisis, 1800–1860*. Washington, DC: The Association for the Study of Negro Life and History, Inc., 1926.

CHAPTER 32

ARCHAEOLOGY AND SLAVERY

THERESA SINGLETON

INTRODUCTION

Archaeology provides an interdisciplinary approach to the study of slavery that combines analyses of archaeological findings with careful readings of traditional primary sources of historiography. Excavations of sites where enslaved people once lived and worked yield residue of things produced, consumed, and discarded by the former occupants of these sites. An archaeological site is a basic unit of archaeological analysis.[1] It can be thought of as an unprocessed archive containing information on diverse aspects of slavery from slaveholder management practices such as provisioning and surveillance to slave self-provisioning, craft production, and clandestine (imbibing, gambling, conjuring) activities. Just as archives vary in the kinds of information contained in them, information obtained through archaeological investigations varies from site to site. Plantations, for example, contain multiple sites such as the great house, manager's house, crop processing area, and slave quarters. Many environmental and human factors can impact the nature of what is retrievable from any one site. For example, objects made primarily from highly perishable plant and animal products may not survive at many sites. At others, activities that occur after the demise of slavery may have greatly disturbed materials from the earlier slave occupation. Field methods used to investigate and collect archaeological information affect the kinds of information collected at all sites. Yet, despite the limitations of archaeological data, every investigation compares to the discovery of an archival record group that offers the potential for yielding new and provocative insights into slavery.

Archaeologists analyze tangible remains of plantation spatial organization, slave housing, household utensils and personal objects, subsistence activities, and so forth in order to understand the intangible—ideas, human action, social relations, and social processes that characterized slavery. Inferring social life from artifacts always presents challenges, but over the past forty or more years, archaeological studies of slavery have moved beyond mere descriptions of the material world of slavery to analyses of planter hegemony, slave resistance, household composition, gender, slave production, consumption and exchange, religious beliefs and practices, and identity formation. Archaeologists interested in slavery have undertaken the vast majority of their research on plantations in the United States and in the English-speaking Caribbean. Outside the anglophone Americas, research on slavery continues apace in Brazil, Cuba, Guadeloupe, and Martinique. In addition to slavery, archaeologists have undertaken research on other African diaspora communities such as slave runaways, urban dwellers, free persons of color, post-emancipation communities, among others in numerous places in the Americas.

PLANTATION SPATIAL ORGANIZATION AND THE BUILT ENVIRONMENT OF SLAVERY

Scholars of diverse disciplines study the spatial organization and built environment of plantations using maps, paintings, prints, photographs along with written descriptions. Archaeology contributes to this scholarship by providing information on the ways in which design principles described in planter essays or depicted on plantation plats (ground plans) were actually implemented on the ground. Through the study of standing ruins, buried foundations, footings, and traces of wooden posts, archaeologists are able to locate buildings and other structures to reconstruct plantation layouts. Although most studies of plantation slavery attempt to recreate the layout of the plantation being investigated as a standard procedure to show the relationship of slave quarters to other parts of the plantation, analysis of the spatial organization of plantations has increasingly become a major research objective. The scholarship on plantation space demonstrates its centrality to understanding how plantations operated and how slavery was organized. In general, plantation layouts were designed to maximize access to fields, enhance productivity, control slave workers, reinforce the social hierarchy of the plantation, and appeal to the aesthetic sensibilities of the slaveholding class at plantations with great houses and landscaped grounds. But planters exercised their control of landscape in varied ways. On some plantations, masters or their surrogates removed or screened slave quarters from the administrative nucleus—the great house, gardens, warehouses, and other buildings. In others, a panopticon—a watchtower or some other kind of elevated structure designed to enhance security—was built into the landscape to observe areas where enslaved people lived and worked at any time. In some parts of the southern United States, slave quarters were dispersed at various locations on the plantation in separate settlements that provided closer access to fields, particularly as the landholding expanded and new fields were opened for planting. Dispersed slave settlements also subdivided a large slaveholding into smaller units that eliminated a large concentration of slave workers in one place and facilitated efficient accounting of slave productivity and distribution of provisions. The placement of slave houses in linear arrangements or grid patterns which permitted easy access and inspection of premises can be found throughout the Americas.

In the Caribbean, several archaeological studies of plantation space illustrate the diverse approaches planters utilized in quartering enslaved workers. At Seville Plantation on the north coast of Jamaica, Douglas Armstrong identified two temporally and spatially distinct slave settlements that show completely different approaches to slave management. The earlier settlement (1670–1760) reflected slaveholder planning of a community wherein the houses were tightly spaced in rows facing a central street with small yard areas. The later slave settlement (1760–1830) was moved to another location, possibly following a hurricane that also damaged the great house. The new location proved closer to provision grounds, and the slave community appears to have exercised choice in the building and arrangement of their own houses. Slaves constructed houses made of various kinds of building materials, oriented on different axes, and loosely organized around a common area—an arrangement of slave houses observed in other slave societies as well.[2] Yard areas doubled in size, and this later village was located at a greater distance from planter and manager residences.[3] Reasons for the permissive attitude of the planter who authorized the later Seville slave settlement are unknown, but he obviously saw advantages in having the slave workforce construct their own slave village on their own terms.

Locating slave settlements at a considerable distance from planter or manager residences posed obstacles to frequent surveillance of slave quarters. At nineteenth-century coffee plantations in the Blue Mountains of Jamaica, James Delle found plantations were intentionally designed for surveillance of slave activities. He observed the overseer's house at the Clydesdale plantation was strategically located to monitor slave activities from two vantage points. From a second-story landing or balcony, the overseer could view the slave village, which was located uphill from the overseer house. The second vantage point, the veranda, provided a view of the coffee dryers and mills located downhill from the overseer's house. The overseer's house, Delle postulates, served as a kind of panopticon because the workers could not tell when they were being watched; therefore, workers could be manipulated into doing what they were told through their own self-discipline.[4]

By far one of harshest methods of quartering slave workers was the notorious *barracón de patio* designed to confine enslaved people to their quarters after work hours and used on many plantations in Brazil and in Cuba. *The barracón de patio* denoted a large rectangular building usually constructed of masonry with a central yard known as a *patio*. The building resembled a prison as it was subdivided into numerous one-room cells and could house large numbers of enslaved workers. Many Cuban slaveholders believed these buildings facilitated better surveillance of slave activities than detached, timber-framed slave houses known as *bohíos*. In 1970, the Cuban Academy of Sciences examined the extant ruins of a *barracón de patio* at Taoro, a sugar plantation outside the city of Havana, and found that it contained sixty cells, each measuring approximately 6.5 × 10 feet, with very small windows and doors located primarily on the interior side of the building facing the patio. Lourdes S. Domínguez, a Cuban archaeologist, estimates that with a slave population of 224 plus Chinese indentured laborers, Taoro had a total of 300 persons living in its *barracón*. Test excavations of the patio yielded a variety of objects— pipes, beads, bone buttons, amulets, ceramic kitchen wares, and tablewares.[5] The recovered artifacts resemble those unearthed at slavery sites found elsewhere in the Americas, and may have been refuse from enslaved people working in the central kitchen, which, according to written sources, was usually located in the patio.

Theresa Singleton's excavations at the nineteenth-century coffee plantation Santa Ana de Biajacas, located approximately forty-eight miles from Havana, uncovered an alternative to the *barracón de patio* that potentially served the same function of restricting slave movement. The slave settlement consisted of slave *bohíos* enclosed within a tall masonry wall measuring eleven feet high. Plantation inventories taken in 1838 and in 1841 describe the wall to be of the same height as it stands today with thirty to forty-five slave *bohíos* located within the wall enclosure. It most likely made running away from the plantation more difficult and kept small bands of *cimarrones*—slave runaways—from entering the slave settlement. Colonial Cuba during its nineteenth-century sugar and coffee booms had an abundance of fugitive slaves ensconced throughout the island in forbidding stretches of swamp, woodland, and mountains. These runaways periodically raided plantations for food and supplies as well as for recruiting or taking a few enslaved people with them.[6] The enclosure also may have served as a way to hide and separate slave houses from the great house. Many planters did not care to live near slave quarters because they perceived slave houses as unsightly, filthy, and disease ridden. The tall wall would have effectively screened slave *bohíos* from various vantage points, particularly from the ground level of the great house or from the main entrance to the plantation. Research remains to be done on whether enclosing a slave village within such a tall wall was widely practiced in Cuba or elsewhere in Latin America and the Caribbean. Recently, Kenneth Kelly reported another enclosed village at Grande Pointe plantation in Guadeloupe. The wall now stands about five feet, but was probably once in excess of 6.5 feet when the plantation was in use. The walled slave village in Guadeloupe is the only one known in the French West Indies.[7]

Planter efforts to control the spaces enslaved people occupied did not go unchallenged. Enslaved people ran away, incited rebellions, or found subtle ways to resist slaveholder power and authority. Documentary sources for Santa Ana de Biajacas, for example, indicate that the slave community living within the walled enclosure harbored on at least one occasion some twenty *cimarrones* until they were discovered by the overseer on Christmas day. Later, shortly after the death of the plantation owner and before a probate inventory of the slave population was taken, four slaves ran away.[8] These actions are difficult, if not impossible, to document from archaeological evidence, but potential forms of everyday resistance or slaveholder accommodation to slave demands can be studied using archaeological resources. Excavations in and around traces of slave *bohíos* within the wall enclosure at Santa Ana de Biajacas suggest that members of the slave community, despite prohibitions, regularly imbibed alcoholic beverages and played gambling games. Numerous round-shaped gaming pieces made from broken pieces of ceramics may have been used to play a game once known in Cuba as *Chinata*. The game's name is derived from small smooth stones known as *china pelonas* originally used as gaming pieces, although the game was also apparently played with pieces made from a wide variety of materials such as iron or wooden fragments.[9] On the one hand, assuming slaveholders and managers were unaware of slave drinking and gambling, these activities could be considered forms of everyday resistance. On the other hand, planters or managers may well have known about these activities but decided to accommodate the slave community by turning a blind eye to these small indulgences.

In other plantation settings, enslaved people made alterations to the interiors of their quarters creating their own sense of space within the slave quarter. The best example of this practice appears on eighteenth-century Virginia plantations in quarters where enslaved people dug pits directly through earthen floors or below wooden floorboards. These pits vary considerably in size from small cubby holes about one to two feet by one to two feet to five by eight feet and at depths of two to four feet. Some pits are lined with brick, stone, or wood, and others are unlined. Slaves used these sub-floor pits for the storage of food and personal items, and a few may have served as ancestral shrines. Many Virginian slave houses had these pits, whatever the purpose, for archaeologists have excavated several hundred of them, and Gary Fesler and Patricia Samford have conducted detailed studies of these curious archaeological features. Some slave quarters have multiple sub-floor pits with one containing twenty pits in one large structure at the Kingsmill estate in James City County, Virginia.[10] A few scattered written references describe slaveholders' suspicions that slaves sometimes used these pits to hide pilfered goods.[11] Yet, the fact that these pits were ubiquitous in Virginian slave houses suggests that slaveholders and overseers more often accommodated rather than opposed slaves' desire to dig and use these sub-floor pits. Perhaps, the pits served as a way for enslaved people to assert their rights to private property decades prior to the Southern Claims Commission during the early years of emancipation.

Archaeological studies of plantation spatial organization and the built environment of slavery provide a wealth of information on plantation layouts, types of buildings used for slave quarters, slave living conditions, and activities within slave quarters. From these findings archaeologists can also draw inferences concerning the dynamics of power between masters and slaves and how these unequal relations were enacted in different times and places.

SLAVE CONSUMPTION, PRODUCTION, AND EXCHANGE

Archaeological studies of slavery since their inception have concerned themselves with slave consumption. The kind, quality, and quantity of objects enslaved people used and how they were acquired identify issues that continue to frame investigations of slave living conditions, household composition, and cultural practices, among other topics. According to John Otto, slaveholders may have provided slave workers with ceramics, which some archaeologists have incorrectly interpreted as documentation that the planter provided enslaved people on the plantation with ceramics. But even though President Andrew Jackson's Hermitage Plantation yielded evidence of such provisioning, written sources that slaveholders provided enslaved people with ceramics or other items found through archaeological investigation remains scarce.[12] With the rise of historical scholarship on slave independent production and marketing activities in the early 1990s, however, the proposition that enslaved people acquired many, if not, most of their household and personal objects on their own became tenable, particularly as archaeologists such as Mark Hauser, Laurie Wilkie, and Paul Farnsworth conducted their own studies of slave markets and informal exchange in the Caribbean.[13] In the southern United States, Barbara Heath analyzed shopkeeper account books that indicate the kinds and frequencies of items enslaved people purchased.[14] Given these research findings, most archaeologists now interpret objects found through excavations of slave quarters as items enslaved people acquired for themselves.

Slave consumption varied from plantation to plantation, and from slave society to slave society. Many of the items enslaved people used and produced for their own use, however, prove remarkably similar throughout the Americas. Pottery, for example, figures among the items found at many slave-occupied sites in South Carolina and Virginia, several Caribbean islands, and some regions of Brazil. This pottery is usually hand-built (potters using their hands to form the shape of the vessel rather than a potter's wheel) and was used primarily for preparing and serving food. Leland Ferguson in the United States and Mark Hauser in the British West Indies have shown that these wares are more commonly found on eighteenth-century sites rather than on later ones, possibly because the Industrial Revolution made the importation of inexpensive, mass-produced British ceramics and iron cooking pots readily available for purchase. The local wares, however, continued to be produced and used, but in smaller quantities in South Carolina until emancipation. On the islands of Antigua, Jamaica, Nevis, and St Lucia, a few Afro-Caribbean potters still produce pottery similar to that found on slavery sites.

Archaeologists have directed a great deal of attention to the study of this pottery because it is the most common, hand-crafted item found on many slave sites. In general, however, there are few written references to enslaved people making or using pottery; therefore, understanding of this artifact has been based almost exclusively on archaeological research. In some places, such as coastal South Carolina and in the Caribbean, enslaved people evidently produced some or all of this pottery, but in others it was produced by other groups—Indians or free communities of diverse racial and cultural backgrounds. Unfortunately archaeologists know very little about the production sites of these wares because they were most likely fired on the ground surface or in shallow pits that leave few archaeological traces compared to the substantial kilns used to make ceramics fired at higher temperatures such as sugar wares (sugar molds and molasses drip jars) or floor and roof tiles produced on many Caribbean sugar plantations. Knowledge of production sites would indicate where this pottery was produced as it is unlikely every plantation where enslaved people used pottery was engaged in pottery production. Location of production sites could also contribute to determining the cultural or racial identities or both of the makers in plantation settings where diverse groups participated in pottery production. Some excavated pottery fragments from colonial plantations in South Carolina, for example, exhibit signs of the pottery-making process itself, demonstrating in fact that the pottery was made on plantations where it was found. Defects in poorly crafted pots or uneven firing conditions can produce fragile pots that easily break, are subsequently discarded, and never used. From studies of these so-called "wasters"—broken, unused fragments of pottery—produced on plantations, archaeologists have built a case for slave-made pottery in South Carolina and, to a lesser extent, on some eighteenth-century sites in Virginia.[15]

Understanding where pottery was produced has been an important question in framing the study of Afro-Caribbean pottery as well. Mark Hauser conducted a study of Afro-Jamaican pottery from eight different sites located in three different regions of Jamaica, the north coast, a central district, and the south coast, in order to obtain evidence to support regional variation in pottery making and local distribution or centralized pottery production and island-wide distribution. Through studies of the mineralogical content and chemical composition of the pottery, Hauser found Afro-Jamaican potters used the same ceramic recipe—the clays and materials added to the clay—to produce pottery in the three regions. This finding, though suggesting that pottery production took place in a limited number of locations on the island, leaves unanswered how and by whom the pottery was distributed to markets located in some cases long distances from production areas. Through analysis of ethno-historical sources, including prints of slave markets and, later, photographs of post-emancipation markets, Hauser demonstrated that female entrepreneurs, oftentimes enslaved, played a key role in the trade of Afro-Jamaican pottery.[16] Hauser's examination of the interrelationship of pottery production, consumption, and exchange stands as the most in-depth analysis of Afro-Caribbean pottery. He is now undertaking a similar study of island-produced pottery in the French Antilles.

Whether or not enslaved people made these earthenwares, Theresa Singleton and Mark Bogard see the consumption of this pottery as a critical factor in understanding cultural practices associated with these wares.[17] Before European trade introduced iron pots and pans to West Africa, Africans, like most preindustrial peoples, prepared their food in clay pots. Slave use of pottery suggests that some traditional African ways of preparing, serving, and consuming foods, beverages, or medicines were practiced on plantations where the pottery is found. Although the culinary practices associated with this pottery use have been lost, some of the slow-simmering soups, stews, or potages once prepared in these vessels became part of cuisines often associated with African diaspora communities. At some sites, archaeologists have found both iron and clay pots, suggesting that clay pots continued to be used, perhaps for preparing or consuming special dishes or medicines. Clay pots apparently kept vegetables like okra (a vegetable indigenous to West Africa) from turning black and added unique seasoning to foods cooked in them. In South Carolina, some pots appear to have been used for ritual purposes, particularly those recovered from underwater sites with crosses etched on them.[18] Much work remains to be done by archaeologists and historians on this pottery's varied usages other than for preparing and serving food in diverse slave societies.

Enslaved people also made items for themselves and for sale from perishable materials: baskets from a variety of plant materials and household utensils such as bowls, ladles, and cups from gourds or calabashes. Although archaeologists seldom recover the finished product of items made from perishable materials, they sometimes find tools used to make such items. One potential, homemade tool that could have been used in the production of crafts was the reuse of broken bottle glass fragments that were reworked and made into tools with razor-sharp cutting edges. It is unknown how slaves used these objects, but they could have employed them in any number of craft or household projects that required a sharp razor-like edge for whittling, delicate scraping, or splitting thin layers from wood or other plant material. Slave-occupied sites in Brazil, Cuba, Jamaica, and Louisiana have yielded these reworked glass shards, and their widespread geographic distribution suggests it was a common practice for enslaved people to make them, although, to be sure, archaeologists have also found such artifacts at sites occupied by both indigenous and European Americans.[19] The presence of recycled glass tools and the absence of similar cutting tools such as blades or pocket knives made of metal suggest that at the sites where glass tools were found enslaved people did not have access to these other kinds of cutting tools. At the previously mentioned site of Santa Ana de Biajacas in Cuba, however, both recycled glass tools as well as numerous machetes and a few knives have been found, suggesting the glass tools had a special function metal knives and other metal tools did not. At slave sites throughout the Americas, archaeologists have observed artifacts that consist of discarded items recycled by slaves into some other kind of object, particularly tools. Some examples include making an awl (a sewing or leather-working implement) from a bone handle of a toothbrush, a chisel from a broken horseshoe, and smoothing or polishing tools from broken pipe bowls.[20]

Not all enslaved craftspersons relied upon the use of homemade tools from recycled objects to fashion craft items. At a few sites, archaeologists have recovered conventional woodworking tools or sewing implements and notions from slave quarters, which possibly served as both slave residences and workshops for craft specialists who made items for plantation use. At the same time, these specialists possibly took advantage of their access to tools and surplus materials to make items for their own independent production. Excavations of a seamstress quarter at Andrew Jackson's Hermitage Plantation outside of Nashville, Tennessee, support such an interpretation. Archaeologists inferred the quarter was occupied by a seamstress or, possibly, an entire household engaged in sewing activities by the abundance of basic sewing equipment (straight pins, scissors, needles, thimbles) as well as a number of specialized tools used to produce fine lacework and to apply elaborate decorative elements to garments. Jillian Galle believes the specialized needleworking equipment and the proximity of the quarter directly behind the mansion are indications that Gracy Bradley, the slave seamstress who made garments for Rachel Jackson, Jackson's wife, and Sarah Yorke Jackson, Jackson's daughter-in-law, occupied the quarter. If Gracy Bradley lived there, it is one of the rare cases in which the name of a slave occupant living in a specific dwelling could be identified. Galle interprets the abundant remains of non-provisioned items—tobacco pipes, medical supplies, toys, beads, hair combs—as evidence Gracy Bradley, or another seamstress, used her skills for her own independent production facilitating her ability to acquire these items. The quantities of these non-provisioned items from the seamstress quarter were found to be well above the quantities recovered from other slave houses at the Hermitage.[21]

Comparative study of slave household production and consumption has also been undertaken in the study of slave foodways—all activities related to food from procurement to preparation and presentation. At St Anne's slave settlement, one of five dispersed slave communities once part of the Hampton Plantation, a sea-island cotton plantation on St Simon, Georgia, analysis of food remains indicates considerable differences between one household and the others in the exploitation of non-domestic food resources. The occupants of one house (identified as House #4) consumed wild birds while occupants in the other three houses did not. This difference suggests that the residents of House #4 may have had access to guns, the most expeditious way to hunt birds, and the other households did not. House #4 also consumed considerably more turtle than the other households, whereas turtle was a minor food item in the other three households.[22] Whether this difference in turtle consumption was also a consequence of not having the proper equipment to capture turtles, or the occupants of House #4 had more access to the habitats where turtles were found, or simply indicates food preferences among the four households, is unknown. Analyses of foodways from St Anne's slave settlement suggest that the ability of enslaved persons to supplement plantation rations by hunting and fishing was perhaps more complicated than archaeologists have previously interpreted. Some slave workers may have had access to guns and traps while others may not. Food preferences and other conditions also influenced the foods enslaved people acquired and consumed.

These examples suggest how archaeologists are increasingly using, when possible, the slave household as a unit of analysis to understand production and consumption. In studies of household composition, for example, archaeologists are attempting to differentiate households that primarily consisted of kin-based social units with adults and children from households that consisted primarily of single, unrelated individuals. Gender has also come under scrutiny. How can archaeology be used to identify slave households composed primarily of males or females? Slave household composition and gender are obviously difficult issues to address from purely archaeological resources, but when combined with records on the make-up of the slave community at specific plantations and the ways in which slave workers were housed, such analyses may be possible.

Gary Fesler examined the transformation of slave households from unrelated co-residents to kin-based residents during a hundred-year period at the Utopia quarter, a slave settlement of an eighteenth-century plantation near Williamsburg, Virginia. He conducted his analyses on ten slave housing units looking at the relationship between types of slave housing (barracks versus family units), sub-floor pits (described previously), and consumption patterns. Using archaeological data, Felser was able to isolate four distinct periods of occupation that corresponded with specific kinds of housing units for slave workers: period 1 (c.1675–1700), period 2 (c.1700–30), period 3 (c.1730–50); period 4 (c.1750–75). Only slave housing of period 1 lacked sub-floor pits; it was therefore eliminated from the analysis. He found that barracks-type quarters used for housing a large group of unrelated individuals during the second and third periods contained more sub-floor pits used for personal storage than in the housing of the fourth period intended to house smaller groups of related individuals. Sub-floor pits are found in the later housing but fewer appear to have been used for personal storage. Fesler reasoned that co-residents stored their personal items individually and therefore needed more sub-floor pits than kin groups who presumably stored their personal items together. He distinguished sub-floor pits used for personal storage from those used as root cellars in that the latter were placed near the hearths of slave houses to take advantage of ambient heat to keep foods from freezing. Root cellars were found in slave houses of all three periods.[23]

Fesler's analyses of consumption patterns and gender did not yield results as straightforward as in his study of sub-floor pits, but he did find some confor-mance with his overall expectations. He anticipated families would generate larger quantities of artifacts compared to co-residents subsisting independently, and he identified several areas of consumption he believed would show these differences such as construction tools, firearms, eating utensils, and kitchen equipment. In a few cases, however, the consumption patterns did not neatly correlate with the type of housing or sub-floor usage which in turn raised questions about the residency of these quarters and the additional uses of these buildings.

As for gender, Fesler attempted to examine gender through the analysis of artifacts associated with women's activities (maintenance and production of clothing and body adornment, and care of children) versus those associated with male activities (hunting, fishing, building and construction, and taking care of livestock). Fesler acknowledged that these characterizations speak to an *ideal* of gendered activities and that men may have had to perform domestic tasks when there was a shortage of women. Conversely, when there were shortages of men, some women probably took on jobs typically handled by men. Despite these caveats, he did find one of the ten slave housing units at Utopia to have a considerably higher proportion of female activities compared to the others, which he suggests may have been a household composed primarily of females.[24]

The archaeological study of gender in slavery studies remains at a very prelimi-nary stage of research. Archaeologists recognize gender as an important aspect in the independent production, consumption, and exchange in slave communities. Enslaved women labored as potters, seamstresses, and market vendors, among other occupations, while enslaved men produced furniture, wooden crafts, hunted and fished, and more often hired out their labor than women. A study of shop-keeper records from several counties in central Virginia revealed that slave men often purchased household and personal items at country stores because store owners extended credit to slave men more often than to slave women.[25] The archaeological study of slave consumption, production, and exchange relies upon the careful study of both archaeological and historical sources. Archaeology allows discernment of the residue of slave independent production and consumption; written sources contain information on perishable objects acquired and details concerning forms of exchange. Together, the two sources can yield insights into the material world of slave life that one source alone cannot.

RELIGIOUS EXPRESSIONS

The study of religion presents one of the most challenging undertakings for archaeologists because religious beliefs and practices are not always expressed in tangible material remains. In the study of slave religion, for example, archaeologists are unlikely to discover evidence of initiation rites, ring shouts, spirit possession, or other forms of religious performance unless these activities were associated with specific objects that were for some reason left behind at the locations where these activities took place. Artifacts recovered from slave sites interpreted as having served a religious purpose are usually small objects such as crosses or pendants, or more often, modified animal bones and teeth, coins, or shells with perforated holes in them suggesting the items were suspended on strings and possibly worn as amulets around the ankle, neck, or wrist. Archaeologists have found amulets of various kinds at slave sites throughout the Americas. But without ethnographic or oral historical sources to provide information as to what these beliefs were, or how the objects were valued or used, the beliefs and practices associated with amulets remain mysteries.

Burials can often provide a context for understanding how objects believed to be of religious significance were used or valued. In Barbados, for example, a burial of an enslaved male who dated from the late seventeenth or early eighteenth century yielded an elaborate necklace made by drilling canine teeth, fish vertebrae, cowrie shells, and beads. Besides the necklace, the burial contained an African-styled clay pipe, metal rings, and bracelets, more grave goods than other slave burials in the cemetery. The objects suggest that the individual may have enjoyed high status within the slave community. The anthropologist Jerome Handler has suggested that the individual was a healer/conjurer and that the necklace could well have been a protective charm imbued with magical or spiritual powers.[26] A similar necklace minus the cowrie shells and the fish vertebrae was found in a slave burial in Cuba from excavations of a nineteenth-century slave cemetery at the previously described Taoro sugar plantation. The Cuban necklace consisted of beads of various sizes, shapes, and materials, coins with pierced holes, and animal canine teeth with drilled holes. Lourdes Domínguez believes it was a religious *collar* (necklace) and, perhaps, a precursor to the beaded *collares* modern-day adherents of Santería wear to be protected by a particular *orisha*—one of the several saints or deities of the Yoruba-derived religion.[27] Excavations in Minas Gerais, Brazil, by Paulo Junqueira of a cemetery once belonging to a mining company that utilized slave labor yielded an assortment of artifacts: a *figa* (a charm in the shape of a hand closed with a fist and worn for centuries in the Mediterranean area by peoples of diverse cultural background), a coin, a figure of a rising sun, and images of the saints and Jesus Christ.[28] Archaeologists call an object that has acquired multiple layers of meaning and symbolism through usage multivalent or polyvalent. Enslaved Mineiros could have used these artifacts in either Catholic or Afro-Brazilian religious practices or both.

Artifacts recovered from the burials provide tantalizing but isolated incidents of religious practices. To understand better the belief systems of which these practices are a part and the symbolism behind object selection, a few archaeologists are studying examples of recurrent practices found at a number of sites in the United States. They hold crystals, polished stones, shells, bone disks, bird skulls and other animal bones, and iron nails and blades. Archaeologists have found these objects together, deliberately placed in caches below floorboards, doorways, or corners of slave quarters, and sometimes in slaveholder houses and other buildings where enslaved people lived or worked. Although there are similarities in the kinds of artifacts found in these caches, they appear to relate to different religious beliefs and practices.

Caches of artifacts found in some sub-floor pits are also thought to be of religious significance. Patricia Samford has rejected the purely functional interpretations of sub-floor pits as either root cellars or as containers for personal storage. From her study of 103 sub-floor pits, she posits that at least nine of them were used as ancestral shrines. She attributes this practice to enslaved people of Igbo heritage who were imported to eighteenth-century Virginia in large numbers from the Bight of Biafra region of what is now southeastern Nigeria. Sub-floor pits identified as shrines contained unbroken or nearly whole items such as bottles, pottery, agricultural tools, shells, resting on the floor surface of the pits. She bases her shrine interpretation on several lines of evidence. Ethnographic accounts describe the shrines of Igbo and other African groups who buried protective charms and poured libations into holes cut into earthen floors within their houses. Samford notes the similarities between the kinds of artifacts, their colors, patterns, and placement within sub-floor pits, and the shrines of Igbo peoples. In one pit, for example, all of the objects were curiously white—fossilized shell, white kaolin pipes, white ceramics, and stones. The color white, she suggests, is a sacred and important symbol in many West African religions as it symbolizes purity and moral ideas. Additionally, white is always used in sacrifices to *Onishe*, an Igbo river spirit.[29] Pollen analysis from one pit indicated high levels of grape pollen, supporting the possibility that libations of wine were poured in the pit. A court case in 1779, in nearby North Carolina, of an enslaved man who was accused of being a conjurer and alleged to have poured brandy into a hole in the earth provides additional support of enslaved people who were pouring libations in holes at the time when they were digging and using sub-floor pits.[30] The court case also helps to establish that enslaved people were observed pouring libations in eighteenth-century North America. Samford was able to build an argument for the use of pits as shrines only when extensive mapping and photography undertaken during the archaeological fieldwork indicated the original placement of objects in the pits. Detection of these and other kinds of religious caches requires careful excavation and willingness for archaeologists to acknowledge the potential of everyday utilitarian objects to reflect religious expressions.

In another study, Christopher Fennell analyzed a variety of artifacts, buried caches, and markings on artifacts attributed to BaKongo culture. He investigated two sites: one in Maryland and one in Texas. Fennell believes adherents of BaKongo religions in the United States resorted to private and covert forms of rituals because they were denied opportunities to practice their faith in public displays or group-oriented rituals as in some other slave societies. At the Carroll House in Annapolis, Maryland, occupied by the Carroll family and as many as nineteen enslaved workers from the mid-1700s to 1821, he interpreted a variety of objects found under the floorboards in the living and work spaces of the slave workers, including quartz crystals, polished stones, glass fragments, disks of white bone, and a mass-produced ceramic bowl of British manufacture with an asterisk mark on it. These items, he maintains, evidence multiple symbols of the BaKongo tradition. Quartz crystals, stone, and glass represent water; disks of bone represent the spirit world of the dead; the disks' circular form represents the cosmic cycle; and the asterisk suggests the imagining of a BaKongo cosmogram.[31]

At a late antebellum slave cabin of a presumed curer/healer from the Levi Jordan plantation in Brazoria, Texas, archaeologists located four caches of artifacts in an alignment of axes possibly demarcating the crossed lines of a BaKongo cosmogram within the space of the cabin. In one area, a cache containing small iron wedges was found close to water-worn pebbles, fragments of mirrors, several seashells, and a part of a small porcelain doll. The investigators of the site and Fennell interpret this cache as part of *nkisi*—a composition used to invoke the spirits. Also adjacent to the iron wedges were two bases of iron kettles with a piece of white chalk, fragments of medicine bottles, a glass thermometer, and two bullet casings which were interpreted as other items used in *nkisi* but also in divination. The thermometer is significant because it once held mercury, a liquid associated by whites as well as by blacks with magical properties and spiritual force. A second cache contained silver coins dated 1853 and 1858 stacked in a line running north–south; a third cache covered with bricks contained a concentrated deposit of burnt items—shells, iron nails and spikes, and white ash. Fennell interprets the coins, glass fragments, burned shell and iron nails, and ash as items that could be used to invoke the spirit world, land of the dead and ancestors, and cycles of the cosmos. The fourth cache, however, did not resemble BaKongo characteristics. It consisted of three nested iron kettles deposited upright. The middle kettle contained soil, bone fragments, seashells, and metal objects, and a heavy chain was wrapped around the circumference of the largest kettle on the bottom. This cache, Fennell believes, is more characteristic of the Yoruba religious practice dedicated to the *orisha* (deity) Ogun or the use of a *prenda* (spiritual offering) used in the Afro-Cuban religious tradition of Palo Monte Mayombe.[32]

The evidence of at least two distinct religious traditions and practices at the slave cabin of the Levi Jordan plantation suggests that there was some kind of interaction or exchange of beliefs and practices between two individual or two groups of practitioners of different religious traditions. Fennell uses this example as well as others to demonstrate his use of the concept "ethnogenic bricolage" as a means for analyzing the process resulting in the creation of new cultural forms. His use of the term bricolage derives from Lévi-Strauss's conceptualization of a *bricoleur*, a social actor who is a practical, innovative manipulator of cultural knowledge.[33] The term ethnogenic derives from the concept ethnogenesis—a process of identity formation resulting in the creation of a new ethnic or cultural group. According to Fennell, in the process of ethnogenic bricolage, individuals of different cultural heritages interact over time, form new social networks, and create new symbols, communicative domains, and cultural practices. Fennell interprets the archaeological findings at the Levi Jordan slave cabin with BaKongo-like characteristics and another African religious tradition (Yoruba or Afro-Cuban Palo Monte) as the blending and negotiation of different African belief systems that took place in many settings throughout the Americas.[34] There are, of course, other possible interpretations such as the occupants of the quarter may have been poly-religious, practicing more than one African religion as well as Christianity, although researchers reported no artifacts identified with Christianity. The Levi Jordan cabin represents a unique find that may require additional study with comparable discoveries to gain a fuller understanding of its religious significance and symbolism.

Fennell and Samford have undertaken innovative archaeological studies of slave religion by grounding their interpretations in detailed analyses of African religions. Their work shows how in North America some African beliefs and practices were transplanted while others were greatly transformed. Additionally, Fennell offers a conceptual framework for understanding how different religious traditions may have been merged into the creation of new religious practices. While some of the authors' interpretations are more compelling than others, their research demonstrates that tangible remains associated with slave beliefs and practices such as conjuring, healing, divination, pouring of libations, or veneration of ancestors and the spirit world are indeed recoverable through archaeology.

SLAVE RESISTANCE

As students of slavery are well aware, enslaved people resisted slavery in many ways. The previous discussion highlighted a few possible examples of everyday resistance discovered through archaeological investigations of slave quarters: digging sub-floor pits, clandestine activities such as imbibing, gambling, conjuring, among others. Leland Ferguson believes even the making of pottery and preparation of African-style foods were forms of unconscious resistance because enslaved people were striving to build their own culture rather than conforming to cultural dictates of their owners.[35] In addition to forms of subtle or covert resistance, archaeologists also study overt slave resistance at the sites of slave runaways or maroons.

Archaeology of maroon communities is a major focus of African diaspora research in Brazil, Cuba, Jamaica, and Suriname. As early as the 1930s, Loureiro Fernandes, a Brazilian archaeologist, excavated burials of slave runaways found in caves of Serra Negra, in southern Brazil. This investigation was possibly the earliest archaeological study of a slave-related site in the Americas. Runaway slave sites range from long-term settlements with complex social structures such as the seventeenth-century runaway polity of Palmares in Brazil to short-term refuges in caves, overhangs, swamps, and other inaccessible terrains.[36] Cuban archaeologists distinguish between *palenques*—substantial runaway settlements with evidence of horticulture—and the sites of *cimarrones*, small groups of runaways who were frequently on the move, foraging wild foods and raiding nearby plantations for food and supplies. Archaeological sites of both types have been investigated in Cuba. Gabino La Rosa studied two *palenques* in the mountains in eastern Cuba where he observed clusters of dwellings laid out to form inner squares and inner paths leading from one cluster of dwellings to another.[37] These inner pathways may have facilitated communication and movement throughout the settlement without the knowledge of outsiders such as slave hunters who were in constant pursuit of runaways. In western Cuba, La Rosa in the mountainous areas of Havana and Matanzas provinces and Enrique Alonso in the Sierra Organos and Sierra del Rosario in the province of Pinar del Rio have conducted investigations of *cimarrón* sites. Located in caves and overhangs, these sites provide glimpses of the Spartan living conditions of maroons who had very few objects: iron cooking pots, pipes, imported ceramics, bottles, and food remains. Analysis of food remains from sites investigated by La Rosa indicate that *cimarrones* consumed both domestic animals—pigs, chicken, cows, and dog as well as non-domestic foods like ducks, *hutías* (a local rodent), and *majá* (Cuban boa). They most likely obtained the domestic animals from raids of nearby plantations and hunted the non-domestic foods. The dog remains present a curiosity. Dogs usually accompanied Cuban slave catchers in their search for slave runaways and perhaps, on occasion, *cimarrones* lured and captured these vicious animals for themselves.[38]

In Jamaica and Suriname where descendants of slave runaways still maintain autonomous communities, archaeologist Kofi Agorsah has collaborated with these present-day groups to locate, identify, and excavate historic maroon sites linking their oral traditions and ethnography with their archaeological heritage. He has observed similarities in the settlement patterns between rural African communities and those of maroon communities.[39]

Studies of maroon sites have also been undertaken in the southeastern United States, but they are fewer in number and at a preliminary stage of research compared to those of Latin America and the Caribbean. The primary goal of the US studies thus far has been to locate, identify, and describe the materials retrieved from sites. In the 1980s, Elaine Nichols conducted an exploratory study of a maroon site on Culpepper Island in the Great Dismal Swamp—a huge expanse of marshland located in both North Carolina and Virginia—once the home of runaway slave communities. More recently, Daniel Sayers conducted excavations of a 20-acre site, demonstrating that communities of slave runaways and disenfranchised Native Americans had occupied this area for over two centuries. In Florida, Kathleen Deagan investigated the town and Fort of Gracia Real de Santa Teresa de Mosé in St Augustine, Florida—a refuge for slave runaways fleeing colonial plantations in South Carolina. The settlement consisted of 87 black males and their families and the archaeology revealed their subsistence patterns more closely resembled those of local Native Americans rather than residents of Spanish St Augustine. At the nineteenth-century Black Seminole site of Pilaklikaha in Central Florida, Terrence Weik found it problematical to sort out differences between the material culture of the Black Seminole and that of the Seminole, but the site provided insights into the process of ethnogenesis—the making of new cultural identities.[40] Despite the preliminary quality of maroon site archaeology in the United States, these investigations have the potential to fill a neglected void in African diaspora archaeology: African interaction with indigenous peoples.

FUTURE DIRECTIONS IN THE ARCHAEOLOGY OF SLAVERY

Slavery continues to be the predominate focus of the archaeological study of the African diaspora in the Americas, and will no doubt continue to be so in the future. It is always difficult to predict what the future holds for any research interest, but some ongoing projects are paving directions for future research. One emerging theme reflects greater emphasis on comparative studies. Comparing archaeological findings from one site with other similar sites is nothing new to slavery studies, but a few ongoing projects are framing questions from comparative perspectives during project initiation rather than comparing research results in the final analysis. A preeminent example of this approach is being undertaken in the French Antilles where the archaeological study of slavery began only in 2001. Kenneth Kelly is conducting a comparative study of plantations on Guadeloupe and Martinique to see how slavery differed on the two islands as each had a different trajectory with regard to the development of slavery. As a consequence of Guadeloupe's participation in the French Revolution, Republican forces under the command of Victor Hughes ousted a British occupation force on the island in 1794 and abolished slavery. But Napoleon, in 1802, subsequently reinstated the institution. Reinstatement of slavery in Guadeloupe involved a degree of renegotiation between slave laborers and landowners. Masters made some concessions to slave laborers such as the elimination of night work in the sugar mills and the protection of free days. Martinique's engagement with the French Revolution differed, however, from Guadeloupe's; slavery remained intact in Martinique until 1848. Kelly believes these differences in the development of slavery between the two islands would be evident in the archaeological record, and he has already found some support for his ideas in slave housing and in slave access to informal markets.[41]

The study of slavery in settings other than plantations is a growing interest. Archaeologists are beginning to study slavery in military forts, missions, and urban areas. When completed these studies of non-plantation slavery will not only provide data for comparison with plantations, but increase our archaeological understanding of slavery in diverse settings. Future comparative studies in the archaeology of slavery will be greatly facilitated by the Digital Archaeological Archive of Comparative Slavery (DAACS), a database of artifacts recovered from slave sites. The Archaeology Department of Thomas Jefferson Monticello Foundation created DAACS initially for comparing sites in the Chesapeake, but researchers have expanded the database to include sites elsewhere in the United States and in the Caribbean.[42] DAACS is the only analytical tool in widespread use that has been specifically developed for analyzing archaeological data recovered from slavery sites.

Another intriguing setting for future research is the archaeological study of the Middle Passage. Study of slave ships lost at sea is receiving increased attention in maritime archaeology—the study of human activities associated with ships and shipbuilding, including remains of ships found in underwater environments. Numerous slave ships were lost at sea, but only a few have been located and identified as slave ships. Identifying a wrecked slave ship can be difficult because without evidence of slave decks, shackles and handcuffs, air vents above the water line of the ship, or other characteristic features, slave ships resemble other cargo ships of the period. Written sources provide crucial corroborating evidence by identifying the name of the ship and its voyage history. Archaeologists have identified, documented, and excavated several former slave ships, but only two excavated wrecks—*Henrietta Marie* and *Fredensborg*—were actively engaged in the slave trade at the time they were lost. Analyses of the excavated vessels and artifacts provide empirical data on the shipboard experiences of both African captives and European crews that expand upon written descriptions. Recovery of a stone mortar on the *Fredensborg* comparable to ones used by Africans and people of African descent in the Americas supports, for example, documentary references that ship captains provided African captives with foods prepared in ways with which they were familiar. Additionally, a few small objects of African origin, possibly used as talismans, suggest Africans carried a few concealed items with them. Several ongoing projects are searching for lost slave ships in Caribbean and South African waters that will greatly enhance findings from these two landmark excavations.[43]

The material evidence uncovered by archaeologists can be used to interpret many aspects of slavery. Early studies focused primarily upon slave living conditions as seen in housing, subsistence, or household possessions. Archaeologists have moved beyond mere descriptions of living conditions to analyze slave independent production and trade, household composition and variation, gender, religious beliefs, and other cultural practices. Archaeology provides more than a method or source of empirical data; also an analytical framework within which various sources of information on the materiality of slavery can be evaluated and interpreted.

Notes

1. A site refers to area of human activity with a distinct spatial clustering of artifacts, structures, organic and environmental remains.
2. Lorena Walsh, From *Calabar to Carter's Grove: The History of a Virginia Slave Community* (Charlottesville, Va., 1997), 103, documents for eighteenth-century Virginia the placement of houses in a square formation that surrounds an open courtyard in eighteenth-century Virginia.
3. Douglas V. Armstrong, "Archaeology and Ethnohistory of the Caribbean Plantation," in Theresa A. Singleton (ed.), *"I, Too, Am America": Archaeological Studies of African-American Life* (Charlottesville, Va., 1999), 179–80; Douglas V. Armstrong and Kenneth G. Kelly, "Settlement Patterns and the Origins of African Jamaican Society: Seville Plantation, St. Ann's Bay, Jamaica," *Ethnohistory*, 47 (2) (Spring 2000): 383–90.
4. James A. Delle, *An Archaeology of Social Space: Analyzing Coffee Plantations in Jamaica's Blue Mountains* (New York, 1998), 159–61.
5. Lourdes S. Domínguez, "Fuentes arqueológicas en el estudio de la esclavitud en Cuba," in Academia de Ciencias de Cuba (ed.), *La esclavitud en Cuba* (Havana, 1986), 276.
6. Theresa A. Singleton, "Slavery and Spatial Dialectics on Cuban Coffee Plantations," *World Archaeology*, 33 (1) (June 2001): 102–4; Theresa A. Singleton, "An Archaeology of Slavery in a Cuban Plantation," in L. Antonio Curet, Shannon Lee Dawdy, and Gabino La Rosa Corzo (eds.), *Dialogues in Cuban Archaeology* (Tuscaloosa, Ala., 2005), 181–6.

7. Kenneth G. Kelly, "Creole Cultures of the Caribbean: Historical Archeology in the French West Indies," *International Journal of Historical Archaeology*, 12 (December 2008): 394–6.

8. For reference to harboring slave runaways within the wall enclosure, see Mariano Paradas, Capitán de Ceiba Mocha, al Antonio García Oña, Gobernador de Matanzas, December 25, 1837. Fondo: Gobierno Provincial O. P. Cimarrones, Legajo 12, Expediente 50, Archivo Historico Provincial de Matanzas, Matanzas, For four slave workers running away after the death of the owner, see Testamentaría del Señor Presbítero Ignacio O'Farril, 1838–9. Fondo: Escribanía Archivo de Galletti, Legajo 245, Expediente 1.

9. *Pichardo novísimo; o odiccinario provincial casi razonado de vozes y frases cubanas*, new edn., rev. Esteban Rodríguez Herrera (Havana, 1953), 248.

10. Gary R. Fesler, "From Houses to Homes: An Archaeological Case Study of Household Formation at the Utopia Slave Quarter, ca.1675 to 1775" (Ph.D. diss., University of Virginia, 2004), 280–350; Patricia M. Samford, *Subfloor Pits and the Archaeology of Slavery in Colonial Virginia* (Tuscaloosa, Ala., 2007), 5, 66–75.

11. Fesler, "Houses to Homes," 280; William M. Kelso, *Kingsmill Plantations, 1619–1800: An Archaeology of Country Life* (Orlando, Fla., 1984), 120; William M. Kelso, "The Archaeology of Slave Life at Thomas Jefferson's Monticello: A Wolf by the Ear," *Journal of New World Archaeology*, 6 (4) (1986): 13.

12. John Otto, *Cannon's Point Plantation 1794–1860: Living Conditions and Status Patterns in the Old South* (Orlando, Fla., 1984), 61–6; Jillian E. Galle, "Designing Women: Measuring Acquisition and Access at the Hermitage Plantation," in Jillian E. Galle and Amy L. Young (eds.), *Engendering African American Archaeology: A Southern Perspective* (Knoxville, Tenn., 2004), 46.

13. Mark W. Hauser, *An Archaeology of Black Markets: Local Ceramics and Economies in Eighteenth-Century Jamaica* (Gainesville, Fla., 2008); Laurie A. Wilkie and Paul Farnsworth, *Sampling Many Pots: An Archaeology of Memory and Tradition at a Bahamian Plantation* (Gainesville, Fla., 2005).

14. Barbara Heath, "Engendering Choice: Slavery and Consumerism in Central Virginia," in Jillian E. Galle and Amy L. Young (eds.), *Engendering African American Archaeology* (Knoxville, Tenn., 2004), 19–38.

15. Leland Ferguson, *Uncommon Ground: Archeology and Early African America, 1650–1800* (Washington, DC, 1992), 29–31, 48–9.

16. Hauser, *Archaeology of Black Markets*, 164–91.

17. Theresa A. Singleton and Mark Bograd, "Breaking Typological Barriers: Looking for Colono in Colonoware," in James A. Delle, Stephan A. Mrozowski, and Robert Paynter (eds.), *Lines that Divide: Historical Archaeologies of Race, Class, and Gender* (Knoxville, Tenn., 2000), 3–21.

18. Anne E. Yentsch, *A Chesapeake Family and their Slaves: A Study in Historical Archaeology* (New York, 1994), 204; Ferguson, *Uncommon Ground*, 110–16; and Ferguson, "The Cross is a Magic Sign": Marks on Eighteenth-Century Bowls from South Carolina," in Singleton (ed.), *"I, Too, Am America,"* 116–31.

19. Theresa A. Singleton and Marcos Torres de Souza, "Archaeologies of the African Diaspora: Brazil, Cuba, and the Unites States," in Teresita Majewski and David Gaimster (eds.), *International Handbook of Historical Archaeology* (London, 2009), 449–69; Cuba, Singleton, "Slavery at a Cuban Coffee Plantation," 195. On Jamaica, Douglas Armstrong, Syracuse University, personal communication; on Louisiana; Laurie Wilkie, "Glass-Knapping at a Louisiana Plantation: African-American Tools?," *Historical Archaeology*, 30 (4) (1996): 37–49.

20. Making tools from broken artifacts has been reported from the following sites: the awl from Andrew Jackson's Hermitage and the chisel, Portici plantation, Virginia, near Washington, DC. See Theresa A. Singleton, "The Archaeology of Slave Life," in Edward D. C. Campbell with Kym Rice (eds.), *Before Freedom Came: African-American Life in the Antebellum South* (Charlottesville, Va., 1991), 162, figs. 138 and 139; broken pipe bowls which appeared to have been used for polishing or buffing objects were found at Santa Ana de Biajacas in Cuba, see Singleton, "Slavery at a Cuban Coffee Plantation," 195.

21. Galle, "Designing Women," 44–62.

22. Scott Butler, "Data Recovery Excavations at the St. Anne's Settlement (9GN197), Glynn County, Georgia," *Early Georgia*, 35 (2) (2008): 126–8.

23. Fesler, "Houses to Homes," 217–350.

24. Ibid. 382–94.

25. Heath, "Engendering Choice," 28–9.

26. Jerome Handler, "An African-Type Healer/Diviner and his Grave Goods: A Burial from a Plantation Slave Cemetery in Barbados, West Indies," *International Journal of Historical Archaeology*, 1 (2) (1997): 114–20.

27. Lourdes S. Domínguez, *Los collares en la santería cubana* (Havana, 1999), 17, 22–3.

28. Singleton and De Souza, "Archaeologies of African Diaspora: Brazil, Cuba, and the United States," 457.

29. Samford, *Subfloor Pits and Archaeology*, 158.

30. Ibid. 150–89.

31. Christopher C. Fennell, *Crossroads and Cosmologies: Diasporas and Ethnogenesis in the New World* (Gainesville, Fla., 2007), 68–9.

32. Ibid. 79–83.

33. Ibid. 129.

34. Ibid. 83.

35. Leland Ferguson, "Struggling with Pots in Colonial South Carolina," in Randall McGuire and Robert Paynter (eds.), *The Archaeology of Inequality* (Cambridge, 1991), 28.

36. Pedro P. A. Funari, "The Archaeology of Palmares and its Contribution to the Understanding of the History of African American Culture," *Historical Archaeology in Latin America*, 7 (1) (1995): 1–41. Charles E. Orser, Jr., and Pedro P. A. Funari, "Archaeology and Slave Resistance and Rebellion," *World Archeology*, 33 (1) (June 2001): 61–72.

37. Gabino La Rosa Corzo, *Runaway Slave Settlements in Cuba: Resistance and Repression*, trans. Mary Todd (Chapel Hill, NC, 2003), 242–3.

38. Gabino La Rosa Corzo, "Subsistence of Cimarrones: An Archaeological Study," in L. Antonio Curet, Shannon Lee Dawdy, and Gabino La Rosa Corzo (eds.), *Dialogues in Cuban Archaeology* (Tuscaloosa, Ala., 2005), 167–79. For a reference, from my own research, to runaways killing dogs belonging to slave catchers, see Comunicación A. D. Cecillo Ayllón, Gobernador de Matanzas sobre ranchería contra un palenque de Negros situado entre la vega de Guerra, espinal y los hatos los alrededores de puerto Escondido y orillas de las Playas, capturando dos negros y una negra. Fondo: Gobierno Provincial O. P. Cimarrones, Legajo 12, Expediente 23 Archivo Histórico Provincial de Matanzas, Matanzas, Cuba.

39. E. Kofi Agorsah (ed.), *Maroon Heritage: Archaeological, Ethnographic, and Historical Perspectives* (Kingston, 1994); E. Kofi Agorsah, "Ethno-archaeogical Consideration of Social Relationship and Settlement Patterning among Africans in the Caribbean Diaspora," in Jay B. Havsier (ed.), *African Sites Archaeology in the Caribbean* (Princeton,

1999), 38–64; E. Kofi Agorsah, "The Other Site of Freedom: The Maroon Trail in Suriname," in *African Re-genesis*, 191–203. E. Kofi Agorsah, "Scars of Brutality: Archaeology of the Maroons in the Caribbean," in Akinwumi Ogundiran and Toyin Falola (eds.), *Archaeology of Atlantic Africa and the African Diaspora* (Bloomington, Ind., 2007), 277–91.

40. Archaeological studies of slave runaways in the United States include: Elaine Nichols, "No Easy Run to Freedom: Maroons in the Great Dismal Swamp of North Carolina and Virginia, 1677–1850" (Ph.D. diss., Department of Anthropology, University of South Carolina, Columbia, 1988); Daniel Sayers, "The Diasporic World of Great Dismal Swamp, 1630–1865" (Ph.D. diss., Department of Anthropology, William and Mary, Virginia, 2008); Kathleen Deagan and Jane Landers, "Fort Mosé: Earliest Free Black Town in the United States," in Singleton (ed.), *"I, Too Am America"*, 261–82. Terrence Weik, "Allies, Adversaries, and Kin in African Seminole Communities of Florida: Archaeology of Pilaklikaha," in Ogundiran and Falola (eds.), *Archaeology of Atlantic Africa and the African Diaspora*, 311–31.

41. Kelly, "Historical Archaeology in the French West Indies," 398–9.

42. Thomas Jefferson Memorial Foundation, Archaeology Department, www.daacs.org.

43. Jane Webster, "Historical Archaeology and the Slave Ship," *International Journal of Historical Archaeology*, 12 (1) (March 2008): 3–5; Jane Webster, "Slave Ships and Maritime Archaeology: An Overview," *International Journal of Historical Archaeology*, 12 (2) (2008): 16–18.

SELECT BIBLIOGRAPHY

ARMSTRONG, DOUGLAS. *The Old Village and the Great House: An Archaeological and Historical Examination of Drax Hall Plantation, St. Ann's Bay, Jamaica.* Blacks in the New World. Urbana, Ill. University of Illinois Press, 1990.

CHAN, ALEXANDRA A. *Slavery in the Age of Reason: Archaeology at a New England Farm.* Knoxville, Tenn.: University of Tennessee Press, 2007.

DELLE, JAMES. *An Archeology of Social Space: Analyzing Coffee Plantations in Jamaica's Blue Mountains.* New York: Plenum Press, 1998.

FERGUSON, LELAND. *Uncommon Ground: Archaeology and Early African America, 1650–1800.* Washington, DC: Smithsonian Institution Press, 1992.

GALLE, JILLIAN E., and AMY L. YOUNG, eds. *Engendering African American Archaeology: A Southern Perspective.* Knoxville, Tenn.: University of Tennessee Press, 2004.

HAUSER, MARK W. *An Archaeology of Black Markets: Local Ceramics and Economies in Eighteenth-Century Jamaica.* Gainesville, Fla.: University Press of Florida, 2008.

OGUNDIRAN, AKINWUMI, and TOYIN FALOLA, eds. *Archaeology of Atlantic Africa and the African Diaspora.* Bloomington, Ind.: Indiana University Press, 2007.

OTTO, JOHN S. *Cannon's Point Plantation: Living Conditions and Status Patterns in the Old South.* Studies in Historical Archaeology. Orlando, Fla.: Academic Press, Inc., 1984.

SAMFORD, PATRICIA M. *Subfloor Pits and the Archaeology of Slavery in Colonial Virginia.* Tuscaloosa, Ala.: University of Alabama Press, 2007.

SINGLETON, THERESA, ed. *"I, Too, Am America": Archaeological Studies of African-American Life*. Charlottesville, Va.: University Press of Virginia, 1999.

——and MARCOS ANDRÉ TORRES DE SOUZA. "Archaeologies of the African Diaspora: Brazil, Cuba, and the United States," in Teresita Majewski and David Gaimster (eds.), *International Handbook of Historical Archaeology*. New York: Springer, 2009, 449–69.

WIKIE, LAURIE A., and PAUL FARNSWORTH. *An Archaeology of Memory and Tradition at a Bahamian Plantation*. Gainesville, Fla.: University of Florida Press, 2005.

EPILOGUE

CHAPTER 33

··

POST-EMANCIPATION ADJUSTMENTS

··

STANLEY L. ENGERMAN

INTRODUCTION

··

Slavery stands as one of the most ubiquitous of all human institutions, existing in almost all societies from the ancient world until, in parts of Africa and Asia, well into the twentieth century. Indeed, it was precisely slavery's ubiquitousness that led some thinkers, ancient and modern, to regard the institution as a product of natural causes, a universal custom of mankind that was to be regulated by positive law but did not originate in it. Slavery existed in the Americas before Columbus and after him in the colonies established by every western European country. Western culture proved unique not in enslaving others, but in giving birth to an organized, sustained ecumenical movement that presented the case for the superiority of free (wage) labor with "liberty and justice for all."

Once the world's first antislavery crusade got under way the demise of slavery in the Western hemisphere unfolded in a remarkably short period of time, in roughly 100 years. Different countries followed different paths to emancipation: slavery ended by revolution in Haiti, by civil war in the United States, by anti-colonial rebellion in Cuba, and by legislated emancipation in the British, French, and Dutch Caribbean. Yet, the various emancipations hardly realized the rosy scenario predicted by their most ardent advocates. The history of post-emancipation societies poses multiple questions—some unanswered, others the matter of continuing debate—about the meaning of freedom and the costs borne by different groups of historical actors.

While the discrete process of emancipation, its causes and its effects, varied from country to country, in most cases, post-emancipation reactions to the new order of things bore some common characteristics.[1] Emancipation entailed new arrangements as governments sought to direct and control the labor of former slaves. Free labor posed a different set of challenges for those in power because freedom brought with it new expectations and a different set of political rights and economic liberties than had existed under slavery. Emancipation typically proceeded gradually, not immediately, whether the state provided slave owners with some additional labor force or, more frequently, mandated a period of adjustment or transition during which slaves would be educated or trained to cope with freedom, although the form the education might take was never specified. In no cases of New World slavery (or of European serfdom) was any compensation in funds or land paid to slaves. Rather, in almost all cases, slaveholders received the compensation. It could take the form of cash, bonds, or land payments or of a compelled labor time or quasi-freedom, more commonly referred to as an apprenticeship. More frequently the compensation to slaveholders occurred through the operation of what in Brazil was called the law of the "free womb." Although it freed no existing slaves, it did emancipate the children of slave mothers but not before subjecting them to a period of apprenticeship that, depending on their location and gender, could vary from fifteen to thirty years. This post-natal provision permitted the slave owners to recapture, in a productive way, the costs of raising the child. The state, for its part, kept the costs of emancipation to taxpayers low, thereby facilitating the political process by which the electorate agreed to the emancipation.

The basic terms of emancipation affected the responses of the ex-slaves to their post-emancipation situation and the overall character of the post-slave society. For the slaves, emancipation seems to have conferred, in addition to legal freedom, several other related benefits: increased leisure time, less intense labor time, and lowered labor force participation rates. Sharecropping and other forms of labor tenancy, however unsatisfactory to modern sensibilities, express negotiation and compromise between former masters and former slaves. To be sure, governments attempted to counter black aspirations by introducing a wide variety of methods to control the labor of ex-slaves. Coercion might take the form of limitations on the ability of former slaves to acquire land for settlement off the plantation, either by artificially elevating prices or by explicit legal prohibition. Taxes might be used to preempt possibilities for slaves to avoid work on the plantation by engaging in subsistence agriculture. No post-emancipation country lacked fresh vagrancy laws to help coerce former slaves into plantation labor. Some schemes provided former slaves with small plots of land insufficient by themselves for subsistence or stoked consumption so as to pressure former slaves to work "voluntarily" on the plantation. Imports of indentured labor had the direct impact of increasing the supply of labor available to planters and the indirect impact of lowering the price of wages. Ex-slaves, generally left with no assets, faced difficult choices. They could not easily become landowners working for themselves; they could not easily avoid the circumstances of poverty that their new-found freedom would usher in. Thus, white officials expected the ex-slaves would need to work for white landowners as wage-earners in a way that would replicate the tightly managed, intensive labor characteristic of the plantation during slavery days. In some cases the government provided magistrates or agents to introduce some equity in contract negotiations, but they were conducted within a framework of ex-slaves as laborers and often led to a favoring of the planters.[2]

THE ENDING OF SLAVERY AND ITS AFTERMATH

At the time of the American Revolution of 1776, as David Brion Davis has pointed out, every western European colony in the Americas from Canada to Chile legally permitted slavery.[3] Slavery's importance varied with crop conditions and climate, not because of any significant difference in morality harbored by the several European colonizers. Not until several of the northeastern states of the United States, beginning with Vermont in 1777, moved to the fore to introduce forms of gradual emancipation did the right to slave ownership in the Americas begin to be restricted. During the colonial period, these northeastern states had proved distinctive in the Americas in their reliance on immigrants from Europe for labor. Only small numbers of Indians inhabited the region, and the demand for slaves exerted a relatively minimal pull. Natural increase determined the essence of the northeastern populations; whites predominated at 85 percent of the population or more. Thus, these northeastern states came to have slaves in small proportions, with none having more than about 6 percent in the total population, and so the early effects of emancipation were limited. Emancipation in Vermont included a period akin to apprenticeship. New Hampshire and Massachusetts, the next two states to follow Vermont's lead, ended slavery immediately without compensation to slave owners. Most northern states after passing laws for gradual emancipation imposed in its aftermath strict restrictions on free black suffrage and the ability of free blacks to obtain an education.

The first major slave emancipation that also achieved political independence for the former slaves began in the French colony of Saint-Domingue. There a slave insurrection in 1791 turned into a social revolution that led to the creation thirteen years later of Haiti. Although scholars have frequently argued for the indirect role of slave resistance in propelling emancipation, only in Haiti did collective slave violence lead directly to emancipation. Prior to 1791, Saint-Domingue ranked as perhaps the richest colony in the world, producing for France and the re-export market in Europe considerable amounts of coffee and sugar. Haiti's economic situation would dramatically change, however, in about two decades after the achievement of slave emancipation and political freedom. The Haitian Constitution prevented whites from owning land. Redistribution programs broke up estates to dole out land as reward to political loyalists. The sugar industry collapsed and coffee production fell to one-third its pre-revolutionary level.[4] To observers on both sides of the Atlantic, Haiti would become a kind of poster child for the failure of emancipation: The "Pearl of the Antilles," as the French colony was called before 1791, had as an independent nation of former slaves sunk into the depths of poverty so severe that by the middle of the twentieth century Haiti would qualify as the only country in the Americas with a level of income comparable to that in sub-Saharan Africa.

Following independence from Spain at the start of the nineteenth century, the former Spanish colonies in South and Central America freed their slaves, generally by gradual means and with compensation to slave owners.[5] Again, the numbers of slaves in these areas were relatively limited in comparison with the number of Indian inhabitants or with the number of slaves in some other American colonies, especially where the cultivation of sugar predominated. Thus the slaves' freedom did not have a significant impact upon production patterns. The ending of slavery became a more significant economic and political issue with the next set of slave emancipations in and after the 1830s, for they dealt with societies in which slaves predominated numerically. For ideological and political reasons the causes and consequences of the British emancipation of slaves have attracted the most attention from scholars as well as contemporaries. After a long series of debates, Parliament passed legislation that ended Britain's slave trade in 1807 and ended slavery throughout the British empire in 1834. But emancipation included a period of apprenticeship (or coerced labor) designed to last for six years and compensation to slave owners in the amount of 20 million pounds, a staggering sum that surpassed the profits earned by British slave traders during the heyday of the traffic in the eighteenth century. Parliament eventually shortened the period of apprenticeship to four years, but paid the compensation to the slave owners in full with a dramatic expansion of the public debt. Slave owners received cash payments that amounted to about 45 percent of the value of slaves in the period 1823 to 1830. Not all British islands accepted or needed a period of apprenticeship to effect an orderly transition to freedom. Planters in Antigua and Bermuda believed that because of their island's high population density and the inability of ex-slaves to find for themselves free land to work or other alternative sources of income, continued apprenticeship served the planters no useful purpose.[6]

A debate continues about the causes of British emancipation and the relative role of economic, political, and ideological factors. Over time interpretations have shifted, from a focus on British morality based on the humanitarian roles of Wilberforce and the Saints, to attention to the role of economic decline in the British Caribbean, as emphasized by the arguments of Eric Williams, the first Prime Minister of Trinidad and Tobago, in *Capitalism & Slavery* (1944). More recent scholarship, most notably that of Seymour Drescher, has disputed the argument for economic decline and returned the focus of research to the role played by non-economic forces, like popular mobilizations, in pressuring Parliament to take action against slavery. In a recent book on the abolition of the British slave trade, David Beck Ryden has attempted to shift the balance back toward Williams's materialist interpretation.[7] These debates are of interest not only for understanding the attack against the slave trade and slavery, but for their insight into the expectations of contemporaries about the shape of post-emancipation events.

In the 1840s the Swedish, French, and Danish islands introduced emancipation schemes, with some form of compensation to slave owners. The Dutch waited until 1863 to end slavery in their West Indian colonies, legislating, like the British, a system of apprenticeship attended by direct compensation to slave owners. After the Dutch emancipation, slavery remained only in Cuba, Puerto Rico, Brazil, and the United States. Emancipation in each of these cases followed a different pattern. In the United States, slavery ended in 1865 at the end of a bloody Civil War with a constitutional amendment but without any period of apprenticeship or compensation to slave owners (or to slaves). Of the two remaining Spanish-American colonies in the Caribbean, Puerto Rico ended slavery in 1873 with a period of apprenticeship plus payment of compensation. Cuba finally ended slavery in 1886, the culmination of a process that began with the Moret Law of 1870, which freed all slaves born to slave mothers after 1868, subject to a period of apprenticeship before full freedom.[8] As with other free womb plans, this one left all slaves at the date of passage still enslaved, pending further legislation. Brazil, independent of Portugal after 1822, passed the Rio Branco Law (Law of the Free Womb) in 1871, and over the next seventeen years passed additional legislation that modified the existence of slavery, until the Golden Law finally abolished slavery in 1888—the last ending of slavery in the Americas. One of the interesting ironies is that while the colonies of the Iberian powers were often touted before emancipation for their relatively benign treatment of slaves, Brazil and Cuba ended slavery some fifty years after the British.[9]

These emancipations, though certainly not congruent, did have several features in common that would influence post-emancipation adjustments. Except for Haiti, the ending of slavery did not lead to substantial changes in political conditions. The other Caribbean colonies remained part of the empire of the European metropolis; Brazil and the United States remained independent nations as did the former Spanish colonies of Central and South America, where the ending of slavery followed political independence. Except for Haiti and the United States, emancipation was generally accomplished either by political actions in the metropolis or, as in the case of Latin America, by political legislation after they became independent countries. In all but the United States and several areas of Latin America, the state compensated slave owners either by direct payments or by compelling labor time, ranging from fifteen to thirty years, from the free born of slave mothers. In no case did slaves receive economic compensation. While economic circumstances did vary among areas at the moment of emancipation, in no case did a prior economic collapse lead to severe economic losses to slave owners. Nor was there a prior weakening of the sugar and other export economies. In general, the international slave trade had ended about a quarter century before the passage of legislation ending slavery, so by the time of emancipation much of the slave population in the emancipating countries had become creole or American born not African born.

Certain similarities existed in most areas regarding the response to the ending of slavery. Based upon the ratio of land to labor and on legislation regarding land ownership and labor control, emancipation led slaves, whenever possible, to move off the plantation. They shifted to working on smaller units, generally producing non-export crops. A related decline in the production of sugar and other export crops and the plantation system as a whole occurred (see Table 33.1). Although the ex-slaves generally lacked political power, the planters were not always able to force their former slaves back onto the plantations. More work remains to be done on the kinds of restraints, moral, political, and economic, that operated on planters in different countries to prevent them from exerting a kind of coercion that more closely approximated slavery. More work also remains to be done on how the nature of slavery in a given area contributed to whatever degree of success ex-slaves experienced in the post-emancipation period. In Britain's colonies landowners attempted to limit the movement of ex-slaves off plantations by controlling the availability of land or by controlling labor mobility using variants of the British Masters and Servants legislation; such methods did not always prove successful. The basic regulations on ex-slave mobility were not unique to the post-emancipation case but derived from previous metropolitan legislation concerning free British workers.

Depending on the availability of land and of alternative local labor supplies, a number of quite different adjustments took place in post-emancipation societies, with the nature of these adjustments clearly varying over time with changes in labor availability and laws relating to land. In some cases, particularly in the West Indies, imports of indentured labor arrived from Asia and Africa; in others, such as Brazil and Cuba, planters came to rely on immigrant labor from Portugal, Spain, and Italy. Other areas drew upon local labor, whether those previously working on plantations (such as Barbados), or else those who had not previously worked on plantations but within the same geographic area (as in the US South). These

Table 33.1. Slave prices, land–labor ratios, and changes in sugar production in the British slave colonies prior to and after emancipation

	(1) Average slave prices 1823 to 1830 (£)	(2) Land–labor ratio (square miles per thousand total population)	(3) Percentage change in average annual sugar production 1824–33 to 1839–46	(4) Period in which pre-emancipation level of sugar production regained	(5) Ratio of sugar production in 1887–96 to sugar production in 1839–46
1. Antigua	33	3.1	+8.7	–	1.5
Barbados	47	1.7	+5.5	–	3.5
St Kitts	36	2.9	+3.8	–	2.7[c]
2. Trinidad	105	47.7	+21.7[a]	–	3.0[b]
British Guiana	115	832.4	−43.0	1857–66	3.4
Mauritius	70	8.0	+54.3	–	3.1
3. Dominica	43	16.3	−6.4	1847–56	0.7
St Lucia	57	15.5	−21.8	1857–66	1.7
Nevis	39	5.0	−43.1	1867–76	–[c]
Montserrat	37	4.6	−43.7	1867–76	2.5
St Vincent	58	5.7	−47.3	Never	0.7
Tobago	46	8.8	−47.5	–[b]	–[b]
Jamaica	45	12.2	−51.2	1930s	0.6
Grenada	59	6.3	−55.9	Never	–[d]

[a] Trinidad output did decline slightly after the end of the apprenticeship, and it was not until 1845 that the 1834 level was regained.
[b] Tobago data merged with Trinidad after 1891. The 1877–86 level of sugar production in Tobago was two-thirds that of 1824–33.
[c] Nevis data merged with St Kitts after 1882.
[d] No sugar output shown after 1888, a year in which only 77 tons were recorded.

Source: Stanley L. Engerman, "Economic Change and Contract Labor in the British Caribbean: The End of Slavery and the Adjustment in Emancipation," Explorations in Economic History, 21 (1984): 133–50. See p. 142 for data on sources and notes.

decisions about labor supply would influence the future levels of output, in some cases permitting recovery of early levels of production of sugar. In other cases where increased labor impact was not economically feasible, areas were left with a permanent shortfall of output relative to the pre-emancipation levels. Interpretations by contemporaries and by some modern historians that emancipation was a failure often point to evidence of declining output to help make their case. In the aftermath of emancipation, declining output generated political debate as to whether the costs associated with the initial transition from slavery to freedom might persist for a much longer time and perhaps even be permanent in the absence of statist interventions.[10]

No crop bears more responsibility than sugar for the growth of the transatlantic slave trade, and sugar output after emancipation opens a strategic window into the basic patterns of adjustment. They can be described more clearly by looking at British West Indian colonies after the ending of slavery in 1834 and of apprenticeship after 1838. The discussion of the effect of emancipation on sugar output remained central to the debates, but such discussion put aside the benefits to the ex-slaves of increased leisure and of more desirable working conditions off the plantation. Three basic patterns resulted.[11] The first (see Table 33.1), seen in Barbados and Antigua, occurred where population density was high, and there was little land available for ex-slaves. Here the plantation system remained strong, sugar output remained high, and economic growth occurred. Antigua's planters, for example, did not believe the compelled labor of the apprenticeship system was needed, and ended coercion in 1834, and once emigration was allowed and encouraged, Barbados became a prime source of emigration elsewhere in the circum-Caribbean region, mainly to Panama, and later to the United States.

Jamaica manifested a different pattern. Sugar exports declined, never to be restored to pre-emancipation levels, but exports of coffee increased and, after 1890, of bananas and logwood as well.[12] The flight of former slaves from the estates in search of land they could call their own contributed to the growth of small family farms in less productive parts of the island. The two areas growing most rapidly and those that had the highest slave prices before emancipation were Trinidad and British Guiana, both acquired by Great Britain at the start of the nineteenth century. These areas, where the third pattern appeared, contained considerable amounts of unsettled land and, with emancipation, the ex-slaves were able to move there to possess it. The plantation system unraveled. For the planters, the availability of highly productive land kindled the desire to reinstall it. After several decades, planters in Trinidad and British Guiana, as well as in Jamaica, effectively reinstituted the plantation system by introducing indentured labor, mainly from India, to work on plantations. In the period from 1838 to 1917 the British colonies brought over about 400,000 indentured laborers, some of whom remained and some of whom returned to their native land, as permitted under the legal provisions of the indenture law (see Table 33.2). This "new system of slavery," as abolitionists in Parliament called it, permitted a return to the plantation production but with a different labor supply and different institutional arrangements than under slavery, a pattern repeated in several other cases. Metropolitan debates developed about whether indentured labor, with its controls and coercion, really differed all that much from slavery, and the attack on the indenture system brought about its generally legislated ending by the early twentieth century.[13]

The French colonies, except Haiti, had patterns of response similar to the growing British areas. Haiti had suffered a permanent decline in the plantation system and export output. Although there were some unsuccessful attempts by the new rulers to reinstate a plantation system two decades after the gaining of

Table 33.2. Estimates of intercontinental flows of contract labor, gross movements, nineteenth and early twentieth centuries

Areas of origin to receiving region	Years	Numbers (thousands)
India: to British Guiana	1838–1918	238.9
Trinidad	1838–1918	143.9
Other British Caribbean	1838–1915	46.8
Mauritius	1834–1910	451.8
French Caribbean	1853–85	about 79.7
Réunion	1826–82	86.9
Suriname	1873–1916	34.0
Saint-Croix	1862	0.4
Fiji	1878–1917	61.0
Natal	1860–1912	152.4
Mombassa	1895–1922	39.5
India: to Malaya	1844–1910	249.8
China: to British Guiana	1852–79	13.5
Trinidad	1852–65	2.6
Other British Caribbean	1852–84	1.7
Peru	1849–74	about 90.0
Cuba	1848–74	124.8
Hawaii	1865–99	33.6
Transvaal	1904–7	63.7
Japan: to Hawaii	1868–99	65.0
Peru	1898–1923	17.8
Java: to Suriname	1890–1939	33.0
Portuguese Islands: to Hawaii	1878–99	10.8
British Guiana	1835–81	32.2
Other British Caribbean	1835–70	8.8
Pacific Islands: to Australia	1863–1904	61.2
Elsewhere in Pacific	1863–1914	about 40.0
Peru	1862–3	3.5
Africa: to British Guiana	1834–67	14.1
Jamaica	1834–67	11.4
Trinidad	1834–67	8.9
Other British Caribbean	1834–67	5.0
French Caribbean	1854–62	18.5
Réunion	1848–61	34.3
Yucatan: to Cuba	1849–71	about 2.0
Angola: to São Tomé and Príncipe	1876–1915	about 96.5

Note: Several intracontinental flows are included: those from India to Malaya, from Yucatan to Cuba, and from Angola to the offshore islands. Also, some relatively minor intercontinental flows of contract labor are omitted, in addition to movements within Africa in the late nineteenth and twentieth centuries. In a few cases there may be small amounts of non-contract labor included, and there may be some differences between numbers registered, numbers departing, and numbers arriving, but these will have only a minor impact on the figures. The years are not in all cases calendar years, and the dates of flows are approximations in some cases, including years in which the trade was prohibited, but, again, these will not have any impact on the interpretations. Finally, there are a number of discrepancies among the various sources (compare, for example, the details of estimates for the Indian emigration in Ferenczi and Willcox, *International Migrations*, with the estimated inflows given in other sources), but, again, these do not alter the basic patterns.

Source: Stanley L. Engerman, "Contract Labor, Sugar, and Technology in the Nineteenth Century," *Journal of Economic History*, 43 (1983): 635–59. See table 1 of that paper for details on sources of data.

freedom, the economic and political collapse of Haiti became permanent despite a growth in population, which, however, added to its economic difficulties. Also complicating Haiti's recovery was the acceptance of French demands for compensation for slave losses as a condition for the reopening of Haitian trade with France in the 1820s, a compensation actually paid by the Haitians. An essentially peasant economy of smallholding, largely subsistence farmers emerged, who if they produced a surplus did so for local markets. Haiti soon became the poorest of the nations in the Caribbean and today ranks as one of the poorest nations in the world.[14]

The two remaining major French islands, Guadeloupe and Martinique, supplemented ex-slave labor with contract labor drawn mainly from Asia, and along with French Guiana, they received close to 100,000 contract workers. The French islands remained part of France, and, even today, have full voting and political rights. The Dutch colonies presented some different patterns. Several, mainly the small tourist islands, have remained colonies of the Netherlands, while the largest of the West Indian colonies, Suriname, remained engaged in the twentieth century in plantation sugar production, employing indentured labor from India and Dutch Java. Not until 1975 did Suriname achieve independence with the help of funds provided by the Netherlands.

The ending of slavery in the United States, Cuba, Puerto Rico, and Brazil provided quite different sets of adjustment. In the United States, the abolition of slavery in the Thirteenth Amendment to the Constitution resulted from the defeat of the Confederacy. A federal policy that would have provided freedmen with forty acres and a mule remains a fascinating counterfactual in contemplating short-term and long-term alternative possible worlds for the postbellum South. That the percentage of blacks in the postbellum South who owned and operated their own farm jumped from nearly nothing in 1860 to more than 20 percent in the 1880s speaks to the question of black initiative after slavery. Whether the existence of pockets of free blacks who owned privately substantial amounts of land had a significant impact on local political and racial questions remains an interesting question. Former slaves also enjoyed for a time a set of political rights—the right to vote, the right to hold political office—unknown to their counterparts in other former slaveholding countries in the Americas. In the immediate aftermath of the Civil War, southern whites used Black Codes with provisions on vagrancy, mobility, and loss of work time to compel blacks into wage labor. Although Congressional Reconstruction overturned these codes, their essence remained to influence legislation in the "redeemed" South once Reconstruction ended. Although whites maintained control of the land, a decline in the plantation system occurred in the postbellum South, particularly for sugar and rice production. Although cotton production also suffered for at least a decade after the war, it eventually recovered rapidly, but on the basis of production on less efficient, smaller units, using both black and white labor, which had considerable geographic mobility within the South. These units were frequently owned by white farmers who had been unable to compete with plantations in the antebellum era. As the share of cotton production in the overall postbellum economy increased, the share of corn production decreased, and southern self-sufficiency declined along the way. The shift to cotton production by white farmers became the basis of economic and political disturbances over the remainder of the century.[15] Although the postbellum South soon regained its position as the world's leading cotton producer around 1875 and kept that status for almost fifty years, income levels did not reach antebellum highs until about a quarter century after the Civil War.

Cuba and Puerto Rico, after 1825 the two remaining Spanish colonies in the Caribbean, experienced rather different patterns of freedom and adjustments to emancipation. The Puerto Rican emancipation in 1873 entailed both payment of compensation to planters and a short period of apprenticeship by the ex-slaves. Given that sugar production accounted for a relatively small share of Puerto Rican output, there was little change in Puerto Rico's output levels and the nature of the labor force. Cuba, the largest of the Spanish islands and one of the wealthiest colonies in the world at the midpoint of the nineteenth century, generated such a demand for labor that the supply of slaves, constricted by British cruisers, proved insufficient. As a supplement Cuban planters between 1847 and 1874 imported into the island more than 100,000 mostly Chinese indentured servants. (A similar stream of Chinese indentures migrated to Peruvian sugar plantations after 1873.) The ending of slavery in Cuba differed from the earlier emancipations in the Caribbean, occurring in 1886 in a period of political instability and a weakening of the plantation system.[16] Sugar production was maintained after slavery, but with a shift away from large plantations to cane farming on small-scale units. Rather than following the British example of bringing in indentured labor, Cuban planters employed immigrants from Spain. Thus after emancipation, Cuba maintained a larger share of whites in the total population than was the case in other areas of the Caribbean and a larger share of whites in sugar production as well.

The final emancipation of slaves in Brazil in 1888 resulted in the growing importance of white labor from southern Europe to replace those ex-slaves who left the plantation. These migrants from Europe were willing to laborers on small-scale coffee units that had replaced the plantation production system. Laborers came, some thanks to a subsidy, from Italy, Spain, and Portugal, whereas the ex-slaves preferred to avoid returning to the plantation system. Coffee production on plantations declined, but Brazil remained the world's leading producer because coffee cultivation could proceed quite efficiently on small units with immigrant labor.[17]

The Dominican Republic, where an invading Haitian army had forced the abolition of slavery in 1822, emerged as a new source of Caribbean sugar production by the end of the nineteenth century. In the twentieth century, Haitian migrants supplied Dominican sugar plantations with the majority of their laborers.

Cuba (at times with the use of migrant labor from Haiti) and Barbados maintained high levels of sugar production in the late nineteenth and twentieth centuries, as did Trinidad and British Guiana, while Jamaica produced some sugar but also shifted to growing bananas. The Caribbean areas maintained agricultural production and a heightened interest in tourism, with only limited production of manufactured goods. In South America there was some development of a manufacturing sector, particularly in Argentina, Chile, and Brazil, but even these areas fell dramatically behind the United States in terms of per capita income and manufacturing production.

POST-EMANCIPATION ECONOMIC PERFORMANCE

Whether from a prolonged period of colonization or from the earlier achievement of independence, those areas of the Americas that formerly held slaves in large numbers demonstrated only limited growth prospects and opportunities for longer-term economic development after emancipation. Even when, in the period after the Second World War, more former colonies achieved political independence, there were few economic gains, and in some areas, such as Suriname, Haiti, and Cuba, political difficulties continued. In the absence of appropriate national income accounts, detailed estimates of emancipation-induced declines in output can be looked at for only two areas—Jamaica 1832–50, and British Guiana 1832–52. In both cases per capita incomes fell by about 20 percent. These figures can be contrasted with an estimate of about a 10 percent decline in the southern United States 1860–80.[18]

In regard to the Caribbean, sugar remained the most important crop, and changing economic fortunes in the region reflected changes in sugar production and prices. The ending of slavery generally meant a large decline in sugar output, one that took a long time to recover since it was based on the ending of the plantation system (see Table 33.3). This decline did not lead to a shift to a new export crop, but to production of foodstuffs for ex-slaves and the general development in the region of a peasantry composed of former slaves and their descendants. The major exceptions were Cuba, British Guiana, Trinidad, and also the three British areas of Antigua, Barbados, and St Kitts, the latter of which had low land–labor ratios that allowed them to maintain sugar production. British Guiana had an initial sharp decline in sugar production from which it recovered once imports of indentured labor was permitted, while Trinidad had only a slight decline with the ending of apprenticeships, but its dramatic recovery did not occur until the mid-1840s.

Table 33.3. Average annual sugar production prior to and after emancipation (000 tons)

	Five years prior to abolition	Five years after end of restrictions[a]	Percentage change	Period in which pre-emancipation level regained
Martinique	29.1	(1847) 20.5	−29.6	1857–61
Guadeloupe	31.9	(1847) 17.7	−44.5	1868–72
Surinam	15.7	(1873) 9.7	−38.2	1927–31
Cuba	595.4	(1886) 745.7	+25.2	—
Puerto Rico	94.0	(1876) 74.4	−20.9	1900–4
Brazil	254.0	(1888) 170.6	−32.8	1905–9
Louisiana[b]	177.1	(1865) 44.0	−75.2	1887–91

[a] Date either of abolition or end of "apprenticeship" controls, except for Martinique and Guadeloupe, where emancipation occurred in April 1848, and Louisiana, where it was the end of the Civil War.
[b] Shown here are the averages for 1857–61 (which include the high output recorded for 1861—the highest of any antebellum year) and 1866–70. The 1856–60 average, which includes the very low output of 1856, was 132.4. If an additional two years were allowed for readjustment, the 1868–72 average was 62.8—still a substantial decline for whatever combination of years is chosen.

Source: Stanley L. Engerman, "Economic Adjustments to Emancipation in the United States and the British West Indies," Journal of Interdisciplinary History, 13 (1982): 191–220. See table 2 on p. 202 for information on sources and notes.

The British maintained the previous tariff system on sugar after emancipation with different rates for colonial- and foreign-grown sugar. After heated debate about the introduction of free trade, Parliament eliminated this differential as well as the extra protection for colonial-grown sugar by legislating the Sugar Duties Act of 1846. Leveling the playing field engendered some rather dramatic changes in the nature of West Indian sugar exports. While the shift in relative prices meant a decline in exports from British West Indian plantations, a concomitant expansion of sugar exports occurred in Cuba and Brazil, still major slave owning areas. Cuba, in particular, became the world's largest cane sugar producer over the second half of the nineteenth century, despite new competition from both beet sugar produced in Europe and North America after the ending of the Napoleonic Wars, and from new areas growing cane sugar, such as Natal (a British colony in southeastern Africa), Hawaii, Fiji, and Queensland, all of which served to limit sugar's expansion in the Caribbean and restrain its prospects for economic growth. In response, some areas of the Caribbean successfully produced other crops. Jamaica turned to coffee, logwood, and bananas; Trinidad looked to rice and cocoa; and several other islands that possessed neither the soil nor the climate for the high-level production of export crops relied on tourism. The one island that was able to generate noteworthy growth after the Second World War was Trinidad, which benefited from the continuing development of oil deposits as well as the location during the war in the Cheguarmas Peninsula of a major United States military base that remained in operation until 1967.

Irony accompanied the poverty that dogged Haiti and many other Caribbean countries in the post-slavery era. Some of the growth in Cuban sugar output during the 1920s stemmed from the relocation of laborers within the Caribbean. Rural regions of Jamaica and Haiti, where former slaves had sought to define the meaning of freedom for themselves by getting away from gang labor in the plantation system, furnished a substantial number of migrant laborers for Cuba's sugar plantations. That the Dominican Republic's sugar industry also drew upon Haitian labor provides another telling sign of the post-slave-era poverty that persisted in Haiti.

EMANCIPATION AND EDUCATION

The rather checkered economic history of ex-slave societies in the Americas raises the question of the relative importance of education and human capital formation in the post-emancipation period. Recent scholarship has underscored the desire of ex-slaves to obtain an education for themselves and their children. The law of slavery throughout the Americas generally prohibited the education of slaves, and thus the number of literate slaves at the moment of emancipation was quite limited, although they frequently rose to positions of leadership in post-emancipation communities. To supporters, free womb laws promised an ordered, tightly supervised process that included formal education of the free born at some stage of apprenticeship. Both the British stipendiary magistrates sent to the Caribbean to supervise emancipation and the agents of the Freedmen's Bureau in the United States had as part of their portfolio the education of freed blacks to prepare them for freedom and a new life that would not turn them into wards of the state. Given the nineteenth-century concern for the development of human capital, and the belief that education could make for an easier, more orderly transition to freedom for both ex-slaves and ex-slave owners, the metropolitan powers expressed concern about providing an education, whether secular or religious, to ex-slaves. The reality of apprenticeship, however, often diverged from the promise. But in the United States at least, a combination of state and federal funding and black self-financing precipitated a surge in black education during Reconstruction.

The British Colonial Office argued for the importance of providing education for the ex-slaves.[19] The Act of Emancipation included provision of grants to religious bodies for the education of ex-slaves, a set of grants that ended in 1845 when each colony was on its own in regard to provision of education. Prior to emancipation, missionaries had been the major source of education, and their educational activities continued after emancipation. The British Colonial Office had been advocating compulsory education, but with limited success. Even with the passage of legislation the enforcement was quite limited, so the ends sought were seldom achieved. Debates on the islands on the desired form of education, secular or religious, persisted. It is estimated that prior to 1865, less than 30 percent of children aged 5–15 received any formal education in the British islands of the Caribbean. Despite the political difficulties, some basic literacy was achieved. By 1871, the literacy of the population over 5 in Jamaica was 16.3 percent, rising to 32.0 percent in 1891. By the first half of the twentieth century, high rates of literacy were achieved in several areas. In 1943 literacy rates were 76.1 percent in Jamaica, 92.7 percent in Barbados, and 70.9 percent in the Windward Islands.[20] Literacy at this time was also high in the former Spanish colonies of Puerto Rico at 68.5 percent and Cuba at 77.9 percent, although the rates for blacks remained far below those of whites. These rates, while below North American mainland levels, compared favorably with those in Asia and eastern Europe. In the French colonies, only religious schools had provided education for freed blacks prior to the imposition of government control over schools in 1886. The level of education until this time was quite low.[21]

Research on the behavior of ex-slaves in educating themselves and in creating a life for themselves in the aftermath of slavery in relation to specific laws and policies should reveal much more about the impact of bondage on the enslaved and its social and psychological toll. Demographic patterns of the former slaves in various countries require much additional research. Why did fertility and mortality rates change so little after emancipation? Birth rates in the West Indies remained relatively unchanged over the course of the nineteenth century, although the areas receiving indentured laborers from India tended to have rates above those of Jamaica and Barbados. Life expectancies did not generally increase until after the start of the twentieth century, with particularly sharp increases after the 1920s.[22] Why do black illegitimacy rates along with the percentage of female-headed households rise in the United States and other countries the further post-emancipation societies distance themselves from slavery?

Post-emancipation patterns of economic and social change did differ widely for different locations. Quite distinct variations existed in the degree of geographic mobility within the Caribbean, to and within the United States, to the United Kingdom, and to other European metropolitan nations. There was little outmigration of ex-slaves from the United States, but after the First World War substantial movement from the South to the states of the North began. In the United States and elsewhere periods of extensive racism and meager economic gains for blacks dragged on insufferably long. The legacy of slavery on post-emancipation adjustments will continue to be a source of intensive and fruitful inquiry by scholars. There needs to be, however, a much more systematic linking of the study of slavery with the study of emancipation to reveal the nature and significance of post-emancipation adjustments. How did, for example, the nature of slavery in a given society relate to the degree of success attained after emancipation by ex-slaves? Greater understanding of post-emancipation adjustments will undoubtedly also further our appreciation of how attitudes toward blacks have changed and of the slow but positive steps taken toward greater equality for many of the world's peoples more than a hundred years after the legal end of slavery in the Americas.

NOTES

1. For a discussion of the different policies that led to slave emancipation, see Stanley L. Engerman, "Emancipation Schemes: Different Ways of Ending Slavery," in Enrico Dal Lago and Constantina Katsari (eds.), *Slave Systems, Ancient and Modern* (New York, 2008), 265–82.
2. On these aspects of emancipation in the United States, see Eric Foner, *Reconstruction: America's Unfinished Revolution, 1863–1877* (New York, 1988). For the Caribbean, see Hilary McD. Beckles and Verene A. Shepherd, *Freedoms Won: Caribbean Emancipations, Ethnicities, and Nationhood* (Cambridge, 2006); Roderick A McDonald, *Between Slavery and Freedom: Special Magistrate John Anderson's Journal of St. Vincent during the Apprenticeship* (Barbados, 2001); and Woodville K Marshall, *The Colthurst Journal: Journal of a Special Magistrate in the Islands of Barbados and St. Vincent, July 1835–September 1838* (Millwood, Va., 1977). Eric Foner, *Nothing But Freedom: Emancipation and its Legacy* (Baton Rouge, La., 1983) provides a concise multi-level analysis of the post-emancipation South that includes a comparative dimension.
3. David Brion Davis, *Inhuman Bondage: The Rise and Fall of Slavery in the New World* (Oxford, 2006), 1.
4. On Haiti, see Mats Lundahl, *Peasants and Poverty: A Study of Haiti* (New York, 1979).
5. Leslie B. Rout, Jr., *The African Experience in Spanish America: 1502 to the Present Day* (Cambridge, 1976), esp.185–322.
6. For the debates on emancipation, see Seymour Drescher, *The Mighty Experiment: Free Labor vs. Slavery in British Emancipation* (New York, 2002). See also Stanley L. Engerman, "Economic Adjustments to Emancipation in the United States and British West Indies," *Journal of Interdisciplinary History*, 13 (Autumn 1982): 191–220; and Stanley L. Engerman, "Economic Change and Contract Labor in the British Caribbean: The End of Slavery and the Adjustment to Emancipation," *Explorations in Economic History*, 21 (April 1984): 133–50.
7. Eric Williams, *Capitalism & Slavery* (Chapel Hill, NC, 1944); Seymour Drescher, *Econocide : British Slavery in the Era of Abolition* (Pittsburgh, 1977); Seymour Drescher, *The Mighty Experiment*; Seymour Drescher, *Abolition: A History of Slavery and Antislavery* (Cambridge, 2009); and David Beck Ryden, *West Indian Slavery and British Abolition, 1783–1807* (Cambridge, 2009). See also Thomas C. Holt, *The Problem of Freedom: Race, Labor, and Politics in Jamaica and Britain, 1832–1938* (Baltimore, 1992); and Barbara L. Solow and Stanley L. Engerman, *British Capitalism and Caribbean Slavery: The Legacy of Eric Williams* (Cambridge, 1987).

8. On Cuban emancipation, see Rebecca J. Scott, *Slave Emancipation in Cuba: The Transition to Free Labor, 1860–1899* (Princeton, 1985). For Cuban emancipation in comparative perspective, see Rebecca J. Scott, *Degrees of Freedom: Louisiana and Cuba after Slavery* (Cambridge, 2005).

9. A good starting point for the growing literature on Brazilian emancipation is Robert E. Conrad, *The Destruction of Brazilian Slavery, 1850–1888* (Berkeley, 1972).

10. For a survey of these changes, see Engerman, "Economic Adjustments to Emancipation," 191–220.

11. Engerman, "Economic Change and Contract Labor," 133–50.

12. Beckles and Shepherd, *Freedoms Won*, 116–18; David Watts, *The West Indies: Patterns of Development, Culture, and Environmental Change since 1492* (Cambridge 1987), 510–11.

13. Stanley L. Engerman, "Contract Labor, Sugar, and Technology in the Nineteenth Century," *Journal of Economic History*, 43 (September 1983): 635–59; Seymour Drescher, "Free Labor vs. Slave Labor: The British and Caribbean Cases," in Stanley L. Engerman (ed.), *Terms of Labor: Slavery, Serfdom, and Free Labor* (Stanford, Calif., 1999), 5–86.

14. Lundahl, *Peasants and Poverty*, esp. 91–120.

15. Engerman, "Economic Adjustments to Emancipation," 191–220.

16. Scott, *Slave Emancipation in Cuba*; Christopher Schmidt-Nowara, *Empire and Antislavery: Spain, Cuba, and Puerto Rico, 1833–1874* (Pittsburgh, 1999), 126–38; Ada Ferrer, *Insurgent Cuba: Race, Nation, and Revolution, 1868–1898* (Chapel Hill, NC, 1999), esp. 94–122.

17. George Reid Andrews, *Blacks & Whites in São Paulo, Brazil, 1888–1988* (Madison, 1991).

18. Michael Moohr, "The Economic Impact of Slave Emancipation in British Guiana, 1832–1852," *Economic History Review*, 25 (November 1972): 588–607; Gisela Eisner, *Jamaica, 1830–1930: A Study in Economic Growth* (Manchester, 1961), 25–59; Engerman, "Economic Adjustments to Emancipation," 191–220.

19. Shirley C. Gordon, *A Century of West Indian Education: A Source Book* (London, 1963).

20. G. W. Roberts, *The Population of Jamaica* (Cambridge, 1957), 78–9.

21. Beckles and Shepherd, *Freedoms Won*, 83–277.

22. Roberts, *Population of Jamaica*, 165–306.

Select Bibliography

ANDREWS, GEORGE REID. *Blacks & Whites in São Paulo, Brazil, 1888–1988*. Madison: University of Wisconsin Press, 1991.

BECKLES, HILARY McD., and VERENE A. SHEPHERD. *Freedoms Won: Caribbean Emancipations, Ethnicities, and Nationhood*. Cambridge: Cambridge University Press, 2006.

DRESCHER, SEYMOUR. *The Mighty Experiment: Free Labor vs. Slavery in British Emancipation*. New York: Oxford University Press, 2002.

ENGERMAN, STANLEY L. "Economic Adjustments to Emancipation in the United States and British West Indies," *Journal of Interdisciplinary History*, 13 (Autumn 1982): 191–220.

——"Contract Labor, Sugar, and Technology in the Nineteenth Century," *Journal of Economic History*, 43 (September 1983): 635–59.

——"Economic Change and Contract Labor in the British Caribbean: The End of Slavery and the Adjustment to Emancipation," *Explorations in Economic History*, 21 (April 1984): 133–50.

FONER, ERIC. *Reconstruction: America's Unfinished Revolution, 1863–1877*. New York: Harper & Row, 1988.

GORDON, SHIRLEY C. *A Century of West Indian Education: A Source Book*. London: Longmans, 1963.

LUNDAHL, MATS. *Peasants and Poverty: A Study of Haiti*. New York: St Martin's Press, 1979.

SCOTT, REBECCA J. *Degrees of Freedom: Louisiana and Cuba after Slavery*. Cambridge, Mass.: Harvard University Press, 2005.

——*Slave Emancipation in Cuba: The Transition to Free Labor, 1860–1899*. Princeton: Princeton University Press, 1985.

INDEX

Ableman v. Booth (1857) 443
abolitionism 11, 38, 97, 146, 166–8, 177, 181,
  240, 556
  African American roles 526, 560, 563,
    564, 569, 571–2
  antislavery activism of 1820s and
    1830s 399
  in Brazil 112, 119, 124
  in Cuba 102–3
  in England 378, 559–60
  gradual approach in British
    Caribbean 563–5, 570
  gradual approach in French
    Caribbean 565–7, 570
  gradual approach in US 558–63, 568–9
  immediate approach 567–70, 572–4
  religious underpinning 575 n.2
  second French emancipation 570–71
  of slave trade 139, 149
  in Spanish South America 72, 80, 81, 83
  in the US North 378, 425
  see also Act for the Abolition of the
    Slave Trade
Accara 164
Act for the Abolition of the Slave Trade 167
Act for the better ordering and governing of
  Negroes (1661) 277–8
Act of Emancipation (British) 740
Adams, John Quincy 610
Adams, John 431, 435
Adams, Willi Paul 431
Adas, Michael 337
Adélaïde-Merlande, Jacques 193
African American Christianity 379–83, 392
African Burial Ground (New York
  City) 216

African Methodist Episcopal Church
  (AME) 389–90
Africanization 276–80, 284, 467
Agency (of slaves) 8, 35, 36, 116–17, 121, 211,
  229–30
Agorash, Kofi 718
Akan/Aja 138, 139, 142
Akans 164
Alabama 241
  Mobile 364
Albert Batista, Celsa 29, 37
Alberta 302
Aldama, Domingo de 98
Alencastro, Luiz Felipe de 586
Allen, Richard 389, 392
Allen, Theodore 492
Altink, Henrice 526
Alvarado, Pedro de 49, 50
Amazon River 156
American and Foreign Anti-Slavery
  Society 573
American Anti-slavery Society 572
American Colonization Society 408, 563
American Freedman's Inquiry
  Commission 242
American Methodist Episcopal Church 389
American Revolution 80, 177, 181, 223–4,
  227, 234, 238, 345, 388–9, 407–8, 424–5,
  430, 432, 447, 450, 535, 547, 560, 673
  effects on antislavery movement 580
  Ethiopian Regiment 580
Amerindians 136, 139
Amistad 573
Anderson, Bonnie 557
Andes 70
Andrés-Gallego, José 69

Anglicans 328, 383, 384, 385
Anglo-Spanish Treaty (1817) 441
Angola 50, 115, 122, 138, 156, 163, 183, 476
angolas 51, 55, 58, 60
Anguilla 136
Annales school 112, 179
Anne I 325
anomie 116–17
Antelope (1825) 441
Anti-Federalists 435
Antigua 138, 145, 146, 149, 300, 454, 459,
    708, 730
  sugar production 734, 738
Antilles 70
Apaches 322, 323, 325
Aponte Rebellion 100–1, 360
Aponte, José Antonio 100, 586
apprenticeship 282
Aptheker, Herbert 9, 246 n.23, 461
Arabs 338
Arawaks 136
archaeology
  plantations and other built
    environments 703–7
  religious expression 712–16
  slave consumption, production, and
    exchange 707–13
  resistance 717–18
Arcos, Marqués de 98
Ardouin, Alexis Beaubrun 177, 185, 190, 612
Argentina 69, 73, 80, 83, 303, 585
  Buenos Aires 8, 71, 72, 78
  Córdoba 77
Arizona 326
Arkansas 323, 366, 371
Armitage, David 671
Armstrong, Douglas 704
Armstrong, George D. 550
Articles of Confederation 434
artisans 10, 74, 366, 455, 515
Aruba 155, 157–8, 162, 169, 315
asiento (slave–trading contract) 50, 71, 72,
    80, 94–5, 97, 157
Aubert, Guillaume 187
Augustinians 73

autonomy 145, 160, 184, 204, 208, 215,
    224, 232, 400, 578
Azoca, don Louis López de 57
Aztecs 48, 313

Bacon, Nathaniel 323, 448
Bacon's Rebellion (1676) 323
Badillo, Jalil Sued 34
Bahamas 136, 151 n.9, 315
Bahamas 651
Bailey, David Thomas 692
Bailyn, Bernard 671
Baiz, Gelpí 34
BaKongo 715–16
Balboa, Vasco Núñez de 50
Bambara 220
Bancroft Prize 13
Bancroft, Frederic 625, 628–9, 630, 631
baptism 382, 388
Baptist, Edward E. 237, 239, 518
Baptists 384, 385, 389, 395–6 n.22, 431
Baralt, Guillermo 31, 37
Barbadian Plantation Complex 207
Barbados 741
Barbados 4, 37, 142, 144, 149, 176, 215,
    299, 300, 360, 357 n.7, 406, 430, 732
  Akan/Aja ethnicities, 138, 139
  Bridgetown 8
  as model for other slave societies 207,
    208, 209, 210, 277, 280, 284
  slave rebellion 146
  slave religion 712
  slavery charter period 134–6, 139–40
  sugar production 135, 141, 143, 206, 208,
    214, 579, 734, 738
  treatment of women 517
Barbuda 136
Barcia, Manuel 90, 101, 638
Barcia, María del Carmen 96, 103
Barickman, B. J. 113
Barry, Boubacar 481
Bastide, Roger 123
Batellas, Angela 83
Baud, J. C. 168
Bautista, Juan 62

Bay, Mia 558
Bayly, Christopher 675, 677
Beard, Charles 556
Becker, Gary 489, 556
Beckles, Hilary 149, 476, 514, 515, 518, 527
Beeldsnijder, Ruud 169
Behrendt, Stephen D. 100
Belize 47, 54, 63
Bellgarde-Smith, Patrick 614
bells 240
Beltrán, Gonzalo Aguirre 46
Benedictines 383
benevolence myth 23, 25–7, 30, 35, 228,
    246 n.23, 293, 362, 393, 403, 405, 408,
    412–13, 414, 537, 538, 541
Benito el Negro 50
Bennett, Herman 56, 60
Bento, Antônio 591
Berbice River 156
Berbice 158, 168
Bergad, Laird W. 504, 637–8, 668
beriberi 303–4, 305
Berkenhead, Isaac 142
Berlin, Ira 134, 202, 205, 216, 220–1, 374,
    433, 472, 475, 476, 574, 668
Bermuda 134, 140, 142, 148, 151 n.9, 730
Berry, Daina Ramey 495, 515, 518
Berry, Mary Frances 470
Biassou, Georges 605, 606
Bierck, Harold, Jr. 83
Biet, Antoine 142
Bight of Benin 100, 115, 120, 122, 137, 180,
    183, 189
Bight of Biafra 51, 100, 115, 137, 138,
    192, 715
Bissette, Cyrille 193, 570–1
Black Code 222, 736
black education 740–2
black Jacobins 607, 675
black Loyalists 450
black majorities 140, 160, 173, 175, 210,
    214, 215, 221, 383, 430, 447, 451, 452,
    473, 599
black Moravians 382, 384
black Seminoles 350, 718

black soldiers 15 n.8, 115, 221, 443, 561
black tongue, see pellagra
Blackburn, Robin 607, 667, 671, 673
Blackstone, William 559–60
Blassingame, John W. 229, 230, 344, 365,
    469, 470, 478, 519, 523, 689–90, 691
Bleby, Henry 148
Bledsoe, Albert Taylor 403
Bloch, Mark 664, 666
Blumenbach, Johann Frederick 342
bodies 239–40
Bogard, Mark 709
Bolívar, Simón 83, 584, 610
Bolivia 69, 71, 72, 80, 318
    Potosí 73, 80, 317
Bolton, Charles C. 365–6
Bonaire 155, 157–8, 162, 169
Bonaparte, Joseph 583
Bonaparte, Josephine 566
Bonaparte, Napoleon 566
Bond, Bradley G. 369, 376 n.25
Bonilla, Raúl Cepero 23
Bonner, Robert 549
Border South 369
Borrego Plá, María del Carmen 79
Botkin, B. A. 469
Botkin, Benjamin 689
Boukman 605
Boulle, Pierre H. 186
Bowman, Shearer Davis 669
Bowser, Frederick 69, 74, 84
Boxer, C. R. 112
Boyer, Jean-Pierre 27
bozales (African-born slaves) 70, 82, 160
Braddick, Lawrence 671
Bradley, Gracy 710
Braithwaite, Edward 138
branding 81, 316
Braude, Benjamin 338
Brazil 4, 5, 6, 10, 13, 40, 52, 83, 99, 102,
    106, 141, 144, 163, 175, 206, 208, 210,
    275, 277, 285, 319, 329, 348–9, 368,
    383, 412, 492, 499, 504, 537, 540, 542,
    549, 575, 579, 586, 587
    Bahia 112, 124, 360, 625, 637, 670, 671, 678

Brazil (*cont.*)
    Bahia Rebellions 360, 458
    barracón de patio 705
    coffee industry 677, 737
    Conservative Party 119
    Dantas-Saraiva-Cotegipe Law (1885) 124
    electoral law (1881) 119
    emancipation 579–80, 584, 586–92,
        593, 728, 731
    Espírito Santo 112
    free(d) people of color 579
    glass 709
    Goiás 125
    Golden Law (1888) 124
    hookworm 301
    immigrant labor 737
    interracial social actions 455
    maroon communities 675, 717
    Matanzas 579
    Mauritsstad 156
    Minas Gerais 112, 113, 115, 118, 119,
        120, 125, 637
    nutrition, 302–3, 305
    Palmares 121–2
    Paraíba Valley 112, 114, 122
    Paraná, 112, 115
    Pernambuco 112, 121, 124, 125, 156,
        587, 591, 637
    Recife 156, 157
    religion 383
    Rio Branco Law (1871) 124
    Rio das Velhas 120
    Rio de Janeiro 112, 113, 115, 119, 120,
        123, 124, 125, 300, 583, 586, 587
    Rio Grande do Sul 112, 113
    Sabará 118
    Salvador 8, 112, 123, 387, 458, 459, 586
    Santa Catarina 112
    São José del Rey 118
    São Paulo 112, 113, 114, 115, 118, 119, 120,
        124, 125, 318, 587, 591
    seventeenth century 381
    slave culture 467, 646, 675, 714
    sugar plantations 360, 494, 579, 582,
        636, 645, 739

Breen, T. H. 340
Brissot, Jacques Pierre 565, 566
Bristol, Joan 55
British America 185
British Caribbean 37, 115, 727
British Colonial Office 740–1
British Guiana 136, 149, 158, 167, 168,
    734, 738
British Honduras 136, 151 n.9
British Virgin Islands 136
British West Indies, *see* Bahamas; Barbados;
        British Guiana; British Honduras;
        Cayman Islands; Jamaica; Leeward
        Islands; Trinidad and Tobago;
        Windward Islands
Broglie, Victor de 566
Brother Thornton 394
Brown Fellowship Society 346
Brown, Christopher 557, 563, 575–6 n.5
Brown, Kathleen 527
Brusone, Julio LeRiverend 23
Bryant, Sherwin 73, 78, 81
Bullet, Jeannot 605
Burke, Edmund 7, 370
Burke, Emily 387
Burnard, Trevor 527
Burton, Richard 613
Bush, Barbara 476, 513, 521
Bush, Michael 669, 670, 672, 676
Butler, Jon 385
Butler, Pierce 433
Buxton, Thomas 567
Byrne, Frank J. 367

cabildos de nación 100
Cabral, Pedro Alvares 156
cacao 8, 54, 59, 73, 80, 175, 183
Cáceres, Alonso de 93
Cáceres, José Núñez de 22
cachaça 114
Cairnes, J. E. 363
Calatrava, José Maria 592
Calhoun, John C. 240, 370, 545
California 326
Calvinism 166, 328

Camp, Stephanie M. H. 237, 238, 239, 519, 520
Campbell, Gwyn 668, 679
Camus, Jean-Yves 195
Canada 7, 321, 326
Candomblé 123, 387
cannibalism 315, 340
Canning, George 567
Canny, Nicholas 671
Cap Français (Saint-Domingue) 8, 183, 188
Cape of Good Hope 137
Cape Verde Islands 114, 300
capitalism 6, 8–9, 229, 230–1, 247 n.28, 280, 456, 475, 490, 539–40, 546, 557, 559
Cardoso, Ciro Flamarion 113
Cardoso, Fernando Henrique 112
Caribs 315
Carmelites 383
Carney, Judith A. 474
Carnot, Lazare 605
Carroll, Patrick 66
Cartagena (New Grenada) 8, 35
cartas de alforria (writs of freedom) 120
Carter, Landon 697
Casas, Bartolomé de las 49, 70, 90, 92, 316, 402
Cassá, Roberto 28, 37
Castañeda, Rodrigo de 48
Caste War (1848, Mexico) 102
castration 76, 523
Castro, Hebe Maria Mattos de 117–18, 119
Castro, Sheila de, 117–18
Catholic Church 142, 348, 379, 380, 383, 401, 402, 617
  in Brazil 123
  in Dutch colonies 156, 161, 162
  in French colonies 185, 186
  in Spanish colonies 25, 27, 28, 30, 35, 73, 75, 96
  in United States 219, 229
  see also Augustinians; Christianity; Dominicans; Jesuits; Mercedarians
Cayman Islands 136
Cecelski, David S. 241
cédula 76

Celestino de Almeida, Maria Regina 125
Central America, see British Honduras; Costa Rica; Guatemala; Honduras; Nicaragua; Panama
Cerezeda, Andrés de 48
Cerrato, Alfonso López de 49
Chagas disease 658
Chalhoub, Sidney 116, 122
Chandler, David 71, 82
Chaplin, Joyce 224, 417
Charles III 81
Charles IV 94
Charles V 70
Charles X 177
Charlestown, see South Carolina, Charleston
charter generation 134
Chase, Salmon 574
Chavannes, Jean-Baptiste 604, 614
Chaves de Resende, Maria de Leônia 125
Cherokees 324, 350
Cheves, Langdon 433
Chickasaws 322–3, 324, 350
children 282, 284, 295, 304–5, 324, 329, 424–5, 432, 439, 478–80, 514, 518, 655–6
  in Brazil 122
  in British colonies 143–4
  and family unity 551
  in French colonies 179
  manumission 589
  in United States 224, 233, 234, 236–7
Childs, Matt D. 100, 360
Chile 7, 72, 76, 80, 83, 316, 317
Chinese laborers 102, 705
Chirac, Jacques 194–5
Chirino, José Leonardo 81
Choctaws 323, 350
cholera 303
Christianity 10–11, 156, 186, 192, 205, 209, 315, 320, 327, 329, 337, 338, 342, 378, 424, 428, 429, 431
  black churches 388
  black versions 378–9, 383–7, 388–9
  in British colonies 142, 147, 148, 150

Christianity (*cont.*)
  critiques of slavery 166
  evangelicalism 11, 135, 146, 148, 224, 228,
    328, 348, 361, 538, 581
  missionaries 162
  and slaves 388, 390, 528, 547
  as slavery sanction 404, 405, 408, 409,
    410, 415, 536–9, 540–1, 543–4, 547, 548,
    550–1
  in Spanish colonies 70, 77
  see also Anglicans; Baptists; Catholicism;
    Methodists; Moravians; Protestantism
Christophe, Henri 583
Churchill, Winston 493
cimarrones (fugitive slave communities) 57,
    61, 204, 706
citizenship 10, 37, 119, 443
Civil Rights Movement 228, 229, 369, 484–5
    n.9, 557, 629
Civil War 227, 234, 235, 238, 242, 313, 361,
    367, 369, 374, 388, 412, 435, 440, 499,
    503–4, 535, 541, 545, 551, 560, 561, 569,
    573, 575, 736
Civique, Gastine de 177
Clarkson, Thomas 556, 565
class 6, 14, 29, 35
  consciousness 28, 358, 360, 361, 370,
    371, 535
  formation 358, 362, 370
  ideology 360, 362, 370
  in slaveholding societies 357–62
  solidarity 28
  tensions 91, 361
Clavière, Etienne 565, 566
Clay, Henry 569
Clinton, Catherine 235
Clitherall, Eliza 542–3
clock time 240
Cluny, Alexander 289 n.23
coartación 579
coartación 95, 97, 105, 106
Cobb, Thomas Reade Rootes 3, 14, 205,
    438–9, 548, 574
cobreros 94
Coclanis, Peter 453

Code Noir (1685) 184, 186–7, 220, 221,
    424, 518
Código Negro Español (Spanish Black
    Code) 81, 82, 98
Codrington, Christopher 142
Coehlo, Philip 655
coffee 4, 8, 12, 564, 645
  in Brazil 112, 113, 114, 117, 121, 124
  in Dutch colonies 158, 159, 163
  in French colonies 176–7189
  in Spanish colonies 32, 97, 99, 100
Coffy 164
cofradías (confraternities) 55–6, 58,
    75, 96
Cohen, David 185, 186
Colfax, Richard 347
Collins, Winfield H. 627–8
Colombia 68, 72, 73, 77, 82, 83, 318, 349,
    495, 585
  Bogotá 82
  Cartagena 71, 77, 79, 300
  Chocó 73, 78
  Comunero rebels 81
  Popayán 73
  Santa Marta 79
colonial era 202, 234, 280, 282
colonialism 12, 313, 320, 557
  English 203
  Spanish 203, 209
  Dutch 154, 427
  French 185, 194, 427
  Portuguese 427
  Spanish 25, 90, 97, 100–1, 102, 104,
    105, 427
Colorado 313, 326
Columbus, Bartolomé 314
Columbus, Christopher 4, 50, 296, 313,
    314, 320, 338, 401
Columbus, Diego 28
Comanches 323, 326
Commonwealth v. Aves (1836) 433
Company of the Indies 220
compensation 63, 168
Compromise of 1850 440
comunidad mulata 21

Concepción Valdés, Gabriel de la,
    see Plácido
Condorcet, Nicolas de 566
Confederacy 542, 551
Confederate Constitution 3, 439
Congo 183
congos 51
Congress of Vienna 581, 586
conjure 382, 702
Connecticut 202, 215, 431, 432
    New London 441
Conrad, Robert 635, 636
consensual sex 369
Constant, Benjamin 566
Constitution of 1824 (Brazil) 119
Constitutional Union Party 369
control 74–7, 112, 135, 138–9, 141–6, 159,
    211, 232–3, 364, 404
convicts 280
Cook, Mercer 185
Cook, Noble David 297
Cooper, James Fennimore 370
Cope, R. Douglas 60
copper 94
Cord, Marcelo Mac 122
Coromantee, see Gold Coast
Coronado Expedition (1540–2) 326
Cortés, Hernando 48, 49, 50
Cortés, Juan 50
Costa Rica 54, 59, 315
    cacao 47
    Cartego 52, 54
    slave trade 50–1
cotton gin 227
cotton 677
cotton 8, 114, 201–2, 494, 499, 501, 504,
    536, 539, 540, 549, 677
    post-Civil War production 736–7
    in British colonies 140
    in Dutch colonies 158, 159
    in Spanish colonies 73
    in United States 205, 206, 215, 223,
        224, 234, 241, 247 n.28
Coupland, Reginald 556
Courlander, Howard 599

Cover, Robert 560
Craton, Michael 208, 558
Craven, Avery 687
Creek War (1813–14) 218
Creeks 218, 322, 324
creoles 360, 384
    in Brazil 115, 117, 122, 123
    in British colonies 134, 136, 135, 139,
        142, 147
    creolization 475–6, 482
    in Dutch colonies 160, 161, 167
    in French colonies 174, 177, 184, 190, 191
    as slaves 343, 537
    in Spanish colonies 35, 47, 55, 57, 60,
        77, 82, 94, 97
    in United States 207, 214, 219
Crosby, Alfred W. 297
Crowther, Samuel Ajayi 480
cruelty 143, 144–5, 163, 186, 208, 220, 229,
    230, 242, 343, 403, 410, 430, 434
    see also branding; mutilation; sexual
        abuse; whipping
Cuba 4–6, 8, 10, 12–13, 21–4, 26, 32, 34, 80,
    90, 124, 144, 185, 299, 303, 315, 322, 412,
    441–2, 499, 504, 575, 579, 637–8, 645,
    667, 678, 741
    agriculture 94–5
    Aponte rebellion 100–1, 360
    barracón de patio 705
    Bemba uprising (1843) 101
    Cárdenas 101, 457
    early modern period 92–6
    El Cobre 94
    emancipation 579–80, 583, 586–92, 593,
        727, 731, 737
    free(d) people of color 579
    gender 35
    glass 709
    Guanajay uprising (1833) 101
    Guamacaro rebellion (1825) 101
    Guantanamo 104
    Hatuey rebellion (1511) 92
    Havana 8, 92, 93, 95, 100, 101, 300, 302,
        303, 457, 583
    indigenous population 91–2

Cuba (*cont.*)
   La Escalera 586
   La Guánabana uprising (1843) 101
   maroons 717
   Matanzas 100, 101, 457
   nineteenth century 96–106, 542
   Puerto Príncipe 104
   race 35
   Santa Ana de Biajacas 706, 709
   Santiago 100, 104
   slave religion 712
   slave uprisings 457
   Spanish conquest 91–2
   sugar plantations 359, 582, 677, 737,
      738, 739
   Ten Years War (1868–78) 103, 104, 105
   Wars for Independence 103
Cuban Revolution (1959) 24, 27, 90
Cubano-Iguina, Astrid 590
Cuffe's Rebellion (1763) 600
Cuguano, Ottaba 480
cultural determinism 185
cultural expression 8
cultural studies 365
culture 15, 35, 36–7, 123, 134, 137–8, 174,
   179, 184–9, 228, 232, 237, 276–7
Curaçao 51, 155, 157–8, 161, 167, 168,
   315, 346
   De Knip plantation insurrection 165
   Hato plantation insurrection 165
   Willemstad 165
curandera (healer) 77, 78
Curet, José 31–2
Curtin, Philip 70, 114–15, 135, 182, 214,
   294, 480, 495, 657, 667, 669
Cushner, Nicholas 73
customary servitude 283
Cyrus Cylinder 559
Cyrus the Great 559

d'Esnambuc, Pierre 173
Daget, Serge 182, 183
Dahomey 192
Danish Virgin Islands 162

Dantas-Saraiva-Cotegipe Law (1885), *see*
   Brazil, Dantas-Saraiva-Cotegipe
   Law (1885)
Darnton, Robert 10
Davidson, Stanley 305
Davies, Samuel 388, 389, 390, 391
Dávila, Pedrarias 48
Davis, David Brion 174, 275, 276, 404,
   436, 557, 559, 667, 669, 671–2, 729
Davis, Hugh 427
day-laborer slavery 26
Daya, Joan 188
De Soto *entrada* 332–3 n.10
Deagan, Kathleen 718
Dean, Warren 112, 116
Debbasch, Yvan 190, 1941
Debien, Gabriel 178–9, 180, 182, 184, 188,
   189, 190, 193, 599
Declaration of Independence 560
Declaration of the Rights of Man and
   Citizen 567
Deep South 369, 371
Degler, Carl N. 340, 341, 369, 666
Deive, Carlos, Esteban 26, 27, 41 n.17
Deken, Aagje 166
Del Monte, Domingo 101
Delaware 223, 425–6, 436, 437, 443, 634
Delgrès, Louis 615
Delisle, Philippe 186
Delle, James 704–5
Demarara 146, 147, 148, 158, 168, 457,
   567–8, 637
Democratic Party 562, 563
Democratic-Republican Party 562, 563
demographics 90, 136, 138–40, 143, 149,
   159–60, 170 n.15, 179, 180, 186, 278–79
   fertility 659–62
   health and mortality 653
   origins of slavery 644–5
   shifts 4, 23, 31
   slave trade 646–8
   sugar plantation conditions 656 –, n.9
   US plantation conditions 654–6
dengue fever 657

Denmark 301
Deschamps Chapeaux, Pedro 91, 96
Dessales, Adrien 177
Dessalines, Jean-Jacques 583, 609, 610
Dew, Thomas Roderick 544, 610
Deyle, Steven 370, 633–4
Díaz Díaz, Rafael Antonio 82
Díaz Soler, Luis M. 30, 31
Díaz, María Chiquinquirá 82
Díaz, María Elena 94
Diego el Negro 49–50
Digital Archaeological Archive of
    Comparative Slavery (DAACS) 719
Diouf, Sylviane 387
disease 125, 279, 294, 296–7, 313, 315, 321,
        325, 329, 493, 516, 543, 609, 644
    in British colonies 143–4
    in Dutch colonies 159–60, 164
    in Spanish colonies 71, 74, 91
    in United States 213, 237
    see also beriberi; cholera; dengue fever;
        malaria; pellagra; pneumonia;
        tetanus; yellow fever
District of Columbia 424, 433, 441, 442
Dixon, Thomas 412, 518
documentary studies 202
Domínguez, Lourdes S. 705, 714
Dominica 151 n.20, 176, 177
Dominican Order 52, 56, 73
Dominican Republic, see Santo Domingo
Dorigny, Marcel 603, 615
Dorsey, Joseph Carroll 34, 39, 638
dos Santos Gomes, Flávio 116, 123
Douglas, Stephen 573
Douglass, Frederick 236, 392, 403, 412,
        564, 569, 574, 612
Downey, Tom 367, 368
Dragtenstein, Frank 169
Drake, Francis 204
Dred Scott v. Sandford (1857) 440, 442,
        443, 573
Drescher, Seymour 155, 504, 557, 667,
        672, 731
drinking 74, 76, 369, 702

Du Bois Institute (Harvard University) 182,
        183
Du Bois, W. E. B. 434, 612, 687
Dubois, Lawrence 192, 193, 557, 601, 603,
        608, 615
Duchet, Michèle 174, 186
Duke's Law (1665) 449
Dunn, Richard S. 208, 361, 671
Dunning, William 414
Dusinberre, William 241
Dutch Caribbean 4, 30
    emancipation 727
Dutch Leeward Islands, see Aruba;
        Bonaire; Curaçao
Dutch West India Company (WIC) 154,
        155, 156, 157, 165, 214
Dutch Windward Islands, see Saba;
        St. Eustatius; St. Maarten
Dutra, Antonio José 587
Duvalier, François ("Papa Doc") 601, 613
Duvalier, Jean-Claude ("Baby Doc") 614

Eaton, Clement 572
Eblen, Jack 646–7
economics of slavery 13, 38, 90, 134
    autarchy 30
    origins of 490, 499, 500, 505
    patterns 493, 504, 505, 506
    profitability 490, 491, 494, 496, 497,
        500–2, 504
    variations 489, 490, 497, 498, 499, 500,
        501, 502, 503
Ecuador 72, 73, 77, 80, 81, 318
    Esmereldas 76–7
    Guayaquil 82, 585
Edelson, Max 210, 213
Edwards, Bryan 146, 610
Edwards, Laura 527
Eguía, Francisco de 50
Eisenberg, Peter 112
El Dorado 69
Eley, Geoff 358, 373
Eliot, T. S. 12
Elizabeth 147

Elkins, Stanley M. 228, 230, 232, 241, 403, 415, 468, 469, 489, 666, 688–9, 694

Eltis, David 94, 97, 100, 137, 138, 149, 208, 285, 599, 637, 670

Emancipation Act (1833) 569

Emancipation League 573

Emancipation Proclamation 561, 574

emancipation 12, 14, 124, 136, 155, 166, 168, 178, 227, 234, 235, 408, 431, 728
    see also Emancipation Act (1833); Emancipation League; Emancipation Proclamation

Emanuel the Negro 428

Emerson, Ralph Waldo 370

Emmer, Piet 154–5

encomienda system 70, 91, 93, 317

Engerman, Stanley L. 144, 230–1, 302, 305, 416, 497–8, 505, 540, 557, 629–30, 668, 695

England 405, 426
    colonialism 333 n.17, 333 n.18, 424
    common law tradition 425

Enlightenment 6, 12

Episcopalians 439

Equiano, Olaudah 480

esclavos de rescate 314

esclavos jornaleros, see day-laborer slavery

Essequibo 158, 164, 168

estancias 94

estate slaves 38

Estevanico 50

ethnicities 4, 7, 9, 29, 90, 112, 139, 180, 182, 220, 474
    Central Africans 123, 381
    East Africans 115, 183
    West Africans 100, 115, 136, 137, 138, 148, 156, 157, 180, 183, 192, 208, 294, 295, 296, 299, 302, 305, 306, 319
    West-Central Africans 51, 55, 115, 117, 120, 121–2, 136, 137, 138, 140, 189, 379, 380, 481

ethnologists 6

Eugenics 413

execution 79

Faesch, Isaac 165

Fallope, Josette 193

families 117, 118, 124, 147, 189, 220, 233, 234, 235, 439–40, 471, 519–20

Faria, Sheila 118, 120

Farnsworth, Paul 707

Faust, Drew Gilpin 526

February Revolution (1848) 571

Federal Republic of Central America 63

Federal Writers' Project 242

Federalist Party 448, 562

Fedon, Julien 151 n20

Fehrenbacher, Don E. 436

Felipe de Alencastro, Luis 114, 115, 125

femininity 37, 522

Fennell, Christopher 715–16

Ferdinand II 314–15

Ferguson, Leland 708, 717

Fernandes, Florestan 112

Fernandes, Loureiro 717

Fernández, José Ramón 590

Ferraz, Lizandra Meyer 120

Ferrer, Ada 103, 104

fertility 159, 305, 306, 342, 493–4, 516–17, 521, 643, 646–7, 653, 659–62
    in British colonies 136, 144, 147, 151 n.14
    in United States 235, 238

Fesler, Gary 706, 711–12

Fett, Sharla M. 237, 239

Few, Martha 55

Fick, Carolyn E. 198–9 n.32, 600, 601, 603, 605, 617

fictive friendships 117

Fields, Barbara Jeanne 338, 558

Figueroa, Luis A. 34–5, 38, 359

Filho, Walter Fraga 122

Finkelman, Paul 432, 436, 434, 442

Finley, Moses 4, 216

First Confiscation Act (1861) 443

First Seminole War (1817–18) 219

Fischer, David Hackett 276–7

Fitzhugh, George 370, 403, 421 n28, 545, 550, 610, 628 n.30

Florentino, Manolo 114

Florida 5, 50, 100, 218, 219, 223, 241, 315,
    318, 321, 322, 350
  St. Augustine 10, 219
  see also Spanish Florida
Floyd-Wilson, Mary 149
Floyd, R. F. 460
Fogel, Robert William 230–1, 302, 305, 416,
    497–8, 540, 557, 629, 630, 651, 695
Follett, Richard 359, 541
Foner, Laura 667
Forbes, Robert 557
forced migration 241
Ford, Lacy K. 365, 411
Forret, Jeff 369, 696
Fort Nassau 156
Forten, James 563
Fouchard, Jean 188, 191, 601
Fourth Anglo-Dutch War (1780–4) 158
Fox-Genovese, Elizabeth 231, 370, 416,
    417, 524–5
Fox, George 142
Fradera, Josep M. 586
France 12, 173, 177, 188, 301, 448, 644
  abolition of slavery 167, 174, 183, 184,
    192–3, 194, 583
  Bordeaux 182, 599
  colonialism 333 n.17, 424
  immigration from 176
  Le Havre 181
  Nantes 182, 599
  Paris 183, 195
  racism 185
  Second Republic 174, 571
  slave treatment 222
  slavery in 178
  Third Republic 177
  see also Franco-Prussian War; French
    Admiralty; French *Annales* school;
    French Antilles; French Canada;
    French Caribbean; French Company
    of the West Indies; French Dominica;
    French Guiana (Cayenne); French
    imperialist historians; French National
    Archives; French Revolution; Société
    des Amis des Noirs

Franco-Prussian War 177
Franco, José Luciano 91
Franco, José Luciano 91, 102
Franco, Maria Sylvia Carvalho 112, 123
Frank, Zephyr 118, 587
Franklin, Benjamin 643, 661
Franklin, Isaac 629
Franklin, John Hope 433, 690
Frazier, E. Franklin 39, 117, 468
Frederickson, George M. 455, 562, 669
Free Dark Men of Color 346
free land hypothesis 279
Free-Soil Party 560, 574
Free-womb laws 82–3, 590, 728, 740
free(d) people of color 5, 342, 344, 360, 366
  blacks 8, 55, 58, 60, 61
  in Brazil 111, 115, 116, 117, 118, 119, 121, 122
  in Dutch colonies 161, 165, 167
  in French colonies 186, 187
  as slaveholders 7, 188
  in Spanish colonies 21, 69, 75, 82, 91,
    94, 95, 96, 100, 101
  in US 204–5, 220, 232, 431, 432, 549
  see also mulattos
Freedman's Bureau 740
Freedmen and Southern Society Proj-
    ect 695
Freedmens' Saving and Trust Bank 242
freedom 12, 37, 75, 105, 135, 150, 164, 168,
    224, 400
Freehling, William W. 369, 436
French Admiralty 182
French Antilles 174
French Canada 187, 449
French Caribbean 6, 30, 727
French Company of the West Indies 181
French Dominica 174
French Guiana (Cayenne) 164, 167, 173,
    178, 194
French imperialist historians 190
French National Archives 195
French Revolution 80, 174, 177–8, 181, 188,
    190, 193, 408, 544, 564, 565, 567, 603
Frey, Sylvia 383, 386, 407, 431
Freyre, Gilberto 112, 119, 121, 467, 471, 667

Frostin, Charles 602
Fuente, Alejandro de la 579
Fuente, Alejandro de la 91, 92, 93, 94
Fugitive Slave Law (1850) 435, 573
Fugitive Slaw Law (1793) 442
Fundamental Constitutions (1669) 209
Furtado, Júnia 118, 122

Gabriel 238, 448, 450–1, 452, 457, 461
Galenson, David 282, 284
Gallay, Alan 217
Galle, Jillian 709
Gama, Luiz 591
gambling 74, 369, 702
Gandano, Magahães de 319
gang labor 207, 208, 213, 215, 232, 285, 539, 678
García Rodriguez, Mercedes 94, 95
García, Gervasio L. 39
Garcia, Gloria 94, 102
Garfield, Evelyn Picon 102
Garofolo, Leo 77
Garraway, Doris 188
Garrido, Juan 50
Garrigus, John 187, 600, 602, 604, 616, 618
Garrison, William Lloyd 202, 240, 393, 572
Gaspar, David Barry 456, 476, 477, 668,
    679, 694, 695
Gautier, Arlette 179, 189
Geggus, David 179–80, 188, 189, 191, 192,
    520, 599, 601, 607, 615, 616, 675
Gehring, Charles 157
Gell, Monday 456
Gemery, Henry A. 280
gender 4, 9, 14, 36, 188, 476, 711–12
    reproduction 516–17
    sexual difference 515–16
    see also labor, gendered divisions, women
Genizaros 326
Genovese, Eugene D. 28, 116, 241, 382, 436,
    450, 457, 460, 557, 607, 666, 667, 672
    on class 359, 364, 365, 366, 367, 370
    on paternalism 403, 416, 417, 524, 677,
        679, 691–2
    on racism 411, 421 n.28
    Roll, Jordan, Roll 470–1

on slavery and capitalism 230–1
on slaves' perspectives 229, 238
George III 450
Georgia 210, 232, 276, 322, 350, 365, 366,
    371, 373, 387, 390, 514, 638
    indigo 645
    rice 500, 645
    St. Simon 711
    Savannah 302, 361, 364, 441, 459
    slave trade 433–4
    Supreme Court 434
    temporary slavery ban 406
Germany 283, 372, 374
Gil-Bermejo García, Juana 34
Gillespie, Michele 366
Gilroy, Paul 668
Ginsberg, Carlo 697
Gisler, Antoine 186
glass 709
Goa 51
Gold Coast 51, 137, 138, 165, 183, 192, 449
gold 27, 73, 78, 91, 93, 112, 315, 645
Golden Law (1888) 592, 731
    see also Brazil, Golden Law
Goldin, Claudia D. 509 n.29
Gomes, Tiago del Melo 119
Gomez, Michael 381, 382, 472, 482
González, José Caridad 612
Goodell, William 556
Gorender, Jacob 113
Gourou, Pierre 503
Gracia Real de Santa Teresa de Mosé 218
Graden, Dale 124
Graham, Martha 613
Graham, Richard 635, 637
Grange movement 371
Grant, U. S. 561
Gray, Lewis 695
Great Awakening 383, 385, 547
Great Britain 12, 83, 95–8, 124, 157, 158,
    166, 173–4, 177, 181, 187, 223, 276, 280,
    282, 301, 644
    American Revolution 450, 580–1
    Anti-slavery movement 167, 171 n.31, 581,
        583, 593, 637, 730

Bristol 284
British America 277, 281, 283, 286 n.6
Emancipation Act (1833) 167, 730
emancipation project 11–12
evangelical Christianity 581
London 277, 284
rise of slavery 340, 342
Greene, Jack 185, 186, 417, 559
Greene, Lorenzo 216
Gregg, William 372
Grégoire, Abbé 566
Grenada 137, 149, 151 n.20, 174, 177
Griffith, D. W. 412, 413
Gronniosaw, James Albert Ukawsa 480
Grotius, Hugo 166
Groves v. Slaughter (1841) 442
Guadeloupe 706
Guadeloupe 30, 192, 193, 194
    free people of color 187, 193, 299, 706
    contract labor 736
    as French colony 173, 175, 176, 177, 178,
        179, 181, 183, 186, 189
    French Revolution 719
guajiros 5
Guatemala 55, 57, 61–2, 313–14
    Amatitlán 60
    Guatemala City 62, 63
    Lake Izabal 57
    San Jerónimo 52, 56
    Santiago de Guatemala 47, 52
    slave trade 50
    Utatlán 48
Gudmestad, Robert, 632–3
Guedes, Roberto 118
Guerra y Sánchez, Ramiro 23
Guerrero, Vicente 63
Guiana 155, 156
Guinea-Bissau 51, 57
Gulf of Guinea 156
Guterl, Matthew Pratt 549
Gutiérrez Brockington, Lolita 78
Gutman, Herbert G. 116, 233, 235, 374,
    471–2, 488, 519, 635
Guyana 158

Hahn, Stephen 365, 416
Haiti 10, 104, 177, 185, 188, 190, 346, 348, 448,
    452, 566, 675, 724, 736, 738, 740
    coffee production 582
    Constitution of 730
    Dominican occupation 27–8
    emancipation 27, 727, 732
    free(d) people of color 582
    Night of Fire 457
    Port-au-Prince 188
    Post-independence 610
    racism 582
    sugar production 582, 730
    US invasion 613
    see also Haitian Revolution
Haitian Ethnographic Society 613
Haitian Revolution (1791–1804) 22, 25, 32,
    97, 99, 124, 178, 180, 181, 185, 188, 190,
    191, 192, 193, 196 n.12, 360, 357 n.7, 434,
    437, 450, 503, 566–7, 575, 673, 675
    colonial background 598–603
    effects on antislavery movement 581–3
Hall, Douglas 475, 694
Hall, Gwendolyn Midlo 98, 185, 186, 219,
    220–1, 474, 481, 482, 666, 668,
    670, 679
Hall, Jacqueline Dowd 518
Hall, Neville T. 475
Hall, Prince 431, 563
Hamilton, Alexander 561
Hammond, James Henry 549
Hancock, John 561
Handler, Jerome 299, 694, 712
Handlin, Mary 340
Handlin, Oscar 340
Harms, Robert 183
Harper, Chancellor 543
Harper, William 345
Harris, J. William 416
Harris, Leslie M. 458, 558
Harrold, Stanley 460
Hartman, Saidiya 558
Hatfield, April 208, 210–11, 277
Hausa 123

Hauser Mark 707, 708, 709
Hay, Denis 337
Haynes, Stephen 391
Heath, Barbara 707
Hegel, G. W. F. 400, 535
Heinl, Nancy 614
Heinl, Robert 614
Helg, Aline 75
Hemmings, Sally 236, 343, 344
Henry, Patrick 450–1
Herskovits, Melville 39, 467, 468, 472,
    599, 613
Heyrick, Elizabeth 568
Heywood, Linda 476, 670, 679
Heywood, Nancy 616
Higman, Barry W. 144, 303, 475, 656–7, 660
Hildalgo y Costilla, Miguel 62
Hilliard, Kathleen 696, 697–8
Hilton, Rodney 460
Hine, Darlene Clark 476, 477, 519,
    668, 679
Hispanola 34, 91, 320
historical memory 194–5
Hobbes, Thomas 7
Hobsbawm, Eric 359
Hoetink, Harry 155
Hofstadter, Richard 687
Hoganson, Kristin 526
Hogendorn, Jan S. 280
Holmes, A. T. 439
Holt, Sharon Ann 521
Holt, Thomas 558
Holton, Woody 407
Hommius, Festus 166
Hondius, Jacobus 166
Honduras 49–50, 62, 315, 316
    exportation of enslaved Indians 48
    Olancho 53
hoodoo 382
Hoogbergen, Wim 163
hookworm 301, 655, 658
Hoover, John 438
Horn, James 283
horns 240
Horton, James 557

Horton, Lois 557
Howard, Philip 100
Howe, Julia Ward 393
Hudson, Larry 459, 696
Hughes, Henry 370
Hughes, Victor 607, 615, 719
Hume, David 643, 661
Hundley, Daniel 546
Hunefeldt, Christine 82
Hunt, Alfred 612
hurricanes 99, 144, 303
husbandry 282
Hutcheson, Francis 11
Hyden, William 345

Ianni, Octávio 112
Ignatiev, Noel 492
Illinois 432
immigration 22, 125, 372, 374
immunology 294–301
Imperial Commission on Slaves 62
imperialism 90, 179, 313, 557
Incas 69, 76
incentives 74
indemnification for masters 104
India 114
Indiana 432
indigo 8, 73, 140, 176, 189, 205, 210, 220,
    223, 536
individuality 401
Industrial Revolution 676, 678, 708
industrialization 367, 501, 509 n.29
    see also Industrial Revolution
infanticide 79
Inikori, Joseph 668
Innes, Stephen 340
Inquisition 55, 77
integrated plantation 141, 142–3, 208
internal slave trade 71–2, 83, 234, 241
    in Brazil 626, 635–7
    in British Caribbean 626, 637–8
    in North America 626, 627–35
interracial alliances 343, 369, 455–6
interracial marriage 184, 187, 205, 205,
    215, 217, 220, 236, 428

interracial sex 30, 218, 427, 428, 429, 437, 475, 514, 518, 519, 522
Ireland 372, 374
Irons, Charles 384, 389, 395–6 n.22
Iroquois Wars (1641–1701) 325
Iroquois 325
Irving, Washington 370
Isabel II 589
Isabella I 314
Islam 379, 387
Iturbide, Agustín de 62

Jabour, Anya 525
Jackson, Andrew 707, 709
Jackson, Rachel 710
Jackson, Sarah Yorke 710
Jakin 183
Jamaica 651
Jamaica 10, 37–8, 51, 71, 135–40, 142–46, 149, 176, 183, 190, 293, 304, 315, 346, 384, 409, 540, 693–4, 708, 738, 741
    Baptist war 569
    Blue Mountains 704
    emancipation 38
    free people of color 187
    glass 709
    Kingston 8, 300
    maroon communities 675, 717, 718
    Montpelier estate 146–7
    pottery 709
    "proto-peasants" 38
    slave economy system 208
    slave revolt 675
    sugar production 579, 734
    treatment of women 518
James River 207
James, C. L. R. 605, 607, 613, 667
Janissaries 326
Jay, John 561
Jefferson, Thomas 236, 343, 344, 426, 435, 440, 547, 560, 607
Jeffrey, Julie Roy 526, 557
jeje 123
Jennings, Lawrence 193, 557
Jennings, Thelma 518

Jesuits 56, 72, 73, 74, 80, 83, 192, 318, 383
Jesup, Thomas 219
Jesús, Ursula de 78
Jews 157, 336
Jezebel stereotype 236
Jim Crow 518, 690
Joe 685, 686, 693, 696
Johnson, Andrew 326
Johnson, Anthony 448
Johnson, Lyman 78
Johnson, Michael 462 n.12
Johnson, Walter 239, 370, 417, 456, 631–2
Johnston, George Milligan 349
Jones v. Van Zandt (1847) 442
Jones, Bernie 433
Jones, C. L. R. 675
Jones, Charles Colcock 390, 547
Jones, Jacqueline 476, 515, 519
Jones, Mary 547
jongos 122
Jordan, Levi 716
Jordan, Winthrop 204, 295, 338, 339, 340, 341, 427
Joyner, Charles W. 241, 365, 471, 689
Juan el Negro 50
Juárez, Benito 102
July Monarchy (1830–48) 570
Junta de Información 103
Junta Piadosa de Indemnización de Esclavos 63

K'iche' Maya 48
Kansas-Nebraska Act (1854) 440, 573
Kapsoli, Wilfredo 80
Karasch, Mary 112, 116, 123
Kaye, Anthony E. 233, 235
Kelly, Kenneth 706, 719
Kennedy, Cynthia 519, 520
Kentucky 443
Kerry, "Irish" Peg 455
Kilbourne, Richard 638
King Philip's War (1675–6) 324, 341
King, James Ferguson 68, 83
King, Rufus 435, 571
King, Stewart 600, 604, 605, 618

King, Wilma 237–8, 488–9
Kinsbruner, Jay 21
Kiple, Kenneth 143, 299, 653, 656–7
Klein, Herbert S. 100, 118, 481, 636, 666,
    667, 668, 670
Knibb, William 148
Knight, Franklin W. 24, 98
Kolchin, Peter 232, 241–2, 417, 465, 485 n.17,
    665, 669, 670, 672, 678–9, 692
Komisaruk, Catherine 61
Kongo, see West-Central Africa
Kongolese Catholicism 10
Konrad, Herman 56
Kortright, Cornelius 38
Ku Klux Klan 412
Kuhrt, Amélie 559
Kupperman, Karen 341

La Escalera (The Ladder) 101–2
La Guyane 178
labor 6, 13, 281
    contractual 69, 318
    domestic 10, 51, 69, 70, 72, 74, 77, 156–7,
        159, 515
    free 6, 52, 106, 111, 124
    gendered divisions 54, 513–16 immigrant
        732
    indentured 102, 140, 149, 203–5, 208,
        214, 216, 276, 277, 280–3, 300, 402,
        729, 732, 734
    internal migration 22
    labor drafts ("repartimiento") 53
    manual 70, 159, 189, 340
    wage 6, 12, 78, 168, 240, 318, 339, 361,
        546, 728
    see also mita
Laing, Annette 380, 383
Landers, Jane 218
Langfur, Hal 125
Laport, Daniel 578
Lara, Silvia Hunold 116, 119
Larrazabal Blanco, Carlos 25–6, 30
Las siete partidas 91, 95
Lasch, Christopher 455
Laurie, Bruce 557

Law, Robin 192, 476, 481
Lawson, John 211
Lay, Benjamin 142
Le Riverend, Julio 92, 94
Leclerc, Charles 608–9
Leeward Islands 136, 140, 141
    see also Antigua; Montserrat; Nevis;
        St. Christopher
Legaré, Hugh Swinton 418
leishmaniasis 658
Lemmon v. The People (1860) 433
Lenders, Maria 162
Lespinasse, Beauvais 185
Lesser Antilles 34, 142, 177, 315
Lévi-Strauss, Claude 716
Levine, Lawrence W. 229, 471
Levine, Lawrence 689
Lewis, Laura 55
Lewis, Matthew Gregory (Monk) 306
Libby, Douglas 118
Liberator, The 572
Liberty Party 560, 573, 574
Lightner, David L. 633
Ligon, Richard 338
Lima, Ivana Stoltz 119
Lincoln, Abraham 411, 443, 573–4
Link, William 373
literacy 232, 284
Littlefield, Daniel C. 474, 481
Livermore, George 561
livestock 27, 29, 53, 73, 80, 94, 113, 158,
    207, 209, 212, 215, 223
Locke, John 405–6, 425
Lockley, Timothy, J. 369
Lokken, Paul 59
Lombardi, John 83
Loncq, Hendrick Corneliszoon 156
London Society for the Abolition of the
    Slave Trade 565, 569
Long, Edward 342, 347
López Cantos, Ángel 34
López Valdés, Rafael 100
López, Narciso 102
Louis XIV 181
Louis XVIII 566

Louisiana 144, 174, 241, 322, 323, 451, 474, 520, 607, 659
  free(d) persons of color 436
  French influence 219–20, 223
  German Coast revolt (1811) 238, 457
  glass 709
  New Orleans 5, 8, 223, 300, 302, 364, 457, 459, 460, 629–31, 632
  sugar plantations 359, 677
Louverture, Toussaint 10, 188, 360, 450, 451, 566, 567, 583, 586, 605–9, 619, 675
Lovejoy, Paul 481, 483–4
Lower Guinea 138
Lower South 223, 224, 285
Luís, see Sanim
Luna, Francisco Vidal 118
Lynch, Thomas 166
lynching 349, 362, 627

Macaulay, Zachary 644
Maceo, Antonio 104, 105
Machado de Assis, Joaquím María 122
Machado, Maria Helena 116
Macumba 122
Madiou, Thomas 177, 185, 612
Madison, James 561, 562
magic 77
Maine 432
maize 158
Majewski, John 553n9
Makandal, François 190, 191–2, 450, 600, 601
malaria 209, 295, 296, 297, 298, 299, 307, 493, 645, 657
Malê rebellion (1835) 124
Malone, Ann 519–20
Malouet, Pierre-Victor 177
Mammy stereotype 236, 522
Mangones, Albert 616
Manigat, Leslie 601
Mann, Kristin 476
Manuel de Céspedes, Carlos 103, 104, 584
Manuel de Lando, Francisco 33
manumission juntas 83
manumission 4, 5, 8, 167, 227, 342, 424–5, 431, 432

of one's sex partner 518
  as reward 578
  in Brazil 112, 116, 117, 119, 121, 120
  in French colonies 185, 187
  in Spanish colonies 59, 61, 68, 78, 95–6
Manzano, Juan Franciso 102
Margarita 181
María 579
Marion, Francis 223
maroons 145, 151 n.20, 163–4, 217–18, 220, 223, 318, 349
  in Brazil 591
  communities of 447, 449, 452
  in Saint-Domingue 601
  in French colonies 190–1
  in Spanish colonies 29, 31, 56, 57, 218
  see also Palmares
Marquese, Rafael de Bivar, 124, 668, 671–2, 677
Marrero, Leví 92
marriage 59–60, 73–4, 82, 98, 117, 124, 233, 234, 439, 519, 525
  see also interracial marriage; slave marriages
Mars, Jean-Price 600, 601
Marshall, John 441
Marshall, Woodville 694
Martin, Gaston 182, 184, 190
Martineau, Alfred 178
Martínez, María Elena 58
Martinez-Fernandez, Luis 361
Martinique 30, 173, 175, 177, 178, 181, 183, 186, 189, 192, 195, 719
  contract labor 736
  free people of color 187
  Saint-Pierre 194
Martins, Roberto Borges 113
Marx, Karl 539, 557
Marxist scholarship 90, 98, 111, 112–13, 124, 280, 470
Maryland 207, 284, 341, 433, 443, 638
  Baltimore 345, 364
  manumission 425–6, 437
  slave religion 715
masculinity 523, 527

Massachusetts 202, 215, 224–5, 431,
    435, 560
  Boston 216, 329, 374, 431
  emancipation 729
masters 111, 363
  absentee ownership 6, 53, 191, 213, 214,
    383, 447, 450, 537, 542
  authority of 6
  paternalism 540–3, 550, 551
  relationship with slaves 400, 403, 457,
    535–6, 537, 539, 541, 552
  residential 6
materialist scholarship 277, 285, 286 n.6
Matos Rodríguez, Félix 37
Mattos de Castro, Hebe Maria 113
Mauritius 174
Maxwell, Kenneth 112
May, Louis-Philippe 178
Mayo Santiago, Raúl 35
Mbundu 381
McCloy, Shelby 185
McCurry, Stephanie 416, 525
McCusker, John 135
McDonald, Lawrence 696, 697
McDonald, Roderick 453–4, 698
McFarlane, Anthony 79
McGuire, Robert 655
McNeill, William 295
McNight, Kathryn Joy 77
Medina, Charles Beatty 76
Meiklejohn, Norman 68
Melish, Joanne Pope 431
Mellafe, Rolando 69
Memminger, Christopher 439
Menard, Russell 135, 140–1, 206, 208, 340
Mendoza, Antonio de 49, 57
Menier, Marie-Antoinette 188
Mennonites 559
mercantilism 111
Mercedarians 73
Mérimée, Prosper 183
mestizaje, see racial mixing
mestizos 47, 53, 55, 59, 115, 121
Metcalf, Alida 125
Methodist General Conference (1784) 547

Methodists 384, 385, 389, 395–6 n.22, 431
Métraux, Alfred 599
Mettas, Jean 182
Mexico 55, 61–2, 69, 205, 223, 299, 314,
    317, 321, 322, 440, 495, 670
  Acapulco 51, 57
  Campeche 51
  Christianity 48, 55–6
  Colima 54
  Córdoba 51, 58, 61, 62–3
  Cuernavaca 49
  esclavos de guerra ("slaves of war") 48
  esclavos de rescate ("slaves of
    rescue") 48
  Guadalajara 57
  Guanajuato 53
  Mérida 52
  Mexico City 47, 49, 50, 51, 55, 56, 57–8
  Michoacán 57
  Morelos 47, 52
  Nuestra Señora de Guadalupe de
    Amapa 58
  Oaxaca 49, 52, 54, 58, 60
  Orizaba 58
  Pánuco 57
  Puebla 57
  Puebla de los Angeles 47, 51
  rise of African slavery 49–51
  San Lorenzos de los Negros 57
  San Luis Potosí 50, 53
  silver mines 53, 57
  slave culture 54–6
  slave flight 57, 61
  slavery myths 46
  slave population 47
  slave resistance 57–8, 61, 62–3
  slave work 51–4
  Tabasco 51
  Taxco 53
  Tenochtitlán 48, 50, 57
  textile industry 53–4
  Tlatelolco 57
  Veracruz 47, 50, 51, 52, 57, 58, 60
  Xalapa 56
  Zacatecas 53, 57

Meyer, Jean 182
Middelburgse Commercie Compagnie
    (MCC) 154, 155
middle class 6, 370, 371, 372
    as slaveholders 367–8
    US South 359–60, 361, 366–7, 370
Middle Colonies 281, 283
Middle Passage 71, 138, 144, 161, 299, 301,
    328, 379, 382, 579, 667, 670, 719–20
midwifery 238, 306, 515
Miers, Suzanne 668, 679
Mill, John Stuart 501
Miller, Christopher 183
Miller, Joseph 481, 668, 679
Milton, John 460
Minchin, Susie 71
mineiro slaves 115, 118
mining 28, 49, 55, 72, 113, 122
Minnesota 440
Mintz, Sidney 116, 137, 474, 475, 481, 557,
    670, 693
miscegenation 22, 30, 215
Misericórdia 497
missionaries 148, 320, 328, 384, 388, 392
Mississippi River 223, 323, 451
Mississippi 5, 241, 366, 376 n.25, 437
    black majority 447
    Natchez 5, 448, 460
    Warren County 247 n.28
Missouri Compromise (1820) 240, 435,
    440, 448, 571
Missouri 371, 409, 443, 547, 561, 571
mita (forced labor system of Indians) 73
Mitchell v. Wells (1859) 437
modernization 372
Moitt, Bernard 476, 520
Monroe, James 451
Montalvo, Juan 101
Monteiro, John 125
monteros 5
Montesquieu 11
Moore v. Illinois (1852) 443
moral economy 148
Morales Carrión, Arturo 30, 31
Moravians 162, 385

Moreau de Saint-Méry, Médéric Louis
    Élie 602, 610, 612
Morelos, José María 62
Moreno Fraginals, Manuel 23, 24, 26, 32,
    33, 35, 91, 98, 99
Moret Law 105, 106, 589–90, 591, 731
Moret, Nistal 35
Moret, Segismundo 105
Morgan, Edmund 204, 208, 407, 427, 340
Morgan, Jennifer L. 476, 477, 513, 517, 521
Morgan, Kenneth 144, 671
Morgan, Philip D. 232, 234, 459, 474–5,
    536–7, 668, 671, 695, 696, 697
moriscos 51
Mormons 326
Mörner, Magnus 25
Morris, Gouverneur 561
Morris, Thomas D. 427, 433
Morrissey, Marietta 515
mortality 284, 294, 305–6, 307, 448, 493–4,
    599, 643, 646–7, 653
    in British colonies 136, 144
    in Dutch colonies 159
    in French colonies 179, 180, 181
Moscoso, Francisco 34
mosquitoes 299
Moya Pons, Frank 26, 27, 28
Moynihan Report 519
Moynihan, Daniel Patrick 233
Mozambique 189
mozambiques 51
mulatizacion 22
mulattos 344, 345, 346, 348
    in Dutch colonies 167
    in French colonies 185
    as slaves 46, 47, 54
    as slaveholders 7, 15 n.8
    in Spanish colonies 57, 58, 59, 60, 61,
        62, 75, 77, 78, 96
    in United States 205, 221
Mullin, Gerald W. 458
Mullin, Michael 202
Mulroy, Kevin 218
munib 47
Muñoz Marín, Luis 24

Murray, David 97
Murray, William (Lord Blackstone) 559–60
Muslims 123, 317, 338, 387, 391, 458, 460, 586
mutilation 79

naborias 316
nagô 123
Napoleonic War 149, 158, 191, 189, 566
narratives 236
Narváez, Pánfilo de 50
Nash, Gary B. 283, 432
Nat Turner revolt (1831) 238, 240, 360, 448,
    452–3, 455, 544, 682 n.23
National Constituent Congress of
    Chilpancingo 62
National Council for Culture and Arts in
    Mexico (CONACULTA) 46
Native Americans 5, 55, 59, 70, 72, 73, 114,
    156, 187, 210, 211, 216, 237, 276, 277,
    280, 289 n.23, 296–7, 299, 301–2, 339,
    492, 493, 513
    as English slaves 320–1, 323, 324, 328, 330
    European attitudes toward 340
    as French slaves 323, 325, 330
    as indentured servants 326
    as peons 326
    population declines 47
    pre-European slavery 313–14
    as Portuguese slaves 318–19, 328, 330
    relations with African Americans 217,
        218, 220
    resistance to slavery 319
    as slaves in American North 324–5
    as slaves in American South 322–4,
        340, 349, 350, 401, 402
    as slaves in the American West 325–6
    as slave owners 321–2
    slave trade 217, 218, 220, 221–2
    as Spanish slaves 314–18, 326, 328, 330
natural scientists 6
Navajos 326
Negro Act (1740) 454
Negro Election Day 217
Negrón, Mariano 35
negros del ray 80

neighborhoods 233, 235
Netherlands 173, 175, 301, 321, 325, 644
    antislavery movement 171 n.31
    Middleburg 155–6
Netscher, P. M. 164
Nevins, Allan 556
Nevis 708
New England 140, 215, 216–17, 281, 321,
    324, 329
New Grenada, *see* Colombia
New Hampshire 224, 431, 729
New Jersey 202, 432
New Laws (1542) 70, 316
New Laws for the Good Treatment and
    Preservation of the Indians 49
New Mexico 316, 323
    Santa Fe 326
New Netherland Project 157
New Netherlands 214, 215, 219, 220, 321, 325
New Social History 229
New York 202, 214, 216, 325, 432, 433, 452,
    459, 638
    Long Island 441
    New York City 374, 431, 447, 448, 449,
        450, 457, 458
    slave rebellion of 1712 430
Newman, Richard 557
Newson, Linda 48, 71
Nicaragua 6, 215, 314, 315, 316
    exportation of enslaved Indians 48
    Granada 52
    Realejo 47, 54
    San Pedro Metapa 60–1
    slave trade 50–1
Nicarao 48
Nichols, Elaine 718
Nicholson, Thomas 11
Nield, Keith 358, 373
Non-white slaveholders 118
nonslaveholding whites 5
North Carolina 241, 303, 323, 373, 438
    Halifax County 451
    Raleigh 374
    slave laws 434
    slave religion 715

Northwest Ordinance 434, 440
Nott, Josiah 347
Nova Scotia 580
Novaes, Fernando 112
Nuestra Tercera Raíz ("Our Third
    Root") 46
Nunn, Nathan 501
nutrition 143–4, 190, 208, 220, 301–6, 329,
    505, 516, 644, 655–6

O'Brien, Michael 370, 372–3, 417, 418, 546
O'Donnell, Leopoldo 98, 101
O'Farrill, Rafael 98, 101
O'Neill, Eugene 613
Oakes, James 231, 367, 368, 411, 416, 417
Oates, Charles 455
Ocaneechi 322
Ogé, Vincent 603–4
Ogilby, John 338
Ohio River 434
Ohio, 432, 437
Ojibwas 325
Olano, Nuflo de 50
Oliveira, Anderson J. 122
Olmstead, Alan 499
Olmsted, Frederick L. 363, 497
One-drop rule 344–5
Oostindie, Gert 155, 169
Orinoco River 156
Ortiz, Fernando 23, 35, 39, 90, 95, 99
Otto, John 707
Oudin-Bastide, Caroline 189
Ouidah 183
Owens, Leslie Howard 488
Ownby, Ted 698
Owsley, Frank 363, 364
Oyos 101

Pacific Northwest 440
Pact of Zanjón 104
Painter, Nell Irvin 236, 635
Paiva, Clothilde de 118
palenques 79, 92
Palmares 5, 318, 450
Palmer, Benjamin Morgan 548

Palmer, Colin 50, 52, 483
Panama Canal 300
Panama 48, 54, 71, 72, 204, 734
    Panama City 51
    Portobello 51
Panis 325
Paquette, Robert 102, 457, 608
Paraguay 68, 69, 72, 76, 83, 317, 318
    abolition 84
Paraguayan War (1864–70) 596 n.33
pardos 118–19
Parés, Luís Nicolau 123
Pares, Richard 135
Parish, Peter 540
paternalism 4, 229, 230–1, 247 n.28, 293,
        368, 391, 399, 403–5, 408, 411–12, 415–16,
        447, 470, 535
    and Christianity 547, 551
    development of 536–9, 546
    master–slave relationship 540–3, 550, 551
    see also Genovese, Eugene
        D., paternalism
patriarchy 4, 158, 212, 447, 536–8, 541, 548
Patriotic Fever, see yellow fever
patrocinados 106
patronato 105
Patterson, Orlando 4, 7, 10, 138, 400,
        557, 694
Paula, A. F. 168
Pawnees 325
Peabody, Sue 192
Peace of Ryswick 598
Pedro I 586
Pedro II 586, 587, 590
pellagra 304
Penningroth, Dylan C. 233, 235, 679,
        696, 697
Pennsylvania 202, 215, 325, 431, 432, 442, 638
    Philadelphia 216, 224, 374, 431
Pequot War (1636–7) 324
Pérez Cabral, Pedro Andrés 21
Pérez de la Riva 91, 92, 94, 99
Pérotin-Dumon, Anne 179, 193
Peru 69, 72–4, 77, 80–4, 316–18, 495, 497,
        585, 670

Peru (*cont.*)
　Chicama Valley 12
　Cuzco 69
　Lima 71, 72, 74, 77, 78, 82
Pétré-Grenouilleau, Olivier 195, 628 n.23
Petrusewicz, Marta 677
Peytraud, Lucien 177–8, 182
Philippines 51
Phillip, John 427
Phillips, Ulrich B. 293, 362–3, 403, 414–17,
　　467–8, 469, 539, 541, 628–9, 686–8,
　　690, 694–5
Phillips, Wendell 572
Phillips, William 669
pica (dirt-eating) 304, 307
Picó, Fernando 36
Pinckney, Charles Cotesworth 435
Pinckney, Charles 561
Pinckney, Thomas 456
Pinkster 217
Pipil 48
Pizarro, Francisco 69
Plá, Josefina 68
Plácido 101
plain folk 363, 364, 365
plantation complex 135, 214
plantation slavery 10, 30, 52, 111
planter class 358–9, 360–1, 366, 367, 368,
　　371, 415
Pluchon, Pierre 191–2, 196 n.12, 615
pneumonia 53, 302
political consciousness 36
political expression 119
political–cultural approach to slavery
　　scholarship 277, 286 n.6
poll tax 514
Polonia 101
Ponce de León, Juan 33, 315
poor whites 6, 8, 338, 340, 346–9, 363,
　　365, 369, 370, 371, 451, 524
Popple, Alured 140
Porter, Kenneth 217
Porteus, Beilby 581
Portugal 5, 50, 51, 111, 114, 156, 157, 163,
　　175, 178, 315, 644

Inquisition 122
rise of slavery 339, 340, 342, 348, 379
slave trade 70, 71, 671
Portuondo, Olga 94
post-freedom mobility 117, 118–19, 121
post-revisionist scholarship 231–42
Post, Elisabeth Maria 166
Postlethwaite, Bill 460
Postma, Johannes 154–5
pottery 708–9
Powell, Henry 136
Praying Towns 320
Presbyterians 384, 385, 388, 390, 392
Price-Mars, Jean 191, 613
Price, Richard 116, 137, 163, 170 n.15, 474, 481
Prigg v. Pennsylvania (1842) 442–3
Prim y Prats, Juan 578
Pritchard, "Gullah" Jack 448
Proctor, Frank T. 52, 53, 56, 59
Progressive Era 413
proslavery thought 6, 14, 240, 347
　colonial period 401–5
　nineteenth century 409–13
　revolutionary period 405–8
Prosser, Thomas 451
prostitution 77
Protest of Baragua 105
Protestantism 378, 383, 384, 402
Proto-peasant adaptation 36, 39
Proto-proletariat adaptation 39
Puerto Rico 21, 22, 24, 80, 97, 100, 315,
　　346, 359, 578, 583, 741
　Bayamón 31
　emancipation 30, 32, 34, 42 n.26, 586–92,
　　593, 595 n.30, 731, 737
　Guayama 32, 35, 38, 40
　Mayagüez 32, 40
　New History 31
　Ponce 31, 32, 36, 40
　rekindled nineteenth-century slave
　　trade 39
　San Juan 34, 35, 36, 37
　slavery 29–36, 38–9
　sugar production 737
Pulliam & Company 633

Punch, John 428
Puritans 166, 215, 324, 328
    as slave owners 321

Quakers 11, 142, 325, 389, 431, 559, 562,
    563, 568
Quamina 148
Quarles, Benjamin 431, 473
Quechua 77
Queen Anne's War (1712) 449
Quiñones, José 578
Quintero Rivera, Angel 39
Quintero Rivera, G. 39

R. G. Dun & Company 634
Raboteau, Albert 394
race 5, 14, 24, 60, 90, 92, 155, 174, 178, 188,
    205, 217, 241, 293–4, 327, 369, 370,
    426–7, 492, 494, 514, 557
    African American inferiority myth 229
    barriers 22, 348–9, 415
    classification 63
    corporatist conception 221
    hair type 295
    mixing 21, 22, 25, 75, 203, 204, 207
    science 178
    skin color 4, 7, 9, 29, 295, 330, 336, 337,
        338, 340, 342, 345, 346, 359
    as slavery defense 339, 348
    social interpretation of 336, 342
racism 119, 312, 331 n.2, 324, 327–30, 369,
    399, 404, 408, 411, 414, 421 n.28, 427,
    453–4, 492, 527, 548–9, 556, 562, 564,
    572, 575, 670
    black biological inferiority myth 12
    egalitarianism 12
    of English 141, 149, 205, 207, 208
    of French 185–8, 194
    Haiti 582
    and slavery 276, 279, 285
    in Spanish colonies 22, 60
    in United States 201, 204, 229, 455
Rael, Patrick 557
railroads 99, 368, 544
Raimond, Julien 602

Ramos Mattei, Andrés 38
Ramsay, James 581
Rankin, John 393
rape 76, 439, 517, 518, 522, 523, 526
Rawick, George P. 469, 470, 689–90, 692
Raynal, Abbé 149, 301, 583
rebellions 4, 5, 7, 9, 10, 12, 22, 28, 31, 100–2,
    105, 122, 160, 164–5, 215, 219, 224, 238,
    240, 246 n.23, 303, 375 n.7
    see also Aponte Rebellion; Haitian
        Revolution; Nat Turner revolt; South
        Carolina, Denmark Vesey conspiracy;
        Stono River revolt; Túpac Amaru
        rebellion; Túpac Katari rebellion;
        Venezuela, Coro rebellion
Rebouças, Antônio Pereira 119
Reconquista 317, 338
Reconstruction 234, 412, 414, 736
Rediker, Marcus 449
Reform Act (1832) 564, 569
Régént, Frédéric 188, 193
Reid, J. H. 685
Reign of Terror 565, 566
Reis, João José 116, 122, 123, 387
religion 122–3, 161–2, 191, 230, 337
    antislavery movement 389, 390–1,
        393, 394
    proslavery movement 378, 390–1,
        392, 394
    see also African American Episcopal
        Church; American Methodist
        Episcopal Church; Anglicans; Baptists;
        Catholicism; Christianity; Methodists;
        Presbyterians
Renkema, W. E. 158
rented slaves 38
repartimiento 317–18
repatriation 408
Republican Party 443, 448, 560, 573
resistance 9, 10, 14, 78–84, 90–1, 92, 135,
    138, 142, 145–6, 148, 150, 151 n.20, 162–4,
    174, 179, 190, 193, 238
    in British Caribbean 456
    everyday variety 37
    in Mexico and Central America 47

resistance (*cont.*)
    use of courts 79
    women 520–1
Restall, Matthew 50, 76
revisionist scholarship 117, 229, 232, 235
Revolution of 1848 102
Rey, Terry 380
Rhode Island 202, 215, 324, 431, 432
    Newport 214, 216
Rhode, Paul 499
Ribbe, Claude 195
rice 8, 10, 201, 210, 211, 223, 227, 232, 406,
    499–500, 536
Rice, Nathan Lewis 627
Richardson, David 100
Ridings, Eugene 368
Rijk, J. C. 168
Rinchon, Dieudonné 182
Rio Branco Law (1871) 106, 590, 592, 731
Río de la Plata 80
Riva, Juan Pérez de la 24
Robeson, Paul 613
Robinson, Armstead 461
Robinson, Donald L. 434, 436
Rockefeller, John D. 301
Rodman, Selden 613
Rodney, Walter 481
Rodríguez Morel, Genaro 28, 34, 37
Roediger, David 351
Rogers, Dominique 187, 188, 600, 604
Roman slave laws 186–7, 427, 540–1
Romero, Fernando 68
Rose, Willie Lee 202, 478
Rosenbloom, Joshua 500
Rousseau, Jean-Jacques 6
Rout, Leslie, Jr. 69
Royal African Company of England 481
royal slaves 93–4
Rufer, Mario 81
Ruffin, Edmund 541–2
runaway slaves 5, 318, 350, 406, 424
    in Brazil 116, 121, 122
    in Dutch colonies 163, 167
    in French colonies 190–1
    in Spanish colonies 60, 62, 76–7, 79, 92, 93

in United States 227, 239
    see also maroons
rural labor 74
Ryan, Thomas 625
Ryden, David Beck 731

Saba 155, 158, 169
Sachs, Jeffrey 503
Saco, José Antonio 3, 14, 90, 103
Saffin, John 215
Saint-Domingue 7, 10, 12, 22, 25, 40, 80–1,
    99, 115, 164–5, 167, 173–9, 181, 183–6, 188,
    191, 408, 450, 503, 520
    African-born slaves 600, 603
    black majority 599, 603
    Cap Français 183, 188
    class 602–3, 604
    Club Massiac 603
    creoles 600, 603
    effect of French Revolution 603–4
    emancipation 729–30
    free people of color 185, 187, 600–1, 603,
        604, 618–19
    Kongo slaves 189
    maroons 601
    see also Saint-Domingue Revolution;
        Santo Domingo
Saint-Domingue Revolution
    (1791–1804) 174, 190, 192, 564, 565, 566,
        570, 581, 645, 667, 675
Saintoyant, Jules 184, 190
Sala-Molin, Louis 186
Salamanca, Miguel 58
Salcedo, Diego López de 48
Salles, Ricardo 121
salt 156, 158, 173
Sambo stereotype 229, 230, 232, 468, 523
Same-sex relationship 427
Samford, Patricia 706, 714–15
Sandoval, Alonso de 35
Santeria 387
Santidade 319
Santo Domingo 583
Santo Domingo 21, 22, 24, 27, 80, 93, 97, 583
    French occupation 22, 27–9

Haitian occupation 22
sugar industry 737, 740
see also Saint-Domingue
São Paulo School of Sociology 111, 112, 115, 117, 118, 119, 124
São Tomé 114
Saraiva-Cotegipe Law (1885) 591
Sarracino, Rodolfo 102
Saskatchewan 302
Saugéra, Eric 182
Savage, John 193
Savannah River 322, 323
sawbuck equality 210
Sayers, Daniel 718
Scarano, Francisco A. 32
Schafer, Judith 436
schistosomiasis 658
Schmidt-Nowara, Christopher 103
Schoelcher, Victor 38, 177, 193–4, 615
Schulman, Ivan A. 102
Schwalm, Leslie 476, 527
Schwartz, Marie Jenkins 237, 476, 489
Schwartz, Stuart 112, 114, 460, 668, 670
scientific racism 391
Scott, Rebecca 103, 105, 106
scrofula, see pneumonia
Searing, James 481
secession 412, 421–2 n.29
Second Confiscation Act (1862) 443
Second Great Awakening 361
Second Seminole War (1835–42) 5, 219
second slavery 22, 115, 119
Second World War 403
Seminoles 218, 219
and runaways 218, 219
see also First Seminole War; Second Seminole War
Sénégal 183, 475
Senegambia 51, 115, 189, 220, 481, 483
Sensbach Jon 382
sensory perception 337, 345
senzala 122
Serna Herrara, Juan Manuel de la 52
Seven Years War (1756–63) 95, 149, 174, 176, 182, 187, 326

Sewall, Samuel 215
Seward, William 574
sexism 527
sexual abuse 144–5, 147, 163, 167, 233, 235, 236, 343, 362, 410, 429, 440, 470, 489, 516, 518
sexuality 71, 76, 77, 83, 522–3, 526, 517–19
see also consensual sex; interracial sex; rape; same-sex relationship; sexual abuse
sharecroppers 365, 376 n.25, 728
Sharp, Samuel 148
Shaw, Lemuel 433
Shawnee 322
Sheller, Mimi 608
Short-staple cotton 227–8
Shugerman, Jed H. 434
Shumpeter, Joseph 539
sickle cell anemia 298
Sierra Leone 137, 138, 294, 580
Siete partidas 222
Sieur de Bienville 220
silicosis 53
Silié, Rubén 26
Silva, Chica de 122
silver 53, 70, 71, 72–3, 74, 80, 93, 317, 495, 645
Singleton, Theresa 705, 709
Sioux 325
Skocpol, Theda 664
slave alliances 116
Slave Coast 51, 183
slave codes 177, 303, 341, 364
see also Code Noir
slave cowboys 53
slave culture: African heritage 466–9, 470–4, 478, 479, 480–4
geographic influences 475–6
as resistance 474–5
slavery's effect on 468, 473, 475
temporal influences 475–6
Westernization 468, 475–6, 479, 480
slave economy system 207, 208, 233
slave law
antebellum period 436–40
colonial period 426–31
revolutionary period 431–6

slave law (*cont.*)
  right of transit 432–3
slave marriages 660–1
slave poisonings 193, 450
slave trade 5, 11, 227, 236, 391, 409, 424
  1808 closing of, 538
  and Brazil 112, 114, 117, 119
  British 135, 137, 142, 149, 183, 203, 214, 564
  closing of 434
  Dutch 154–5, 156, 157, 170 n.7, 181, 203, 206, 214
  French 178, 179, 181–4, 188, 189, 195
  internal 71–2, 83, 234, 241
  Portuguese 183, 214
  Spanish 23, 214
  trade clause 435
  transatlantic 96, 97, 99–100, 732
  see also internal slave trade
slavery 46, 54, 55, 69, 70, 111
  see also slave codes; slave cowboys; slave culture; slave economy system; slave law; slave marriages; slave poisonings; slave trade
Slenes, Robert, 122, 124, 635, 636
Small-scale planters 149, 277
smallpox 50
Smallwood, Stephanie 668, 670
Smith, Adam 9, 11, 540
Smith, George 457
Smith, Gerrit 572–73
Smith, John 148
Smith, Mark M. 240, 337, 380, 417
Smith, Samuel Stanhope 343
Smith, Venture 480
Smolenski, John 697
smuggling 70, 71
Smytegelt, Bernard 166
Soares, Mariza de Carvalho 122
Sobel, Mechal 385, 386
social mobility 455
Société des Amis des Noirs 565, 582, 603
Society for Effecting the Abolition of the Slave Trade 564
Society of West Indian Planters and Merchants 567

Soderlund, Jean R. 432
Sokoloff, Kenneth 505
Solow, Barbara 668
Somers, Margaret 664
Somerset case 559–60
Sommerville, Diane Miller 523
Soto, Hernando de 92
Soulodre-La France, Renée 79, 81
South America 100, 156
South Carolina Society 497
South Carolina 100, 156, 206–9, 215, 217, 220, 276–7, 280, 297–8, 322–3, 343, 350, 371, 373, 409, 411, 459, 631
  Anderson Courthouse 685, 693
  Barnwell District 368
  black majority 447, 473
  Charleston 8, 213, 217, 221, 224, 302, 346, 389–90, 406, 437, 448, 452, 453, 457, 458, 459, 625, 628
  Columbia 460
  Constitution 406
  Court of Magistrates and Freeholders 685–6, 697
  Denmark Vesey conspiracy 437
  Edgefield District 368
  free(d) people of color 221, 437
  indigo production 645
  Native Americans 349, 353 n.17
  Negro Act (1740) 406
  pottery 708
  rice production 211, 212, 213, 500, 645, 671
  slave laws 210, 430
  slave rebellions 452, 454, 457, 458, 460–1
  slave-related statutes 450, 454
  slave trade 433–4
  treatment of women 517
  upcountry 365
  see also Stono Rebellion; Vesey, Denmark
South Province 7
South Sea Company 95
Souther v. Commonwealth (1851) 438
Southern Claims Commission 232, 234, 242, 695, 696, 697, 707
Southwest Ordinance 440

Sovereign Constituent Congress of
    Mexico 62
Spain 26, 47, 55, 97, 103, 156, 157, 164, 174,
    175–6, 181, 185, 205, 297, 301, 314–18,
    448, 583, 598, 644–5
    antislavery movement 583–5
    emancipation 22
    rise of slavery 340, 341, 342, 348
    runaway slave policy 350
    Santo Domingo 583
    slave treatment 222
    see also Spanish Abolitionist Society;
        Spanish Buck; Spanish Florida
Spanish Abolitionist Society 589
Spanish Buck 161
Spanish Florida 10, 447, 449–50
Spruill, Julia Cherry 525
St. Christopher 136, 173, 175, 299, 738
St. Croix 30
St. Eustatius (Statia) 155, 157, 158, 169
St. John 449
St. Kitts, see St. Christopher
St. Lucia 174, 176, 177, 708
St. Maarten 155, 158, 168, 169, 173
St. Thomas 384
St. Vincent 151 n.20, 176, 177
Stäel-Holstein family 566
Stampp, Kenneth M. 228–9, 293, 294, 415,
    468, 629, 687–8, 694, 690
Stanton, William 342
Stark, David M. 43 n.44
State v. Hale (1823) 438
State v. Hoover (1839) 438
State v. Moran (1829) 438
states' rights 411
Stauffer, John 557
Steckel, Richard 302, 305, 505, 516, 653,
    659, 660
Stedman, John Gabriel 159
Stein, Robert Louis 182, 196n12
Stein, Stanley 112, 116, 122
Stephenson, Wendell Holmes 629
Stevens, Brenda 241, 488, 520
Stewart, James Brewer 557

Stibbs, Bartholomew 337
Stolcke, Verena 24, 35
Stono Rebellion (1739) 10, 219, 360, 380,
    406, 447, 449, 454, 600, 682 n.23
Storey, Margaret M. 370
Story, Joseph 442, 443
Stowe, Harriet Beecher 403, 438, 573
Strangers Fever, see yellow fever
Stuckey, Sterling 688–9
Studer, Elena de 80
Sugar Duties Act (1846) 739
sugar 4, 8, 9, 10, 12, 277, 299, 318, 319, 320,
    493–5, 677
    Barbadian production 208
    Brazilian production 112, 113, 121, 125, 537
    demographics 626
    Dutch production 156, 157, 158, 159, 163
    English production 140–1, 142, 146, 207
    French production 175, 176, 177, 183
    Jamaican production 453, 540
    Portuguese production 207
    Spanish production 22, 23, 27–35, 38,
        52, 55, 49, 61, 73, 90, 91, 93–5, 96–8,
        99–100, 102, 104, 207
    United States production 201, 206, 207,
        210, 214, 227, 453
suicide 165
Sumpter Thomas, 223
superstition 230
Suriname 155, 158, 159, 161, 162, 163–4, 167,
    168–9, 346, 348, 349, 738
    Berbice slave revolts 164
    Bethlehem plantation insurrection 163
    Commewijne River 163
    maroons 717, 718
    Paramaribo 163, 168
    sugar production 736
Sweden 644
Sweet, James H. 122, 139, 338, 380–1, 481
Sweet, John 216, 217

Tadman, Michael 630–1, 634, 635, 640 n.15
Tagaki, Midori 456
tamemes 316

Tannenbaum, Frank 23, 25, 30, 32, 33, 35, 43
    n.44, 68, 69, 185, 354–5 n.43, 415, 417,
    579, 580, 666, 688
Tapuya 5
Tardieu, Jean-Pierre 73, 76, 80
tariffs 240
task system 213–14, 215, 232, 298
taxes 70, 124, 374, 433, 636
Taylor, Elizabeth 613
telegraph 373
ten Haeff, Adriaen 155–6
tenant farming 141, 366
Tennessee 373, 635
tetanus 306, 516
Texas 316, 323, 326, 366, 371, 435, 440, 715
textile manufacturing 55
Thésée, Françoise 189
Third Anglo-Dutch War (1672–4) 166
third root 41 n.7
Thirteenth Amendment 443, 736
Thistlewood, Thomas 144–5
Thompson, E. P. 116, 358
Thompson, Maurice 136
Thoreau, Henry David 370
Thornton, J. Mills, III 365
Thornton, John 138, 379, 380, 381, 476,
    480–81, 606, 616, 617, 619, 668, 670, 679
Thornwell, James Henley 543, 550
three-fifths clause 434–5
tlacotin 47
Tobacco Age 205–6
tobacco 8, 140, 283, 487 n.47, 536, 537, 645
    Brazilian production 113, 114
    French production 173, 175, 176
    Spanish production 28, 94–5, 96, 97, 99
    United States production 201, 203, 205,
        207, 211, 212, 215, 220, 223, 227
Tobago 136
Tomich, Dale 115, 183, 475, 669, 676
Torre, Miguel de la 31
Toubira Law 194
Toubira, Christiane 194
Tradieu, Jeanne-Pierre 98
trapiches 52
trash gangs 515

Treaty of Guadalupe Hidalgo (1848) 440
Treaty of London (1814) 158
Treaty of Madrid (1817) 97
Treaty of Paris (1763) 95
tributary peasants 47
Trinidad 136, 139, 315, 637, 734, 738, 739
Trouillot, Michel-Rolph 607
trujillista 26, 27
Trujillo, Rafael L. 24, 25
trypanosomes 306
tuberculosis 302
Tucker, St. George 426
Tula 165
Tunica trackers 5
Túpac Amaru rebellion 81
Túpac Katari rebellion 81
Turnbull, David 101
Turner, Dale 694
Turner, Lorenzo Dow 467
Turner, Mary 385, 695
Tuscarora War (1711) 323
Tuscaroras 323
Tushnet, Mark V. 438
Twelve Years True (1621) 156
Tyler, Watt 460

Umbanda 122
Uncle Tom stereotype 523
UNESCO Slave Route Project 46
Unger, W. S. 154
United Provinces of Central America 63
United States v. The Amistad (1841) 441–2
United States 4, 6, 96, 102, 185
    emancipation 727, 731, 732
    slave religion 714–17
    slave trade 646
    see also Alabama; Arizona; Arkansas;
        Connecticut; Delaware; Florida;
        Georgia; Kentucky; Louisiana; Maine;
        Maryland; Massachusetts; Missouri;
        New Jersey; New Mexico; New York;
        North Carolina; Ohio; Pennsylvania;
        South Carolina; Tennessee; Texas;
        Utah; Vermont; Virginia
Upper Guinea 137

Upper Peru, *see* Bolivia
Upper South 224, 234, 285, 323, 345, 371, 437, 524
urban black religious brotherhoods 122
urban slavery 59, 73, 78, 81, 90, 157, 364
Ursinius, Zacharias 166
Uruguay 69, 83, 585
US Civil War 11, 12, 13
US Coast Guard 441
US Colored Troops 242
US Congress 424, 435
    fugitive slave laws 440, 442, 443
    slave trade laws 440
US Constitution 424, 426, 436, 561
    see also Thirteenth Amendment
US Supreme Court 440–1
    under John Marshall 441
    under Roger Taney 441
Utah 313, 326
Utes 326

Vaissière, Pierre de 174, 184, 602
Valdés, Dennis 61
Valdés, Gerónimo 98
Valencia Villa, Carlos Eduardo 78
van Deusen, Nancy 78
van Hoëvell, W. R. 168
Van Hogenheim, W. S. 164
van Pere, Abraham 156
van Poudroyen, Cornelius 166
van Stipriaan, Alex 169
Vanhee, Hein 380
Vanony-Frisch, Nichole 189
Vansina, Jan 616
Varick, Caesar 447–8, 449, 455
Varon, Elizabeth 526
Vastey, Baron de 177
Vaughan, Alden T. 204, 338, 340
Vaughan, Virginia Mason 338
Velasco, don Luis de 57
Velázquez, Diego 91
venereal disease 516
Venezuela 69, 72, 73, 76, 77, 80, 97, 157, 181, 315, 317
    abolition 84

Coro rebellion 81, 83, 583
    emancipation 579–80, 583
    free(d) people of color 579
Vermont 432, 560, 729
Vernon, Edward 300
Vesey, Denmark 238, 240, 390, 448, 452, 453, 462 n.12
Vestry of St. Thomas and St. Denis 497
Vianna, Larissa 119
Victoria, Guadalupe 62
Villa-Flores, Javier 53
Vincentians 383
Vinson, Ben 61, 570, 668
Viotti da Costa, Emília 112, 148
Virginia Company 281
Virginia Slave Code of 1705 448
Virginia 140, 203–6, 208–10, 215, 227, 241, 277, 280, 283, 285, 322, 388, 406, 409, 426–7, 459, 514, 520, 638, 671
    colonial period 339, 580
    colonial slave laws 207
    eighteenth century 384
    Elizabeth City 451
    House of Burgesses 428, 429, 430
    James City County 706–7
    Jamestown 321, 448
    manumission 425, 433, 436–7
    Native Americans 340
    Norfolk 451, 457
    Race-related laws 341, 344–5
    Richmond 8, 364, 437, 451, 456, 457, 458
    slave laws 428–30, 448
    slave rebellions 448, 451
    Southampton County 453
    Williamsburg 406, 455, 482–3
    see also Nat Turner rebellion
vodou 188, 189, 191, 192, 380, 382, 387, 604, 605
Voetius, Gisbertus 166
Voltaire 370
voluntary servitude 283
von Germeten, Nicole 55
von Humboldt, Alexander 90, 497
voting rights 119

Wade, Richard C. 364, 459
Walcott, Derek 149
Walker, David 240
Walker, William 6, 549
Walkowitz, Daniel J. 358
Wallerstein, Immanuel 280, 492, 670, 672, 677
Walsh, Lorena 277, 482–3
Walvin, James 668
War of 1812218, 433, 448, 451
War of Jenkins Ear (1739–42) 300
War of Spanish Succession (1701–14) 95, 157, 173
War of the Grand Alliance (1688–97) 598
War of the Triple Alliance (1864–70) 84
Washington, George 547, 561, 580, 586
Watson, Alan 186, 427
Watts, Sheldon 299
Weaver, Karol 192
Webber, Thomas 488
Weik, Terrence 718
Weld, Theodore 644
Wells, Jonathan Daniel 366–7
Wesley, Charles H. 362
West Indies 69, 203, 215, 281, 283, 285, 297, 301, 315, 323, 329
West Nile Virus 300
West Virginia 574
Weston, George M. 363
Westos 322, 323
Wet-nurses 77
Wheatley, Phillis 480
Whig Party 526, 562
whipping 75–6, 79, 81, 141, 142, 144, 161, 163, 207, 208, 211, 233, 240, 427, 430, 685, 686
Whit, William 466
white distraction 9
white elites 22, 277, 285, 348, 416, 524
white nostalgia 412
white slavery 275
white supremacy myth 295, 410, 525, 549, 557, 628
White, Charles 342
White, Deborah Gray 235, 236, 476, 515, 518, 519, 521

Whitefield, George 384, 391
whiteness 187, 337, 344, 345, 346, 347, 351, 527
whitening 25, 26, 59
Wiecek, William M. 436
Wilberforce, William 564, 567, 731
Wild Coast 156, 158, 159, 160
Wilentz, Sean 558
Wilkie, Laura 707
Willem I 167
Williams, Eric 340, 501, 557, 637, 667, 672, 731
Williams, Robert 453
Williams, Roger 324
Williamson, John 293
Wilson, George 456
Wilson, Henry 556
Wilson, Woodrow 413
Winch, Julie 557
Windward Islands 136
    see also Dominica; Grenada; Grenadines; St. Lucia; St. Vincent
Winti 161, 162
Wirkus, Faustin 613
witchcraft 77
Wolf, Eric 670, 677
Wolff, Betje 166
Wolofs 28
women (enslaved) 304, 471, 513–14, 516, 520–4, 527
    in Brazil 115, 124
    in British colonies 144–5
    in French Caribbean 179
    sexuality 517–18
    in Spanish colonies 27, 29, 36, 37, 51, 52, 53, 54, 55, 58, 59, 62, 70–1, 74, 76–8, 82, 83, 93–5, 101, 317
    in United States 204, 208, 213, 233, 235, 238–9, 324, 450, 476–8
women (free) 504, 514, 525
    in Brazil 120, 122
    in Spanish colonies 60, 76, 95–6
    in United States 217, 221
Wood, Betty 383, 386, 477–8
Wood, Gordon 548

Wood, Kirsten 525
Wood, Peter H. 202, 209–10, 297–8, 430,
    473, 474
Woodbury, Levi 442
Woodson, Carter 687
Woodward, C. Vann 470, 485 n.10, 692
Works Progress Administration 229, 242,
    469, 470, 471, 472, 473, 689–90, 692, 696
World War II 178, 229
Wright, Donald R. 455
Wright, Gavin 500
Wright, Henry C. 393
Wright, Joseph 480
Wyatt-Brown, Bertram 523

Yamasee War (1715–17) 323, 324, 353 n.17
Yamasees 322

yanaconaje 316–17
Yanga 57
Yellin, Jean Fagin 557
yellow fever 209, 295, 296, 297, 299, 300,
    307, 493, 645, 657
yeomen farmers 5, 365, 367, 368, 371, 376
    n.25, 416, 524
Yetman, Norman 470, 689
Yoruba 34, 139
Yucatec 48

Zaire River 115, 122
Zamba 480
zambo (mixed black-Indian) 77, 81
Zedong, Mao 619
Zeuske, Michael 671, 677
Zilversmit, Arthur 432

Lightning Source UK Ltd.
Milton Keynes UK
UKOW05f0735200116

266741UK00003B/3/P